MW00786165

The New Frontiers of Civil Rights Litigation

The New Frontiers of Civil Rights Litigation

Michèle Alexandre
PROFESSOR OF LAW
UNIVERSITY OF MISSISSIPPI SCHOOL OF LAW

CAROLINA ACADEMIC PRESS
Durham, North Carolina

ISBN: 978-1-61163-416-7
LCCN: 2018952158

Carolina Academic Press, LLC
700 Kent Street
Durham, North Carolina 27701
Telephone (919) 489-7486
Fax (919) 493-5668
www.cap-press.com

Printed in the United States of America

To my family, friends, and, to all
civil rights attorneys, teachers, and activists working hard
to bring equity to all aspects of our society.

Contents

PART II
**IMPACT OF POST-*BROWN* GAINS BENEFITING
DIVERSE GROUPS—ONGOING LIMITATIONS**

Table of Cases

Preface

The purpose of this book is to provide students with a survey of current and emerging issues in American civil rights litigation. It defines civil rights broadly and incorporates issues related to food justice as well as traditional doctrines addressing discrimination based on race, gender and other identities. As a start, the materials on racial discrimination serve as an anchor. The foundational framework for our civil rights laws is directly related to our racially discriminatory laws. For that reason, the textbook starts with landmark cases and historical developments impacting the social and legal treatment of blacks and other communities of color. Additionally, it asks students to think about what law is, what law is doing, and what it should be.

The coverage, then, expands to the diverse areas of civil rights laws. Throughout, students will learn the contours of each doctrine, the principles that form it and their practical relevance. This begins with a discussion of racial discrimination as the catalyst for civil rights jurisprudence in America. The Civil Rights Act and relevant doctrines of the 14th Amendment, are important to understanding the development of civil rights litigation. Ongoing and emerging issues affecting gay, transgender, women, nonconforming individuals and poor classes are also covered as vibrant parts of civil rights jurisprudence.

To this end, the book is divided into three parts: the first part deals with foundational and historical issues that impact today's jurisprudence. Chapters in this first section examine the road to *Brown* and the struggle for desegregation in school systems nationally. It also discusses pre and post Reconstruction cases and statutes still relevant today.

The second part of this text examines in detail the cases and laws that make up the modern civil rights landscape. As such, it starts with the Civil Rights Act and a close examination of Title VII, Tile IX and Title VI. This section also includes cases that make up the voting rights canon as well as chapters on disability law, language minorities, Section 1989, and gender discrimination.

Finally, the third section delves into a study of emerging issues in the twenty-first century. In these chapters, relevant issues include food rights and the struggle for sustainability as civil rights issues, food justice, gender identity, sexual orientation and same sex marriage, as well as litigation and models for educational equality beyond affirmative action.

To introduce these concepts, we ask students to consider and define what is and should be the role of law. Should law simply reflect the status quo or should it continuously work to serve disadvantaged groups? Depending on the identified role of law, what are the most effective means to achieve these goals? Similarly, each chapter opens by asking students to consider the role and operation of law in the specific doctrines and facts discussed.

Introduction

A. The Role of Law: Logic or Power?

The modern foundations of civil rights were laid in the last decades of the twentieth century. Those last decades ushered in a shift from color centric jurisprudence to the now accepted color blindness. That gargantuan process understandably appropriated jurisprudential energy and resources. Civil rights attorneys and activists remained busy with efforts to dismantle Jim Crow and to implement policies promoting integration. Desegregation, however, turned out to be a difficult task. *See Stout v. Jefferson Cty. Bd. of Educ.*, 250 F. Supp. 3d 1092 (N.D. Ala. May 9, 2017) (finding intentional discrimination, but still allowing the creation of a separate school system); *see also* U.S. GOVERNMENT ACCOUNTABILITY OFFICE, K–12 EDUCATION: BETTER USE OF INFORMATION COULD HELP AGENCIES IDENTIFY DISPARITIES AND ADDRESS RACIAL DISCRIMINATION (May 17, 2016), http://www.gao.gov/assets/680/676745.pdf (finding impoverished schools are concentrated with at least 75% Black or Hispanic children). In time, courts and judges seemed weighed down by it. The move from color consciousness to color blindness was painstaking and took much of the resources of those last decades. Looking back, it is, thus, not surprising that less thought was devoted to crafting a plan for implementing post-de jure desegregation. Much of the last 50 years has been dedicated to remedying and attempting to eradicate formal discrimination. Still, it persists in overt and covert forms.

Think of the shootings of Rodney King, Abner Louima, Michael Brown, and Alton Sterling, just to name a few, and, already, you'll conjure up a picture of some of the ongoing inequities persisting in the United States. *See* Chelsea Matiash & Lily Rothman, *The Beating that Changed America: What Happened to Rodney King 25 Years* Ago, TIME (Mar. 3, 2016), http://time.com/4245175/rodney-king-la-riots-anniversary/; Sewell Chan, *The Abner Louima Case, 10 Years Later*, N.Y. TIMES (Aug. 9, 2007), https://cityroom.blogs.nytimes.com/ 2007/08/09/the-abner-louima-case-10-years-later/; Larry Buchanan et al., *Q&A: What Happened in Ferguson?*, N.Y. TIMES (Aug. 10, 2015), https://www.nytimes.com/interactive/2014/08/13/us/ferguson-missouri-town-under-siege-after-police-shooting.html; Leah Donnella, *Two Days, Two Deaths: The Police Shootings of Alton Sterling and Philando Castile*, NPR (July 7, 2016), https://www.npr.org/sections/codeswitch/2016/07/07/485078670/two-days-two-deaths-the-police-shootings-of-alton-sterling-and-philando-castile. Racial bias, despite anti-discrimination statutes, remains an ongoing ill. Since 2006, for example, black men have died at the hands of the police at the rate of two a week. *See* Kevin Johnson, Meghan Hoyer & Brad Heath, *Local police involved in 400 killings per year*, USA TODAY (Aug. 15, 2014), https://www.usatoday.com/story/news /nation/2014/08/14/police-killings-data/14060357/ (reviewing FBI report of justifiable homicides for a seven-year period ending in 2012); *see also* Michelle Ye Hee Lee, *The viral claim that a black person is killed by police 'every 28 hours'*, WASH. POST (Dec. 24, 2014), https://www.washingtonpost.com/news/fact-checker/wp/2014/12 /24/the-viral-claim-that-a-black-person-is-killed-by-police-every-28-hours/?utm _term=.b4f013560bb6 (citing USA Today's "review of the most recent accounts of justifiable homicide reported to the FBI"). Furthermore, the rate of income inequality is increasing in this country faster than even during the great depression. Additionally, sexual assault cases proliferate, both in higher education, in K-12 settings and in the streets of America, each day, each passing week, revealing a new failure and throwback to gender stereotypes. Recent and ongoing allegations of gender based harassment in virtually all sectors of society bring these realities to the mainstream's consciousness. In the midst of it all, law and courts still struggle to fully grasp the pervasiveness and complexities of these issues.

In 2014, for example, the Department of Education identified at least 50 colleges and universities accused of disregarding sexual assault complaints and of overlooking complaints by victims in contravention of Title IX of the Civil Rights Act. As a result, the Department undertook massive investigation of these schools and of the handling of sexual assault in education. Sadly, this pattern is duplicated in practically every sphere of society. The military, for example, has been under scrutiny for failing to investigate and litigate complaints of sexual abuse, with only 2,892 of the reported 6,172 sexual abuse cases considered for possible action by the Department of Defense. DEP'T OF DEFENSE, ANNUAL REPORT ON SEXUAL ASSAULT IN THE MILITARY, App. B: Statistical Data on Sexual Assault (2016) http://www .sapr.mil/public/docs/reports/FY16_Annual/FY16_SAPRO_Annual_Report.pdf (reporting 14,900 service members experienced some type of sexual assault in 2016). Still more cases of sexual abuse remain unreported due to this hostile climate. In the private sphere, domestic abuse remains one of the leading causes of death for women. *See* Emiko Petrosky et al., *Racial and Ethnic Differences in Homicides of Adult Women and the Role of Intimate Partner Violence — United States, 2003–2014*, CDC (July 21, 2017), https://www.cdc.gov/mmwr/volumes/66/wr /mm6628a1.htm?s_cid=mm6628a1_ w#suggestedcitation (citing a CDC report finding that one leading cause of death for women is homicide, and nearly half of the victims are killed by current or former intimate partners); *see also* Melissa Jeltsen, *Who Is Killling American Women? Their Husbands And Boyfriends, CDC Confirms.*, HUFFINGTON POST (July 21, 2017), https://www.huffingtonpost.com/entry /most-murders-of-american-women-involve-domestic-violence_us_5971fc f6e4b09e5f6cceba87. Similarly, ongoing sexual assault and domestic abuse cases involving the NFL and other athletic contexts are staunch reminders of that reality.

After reading about these reports, you might be asking yourself why the inequities, inherited from past centuries with blatant discriminatory structures, still persist today. That is the right question to ask. Tracing the historical root of specific inequities and interrogating legal doctrines designed to address them are instrumental steps to mastering civil rights law. These steps are also pre-requisites to devising potential solutions to these problems.

Students of the law often feel consternation about the fact that legal rules do not meet their vision of justice; that laws often reveal themselves to be imperfect, and even, that law can cause new problems. While we think of law as a tool for problem solving in helping to create law and order, in the civil and human rights field, there remains constant frustration with the discrepancy between the spirit of justice and the practicality of rulemaking and implementation. *See Gloucester Cty. Sch. Bd. v. G.G.*, 137 S. Ct. 1239 (2017) (remanding the case to the Fourth Circuit for further consideration in light of the guidance document issued by the Department of Education and Department of Justice on Feb. 22, 2017); *Stout v. Jefferson Cty. Bd. of Educ.*, 250 F. Supp. 3d 1092 (N.D. Ala. May 9, 2017) (finding intentional discrimination, but still allowing the creation of a separate school system); *see also* Hiba Hafiz, *How Legal Agreements Can Silence Victims of Workplace Sexual Assault*, THE ATLANTIC (Oct. 18, 2017), https://www.theatlantic.com/business/archive/2017/10/legal -agreements-sexual-assault-ndas/543252/. Why is that? Why is it so difficult for society and legal institutions to reach the ideal of justice espoused, for example, in our Constitution? In other words, what is the nature and role of law? And, how could we work to further meet its promise?

As we go forth into the twenty-first century, the limitations of the civil rights gains of the twentieth century have become a hotly debated issue. The fact is that, despite anti-discrimination laws, inequality rages on. For example, the gender wage gap persists, the American educational system remains de facto segregated, brutality against vulnerable bodies occurs routinely, economic inequalities are higher than in decades prior, and tensions in American society are at a higher rate than in recent memory. *See* Camille Patti, *Hively v. Ivy Tech Community College: Losing the Battle but Winning the War for Title VII Sexual Orientation Discrimination Protection*, 26 TUL. J.L. & SEXUALITY 133 (2017) (discussing circuit courts' unanimous holdings that Title VII does not prohibit discrimination based on sexual orientation); *see also Barber v. Bryant*, 860 F.3d 345 (5th Cir. 2017) (reversing an injunction on HB1523, and reinstating Mississippi's "Protecting Freedom of Conscience from Government Discrimination Act"); *Gloucester Cty. Sch. Bd. v. G.G.*, 137 S. Ct. 1239 (2017) (remanding the case to the Fourth Circuit for further consideration in light of the guidance document issued by the Department of Education and Department of Justice on Feb. 22, 2017). In addition, the gains of the twentieth century seem to have reached an impasse as the ranks of the marginalized are steadily increasing. *See* Claire Zillman, *Law Firms' Gender Diversity Programs Aren't Keeping Women in the Industry*, FORTUNE (April 19, 2017), http://fortune.com/2017/04/19/ big-law-firms-women/ (citing an ALM Legal Intelligence report finding that women make up 30% of lawyers at the nation's 200 largest law firms, and women account for 17% of equity partners and 25% of non-equity partners); Laura Kann, *Sexual Identity, Sex of Sexual Contacts, and Health-Related Behaviors Among Students in Grades 9–12 — United States and Selected Sites, 2015*, U.S. Dept. of Health and Human Servs. & Centers for Disease Control and Prevention (Aug. 12, 2016), https://www.cdc.gov/mmwr/volumes/65/ ss/pdfs/ss6509.pdf (finding 29.4% of LGBTQ students had attempted suicide one or more times in the year preceeding the survey); Ann P. Haas, Philip L. Rodgers & Jody L. Herman, *Suicide Attempts among Transgender and Gender Non-Conforming Adults: Findings of the National Transgender Discrimination Survey*, American Foundation for Suicide Prevention & The Williams Institute (Jan. 2014), http://williamsinstitute.law.ucla.edu /wp-content/uploads/AFSP-Williams-Suicide-Report-Final.pdf (reporting that 41% of transgender survey respondents had attempted suicide in their lifetime); NAACP, Criminal Justice Fact Sheet (last visited Nov. 8, 2017), http://www .naacp.org/criminal-justice-fact-sheet/ (reporting that, in 2014, African Americans constituted 34% of the total correctional population and are incarcerated at more than five times the rate of whites). Further, it is becoming more apparent that our laws need to be ameliorated and expanded to address new realities and the interests of those neglected for far too long. Still, what of the civil rights movement that ushered in these twentieth century laws? Why were its efforts and laws not enough to cure past and present problems? More specifically, what could we learn from its invaluable contributions to craft a successful twenty-first century civil rights movement? To answer these questions, it is imperative to investigate the underlying ideals and structures promoted by our legal system.

In this task, consider philosopher Jacques Derrida's description of law formation as inherently external:

> La loi, est la décision d'un autre, extérieur à ce qu'il instaure. Cette décision peut toujours arriver. Elle se présente comme un coup de force, un événement imprévisible, hors-la-loi, irréductible à la pensée de l'être, irracontable. Le droit qui en résulte est incalculable. Il excède, il disloque, il altère. Il n'a pas d'histoire, de genèse, de dérivation possible: c'est la loi de la loi, une loi qu'on ne peut ni approcher, ni représenter, dont on ne peut pas connaître l'origine, et pourtant qui s'impose, qui s'enforce, comme on dit en anglais (*to enforce the law*), dont la légitimité tient à une force interne, performative, mystique, à la fois justifiée et injustifiable.

> [Law is the decision of another, external to what it institutes. This decision can always come to fruition. Law presents itself like a blow, an unpredictable event, outside of the law, incapable of being reduced in one's thought, impossible to explain. The right that results is immeasurable. It exceeds, it displaces, it changes. There is no past, no genesis possible. It's law's law, a rule to which one cannot get close, nor represent or know its origin, but which nonetheless imposes itself, as it is said in English (*to enforce the law*),

its legitimacy deriving from an internal force, performance based, mystical, both justified and unjustified.][1]

As Jacques Derrida captures so well, law has two components that often come into conflict: the big ideas motivating it and its practical manifestation. The two can seem quite contradictory. One way to think of it is to imagine law *as simultaneously capturing the essence of justice, the whole structure so to speak, with legislation acting as parts of that whole.* Sometimes, ideas of what things should be are much more perfect than the steps we create to get to that image. So also are law's illustrations of steps created to reach the ideal, the essence of a fair world. Still, when looking at law via legal rules and manifestations, it is sometimes impossible to trace its origins to a big ideal, to a uniform concept of justice. Instead, law with a small "l" often results from political wrangling and backroom compromises. As a result, linking lawmaking, the big "L," to an ideal of justice often seems like a farfetched endeavor. These are the inherent conflicts and contradictions present in the legal system.

For Derrida, then, justice is both unknowable in its ideal form and knowable through processes of deconstruction that lead to the enactment of rules. In that process, though, Derrida sees violence and imposition of hierarchy that comes from the deference to law and enforcement. Visualize your idea of how laws should be enforced. Is the image inextricable from force? Do you see Derrida's criticism play out in your vision? Is it really impossible for law, law with a small "l" or justice with a small "j," to be enforced without force? Is our interaction with law enforcement laden with fears?

Alternatively, take any of the legal changes we ushered in during the twentieth century. The process of racial integration, for instance, involved force and violence by law enforcement and private resisters alike.

Integration is a perfect illustration of Derrida's point. Due to its dual nature, then, law becomes a powerful sovereign which, when unexamined, could run counter to the spirit of justice.

> On ne peut faire la loi, fonder, inaugurer ou justifier le droit que par un coup de force, un acte violent à la fois performatif et interprétatif. C'est une loi de structure: un pouvoir souverain ne se pose qu'en distinguant *lui-même* entre violence légale ou illégale. Sa structure fondamentale est tautologique. Si l'on obéit à ses lois, ce n'est pas parce qu'elles sont justes, mais parce qu'elles sont lois; si l'on y croit, ce n'est pas sur un fondement légal, mais mystique . . . Le pouvoir du souverain tient à la parole: c'est un effet de fable, de fiction. Il lui suffit de s'avancer silencieusement, à pas de loup, ou de se montrer dans son évidence visible, éclatante, dans la toute-puissance de son savoir, pour légitimer la violence.

---

1. Force de Loi — Le "Fondement Mystique de l'autorité" (Jacques Derrida, 1994) [FDL].

[Law cannot be created, right cannot be instituted or justified but by a strike of violence, a sort of violent act both performative and interpretative. That is a structural rule: dominating power only asserts itself by making a distinction between legal and illegal violence. It is a tautological structural foundation. If one obeys its rules, it's not because they are just, but because they are the laws; if one believes in them, it is not based on a legal foundation, but of a mystical one . . . Sovereign power is deeply attached to speech: it's a product fantasy and fiction. To legitimize violence, a powerful sovereign is equally contented to, either move silently, stealthily, or, to move ostensibly in all its resplendence, its all knowing power.]

Jim Crow, and its rules and cultural implementation, are vivid illustrations of the danger that law could evolve to be an unexamined sovereign maintained through violence and rigid implementation. Law can be tyrannical and wholly unreasonable in its enforcement. Consequently, just laws require thoughtfulness and work. They don't just happen. The fiction of inferiority underlying Jim Crow laws and practice further crystallizes the importance of constant deconstruction and interrogation in law making. If force and violence are inevitable in law making, it is incumbent on all to re-evaluate relevant laws and their by-products to ensure that they remain closer to the ideal of justice rather than based on contingent and subjugating biases.

Together with that process, then, is the reality that law making and interpretation are often conducted by those already in power. Thus, deconstruction and analysis are not enough. Inclusion and periodic re-evaluation are also necessary.

Not surprisingly, and because of this violent tendency inherent in law, the relationship of law to civil rights has been, at times, a contentious one. In fact, at various times in our history, law has been overtly hostile to civil rights. *See* Defense of Marriage Act, 1 U.S.C. § 7 (1996) (defining marriage as between a husband and wife, but later held unconstitutional by *United States v. Windsor*, 133 S. Ct. 2675 (2013); Public Law 503, 18 U.S.C. § 97a (1942) (permitting Japanese internment camps in the United States during World War II); Fugitive Slave Act of 1850, Ch. 60, 9 Stat. 462 (1850) (requiring escaped slaves to be returned to their owners); *see also* Plessy v. Ferguson, 163 U.S. 537 (1896); *Dred Scott v. Sandford*, 60 U.S. 393 (1857). Still, with all its contradictions, the promise of equity has always resided in the foundation of a progressive legal system structurally and textually (See generally the Bill of Rights, specifically the Due Process Clause of the U.S. Constitution, etc.). The tension creates a complex legacy of repression with a promise of liberty. For this reason, we must constantly take stock, re-evaluate our journey toward our democratic ideals and implement whatever new equity models are needed for evolving times. We are a nation of constant evolution; therein lies our greatest strength and discomfort.

We are at that re-evaluation point again today. The beginning of the twenty-first century marked just fifty years of civil rights reform in America. Though fifty years seem short, an exploration of the landscape reveals clearly that this is the perfect landmark for evaluation. A time to reconsider old strategies and devise new ones.

This type of introspection is a necessary part of progress. Legal reforms, when neglected, risk stagnation and paralysis. Further, key cases in the last 10 years indicate that current civil rights frameworks have reached an impasse. *See Masterpiece Cakeshop, Ltd. v. Colorado Civil Rights Comm'n*, 137 S. Ct. 2290 (2017); *Gloucester Cty. Sch. Bd. v. G.G.*, 137 S. Ct. 1239 (2017); *Burwell v. Hobby Lobby Stores, Inc.*, 134 S. Ct. 2751 (2014); *Town of Greece v. Galloway*, 134 S. Ct. 1811 (2014); *Shelby Cty. v. Holder*, 133 S. Ct. 2612 (2013); *Hosanna-Tabor Evangelical Lutheran Church & Sch. v. E.E.O.C.*, 565 U.S. 171 (2012). Still, it is one thing to know that methods have lost their luster and efficacy, but it is yet another to create and test new frameworks, to galvanize individuals and groups toward common interests. Those efforts and that task are yet to be concretized in the second phase of the long civil rights movement.

In light of the above discussion about the violence inherent in unchecked law making, consider the following questions: How is enforcement of the existing laws dependent on or comingled with violence, in the materials below? In the face of resistance, how easily did violence rear its head? Think, for example, of efforts to integrate the University of Mississippi with the admission of James Meredith. Think of the standoff between federal law enforcement and protestors resistant to integration. Think also of the role of the state law enforcement, of the Governor of Mississippi, defending the discriminatory state laws of the time. These events presented a classic clash between two entities trying to enforce two opposite laws, both demonstrating that lawmaking can lead to violence when met with resistance. Knowing this, how do we check laws and push them to manifest their most redemptive and transformative potential without devolving into repression? How could we inspire governments to curb their impulse to utilize violence in the name of efficiency? And, how do we, individually, resist modeling violence in our every day life, so we may live up to the ideals of justice that we want states and institutions to emulate?

B. If Law Is Power, Then What?

Using Derrida's concept of law as power and violence, much could be learned from the twentieth century's civil rights models and implementation. Equally as important are their limitations and shortcomings. Consequently, this book is a call for understanding the legacy of the civil rights movement, the deliberate application of these twentieth century seeds, and their import for emerging and current issues. A modern twenty-first century civil rights movement could learn from them and include, as part of its agenda: 1) relentless critical evaluations of laws' underpinnings to denounce and unearth patterns of marginalization; and 2) deliberate incorporation of *Brown*-based coalition building to secure consensus and solidify coalitions across groups. As we face the impasse caused by the limitations of the twentieth century identity-based laws, consider whether this two-prong model might prove more effective today. In so doing, think about current twenty-first century issues.

How could maximizing interests across differences and questioning the law's relationship to power help overcome current impasses?

To answer this question, twenty-first century activism and legal scholarship could benefit from a focus on life and inequities present at the margins of society. Further introspection could also include a strict review of past and existing civil rights cases. In so doing, a twenty-first century vision of the role of law could be extrapolated. In the twenty-first century, the role of law should be to address inequities by taking into account the lived realities of those at the margins of society. That translation and transposition from margin to mainstream is crucial to creating the type of understanding and empathy necessary to bridge the current gaps present in society today. Law and activism, thus, could move beyond social interests to incentive building.

Redefining the role of law as margin identifying would allow justice work to address current issues. As it stands, one of the perpetual complaints of law is its failure to systematically reflect subjugated interests. Rather, for most of its existence, American law has tended to reflect positions of power rather than that of the marginalized. As a consequence, those advocating for the interests of the excluded often feel like they are playing with inadequate tools. As Justice Holmes pointed out:

> The life of the law has not been logic: it has been experience. The felt necessities of the time, the prevalent moral and political theories, intuitions of public policy, avowed or unconscious, even prejudices which judges share with their fellow-men, have had a good deal more to do than the syllogism in determining the rules by which men should be governed.[2]

Thus, tackling legal precepts armed only with jurisprudential doctrines and individual fact patterns only maintains the stagnant status quo.

Lessons and deconstruction of twentieth century civil rights laws deepen understanding of the contributions of this prior movement. For example, the famed scholar, Derrick Bell, affirmed that civil rights lawyers working on desegregation were "serving two masters."[3] By this, Bell meant that the dual goals of integration and educational equality were often at odds with each other during litigation of the desegregation cases. As such, sometimes, the desire to achieve integration might have caused attorneys to evaluate proposed integration models inadequately, instead of making quality education for the plaintiffs the sole priority. Indubitably, it is easier 50 years after *Brown* to see the danger of an exclusive focus on integration. At the time, the emergency and the dire conditions of segregation often blurred the lines. As a result, Bell's observation or discussion of the twentieth century's shortcomings should not be viewed as an indictment of the civil rights attorneys then. Instead, Bell simply reminds us all with these words of the importance of critical analysis at

---

2. OLIVER WENDELL HOLMES, THE COMMON LAW 1 (Boston: Little, Brown, & Co. 1881).

3. Derrick Bell, *Serving Two Masters: Integration Ideals and Client Interests in School Desegregation Litogation* 85 YALE L.J., 470–516 (1976).

in every stage of a movement. Critical evaluation is crucial to tweaking and improving models inherited from prior generations. After all, as Frantz Fanon so aptly observed, "each generation must, out of relative obscurity, discover its mission, fulfill it, or betray it." Frantz Fanon, *On National Culture, in* THE WRETCHED OF THE EARTH (trans. Constance Farrington, Penguin: Harmondsworth 36 (1967). What is then our generation's task? How should we fulfill the promise inherited from twentieth century civil rights activists and scholars? To fully grapple with these issues, one must engage constantly with the foundational doctrines and structure of civil rights jurisprudence. This book starts this process by discussing key cases. To start, it examines cases that serve as the cornerstone of our civil rights jurisprudence so that students can understand the substance and methodology of today's litigation landscape. In so doing, it asks students to consider the efficacy of current standards and their effectiveness in promoting identified purposes. For example, our discrimination laws, as students will see here, are based on harm done to others based on race, sex, religion, etc. While these protections provide a good starting point, endorsement of these laws becomes restricted to those who fit these types of identity. What more, these laws constitute such a blueprint that most of activism around civil rights issues tends to follow the identity points. How much more powerful would it be if, instead of more routine single cause and identity movements, more models designed to serve multiple intersecting interests were crafted? What effects could that coalition building and merging of interests have on civil rights movements' lasting success?

Desegregation cases and the regression of twentieth century civil rights gains illustrate, partly, the limitations of the jurisprudence's reliance on singular characteristics like race, gender, religion, etc. *Brown v. Board of Education*, for example, remains often identified in the legal narrative, as a decision beneficial for African Americans, or protecting against racial discrimination generally. Nonetheless, a closer look at *Brown* and its progeny makes clear that its tenets ushered in laws that provided legal protections across racial, gender, ability, and orientation. Furthermore, the grassroots activism leading to *Brown* also demonstrates deep benefits stemming from coalition building across racial groups. Such coalition building at the grassroots level changed the conscience of a nation as well as, eventually, that of the Supreme Court.

As you study the foundational cases and literature, think about an alternative model for advancing the ball in civil rights litigation. Perhaps, this alternative perspective could be two-fold. It could (1) define the purpose of civil rights laws then, now, and in the future, as protecting the marginalized. If, as we discussed above, law tends to organically reflects existing hierarchies, then it is always at risk of being a conduit for marginalization. Thus, all in society have a vested interest in preventing its potential negative effects. This means that there might be a danger of marginalization and fear of marginalization that unites, rather than divides. This realization should lead to the second step, which is: (2) to continuously identify sites in society of unchecked power and marginalization. This should be understood as

xxviii   INTRODUCTION

an ongoing process. Sites of power shift, develop, and evolve periodically depending on circumstances, context, and resources. Law tends to reflect these shifts. The result could be a sort of unified vigilance, a common awareness of issues that build bridges, causing an ongoing critical evaluation of law.

What about you? What would you suggest as a solution or methodology to prevent the type of destruction that oppressive legal structures can wreak on individuals' civil rights? Do you agree that law is inherently based on power and opposed to civil rights, when not deconstructed and checked? What model might you propose to address its limitations?

Part I

Foundations: Historical, Social, and Legal

Chapter 1

Historical Background

A. From Ideals to Reality

A free negro of the African race, whose ancestors were brought to this country and sold as slaves, is not a "citizen" within the meaning of the Constitution of the United States . . . When the Constitution was adopted, they were not regarded in any of the States as members of the community which constituted the State, and were not numbered among its "people or citizens." Consequently, the special rights and immunities guarantied to citizens do not apply to them. And not being "citizens" within the meaning of the Constitution, they are not entitled to sue in that character in a court of the United States, and the Circuit Court has no jurisdiction in such a suit.

—Justice Taney, *Dred Scott vs. Stanford*, 60 U.S. 393 (1857)

Representatives and direct taxes shall be apportioned among the several states which may be included within this union, according to their respective numbers, which shall be determined by adding to the whole number of free persons, including those bound to service for a term of years, and excluding Indians not taxed, three fifths of all other Persons.

—United States Constitution, Article 1, Section 2, Paragraph 3

In general, their existence appears to participate more of sensation than reflection. To this must be ascribed to their disposition to sleep when abstracted from their diversions, and unemployed in labour. An animal whose body is at rest, and who does not reflect, must be disposed to sleep of course. Comparing them by their faculties of memory, reason, and imagination, it appears to me, that in memory they are equal to the whites; in reason much inferior, as I think one could scarcely be found capable of tracing and comprehending the investigations of Euclid; and that in imagination they are dull, tasteless, and anomalous.

—THOMAS JEFFERSON, NOTES ON THE STATE OF VIRGINIA 138–43 (William Peden ed., 1954).

We hold these truths to be self-evident, that all men are created equal, that they are endowed by their Creator with certain unalienable Rights, that among these are Life, Liberty and the pursuit of Happiness. — That to secure these rights, Governments are instituted among Men, deriving their just powers from the consent of the governed, — That whenever any Form of

Government becomes destructive of these ends, it is the Right of the People to alter or to abolish it, and to institute new Government, laying its foundation on such principles and organizing its powers in such form, as to them shall seem most likely to effect their Safety and Happiness.

—The Declaration of Independence para. 2 (U.S. 1776).

How do we reconcile these contrasting legacies and views of the role of law inherited from our country's framers and prior jurists? On the one hand, the Declaration of Independence portrays justice as transcendent, applying the notion of equality to all.[1] On the other, in *Dred Scott*, justice is hierarchical and violent.[2] Dred Scott, an enslaved African, could not enforce contractual terms against a white man because the law considered him inferior.[3]

As daunting as these inconsistencies and injustices might be, the first step for any American legal scholar is to understand the role they play in our legal system. Law does not exist in a vacuum. On the contrary, legal rules and legislative enactments are very much impacted by context, individuals, and the political realities of the time.[4] Attention to these factors in legal reasoning can help students to comprehend relevant legal foundations.

B. Theoretical and Legal Foundations of the Modern Civil Rights Movement

The Nation's founding is based on some of the most progressive ideals of their time. Influenced by Enlightenment philosophers, the Declaration of Independence and its accompanying debates capture some of the most pivotal and basic human yearnings for protection that existed. Unfortunately, in making a break from the monarchy, the Constitution failed to provide freedoms for all members of its society, namely enslaved Africans, women and the poor.[5] As a result, despite the promise

---

1. Declaration of Independence para. 2 (U.S. 1776).

2. Dred Scott v. Sandford, 60 U.S. 393, 407–27 (1856).

3. *Id.*

4. Mark A. Graber, *Desperately Ducking Slavery: Dred Scott and Contemporary Constitutional Theory*, 14 Const. Comment. 271, 286–87 (1997). Political pressures of the time influenced several Justices in the *Dred Scott* majority. Justice Wayne thought that "the peace and harmony of the country required the settlement" of the status of slavery in the territories "by judicial decision." *Dred Scott*, 60 U.S. at 455 (Wayne, J., concurring). Justice Campbell maintained that he filed a separate opinion because of "the importance of the cause, the expectation and interest it has awakened, and the responsibility involved in its determination . . . ." *Dred Scott*, 60 U.S. at 493 (Campbell, J., concurring).

5. U.S. Const. art 1, § 9, cl. 1 (Constitution forbade Congress from stopping the importation of slaves from Africa for at least twenty years); U.S. Const. art. I, § 2, cl. 3 (Constitution counted slaves as only three-fifths of a person for purposes of apportioning representation and taxation); U.S. Const. art. 4, § 2, cl. 3 (Constitution still requires persons in the North to return runaway slaves).

inherent in the U.S. Constitution, the United States initially forged an incomplete social contract, one that said that the government only bore responsibility to some members of society. Over time, however, this contract was refined and revisited, with sometimes-painful strokes.[6]

As Dr. Martin Luther King, Jr. once said, "We have come to cash this check—a check that will give us upon demand the riches of freedom and the security of justice."[7] This statement captures the incomplete nature of the American experiment. The framers themselves knew that it was incomplete at the time of framing. This understanding is revealed in their agreement to classify enslaved Africans as three-fifths of people.[8] Though much progress has resulted in the last part of the twentieth century, this initial, imperfect, contract still influences current relationships and debates.

> The clauses that [Southerners] worked hard to create set the stage for a government that both protected slavery and was deeply influenced by it. This, in turn, shaped American race relations, not only in the antebellum period, but also during Reconstruction and beyond. In addition, the jurisprudence of slavery had long-term implications for American constitutional law. Some clauses that were inserted into the Constitution to specifically protect slavery, such as the Electoral College, continue to haunt the political structure. Other clauses inserted to protect slavery, such as the two prohibiting export taxes, remain lurking in our Constitution, perhaps to rear their heads to prevent some useful public policy initiative in the future. To this day, inequities associated with race, racism, and racial separation trouble our society and our legal system. Race remains America's greatest social problem, as it has been since the nation's founding. Since 1776, Americans have repeatedly failed to implement our national credo, that all people "are created equal, that they are endowed by their Creator with certain unalienable Rights, that among these are Life, Liberty, and the Pursuit of Happiness."[9]

It is significant that, despite the weight of this legacy, and perhaps because of it, the words slavery and slaves does not appear in the original Constitution. Slavery is mentioned once in the Thirteenth Amendment, one of the Reconstruction Amendments.[10] This reluctance to face the inequitable realities is often reflected in current national discourse around civil rights issues. To a certain extent, this discomfort around race trickles down to other excluded groups, like women and disabled

---

6. Civil Rights Act of 1964; Voting Rights Act of 1965; Housing Rights Act of 1968; Civil Rights Act of 1990.

7. Martin Luther King, "I Have a Dream" (speech, Civil Rights March in Washington, DC, August 28, 1963).

8. U.S. Const. art. I, §2, cl. 3.

9. Paul Finkelman, *How the Proslavery Constitution Led to the Civil War*, 43 RUTGERS L.J. 405, 412–13 (Fall/Winter 2013).

10. U.S. Const. amend. XII.

persons, who were similarly neglected in the framers' promulgation of rights.[11] The American community, "in its 'process of . . . self-definition'—the making of citizenship determinations—often has perverted settled and clear legal principles, as well as the ideological underpinnings of the nation, to exclude groups perceived as racially and culturally inferior to avoid 'degrading' the national community and collective national character."[12] Consider the criticisms levied against current civil rights doctrines and consider whether vestiges of inequities traceable to the framing of our Constitution still play a role in today's implementation of equity models.

In this section, you will cover statutes and constitutional amendments designed to undo the harm and mistakes that burdened the original Constitution. The Civil Rights Act of 1964,[13] Voting Rights Act of 1965,[14] and the American with Disabilities Act of 1990[15] are all mammoth statutes that attempt to remedy the harm perpetuated in the first centuries of the United States. It is significant, also, to note that these statutes, in many ways, attempt to revisit the original agreement negotiated by the framers of our Constitution in relation to equity by placing burdens on states and private individuals; burdens that even today are heavily contested. The Civil Rights Act of 1964, for example, imposes obligations not to discriminate based on race or gender using incentives under the Spending Clause of the Constitution in Title VI[16] and Title IX.[17] Also, consider that Title VII of the Civil Rights Act imposes non-discriminatory restrictions. Title VII applies to states as employers, as well as to private entities. The ADA explicitly burdens states in Title II of the Act.[18] These measures expand the scope and contour of the American contract; not only between the government and its citizens, but also between the federal government and the now fifty states.

---

11. Jonathan C. Drimmer, *The Nephews of Uncle Sam: The History, Evolution, and Application of Birthright Citizenship in the United States*, 9 Geo. Immigr. L.J. 667, 668–69 (1995) (quoting Gerald L. Neuman, *Justifying U.S. Naturalization Policies*, 35 Va. J. Int'l L. 237, 251 (1994).

12. *Id.*

13. Civil Rights Act of 1964, Pub. L. No. 88-352, 78 Stat. 241 (codified as amended in scattered sections of 2 U.S.C., 28 U.S.C., and 42 U.S.C.).

14. Voting Rights Act of 1965, Pub. L. No. 89-110, 79 Stat. 445 (codified as amended at 42 U.S.C. §§ 1971, 1973 to 1973bb-1 (1994)).

15. Americans with Disabilities Act of 1990 (ADA), 42 U.S.C. §§ 12101–12213 (amended 2008).

16. 42 U.S.C. § 2000d *et seq.*

17. 20 U.S.C. § 1681 *et seq.*

18. 42 U.S.C. § 2000e *et seq.*

Chapter 2

From the Civil Rights Act to Today

Law As Power

I urge you again, as I did in 1957 and again in 1960, to enact a civil rights law so that we can move forward to eliminate from this Nation every trace of discrimination and oppression that is based upon race or color. There could be no greater source of strength to this Nation both at home and abroad.

We have talked long enough in this country about equal rights. We have talked for one hundred years or more. It is time now to write the next chapter, and to write it in the books of law.[1]

—President Lyndon Johnson

Brown vs. Board of Education is often referred to as ending legal segregation in the United States. This is so because, as you will see below, the Court, in that case, declared for the first time that separation of the races could never be equal. Still, in practicality, the *Brown* opinion did not automatically end segregation. Subsequent litigation was necessary to desegregate other spheres of society, such as housing, public transportation, marriage, etc. In addition, even in education, desegregation did not take effect easily after *Brown*. Despite the ruling, efforts to desegregate were met with resistance and often violence.

That reality demonstrates the importance of a consistent and focused legal strategy when attempting to change legal structures. The legal strategy that led to *Brown* had to be followed up by similar litigation in all contexts to fully dismantle legal segregation. The Road to *Brown* is a term often used as shorthand by legal historians to describe the long quest to dismantle Jim Crow. Specifically, it captures the legal assault conducted by Charles Hamilton Houston and Attorney Thurgood Marshall, who together chipped away at the theoretical foundations of the "separate but equal" mandate in education through continuous litigation.[2] That quest reached

---

1. Address to a joint session of Congress on November 27, 1963. President Lyndon Johnson requested quick action on a civil rights bill.
2. *Id.*

its apogee with *Brown*.[3] Still, after *Brown*, practical enforcement of anti-segregation mandates was needed in all sectors.[4]

Particularly, it became quickly apparent, that despite *Brown*, a discrimination-free society could not be achieved without a system wide overhaul. For example, it became obvious that social attitudes and bias in employment, and in private accommodations, played very important roles in maintaining the myth of racial inferiority. Rhetoric and impleaders to goodwill would not be enough. In the years after *Brown*, hostility and resistance to integration required specific action from the federal government.[5] Still, action did not come swiftly.

During the years following *Brown*, visuals of horrific and dehumanizing attacks against African Americans via water hoses and attack dogs were routinely broadcast. With the advent of television in most homes at the time, the world and the country took notice. The sight, for example, of representative John Lewis, then 25 years old, getting clobbered by police officers[6] and the bloody faces of women, men and teenagers on the Edmund Pettus Bridge in Selma, Alabama attacked by the Alabama Police,[7] sent a clear message to the rest of the United States. Americans realized that the violence could no longer be ignored.

On May 2, 1963, a horrified country watched on television as the public safety commissioner of Birmingham, Alabama, T. Eugene "Bull" Connor, and his policemen and firemen descended on hundreds of African American marchers, including schoolchildren, with attack dogs, nightsticks, and fire hoses. In response to the resulting national uproar, on June 11, President Kennedy announced on national television that he was sending a tough civil rights bill to Congress. A few hours later, Medgar Evers, director of the Mississippi National Association for the Advancement of Colored People (NAACP), was murdered in the driveway of his house.[8]

And, perhaps an even more compelling argument for the federal government, these images raised deep questions as to the purported authority of the United States to taunt democracy as the opposite of communism when democracy did not exist within that country's borders at the time. This is what scholar Derrick Bell calls a perfect instance of interest convergence. In the second half of twentieth century,

---

3. U.W. Clemon & Stephanie Y. Moore, *Justice Clarence Thomas: The Burning of Civil Rights Bridges*, 1 Ala. C.R. & C.L. L. Rev. 49, 51 (2011).

4. Brando Simeo Starkey, *Jim Crow, Social Norms, and the Birth of Uncle Tom*, 3 Ala. C.R. & C.L. L. Rev. 69, 76–85 (2013).

5. Ian F. Haney, *"A Nation of Minorities": Race Ethnicity, and Reactionary Colorblindness*, 59 Stan. L. Rev. 985, 1001, 1002 (2007) ("Even a decade after *Brown* . . . virtually no southern school systems had actually desegregated.").

6. Margaret Burnham, *The Long Civil Rights Act and Criminal Justice*, 95 B.U. L. Rev. 687, 706 (2015).

7. James D. Wascher, *"I Feel the Pain of Racism in My Bones": Richard F. Morrisroe's Story*, 15-May CBA Rec. 46 (2001).

8. LBJ Champions the Civil Rights Act of 1964, Part I, http://www.archives.gov/publications/prologue/2004/summer/civil-rights-act-1.html.

then, America's global position as a champion of democracy was deeply endangered by Jim Crow and its oppressive structures. So it is, then, that in the years following *Brown*, the federal government was straddled by these various dynamics, hesitating as to the best cause of action and hoping to avoid conflicts. Images from Selma and terror tactics like the bombing and the death of four little girls in Birmingham,[9] made the hope of a conflict-free transition to integration a chimera. Enter President Lyndon Johnson, who had to, after the assassination of President Kennedy, decide on a course of action for systemic resolution of these issues. From these legal, social and political realities came the Civil Rights Act of 1964.

The political wrangling leading to the bill tells the story of a time where it became necessary for unlikely allies to combine forces to move the country forward. It also demonstrates that revolutionary changes, ironically, can be very much interest driven. For example, before his death, President Kennedy purposefully ordered the civil rights bill to be held back because of his desire to pass a tax reduction bill that, at the time, took priority for him.[10] That decision delayed the passage of the Act. President Kennedy did not live to see the Act come to fruition.

Another example of interest convergence lies in the passage of the earlier, weaker civil rights bills. These bills were hollow and ineffective. Still, then-Senator Lyndon Johnson's political maneuvering in convincing Southern representatives to pass these bills provides a window as to the comingling of interests often needed for political change. Then-Senator Johnson's success in passing the much-forgotten earlier versions of the civil rights bills reveals an emphasis on individual and political interest as a primary tool for achieving reform.

For example, one key to Johnson's success in passing these two bills was his maximizing of two unrelated interests: civil rights and dam construction in Hells Canyon in the Sawtooth Mountains of America's far Northwest. Western senators were eager for the dam, which would produce enormous amounts of electricity. For years, the advocates of public power and private power interests had fought to determine whether the dams would be built by government or private companies. Those favoring public power were generally liberals from the Northwest states. They were liberal on civil rights as well, but they had no large numbers of African American voters in their states to answer to, so a vote against civil rights would not have hurt them very much. President Johnson brokered an agreement that traded some of their votes to support the southern, conservative position favoring a weak civil rights bill. In return, southerners voted for public power at Hells Canyon.[11] Note, however, the limited civil rights gains here. In this example, civil rights

---

9. S. Willoughby Anderson, *The Past on Trial: Birmingham, The Bombing, and Restorative Justice*, 96 CAL. L. REV. 471 (2008).

10. Burnham, *supra*, at 688.

11. Ted Gittinger & Allen Fisher, *LBJ Champions the Civil Rights Act of 1964*, NATIONAL ARCHIVES, available at http://www.archives.gov/publications/prologue/2004/summer/civil-rights -act-1.html.

interests were greatly sacrificed for the political and personal desires of the Western representatives.

They got the dam by agreeing to a weaker bill. In turn, Southern representatives were able to maintain the political power and repression in their states because they succeeded in weakening the proposed legislation. This is a cautionary tale. Interest convergence provides a pragmatic, legally realistic lens for understanding legal and institutional limitations. While it does show interest maximization as an important step for political progress, it does also warn about personal limitations and ambitions overtaking social and equitable interests during negotiations.

In light of this, the long view of civil rights legislation requires a realistic understanding of the practical manifestations of these power dynamics. This realization that progress does not traditionally occur from a mere moral imperative, but rather from self-interest or from a driving thirst for exercise of power, might cause law students to feel despondent. Yet, it is that flawed reality which could present the greatest hope for progressive concretization of justice based ideals. It will not, however, happen in a vacuum and without checks and balances. And, to offset backroom deals and personal motivations, one of the strongest checks will have to take the form of unwavering allyship.

The convergence of interests and push to pass what ultimately became the Civil Rights Act of 1964 speaks to the possibility of progressive transformation using all of these available tools. In retrospect, though the two earlier versions of the Act are generally considered toothless, they served a specific purpose:

> . . . [T]he 1957 Civil Rights Act was nearly toothless legislation—which is one reason it was able to win Senate approval. Still, it had significance. George Reedy, an assistant to President Johnson for many years, anticipated later authors with his evaluation of the 1957 Civil Rights Act, when he wrote in 1983:
>
>> "This is the point which has probably caused the most confusion among students of the political process. Their mistake has been to examine the 1957 bill *solely on the basis of its merits. The more important reality is that it broke down the barriers to civil rights legislation and made possible more sweeping acts which followed later. . . . [T]he Senate is an on-going body* and its acts must be analyzed not just in terms of what they do but how they pave the way for doing other things."[12] [Emphasis in the original.]

In his oral history, Representative Emanuel Celler of New York, then chairman of the House Judiciary Committee, who wrote the 1957 bill, may have

---

12. Oral history transcript, George E. Reedy, interview 4 (IV), 5/21/1982, by Michael L. Gillette, *LBJ Library Oral Histories*, LBJ Presidential Library, accessed October 28, 2017, http://www.discoverlbj.org:443/item/oh-reedyg-19820521-4-84-40.

overstated his case when he said that the finished Civil Rights Act "was a revolutionary bill . . . it was worth the compromise. . . . I think the liberals were pretty jubilant that we had this breakthrough."[13]

To label the 1957 Act revolutionary is clearly an overstatement. For example, the Act did not include an anti-lynching provision.[14] Still, it is a useful look at the role of political negotiations and backdoor channels in lawmaking. It also signaled to the most recalcitrant opponents of a civil rights act that a change, in a not too remote future, was inevitable. Ultimately a better and more equitable version was passed in 1964, including more sweeping measures than those negotiated in 1957 and 1960.[15] Contrary to the prior acts which focused on voting, the 1964 Act, while making some provisions for voting, mainly leaves that task for the subsequent Voting Rights Act of 1965. Still, the impact of the Civil Rights Act of 1964 is long lasting and ongoing, particularly in its use of the spending power to promote antidiscrimination.

In Title VI of the Act,[16] for example, entities and states receiving federal funding undertake not to discriminate.[17] In addition, the Act resulted in more sweeping coverage because of a failed gamble by Congressman Smith, who included "sex" as a last-minute part of Title VII[18] in the hope that such inclusion would derail its pas-

---

13. Ted Gittinger and Allen Fisher, *LBJ Champions the Civil Rights Act of 1964* Summer 2004, Vol. 36, No. 2 https://www.archives.gov/publications/prologue/2004/summer/civil-rights-act-1.html

14. Burnham, *supra*, at 698.

15. Burnham, *supra*, at 705 ("Its provisions addressed the right to vote, public accommodations, public education, discrimination in federal programs, and equal employment opportunities.").

16. 42 U.S.C. § 2000d.

17. See http://www.archives.gov/publications/prologue/2004/summer/civil-rights-act-2.html stating "The real hammer that broke segregated school systems, however, was Title VI, which barred discrimination in "any program or activity receiving Federal financial assistance." Gary Orfield has written that fund cutoffs accomplished more by the end of the Johnson administration than had a decade of litigation following the *Brown v. Board of Education* decision, giving the Civil Rights Act "more impact on American education than any of the Federal education laws of the twentieth century." Beyond its effect against racial discrimination, the language in this title was the model for subsequent anti-discrimination legislation affecting gender, disabilities, and age. And Hugh Davis Graham has argued that Title VI, not Titles II or VII, which appeared to be the most important at the time, was actually the most significant because of its application in succeeding years to other institutions that had come to rely on federal money. In the 1964 legislation, employment discrimination was addressed in Title VII, the only one in the 1964 act to include gender as a protected category, owing to Judge Smith's miscalculation. The principal objects of attention and controversy in 1964 were the provisions mandating desegregation of public accommodations and facilities. Title II contained the prohibition against discrimination on the basis of race, color, religion or national origin in public accommodations such as restaurants, lodgings, and entertainment venues if their operation "affect[ed] commerce" or if such discrimination was "supported by State action" such as Jim Crow laws. Title III permitted the Justice Department, upon receipt of a "meritorious" complaint, to sue to desegregate public facilities, other than schools, owned or operated by state or local governments. Title IV permitted the attorney general to file suit to desegregate public schools or colleges under certain conditions, but it explicitly did not empower any federal official or court to require transportation of students to achieve racial balance.

18. 42 U.S.C. § 2000e.

sage. In essence, the 1964 Act thus covered sex, religion and race, forcing the nation to grapple with what anti-discrimination should look like in these areas. Title VII, another part of the Civil Rights Act, regulates the employment sector. The following section explores the issues and questions faced by courts, legislators and society regarding the application of Title VII. We will explore Title VI and Title IX in subsequent chapters.

Consider the employment context discussed below. In what way, are there still discrepancies in case law between idealism and implementation? How would you change the current approach to achieve your vision of equity?

A. Employment

1. Title VII of the Civil Rights Act of 1964

Title VII of the Civil Rights Act of 1964 serves as foundation for many subsequent anti-discrimination statutes. As the precursor to many statutes, litigation under Title VII has fleshed out important issues in judicial interpretation of the statute, like scope of liability, burdens of proof, role of judiciary, etc. Furthermore, Title VII's racial discrimination jurisprudence is an important turning point in affording equal opportunity for marginalized groups including women, religious minorities, etc. *See Oncale v. Sundowner Offhore Servs.*, 523 U.S. 75 (1998) (prohibiting same-sex sexual harassment under Title VII); *Price Waterhouse v. Hopkins*, 490 U.S. 228 (1989) (finding a violation of Title VII when a woman was not given partnership because she acted too much like a man); *Meritor Savings Bank v. Vinson*, 477 U.S. 57 (1986) (finding sexual harassment that creates a hostile work environment prohibited under Title VII as a form of sex discrimination); *see also EEOC v. Abercrombie & Fitch Stores, Inc.*, 135 S. Ct. 2028 (2015) (holding a showing of the need for religious accommodation as a motivating factor in an employer's adverse employment decision sufficient to prove Title VII disparate treatment claims); *Trans World Airlines, Inc. v. Hardison*, 432 U.S. 63 (1977) (stating that Title VII requires employers to provide reasonable accommodations for employees' religious exercise). Title VII prohibits discrimination based on race, sex, religion and national origin. Note that the statute could be amended to expand protections to other groups, such as members of the LGBTQ community. As it stands, proposed amendments to the statute were passed by the U.S. Senate, but have failed to pass the House of Representatives. As a result, Title VII's protections do not reach discrimination based on sexual orientation. Consider, however, whether the sexual stereotyping doctrine, discussed below might, serve as an alternate source of protection for LGBTQ victims of discrimination.

Post-Civil Rights Movement litigation has exposed a number of issues: the Supreme Court struggled to balance anti-discrimination goals with market concerns, eventually causing substantial retrenchment and regression from protecting civil rights. Additionally, interpretation of civil rights statutes like Title VII have triggered some of the most vigorous back and forth between Congress and federal courts. Title VII litigation makes up a recurring part of the Supreme Court's docket and a substantial part of all federal courts'. At various times in the history of the statute, in 1991 and in 2008, Congress has directly responded to Supreme Court's narrowed interpretation of the statute by enacting specific amendments to Title VII. Conversely, Congress has also enacted amendments recognizing and validating judicial interpretations of Title VII that went beyond the four corners of the statute. For example, the viability of a disparate impact claim under Title VII was first recognized judicially, based on the Court's interpretation of the statute's legislative history, well before that right was codified by Congress in the statute.

So, what does Title VII provide and how exactly might one bring a claim under the statute? Imagine that your neighbor, Sue E., comes to you complaining that her work environment at Corporation X has become unbearable. She explains that, each time she has applied for an advertised management position at the Corporation, she has been passed over in favor of male employees although she is more qualified than most of them. In addition, she mentions comments made by her supervisors about women not being suited for leadership positions.

These facts alone do not automatically make a case of discrimination. However, they do provide the starting point for thinking about implementation of Title VII of the Civil Rights Act in all its nuances.

Title VII litigation is divided into disparate treatment and disparate intent litigation. This distinction has been delineated by the Court based on 703(1) and 703(2) of the statute. The first is deemed to regulate intentional discrimination and the second, impact litigation. Specifically, Section 703 states:

> It shall be an unlawful employment practice for an employer—
>
> (1) to fail or refuse to hire or to discharge any individual, or otherwise to discriminate against any individual with respect to his compensation, terms, conditions, or privileges of employment, because of such individual's race, color, religion, sex, or national origin; or
>
> (2) to limit, segregate, or classify his employees or applicants for employment in any way, which would deprive or tend to deprive any individual of employment opportunities or otherwise adversely affect his status as an employee, because of such individual's race, color, religion, sex, or national origin.

As a prerequisite, Title VII claims can only be brought against employers with 15 or more employees for 20 or more calendar weeks.[19] Consequently, small businesses with less than 15 employees are not covered. Additionally, litigation arises as to whether someone qualifies as an employee for the sake of meeting the threshold requirement for coverage. Cases trying to determine whether someone classifies as

---

19. 42 U.S.C. § 2000e(b).

an employee have traditionally revolved around common law notions of control and master servant relationship.[20]

Title VII is administered by the Equal Employment Opportunity Commission ("EEOC"). The EEOC issues rules and regulations regarding the litigation of Title VII claims. Under the statute, to file an employment discrimination claim plaintiffs must file a complaint with the EEOC within 180 days of the adverse employment action in question. The EEOC in turn investigates the claim and issues what is called "a right to sue letter," a letter informing the plaintiffs as to the result of the EEOC investigation. These steps pose tremendous hurdles for plaintiffs. Only about 10% of right to sue letters end up in a finding of discrimination. A right to sue letter triggers the timeline for plaintiffs to file a claim in federal court. Plaintiffs must file their claim within 90 days of receipt of that letter.

Federal and state discrimination offices often have concurrent offices handling discrimination claims. For that purpose, many states have created deferral and non-deferral structures for determining the statute of limitations for a discrimination claim. Whether in a deferral or non-deferral state, for example, plaintiffs might have 300 days, taking in consideration the state agency's role in investigating discrimination claims. Others, in contrast, abide by the 180-day federal deadline, with the EEOC shouldering the investigation.

These procedural issues, whether a plaintiff filed a timely claim under the statute and when they knew or should have known of the employment action, often derail plaintiffs' pursuit of discriminatory claims. This fact prompted the enactment of the Lilly Ledbetter Act of 2009, which reversed the Supreme Court's decision in *Ledbetter v. Goodyear Tire & Rubber Co., Inc.*[21] In *Ledbetter*, the Supreme Court substantially restricted the time limit for filing a complaint of discrimination regarding compensation. The act of Congress reversing that ruling is named after the named plaintiff in that case. The Lilly Ledbetter Fair Pay Act of 2009[22] allows plaintiffs' limitations periods to extend to the time they discover the discrimination. For that reason, that statue contains an "explicit retroactivity provision."[23] Furthermore, preliminary issues, like whether "an employment contract" existed, further impact the

---

20. 46 Am Jur 2d Job Discrimination § 109; Farlow v. Wachovia Bank of North Carolina, N.A., 259 F.3d 309 (4th Cir. 2001) (even though the bank provided the attorney with a computer and exercised control over some administrative details, the attorney was not paid a salary, the bank did not withhold taxes, the attorney did not receive benefits, the attorney filed tax returns under a self-employed status, the attorney and bank had a written contract labeling the attorney as an independent contractor, the attorney had other clients, and the bank did not exercise control over the manner of the attorney's work); Pisharodi v. Valley Baptist Medical Center, 393 F. Supp. 2d 561 (S.D. Tex. 2005) (noting that hospital did not have the right to supervise neurosurgeon, beyond ensuring that he was not engaging in malpractice, or to control his work schedule).

21. 550 U.S. 618 (2007).

22. Lilly Ledbetter Fair Pay Act of 2009, Pub. L. No. 111-2, § 3, 123 Stat. 5 (to be codified at 42 U.S.C. § 2000e-5(e)(3)).

23. EEOC, Equal Pay Act of 1963 and Lilly Ledbetter Fair Pay Act of 2009, https://www.eeoc.gov/eeoc/publications/brochure-equal_pay_and_ledbetter_act.cfm.

success of claims. Additional issues, as to whom Title VII covers and whether claims of discrimination by transgender claimants would fit the definition of "sex" discrimination under Title VII, are the subject of ongoing debate and litigation.

The first section of this chapter explores the disparate treatment doctrine and its various components (disparate treatment and systemic disparate treatment and the forms of proof delineated by the Court for proving a case under Title VII's intentional discrimination in the racial context). It also examines how these issues play out in litigation, using lower court debates and splits in their review of summary judgment motions. This section then reviews the issues raised by disparate impact doctrine, the particular difficulties inherent in proving these types of cases, along with the defenses available under each branch of the Title VII doctrine. Cases involving claims of employment discrimination based on gender are explored in Chapter 3. Chapter 3 evaluates gender discrimination jurisprudence by reviewing claims brought under Title VII, as well as other anti-discrimination doctrines like Title IX and the Fourteenth Amendment. It focuses on specific issues and peculiarities inherent to the intentional gender discrimination context, with namely the sexual harassment, grooming and sex stereotyping lines of cases.

In the above hypo, Sue would have to satisfy a number of additional procedural requirements in order to bring a claim. A second preliminary step for addressing Sue's concerns would involve investigating the nature and scope of her employment contract in order to determine whether the contractual terms at issue or the subject of discrimination fit the Court's interpretation of what is meant by "terms of employment" in section 703(a). *Hishon v. Spaulding* below illustrates the type of analysis required when assessing "terms" of employment. As you review this case, try to determine how courts interpret the "terms, conditions, or privileges of employment." For example, what could "terms" of employment entail? Does partnership fit what we consider as a "term" of employment?

Hishon v. King & Spaulding

467 U.S. 69 (1984)

Chief Justice BURGER delivered the opinion of the Court.

We granted certiorari to determine whether the District Court properly dismissed a Title VII complaint alleging that a law partnership discriminated against petitioner, a woman lawyer employed as an associate, when it failed to invite her to become a partner.

I

In 1972 petitioner Elizabeth Anderson Hishon accepted a position as an associate with respondent, a large Atlanta law firm established as a general partnership. When this suit was filed in 1980, the firm had more than 50 partners and employed approximately 50 attorneys as associates. Up to that time, no woman had ever served as a partner at the firm.

Petitioner alleges that the prospect of partnership was an important factor in her initial decision to accept employment with respondent. She alleges that respondent used the possibility of ultimate partnership as a recruiting device to induce petitioner and other young lawyers to become associates at the firm. According to the complaint, respondent represented that advancement to partnership after five or six years was "a matter of course" for associates "who receive[d] satisfactory evaluations" and that associates were promoted to partnership "on a fair and equal basis." Petitioner alleges that she relied on these representations when she accepted employment with respondent. The complaint further alleges that respondent's promise to consider her on a "fair and equal basis" created a binding employment contract.

In May 1978 the partnership considered and rejected Hishon for admission to the partnership; one year later, the partners again declined to invite her to become a partner. Once an associate is passed over for partnership at respondent's firm, the associate is notified to begin seeking employment elsewhere. Petitioner's employment as an associate terminated on December 31, 1979.

Hishon filed a charge with the Equal Employment Opportunity Commission on November 19, 1979, claiming that respondent had discriminated against her on the basis of her sex in violation of Title VII of the Civil Rights Act of 1964, 78 Stat. 241, as amended, 42 U.S.C. § 2000e et seq. Ten days later the Commission issued a notice of right to sue, and on February 27, 1980, Hishon brought this action in the United States District Court for the Northern District of Georgia. She sought declaratory and injunctive relief, back pay, and compensatory damages "in lieu of reinstatement and promotion to partnership." . . .

The District Court dismissed the complaint on the ground that Title VII was inapplicable to the selection of partners by a partnership. 24 FEP Cases 1303 (1980). A divided panel of the United States Court of Appeals for the Eleventh Circuit affirmed. 678 F.2d 1022 (1982). We granted certiorari . . .

. . .

At this stage of the litigation, we must accept petitioner's allegations as true. A court may dismiss a complaint only if it is clear that no relief could be granted under any set of facts that could be proved consistent with the allegations. *Conley v. Gibson,* 355 U.S. 41, 45–46 (1957). The issue before us is whether petitioner's allegations state a claim under Title VII, the relevant portion of which provides as follows:

(a) *It shall be an unlawful employment practice for an employer —*

(1) to fail or refuse to hire or to discharge any individual, or otherwise *to discriminate against any individual with respect to his compensation, terms, conditions, or privileges of employment, because of such individual's* race, color, religion, *sex,* or national origin

. . . .

[R]espondent argues that Title VII categorically exempts partnership decisions from scrutiny. However, respondent points to nothing in the statute or the legislative history that would support such a per se exemption. When Congress wanted to grant an employer complete immunity, it expressly did so.

. . .

. . . Petitioner alleges that respondent is an "employer" to whom Title VII is addressed. She then asserts that consideration for partnership was one of the "terms, conditions, or privileges of employment" as an associate with respondent. . . .

Once a contractual relationship of employment is established, the provisions of Title VII attach and govern certain aspects of that relationship. . . . In the context of Title VII, the contract of employment may be written or oral, formal or informal; an informal contract of employment may arise by the simple act of handing a job applicant a shovel and providing a workplace. The contractual relationship of employment triggers the provision of Title VII governing "terms, conditions, or privileges of employment." Title VII in turn forbids discrimination on the basis of "race, color, religion, sex, or national origin."

Because the underlying employment relationship is contractual, it follows that the "terms, conditions, or privileges of employment" clearly include benefits that are part of an employment contract. Here, petitioner in essence alleges that respondent made a contract to consider her for partnership. . . . Indeed, this promise was allegedly a key contractual provision which induced her to accept employment. If the evidence at trial establishes that the parties contracted to have petitioner considered for partnership, that promise clearly was a term, condition, or privilege of her employment. Title VII would then bind respondent to consider petitioner for partnership as the statute provides, *i.e.,* without regard to petitioner's sex. The contract she alleges would lead to the same result.

Petitioner's claim that a contract was made, however, is not the only allegation that would qualify respondent's consideration of petitioner for partnership as a term, condition, or privilege of employment. An employer may provide its employees with many benefits that it is under no obligation to furnish by any express or implied contract. Such a benefit, though not a contractual right of employment, may qualify as a "privileg[e]" of employment under Title VII. A benefit that is part and parcel of the employment relationship may not be doled out in a discriminatory fashion, even if the employer would be free under the employment contract simply not to provide the benefit at all. We conclude that petitioner's complaint states a claim cognizable under Title VII. Petitioner therefore is entitled to her day in court to prove her allegations. The judgment of the Court of Appeals is reversed, and the case is remanded for further proceedings consistent with this opinion.

It is so ordered.

Notes and Questions

1. The opinion states, "At this stage of the litigation, we must accept petitioner's allegations as true." This statement indicates at what stage of litigation the issue arose. More importantly, it reminds us of an important rule you might recall learning in civil procedure: Rule 12(b)(6) of the Federal Rules of Civil Procedure, i.e., the motion to dismiss stage. A motion to dismiss filed pursuant to Rule 12(b)(6) can foil a plaintiff's lawsuit, if their complaint is not properly drafted. At the point where parties are filing and/or responding to motion to dismiss, the complaint has already been filed with claims asserted based on relevant doctrine. As the majority indicates, this stage is most favorable to plaintiffs, because it comes with a presumption that allegations properly claimed are accepted as true. Still, the key is that the allegations must be coherent, framed within a cognizable relevant doctrine supported by sufficient facts. If these elements are not present, then a defendant's motion to dismiss could successfully allege that the Plaintiff failed to satisfy Rule 12(b)(6). The discovery process (interrogatories, depositions, etc.) is also key to helping plantiffs gather support for their claims, as well as help defendants support counter claims and defenses.

2. In *Hishon*, the majority determined that the Plaintiff alleged sufficient facts in the complaint to survive a motion to dismiss based on Rule 12(b)(6) of the Federal Rules of Civil Procedure. What kind of allegations should plaintiffs include in complaints in order to increase the likelihood of surviving that standard?

The issue in *Hishon* very much revolves around whether the privilege that she is seeking, "partnership," is connected and part of parcel of the terms of her employment. In *Hishon*, because the employer undertook to make partnership part of the terms of employment, i.e., that employees could be eligible for partnership if they meet the requirements, the employer was estopped from denying partnership if denial was based on characteristics protected by Title VII. Hishon argued that denial of partnership was based on sex. She was able to proceed with her suit and survive a motion to dismiss because her allegation satisfied the requirement for making a prima facie case and the basis of her suit, partnership, concerned a term of employment.[24]

3. To make a prima facie case under Title VII and survive a 12(b)(6) or summary judgment motion, Plaintiff must allege: 1) that Plaintiff is a member of a protected class (based on race, gender, religion, national origin); 2) that Plaintiff suffered an adverse employment action (e.g., the employee was qualified for the position, but

---

24. In 1984, the Supreme Court held that King & Spalding was subject to Title VII of the Civil Rights Act of 1964. Hishon v. King & Spalding, 104 S. Ct. 2229 (1984). The discrimination case was never tried, however, because the case was ultimately settled for an undisclosed amount. *See* Ann Hopkins, *Price Waterhouse v. Hopkins: A Personal Account of a Sexual Discrimination Plaintiff*, 22 Hofstra Labor & Emp. L.J. 357, 362 (2005).

did not get it); and 3) that the adverse action was caused by the employer's impermissible motive (e.g., Plaintiff was rejected because of her gender).[25]

Alleging these claims and meeting the prima facie case are only the beginning, however. Plaintiff carries the burden of proving them, and the means available to do so have been the subject of litigation and some confusion in the Court's treatment of these issues. These issues are discussed below.

4. Justice Powell seemed to correlate success of women in law firms with likelihood of non-discriminatory motive. "In admission decisions made by law firms, it is now widely recognized—as it should be—that in fact neither race nor sex is relevant. The qualities of mind, capacity to reason logically, ability to work under pressure, leadership, and the like are unrelated to race or sex. This is demonstrated by the success of women and minorities in law schools, in the practice of law, on the bench, and in positions of community, state, and national leadership. Law firms— and, of course, society—are the better for these changes." Consider the statistics about dearth of diversity in managing positions at law firms in the country.[26] Was Powell overly optimistic? Should lack of diversity in law firms serve as an indication of discrimination? (See reports stating that black women make up .56% of law firms).

---

25. McDonnell Douglas Corp. v. Green, 411 U.S. 792, 802 (1973).

26. *See* Elizabeth Olson, *"A Bleak Picture" for Women Trying to Rise at Law Firms*, N.Y. Times (July 24, 2017), https://www.nytimes.com/2017/07/24/bus iness/dealbook/women-law-firm -partners.html (stating a successful careers at law firms for women "remains an uphill endeavor," and "female lawyers largely remain boxed into the lower-ranking and lesser-paying jobs"); Claire Zillman, *Law Firms' Gender Diversity Programs Aren't Keeping Women in the Industry*, Fortune (April 19, 2017), http://fortune.com/2017/04/19/ big-law-firms-women/ (citing an ALM Legal Intelligence report finding that women make up 30% of lawyers at the nation's 200 largest law firms, and women account for 17% of equity partners and 25% of non-equity partners); Catherine Ho, *Women in charge of law firms a rarity*, Wash. Post (Sept. 22, 2013), https://www.washingtonpost .com/business/capitalbusiness/women-in-charge-of-law-firms-a-rarity/2013/09/20/97e37952-1f19 -11e3-8459-657e0c72fec8_story.html (reporting four percent of law firms are led by women and fifteen percent of equity partners in America's 200 largest law firms are women); *see also* Stephanie Russell-Kraft, *Top Lawyer to Investigate Legal Profession's Gender Problem*, Bloomberg (Sept. 19, 2017), https://biglawbusiness.com/lawyer-to-investigate-legal-professions-gender-problem/ (discussing a new project, *Achieving Long-Term Careers for Women in the Law*, to conduct national research determine the cause of women leaving their legal careers). The National Association of Women Lawyers (NAWL) reports that the number of female equity partners has increased by only 3% over the past ten years, the gender pay gap persists across all levels of attorneys, and women make up 25% of firm governance roles. Destiny Peery, *Number of women equity partners in law firms maintains a slow and steady pace*, NWLA (Sept. 19, 2017), file:///Users/kayleebeauchamp /Downloads/2017%20NAWL%20Survey%20Report.pdf. As of April 2016, the American Bar Association's Market Research Department calculated that women make up 36% of the legal profession. Commission on Women in the Profession, *A Current Glance at Women in the Law*, ABA (Jan. 2017), https://www.americanbar.org/content/dam/aba/marketing/women/current_glance_statistics _january2017.authcheckdam.pdf.

5. In an omitted portion of the opinion, King & Spalding argued that Title VII infringed on their First Amendment rights. How do you assess this argument? Note the majority's response:

> Moreover, as we have held in another context, "[i]nvidious private discrimination may be characterized as a form of exercising freedom of association protected by the First Amendment, but it has never been accorded affirmative constitutional protections." *Norwood v. Harrison*, 413 U.S. 455, 470, 93 S.Ct. 2804, 2813, 37 L.Ed.2d 723 (1973). There is no constitutional right, for example, to discriminate in the selection of who may attend a private school or join a labor union. *Runyon v. McCrary*, 427 U.S. 160, 96 S.Ct. 2586, 49 L.Ed.2d 415 (1976); *Railway Mail Assn. v. Corsi*, 326 U.S. 88, 93–94, 65 S. Ct. 1483, 1487–1488, 89 L.Ed. 2072 (1945).

6. In order to trigger protection under Title VII, the Court emphasizes that there must be an employment contract. The opinion, however, notes that the contract may be "oral, written, etc." This is, of course, in addition to falling under the Title VII coverage requirement for employers and employees. Recall that Title VII only protects employees working for employers with "15 or more employees" who work "20 or more calendar weeks." For example, in *Slack v. Havens* below, defendants unsuccessfully tried to argue that they did not qualify as employers under the statute. They claimed that the standard to use is a notion of "critical mass" in counting the number of employees. The Court quickly rejected that claim and concluded that the plain meaning of the language prevails. In other words, "Congress meant what it said and that Havens is indeed an 'employer' within the terms of the statute."[27]

Based on these specific parameters, not all employers can be sued under Title VII automatically, even if there exists an employment contract. The preliminary issue of whether King & Spaulding is "covered" under Title VII is not present in *Havens* because King & Spaulding is a large law firm with a well established roster

---

27. Slacks v. Havens: "Havens first argues that he is not an 'employer' within the meaning of the Civil Rights Act and that, consequently, the district court should have dismissed the action for lack of subject matter jurisdiction. According to his interpretation, the statute requires the existence of a 'critical mass' of 50 employees for a total of 20 weeks during the prior calendar year and only those months of the current year preceding the incident at issue. Such a reading, he contends, is required to give employers notice of their potential liability under Title VII before a discriminatory incident occurs, and to prevent after-the-fact divestiture of jurisdiction by an employer's reduction of the size of his work force to fall outside the statutory limit. These arguments are unpersuasive. Employers have had notice of the requirements of the Civil Rights Act since the time of its passage. Whether they could attempt to circumvent its provisions by manipulating the number of persons they employ is irrelevant to the problem of statutory construction facing us. The language of the statute is plain: Congress clearly spoke in terms of 'calendar years.' Although it would have been easy to incorporate appellants' 'critical mass' idea by measuring the relevant number of employees over the 24 months preceding the incident, the statute gives no evidence of such intent. We can therefore only conclude that Congress meant what it said and that Havens is indeed an 'employer' within the terms of the statute. (See, e.g., *Culpepper v. Reynolds Metals Co.* (5th Cir. 1970) 421 F.2d 888, 891.)"

of over 15 or more employees. *Hishon's* preliminary issues involved the nature of the contract and whether consideration for partnership was part of its terms. The lesson in *Hishon* is that if Plaintiff successfully proves that certain expectations and privileges were part of the contract, then, those terms could become subject to Title VII regulation. On the one hand, this expands protection for employees so that employment related terms other than hours of work, title, etc. can provide the basis of a Title VII claim. On the other hand, fear of litigation incentivizes employers who can to keep their roster below the requisite formula for qualifying as "employer" and "employee" for purposes of Title VII protection. For example, what protections remain available for employees working for employers with 14 employees and part time employees all below the 20-hour a week per calendar year benchmark? None under Title VII, though there might be available state claims to provide a remedy for alleged wrongs.

7. Based on the Court's rationale, what factors might you look at to determine if an alleged discrimination relates to "terms of employment"? Do all terms in a contract potentially subject an employer to liability if not given to all employees? How do we distinguish between those that might trigger liability and those that might not? Imagine that you are counsel for Wal-Mart, who is a major employer. What advice should you provide regarding how to best insulate the company from lawsuits like Hishon's? Does that create a loophole for employers to escape liability under Title VII?

8. In 1984, King & Spaulding, the defendant in *Hishon* had not yet had any woman partners. Does that seem odd for that time? Consider current statistics regarding gender breakdown at law firms cited in Note 2 above. Would you have expected greater representation by that time?

2. Forms of Proof

The next big hurdle a plaintiff might face after surviving a motion to dismiss is a defendant's motion for summary judgment. The first rule all attorneys must remember is that a plaintiif is responsible for convincing judge and, eventually a jury, from the beginning in most cases, until the very end of the lawsuit. You saw that responsibility at play in *Hishon* in reference to allegations in the complaint. That means that plaintiffs have to allege, adequately, facts that fit the required elements of a Title VII claim, i.e., that: 1) she is protected by Title VII; 2) suffered an adverse employment action; and 3) that the employment action was caused by the employer's impermissible motive. That has to be clear in the complaint. For example, imagine that someone files a complaint alleging: discrimination based on religion. They state that because they are Hindu, they were treated differently and were promoted and awarded more money because of that difference in treatment. That complaint might be dismissed based on those allegations, since this would-be-plaintiff would likely fail to meet the third element of a Title VII claim, "an adverse employment action." These facts fail to demonstrate any action detrimental to the employee, much less allege facts sufficient enough to withstand the 12(b)(6)motion. Thus, Title VII prohibits discriminatory actions by the employer that caused detriment to the employee. This means that the employee, to prove the case, not only has to prove the motive, but she also has to prove harm and a causal link between the harm and the impermissible motive.

Thus, in practice, since it is their duty to convince the trier of fact that discrimination did occur, the plaintiff has to surmount another tough hurdle: proving a discrimination claim. At the motion to dismiss stage, an employee might be able to allege enough facts to survive a motion to dismiss (Fed. R. Civ. P. 12(b)(6)) because plaintiffs need only allege enough facts which would be interpreted in the light most favorable to the nonmoving party, *see Ashcroft v. Iqbal*, 556 U.S. 662 (2009); *Bell Atlantic Corp. v. Twombly*, 550 U.S. 544 (2007)), but encounter greater difficulties at the summary judgment stage of litigation. As the litigation proceeds, parties should be busy with the process of discovery to unearth any potential additional evidence that supports their claim. Discovery itself can lead to substantial conflicts between parties, with defendant for example, being unwilling to produce relevant records, or a plaintiff being uncooperative at a particular deposition. Navigating the discovery process and knowing the landscape of the employment context well enough to know what documents to request is a skill that needs to be acquired swiftly by any employment discrimination attorney. One of the best ways to learn about the context that is the subject of the lawsuit is to travel to the actual location and interview as many employees as possible. Also, long and probing conversations with your employee-plaintiff are crucial in order to fully grasp all of the idiosyncrecies and patterns of that particular workplace. Imagine filing a claim of sex discrimination based on violation of the Equal Pay Act where your client claims to have systematically been underpaid by 20% less than her male counterparts for the last 15 years. Information regarding pay structures and merit measurements in the private workforce are some of the hardest to unearth. Moreover, much of the private companies' information on the issue is not public. In order to actively prepare for the discovery process and obtain useful and relevant records that can help prove the claim that an employer violates the Equal Pay Act, an attorney has to spend a tremendous amount of time investigating the employment context, understanding its culture by talking to as many employees as possible. This information informs better crafted and effective sets of interrogatories and depositions.

These are just the beginning preparations required to withstand a summary judgment motion by a defendant. In order to understand why this investigation matters even more for plaintiffs, we must turn to the standard of proof required for plaintiffs to prevail in Title VII disparate treatment claims. Again, recall that plaintiffs have the duty to pursuade the trier of fact using both arguments based on the doctrine and case law as well as produce documents/evidence. The Supreme Court over time has fleshed out the process for proving treatment based employment discrimination claims, once plaintiff has met the basic elements, cited above, of a Title VII allegation.

Rule 56 of the Federal Rules of Civil Procedure directs that summary judgment may be granted in favor of a moving party if there are no genuine issues of fact that would warrant submission to the jury. In other words, if a plaintiff fails to properly support its allegations in the manner mandated by the courts, their claim might fail on summary judgment. In order to create an evidentiary issue for Title VII disparate treatment claims, the Court used as foundation Rule 301 of the Federal Rules of Evidence. Rule 301 states: "In a civil case, unless a federal statute or these rules provide otherwise, the party against whom a presumption is directed has the burden of producing evidence to rebut the presumption." This rule encapsulates the burden of proof requirement which is essential to Title VII's evidentiary scheme.

Generally, the burden of proof shouldered by the parties is divided into burden of production and persuasion: 1) The burden of production refers to who has the obligation to submit evidence (or who gets to move forward with the evidence). In other words, it determines who has the obligation to come forward with the necessary factual evidence to support the claim (in some cases, defense) being asserted. 2) The burden of persuasion has to do with who has the obligation to convince the trier of fact. It has been described as the burden to persuade the trier of fact that the facts proposed are indeed true or more probable than not.

The specific contours of their applicability in various contexts are fleshed out by courts, state laws and federal statutes. Under Title VII, plaintiffs and defendants shoulder different burdens depending on whether the case rests on direct, circumstantial or mixed evidence. Direct evidence involves uncontroverted, first hand evidence of bad intent. Circumstantial evidence comes in when such uncontroverted evidence is lacking, but when the totality of the evidence can support an inference of discrimination. A mixed evidence case involves cases in which there exist both the presence of discriminatory motive on the part of the employer and bad performance by the employee that could justify the adverse employment action. To illustrate, let's consider Sue's case discussed above:

Assume Sue comes to you with information revealing that male employees junior to her are paid more than her. Assume that, when you investigate, you find wage increases and payroll records confirming this.

This type of information of comparative inequity is a form of circumstantial evidence. Attorneys must plough through records to determine if enough evidence exists of unequal treatment to make an inference of bad intent.

In contrast, if Sue comes to you with copies of emails or recordings involving her employers discussing deliberately paying her less than her male counterparts, such documents would constitute direct evidence.

In short, direct evidence is actual evidence that employer did because of discriminatory intent (like email saying: "I won't let a woman be a manager because they take maternity leave too often or cry too much" or witnesses testifying that manager said "I'm not letting Hispanics get the overtime when white people need it" or "black people clean better," as in *Slack v. Havens* below).

With this type of evidence, we start with the burden of production/persuasion on plaintiff, but once plantiff successfully submits irrefutable direct evidence, the burden of production and persuasion shift to defendant. This is so because no inference of motive is needed. In the face of uncontroverted evidence of discrimination, the defendant becomes the one in the hot seat with the obligation to convince the court that they derserve to prevail and that they were not motivated by bias.

The Direct Evidence structure, as amended by the Civil Rights Act, is more favorable to plaintiffs. 42 U.S.C. §2000e-2(m). *See Desert Palace v. Costa, Inc.*, 539 U.S. 90 (2003); *see also* Joel Wm. Friedman, *Gender Nonconformity and the Unfulfilled Promise of Price Waterhouse v. Hopkins*, 14 Duke J. Gender L. & Pol'y 205, 214 n. 64 (2007). If direct evidence is presented, it shifts the burden to the employer to show that it would have made the same decision in the absence of discriminatory intent.

Indirect/circumstantial on the other hand, requires that:

> 1. Plaintiff makes prima facie case (which is: (a) member of protected class, (b) adverse employment action/decision, (c) members outside protected class treated more favorably). Throughout plaintiff has burden of production on all of these items, which creates an inference of forbidden intent (i.e., adverse action was caused by or product of discriminatory intent), which satisfies burden of persuasion on intent issue if defendant does nothing more.

> 2. In turn, defendant can present legitimate non-discriminatory reason for its action. Defendant has burden of production at that point. If successful, this rebuts the presumption of discriminatory intent.

> 3. With presumption of discriminatory intent gone, plaintiff has burden of persuasion on that issue without benefit of presumption. The only option left to plaintiff at that stage is to show pretext, i.e., that the alleged legitimate reason was just a cover up for an actual discriminatory reason.

Thus, under Title VII, claimants start out having to shoulder both the burden of production and of persuasion. This means that the plaintiff has to convince the court of all the required elements for a prima facie case of discrimination and provide evidence that can support her claim of discrimination. If she is successful in proving bad intent with uncontroverted and irrefutable direct evidence, then plaintiff has satisfied her burdens and made a prima facie case of discrimination. At that point, the burden of persuasion will shift to defendant to demonstrate that the defendant's actions were not motivated by a bad motive. This is the strongest evidentiary position for a plaintiff. Due to the strength of direct evidence, it places plaintiff's claims in the best light and increases the likelihood of success. Unlike with cases involving circumstantial evidence discussed below, cases establishing direct evidence of discriminatory intent constitute rare times when the defendant might shoulder a more demanding burden of proof than plaintiffs.

In contrast, under the framework for circumstantial evidence, the burden of persuasion remains on the plaintiff. Plaintiff shoulders the burden of persuasion at all times, leaving defendant with only the burden to produce evidence of non-discriminatory reasons for the decision in question. Since cases alleging discrimination based on circumstantial evidence are more labored and rely on the totality of circumstances, this evidentiary framework requires the plaintiff to demonstrate and persuade the court that the circumstances amount in fact to discrimination. If the defendant is successful in producing non-discriminatory support for the employment decision, such as plaintiff-employee's record of tardiness, such production might then be enough to derail plaintiff's claim. Unlike in direct evidence claims, defendants are not required to persuade the court that they are not biased. They need only prove that they had good non-discriminatory reasons to make their decision. With such a low bar for defendants, plaintiff's only chance under the circumstantial framework is to persuade the court that defendant's alleged non-discriminatory reasons are pretextual and a cover for actual bias. Consequently, courts recognize the following evidentiary steps to support claims of discrimination based on circumstantial evidence. First, a plaintiff must convince the court and submit evidence proving that employer's biased motive, prohibited by Title VII, caused an adverse employment action (ex. firing, demotion, unequal pay, etc.). Once the plaintiff successfully makes this claim, the burden of production shifts to defendant to demonstrate via sufficient evidence that the decision was based on a legitimate employment reason. If defendant, is successful in doing so, plaintiff loses unless they are successful in convincing the court using arguments and documents demonstrating that defendant's reason is a pretext. If plaintiff is successful in showing pretext, only then might they win; if not, defendant will likely still prevail.

The above steps were constructed by the Court based on Rule 301 of the Federal Rules of Evidence. (This evidentiary standard is referred to as the *McDonnell Douglas* test—named after the precedent that formulated it.). So, under the above hypo involving Sue, Sue would shoulder both the burden of production and persuasion of proving her claim of discrimination. Only after she is successful in proving all of the prongs of her prima facie case, would the burden shift to the employer. *See Texas Dept. Comm. Affairs v. Burdine*, 450 U.S. 248 (1981) (finding that once the employee proved a prima facie case of employment discrimination, the employer bore the burden of proving nondiscriminatory reasons for its actions); *McDonnell Douglas Corp. v. Green*, 411 U.S. 792 (1973) (adopting the evidentiary standards that apply in Title VII discriminatory treatment cases).

Subsequently, the employer only has the burden/obligation of producing evidence showing that it had a non-discriminatory reason for its action. That burden is lower because it only requires providing evidence of a legitimate reason. Such legitimate reason could be evidence of tardiness, bad performance, etc. In other words, the employer only has to produce just enough evidence to convince the trier of fact that there could be a permissible reason. The employer does not have an obligation to persuade the trier of fact that it was not guilty of the discrimination alleged. It is, instead, the plaintiff's responsibility to show that the employer did commit the alleged wrongdoing.

Imagining the allegations that you would make in drafting the initial complaint is helpful here. How would you draft Sue's complaint? What facts would you need to know? Subsequently, try to determine what you would need in order to prove the allegations in the complaint. *Slack v. Havens* provides a blueprint for cases where the evidence of discrimination is clear and uncontroverted. It illustrates the operation of direct evidence, this most effective form of evidence in Title VII cases.

Slack v. Havens

522 F.2d 1091 (9th Cir. 1975)

HUFSTEDLER, Circuit Judge:

Four black women brought an action against their former employers under Title VII of the Civil Rights Act of 1964, charging discriminatory discharge and seeking damages. They prevailed below, and the employers Glenn C. Havens ("Havens") and Havens International ("International") appealed. Havens and International contend that: (1) Havens was not an "employer" within the meaning of the Act because the period of the employment of these women and the number of his employees did not bring him within the purview of the Act; (2) their request for a jury trial was improperly denied; (3) International was not jointly liable because it was not a party to the antecedent EEOC proceeding, was not in existence when the discriminatory acts occurred, and had been dissolved before the complaint was filed; and (4) the evidence was insufficient to support the findings upon which the award was based.

Appellees Slack, Matthews, Hampton and Hale were employed in the bonding and coating department of Havens. On January 31, 1968, Matthews, Hampton and Slack were working with a white co-worker, Murphy. Their immediate supervisor, Pohasky, at that time informed them that they would be expected to undertake a general heavy cleaning of their department on the following morning. They protested. The next day, Pohasky excused Ms. Murphy to another assignment and called Hale back from another department where she had been on loan in order to have her join the cleaning. Appellees again protested that they had not been hired to do janitorial work, and inquired as to why Ms. Murphy had been excused. Pohasky insisted that they perform the work, remarking that "Colored people should stay in their places," and "Colored people are hired to clean because they clean better," or words to that effect. When appellees persisted in refusing to do the work, they were given their final paychecks. After pursuing state remedies, they filed charges with the Equal Employment Opportunity Commission (EEOC) and, upon receiving right to sue letters, brought this action seeking an injunction, back pay, and exemplary damages. The court denied injunctive relief because the only named defendant currently carrying on the business was Calgon Corporation, against whom the action had been dismissed with prejudice. Punitive damages were denied because they are not authorized by statute. The court awarded Matthews and Hampton six weeks' pay because they had thereafter refused to consider reemployment until all four women were reinstated; no issue is raised on appeal concerning the propriety of the limited award to them. Slack and Hale were awarded damages for back pay from February 1, 1968 to January 17, 1972, reduced by the amounts they could have earned by reasonable diligence elsewhere, pursuant to 42 U.S.C. § 2000e-5(g).

. . .

. . . Appellants finally contend that the district court's finding of discrimination was clearly erroneous. We cannot agree. In a case such as this, the trier of fact must make the necessary determination based upon "reasonable inferences drawn from the totality of facts, the conglomerate of activities, and the entire web of circumstances presented by the evidence on the record as a whole." (*Aeronca Manufacturing Co. v. NLRB* (9th Cir. 1967) 385 F.2d 724, 728.)

As mandated by *Griggs v. Duke Power Co.* (1971) 401 U.S. 424, 91 S.Ct. 849, 28 L. Ed.2d 158, the court correctly looked beyond appellants' alleged lack of intent to discriminate and considered the consequences of the employment practices in question. Based on the evidence, we think that the district court reasonably found discrimination in the terms and conditions of employment applied to the appellees.

The cause is remanded for the purpose of correcting the amount of back pay awarded to Slack and Hale; in all other respects the judgment is affirmed. Appellees shall have their costs on appeal.

. . . .

Consider when plaintiffs do not have direct and uncontroverted evidence as seen in *Slack*, but instead are forced to rely on circumstantial evidence. How do the burdens on plaintiffs and defendants differ? See below.

a. Pretext and Circumstantial Evidence

As stated above, when a plaintiff must rely on circumstantial evidence to prove a case of discrimination, a burden-shifting model governs the inquiry. This standard was fleshed out in *McDonnell Douglas Corporation v. Green*.[27] Recall that under this model, the plaintiff first has the burden of proving by the preponderance of the evidence a prima facie case of discrimination, as discussed above.[28] Second, if the plaintiff succeeds in proving the prima facie case, the burden shifts to the defendant "to articulate some legitimate, nondiscriminatory reason for the employee's rejection."[29] Third, should the defendant carry this burden, the plaintiff must then have an opportunity to prove by a preponderance of the evidence that the legitimate

---

27. 411 U.S. 792 (1973).
28. *Id.* at 802.
29. *Id.*

reasons offered by the defendant were not its true reasons, but were a pretext for discrimination.[30]

The defendant need not persuade the court that it was actually motivated by the proffered reasons, but it is sufficient if the defendant's evidence raises a genuine issue of fact as to whether it discriminated against the plaintiff.[31] To accomplish this, the defendant must clearly set forth, through the introduction of admissible evidence, the reasons for the plaintiff's rejection.[32]

Under this analysis, how may the plaintiff show that the defendant's proffered reasons for the adverse action are merely pretext? The decision of *Texas Department of Community Affairs v. Burdine* provides the answer.

Texas Dept. of Community Affairs v. Burdine
450 U.S. 248 (1981)

Justice POWELL delivered the opinion of the Court.

This case requires us to address again the nature of the evidentiary burden placed upon the defendant in an employment discrimination suit brought under Title VII of the Civil Rights Act of 1964, 42 U.S.C. § 2000e *et seq.* The narrow question presented is whether, after the plaintiff has proved a prima facie case of discriminatory treatment, the burden shifts to the defendant to persuade the court by a preponderance of the evidence that legitimate, nondiscriminatory reasons for the challenged employment action existed.

I

Petitioner, the Texas Department of Community Affairs (TDCA), hired respondent, a female, in January 1972, for the position of accounting clerk in the Public Service Careers Division (PSC). PSC provided training and employment opportunities in the public sector for unskilled workers. When hired, respondent possessed several years' experience in employment training. She was promoted to Field Services Coordinator in July 1972. Her supervisor resigned in November of that year, and respondent was assigned additional duties. Although she applied for the supervisor's position of Project Director, the position remained vacant for six months.

PSC was funded completely by the United States Department of Labor. The Department was seriously concerned about inefficiencies at PSC. In February 1973, the Department notified the Executive Director of TDCA, B.R. Fuller, that it would terminate PSC the following month. TDCA officials, assisted by respondent, persuaded the Department to continue funding the program, conditioned upon PSC's reforming its operations. Among the agreed conditions were the appointment of a permanent Project Director and a complete reorganization of the PSC staff.

---

30. *Id.* at 803.
31. *Id.* at 805.
32. *Id.* at 804.

After consulting with personnel within TDCA, Fuller hired a male from another division of the agency as Project Director. In reducing the PSC staff, he fired respondent along with two other employees, and retained another male, Walz, as the only professional employee in the division. It is undisputed that respondent had maintained her application for the position of Project Director and had requested to remain with TDCA. Respondent soon was rehired by TDCA and assigned to another division of the agency. She received the exact salary paid to the Project Director at PSC, and the subsequent promotions she has received have kept her salary and responsibility commensurate with what she would have received had she been appointed Project Director.

Respondent filed this suit in the United States District Court for the Western District of Texas. She alleged that the failure to promote and the subsequent decision to terminate her had been predicated on gender discrimination in violation of Title VII. After a bench trial, the District Court held that neither decision was based on gender discrimination. The court relied on the testimony of Fuller that the employment decisions necessitated by the commands of the Department of Labor were based on consultation among trusted advisers and a nondiscriminatory evaluation of the relative qualifications of the individuals involved. He testified that the three individuals terminated did not work well together, and that TDCA thought that eliminating this problem would improve PSC's efficiency. The court accepted this explanation as rational and, in effect, found no evidence that the decisions not to promote and to terminate respondent were prompted by gender discrimination.

The Court of Appeals for the Fifth Circuit reversed in part. 608 F.2d 563 (1979). The court held that the District Court's "implicit evidentiary finding" that the male hired as Project Director was better qualified for that position than respondent was not clearly erroneous. Accordingly, the court affirmed the District Court's finding that respondent was not discriminated against when she was not promoted. The Court of Appeals, however, reversed the District Court's finding that Fuller's testimony sufficiently had rebutted respondent's prima facie case of gender discrimination in the decision to terminate her employment at PSC. We now vacate the Fifth Circuit's decision and remand for application of the correct standard.

II

In *McDonnell Douglas Corp. v. Green*, 411 U.S. 792, 93 S.Ct. 1817, 36 L.Ed.2d 668 (1973), we set forth the basic allocation of burdens and order of presentation of proof in a Title VII case alleging discriminatory treatment. First, the plaintiff has the burden of proving by the preponderance of the evidence a prima facie case of discrimination. Second, if the plaintiff succeeds in proving the prima facie case, the burden shifts to the defendant "to articulate some legitimate, nondiscriminatory reason for the employee's rejection." *Id.*, at 802, 93 S.Ct., at 1824. Third, should the defendant carry this burden, the plaintiff must then have an opportunity to prove by a preponderance of the evidence that the legitimate reasons offered by the defendant were not its true reasons, but were a pretext for discrimination. *Id.*, at 804, 93 S. Ct., at 1825.

The nature of the burden that shifts to the defendant should be understood in light of the plaintiff's ultimate and intermediate burdens. The ultimate burden of persuading the trier of fact that the defendant intentionally discriminated against the plaintiff remains at all times with the plaintiff. See *Board of Trustees of Keene State College v. Sweeney*, 439 U.S. 24, 25, n. 2, 99 S.Ct. 295, 296, n. 2, 58 L.Ed.2d 216 (1978); *id.*, at 29, 99 S.Ct., at 297 (Stevens, J., dissenting). See generally 9 J. Wigmore, Evidence § 2489 (3d ed. 1940) (the burden of persuasion "never shifts"). The *McDonnell Douglas* division of intermediate evidentiary burdens serves to bring the litigants and the court expeditiously and fairly to this ultimate question.

The burden of establishing a prima facie case of disparate treatment is not onerous. The plaintiff must prove by a preponderance of the evidence that she applied for an available position for which she was qualified, but was rejected under circumstances which give rise to an inference of unlawful discrimination. The prima facie case serves an important function in the litigation: it eliminates the most common nondiscriminatory reasons for the plaintiff's rejection. See *Teamsters v. United States*, 431 U.S. 324, 358, and n. 44, 97 S.Ct. 1843, 1866, n. 44, 52 L.Ed.2d 396 (1977). As the Court explained in *Furnco Construction Corp. v. Waters*, 438 U.S. 567, 577, 98 S.Ct. 2943, 2949, 57 L.Ed.2d 957 (1978), the prima facie case "raises an inference of discrimination only because we presume these acts, if otherwise unexplained, are more likely than not based on the consideration of impermissible factors." Establishment of the prima facie case in effect creates a presumption that the employer unlawfully discriminated against the employee. If the trier of fact believes the plaintiff's evidence, and if the employer is silent in the face of the presumption, the court must enter judgment for the plaintiff because no issue of fact remains in the case.

The burden that shifts to the defendant, therefore, is to rebut the presumption of discrimination by producing evidence that the plaintiff was rejected, or someone else was preferred, for a legitimate, nondiscriminatory reason. The defendant need not persuade the court that it was actually motivated by the proffered reasons. See *Sweeney, supra*, at 25, 99 S.Ct., at 296. It is sufficient if the defendant's evidence raises a genuine issue of fact as to whether it discriminated against the plaintiff to accomplish this, the defendant must clearly set forth, through the introduction of admissible evidence, the reasons for the plaintiff's rejection. The explanation provided must be legally sufficient to justify a judgment for the defendant. If the defendant carries this burden of production, the presumption raised by the prima facie case is rebutted, and the factual inquiry proceeds to a new level of specificity. Placing this burden of production on the defendant thus serves simultaneously to meet the plaintiff's prima facie case by presenting a legitimate reason for the action and to frame the factual issue with sufficient clarity so that the plaintiff will have a full and fair opportunity to demonstrate pretext. The sufficiency of the defendant's evidence should be evaluated by the extent to which it fulfills these functions.

The plaintiff retains the burden of persuasion. She now must have the opportunity to demonstrate that the proffered reason was not the true reason for the employment decision. This burden now merges with the ultimate burden of persuading the court that she has been the victim of intentional discrimination. She may succeed in this either directly by persuading the court that a discriminatory reason more likely motivated the employer or indirectly by showing that the employer's proffered explanation is unworthy of credence. See *McDonnell Douglas*, 411 U.S., at 804–805, 93 S.Ct., at 1825–1826.

III

. . .

A

The Court of Appeals has misconstrued the nature of the burden that *McDonnell Douglas* and its progeny place on the defendant. See Part II, *supra*. We stated in *Sweeney* that "the employer's burden is satisfied if he simply 'explains what he has done' or 'produc[es] evidence of legitimate nondiscriminatory reasons.'" 439 U.S., at 25, n. 2, 99 S.Ct., at 296 n. 2, quoting *id.*, at 28, 29, 99 S.Ct., at 297–298 (Stevens, J., dissenting). It is plain that the Court of Appeals required much more: it placed on the defendant the burden of persuading the court that it had convincing, objective reasons for preferring the chosen applicant above the plaintiff.

We have stated consistently that the employee's prima facie case of discrimination will be rebutted if the employer articulates lawful reasons for the action; that is, to satisfy this intermediate burden, the employer need only produce admissible evidence which would allow the trier of fact rationally to conclude that the employment decision had not been motivated by discriminatory animus. The Court of Appeals would require the defendant to introduce evidence which, in the absence of any evidence of pretext, would *persuade* the trier of fact that the employment action was lawful. This exceeds what properly can be demanded to satisfy a burden of production.

. . .

B

The Court of Appeals also erred in requiring the defendant to prove by objective evidence that the person hired or promoted was more qualified than the plaintiff. *McDonnell Douglas* teaches that it is the plaintiff's task to demonstrate that similarly situated employees were not treated equally. 411 U.S., at 804, 93 S.Ct., at 1825. The Court of Appeals' rule would require the employer to show that the plaintiff's objective qualifications were inferior to those of the person selected. If it cannot, a court would, in effect, conclude that it has discriminated.

The views of the Court of Appeals can be read, we think, as requiring the employer to hire the minority or female applicant whenever that person's objective qualifications were equal to those of a white male applicant. But Title VII does not obligate an employer to accord this preference. Rather, the employer has discretion to choose among equally qualified candidates, provided the decision is not based upon unlawful criteria. The fact that a court may think that the employer misjudged the qualifications of the applicants does not in itself expose him to Title VII liability, although this may be probative of whether the employer's reasons are pretexts for discrimination. *Loeb v. Textron, Inc., supra,* at 1012, n. 6; see *Lieberman v. Gant,* 630 F.2d 60, 65 (CA2 1980).

IV

In summary, the Court of Appeals erred by requiring the defendant to prove by a preponderance of the evidence the existence of nondiscriminatory reasons for terminating the respondent and that the person retained in her stead had superior objective qualifications for the position. When the plaintiff has proved a prima facie case of discrimination, the defendant bears only the burden of explaining clearly the nondiscriminatory reasons for its actions. The judgment of the Court of Appeals is vacated, and the case is remanded for further proceedings consistent with this opinion.

It is so ordered.

Note and Questions

1. Title VII places a minimal burden on the employer in discrimination claims relying on circumstantial evidence. Employers only have to produce evidence (employment record showing that plaintiff was habitually late, for example) to demonstrate a non-discriminatory motive. If an employer were indeed motivated by racial or gender animus, but was still able to produce evidence that the plaintiff had been an imperfect employee, what options would remain for the plaintiff?

2. Title VII does provide wide discretion to employers to choose among qualified individuals. See data regarding the role of implicit bias in hiring and employment.[33] In light of the limitations inherent in the statute, is law enough to resolve these problems?

3. Consider the validity of the Court of Appeals' concerns and reasons for imposing such a low burden for proving defendant's justifications.

> The court placed the burden of persuasion on the defendant apparently because it feared that "[i]f an employer need only articulate — not *prove* — a legitimate, nondiscriminatory reason for his action, he may compose fictitious, but legitimate, reasons for his actions." *Turner v. Texas Instruments, Inc., supra,* at 1255 (emphasis in original). We do not believe, however, that limiting the defendant's evidentiary obligation to a burden of production

---

33. *See* Marianne Bertrand & Sendhil Mullainathan, *Are Emily and Greg More Employable Than Lakisha and Jamal? A Field Experiment on Labor Market Discrimination*, 94 AMERICAN ECON. REV. 991 (2004) (finding that identical resumes with applicant's name manipulated to be either a stereotypical African-American name or white name had a 50% higher chance to result in a callback interview if resume had a "white" name); Devah Pager, Bruce Western & Bart Bonikowski, *Discrimination in a Low-Wage LaborMarket: A Field Experiment*, 74 AMERICAN SOCIOLOGICAL REV. 777 (2009) (finding African-Americans applying for low-wage jobs with no criminal record, identical resumes and interview training as white applicants were offered jobs at the same rate as white applicants with criminal records).

will unduly hinder the plaintiff. First, as noted above, the defendant's explanation of its legitimate reasons must be clear and reasonably specific. *See Loeb v. Textron, Inc.*, 600 F.2d 1003, 1011–1012, n. 5 (CA1 1979). This obligation arises both from the necessity of rebutting the inference of discrimination arising from the prima facie case and from the requirement that the plaintiff be afforded "a full and fair opportunity" to demonstrate pretext. Second, although the defendant does not bear a formal burden of persuasion, the defendant nevertheless retains an incentive to persuade the trier of fact that the employment decision was lawful. Thus, the defendant normally will attempt to prove the factual basis for its explanation. Third, the liberal discovery rules applicable to any civil suit in federal court are supplemented in a Title VII suit by the plaintiff's access to the Equal Employment Opportunity Commission's investigatory files concerning her complaint. *See EEOC v. Associated Dry Goods Corp.*, 449 U.S. 590, 101 S.Ct. 817, 66 L.Ed.2d 762 (1981). Given these factors, we are unpersuaded that the plaintiff will find it particularly difficult to prove that a proffered explanation lacking a factual basis is a pretext. We remain confident that the *McDonnell Douglas* framework permits the plaintiff meriting relief to demonstrate intentional discrimination.

St. Mary's Honor Center v. Hicks

509 U.S. 502 (1993)

Justice SCALIA delivered the opinion of the Court.

Petitioner St. Mary's Honor Center (St. Mary's) is a halfway house operated by the Missouri Department of Corrections and Human Resources (MDCHR). Respondent Melvin Hicks, a black man, was hired as a correctional officer at St. Mary's in August 1978 and was promoted to shift commander, one of six supervisory positions, in February 1980.

In 1983 MDCHR conducted an investigation of the administration of St. Mary's, which resulted in extensive supervisory changes in January 1984. Respondent retained his position, but John Powell became the new chief of custody (respondent's immediate supervisor) and petitioner Steve Long the new superintendent. Prior to these personnel changes respondent had enjoyed a satisfactory employment record, but soon thereafter became the subject of repeated, and increasingly severe, disciplinary actions. He was suspended for five days for violations of institutional rules by his subordinates on March 3, 1984. He received a letter of reprimand for alleged failure to conduct an adequate investigation of a brawl between inmates that occurred during his shift on March 21. He was later demoted from shift commander to correctional officer for his failure to ensure that his subordinates entered their use of a St. Mary's vehicle into the official log book on March 19, 1984. Finally, on June 7, 1984, he was discharged for threatening Powell during an exchange of heated words on April 19.

Respondent brought this suit in the United States District Court for the Eastern District of Missouri, alleging that petitioner St. Mary's violated § 703(a)(1) of Title VII of the Civil Rights Act of 1964, 42 U.S.C. § 2000e-2(a)(1), and that petitioner Long violated Rev. Stat. § 1979, 42 U.S.C. § 1983 by demoting and then discharging him because of his race. After a full bench trial, the District Court found for petitioners. 756 F. Supp. 1244 (ED Mo. 1991). The United States Court of Appeals for the Eighth Circuit reversed and remanded, 970 F.2d 487 (1992), and we granted certiorari, 506 U.S. ___ (1993).

Section 703(a)(1) of Title VII of the Civil Rights Act of 1964 provides in relevant part:

"It shall be an unlawful employment practice for an employer —

"(1) . . . to discharge any individual, or otherwise to discriminate against any individual with respect to his compensation, terms, conditions, or privileges of employment, because of such individual's race . . . ." 42 U.S.C. § 2000e-2(a).

. . . [O]ur opinion in *McDonnell Douglas Corp. v. Green*, 411 U.S. 792 (1973), established an allocation of the burden of production and an order for the presentation of proof in Title VII discriminatory treatment cases. The plaintiff in such a case, we said, must first establish, by a preponderance of the evidence, a "prima facie" case of racial discrimination. *Burdine, supra,* at 252–253. Petitioners do not challenge the District Court's finding that respondent satisfied the minimal requirements of such a prima facie case (set out in *McDonnell Douglas, supra,* at 802) by proving (1) that he is black, (2) that he was qualified for the position of shift commander, (3) that he was demoted from that position and ultimately discharged, and (4) that the position remained open and was ultimately filled by a white man. 756 F. Supp., at 1249–1250.

Under the *McDonnell Douglas* scheme, "[e]stablishment of the prima facie case in effect creates a presumption that the employer unlawfully discriminated against the employee." *Burdine, supra,* at 254. To establish a "presumption" is to say that a finding of the predicate fact (here, the prima facie case) produces "a required conclusion in the absence of explanation" (here, the finding of unlawful discrimination). 1 D. Louisell & C. Mueller, Federal Evidence § 67, p. 536 (1977). Thus, the *McDonnell Douglas* presumption places upon the defendant the burden of producing an explanation to rebut the prima facie case — *i.e.,* the burden of "producing evidence" that the adverse employment actions were taken "for a legitimate, nondiscriminatory reason." *Burdine,* 450 U. S., at 254. "[The defendant must clearly set forth, through the introduction of admissible evidence," reasons for its actions which, *if believed by the trier of fact,* would support a finding that unlawful discrimination was not the cause of the employment action. *Id.,* at 254–255, and n. 8. It is important to note, however, that although the *McDonnell Douglas* presumption shifts the burden of *production* to the defendant, "[t]he ultimate burden of persuading the trier of fact that the defendant intentionally discriminated against the plaintiff remains at all times with the plaintiff," *id.*, at 253. In this regard it operates like all presumptions, as described in Rule 301 of the Federal Rules of Evidence:

> "In all civil actions and proceedings not otherwise provided for by Act of Congress or by these rules, a presumption imposes on the party against whom it is directed the burden of going forward with evidence to rebut or meet the presumption, but does not shift to such party the burden of proof in the sense of the risk of nonpersuasion, which remains throughout the trial upon the party on whom it was originally cast."

Respondent does not challenge the District Court's finding that petitioners sustained their burden of production by introducing evidence of two legitimate, nondiscriminatory reasons for their actions: the severity and the accumulation of rules violations committed by respondent. 756 F. Supp., at 1250. Our cases make clear that at that point the shifted burden of production became irrelevant: "If the defendant carries this burden of production, the presumption raised by the prima facie case is rebutted," *Burdine*, 450 U.S., at 255, and "drops from the case," *id.*, at 255, n. 10. The plaintiff then has "the full and fair opportunity to demonstrate," through presentation of his own case and through cross examination of the defendant's witnesses, "that the proffered reason was not the true reason for the employment decision," *id.*, at 256, and that race was. He retains that "ultimate burden of persuading the [trier of fact] that [he] has been the victim of intentional discrimination." *Ibid.*

The District Court, acting as trier of fact in this bench trial, found that the reasons petitioners gave were not the real reasons for respondent's demotion and discharge. It found that respondent was the only supervisor disciplined for violations committed by his subordinates; that similar and even more serious violations committed by respondent's coworkers were either disregarded or treated more leniently; and that Powell manufactured the final verbal confrontation in order to provoke respondent into threatening him. 756 F. Supp., at 1250–1251. It nonetheless held that respondent had failed to carry his ultimate burden of proving that *his race* was the determining factor in petitioners' decision first to demote and then to dismiss him. In short, the District Court concluded that "although [respondent] has proven the existence of a crusade to terminate him, he has not proven that the crusade was racially rather than personally motivated." *Id.*, at 1252.

The Court of Appeals set this determination aside on the ground that "[o]nce [respondent] proved all of [petitioners'] proffered reasons for the adverse employment actions to be pretextual, [respondent] was entitled to judgment as a matter of law." 970 F.2d, at 492. The Court of Appeals reasoned:

> "Because all of defendants' proffered reasons were discredited, defendants were in a position of having offered no legitimate reason for their actions. In other words, defendants were in no better position than if they had remained silent, offering no rebuttal to an established inference that they had unlawfully discriminated against plaintiff on the basis of his race." *Ibid.*

That is not so. By producing *evidence* (whether ultimately persuasive or not) of non-discriminatory reasons, petitioners sustained their burden of production, and thus placed themselves in a "better position than if they had remained silent."

In the nature of things, the determination that a defendant has met its burden of production (and has thus rebutted any legal presumption of intentional discrimination) can involve no credibility assessment. For the burden of production determination necessarily *precedes* the credibility assessment stage. At the close of the defendant's case, the court is asked to decide whether an issue of fact remains for the trier of fact to determine. None does if, on the evidence presented, (1) any rational person would have to find the existence of facts constituting a prima facie case, and (2) the defendant has failed to meet its burden of production—*i.e.*, has failed to introduce evidence which, *taken as true*, would *permit* the conclusion that there was a nondiscriminatory reason for the adverse action. In that event, the court must award judgment to the plaintiff as a matter of law under Federal Rule of Civil Procedure 50(a)(1) (in the case of jury trials) or Federal Rule of Civil Procedure 52(c) (in the case of bench trials). See F. James & G. Hazard, Civil Procedure §7.9, p. 327 (3d ed. 1985); 1 Louisell & Mueller, Federal Evidence §70, at 568. If the defendant has failed to sustain its burden but reasonable minds could *differ* as to whether a preponderance of the evidence establishes the facts of a prima facie case, then a question of fact *does* remain, which the trier of fact will be called upon to answer.

If, on the other hand, the defendant has succeeded in carrying its burden of production, the *McDonnell Douglas* framework—with its presumptions and burdens—is no longer relevant. To resurrect it later, after the trier of fact has determined that what was "produced" to meet the burden of production is not credible, flies in the face of our holding in *Burdine* that to rebut the presumption "[t]he defendant need not persuade the court that it was actually motivated by the proffered reasons." 450 U.S., at 254. The presumption, having fulfilled its role of forcing the defendant to come forward with some response, simply drops out of the picture. *Id.*, at 255. The defendant's "production" (whatever its persuasive effect) having been made, the trier of fact proceeds to decide the ultimate question: whether plaintiff has proven "that the defendant intentionally discriminated against [him]" because of his race, *id.*, at 253. The factfinder's disbelief of the reasons put forward by the defendant (particularly if disbelief is accompanied by a suspicion of mendacity) may, together with the elements of the prima facie case, suffice to show intentional discrimination. Thus, rejection of the defendant's proffered reasons, will *permit* the trier of fact to infer the ultimate fact of intentional discrimination, and the Court of Appeals was correct when it noted that, upon such rejection, "[n]o additional proof of discrimination is *required*," 970 F.2d, at 493 (emphasis added). But the Court of Appeals' holding that rejection of the defendant's proffered reasons *compels* judgment for the plaintiff disregards the fundamental principle of Rule 301 that a presumption does not shift the burden of proof, and ignores our repeated admonition that the Title VII plaintiff at all times bears the "ultimate burden of persuasion." See, *e.g.*, *United States Postal Service Bd. of Governors v. Aikens*, 460 U.S. 711, 716 (1983) (citing *Burdine, supra*, at 256); *Patterson v. McLean Credit Union*, 491 U.S. 164, 187 (1989); . . .

Only one unfamiliar with our case law will be upset by the dissent's alarum that we are today setting aside "settled precedent," *post*, at 2, "two decades of stable law in this Court," *post*, at 1, "a framework carefully crafted in precedents as old as 20 years," *post*, at 17, which "Congress is [aware]" of and has implicitly approved, *post*, at 19. Panic will certainly not break out among the courts of appeals, whose divergent views concerning the nature of the supposedly "stable law in this Court" are precisely what prompted us to take this case — a divergence in which the dissent's version of "settled precedent" cannot remotely be considered the "prevailing view." Compare, *e.g.*, *EEOC v. Flasher Co.*, 986 F.2d 1312, 1321 (CA10 1992) (finding of pretext does not mandate finding of illegal discrimination); *Galbraith v. Northern Telecom, Inc.*, 944 F.2d 275, 282–283 (CA6 1991) (same) (opinion of Boggs, J.), cert. denied, 503 U.S. ___ (1992); 944 F.2d, at 283 (same) (opinion of Guy, J., concurring in result); *Samuels v. Raytheon Corp.*, 934 F.2d 388, 392 (CA1 1991) (same); *Holder v. City of Raleigh*, 867 F.2d 823, 827–828 (CA4 1989) (same); *Benzies v. Illinois Dept. of Mental Health and Developmental Disabilities*, 810 F.2d 146, 148 (CA7) (same) *(dictum)*, cert. denied, 483 U.S. 1006 (1987) . . . .

. . . .

We reaffirm today what we said in *Aikens*:

> "[T]he question facing triers of fact in discrimination cases is both sensitive and difficult. The prohibitions against discrimination contained in the Civil Rights Act of 1964 reflect an important national policy. There will seldom be 'eyewitness' testimony as to the employer's mental processes. But none of this means that trial courts or reviewing courts should treat discrimination differently from other ultimate questions of fact. Nor should they make their inquiry even more difficult by applying legal rules which were devised to govern 'the basic allocation of burdens and order of presentation of proof,' *Burdine*, 450 U.S., at 252, in deciding this ultimate question." *Aikens*, 460 U.S., at 716.

The judgment of the Court of Appeals is reversed, and the case is remanded for further proceedings consistent with this opinion.

It is so ordered.

Notes and Questions

1. Note the quintessential issue in *St Mary's*: "it is up to Plaintiff to prove that Plaintiff discriminated against them because of their race." This task must be accomplished independent of whatever defense is put forth by defendant in response to plaintiff's claims." Concerns that the *McDonnell Douglas* standard might lean too much in favor of employers persist in *St. Mary's*. The *McDonnell Douglas* standard has had its share of critics stating that it errs in favor of defendants and places too

onerous a burden on plaintiffs. Note the operation of the *McDonnell Douglas* evidentiary standard in litigation, as described by the Court:

> If the finder of fact answers affirmatively—if it finds that the prima facie case *is* supported by a preponderance of the evidence—it *must* find the existence of the presumed fact of unlawful discrimination and *must*, therefore, render a verdict for the plaintiff. See *Texas Dept. of Community Affairs v. Burdine*, 450 U.S. 248, 254, and n. 7 (1981); F. James & G. Hazard, Civil Procedure § 7.9, p. 327 (3d ed. 1985); 1 D. Louisell & C. Mueller, Federal Evidence § 70, pp. 568–569 (1977). Thus, the *effect* of failing to produce evidence to rebut the *McDonnell Douglas Corp. v. Green*, 411 U.S. 792 (1973), presumption is not felt until the prima facie case has been *established*, either as a matter of law (because the plaintiff's facts are uncontested) or by the factfinder's determination that the plaintiff's facts are supported by a preponderance of the evidence. It is thus technically accurate to describe the sequence as we did in *Burdine*: "First, the plaintiff has the burden of proving by the preponderance of the evidence a prima facie case of discrimination. Second, if the plaintiff succeeds in proving the prima facie case, the burden shifts to the defendant to articulate some legitimate, nondiscriminatory reason for the employee's rejection." 450 U.S., at 252–253 (internal quotation omitted).
>
> As a practical matter, however, and in the real-life sequence of a trial, the defendant *feels* the "burden" not when the plaintiff's prima facie case is *proved*, but as soon as evidence of it is *introduced*. The defendant then knows that its failure to introduce evidence of a nondiscriminatory reason will cause judgment to go against it *unless* the plaintiff's prima facie case is held to be inadequate in law or fails to convince the factfinder. It is this practical coercion which causes the *McDonnell Douglas* presumption to function as a means of "arranging the presentation of evidence," *Watson v. Fort Worth Bank & Trust*, 487 U.S. 977, 986 (1988).

2. The majority and dissent disagreed on the import of defendant's burden of production. The dissent accused the majority's interpretation of encouraging impunity for lying employers. Is the dissent's fear founded?

3. Imagine the sequence of events described in note 1, as it plays out at trial. Does it provide more chances for bias-motivated employers to escape accountability? What justifies a lower evidentiary standard on the defendant at this stage of the litigation?

b. Title VII Cases and Summary Judgment

1. The majority of Title VII cases in lower courts get resolved at the summary judgment stage, with many not surviving defendants' Rule 56 motions. For example, see the following cases litigated after *St. Mary's*: *Cofield v. Goldkist*, 267 F.3d 1264 (11th Cir. 2001) (Finding in favor of the employer even if plaintiff was more

qualified than the person actually promoted. Plaintiff was not more qualified in a way that created an inference of pretext for discrimination. Specifically, the court stated that "plaintiff must adduce evidence that the disparity in qualifications 'is so apparent as virtually to jump off the page and slap you in the face.'"); *Maynard v. Board of Regents*, 342 F.3d 1281, 1289 (11th Cir. 2003) (for plaintiff to "satisfy the prima facie requirement, [plaintiff] must show that a [white employee] in similar circumstances was retained . . ."); *Knight v. Baptist Hosp. of Miami, Inc.*, 330 F.3d 1313, 1316 (11th Cir. 2003) (plaintiff did not make a "a prima facie case because [plaintiff did not] not show that similarly situated employees of other races were treated better"); *Holifield v. Reno*, 115 F.3d 1555, 1562 (11th Cir. 1997) (another case demonstrating the requirement that plaintiffs prove that similarly situated employees not protected by Titl VII were treated better than plaintiffs.).

2. For better news for plaintiffs, cases involving discrimination based on pregnancy are not as constrained by the requirement that plaintiffs demonstrate better treatment for similarly situated individuals not protected by Title VII. For example, in *EEOC v. Houston Funding II, Ltd.* (5th Cir. May 30, 2013), the Fifth Circuit ruled that an adverse employment decision based on the fact that plaintiff was lactating is a violation of Title VII. *See also Fischer vs. City of Donna, S.D. District of Texas* (2013), for a finding against defendants' motion for summary judgment ("In this case, Fischer has produced evidence that Councilman/Mayor Pro-Tem Simon Sauceda made a comment to Councilwoman Muñoz which on its face shows that improper criteria served as bases for Defendant's decision to not hire Fischer."); *Haire v. Board of Supervisors of Louisiana State University* (5th Cir. May 21, 2013) (denying defendant's motion for summary judgment finding that plaintiff raised a genuine issue of fact as to whether "LSU's alleged non-discriminatory reason for not promoting Haire is pretextual" as well as showing "substantial conflict as to whether she was a victim of retaliation.").

B. Systemic Disparate Treatment

In addition to simple disparate treatment claims Title VII provides an avenue for mass or individual claims alleging a pattern of discriminatory behavior by the employer. In these types of cases, employees, typically, sue alleging that the employer is guilty of promoting a practice of discrimination in the workplace. Failure to hire or promote claims, for example, depend, in those cases, not necessarily on demonstration of adverse employment action against plaintiff, but on a record of adverse employment action against similarly situated individuals of one race, sex, national origin or religion compared to those who are not. Section 707(a) of the Civil Rights Act also authorizes the Attorney General of the United States to sue employers for injunctive relief to rectify patterns or practices of discrimination. This portion of the statute is designed to protect consistent and chronic practices of discrimination in the workforce. To make a claim of discrimination, the government or plaintiffs must prove system wide behavior by the employer. Under this theory, even when plaintiffs cannot point to a facially discriminatory policy adopted by the employer, they can still establish liability by using statistics and other evidence to show that discrimination within the organization was or is so widespread that it is, in the Court's words, "the regular rather than the unusual practice." Systemic disparate treatment theory, which requires proof of different treatment within the defendant's organization based on sex or race or other protected characteristics, is distinct from disparate impact theory, which we will see later. Under disparate impact theory, employers' polices that are neutral, but affect protected groups disproportionately, may be deemed discriminatory. Such allegations of disparate impact discrimination may be refuted if employers successfully demonstrate business necessity. (Kristen K. Green, *The Future of Systemic Disparate Treatment Law*, 32 BERKLEY J. EMP. & LABOR L. 395 (2011).

Title VII also provides for specific exemptions that would protect the employer from liability, if triggered. *International Brotherhood of Teamsters* below shows the role that one of these exemptions—seniority systems—plays in findings of pattern and practice of discriminatory behavior. For example, is a seniority system that perpetuates pre-Title VII discrimination still exempted from the reach of Title VII? What about seniority systems operating as cover for discriminatory behavior? In proving claims of systemic disparate treatment, notice the importance of statistical evidence in demonstrating that the policies caused the alleged detriment. For plaintiffs, this can be an arduous task, as courts have increasingly demanded that such statistical proofs also rule out other potential causes. The cases below demonstrate how courts evaluate such evidence.

International Brotherhood of Teamsters v. United States
431 U.S. 324 (1977)

Mr. Justice STEWART delivered the opinion of the Court.

This litigation brings here several important questions under Title VII of the Civil Rights Act of 1964, 78 Stat. 253, as amended, 42 U.S.C. 2000e et seq. (1970 ed. and Supp. V). The issues grow out of alleged unlawful employment practices engaged in by an employer and a union. The employer is a common carrier of motor freight with nationwide operations, and the union represents a large group of its employees. The District Court and the Court of Appeals held that the employer had violated Title VII by engaging in a pattern and practice of employment discrimination against Negroes and Spanish-surnamed Americans, and that the union had violated the Act by agreeing with the employer to create and maintain a seniority system that perpetuated the effects of past racial and ethnic discrimination. . . .

. . . The United States brought an action in a Tennessee federal court against the petitioner T.I.M.E.-D.C., Inc. (company), pursuant to § 707(a) of the Civil Rights Act of 1964, 42 U.S.C. 2000e-6(a). The complaint charged that the company had followed discriminatory hiring, assignment, and promotion policies against Negroes at its terminal in Nashville, Tenn. The Government brought a second action against the company almost three years later in a Federal District Court in Texas, charging a pattern and practice of employment discrimination against Negroes and Spanish-surnamed persons throughout the company's transportation system. The petitioner International Brotherhood of Teamsters (union) was joined as a defendant in that suit. The two actions were consolidated for trial in the Northern District of Texas.

The central claim in both lawsuits was that the company had engaged in a pattern or practice of discriminating against minorities in hiring so-called line drivers. Those Negroes and Spanish-surnamed persons who had been hired, the Government alleged, were given lower paying, less desirable jobs as servicemen or local city drivers, and were thereafter discriminated against with respect to promotions and transfers. In this connection the complaint also challenged the seniority system established by the collective-bargaining agreements between the employer and the union. The Government sought a general injunctive remedy and specific "make whole" relief for all individual discriminatees, which would allow them an opportunity to transfer to line-driver jobs with full company seniority for all purposes.

The cases went to trial and the District Court found that the Government had shown "by a preponderance of the evidence that T.I.M.E.-D.C. and its predecessor companies were engaged in a plan and practice of discrimination in violation of Title VII . . . ." The court further found that the seniority system contained in the collective-bargaining contracts between the company and the union violated Title VII because it "operate(d) to impede the free transfer of minority groups into and within the company." Both the company and the union were enjoined from committing further violations of Title VII.

With respect to individual relief the court accepted the Government's basic contention that the "affected class" of discriminatees included all Negro and Spanish-surnamed incumbent employees who had been hired to fill city operations or serviceman jobs at every terminal that had a line-driver operation. All of these employees, whether hired before or after the effective date of Title VII, thereby became entitled to preference over all other applicants with respect to consideration for future vacancies in line-driver jobs. . . .

The Court of Appeals for the Fifth Circuit agreed with the basic conclusions of the District Court: that the company had engaged in a pattern or practice of employment discrimination and that the seniority system in the collective-bargaining agreements violated Title VII as applied to victims of prior discrimination. 517 F.2d 299. The appellate court held, however, that the relief ordered by the District Court was inadequate. Rejecting the District Court's attempt to trisect the affected class, the Court of Appeals held that all Negro and Spanish-surnamed incumbent employees were entitled to bid for future line-driver jobs on the basis of their company seniority, and that once a class member had filled a job, he could use his full company seniority even if it predated the effective date of Title VII for all purposes, including bidding and layoff. This award of retroactive seniority was to be limited only by a "qualification date" formula, under which seniority could not be awarded for periods prior to the date when (1) a line-driving position was vacant, and (2) the class member met (or would have met, given the opportunity) the qualifications for employment as a line driver. Finally, the Court of Appeals modified that part of the District Court's decree. . . .

II

In this Court the company and the union contend that their conduct did not violate Title VII in any respect, asserting first that the evidence introduced at trial was insufficient to show that the company engaged in a "pattern or practice" of employment discrimination. The union further contends that the seniority system contained in the collective-bargaining agreements in no way violated Title VII. If these contentions are correct, it is unnecessary, of course, to reach any of the issues concerning remedies that so occupied the attention of the Court of Appeals.

Consideration of the question whether the company engaged in a pattern or practice of discriminatory hiring practices involves controlling legal principles that are relatively clear. The Government's theory of discrimination was simply that the company, in violation of § 703(a) of Title VII, regularly and purposefully treated Negroes and Spanish-surnamed Americans less favorably than white persons. The disparity in treatment allegedly involved the refusal to recruit, hire, transfer, or promote minority group members on an equal basis with white people, particularly with respect to line-driving positions. The ultimate factual issues are thus simply whether there was a pattern or practice of such disparate treatment and, if so, whether the differences were "racially premised." *McDonnell Douglas Corp. v. Green*, 411 U.S. 792, 805 n. 18, 93 S.Ct. 1817, 1825, 36 L.Ed.2d 668.

As the plaintiff, the Government bore the initial burden of making out a prima facie case of discrimination. *Albemarle Paper Co. v. Moody*, 422 U.S. 405, 425, 95 S. Ct. 2362, 2375, 45 L.Ed.2d 280; *McDonnell Douglas Corp. v. Green, supra*, 411 U.S., at 802, 93 S.Ct., at 1824. And, because it alleged a system wide pattern or practice of resistance to the full enjoyment of Title VII rights, the Government ultimately had to prove more than the mere occurrence of isolated or "accidental" or sporadic discriminatory acts. It had to establish by a preponderance of the evidence that racial discrimination was the company's standard operating procedure the regular rather than the unusual practice.

We agree with the District Court and the Court of Appeals that the Government carried its burden of proof. As of March 31, 1971, shortly after the Government filed its complaint alleging system wide discrimination, the company had 6,472 employees. Of these, 314 (5%) were Negroes and 257 (4%) were Spanish-surnamed Americans. Of the 1,828 line drivers, however, there were only 8 (0.4%) Negroes and 5 (0.3%) Spanish-surnamed persons, and all of the Negroes had been hired after the litigation had commenced. With one exception a man who worked as a line driver at the Chicago terminal from 1950 to 1959 the company and its predecessors did not employ a Negro on a regular basis as a line driver until 1969. And, as the Government showed, even in 1971 there were terminals in areas of substantial Negro population where all of the company's line drivers were white. A great majority of the Negroes (83%) and Spanish-surnamed Americans (78%) who did work for the company held the lower paying city operations and serviceman jobs, whereas only 39% of the nonminority employees held jobs in those categories.

The Government bolstered its statistical evidence with the testimony of individuals who recounted over 40 specific instances of discrimination. Upon the basis of this testimony the District Court found that "[n]umerous qualified black and Spanish-surnamed American applicants who sought line driving jobs at the company over the years, either had their requests ignored, were given false or misleading information about requirements, opportunities, and application procedures, or were not considered and hired on the same basis that whites were considered and hired." Minority employees who wanted to transfer to line-driver jobs met with similar difficulties.

The company's principal response to this evidence is that statistics can never in and of themselves prove the existence of a pattern or practice of discrimination, or even establish a prima facie case shifting to the employer the burden of rebutting the inference raised by the figures. But, as even our brief summary of the evidence shows, this was not a case in which the Government relied on "statistics alone." The individuals who testified about their personal experiences with the company brought the cold numbers convincingly to life.

In any event, our cases make it unmistakably clear that "[s]tatistical analyses have served and will continue to serve an important role" in cases in which the existence of discrimination is a disputed issue. *Mayor of Philadelphia v. Educational Equality League*, 415 U.S. 605, 620, 94 S.Ct. 1323, 1333, 39 L.Ed.2d 630. See also *McDonnell Douglas Corp. v. Green*, 411 U.S., at 805, 93 S.Ct., at 1825. Cf. *Washington v. Davis*, 426 U.S. 229, 241–242, 96 S.Ct. 2040, 2048–2049, 48 L.Ed.2d 597. We have repeatedly approved the use of statistical proof, where it reached proportions comparable to those in this case, to establish a prima facie case of racial discrimination in jury selection cases, see, e.g., *Turner v. Fouche*, 396 U.S. 346, 90 S.Ct. 532, 24 L. Ed.2d 567; *Hernandez v. Texas*, 347 U.S. 475, 74 S.Ct. 667, 98 L.Ed. 866; *Norris v. Alabama*, 294 U.S. 587, 55 S.Ct. 579, 79 L.Ed. 1074. Statistics are equally competent in proving employment discrimination. We caution only that statistics are not irrefutable; they come in infinite variety and, like any other kind of evidence, they may be rebutted. In short, their usefulness depends on all of the surrounding facts and circumstances. See, e.g., *Hester v. Southern R. Co.*, 497 F.2d 1374, 1379–1381 (CA5).

In addition to its general protest against the use of statistics in Title VII cases, the company claims that in this case the statistics revealing racial imbalance are misleading because they fail to take into account the company's particular business situation as of the effective date of Title VII. The company concedes that its line drivers were virtually all white in July 1965, but it claims that thereafter business conditions were such that its work force dropped. Its argument is that low personnel turnover, rather than post-Act discrimination, accounts for more recent statistical disparities. It points to substantial minority hiring in later years, especially after 1971, as showing that any pre-Act patterns of discrimination were broken.

The argument would be a forceful one if this were an employer who, at the time of suit, had done virtually no new hiring since the effective date of Title VII. But it is not. Although the company's total number of employees apparently dropped somewhat during the late 1960's, the record shows that many line drivers continued to be hired throughout this period, and that almost all of them were white. To be sure, there were improvements in the company's hiring practices. . . .

The District Court and the Court of Appeals also found that the seniority system contained in the collective-bargaining agreements between the company and the union operated to violate Title VII of the Act.

For purposes of calculating benefits, such as vacations, pensions, and other fringe benefits, an employee's seniority under this system runs from the date he joins the company, and takes into account his total service in all jobs and bargaining units. For competitive purposes, however, such as determining the order in which employees may bid for particular jobs, are laid off, or are recalled from layoff, it is bargaining-unit seniority that controls. Thus, a line driver's seniority, for purposes of bidding for particular runs and protection against layoff, takes into account only the length of time he has been a line driver at a particular terminal. The practical effect is that a city driver or serviceman who transfers to a line-driver job must forfeit all the competitive seniority he has accumulated in his previous bargaining unit and start at the bottom of the line drivers' "board."

The vice of this arrangement, as found by the District Court and the Court of Appeals, was that it "locked" minority workers into inferior jobs and perpetuated prior discrimination by discouraging transfers to jobs as line drivers. While the disincentive applied to all workers, including whites, it was Negroes and Spanish-surnamed persons who, those courts found, suffered the most because many of them had been denied the equal opportunity to become line drivers when they were initially hired, whereas whites either had not sought or were refused line-driver positions for reasons unrelated to their race or national origin.

The linchpin of the theory embraced by the District Court and the Court of Appeals was that a discriminatee who must forfeit his competitive seniority in order finally to obtain a line-driver job will never be able to "catch up" to the seniority level of his contemporary who was not subject to discrimination. Accordingly, this continued, built-in disadvantage to the prior discriminatee who transfers to a line-driver job was held to constitute a continuing violation of Title VII, for which both the employer and the union who jointly created and maintain the seniority system were liable.

The union, while acknowledging that the seniority system may in some sense perpetuate the effects of prior discrimination, asserts that the system is immunized from a finding of illegality by reason of §703(h) of Title VII, 42 U.S.C. 2000e-2(h), which provides in part:

> "Notwithstanding any other provision of this subchapter, it shall not be an unlawful employment practice for an employer to apply different standards

of compensation, or different terms, conditions, or privileges of employment pursuant to a bona fide seniority . . . system, . . . provided that such differences are not the result of an intention to discriminate because of race . . . or national origin . . . ."

It argues that the seniority system in this case is "bona fide" within the meaning of § 703(h) when judged in light of its history, intent, application, and all of the circumstances under which it was created and is maintained. More specifically, the union claims that the central purpose of § 703(h) is to ensure that mere perpetuation of pre-Act discrimination is not unlawful under Title VII. And, whether or not § 703(h) immunizes the perpetuation of post-Act discrimination, the union claims that the seniority system in this litigation has no such effect. Its position in this Court, as has been its position throughout this litigation, is that the seniority system presents no hurdle to post-Act discriminatees who seek retroactive seniority to the date they would have become line drivers but for the company's discrimination. Indeed, the union asserts that under its collective-bargaining agreements the union will itself take up the cause of the post-Act victim and attempt, through grievance procedures, to gain for him full "make whole" relief, including appropriate seniority.

The Government responds that a seniority system that perpetuates the effects of prior discrimination pre-Act or post-Act can never be "bona fide" under § 703(h); at a minimum Title VII prohibits those applications of a seniority system that perpetuate the effects on incumbent employees of prior discriminatory job assignments.

The issues thus joined are open ones in this Court. We considered § 703(h) in *Franks v. Bowman Transportation Co.*, 424 U.S. 747, 96 S.Ct. 1251, 47 L.Ed.2d 444, but there decided only that § 703(h) does not bar the award of retroactive seniority to job applicants who seek relief from an employer's post-Act hiring discrimination. We stated that "the thrust of [§ 703(h)] is directed toward defining what is and what is not an illegal discriminatory practice in instances in which the post-Act operation of a seniority system is challenged as perpetuating the effects of discrimination occurring prior to the effective date of the Act." 424 U.S., at 761, 96 S.Ct., at 1263. Beyond noting the general purpose of the statute, however, we did not undertake the task of statutory construction required in this litigation.

(1)

Because the company discriminated both before and after the enactment of Title VII, the seniority system is said to have operated to perpetuate the effects of both pre- and post-Act discrimination. Post-Act discriminatees, however, may obtain full "make whole" relief, including retroactive seniority under *Franks v. Bowman, supra*, without attacking the legality of the seniority system as applied to them. Franks made clear and the union acknowledges that retroactive seniority may be awarded as relief from an employer's discriminatory hiring and assignment policies even if the seniority system agreement itself makes no provision for such relief. 424 U.S., at 778–779, 96 S.Ct., at 1271. Here the Government has proved that the company engaged in a post-Act pattern of discriminatory hiring, assignment, transfer and promotion policies. Any Negro or Spanish-surnamed American injured by those policies may receive all appropriate relief as a direct remedy for this discrimination.

(2)

What remains for review is the judgment that the seniority system unlawfully perpetuated the effects of pre-Act discrimination. We must decide, in short, whether § 703(h) validates otherwise bona fide seniority systems that afford no constructive seniority to victims discriminated against prior to the effective date of Title VII, and it is to that issue that we now turn.

The primary purpose of Title VII was "to assure equality of employment opportunities and to eliminate those discriminatory practices and devices which have fostered racially stratified job environments to the disadvantage of minority citizens. . . . One kind of practice "fair in form, but discriminatory in operation" is that which perpetuates the effects of prior discrimination. As the Court held in *Griggs*: "Under the Act, practices, procedures, or tests neutral on their face, and even neutral in terms of intent, cannot be maintained if they operate to 'freeze' the status quo of prior discriminatory employment practices." 401 U.S., at 430, 91 S. Ct., at 853.

Were it not for § 703(h), the seniority system in this case would seem to fall under the *Griggs* rationale. The heart of the system is its allocation of the choicest jobs, the greatest protection against layoffs, and other advantages to those employees who have been line drivers for the longest time. Where, because of the employer's prior intentional discrimination, the line drivers with the longest tenure are without exception white, the advantages of the seniority system flow disproportionately to them and away from Negro and Spanish-surnamed employees who might by now have enjoyed those advantages had not the employer discriminated before the passage of the Act. This disproportionate distribution of advantages does in a very real sense "operate to 'freeze' the status quo of prior discriminatory employment practices." *But both the literal terms of § 703(h) and the legislative history of Title VII demonstrate that Congress considered this very effect of many seniority systems extended a measure of immunity to them.* [Emphasis added—Ed.]

Throughout the initial consideration of H.R. 7152, later enacted as the Civil Rights Act of 1964, critics of the bill charged that it would destroy existing seniority rights. The consistent response of Title VII's congressional proponents and of the Justice Department was that seniority rights would not be affected, even where the employer had discriminated prior to the Act. An interpretive memorandum placed in the Congressional Record by Senators Clark and Case stated:

"Title VII would have no effect on established seniority rights. Its effect is prospective and not retrospective. Thus, for example, *if a business has been discriminating in the past and as a result has an all-white working force, when the title comes into effect the employer's obligation would be simply to fill future vacancies on a non-discriminatory basis.* He would not be obliged or indeed, permitted to fire whites in order to hire Negroes or to prefer Negroes for future vacancies, or, once Negroes are hired to give them special seniority rights at the expense of the white workers hired earlier." 110 Cong.Rec. 7213 (1964) (emphasis added).

A Justice Department statement concerning Title VII placed in the Congressional Record by Senator Clark, voiced the same conclusion:

> "Title VII would have no effect on seniority rights existing at the time it takes effect. If, for example, a collective bargaining contract provides that in the event of layoffs, those who were hired last must be laid off first, such a provision would not be affected in the least by title VII. *This would be true even in the case where owing to discrimination prior to the effective date of the title, white workers had more seniority than Negroes."* Id., at 7207 (emphasis added).

While these statements were made before § 703(h) was added to Title VII, they are authoritative indicators of that section's purpose. Section 703(h) was enacted as part of the Mansfield-Dirksen compromise substitute bill that cleared the way for the passage of Title VII. The drafters of the compromise bill stated that one of its principal goals was to resolve the ambiguities in the House-passed version of H.R. 7152. See, e.g., 110 Cong.Rec. 11935–11937 (1964) (remarks of Sen. Dirksen); *id.*, at 12707 (remarks of Sen. Humphrey). As the debates indicate, one of those ambiguities concerned Title VII's impact on existing collectively bargained seniority rights. It is apparent that § 703(h) was drafted with an eye toward meeting the earlier criticism on this issue with an explicit provision embodying the understanding and assurances of the Act's proponents, namely, that Title VII would not outlaw such differences in treatment among employees as flowed from a bona fide seniority system that allowed for full exercise of seniority accumulated before the effective date of the Act. . . .

In sum, the unmistakable purpose of § 703(h) was to make clear that the routine application of a bona fide seniority system would not be unlawful under Title VII. [However], § 703(h) does not immunize all seniority systems. It refers only to "bona fide" systems, and a proviso requires that any differences in treatment not be "the result of an intention to discriminate because of race . . . or national origin . . . ." But our reading of the legislative history compels us to reject the Government's broad argument that no seniority system that tends to perpetuate pre-Act discrimination can be "bona fide." To accept the argument would require us to hold that a seniority system becomes illegal simply because it allows the full exercise of the pre-Act seniority rights of employees of a company that discriminated before Title VII was enacted. It would place an affirmative obligation on the parties to the seniority agreement to subordinate those rights in favor of the claims of pre-Act discriminatees without seniority. The consequence would be a perversion of the congressional purpose. We cannot accept the invitation to disembowel § 703(h) by reading the words "bona fide" as the Government would have us do. Accordingly, we hold that an otherwise neutral, legitimate seniority system does not become unlawful under Title VII simply because it may perpetuate pre-Act discrimination. Congress did not intend to make it illegal for employees with vested seniority rights to continue to exercise those rights, even at the expense of pre-Act discriminatees.

That conclusion is inescapable even in a case, such as this one, where the pre-Act discriminatees are incumbent employees who accumulated seniority in other bargaining units.

(3)

The seniority system in this litigation is entirely bona fide. It applies equally to all races and ethnic groups. To the extent that it "locks" employees into non-line-driver jobs, it does so for all. The city drivers and servicemen who are discouraged from transferring to line-driver jobs are not all Negroes or Spanish-surnamed Americans; to the contrary, the overwhelming majority are white. The placing of line drivers in a separate bargaining unit from other employees is rational in accord with the industry practice, and consistent with National Labor Relations Board precedents. It is conceded that the seniority system did not have its genesis in racial discrimination, and that it was negotiated and has been maintained free from any illegal purpose. In these circumstances, the single fact that the system extends no retroactive seniority to pre-Act discriminatees does not make it unlawful.

Because the seniority system was protected by § 703(h), the union's conduct in agreeing to and maintaining the system did not violate Title VII. On remand, the District Court's injunction against the union must be vacated.

. . . . In Part II-A, *supra*, we have held that the District Court and Court of Appeals were not in error in finding that the Government had proved a system wide pattern and practice of racial and ethnic discrimination on the part of the company. On remand, therefore, every post-Act minority group applicant for a line-driver position will be presumptively entitled to relief, subject to a showing by the company that its earlier refusal to place the applicant in a line-driver job was not based on its policy of discrimination.

. . .

It is so ordered.

Notes and Questions:

1. Based on the facts, what did the Government prove to make a successful claim of systemic disparate treatment. Why was the government the entity to bring this lawsuit? Under what authority?

2. How does Title VII treat seniority systems according to *Teamsters*? What is the Court's interpretation of the legislative intent guiding its reading of Title VII?

3. What facts were significant to the Court's finding of non-discrimination? Could the seniority system had been found discriminatory had the findings been different?

4. Compare the use of statistics in *Teamsters* compared to the way they are used and analyzed in the disparate impact cases.

Hazelwood Sch. Dist. v. United States
433 US. 299 (1977)

MR. JUSTICE STEWART delivered the opinion of the Court.

The petitioner Hazelwood School District covers 78 square miles in the northern part of St. Louis County, Mo. In 1973, the Attorney General brought this lawsuit against Hazelwood and various of its officials, alleging that they were engaged in a "pattern or practice" of employment discrimination in violation of Title VII of the Civil Rights Act of 1964, 78 Stat. 253, as amended, 42 U.S.C. § 2000e *et seq.* (1970 ed. and Supp. V). The complaint asked for an injunction requiring Hazelwood to cease its discriminatory practices, to take affirmative steps to obtain qualified Negro faculty members, and to offer employment and give back pay to victims of past illegal discrimination.

Hazelwood was formed from 13 rural school districts between 1949 and 1951 by a process of annexation. By the 1967–1968 school year, 17,550 students were enrolled in the district, of whom only 59 were Negro; the number of Negro pupils increased to 576 of 25,166 in 1972–1973, a total of just over 2%.

From the beginning, Hazelwood followed relatively unstructured procedures in hiring its teachers. Every person requesting an application for a teaching position was sent one, and completed applications were submitted to a central personnel office, where they were kept on file. During the early 1960's, the personnel office notified all applicants whenever a teaching position became available, but, as the number of applications on file increased in the late 1960's and early 1970's, this practice was no longer considered feasible. The personnel office thus began the practice of selecting anywhere from 3 to 10 applicants for interviews at the school where the vacancy existed. The personnel office did not substantively screen the applicants in determining which of them to send for interviews, other than to ascertain that each applicant, if selected, would be eligible for state certification by the time he began the job. Generally, those who had most recently submitted applications were most likely to be chosen for interviews.

Interviews were conducted by a department chairman, program coordinator, or the principal at the school where the teaching vacancy existed. Although those conducting the interviews did fill out forms rating the applicants in a number of respects, it is undisputed that each school principal possessed virtually unlimited discretion in hiring teachers for his school. The only general guidance given to the principals was to hire the "most competent" person available, and such intangibles as "personality, disposition, appearance, poise, voice, articulation, and ability to deal with people" counted heavily. The principal's choice was routinely honored by Hazelwood's Superintendent and the Board of Education.

In the early 1960's Hazelwood found it necessary to recruit new teachers, and, for that purpose, members of its staff visited a number of colleges and universities in Missouri and bordering States. All the institutions visited were predominantly white, and Hazelwood did not seriously recruit at either of the two predominantly Negro four-year colleges in Missouri. As a buyer's market began to develop for public school teachers, Hazelwood curtailed its recruiting efforts. For the 1971–1972 school year, 3,127 persons applied for only 234 teaching vacancies; for the 1972–1973 school year, there were 2,373 applications for 282 vacancies. A number of the applicants who were not hired were Negroes.

Hazelwood hired its first Negro teacher in 1969. The number of Negro faculty members gradually increased in successive years: 6 of 957 in the 1970 school year; 16 of 1,107 by the end of the 1972 school year; 22 of 1,231 in the 1973 school year. By comparison, according to 1970 census figures, of more than 19,000 teachers employed in that year in the St. Louis area, 15.4% were Negro. That percentage figure included the St. Louis City School District, which in recent years has followed a policy of attempting to maintain a 50% Negro teaching staff. Apart from that school district, 5.7% of the teachers in the county were Negro in 1970.

Drawing upon these historic facts, the Government mounted its "pattern or practice" attack in the District Court upon four different fronts. It adduced evidence of (1) a history of alleged racially discriminatory practices, (2) statistical disparities in hiring, (3) the standard less and largely subjective hiring procedures, and (4) specific instances of alleged discrimination against 55 unsuccessful Negro applicants for teaching jobs. Hazelwood offered virtually no additional evidence in response, relying instead on evidence introduced by the Government, perceived deficiencies in the Government's case, and its own officially promulgated policy "to hire all teachers on the basis of training, preparation and recommendations, regardless of race, color or creed."

The District Court ruled that the Government had failed to establish a pattern or practice of discrimination. The court was unpersuaded by the alleged history of discrimination, noting that no dual school system had ever existed in Hazelwood. The statistics showing that relatively small numbers of Negroes were employed as teachers were found nonprobative, on the ground that the percentage of Negro pupils in Hazelwood was similarly small. The court found nothing illegal or suspect in the teacher hiring procedures that Hazelwood had followed. Finally, the court reviewed the evidence in the 55 cases of alleged individual discrimination, and after stating that the burden of proving intentional discrimination was on the Government, it found that this burden had not been sustained in a single instance. Hence, the court entered judgment for the defendants. 392 F.Supp. 1276 (ED Mo.).

The Court of Appeals for the Eighth Circuit reversed. 534 F.2d 805. After suggesting that the District Court had assigned inadequate weight to evidence of discriminatory conduct on the part of Hazelwood before the effective date of Title VII, the Court of Appeals rejected the trial court's analysis of the statistical data as resting on an irrelevant comparison of Negro teachers to Negro pupils in Hazelwood. The proper comparison, in the appellate court's view, was one between Negro teachers in Hazelwood and Negro teachers in the relevant labor market area. Selecting St. Louis County and St. Louis City as the relevant area, the Court of Appeals compared the 1970 census figures, showing that 15.4% of teachers in that area were Negro, to the racial composition of Hazelwood's teaching staff. In the 1972–1973 and 1973–1974 school years, only 1.4% and 1.8%, respectively, of Hazelwood's teachers were Negroes. This statistical disparity, particularly when viewed against the background of the teacher hiring procedures that Hazelwood had followed, was held to constitute a *prima facie* case of a pattern or practice of racial discrimination.

In addition, the Court of Appeals reasoned that the trial court had erred in failing to measure the 55 instances in which Negro applicants were denied jobs against the four-part standard for establishing a *prima facie* case of individual discrimination set out in this Court's opinion in *McDonnell Douglas Corp. v. Green*, 411 U.S. 792, 802. Applying that standard, the appellate court found 16 cases of individual discrimination, which "buttressed" the statistical proof. Because Hazelwood had not rebutted the Government's *prima facie* case of a pattern or practice of racial discrimination, the Court of Appeals directed judgment for the Government and prescribed the remedial order to be entered.

We granted certiorari, 429 U.S. 1037, to consider a substantial question affecting the enforcement of a pervasive federal law.

The petitioners primarily attack the judgment of the Court of Appeals for its reliance on "undifferentiated workforce statistics to find an unrebutted *prima facie* case of employment discrimination." The question they raise, in short, is whether a basic component in the Court of Appeals' finding of a pattern or practice of discrimination—the comparatively small percentage of Negro employees on Hazelwood's teaching staff—was lacking in probative force.

This Court's recent consideration in *Teamsters v. United States*, 431 U.S. 324, of the role of statistics in "pattern or practice" suits under Title VII provides substantial guidance in evaluating the arguments advanced by the petitioners. In that case, we stated that it is the Government's burden to "establish by a preponderance of the evidence that racial discrimination was the [employer's] standard operating procedure—the regular, rather than the unusual, practice." *Id.* at 336. We also noted that statistics can be an important source of proof in employment discrimination cases, since, "absent explanation, it is ordinarily to be expected that nondiscriminatory hiring practices will, in time, result in a workforce more or less representative of the racial and ethnic composition of the population in the community from which employees are hired. Evidence of long-lasting and gross disparity between the composition of a workforce and that of the general population thus may be significant even though § 703(j) makes clear that Title VII imposes no requirement that a workforce mirror the general population." *Id.* at 340 n. 20. *See also Arlington Heights v. Metropolitan Housing Dev. Corp.*, 429 U.S. 252, 266; *Washington v. Davis*, 426 U.S.

229, 241–242. Where gross statistical disparities can be shown, they alone may, in a proper case, constitute *prima facie* proof of a pattern or practice of discrimination. *Teamsters, supra* at 339.

There can be no doubt, in light of the *Teamsters* case, that the District Court's comparison of Hazelwood's teacher workforce to its student population fundamentally misconceived the role of statistics in employment discrimination cases. The Court of Appeals was correct in the view that a proper comparison was between the racial composition of Hazelwood's teaching staff and the racial composition of the qualified public-school teacher population in the relevant labor market. *See Teamsters, supra* at 337–338, and n. 17. The percentage of Negroes on Hazelwood's teaching staff in 1972–1973 was 1.4%, and in 1973–1974 it was 1.8%. By contrast, the percentage of qualified Negro teachers in the area was, according to the 1970 census, at least 5.7%. Although these differences were, on their face, substantial, the Court of Appeals erred in substituting its judgment for that of the District Court and holding that the Government had conclusively proved its "pattern or practice" lawsuit.

The Court of Appeals totally disregarded the possibility that this *prima facie* statistical proof in the record might at the trial court level be rebutted by statistics dealing with Hazelwood's hiring after it became subject to Title VII. Racial discrimination by public employers was not made illegal under Title VII until March 24, 1972. A public employer who from that date forward made all its employment decisions in a wholly nondiscriminatory way would not violate Title VII even if it had formerly maintained an all-white workforce by purposefully excluding Negroes. For this reason, the Court cautioned in the *Teamsters* opinion that, once a *prima facie* case has been established by statistical workforce disparities, the employer must be given an opportunity to show that "the claimed discriminatory pattern is a product of pre-Act hiring, rather than unlawful post-Act discrimination." 431 U.S. at 360.

The record in this case showed that, for the 1972–1973 school year, Hazelwood hired 282 new teachers, 10 of whom (3.5%) were Negroes; for the following school year, it hired 123 new teachers, 5 of whom (4.1%) were Negroes. Over the two-year period, Negroes constituted a total of 15 of the 405 new teachers hired (3.7%). Although the Court of Appeals briefly mentioned these data in reciting the facts, it wholly ignored them in discussing whether the Government had shown a pattern or practice of discrimination. And it gave no consideration at all to the possibility that post-Act data as to the number of Negroes hired compared to the total number of Negro applicants might tell a totally different story.

What the hiring figures prove obviously depends upon the figures to which they are compared. The Court of Appeals accepted the Government's argument that the relevant comparison was to the labor market area of St. Louis County and the city of St. Louis, in which, according to the 1970 census, 15.4% of all teachers were Negro. The propriety of that comparison was vigorously disputed by the petitioners, who urged that, because the city of St. Louis has made special attempts to maintain a 50% Negro teaching staff, inclusion of that school district in the relevant market area distorts the comparison. Were that argument accepted, the percentage of Negro teachers in the relevant labor market area (St. Louis County alone) as shown in the 1970 census would be 5.7%, rather than 15.4%.

The difference between these figures may well be important; the disparity between 3.7% (the percentage of Negro teachers hired by Hazelwood in 1972–1973 and 1973–1974) and 5.7% may be sufficiently small to weaken the Government's other proof, while the disparity between 3.7% and 15.4% may be sufficiently large to reinforce it. In determining which of the two figures—or, very possibly, what intermediate figure—provides the most accurate basis for comparison to the hiring figures at Hazelwood, it will be necessary to evaluate such considerations as (i) whether the racially based hiring policies of the St. Louis City School District were in effect as far back as 1970, the year in which the census figures were taken; (ii) to what extent those policies have changed the racial composition of that district's teaching staff from what it would otherwise have been; (iii) to what extent St. Louis' recruitment policies have diverted to the city, teachers who might otherwise have applied to Hazelwood; (iv) to what extent Negro teachers employed by the city would prefer employment in other districts such as Hazelwood; and (v) what the experience in other school districts in St. Louis County indicates about the validity of excluding the City School District from the relevant labor market.

It is thus clear that a determination of the appropriate comparative figures in this case will depend upon further evaluation by the trial court. As this Court admonished in *Teamsters:* "[S]tatistics . . . come in infinite variety. . . . [T]heir usefulness depends on all of the surrounding facts and circumstances." 431 U.S. at 340. Only the trial court is in a position to make the appropriate determination after further findings. And only after such a determination is made can a foundation be established for deciding whether or not Hazelwood engaged in a pattern or practice of racial discrimination in its employment practices in violation of the law.

We hold, therefore, that the Court of Appeals erred in disregarding the post-Act hiring statistics in the record, and that it should have remanded the case to the District Court for further findings as to the relevant labor market area and for an ultimate determination of whether Hazelwood engaged in a pattern or practice of employment discrimination after March 24, 1972. Accordingly, the judgment is vacated, and the case is remanded to the District Court for further proceedings consistent with this opinion.

It is so ordered.

C. Disparate Impact

The cases below usher in the doctrine of disparate impact discrimination, now accepted as part of Title VII. Unlike systemic discrimination claims, disparate impact targets otherwise neutral policies that operate or are implemented in a discriminatory manner. For example, though requiring a particular degree or results from standardized tests is perfectly legal, it can be found to be illegal if shown to cause disproportionate negative effects on employees protected by Title VII. This is most likely to be so if the requirement cannot be justified by business necessity. Causation, as the jurisprudence progressed, became the linchpin of these cases. Proving that a neutral policy caused a particular impact requires tailored statistical analysis. Progressively, the courts seem to have moved toward a "but for" view of causation for these kinds of cases. The expense and level of expertise required for that type of analysis has made these claims less likely to prevail. *See* Tom Tinkham, *The Uses and Misuses of Statistical Proof in Age Discrimination Claims*, 27 HOFSTRA LAB. & EMP. L.J. 357 (2010); Jennifer L. Peresie, *Toward a Coherent Test for Disparate Impact Discrimination*, 84 IND. L.J. 773 (2009).

Griggs v. Duke Power Co.
401 U.S. 424 (1971)

MR. CHIEF JUSTICE BURGER delivered the opinion of the Court.

We granted the writ in this case to resolve the question whether an employer is prohibited by the Civil Rights Act of 1964, Title VII, from requiring a high school education or passing of a standardized general intelligence test as a condition of employment in or transfer to jobs when (a) neither standard is shown to be significantly related to successful job performance, (b) both requirements operate to disqualify Negroes at a substantially higher rate than white applicants, and (c) the jobs in question formerly had been filled only by white employees as part of a long-standing practice of giving preference to whites.

Congress provided, in Title VII of the Civil Rights Act of 1964, for class actions for enforcement of provisions of the Act, and this proceeding was brought by a group of incumbent Negro employees against Duke Power Company. All the petitioners are employed at the Company's Dan River Steam Station, a power generating facility located at Draper, North Carolina. At the time this action was instituted, the Company had 95 employees at the Dan River Station, 14 of whom were Negroes; 13 of these are petitioners here.

The District Court found that, prior to July 2, 1965, the effective date of the Civil Rights Act of 1964, the Company openly discriminated on the basis of race in the hiring and assigning of employees at its Dan River plant. The plant was organized into five operating departments: (1) Labor, (2) Coal Handling, (3) Operations, (4) Maintenance, and (5) Laboratory and Test. Negroes were employed only in the Labor Department, where the highest paying jobs paid less than the lowest paying jobs in the other four "operating" departments, in which only whites were employed. Promotions were normally made within each department on the basis of job seniority. Transferees into a department usually began in the lowest position.

In 1955, the Company instituted a policy of requiring a high school education for initial assignment to any department except Labor, and for transfer from the

Coal Handling to any "inside" department (Operations, Maintenance, or Laboratory). When the Company abandoned its policy of restricting Negroes to the Labor Department in 1965, completion of high school also was made a prerequisite to transfer from Labor to any other department. From the time the high school requirement was instituted to the time of trial, however, white employees hired before the time of the high school education requirement continued to perform satisfactorily and achieve promotions in the "operating" departments. Findings on this score are not challenged.

The Company added a further requirement for new employees on July 2, 1965, the date on which Title VII became effective. To qualify for placement in any but the Labor Department, it became necessary to register satisfactory scores on two professionally prepared aptitude tests, as well as to have a high school education. Completion of high school alone continued to render employees eligible for transfer to the four desirable departments from which Negroes had been excluded if the incumbent had been employed prior to the time of the new requirement. In September 1965, the Company began to permit incumbent employees who lacked a high school education to qualify for transfer from Labor or Coal Handling to an "inside" job by passing two tests—the Wonderlic Personnel Test, which purports to measure general intelligence, and the Bennett Mechanical Comprehension Test. Neither was directed or intended to measure the ability to learn to perform a particular job or category of jobs. The requisite scores used for both initial hiring and transfer approximated the national median for high school graduates. [The lower courts struggled unsatisfactorily based their analysis on intent. The Court of Appeals found that the policies had been applied fairly to blacks and whites.] We granted the writ on these claims. 399 U.S. 926.

The objective of Congress in the enactment of Title VII is plain from the language of the statute. It was to achieve equality of employment opportunities and remove barriers that have operated in the past to favor an identifiable group of white employees over other employees. Under the Act, practices, procedures, or tests neutral on their face, and even neutral in terms of intent, cannot be maintained if they operate to "freeze" the *status quo* of prior discriminatory employment practices.

The Court of Appeals' opinion, and the partial dissent, agreed that, on the record in the present case, "whites register far better on the Company's alternative requirements" than Negroes. 420 F.2d 1225, 1239 n. 6. This consequence would appear to be directly traceable to race. Basic intelligence must have the means of articulation to manifest itself fairly in a testing process. Because they are Negroes, petitioners have long received inferior education in segregated schools, and this Court expressly recognized these differences in *Gaston County v. United States*, 395 U.S. 285 (1969). There, because of the inferior education received by Negroes in North Carolina, this Court barred the institution of a literacy test for voter registration on the ground that the test would abridge the right to vote indirectly on account of race. Congress did not intend by Title VII, however, to guarantee a job to every person regardless of qualifications. In short, the Act does not command that any person be hired simply because he was formerly the subject of discrimination, or because he is a member of a minority group. Discriminatory preference for any group, minority or majority, is precisely and only what Congress has proscribed. What is required by Congress is the removal of artificial, arbitrary, and unnecessary barriers to employment when the barriers operate invidiously to discriminate on the basis of racial or other impermissible classification.

Congress has now provided that tests or criteria for employment or promotion may not provide equality of opportunity merely in the sense of the fabled offer of milk to the stork and the fox. On the contrary, Congress has now required that the posture and condition of the job seeker be taken into account. It has—to resort again to the fable—provided that the vessel in which the milk is proffered be one all seekers can use. The Act proscribes not only overt discrimination, but also practices that are fair in form, but discriminatory in operation. The touchstone is business necessity. If an employment practice which operates to exclude Negroes cannot be shown to be related to job performance, the practice is prohibited.

On the record before us, neither the high school completion requirement nor the general intelligence test is shown to bear a demonstrable relationship to successful performance of the jobs for which it was used. Both were adopted, as the Court of Appeals noted, without meaningful study of their relationship to job performance ability. Rather, a vice-president of the Company testified, the requirements were instituted on the Company's judgment that they generally would improve the overall quality of the workforce.

The evidence, however, shows that employees who have not completed high school or taken the tests have continued to perform satisfactorily, and make progress in departments for which the high school and test criteria are now used. The promotion record of present employees who would not be able to meet the new criteria thus suggests the possibility that the requirements may not be needed even for the limited purpose of preserving the avowed policy of advancement within the Company. In the context of this case, it is unnecessary to reach the question whether testing requirements that take into account capability for the next succeeding position or related future promotion might be utilized upon a showing that such long-range requirements fulfill a genuine business need. In the present case, the Company has made no such showing.

. . . The Company's lack of discriminatory intent is suggested by special efforts to help the undereducated employees through Company financing of two-thirds the cost of tuition for high school training. But Congress directed the thrust of the Act to the consequences of employment practices, not simply the motivation. More than that, Congress has placed on the employer the burden of showing that any given requirement must have a manifest relationship to the employment in question.

The facts of this case demonstrate the inadequacy of broad and general testing devices, as well as the infirmity of using diplomas or degrees as fixed measures of capability. History is filled with examples of men and women who rendered highly effective performance without the conventional badges of accomplishment in terms of certificates, diplomas, or degrees. Diplomas and tests are useful servants, but Congress has mandated the common-sense proposition that they are not to become masters of reality.

The Company contends that its general intelligence tests are specifically permitted by §703(h) of the Act. That section authorizes the use of "any professionally developed ability test" that is not "designed, intended *or used* to discriminate because of race. . . ." (Emphasis added.)

The Equal Employment Opportunity Commission, having enforcement responsibility, has issued guidelines interpreting §703(h) to permit only the use of job-related tests. The administrative interpretation of the Act by the enforcing agency is entitled to great deference. See, *e.g., United States v. City of Chicago,* 400 U.S. 8 (1970); *Udall v. Tallman,* 380 U.S. 1 (1965); *Power Reactor Co. v. Electricians,* 367 U.S. 396 (1961). Since the Act and its legislative history support the Commission's construction, this affords good reason to treat the guidelines as expressing the will of Congress.

Section 703(h) was not contained in the House version of the Civil Rights Act, but was added in the Senate during extended debate. For a period, debate revolved around claims that the bill, as proposed, would prohibit all testing and force employers to hire unqualified persons simply because they were part of a group formerly subject to job discrimination. Proponents of Title VII sought throughout the debate to assure the critics that the Act would have no effect on job-related tests. Senators Case of New Jersey and Clark of Pennsylvania, comanagers of the bill on the Senate floor, issued a memorandum explaining that the proposed Title VII "expressly protects the employer's right to insist that any prospective applicant, Negro or white, *must meet the applicable job qualifications.* Indeed, the very purpose of title VII is to promote hiring on the basis of job qualifications, rather than on the basis of race or color." 110 Cong.Rec. 7247. (Emphasis added.) Despite these assurances, Senator Tower of Texas introduced an amendment authorizing "professionally developed ability tests." Proponents of Title VII opposed the amendment because, as written, it would permit an employer to give any test "whether it was a good test or not, so long as it was professionally designed. Discrimination could actually exist under the guise of compliance with the statute." 110 Cong.Rec. 13504 (remarks of Sen. Case).

The amendment was defeated, and, two days later, Senator Tower offered a substitute amendment which was adopted verbatim, and is now the testing provision of §703(h). Speaking for the supporters of Title VII, Senator Humphrey, who had vigorously opposed the first amendment, endorsed the substitute amendment, stating: "Senators on both sides of the aisle who were deeply interested in title VII have examined the text of this amendment, and have found it to be in accord with the intent and purpose of that title." 110 Cong.Rec. 13724. The amendment was then adopted. From the sum of the legislative history relevant in this case, the conclusion is inescapable that the EEOC's construction of § 703(h) to require that employment tests be job-related comports with congressional intent.

Nothing in the Act precludes the use of testing or measuring procedures; obviously they are useful. What Congress has forbidden is giving these devices and mechanisms controlling force unless they are demonstrably a reasonable measure of job performance. Congress has not commanded that the less qualified be preferred over the better qualified simply because of minority origins. Far from disparaging job qualifications as such, Congress has made such qualifications the controlling factor, so that race, religion, nationality, and sex become irrelevant. What Congress has commanded is that any tests used must measure the person for the job, and not the person in the abstract.

The judgment of the Court of Appeals is, as to that portion of the judgment appealed from, reversed.

Ward's Cove Packing Co., Inc. v. Antonio
490 U.S. 642 (1989)

Justice WHITE delivered the opinion of the Court.

Title VII of the Civil Rights Act of 1964, 78 Stat. 253, *as amended*, 42 U.S.C. § 2000e *et seq.*, makes it an unfair employment practice for an employer to discriminate against any individual with respect to hiring or the terms and condition of employment because of such individual's race, color, religion, sex, or national origin; or to limit, segregate, or classify his employees in ways that would adversely affect any employee because of the employee's race, color, religion, sex, or national origin. § 2000e-2(a). *Griggs v. Duke Power Co.*, 401 U.S. 424, 431 (1971), construed Title VII to proscribe "not only overt discrimination, but also practices that are fair in form, but discriminatory in practice." Under this basis for liability, which is known as the "disparate impact" theory and which is involved in this case, a facially neutral employment practice may be deemed violative of Title VII without evidence of the employer's subjective intent to discriminate that is required in a "disparate treatment" case.

I

The claims before us are disparate impact claims, involving the employment practices of petitioners, two companies that operate salmon canneries in remote and widely separated areas of Alaska. The canneries operate only during the salmon runs in the summer months. They are inoperative and vacant for the rest of the year. In May or June of each year, a few weeks before the salmon runs begin, workers arrive and prepare the equipment and facilities for the canning operation. Most of these workers possess a variety of skills. When salmon runs are about to begin, the workers who will operate the cannery lines arrive, remain as long as there are fish to can, and then depart. The canneries are then closed down, winterized, and left vacant until the next spring. During the off-season, the companies employ only a small number of individuals at their headquarters in Seattle and Astoria, Oregon, plus some employees at the winter shipyard in Seattle.

The length and size of salmon runs vary from year to year, and hence the number of employees needed at each cannery also varies. Estimates are made as early in the winter as possible; the necessary employees are hired, and when the time comes, they are transported to the canneries. Salmon must be processed soon after they are caught, and the work during the canning season is therefore intense. For this reason, and because the canneries are located in remote regions, all workers are housed at the canneries and have their meals in company-owned mess halls.

Jobs at the canneries are of two general types: "cannery jobs" on the cannery line, which are unskilled positions; and "noncannery jobs," which fall into a variety of classifications. Most noncannery jobs are classified as skilled positions. Cannery jobs are filled predominantly by nonwhites: Filipinos and Alaska Natives. The Filipinos are hired through, and dispatched by, Local 37 of the International Longshoremen's and Warehousemen's Union pursuant to a hiring hall agreement with the local. The Alaska Natives primarily reside in villages near the remote cannery locations. Noncannery jobs are filled with predominantly white workers, who are hired during the winter months from the companies' offices in Washington and Oregon. Virtually all of the noncannery jobs pay more than cannery positions. The predominantly white noncannery workers and the predominantly nonwhite cannery employees live in separate dormitories and eat in separate mess halls.

In 1974, respondents, a class of nonwhite cannery workers who were (or had been) employed at the canneries, brought this Title VII action against petitioners. Respondents alleged that a variety of petitioners' hiring/promotion practices—e.g., nepotism, a rehire preference, a lack of objective hiring criteria, separate hiring channels, a practice of not promoting from within—were responsible for the racial stratification of the workforce, and had denied them and other nonwhites employment as noncannery workers on the basis of race. Respondents also complained of petitioners' racially segregated housing and dining facilities. All of respondents' claims were advanced under both the disparate treatment and disparate impact theories of Title VII liability.

The District Court held a bench trial, after which it entered 172 findings of fact. App. to Pet. for Cert. I-1 to I-94. It then rejected all of respondents' disparate treatment claims. It also rejected the disparate impact challenges involving the subjective employment criteria used by petitioners to fill these noncannery positions, on the ground that those criteria were not subject to attack under a disparate impact theory. *Id.* at I-102. Petitioners' "objective" employment practices (*e.g.,* an English language requirement, alleged nepotism in hiring, failure to post noncannery openings, the rehire preference, etc.) were found to be subject to challenge under the disparate impact theory, but these claims were rejected for failure of proof. Judgment was entered for petitioners.

On appeal, a panel of the Ninth Circuit affirmed, 768 F.2d 1120 (1985), but that decision was vacated when the Court of Appeals agreed to hear the case *en banc,*787 F.2d 462 (1985). The *en banc* hearing was ordered to settle an intracircuit conflict over the question whether subjective hiring practices could be analyzed under a disparate impact model; the Court of Appeals held — as this Court subsequently ruled in *Watson v. Fort Worth Bank & Trust,* 487 U.S. 977 (1988) — that disparate impact analysis could be applied to subjective hiring practices. 810 F.2d 1477, 1482 (1987). The Ninth Circuit also concluded that, in such a case, "[o]nce the plaintiff class has shown disparate impact caused by specific, identifiable employment practices or criteria, the burden shifts to the employer," *id.* at 1485, to "prov[e the] business necessity" of the challenged practice, *id.* at 1486. Because the *en banc* holding on subjective employment practices reversed the District Court's contrary ruling, the *en banc* Court of Appeals remanded the case to a panel for further proceedings.

On remand, the panel applied the *en banc* ruling to the facts of this case. 827 F.2d 439 (1987). It held that respondents had made out a *prima facie* case of disparate impact in hiring for both skilled and unskilled noncannery positions. The panel remanded the case for further proceedings, instructing the District Court that it was the employer's burden to prove that any disparate impact caused by its hiring and employment practices was justified by business necessity. Neither the *en banc* court nor the panel disturbed the District Court's rejection of the disparate treatment claims.

Petitioners sought review of the Court of Appeals' decision in this Court, challenging it on several grounds. Because some of the issues raised by the decision below were matters on which this Court was evenly divided in *Watson v. Fort Worth Bank & Trust, supra,* we granted certiorari, 487 U.S. 1264 (1988), for the purpose of addressing these disputed questions of the proper application of Title VII's disparate impact theory of liability.

II

In holding that respondents had made out a *prima facie* case of disparate impact, the Court of Appeals relied solely on respondents' statistics showing a high percentage of nonwhite workers in the cannery jobs and a low percentage of such workers in the noncannery positions. Although statistical proof can alone make out a *prima facie* case, see *Teamsters v. United States,* 431 U.S. 324, 339 (1977); *Hazelwood School Dist. v. United States,* 433 U.S. 299, 307–308 (1977), the Court of Appeals' ruling here misapprehends our precedents and the purposes of Title VII, and we therefore reverse.

"There can be no doubt," as there was when a similar mistaken analysis had been undertaken by the courts below in *Hazelwood, supra,* at 308, "that the . . . comparison . . . fundamentally misconceived the role of statistics in employment discrimination cases." The "proper comparison [is] between the racial composition of [the at-issue jobs] and the racial composition of the qualified . . . population in the relevant labor market." *Ibid.* It is such a comparison — between the racial composition of the qualified persons in the labor market and the persons holding at-issue jobs — that generally forms the proper basis for the initial inquiry in a disparate impact case. Alternatively, in cases where such labor market statistics will be difficult if not impossible to ascertain, we have recognized that certain other statistics — such as measures indicating the racial composition of "otherwise-qualified applicants" for at-issue jobs — are equally probative for this purpose. See, *e.g., New York City Transit Authority v. Beazer,* 440 U.S. 568, 585 (1979).

It is clear to us that the Court of Appeals' acceptance of the comparison between the racial composition of the cannery workforce and that of the noncannery workforce, as probative of a *prima facie* case of disparate impact in the selection of the latter group of workers, was flawed for several reasons. Most obviously, with respect to the skilled noncannery jobs at issue here, the cannery workforce in no way reflected "the pool of *qualified* job applicants" or the "*qualified* population in the labor force." Measuring alleged discrimination in the selection of accountants, managers, boat captains, electricians, doctors, and engineers — and the long list of other "skilled" noncannery positions found to exist by the District Court, See App. to Pet. for Cert. I-56 to I-58 — by comparing the number of nonwhites occupying these jobs to the number of nonwhites filling cannery worker positions is nonsensical. If the absence of minorities holding such skilled positions is due to a dearth of qualified nonwhite applicants (for reasons that are not petitioners' fault), petitioners' selection methods or employment practices cannot be said to have had a "disparate impact" on nonwhites.

One example illustrates why this must be so. Respondents' own statistics concerning the noncannery workforce at one of the canneries at issue here indicate that approximately 17% of the new hires for medical jobs, and 15% of the new hires for officer worker positions, were nonwhite. See App. to Brief for Respondents B-l. If it were the case that less than 15 to 17% of the applicants for these jobs were nonwhite and that nonwhites made up a lower percentage of the relevant qualified labor market, it is hard to see how respondents, without more, cf. *Connecticut v. Teal,* 457 U.S. 440 (1982), would have made out a *prima facie* case of disparate impact. Yet, under the Court of Appeals' theory, simply because nonwhites comprise 52% of the cannery workers at the cannery in question, *see* App. to Brief for Respondents B-1, respondents would be successful in establishing a *prima facie* case of racial discrimination under Title VII.

Such a result cannot be squared with our cases or with the goals behind the statute. The Court of Appeals' theory, at the very least, would mean that any employer who had a segment of his workforce that was — for some reason — racially imbalanced, could be haled into court and forced to engage in the expensive and time-consuming task of defending the "business necessity" of the methods used to select the other members of his workforce. The only practicable option for many employers would be to adopt racial quotas, insuring that no portion of their workforces deviated in racial composition from the other portions thereof; this is a result that Congress expressly rejected in drafting Title VII. See 42 U.S.C. §2000e-2(j); see also *Watson v. Fort Worth Bank & Trust,* 487 U.S. at 922–994, and n. 2 (opinion of O'Connor, J.). The Court of Appeals' theory would "leave the employer little choice . . . but to engage in a subjective quota system of employment selection. This, of course, is far from the intent of Title VII." *Albemarle Paper Co. v. Moody,* 422 U.S. 405, 449 (1975) (Blackmun, J., concurring in judgment).

The Court of Appeals also erred with respect to the unskilled noncannery positions. Racial imbalance in one segment of an employer's workforce does not, without more, establish a *prima facie* case of disparate impact with respect to the selection of workers for the employer's other positions, even where workers for the different positions may have somewhat fungible skills (as is arguably the case for cannery and unskilled noncannery workers). As long as there are no barriers or practices deterring qualified nonwhites from applying for noncannery positions, if the percentage of selected applicants who are nonwhite is not significantly less than the percentage of qualified applicants who are nonwhite, the employer's selection mechanism probably does not operate with a disparate impact on minorities. Where this is the case, the percentage of nonwhite workers found in other positions in the employer's labor force is irrelevant to the question of a *prima facie* statistical case of disparate impact. As noted above, a contrary ruling on this point would almost inexorably lead to the use of numerical quotas in the workplace, a result that Congress and this Court have rejected repeatedly in the past.

Moreover, isolating the cannery workers as the potential "labor force" for unskilled noncannery positions is at once both too broad and too narrow in its focus. It is too broad because the vast majority of these cannery workers did not seek jobs in unskilled noncannery positions; there is no showing that many of them would have done so even if none of the arguably "deterring" practices existed. Thus, the pool of cannery workers cannot be used as a surrogate for the class of qualified job applicants, because it contains many persons who have not (and would not) be noncannery job applicants. Conversely, if respondents propose to use the cannery workers for comparison purposes because they represent the "qualified labor population" generally, the group is too narrow, because there are obviously many qualified persons in the labor market for noncannery jobs who are not cannery workers.

The peculiar facts of this case further illustrate why a comparison between the percentage of nonwhite cannery workers and nonwhite noncannery workers is an improper basis for making out a claim of disparate impact. Here, the District Court found that nonwhites were "overrepresent[ed]" among cannery workers because petitioners had contracted with a predominantly nonwhite union (Local 37) to fill these positions. See App. to Pet. for Cert. I-42. As a result, if petitioners (for some permissible reason) ceased using local 37 as its hiring channel for cannery positions, it appears (according to the District Court's findings) that the racial stratification between the cannery and noncannery workers might diminish to statistical insignificance. Under the Court of Appeals' approach, therefore, it is possible that, *with no change whatsoever* in their hiring practices for noncannery workers—the jobs at issue in this lawsuit—petitioners could make respondents' *prima facie* case of disparate impact "disappear." But if there would be no *prima facie* case of disparate impact in the selection of noncannery workers absent petitioners' use of local 37 to hire cannery workers, surely petitioners' reliance on the union to fill the cannery jobs not at issue here (and its resulting "overrepresentation" of nonwhites in those positions) does not—standing alone—make out a *prima facie* case of disparate impact. Yet it is precisely such an ironic result that the Court of Appeals reached below.

Consequently, we reverse the Court of Appeals' ruling that a comparison between the percentage of cannery workers who are nonwhite and the percentage of noncannery workers who are nonwhite makes out a *prima facie* case of disparate impact. Of course, this leaves unresolved whether the record made in the District Court will support a conclusion that a *prima facie* case of disparate impact has been established on some basis other than the racial disparity between cannery and noncannery workers. This is an issue that the Court of Appeals or the District Court should address in the first instance.

III

Since the statistical disparity relied on by the Court of Appeals did not suffice to make out a *prima facie* case, any inquiry by us into whether the specific challenged employment practices of petitioners caused that disparity is pretermitted, as is any inquiry into whether the disparate impact that any employment practice may have had was justified by business considerations. Because we remand for further proceedings, however, on whether a *prima facie* case of disparate impact has been made in defensible fashion in this case, we address two other challenges petitioners have made to the decision of the Court of Appeals.

A

First is the question of causation in a disparate impact case. The law in this respect was correctly stated by Justice O'Connor's opinion last Term in *Watson v. Fort Worth Bank & Trust*, 487 U.S. at 994:

> "[W]e note that the plaintiff's burden in establishing a *prima facie* case goes beyond the need to show that there are statistical disparities in the employer's workforce. The plaintiff must begin by identifying the specific employment practice that is challenged. . . . Especially in cases where an employer combines subjective criteria with the use of more rigid standardized rules or tests, the plaintiff is in our view responsible for isolating and identifying the specific employment practices that are allegedly responsible for any observed statistical disparities."

. . .

It is so ordered.

D. When Disparate Impact and Disparate Treatment Collide

Note the appropriate standard for defenses under disparate impact and disparate treatment. Under disparate impact theory, even if a plaintiff is successful in proving that an employer's neutral policy causes discriminatory effects, with the exact statistical accuracy required by *Wards Cove*, the defendant still might prevail by demonstrating business necessity. The business necessity defense requires that the defendant show that the policy was necessary to the nature of the business. In comparison, in the disparate treatment, defendants can only justify a discriminatory element by showing that such element is a boni fide occupational qualification (commonly referred to as the BFOQ defense). These two standards collide in *AUW vs. Johnson Controls*. The biggest warning coming from *UAW v. Johnson Controls* is never to confuse the two theories. The reasoning below should also prove quite interesting to students as it constitutes one of the rare instances where the Supreme Court openly chastises a lower court.

International Union, United Automobile, Aerospace & Agricultural Implement Workers of America, UAW v. Johnson Controls, Inc.

499 U.S. 187 (1991)

JUSTICE BLACKMUN delivered the opinion of the Court.

In this case we are concerned with an employer's gender based fetal-protection policy. May an employer exclude a fertile female employee from certain jobs because of its concern for the health of the fetus the woman might conceive?

I

Respondent Johnson Controls, Inc., manufactures batteries. In the manufacturing process, the element lead is a primary ingredient. Occupational exposure to lead entails health risks, including the risk of harm to any fetus carried by a female employee.

Before the Civil Rights Act of 1964, 78 Stat. 241, became law, Johnson Controls did not employ any woman in a battery-manufacturing job. In June 1977, however, it announced its first official policy concerning its employment of women in lead-exposure work:

> "[P]rotection of the health of the unborn child is the immediate and direct responsibility of the prospective parents. While the medical profession and the company can support them in the exercise of this responsibility, it cannot assume it for them without simultaneously infringing their rights as persons.

> . . . .

> "... Since not all women who can become mothers wish to become mothers (or will become mothers), it would appear to be illegal

discrimination to treat all who are capable of pregnancy as though they will become pregnant." App. 140.

Consistent with that view, Johnson Controls "stopped short of excluding women capable of bearing children from lead exposure," *id.*, at 138, but emphasized that a woman who expected to have a child should not choose a job in which she would have such exposure. The company also required a woman who wished to be considered for employment to sign a statement that she had been advised of the risk of having a child while she was exposed to lead. The statement informed the woman that although there was evidence "that women exposed to lead have a higher rate of abortion," this evidence was "not as clear . . . as the relationship between cigarette smoking and cancer," but that it was, "medically speaking, just good sense not to run that risk if you want children and do not want to expose the unborn child to risk, however small . . . ." *Id.*, at 142–143.

Five years later, in 1982, Johnson Controls shifted from a policy of warning to a policy of exclusion. Between 1979 and 1983, eight employees became pregnant while maintaining blood lead levels in excess of 30 micrograms per deciliter. Tr. of Oral Arg. 25, 34. This appeared to be the critical level noted by the Occupational Health and Safety Administration (OSHA) for a worker who was planning to have a family. See 29 CFR 1910.1025 (1989). The company responded by announcing a broad exclusion of women from jobs that exposed them to lead:

> ". . . [I]t is [Johnson Controls'] policy that women who are pregnant or who are capable of bearing children will not be placed into jobs involving lead exposure or which could expose them to lead through the exercise of job bidding, bumping, transfer or promotion rights." App. 85–86.

The policy defined "women . . . capable of bearing children" as "[a]ll women except those whose inability to bear children is medically documented." *Id.*, at 81. It further stated that an unacceptable work station was one where, "over the past year," an employee had recorded a blood lead level of more than 30 micrograms per deciliter or the work site had yielded an air sample containing a lead level in excess of 30 micrograms per cubic meter. *Ibid.*

II

In April 1984, petitioners filed in the United States District Court for the Eastern District of Wisconsin a class action challenging Johnson Controls' fetal-protection policy as sex discrimination that violated Title VII of the Civil Rights Act of 1964, as amended, 42 U.S.C. 2000e *et seq.* Among the individual plaintiffs were petitioners Mary Craig, who had chosen to be sterilized in order to avoid losing her job, Elsie Nason, a 50-year-old divorcee, who had suffered a loss in compensation when she was transferred out of a job where she was exposed to lead, and Donald Penney, who had been denied a request for a leave of absence for the purpose of lowering his lead level because he intended to become a father. Upon stipulation of the parties, the District Court certified a class consisting of "all past, present and future production and maintenance employees" in United Auto Workers bargaining units at nine of Johnson Controls' plants "who have been and continue to be affected by [the employer's] Fetal Protection Policy implemented in 1982." Order of Feb. 25, 1985.

The District Court granted summary judgment for defendant-respondent Johnson Controls. 680 F. Supp. 309 (1988). Applying a three-part business necessity defense derived from fetal-protection cases in the Courts of Appeals for the Fourth and Eleventh Circuits, the District Court concluded that while "there is a disagreement among the experts regarding the effect of lead on the fetus," the hazard to the fetus through exposure to lead was established by "a considerable body of opinion"; that although "[e]xpert opinion has been provided which holds that lead also affects the reproductive abilities of men and women . . . [and] that these effects are as great as the effects of exposure of the fetus . . . a great body of experts are of the opinion that the fetus is more vulnerable to levels of lead that would not affect adults"; and that petitioners had "failed to establish that there is an acceptable alternative policy which would protect the fetus." *Id.*, at 315–316. The court stated that, in view of this disposition of the business necessity defense, it did not "have to undertake a bona fide occupational qualification's (BFOQ) analysis." *Id.*, at 316, n. 5.

The Court of Appeals for the Seventh Circuit, sitting en banc, affirmed the summary judgment by a 7 to 4 vote. 886 F.2d 871 (1989). The majority held that the proper standard for evaluating the fetal-protection policy was the defense of business necessity; that Johnson Controls was entitled to summary judgment under that defense; and that even if the proper standard was a BFOQ, Johnson Controls still was entitled to summary judgment.

. . . .

Applying this business necessity defense, the Court of Appeals ruled that Johnson Controls should prevail. Specifically, the court concluded that there was no genuine issue of material fact about the substantial health-risk factor because the parties agreed that there was a substantial risk to a fetus from lead exposure. 886 F.2d, at 888–889. The Court of Appeals also concluded that, unlike the evidence of risk to the fetus from the mother's exposure, the evidence of risk from the father's exposure, which petitioners presented, "is, at best, speculative and unconvincing." *Id.*, at 889. Finally, the court found that petitioners had waived the issue of less discriminatory alternatives by not adequately presenting it. It said that, in any event, petitioners had not produced evidence of less discriminatory alternatives in the District Court. *Id.*, at 890–893.

Having concluded that the business necessity defense was the appropriate framework and that Johnson Controls satisfied that standard, the court proceeded to discuss the BFOQ defense and concluded that Johnson Controls met that test, too. *Id.*, at 893–894. The en banc majority ruled that industrial safety is part of the essence of respondent's business, and that the fetal-protection policy is reasonably necessary to further that concern. Quoting *Dothard v. Rawlinson*, 433 U.S. 321, 335 (1977), the majority emphasized that, in view of the goal of protecting the unborn, "more is at stake" than simply an individual woman's decision to weigh and accept the risks of employment. 886 F.2d, at 898.

. . . .

III

... The bias in Johnson Controls' policy is obvious. Fertile men, but not fertile women, are given a choice as to whether they wish to risk their reproductive health for a particular job. Section 703(a) of the Civil Rights Act of 1964, 78 Stat. 255, as amended, 42 U.S.C. 2000e-2(a), prohibits sex based classifications in terms and conditions of employment, in hiring and discharging decisions, and in other employment decisions that adversely affect an employee's status. Respondent's fetal-protection policy explicitly discriminates against women on the basis of their sex. The policy excludes women with childbearing capacity from lead-exposed jobs and so creates a facial classification based on gender. Respondent assumes as much in its brief before this Court. Brief for Respondent 17, n. 24.

Nevertheless, the Court of Appeals assumed, as did the two appellate courts who already had confronted the issue, that sex-specific fetal-protection policies do not involve facial discrimination. 886 F.2d, at 886–887; *Hayes*, 726 F.2d, at 1547; *Wright*, 697 F.2d, at 1190. These courts analyzed the policies as though they were facially neutral, and had only a discriminatory effect upon the employment opportunities of women. Consequently, the courts looked to see if each employer in question had established that its policy was justified as a business necessity.

[T]he business necessity standard is more lenient for the employer than the statutory BFOQ defense. The Court of Appeals here went one step further and invoked the burden-shifting framework set forth in *Wards Cove Packing Co. v. Atonio*, 490 U.S. 642 (1989), thus requiring petitioners to bear the burden of persuasion on all questions. 886 F.2d, at 887–888. The court assumed that because the asserted reason for the sex-based exclusion (protecting women's unconceived offspring) was ostensibly benign, the policy was not sex-based discrimination. That assumption, however, was incorrect.

First, Johnson Controls' policy classifies on the basis of gender and childbearing capacity, rather than fertility alone. Respondent does not seek to protect the unconceived children of all its employees. Despite evidence in the record about the debilitating effect of lead exposure on the male reproductive system, Johnson Controls is concerned only with the harms that may befall the unborn offspring of its female employees. Accordingly, it appears that Johnson Controls would have lost in the Eleventh Circuit under *Hayes* because its policy does not "effectively and equally protec[t] the offspring of all employees." 726 F.2d, at 1548. This Court faced a conceptually similar situation in *Phillips v. Martin Marietta Corp.*, 400 U.S. 542 (1971), and found sex discrimination because the policy established "one hiring policy for women and another for men—each having pre-school-age children." *Id.*, at 544. Johnson Controls' policy is facially discriminatory because it requires only a female employee to produce proof that she is not capable of reproducing.

Our conclusion is bolstered by the Pregnancy Discrimination Act of 1978 (PDA), 92 Stat. 2076, 42 U.S.C. 2000e(k), in which Congress explicitly provided that, for purposes of Title VII, discrimination "on the basis of sex" includes discrimination "because of or on the basis of pregnancy, childbirth, or related medical conditions." "The Pregnancy Discrimination Act has now made clear that, for all Title VII purposes, discrimination based on a woman's pregnancy is, on its face, discrimination because of her sex." *Newport News Shipbuilding & Dry Dock Co. v. EEOC*, 462 U.S. 669, 684 (1983). In its use of the words "capable of bearing children" in the 1982 policy statement as the criterion for exclusion, Johnson Controls explicitly classifies on the basis of potential for pregnancy. Under the PDA, such a classification must be regarded, for Title VII purposes, in the same light as explicit sex discrimination. Respondent has chosen to treat all its female employees as potentially pregnant; that choice evinces discrimination on the basis of sex.

We concluded above that Johnson Controls' policy is not neutral because it does not apply to the reproductive capacity of the company's male employees in the same way as it applies to that of the females. Moreover, the absence of a malevolent motive does not convert a facially discriminatory policy into a neutral policy with a discriminatory effect. Whether an employment practice involves disparate treatment through explicit facial discrimination does not depend on why the employer discriminates but rather on the explicit terms of the discrimination. In *Martin Marietta, supra,* the motives underlying the employers' express exclusion of women did not alter the intentionally discriminatory character of the policy. Nor did the arguably benign motives lead to consideration of a business necessity defense. The question in that case was whether the discrimination in question could be justified under 703(e) as a BFOQ. The beneficence of an employer's purpose does not undermine the conclusion that an explicit gender-based policy is sex discrimination under 703(a) and thus may be defended only as a BFOQ.

The enforcement policy of the Equal Employment Opportunity Commission accords with this conclusion. On January 24, 1990, the EEOC issued a Policy Guidance in the light of the Seventh Circuit's decision in the present case. App. to Pet. for Cert. 127a. The document noted: "For the plaintiff to bear the burden of proof in a case in which there is direct evidence of a facially discriminatory policy is wholly inconsistent with settled Title VII law." *Id.*, at 133a. The Commission concluded: "[W]e now think BFOQ is the better approach." *Id.*, at 134a.

In sum, Johnson Controls' policy "does not pass the simple test of whether the evidence shows 'treatment of a person in a manner which but for that person's sex would be different.' " *Los Angeles Dept. of Water & Power v. Manhart*, 435 U.S. 702, 711 (1978), quoting *Developments in the Law, Employment Discrimination and Title VII of the Civil Rights Act of 1964*, 84 Harv. L. Rev. 1109, 1170 (1971). We hold that Johnson Controls' fetal-protection policy is sex discrimination forbidden under Title VII unless respondent can establish that sex is a "bona fide occupational qualification."

IV

Under 703(e)(1) of Title VII, an employer may discriminate on the basis of "religion, sex, or national origin in those certain instances where religion, sex, or national origin is a bona fide occupational qualification reasonably necessary to the normal operation of that particular business or enterprise."42 U.S.C. 2000e-2(e)(1). We therefore turn to the question whether Johnson Controls' fetal-protection policy is one of those "certain instances" that come within the BFOQ exception.

The BFOQ defense is written narrowly, and this Court has read it narrowly. See, *e.g.*, *Dothard v. Rawlinson*, 433 U.S. 321, 332–337 (1977); *Trans World Airlines, Inc. v. Thurston*, 469 U.S. 111, 122–125 (1985). We have read the BFOQ language of 4(f) of the Age Discrimination in Employment Act of 1967 (ADEA), 81 Stat. 603, as amended, 29 U.S.C. 623(f)(1), which tracks the BFOQ provision in Title VII, just as narrowly. See *Western Air Lines, Inc. v. Criswell*, 472 U.S. 400 (1985). Our emphasis on the restrictive scope of the BFOQ defense is grounded on both the language and the legislative history of 703.

The wording of the BFOQ defense contains several terms of restriction that indicate that the exception reaches only special situations. The statute thus limits the situations in which discrimination is permissible to "certain instances" where sex discrimination is "reasonably necessary" to the "normal operation" of the "particular" business. Each one of these terms — certain, normal, particular — prevents the use of general subjective standards and favors an objective, verifiable requirement. But the most telling term is "occupational"; this indicates that these objective, verifiable requirements must concern job-related skills and aptitudes.

. . . .

Johnson Controls argues that its fetal-protection policy falls within the so-called safety exception to the BFOQ. Our cases have stressed that discrimination on the basis of sex because of safety concerns is allowed only in narrow circumstances. In *Dothard v. Rawlinson*, this Court indicated that danger to a woman herself does not justify discrimination. 433 U.S., at 335. We there allowed the employer to hire only male guards in contact areas of maximum-security male penitentiaries only because more was at stake than the "individual woman's decision to weigh and accept the risks of employment." *Ibid.* We found sex to be a BFOQ inasmuch as the employment of a female guard would create real risks of safety to others if violence broke out because the guard was a woman. Sex discrimination was tolerated because sex was related to the guard's ability to do the job — maintaining prison security. We also required in *Dothard* a high correlation between sex and ability to perform job functions and refused to allow employers to use sex as a proxy for strength although it might be a fairly accurate one.

Similarly, some courts have approved airlines' layoffs of pregnant flight attendants at different points during the first five months of pregnancy on the ground that the employer's policy was necessary to ensure the safety of passengers. See *Harriss v. Pan*

American World Airways, Inc., 649 F.2d 670 (CA9 1980); *Burwell v. Eastern Air Lines, Inc.*, 633 F.2d 361 (CA4 1980), cert. denied, 450 U.S. 965 (1981); *Condit v. United Air Lines, Inc.*, 558 F.2d 1176 (CA4 1977), cert. denied, 435 U.S. 934 (1978); *In re National Airlines, Inc.*, 434 F. Supp. 249 (SD Fla. 1977). In two of these cases, the courts pointedly indicated that fetal, as opposed to passenger, safety was best left to the mother. *Burwell*, 633 F.2d, at 371; *National Airlines*, 434 F. Supp., at 259.

We considered safety to third parties in *Western Airlines, Inc. v. Criswell*, *supra*, in the context of the ADEA. We focused upon "the nature of the flight engineer's tasks," and the "actual capabilities of persons over age 60" in relation to those tasks. 472 U. S., at 406. Our safety concerns were not independent of the individual's ability to perform the assigned tasks, but rather involved the possibility that, because of age-connected debility, a flight engineer might not properly assist the pilot, and might thereby cause a safety emergency. Furthermore, although we considered the safety of third parties in *Dothard* and *Criswell*, those third parties were indispensable to the particular business at issue. In *Dothard*, the third parties were the inmates; in *Criswell*, the third parties were the passengers on the plane. We stressed that in order to qualify as a BFOQ, a job qualification must relate to the "essence," *Dothard*, 433 U.S., at 333, or to the "central mission of the employer's business," *Criswell*, 472 U.S., at 413.

The concurrence ignores the "essence of the business" test and so concludes that "the safety to fetuses in carrying out the duties of battery manufacturing is as much a legitimate concern as is safety to third parties in guarding prisons (*Dothard*) or flying airplanes (*Criswell*)." *Post*, at 6. By limiting its discussion to cost and safety concerns and rejecting the "essence of the business" test that our case law has established, the concurrence seeks to expand what is now the narrow BFOQ defense. Third-party safety considerations properly entered into the BFOQ analysis in *Dothard* and *Criswell* because they went to the core of the employee's job performance. Moreover, that performance involved the central purpose of the enterprise. *Dothard*, 433 U.S., at 335 . . . . No one can disregard the possibility of injury to future children; the BFOQ, however, is not so broad that it transforms this deep social concern into an essential aspect of battery-making.

Our case law, therefore, makes clear that the safety exception is limited to instances in which sex or pregnancy actually interferes with the employee's ability to perform the job. This approach is consistent with the language of the BFOQ provision itself, for it suggests that permissible distinctions based on sex must relate to ability to perform the duties of the job. Johnson Controls suggests, however, that we expand the exception to allow fetal-protection policies that mandate particular standards for pregnant or fertile women. We decline to do so. Such an expansion contradicts not only the language of the BFOQ and the narrowness of its exception but the plain language and history of the Pregnancy Discrimination Act.

The PDA's amendment to Title VII contains a BFOQ standard of its own: unless pregnant employees differ from others "in their ability or inability to work," they must be "treated the same" as other employees "for all employment related purposes." 42 U.S.C. 2000e(k). This language clearly sets forth Congress' remedy for discrimination on the basis of pregnancy and potential pregnancy. Women who are either pregnant or potentially pregnant must be treated like others "similar in their ability . . . to work." *Ibid.* In other words, women as capable of doing their jobs as their male counterparts may not be forced to choose between having a child and having a job.

. . . .

The legislative history confirms what the language of the Pregnancy Discrimination Act compels. Both the House and Senate Reports accompanying the legislation indicate that this statutory standard was chosen to protect female workers from being treated differently from other employees simply because of their capacity to bear children. See Amending Title VII, Civil Rights Act of 1964, S. Rep. No. 95-331, pp. 4–6 (1977):

> "Under this bill, the treatment of pregnant women in covered employment must focus not on their condition alone but on the actual effects of that condition on their ability to work. Pregnant women who are able to work must be permitted to work on the same conditions as other employees . . . .
>
> . . . . .
>
> ". . . [U]nder this bill, employers will no longer be permitted to force women who become pregnant to stop working regardless of their ability to continue."

See also Prohibition of Sex Discrimination Based on Pregnancy, H. R. Rep. No. 95-948, pp. 3–6 (1978).

This history counsels against expanding the BFOQ to allow fetal-protection policies. The Senate Report quoted above states that employers may not require a pregnant woman to stop working at any time during her pregnancy unless she is unable to do her work. Employment late in pregnancy often imposes risks on the unborn child, see Chavkin, Walking a Tightrope: Pregnancy, Parenting, and Work, in Double Exposure 196, 196–202 (W. Chavkin ed. 1984), but Congress indicated that the employer may take into account only the woman's ability to get her job done. See Becker, *From Muller v. Oregon to Fetal Vulnerability Policies*, 53 U. Chi. L. Rev. 1219, 1255–1256 (1986). With the PDA, Congress made clear that the decision to become pregnant or to work while being either pregnant or capable of becoming pregnant was reserved for each individual woman to make for herself.

We conclude that the language of both the BFOQ provision and the PDA which amended it, as well as the legislative history and the case law, prohibit an employer from discriminating against a woman because of her capacity to become pregnant unless her reproductive potential prevents her from performing the duties of her job. We reiterate our holdings in *Criswell* and *Dothard* that an employer must direct its concerns about a woman's ability to perform her job safely and efficiently to those aspects of the woman's job-related activities that fall within the "essence" of the particular business.

V

We have no difficulty concluding that Johnson Controls cannot establish a BFOQ. Fertile women, as far as appears in the record, participate in the manufacture of batteries as efficiently as anyone else. Johnson Controls' professed moral and ethical concerns about the welfare of the next generation do not suffice to establish a BFOQ of female sterility. Decisions about the welfare of future children must be left to the parents who conceive, bear, support, and raise them rather than to the employers who hire those parents. Congress has mandated this choice through Title VII, as amended by the Pregnancy Discrimination Act. Johnson Controls has attempted to exclude women because of their reproductive capacity. Title VII and the PDA simply do not allow a woman's dismissal because of her failure to submit to sterilization.

Nor can concerns about the welfare of the next generation be considered a part of the "essence" of Johnson Controls' business. Judge Easterbrook in this case pertinently observed: "It is word play to say that 'the job' at Johnson [Controls] is to make batteries without risk to fetuses in the same way 'the job' at Western Air Lines is to fly planes without crashing." 886 F.2d, at 913.

Johnson Controls argues that it must exclude all fertile women because it is impossible to tell which women will become pregnant while working with lead. This argument is somewhat academic in light of our conclusion that the company may not exclude fertile women at all; it perhaps is worth noting, however, that Johnson Controls has shown no "factual basis for believing that all or substantially all women would be unable to perform safely and efficiently the duties of the job involved." *Weeks v. Southern Bell Tel. & Tel. Co.*, 408 F.2d 228, 235 (CA5 1969), quoted with approval in *Dothard*, 433 U.S., at 333. Even on this sparse record, it is apparent that Johnson Controls is concerned about only a small minority of women. Of the eight pregnancies reported among the female employees, it has not been shown that any of the babies have birth defects or other abnormalities. The record does not reveal the birth rate for Johnson Controls' female workers but national statistics show that approximately nine percent of all fertile women become pregnant each year. The birthrate drops to two percent for blue collar workers over age 30. See Becker, 53 U. Chi. L. Rev., at 1233. Johnson Controls' fear of prenatal injury, no matter how sincere, does not begin to show that substantially all of its fertile women employees are incapable of doing their jobs . . .

VI

. . . Our holding today that Title VII, as so amended, forbids sex-specific fetal-protection policies is neither remarkable nor unprecedented. Concern for a woman's existing or potential offspring historically has been the excuse for denying women equal employment opportunities. See, *e.g., Muller v. Oregon*, 208 U.S. 412 (1908). Congress in the PDA prohibited discrimination on the basis of a woman's ability to become pregnant. We do no more than hold that the Pregnancy Discrimination Act means what it says.

It is no more appropriate for the courts than it is for individual employers to decide whether a woman's reproductive role is more important to herself and her family than her economic role. Congress has left this choice to the woman as hers to make.

The judgment of the Court of Appeals is reversed and the case is remanded for further proceedings consistent with this opinion.

It is so ordered.

E. Business Necessity Defense and the Bottom Line Defense

Connecticut v. Teal

457 U.S. 440 (1982)

Justice Brennan delivered the opinion of the Court.

We consider here whether an employer sued for violation of Title VII of the Civil Rights Act of 1964 may assert a "bottom-line" theory of defense. Under that theory, as asserted in this case, an employer's acts of racial discrimination in promotions— effected by an examination having disparate impact would not render the employer liable for the racial discrimination suffered by employees barred from promotion if the "bottom-line" result of the promotional process was an appropriate racial balance. We hold that the "bottom line" does not preclude respondent employees from establishing a prima facie case, nor does it provide petitioner employer with a defense to such a case.

Four of the respondents, Winnie Teal, Rose Walker, Edith Latney, and Grace Clark, are black employees of the Department of Income Maintenance of the State of Connecticut. Each was promoted provisionally to the position of Welfare Eligibility Supervisor and served in that capacity for almost two years. To attain permanent status as supervisors, however, respondents had to participate in a selection process that required, as the first step, a passing score on a written examination. This written test was administered on December 2, 1978, to 329 candidates. Of these candidates, 48 identified themselves as black and 259 identified themselves as white. The results of the examination were announced in March 1979. With the passing score set at 65, 54.17 percent of the identified black candidates passed. This was approximately 68 percent of the passing rate for the identified white candidates. The four respondents were among the blacks who failed the examination, and they were thus excluded from further consideration for permanent supervisory positions. In April 1979, respondents instituted this action in the United States District Court for the District of Connecticut against petitioners, the State of Connecticut, two state agencies, and two state officials. Respondents alleged, inter alia, that petitioners violated Title VII by imposing, as an absolute condition for consideration for

promotion, that applicants pass a written test that excluded blacks in disproportionate numbers and that was not job related.

More than a year after this action was instituted, and approximately one month
before trial, petitioners made promotions from the eligibility list generated by the
written examination. In choosing persons from that list, petitioners considered past
work performance, recommendations of the candidates' supervisors and, to a lesser
extent, seniority. Petitioners then applied what the Court of Appeals characterized
as an affirmative-action program in order to ensure a significant number of minority supervisors. Forty-six persons were promoted to permanent supervisory positions, 11 of whom were black and 35 of whom were white. The overall result of the
selection process was that, of the 48 identified black candidates who participated in
the selection process, 22.9 percent were promoted and of the 259 identified white
candidates, 13.5 percent were promoted. It is this "bottom-line" result, more favorable to blacks than to whites, that petitioners urge should be adjudged to be a complete defense to respondents' suit.

After trial, the District Court entered judgment for petitioners. . . . The United
States Court of Appeals for the Second Circuit reversed, holding that the District
Court erred in ruling that the results of the written examination alone were insufficient to support a prima facie case of disparate impact in violation of Title VII.
645 F.2d 133 (1981) . . . We granted certiorari, 454 U.S. 813, 102 S.Ct. 89, 70 L.Ed.2d
82 (1981), and now affirm.

I

We must first decide whether an examination that bars a disparate number of
black employees from consideration for promotion, and that has not been shown to
be job related, presents a claim cognizable under Title VII. Section 703(a)(2) of Title
VII provides in pertinent part:

> "It shall be an unlawful employment practice for an employer—
>
> * * *
>
> "(2) to limit, segregate, or classify his employees or applicants for
> employment in any way which would deprive or tend to deprive any indi-
> vidual of employment opportunities or otherwise adversely affect his status
> as an employee, because of such individual's race, color, religion, sex, or
> national origin." 78 Stat. 255, as amended, 42 U.S.C. 2000e-2(a)(2).

Respondents base their claim on our construction of this provision in *Griggs v.
Duke Power Co., supra*. Prior to the enactment of Title VII, the Duke Power Co.
restricted its black employees to the labor department. Beginning in 1965, the company required all employees who desired a transfer out of the labor department to
have either a high school diploma or to achieve a passing grade on two professionally prepared aptitude tests. New employees seeking positions in any department
other than labor had to possess both a high school diploma and a passing grade on

these two examinations. Although these requirements applied equally to white and black employees and applicants, they barred employment opportunities to a disproportionate number of blacks. While there was no showing that the employer had a racial purpose or invidious intent in adopting these requirements, this Court held that they were invalid because they had a disparate impact and were not shown to be related to job performance...

Griggs and its progeny have established a three-part analysis of disparate-impact claims. To establish a prima facie case of discrimination, a plaintiff must show that the facially neutral employment practice had a significantly discriminatory impact. If that showing is made, the employer must then demonstrate that "any given requirement has a manifest relationship to the employment in question," in order to avoid a finding of discrimination. *Griggs, supra*, at 432, 91 S.Ct., at 854. Even in such a case, however, the plaintiff may prevail, if he shows that the employer was using the practice as a mere pretext for discrimination. See *Albemarle Paper Co., supra*, 422 U.S., at 425, 95 S.Ct., at 2375; *Dothard, supra*, 433 U.S., at 329, 97 S.Ct., at 2726–2727.

Griggs recognized that in enacting Title VII, Congress required "the removal of artificial, arbitrary, and unnecessary barriers to employment" and professional development that had historically been encountered by women and blacks as well as other minorities. 401 U.S., at 431, 91 S.Ct., at 853. See also *Dothard v. Rawlinson, supra*...

Petitioners' examination, which barred promotion and had a discriminatory impact on black employees, clearly falls within the literal language of § 703(a)(2), as interpreted by *Griggs*. The statute speaks, not in terms of jobs and promotions, but in terms of limitations and classifications that would deprive any individual of employment opportunities. A disparate-impact claim reflects the language of § 703(a)(2) and Congress' basic objectives in enacting that statute: "to achieve equality of employment *opportunities* and remove barriers that have operated in the past to favor an identifiable group of white employees over other employees." 401 U.S., at 429–430, 91 S.Ct., at 852–853 (emphasis added). When an employer uses a nonjob-related barrier in order to deny a minority or woman applicant employment or promotion, and that barrier has a significant adverse effect on minorities or women, then the applicant has been deprived of an employment opportunity "because of... race, color, religion, sex, or national origin." In other words, § 703(a)(2) prohibits discriminatory "artificial, arbitrary, and unnecessary barriers to employment," 401 U.S., at 431, 91 S.Ct., at 853, that "limit... or classify... applicants for employment... in any way which would deprive or tend to deprive any individual of employment *opportunities*." (Emphasis added.)

Relying on § 703(a)(2), *Griggs* explicitly focused on employment "practices, procedures, or tests," 401 U.S., at 430, 91 S.Ct., at 853, that deny equal employment "opportunity," *id.*, at 431, 91 S.Ct., at 853. We concluded that Title VII prohibits "procedures or testing mechanisms that operate as 'built-in headwinds' for minority groups." *Id.*, at 432, 91 S.Ct., at 854. We found that Congress' primary purpose was the prophylactic one of achieving equality of employment "opportunities" and removing "barriers" to such equality. *Id.*, at 429–430, 91 S.Ct., at 852–853. See *Albemarle Paper Co. v. Moody*, 422 U.S., at 417, 95 S.Ct., at 2371. The examination given to respondents in this case surely constituted such a practice and created such a barrier.

Our conclusion that §703(a)(2) encompasses respondents' claim is reinforced by the terms of Congress' 1972 extension of the protections of Title VII to state and municipal employees. Although Congress did not explicitly consider the viability of the defense offered by the state employer in this case, the 1972 amendments to Title VII do reflect Congress' intent to provide state and municipal employees with the protection that Title VII, as interpreted by *Griggs*, had provided to employees in the private sector: equality of opportunity and the elimination of discriminatory barriers to professional development. The Committee Reports and the floor debates stressed the need for equality of opportunity for minority applicants seeking to obtain governmental positions. E.g., S.Rep. No. 92-415, p. 10 (1971); 118 Cong. Rec. 1815 (1972) (remarks of Sen. Williams). Congress voiced its concern about the widespread use by state and local governmental agencies of "invalid selection techniques" that had a discriminatory impact. S.Rep. No. 92-415, *supra*, at 10; H.R.Rep. No. 92-238, p. 17 (1971); 117 Cong.Rec. 31961 (1971) (remarks of Rep. Perkins).

The decisions of this Court following *Griggs* also support respondents' claim. In considering claims of disparate impact under §703(a)(2) this Court has consistently focused on employment and promotion requirements that create a discriminatory bar to opportunities. This Court has never read §703(a)(2) as requiring the focus to be placed instead on the overall number of minority or female applicants actually hired or promoted. . .

In short, the District Court's dismissal of respondents' claim cannot be supported on the basis that respondents failed to establish a prima facie case of employment discrimination under the terms of §703(a)(2). The suggestion that disparate impact should be measured only at the bottom line ignores the fact that Title VII guarantees these individual respondents the opportunity to compete equally with white workers on the basis of job-related criteria. Title VII strives to achieve equality of opportunity by rooting out "artificial, arbitrary, and unnecessary" employer-created barriers to professional development that have a discriminatory impact upon individuals. Therefore, respondents' rights under §703(a)(2) have been violated, unless petitioners can demonstrate that the examination given was not an artificial, arbitrary, or unnecessary barrier, because it measured skills related to effective performance in the role of Welfare Eligibility Supervisor.

The United States, in its brief as amicus curiae, apparently recognizes that respondents' claim in this case falls within the affirmative commands of Title VII. But it seeks to support the District Court's judgment in this case by relying on the defenses provided to the employer in §703(h). Section 703(h) provides in pertinent part:

"Notwithstanding any other provision of this subchapter, it shall not be an unlawful employment practice for an employer . . . to give and to act upon the results of any professionally developed ability test provided that such test, its administration or action upon the results is not designed, intended or used to discriminate because of race, color, religion, sex or national origin." 78 Stat. 257, as amended, 42 U.S.C. 2000e-2(h).

The Government argues that the test administered by the petitioners was not "used to discriminate" because it did not actually deprive disproportionate numbers of blacks of promotions. But the Government's reliance on § 703(h) as offering the employer some special haven for discriminatory tests is misplaced. We considered the relevance of this provision in *Griggs*. After examining the legislative history of § 703(h), we concluded that Congress, in adding § 703(h), intended only to make clear that tests that were job related would be permissible despite their disparate impact. 401 U.S., at 433–436, 91 S.Ct., at 854–856. As the Court recently confirmed, § 703(h), which was introduced as an amendment to Title VII on the Senate floor, "did not alter the meaning of Title VII, but 'merely clarified its present intent and effect.'" *American Tobacco Co. v. Patterson*, 456 U.S. 63, 73, n. 11, 102 S.Ct. 1534, 1539, n. 11, 71 L.Ed.2d 748 (1982), quoting 110 Cong.Rec. 12723 (1964) (remarks of Sen. Humphrey). . .

In sum, respondents' claim of disparate impact from the examination, a pass-fail barrier to employment opportunity, states a prima facie case of employment discrimination under § 703(a)(2), despite their employer's nondiscriminatory "bottom line," and that "bottom line" is no defense to this prima facie case under § 703(h).

II

Having determined that respondents' claim comes within the terms of Title VII, we must address the suggestion of petitioners and some amici curiae that we recognize an exception, either in the nature of an additional burden on plaintiffs seeking to establish a prima facie case or in the nature of an affirmative defense, for cases in which an employer has compensated for a discriminatory pass-fail barrier by hiring or promoting a sufficient number of black employees to reach a nondiscriminatory "bottom line." We reject this suggestion, which is in essence nothing more than a request that we redefine the protections guaranteed by Title VII.

Section 703(a)(2) prohibits practices that would deprive or tend to deprive "any individual of employment opportunities." The principal focus of the statute is the protection of the individual employee, rather than the protection of the minority group as a whole. Indeed, the entire statute and its legislative history are replete with references to protection for the individual employee. See, e.g., §§ 703(a)(1), (b), (c), 704(a), 78 Stat. 255–257, as amended, 42 U.S.C. 2000e-2(a)(1), (b), (c), 2000e-3(a); 110 Cong.Rec. 7213 (1964) (interpretive memorandum of Sens. Clark and Case) ("discrimination is prohibited as to any individual"); *id.*, at 8921 (remarks of Sen. Williams) ("Every man must be judged according to his ability. In that respect, all men are to have an equal opportunity to be considered for a particular job").

In suggesting that the "bottom line" may be a defense to a claim of discrimination against an individual employee, petitioners and amici appear to confuse unlawful discrimination with discriminatory intent. The Court has stated that a nondiscriminatory "bottom line" and an employer's good-faith efforts to achieve a nondiscriminatory work force, might in some cases assist an employer in rebutting the inference that particular action had been intentionally discriminatory: "Proof that a work force was racially balanced or that it contained a disproportionately high percentage of minority employees is not wholly irrelevant on the issue of intent when that issue is yet to be decided." *Furnco Construction Corp. v. Waters*, 438 U.S. 567, 580, 98 S.Ct. 2943, 2951, 57 L.Ed.2d 957 (1978). See also *Teamsters v. United States*, 431 U.S. 324, 340, n. 20, 97 S.Ct. 1843, 1856–1857, n. 20, 52 L.Ed.2d 396 (1977). But resolution of the factual question of intent is not what is at issue in this case. Rather, petitioners seek simply to justify discrimination against respondents on the basis of their favorable treatment of other members of respondents' racial group. Under Title VII, "a racially balanced work force cannot immunize an employer from liability for specific acts of discrimination." *Furnco Construction Corp. v. Waters*, 438 U.S., at 579, 98 S.Ct., at 2950–2951.

> "It is clear beyond cavil that the obligation imposed by Title VII is to provide an equal opportunity for *each* applicant regardless of race, without regard to whether members of the applicant's race are already proportionately represented in the work force. See *Griggs v. Duke Power Co.*, 401 U.S., at 430 91 S. Ct., at 853; *McDonald v. Santa Fe Trail Transportation Co.*, 427 U.S. 273, 279 96 S.Ct. 2574, 2578, 49 L.Ed.2d 493 (1976)." *Ibid.* (emphasis in original).

It is clear that Congress never intended to give an employer license to discriminate against some employees on the basis of race or sex merely because he favorably treats other members of the employees' group. We recognized in *Los Angeles Dept. of Water & Power v. Manhart*, 435 U.S. 702, 98 S.Ct. 1370, 55 L.Ed.2d 657 (1978), that fairness to the class of women employees as a whole could not justify unfairness to the individual female employee because the "statute's focus on the individual is unambiguous." *Id.*, at 708, 98 S.Ct., at 1375. Similarly, in *Phillips v. Martin Marietta Corp.*, 400 U.S. 542, 91 S.Ct. 496, 27 L.Ed.2d 613 (1971) (per curiam), we recognized that a rule barring employment of all married women with preschool children, if not a bona fide occupational qualification under § 703(e), violated Title VII, even though female applicants without preschool children were hired in sufficient numbers that they constituted 75 to 80 percent of the persons employed in the position plaintiff sought.

... Title VII does not permit the victim of a facially discriminatory policy to be told that he has not been wronged because other persons of his or her race or sex were hired. That answer is no more satisfactory when it is given to victims of a policy that is facially neutral but practically discriminatory. Every individual employee is protected against both discriminatory treatment and "practices that are fair in form, but discriminatory in operation." *Griggs v. Duke Power Co.*, 401 U.S., at 431, 91 S.Ct., at 853. Requirements and tests that have a discriminatory impact are merely some of the subtler, but also the more pervasive, of the "practices and devices which have fostered racially stratified job environments to the disadvantage of minority citizens." *McDonnell Douglas Corp. v. Green*, 411 U.S., at 800, 93 S.Ct., at 1823.

. . . .

In sum, petitioners' nondiscriminatory "bottom line" is no answer, under the terms of Title VII, to respondents' prima facie claim of employment discrimination. Accordingly, the judgment of the Court of Appeals for the Second Circuit is affirmed, and this case is remanded to the District Court for further proceedings consistent with this opinion.

F. Scope of the Anti-Retaliation Mandate

Burlington Northern and Santa Fe Railway v. White

448 U.S. 53 (2006)

Justice BREYER delivered the opinion of the Court.

Title VII of the Civil Rights Act of 1964 forbids employment discrimination against "any individual" based on that individual's "race, color, religion, sex, or national origin." Pub. L. 88-352, §704, 78 Stat. 257, as amended, 42 U.S.C. §2000e-2(a). A separate section of the Act—its anti-retaliation provision—forbids an employer from "discriminat[ing] against" an employee or job applicant because that individual "opposed any practice" made unlawful by Title VII or "made a charge, testified, assisted, or participated in" a Title VII proceeding or investigation. §2000e-3(a).

The Courts of Appeals have come to different conclusions about the scope of the Act's anti-retaliation provision, particularly the reach of its phrase "discriminate against." Does that provision confine actionable retaliation to activity that affects the terms and conditions of employment? And how harmful must the adverse actions be to fall within its scope?

We conclude that the anti-retaliation provision does not confine the actions and harms it forbids to those that are related to employment or occur at the workplace. We also conclude that the provision covers those (and only those) employer actions that would have been materially adverse to a reasonable employee or job applicant. In the present context that means that the employer's actions must be harmful to the point that they could well dissuade a reasonable worker from making or supporting a charge of discrimination.

I

A

This case arises out of actions that supervisors at petitioner Burlington Northern & Santa Fe Railway Company took against respondent Sheila White, the only woman working in the Maintenance of Way department at Burlington's Tennessee Yard. In June 1997, Burlington's road master, Marvin Brown, interviewed White and expressed interest in her previous experience operating forklifts. Burlington hired White as a "track laborer," a job that involves removing and replacing track components, transporting track material, cutting brush, and clearing litter and cargo spillage from the right-of-way. Soon after White arrived on the job, a co-worker who had previously operated the forklift chose to assume other responsibilities. Brown immediately assigned White to operate the forklift. While she also performed some of the other track laborer tasks, operating the forklift was White's primary responsibility.

In September 1997, White complained to Burlington officials that her immediate supervisor, Bill Joiner, had repeatedly told her that women should not be working in the Maintenance of Way department. Joiner, White said, had also made insulting and inappropriate remarks to her in front of her male colleagues. After an internal investigation, Burlington suspended Joiner for 10 days and ordered him to attend a sexual-harassment training session.

On September 26, Brown told White about Joiner's discipline. At the same time, he told White that he was removing her from forklift duty and assigning her to perform only standard track laborer tasks. Brown explained that the reassignment reflected co-worker's complaints that, in fairness, a "'more senior man'" should have the "less arduous and cleaner job" of forklift operator. 364 F.3d 789, 792 (CA6 2004) (case below).

On October 10, White filed a complaint with the Equal Employment Opportunity Commission (EEOC or Commission). She claimed that the reassignment of her duties amounted to unlawful gender-based discrimination and retaliation for her having earlier complained about Joiner. In early December, White filed a second retaliation charge with the Commission, claiming that Brown had placed her under surveillance and was monitoring her daily activities. That charge was mailed to Brown on December 8.

A few days later, White and her immediate supervisor, Percy Sharkey, disagreed about which truck should transport White from one location to another. The specific facts of the disagreement are in dispute, but the upshot is that Sharkey told Brown later that afternoon that White had been insubordinate. Brown immediately suspended White without pay. White invoked internal grievance procedures. Those procedures led Burlington to conclude that White had *not* been insubordinate. Burlington reinstated White to her position and awarded her back pay for the 37 days she was suspended. White filed an additional retaliation charge with the EEOC based on the suspension.

B

After exhausting administrative remedies, White filed this Title VII action against Burlington in federal court. As relevant here, she claimed that Burlington's actions—(1) changing her job responsibilities, and (2) suspending her for 37 days without pay—amounted to unlawful retaliation in violation of Title VII.

§ 2000e-3(a). A jury found in White's favor on both of these claims. It awarded her $43,500 in compensatory damages, including $3,250 in medical expenses. The District Court denied Burlington's post-trial motion for judgment as a matter of law. See Fed. Rule Civ. Proc. 50(b).

Initially, a divided Sixth Circuit panel reversed the judgment and found in Burlington's favor on the retaliation claims. 310 F.3d 443 (2002). The full Court of Appeals vacated the panel's decision, however, and heard the matter en banc. The court then affirmed the District Court's judgment in White's favor on both retaliation claims. While all members of the en banc court voted to uphold the District Court's judgment, they differed as to the proper standard to apply. Compare 364 F.3d, at 795–800, with *id.*, at 809 (Clay, J., concurring).

II

Title VII's anti-retaliation provision forbids employer actions that "discriminate against" an employee (or job applicant) because he has "opposed" a practice that Title VII forbids or has "made a charge, testified, assisted, or participated in" a Title VII "investigation, proceeding, or hearing." § 2000e-3(a). No one doubts that the term "discriminate against" refers to distinctions or differences in treatment that injure protected individuals. See *Jackson v. Birmingham Bd. of Ed.*, 544 U.S. 167, 174 (2005); *Price Waterhouse v. Hopkins*, 490 U.S. 228, 244 (1989) (plurality opinion); see also 4 Oxford English Dictionary 758 (2d ed. 1989) (def. 3b). But different Circuits have come to different conclusions about whether the challenged action has to be employment or workplace related and about how harmful that action must be to constitute retaliation.

Some Circuits have insisted upon a close relationship between the retaliatory action and employment. . . . Other Circuits have not so limited the scope of the provision. . . .

We granted certiorari to resolve this disagreement. To do so requires us to decide whether Title VII's anti-retaliation provision forbids only those employer actions and resulting harms that are related to employment or the workplace. And we must characterize how harmful an act of retaliatory discrimination must be in order to fall within the provision's scope.

A

Petitioner and the Solicitor General both argue that the Sixth Circuit is correct to require a link between the challenged retaliatory action and the terms, conditions, or status of employment. They note that Title VII's substantive anti-discrimination provision protects an individual only from employment-related discrimination. They add that the anti-retaliation provision should be read *in pari materia* with the anti-discrimination provision. And they conclude that the employer actions prohibited by the anti-retaliation provision should similarly be limited to conduct that "affects the employee's 'compensation, terms, conditions, or privileges of employment.'" Brief for United States as *Amicus Curiae* 13 (quoting § 2000e-2(a)(1)); see Brief for Petitioner 13 (same).

We cannot agree. The language of the substantive provision differs from that of the anti-retaliation provision in important ways. Section 703(a) sets forth Title VII's core anti-discrimination provision in the following terms:

"It shall be an unlawful employment practice for an employer—

"(1) *to fail or refuse to hire or to discharge* any individual, or otherwise to discriminate against any individual *with respect to his compensation, terms, conditions, or privileges of employment*, because of such individual's race, color, religion, sex, or national origin; or

"(2) to limit, segregate, or classify his employees or applicants for employment in any way *which would deprive or tend to deprive any individual of employment opportunities or otherwise adversely affect his status as an employee*, because of such individual's race, color, religion, sex, or national origin." § 2000e-2(a) (emphasis added).

Section 704(a) sets forth Title VII's anti-retaliation provision in the following terms:

"It shall be an unlawful employment practice for an employer *to discriminate against* any of his employees or applicants for employment . . . because he has opposed any practice made an unlawful employment practice by this subchapter, or because he has made a charge, testified, assisted, or participated in any manner in an investigation, proceeding, or hearing under this subchapter." § 2000e-3(a) (emphasis added).

The underscored words in the substantive provision—"hire," "discharge," "compensation, terms, conditions, or privileges of employment," "employment opportunities," and "status as an employee"—explicitly limit the scope of that provision to actions that affect employment or alter the conditions of the workplace. No such limiting words appear in the anti-retaliation provision. Given these linguistic differences, the question here is not whether identical or similar words should be read *in pari materia* to mean the same thing. See, *e.g., Pasquantino v. United States,* 544 U.S. 349, n. 2 (2005); *McFarland v. Scott,* 512 U.S. 849, 858 (1994); *Sullivan v. Everhart,* 494 U.S. 83, 92 (1990). Rather, the question is whether Congress intended its different words to make a legal difference. We normally presume that, where words differ as they differ here, "'Congress acts intentionally and purposely in the disparate inclusion or exclusion.'" *Russello v. United States,* 464 U.S. 16, 23 (1983).

There is strong reason to believe that Congress intended the differences that its language suggests, for the two provisions differ not only in language but in purpose as well. The anti-discrimination provision seeks a workplace where individuals are not discriminated against because of their racial, ethnic, religious, or gender-based status. See *McDonnell Douglas Corp. v. Green,* 411 U.S. 792, 800–801 (1973). The anti-retaliation provision seeks to secure that primary objective by preventing an employer from interfering (through retaliation) with an employee's efforts to secure or advance enforcement of the Act's basic guarantees. The substantive provision seeks to prevent injury to individuals based on who they are, *i.e.*, their status. The anti-retaliation provision seeks to prevent harm to individuals based on what they do, *i.e.*, their conduct.

To secure the first objective, Congress did not need to prohibit anything other than employment-related discrimination. The substantive provision's basic objective of "equality of employment opportunities" and the elimination of practices that tend to bring about "stratified job environments," *id.*, at 800, would be achieved were all employment-related discrimination miraculously eliminated.

But one cannot secure the second objective by focusing only upon employer actions and harm that concern employment and the workplace. Were all such actions and harms eliminated, the anti-retaliation provision's objective would *not* be achieved. An employer can effectively retaliate against an employee by taking actions not directly related to his employment or by causing him harm *outside* the workplace. See, *e.g.*, *Rochon v. Gonzales*, 438 F.3d, at 1213 (FBI retaliation against employee "took the form of the FBI's refusal, contrary to policy, to investigate death threats a federal prisoner made against [the agent] and his wife"); *Berry v. Stevinson Chevrolet*, 74 F.3d 980, 984, 986 (CA10 1996) (finding actionable retaliation where employer filed false criminal charges against former employee who complained about discrimination). A provision limited to employment-related actions would not deter the many forms that effective retaliation can take. Hence, such a limited construction would fail to fully achieve the anti-retaliation provision's "primary purpose," namely, "[m]aintaining unfettered access to statutory remedial mechanisms." *Robinson v. Shell Oil Co.*, 519 U.S. 337, 346 (1997).

Thus, purpose reinforces what language already indicates, namely, that the anti-retaliation provision, unlike the substantive provision, is not limited to discriminatory actions that affect the terms and conditions of employment. Cf. *Wachovia Bank, N.A. v. Schmidt*, 546 U.S. ___ (2006) (slip op., at 14) (rejecting statutory construction that would "trea[t] venue and subject-matter jurisdiction prescriptions as *in pari materia*" because doing so would "overloo[k] the discrete offices of those concepts").

Our precedent does not compel a contrary conclusion. Indeed, we have found no case in this Court that offers petitioner or the United States significant support. *Burlington Industries, Inc. v. Ellerth*, 524 U.S. 742 (1998), as petitioner notes, speaks of a Title VII requirement that violations involve "tangible employment action" such as "hiring, firing, failing to promote, reassignment with significantly different responsibilities, or a decision causing a significant change in benefits." *Id.*, at 761. But *Ellerth* does so only to "identify a class of [hostile work environment] cases" in which an employer should be held vicariously liable (without an affirmative defense) for the acts of supervisors. *Id.*, at 760; see also *Pennsylvania State Police v. Suders*, 542 U.S. 129, 143 (2004) (explaining holdings in *Ellerth* and *Faragher v. Boca Raton*, 524 U.S. 775 (1998), as dividing hostile work environment claims into two categories, one in which the employer is strictly liable because a tangible employment action is taken and one in which the employer can make an affirmative defense). *Ellerth* did not discuss the scope of the general anti-discrimination provision. See 524 U.S., at 761 (using "concept of a tangible employment action [that] appears in numerous cases in the Courts of Appeals" only "for resolution of the vicarious liability issue"). And *Ellerth* did not mention Title VII's anti-retaliation provision at all. At most, *Ellerth* sets forth a standard that petitioner and the Solicitor General believe the anti-retaliation provision ought to contain. But it does not compel acceptance of their view.

Nor can we find significant support for their view in the EEOC's interpretations of the provision. We concede that the EEOC stated in its 1991 and 1988 Compliance Manuals that the anti-retaliation provision is limited to "adverse employment-related action." 2 EEOC Compliance Manual §614.1(d), p. 614–5 (1991) (hereinafter EEOC 1991 Manual); EEOC Compliance Manual §614.1(d), p. 614–5 (1988) (hereinafter EEOC 1988 Manual). But in those same manuals the EEOC lists the "[e]ssential [e]lements" of a retaliation claim along with language suggesting a broader interpretation. EEOC 1991 Manual §614.3(d), pp. 614–8 to 614–9 (complainant must show "that [s]he was in some manner subjected to adverse treatment by the respondent because of the protest or opposition"); EEOC 1988 Manual §614.3(d), pp. 614–8 to 614–9 (same).

Moreover, both before and after publication of the 1991 and 1988 manuals, the EEOC similarly expressed a broad interpretation of the anti-retaliation provision. Compare EEOC Interpretive Manual, Reference Manual to Title VII Law for Compliance Personnel §491.2 (1972) (hereinafter 1972 Reference Manual) (§704(a) "is intended to provide 'exceptionally broad protection' for protestors of discriminatory employment practices"), with 2 EEOC Compliance Manual §8, p. 8–13 (1998) (hereinafter EEOC 1998 Manual), available at http://www.eeoc.gov/policy/docs/retal.html (as visited June 20, 2006, and available in Clerk of Court's case file) (§704(a) "prohibit[s] any adverse treatment that is based on a retaliatory motive and is reasonably likely to deter the charging party or others from engaging in protected activity"). And the EEOC 1998 Manual, which offers the Commission's *only* direct statement on the question of whether the anti-retaliation provision is limited to the same employment-related activity covered by the anti-discrimination provision, answers that question in the negative—directly contrary to petitioner's reading of the Act. *Ibid.*

Finally, we do not accept the petitioner's and Solicitor General's view that it is "anomalous" to read the statute to provide broader protection for victims of retaliation than for those whom Title VII primarily seeks to protect, namely, victims of race-based, ethnic-based, religion-based, or gender-based discrimination. Brief for Petitioner 17; Brief for United States as *Amicus Curiae* 14–15. Congress has provided similar kinds of protection from retaliation in comparable statutes without any judicial suggestion that those provisions are limited to the conduct prohibited by the primary substantive provisions. The National Labor Relations Act, to which this Court has "drawn analogies . . . in other Title VII contexts," *Hishon v. King & Spalding,* 467 U.S. 69, n. 8 (1984), provides an illustrative example. Compare 29

U.S.C. § 158(a)(3) (substantive provision prohibiting employer "discrimination in regard to . . . any term or condition of employment to encourage or discourage membership in any labor organization") with § 158(a)(4) (retaliation provision making it unlawful for an employer to "discharge or otherwise discriminate against an employee because he has filed charges or given testimony under this subchapter"); see also *Bill Johnson's Restaurants, Inc. v. NLRB,* 461 U.S. 731, 740 (1983) (construing anti-retaliation provision to "prohibi[t] a wide variety of employer conduct that is intended to restrain, or that has the likely effect of restraining, employees in the exercise of protected activities," including the retaliatory filing of a lawsuit against an employee); *NLRB v. Scrivener,* 405 U.S. 117, 121–122 (1972) (purpose of the anti-retaliation provision is to ensure that employees are "'completely free from coercion against reporting'" unlawful practices).

In any event, as we have explained, differences in the purpose of the two provisions remove any perceived "anomaly," for they justify this difference of interpretation. . . .

For these reasons, we conclude that Title VII's substantive provision and its anti-retaliation provision are not coterminous. The scope of the anti-retaliation provision extends beyond workplace-related or employment-related retaliatory acts and harm. We therefore reject the standards applied in the Courts of Appeals that have treated the anti-retaliation provision as forbidding the same conduct prohibited by the anti-discrimination provision and that have limited actionable retaliation to so-called "ultimate employment decisions." See *supra,* at 5.

B

The anti-retaliation provision protects an individual not from all retaliation, but from retaliation that produces an injury or harm. As we have explained, the Courts of Appeals have used differing language to describe the level of seriousness to which this harm must rise before it becomes actionable retaliation. We agree with the formulation set forth by the Seventh and the District of Columbia Circuits. In our view, a plaintiff must show that a reasonable employee would have found the challenged action materially adverse, "which in this context means it well might have 'dissuaded a reasonable worker from making or supporting a charge of discrimination.'" *Rochon,* 438 F.3d, at 1219 (quoting *Washington,* 420 F.3d, at 662).

We speak of *material* adversity because we believe it is important to separate significant from trivial harms. Title VII, we have said, does not set forth "a general civility code for the American workplace." *Oncale v. Sundowner Offshore Services, Inc.,* 523 U.S. 75, 80 (1998); See *Faragher,* 524 U.S., at 788 (judicial standards for sexual harassment must "filter out complaints attacking 'the ordinary tribulations of the workplace, such as the sporadic use of abusive language, gender-related jokes, and occasional teasing'"). . . . The anti-retaliation provision seeks to prevent employer interference with "unfettered access" to Title VII's remedial mechanisms. *Robinson,* 519 U.S., at 346. It does so by prohibiting employer actions that are likely "to deter victims of discrimination from complaining to the EEOC," the courts, and their employers. *Ibid.* And normally petty slights, minor annoyances, and simple lack of good manners will not create such deterrence. See 2 EEOC 1998 Manual § 8, p. 8–13.

We refer to reactions of a *reasonable* employee because we believe that the provision's standard for judging harm must be objective. An objective standard is judicially administrable. It avoids the uncertainties and unfair discrepancies that can plague a judicial effort to determine a plaintiff's unusual subjective feelings. We have emphasized the need for objective standards in other Title VII contexts, and those same concerns animate our decision here. See, *e.g.*, *Suders*, 542 U.S., at 141 (constructive discharge doctrine); *Harris v. Forklift Systems, Inc.*, 510 U.S. 17, 21 (1993) (hostile work environment doctrine).

We phrase the standard in general terms because the significance of any given act of retaliation will often depend upon the particular circumstances. Context matters. . . .

Finally, we note that contrary to the claim of the concurrence, this standard does *not* require a reviewing court or jury to consider "the nature of the discrimination that led to the filing of the charge." *Post*, at 6 (Alito, J., concurring in judgment). Rather, the standard is tied to the challenged retaliatory act, not the underlying conduct that forms the basis of the Title VII complaint. By focusing on the materiality of the challenged action and the perspective of a reasonable person in the plaintiff's position, we believe this standard will screen out trivial conduct while effectively capturing those acts that are likely to dissuade employees from complaining or assisting in complaints about discrimination.

III

Applying this standard to the facts of this case, we believe that there was a sufficient evidentiary basis to support the jury's verdict on White's retaliation claim. See *Reeves v. Sanderson Plumbing Products, Inc.*, 530 U.S. 133, 150–151 (2000). The jury found that two of Burlington's actions amounted to retaliation: the reassignment of White from forklift duty to standard track laborer tasks and the 37-day suspension without pay.

Burlington does not question the jury's determination that the motivation for these acts was retaliatory. But it does question the statutory significance of the harm these acts caused. . . .

First, Burlington argues that a reassignment of duties cannot constitute retaliatory discrimination where, as here, both the former and present duties fall within the same job description. Brief for Petitioner 24–25. We do not see why that is so. Almost every job category involves some responsibilities and duties that are less desirable than others. Common sense suggests that one good way to discourage an employee such as White from bringing discrimination charges would be to insist that she spend more time performing the more arduous duties and less time performing those that are easier or more agreeable. That is presumably why the EEOC has consistently found "[r]etaliatory work assignments" to be a classic and "widely recognized" example of "forbidden retaliation." 2 EEOC 1991 Manual § 614.7, pp. 614–31 to 614–32; see also 1972 Reference Manual § 495.2 (noting Commission decision involving an employer's ordering an employee "to do an unpleasant work assignment in retaliation" for filing racial discrimination complaint); EEOC Dec. No. 74–77, 1974 WL 3847, *4 (Jan. 18, 1974) ("Employers have been enjoined" under Title VII "from imposing unpleasant work assignments upon an employee for filing charges").

To be sure, reassignment of job duties is not automatically actionable. Whether a particular reassignment is materially adverse depends upon the circumstances of the particular case, and "should be judged from the perspective of a reasonable person in the plaintiff's position, considering 'all the circumstances.'" *Oncale*, 523 U. S., at 81. But here, the jury had before it considerable evidence that the track labor duties were "by all accounts more arduous and dirtier"; that the "forklift operator position required more qualifications, which is an indication of prestige"; and that "the forklift operator position was objectively considered a better job and the male employees resented White for occupying it." 364 F.3d, at 803 (internal quotation marks omitted). Based on this record, a jury could reasonably conclude that the reassignment of responsibilities would have been materially adverse to a reasonable employee.

Second, Burlington argues that the 37-day suspension without pay lacked statutory significance because Burlington ultimately reinstated White with back pay. Burlington says that "it defies reason to believe that Congress would have considered a rescinded investigatory suspension with full back pay" to be unlawful, particularly because Title VII, throughout much of its history, provided no relief in an equitable action for victims in White's position. Brief for Petitioner 36.

We do not find Burlington's last-mentioned reference to the nature of Title VII's remedies convincing. . . . [W]e have no reason to believe that a court could not have issued an injunction where an employer suspended an employee for retaliatory purposes, even if that employer later provided back pay. In any event, Congress amended Title VII in 1991 to permit victims of intentional discrimination to recover compensatory (as White received here) and punitive damages, concluding that the additional remedies were necessary to "'help make victims whole.'" *West v. Gibson*, 527 U.S. 212, 219 (1999) (quoting H.R. Rep. No. 102-40, pt. 1, pp. 64–65 (1991)); See 42 U.S.C. §§ 1981a(a)(1), (b). We would undermine the significance of that congressional judgment were we to conclude that employers could avoid liability in these circumstances.

Neither do we find convincing any claim of insufficient evidence. White did receive back pay. But White and her family had to live for 37 days without income. They did not know during that time whether or when White could return to work. Many reasonable employees would find a month without a paycheck to be a serious hardship. And White described to the jury the physical and emotional hardship that 37 days of having "no income, no money" in fact caused. 1 Tr. 154 ("That was the worst Christmas I had out of my life. No income, no money, and that made all of us feel bad. . . . I got very depressed"). Indeed, she obtained medical treatment for her emotional distress. A reasonable employee facing the choice between retaining her job (and paycheck) and filing a discrimination complaint might well choose the former. That is to say, an indefinite suspension without pay could well act as a deterrent, even if the suspended employee eventually received back pay. Cf. *Mitchell,* 361 U.S., at 292 ("[I]t needs no argument to show that fear of economic retaliation might often operate to induce aggrieved employees quietly to accept substandard conditions"). Thus, the jury's conclusion that the 37-day suspension without pay was materially adverse was a reasonable one.

IV

For these reasons, the judgment of the Court of Appeals is affirmed.

It is so ordered.

Chapter 3

Gender Discrimination

A. Title VII and Sexual Harassment

Congress heatedly debated the passage of the Civil Rights Act of 1964. So much so that, at the last hour, the term "sex" was included in an amendment by detractors in the hope of foiling the statute's enactment. The attempt failed and the statute passed, including protections from discrimination based on sex. Since then, gender discrimination litigation has been a common and vibrant part of the anti-discrimination landscape. *See* Jo Freeman, *How "Sex" Got Into Title VII: Persistent Opportunism as a Maker of Public Policy*, 9 LAW & INEQ. 163 (1991) (referring to the hours of debate over adding "sex" to the bill as "Ladies Day in the House"). The debate around the meaning of "sex" and what should be included as part of sex discrimination still remains, however. We start this section with sexual harassment, as an important extension of discrimination based on sex. Sexual harassment law began in 1986 with the landmark case *Meritor Savings Bank v. Vinson*, 477 U.S. 57 (1986) (finding sexual harassment to be a violation of Title VII.) Later the Congressional hearings with Professor Anita Hill and then-Judge Thomas, further helped to change the face of the workplace. *See* Julia Carpenter, *How Anita Hill forever changed the way we talk about sexual harassment*, CNN Money (Nov. 9, 2017), http://money .cnn.com/2017/10/30/pf/anita-hill-sexual-harassment/index.html (reporting that the media attention given to the Anita Hill hearings resulted in national attention to sexual harassment in the workplace, more than doubling the number of EEOC sexual harassment complaint filings). Sexual harassment law is a vibrant part of Title VII litigation. Though limited and tweaked over the decades, it still remains a strong protection against acts creating a hostile environment in the workplace. We then end the chapter with grooming standards and protections for breastfeeding under the Affordable Care Act, as ongoing issues. See *Harris v. Forklift* below, laying out the standard and requirements for a sexual harassment claim, and *Farragher*, discussing the scope of employer liability for violations committed by employees.

Recently renewed focus on sexual harassment in the workplace nationwide demonstrates that decades long legal changes prohibiting harassment have not worked to eradicate it. As the cultural evolution continues, it remains incumbent on attorneys to educate all sectors about the harmful effects of of harassment in the workplace. As you read the cases below, consider the following hypo and the mock sexual harassment claim. Would this plaintiff be deemed to have alleged facts sufficient to support a claim of sexual harassment? What would you add or change?

Mock Claim

GENERAL ALLEGATIONS

Charlie X is a a twenty-two year old Native American woman.

Mr. Angel X is a fifty year old white male casting director and supervisor directly employed by Disney Channels.

Over one year ago, Charlie began working at Disney Channels as an assistant to Mr. Angel doing primarily secretarial work. She aspires to be an actress.

Not long after being hired, Charlie informed her boss, Mr. Angel, of her acting aspirations in hopes that he would consider casting her in an upcoming Disney project. She felt that her experiences as a Native American woman would add depth to her characters.

Approximately one year into her employment, Angel informed her that he had a potential role for her, and invited her out to dinner to discuss it.

Charlie had never been romantically involved with Angel, nor given him any indication that she was interested in being romantically or sexually involved with him. He was her supervisor.

Thinking, however, that this may be a terrific opportunity for her, Charlie accepted his offer solely for the promise of a potential acting job. The dinner progressed smoothly with no indication that its purpose was anything other than business related.

Afterward, Angel informed Charlie that he wanted to offer her a chance to audition as a main character's sister in a movie, and invited her to come home with him in order to show her the script and help her prepare. Still excited that this may be her first shot at landing a substantial role, which Angel assured her he thought she was "perfect" for, Charlie accepted.

They arrived at his substantial estate at approximately 10:30 in the evening, at which point Charlie was thoroughly impressed, and hopeful that the occasion would be her break into acting. When Angel offered her a drink, she accepted, and drank it.

At no point prior to this did Angel make any sexual advances or propositions, nor did Charlie consent to anything of the sort.

Hours later, Charlie awoke naked, disoriented, cotton mouthed, and lethargic with her clothes torn from her body and no sense of how much time had passed or where she was. When she regained her senses enough to move, she fled the room in a panic.

Eventually, she found Angel in the dining room, and accused him of assaulting her, to which he replied, "You didn't expect me to help you for nothing, did you? I put something in your drink to make things easier. I can't stand doing the small talk." He also emphasized that she should not bother telling anyone about the incident because, "No one will believe you."

Shocked and traumatized, Charlie returned home, and later—with difficulty—returned to work. The promised acting role never materialized. Quite the contrary, afterward Angel reacted with chilly distance towards her "as though she didn't exist."

In the aftermath of her trauma, Charlie has suffered repeated stress headaches and anxiety. She tried to get another position within the company so as to avoid future contact with Angel.

His action was so severe and pervasive that she can no longer function in the current work environment, and she is still experiencing repercussions from that night.

Finally, soon after this trauma, Charlie applied for a promotion within her department, but was denied. Instead the position was given to a newly hired, white male colleague with less experience and qualifications than her.

This colleague had been working for the company for a couple of weeks at most, whereas Charlie had been with them for over a year, during which period she had never received any disciplinary action.

When she inquired as to why she had been passed over for the position, the head of the department informed her that she "did not act like the type of woman who should be in that position" and that she was "too girly and pretty."

Three months ago, on advice of counsel, Charlie reported Angel's infraction to her Human Resources department. Disney Channels has yet to take corrective action.

COUNT
Gender Discrimination: Sexual Harassment

As set forth above, the Plaintiff, Charlie, is a woman employed at Disney, and, thus, a member of a protected class as defined by Title VII of the Civil Rights Act of 1964. She was in a subordinate position to Defendant, Angel X.

On the evening described above, Charlie accepted her supervisor Angel X's invitation to dinner only on the premise that he presented it as a work opportunity for her as an actress. The same applies to her decision to visit his home.

The assault that followed was not only uninvited and without her consent, but performed without ever presenting her with the chance to give such consent, and instead carried out forcibly by means of narcotics.

Angel X's behavior amounted to sexual assault and sexual harassment. His conduct was not only subjectively traumatizing, humiliating, and demeaning to Charlie, but would have been considered hostile to a reasonable person.

In addition, the hostile work environment left in the wake of the event continued to be objectionable and traumatizing.

Title VII is violated when a workplace is permeated with discriminatory intimidation, that is sufficiently severe or pervasive to alter conditions of victim's employment and create abusive working environment.

Angel X's behavior was severe and pervasive enough to cause Charlie continuing stress headaches, anxiety, and continuing, constant discomfort in the workplace.

The *Meritor* standard for determining whether conduct is actionable under Title VII as "abusive work environment" harassment requires an objectively hostile or abusive environment — one that reasonable person would find hostile or abusive — as well as victim's subjective perception that the environment is abusive.

Charlie has stated that she feels her work environment is changed and hostile, and in the wake of such severe trauma, a reasonable person would find this to be so.

Harris v. Forklift Sys.

510 U.S. 17 (1993)

Justice O'Connor delivered the opinion of the Court.

In this case we consider the definition of a discriminatorily "abusive work environment" (also known as a "hostile work environment") under Title VII of the Civil Rights Act of 1964, 78 Stat. 253, as amended, 42 U.S.C. § 2000e *et seq.* (1988 ed., Supp. III).

I

Teresa Harris worked as a manager at Forklift Systems, Inc., an equipment rental company, from April 1985 until October 1987. Charles Hardy was Forklift's president.

The Magistrate found that, throughout Harris' time at Forklift, Hardy often insulted her because of her gender and often made her the target of unwanted sexual innuendos. Hardy told Harris on several occasions, in the presence of other employees, "You're a woman, what do you know" and "We need a man as the rental manager"; at least once, he told her she was "a dumb ass woman." App. to Pet. for Cert. A-13. Again in front of others, he suggested that the two of them "go to the Holiday Inn to negotiate [Harris'] raise." *Id.,* at A-14. Hardy occasionally asked Harris and other female employees to get coins from his front pants pocket. *Ibid.* He threw objects on the ground in front of Harris and other women, and asked them to pick the objects up. *Id.,* at A-14 to A-15. He made sexual innuendos about Harris' and other women's clothing. *Id.,* at A-15.

In mid-August 1987, Harris complained to Hardy about his conduct. Hardy said he was surprised that Harris was offended, claimed he was only joking, and apologized. *Id.,* at A-16. He also promised he would stop, and based on this assurance Harris stayed on the job. *Ibid.* But in early September, Hardy began anew: While Harris was arranging a deal with one of Forklift's customers, he asked her, again in front of other employees, "What did you do, promise the guy . . . some [sex] Saturday night?" *Id.,* at A-17. On October 1, Harris collected her paycheck and quit.

Harris then sued Forklift, claiming that Hardy's conduct had created an abusive work environment for her because of her gender. The United States District Court for the Middle District of Tennessee, adopting the report and recommendation of the Magistrate, found this to be "a close case," *id.*, at A-31, but held that Hardy's conduct did not create an abusive environment. The court found that some of Hardy's comments "offended [Harris], and would offend the reasonable woman," *id.*, at A-33, but that they were not

> "so severe as to be expected to seriously affect [Harris'] psychological well-being. A reasonable woman manager under like circumstances would have been offended by Hardy, but his conduct would not have risen to the level of interfering with that person's work performance.
>
> "Neither do I believe that [Harris] was subjectively so offended that she suffered injury.... Although Hardy may at times have genuinely offended [Harris], I do not believe that he created a working environment so poisoned as to be intimidating or abusive to [Harris]." *Id.*, at A-34 to A-35.

In focusing on the employee's psychological well-being, the District Court was following Circuit precedent. See *Rabidue v. Osceola Refining Co.*, 805 F.2d 611, 620 (CA6 1986), cert. denied, 481 U.S. 1041, 107 S.Ct. 1983, 95 L.Ed.2d 823 (1987). The United States Court of Appeals for the Sixth Circuit affirmed in a brief unpublished decision, 976 F.2d 733. (1992)

We granted certiorari, 507 U.S. 959, 113 S.Ct. 1382, 122 L.Ed.2d 758 (1993), to resolve a conflict among the Circuits on whether conduct, to be actionable as "abusive work environment" harassment (no *quid pro quo* harassment issue is present here), must "seriously affect [an employee's] psychological well-being" or lead the plaintiff to "suffe[r] injury." Compare *Rabidue* (requiring serious effect on psychological well-being). . . .

II

Title VII of the Civil Rights Act of 1964 makes it "an unlawful employment practice for an employer . . . to discriminate against any individual with respect to his compensation, terms, conditions, or privileges of employment, because of such individual's race, color, religion, sex, or national origin." 42 U.S.C. § 2000e-2(a)(1). As we made clear in *Meritor Savings Bank, FSB v. Vinson*, 477 U.S. 57, 106 S.Ct. 2399, 91 L.Ed.2d 49 (1986), this language "is not limited to 'economic' or 'tangible' discrimination. The phrase 'terms, conditions, or privileges of employment' evinces a congressional intent 'to strike at the entire spectrum of disparate treatment of men and women' in employment," which includes requiring people to work in a discriminatorily hostile or abusive environment. *Id.*, at 64, 106 S.Ct., at 2404, quoting *Los Angeles Dept. of Water and Power v. Manhart*, 435 U.S. 702, 707, n. 13, 98 S.Ct. 1370, 1374, 55 L.Ed.2d 657 (1978) (some internal quotation marks omitted). When the workplace is permeated with "discriminatory intimidation, ridicule, and insult," 477 U.S., at 65, 106 S.Ct., at 2405, that is "sufficiently severe or pervasive to alter the conditions of the victim's employment and create an abusive working environment," *id.,* at 67, 106 S.Ct., at 2405 (internal brackets and quotation marks omitted), Title VII is violated.

This standard, which we reaffirm today, takes a middle path between making actionable any conduct that is merely offensive and requiring the conduct to cause a tangible psychological injury. As we pointed out in *Meritor,* "mere utterance of an . . . epithet which engenders offensive feelings in a[n] employee," *ibid.* (internal quotation marks omitted) does not sufficiently affect the conditions of employment to implicate Title VII. Conduct that is not severe or pervasive enough to create an objectively hostile or abusive work environment—an environment that a reasonable person would find hostile or abusive—is beyond Title VII's purview. Likewise, if the victim does not subjectively perceive the environment to be abusive, the conduct has not actually altered the conditions of the victim's employment, and there is no Title VII violation.

But Title VII comes into play before the harassing conduct leads to a nervous breakdown. A discriminatorily abusive work environment, even one that does not seriously affect employees' psychological well-being, can and often will detract from employees' job performance, discourage employees from remaining on the job, or keep them from advancing in their careers. Moreover, even without regard to these tangible effects, the very fact that the discriminatory conduct was so severe or pervasive that it created a work environment abusive to employees because of their race, gender, religion, or national origin offends Title VII's broad rule of workplace equality. The appalling conduct alleged in *Meritor,* and the reference in that case to environments "'so heavily polluted with discrimination as to destroy completely the emotional and psychological stability of minority group workers,'" *id.,* at 66, 106 S.Ct., at 2405, quoting *Rogers v. EEOC,* 454 F.2d 234, 238 (CA5 1971), cert. denied, 406 U.S. 957, 92 S.Ct. 2058, 32 L.Ed.2d 343 (1972), merely present some especially egregious examples of harassment. They do not mark the boundary of what is actionable.

We therefore believe the District Court erred in relying on whether the conduct "seriously affect[ed] plaintiff's psychological well-being" or led her to "suffe[r] injury." Such an inquiry may needlessly focus the factfinder's attention on concrete psychological harm, an element Title VII does not require. Certainly Title VII bars conduct that would seriously affect a reasonable person's psychological well-being, but the statute is not limited to such conduct. So long as the environment would reasonably be perceived, and is perceived, as hostile or abusive, *Meritor, supra,* 477 U.S., at 67, 106 S.Ct., at 2405, there is no need for it also to be psychologically injurious.

This is not, and by its nature cannot be, a mathematically precise test. We need not answer today all the potential questions it raises, nor specifically address the Equal Employment Opportunity Commission's new regulations on this subject, see 58 Fed.Reg. 51266 (1993) (proposed 29 CFR §§ 1609.1, 1609.2); see also 29 CFR § 1604.11 (1993). But we can say that whether an environment is "hostile" or "abusive" can be determined only by looking at all the circumstances. These may include the frequency of the discriminatory conduct; its severity; whether it is physically threatening or humiliating, or a mere offensive utterance; and whether it unreasonably interferes with an employee's work performance. The effect on the employee's psychological well-being is, of course, relevant to determining whether the plaintiff actually found the environment abusive. But while psychological harm, like any other relevant factor, may be taken into account, no single factor is required.

III

Forklift, while conceding that a requirement that the conduct seriously affect psychological well-being is unfounded, argues that the District Court nonetheless correctly applied the *Meritor* standard. We disagree. Though the District Court did conclude that the work environment was not "intimidating or abusive to [Harris]," App. to Pet. for Cert. A-35, it did so only after finding that the conduct was not "so severe as to be expected to seriously affect plaintiff's psychological well-being," *id.,* at A-34, and that Harris was not "subjectively so offended that she suffered injury," *ibid.* The District Court's application of these incorrect standards may well have influenced its ultimate conclusion, especially given that the court found this to be a "close case," *id.,* at A-31.

We therefore reverse the judgment of the Court of Appeals, and remand the case for further proceedings consistent with this opinion.

So ordered.

JUSTICE GINSBURG, concurring.

Today the Court reaffirms the holding of *Meritor Savings Bank, FSB v. Vinson,* 477 U.S. 57, 66, 106 S.Ct. 2399, 2405, 91 L.Ed.2d 49 (1986): "[A] plaintiff may establish a violation of Title VII by proving that discrimination based on sex has created a hostile or abusive work environment." The critical issue, Title VII's text indicates, is whether members of one sex are exposed to disadvantageous terms or conditions of employment to which members of the other sex are not exposed. See 42 U.S.C. §2000e-2(a)(1) (declaring that it is unlawful to discriminate with respect to, *inter alia,* "terms" or "conditions" of employment). As the Equal Employment Opportunity Commission emphasized, see Brief for United States and Equal Employment Opportunity Commission as *Amici Curiae* 9–14, the adjudicator's inquiry should center, dominantly, on whether the discriminatory conduct has unreasonably interfered with the plaintiff's work performance. To show such interference, "the plaintiff need not prove that his or her tangible productivity has declined as a result of the harassment." *Davis v. Monsanto Chemical Co.,* 858 F.2d 345, 349 (CA6 1988). It suffices to prove that a reasonable person subjected to the discriminatory conduct would find, as the plaintiff did, that the harassment so altered working conditions as to "ma[k]e it more difficult to do the job." See *ibid. Davis* concerned race-based discrimination, but that difference does not alter the analysis; except in the rare case in which a bona fide occupational qualification is shown, see *Automobile Workers v. Johnson Controls, Inc.,* 499 U.S. 187, 200–207, 111 S.Ct. 1196, 1204–1208, 113 L.Ed.2d 158 (1991) (construing 42 U.S.C. §2000e-2(e)(1)), Title VII declares discriminatory practices based on race, gender, religion, or national origin equally unlawful.

The Court's opinion, which I join, seems to me in harmony with the view expressed in this concurring statement.

Faragher v. City of Boca Raton
524 U.S. 775 (1998)

JUSTICE SOUTER delivered the opinion of the Court.

This case calls for identification of the circumstances under which an employer may be held liable under Title VII of the Civil Rights Act of 1964, 78 Stat. 253, as amended, 42 U.S.C. § 2000e *et seq.,* for the acts of a supervisory employee whose sexual harassment of subordinates has created a hostile work environment amounting to employment discrimination. We hold that an employer is vicariously liable for actionable discrimination caused by a supervisor, but subject to an affirmative defense looking to the reasonableness of the employer's conduct as well as that of a plaintiff victim.

I

Between 1985 and 1990, while attending college, petitioner Beth Ann Faragher worked part time and during the summers as an ocean lifeguard for the Marine Safety Section of the Parks and Recreation Department of respondent, the City of Boca Raton, Florida (City). During this period, Faragher's immediate supervisors were Bill Terry, David Silverman, and Robert Gordon. In June 1990, Faragher resigned.

In 1992, Faragher brought an action against Terry, Silverman, and the City, asserting claims under Title VII, Rev.Stat. § 1979, 42 U.S.C. § 1983, and Florida law. So far as it concerns the Title VII claim, the complaint alleged that Terry and Silverman created a "sexually hostile atmosphere" at the beach by repeatedly subjecting Faragher and other female lifeguards to "uninvited and offensive touching," by making lewd remarks, and by speaking of women in offensive terms. The complaint contained specific allegations that Terry once said that he would never promote a woman to the rank of lieutenant, and that Silverman had said to Faragher, "Date me or clean the toilets for a year." Asserting that Terry and Silverman were agents of the City, and that their conduct amounted to discrimination in the "terms, conditions, and privileges" of her employment, 42 U.S.C. § 2000e-2(a)(1), Faragher sought a judgment against the City for nominal damages, costs, and attorney's fees.

Following a bench trial, the United States District Court for the Southern District of Florida found that throughout Faragher's employment with the City, Terry served as Chief of the Marine Safety Division, with authority to hire new lifeguards (subject to the approval of higher management), to supervise all aspects of the lifeguards' work assignments, to engage in counseling, to deliver oral reprimands, and to make a record of any such discipline. 864 F.Supp. 1552, 1563–1564 (1994).

Silverman was a Marine Safety lieutenant from 1985 until June 1989, when he became a captain. *Id.,* at 1555. Gordon began the employment period as a lieutenant and at some point was promoted to the position of training captain. In these positions, Silverman and Gordon were responsible for making the lifeguards' daily assignments, and for supervising their work and fitness training. *Id.,* at 1564.

The lifeguards and supervisors were stationed at the city beach and worked out of the Marine Safety Headquarters, a small one-story building containing an office, a meeting room, and a single, unisex locker room with a shower. *Id.,* at 1556. Their work routine was structured in a "paramilitary configuration," *id.,* at 1564, with a clear chain of command. Lifeguards reported to lieutenants and captains, who reported to Terry. He was supervised by the Recreation Superintendent, who in turn reported to a Director of Parks and Recreation, answerable to the City Manager. *Id.,* at 1555. The lifeguards had no significant contact with higher city officials like the Recreation Superintendent. *Id.,* at 1564.

In February 1986, the City adopted a sexual harassment policy, which it stated in a memorandum from the City Manager addressed to all employees. *Id.,* at 1560. In May 1990, the City revised the policy and reissued a statement of it. *Ibid.* Although the City may actually have circulated the memos and statements to some employees, it completely failed to disseminate its policy among employees of the Marine Safety Section, with the result that Terry, Silverman, Gordon, and many lifeguards were unaware of it. *Ibid.*

From time to time over the course of Faragher's tenure at the Marine Safety Section, between 4 and 6 of the 40 to 50 lifeguards were women. *Id.,* at 1556. During that 5-year period, Terry repeatedly touched the bodies of female employees without invitation, *ibid.,* would put his arm around Faragher, with his hand on her buttocks, *id.,* at 1557, and once made contact with another female lifeguard in a motion of sexual simulation, *id.,* at 1556. He made crudely demeaning references to women generally, *id.,* at 1557, and once commented disparagingly on Faragher's shape, *ibid.* During a job interview with a woman he hired as a lifeguard, Terry said that the female lifeguards had sex with their male counterparts and asked whether she would do the same. *Ibid.*

Silverman behaved in similar ways. He once tackled Faragher and remarked that, but for a physical characteristic he found unattractive, he would readily have had sexual relations with her. *Ibid.* Another time, he pantomimed an act of oral sex. *Ibid.* Within earshot of the female lifeguards, Silverman made frequent, vulgar references to women and sexual matters, commented on the bodies of female lifeguards and beachgoers, and at least twice told female lifeguards that he would like to engage in sex with them. *Id.,* at 1557–1558.

Faragher did not complain to higher management about Terry or Silverman. Although she spoke of their behavior to Gordon, she did not regard these discussions as formal complaints to a supervisor but as conversations with a person she held in high esteem. *Id.,* at 1559. Other female lifeguards had similarly informal talks with Gordon, but because Gordon did not feel that it was his place to do so, he did not report these complaints to Terry, his own supervisor, or to any other city official. *Id.*, at 1559–1560. Gordon responded to the complaints of one lifeguard by saying that "the City just [doesn't] care." *Id.*, at 1561.

In April 1990, however, two months before Faragher's resignation, Nancy Ewanchew, a former lifeguard, wrote to Richard Bender, the City's Personnel Director, complaining that Terry and Silverman had harassed her and other female lifeguards. *Id.*, at 1559. Following investigation of this complaint, the City found that Terry and Silverman had behaved improperly, reprimanded them, and required them to choose between a suspension without pay or the forfeiture of annual leave. *Ibid.*

On the basis of these findings, the District Court concluded that the conduct of Terry and Silverman was discriminatory harassment sufficiently serious to alter the conditions of Faragher's employment and constitute an abusive working environment. *Id.*, at 1562–1563. The District Court then ruled that there were three justifications for holding the City liable for the harassment of its supervisory employees. First, the court noted that the harassment was pervasive enough to support an inference that the City had "knowledge, or constructive knowledge," of it. *Id.*, at 1563. Next, it ruled that the City was liable under traditional agency principles because Terry and Silverman were acting as its agents when they committed the harassing acts. *Id.*, at 1563–1564. Finally, the court observed that Gordon's knowledge of the harassment, combined with his inaction, "provides a further basis for imputing liability on [*sic*] the City." *Id.*, at 1564. The District Court then awarded Faragher $1 in nominal damages on her Title VII claim. *Id.*, at 1564–1565.

Since our decision in *Meritor,* Courts of Appeals have struggled to derive manageable standards to govern employer liability for hostile environment harassment perpetrated by supervisory employees. . . . We granted certiorari to address the divergence, 522 U.S. 978, 118 S.Ct. 438, 139 L.Ed.2d 337 (1997), and now reverse the judgment of the Eleventh Circuit and remand for entry of judgment in Faragher's favor.

II

A

Under Title VII of the Civil Rights Act of 1964, "[i]t shall be an unlawful employment practice for an employer . . . to fail or refuse to hire or to discharge any individual, or otherwise to discriminate against any individual with respect to his compensation, terms, conditions, or privileges of employment, because of such individual's race, color, religion, sex, or national origin." 42 U.S.C. § 2000e-2(a)(1). We have repeatedly made clear that although the statute mentions specific employment decisions with immediate consequences, the scope of the prohibition "'is not limited to "economic" or "tangible" discrimination,'" *Harris v. Forklift Systems, Inc.,* 510 U.S. 17, 21, 114 S.Ct. 367, 370, 126 L.Ed.2d 295 (1993) (quoting *Meritor Savings Bank, FSB v. Vinson, supra,* at 64, 106 S.Ct., at 2404), and that it covers more than "'terms' and 'conditions' in the narrow contractual sense." *Oncale v. Sundowner*

Offshore Services, Inc., 523 U.S. 75, 78, 118 S.Ct. 998, 1001, 140 L.Ed.2d 201 (1998). Thus, in *Meritor* we held that sexual harassment so "severe or pervasive" as to "'alter the conditions of [the victim's] employment and create an abusive working environment'" violates Title VII. 477 U.S., at 67, 106 S.Ct., at 2405–2406 (quoting *Henson v. Dundee,* 682 F.2d 897, 904 (C.A.11 1982)).

. . .

. . . While indicating the substantive contours of the hostile environments forbidden by Title VII, our cases have established few definite rules for determining when an employer will be liable for a discriminatory environment that is otherwise actionably abusive. Given the circumstances of many of the litigated cases, including some that have come to us, it is not surprising that in many of them, the issue has been joined over the sufficiency of the abusive conditions, not the standards for determining an employer's liability for them. There have, for example, been myriad cases in which District Courts and Courts of Appeals have held employers liable on account of actual knowledge by the employer, or high-echelon officials of an employer organization, of sufficiently harassing action by subordinates, which the employer or its informed officers have done nothing to stop. See, *e.g., Katz v. Dole,* 709 F.2d 251, 256 (C.A.4 1983) (upholding employer liability because the "employer's supervisory personnel manifested unmistakable acquiescence in or approval of the harassment"); *EEOC v. Hacienda Hotel,* 881 F.2d 1504, 1516 (C.A.9 1989) (employer liable where hotel manager did not respond to complaints about supervisors' harassment); *Hall v. Gus Constr. Co.,* 842 F.2d 1010, 1016 (C.A.8 1988) (holding employer liable for harassment by co-workers because supervisor knew of the harassment but did nothing). In such instances, the combined knowledge and inaction may be seen as demonstrable negligence, or as the employer's adoption of the offending conduct and its results, quite as if they had been authorized affirmatively as the employer's policy. Cf. *Oncale, supra,* at 77, 118 S.Ct., at 1001 (victim reported his grounds for fearing rape to company's safety supervisor, who turned him away with no action on complaint).

Nor was it exceptional that standards for binding the employer were not in issue in *Harris, supra.* In that case of discrimination by hostile environment, the individual charged with creating the abusive atmosphere was the president of the corporate employer, 510 U.S., at 19, 114 S.Ct., at 369, who was indisputably within that class of an employer organization's officials who may be treated as the organization's proxy. *Burns* v. *McGregor Electronic Industries, Inc.,* 955 F.2d 559, 564 (C.A.8 1992) (employer-company liable where harassment was perpetrated by its owner); see *Torres v. Pisano,* 116 F.3d 625, 634–635, and n. 11 (C.A.2) (noting that a supervisor may hold a sufficiently high position "in the management hierarchy of the company for his actions to be imputed automatically to the employer"), cert. denied, 522 U.S. 997, 118 S.Ct. 563, 139 L.Ed.2d 404 (1997); cf. *Katz, supra,* at 255 ("Except in situations where a proprietor, partner or corporate officer participates personally in the harassing behavior," an employee must "demonstrat[e] the propriety of holding the employer liable").

Finally, there is nothing remarkable in the fact that claims against employers for discriminatory employment actions with tangible results, like hiring, firing, promotion, compensation, and work assignment, have resulted in employer liability once the discrimination was shown. See *Meritor,* 477 U.S., at 70–71, 106 S.Ct., at 2407–2408 (noting that "courts have consistently held employers liable for the discriminatory discharges of employees by supervisory personnel, whether or not the employer knew, should have known, or approved of the supervisor's actions"); *id.,* at 75, 106 S.Ct., at 2409–2410 (Marshall, J., concurring in judgment) ("[W]hen a supervisor discriminatorily fires or refuses to promote a black employee, that act is, without more, considered the act of the employer"); see also *Anderson v. Methodist Evangelical Hospital, Inc.,* 464 F.2d 723, 725 (C.A.6 1972) (imposing liability on employer for racially motivated discharge by low-level supervisor, although the "record clearly shows that [its] record in race relations . . . is exemplary").

A variety of reasons have been invoked for this apparently unanimous rule. Some courts explain, in a variation of the "proxy" theory discussed above, that when a supervisor makes such decisions, he "merges" with the employer, and his act becomes that of the employer. See, *e.g., Kotcher v. Rosa and Sullivan Appliance Ctr., Inc.,* 957 F.2d 59, 62 (C.A.2 1992) ("The supervisor is deemed to act on behalf of the employer when making decisions that affect the economic status of the employee. From the perspective of the employee, the supervisor and the employer merge into a single entity"); *Steele v. Offshore Shipbuilding, Inc.,* 867 F.2d 1311, 1316 (C.A.11 1989) ("When a supervisor requires sexual favors as a *quid pro quo* for job benefits, the supervisor, by definition, acts as the company"); see also Lindemann & Grossman 776 (noting that courts hold employers "automatically liable" in *quid pro quo* cases because the "supervisor's actions, in conferring or withholding employment benefits, are deemed as a matter of law to be those of the employer"). Other courts have suggested that vicarious liability is proper because the supervisor acts within the scope of his authority when he makes discriminatory decisions in hiring, firing, promotion, and the like. See, *e.g., Shager v. Upjohn Co.,* 913 F.2d 398, 405 (C.A.7 1990) ("[A] supervisory employee who fires a subordinate is doing the kind of thing that he is authorized to do, and the wrongful intent with which he does it does not carry his behavior so far beyond the orbit of his responsibilities as to excuse the employer" (citing Restatement § 228)). Others have suggested that vicarious liability is appropriate because the supervisor who discriminates in this manner is aided by the agency relation. See, *e.g., Nichols v. Frank,* 42 F.3d 503, 514 (C.A.9 1994). Finally, still other courts have endorsed both of the latter two theories. See, *e.g., Harrison,* 112 F.3d, at 1443; *Henson,* 682 F.2d, at 910.

The soundness of the results in these cases (and their continuing vitality), in light of basic agency principles, was confirmed by this Court's only discussion to date of standards of employer liability, in *Meritor, supra,* which involved a claim of discrimination by a supervisor's sexual harassment of a subordinate over an extended period.

. . . .

1

. . . In the case before us, a justification for holding the offensive behavior within the scope of Terry's and Silverman's employment was well put in Judge Barkett's dissent: "[A] pervasively hostile work environment of sexual harassment is never (one would hope) authorized, but the supervisor is clearly charged with maintaining a productive, safe work environment. The supervisor directs and controls the conduct of the employees, and the manner of doing so may inure to the employer's benefit or detriment, including subjecting the employer to Title VII liability." 111 F.3d, at 1542 (opinion dissenting in part and concurring in part). It is by now well recognized that hostile environment sexual harassment by supervisors (and, for that matter, coemployees) is a persistent problem in the workplace. See Lindemann & Kadue 4–5 (discussing studies showing prevalence of sexual harassment); *Ellerth*, 123 F.3d, at 511 (Posner, C.J., concurring and dissenting) ("*[E]veryone knows by now that sexual harassment is a common problem in the American workplace*"). [Emphasis added.] An employer can, in a general sense, reasonably anticipate the possibility of such conduct occurring in its workplace, and one might justify the assignment of the burden of the untoward behavior to the employer as one of the costs of doing business, to be charged to the enterprise rather than the victim. As noted, *supra*, at 2287–2288, developments like this occur from time to time in the law of agency.

Two things counsel us to draw the contrary conclusion. First, there is no reason to suppose that Congress wished courts to ignore the traditional distinction between acts falling within the scope and acts amounting to what the older law called frolics or detours from the course of employment. Such a distinction can readily be applied to the spectrum of possible harassing conduct by supervisors, as the following examples show. First, a supervisor might discriminate racially in job assignments in order to placate the prejudice pervasive in the labor force. Instances of this variety of the heckler's veto would be consciously intended to further the employer's interests by preserving peace in the workplace. Next, supervisors might reprimand male employees for workplace failings with banter, but respond to women's shortcomings in harsh or vulgar terms. A third example might be the supervisor who, as here, expresses his sexual interests in ways having no apparent object whatever of serving an interest of the employer. If a line is to be drawn between scope and frolic, it would lie between the first two examples and the third, and it thus makes sense in terms of traditional agency law to analyze the scope issue, in cases like the third example, just as most federal courts addressing that issue have done, classifying the harassment as beyond the scope of employment.

The second reason goes to an even broader unanimity of views among the holdings of District Courts and Courts of Appeals thus far. Those courts have held not only that the sort of harassment at issue here was outside the scope of supervisors' authority, but, by uniformly judging employer liability for co-worker harassment under a negligence standard, they have also implicitly treated such harassment as outside the scope of common employees' duties as well. . . .

. . . .

2

. . . .

We therefore agree with Faragher that in implementing Title VII it makes sense to hold an employer vicariously liable for some tortious conduct of a supervisor made possible by abuse of his supervisory authority, and that the aided-by-agency-relation principle embodied in § 219(2)(d) of the Restatement provides an appropriate starting point for determining liability for the kind of harassment presented here. Several courts, indeed, have noted what Faragher has argued, that there is a sense in which a harassing supervisor is always assisted in his misconduct by the supervisory relationship. . . . Recognition of employer liability when discriminatory misuse of supervisory authority alters the terms and conditions of a victim's employment is underscored by the fact that the employer has a greater opportunity to guard against misconduct by supervisors than by common workers; employers have greater opportunity and incentive to screen them, train them, and monitor their performance.

In sum, there are good reasons for vicarious liability for misuse of supervisory authority. That rationale must, however, satisfy one more condition. We are not entitled to recognize this theory under Title VII unless we can square it with *Meritor*'s holding that an employer is not "automatically" liable for harassment by a supervisor who creates the requisite degree of discrimination, and there is obviously some tension between that holding and the position that a supervisor's misconduct aided by supervisory authority subjects the employer to liability vicariously; if the "aid" may be the unspoken suggestion of retaliation by misuse of supervisory authority, the risk of automatic liability is high.

[T]o counter it, we think there are two basic alternatives, one being to require proof of some affirmative invocation of that authority by the harassing supervisor, the other to recognize an affirmative defense to liability in some circumstances, even when a supervisor has created the actionable environment.

There is certainly some authority for requiring active or affirmative, as distinct from passive or implicit, misuse of supervisory authority before liability may be imputed. That is the way some courts have viewed the familiar cases holding the employer liable for discriminatory employment action with tangible consequences, like firing and demotion. See *supra,* at 2284. And we have already noted some examples of liability provided by the Restatement itself, which suggest that an affirmative misuse of power might be required. See *supra,* at 2290 (telegraph operator sends false messages, a store manager cheats customers, editor publishes libelous editorial). . . .

The other basic alternative to automatic liability would avoid this particular temptation to litigate, but allow an employer to show as an affirmative defense to liability that the employer had exercised reasonable care to avoid harassment and to eliminate it when it might occur, and that the complaining employee had failed to act with like reasonable care to take advantage of the employer's safeguards and otherwise to prevent harm that could have been avoided. This composite defense would, we think, implement the statute sensibly, for reasons that are not hard to fathom.

Although Title VII seeks "to make persons whole for injuries suffered on account of unlawful employment discrimination," *Albemarle Paper Co. v. Moody,* 422 U.S. 405, 418, 95 S.Ct. 2362, 2372, 45 L.Ed.2d 280 (1975), its "primary objective," like that of any statute meant to influence primary conduct, is not to provide redress but to avoid harm. *Id.,* at 417, 95 S.Ct., at 2371. As long ago as 1980, the EEOC, charged with the enforcement of Title VII, 42 U.S.C. § 2000e-4, adopted regulations advising employers to "take all steps necessary to prevent sexual harassment from occurring, such as . . . informing employees of their right to raise and how to raise the issue of harassment." 29 CFR § 1604.11(f) (1997). . . . It would therefore implement clear statutory policy and complement the Government's Title VII enforcement efforts to recognize the employer's affirmative obligation to prevent violations and give credit here to employers who make reasonable efforts to discharge their duty. Indeed, a theory of vicarious liability for misuse of supervisory power would be at odds with the statutory policy if it failed to provide employers with some such incentive.

The requirement to show that the employee has failed in a coordinate duty to avoid or mitigate harm reflects an equally obvious policy imported from the general theory of damages, that a victim has a duty "to use such means as are reasonable under the circumstances to avoid or minimize the damages" that result from violations of the statute. *Ford Motor Co. v. EEOC,* 458 U.S. 219, 231, n. 15, 102 S.Ct. 3057, 3065, n. 15, 73 L.Ed.2d 721 (1982) . . . .

In order to accommodate the principle of vicarious liability for harm caused by misuse of supervisory authority, as well as Title VII's equally basic policies of encouraging forethought by employers and saving action by objecting employees, we adopt the following holding in this case and in *Burlington Industries, Inc. v. Ellerth,* 524 U.S. 742, 118 S.Ct. 2257, 141 L.Ed.2d 633 (1998), also decided today. An employer is subject to vicarious liability to a victimized employee for an actionable hostile environment created by a supervisor with immediate (or successively higher) authority over the employee. When no tangible employment action is taken, a defending employer may raise an affirmative defense to liability or damages, subject to proof by a preponderance of the evidence, see Fed. Rule Civ. Proc. 8(c). The defense comprises two necessary elements: (a) that the employer exercised reasonable care to prevent and correct promptly any sexually harassing behavior, and (b) that the plaintiff employee unreasonably failed to take advantage of any preventive or corrective opportunities provided by the employer or to avoid harm otherwise. While proof that an employer had promulgated an anti-harassment policy with complaint procedure is not necessary in every instance as a matter of law, the need for a stated policy suitable to the employment circumstances may appropriately be addressed in any case when litigating the first element of the defense. And while proof that an employee failed to fulfill the corresponding obligation of reasonable care to avoid harm is not limited to showing an unreasonable failure to use any complaint procedure provided by the employer, a demonstration of such failure will normally suffice to satisfy the employer's burden under the second element of the defense. No affirmative defense is available, however, when the supervisor's harassment culminates in a tangible employment action, such as discharge, demotion, or undesirable reassignment. See *Burlington*, 524 U.S., at 762–763, 118 S.Ct., at 2269.

Applying these rules here, we believe that the judgment of the Court of Appeals must be reversed. The District Court found that the degree of hostility in the work environment rose to the actionable level and was attributable to Silverman and Terry. It is undisputed that these supervisors "were granted virtually unchecked authority" over their subordinates, "directly controll[ing] and supervis[ing] all aspects of [Faragher's] day-to-day activities." 111 F.3d, at 1544 (Barkett, J., dissenting in part and concurring in part). It is also clear that Faragher and her colleagues were "completely isolated from the City's higher management." *Ibid.* The City did not seek review of these findings.

While the City would have an opportunity to raise an affirmative defense if there were any serious prospect of its presenting one, it appears from the record that any such avenue is closed. The District Court found that the City had entirely failed to disseminate its policy against sexual harassment among the beach employees and that its officials made no attempt to keep track of the conduct of supervisors like Terry and Silverman. The record also makes clear that the City's policy did not include any assurance that the harassing supervisors could be bypassed in registering complaints. App. 274. Under such circumstances, we hold as a matter of law that the City could not be found to have exercised reasonable care to prevent the supervisors' harassing conduct. Unlike the employer of a small work force, who might expect that sufficient care to prevent tortious behavior could be exercised informally, those responsible for city operations could not reasonably have thought that precautions against hostile environments in any one of many departments in far-flung locations could be effective without communicating some formal policy against harassment, with a sensible complaint procedure.

The second possible ground for pursuing a defense was asserted by the City in its argument addressing the possibility of negligence liability in this case. It said that it should not be held liable for failing to promulgate an anti-harassment policy, because there was no apparent duty to do so in the 1985–1990 period. The City purports to rest this argument on the position of the EEOC during the period mentioned, but it turns out that the record on this point is quite against the City's position. Although the EEOC issued regulations dealing with promulgating a statement of policy and providing a complaint mechanism in 1990, see *supra,* at 2292, ever since 1980 its regulations have called for steps to prevent violations, such as informing employees of their rights and the means to assert them, *ibid.* The City, after all, adopted an anti-harassment policy in 1986.

The City points to nothing that might justify a conclusion by the District Court on remand that the City had exercised reasonable care. Nor is there any reason to remand for consideration of Faragher's efforts to mitigate her own damages, since the award to her was solely nominal.

III

The judgment of the Court of Appeals for the Eleventh Circuit is reversed, and the case is remanded for reinstatement of the judgment of the District Court.

It is so ordered.

JUSTICE THOMAS, with whom JUSTICE SCALIA joins, dissenting.

For the reasons given in my dissenting opinion in *Burlington Industries, Inc. v. Ellerth,* 524 U.S. 742, 118 S.Ct. 2257, 141 L.Ed.2d 633 (1998), absent an adverse employment consequence, an employer cannot be held vicariously liable if a supervisor creates a hostile work environment. Petitioner suffered no adverse employment consequence; thus the Court of Appeals was correct to hold that the City of Boca Raton (City) is not vicariously liable for the conduct of Chief Terry and Lieutenant Silverman. Because the Court reverses this judgment, I dissent.

As for petitioner's negligence claim, the District Court made no finding as to the City's negligence, and the Court of Appeals did not directly consider the issue. I would therefore remand the case to the District Court for further proceedings on this question alone. I disagree with the Court's conclusion that merely because the City did not disseminate its sexual harassment policy, it should be liable as a matter of law. See *ante,* at 2293. The City should be allowed to show either that: (1) there was a reasonably available avenue through which petitioner could have complained to a City official who supervised both Chief Terry and Lieutenant Silverman, see Brief for United States and EEOC as *Amici Curiae* in *Meritor Savings Bank, FSB v. Vinson,* O.T.1985, No. 84-1979, p. 26, or (2) it would not have learned of the harassment even if the policy had been distributed. Petitioner, as the plaintiff, would of course bear the burden of proving the City's negligence.

Notes and Questions

1. In *Vance v. Ball State University,* 133 S. Ct. 2434 (2013), the Supreme Court narrowed the definition of the term supervisor to someone who has the actual title on record, rather than individuals who for all purposes operate as such. Thus, someone committing sexual harassment while having assumed the duties of a supervisor, but without the official title (as often happens in the workplace), might not trigger employer liability for their employment actions. This makes it harder for plaintiffs' claims to reach the employer, if notice of actions by this individual cannot be imputed to the employer without additional proof. Justice Ginsburg, in her dissent, accused the Court of ignoring the realities of the workplace:

> The Court today strikes from the supervisory category employees who control the day-to-day schedules and assignments of others, confining the category to those formally empowered to take tangible employment actions. The limitation the Court decrees diminishes the force of *Faragher* and *Ellerth,*

ignores the conditions under which members of the work force labor, and disserves the objective of Title VII to prevent discrimination from infecting the Nation's workplaces. I would follow the EEOC's Guidance and hold that the authority to direct an employee's daily activities establishes supervisory status under Title VII.

Vance v. Ball State Univ., 133 S. Ct. 2434, 2455 (2013) (Ginsburg, J., dissenting).

2. What does Justice Ginsburg mean by this? How does her argument match your own experience in the workplace? Do recent reports and debates on the pervasiveness of sexual harassment today prove her point?

3. Is the legal approach to sexual harassment in the above cases enough to eliminate these behaviors? If not, what else might be needed?

B. Gender Discrimination: Grooming and Sex Stereotyping

Craft v. Metromedia Inc.

766 F.2d 1205 (8th Cir. 1985)

Christine Craft was reassigned from co-anchor to reporter by KMBC-TV in Kansas City, Missouri, and as a result brought this action against the station's owner and operator, Metromedia, Inc. Craft alleged that she had been discriminated against on the basis of sex in violation of both Title VII of the Civil Rights Act of 1964, 42 U.S.C. § 2000e et seq. (1982), and the Equal Pay Act of 1963, 29 U.S.C. § 206(d) (1982), and that she had been fraudulently induced into accepting the KMBC employment. The primary focus of the suit was KMBC's concern with appearance—whether the station's standards for on-air personnel were stricter and more strictly enforced as to females than as to males and whether the station misrepresented to Craft its intentions as to changing her appearance to persuade her to accept the anchor job. The district court found against Craft on her Title VII sex discrimination claim and refused a new trial as to the jury verdict against her on her equal pay claim. . . .

Christine Craft commenced her television career in mid-1975 as a weeknight weather reporter at a small station in Salinas, California. After about a year and a half, during which she also worked as an announcer, reporter, and substitute sportscaster, she became the weekend weather anchor at a San Francisco television station. She spent a year there, again handling some additional news and substitute sports assignments.

Craft then was hired by Columbia Broadcasting System to host the "Women In Sports" portion of its network television program "CBS Sports Spectacular." At the network's behest she had her hair cut short and bleached blond. She was required to use black eyebrow pencil and dark red lipstick, and a CBS technician applied heavy makeup before every on-air appearance. "Women in Sports" was discontinued after thirty weeks, and Craft returned to California.

About a year later Craft resumed her television career as a reporter at a station in Santa Barbara, California. She remained there, also serving as coanchor of the late news and occasionally doing sports and weather, until December 1980, when she began work at KMBC.

KMBC, having slipped in its local news ratings, had determined to adopt the coanchor format used by its two major competitors in Kansas City. Furthermore, it had determined that, because of the perceived "coldness" of its anchor, Scott Feldman, the new position was to be filled by a female to "soften" its news presentation. The station obtained tapes of a number of performers, including Craft, from Media Associates of Dallas. After studying these tapes, KMBC news director Ridge Shannon contacted Craft, among other individuals, to see if she was interested in auditioning for the job. Craft described her unpleasant experience at CBS and made plain that she was not interested if KMBC intended a "makeover" of her appearance. She continued to stress this point while in Kansas City for the audition, and Shannon and R. Kent Replogle, vice president and general manager of KMBC, assured her they planned no changes such as those at CBS. Shannon did mention that KMBC made some use of consultants, and Craft indicated some willingness to work on her appearance and dress.

Craft accepted the coanchor position at KMBC and at the station's request stopped in Dallas for a meeting with Lynn Wilford of Media Associates before reporting to Kansas City. She made her debut as coanchor on January 5, 1981, and the testimony is essentially uncontradicted that Shannon and Replogle immediately began having concerns about her clothing and makeup. Wilford came to Kansas City on January 14 to work with Craft on dress as well as on various aspects of her presentation technique. It was during this visit that Wilford for the only time applied Craft's makeup, and the results on the 6 p.m. news were so unsatisfactory that Craft was allowed to remove the makeup before the 10 p.m. broadcast.

In the following months Shannon continued to make occasional suggestions or criticisms as to certain articles of Craft's clothing, and Craft was provided with materials, including the book Women's Dress for Success, on wardrobe and makeup. Then, beginning in April, KMBC arranged for Macy's Department Store to provide clothing for Craft in exchange for advertising time. Craft was assisted by a consultant from Macy's in selecting outfits. She would then return to the KMBC studio, try on the clothing, and appear before camera so tapes could be made to send to Wilford for review.

On May 19 and 20, 1981, Media Associates initiated some research of viewer perceptions of KMBC's newscasts by conducting four "focus group" discussions. By this technique groups of ten individuals viewed sample video tapes of local news programs and then gave their reactions in sessions moderated by a Media Associates representative. The response to Craft's appearance was, as summed up by the district court, "overwhelmingly negative." 572 F. Supp. at 873. When Replogle and Shannon met with Craft the following day to discuss this result, Craft at first wanted to be let out of her contract to return to California. Replogle, however, stated that management was ready to work with her to overcome the problems, and Craft ultimately agreed to cooperate. Thereafter, her wardrobe was more closely supervised, and the "clothing calendar" then mentioned by Replogle was eventually instituted in late July or early August.

As a further follow-up, KMBC and Media Associates in late June conducted a telephone survey of some 400 randomly selected persons in the greater Kansas City viewing area. These persons were asked to respond to a questionnaire specifically drafted to pursue issues raised in the focus group discussions. For example in one segment the survey participants were asked to rank Craft in comparison with the female coanchors at KMBC's competitors in response to some fourteen statements, four of which dealt with "good looks" or the dress of and image of a "professional anchor woman." Craft came out trailing in almost every category. Media Associates' report on the results of this survey, which was conveyed to Shannon and Replogle on August 3, 1981, suggested that Craft was having an extremely adverse impact on KMBC's acceptance among Kansas City viewers. On August 13 Media Associates recommended that Craft be replaced, and KMBC, after initial resistance, agreed.

The next day Shannon told Craft she was being reassigned to reporter at no loss of pay or contractual benefits. He characterized the results of the research, in the language of the district court, as "devastating and unprecedented in the history of the consultants of Media Associates." 572 F. Supp. at 874. Craft states that Shannon also told her she was being reassigned because the audience perceived her as too old, too unattractive, and not deferential enough to men. Shannon, however, specifically denies making such a statement, and the district court believed his version of the conversation. *Id.*

After the weekend Craft sent a telegram to KMBC refusing to accept reassignment, and when further discussions failed to resolve the matter, she returned to Santa Barbara where on September 1, 1981, she commenced work as a coanchor at the television station at which she previously had been employed. This suit followed in four counts: the Title VII sex discrimination and the fraud counts, the allegation of violation of the Equal Pay Act based on the differential between Craft's and Scott Feldman's salaries, and an allegation of prima facie tort based on an intent by KMBC to injure Craft. This last count was abandoned during the first trial in Kansas City.

Following that first trial the district court rejected the findings of the advisory jury on the Title VII sex discrimination claim and entered judgment for Metromedia on that issue. The district court found that KMBC required both male and female on-air personnel to maintain professional, businesslike appearances "consistent with community standards" and that the station enforced that requirement in an evenhanded, nondiscriminatory manner. 572 F. Supp. at 877–78. Any greater attention to Craft's appearance, the court concluded, was "tailored to fit her individual needs" and was necessary because of her "below-average aptitude" in matters of clothing and makeup. *Id.* at 878. The district court also found that Craft had not been constructively discharged because there was insufficient evidence that her working conditions had become so intolerable that she had no choice but to quit or that KMBC had intended to force her resignation. *Id.* at 879. Finally, the court concluded that the telephone survey conducted by Media Associates had not been discriminatory or designed to effect Craft's removal as coanchor and that KMBC had reasonably relied on the survey results as the basis for the personnel change. *Id.* at 873, 878–79.

. . . .

Craft's attacks on the district court's disposition of her Title VII sex discrimination claim are essentially factual, rather than legal as she contends. Her central position is that KMBC's appearance standards were based on stereotyped characterizations of the sexes and were applied to women more constantly and vigorously than they were applied to men. Her further contentions that the district court erred in finding certain grooming cases controlling and in allowing Metromedia to rebut her prima facie case with stereotypical customer preferences follow only if we accept her central factual position.

As an initial matter Craft argues that, since her case was one involving direct evidence of discrimination, the district court erred in failing to shift the burden to Metromedia to prove by a preponderance of the evidence that it would have taken the challenged actions even in the absence of gender bias. E.g., *Bell v. Birmingham Linen Service*, 715 F.2d 1552, 1557 (11th Cir. 1983), cert. denied, — U.S. —, 104 S. Ct. 2385, 81 L. Ed. 2d 344 (1984); *Lee v. Russell County Board of Education*, 684 F.2d 769, 774 (11th Cir. 1982). The cases relied on by Craft, however, involved direct testimony of discrimination accepted by the trier of fact. *Bell*, 715 F.2d at 1557; *Lee*, 684 F.2d at 774–75. It is apparent that the district court did not accept any such testimony in this case. Thus, the burden-shifting rule for which Craft argues could have no application here, and we need not give further consideration to whether it should be adopted by this circuit . . .

Craft [also] argues that the district court erred in finding her claim of discrimination in employment conditions controlled by grooming cases such as *Knott v. Missouri Pacific Railroad*, 527 F.2d 1249 (8th Cir. 1975). In *Knott* we held that appearance regulations making distinctions on the basis of sex will not support allegations of discrimination when the standards are reasonable and are enforced as to both sexes in an evenhanded manner. *Id.* at 1252. Again what Craft really contests is the district court's factual determination that KMBC's actions concerning the appearance of its on-air personnel fell within the *Knott* guidelines.

Because many of Craft's arguments boldly seek reevaluation of the evidence and rejection of the district court's factual findings, we make clear our limited standard of review in such cases. Factual findings may be set aside only when clearly erroneous. . . . Furthermore, we have stated that the burden is on the objecting party to clearly demonstrate error in the factual findings. *Aetna Casualty & Surety Co. v. General Electric Co.*, 758 F.2d 319, 323 (8th Cir. 1985); *Hunt v. Pan American Energy*, 540 F.2d 894, 901 (8th Cir. 1976), cert. denied, 429 U.S. 1062 (1977); *Reilly v. United States*, 513 F.2d 147, 150 n. 2 (8th Cir. 1975). The evidence is to be construed in the light most favorable to the party prevailing below. *Tautfest v. City of Lincoln*, 742 F.2d 477, 481 (8th Cir. 1984); *United Barge Co. v. Notre Dame Fleeting & Towing Service*, 568 F.2d 599, 602 (8th Cir. 1978).

We turn first to the most prominent factual element of Craft's case—her testimony that Shannon told her she was being reassigned because she was too old, too unattractive, and not deferential enough to men or because the audience perceived her as such. Shannon, however, specifically denied making that statement. The only additional evidence was that of Feldman, who testified on the stand at trial that he did not recall Shannon making such a comment but who had said in his deposition that Shannon had done so—again diametrically opposite testimony, this time from one witness. Credibility thus was central to the district court's finding on this point.

Respect for the role of the district court is especially crucial as to determinations which rest on "variations in demeanor and tone of voice" of the witnesses and "the listener's understanding of and belief in what is said." *Anderson*, 105 S. Ct. at 1512. The Supreme Court has cautioned:

> [W]hen a trial judge's finding is based on his decision to credit the testimony of one of two or more witnesses, each of whom has told a coherent and facially plausible story that is not contradicted by extrinsic evidence, that finding, if not internally inconsistent, can virtually never be clear error.

Id. at 1513. The district court was in the best position to determine whether to believe Shannon or Craft, and there are no circumstances suggesting any basis for finding clear error in the district court's choice in favor of Shannon.

Craft next argues, as do the amici curiae, that the district court clearly erred in failing to find that KMBC enforced appearance standards more strictly as to female than as to male on-air personnel. In support of her position she points to the evidence most favorable to her, which shows that only females were subject to daily scrutiny of their appearance or were ever required to change clothes at the station before going on the air and that no male was ever directed to take time from his journalistic duties to select clothing, with the help of a consultant, from Macy's and to test that clothing on camera for the approval of another consultant. The district court, however, concluded that such facts, in light of other evidence, showed only that KMBC was concerned with the appearance of all its on-air personnel and that it took measures appropriate to individual situations, characteristics, and shortcomings. *Craft*, 572 F. Supp. at 875, 876, 878. The court found that KMBC had only gradually increased its attentions to Craft's appearance, with the institution of the clothing calendar representing the culmination of efforts made necessary when lesser suggestions, such as those complied with by other personnel, proved ineffective. *Id*. at 878.

The evidence shows that one female, Brenda Williams, had never been the subject of criticism for her appearance while numerous males on occasion had been given specific directions as to their individual shortcomings. Mike Placke, for example, had been told to lose weight, to get better-fitting clothes, to refrain from wearing sweaters under jackets, and to tie his necktie in a certain manner. Similarly, Michael Mahoney had been told to lose weight and to pay more attention to his wardrobe and hairstyle, while Bob Werley had been told to try wearing contact lenses and to get a hair piece and had been given a makeup chart on a form similar to that used with Craft. Shannon had discussed hair or moustache problems with Tim Richardson, Dave Dusik, Stan Carmack, and Corrice Collins, and Craig Sager had been advised to improve his wardrobe. Even Feldman on at least two occasions had received specific directives regarding his choice of shirts, and the Macy's clothing consultant who worked with Craft testified that she had also met with Feldman and Dusik. Media Associates eventually prepared wardrobe "dos" and "don'ts" for male as well as female newscasters. The district court found that the male personnel generally complied with grooming suggestions.

An interpretation of this record as showing that KMBC enforced its appearance standards equally as to males and females in response to individual problems is neither "illogical" nor "implausible" and has "support in inferences that may be drawn from the facts." *Anderson*, 105 S. Ct. at 1513. We cannot conclude that the district court erred in this respect.

Our determination is not altered by the testimony, cited by Craft, of the consultant Wilford or of other female KMBC employees to the effect that the station put more emphasis on the appearance of females. This testimony represents only the opinions and impressions of the witnesses as to KMBC's policy, and the district court by implication rejected such opinions, making its own finding to the contrary on the record. The court also apparently chose not to believe testimony by Pam Whiting that Shannon had said it was more important for she and Craft than for Feldman to look good on the air; Whiting herself had been subject to a great deal of attention as to her appearance and had eventually left the station, and on the stand she expressed the opinion that appearance was overemphasized in television news and said she hoped Craft prevailed. Finally, the district court attributed the use in the survey of questions on appearance and good looks only as to female anchors as prompted not by sexual bias but by the concerns raised as to Craft by the focus groups. *Craft*, 572 F. Supp. at 873. The viewers were asked to rank the male anchors on more points concerning personality and "coldness," Feldman's perceived weaknesses. The inclusion of a makeup criterion and a requirement that Craft not deviate from her clothing calendar in the "standards of performance" by which her work was to be evaluated, in contrast to the absence of any appearance objectives in Feldman's "standards of performance," similarly just reflected management's efforts to pursue with personnel their individual weaknesses.

Craft further argues, however, again joined by the amici curiae, that even if KMBC was evenhanded in applying its appearance standards, the district court erred in failing to recognize that the standards themselves were discriminatory. She contends that she was forced to conform to a stereotypical image of how a woman anchor should appear. The evidence included a communication from the consultant, Wilford, to Shannon suggesting that Craft purchase more blouses with "feminine touches," such as bows and ruffles, because many of her clothes were "too masculine." The general wardrobe hints for females developed by Media Associates warned that women with "soft" hairstyles and looks should wear blazers to establish their authority and credibility while women with short "masculine" hairstyles shouldn't wear "masculine" clothing in dark colors and with strong lines because they would appear too "aggressive." The district court found that Craft had been hired to "soften" KMBC's news presentation. *Id.* at 871.

The "dos" and "don'ts" for anchors suggested that while males should remember "professional image," female anchors were to remember "professional elegance." The outfits on the clothing calendar given to Craft were dominated by recognized fashion labels. Wilford testified that in April she had told Craft not to wear the same outfit more than once every three to four weeks because people would start calling in about it; males, however, Wilford said, could wear an outfit every week and a suit even twice within the same week if combined with a different tie. Wilford further testified that viewers—particularly other women—criticize women more severely than men for their appearance on camera and that women's dress is more complex and demanding because "society has made it that way." Craft's argument is that these differing standards as to females reflect customer preferences, which a number of cases have held cannot justify discriminatory practices. E.g., *Diaz v. Pan American World Airways*, 442 F.2d 385, 389 (5th Cir.), cert. denied, 404 U.S. 950 (1971); see also *Gerdom v. Continental Airlines*, 692 F.2d 602, 609 (9th Cir. 1982), cert. dismissed, 460 U.S. 1074 (1983); *Fernandez v. Wynn Oil Co.*, 653 F.2d 1273, 1276–77 (9th Cir. 1981).

The district court, however, found that KMBC's appearance standards were based instead on permissible factors. 572 F. Supp. at 877. While there may have been some emphasis on the feminine stereotype of "softness" and bows and ruffles and on the fashionableness of female anchors, the evidence suggests such concerns were incidental to a true focus on consistency of appearance, proper coordination of colors and textures, the effects of studio lighting on clothing and makeup, and the greater degree of conservatism thought necessary in the Kansas City market. The "dos" and "don'ts" for female anchors addressed the need to avoid, for example, tight sweaters or overly "sexy" clothing and extreme "high fashion" or "sporty" outfits while the male "dos" and "don'ts" similarly cautioned against "frivolous" colors and "extreme" textures and styles as damaging to the "authority" of newscasters. These criteria do not implicate the primary thrust of Title VII, which is to prompt employers to "discard outmoded sex stereotypes posing distinct employment disadvantages for one sex." *Knott v. Missouri Pacific Railroad*, 527 F.2d 1249, 1251 (8th Cir. 1975); see generally Note, *Title VII Limits on Discrimination Against Television Anchorwomen on the Basis of Age-Related Appearance*, 85 Colum. L. Rev. 190, 201 (1985).

Courts have recognized that the appearance of a company's employees may contribute greatly to the company's image and success with the public and thus that a reasonable dress or grooming code is a proper management prerogative. E.g., *Fagan v. National Cash Register Co.*, 481 F.2d 1115, 1124–25 (D.C. Cir. 1973); *La Von Lanigan v. Bartlett & Co. Grain*, 466 F. Supp. 1388, 1392 (W.D. Mo. 1979). Evidence showed a particular concern with appearance in television; the district court stated that reasonable appearance requirements were "obviously critical" to KMBC's economic well-being; and even Craft admitted she recognized that television was a visual medium and that on-air personnel would need to wear appropriate clothes and makeup. *Craft*, 572 F. Supp. at 877; see Note, *supra*, at 201 ("As television is a visual medium, television networks and local stations clearly have a right to require both male and female anchors to maintain a professional appearance while on camera."). While we believe the record shows an overemphasis by KMBC on appearance, we are not the proper forum in which to debate the relationship between newsgathering and dissemination and considerations of appearance and presentation—i.e., questions of substance versus image—in television journalism. The record does not leave us with the "definite and firm conviction" that the district court erred or adopted an impermissible view of the evidence when it concluded that KMBC's appearance standards were shaped only by neutral professional and technical considerations and not by any stereotypical notions of female roles and images.

We further reject the argument of Craft that the perception, discussed above, that she would add warmth and "comfortability" to the newscast defined a stereotypical "female" role, secondary to that of the male anchor, into which she was forced in terms of story assignments and division of duties. First, we observe that the research survey asked participants to rank both male and female anchors in response to the statement "comfortable to watch." In addition, the district court rejected Craft's factual contention that Feldman was assigned the lead story more frequently and was given more live stories while she was assigned the human interest, personal, and humorous stories. The court, for example, while acknowledging the testimony of news producer Sandra Woodward that she initially was instructed to give Feldman about two-thirds of the lead stories, also accepted testimony of Shannon that that policy had been designed to ease the transition to coanchors for Craft and the viewers and was discontinued after a few weeks, after which time the lead stories were equitably divided. *Craft*, 572 F. Supp. at 872, 875. The court further found that the on-site reporting and hard news stories were equitably distributed. *Id.* at 875. Finally, Shannon testified that Craft herself suggested her Thursday arts and entertainment segment to take advantage of her cultural background and her contacts from Santa Barbara with various Hollywood personalities. Craft cites no facts sufficient for us to find the district court's interpretation of the record in this regard clearly erroneous.

We also cannot conclude that the district court erred when it held that Craft was not impermissibly removed as anchor on the basis of gender. While we disposed earlier of the alleged "too old, too unattractive" statement and have also already discussed the legitimate reasons why the survey questions focused on appearance only as to the female and not as to the male anchors, Craft further argues that her reassignment was based on a discriminatory interpretation of the survey results. She contends that discrimination may be inferred in that KMBC attributed all the negative viewer reaction to her despite Feldman's earlier problems in the ratings and the failure of most respondents to name him as a positive reason for watching the station. She further alleges that she was unfairly burdened with having to offset Feldman's weaknesses. The inferences on which she relies, however, are insufficient to justify setting aside the conclusions of the district court.

Craft essentially is asking us to reject the district court's findings accepting Media Associate's interpretation of the survey data and to substitute our own interpretation thereof. The evaluation of expert testimony, however, is primarily the function of the district court. *Hoefelman v. Conservation Commission of Missouri*, 718 F.2d 281, 284–85 (8th Cir. 1983). The court here specifically found that the survey had been "conducted in accordance with generally accepted principles of survey research" and that its results were "trustworthy." *Craft*, 572 F. Supp. at 873. Craft scored low on many neutral points such as knowledge of Kansas City, journalism ability, and apparent enjoyment of her job, and the court found "simply no evidence" that the survey had been designed to effect her removal because of her gender. *Id.* at 878. It concluded that KMBC was entitled to—and did—rely on the Media Associates report. *Id.* at 879.

We further reject Craft's argument that even if the survey was objective, KMBC's reliance on it was merely a pretext because the station ignored improved ratings and profits during her tenure: This shows only that broadcast market research is an inexact science and does not make clearly erroneous the district court's conclusion that KMBC still relied upon the survey in good faith. The court in addition found that the ratings cited by Craft were "equivocal at best" and were not yet available when she was reassigned. *Id.* at 876. KMBC's failure to delay its decision a few days until the ratings did come out may just be testament to the unprecedented negative reaction to Craft suggested by the survey. Finally, KMBC's allegedly differing treatment of two males who also were criticized in the survey is insufficient to raise an inference of discrimination because of the more extreme nature of Craft's difficulties and Craft's pivotal role on the newscast as coanchor.

Our conclusion that Craft was not subject to sex discrimination either in KMBC's application of its appearance standards or in its reassignment of her to reporter effectively determines the outcome of her claim of constructive discharge.

. . . .

Price Waterhouse v. Hopkins

490 U.S. 228 (1989)

JUSTICE BRENNAN announced the judgment of the Court and delivered an opinion, in which JUSTICE MARSHALL, JUSTICE BLACKMUN, and JUSTICE STEVENS join.

Ann Hopkins was a senior manager in an office of Price Waterhouse when she was proposed for partnership in 1982. She was neither offered nor denied admission to the partnership; instead, her candidacy was held for reconsideration the following year. When the partners in her office later refused to repropose her for partnership, she sued Price Waterhouse under Title VII of the Civil Rights Act of 1964, 78 Stat. 253, *as amended,* 42 U.S.C. § 2000e *et seq.,*charging that the firm had discriminated against her on the basis of sex in its decisions regarding partnership. Judge Gesell in the Federal District Court for the District of Columbia ruled in her favor on the question of liability, 618 F.Supp. 1109 (1985), and the Court of Appeals for the District of Columbia Circuit affirmed. 263 U.S.App.D.C. 321, 825 F.2d 458 (1987). We granted certiorari to resolve a conflict among the Courts of Appeals concerning the respective burdens of proof of a defendant and plaintiff in a suit under Title VII when it has been shown that an employment decision resulted from a mixture of legitimate and illegitimate motives. 485 U.S. 933 (1988).

I

At Price Waterhouse, a nationwide professional accounting partnership, a senior manager becomes a candidate for partnership when the partners in her local office submit her name as a candidate. All of the other partners in the firm are then invited to submit written comments on each candidate—either on a "long" or a "short" form, depending on the partner's degree of exposure to the candidate. Not every partner in the firm submits comments on every candidate. After reviewing the comments and interviewing the partners who submitted them, the firm's Admissions Committee makes a recommendation to the Policy Board. This recommendation will be either that the firm accept the candidate for partnership, put her application on "hold," or deny her the promotion outright. The Policy Board then decides whether to submit the candidate's name to the entire partnership for a vote, to "hold" her candidacy, or to reject her. The recommendation of the Admissions Committee, and the decision of the Policy Board, are not controlled by fixed guidelines: a certain number of positive comments from partners will not guarantee a candidate's admission to the partnership, nor will a specific quantity of negative comments necessarily defeat her application. Price Waterhouse places no limit on the number of persons whom it will admit to the partnership in any given year.

Ann Hopkins had worked at Price Waterhouse's Office of Government Services in Washington, D.C., for five years when the partners in that office proposed her as a candidate for partnership. Of the 662 partners at the firm at that time, 7 were women. Of the 88 persons proposed for partnership that year, only 1—Hopkins— was a woman. Forty-seven of these candidates were admitted to the partnership, 21 were rejected, and 20—including Hopkins—were "held" for reconsideration the following year. Thirteen of the 32 partners who had submitted comments on Hopkins supported her bid for partnership. Three partners recommended that her candidacy be placed on hold, eight stated that they did not have an informed opinion about her, and eight recommended that she be denied partnership.

In a jointly prepared statement supporting her candidacy, the partners in Hopkins' office showcased her successful 2-year effort to secure a $25 million contract with the Department of State, labeling it "an outstanding performance" and one that Hopkins carried out "virtually at the partner level." . . . The partners in Hopkins' office praised her character as well as her accomplishments, describing her in their joint statement as "an outstanding professional" who had a "deft touch," a "strong character, independence and integrity." Plaintiff's Exh. 15. Clients appear to have agreed with these assessments. At trial, one official from the State Department described her as "extremely competent, intelligent," "strong and forthright, very productive, energetic and creative." Tr. 150. Another high-ranking official praised Hopkins' decisiveness, broadmindedness, and "intellectual clarity"; she was, in his words, "a stimulating conversationalist." *Id.* at 156–157. Evaluations such as these led Judge Gesell to conclude that Hopkins "had no difficulty dealing with clients and her clients appear to have been very pleased with her work" and that she was generally viewed as a highly competent project leader who worked long hours, pushed vigorously to meet deadlines and demanded much from the multidisciplinary staffs with which she worked.

On too many occasions, however, Hopkins' aggressiveness apparently spilled over into abrasiveness. Staff members seem to have borne the brunt of Hopkins' brusqueness.

Long before her bid for partnership, partners evaluating her work had counseled her to improve her relations with staff members. Although later evaluations indicate an improvement, Hopkins' perceived shortcomings in this important area eventually doomed her bid for partnership. Virtually all of the partners' negative remarks about Hopkins — even those of partners supporting her — had to do with her "interpersonal skills." Both "[s]upporters and opponents of her candidacy," stressed Judge Gesell, "indicated that she was sometimes overly aggressive, unduly harsh, difficult to work with, and impatient with staff." *Id.* at 1113.

There were clear signs, though, that some of the partners reacted negatively to Hopkins' personality because she was a woman. One partner described her as "macho" (Defendant's Exh. 30); another suggested that she "overcompensated for being a woman" (Defendant's Exh. 31); a third advised her to take "a course at charm school" (Defendant's Exh. 27). Several partners criticized her use of profanity; in response, one partner suggested that those partners objected to her swearing only "because it's a lady using foul language." Tr. 321. Another supporter explained that Hopkins ha[d] matured from a tough-talking somewhat masculine hard-nosed mgr to an authoritative, formidable, but much more appealing lady ptr candidate . . . But it was the man who, as Judge Gesell found, bore responsibility for explaining to Hopkins the reasons for the Policy Board's decision to place her candidacy on hold who delivered the *coup de grace:* in order to improve her chances for partnership, Thomas Beyer advised, Hopkins should "walk more femininely, talk more femininely, dress more femininely, wear make-up, have her hair styled, and wear jewelry." 618 F.Supp. at 1117.

Dr. Susan Fiske, a social psychologist and Associate Professor of Psychology at Carnegie-Mellon University, testified at trial that the partnership selection process at Price Waterhouse was likely influenced by sex stereotyping. Her testimony focused not only on the overtly sex-based comments of partners but also on gender-neutral remarks, made by partners who knew Hopkins only slightly, that were intensely critical of her. One partner, for example, baldly stated that Hopkins was "universally disliked" by staff (Defendant's Exh. 27), and another described her as "consistently annoying and irritating" (*ibid.*); yet these were people who had had very little contact with Hopkins. According to Fiske, Hopkins' uniqueness (as the only woman in the pool of candidates) and the subjectivity of the evaluations made it likely that sharply critical remarks such as these were the product of sex stereotyping—although Fiske admitted that she could not say with certainty whether any particular comment was the result of stereotyping. Fiske based her opinion on a review of the submitted comments, explaining that it was commonly accepted practice for social psychologists to reach this kind of conclusion without having met any of the people involved in the decisionmaking process.

In previous years, other female candidates for partnership also had been evaluated in sex-based terms. As a general matter, Judge Gesell concluded, "[c]andidates were viewed favorably if partners believed they maintained their femin[in]ity while becoming effective professional managers"; in this environment, "[t]o be identified as a 'women's lib[b]er' was regarded as [a] negative comment." 618 F.Supp. at 1117 . . .

In passing Title VII, Congress made the simple but momentous announcement that sex, race, religion, and national origin are not relevant to the selection, evaluation, or compensation of employees. Yet the statute does not purport to limit the other qualities and characteristics that employers may take into account in making employment decisions. The converse, therefore, of "for cause" legislation, Title VII eliminates certain bases for distinguishing among employees while otherwise preserving employers' freedom of choice. This balance between employee rights and employer prerogatives turns out to be decisive in the case before us.

Congress' intent to forbid employers to take gender into account in making employment decisions appears on the face of the statute. In now-familiar language, the statute forbids an employer to fail or refuse to hire or to discharge any individual, or otherwise to discriminate with respect to his compensation, terms, conditions, or privileges of employment, or to limit, segregate, or classify his employees or applicants for employment in any way which would deprive or tend to deprive any individual of employment opportunities or otherwise adversely affect his status as an employee, *because of* such individual's . . . sex . . .

We have, in short, been here before. Each time, we have concluded that the plaintiff who shows that an impermissible motive played a motivating part in an adverse employment decision has thereby placed upon the defendant the burden to show that it would have made the same decision in the absence of the unlawful motive. Our decision today treads this well-worn path.

B

In saying that gender played a motivating part in an employment decision, we mean that, if we asked the employer at the moment of the decision what its reasons were and if we received a truthful response, one of those reasons would be that the applicant or employee was a woman. In the specific context of sex stereotyping, an employer who acts on the basis of a belief that a woman cannot be aggressive, or that she must not be, has acted on the basis of gender.

Although the parties do not overtly dispute this last proposition, the placement by Price Waterhouse of "sex stereotyping" in quotation marks throughout its brief seems to us an insinuation either that such stereotyping was not present in this case or that it lacks legal relevance. We reject both possibilities.] As to the existence of sex stereotyping in this case, we are not inclined to quarrel with the District Court's conclusion that a number of the partners' comments showed sex stereotyping at work. *See infra* at 255–256. As for the legal relevance of sex stereotyping, we are beyond the day when an employer could evaluate employees by assuming or insisting that they matched the stereotype associated with their group, for, "[i]n forbidding employers to discriminate against individuals because of their sex, Congress intended to strike at the entire spectrum of disparate treatment of men and women resulting from sex stereotypes. *Los Angeles Dept. of Water & Power v. Manhart,* 435 U.S. 702, 707, n. 13 (1978), quoting *Sprogis v. United Air Lines, Inc.,* 444 F.2d 1194, 1198 (CA7 1971). An employer who objects to aggressiveness in women but whose positions require this trait places women in an intolerable and impermissible Catch-22: out of a job if they behave aggressively and out of a job if they do not. Title VII lifts women out of this bind.

Remarks at work that are based on sex stereotypes do not inevitably prove that gender played a part in a particular employment decision. The plaintiff must show that the employer actually relied on her gender in making its decision. In making this showing, stereotyped remarks can certainly be evidence that gender played a part. In any event, the stereotyping in this case did not simply consist of stray remarks. On the contrary, Hopkins proved that Price Waterhouse invited partners to submit comments; that some of the comments stemmed from sex stereotypes; that an important part of the Policy Board's decision on Hopkins was an assessment of the submitted comments; and that Price Waterhouse in no way disclaimed reliance on the sex-linked evaluations. This is not, as Price Waterhouse suggests, "discrimination in the air"; rather, it is, as Hopkins puts it, "discrimination brought to ground and visited upon" an employee. Brief for Respondent 30 . . .

As to the employer's proof, in most cases, the employer should be able to present some objective evidence as to its probable decision in the absence of an impermissible motive. Moreover, proving "'that the same decision would have been justified . . . is not the same as proving that the same decision would have been made.'" *Givhan,* 439 U.S. at 416, quoting *Ayers v. Western Line Consolidated School District,* 555 F.2d 1309, 1315 (CA5 1977). An employer may not, in other words, prevail by offering a legitimate and sufficient reason for its decision if that reason did not motivate it at the time of the decision. Finally, an employer may not meet its burden in such a case by merely showing that, at the time of the decision, it was motivated only in part by a legitimate reason. . . . The employer instead must show that its legitimate reason, standing alone, would have induced it to make the same decision.

II

. . . Indeed, we are tempted to say that Dr. Fiske's expert testimony was merely icing on Hopkins' cake. It takes no special training to discern sex stereotyping in a description of an aggressive female employee as requiring "a course at charm school." Nor, turning to Thomas Beyer's memorable advice to Hopkins, does it require expertise in psychology to know that, if an employee's flawed "interpersonal skills" can be corrected by a soft-hued suit or a new shade of lipstick, perhaps it is the employee's sex, and not her interpersonal skills, that has drawn the criticism.

Price Waterhouse also charges that Hopkins produced no evidence that sex stereotyping played a role in the decision to place her candidacy on hold. As we have stressed, however, Hopkins showed that the partnership solicited evaluations from all of the firm's partners; that it generally relied very heavily on such evaluations in making its decision; that some of the partners' comments were the product of stereotyping; and that the firm in no way disclaimed reliance on those particular comments, either in Hopkins' case or in the past. Certainly a plausible—and, one might say, inevitable—conclusion to draw from this set of circumstances is that the Policy Board, in making its decision, did in fact take into account all of the partners' comments, including the comments that were motivated by stereotypical notions about women's proper deportment.

. . . Nor is the finding that sex stereotyping played a part in the Policy Board's decision undermined by the fact that many of the suspect comments were made by supporters, rather than detractors, of Hopkins. A negative comment, even when made in the context of a generally favorable review, nevertheless may influence the decisionmaker to think less highly of the candidate; the Policy Board, in fact, did not simply tally the "yesses" and "noes" regarding a candidate, but carefully reviewed the content of the submitted comments. The additional suggestion that the comments were made by "persons outside the decisionmaking chain" (Brief for Petitioner 48)—and therefore could not have harmed Hopkins—simply ignores the critical role that partners' comments played in the Policy Board's partnership decisions.

. . . Even if we knew that Hopkins had "personality problems," this would not tell us that the partners who cast their evaluations of Hopkins in sex-based terms would have criticized her as sharply (or criticized her at all) if she had been a man. It is not our job to review the evidence and decide that the negative reactions to Hopkins were based on reality; our perception of Hopkins' character is irrelevant. We sit not to determine whether Ms. Hopkins is nice, but to decide whether the partners reacted negatively to her personality because she is a woman.

III

We hold that, when a plaintiff in a Title VII case proves that her gender played a motivating part in an employment decision, the defendant may avoid a finding of liability only by proving by a preponderance of the evidence that it would have made the same decision even if it had not taken the plaintiff's gender into account. Because the courts below erred by deciding that the defendant must make this proof by clear and convincing evidence, we reverse the Court of Appeals' judgment against Price Waterhouse on liability and remand the case to that court for further proceedings.

Jespersen v. Harrah's Operating Company, Inc.

No. 03-15045
United States Court of Appeals, Ninth Circuit, en banc.
Filed April 14, 2006.

We took this sex discrimination case en banc in order to reaffirm our circuit law concerning appearance and grooming standards, and to clarify our evolving law of sex stereotyping claims.

The plaintiff, Darlene Jespersen, was terminated from her position as a bartender at the sports bar in Harrah's Reno casino not long after Harrah's began to enforce its comprehensive uniform, appearance and grooming standards for all bartenders. The standards required all bartenders, men and women, to wear the same uniform of black pants and white shirts, a bow tie, and comfortable black shoes. The standards also included grooming requirements that differed to some extent for men and women, requiring women to wear some facial makeup and not permitting men to wear any. Jespersen refused to comply with the makeup requirement and was effectively terminated for that reason.

The district court granted summary judgment to Harrah's on the ground that the appearance and grooming policies imposed equal burdens on both men and women bartenders because, while women were required to use makeup and men were forbidden to wear makeup, women were allowed to have long hair and men were required to have their hair cut to a length above the collar. *Jespersen v. Harrah's Operating Co.*, 280 F.Supp.2d 1189, 1192–93 (D.Nev.2002). The district court also held that the policy could not run afoul of Title VII because it did not discriminate against Jespersen on the basis of the "immutable characteristics" of her sex. *Id.* In *Price Waterhouse v. Hopkins*, 490 U.S. 228, 109 S.Ct. 1775, 104 L.Ed.2d 268 (1989) (plurality opinion), prohibiting discrimination on the basis of sex stereotyping, did not apply to this case because in the district court's view, the Ninth Circuit had excluded grooming standards from the reach of *Price Waterhouse. Jespersen*, 280 F.Supp.2d at 1193. In reaching that conclusion, the district court relied on *Nichols v. Azteca Restaurant Enters., Inc.*, 256 F.3d 864, 875 n. 7 (9th Cir.2001) ("We do not imply that all gender-based distinctions are actionable under Title VII. For example, our decision does not imply that there is any violation of Title VII occasioned by reasonable regulations that require male and female employees to conform to different dress and grooming standards."). *Jespersen*, 280 F.Supp.2d at 1193. The district court granted summary judgment to Harrah's on all claims.

The three-judge panel affirmed, but on somewhat different grounds. *Jespersen v. Harrah's Operating Co.*, 392 F.3d 1076 (9th Cir.2004). The panel majority held that Jespersen, on this record, failed to show that the appearance policy imposed a greater burden on women than on men. *Id.* twenty years and compiled what by all accounts was an exemplary record. During Jespersen's entire tenure with Harrah's, the company maintained a policy encouraging female beverage servers to wear makeup. The parties agree, however, that the policy was not enforced until 2000. In February 2000, Harrah's implemented a "Beverage Department Image Transformation" program at twenty Harrah's locations, including its casino in Reno. Part of the program consisted of new grooming and appearance standards, called the "Personal Best" program. The program contained certain appearance standards that applied equally to both sexes, including a standard uniform of black pants, white shirt, black vest, and black bow tie. Jespersen has never objected to any of these policies. The program also contained some sex-differentiated appearance requirements as to hair, nails, and makeup.

In April 2000, Harrah's amended that policy to require that women wear makeup. Jespersen's only objection here is to the makeup requirement. The amended policy provided in relevant part:

> All Beverage Service Personnel, in addition to being friendly, polite, courteous and responsive to our customer's needs, must possess the ability to physically perform the essential factors of the job as set forth in the standard job descriptions. They must be well groomed, appealing to the eye, be firm and body toned, and be comfortable with maintaining this look while wearing the specified uniform. Additional factors to be considered include, but are not limited to, hair styles, overall body contour, and degree of comfort the employee projects while wearing the uniform.
>
> * * *
>
> Beverage Bartenders and Barbacks will adhere to these additional guidelines:
>
> • Overall Guidelines (applied equally to male/ female):
> • Appearance: Must maintain Personal Best image portrayed at time of hire.
> • Jewelry, if issued, must be worn. Otherwise, tasteful and simple jewelry is permitted; no large chokers, chains or bracelets.
> • No faddish hairstyles or unnatural colors are permitted.
> • Males:
>> • Hair must not extend below top of shirt collar. Ponytails are prohibited.
>> • Hands and fingernails must be clean and nails neatly trimmed at all times. No colored polish is permitted.

- Eye and facial makeup is not permitted.
- Shoes will be solid black leather or leather type with rubber (non skid) soles.

- Females:
  - Hair must be teased, curled, or styled every day you work. Hair must be worn down at all times, no exceptions.
  - Stockings are to be of nude or natural color consistent with employee's skin tone. No runs.
  - Nail polish can be clear, white, pink or red color only. No exotic nail art or length.
  - Shoes will be solid black leather or leather type with rubber (non skid) soles.
  - *Make up (face powder, blush and mascara) must be worn and applied neatly in complimentary colors. Lip color must be worn at all times.* (emphasis added).

Jespersen did not wear makeup on or off the job, and in her deposition stated that wearing it would conflict with her self image. It is not disputed that she found the makeup requirement offensive, and felt so uncomfortable wearing makeup that she found it interfered with her ability to perform as a bartender. Unwilling to wear the makeup, and not qualifying for any open positions at the casino with a similar compensation scale, Jespersen left her employment with Harrah's.

After exhausting her administrative remedies with the Equal Employment Opportunity Commission and obtaining a right to sue notification, Jespersen filed this action in July 2001. In her complaint, Jespersen sought damages as well as declaratory and injunctive relief for discrimination and retaliation for opposition to discrimination, alleging that the "Personal Best" policy discriminated against women by "(1) subjecting them to terms and conditions of employment to which men are not similarly subjected, and (2) requiring that women conform to sex-based stereotypes as a term and condition of employment."

Harrah's moved for summary judgment, supporting its motion with documents giving the history and purpose of the appearance and grooming policies. Harrah's argued that the policy created similar standards for both men and women, and that where the standards differentiated on the basis of sex, as with the face and hair standards, any burdens imposed fell equally on both male and female bartenders.

In her deposition testimony, attached as a response to the motion for summary judgment, Jespersen described the personal indignity she felt as a result of attempting to comply with the makeup policy. Jespersen testified that when she wore the makeup she "felt very degraded and very demeaned." In addition, Jespersen testified that "it prohibited [her] from doing [her] job" because "[i]t affected [her] self-dignity . . . [and] took away [her] credibility as an individual and as a person."

Jespersen made no cross-motion for summary judgment, taking the position that the case should go to the jury. Her response to Harrah's motion for summary judgment relied solely on her own deposition testimony regarding her subjective reaction to the makeup policy, and on favorable customer feedback and employer evaluation forms regarding her work.

The record therefore does not contain any affidavit or other evidence to establish that complying with the "Personal Best" standards caused burdens to fall unequally on men or women, and there is no evidence to suggest Harrah's motivation was to stereotype the women bartenders. Jespersen relied solely on evidence that she had been a good bartender, and that she had personal objections to complying with the policy, in order to support her argument that Harrah's "'sells' and exploits its women employees." Jespersen contended that as a matter of law she had made a prima facie showing of gender discrimination, sufficient to survive summary judgment on both of her claims.

The district court granted Harrah's motion for summary judgment on all of Jespersen's claims. *Jespersen,* 280 F.Supp.2d at 1195–96. In this appeal, Jespersen maintains that the record before the district court was sufficient to create triable issues of material fact as to her unlawful discrimination claims of unequal burdens and sex stereotyping. We deal with each in turn.

II. UNEQUAL BURDENS

In order to assert a valid Title VII claim for sex discrimination, a plaintiff must make out a prima facie case establishing that the challenged employment action was either intentionally discriminatory or that it had a discriminatory effect on the basis of gender. *McDonnell Douglas Corp. v. Green,* 411 U.S. 792, 802, 93 S.Ct. 1817, 36 L.Ed.2d 668 (1973); *Harriss v. Pan Am. World Airways, Inc.,* 649 F.2d 670, 673 (9th Cir.1980). Once a plaintiff establishes such a prima facie case, "[t]he burden then must shift to the employer to articulate some legitimate, nondiscriminatory reason for the employee's rejection." *McDonnell,* 411 U.S. at 802, 93 S.Ct. 1817.

In this case, Jespersen argues that the makeup requirement itself establishes a prima facie case of discriminatory intent and must be justified by Harrah's as a bona fide occupational qualification. *See* 42 U.S.C. § 2000e-2(e)(1).[1] Our settled law in this circuit, however, does not support Jespersen's position that a sex-based difference in appearance standards alone, without any further showing of disparate effects, creates a prima facie case.

In *Gerdom v. Cont'l Airlines, Inc.,* 692 F.2d 602 (9th Cir.1982), we considered the Continental Airlines policy that imposed strict weight restrictions on female flight attendants, and held it constituted a violation of Title VII. We did so because the airline imposed no weight restriction whatsoever on a class of male employees who performed the same or similar functions as the flight attendants. *Id.* at 610. Indeed, the policy was touted by the airline as intended to "create the public image of an airline which offered passengers service by thin, attractive women, whom executives referred to as Continental's 'girls.'" *Id.* at 604. In fact, Continental specifically argued that its policy was justified by its "desire to compete [with other airlines] by featuring attractive female cabin attendants[,]" a justification which this court recognized as "discriminatory on its face." *Id.* at 609. The weight restriction was part of an overall program to create a sexual image for the airline. *Id.* at 604.

In contrast, this case involves an appearance policy that applied to both male and female bartenders, and was aimed at creating a professional and very similar look for all of them. All bartenders wore the same uniform. The policy only differentiated as to grooming standards.

In *Frank v. United Airlines, Inc.*, 216 F.3d 845 (9th Cir.2000), we dealt with a weight policy that applied different standards to men and women in a facially unequal way. The women were forced to meet the requirements of a medium body frame standard while men were required to meet only the more generous requirements of a large body frame standard. *Id.* at 854. In that case, we recognized that "[a]n appearance standard that imposes different but essentially equal burdens on men and women is not disparate treatment." *Id.* The United weight policy, however, did not impose equal burdens. On its face, the policy embodied a requirement that categorically "'applie[d] less favorably to one gender[,]'" and the burdens imposed upon that gender were obvious from the policy itself. *Id.* (quoting *Gerdom*, 692 F.2d at 608 (alteration omitted)).

This case stands in marked contrast, for here we deal with requirements that, on their face, are not more onerous for one gender than the other. Rather, Harrah's "Personal Best" policy contains sex-differentiated requirements regarding each employee's hair, hands, and face. While those individual requirements differ according to gender, none on its face places a greater burden on one gender than the other. Grooming standards that appropriately differentiate between the genders are not facially discriminatory.

We have long recognized that companies may differentiate between men and women in appearance and grooming policies, and so have other circuits. *See, e.g., Fountain v. Safeway Stores, Inc.*, 555 F.2d 753, 755 (9th Cir.1977); *Barker v. Taft Broad. Co.*, 549 F.2d 400, 401 (6th Cir.1977); *Earwood v. Cont'l Southeastern Lines, Inc.*, 539 F.2d 1349, 1350 (4th Cir.1976); *Longo v. Carlisle DeCoppet & Co.*, 537 F.2d 685, 685 (2d Cir.1976) (per curiam); *Knott v. Mo. Pac. R.R. Co.*, 527 F.2d 1249, 1252 (8th Cir.1975); *Willingham v. Macon Tel. Publ'g Co.*, 507 F.2d 1084, 1092 (5th Cir. 1975) (en banc); *Baker v. Cal. Land Title Co.*, 507 F.2d 895, 896 (9th Cir.1974); *Dodge v. Giant Food, Inc.*, 488 F.2d 1333, 1337 (D.C.Cir.1973). The material issue under our settled law is not whether the policies are different, but whether the policy imposed on the plaintiff creates an "unequal burden" for the plaintiff's gender. *See Frank*, 216 F.3d at 854–55; *Gerdom*, 692 F.2d at 605–06; *see also Fountain*, 555 F.2d at 755–56.

Not every differentiation between the sexes in a grooming and appearance policy creates a "significantly greater burden of compliance[.]" *Gerdom*, 692 F.2d at 606. For example, in *Fountain*, this court upheld Safeway's enforcement of its sex-differentiated appearance standard, including its requirement that male employees wear ties, because the company's actions in enforcing the regulations were not "overly burdensome to its employees[.]" 555 F.2d at 756; *see also Baker,* 507 F.2d at 898. Similarly, as the Eighth Circuit has recognized, "[w]here, as here, such [grooming and appearance] policies are reasonable and are imposed in an even-handed manner on all employees, slight differences in the appearance requirements for males and females have only a negligible effect on employment opportunities." *Knott,* 527 F.2d at 1252. Under established equal burdens analysis, when an employer's grooming and appearance policy does not unreasonably burden one gender more than the other, that policy will not violate Title VII.

Jespersen asks us to take judicial notice of the fact that it costs more money and takes more time for a woman to comply with the makeup requirement than it takes for a man to comply with the requirement that he keep his hair short, but these are not matters appropriate for judicial notice. Judicial notice is reserved for matters "generally known within the territorial jurisdiction of the trial court" or "capable of accurate and ready determination by resort to sources whose accuracy cannot reasonably be questioned." Fed. R.Evid. 201. The time and cost of makeup and haircuts is in neither category. The facts that Jespersen would have this court judicially notice are not subject to the requisite "high degree of indisputability" generally required for such judicial notice. Fed.R.Evid. 201 advisory committee's note.

Our rules thus provide that a plaintiff may not cure her failure to present the trial court with facts sufficient to establish the validity of her claim by requesting that this court take judicial notice of such facts. *See id.; see also* Fed. R. Civ. Proc. 56(e). Those rules apply here. Jespersen did not submit any documentation or any evidence of the relative cost and time required to comply with the grooming requirements by men and women. As a result, we would have to speculate about those issues in order to then guess whether the policy creates unequal burdens for women. This would not be appropriate. *See, e.g.,* Anderson v. Liberty Lobby, Inc., 477 U.S. 242, 249, 106 S.Ct. 2505, 91 L.Ed.2d 202 (1986) ("[T]here is no issue for trial unless there is sufficient evidence favoring the nonmoving party for a jury to return a verdict for that party."); Steckl v. Motorola, Inc., 703 F.2d 392, 393 (9th Cir.1983) ("A party opposing a summary judgment motion must produce *specific* facts showing that there remains a genuine factual issue for trial and evidence significantly probative as to any material fact claimed to be disputed.") (internal quotation marks and alteration omitted); *cf.* Lindahl v. Air France, 930 F.2d 1434, 1437 (9th Cir. 1991) (In a Title VII case, "a plaintiff cannot defeat summary judgment simply by making out a prima facie case.").

Having failed to create a record establishing that the "Personal Best" policies are more burdensome for women than for men, Jespersen did not present any triable issue of fact. The district court correctly granted summary judgment on the record before it with respect to Jespersen's claim that the makeup policy created an unequal burden for women.

III. SEX STEREOTYPING

In *Price Waterhouse,* the Supreme Court considered a mixed-motive discrimination case. 490 U.S. 228, 109 S.Ct. 1775, 104 L.Ed.2d 268 (1989). There, the plaintiff, Ann Hopkins, was denied partnership in the national accounting firm of Price Waterhouse because some of the partners found her to be too aggressive. *Id.* at 234–36, 109 S.Ct. 1775. While some partners praised Hopkins's "'strong character, independence and integrity[,]'" others commented that she needed to take "'a course at charm school[.]'" *Id.* at 234–35, 109 S.Ct. 1775. The Supreme Court determined that once a plaintiff has established that gender played "a motivating part in an employment decision, the defendant may avoid a finding of liability only by proving by a preponderance of the evidence that it would have made the same decision even if it had not taken the plaintiff's gender into account." *Id.* at 258, 109 S.Ct. 1775.

Consequently, in establishing that "gender played a motivating part in an employment decision," a plaintiff in a Title VII case may introduce evidence that the employment decision was made in part because of a sex stereotype. *Id.* at 250–51, 109 S.Ct. 1775. According to the Court, this is because "we are beyond the day when an employer could evaluate employees by assuming or insisting that they matched the stereotype associated with their group, for 'in forbidding employers to discriminate against individuals because of their sex, Congress intended to strike at the entire spectrum of disparate treatment of men and women resulting from sex stereotypes.'" *Id.* at 251, 109 S.Ct. 1775 (quoting Los Angeles Dept. of Water & Power v. Manhart, 435 U.S. 702, 707 n. 13, 98 S.Ct. 1370, 55 L.Ed.2d 657 (1978) (alteration omitted)). It was therefore impermissible for Hopkins's employer to place her in an untenable Catch-22: she needed to be aggressive and masculine to excel at her job, but was denied partnership for doing so because of her employer's gender stereotype. Instead, Hopkins was advised to "'walk more femininely, talk more femininely, dress more femininely, wear make up, have her hair styled, and wear jewelry.'" *Id.* at 235, 109 S.Ct. 1775.

The stereotyping in *Price Waterhouse* interfered with Hopkins' ability to perform her work; the advice that she should take "a course at charm school" was intended to discourage her use of the forceful and aggressive techniques that made her successful in the first place. *Id.* at 251, 109 S.Ct. 1775. Impermissible sex stereotyping was clear because the very traits that she was asked to hide were the same traits considered praiseworthy in men.

Harrah's "Personal Best" policy is very different. The policy does not single out Jespersen. It applies to all of the bartenders, male and female. It requires all of the bartenders to wear exactly the same uniforms while interacting with the public in the context of the entertainment industry. It is for the most part unisex, from the black tie to the non-skid shoes. There is no evidence in this record to indicate that the policy was adopted to make women bartenders conform to a commonly-accepted stereotypical image of what women should wear. The record contains nothing to suggest the grooming standards would objectively inhibit a woman's ability to do the job. The only evidence in the record to support the stereotyping claim is Jespersen's own subjective reaction to the makeup requirement.

. . . .

We emphasize that we do not preclude, as a matter of law, a claim of sex-stereotyping on the basis of dress or appearance codes. Others may well be filed, and any bases for such claims refined as law in this area evolves. This record, however, is devoid of any basis for permitting this particular claim to go forward, as it is limited to the subjective reaction of a single employee, and there is no evidence of a stereotypical motivation on the part of the employer. This case is essentially a challenge to one small part of what is an overall apparel, appearance, and grooming policy that applies largely the same requirements to both men and women. As we said in *Nichols*, in commenting on grooming standards, the touch-stone is reasonableness. A makeup requirement must be seen in the context of the overall standards imposed on employees in a given workplace.

AFFIRMED.

Notes and Questions:

1. How does the Court respond to Craft's argument that the lower court should have shifted the burden to Metromedia to show that they would have taken "the alleged actions in the absence of gender bias"?

2. Recall our coverage of Title VII's evidentiary scheme in chapter 2. Was Craft arguing that she should have been entitled to the benefit of the *McDonnell Douglas* standard? If so, how do you evaluate her argument based on the facts?

3. Is the Court ultimately classifying Craft's evidence as circumstantial or direct? What is the basis for the Court's conclusion that the lower court had no obligation to shift the burden to the employer?

In light of the ruling and analysis in the above cases, would an employer commit gender discrimination if they fire an employee for being too attractive and a threat to their marriage?

Nelson v. Knight

In The Supreme Court Of Iowa

No. 11-1857 Filed July 12, 2013

MANSFIELD, JUSTICE.

Can a male employer terminate a long-time female employee because the employer's wife, due to no fault of the employee, is concerned about the nature of the relationship between the employer and the employee? This is the question we are required to answer today. For the reasons stated herein, we ultimately conclude the conduct does not amount to unlawful sex discrimination in violation of the Iowa Civil Rights Act.

We emphasize the limits of our decision. The employee did not bring a sexual harassment or hostile work environment claim; we are not deciding how such a claim would have been resolved in this or any other case. Also, when an employer takes an adverse employment action against a person or persons because of a gender-specific characteristic, that can violate the civil rights laws. The record in this case, however, does not support such an allegation.

I. Facts and Procedural Background.

Because this case was decided on summary judgment, we set forth the facts in the light most favorable to the plaintiff, Melissa Nelson.

In 1999, Dr. Knight hired Nelson to work as a dental assistant in his dental office. At that time, Nelson had just received her community college degree and was twenty years old.

Over the next ten-and-a-half years, Nelson worked as a dental assistant for Dr. Knight. Dr. Knight admits that Nelson was a good dental assistant. Nelson in turn acknowledges that Dr. Knight generally treated her with respect, and she believed him to be a person of high integrity.

On several occasions during the last year and a half when Nelson worked in the office, Dr. Knight complained to Nelson that her clothing was too tight and revealing and "distracting." Dr. Knight at times asked Nelson to put on her lab coat. Dr. Knight later testified that he made these statements to Nelson because "I don't think it's good for me to see her wearing things that accentuate her body." Nelson denies that her clothing was tight or in any way inappropriate.

During the last six months or so of Nelson's employment, Dr. Knight and Nelson started texting each other on both work and personal matters outside the workplace. Both parties initiated texting. Neither objected to the other's texting. Both Dr. Knight and Nelson have children, and some of the texts involved updates on the kids' activities and other relatively innocuous matters. Nelson considered Dr. Knight to be a friend and father figure, and she denies that she ever flirted with him or sought an intimate or sexual relationship with him. At the same time, Nelson admits that a coworker was "jealous that we got along." At one point, Nelson *66 texted Dr. Knight that "[t]he only reason I stay is because of you."

Dr. Knight acknowledges he once told Nelson that if she saw his pants bulging, she would know her clothing was too revealing. On another occasion, Dr. Knight texted Nelson saying the shirt she had worn that day was too tight. After Nelson responded that she did not think he was being fair, Dr. Knight replied that it was a good thing Nelson did not wear tight pants too because then he would get it coming and going. Dr. Knight also recalls that after Nelson allegedly made a statement regarding infrequency in her sex life, he responded to her, "[T]hat's like having a Lamborghini in the garage and never driving it." Nelson recalls that Dr. Knight once texted her to ask how often she experienced an orgasm. Nelson did not answer the text. However, Nelson does not remember ever telling Dr. Knight not to text her or telling him that she was offended.

In late 2009, Dr. Knight took his children to Colorado for Christmas vacation. Dr. Knight's wife Jeanne, who was also an employee in the dental practice, stayed home. Jeanne Knight found out that her husband and Nelson were texting each other during that time. When Dr. Knight returned home, Jeanne Knight confronted her husband and demanded that he terminate Nelson's employment. Both of them consulted with the senior pastor of their church, who agreed with the decision.

Jeanne Knight insisted that her husband terminate Nelson because "she was a big threat to our marriage." According to her affidavit and her deposition testimony, she had several complaints about Nelson. These included Nelson's texting with Dr. Knight, Nelson's clothing, Nelson's alleged flirting with Dr. Knight, Nelson's alleged coldness at work toward her (Jeanne Knight), and Nelson's ongoing criticism of another dental assistant. She added that

> [Nelson] liked to hang around after work when it would be just her and [Dr. Knight] there. I thought it was strange that after being at work all day and away from her kids and husband that she would not be anxious to get home like the other [women] in the office.

At the end of the workday on January 4, 2010, Dr. Knight called Nelson into his office. He had arranged for another pastor from the church to be present as an observer. Dr. Knight, reading from a prepared statement, told Nelson he was firing her. The statement said, in part, that their relationship had become a detriment to Dr. Knight's family and that for the best interests of both Dr. Knight and his family and Nelson and her family, the two of them should not work together. Dr. Knight handed Nelson an envelope which contained one month's severance pay. Nelson started crying and said she loved her job.

Nelson's husband Steve phoned Dr. Knight after getting the news of his wife's firing. Dr. Knight initially refused to talk to Steve Nelson, but later called back and invited him to meet at the office later that same evening. Once again, the pastor was present. In the meeting, Dr. Knight told Steve Nelson that Melissa Nelson had not done anything wrong or inappropriate and that she was the best dental assistant he ever had. However, Dr. Knight said he was worried he was getting too personally attached to her. Dr. Knight told Steve Nelson that nothing was going on but that he feared he would try to have an affair with her down the road if he did not fire her.

Dr. Knight replaced Nelson with another female. Historically, all of his dental assistants have been women. After timely filing a civil rights complaint and getting a "right to sue" letter from the Iowa Civil Rights Commission, Nelson brought this action against Dr. Knight on August 12, 2010. Nelson's one-count petition alleges that Dr. Knight discriminated against her on the basis of sex. Nelson does not contend that her employer committed sexual harassment. See McElroy v. State, 637 N.W.2d 488, 499–500 (Iowa 2001) (discussing when sexual harassment amounts to unlawful sex discrimination and restating the elements of both quid pro quo and hostile work environment sexual harassment). Her argument, rather, is that

Dr. Knight terminated her because of her gender and would not have terminated her if she was male.

Dr. Knight moved for summary judgment. After briefing and oral argument, the district court sustained the motion. The court reasoned in part, "Ms. Nelson was fired not because of her gender but because she was a threat to the marriage of Dr. Knight." Nelson appeals.

II. Standard of Review.

We review the district court's summary judgment ruling for correction of errors at law. *Pecenka v. Fareway Stores, Inc.*, 672 N.W.2d 800, 802 (Iowa 2003). We view the factual record in the light most favorable to the nonmoving party, affording that party all reasonable inferences. *Id.* Summary judgment is proper only if the record, so viewed, entitles the moving party to judgment as a matter of law. *Id.*

III. Analysis.

Section 216.6(1)(a) of the Iowa Code makes it generally unlawful to discharge or otherwise discriminate against an employee because of the employee's sex. Iowa Code § 216.6(1)(a) (2009). "When interpreting discrimination claims under Iowa Code chapter 216, we turn to federal law, including Title VII of the United States Civil Rights Act. . . ." *Deboom v. Raining Rose, Inc.*, 772 N.W.2d 1, 7 (Iowa 2009). Generally, an employer engages in unlawful sex discrimination when the employer takes adverse employment action against an employee and sex is a motivating factor in the employer's decision. See *Channon v. United Parcel Serv., Inc.*, 629 N.W.2d 835, 861 (Iowa 2001).

Nelson argues that her gender was a motivating factor in her termination because she would not have lost her job if she had been a man. See, e.g., *Watson v. Se. Pa. Transp. Auth.*, 207 F.3d 207, 213, 222 (3d Cir.2000) (affirming a jury verdict in a Title VII case because the charge, taken as a whole, adequately informed the jury that sex had to be a but-for cause of the adverse employment action). Dr. Knight responds that Nelson was terminated not because of her sex—after all, he only employs women—but because of the nature of their relationship and the perceived threat to Dr. Knight's marriage. Yet Nelson rejoins that neither the relationship nor the alleged threat would have existed if she had not been a woman.

Several cases, including a decision of the United States Court of Appeals for the Eighth Circuit, have found that an employer does not engage in unlawful gender discrimination by discharging a female employee who is involved in a consensual relationship that has triggered personal jealousy. This is true even though the relationship and the resulting jealousy presumably would not have existed if the employee had been male.

Tenge v. Phillips Modern Ag Co., like the present case, centered on a personal relationship between the owner of a small business and a valued employee of the business that was seen by the owner's wife as a threat to their marriage. 446 F.3d 903, 905–06 (8th Cir.2006). In that case, unlike here, the plaintiff had pinched the owner's rear. *Id.* at 906. She admitted that the owner's wife "could have suspected the two had an intimate relationship." *Id.* Further, the plaintiff acknowledged she wrote "notes of a sexual or intimate nature" to the owner and put them in a location where others could see them. *Id.* In the end, the owner fired the plaintiff, stating that his wife was "'making me choose between my best employee or her and the kids.'" *Id.*

Reviewing this series of events, the Eighth Circuit affirmed the summary judgment in favor of the defendants. *Id.* at 911. The Eighth Circuit first noted the considerable body of authority that "'sexual favoritism,' where one employee was treated more favorably than members of the opposite sex because of a consensual relationship with the boss," does not violate Title VII. *Id.* at 908–09. The court distilled that law as follows:

> "[T]he principle that emerges from the above cases is that absent claims of coercion or widespread sexual favoritism, where an employee engages in consensual sexual conduct with a supervisor and an employment decision is based on this conduct, Title VII is not implicated because any benefits of the relationship are due to the sexual conduct, rather than the gender, of the employee.: *Id.* at 909.

The Eighth Circuit believed these sexual favoritism precedents were relevant. The court's unstated reasoning was that if a specific instance of sexual favoritism does not constitute gender discrimination, treating an employee unfavorably because of such a relationship does not violate the law either.

Yet the court acknowledged that cases where the employee was treated less favorably would be "more directly analogous." *Id.* The court then discussed a decision of the Eleventh Circuit where an employee had been terminated for being a perceived threat to the marriage of the owner's son. *Id.* (discussing *Platner v. Cash & Thomas Contractors, Inc.*, 908 F.2d 902, 903–05 (11th Cir.1990)). It also cited three federal district court cases, each of which had "concluded that terminating an employee based on the employee's consensual sexual conduct does not violate Title VII absent allegations that the conduct stemmed from unwelcome sexual advances or a hostile work environment." *Id.* (citing *Kahn v. Objective Solutions, Int'l*, 86 F.Supp.2d 377, 382 (S.D.N.Y.2000); *Campbell v. Masten*, 955 F.Supp. 526, 529 (D.Md.1997); *Freeman v. Cont'l Technical Serv., Inc.*, 710 F.Supp. 328, 331 (N.D.Ga.1988)).

After reviewing these precedents, the Eighth Circuit found the owner had not violated Title VII in terminating the employee at his wife's behest. As the court explained, "The ultimate basis for Tenge's dismissal was not her sex, it was Scott's desire to allay his wife's concerns over Tenge's admitted sexual behavior with him." *Id.* at 910.

In our case, the district court quoted at length from *Tenge*, stating it found that decision "persuasive." However, Nelson argues there is a significant factual difference between the two cases. As the Eighth Circuit put it, "Tenge was terminated due to the consequences of her own admitted conduct with her employer, not because of her status as a woman." *Id.* . . .

The question we must answer is the one left open in *Tenge*—whether an employee who has not engaged in flirtatious conduct may be lawfully terminated simply because the boss's spouse views the relationship between the boss and the employee as a threat to her marriage. Notwithstanding the Eighth Circuit's care to leave that question unanswered, it seems odd at first glance to have the question of whether the employer engaged in unlawful discrimination turn on the employee's conduct, assuming that such conduct (whatever it is) would not typically be a firing offense. Usually our legal focus is on the employer's motivation, not on whether the discharge in a broader sense is fair. Title VII and the Iowa Civil Rights Act are not general fairness laws, and an employer does not violate them by treating an employee unfairly so long as the employer does not engage in discrimination based upon the employee's protected status.

In some respects, the present case resembles *Platner*. There a business owner chose to terminate a female employee who worked on the same crew as the business owner's son, after the wife of the business owner's son became "extremely jealous" of her. *Platner*, 908 F.2d at 903. The district court found that the son was "largely to blame for fueling [the wife's] jealousy," and that the plaintiff's conduct was "basically blameless and no different from that of the male employees." *Id*. Nonetheless, the Eleventh Circuit found no unlawful discrimination had occurred:

> It is evident that Thomas, faced with a seemingly insoluble conflict within his family, felt he had to make a choice as to which employee to keep. He opted to place the burden of resolving the situation on Platner, to whom he was not related, and whose dismissal would not, as firing Steve obviously would, fracture his family and its relationships. It is thus clear that the ultimate basis for Platner's dismissal was not gender but simply favoritism for a close relative . . .

Significantly, although Dr. Knight discusses *Platner* at some length in his briefing, Nelson does not refer to the decision in her briefing or attempt to distinguish it.

Nelson does, however, have three responses to Dr. Knight's overall position. First, she does not necessarily agree with Tenge. She argues that any termination because of a supervisor's interest in an employee amounts to sex discrimination: "Plaintiff's sex is implicated by the very nature of the reason for termination." Second, she suggests that without some kind of employee misconduct requirement, Dr. Knight's position becomes simply a way of enforcing stereotypes and permitting pretexts: The employer can justify a series of adverse employment actions against persons of one gender by claiming, "My spouse was jealous." Third, she argues that if Dr. Knight would have been liable to Nelson for sexually harassing her, he should not be able to avoid liability for terminating her out of fear that he was going to harass her.

Nelson's arguments warrant serious consideration, but we ultimately think a distinction exists between (1) an isolated employment decision based on personal relations (assuming no coercion or quid pro quo), even if the relations would not have existed if the employee had been of the opposite gender, and (2) a decision based on gender itself. In the former case, the decision is driven entirely by individual feelings and emotions regarding a specific person. Such a decision is not gender-based, nor is it based on factors that might be a proxy for gender.

The civil rights laws seek to insure that employees are treated the same regardless of their sex or other protected status. Yet even taking Nelson's view of the facts, Dr. Knight's unfair decision to terminate Nelson (while paying her a rather ungenerous one month's severance) does not jeopardize that goal. As the Platner court observed, "'[W]e do not believe that Title VII authorizes courts to declare unlawful every arbitrary and unfair employment decision.'" *Id.* at 905 (quoting *Holder v. City of Raleigh*, 867 F.2d 823, 825–26 (4th Cir.1989)).

Nelson's viewpoint would allow any termination decision related to a consensual relationship to be challenged as a discriminatory action because the employee could argue the relationship would not have existed but for her or his gender. This logic would contradict federal caselaw to the effect that adverse employment action stemming from a consensual workplace relationship (absent sexual harassment) is not actionable under Title VII. See, e.g., *Benders v. Bellows & Bellows*, 515 F.3d 757, 768 (7th Cir.2008) (holding that allegations that an employee's termination was based on the owner's desire to hide a past consensual relationship from his wife were "insufficient to support a cause of action for sex discrimination"); see also *Blackshear v. Interstate Brands Corp.*, No. 10–3696, 2012 WL 3553499, at *3 (6th Cir.2012) (affirming summary judgment for the employer where the employee presented evidence that she was treated unfairly due to her supervisor's jealousy of her relationship with another employee, and noting that such "personal animus . . . cannot be the basis of a discrimination claim under federal or Ohio law"); *West v. MCI Worldcom, Inc.*, 205 F.Supp.2d 531, 544–45 (E.D.Va.2002) (granting summary judgment to an employer when an employee was removed from a project because of a supervisor's animosity toward the employee over her termination of their consensual relationship but there was no evidence the supervisor had made unwanted advances to the employee following the termination of that relationship).

Nelson raises a legitimate concern about a slippery slope. What if Jeanne Knight demanded that her spouse terminate the employment of several women? Of course, a pretext does not prevail in a discrimination case. See *St. Mary's Honor Ctr. v. Hicks*, 509 U.S. 502, 515 (1993) (discussing how a plaintiff can prove that an employer's reason for a firing was not legitimate, but a pretext for discrimination). If an employer repeatedly took adverse employment actions against persons of a particular gender, that would make it easier to infer that gender and not a relationship was a motivating factor. Here, however, it is not disputed that Jeanne Knight objected to this particular relationship as it had developed after Nelson had already been working at the office for over ten years.

It is likewise true that a decision based on a gender stereotype can amount to unlawful sex discrimination. *Price Waterhouse v. Hopkins*, 490 U.S. 228, 251, 109 S. Ct. 1775, 1791, 104 L.Ed.2d 268, 288 (1989) . . . . If Nelson could show that she had been terminated because she did not conform to a particular stereotype, this might be a different case. But the record here does not support that conclusion. It is undisputed, rather, that Nelson was fired because Jeanne Knight, unfairly or not, viewed her as a threat to her marriage.

The present case can be contrasted with another recent Eighth Circuit decision. In *Lewis v. Heartland Inns of America, L.L.C.*, a female front desk employee at a hotel claimed she lost her job because she did not have the "Midwestern girl look." 591 F.3d 1033, 1037 (8th Cir. 2010). As the court explained, "The theory of [Lewis's] case is that the evidence shows Heartland enforced a de facto requirement that a female employee conform to gender stereotypes in order to work the A shift." *Id.* In fact, the evidence showed that motel management later procured video equipment so they could observe the appearance of front desk applicants prior to hiring. *Id.* at 1042. The Eighth Circuit reversed the district court's grant of summary judgment to the employer and remanded for trial. *Id.* However, the critical difference between *Lewis* and this case is that Nelson indisputably lost her job because Dr. Knight's spouse objected to the parties' relationship. In *Lewis*, by contrast, no relationship existed.

Nelson also raises a serious point about sexual harassment. Given that sexual harassment is a violation of antidiscrimination law, Nelson argues that a firing by a boss to avoid committing sexual harassment should be treated similarly. But sexual harassment violates our civil rights laws because of the "hostile work environment" or "abusive atmosphere" that it has created for persons of the victim's sex. See, e.g., *Faragher v. City of Boca Raton*, 524 U.S. 775, 786–90 (1998). On the other hand, an isolated decision to terminate an employee before such an environment arises, even if the reasons for termination are unjust, by definition does not bring about that atmosphere.

As a Michigan appellate court observed regarding a male employee's claim that he had been subjected to sex discrimination:

> We do not read the [Michigan Civil Rights Act or CRA] to prohibit conduct based on romantic jealousy. . . . Interpreting the CRA's prohibition of discrimination based on sex to prohibit conduct based on romantic jealousy turns the CRA on its head. The CRA was enacted to prevent discrimination because of classifications specifically enumerated by the Legislature and to eliminate the effects of offensive or demeaning stereotypes, prejudices, and biases. It is beyond reason to conclude that plaintiff's status as the romantic competition to the woman Vajda sought to date places plaintiff within the class of individuals the Legislature sought to protect when it prohibited discrimination based on sex under the CRA.
>
> Plaintiff proceeded to trial on a theory of discrimination based on romantic jealousy. Plaintiff did not claim and the evidence did not establish that plaintiff was required to submit to sexually-based harassment as a condition of employment. Nor did the evidence presented at trial support a theory of gender-based discrimination. Plaintiff established, at most, that

Vajda's alleged adverse treatment of plaintiff was based on plaintiff's relationship with Goshorn, not plaintiff's gender . . .

IV. Conclusion.

As we have indicated above, the issue before us is not whether a jury could find that Dr. Knight treated Nelson badly. We are asked to decide only if a genuine fact issue exists as to whether Dr. Knight engaged in unlawful gender discrimination when he fired Nelson at the request of his wife. For the reasons previously discussed, we believe this conduct did not amount to unlawful discrimination, and therefore we affirm the judgment of the district court.

C. Gender Discrimination and Title IX

Title IX is a companion statute to Title VII in the educational context. As litigation regarding workplace harassment has proliferated, so have issues affecting the quality of education for women and gender non-conforming persons in the K-12 context as well as in higher education. Title IX is a post-civil rights movement statute, which is now part of the Civil Rights Act of 1964. It states: "[n]o person in the United States shall, on the basis of sex, be excluded from participation in, be denied the benefits of, or be subjected to discrimination under any education program or activity receiving Federal financial assistance." 20 U.S.C. § 1681(a). The statute was enacted to eradicate sex discrimination in education. It binds institutions receiving federal funding from discriminating on the basis of sex.

Unlike Title VII, the statute is based on the Spending Clause's understanding that states/local governments, as well as private individuals, can contract with the federal governments to accomplish certain goals in exchange for federal funding. Once institutions accept Title IX funds, the prohibition against discrimination applies to all programs within the institution. Like with Title VII, however, the scope of protection against sex discrimination is still the subject of ongoing debate. A literal definition of sex discrimination might leave out LGBTQIA students, for example, whose struggles in schools and employment continue. *See Gloucester Cty. Sch. Bd. v. G.G.*, 137 S. Ct. 1239 (2017) (remanding the case to the Fourth Circuit for further consideration in light of the guidance issued by the Department of Education and Department of Justice on Feb. 22, 2017); *see also Lakoski v. James*, 66 F.3d 751 (11th Cir. 1995) (holding that Title VII provides the exclusive remedy for employment discrimination based on sex in federally funded educational institutions, therefore excluding potential remedies under Title IX). Recently, waves of legislation, colloquially known as bathroom bills, directing access to public facilities on the basis of gender classification at birth raise these issues. As you see below, these issues continue to be heavily litigated. These types of litigation have been crucial to moving the gender debate forward, pushing the law to slowly eliminate classifications based on stereotypes and gender roles. They also progressively have pushed the envelope on what constitutes sex discrimination.

In the chapter following, we chronicle the history of segregation and desegregation in school systems across the United States, culminating in *Brown v. Board of
Education*, which also contributed to statutes like Title IX. However, we place our
discussion of Title IX in this section, rather than the next chapter, to chronicle the
gains and limitations in the gender context. The cases below demonstrate the scope
and application of Title IX, who it protects, as well as highlight the controversies
regarding how far these protections extend. For example, foundational cases, like
Cannon v. University of Chicago and *North Haven Board of Education v. Bell* serve as
the propelling bedrock of Title IX jurisprudence. *Cannon v. University of Chicago*
provides for a private right of action under Title IX, based on the Court's interpretation of the statute and the legislative intent underlying it. *North Haven Board of Education v. Bell* extends protection against discrimination to all programs and all parts
of a funding recipient under the statute.

Cannon v. University of Chicago

441 U.S. 677 (1979)

Mr. Justice Stevens delivered the opinion of the Court.

Petitioner's complaints allege that her applications for admission to medical
school were denied by the respondents because she is a woman. Accepting the truth
of those allegations for the purpose of its decision, the Court of Appeals held that
petitioner has no right of action against respondents that may be asserted in a federal court. 559 F.2d 1063. We granted certiorari to review that holding. 438 U.S. 914,
98 S.Ct. 3142, 57 L.Ed.2d 1159.

Only two facts alleged in the complaints are relevant to our decision. First, petitioner was excluded from participation in the respondents' medical education programs because of her sex. Second, these education programs were receiving federal
financial assistance at the time of her exclusion. These facts, admitted *arguendo* by
respondents' motion to dismiss the complaints, establish a violation of §901(a) of
Title IX of the Education Amendments of 1972 hereinafter Title IX).

That section, in relevant part, provides:

> "No person in the United States shall, on the basis of sex, be excluded from
> participation in, be denied the benefits of, or be subjected to discrimina-
> tion under any education program or activity receiving Federal financial
> assistance . . . ."

The statute does not, however, expressly authorize a private right of action by a person injured by a violation of §901. For that reason, and because it concluded that
no private remedy should be inferred, the District Court granted the respondents'
motions to dismiss. 406 F.Supp. 1257, 1259.

The Court of Appeals agreed that the statute did not contain an implied private
remedy. Noting that §902 of Title IX establishes a procedure for the termination

of federal financial support for institutions violating § 901, the Court of Appeals concluded that Congress intended that remedy to be the exclusive means of enforcement. It recognized that the statute was patterned after Title VI of the Civil Rights Act of 1964 (hereinafter Title VI), but rejected petitioner's argument that Title VI included an implied private cause of action. 559 F.2d, at 1071–1075.

. . . .

The court also noted that the Department of Health, Education, and Welfare had taken the position that a private cause of action under Title IX should be implied, but the court disagreed with that agency's interpretation of the Act. In sum, it adhered to its original view, 559 F.2d, at 1077–1080.

The Court of Appeals quite properly devoted careful attention to this question of statutory construction. As our recent cases—particularly *Cort v. Ash,* 422 U.S. 66, 95 S.Ct. 2080, 45 L.Ed.2d 26—demonstrate, the fact that a federal statute has been violated and some person harmed does not automatically give rise to a private cause of action in favor of that person. Instead, before concluding that Congress intended to make a remedy available to a special class of litigants, a court must carefully analyze the four factors that *Cort* identifies as indicative of such an intent. Our review of those factors persuades us, however, that the Court of Appeals reached the wrong conclusion and that petitioner does have a statutory right to pursue her claim that respondents rejected her application on the basis of her sex. After commenting on each of the four factors, we shall explain why they are not overcome by respondents' countervailing arguments.

I

First, the threshold question under *Cort* is whether the statute was enacted for the benefit of a special class of which the plaintiff is a member. That question is answered by looking to the language of the statute itself. Thus, the statutory reference to "any employee of any such common carrier" in the 1893 legislation requiring railroads to equip their cars with secure "grab irons or handholds," see 27 Stat. 532, 531, made "irresistible" the Court's earliest "inference of a private right of action"—in that case in favor of a railway employee who was injured when a grab iron gave way. *Texas & Pacific R. Co. v. Rigsby,* 241 U.S. 33, 40, 36 S.Ct. 482, 484, 60 L.Ed. 874.

Similarly, it was statutory language describing the special class to be benefited by § 5 of the Voting Rights Act of 1965 that persuaded the Court that private parties within that class were implicitly authorized to seek a declaratory judgment against a covered State. *Allen v. State Board of Elections,* 393 U.S. 544, 554–555, 89 S.Ct. 817, 825–826, 22 L.Ed.2d 1. The dispositive language in that statute—"no person shall be denied the right to vote for failure to comply with [a new state enactment covered by, but not approved under, § 5]"—is remarkably similar to the language used by Congress in Title IX.

The language in these statutes—which expressly identifies the class Congress intended to benefit—contrasts sharply with statutory language customarily found in criminal statutes, such as that construed in *Cort, supra,* and other laws enacted for the protection of the general public. . . .

Unquestionably, therefore, the first of the four factors identified in *Cort* favors the implication of a private cause of action. Title IX explicitly confers a benefit on persons discriminated against on the basis of sex, and petitioner is clearly a member of that class for whose special benefit the statute was enacted.

Second, the *Cort* analysis requires consideration of legislative history. We must recognize, however, that the legislative history of a statute that does not expressly create or deny a private remedy will typically be equally silent or ambiguous on the question. Therefore, in situations such as the present one "in which it is clear that federal law has granted a class of persons certain rights, it is not necessary to show an intention to *create* a private cause of action, although an explicit purpose to *deny* such cause of action would be controlling." *Cort,* 422 U.S., at 82, 95 S.Ct., at 2090 (emphasis in original). But this is not the typical case. Far from evidencing any purpose to *deny* a private cause of action, the history of Title IX rather plainly indicates that Congress intended to create such a remedy.

Title IX was patterned after Title VI of the Civil Rights Act of 1964. Except for the substitution of the word "sex" in Title IX to replace the words "race, color, or national origin" in Title VI, the two statutes use identical language to describe the benefited class. Both statutes provide the same administrative mechanism for terminating federal financial support for institutions engaged in prohibited discrimination. Neither statute expressly mentions a private remedy for the person excluded from participation in a federally funded program. The drafters of Title IX explicitly assumed that it would be interpreted and applied as Title VI had been during the preceding eight years.

In 1972 when Title IX was enacted, the critical language in Title VI had already been construed as creating a private remedy. . . . Moreover, in 1969, in Allen v. State Board of Elections, 393 U.S. 544, 89 S.Ct. 817, 22 L.Ed.2d 1, this Court had interpreted the comparable language in §5 of the Voting Rights Act as sufficient to authorize a private remedy. Indeed, during the period between the enactment of Title VI in 1964 and the enactment of Title IX in 1972, this Court had consistently found implied remedies—often in cases much less clear than this. It was *after* 1972 that this Court decided *Cort v. Ash* and the other cases cited by the Court of Appeals in support of its strict construction of the remedial aspect of the statute. We, of course, adhere to the strict approach followed in our recent cases, but our evaluation of congressional action in 1972 must take into account its contemporary legal context. In sum, it is not only appropriate but also realistic to presume that Congress was thoroughly familiar with these unusually important precedents from this and other federal courts and that it expected its enactment to be interpreted in conformity with them.

It is not, however, necessary to rely on these presumptions. The package of statutes of which Title IX is one part also contains a provision whose language and history demonstrate that Congress itself understood Title VI, and thus its companion, Title IX, as creating a private remedy. Section 718 of the Education Amendments authorizes federal courts to award attorney's fees to the prevailing parties, other than the United States, in private actions brought against public educational agencies to enforce Title VI in the context of elementary and secondary education. The language of this provision explicitly presumes the availability of private suits to enforce Title VI in the education context. For many such suits, no express cause of action was then available; hence Congress must have assumed that one could be implied under Title VI itself. That assumption was made explicit during the debates on §718. It was also aired during the debates on other provisions in the Education Amendments of 1972 and on Title IX itself, and is consistent with the Executive Branch's apparent understanding of Title VI at the time.

. . . .

Third, under *Cort*, a private remedy should not be implied if it would frustrate the underlying purpose of the legislative scheme. On the other hand, when that remedy is necessary or at least helpful to the accomplishment of the statutory purpose, the Court is decidedly receptive to its implication under the statute.

Title IX, like its model Title VI, sought to accomplish two related, but nevertheless somewhat different, objectives. First, Congress wanted to avoid the use of federal resources to support discriminatory practices; second, it wanted to provide individual citizens effective protection against those practices. Both of these purposes were repeatedly identified in the debates on the two statutes.

The first purpose is generally served by the statutory procedure for the termination of federal financial support for institutions engaged in discriminatory practices. That remedy is, however, severe and often may not provide an appropriate means of accomplishing the second purpose if merely an isolated violation has occurred. In that situation, the violation might be remedied more efficiently by an order requiring an institution to accept an applicant who had been improperly excluded. Moreover, in that kind of situation it makes little sense to impose on an individual, whose only interest is in obtaining a benefit for herself, or on HEW, the burden of demonstrating that an institution's practices are so pervasively discriminatory that a complete cut-off of federal funding is appropriate. The award of individual relief to a private litigant who has prosecuted her own suit is not only sensible but is also fully consistent with — and in some cases even necessary to — the orderly enforcement of the statute.

The Department of Health, Education, and Welfare, which is charged with the responsibility for administering Title IX, perceives no inconsistency between the private remedy and the public remedy. On the contrary, the agency takes the unequivocal position that the individual remedy will provide effective assistance to achieving the statutory purposes. The agency's position is unquestionably correct.

Fourth, the final inquiry suggested by *Cort* is whether implying a federal remedy is inappropriate because the subject matter involves an area basically of concern to the States. No such problem is raised by a prohibition against invidious discrimination of any sort, including that on the basis of sex. Since the Civil War, the Federal Government and the federal courts have been the "'*primary* and powerful reliances'" in protecting citizens against such discrimination. *Steffel v. Thompson*, 415 U.S. 452, 464, 94 S.Ct. 1209, 1218, 39 L.Ed.2d 505 (emphasis in original), quoting F. Frankfurter & J. Landis, The Business of the Supreme Court 65 (1928)....

In sum, there is no need in this case to weigh the four *Cort* factors; all of them support the same result. Not only the words and history of Title IX, but also its subject matter and underlying purposes, counsel implication of a cause of action in favor of private victims of discrimination.

. . . .

. . .

IV

When Congress intends private litigants to have a cause of action to support their statutory rights, the far better course is for it to specify as much when it creates those rights. But the Court has long recognized that under certain limited circumstances the failure of Congress to do so is not inconsistent with an intent on its part to have such a remedy available to the persons benefited by its legislation. Title IX presents the atypical situation in which *all* of the circumstances that the Court has previously identified as supportive of an implied remedy are present. We therefore conclude that petitioner may maintain her lawsuit, despite the absence of any express authorization for it in the statute.

The judgment of the Court of Appeals is reversed, and the case is remanded for further proceedings consistent with this opinion.

It is so ordered.

North Haven Board of Education v. Bell

456 U.S. 512 (1982)

Justice Blackmun delivered the opinion of the Court.

At issue here is the validity of regulations promulgated by the Department of Education pursuant to Title IX of the Education Amendments of 1972, Pub.L.92-318, 86 Stat. 373, as amended, 20 U.S.C. §1681 *et seq.* These regulations prohibit federally funded education programs from discriminating on the basis of gender with respect to employment.

I

Title IX proscribes gender discrimination in education programs or activities receiving federal financial assistance. Patterned after Title VI of the Civil Rights Act of 1964, Pub.L.88-352, 78 Stat. 252, 42 U.S.C. §2000d *et seq.* (1976 ed. and Supp.IV), Title IX, as amended, contains two core provisions. The first is a "program-specific" prohibition of gender discrimination:

"No person in the United States shall, on the basis of sex, be excluded from
participation in, be denied the benefits of, or be subjected to discrimination
under any education program or activity receiving Federal financial assistance . . . ." § 901(a), 20 U.S.C. § 1681(a).

Nine statutory exceptions to § 901(a)'s coverage follow. See §§ 901(a)(1)-(9).

The second core provision relates to enforcement. Section 902, 20 U.S.C. § 1682,
authorizes each agency awarding federal financial assistance to any education program to promulgate regulations ensuring that aid recipients adhere to § 901(a)'s
mandate. The ultimate sanction for noncompliance is termination of federal funds
or denial of future grants. Like § 901, § 902 is program-specific:

"[S]uch termination or refusal shall be limited to the particular political
entity, or part thereof, or other recipient as to whom such a finding [of non-
compliance] has been made, and shall be limited in its effect to the particular program, or part thereof, in which such noncompliance has been so
found . . . ."

In 1975, the Department of Health, Education, and Welfare (HEW) invoked its
§ 902 authority to issue regulations governing the operation of federally funded
education programs. These regulations extend, for example, to policies involving admissions, textbooks, and athletics. See 34 CFR pt. 106 (1980). Interpreting
the term "person" in § 901(a) to encompass employees as well as students, HEW
included among the regulations a series entitled "Subpart E," which deals with
employment practices, ranging from job classifications to pregnancy leave. See 34
CFR §§ 106.51-106.61 (1980). Subpart E's general introductory section provides:

"No person shall, on the basis of sex, be excluded from participation in, be
denied the benefits of, or be subjected to discrimination in employment,
or recruitment, consideration, or selection therefor, whether full-time or
part-time, under any education program or activity operated by a recipient
which receives or benefits from Federal financial assistance." § 106.51(a)(1).

II

Petitioners are two Connecticut public school boards that brought separate suits
challenging HEW's authority to issue the Subpart E regulations. Petitioners contend that Title IX was not meant to reach the employment practices of educational
institutions.

A. *The North Haven case.*

The North Haven Board of Education (North Haven) receives federal funds for
its education programs and activities and is therefore subject to Title IX's prohibition of gender discrimination. Since the 1975–1976 school year, North Haven has
devoted between 46.8% and 66.9% of its federal assistance to the salaries of its
employees; this practice is expected to continue.

In January 1978, Elaine Dove, a tenured teacher in the North Haven public school
system, filed a complaint with HEW, alleging that North Haven had violated Title IX

by refusing to rehire her after a one-year maternity leave. In response to this complaint, HEW began to investigate the school board's employment practices and sought from petitioner information concerning its policies on hiring, leaves of absence, seniority, and tenure. Asserting that HEW lacked authority to regulate employment practices under Title IX, North Haven refused to comply with the request.

When HEW then notified petitioner that it was considering administrative enforcement proceedings, North Haven brought this action in the United States District Court for the District of Connecticut. The complaint sought a declaratory judgment that the Subpart E regulations exceeded the authority conferred on HEW by Title IX, and an injunction prohibiting HEW from attempting to terminate the school district's federal funds on the basis of those regulations. The parties filed cross-motions for summary judgment, and on April 24, 1979, the District Court granted North Haven's motion. App. to Pet. for Cert. 51A. Agreeing with petitioner that Title IX was not intended to apply to employment practices, the court invalidated the employment regulations and permanently enjoined HEW from interfering with North Haven's federal funds because of noncompliance with those regulations.

B. *The Trumbull case.*

The Trumbull Board of Education (Trumbull) likewise receives financial support from the Federal Government and must therefore adhere to the requirements of Title IX and appropriate implementing regulations. In October 1977, HEW began investigating a complaint filed by respondent Linda Potz, a former guidance counselor in the Trumbull school district. Potz alleged that Trumbull had discriminated against her on the basis of gender with respect to job assignments, working conditions, and the failure to renew her contract. In September 1978, HEW notified Trumbull that it had violated Title IX and warned that corrective action, including respondent's reinstatement, must be taken.

Trumbull then filed suit in the United States District Court for the District of Connecticut, contending that HEW's Title IX employment regulations were invalid and seeking declaratory and injunctive relief. On the basis of its decision in *North Haven*, the District Court granted Trumbull's motion for summary judgment on May 24, 1979. App. to Pet. for Cert. 76A. The court subsequently amended the judgment, on Trumbull's request, to include injunctive and declaratory relief similar to that ordered in North Haven's case. *Id.*, at 77A, 91A-92A.

C. *The appeal.*

The two cases were consolidated on appeal, and the Court of Appeals for the Second Circuit reversed.

. . .

Because other federal courts have invalidated the employment regulations as unauthorized by Title IX, we granted certiorari to resolve the conflict. 450 U.S. 909, 101 S.Ct. 1345, 67 L.Ed.2d 332 (1981).

III

A

Our starting point in determining the scope of Title IX is, of course, the statutory language. See *Greyhound Corp. v. Mt. Hood Stages, Inc.*, 437 U.S. 322, 330, 98 S.Ct. 2370, 2375, 57 L.Ed.2d 239 (1978). Section 901(a)'s broad directive that "no person" may be discriminated against on the basis of gender appears, on its face, to include employees as well as students. Under that provision, employees, like other "persons," may not be "excluded from participation in," "denied the benefits of," or "subjected to discrimination under" education programs receiving federal financial support.

Employees who directly participate in federal programs or who directly benefit from federal grants, loans, or contracts clearly fall within the first two protective categories described in § 901(a). See *Islesboro School Comm. v. Califano*, 593 F.2d 424, 426 (CA1), cert. denied, 444 U.S. 972, 100 S.Ct. 467, 62 L.Ed.2d 387 (1979). In addition, a female employee who works in a federally funded education program is "subjected to discrimination under" that program if she is paid a lower salary for like work, given less opportunity for promotion, or forced to work under more adverse conditions than are her male colleagues. See *Dougherty Cty. School System v. Harris*, 622 F.2d 735, 737–738 (CA5 1980), cert. pending *sub nom. Bell v. Dougherty Cty. School System*, No. 80-1023.

There is no doubt that "if we are to give [Title IX] the scope that its origins dictate, we must accord it a sweep as broad as its language." *United States v. Price*, 383 U.S. 787, 801, 86 S.Ct. 1152, 1160, 16 L.Ed.2d 267 (1966); see also *Griffin v. Breckenridge*, 403 U.S. 88, 97, 91 S.Ct. 1790, 1795, 29 L.Ed.2d 338 (1971); *Daniel v. Paul*, 395 U.S. 298, 307–308, 89 S.Ct. 1697, 1702, 23 L.Ed.2d 318 (1969); *Jones v. Alfred H. Mayer Co.*, 392 U.S. 409, 437, 88 S.Ct. 2186, 2202, 20 L.Ed.2d 1189 (1968); *Piedmont & Northern R. Co. v. ICC*, 286 U.S. 299, 311–312, 52 S.Ct. 541, 545, 76 L.Ed. 1115 (1932). Because § 901(a) neither expressly nor impliedly excludes employees from its reach, we should interpret the provision as covering and protecting these "persons" unless other considerations counsel to the contrary. After all, Congress easily could have substituted "student" or "beneficiary" for the word "person" if it had wished to restrict the scope of § 901(a).

Petitioners, however, point to the nine exceptions to § 901(a)'s coverage set forth in §§ 901(a)(1)-(9). The exceptions, the school boards argue, are directed only at students, and thus indicate that § 901(a) similarly applies only to students. But the exceptions are not concerned solely with students and student activities: two of them exempt an entire class of institutions—religious and military schools—and are not limited to student-related activities at such schools. See §§ 901(a)(3), (4). Moreover, petitioners' argument rests on an inference that is by no means compelled; in fact, the absence of a specific exclusion for employment among the list of exceptions tends to support the Court of Appeals' conclusion that Title IX's broad protection of "person[s]" does extend to employees of educational institutions. See

Andrus v. Glover Construction Co., 446 U.S. 608, 616–617, 100 S.Ct. 1905, 1910, 64 L. Ed.2d 548 (1980).

Although the statutory language thus seems to favor inclusion of employees, nevertheless, because Title IX does not expressly include or exclude employees from its scope, we turn to the Act's legislative history for evidence as to whether Congress meant somehow to limit the expansive language of §901.

B

. . . .

Petitioners observe that the discussion of this portion of the amendment appears under the heading "A. Prohibition of Sex Discrimination in Federally Funded Education Programs," while the provisions involving Title VII and the Equal Pay Act are summarized under the heading "B. Prohibition of Education-Related Employment Discrimination." But we are not willing to ascribe any particular significance to these headings. The Title VII and Equal Pay Act portions of the Bayh amendment are more narrowly focused on employment discrimination than is the general ban on gender discrimination, and the headings reflect that difference. . . .

. . . .

This focus on the history of Title VI—urged by petitioners and adopted by the dissent—is misplaced. It is Congress' intention in 1972, not in 1964, that is of significance in interpreting Title IX. See *Cannon v. University of Chicago*, 441 U.S. 677, 710–711, 99 S.Ct. 1946, 1964–1965, 60 L.Ed.2d 560 (1979). The meaning and applicability of Title VI are useful guides in construing Title IX, therefore, only to the extent that the language and history of Title IX do not suggest a contrary interpretation. Moreover, whether §604 clarified or altered the scope of Title VI, it is apparent that §601 alone was not considered adequate to exclude employees from the statute's coverage. If Congress had intended that Title IX have the same reach as Title VI, therefore, we assume that it would have enacted counterparts to both §601 and §604. For although two statutes may be similar in language and objective, we must not fail to give effect to the differences between them. See *Lorillard v. Pons*, 434 U.S. 575, 584–585, 98 S.Ct. 866, 872, 55 L.Ed.2d 40 (1978).

In our view, the legislative history thus corroborates our reading of the statutory language and verifies the Court of Appeals' conclusion that employment discrimination comes within the prohibition of Title IX.

. . . .

IV

Although we agree with the Second Circuit's conclusion that Title IX proscribes employment discrimination in federally funded education programs, we find that the Court of Appeals paid insufficient attention to the "program-specific" nature of the statute. The court acknowledged that, under §902, termination of funds "shall be limited in its effect to the particular program, or part thereof, in which . . .

noncompliance has been . . . found," but implied that the Department's authority to issue regulations is considerably broader. See 629 F.2d, at 785–786. We disagree.

It is not only Title IX's funding termination provision that is program-specific. The portion of §902 authorizing the issuance of implementing regulations also provides:

> "Each Federal department and agency which is empowered to extend Federal financial assistance to any education program or activity . . . is authorized and directed to effectuate the provisions of section 901 *with respect to such program or activity* by issuing rules, regulations, or orders of general applicability which shall be consistent with achievement of the objectives of the statute authorizing the financial assistance in connection with which the action is taken." (Emphasis added.)

Certainly, it makes little sense to interpret the statute, as respondents urge, to authorize an agency to promulgate rules that it cannot enforce. And §901(a) itself has a similar program-specific focus: it forbids gender discrimination "under any education program or activity receiving Federal financial assistance . . . ."

Title IX's legislative history corroborates its general program-specificity. Congress failed to adopt proposals that would have prohibited *all* discriminatory practices of an institution that receives federal funds. See 117 Cong.Rec. 30155–30157, 30408 (1971) (Sen. Bayh's 1971 amendment); H.R. 5191, 92d Cong., 1st Sess., §1001(b) (1971) (administration proposal); 1970 Hearings 690–691 (Dept. of Justice's proposed alternative to §805 of H.R. 16098); cf. Title IX, §904 (proscribing discrimination against the blind by a recipient of federal assistance with no program-specific limitation). In contrast, Senator Bayh indicated that his 1972 amendment, which in large part was ultimately adopted, was program-specific. See 118 Cong.Rec. 5807 (1972) (observing that the amendment "prohibit[s] discrimination on the basis of sex in federally funded education programs," and that "[t]he effect of termination of funds is limited to the particular entity and program in which such noncompliance has been found . . ."); cf. 117 Cong.Rec. 39256 (1971) (colloquies between Reps. Green and Waggoner and between Reps. Green and Steiger). Finally, we note that language in §§601 and 602 of Title VI, virtually identical to that in §§901 and 902 and on which Title IX was modeled, has been interpreted as being program-specific. See *Board of Public Instruction v. Finch*, 414 F.2d 1068 (CA5 1969). We conclude, then, that an agency's authority under Title IX both to promulgate regulations and to terminate funds is subject to the program-specific limitation of §§901 and 902. Cf. *Cannon v. University of Chicago*, 441 U.S., at 690–693, 99 S.Ct., at 1954–1955.

Examining the employment regulations with this restriction in mind, we nevertheless reject petitioners' contention that the regulations are facially invalid. Although their import is by no means unambiguous, we do not view them as inconsistent with Title IX's program-specific character. The employment regulations do speak in general terms of an educational institution's employment practices, but they are limited by the provision that states their general purpose: "to effectuate title IX . . . [,] which is designed to eliminate (with certain exceptions) discrimination on the basis of sex in any education *program or activity* receiving Federal financial assistance . . . ." 34 CFR § 106.1 (1980) (emphasis added).

HEW's comments accompanying publication of its final Title IX regulations confirm our view that Subpart E is consistent with the Act's program-specificity. The Department recognized that § 902 limited its authority to terminate funds to particular programs that were found to have violated Title IX, and it continued:

> "Therefore, an education program or activity or part thereof operated by a recipient of Federal financial assistance administered by the Department will be subject to the requirements of this regulation if it receives or benefits from such assistance. This interpretation is consistent with the only case specifically ruling on the language contained in title VI, which holds that Federal funds may be terminated under title VI upon a finding that they 'are infected by a discriminatory environment . . .' *Board of Public Instruction of Taylor County, Florida v. Finch*, 414 F.2d 1068, 1078–79 (5th Cir. 1969)." 40 Fed.Reg. 24128 (1975).

By expressly adopting the Fifth Circuit opinion construing Title VI as program-specific, HEW apparently indicated its intent that the Title IX regulations be interpreted in like fashion. So read, the regulations conform with the limitations Congress enacted in §§ 901 and 902.

Whether termination of petitioners' federal funds is permissible under Title IX is a question that must be answered by the District Court in the first instance. Similarly, we do not undertake to define "program" in this opinion. Neither of the cases before us advanced beyond a motion for summary judgment, and the record therefore does not reflect whether petitioners' employment practices actually discriminated on the basis of gender or whether any such discrimination comes within the prohibition of Title IX. Neither school board opposed HEW's investigation into its employment practices on the grounds that the complaining employees' salaries were not funded by federal money, that the employees did not work in an education program that received federal assistance, or that the discrimination they allegedly suffered did not affect a federally funded program. Instead, petitioners disputed the Department's authority to regulate any employment practices whatsoever, and the District Court adopted that view, which we find to be error. Accordingly, we affirm the judgment of the Court of Appeals but remand the case for further proceedings consistent with this opinion.

It is so ordered.

Notes and Questions

1. The dissent disagreed with the majority, arguing that Title IX could not be interpreted to extend as far and as broadly as the majority's interpretation:

> A natural reading of these words would limit the statute's scope to discrimination against those who are enrolled in, or who are denied the benefits of,

programs or activities receiving federal funding. It tortures the language chosen by Congress to conclude that not only teachers and administrators, but also secretaries and janitors, who are discriminated against on the basis of sex in employment, are thereby (i) denied *participation* in a program or activity; (ii) denied the *benefits* of a program or activity; or (iii) subject to discrimination *under* an education program or activity. Moreover, Congress made no reference whatever to employers or employees in Title IX, in sharp contrast to quite explicit language in other statutes regulating employment practices.

How do you assess the majority's interpretation?

2. Why did the Court determine the regulations at issue not to be inconsistent with the "program specific character of Title IX"? What policy considerations can you formulate to support this determination?

3. Consider the facts alleged in the complaint below:

Complaint

Jane Doe, Individually and as Mother and Next Friend of John Doe, a Minor, By: /s/ Katrina M. Taraska, one of her attorneys, Katrina M. Taraska, M. Michael Waters, Vonachen, Lawless, Trager & Slevin, 111 Fulton, Suite 111, Peoria, IL 61602, Telephone: 309/111-1111, Facsimile: 309/111-1111.

JURISDICTION AND VENUE

1. That this Court has jurisdiction of Counts I, II and III pursuant to 28 U.S.C. 1331 and Counts IV, V and VI pursuant to 28 U.S.C. 1367.

2. That the action properly lies in this district pursuant to 28 U.S.C. Section 1391(b), as the events giving rise to the claim occurred in Brimfield, Illinois, which is encompassed within the particular judicial district.

THE PARTIES

3. The Plaintiffs, JOHN DOE (a minor), and his mother, JANE DOE, are citizens of the United States and the State of Illinois.

4. The Defendant, BRIMFIELD GRADE SCHOOL and BRIMFIELD SCHOOL DISTRICT #309 (hereinafter "BRIMFIELD"), are a public elementary school and a public school district located in Brimfield, Illinois.

5. The Defendant, ALLEN ABLE, a minor, was at all relevant times a student at BRIMFIELD GRADE SCHOOL.

6. The Defendant, ABBY ABLE, was at all times the parent of ALLEN ABLE.

7. The Defendant, BRIAN BAKER, a minor, was at all relevant times a student at BRIMFIELD GRADE SCHOOL.

8. The Defendants, BETTY BAKER and BARRY BAKER, were at all times the parents of BRIAN BAKER.

9. The Defendant, CONNER CHARLIE, a minor, was at all relevant times a student at BRIMFIELD GRADE

10. The Defendants, CONNIE CHARLIE and CHESTER CHARLIE, were at all times the parents of CONNER CHARLIE.

11. The Defendant, DAVID DOG, a minor, was at all relevant times a student at BRIMFIELD GRADE SCHOOL.

12. The Defendant, DONALD DOG, was at all times the parent of DAVID DOG.

13. The Defendant, ELWARD EASY, a minor, was at all relevant times a student at BRIMFIELD GRADE SCHOOL.

14. The Defendants, EDWARD EASY and ELLEN EASY, were at all times the parents of ELWARD EASY.

15. The Defendant, FRANK FOX, a minor, was at all relevant times a student at BRIMFIELD GRADE SCHOOL.

16. The Defendant, FRANCINE FOX, was at all times the parent of FRANK FOX.

COUNT I.
SEXUAL HARASSMENT AND RETALIATION IN VIOLATION OF TITLE IX
(Title IX of the Education Amendment of 1972)
(*John Doe v. Brimfield Grade School and Brimfield School District #309*)

NOW COMES the Plaintiff, JANE DOE, Individually and as Mother and Next Friend of JOHN DOE, a minor, by KATRINA M. TARASKA and M. MICHAEL WATERS, and the law firm of VONACHEN, LAWLESS, TRAGER & SLEVIN, and for her Complaint against the various Defendants, states as follows:

1. JOHN DOE (hereinafter "JOHN") is a minor whose date of birth is XX/XX/1992, and he brings this action by JANE DOE (hereinafter "JANE"), his Mother and Next Friend.

2. That at the time of the events described herein, related to the allegations of this Complaint, BRIMFIELD was the recipient of Federal funds for the school's operations, including but not limited to, educational programs and activities.

3. That at all relevant times herein DENNIS McNAMARA (hereinafter "McNAMARA") was the school Superintendent and Principal of BRIMFIELD.

4. That JOHN was at all relevant times referred to herein a student at BRIMFIELD.

5. That commencing on and prior to November 2004, and occurring thereafter on a regular and consistent basis, JOHN was subjected to physical and verbal misconduct of a sexual nature, by other male students at BRIMFIELD.

6. That the above-described sexual misconduct consisted predominantly of grabbing, twisting, and hitting JOHN's testicles.

7. That the above-described sexual misconduct to which the Plaintiff was subjected, was at all times unwelcome.

8. That said sexual and physical misconduct, to which JOHN was repeatedly subjected, was sufficiently severe so as to create a hostile and abusive educational environment, thus denying JOHN equal access to his education.

9. That the above described sexual misconduct, to which JOHN was subjected to was committed by the following students: ALLAN ABLE, BRIAN BAKER, CONNER CHARLIE, DAVID DOG, ELWARD EASY and FRANK FOX.

10. That JOHN repeatedly objected to said misconduct verbally and in his physical response to said misconduct.

11. That as a direct and proximate cause of the repeated trauma to JOHN'S testicles, this minor child experienced pain, swelling, and further aggravation to a preexisting condition of left testicular varicocele in addition to significant mental and emotional distress.

Notice of Sexual Harassment to School Officials

12. That in November 2004, while at school, JOHN spoke to McNAMARA about the ongoing sexual harassment.

13. That during the conversation between JOHN and McNAMARA, JOHN advised McNAMARA that he was being repeatedly hit in the testicles.

14. That further, during the conversation between JOHN and McNAMARA, JOHN advised McNAMARA that the above described physical misconduct was being perpetuated by several male students, including, DAVID DOG, who was in JOHN'S Physical Education class.

15. That in response to the information provided by JOHN to McNAMARA, McNAMARA directed JOHN to speak to JOHN'S Physical Education teacher, MR. FARQUER ("FARQUER").

16. That at no time during the conversation between JOHN and McNAMARA, or any time thereafter, did McNAMARA verify that JOHN or his parents were provided a sexual harassment policy promulgated by the school.

17. That at no time during the conversation between JOHN and McNAMARA, or any time thereafter, did McNAMARA advise JOHN of any existing Title IX Grievance Procedures adopted and published by BRIMFIELD GRADE SCHOOL, as mandated by Federal Regulation.

18. That at no time during the conversation between JOHN and McNAMARA, or any time thereafter, did McNAMARA request that JOHN provide the school with further and more specific details of the harassment described by JOHN, in an effort to obtain the specific identity of all of the male students involved in the alleged misconduct, in order to prevent further harassment.

19. That at no time during the conversation between JOHN and McNAMARA, or any time thereafter, did McNAMARA advise JOHN of any existing policy for JOHN to file a Complaint for such misconduct.

20. That at no time during the conversation between JOHN and McNAMARA, or any time thereafter, did McNAMARA identify for JOHN, or arrange a meeting with, the school's Nondiscrimination Coordinator, whose responsibilities included the investigation of Complaints communicated to the school which allege potential discrimination based upon sexual harassment, pursuant to Federal Regulation.

21. That said sexual and physical misconduct, to which JOHN was repeatedly subjected, was sufficiently severe so as to create a hostile and abusive educational environment, thus denying JOHN equal access to his education.

22. That the above described sexual misconduct, to which JOHN was subjected to was committed by the following students: ALLEN ABLE, BRIAN BAKER, CONNER CHARLIE, DAVID DOG, ELWARD EASY and FRANK FOX.

23. That JOHN repeatedly objected to said misconduct verbally and in his physical response to said misconduct.

24. That as a direct and proximate cause of the repeated trauma to JOHN'S testicles, this minor child experienced pain, swelling, and further aggravation to a preexisting condition of left testicular varicocele in addition to significant mental and emotional distress.

. . . .

Note

How do the facts alleged above support the standard enunciated in *Franklin vs. Gwinnett County Public Schools* and *Gebser vs. Lago Vista Independent School District* below?

Franklin v. Gwinnett County Public Schools
503 U.S. 60 (1992)

JUSTICE WHITE delivered the opinion of the Court.

This case presents the question whether the implied right of action under Title IX of the Education Amendments of 1972, 20 U.S.C. §§ 1681–1688 (Title IX), which this Court recognized in *Cannon v. University of Chicago,* 441 U.S. 677, 99 S.Ct. 1946, 60 L.Ed.2d 560 (1979), supports a claim for monetary damages.

I

Petitioner Christine Franklin was a student at North Gwinnett High School in Gwinnett County, Georgia, between September 1985 and August 1989. Respondent Gwinnett County School District operates the high school and receives federal funds. According to the complaint filed on December 29, 1988, in the United States District Court for the Northern District of Georgia, Franklin was subjected to continual sexual harassment beginning in the autumn of her tenth-grade year (1986) from Andrew Hill, a sports coach and teacher employed by the district. Among other allegations, Franklin avers that Hill engaged her in sexually oriented conversations in which he asked about her sexual experiences with her boyfriend and whether she would consider having sexual intercourse with an older man, Complaint ¶ 10; First Amended Complaint, Exh. A, p. 3; that Hill forcibly kissed her on the mouth in the school parking lot, Complaint ¶ 17; that he telephoned her at her home and asked if she would meet him socially, Complaint ¶ 21; First Amended Complaint, Exh. A, pp. 4–5; and that, on three occasions in her junior year, Hill interrupted a class, requested that the teacher excuse Franklin, and took her to a private office where he subjected her to coercive intercourse,. . . . The complaint further alleges that though they became aware of and investigated Hill's sexual harassment of Franklin and other female students, teachers and administrators took no action to halt it and discouraged Franklin from pressing charges against Hill. Complaint ¶¶ 23, 24, 35. On April 14, 1988, Hill resigned on the condition that all matters pending against him be dropped. Complaint ¶¶ 36, 37. The school thereupon closed its investigation. Complaint ¶ 37.

In this action, the District Court dismissed the complaint on the ground that Title IX does not authorize an award of damages. The Court of Appeals affirmed. 911 F.2d 617 (CA11 1990). . .

Because this opinion conflicts with a decision of the Court of Appeals for the Third Circuit, see *Pfeiffer v. Marion Center Area School Dist.,* 917 F.2d 779, 787–789 (1990), we granted certiorari, 501 U.S. 1204, 111 S.Ct. 2795, 115 L.Ed.2d 969 (1991). We reverse.

II

In *Cannon v. University of Chicago,* 441 U.S. 677, 99 S.Ct. 1946, 60 L.Ed.2d 560 (1979), the Court held that Title IX is enforceable through an implied right of action. We have no occasion here to reconsider that decision. Rather, in this case we must decide what remedies are available in a suit brought pursuant to this implied right. As we have often stated, the question of what remedies are available under a statute that provides a private right of action is "analytically distinct" from the issue of whether such a right exists in the first place. *Davis v. Passman,* 442 U.S. 228, 239, 99 S.Ct. 2264, 2274, 60 L.Ed.2d 846 (1979). Thus, although we examine the text and history of a statute to determine whether Congress intended to create a right of action, *Touche Ross & Co. v. Redington,* 442 U.S. 560, 575–576, 99 S.Ct. 2479, 2489, 61 L.Ed.2d 82 (1979), we presume the availability of all appropriate remedies unless Congress has expressly indicated otherwise. *Davis, supra,* 442 U.S., at 246–247, 99 S. Ct., at 2277–2278. This principle has deep roots in our jurisprudence.

A

"[W]here legal rights have been invaded, and a federal statute provides for a general right to sue for such invasion, federal courts may use any available remedy to make good the wrong done." *Bell v. Hood,* 327 U.S. 678, 684, 66 S.Ct. 773, 777, 90 L. Ed. 939 (1946). The Court explained this longstanding rule as jurisdictional and upheld the exercise of the federal courts' power to award appropriate relief so long as a cause of action existed under the Constitution or laws of the United States. *Ibid.*

The *Bell* Court's reliance on this rule was hardly revolutionary. From the earliest years of the Republic, the Court has recognized the power of the Judiciary to award appropriate remedies to redress injuries actionable in federal court, although it did not always distinguish clearly between a right to bring suit and a remedy available under such a right. In *Marbury v. Madison,* 5 U.S. (1 Cranch) 137, 163, 2 L.Ed. 60 (1803), for example, Chief Justice Marshall observed that our Government "has been emphatically termed a government of laws, and not of men. It will certainly cease to deserve this high appellation, if the laws furnish no remedy for the violation of a vested legal right." This principle originated in the English common law, and Blackstone described it as "a general and indisputable rule, that where there is a legal right, there is also a legal remedy, by suit or action at law, whenever that right is invaded." 3 W. Blackstone, Commentaries 23 (1783). See also *Ashby v. White,* 1 Salk. 19, 21, 87 Eng.Rep. 808, 816 (Q.B.1702) ("If a statute gives a right, the common law will give a remedy to maintain that right . . .").

In *Kendall v. United States ex rel. Stokes,* 37 U.S. (12 Pet.) 524, 9 L.Ed. 1181 (1838), the Court applied these principles to an Act of Congress that accorded a right of action in mail carriers to sue for adjustment and settlement of certain claims for extra services but which did not specify the precise remedy available to the carriers. After surveying possible remedies, which included an action against the Postmaster General for monetary damages, the Court held that the carriers were entitled to a writ of mandamus compelling payment under the terms of the statute. "It cannot be denied but that congress had the power to command that act to be done," the Court stated; "and the power to enforce the performance of the act must rest somewhere, or it will present a case which has often been said to involve a monstrous absurdity in a well-organized government, that there should be no remedy, although a clear and undeniable right should be shown to exist. And if the remedy cannot be applied by the circuit court of this district, it exists nowhere." *Id.,* at 624. *Dooley v. United States,* 182 U.S. 222, 229, 21 S.Ct. 762, 764, 45 L.Ed. 1074 (1901), also restated "the principle that a liability created by statute without a remedy may be enforced by a common-law action."

The Court relied upon this traditional presumption again after passage of the Federal Safety Appliance Act of 1893, ch. 196, 27 Stat. 531. In *Texas & Pacific R. Co. v. Rigsby,* 241 U.S. 33, 36 S.Ct. 482, 60 L.Ed. 874 (1916), the Court first had to determine whether the Act supported an implied right of action. After answering that question in the affirmative, the Court then upheld a claim for monetary damages. . . .

B

Respondents and the United States as *amicus curiae,* however, maintain that whatever the traditional presumption may have been when the Court decided *Bell v. Hood,* it has disappeared in succeeding decades. We do not agree. In *J.I. Case Co. v. Borak,* 377 U.S. 426, 84 S.Ct. 1555, 12 L.Ed.2d 423 (1964), the Court adhered to the general rule that all appropriate relief is available in an action brought to vindicate a federal right when Congress has given no indication of its purpose with respect to remedies. Relying on *Bell v. Hood,* the *Borak* Court specifically rejected an argument that a court's remedial power to redress violations of the Securities Exchange Act of 1934 was limited to a declaratory judgment. 377 U.S., at 433–434, 84 S.Ct., at 1560. The Court concluded that the federal courts "have the power to grant all necessary remedial relief" for violations of the Act. *Id.,* at 435, 84 S.Ct., at 1561. As Justice Clark's opinion for the Court observed, this holding closely followed the reasoning of a similar case brought under the Securities Act of 1933, in which the Court had stated:

> "'The power *to enforce* implies the power to make effective the right of recovery afforded by the Act. And the power to make the right of recovery effective implies the power to utilize any of the procedures or actions normally available to the litigant according to the exigencies of the particular case.'" *Id.,* at 433–434, 84 S.Ct., at 1560 (quoting *Deckert v. Independence Shares Corp.,* 311 U.S. 282, 288, 61 S.Ct. 229, 233, 85 L.Ed. 189 (1940)).

That a statute does not authorize the remedy at issue "in so many words is no more significant than the fact that it does not in terms authorize execution to issue on a judgment." *Id.,* at 288, 61 S.Ct., at 233. Subsequent cases have been true to this position. See, *e.g., Sullivan v. Little Hunting Park, Inc.,* 396 U.S. 229, 239, 90 S.Ct. 400, 405, 24 L.Ed.2d 386 (1969), stating that the "existence of a statutory right implies the existence of all necessary and appropriate remedies"; *Carey v. Piphus,* 435 U.S. 247, 255, 98 S.Ct. 1042, 1048, 55 L.Ed.2d 252 (1978), upholding damages remedy under Rev.Stat. § 1979, 42 U.S.C. § 1983, even though the enacting Congress had not specifically provided such relief.

. . . Whether Congress may limit the class of persons who have a right of action under Title IX is irrelevant to the issue in this lawsuit. To reiterate, "the question whether a litigant has a 'cause of action' is analytically distinct and prior to the question of what relief, if any, a litigant may be entitled to receive." *Id.,* at 239, 99 S. Ct., at 2274. *Davis,* therefore, did nothing to interrupt the long line of cases in which the Court has held that if a right of action exists to enforce a federal right and Congress is silent on the question of remedies, a federal court may order any appropriate relief. See *id.,* at 247, n. 26, 99 S.Ct., at 2278, n. 26 (contrasting *Brown v. GSA,* 425 U.S. 820, 96 S.Ct. 1961, 48 L.Ed.2d 402 (1976)).

Contrary to arguments by respondents and the United States that *Guardians Assn. v. Civil Service Comm'n of New York City,* 463 U.S. 582, 103 S.Ct. 3221, 77 L. Ed.2d 866 (1983), and *Consolidated Rail Corporation v. Darrone,* 465 U.S. 624, 104 S. Ct. 1248, 79 L.Ed.2d 568 (1984), eroded this traditional presumption, those cases in fact support it. Though the multiple opinions in *Guardians* suggest the difficulty of inferring the common ground among the Justices in that case, a clear majority expressed the view that damages were available under Title VI in an action seeking remedies for an intentional violation, and no Justice challenged the traditional presumption in favor of a federal court's power to award appropriate relief in a cognizable cause of action . . .

The general rule, therefore, is that absent clear direction to the contrary by Congress, the federal courts have the power to award any appropriate relief in a cognizable cause of action brought pursuant to a federal statute.

III

We now address whether Congress intended to limit application of this general principle in the enforcement of Title IX. See *Bush v. Lucas,* 462 U.S. 367, 378, 103 S. Ct. 2404, 2411–2412, 76 L.Ed.2d 648 (1983); *Wyandotte Transportation Co. v. United States,* 389 U.S. 191, 200, 88 S.Ct. 379, 385, 19 L.Ed.2d 407 (1967). Because the cause of action was inferred by the Court in *Cannon,* the usual recourse to statutory text and legislative history in the period prior to that decision necessarily will not enlighten our analysis. Respondents and the United States fundamentally misunderstand the nature of the inquiry, therefore, by needlessly dedicating large portions of their briefs to discussions of how the text and legislative intent behind Title IX are "silent" on the issue of available remedies. Since the Court in *Cannon* concluded that this statute supported no express right of action, it is hardly surprising that Congress also said nothing about the applicable remedies for an implied right of action.

During the period prior to the decision in *Cannon,* the inquiry in any event is *not* "'basically a matter of statutory construction,'" as the United States asserts. Brief for United States as *Amicus Curiae* 8 (quoting *Transamerica Mortgage Advisors, Inc. v. Lewis,* 444 U.S. 11, 15, 100 S.Ct. 242, 245, 62 L.Ed.2d 146 (1979)). Rather, in determining Congress' intent to limit application of the traditional presumption in favor of all appropriate relief, we evaluate the state of the law when the Legislature passed Title IX. Cf. *Merrill Lynch, Pierce, Fenner & Smith, Inc. v. Curran,* 456 U.S. 353, 378, 102 S.Ct. 1825, 1839, 72 L.Ed.2d 182 (1982). In the years before and after Congress enacted this statute, the Court "follow[ed] a common-law tradition [and] regarded the denial of a remedy as the exception rather than the rule." *Id.,* at 375, 102 S.Ct., at 1837 (footnote omitted). As we outlined in Part II, this has been the prevailing presumption in our federal courts since at least the early 19th century. In *Cannon,* the majority upheld an implied right of action in part because in the decade immediately preceding enactment of Title IX in 1972, this Court had found implied rights of action in six cases. In three of those cases, the Court had approved a damages remedy. See, *e.g., J.I. Case Co.,* 377 U.S., at 433, 84 S.Ct., at 1560; *Wyandotte Transportation Co., supra,* 389 U.S., at 207, 88 S.Ct., at 389; *Sullivan v. Little Hunting Park, Inc.,* 396 U.S. 229, 90 S.Ct. 400, 24 L.Ed.2d 386 (1969). Wholly apart from the wisdom of the *Cannon* holding, therefore, the same contextual approach used to justify an implied right of action more than amply demonstrates the lack of any legislative intent to abandon the traditional presumption in favor of all available remedies.

In the years *after* the announcement of *Cannon,* on the other hand, a more traditional method of statutory analysis is possible, because Congress was legislating with full cognizance of that decision. Our reading of the two amendments to Title IX enacted after *Cannon* leads us to conclude that Congress did not intend to limit the remedies available in a suit brought under Title IX. In the Rehabilitation Act Amendments of 1986, 100 Stat. 1845, 42 U.S.C. § 2000d-7, Congress abrogated the States' Eleventh Amendment immunity under Title IX, Title VI, § 504 of the Rehabilitation Act of 1973, and the Age Discrimination Act of 1975. This statute cannot be read except as a validation of *Cannon*'s holding. A subsection of the 1986 law provides that in a suit against a State, "remedies (including remedies both at law and in equity) are available for such a violation to the same extent as such remedies are available for such a violation in the suit against any public or private entity other than a State." 42 U.S.C. § 2000d-7(a)(2). While it is true that this saving clause says nothing about the nature of those other available remedies, cf. *Milwaukee v. Illinois,* 451 U.S. 304, 329, n. 22, 101 S.Ct. 1784, 1798–1799, n. 22, 68 L.Ed.2d 114 (1981), absent any contrary indication in the text or history of the statute, we presume Congress enacted this statute with the prevailing traditional rule in mind.

In addition to the Rehabilitation Act Amendments of 1986, Congress also enacted the Civil Rights Restoration Act of 1987, Pub.L. 100-259, 102 Stat. 28. Without in any way altering the existing rights of action and the corresponding remedies permissible under Title IX, Title VI, § 504 of the Rehabilitation Act, and the Age Discrimination Act, Congress broadened the coverage of these antidiscrimination provisions in this legislation. In seeking to correct what it considered to be an unacceptable decision on our part in *Grove City College v. Bell,* 465 U.S. 555, 104 S.Ct. 1211, 79 L.Ed.2d 516 (1984), Congress made no effort to restrict the right of action recognized in *Cannon* and ratified in the 1986 Act or to alter the traditional presumption in favor of any appropriate relief for violation of a federal right. We cannot say, therefore, that Congress has limited the remedies available to a complainant in a suit brought under Title IX.

IV

Respondents and the United States nevertheless suggest three reasons why we should not apply the traditional presumption in favor of appropriate relief in this case.

. . . .

B

Next, consistent with the Court of Appeals' reasoning, respondents and the United States contend that the normal presumption in favor of all appropriate remedies should not apply because Title IX was enacted pursuant to Congress' Spending Clause power. In *Pennhurst State School and Hospital v. Halderman,* 451 U.S. 1, 28–29, 101 S.Ct. 1531, 1545–1546, 67 L.Ed.2d 694 (1981), the Court observed that remedies were limited under such Spending Clause statutes when the alleged violation was *unintentional.* Respondents and the United States maintain that this presumption should apply equally to *intentional* violations. We disagree. The point of not permitting monetary damages for an unintentional violation is that the receiving entity of federal funds lacks notice that it will be liable for a monetary award. See *id.,* at 17, 101 S.Ct., at 1540. This notice problem does not arise in a case such as this, in which intentional discrimination is alleged. Unquestionably, Title IX placed on the Gwinnett County Public Schools the duty not to discriminate on the basis of sex, and "when a supervisor sexually harasses a subordinate because of the subordinate's sex, that supervisor 'discriminate[s]' on the basis of sex." *Meritor Sav. Bank, FSB v. Vinson,* 477 U.S. 57, 64, 106 S.Ct. 2399, 2404, 91 L.Ed.2d 49 (1986). We believe the same rule should apply when a teacher sexually harasses and abuses a student. Congress surely did not intend for federal moneys to be expended to support the intentional actions it sought by statute to proscribe. Moreover, the notion that Spending Clause statutes do not authorize monetary awards for intentional violations is belied by our unanimous holding in *Darrone.* See 465 U.S., at 628, 104 S. Ct., at 1251. Respondents and the United States characterize the back pay remedy in *Darrone* as equitable relief, but this description is irrelevant to their underlying objection: that application of the traditional rule in this case will require state entities to pay monetary awards out of their treasuries for intentional violations of federal statutes.

C

Finally, the United States asserts that the remedies permissible under Title IX should nevertheless be limited to backpay and prospective relief. In addition to diverging from our traditional approach to deciding what remedies are available for violation of a federal right, this position conflicts with sound logic. First, both remedies are equitable in nature, and it is axiomatic that a court should determine the adequacy of a remedy in law before resorting to equitable relief. Under the ordinary convention, the proper inquiry would be whether monetary damages provided an adequate remedy, and if not, whether equitable relief would be appropriate. *Whitehead v. Shattuck,* 138 U.S. 146, 150, 11 S.Ct. 276, 276, 34 L.Ed. 873 (1891). See generally C. McCormick, Damages 1 (1935). Moreover, in this case the equitable remedies suggested by respondent and the Federal Government are clearly inadequate. Backpay does nothing for petitioner, because she was a student when the alleged discrimination occurred. Similarly, because Hill—the person she claims subjected her to sexual harassment—no longer teaches at the school and she herself no longer attends a school in the Gwinnett system, prospective relief accords her no remedy at all. The Government's answer that administrative action helps other similarly situated students in effect acknowledges that its approach would leave petitioner remediless.

V

In sum, we conclude that a damages remedy is available for an action brought to enforce Title IX. The judgment of the Court of Appeals, therefore, is reversed, and the case is remanded for further proceedings consistent with this opinion.

So ordered.

Note

Consider the case of Gavin Grimm, challenging Virginia's bathroom laws, and potential legal challenges to Mississippi's HB 1523 regarding the expansion of the meaning of gender discrimination to include protection based on gender identity under Title IX. Consider the agencies' role in implementing these provisions. As seen when we discussed Title VII, statutes like Title IX and Title VII are enforced by designated executive agencies. In the case of Title IX, the Department of Justice and the Department of Education promulgate regulations to ensure that grant recipients comply with the statute. *See* Catherine E. Lhamon & Vanita Gupta, *Dear Colleague Letter*, U.S. Dep't of Educ., Office for Civil Rights 1 (Jan. 7, 2015), https://www2.ed.gov/about/offices/list/ocr/letters/colleague-el-201501.pdf; Catherine E. Lhamon, *Dear Colleague Letter*, U.S. Dep't of Educ., Office for Civil Rights 1 (Apr. 24, 2015), https://www2.ed.gov/about/offices/list/ocr/letters/ colleague-201504-title-ix-coordinators.pdf;Russlynn Ali, *Dear Colleague Letter*, U.S. Dep't of Educ., Office for Civil Rights 1 (Apr. 4, 2011), https://www2.ed.gov /about/offices/list/ocr/letters/colleague-201104.pdf; *see also* Sandra Battle & T.E. Wheeler, II, *Dear Colleague* Letter, U.S. Dep't of Educ., Office for Civil Rights 1 (Feb. 22, 2017), https://www2.ed.gov/about /offices/list/ocr/letters/colleague-201702-title-ix.pdf. What are the agencies' proper role in promoting and enforcing the goals of Title IX? Should a government agency join to limit the scope of an anti-discrimination statute rather than to expand it?

See below for the Court's interpretation of school districts liability regarding student-teacher harassment and student-on-student harassment. Sexual harassment by teachers and adults in the school system, as well as students bullying and harassing other students, are major and ongoing problems in the K-12 context. Vulnerable students and those who do not conform to gender norms are the most at risk in that context. In light of this, what role should school districts play in preventing harm to these students? Should school districts be held responsible for violations by faculty, staff and other students? What responsibility do school systems and agencies enforcing Title IX bear regarding a duty to create regulations and policies that are designed to change cultural attitudes around gender and harrassment?

Gebser v. Lago Vista Independent School District

524 U.S. 274 (1998)

Justice O'Connor delivered the opinion of the Court.

The question in this case is when a school district may be held liable in damages in an implied right of action under Title IX of the Education Amendments of 1972, 86 Stat. 373, as amended, 20 U.S.C. § 1681 *et seq.* (Title IX), for the sexual harassment of a student by one of the district's teachers. We conclude that damages may not be recovered in those circumstances unless an official of the school district who at a minimum has authority to institute corrective measures on the district's behalf has actual notice of, and is deliberately indifferent to, the teacher's misconduct.

I

In the spring of 1991, when petitioner Alida Star Gebser was an eighth-grade student at a middle school in respondent Lago Vista Independent School District (Lago Vista), she joined a high school book discussion group led by Frank Waldrop, a teacher at Lago Vista's high school. Lago Vista received federal funds at all pertinent times. During the book discussion sessions, Waldrop often made sexually suggestive comments to the students. Gebser entered high school in the fall and was assigned to classes taught by Waldrop in both semesters. Waldrop continued to make inappropriate remarks to the students, and he began to direct more of his suggestive comments toward Gebser, including during the substantial amount of time that the two were alone in his classroom. He initiated sexual contact with Gebser in the spring, when, while visiting her home ostensibly to give her a book, he kissed and fondled her. The two had sexual intercourse on a number of occasions during the remainder of the school year. Their relationship continued through the summer and into the following school year, and they often had intercourse during class time, although never on school property.

Gebser did not report the relationship to school officials, testifying that while she realized Waldrop's conduct was improper, she was uncertain how to react and she wanted to continue having him as a teacher. In October 1992, the parents of two other students complained to the high school principal about Waldrop's comments in class. The principal arranged a meeting, at which, according to the principal, Waldrop indicated that he did not believe he had made offensive remarks but apologized to the parents and said it would not happen again. The principal also advised Waldrop to be careful about his classroom comments and told the school guidance counselor about the meeting, but he did not report the parents' complaint to Lago Vista's superintendent, who was the district's Title IX coordinator. A couple of months later, in January 1993, a police officer discovered Waldrop and Gebser engaging in sexual intercourse and arrested Waldrop. Lago Vista terminated his employment, and subsequently, the Texas Education Agency revoked his teaching license. During this time, the district had not promulgated or distributed an official grievance procedure for lodging sexual harassment complaints; nor had it issued a formal anti-harassment policy.

Gebser and her mother filed suit against Lago Vista and Waldrop in state court in November 1993, raising claims against the school district under Title IX, Rev. Stat. § 1979, 42 U.S.C. § 1983, and state negligence law, and claims against Waldrop primarily under state law. They sought compensatory and punitive damages from both defendants. After the case was removed, the United States District Court for the Western District of Texas granted summary judgment in favor of Lago Vista on all claims, and remanded the allegations against Waldrop to state court. In rejecting the Title IX claim against the school district, the court reasoned that the statute "was enacted to counter *policies* of discrimination . . . in federally funded education programs," and that "[o]nly if school administrators have some type of notice of the gender discrimination and fail to respond in good faith can the discrimination be interpreted as a *policy* of the school district." App. to Pet. for Cert. 6a-7a. Here, the court determined, the parents' complaint to the principal concerning Waldrop's comments in class was the only one Lago Vista had received about Waldrop, and that evidence was inadequate to raise a genuine issue on whether the school district had actual or constructive notice that Waldrop was involved in a sexual relationship with a student.

Petitioners appealed only on the Title IX claim. The Court of Appeals for the Fifth Circuit affirmed, *Doe v. Lago Vista Independent School Dist.*, 106 F.3d 1223 (1997), relying in large part on two of its recent decisions, *Rosa H. v. San Elizario Independent School Dist.*, 106 F.3d 648 (1997), and *Canutillo Independent School Dist. v. Leija*, 101 F.3d 393 (1996), cert. denied, 520 U.S. 1265, 117 S.Ct. 2434, 138 L. Ed.2d 195 (1997). . . . We granted certiorari to address the issue, 522 U.S. 1011, 118 S. Ct. 595, 139 L.Ed.2d 431 (1997), and we now affirm.

II

Title IX provides in pertinent part: "No person . . . shall, on the basis of sex, be excluded from participation in, be denied the benefits of, or be subjected to discrimination under any education program or activity receiving Federal financial assistance." 20 U.S.C. § 1681(a). The express statutory means of enforcement is administrative: The statute directs federal agencies that distribute education funding to establish requirements to effectuate the nondiscrimination mandate, and permits the agencies to enforce those requirements through "any . . . means authorized by law," including ultimately the termination of federal funding. § 1682. The Court held in *Cannon v. University of Chicago*, 441 U.S. 677, 99 S.Ct. 1946, 60 L. Ed.2d 560 (1979), that Title IX is also enforceable through an implied private right of action, a conclusion we do not revisit here. We subsequently established in *Franklin v. Gwinnett County Public Schools*, 503 U.S. 60, 112 S.Ct. 1028, 117 L.Ed.2d 208 (1992), that monetary damages are available in the implied private action.

In *Franklin*, a high school student alleged that a teacher had sexually abused her on repeated occasions and that teachers and school administrators knew about the harassment but took no action, even to the point of dissuading her from initiating charges. See *id.*, at 63–64, 112 S.Ct., at 1031–1032. . . . *Franklin* thereby establishes that a school district can be held liable in damages in cases involving a teacher's sexual harassment of a student; the decision, however, does not purport to define the contours of that liability.

We face that issue squarely in this case. Petitioners, joined by the United States as *amicus curiae*, would invoke standards used by the Courts of Appeals in Title VII cases involving a supervisor's sexual harassment of an employee in the workplace. In support of that approach, they point to a passage in *Franklin* in which we stated: "Unquestionably, Title IX placed on the Gwinnett County Public Schools the duty not to discriminate on the basis of sex, and 'when a supervisor sexually harasses a subordinate because of the subordinate's sex, that supervisor "discriminate[s]" on the basis of sex.' *Meritor Sav. Bank, FSB v. Vinson,* 477 U.S. 57, 64, 106 S.Ct. 2399, 2404, 91 L.Ed.2d 49 (1986). We believe the same rule should apply when a teacher sexually harasses and abuses a student." *Id.,* at 75, 112 S.Ct., at 1037. . . .

In this case, moreover, petitioners seek not just to establish a Title IX violation but to recover *damages* based on theories of *respondeat superior* and constructive notice. It is that aspect of their action, in our view, that is most critical to resolving the case. Unlike Title IX, Title VII contains an express cause of action, § 2000e-5(f), and specifically provides for relief in the form of monetary damages, § 1981a. Congress therefore has directly addressed the subject of damages relief under Title VII and has set out the particular situations in which damages are available as well as the maximum amounts recoverable. § 1981a(b). With respect to Title IX, however, the private right of action is judicially implied, see *Cannon,* 441 U.S., at 717, 99 S.Ct., at 1968, and there is thus no legislative expression of the scope of available remedies, including when it is appropriate to award monetary damages. In addition, although the general presumption that courts can award any appropriate relief in an established cause of action, *e.g., Bell v. Hood,* 327 U.S. 678, 684, 66 S.Ct. 773, 776–777, 90 L.Ed. 939 (1946), coupled with Congress' abrogation of the States' Eleventh Amendment immunity under Title IX, see 42 U.S.C. § 2000d-7, led us to conclude in *Franklin* that Title IX recognizes a damages remedy, 503 U.S., at 68–73, 112 S.Ct., at 1033–1037; see *id.,* at 78, 112 S.Ct., at 1039 (Scalia, J., concurring in judgment), we did so in response to lower court decisions holding that Title IX does not support damages relief at all. We made no effort in *Franklin* to delimit the circumstances in which a damages remedy should lie.

III

Because the private right of action under Title IX is judicially implied, we have a measure of latitude to shape a sensible remedial scheme that best comports with the statute. . . . Those considerations, we think, are pertinent not only to the scope of the implied right, but also to the scope of the available remedies.

. . . .

As a general matter, it does not appear that Congress contemplated unlimited recovery in damages against a funding recipient where the recipient is unaware of discrimination in its programs. When Title IX was enacted in 1972, the principal civil rights statutes containing an express right of action did not provide for recovery of monetary damages at all, instead allowing only injunctive and equitable relief. See 42 U.S.C. § 2000a-3(a) (1970 ed.); §§ 2000e-5(e), (g) (1970 ed., Supp. II). It was not until 1991 that Congress made damages available under Title VII, and even then, Congress carefully limited the amount recoverable in any individual case, calibrating the maximum recovery to the size of the employer. See 42 U.S.C. § 1981a(b)(3). Adopting petitioners' position would amount, then, to allowing unlimited recovery of damages under Title IX where Congress has not spoken on the subject of either the right or the remedy, and in the face of evidence that when Congress expressly considered both in Title VII it restricted the amount of damages available.

Congress enacted Title IX in 1972 with two principal objectives in mind: "[T] o avoid the use of federal resources to support discriminatory practices" and "to provide individual citizens effective protection against those practices." *Cannon, supra,* at 704, 99 S.Ct., at 1961–1962. The statute was modeled after Title VI of the Civil Rights Act of 1964, see 441 U.S., at 694–696, 99 S.Ct., at 1956–1958; *Grove City College v. Bell,* 465 U.S. 555, 566, 104 S.Ct. 1211, 1217–1218, 79 L.Ed.2d 516 (1984), which is parallel to Title IX except that it prohibits race discrimination, not sex discrimination, and applies in all programs receiving federal funds, not only in education programs. See 42 U.S.C. § 2000d *et seq.* The two statutes operate in the same manner, conditioning an offer of federal funding on a promise by the recipient not to discriminate, in what amounts essentially to a contract between the Government and the recipient of funds. See *Guardians,* 463 U.S., at 599, 103 S.Ct., at 3231 (opinion of White, J.); *id.,* at 609, 103 S.Ct., at 3236 (Powell, J., concurring in judgment); cf. *Pennhurst State School and Hospital v. Halderman,* 451 U.S. 1, 17, 101 S.Ct. 1531, 1539–1540, 67 L.Ed.2d 694 (1981).

That contractual framework distinguishes Title IX from Title VII, which is framed in terms not of a condition but of an outright prohibition. Title VII applies to all employers without regard to federal funding and aims broadly to "eradicat[e] discrimination throughout the economy." *Landgraf v. USI Film Products,* 511 U.S. 244, 254, 114 S.Ct. 1483, 1491, 128 L.Ed.2d 229 (1994) (internal quotation marks omitted). Title VII, moreover, seeks to "make persons whole for injuries suffered through past discrimination." *Ibid.* (internal quotation marks omitted). Thus, whereas Title VII aims centrally to compensate victims of discrimination, Title IX focuses more on "protecting" individuals from discriminatory practices carried out by recipients of federal funds. *Cannon, supra,* at 704, 99 S.Ct., at 1961–1962. That might explain why, when the Court first recognized the implied right under Title IX in *Cannon,* the opinion referred to injunctive or equitable relief in a private action, see 441 U.S., at 705, and n. 38, 710, n. 44, 711, 99 S.Ct., at 1962, and n. 38, 1964, n. 44, 1965, but not to a damages remedy.

Title IX's contractual nature has implications for our construction of the scope of available remedies. When Congress attaches conditions to the award of federal funds under its spending power, U.S. Const., Art. I, § 8, cl. 1, as it has in Title IX and Title VI, we examine closely the propriety of private actions holding the recipient liable in monetary damages for noncompliance with the condition. See *Franklin, supra,* at 74–75, 112 S.Ct., at 1037; *Guardians, supra,* at 596–603, 103 S.Ct., at 3229–3230 (White, J.); see generally *Pennhurst, supra,* at 28–29, 101 S.Ct., at 1545–1546. Our central concern in that regard is with ensuring that "the receiving entity of federal funds [has] notice that it will be liable for a monetary award." *Franklin, supra,* at 74, 112 S.Ct., at 1037. Justice White's opinion announcing the Court's judgment in *Guardians Assn. v. Civil Serv. Comm'n of New York City,* for instance, concluded that the relief in an action under Title VI alleging unintentional discrimination should be prospective only, because where discrimination is unintentional, "it is surely not obvious that the grantee was aware that it was administering the program in violation of the [condition]." 463 U.S., at 598, 103 S.Ct., at 3230. We confront similar concerns here. If a school district's liability for a teacher's sexual harassment rests on principles of constructive notice or *respondeat superior,* it will likewise be the case that the recipient of funds was unaware of the discrimination. It is sensible to assume that Congress did not envision a recipient's liability in damages in that situation. See *Rosa H.,* 106 F.3d, at 654 ("When the school board accepted federal funds, it agreed not to discriminate on the basis of sex. We think it unlikely that it further agreed to suffer liability whenever its employees discriminate on the basis of sex").

Most significantly, Title IX contains important clues that Congress did not intend to allow recovery in damages where liability rests solely on principles of vicarious liability or constructive notice. Title IX's express means of enforcement—by administrative agencies—operates on an assumption of actual notice to officials of the funding recipient. The statute entitles agencies who disburse education funding to enforce their rules implementing the nondiscrimination mandate through proceedings to suspend or terminate funding or through "other means authorized by law." 20 U.S.C. § 1682. Significantly, however, an agency may not initiate enforcement proceedings until it "has advised the appropriate person or persons of the failure to comply with the requirement and has determined that compliance cannot be secured by voluntary means." *Ibid.* The administrative regulations implement that obligation, requiring resolution of compliance issues "by informal means whenever possible," 34 CFR § 100.7(d) (1997), and prohibiting commencement of enforcement proceedings until the agency has determined that voluntary compliance is unobtainable and "the recipient . . . has been notified of its failure to comply and of the action to be taken to effect compliance," § 100.8(d); see § 100.8(c).

     . . . .

Presumably, a central purpose of requiring notice of the violation "to the appropriate person" and an opportunity for voluntary compliance before administrative enforcement proceedings can commence is to avoid diverting education funding from beneficial uses where a recipient was unaware of discrimination in its programs and is willing to institute prompt corrective measures. The scope of private damages relief proposed by petitioners is at odds with that basic objective. When a teacher's sexual harassment is imputed to a school district or when a school district is deemed to have "constructively" known of the teacher's harassment, by assumption the district had no actual knowledge of the teacher's conduct. Nor, of course, did the district have an opportunity to take action to end the harassment or to limit further harassment.

It would be unsound, we think, for a statute's *express* system of enforcement to require notice to the recipient and an opportunity to come into voluntary compliance while a judicially *implied* system of enforcement permits substantial liability without regard to the recipient's knowledge or its corrective actions upon receiving notice. Cf. *Central Bank of Denver, N.A. v. First Interstate Bank of Denver, N. A.,* 511

U.S., at 180, 114 S.Ct., at 1449 ("[I]t would be 'anomalous to impute to Congress an intention to expand the plaintiff class for a judicially implied cause of action beyond the bounds it delineated for comparable express causes of action'"), quoting *Blue Chip Stamps v. Manor Drug Stores*, 421 U.S. 723, 736, 95 S.Ct. 1917, 1925–1926, 44 L. Ed.2d 539 (1975). Moreover, an award of damages in a particular case might well exceed a recipient's level of federal funding. See Tr. of Oral Arg. 35 (Lago Vista's federal funding for 1992–1993 was roughly $120,000). Where a statute's express enforcement scheme hinges its most severe sanction on notice and unsuccessful efforts to obtain compliance, we cannot attribute to Congress the intention to have implied an enforcement scheme that allows imposition of greater liability without comparable conditions.

IV

Because the express remedial scheme under Title IX is predicated upon notice to an "appropriate person" and an opportunity to rectify any violation, 20 U.S.C. § 1682, we conclude, in the absence of further direction from Congress, that the implied damages remedy should be fashioned along the same lines. An "appropriate person" under § 1682 is, at a minimum, an official of the recipient entity with authority to take corrective action to end the discrimination. Consequently, in cases like this one that do not involve official policy of the recipient entity, we hold that a damages remedy will not lie under Title IX unless an official who at a minimum has authority to address the alleged discrimination and to institute corrective measures on the recipient's behalf has actual knowledge of discrimination in the recipient's programs and fails adequately to respond.

We think, moreover, that the response must amount to deliberate indifference to discrimination. The administrative enforcement scheme presupposes that an official who is advised of a Title IX violation refuses to take action to bring the recipient into compliance. The premise, in other words, is an official decision by the recipient not to remedy the violation. That framework finds a rough parallel in the standard of deliberate indifference. Under a lower standard, there would be a risk that the recipient would be liable in damages not for its own official decision but instead for its employees' independent actions. Comparable considerations led to our adoption of a deliberate indifference standard for claims under § 1983 alleging that a municipality's actions in failing to prevent a deprivation of federal rights was the cause of the violation. See *Board of Comm'rs of Bryan Cty. v. Brown*, 520 U.S. 397, 117 S.Ct. 1382, 137 L.Ed.2d 626 (1997); *Canton v. Harris*, 489 U.S. 378, 388–392, 109 S.Ct. 1197, 1204–1207, 103 L.Ed.2d 412 (1989); see also *Collins v. Harker Heights*, 503 U.S. 115, 123–124, 112 S.Ct. 1061, 1067–1068, 117 L.Ed.2d 261 (1992).

Applying the framework to this case is fairly straightforward, as petitioners do not contend they can prevail under an actual notice standard. The only official alleged to have had information about Waldrop's misconduct is the high school principal. That information, however, consisted of a complaint from parents of other students charging only that Waldrop had made inappropriate comments during class, which was plainly insufficient to alert the principal to the possibility that Waldrop was involved in a sexual relationship with a student. Lago Vista, moreover, terminated Waldrop's employment upon learning of his relationship with Gebser. Justice Stevens points out in his dissenting opinion that Waldrop of course had knowledge of his own actions. See *post*, at 2003, n. 8. Where a school district's liability rests on actual notice principles, however, the knowledge of the wrongdoer himself is not pertinent to the analysis. See Restatement § 280.

Petitioners focus primarily on Lago Vista's asserted failure to promulgate and publicize an effective policy and grievance procedure for sexual harassment claims. They point to Department of Education regulations requiring each funding recipient to "adopt and publish grievance procedures providing for prompt and equitable resolution" of discrimination complaints, 34 C.F.R. § 106.8(b) (1997), and to notify students and others that "it does not discriminate on the basis of sex in the educational programs or activities which it operates," § 106.9(a). Lago Vista's alleged failure to comply with the regulations, however, does not establish the requisite actual notice and deliberate indifference. And in any event, the failure to promulgate a grievance procedure does not itself constitute "discrimination" under Title IX. Of course, the Department of Education could enforce the requirement administratively: Agencies generally have authority to promulgate and enforce requirements that effectuate the statute's nondiscrimination mandate, 20 U.S.C. § 1682, even if those requirements do not purport to represent a definition of discrimination under the statute. *E.g., Grove City*, 465 U.S., at 574–575, 104 S.Ct., at 1221–1222 (permitting administrative enforcement of regulation requiring college to execute an "Assurance of Compliance" with Title IX). We have never held, however, that the implied private right of action under Title IX allows recovery in damages for violation of those sorts of administrative requirements.

V

The number of reported cases involving sexual harassment of students in schools confirms that harassment unfortunately is an all too common aspect of the educational experience. No one questions that a student suffers extraordinary harm when subjected to sexual harassment and abuse by a teacher, and that the teacher's conduct is reprehensible and undermines the basic purposes of the educational system. The issue in this case, however, is whether the independent misconduct of a teacher is attributable to the school district that employs him under a specific federal statute designed primarily to prevent recipients of federal financial assistance from using the funds in a discriminatory manner. Our decision does not affect any right of recovery that an individual may have against a school district as a matter of state law or against the teacher in his individual capacity under state law or under 42 U.S.C. § 1983. Until Congress speaks directly on the subject, however, we will not hold a school district liable in damages under Title IX for a teacher's sexual harassment of a student absent actual notice and deliberate indifference. We therefore affirm the judgment of the Court of Appeals.

It is so ordered.

Notes and Questions

1. Consider the prevalence of sexual abuse and teacher on student harassment in schools. Is the "deliberate indifference" requirement too high for imposing damages against school districts? What specific type of actions could likely trigger liability against the school district? Should school districts be absolved of liability under Title IX, even when aware of the harassment?

2. Are you convinced by the argument that the recipient school districts did not have enough notice that these types of liability would be part of the responsibility of compliance with Title IX? Would you classify that as part of the inherent risk and burden funding recipients should bear under the Spending Clause?

3. Is it part of the Court's duties to worry about the damage award being higher than the amount of Title IX funding? Read the desegregation cases in Chapter 4 and note the Court's eventual reluctance to delve into budgetary issues in that context. Is the Court consistent on this in both contexts?

4. See *Davis* below for the Court's different approach regarding notice in the context of student on student harassment. Note also the drastically different approaches espoused by the majority and the dissent in that case.

5. Note the Court statement that: "Because the private right of action under Title IX is judicially implied, we have a measure of latitude to shape a sensible remedial scheme that best comports with the statute." Is the Court too flexible when assessing its own authority?

Davis v. Monroe County Board of Education
526 U.S. 629 (1999)

JUSTICE O'CONNOR delivered the opinion of the Court.

Petitioner brought suit against the Monroe County Board of Education and other defendants, alleging that her fifth-grade daughter had been the victim of sexual harassment by another student in her class. Among petitioner's claims was a claim for monetary and injunctive relief under Title IX of the Education Amendments of 1972 (Title IX), 86 Stat. 373, as amended, 20 U.S.C. § 1681 *et seq.* The District Court dismissed petitioner's Title IX claim on the ground that "student-on-student," or peer, harassment provides no ground for a private cause of action under the statute. The Court of Appeals for the Eleventh Circuit, sitting en banc, affirmed. We consider here whether a private damages action may lie against the school board in cases of student-on-student harassment. We conclude that it may, but only where the funding recipient acts with deliberate indifference to known acts of harassment in its programs or activities. Moreover, we conclude that such an action will lie only for harassment that is so severe, pervasive, and objectively offensive that it effectively bars the victim's access to an educational opportunity or benefit.

. . . .

I.

A

Petitioner's minor daughter, LaShonda, was allegedly the victim of a prolonged pattern of sexual harassment by one of her fifth-grade classmates at Hubbard Elementary School, a public school in Monroe County, Georgia. According to petitioner's complaint, the harassment began in December 1992, when the classmate, G.F., attempted to touch LaShonda's breasts and genital area and made vulgar statements such as "'I want to get in bed with you'" and "'I want to feel your boobs.'" Complaint 7. Similar conduct allegedly occurred on or about January 4 and January 20, 1993. *Ibid.* LaShonda reported each of these incidents to her mother and to her classroom teacher, Diane Fort. *Ibid.* Petitioner, in turn, also contacted Fort, who allegedly assured petitioner that the school principal, Bill Querry, had been informed of the incidents. *Ibid.* Petitioner contends that, notwithstanding these reports, no disciplinary action was taken against G.F. *Id.*, 16.

G.F.'s conduct allegedly continued for many months. In early February, G.F. purportedly placed a door stop in his pants and proceeded to act in a sexually suggestive manner toward LaShonda during physical education class. *Id.*, 8. LaShonda reported G.F.'s behavior to her physical education teacher, Whit Maples. *Ibid.* Approximately one week later, G.F. again allegedly engaged in harassing behavior, this time while under the supervision of another classroom teacher, Joyce Pippin. *Id.*, 9. Again, LaShonda allegedly reported the incident to the teacher, and again petitioner contacted the teacher to follow up. *Ibid.*

Petitioner alleges that G.F. once more directed sexually harassing conduct toward LaShonda in physical education class in early March, and that LaShonda reported the incident to both Maples and Pippen. *Id.*, 10. In mid-April 1993, G.F. allegedly rubbed his body against LaShonda in the school hallway in what LaShonda considered a sexually suggestive manner, and LaShonda again reported the matter to Fort. *Id.*

The string of incidents finally ended in mid-May, when G.F. was charged with, and pleaded guilty to, sexual battery for his misconduct. *Id.*,. The complaint alleges that LaShonda had suffered during the months of harassment, however; specifically, her previously high grades allegedly dropped as she became unable to concentrate on her studies, *id.*, ¶ 15, and, in April 1993, her father discovered that she had written a suicide note, *ibid*. The complaint further alleges that, at one point, LaShonda told petitioner that she "'didn't know how much longer she could keep [G.F.] off her.'" *Id.*, ¶ 12.

Nor was LaShonda G.F.'s only victim; it is alleged that other girls in the class fell prey to G.F.'s conduct. *Id.*, ¶ 16. At one point, in fact, a group composed of LaShonda and other female students tried to speak with Principal Querry about G.F.'s behavior. *Id.*, ¶ 10. According to the complaint, however, a teacher denied the students' request with the statement, "'If [Querry] wants you, he'll call you.'" *Ibid.*

Petitioner alleges that no disciplinary action was taken in response to G.F.'s behavior toward LaShonda. *Id.,* ¶ 16. In addition to her conversations with Fort and Pippen, petitioner alleges that she spoke with Principal Querry in mid-May 1993. When petitioner inquired as to what action the school intended to take against G.F., Querry simply stated, "'I guess I'll have to threaten him a little bit harder.'" *Id.,* ¶ 12. Yet, petitioner alleges, at no point during the many months of his reported misconduct was G.F. disciplined for harassment. *Id.,* ¶ 16. Indeed, Querry allegedly asked petitioner why LaShonda "'was the only one complaining.'"

Nor, according to the complaint, was any effort made to separate G.F. and LaShonda. *Id.,* ¶ 16. On the contrary, notwithstanding LaShonda's frequent complaints, only after more than three months of reported harassment was she even permitted to change her classroom seat so that she was no longer seated next to G.F. *Id.,* ¶ 13. Moreover, petitioner alleges that, at the time of the events in question, the Monroe County Board of Education (Board) had not instructed its personnel on how to respond to peer sexual harassment and had not established a policy on the issue. *Id.,* ¶ 17.

. . . .

II

Title IX provides, with certain exceptions not at issue here, that

"[n]o person in the United States shall, on the basis of sex, be excluded from participation in, be denied the benefits of, or be subjected to discrimination under any education program or activity receiving Federal financial assistance." 20 U.S.C. § 1681(a).

There is no dispute here that the Board is a recipient of federal education funding for Title IX purposes. 74 F.3d, at 1189. Nor do respondents support an argument that student-on-student harassment cannot rise to the level of "discrimination" for purposes of Title IX. Rather, at issue here is the question whether a recipient of federal education funding may be liable for damages under Title IX under any circumstances for discrimination in the form of student-on-student sexual harassment.

A

Petitioner urges that Title IX's plain language compels the conclusion that the statute is intended to bar recipients of federal funding from permitting this form of discrimination in their programs or activities. She emphasizes that the statute prohibits a student from being *"subjected to discrimination* under any education program or activity receiving Federal financial assistance." 20 U.S.C. § 1681(a) (emphasis added). It is Title IX's "unmistakable focus on the benefited class," *Cannon v. University of Chicago,* 441 U.S. 677, 691, 99 S.Ct. 1946, 60 L.Ed.2d 560 (1979), rather than the perpetrator, that, in petitioner's view, compels the conclusion that the statute works to protect students from the discriminatory misconduct of their peers.

Here, however, we are asked to do more than define the scope of the behavior that Title IX proscribes. We must determine whether a district's failure to respond to student-on-student harassment in its schools can support a private suit for money damages. See *Gebser v. Lago Vista Independent School Dist.,* 524 U.S. 274, 283, 118 S. Ct. 1989, 141 L.Ed.2d 277 (1998) ("In this case, . . . petitioners seek not just to establish a Title IX violation but to recover *damages* . . ."). This Court has indeed recognized an implied private right of action under Title IX, see *Cannon v. University of Chicago, supra,* and we have held that money damages are available in such suits, *Franklin v. Gwinnett County Public Schools,* 503 U.S. 60, 112 S.Ct. 1028, 117 L.Ed.2d 208 (1992). Because we have repeatedly treated Title IX as legislation enacted pursuant to Congress' authority under the Spending Clause, however, see, *e.g., Gebser v. Lago Vista Independent School Dist., supra,* at 287, 118 S.Ct. 1989 (Title IX); *Franklin v. Gwinnett County Public Schools, supra,* at 74–75, and n. 8, 112 S.Ct. 1028 (Title IX); see also *Guardians Assn. v. Civil Serv. Comm'n of New York City,* 463 U.S. 582, 598–599, 103 S.Ct. 3221, 77 L.Ed.2d 866 (1983) (opinion of White, J.) (Title VI), private damages actions are available only where recipients of federal funding had adequate notice that they could be liable for the conduct at issue. When Congress acts pursuant to its spending power, it generates legislation "much in the nature of a contract: in return for federal funds, the States agree to comply with federally imposed conditions." *Pennhurst State School and Hospital v. Halderman,* 451 U.S. 1, 17, 101 S.Ct. 1531, 67 L.Ed.2d 694 (1981). In interpreting language in spending legislation, we thus "insis[t] that Congress speak with a clear voice," recognizing that "[t]here can, of course, be no knowing acceptance [of the terms of the putative contract] if a State is unaware of the conditions [imposed by the legislation] or is unable to ascertain what is expected of it." *Ibid.;* see also *id.,* at 24–25, 101 S.Ct. 1531.

. . . .

Gebser thus established that a recipient intentionally violates Title IX, and is subject to a private damages action, where the recipient is deliberately indifferent to known acts of teacher-student discrimination. Indeed, whether viewed as "discrimination" or "subject[ing]" students to discrimination, Title IX "[u]nquestionably . . . placed on [the Board] the duty not" to permit teacher-student harassment in its schools, *Franklin v. Gwinnett County Public Schools, supra,* at 75, 112 S.Ct. 1028, and recipients violate Title IX's plain terms when they remain deliberately indifferent to this form of misconduct.

We consider here whether the misconduct identified in *Gebser*—deliberate indifference to known acts of harassment—amounts to an intentional violation of Title IX, capable of supporting a private damages action, when the harasser is a student rather than a teacher. We conclude that, in certain limited circumstances, it does. As an initial matter, in *Gebser* we expressly rejected the use of agency principles in the Title IX context, noting the textual differences between Title IX and Title VII. 524

U.S., at 283, 118 S.Ct. 1989; cf. *Faragher v. City of Boca Raton,* 524 U.S. 775, 791–792, 118 S.Ct. 2275, 141 L.Ed.2d 662 (1998) (invoking agency principles on ground that definition of "employer" in Title VII includes agents of employer); *Meritor Savings Bank, FSB v. Vinson,* 477 U.S. 57, 72, 106 S.Ct. 2399, 91 L.Ed.2d 49 (1986) (same). Additionally, the regulatory scheme surrounding Title IX has long provided funding recipients with notice that they may be liable for their failure to respond to the discriminatory acts of certain nonagents. The Department of Education requires recipients to monitor third parties for discrimination in specified circumstances and to refrain from particular forms of interaction with outside entities that are known to discriminate. See, *e.g.,* 34 CFR §§ 106.31(b)(6), 106.31(d), 106.37(a)(2), 106.38(a), 106.51(a)(3) (1998).

The common law, too, has put schools on notice that they may be held responsible under state law for their failure to protect students from the tortious acts of third parties. See Restatement (Second) of Torts § 320, and Comment *a* (1965). In fact, state courts routinely uphold claims alleging that schools have been negligent in failing to protect their students from the torts of their peers. See, *e.g., Rupp v. Bryant,* 417 So.2d 658, 666–667 (Fla.1982); *Brahatcek v. Millard School Dist.,* 202 Neb. 86, 99–100, 273 N.W.2d 680, 688 (1979); *McLeod v. Grant County School Dist. No. 128,* 42 Wash.2d 316, 320, 255 P.2d 360, 362–363 (1953).

This is not to say that the identity of the harasser is irrelevant. On the contrary, both the "deliberate indifference" standard and the language of Title IX narrowly circumscribe the set of parties whose known acts of sexual harassment can trigger some duty to respond on the part of funding recipients. Deliberate indifference makes sense as a theory of direct liability under Title IX only where the funding recipient has some control over the alleged harassment. A recipient cannot be directly liable for its indifference where it lacks the authority to take remedial action.

The language of Title IX itself—particularly when viewed in conjunction with the requirement that the recipient have notice of Title IX's prohibitions to be liable for damages—also cabins the range of misconduct that the statute proscribes. The statute's plain language confines the scope of prohibited conduct based on the recipient's degree of control over the harasser and the environment in which the harassment occurs. If a funding recipient does not engage in harassment directly, it may not be liable for damages unless its deliberate indifference "subject[s]" its students to harassment. That is, the deliberate indifference must, at a minimum, "cause [students] to undergo" harassment or "make them liable or vulnerable" to it. Random House Dictionary of the English Language 1415 (1966) . . . .

These factors combine to limit a recipient's damages liability to circumstances wherein the recipient exercises substantial control over both the harasser and the context in which the known harassment occurs. Only then can the recipient be said to "expose" its students to harassment or "cause" them to undergo it "under" the recipient's programs. We agree with the dissent that these conditions are satisfied most easily and most obviously when the offender is an agent of the recipient. *Post,* at 1680. We rejected the use of agency analysis in *Gebser,* however, and we disagree that the term "under" somehow imports an agency requirement into Title IX. See *post,* at 1679–1680. As noted above, the theory in *Gebser* was that the recipient was *directly* liable for its deliberate indifference to discrimination. See *supra,* at 1671. Liability in that case did not arise because the "teacher's actions [were] treated" as those of the funding recipient, *post,* at 1680; the district was directly liable for its *own* failure to act. The terms "subjec[t]" and "under" impose limits, but nothing about these terms requires the use of agency principles.

Where, as here, the misconduct occurs during school hours and on school grounds—the bulk of G.F.'s misconduct, in fact, took place in the classroom—the misconduct is taking place "under" an "operation" of the funding recipient. See *Doe v. University of Illinois,* 138 F.3d, at 661 (finding liability where school fails to respond properly to "student-on-student sexual harassment that takes place while the students are involved in school activities or otherwise under the supervision of school employees"). In these circumstances, the recipient retains substantial control over the context in which the harassment occurs. More importantly, however, in this setting the Board exercises significant control over the harasser. . . .

At the time of the events in question here, in fact, school attorneys and administrators were being told that student-on-student harassment could trigger liability under Title IX. In March 1993, even as the events alleged in petitioner's complaint were unfolding, the National School Boards Association issued a publication, for use by "school attorneys and administrators in understanding the law regarding sexual harassment of employees and students," which observed that districts could be liable under Title IX for their failure to respond to student-on-student harassment. See National School Boards Association Council of School Attorneys, Sexual Harassment in the Schools: Preventing and Defending Against Claims v, 45 (rev. ed.). Drawing on Equal Employment Opportunity Commission guidelines interpreting Title VII, the publication informed districts that, "if [a] school district has constructive notice of severe and repeated acts of sexual harassment by fellow students, that may form the basis of a [T]itle IX claim." *Ibid.* The publication even correctly anticipated a form of *Gebser's* actual notice requirement: "It is unlikely that courts will hold a school district liable for sexual harassment by students against students in the absence of actual knowledge or notice to district employees." Sexual Harassment in the Schools, *supra,* at 45. Although we do not rely on this publication as an "indicium of congressional notice," see *post,* at 1685, we do find support for our reading of Title IX in the fact that school attorneys have rendered an analogous interpretation.

Likewise, although they were promulgated too late to contribute to the Board's notice of proscribed misconduct, the Department of Education's Office for Civil Rights (OCR) has recently adopted policy guidelines providing that student-on-student harassment falls within the scope of Title IX's proscriptions. See Department of Education, Office of Civil Rights, Sexual Harassment Guidance: Harassment of Students by School Employees, Other Students, or Third Parties, 62 Fed.Reg. 12034,

12039–12040 (1997) (OCR Title IX Guidelines); see also Department of Education, Racial Incidents and Harassment Against Students at Educational Institutions, 59 Fed.Reg. 11448, 11449 (1994).

We stress that our conclusion here—that recipients may be liable for their deliberate indifference to known acts of peer sexual harassment—does not mean that recipients can avoid liability only by purging their schools of actionable peer harassment or that administrators must engage in particular disciplinary action. We thus disagree with respondents' contention that, if Title IX provides a cause of action for student-on-student harassment, "nothing short of expulsion of every student accused of misconduct involving sexual overtones would protect school systems from liability or damages." See Brief for Respondents 16; see also 120 F.3d, at 1402 (Tjoflat, J.) ("[A] school must immediately suspend or expel a student accused of sexual harassment"). Likewise, the dissent erroneously imagines that victims of peer harassment now have a Title IX right to make particular remedial demands. See post, at 1691 (contemplating that victim could demand new desk assignment). In fact, as we have previously noted, courts should refrain from second-guessing the disciplinary decisions made by school administrators. New Jersey v. T.L.O., supra, at 342–343, n. 9, 105 S.Ct. 733.

School administrators will continue to enjoy the flexibility they require so long as funding recipients are deemed "deliberately indifferent" to acts of student-on-student harassment only where the recipient's response to the harassment or lack thereof is clearly unreasonable in light of the known circumstances. . . .

Like the dissent, see post, at 1681–1683, we acknowledge that school administrators shoulder substantial burdens as a result of legal constraints on their disciplinary authority. To the extent that these restrictions arise from federal statutes, Congress can review these burdens with attention to the difficult position in which such legislation may place our Nation's schools. We believe, however, that the standard set out here is sufficiently flexible to account both for the level of disciplinary authority available to the school and for the potential liability arising from certain forms of disciplinary action. A university might not, for example, be expected to exercise the same degree of control over its students that a grade school would enjoy, see post, at 1682–1683, and it would be entirely reasonable for a school to refrain from a form of disciplinary action that would expose it to constitutional or statutory claims.

While it remains to be seen whether petitioner can show that the Board's response to reports of G.F.'s misconduct was clearly unreasonable in light of the known circumstances, petitioner may be able to show that the Board "subject[ed]" LaShonda to discrimination by failing to respond in any way over a period of five months to complaints of G.F.'s in-school misconduct from LaShonda and other female students.

B

The requirement that recipients receive adequate notice of Title IX's proscriptions also bears on the proper definition of "discrimination" in the context of a private damages action. We have elsewhere concluded that sexual harassment is a form of discrimination for Title IX purposes and that Title IX proscribes harassment with sufficient clarity to satisfy *Pennhurst*'s notice requirement and serve as a basis for a damages action. See *Gebser v. Lago Vista Independent School Dist.*, 524 U.S., at 281, 118 S.Ct. 1989; *Franklin v. Gwinnett County Public Schools*, 503 U.S., at 74–75, 112 S.Ct. 1028. Having previously determined that "sexual harassment" is "discrimination" in the school context under Title IX, we are constrained to conclude that student-on-student sexual harassment, if sufficiently severe, can likewise rise to the level of discrimination actionable under the statute. . . . The statute's other prohibitions, moreover, help give content to the term "discrimination" in this context. Students are not only protected from discrimination, but also specifically shielded from being "excluded from participation in" or "denied the benefits of" any "education program or activity receiving Federal financial assistance." § 1681(a). The statute makes clear that, whatever else it prohibits, students must not be denied access to educational benefits and opportunities on the basis of gender. We thus conclude that funding recipients are properly held liable in damages only where they are deliberately indifferent to sexual harassment, of which they have actual knowledge, that is so severe, pervasive, and objectively offensive that it can be said to deprive the victims of access to the educational opportunities or benefits provided by the school.

The most obvious example of student-on-student sexual harassment capable of triggering a damages claim would thus involve the overt, physical deprivation of access to school resources. Consider, for example, a case in which male students physically threaten their female peers every day, successfully preventing the female students from using a particular school resource—an athletic field or a computer lab, for instance. District administrators are well aware of the daily ritual, yet they deliberately ignore requests for aid from the female students wishing to use the resource. The district's knowing refusal to take any action in response to such behavior would fly in the face of Title IX's core principles, and such deliberate indifference may appropriately be subject to claims for monetary damages. It is not necessary, however, to show physical exclusion to demonstrate that students have been deprived by the actions of another student or students of an educational opportunity on the basis of sex. Rather, a plaintiff must establish sexual harassment of students that is so severe, pervasive, and objectively offensive, and that so undermines and detracts from the victims' educational experience, that the victim-students are effectively denied equal access to an institution's resources and opportunities. Cf. *Meritor Savings Bank, FSB v. Vinson*, 477 U.S., at 67, 106 S.Ct. 2399.

Whether gender-oriented conduct rises to the level of actionable "harassment" thus "depends on a constellation of surrounding circumstances, expectations, and relationships," *Oncale v. Sundowner Offshore Services, Inc.*, 523 U.S. 75, 82, 118 S.Ct. 998, 140 L.Ed.2d 201 (1998), including, but not limited to, the ages of the harasser and the victim and the number of individuals involved, see OCR Title IX Guidelines 12041–12042. Courts, moreover, must bear in mind that schools are unlike the adult workplace and that children may regularly interact in a manner that would be unacceptable among adults. See, *e.g.,* Brief for National School Boards Association et al. as *Amici Curiae* 11 (describing "dizzying array of immature . . . behaviors by students"). Indeed, at least early on, students are still learning how to interact appropriately with their peers. It is thus understandable that, in the school setting, students often engage in insults, banter, teasing, shoving, pushing, and gender-specific conduct that is upsetting to the students subjected to it. Damages are not available for simple acts of teasing and name-calling among school children, however, even where these comments target differences in gender. Rather, in the context of student-on-student harassment, damages are available only where the behavior is so severe, pervasive, and objectively offensive that it denies its victims the equal access to education that Title IX is designed to protect.

. . . . Moreover, the provision that the discrimination occur "under any education program or activity" suggests that the behavior be serious enough to have the systemic effect of denying the victim equal access to an educational program or activity. Although, in theory, a single instance of sufficiently severe one-on-one peer harassment could be said to have such an effect, we think it unlikely that Congress would have thought such behavior sufficient to rise to this level in light of the inevitability of student misconduct and the amount of litigation that would be invited by entertaining claims of official indifference to a single instance of one-on-one peer harassment. By limiting private damages actions to cases having a systemic effect on educational programs or activities, we reconcile the general principle that Title IX prohibits official indifference to known peer sexual harassment with the practical realities of responding to student behavior, realities that Congress could not have meant to be ignored. Even the dissent suggests that Title IX liability may arise when a funding recipient remains indifferent to severe, gender-based mistreatment played out on a "widespread level" among students. *Post,* at 1690.

The fact that it was a teacher who engaged in harassment in *Franklin* and *Gebser* is relevant. The relationship between the harasser and the victim necessarily affects the extent to which the misconduct can be said to breach Title IX's guarantee of equal access to educational benefits and to have a systemic effect on a program or activity. Peer harassment, in particular, is less likely to satisfy these requirements than is teacher-student harassment.

C

Applying this standard to the facts at issue here, we conclude that the Eleventh Circuit erred in dismissing petitioner's complaint. Petitioner alleges that her daughter was the victim of repeated acts of sexual harassment by G.F. over a 5-month period, and there are allegations in support of the conclusion that G.F.'s misconduct was severe, pervasive, and objectively offensive. The harassment was not only verbal; it included numerous acts of objectively offensive touching, and, indeed, G.F. ultimately pleaded guilty to criminal sexual misconduct. Moreover, the complaint alleges that there were multiple victims who were sufficiently disturbed by G.F.'s misconduct to seek an audience with the school principal. Further, petitioner contends that the harassment had a concrete, negative effect on her daughter's ability to receive an education. The complaint also suggests that petitioner may be able to show both actual knowledge and deliberate indifference on the part of the Board, which made no effort whatsoever either to investigate or to put an end to the harassment.

On this complaint, we cannot say "beyond doubt that [petitioner] can prove no set of facts in support of [her] claim which would entitle [her] to relief." *Conley v. Gibson,* 355 U.S. 41, 45–46, 78 S.Ct. 99, 2 L.Ed.2d 80 (1957). See also *Scheuer v. Rhodes,* 416 U.S. 232, 236, 94 S.Ct. 1683, 40 L.Ed.2d 90 (1974) ("The issue is not whether a plaintiff will ultimately prevail but whether the claimant is entitled to offer evidence to support the claims"). Accordingly, the judgment of the United States Court of Appeals for the Eleventh Circuit is reversed, and the case is remanded for further proceedings consistent with this opinion.

It is so ordered.

Notes and Questions

1. The dissent, in an omitted portion of the opinion, states:

In the final analysis, this case is about federalism. Yet the majority's decision today says not one word about the federal balance. Preserving our federal system is a legitimate end in itself. It is, too, the means to other ends. It ensures that essential choices can be made by a government more proximate to the people than the vast apparatus of federal power. Defining the appropriate role of schools in teaching and supervising children who are beginning to explore their own sexuality and learning how to express it to others is one of the most complex and sensitive issues our schools face. Such decisions are best made by parents and by the teachers and school administrators who can counsel with them. The delicacy and immense significance of teaching children about sexuality should cause the Court to act with great restraint before it displaces state and local governments.

How do you evaluate the dissent's definition of federalism in this context? Does it fit the definition used by the Court in other area? Keep this assessment in mind as you proceed through the coverage. Particularly, as you review *Shelby County vs. Holder* in the chapter on Voting Rights, determine whether the above definition is consistent with the Court's approach to federalism in that case.

2. In contrast to the dissent, the majority views school districts as having more control over students and being able to administer light punishment to curtail harmful behavior. Compared to universities where control of third party behavior and of students is limited, K-12 schools are able to send a message regarding acceptable behavior. Both opinions cite state laws as alternative actions and concede that state laws might prohibit harassment. Should the fact that state law makes a particular behavior illegal serve as notice to federal recipients that encroachments that fit the purpose of the statutes will trigger liability?

3. Note the dissent's definition of the basis for liability:

> It is not enough, then, that the alleged discrimination occur in a "context subject to the school district's control." *Ante,* at 1672. The discrimination must actually be "controlled by"—that is, be authorized by, pursuant to, or in accordance with, school policy or actions. Compare *ante,* at 1672 (defining "under" as "*in* or into *a condition of* subjection, regulation, or subordination" (emphasis added)), with *ibid.* (defining "under" as "*subject to* the guidance and instruction of" (emphasis added)).

> This reading is also consistent with the fact that the discrimination must be "under" the "operations" of the grant recipient. The term "operations" connotes active and affirmative participation by the grant recipient, not merely inaction or failure to respond. See Black's Law Dictionary 1092 (6th ed.1990) (defining "operation" as an "[e]xertion of power; the process of operating or mode of action; an effect brought about in accordance with a definite plan; action; activity"). Teacher sexual harassment of students is "under" the school's program or activity in certain circumstances, but student harassment is not. Our decision in *Gebser* recognizes that a grant recipient acts through its agents and thus, under certain limited circumstances, even tortious acts by teachers may be attributable to the school. We noted in *Gebser* that, in contrast to Title VII, which defines "employer" to include "any agent"—Title IX "contains no comparable reference to an educational institution's 'agents,' and so does not expressly call for application of agency principles." 524 U.S., at 283, 118 S.Ct. 1989. As a result, we declined to incorporate principles of agency liability, such as a strict application of vicarious liability, that would conflict with the Spending Clause's notice requirement and Title IX's express administrative enforcement scheme.

Why does the dissent not think the student's behavior is "under the operations" of a school? Are all occurrences in classrooms and schoolyards within the dominion of the school?

4. Notice the Court's emphasis that the deliberate indifference standard acts to trigger liability for the school disticts's disregard of its Title IX obligations once it has received notice of a violation, not for the actual harassment. How does that limit potential liability in the run of the mill cases?

D. Gender Discrimination and the Fourteenth Amendment

United States v. Virginia tackles eradication of sex stereotypes and assumptions relating to gender roles under the Fourteenth Amendment of the Constitution. How are the issues under this constitutional doctrine, different than or similar to those litigated under Title IX and Title VII?

United States v. Virginia

518 U.S. 515 (1996)

JUSTICE GINSBURG delivered the opinion of the Court.

Virginia's public institutions of higher learning include an incomparable military college, Virginia Military Institute (VMI). The United States maintains that the Constitution's equal protection guarantee precludes Virginia from reserving exclusively to men the unique educational opportunities VMI affords. We agree.

I

Founded in 1839, VMI is today the sole single-sex school among Virginia's 15 public institutions of higher learning. VMI's distinctive mission is to produce "citizen-soldiers," men prepared for leadership in civilian life and in military service. VMI pursues this mission through pervasive training of a kind not available anywhere else in Virginia. Assigning prime place to character development, VMI uses an "adversative method" modeled on English public schools and once characteristic of military instruction. VMI constantly endeavors to instill physical and mental discipline in its cadets and impart to them a strong moral code. The school's graduates leave VMI with heightened comprehension of their capacity to deal with duress and stress, and a large sense of accomplishment for completing the hazardous course.

VMI has notably succeeded in its mission to produce leaders; among its alumni are military generals, Members of Congress, and business executives. The school's alumni overwhelmingly perceive that their VMI training helped them to realize their personal goals. VMI's endowment reflects the loyalty of its graduates; VMI has the largest per-student endowment of all public undergraduate institutions in the Nation.

Neither the goal of producing citizen-soldiers nor VMI's implementing methodology is inherently unsuitable to women. And the school's impressive record in producing leaders has made admission desirable to some women. Nevertheless, Virginia has elected to preserve exclusively for men the advantages and opportunities a VMI education affords.

II

A

From its establishment in 1839 as one of the Nation's first state military colleges, see 1839 Va. Acts, ch. 20, VMI has remained financially supported by Virginia and "subject to the control of the [Virginia] General Assembly," Va.Code Ann. § 23-92 (1993). First southern college to teach engineering and industrial chemistry, see H. Wise, Drawing Out the Man: The VMI Story 13 (1978) (The VMI Story), VMI once provided teachers for the Commonwealth's schools, see 1842 Va. Acts, ch. 24, § 2 (requiring every cadet to teach in one of the Commonwealth's schools for a 2-year period). Civil War strife threatened the school's vitality, but a resourceful superintendent regained legislative support by highlighting "VMI's great potential[,] through its technical know-how," to advance Virginia's postwar recovery. The VMI Story 47.

VMI today enrolls about 1,300 men as cadets. Its academic offerings in the liberal arts, sciences, and engineering are also available at other public colleges and universities in Virginia. But VMI's mission is special. It is the mission of the school

> "'to produce educated and honorable men, prepared for the varied work of civil life, imbued with love of learning, confident in the functions and attitudes of leadership, possessing a high sense of public service, advocates of the American democracy and free enterprise system, and ready as citizen-soldiers to defend their country in time of national peril.'" 766 F.Supp. 1407, 1425 (W.D.Va.1991) (quoting Mission Study Committee of the VMI Board of Visitors, Report, May 16, 1986).

In contrast to the federal service academies, institutions maintained "to prepare cadets for career service in the armed forces," VMI's program "is directed at preparation for both military and civilian life"; "[o]nly about 15% of VMI cadets enter career military service." 766 F.Supp., at 1432.

VMI produces its "citizen-soldiers" through "an adversative, or doubting, model of education" which features "[p]hysical rigor, mental stress, absolute equality of treatment, absence of privacy, minute regulation of behavior, and indoctrination in desirable values." *Id.*, at 1421. As one Commandant of Cadets described it, the adversative method "'dissects the young student,'" and makes him aware of his "'limits and capabilities,'" so that he knows "'how far he can go with his anger, . . . how much he can take under stress, . . . exactly what he can do when he is physically exhausted.'" *Id.*, at 1421–1422 (quoting Col. N. Bissell).

VMI cadets live in spartan barracks where surveillance is constant and privacy nonexistent; they wear uniforms, eat together in the mess hall, and regularly participate in drills. *Id.*, at 1424, 1432. Entering students are incessantly exposed to the rat line, "an extreme form of the adversative model," comparable in intensity to Marine Corps boot camp. *Id.*, at 1422. Tormenting and punishing, the rat line bonds new cadets to their fellow sufferers and, when they have completed the 7-month experience, to their former tormentors. *Ibid.*

VMI's "adversative model" is further characterized by a hierarchical "class system" of privileges and responsibilities, a "dyke system" for assigning a senior class mentor to each entering class "rat," and a stringently enforced "honor code," which prescribes that a cadet "'does not lie, cheat, steal nor tolerate those who do.'" *Id.*, at 1422–1423.

VMI attracts some applicants because of its reputation as an extraordinarily challenging military school, and "because its alumni are exceptionally close to the school." *Id.*, at 1421. "[W]omen have no opportunity anywhere to gain the benefits of [the system of education at VMI]." *Ibid.*

B

In 1990, prompted by a complaint filed with the Attorney General by a female high-school student seeking admission to VMI, the United States sued the Commonwealth of Virginia and VMI, alleging that VMI's exclusively male admission policy violated the Equal Protection Clause of the Fourteenth Amendment. *Id.,* at 1408.Trial of the action consumed six days and involved an array of expert witnesses on each side. *Ibid.*

In the two years preceding the lawsuit, the District Court noted, VMI had received inquiries from 347 women, but had responded to none of them. *Id.,* at 1436. "[S]ome women, at least," the court said, "would want to attend the school if they had the opportunity." *Id.,* at 1414. The court further recognized that, with recruitment, VMI could "achieve at least 10% female enrollment"—"a sufficient 'critical mass' to provide the female cadets with a positive educational experience." *Id.,* at 1437–1438. And it was also established that "some women are capable of all of the individual activities required of VMI cadets." *Id.,* at 1412. In addition, experts agreed that if VMI admitted women, "the VMI ROTC experience would become a better training program from the perspective of the armed forces, because it would provide training in dealing with a mixed-gender army." *Id.,* at 1441.

The District Court ruled in favor of VMI, however, and rejected the equal protection challenge pressed by the United States. That court correctly recognized that *Mississippi Univ. for Women v. Hogan,* 458 U.S. 718, 102 S.Ct. 3331, 73 L.Ed.2d 1090 (1982), was the closest guide. 766 F.Supp., at 1410. There, this Court underscored that a party seeking to uphold government action based on sex must establish an "exceedingly persuasive justification" for the classification. *Mississippi Univ. for Women,* 458 U.S., at 724, 102 S.Ct., at 3336 (internal quotation marks omitted). To succeed, the defender of the challenged action must show "at least that the classification serves important governmental objectives and that the discriminatory means employed are substantially related to the achievement of those objectives." *Ibid.* (internal quotation marks omitted).

. . . .

The Court of Appeals for the Fourth Circuit disagreed and vacated the District Court's judgment. The appellate court held: "The Commonwealth of Virginia has not . . . advanced any state policy by which it can justify its determination, under an announced policy of diversity, to afford VMI's unique type of program to men and not to women." 976 F.2d 890, 892 (1992).

The appeals court greeted with skepticism Virginia's assertion that it offers single-sex education at VMI as a facet of the Commonwealth's overarching and undisputed policy to advance "autonomy and diversity." . . . In short, the court concluded, "[a] policy of diversity which aims to provide an array of educational opportunities, including single-gender institutions, must do more than favor one gender." *Ibid.*

The parties agreed that "*some* women can meet the physical standards now imposed on men," *id.,* at 896, and the court was satisfied that "neither the goal of producing citizen soldiers nor VMI's implementing methodology is inherently unsuitable to women," *id.,* at 899. The Court of Appeals, however, accepted the District Court's finding that "at least these three aspects of VMI's program—physical training, the absence of privacy, and the adversarial approach—would be materially affected by coeducation." *Id.,* at 896–897. Remanding the case, the appeals court assigned to Virginia, in the first instance, responsibility for selecting a remedial course. The court suggested these options for the Commonwealth: Admit women to VMI; establish parallel institutions or programs; or abandon state support, leaving VMI free to pursue its policies as a private institution. *Id.,* at 900. In May 1993, this Court denied certiorari. See 508 U.S. 946, 113 S.Ct. 2431, 124 L.Ed.2d 651; see also *ibid.* (opinion of Scalia, J., noting the interlocutory posture of the litigation).

C

In response to the Fourth Circuit's ruling, Virginia proposed a parallel program for women: Virginia Women's Institute for Leadership (VWIL). The 4-year, state-sponsored undergraduate program would be located at Mary Baldwin College, a private liberal arts school for women, and would be open, initially, to about 25 to 30 students. Although VWIL would share VMI's mission—to produce "citizen-soldiers"—the VWIL program would differ, as does Mary Baldwin College, from VMI in academic offerings, methods of education, and financial resources. See 852 F.Supp. 471, 476–477 (W.D.Va.1994).

The average combined SAT score of entrants at Mary Baldwin is about 100 points lower than the score for VMI freshmen. See *id.,* at 501. Mary Baldwin's faculty holds "significantly fewer Ph.D.'s than the faculty at VMI," *id.,* at 502, and receives significantly lower salaries, see Tr. 158 (testimony of James Lott, Dean of Mary Baldwin College), reprinted in 2 App. in Nos. 94-1667 and 94-1717(CA4) (hereinafter Tr.). While VMI offers degrees in liberal arts, the sciences, and engineering, Mary Baldwin, at the time of trial, offered only bachelor of arts degrees. See 852 F.Supp., at 503. A VWIL student seeking to earn an engineering degree could gain one, without public support, by attending Washington University in St. Louis, Missouri, for two years, paying the required private tuition. See *ibid.*

Experts in educating women at the college level composed the Task Force charged with designing the VWIL program; Task Force members were drawn from Mary Baldwin's own faculty and staff. *Id.,* at 476. Training its attention on methods of instruction appropriate for "most women," the Task Force determined that a military model would be "wholly inappropriate" for VWIL. *Ibid.;* see 44 F.3d 1229, 1233 (C.A.4 1995).

VWIL students would participate in ROTC programs and a newly established, "largely ceremonial" Virginia Corps of Cadets, *id.,* at 1234, but the VWIL House would not have a military format, 852 F.Supp., at 477, and VWIL would not require its students to eat meals together or to wear uniforms during the school day, *id.,* at 495. In lieu of VMI's adversative method, the VWIL Task Force favored "a cooperative method which reinforces self-esteem." *Id.,* at 476. In addition to the standard bachelor of arts program offered at Mary Baldwin, VWIL students would take courses in leadership, complete an off-campus leadership externship, participate in community service projects, and assist in arranging a speaker series. See 44 F.3d, at 1234.

Virginia represented that it will provide equal financial support for in-state VWIL students and VMI cadets, 852 F.Supp., at 483, and the VMI Foundation agreed to supply a $5.4625 million endowment for the VWIL program, *id.,* at 499. Mary Baldwin's own endowment is about $19 million; VMI's is $131 million. *Id.,* at 503. Mary Baldwin will add $35 million to its endowment based on future commitments; VMI will add $220 million. *Ibid.* The VMI Alumni Association has developed a network of employers interested in hiring VMI graduates. The Association has agreed to open its network to VWIL graduates, *id.,* at 499, but those graduates will not have the advantage afforded by a VMI degree.

D

Virginia returned to the District Court seeking approval of its proposed remedial plan, and the court decided the plan met the requirements of the Equal Protection Clause. *Id.,* at 473. . . .

A divided Court of Appeals affirmed the District Court's judgment. 44 F.3d 1229 (C.A.4 1995). . . .

. . . .

III

The cross-petitions in this suit present two ultimate issues. First, does Virginia's exclusion of women from the educational opportunities provided by VMI— extraordinary opportunities for military training and civilian leadership development—deny to women "capable of all of the individual activities required of VMI cadets," 766 F.Supp., at 1412, the equal protection of the laws guaranteed by the Fourteenth Amendment? Second, if VMI's "unique" situation, *id.,* at 1413—as Virginia's sole single-sex public institution of higher education—offends the Constitution's equal protection principle, what is the remedial requirement?

IV

We note, once again, the core instruction of this Court's path marking decisions in *J.E.B. v. Alabama ex rel. T. B.,* 511 U.S. 127, 136–137, and n. 6, 114 S.Ct. 1419, 1425–1426, and n. 6, 128 L.Ed.2d 89 (1994), and *Mississippi Univ. for Women,* 458 U.S., at 724, 102 S.Ct., at 3336 (internal quotation marks omitted): Parties who seek to defend gender-based government action must demonstrate an "exceedingly persuasive justification" for that action.

Today's skeptical scrutiny of official action denying rights or opportunities based on sex responds to volumes of history. As a plurality of this Court acknowledged a generation ago, "our Nation has had a long and unfortunate history of sex discrimination." *Frontiero v. Richardson,* 411 U.S. 677, 684, 93 S.Ct. 1764, 1769, 36 L. Ed.2d 583 (1973). Through a century plus three decades and more of that history, women did not count among voters composing "We the People"; not until 1920 did women gain a constitutional right to the franchise. *Id.,* at 685, 93 S.Ct., at 1769–1770. And for a half century thereafter, it remained the prevailing doctrine that government, both federal and state, could withhold from women opportunities accorded men so long as any "basis in reason" could be conceived for the discrimination. See, *e.g., Goesaert v. Cleary,* 335 U.S. 464, 467, 69 S.Ct. 198, 200, 93 L.Ed. 163 (1948) (rejecting challenge of female tavern owner and her daughter to Michigan law denying bartender licenses to females—except for wives and daughters of male tavern owners; Court would not "give ear" to the contention that "an unchivalrous desire of male bartenders to . . . monopolize the calling" prompted the legislation).

. . . .

"Inherent differences" between men and women, we have come to appreciate, remain cause for celebration, but not for denigration of the members of either sex or for artificial constraints on an individual's opportunity. Sex classifications may be used to compensate women "for particular economic disabilities [they have] suffered," *Califano v. Webster,* 430 U.S. 313, 320, 97 S.Ct. 1192, 1196, 51 L.Ed.2d 360 (1977) *(per curiam),* to "promot[e] equal employment opportunity," see *California Fed. Sav. & Loan Assn. v. Guerra,* 479 U.S. 272, 289, 107 S.Ct. 683, 693–694, 93 L. Ed.2d 613 (1987), to advance full development of the talent and capacities of our Nation's people. But such classifications may not be used, as they once were, see *Goesaert,* 335 U.S., at 467, 69 S.Ct., at 200, to create or perpetuate the legal, social, and economic inferiority of women.

Measuring the record in this case against the review standard just described, we conclude that Virginia has shown no "exceedingly persuasive justification" for excluding all women from the citizen-soldier training afforded by VMI. We therefore affirm the Fourth Circuit's initial judgment, which held that Virginia had violated the Fourteenth Amendment's Equal Protection Clause. Because the remedy proffered by Virginia—the Mary Baldwin VWIL program—does not cure the constitutional violation, *i.e.,* it does not provide equal opportunity, we reverse the Fourth Circuit's final judgment in this case.

V

The Fourth Circuit initially held that Virginia had advanced no state policy by which it could justify, under equal protection principles, its determination "to afford VMI's unique type of program to men and not to women." 976 F.2d, at 892. Virginia challenges that "liability" ruling and asserts two justifications in defense of VMI's exclusion of women. First, the Commonwealth contends, "single-sex education provides important educational benefits," Brief for Cross-Petitioners 20, and the option of single-sex education contributes to "diversity in educational approaches," *id.,* at 25. Second, the Commonwealth argues, "the unique VMI method of character development and leadership training," the school's adversative approach, would have to be modified were VMI to admit women. *Id.*, at 33–36 (internal quotation marks omitted). We consider these two justifications in turn.

A

. . . Virginia has not shown that VMI was established, or has been maintained, with a view to diversifying, by its categorical exclusion of women, educational opportunities within the Commonwealth. In cases of this genre, our precedent instructs that "benign" justifications proffered in defense of categorical exclusions will not be accepted automatically; a tenable justification must describe actual state purposes, not rationalizations for actions in fact differently grounded. . . .

Mississippi Univ. for Women is immediately in point. There the State asserted, in justification of its exclusion of men from a nursing school, that it was engaging in "educational affirmative action" by "compensat[ing] for discrimination against women." 458 U.S., at 727, 102 S.Ct., at 3337. Undertaking a "searching analysis," *id.*, at 728, 102 S.Ct., at 3338, the Court found no close resemblance between "the alleged objective" and "the actual purpose underlying the discriminatory classification," *id.*, at 730, 102 S.Ct., at 3339. Pursuing a similar inquiry here, we reach the same conclusion.

Neither recent nor distant history bears out Virginia's alleged pursuit of diversity through single-sex educational options. In 1839, when the Commonwealth established VMI, a range of educational opportunities for men and women was scarcely contemplated. Higher education at the time was considered dangerous for women; reflecting widely held views about women's proper place, the Nation's first universities and colleges—for example, Harvard in Massachusetts, William and Mary in Virginia—admitted only men. See E. Farello, A History of the Education of Women in the United States 163 (1970). VMI was not at all novel in this respect: In admitting no women, VMI followed the lead of the Commonwealth's flagship school, the University of Virginia, founded in 1819.

"[N]o struggle for the admission of women to a state university," a historian has recounted, "was longer drawn out, or developed more bitterness, than that at the University of Virginia." 2 T. Woody, A History of Women's Education in the United States 254 (1929) (History of Women's Education). In 1879, the State Senate resolved to look into the possibility of higher education for women, recognizing that Virginia "'has never, at any period of her history,'" provided for the higher education of her daughters, though she "'has liberally provided for the higher education of her sons.'" *Ibid.* (quoting 10 Educ. J. Va. 212 (1879)). Despite this recognition, no new opportunities were instantly open to women.

Virginia eventually provided for several women's seminaries and colleges. Farmville Female Seminary became a public institution in 1884. See *supra*, at 2270, n. 2. Two women's schools, Mary Washington College and James Madison University, were founded in 1908; another, Radford University, was founded in 1910. 766 F. Supp., at 1418–1419. By the mid-1970's, all four schools had become coeducational. *Ibid.*

. . . .

Ultimately, in 1970, "the most prestigious institution of higher education in Virginia," the University of Virginia, introduced coeducation and, in 1972, began to admit women on an equal basis with men. See *Kirstein v. Rector and Visitors of Univ. of Virginia,* 309 F.Supp. 184, 186 (E.D.Va.1970). . . .

Virginia describes the current absence of public single-sex higher education for women as "an historical anomaly." Brief for Cross-Petitioners 30. But the historical record indicates action more deliberate than anomalous: First, protection of women against higher education; next, schools for women far from equal in resources and stature to schools for men; finally, conversion of the separate schools to coeducation. The state legislature, prior to the advent of this controversy, had repealed "[a]ll Virginia statutes requiring individual institutions to admit only men or women." 766 F.Supp., at 1419. And in 1990, an official commission, "legislatively established to chart the future goals of higher education in Virginia," reaffirmed the policy "'of affording broad access'" while maintaining "'autonomy and diversity.'" 976 F.2d, at 898–899 (quoting Report of the Virginia Commission on the University of the 21st Century). Significantly, the commission reported:

> "'Because colleges and universities provide opportunities for students to develop values and learn from role models, it is extremely important that they deal with faculty, staff, and students *without regard to sex, race, or ethnic origin.*'" *Id.,* at 899 (emphasis supplied by Court of Appeals deleted).

This statement, the Court of Appeals observed, "is the only explicit one that we have found in the record in which the Commonwealth has expressed itself with respect to gender distinctions." *Ibid.*

[W]e find no persuasive evidence in this record that VMI's male-only admission policy "is in furtherance of a state policy of 'diversity.'" See 976 F.2d, at 899. No such policy, the Fourth Circuit observed, can be discerned from the movement of all other public colleges and universities in Virginia away from single-sex education. See *ibid.* That court also questioned "how one institution with autonomy, but with no authority over any other state institution, can give effect to a state policy of diversity among institutions." *Ibid.* A purpose genuinely to advance an array of educational options, as the Court of Appeals recognized, is not served by VMI's historic and constant plan—a plan to "affor[d] a unique educational benefit only to males." *Ibid.* However "liberally" this plan serves the Commonwealth's sons, it makes no provision whatever for her daughters. That is not *equal* protection.

B

Virginia next argues that VMI's adversative method of training provides educational benefits that cannot be made available, unmodified, to women. Alterations to accommodate women would necessarily be "radical," so "drastic," Virginia asserts, as to transform, indeed "destroy," VMI's program. See Brief for Cross-Petitioners 34–36. Neither sex would be favored by the transformation, Virginia maintains: Men would be deprived of the unique opportunity currently available to them; women would not gain that opportunity because their participation would "eliminat[e] the very aspects of [the] program that distinguish [VMI] from . . . other institutions of higher education in Virginia." *Id.,* at 34.

. . . .

The United States does not challenge any expert witness estimation on average capacities or preferences of men and women. Instead, the United States emphasizes that time and again since this Court's turning point decision in *Reed v. Reed,* 404 U.S. 71, 92 S.Ct. 251, 30 L.Ed.2d 225 (1971), we have cautioned reviewing courts to take a "hard look" at generalizations or "tendencies" of the kind pressed by Virginia, and relied upon by the District Court. See O'Connor, *Portia's Progress,* 66 N.Y.U.L.Rev. 1546, 1551 (1991). State actors controlling gates to opportunity, we have instructed, may not exclude qualified individuals based on "fixed notions concerning the roles and abilities of males and females." *Mississippi Univ. for Women,* 458 U.S., at 725, 102 S.Ct., at 3336; see *J.E.B.,* 511 U.S., at 139, n. 11, 114 S.Ct., at 1427, n. 11 (equal protection principles, as applied to gender classifications, mean state actors may not rely on "overbroad" generalizations to make "judgments about people that are likely to . . . perpetuate historical patterns of discrimination").

It may be assumed, for purposes of this decision, that most women would not choose VMI's adversative method. As Fourth Circuit Judge Motz observed, however, in her dissent from the Court of Appeals' denial of rehearing en banc, it is also probable that "many men would not want to be educated in such an environment." 52 F.3d, at 93. (On that point, even our dissenting colleague might agree.) . . . The notion that admission of women would downgrade VMI's stature, destroy the adversative system and, with it, even the school, is a judgment hardly proved, a prediction hardly different from other "self-fulfilling prophec[ies]," see *Mississippi Univ. for Women,* 458 U.S., at 730, 102 S.Ct., at 3339, once routinely used to deny rights or opportunities. When women first sought admission to the bar and access to legal education, concerns of the same order were expressed. For example, [a] like fear, according to a 1925 report, accounted for Columbia Law School's resistance to women's admission, although

> "[t]he faculty . . . never maintained that women could not master legal learning. . . . No, its argument has been . . . more practical. If women were admitted to the Columbia Law School, [the faculty] said, then the choicer, more manly and red-blooded graduates of our great universities would go to the Harvard Law School!" The Nation, Feb. 18, 1925, p. 173.

Medical faculties similarly resisted men and women as partners in the study of medicine. . . .

Women's successful entry into the federal military academies, and their participation in the Nation's military forces, indicate that Virginia's fears for the future of VMI may not be solidly grounded. The Commonwealth's justification for excluding all women from "citizen-soldier" training for which some are qualified, in any event, cannot rank as "exceedingly persuasive," as we have explained and applied that standard.

Virginia and VMI trained their argument on "means" rather than "end," and thus misperceived our precedent. Single-sex education at VMI serves an "important governmental objective," they maintained, and exclusion of women is not only "substantially related," it is essential to that objective. By this notably circular argument, the "straightforward" test *Mississippi Univ. for Women* described, see 458 U.S., at 724–725, 102 S.Ct., at 3336–3337, was bent and bowed.

. . . .

VI

In the second phase of the litigation, Virginia presented its remedial plan— maintain VMI as a male-only college and create VWIL as a separate program for women. The plan met District Court approval. The Fourth Circuit, in turn, deferentially reviewed the Commonwealth's proposal and decided that the two single-sex programs directly served Virginia's reasserted purposes: single-gender education, and "achieving the results of an adversative method in a military environment." See 44 F.3d, at 1236, 1239. Inspecting the VMI and VWIL educational programs to determine whether they "afford[ed] to both genders benefits comparable in substance, [if] not in form and detail," *id.*, at 1240, the Court of Appeals concluded that Virginia had arranged for men and women opportunities "sufficiently comparable" to survive equal protection evaluation, *id.*, at 1240–1241. The United States challenges this "remedial" ruling as pervasively misguided.

A

A remedial decree, this Court has said, must closely fit the constitutional violation; it must be shaped to place persons unconstitutionally denied an opportunity or advantage in "the position they would have occupied in the absence of [discrimination]." See *Milliken v. Bradley,* 433 U.S. 267, 280, 97 S.Ct. 2749, 2757, 53 L. Ed.2d 745 (1977) (internal quotation marks omitted). The constitutional violation in this suit is the categorical exclusion of women from an extraordinary educational opportunity afforded men. A proper remedy for an unconstitutional exclusion, we have explained, aims to "eliminate [so far as possible] the discriminatory effects of the past" and to "bar like discrimination in the future." *Louisiana v. United States,* 380 U.S. 145, 154, 85 S.Ct. 817, 822, 13 L.Ed.2d 709 (1965).

Virginia chose not to eliminate, but to leave untouched, VMI's exclusionary policy. For women only, however, Virginia proposed a separate program, different in kind from VMI and unequal in tangible and intangible facilities. Having violated the Constitution's equal protection requirement, Virginia was obliged to show that its remedial proposal "directly address[ed] and relate[d] to" the violation, see *Milliken,* 433 U.S., at 282, 97 S.Ct., at 2758, *i.e.,* the equal protection denied to women ready, willing, and able to benefit from educational opportunities of the kind VMI offers.

Virginia described VWIL as a "parallel program," and asserted that VWIL shares VMI's mission of producing "citizen-soldiers" and VMI's goals of providing "education, military training, mental and physical discipline, character . . . and leadership development." Brief for Respondents 24 (internal quotation marks omitted). If the VWIL program could not "eliminate the discriminatory effects of the past," could it at least "bar like discrimination in the future"? See *Louisiana*, 380 U.S., at 154, 85 S. Ct., at 822. A comparison of the programs said to be "parallel" informs our answer. In exposing the character of, and differences in, the VMI and VWIL programs, we recapitulate facts earlier presented. See *supra*, at 2269–2271, 2272–2273.

VWIL affords women no opportunity to experience the rigorous military training for which VMI is famed. . . . VWIL students participate in ROTC and a "largely ceremonial" Virginia Corps of Cadets, see 44 F.3d, at 1234, but Virginia deliberately did not make VWIL a military institute. . . . VWIL students receive their "leadership training" in seminars, externships, and speaker series, see 852 F.Supp., at 477, episodes and encounters lacking the "[p]hysical rigor, mental stress, . . . minute regulation of behavior, and indoctrination in desirable values" made hallmarks of VMI's citizen-soldier training, see 766 F.Supp., at 1421. Kept away from the pressures, hazards, and psychological bonding characteristic of VMI's adversative training, see *id.*, at 1422, VWIL students will not know the "feeling of tremendous accomplishment" commonly experienced by VMI's successful cadets, *id.*, at 1426.

Virginia maintains that these methodological differences are "justified pedagogically," based on "important differences between men and women in learning and developmental needs," "psychological and sociological differences" Virginia describes as "real" and "not stereotypes." Brief for Respondents 28 (internal quotation marks omitted). . . .

As earlier stated, see *supra*, at 2280, generalizations about "the way women are," estimates of what is appropriate for *most women*, no longer justify denying opportunity to women whose talent and capacity place them outside the average description. Notably, Virginia never asserted that VMI's method of education suits *most men*. It is also revealing that Virginia accounted for its failure to make the VWIL experience "the entirely militaristic experience of VMI" on the ground that VWIL "is planned for women who do not necessarily expect to pursue military careers." 852 F.Supp., at 478. By that reasoning, VMI's "entirely militaristic" program would be inappropriate for men in general or *as a group*, for "[o]nly about 15% of VMI cadets enter career military service." See 766 F.Supp., at 1432.

In contrast to the generalizations about women on which Virginia rests, we note again these dispositive realities: VMI's "implementing methodology" is not "inherently unsuitable to women," 976 F.2d, at 899; "some women . . . do well under [the] adversative model," 766 F.Supp., at 1434 (internal quotation marks omitted); "some women, at least, would want to attend [VMI] if they had the opportunity," *id.*, at 1414; "some women are capable of all of the individual activities required of VMI cadets," *id.*, at 1412, and "can meet the physical standards [VMI] now impose[s] on men," 976 F.2d, at 896. It is on behalf of these women that the United States has instituted this suit, and it is for them that a remedy must be crafted, a remedy that will end their exclusion from a state-supplied educational opportunity for which they are fit, a decree that will "bar like discrimination in the future." *Louisiana,* 380 U.S., at 154, 85 S.Ct., at 822.

B

In myriad respects other than military training, VWIL does not qualify as VMI's equal. VWIL's student body, faculty, course offerings, and facilities hardly match VMI's. Nor can the VWIL graduate anticipate the benefits associated with VMI's 157-year history, the school's prestige, and its influential alumni network.

. . . [For example,] the VWIL student does not graduate with the advantage of a VMI degree. Her diploma does not unite her with the legions of VMI "graduates [who] have distinguished themselves" in military and civilian life. See 976 F.2d, at 892–893. "[VMI] alumni are exceptionally close to the school," and that closeness accounts, in part, for VMI's success in attracting applicants. See 766 F.Supp., at 1421. A VWIL graduate cannot assume that the "network of business owners, corporations, VMI graduates and non-graduate employers . . . interested in hiring VMI graduates," 852 F.Supp., at 499, will be equally responsive to her search for employment see 44 F.3d, at 1250 (Phillips, J., dissenting) ("the powerful political and economic ties of the VMI alumni network cannot be expected to open" for graduates of the fledgling VWIL program).

Virginia, in sum, while maintaining VMI for men only, has failed to provide any "comparable single-gender women's institution." *Id.,* at 1241. Instead, the Commonwealth has created a VWIL program fairly appraised as a "pale shadow" of VMI in terms of the range of curricular choices and faculty stature, funding, prestige, alumni support and influence.

. . . .

C

When Virginia tendered its VWIL plan, the Fourth Circuit did not inquire whether the proposed remedy, approved by the District Court, placed women denied the VMI advantage in "the position they would have occupied in the absence of [discrimination]." *Milliken,* 433 U.S., at 280, 97 S.Ct., at 2757 (internal quotation marks omitted). Instead, the Court of Appeals considered whether the Commonwealth could provide, with fidelity to the equal protection principle, separate and unequal educational programs for men and women.

The Fourth Circuit acknowledged that "the VWIL degree from Mary Baldwin College lacks the historical benefit and prestige of a degree from VMI." 44 F.3d, at 1241. The Court of Appeals further observed that VMI is "an ongoing and successful institution with a long history," and there remains no "comparable single-gender women's institution." *Ibid.* Nevertheless, the appeals court declared the substantially different and significantly unequal VWIL program satisfactory. The court reached that result by revising the applicable standard of review. The Fourth Circuit displaced the standard developed in our precedent, see *supra*, at 2275–2276, and substituted a standard of its own invention.

We have earlier described the deferential review in which the Court of Appeals engaged, see *supra*, at 2273–2274, a brand of review inconsistent with the more exacting standard our precedent requires, see *supra*, at 2275–2276. Quoting in part from *Mississippi Univ. for Women,* the Court of Appeals candidly described its own analysis as one capable of checking a legislative purpose ranked as "pernicious," but generally according "deference to [the] legislative will." 44 F.3d, at 1235, 1236. Recognizing that it had extracted from our decisions a test yielding "little or no scrutiny of the effect of a classification directed at [single-gender education]," the Court of Appeals devised another test, a "substantive comparability" inquiry, *id.,* at 1237, and proceeded to find that new test satisfied, *id.,* at 1241.

The Fourth Circuit plainly erred in exposing Virginia's VWIL plan to a deferential analysis, for "all gender-based classifications today" warrant "heightened scrutiny." See *J.E.B.,* 511 U.S., at 136, 114 S.Ct., at 1425. Valuable as VWIL may prove for students who seek the program offered, Virginia's remedy affords no cure at all for the opportunities and advantages withheld from women who want a VMI education and can make the grade. See *supra*, at 2282–2286. In sum, Virginia's remedy does not match the constitutional violation; the Commonwealth has shown no "exceedingly persuasive justification" for withholding from women qualified for the experience premier training of the kind VMI affords.

VII

A generation ago, "the authorities controlling Virginia higher education," despite long established tradition, agreed "to innovate and favorably entertain[ed] the [then] relatively new idea that there must be no discrimination by sex in offering educational opportunity." *Kirstein,* 309 F.Supp., at 186. Commencing in 1970, Virginia opened to women "educational opportunities at the Charlottesville campus that [were] not afforded in other [state-operated] institutions." *Id.,* at 187; see *supra*, at 2278. A federal court approved the Commonwealth's innovation, emphasizing that the University of Virginia "offer[ed] courses of instruction . . . not available elsewhere." 309 F.Supp., at 187. The court further noted: "[T]here exists at Charlottesville a 'prestige' factor [not paralleled in] other Virginia educational institutions." *Ibid.*

VMI, too, offers an educational opportunity no other Virginia institution provides, and the school's "prestige"—associated with its success in developing "citizen-soldiers"—is unequaled. Virginia has closed this facility to its daughters and, instead, has devised for them a "parallel program," with a faculty less impressively credentialed and less well paid, more limited course offerings, fewer opportunities for military training and for scientific specialization. Cf. *Sweatt,* 339 U.S., at 633, 70 S.Ct., at 849–850. VMI, beyond question, "possesses to a far greater degree" than the VWIL program "those qualities which are incapable of objective measurement but which make for greatness in a . . . school," including "position and influence of the alumni, standing in the community, traditions and prestige." *Id.*, at 634, 70 S.Ct., at 850. Women seeking and fit for a VMI-quality education cannot be offered anything less, under the Commonwealth's obligation to afford them genuinely equal protection.

A prime part of the history of our Constitution, historian Richard Morris recounted, is the story of the extension of constitutional rights and protections to people once ignored or excluded. VMI's story continued as our comprehension of "We the People" expanded. See *supra*, at 2282, n. 16. There is no reason to believe that the admission of women capable of all the activities required of VMI cadets would destroy the Institute rather than enhance its capacity to serve the "more perfect Union."

For the reasons stated, the initial judgment of the Court of Appeals, 976 F.2d 890 (C.A.4 1992), is affirmed, the final judgment of the Court of Appeals, 44 F.3d 1229 (C.A.4 1995), is reversed, and the case is remanded for further proceedings consistent with this opinion.

It is so ordered.

Note

U.S. v. Virginia also serves as a precursor to our materials and cases on equal protection in education, discussed later in this book. Those early Fourteenth Amendment cases created a basis for adjudicating claims of segregation by race and then by sex, in education. Aptly, in a portion omitted here, the Court acknowledges this history and the relevance of the racial discrimination jurisprudence to the gender context.

> Virginia's VWIL solution is reminiscent of the remedy Texas proposed 50 years ago, in response to a state trial court's 1946 ruling that, given the equal protection guarantee, African-Americans could not be denied a legal education at a state facility. See *Sweatt v. Painter,* 339 U.S. 629, 70 S.Ct. 848, 94 L.Ed. 1114 (1950). Reluctant to admit African-Americans to its flagship University of Texas Law School, the State set up a separate school for Heman Sweatt and other black law students. *Id.*, at 632, 70 S.Ct., at 849. As originally opened, the new school had no independent faculty or library, and it lacked accreditation. *Id.*, at 633, 70 S.Ct., at 849–850. Nevertheless, the state trial and appellate courts were satisfied that the new school offered Sweatt opportunities for the study of law "substantially equivalent to those offered by the State to white students at the University of Texas." *Id.*, at 632, 70 S.Ct., at 849 (internal quotation marks omitted).

> Before this Court considered the case, the new school had gained "a faculty of five full-time professors; a student body of 23; a library of some 16,500 volumes serviced by a full-time staff; a practice court and legal aid association; and one alumnus who ha[d] become a member of the Texas Bar." *Id.*, at 633, 70 S.Ct., at 850. This Court contrasted resources at the new

school with those at the school from which Sweatt had been excluded. The University of Texas Law School had a full-time faculty of 16, a student body of 850, a library containing over 65,000 volumes, scholarship funds, a law review, and moot court facilities. *Id.,* at 632–633, 70 S.Ct., at 849–850.

More important than the tangible features, the Court emphasized, are "those qualities which are incapable of objective measurement but which make for greatness" in a school, including "reputation of the faculty, experience of the administration, position and influence of the alumni, standing in the community, traditions and prestige." *Id.,* at 634, 70 S.Ct., at 850. Facing the marked differences reported in the *Sweatt* opinion, the Court unanimously ruled that Texas had not shown "substantial equality in the [separate] educational opportunities" the State offered. *Id.,* at 633, 70 S.Ct., at 850. Accordingly, the Court held, the Equal Protection Clause required Texas to admit African-Americans to the University of Texas Law School. *Id.,* at 636, 70 S.Ct., at 851. In line with *Sweatt,* we rule here that Virginia has not shown substantial equality in the separate educational opportunities the Commonwealth supports at VWIL and VMI.

Note

In the section of affirmative action, covered later in this book, consider whether we have moved away from seeing the legal connections between gender and racial discrimination. Are there commonalities between discrimination based on sex and discrimination based on race? Should different standards be used under the 14th Amendment to remedy past inequities faced by both groups?

Chapter 4

Educational Opportunity

This chapter on educational opportunity illustrates most tangibly the dangers presented when law replicates power structures. When states and the other branches of the federal governments seemed lackluster in implementing the mandates of integration, civil rights lawyers turned to the federal courts. Despite limitations, the cases below demonstrate a potential for law as a change agent when combined with lawyers' understanding of the realities on the ground. First in the racial desegregation context, and, then in interpreting civil rights statutes, the Supreme Court has become acutely aware of, and somewhat ambivalent about, its role in dismantling de jure segregation. Consequently, as time progressed away from de jure segregation, federal courts simultaneously began a retrenchment away from civil rights gains.

As you read the pre-integration cases below, try to map out the march from *Plessy* to *Brown*. What is the significance of references to the badge of inferiority in *Plessy* and *Brown*? How is this concept interpreted differently by the Court from *Plessy* to *Brown*?

A. Law as Power

There is no better illustration of the uses of law as replication of power than the Slavery and Jim Crow eras. As captured by Professor Chemerinsky in *The Case Against the Supreme Court*, the legitimacy of the Court as a democratic and fairness-based institution took a huge blow when it penned such infamous and deplorable decisions as *Dred Scott v. Sanford*, 60 U.S. 393 (1857) (maintaining that African Americans could not be considered citizens with rights equal to whites and invalidating the Missouri compromise), *Plessy v. Fergusson*, 163 U.S. 537 (1896) (upholding the doctrine of separate but equal as constitutional), *Buck v. Bell*, 274 U.S. 200 (1927) (upholding state decision to sterilize a woman deemed mentally challenged with the infamous pronouncement that "three generations of idiots are enough"). Erwin Chemerinsky, The Case Against the Supreme Court 1–38 (2014). We cover *Buck v. Bell* in the chapter on disability law.

The common denominator tying these cases is the Court's prevailing sentiments of the time rather than attempting to transcend them. This judicial legacy in the context of education, particularly, serves as a painful reminder of the failures of laws to protect the vulnerable. Still, even in the midst of this context, there exist documented examples of law affirming democratic aspirations. One occured in

Massachusetts when the Massachusetts Supreme Court held, in *Roberts v. City of Boston*, 59 Mass. 198 (1849), that the city of Boston could continue segregation despite that state's equal protection clause. This caused such outrage among the state's citizens that the Massachusetts legislature outlawed segregated education six years later (similar to Massachusetts's Supreme Court, the highest courts in California and Ohio opted for solid segregation in their respective states—Ohio Supreme Court in *State ex rel. Garnes v. McCann*, 21 Ohio St. 198 (1871), and Supreme Court of California in *Ward v. Flood*, 48 Cal. 36 (1874)).

In a few other states, state courts transcended prevailing discriminatory sentiments. In *Clark v. Board of Directors*, 24 Iowa 266 (1868), and *Board of Education v. Tinnon*, 26 Kan. 1 (1881), for example, the courts refused to succumb to pressure from legislature or to public resistance and interpreted their color-blind statutes to prohibit segregated schools.

In this chapter, we will track the road to federal judicial awareness of the harms of segregation in education and courts' active involvement in promoting educational integration after *Brown*. This chapter begins with the struggle for equal education and describes the road to *Brown*, the seminal integration case. The next section focuses on constitutional issues tackled by the Court during the long period of desegregation and the persisting hurdles created by the de facto segregation that replaced Jim Crow. The third section centers around the remedies available under Title VI for challenging racial inequities in education.

B. Historical Background

The right to equal education has a tortured history. First, public schools are a fairly recent phenomenon. They were not prevalent during the framing of the Constitution or even during the passing of the Reconstruction Amendments. For a long time, educational opportunities were contingent on region and subjective to background. For example, states like Massachusetts began to open schools in the seventeenth century. These early schools were integrated, but African Americans in those schools were subject to such mistreatment and isolation that members of the African communities in Massachusetts lobbied for publicly supported separate schools. Separate schools were opened in the early nineteenth century, and leading members of the black community were finally successful in obtaining state funded African American schools in 1820, 10 years before public schools became the norm throughout the nation. Unfortunately, state sponsored separate schools for blacks became institutionalized with racism and inequality. Parents and activists soon realized that the schools were unequal to those of their white counterparts. In addition, control of the schools was removed from the hands of parents, so that their complaints of mismanagement and abuse of pupils by certain educators fell on deaf ears. These generalities varied depending on the locale. A few states progressively made public education available very early. An even fewer number in the North allowed black students access to integrated school systems. Options were more limited in the South. Until the Civil War, it was illegal to educate African Americans. As a result, the struggle for education during that time was a subversive act tantamount to attempting to escaping slavery. Fairly soon after the Civil War, this criminalization was replaced by separate but equal, a system which *Plessy v. Fergusson* institutionalized when it declared the separate but equal doctrine constitutional. In the Southern reality, inequalities loomed large for nearly 100 years.

Plessy vs. Fergusson (1896), below, illustrates the extent of harm accomplished when the judiciary chooses to reflect power uncritically. Subsection (b) continues with an exploration of the cases that led to *Brown*.

Plessy v. Ferguson came at a time when gains made during Reconstruction were actively being pulled back. The federal government agreed to withdraw from the South and cease oversight of equal administration of the laws in former seceding and slave holding states. From that time, efforts to provide substantive public education to newly emancipated blacks were impeded by formal Jim Crow laws mandating segregation based on color. Thus, blacks' education depended on a fraction of the resources for whites, and on the benevolence of philanthropic whites (Spelman, Tuskegee). It was not unusual, then, for black communities to lack schools or to have schools reaching only up to 6th grade, without access to any high schools within a hundred mile radius.

Plessy v. Ferguson
163 U.S. 537 (1986)

Brown, J., Opinion of the Court

This case turns upon the constitutionality of an act of the General Assembly of the State of Louisiana, passed in 1890, providing for separate railway carriages for the white and colored races. Acts 1890, No. 111, p. 152.

The first section of the statute enacts that all railway companies carrying passengers in their coaches in this State shall provide equal but separate accommodations for the white and colored races by providing two or more passenger coaches for each passenger train, or by dividing the passenger coaches by a partition so as to secure separate accommodations: *Provided,* That this section shall not be construed to apply to street railroads. No person or persons, shall be admitted to occupy seats in coaches other than the ones assigned to them on account of the race they belong to.

By the second section, it was enacted that the officers of such passenger trains shall have power and are hereby required to assign each passenger to the coach or compartment used for the race to which such passenger belongs; any passenger insisting on going into a coach or compartment to which by race he does not belong shall be liable to a fine of twenty-five dollars, or in lieu thereof to imprisonment for a period of not more than twenty days in the parish prison, and any officer of any railroad insisting on assigning a passenger to a coach or compartment other than the one set aside for the race to which said passenger belongs shall be liable to a fine of twenty-five dollars, or in lieu thereof to imprisonment for a period of not more than twenty days in the parish prison; and should any passenger refuse to occupy the coach or compartment to which he or she is assigned by the officer of such railway, said officer shall have power to refuse to carry such passenger on his train, and for such refusal neither he nor the railway company which he represents shall be liable for damages in any of the courts of this State.

The third section provides penalties for the refusal or neglect of the officers, directors, conductors, and employees of railway companies to comply with the act, with a proviso that "nothing in this act shall be construed as applying to nurses attending children of the other race." The fourth section is immaterial.

. . . The petition for the writ of prohibition averred that petitioner was seven-eighths Caucasian and one eighth African blood; that the mixture of colored blood was not discernible in him, and that he was entitled to every right, privilege and immunity secured to citizens of the United States of the white race; and that, upon such theory, he took possession of a vacant seat in a coach where passengers of the white race were accommodated, and was ordered by the conductor to vacate said coach and take a seat in another assigned to persons of the colored race, and, having refused to comply with such demand, he was forcibly ejected with the aid of a police officer, and imprisoned in the parish jail to answer a charge of having violated the above act.

The constitutionality of this act is attacked upon the ground that it conflicts both with the Thirteenth Amendment of the Constitution, abolishing slavery, and the Fourteenth Amendment, which prohibits certain restrictive legislation on the part of the States.

1. That it does not conflict with the Thirteenth Amendment, which abolished slavery and involuntary servitude, except as a punishment for crime, is too clear for argument. . . . This amendment was said in the *Slaughterhouse Cases,* 16 Wall. 36, to have been intended primarily to abolish slavery as it had been previously known in this country, and that it equally forbade Mexican peonage or the Chinese coolie trade when they amounted to slavery or involuntary servitude, and that the use of the word "servitude" was intended to prohibit the use of all forms of involuntary slavery, of whatever class or name. It was intimated, however, in that case that this amendment was regarded by the statesmen of that day as insufficient to protect the colored race from certain laws which had been enacted in the Southern States, imposing upon the colored race onerous disabilities and burdens and curtailing their rights in the pursuit of life, liberty and property to such an extent that their freedom was of little value; and that the Fourteenth Amendment was devised to meet this exigency.

So, too, in the *Civil Rights Cases,* 109 U.S. 3, 24, it was said that the act of a mere individual, the owner of an inn, a public conveyance or place of amusement, refusing accommodations to colored people cannot be justly regarded as imposing any badge of slavery or servitude upon the applicant, but only as involving an ordinary civil injury, properly cognizable by the laws of the State and presumably subject to redress by those laws until the contrary appears. . . .

A statute which implies merely a legal distinction between the white and colored races—a distinction which is founded in the color of the two races and which must always exist so long as white men are distinguished from the other race by color—has no tendency to destroy the legal equality of the two races, or reestablish a state of involuntary servitude. Indeed, we do not understand that the Thirteenth Amendment is strenuously relied upon by the plaintiff in error in this connection.

2. By the Fourteenth Amendment, all persons born or naturalized in the United States and subject to the jurisdiction thereof are made citizens of the United States and of the State wherein they reside, and the States are forbidden from making or enforcing any law which shall abridge the privileges or immunities of citizens of the United States, or shall deprive any person of life, liberty, or property without due process of law, or deny to any person within their jurisdiction the equal protection of the laws.

The proper construction of this amendment was first called to the attention of this court in the *Slaughterhouse Cases,* 16 Wall. 36, which involved, however, not a question of race, but one of exclusive privileges. The case did not call for any expression of opinion as to the exact rights it was intended to secure to the colored race, but it was said generally that its main purpose was to establish the citizenship of the negro, to give definitions of citizenship of the United States and of the States, and to protect from the hostile legislation of the States the privileges and immunities of citizens of the United States, as distinguished from those of citizens of the States.

The object of the amendment was undoubtedly to enforce the absolute equality of the two races before the law, but, in the nature of things, it could not have been intended to abolish distinctions based upon color, or to enforce social, as distinguished from political, equality, or a commingling of the two races upon terms unsatisfactory to either. Laws permitting, and even requiring, their separation in places where they are liable to be brought into contact do not necessarily imply the inferiority of either race to the other, and have been generally, if not universally, recognized as within the competency of the state legislatures in the exercise of their police power. The most common instance of this is connected with the establishment of separate schools for white and colored children, which has been held to be a valid exercise of the legislative power even by courts of States where the political rights of the colored race have been longest and most earnestly enforced.

One of the earliest of these cases is that of *Roberts v. City of Boston,* 5 Cush. 19, in which the Supreme Judicial Court of Massachusetts held that the general school committee of Boston had power to make provision for the instruction of colored children in separate schools established exclusively for them, and to prohibit their attendance upon the other schools. "The great principle," said Chief Justice Shaw, p. 206, "advanced by the learned and eloquent advocate for the plaintiff" (Mr. Charles Sumner), is that, by the constitution and laws of Massachusetts, all persons without distinction of age or sex, birth or color, origin or condition, are equal before the law. . . . But when this great principle comes to be applied to the actual and various conditions of persons in society, it will not warrant the assertion that men and women are legally clothed with the same civil and political powers, and that children and adults are legally to have the same functions and be subject to the same treatment, but only that the rights of all, as they are settled and regulated by law, are equally entitled to the paternal consideration and protection of the law for their maintenance and security.

It was held that the powers of the committee extended to the establishment of separate schools for children of different ages, sexes and colors, and that they might also establish special schools for poor and neglected children, who have become too old to attend the primary school and yet have not acquired the rudiments of learning to enable them to enter the ordinary schools. Similar laws have been enacted by Congress under its general power of legislation over the District of Columbia, Rev.Stat. D.C. §§ 281, 282, 283, 310, 319, as well as by the legislatures of many of the States, and have been generally, if not uniformly, sustained by the courts. *State v. McCann,* 21 Ohio St. 198; *Lehew v. Brummell,* 15 S.W.Rep. 765; *Ward v. Flood,* 48 California 36; *Bertonneau v. School Directors,* 3 Woods 177; *People v. Gallagher,* 93 N.Y. 438; *Cory v. Carter,* 48 Indiana 897; *Dawson v. Lee,* 3 Kentucky 49.

Laws forbidding the intermarriage of the two races may be said in a technical sense to interfere with the freedom of contract, and yet have been universally recognized as within the police power of the State. *State v. Gibson,* 36 Indiana 389.

. . . .

In the *Civil Rights Case,* 109 U.S. 3, it was held that an act of Congress entitling all persons within the jurisdiction of the United States to the full and equal enjoyment of the accommodations, advantages, facilities and privileges of inns, public conveyances, on land or water, theatres and other places of public amusement, and made applicable to citizens of every race and color, regardless of any previous condition of servitude, was unconstitutional and void upon the ground that the Fourteenth Amendment was prohibitory upon the States only, and the legislation authorized to be adopted by Congress for enforcing it was not direct legislation on matters respecting which the States were prohibited from making or enforcing certain laws, or doing certain acts, but was corrective legislation such as might be necessary or proper for counteracting and redressing the effect of such laws or acts.

. . . .

It is claimed by the plaintiff in error that, in any mixed community, the reputation of belonging to the dominant race, in this instance the white race, is property in the same sense that a right of action or of inheritance is property. Conceding this to be so for the purposes of this case, we are unable to see how this statute deprives him of, or in any way affects his right to, such property. If he be a white man and assigned to a colored coach, he may have his action for damages against the company for being deprived of his so-called property. Upon the other hand, if he be a colored man and be so assigned, he has been deprived of no property, since he is not lawfully entitled to the reputation of being a white man.

In this connection, it is also suggested by the learned counsel for the plaintiff in error that the same argument that will justify the state legislature in requiring railways to provide separate accommodations for the two races will also authorize them to require separate cars to be provided for people whose hair is of a certain color, or who are aliens, or who belong to certain nationalities, or to enact laws requiring colored people to walk upon one side of the street and white people upon the other, or requiring white men's houses to be painted white and colored men's black, or their vehicles or business signs to be of different colors, upon the theory that one side of the street is as good as the other, or that a house or vehicle of one color is as good as one of another color. The reply to all this is that every exercise of the police power must be reasonable, and extend only to such laws as are enacted in good faith for the promotion for the public good, and not for the annoyance or oppression of a particular class. Thus, in *Yick Wo v. Hopkins,* 118 U.S. 356, it was held by this court that a municipal ordinance of the city of San Francisco to regulate the carrying on of public laundries within the limits of the municipality violated the provisions of the Constitution of the United States if it conferred upon the municipal authorities arbitrary power, at their own will and without regard to discretion, in the legal sense of the term, to give or withhold consent as to persons or places without regard to the competency of the persons applying or the propriety of the places selected for the carrying on of the business. It was held to be a covert attempt on the part of the municipality to make an arbitrary and unjust discrimination against the Chinese race. While this was the case of a municipal ordinance, a like principle has been held to apply to acts of a state legislature passed in the exercise of the police power. *Railroad Company v. Husen,* 95 U.S. 465; *Louisville & Nashville Railroad v. Kentucky,* 161 U.S. 677, and cases cited on p. 700; *Duggett v. Hudson,* 43 Ohio St. 548; *Capen v. Foster,* 12 Pick. 48; *State ex rel. Wood v. Baker,* 38 Wisconsin 71; *Monroe v. Collins,* 17 Ohio St. 66; *Hulseman v. Rems,* 41 Penn. St. 396; *Orman v. Riley,* 1 California 48.

So far, then, as a conflict with the Fourteenth Amendment is concerned, the case reduces itself to the question whether the statute of Louisiana is a reasonable regulation, and, with respect to this, there must necessarily be a large discretion on the part of the legislature. In determining the question of reasonableness, it is at liberty to act with reference to the established usages, customs, and traditions of the people, and with a view to the promotion of their comfort and the preservation of the public peace and good order. Gauged by this standard, we cannot say that a law which authorizes or even requires the separation of the two races in public conveyances is unreasonable, or more obnoxious to the Fourteenth Amendment than the acts of Congress requiring separate schools for colored children in the District of Columbia, the constitutionality of which does not seem to have been questioned, or the corresponding acts of state legislatures.

We consider the underlying fallacy of the plaintiff's argument to consist in the assumption that the enforced separation of the two races stamps the colored race with a badge of inferiority. If this be so, it is not by reason of anything found in the act, but solely because the colored race chooses to put that construction upon it. The argument necessarily assumes that if, as has been more than once the case and is not unlikely to be so again, the colored race should become the dominant power in the state legislature, and should enact a law in precisely similar terms, it would thereby relegate the white race to an inferior position. We imagine that the white race, at least, would not acquiesce in this assumption. The argument also assumes that social prejudices may be overcome by legislation, and that equal rights cannot be secured to the negro except by an enforced commingling of the two races. We cannot accept this proposition. If the two races are to meet upon terms of social equality, it must be the result of natural affinities, a mutual appreciation of each other's merits, and a voluntary consent of individuals. As was said by the Court of Appeals of New York in *People v. Gallagher,* 93 N. Y. 438, 448,

> this end can neither be accomplished nor promoted by laws which conflict with the general sentiment of the community upon whom they are designed to operate. When the government, therefore, has secured to each of its citizens equal rights before the law and equal opportunities for improvement and progress, it has accomplished the end for which it was organized, and performed all of the functions respecting social advantages with which it is endowed.

Legislation is powerless to eradicate racial instincts or to abolish distinctions based upon physical differences, and the attempt to do so can only result in accentuating the difficulties of the present situation. If the civil and political rights of both races be equal, one cannot be inferior to the other civilly or politically. If one race be inferior to the other socially, the Constitution of the United States cannot put them upon the same plane.

It is true that the question of the proportion of colored blood necessary to constitute a colored person, as distinguished from a white person, is one upon which there is a difference of opinion in the different States, some holding that any visible admixture of black blood stamps the person as belonging to the colored race (*State v. Chaver,* 5 Jones [N.C.] 1, p. 11); others that it depends upon the preponderance of blood (*Gray v. State,* 4 Ohio 354; *Monroe v. Collins,* 17 Ohio St. 665); and still others that the predominance of white blood must only be in the proportion of three-fourths. (*People v. Dean,* 4 Michigan 406; *Jones v. Commonwealth,* 80 Virginia 538). But these are questions to be determined under the laws of each State, and are not properly put in issue in this case. Under the allegations of his petition, it may undoubtedly become a question of importance whether, under the laws of Louisiana, the petitioner belongs to the white or colored race.

The judgment of the court below is, therefore,

Affirmed.

Notes and Questions

1. Consider the following statement in Justice Harlan's dissent. How do you interpret it? Does it shed light on the factors that might have influenced his own judicial interpretation of the issues?

There is a race so different from our own that we do not permit those belonging to it to become citizens of the United States. Persons belonging to it are, with few exceptions, absolutely excluded from our country. I allude to the Chinese race. But, by the statute in question, a Chinaman can ride in the same passenger coach with white citizens of the United States, while citizens of the black race in Louisiana, many of whom, perhaps, risked their lives for the preservation of the Union, who are entitled, by law, to participate in the political control of the State and nation, who are not excluded, by law or by reason of their race, from public stations of any kind, and who have all the legal rights that belong to white citizens, are yet declared to be criminals, liable to imprisonment, if they ride in a public coach occupied by citizens of the white race. It is scarcely just to say that a colored citizen should not object to occupying a public coach assigned to his own race. He does not object, nor, perhaps, would he object to separate coaches for his race if his rights under the law were recognized. But he is objecting, and ought never to cease objecting, to the proposition that citizens of the white and black race can be adjudged criminals because they sit, or claim the right to sit, in the same public coach on a public highway. . . .

163 U.S. at 561 (Harlan, J., dissenting).

2. How does the Court distinguish *Plessy* from *Yick Wo v. Hopkins*? Though *Plessy* is no longer good law, it still informs the way we litigate Fourteenth Amendment claims. Consider the following roadmap for alleging a Fourteenth Amendment violation.

Plessy, and later, *Brown* and *Korematsu*, ushered in the idea of a characteristic as requiring special scrutiny under the Fourteenth Amendment. Although the Fourteenth Amendment was not correctly interpreted for a long time, the Supreme Court could never deny the importance of race as a characteristic for the framers of the Fourteenth Amendment. After *Brown*, that awareness eventually evolved into a prohibition against any discrimination targeting specific characteristics worthy of added protection in our society. This is how the doctrine evolved to protect against governmental actions that target race, gender, legitimacy, alienage, and national origin under the various standards referred to as the three tiers of scrutiny. The Court came to include protections for these characteristics using a standard called the *Carolene* factors test. The *Carolene* factors test came to be a shorthand for determination of whether a particular characteristic/group could make a successful claim for special protection under the Equal Protection Clause. Under this test: the characteristic must be immutable; there must be a history of discrimination; the group with the characteristic must be legislatively powerless; and the group with the characteristic must be discrete and insular.

Consider these standards using the following hypo. Assume that a law passed by State X provides that women and men bathrooms must be used by those who were born as "men" and "women" and not by anyone else. A transgender woman, born a man, but now identifying as a woman, sues State X claiming that this law violates the Equal Protection Clause. As you might remember from constitutional law, the following steps will be crucial to successful adjudication of the claim. First, the plaintiff has to show that she has standing (that she is injured in fact, that law caused the injury and that the court can provide a remedy). Then, the plaintiff has to adequately make a claim under the Equal Protection Clause. To make a claim, she has to demonstrate that the law classifies her and people like her in a way that constitutes illegal discrimination.

This is where the issues get more complex. At this point, the attorney for the plaintiff will have to identify the characteristic that forms the basis of the illegal classification. Here, there are two possibilities. First, the plaintiff could allege that the characteristic targeted by the law is sex. In that case, the plaintiff would frame her claim using the intermediate scrutiny standard applicable to sex discrimination. The issue there would be whether a law that separates individuals based on their sex at birth violates the intermediate standard requiring that governments demonstrate an important government interest (with justification having to be exceedingly persuasive) substantially related to achieve that interest. Recall the application of that standard in *U.S. v. Virginia*, covered in Chapter 3.

Another avenue for the plaintiff is to argue that the law targets gender identity and to demonstrate that transgender individuals should qualify for protected status under the *Carolene* factors test. How would the plaintiff fare under this analysis based on your knowledge of gender identity so far? How do you assess the likelihood of success under either alternative?

———————

But, before that evolution in equal protection doctrine, we had to overcome the effects of *Plessy* on Fourteenth Amendment's jurisprudence on race. *Plessy*'s holding that separate could be equal came under direct attack in *Sweat* and *McLaurin* [cited in *Sweatt* below]. Subsequent cases eroded *Plessy*'s holding, setting the stage for *Brown vs. Board of Ed.*, invalidating segregation in education.

Sweatt v. Painter

339 U.S. 629 (1950)

MR. CHIEF JUSTICE VINSON delivered the opinion of the Court.

This case and *McLaurin v. Oklahoma State Regents*, 339 U.S. 637, 70 S.Ct. 851, present different aspects of this general question: To what extent does the Equal Protection Clause of the Fourteenth Amendment limit the power of a state to distinguish between students of different races in professional and graduate education in a state university? Broader issues have been urged for our consideration, but we adhere to the principle of deciding constitutional questions only in the context of the particular case before the Court. We have frequently reiterated that this Court will decide constitutional questions only when necessary to the disposition of the case at hand, and that such decisions will be drawn as narrowly as possible. *Rescue Army v. Municipal Court*, 1947, 331 U.S. 549, 67 S.Ct. 1409, 91 L.Ed. 1666, and cases cited therein. Because of this traditional reluctance to extend constitutional interpretations to situations or facts which are not before the Court, much of the excellent research and detailed argument presented in these cases is unnecessary to their disposition.

In the instant case, petitioner filed an application for admission to the University of Texas Law School for the February 1946 term. His application was rejected solely because he is a Negro. Petitioner thereupon brought this suit for mandamus against the appropriate school officials, respondents here, to compel his admission. At that time, there was no law school in Texas which admitted Negroes.

The State trial court recognized that the action of the State in denying petitioner the opportunity to gain a legal education while granting it to others deprived him of the equal protection of the laws guaranteed by the Fourteenth Amendment. The court did not grant the relief requested, however, but continued the case for six months to allow the State to supply substantially equal facilities. At the expiration of the six months, in December 1946, the court denied the writ on the showing that the authorized university officials had adopted an order calling for the opening of a law school for Negroes the following February. While petitioner's appeal was pending, such a school was made available, but petitioner refused to register therein. The Texas Court of Civil Appeals set aside the trial court's judgment and ordered the cause 'remanded generally to the trial court for further proceedings without prejudice to the rights of any party to this suit.'

On remand, a hearing was held on the issue of the equality of the educational facilities at the newly established school as compared with the University of Texas Law School. Finding that the new school offered petitioner 'privileges, advantages, and opportunities for the study of law substantially equivalent to those offered by the State to white students at the University of Texas,' the trial court denied mandamus. The Court of Civil Appeals affirmed. 1948, 210 S.W.2d 442. Petitioner's application for a writ of error was denied by the Texas Supreme Court. We granted certiorari, 1949, 338 U.S. 865, 70 S.Ct. 139, because of the manifest importance of the constitutional issues involved.

The University of Texas Law School, from which petitioner was excluded, was staffed by a faculty of sixteen full-time and three part-time professors, some of whom are nationally recognized authorities in their field. Its student body numbered 850. The library contained over 65,000 volumes. Among the other facilities available to the students were a law review, moot court facilities, scholarship funds, and Order of the Coif affiliation. The school's alumni occupy the most distinguished positions in the private practice of the law and in the public life of the State. It may properly be considered one of the nation's ranking law schools.

The law school for Negroes which was to have opened in February 1947, would have had no independent faculty or library. The teaching was to be carried on by four members of the University of Texas Law School faculty, who were to maintain their offices at the University of Texas while teaching at both institutions. Few of the 10,000 volumes ordered for the library had arrived; nor was there any full-time librarian. The school lacked accreditation.

Since the trial of this case, respondents report the opening of a law school at the Texas State University for Negroes. It is apparently on the road to full accreditation. It has a faculty of five full-time professors; a student body of 23; a library of some 16,500 volumes serviced by a full-time staff; a practice court and legal aid association; and one alumnus who has become a member of the Texas Bar.

Whether the University of Texas Law School is compared with the original or the new law school for Negroes, we cannot find substantial equality in the educational opportunities offered white and Negro law students by the State. In terms of number of the faculty, variety of courses and opportunity for specialization, size of the student body, scope of the library, availability of law review and similar activities, the University of Texas Law School is superior. What is more important, the University of Texas Law School possesses to a far greater degree those qualities which are incapable of objective measurement but which make for greatness in a law school. Such qualities, to name but a few, include reputation of the faculty, experience of the administration, position and influence of the alumni, standing in the community, traditions and prestige. It is difficult to believe that one who had a free choice between these law schools would consider the question close.

Moreover, although the law is a highly learned profession, we are well aware that it is an intensely practical one. The law school, the proving ground for legal learning and practice, cannot be effective in isolation from the individuals and institutions with which the law interacts. Few students and no one who has practiced law would choose to study in an academic vacuum, removed from the interplay of ideas and the exchange of views with which the law is concerned. The law school to which Texas is willing to admit petitioner excludes from its student body members of the racial groups which number 85% of the population of the State and include most of the lawyers, witnesses, jurors, judges and other officials with whom petitioner will inevitably be dealing when he becomes a member of the Texas Bar. With such a substantial and significant segment of society excluded, we cannot conclude that the education offered petitioner is substantially equal to that which he would receive if admitted to the University of Texas Law School.

It may be argued that excluding petitioner from that school is no different from excluding white students from the new law school. This contention overlooks realities. It is unlikely that a member of a group so decisively in the majority, attending a school with rich traditions and prestige which only a history of consistently maintained excellence could command, would claim that the opportunities afforded him for legal education were unequal to those held open to petitioner. That such a claim, if made, would be dishonored by the State, is no answer. 'Equal protection of the laws is not achieved through indiscriminate imposition of inequalities.' *Shelley v. Kraemer*, 1948, 334 U.S. 1, 22, 68 S.Ct. 836, 846, 92 L.Ed. 1161, 3 A.L.R.2d 441.

It is fundamental that these cases concern rights which are personal and present. This Court has stated unanimously that 'The State must provide [legal education] for [petitioner] in conformity with the equal protection clause of the Fourteenth Amendment and provide it as soon as it does for applicants of any other group.' *Sipuel v. Board of Regents*, 1948, 332 U.S. 631, 633, 68 S.Ct. 299, 92 L.Ed. 247. That case 'did not present the issue whether a state might not satisfy the equal protection clause of the Fourteenth Amendment by establishing a separate law school for Negroes.' *Fisher v. Hurst*, 1948, 333 U.S. 147, 150, 68 S.Ct. 389, 390, 92 L.Ed. 604. In *State of Missouri ex rel. Gaines v. Canada*, 1938, 305 U.S. 337, 351, 59 S.Ct. 232, 237, 83 L.Ed. 208, the Court, speaking through Chief Justice Hughes, declared that 'petitioner's right was a personal one. It was as an individual that he was entitled to the equal protection of the laws, and the State was bound to furnish him within its borders facilities for legal education substantially equal to those which the State there afforded for persons of the white race, whether or not other Negroes sought the same opportunity.' These are the only cases in this Court which present the issue of the constitutional validity of race distinctions in state-supported graduate and professional education.

In accordance with these cases, petitioner may claim his full constitutional right: legal education equivalent to that offered by the State to students of other races. Such education is not available to him in a separate law school as offered by the State. We cannot, therefore, agree with respondents that the doctrine of *Plessy v. Ferguson*, 1896, 163 U.S. 537, 16 S.Ct. 1138, 41 L.Ed. 256, requires affirmance of the judgment below. Nor need we reach petitioner's contention that *Plessy v. Ferguson* should be reexamined in the light of contemporary knowledge respecting the purposes of the Fourteenth Amendment and the effects of racial segregation. See *supra*, 339 U.S. 631, 70 S.Ct. 849.

We hold that the Equal Protection Clause of the Fourteenth Amendment requires that petitioner be admitted to the University of Texas Law School. The judgment is reversed and the cause is remanded for proceedings not inconsistent with this opinion.

Reversed.

Brown v. Board of Education of Topeka [*Brown I*]

347 U.S. 483

(1954)

MR. CHIEF JUSTICE WARREN delivered the opinion of the Court.

These cases come to us from the States of Kansas, South Carolina, Virginia, and Delaware. They are premised on different facts and different local conditions, but a common legal question justifies their consideration together in this consolidated opinion.

In each of the cases, minors of the Negro race, through their legal representatives, seek the aid of the courts in obtaining admission to the public schools of their community on a nonsegregated basis. In each instance, they have been denied admission to schools attended by white children under laws requiring or permitting segregation according to race. This segregation was alleged to deprive the plaintiffs of the equal protection of the laws under the Fourteenth Amendment. In each of the cases other than the Delaware case, a three-judge federal district court denied relief to the plaintiffs on the so-called 'separate but equal' doctrine announced by this Court in *Plessy v. Ferguson*, 163 U.S. 537, 16 S.Ct. 1138, 41 L. Ed. 256. Under that doctrine, equality of treatment is accorded when the races are provided substantially equal facilities, even though these facilities be separate. In the Delaware case, the Supreme Court of Delaware adhered to that doctrine, but ordered that the plaintiffs be admitted to the white schools because of their superiority to the Negro schools.

The plaintiffs contend that segregated public schools are not 'equal' and cannot be made 'equal,' and that hence they are deprived of the equal protection of the laws. Because of the obvious importance of the question presented, the Court took jurisdiction. Argument was heard in the 1952 Term, and reargument was heard this Term on certain questions propounded by the Court.

Reargument was largely devoted to the circumstances surrounding the adoption of the Fourteenth Amendment in 1868. It covered exhaustively consideration of the Amendment in Congress, ratification by the states, then existing practices in racial segregation, and the views of proponents and opponents of the Amendment. This discussion and our own investigation convince us that, although these sources cast some light, it is not enough to resolve the problem with which we are faced. At best, they are inconclusive. The most avid proponents of the post-War Amendments undoubtedly intended them to remove all legal distinctions among 'all persons born or naturalized in the United States.' Their opponents, just as certainly, were antagonistic to both the letter and the spirit of the Amendments and wished them to have the most limited effect. What others in Congress and the state legislatures had in mind cannot be determined with any degree of certainty.

An additional reason for the inconclusive nature of the Amendment's history, with respect to segregated schools, is the status of public education at that time. In the South, the movement toward free common schools, supported by general taxation, had not yet taken hold. Education of white children was largely in the hands of private groups. Education of Negroes was almost nonexistent, and practically all of the race were illiterate. In fact, any education of Negroes was forbidden by law in some states. Today, in contrast, many Negroes have achieved outstanding success in the arts and sciences as well as in the business and professional world. It is true that public school education at the time of the Amendment had advanced further in the North, but the effect of the Amendment on Northern States was generally ignored in the congressional debates. Even in the North, the conditions of public education did not approximate those existing today. The curriculum was usually rudimentary; ungraded schools were common in rural areas; the school term was but three months a year in many states; and compulsory school attendance was virtually unknown. As a consequence, it is not surprising that there should be so little in the history of the Fourteenth Amendment relating to its intended effect on public education.

In the first cases in this Court construing the Fourteenth Amendment, decided shortly after its adoption, the Court interpreted it as proscribing all state-imposed discriminations against the Negro race. The doctrine of "separate but equal" did not make its appearance in this court until 1896 in the case of Plessy v. Ferguson, supra, involving not education but transportation. American courts have since labored with the doctrine for over half a century. In this Court, there have been six cases involving the 'separate but equal' doctrine in the field of public education. In *Cumming v. Board of Education of Richmond County*, 175 U.S. 528, 20 S.Ct. 197, 44 L. Ed. 262, and *Gong Lum v. Rice*, 275 U.S. 78, 48 S.Ct. 91, 72 L.Ed. 172, the validity of the doctrine itself was not challenged. In more recent cases, all on the graduate school level, inequality was found in that specific benefits enjoyed by white students were denied to Negro students of the same educational qualifications. *State of Missouri ex rel. Gaines v. Canada*, 305 U.S. 337, 59 S.Ct. 232, 83 L.Ed. 208; *Sipuel v. Board of Regents of University of Oklahoma*, 332 U.S. 631, 68 S.Ct. 299, 92 L.Ed. 247; *Sweatt v. Painter*, 339 U.S. 629, 70 S.Ct. 848, 94 L.Ed. 1114; *McLaurin v. Oklahoma State Regents*, 339 U.S. 637, 70 S.Ct. 851, 94 L.Ed. 1149. In none of these cases was it necessary to re-examine the doctrine to grant relief to the Negro plaintiff. And in *Sweatt v. Painter, supra*, the Court expressly reserved decision on the question whether *Plessy v. Ferguson* should be held inapplicable to public education.

In the instant cases, that question is directly presented. Here, unlike Sweatt v. Painter, there are findings below that the Negro and white schools involved have been equalized, or are being equalized, with respect to buildings, curricula, qualifications and salaries of teachers, and other 'tangible' factors. Our decision, therefore, cannot turn on merely a comparison of these tangible factors in the Negro and white schools involved in each of the cases. We must look instead to the effect of segregation itself on public education.

In approaching this problem, we cannot turn the clock back to 1868 when the Amendment was adopted, or even to 1896 when *Plessy v. Ferguson* was written. We must consider public education in the light of its full development and its present place in American life throughout the Nation. Only in this way can it be determined if segregation in public schools deprives these plaintiffs of the equal protection of the laws.

Today, education is perhaps the most important function of state and local governments. Compulsory school attendance laws and the great expenditures for education both demonstrate our recognition of the importance of education to our democratic society. It is required in the performance of our most basic public responsibilities, even service in the armed forces. It is the very foundation of good citizenship. Today it is a principal instrument in awakening the child to cultural values, in preparing him for later professional training, and in helping him to adjust normally to his environment. In these days, it is doubtful that any child may reasonably be expected to succeed in life if he is denied the opportunity of an education. Such an opportunity, where the state has undertaken to provide it, is a right which must be made available to all on equal terms.

We come then to the question presented: Does segregation of children in public schools solely on the basis of race, even though the physical facilities and other 'tangible' factors may be equal, deprive the children of the minority group of equal educational opportunities? We believe that it does.

In *Sweatt v. Painter, supra* (339 U.S. 629, 70 S.Ct. 850), in finding that a segregated law school for Negroes could not provide them equal educational opportunities, this Court relied in large part on 'those qualities which are incapable of objective measurement but which make for greatness in a law school.' In *McLaurin v. Oklahoma State Regents, supra* (339 U.S. 637, 70 S.Ct. 853), the Court, in requiring that a Negro admitted to a white graduate school be treated like all other students, again resorted to intangible considerations: 'his ability to study, to engage in discussions and exchange views with other students, and, in general, to learn his profession.' Such considerations apply with added force to children in grade and high schools. To separate them from others of similar age and qualifications solely because of their race generates a feeling of inferiority as to their status in the community that may affect their hearts and minds in a way unlikely ever to be undone. The effect of this separation on their educational opportunities was well stated by a finding in the Kansas case by a court which nevertheless felt compelled to rule against the Negro plaintiffs:

> 'Segregation of white and colored children in public schools has a detrimental effect upon the colored children. The impact is greater when it has the sanction of the law; for the policy of separating the races is usually interpreted as denoting the inferiority of the negro group. A sense of inferiority affects the motivation of a child to learn. Segregation with the sanction of law, therefore, has a tendency to [retard] the educational and mental development of Negro children and to deprive them of some of the benefits they would receive in a racial[ly] integrated school system.'

Whatever may have been the extent of psychological knowledge at the time of *Plessy v. Ferguson*, this finding is amply supported by modern authority. Any language in *Plessy v. Ferguson* contrary to this finding is rejected.

We conclude that in the field of public education the doctrine of 'separate but equal' has no place. Separate educational facilities are inherently unequal. Therefore, we hold that the plaintiffs and others similarly situated for whom the actions have been brought are, by reason of the segregation complained of, deprived of the equal protection of the laws guaranteed by the Fourteenth Amendment. This disposition makes unnecessary any discussion whether such segregation also violates the Due Process Clause of the Fourteenth Amendment.

Because these are class actions, because of the wide applicability of this decision, and because of the great variety of local conditions, the formulation of decrees in these cases presents problems of considerable complexity. On reargument, the consideration of appropriate relief was necessarily subordinated to the primary question—the constitutionality of segregation in public education. We have now announced that such segregation is a denial of the equal protection of the laws. In order that we may have the full assistance of the parties in formulating decrees, the cases will be restored to the docket, and the parties are requested to present further argument on Questions 4 and 5 previously propounded by the Court for the reargument this Term. The Attorney General of the United States is again invited to participate. The Attorneys General of the states requiring or permitting segregation in public education will also be permitted to appear as amici curiae upon request to do so by September 15, 1954, and submission of briefs by October 1, 1954.

It is so ordered.

C. The Aftermath

Brown's desegregation order proved inefficient due to its vagueness. Initially, it was met with massive resistance from a number of states. As the Supreme Court quickly learned, firm directives should have been incorporated at the onset. In reality, in the aftermath of *Brown*, comprehensive desegregation took place in a piecemeal manner, eventually requiring the aid of all arms of the federal government. *See* Michael J. Klarman, *Brown, Racial Change, and the Civil Rights Movement*, 80 Va. L. Rev. 7 (1994); Lina Mai, *'I Had a Right to Be at Central': Remembering Little Rock's Integration Battle*, Time (Sept. 22, 2017), http://time.com/4948704/little-rock-nine -anniversary/ (discussing President Eisenhower's sending of 1,200 soldiers to protect the nine black students after mobs and the Arkansas Netional Guardsmen prevented them from entering the school); Debbie Elliott, *Integrating Ole Miss: A Transformative, Deadly Riot*, NPR (Oct. 1, 2012), https://www.npr.org/2012/10/01/161573289 /integrating-ole-miss-a-transformative-deadly-riot (recalling President Kennedy's deployment of 30,000 U.S. troops, federal marshals and national guardsmen to get

James Meredith to class at Ole Miss); Debra Bell, *George Wallace Stood in a Doorway at the University of Alabama 50 Years Ago Today,* U.S. News (June 11, 2013), https://www.usnews.com/news/blogs/press-past/2013/06/11/george-wallace-stood-in-a-doorway-at-the-university-of-alabama-50-years-ago-today (noting President Kennedy's calling of 100 troops from the Alabama National Guard to assist federal authorities in trying to allow black students to enter the university); *see also* Paulette Brown, *The Civil Rights Act of 1964*, 92 Wash. U. L. Rev. 527, 532–34 (2014) (discussing the Civil Rights Act of 1964, which was prompted by the desegregation crisis at the University of Alabama).

Ironically, the federal government itself was also called to comply with *Brown's* mandate and to desegregate schools within the District of Columbia. The Court in *Bolling vs. Sharpe* below ruled that the equal protection mandate of the Fourteenth Amendment also applied to the federal government, via the Fifth Amendment of the Constitution. This is referred to as reverse incorporation.

Bolling v. Sharpe
347 U.S. 497 (1954)

Mr. Chief Justice Warren delivered the opinion of the Court.

This case challenges the validity of segregation in the public schools of the District of Columbia. The petitioners, minors of the Negro race, allege that such segregation deprives them of due process of law under the Fifth Amendment. They were refused admission to a public school attended by white children solely because of their race. They sought the aid of the District Court for the District of Columbia in obtaining admission. That court dismissed their complaint. The Court granted a writ of certiorari before judgment in the Court of Appeals because of the importance of the constitutional question presented. 344 U.S. 873, 73 S.Ct. 173, 97 L.Ed. 676.

We have this day held that the Equal Protection Clause of the Fourteenth Amendment prohibits the states from maintaining racially segregated public schools. The legal problem in the District of Columbia is somewhat different, however. The Fifth Amendment, which is applicable in the District of Columbia, does not contain an equal protection clause as does the Fourteenth Amendment which applies only to the states. But the concepts of equal protection and due process, both stemming from our American ideal of fairness, are not mutually exclusive. The 'equal protection of the laws' is a more explicit safeguard of prohibited unfairness than 'due process of law,' and, therefore, we do not imply that the two are always interchangeable phrases. But, as this Court has recognized, discrimination may be so unjustifiable as to be violative of due process.

Classifications based solely upon race must be scrutinized with particular care, since they are contrary to our traditions and hence constitutionally suspect. As long ago as 1896, this Court declared the principle 'that the constitution of the United States, in its present form, forbids, so far as civil and political rights are concerned, discrimination by the general government, or by the states, against any citizen because of his race.' And in *Buchanan v. Warley*, 245 U.S. 60, 38 S.Ct. 16, 62 L.Ed. 149, the Court held that a statute which limited the right of a property owner to convey his property to a person of another race was, as an unreasonable discrimination, a denial of due process of law.

Although the Court has not assumed to define 'liberty' with any great precision, that term is not confined to mere freedom from bodily restraint. Liberty under law extends to the full range of conduct which the individual is free to pursue, and it cannot be restricted except for a proper governmental objective. Segregation in public education is not reasonably related to any proper governmental objective, and thus it imposes on Negro children of the District of Columbia a burden that constitutes an arbitrary deprivation of their liberty in violation of the Due Process Clause.

In view of our decision that the Constitution prohibits the states from maintaining racially segregated public schools, it would be unthinkable that the same Constitution would impose a lesser duty on the Federal Government. We hold that racial segregation in the public schools of the District of Columbia is a denial of the due process of law guaranteed by the Fifth Amendment to the Constitution.

For the reasons set out in *Brown v. Board of Education*, this case will be restored to the docket for reargument on Questions 4 and 5 previously propounded by the Court. 345 U.S. 972, 73 S.Ct. 1114, 97 L.Ed. 1388.

It is so ordered.

D. *Brown* and Constitutional Remedies

Brown's mandate of desegregation was patently unclear. Initially, the Court ordered states to desegregate with "all deliberate speed" without any more guidance. Without a clear implementation model for desegregation; it was all left to the states. This had to be rectified. Upon resistance from states, the Court then attempted to build and recognize remedial structures necessary for successful desegregation. The cases below illustrate the scope of these remedies, and later, the Court's retrenchment from this remedial commitment, leaving room for de facto segregation to flourish.

Brown v. Board of Education of Topeka [*Brown II*]
349 U.S. 294 (1955)

MR. CHIEF JUSTICE WARREN delivered the opinion of the Court.

These cases were decided on May 17, 1954. The opinions of that date, declaring the fundamental principle that racial discrimination in public education is unconstitutional, are incorporated herein by reference. All provisions of federal, state, or local law requiring or permitting such discrimination must yield to this principle. There remains for consideration the manner in which relief is to be accorded.

Because these cases arose under different local conditions and their disposition will involve a variety of local problems, we requested further argument on the question of relief. In view of the nationwide importance of the decision, we invited the Attorney General of the United States and the Attorneys General of all states requiring or permitting racial discrimination in public education to present their views on that question. The parties, the United States, and the States of Florida, North Carolina, Arkansas, Oklahoma, Maryland, and Texas filed briefs and participated in the oral argument.

These presentations were informative and helpful to the Court in its consideration of the complexities arising from the transition to a system of public education freed of racial discrimination. The presentations also demonstrated that substantial steps to eliminate racial discrimination in public schools have already been taken, not only in some of the communities in which these cases arose, but in some of the states appearing as amici curiae, and in other states as well. Substantial progress has been made in the District of Columbia and in the communities in Kansas and Delaware involved in this litigation. The defendants in the cases coming to us from South Carolina and Virginia are awaiting the decision of this Court concerning relief.

Full implementation of these constitutional principles may require solution of varied local school problems. School authorities have the primary responsibility for elucidating, assessing, and solving these problems; courts will have to consider whether the action of school authorities constitutes good faith implementation of the governing constitutional principles. Because of their proximity to local conditions and the possible need for further hearings, the courts which originally heard these cases can best perform this judicial appraisal. Accordingly, we believe it appropriate to remand the cases to those courts.

In fashioning and effectuating the decrees, the courts will be guided by equitable principles. Traditionally, equity has been characterized by a practical flexibility in shaping its remedies and by a facility for adjusting and reconciling public and private needs. These cases call for the exercise of these traditional attributes of equity power. At stake is the personal interest of the plaintiffs in admission to public schools as soon as practicable on a nondiscriminatory basis. To effectuate this interest may call for elimination of a variety of obstacles in making the transition to school systems operated in accordance with the constitutional principles set forth in our May 17, 1954, decision. Courts of equity may properly take into account the public interest in the elimination of such obstacles in a systematic and effective manner. But it should go without saying that the vitality of these constitutional principles cannot be allowed to yield simply because of disagreement with them.

While giving weight to these public and private considerations, the courts will require that the defendants make a prompt and reasonable start toward full compliance with our May 17, 1954, ruling. Once such a start has been made, the courts may find that additional time is necessary to carry out the ruling in an effective manner. The burden rests upon the defendants to establish that such time is necessary in the public interest and is consistent with good faith compliance at the earliest practicable date. To that end, the courts may consider problems related to administration, arising from the physical condition of the school plant, the school transportation system, personnel, revision of school districts and attendance areas into compact units to achieve a system of determining admission to the public schools on a nonracial basis, and revision of local laws and regulations which may be necessary in solving the foregoing problems. They will also consider the adequacy of any plans the defendants may propose to meet these problems and to effectuate a transition to a racially nondiscriminatory school system. During this period of transition, the courts will retain jurisdiction of these cases.

The judgments below, except that in the Delaware case, are accordingly reversed and the cases are remanded to the District Courts to take such proceedings and enter such orders and decrees consistent with this opinion as are necessary and proper to admit to public schools on a racially nondiscriminatory basis with all deliberate speed the parties to these cases. The judgment in the Delaware case—ordering the immediate admission of the plaintiffs to schools previously attended only by white children—is affirmed on the basis of the principles stated in our May 17, 1954, opinion, but the case is remanded to the Supreme Court of Delaware for such further proceedings as that Court may deem necessary in light of this opinion.

It is so ordered.

Notes

1. For further evidence as to why litigation and civil rights attorneys matter, see some of the cases that dismantled segregration in other areas of society: *Bailey v. Patterson*, 369 U.S. 31 (1962) (holding "that any claim that a state statute requiring racial segregation on common carriers or facilities maintained by them were constitutional was frivolous"); *Dawson v. Mayor & City Council of Baltimore City*, 220 F.2d 386 (4th Cir. 1955), *aff'd*, 350 U.S. 877 (1955) (enjoining segregation at public bathing beaches, bathhouses, and swimming pools); *Holmes v. Atlanta*, 350 U.S. 879 (1955) (holding it improper for Atlanta to restrict use of public golf courses or city parks based on race); *Brown v. Board of Education*, 347 U.S. 483, 873 (1954) (holding segregation of schools based on race).

2. "All deliberate speed" and its aftermath: In *Cooper v. Aaron*, below, the Court reiterates the judiciary's power to mandate compliance with the desegregation mandate. Recall that *Marbury v. Madison*, 5 U.S. (1 Cranch) 137 (1803), established that federal courts have the power to review governmental actions and laws raising constitutional issues. In *Cooper*, the Court's impatience with non-complying states becomes palpable.

Cooper v. Aaron

358 U.S. 1 (1958)

Opinion of the Court by The Chief Justice, Mr. Justice Black, Mr. Justice Frankfurter, Mr. Justice Douglas, Mr. Justice Burton, Mr. Justice Clark, Mr. Justice Harlan, Mr. Justice Brennan, and Mr. Justice Whittaker.

As this case reaches us it raises questions of the highest importance to the maintenance of our federal system of government. It necessarily involves a claim by the Governor and Legislature of a State that there is no duty on state officials to obey federal court orders resting on this Court's considered interpretation of the United States Constitution. Specifically it involves actions by the Governor and Legislature of Arkansas upon the premise that they are not bound by our holding in *Brown v. Board of Education*, 347 U.S. 483, 74 S.Ct. 686, 98 L.Ed. 873. That holding was that the Fourteenth Amendment forbids States to use their governmental powers to bar children on racial grounds from attending schools where there is state participation through any arrangement, management, funds or property. We are urged to uphold a suspension of the Little Rock School Board's plan to do away with segregated public schools in Little Rock until state laws and efforts to upset and nullify our holding in Brown v. Board of Education have been further challenged and tested in the courts. We reject these contentions.

The case was argued before us on September 11, 1958. On the following day we unanimously affirmed the judgment of the Court of Appeals for the Eighth Circuit, 257 F.2d 33, which had reversed a judgment of the District Court for the Eastern District of Arkansas, 163 F.Supp. 13. The District Court had granted the application of the petitioners, the Little Rock School Board and School Superintendent, to suspend for two and one-half years the operation of the School Board's court-approved desegregation program. In order that the School Board might know, without doubt, its duty in this regard before the opening of school, which had been set for the following Monday, September 15, 1958, we immediately issued the judgment, reserving the expression of our supporting views to a later date. This opinion of all of the members of the Court embodies those views.

The following are the facts and circumstances so far as necessary to show how the legal questions are presented.

On May 17, 1954, this Court decided that enforced racial segregation in the public schools of a State is a denial of the equal protection of the laws enjoined by the Fourteenth Amendment. Brown v. Board of Education, 347 U.S. 483, 74 S.Ct. 686. The Court postponed, pending further argument, formulation of a decree to effectuate this decision. That decree was rendered May 31, 1955. *Brown v. Board of Education*, 349 U.S. 294, 75 S.Ct. 753, 756. In the formulation of that decree the Court recognized that good faith compliance with the principles declared in *Brown* might in some situations 'call for elimination of a variety of obstacles in making the transition to school systems operated in accordance with the constitutional principles set forth in our May 17, 1954, decision.' 349 U.S. at page 300, 75 S.Ct. at page 756. . . .

Under such circumstances, the District Courts were directed to require 'a prompt and reasonable start toward full compliance,' and to take such action as was necessary to bring about the end of racial segregation in the public schools 'with all deliberate speed.' *Ibid*. Of course, in many locations, obedience to the duty of desegregation would require the immediate general admission of Negro children, otherwise qualified as students for their appropriate classes, at particular schools. On the other hand, a District Court, after analysis of the relevant factors (which, of course, excludes hostility to racial desegregation), might conclude that justification existed for not requiring the present nonsegregated admission of all qualified Negro children. In such circumstances, however, the Court should scrutinize the program of the school authorities to make sure that they had developed arrangements pointed toward the earliest practicable completion of desegregation, and had taken appropriate steps to put their program into effective operation. It was made plain that delay in any guise in order to deny the constitutional rights of Negro children could not be countenanced, and that only a prompt start, diligently and earnestly pursued, to eliminate racial segregation from the public schools could constitute good faith compliance. State authorities were thus duty bound to devote every effort toward initiating desegregation and bringing about the elimination of racial discrimination in the public-school system.

On May 20, 1954, three days after the first *Brown* opinion, the Little Rock District School Board adopted, and on May 23, 1954, made public, a statement of policy entitled 'Supreme Court Decision — Segregation in Public Schools.' In this statement the Board recognized that

> 'It is our responsibility to comply with Federal Constitutional Requirements and we intend to do so when the Supreme Court of the United States outlines the method to be followed.'

Thereafter the Board undertook studies of the administrative problems confronting the transition to a desegregated public-school system at Little Rock. It instructed the Superintendent of Schools to prepare a plan for desegregation, and approved such a plan on May 24, 1955, seven days before the second *Brown* opinion. The plan provided for desegregation at the senior high school level (grades 10 through 12) as the first stage. Desegregation at the junior high and elementary levels was to follow. It was contemplated that desegregation at the high school level would commence in the fall of 1957, and the expectation was that complete desegregation of the school system would be accomplished by 1963. Following the adoption of this plan, the Superintendent of Schools discussed it with a large number of citizen groups in the city. As a result of these discussions, the Board reached the conclusion that 'a large majority of the residents' of Little Rock were of 'the belief that the Plan, although objectionable in principle,' from the point of view of those supporting segregated schools, 'was still the best for the interests of all pupils in the District.'

Upon challenge by a group of Negro plaintiffs desiring more rapid completion of the desegregation process, the District Court upheld the School Board's plan, *Aaron v. Cooper*, 143 F.Supp. 855. The Court of Appeals affirmed, 8 Cir., 243 F.2d 361. Review of that judgment was not sought here.

While the School Board was thus going forward with its preparation for desegregating the Little Rock school system, other state authorities, in contrast, were actively pursuing a program designed to perpetuate in Arkansas the system of racial segregation which this Court had held violated the Fourteenth Amendment. First came, in November 1956, an amendment to the State Constitution flatly commanding the Arkansas General Assembly to oppose 'in every Constitutional manner the Un-constitutional desegregation decisions of May 17, 1954 and May 31, 1955 of the United States Supreme Court,' Ark.Const.Amend. 44, and, through the initiative, a pupil assignment law, Ark.Stats. §§ 80-1519 to 80-1524. Pursuant to this state constitutional command, a law relieving school children from compulsory attendance at racially mixed schools, Ark.Stats. § 80-1525, and a law establishing a State Sovereignty Commission, Ark.Stats. §§ 6-801 to 6-824, were enacted by the General Assembly in February 1957.

The School Board and the Superintendent of Schools nevertheless continued with preparations to carry out the first stage of the desegregation program. Nine Negro children were scheduled for admission in September 1957 to Central High School, which has more than two thousand students. Various administrative measures, designed to assure the smooth transition of this first stage of desegregation, were undertaken.

On September 2, 1957, the day before these Negro students were to enter Central High, the school authorities were met with drastic opposing action on the part of the Governor of Arkansas who dispatched units of the Arkansas National Guard to the Central High School grounds and placed the school 'off limits' to colored students. As found by the District Court in subsequent proceedings, the Governor's action had not been requested by the school authorities, and was entirely unheralded. . . .

On the morning of the next day, September 4, 1957, the Negro children attempted to enter the high school but, as the District Court later found, units of the Arkansas National Guard 'acting pursuant to the Governor's order, stood shoulder to shoulder at the school grounds and thereby forcibly prevented the 9 Negro students from entering,' as they continued to do every school day during the following three weeks. 156 F.Supp. at page 225.

That same day, September 4, 1957, the United States Attorney for the Eastern District of Arkansas was requested by the District Court to begin an immediate investigation in order to fix responsibility for the interference with the orderly implementation of the District Court's direction to carry out the desegregation program. Three days later, September 7, the District Court denied a petition of the School Board and the Superintendent of Schools for an order temporarily suspending continuance of the program.

Upon completion of the United States Attorney's investigation, he and the Attorney General of the United States, at the District Court's request, entered the proceedings and filed a petition on behalf of the United States, as *amicus curiae*, to enjoin the Governor of Arkansas and officers of the Arkansas National Guard from further attempts to prevent obedience to the court's order. After hearings on the petition, the District Court found that the School Board's plan had been obstructed by the Governor through the use of National Guard troops, and granted a preliminary injunction on September 20, 1957, enjoining the Governor and the officers of the Guard from preventing the attendance of Negro children at Central High School, and from otherwise obstructing or interfering with the orders of the court in connection with the plan. 156 F.Supp. 220, affirmed, *Faubus v. United States*, 8 Cir., 254 F.2d 797. The National Guard was then withdrawn from the school.

The next school day was Monday, September 23, 1957. The Negro children entered the high school that morning under the protection of the Little Rock Police Department and members of the Arkansas State Police. But the officers caused the children to be removed from the school during the morning because they had difficulty controlling a large and demonstrating crowd which had gathered at the high school. 163 F.Supp. at page 16. On September 25, however, the President of the United States dispatched federal troops to Central High School and admission of the Negro students to the school was thereby effected. Regular army troops continued at the high school until November 27, 1957. They were then replaced by federalized National Guardsmen who remained throughout the balance of the school year. Eight of the Negro students remained in attendance at the school throughout the school year.

We come now to the aspect of the proceedings presently before us. On February 20, 1958, the School Board and the Superintendent of Schools filed a petition in the District Court seeking a postponement of their program for desegregation. Their position in essence was that because of extreme public hostility, which they stated had been engendered largely by the official attitudes and actions of the Governor and the Legislature, the maintenance of a sound educational program at Central High School, with the Negro students in attendance, would be impossible. The Board therefore proposed that the Negro students already admitted to the school be withdrawn and sent to segregated schools, and that all further steps to carry out the Board's desegregation program be postponed for a period later suggested by the Board to be two and one-half years.

... We ... have accepted the findings of the District Court as to the conditions at Central High School during the 1957–1958 school year, and also the findings that the educational progress of all the students, white and colored, of that school has suffered and will continue to suffer if the conditions which prevailed last year are permitted to continue.

The significance of these findings, however, is to be considered in light of the fact, indisputably revealed by the record before us, that the conditions they depict are directly traceable to the actions of legislators and executive officials of the State of Arkansas, taken in their official capacities, which reflect their own determination to resist this Court's decision in the Brown case and which have brought about violent resistance to that decision in Arkansas. In its petition for certiorari filed in this Court, the School Board itself describes the situation in this language: 'The legislative, executive, and judicial departments of the state government opposed the desegregation of Little Rock schools by enacting laws, calling out troops, making statements vilifying federal law and federal courts, and failing to utilize state law enforcement agencies and judicial processes to maintain public peace.'

One may well sympathize with the position of the Board in the face of the frustrating conditions which have confronted it, but, regardless of the Board's good faith, the actions of the other state agencies responsible for those conditions compel us to reject the Board's legal position. Had Central High School been under the direct management of the State itself, it could hardly be suggested that those immediately in charge of the school should be heard to assert their own good faith as a legal excuse for delay in implementing the constitutional rights of these respondents, when vindication of those rights was rendered difficult of impossible by the actions of other state officials. The situation here is in no different posture because the members of the School Board and the Superintendent of Schools are local officials; from the point of view of the Fourteenth Amendment, they stand in this litigation as the agents of the State.

The constitutional rights of respondents are not to be sacrificed or yielded to the violence and disorder which have followed upon the actions of the Governor and Legislature. As this Court said some 41 years ago in a unanimous opinion in a case involving another aspect of racial segregation: 'It is urged that this proposed segregation will promote the public peace by preventing race conflicts. Desirable as this is, and important as is the preservation of the public peace, this aim cannot be accomplished by laws or ordinances which deny rights created or protected by the federal Constitution.' *Buchanan v. Warley*, 245 U.S. 60, 81, 38 S.Ct. 16, 20, 62 L. Ed. 149. Thus law and order are not here to be preserved by depriving the Negro children of their constitutional rights. The record before us clearly establishes that the growth of the Board's difficulties to a magnitude beyond its unaided power to control is the product of state action. Those difficulties, as counsel for the Board forthrightly conceded on the oral argument in this Court, can also be brought under control by state action.

The controlling legal principles are plain. The command of the Fourteenth Amendment is that no 'State' shall deny to any person within its jurisdiction the equal protection of the laws. 'A State acts by its legislative, its executive, or its judicial authorities. It can act in no other way. The constitutional provision, therefore, must mean that no agency of the State, or of the officers or agents by whom its powers are exerted, shall deny to any person within its jurisdiction the equal protection of the laws. Whoever, by virtue of public position under a State government, * * * denies or takes away the equal protection of the laws, violates the constitutional inhibition; and as he acts in the name and for the State, and is clothed with the State's power, his act is that of the State. This must be so, or the constitutional prohibition has no meaning.' *Ex parte Virginia*, 100 U.S. 339, 347, 25 L.Ed. 676. Thus the prohibitions of the Fourteenth Amendment extend to all action of the State denying equal protection of the laws; whatever the agency of the State taking the action. . . .

What has been said, in the light of the facts developed, is enough to dispose of the case. However, we should answer the premise of the actions of the Governor and Legislature that they are not bound by our holding in the *Brown* case. It is necessary only to recall some basic constitutional propositions which are settled doctrine.

Article VI of the Constitution makes the Constitution the 'supreme Law of the Land.' In 1803, Chief Justice Marshall, speaking for a unanimous Court, referring to the Constitution as 'the fundamental and paramount law of the nation,' declared in the notable case of *Marbury v. Madison*, 1 Cranch 137, 177, 2 L.Ed. 60, that 'It is emphatically the province and duty of the judicial department to say what the law is.' This decision declared the basic principle that the federal judiciary is supreme in the exposition of the law of the Constitution, and that principle has ever since been respected by this Court and the Country as a permanent and indispensable feature of our constitutional system. It follows that the interpretation of the Fourteenth Amendment enunciated by this Court in the *Brown* case is the supreme law of the land, and Art. VI of the Constitution makes it of binding effect on the States 'any Thing in the Constitution or Laws of any State to the Contrary notwithstanding.' Every state legislator and executive and judicial officer is solemnly committed by oath taken pursuant to Art. VI, ¶3 'to support this Constitution.' Chief Justice Taney, speaking for a unanimous Court in 1859, said that this requirement reflected the framers' 'anxiety to preserve it [the Constitution] in full force, in all its powers, and to guard against resistance to or evasion of its authority, on the part of a State.' *Ableman v. Booth*, 21 How. 506, 524, 16 L.Ed. 169.

No state legislator or executive or judicial officer can war against the Constitution without violating his undertaking to support it. Chief Justice Marshall spoke for a unanimous Court in saying that: 'If the legislatures of the several states may, at will, annul the judgments of the courts of the United States, and destroy the rights acquired under those judgments, the constitution itself becomes a solemn mockery.' *United States v. Peters*, 5 Cranch 115, 136, 3 L.Ed. 53. A Governor who asserts a power to nullify a federal court order is similarly restrained. If he had such power, said Chief Justice Hughes, in 1932, also for a unanimous Court, 'it is manifest that the fiat of a state Governor, and not the Constitution of the United States, would be the supreme law of the land; that the restrictions of the Federal Constitution upon the exercise of state power would be but impotent phrases.' *Sterling v. Constantin*, 287 U.S. 378, 397–398, 53 S.Ct. 190, 195, 77 L.Ed. 375.

... The right of a student not to be segregated on racial grounds in schools so maintained is indeed so fundamental and pervasive that it is embraced in the concept of due process of law. *Bolling v. Sharpe*, 347 U.S. 497, 74 S.Ct. 693, 98 L.Ed. 884. The basic decision in *Brown* was unanimously reached by this Court only after the case had been briefed and twice argued and the issues had been given the most serious consideration. Since the first *Brown* opinion three new Justices have come to the Court. They are at one with the Justices still on the Court who participated in that basic decision as to its correctness, and that decision is now unanimously reaffirmed. The principles announced in that decision and the obedience of the States to them, according to the command of the Constitution, are indispensable for the protection of the freedoms guaranteed by our fundamental charter for all of us. Our constitutional ideal of equal justice under law is thus made a living truth.

Notes and Questions

1. In today's modern landscape, school choice continues to stir ongoing debates. Is the best way to foster educational equality to provide vouchers, and school choice programs to parents? Does this allow the best students to compete for admission in the best school systems, or do these programs doom the public education system to failure?

2. As *Green v. County School Board of New Kent County* illustrates, school choice is far from a lightning rod solution for systemic segregation, de facto or otherwise. White flight and the creation of private schools as alternatives to integrated public schools created a dearth of resources in many public school districts across the nation. Furthermore, new hybrid public/private schools have been found to have their own problems. Education scholars have identified similar patterns, in these educational enterprises, as those seen in the public schools. Charter schools, for example, are accused by some of neglecting or failing low performing students. *See* Heather Vogell & Hannah Fresques, *'Altenative' Education: Using Charter Schools to Hide Dropouts and Game the System*, PROPUBLICA (Feb. 21, 2017), https://www .propublica.org/article/alternative-education-using-charter-schools-hide-dropouts -and-game-system (reporting Florida public schools use alternative charter schools to send poor-performing students). This can prove dangerous for low performing students, leaving them in the same position as in failing public schools. This pattern, in turn, makes them more at risk for the school to prison pipeline.

1. Inadequate Means of Desegregation

Green v. County School Board of New Kent County, Virginia
391 U.S. 430 (1968)

Mr. Justice BRENNAN delivered the opinion of the Court.

The question for decision is whether, under all the circumstances here, respondent School Board's adoption of a 'freedom-of-choice' plan which allows a pupil to choose his own public school constitutes adequate compliance with the Board's responsibility 'to achieve a system of determining admission to the public schools on a non-racial basis * * *.' *Brown v. Board of Education of Topeka, Kan.*, 349 U.S. 294, 300–301, 75 S.Ct. 753, 756, 99 L.Ed. 1083 (*Brown II*).

Petitioners brought this action in March 1965 seeking injunctive relief against respondent's continued maintenance of an alleged racially segregated school system. New Kent County is a rural county in Eastern Virginia. About one-half of its population of some 4,500 are Negroes. There is no residential segregation in the county; persons of both races reside throughout. The school system has only two schools, the New Kent school on the east side of the county and the George W. Watkins school on the west side. In a memorandum filed May 17, 1966, the District Court found that the 'school system serves approximately 1,300 pupils, of which 740 are Negro and 550 are White. The School Board operates one white combined elementary and high school (New Kent), and one Negro combined elementary and high school (George W. Watkins). There are no attendance zones. Each school serves the entire county.' The record indicates that 21 school buses — 11 serving the Watkins school and 10 serving the New Kent school — travel overlapping routes throughout the county to transport pupils to and from the two schools.

The segregated system was initially established and maintained under the compulsion of Virginia constitutional and statutory provisions mandating racial segregation in public education, Va.Const., Art. IX, § 140 (1902); Va.Code § 22-221 (1950). These provisions were held to violate the Federal Constitution in *Davis v. County School Board of Prince Edward County*, decided with *Brown v. Board of Education of Topeka*, 347 U.S. 483, 487, 74 S.Ct. 686, 688, 98 L.Ed. 873 (*Brown I*). The respondent School Board continued the segregated operation of the system after the *Brown* decisions, presumably on the authority of several statutes enacted by Virginia in resistance to those decisions. Some of these statutes were held to be unconstitutional on their face or as applied. One statute, the Pupil Placement Act, Va.Code § 22-232.1 et seq. (1964), not repealed until 1966, divested local boards of authority to assign children to particular schools and placed that authority in a State Pupil Placement Board. Under that Act children were each year automatically reassigned to the school previously attended unless upon their application the State Board assigned them to another school; students seeking enrollment for the first time were also assigned at the discretion of the State Board. To September 1964, no Negro pupil had applied for admission to the New Kent school under this statute and no white pupil had applied for admission to the Watkins school.

The School Board initially sought dismissal of this suit on the ground that petitioners had failed to apply to the State Board for assignment to New Kent school. However on August 2, 1965, five months after the suit was brought, respondent School Board, in order to remain eligible for federal financial aid, adopted a 'freedom-of-choice' plan for desegregating the schools. Under that plan, each pupil, except those entering the first and eighth grades, may annually choose between the New Kent and Watkins schools and pupils not making a choice are assigned to the school previously attended; first and eighth grade pupils must affirmatively choose a school. . . .

The pattern of separate 'white' and 'Negro' schools in the New Kent County school system established under compulsion of state laws is precisely the pattern of segregation to which *Brown I* and *Brown II* were particularly addressed, and which *Brown I* declared unconstitutionally denied Negro school children equal protection of the laws. Racial identification of the system's schools was complete, extending not just to the composition of student bodies at the two schools but to every facet of school operations—faculty, staff, transportation, extracurricular activities and facilities. In short, the State, acting through the local school board and school officials, organized and operated a dual system, part 'white' and part 'Negro.'

It was such dual systems that 14 years ago *Brown I* held unconstitutional and a year later *Brown II* held must be abolished; school boards operating such school systems were required by *Brown II* 'to effectuate a transition to a racially nondiscriminatory school system.' 349 U.S., at 301, 75 S.Ct. at 756. It is of course true that for the time immediately after *Brown II* the concern was with making an initial break in a long-established pattern of excluding Negro children from schools attended by white children. The principal focus was on obtaining for those Negro children courageous enough to break with tradition a place in the 'white' schools. See, e.g., *Cooper v. Aaron*, 358 U.S. 1, 78 S.Ct. 1401, 3 L.Ed.2d 5. Under *Brown II* that immediate goal was only the first step, however. The transition to a unitary, nonracial system of public education was and is the ultimate end to be brought about; it was because of the 'complexities arising from the transition to a system of public education freed of racial discrimination' that we provided for 'all deliberate speed' in the implementation of the principles of *Brown I*. 349 U.S., at 299–301, 75 S.Ct. at 755. Thus we recognized the task would necessarily involve solution of 'varied local school problems.' *Id.*, at 299, 75 S.Ct. at 756. In referring to the 'personal interest of the plaintiffs in admission to public schools as soon as practicable on a nondiscriminatory basis,' we also noted that '[t]o effectuate this interest may call for elimination of a variety of obstacles in making the transition * * *.' *Id.*, at 300, 75 S.Ct. at 756. Yet we emphasized that the constitutional rights of Negro children required school officials to bear the burden of establishing that additional time to carry out the ruling in an effective manner 'is necessary in the public interest and is consistent with good faith compliance at the earliest practicable date. . . .

It is against this background that 13 years after *Brown II* commanded the abolition of dual systems we must measure the effectiveness of respondent School Board's 'freedom-of-choice' plan to achieve that end. . . . School boards such as the respondent then operating state-compelled dual systems were nevertheless clearly charged with the affirmative duty to take whatever steps might be necessary to convert to a unitary system in which racial discrimination would be eliminated root and branch. See *Cooper v. Aaron, supra*, 358 U.S. at 7, 78 S.Ct. at 1404; *Bradley v. School Board of City of Richmond, Va.*, 382 U.S. 103, 86 S.Ct. 224, 15 L.Ed.2d 187; cf. *Watson v. City of Memphis*, 373 U.S. 526, 83 S.Ct. 1314, 10 L.Ed.2d 529. The constitutional rights of

Negro school children articulated in *Brown I* permit no less than this; and it was to this end that *Brown II* commanded school boards to bend their efforts.

In determining whether respondent School Board met that command by adopting its 'freedom-of-choice' plan, it is relevant that this first step did not come until some 11 years after *Brown I* was decided and 10 years after *Brown II* directed the making of a 'prompt and reasonable start.' This deliberate perpetuation of the unconstitutional dual system can only have compounded the harm of such a system. Such delays are no longer tolerable, for 'the governing constitutional principles no longer bear the imprint of newly enunciated doctrine.' *Watson v. City of Memphis, supra*, 373 U.S. at 529, 83 S.Ct. at 1316; see *Bradley v. School Board, City of Richmond, Va., supra*; *Rogers v. Paul*, 382 U.S. 198, 86 S.Ct. 358, 15 L.Ed.2d 265. Moreover, a plan that at this late date fails to provide meaningful assurance of prompt and effective disestablishment of a dual system is also intolerable. 'The time for mere "deliberate speed" has run out,' *Griffin v. County School Board of Prince Edward County*, 377 U.S. 218, 234, 84 S.Ct. 1226, 1235, 12 L.Ed.2d 256, 'the context in which we must interpret and apply this language (of *Brown II*) to plans for desegregation has been significantly altered.' *Goss v. Board of Education of City of Knoxville, Tenn.*, 373 U.S. 683, 689, 83 S.Ct. 1405, 1409, 10 L.Ed.2d 632. See *Calhoun v. Latimer*, 377 U.S. 263, 84 S.Ct. 1235, 12 L.Ed.2d 288. The burden on a school board today is to come forward with a plan that promises realistically to work, and promises realistically to work now.

The obligation of the district courts, as it always has been, is to assess the effectiveness of a proposed plan in achieving desegregation. There is no universal answer to complex problems of desegregation; there is obviously no one plan that will do the job in every case. The matter must be assessed in light of the circumstances present and the options available in each instance. It is incumbent upon the school board to establish that its proposed plan promises meaningful and immediate progress toward disestablishing state-imposed segregation. It is incumbent upon the district court to weigh that claim in light of the facts at hand and in light of any alternatives which may be shown as feasible and more promising in their effectiveness. Where the court finds the board to be acting in good faith and the proposed plan to have real prospects for dismantling the state-imposed dual system 'at the earliest practicable date,' then the plan may be said to provide effective relief. Of course, the availability to the board of other more promising courses of action may indicate a lack of good faith; and at the least it places a heavy burden upon the board to explain its preference for an apparently less effective method. Moreover, whatever plan is adopted will require evaluation in practice, and the court should retain jurisdiction until it is clear that state-imposed segregation has been completely removed. See *Raney v. Board of Education of Gould School District*, 391 U.S. 443, at 449, 88 S.Ct. 1697, at 1700, 20 L.Ed.2d 727.

We do not hold that 'freedom of choice' can have no place in such a plan. We do not hold that a 'freedom-of-choice' plan might of itself be unconstitutional, although that argument has been urged upon us. Rather, all we decide today is that in desegregating a dual system a plan utilizing 'freedom of choice' is not an end in itself.

. . . Although the general experience under 'freedom of choice' to date has been such as to indicate its ineffectiveness as a tool of desegregation, there may well be instances in which it can serve as an effective device. Where it offers real promise of aiding a desegregation program to effectuate conversion of a state-imposed dual system to a unitary, non-racial system there might be no objection to allowing such a device to prove itself in operation. On the other hand, if there are reasonably available other ways, such for illustration as zoning, promising speedier and more effective conversion to a unitary, nonracial school system, 'freedom of choice' must be held unacceptable.

The New Kent School Board's 'freedom-of-choice' plan cannot be accepted as a sufficient step to 'effectuate a transition' to a unitary system. In three years of operation not a single white child has chosen to attend Watkins school and although 115 Negro children enrolled in New Kent school in 1967 (up from 35 in 1965 and 111 in 1966) 85% of the Negro children in the system still attend the all-Negro Watkins school. In other words, the school system remains a dual system. Rather than further the dismantling of the dual system, the plan has operated simply to burden children and their parents with a responsibility which *Brown II* placed squarely on the School Board. The Board must be required to formulate a new plan and, in light of other courses which appear open to the Board, such as zoning, fashion steps which promise realistically to convert promptly to a system without a 'white' school and a 'Negro' school, but just schools.

The judgment of the Court of Appeals is vacated insofar as it affirmed the District Court and the case is remanded to the District Court for further proceedings consistent with this opinion. It is so ordered.

Notes and Questions

As seen above, in striving for a unitary system, a freedom of choice plan is not sufficient. This is of particular importance in post de jure segregated systems. The validity of freedom of choice plans was the subject of recent litigation in Cleveland, Mississippi, a school system still under consent decree tracing back to Jim Crow laws. *See Cowan v. Bolivar County Board of Educ.*, 2017 WL 988411 (N.D. Miss. 2017), available at: http://i2.cdn.turner.com/cnn/2017/images/03/14/cleveland .school.order.pdf; *Cowan by Johnson v. Bolivar County Board of Education*, 2015 WL 13048874 (N.D. Miss. 2015) (denying the motion to dismiss); *see also* Aria Bendix, *A Mississippi School District Is Finally Getting* Desegregated, THE ATLANTIC (Mar, 14, 2017), https://www.theatlantic.com/education/archive/2017/03/a-mississippi -school-district-is-finally-getting-desegregated/519573/; Christine Hauser, *Mississippi District Ordered to Desegregate Its Schools*, N.Y. TIMES (May 17, 2016), https://www.nytimes.com/2016/05/18/us/cleveland-mississippi-school-district -desegregate.html?mtrref=www.google.com&gwh=AA707 E04ED0E1D6E098E869

2915BCEF7&gwt=pay. Still of import are the choice plans adopted by schools now considered unitary and schools post-consent decrees. See Danielle Holley Walker's article on challenges and options post-desegregation. Danielle Holley-Walker, *A New Era for Desegregation*, 28 GA. ST. U. L. REV. 423 (2012). *See also* Danielle Holley-Walker, *After Unitary Status: Examining Voluntary Integration Strategies for Southern School Districts*, 88 N.C. L. REV. 877 (2010); Danielle Holley-Walker, *Educating at the Crossroads: Parents Involved, No Child Left Behind, and School Choice*, 69 OHIO STATE L.J. 911 (2008); Erica Frankenberg & Genevieve Siegel-Hawley, *Public Decisions and Private Choices: Reassessing the School-Housing Segregation Link in the Post-Parents Involved Era*, 48 WAKE FOREST L. REV. 397 (2013); Meera E. Deo, *Separate, Unequal, and Seeking Support*, 28 HARV. J. RACIAL & ETHNIC JUST. 9 (2012); Derek W. Black, *Education's Elusive Future, Storied Past, and the Fundamental Inequities Between*, 46 GA. L. REV. 557, 558 (2012); Jim Hilbert, *Restoring the Promise of Brown: Using State Constitutional Law to Challenge School Segregation*, 46 J.L. & EDUC. 1 (2017); Erica Frankenberg, *Assessing the Status of School Desegregation Sixty Years After Brown*, 2014 MICH. ST. L. REV. 677 (2014); Jennifer Reboul Rust, *Investing in Integration: A Case for "Promoting Diversity" in Federal Education Funding Priorities*, 59 LOY. L. REV. 623 (2013); Nicholas O. Stephanopoulos, *Civil Rights in A Desegregating America*, 83 U. CHI. L. REV. 1329 (2016); Erwin Chemerinsky, *Making Schools More Separate and Unequal:Parents Involved in Community Schools v. Seattle School District No. 1*, 2014 MICH. ST. L. REV. 633 (2014); Kimberly Jenkins Robinson, *Resurrecting the Promise of Brown: Understanding and Remedying How the Supreme Court Reconstitutionalized Segregated Schools*, 88 N.C. L. REV. 787 (2010).

On the road to de jure desegregation, in *Keyes vs. School District* the Supreme Court warned school districts that evidence of intent to discriminate could be construed as intent to discriminate system-wide. *Keyes v. Sch. Dist. No. 1*, 413 U.S. 189, 208 (1973) (shifting the burden of showing no segregative intent on the school authorities for all other segregated schools when school authorities have practiced purposeful segregation in part of the school system). This constituted a win for plaintiffs attempting to establish district wide liability for discriminatory practices, without adequate discovery to find proof for the entire system.

Still the Court struggled with its responsibility to steer desegregation plans, as time progressed. As schools' plans became more removed from *Brown*, *Keyes*'s admonishment became more attenuated in later cases. Thus, in *Missouri vs. Jenkins* began a diminishment in the Court's role in demanding accountability from school boards.

2. The Scope of "Desegregative Relief"

The cases below outline the forms of remedies recognized as adequate desegregation relief in the aftermath of *Brown*. Trace these remedies and their limits, as time has progressed. Would the promise of desegregation have been fulfilled more fully had these remedies not been limited so quickly by the Court?

By 1976, the Court's retrenchment began. School districts began to seek a reprieve from desegregation orders, citing demographic shifts. *Pasadena City Board Education v. Spangler*, 427 U.S. 424 (1976), for example, ruled that shifts in demographics was a suitable justification for release from desegregation orders. Considering that white flight and shifting demographics are recognized as root causes for de facto and reorganized informal segregation, this seems like a circular argument.

In *Swann v. Charlotte-Mecklenburg Bd. of Ed.*, 402 U.S. 1 (1971), the Supreme Court enunciated potential remedies suitable to achieve desegregation goals. Such remedies include school reassignments, busing, etc. In *Milliken II*, below, the Court reiterated, "in *Swann* we reaffirmed the principle laid down in *Green v. County School Board*, 391 U.S. 430, 88 S.Ct. 1689, 20 L.Ed.2d 716 (1968), that 'existing policy and practice with regard to faculty, staff, transportation, extracurricular activities, and facilities were among the most important indicia of a segregated system.' 402 U.S., at 18, 91 S.Ct., at 1277. In a word, discriminatory student assignment policies can themselves manifest and breed other inequalities built into a dual system founded on racial discrimination. Federal courts need not, and cannot, close their eyes to inequalities, shown by the record, which flow from a longstanding segregated system." Nonetheless, gradually, the remedies considered as imperative in early desegregation began to lose their appeal.

After *Swann,* the Court began to frame desegregation remedies as temporary. The complexities inherent in judicial oversight of local governments' operation of their school's system led to ambivalence. As as a result, the Supreme Court began to question the judiciary's power to mandate certain remedies. *Milliken* and *Jenkins,* below, showcase that ambivalence. In limiting its power to command interdistrict remedies, for example, the Court re-affirmed the limits of law as a tool for educational equality. As school districts around the nation are documented as de facto re-segregated, overreliance on judicially-provided desegregation avenues has been criticized by some as shortsighted (Derrick A. Bell, Jr., *Serving Two Masters: Integration Ideals and Client Interests in School Desegregation Litigation*, 85 YALE L.J. 470 (1976)).

Milliken v. Bradley [*Milliken II*]

433 U.S. 267 (1977)

MR. CHIEF JUSTICE BURGER delivered the opinion of the Court.

We granted certiorari in this case to consider two questions concerning the remedial powers of federal district courts in school desegregation cases, namely, whether a District Court can, as part of a desegregation decree, order compensatory or remedial educational programs for schoolchildren who have been subjected to past acts of de jure segregation, and whether, consistent with the Eleventh Amendment, a federal court can require state officials found responsible for constitutional violations to bear part of the costs of those programs.

I

This case is before the Court for the second time, following our remand, *Milliken v. Bradley*, 418 U.S. 717, 94 S.Ct. 3112, 41 L.Ed.2d 1069 (1974) (*Milliken I*); it marks the culmination of seven years of litigation over de jure school segregation in the Detroit public school system. For almost six years, the litigation has focused exclusively on the appropriate remedy to correct official acts of racial discrimination committed by both the Detroit School Board and the State of Michigan. No challenge is now made by the State or the local School Board to the prior findings of de jure segregation.

A

In the first stage of the remedy, proceedings which we reviewed in *Milliken I, supra*, the District Court, after reviewing several 'Detroit-only' desegregation plans, concluded that an interdistrict plan was required to 'achieve the greatest degree of actual desegregation . . . [so that] no school, grade or classroom [would be] substantially disproportionate to the overall pupil racial composition.' 345 F.Supp. 914, 918 (E.D.Mich.1972), quoted in *Milliken I, supra*, 418 U.S., at 734, 94 S.Ct., at 3122. . . . We reversed, holding that the order exceeded appropriate limits of federal equitable authority as defined in *Swann v. Charlotte-Mecklenburg Board of Education*, 402 U.S. 1, 24, 91 S.Ct. 1267, 1280, 28 L.Ed.2d 554 (1971), by concluding that 'as a matter of substantive constitutional right, [a] particular degree of racial balance' is required, and by subjecting other school districts, uninvolved with and unaffected by any constitutional violations, to the court's remedial powers. *Milliken I, supra*. Proceeding from the *Swann* standard 'that the scope of the remedy is determined by the nature and extent of the constitutional violation,' we held that, on the record before us, there was no interdistrict violation calling for an interdistrict remedy. Because the District Court's 'metropolitan remedy' went beyond the constitutional violation, we remanded the case for further proceedings 'leading to prompt formulation of a decree directed to eliminating the segregation found to exist in the Detroit city schools, a remedy which has been delayed since 1970.' 418 U.S., at 753, 94 S.Ct., at 3131.

B

. . . [On remand, the District Court] promptly ordered respondent Bradley and the Detroit Board to submit desegregation plans limited to the Detroit school system. On April 1, 1975, both parties submitted their proposed plans. Respondent Bradley's plan was limited solely to pupil reassignment; the proposal called for extensive transportation of students to achieve the plan's ultimate goal of assuring that every school within the district reflected, within 15 percentage points, the racial ratio of the school district as a whole. In contrast to respondent Bradley's proposal, the Detroit Board's plan provided for sufficient pupil reassignment to eliminate 'racially identifiable white elementary schools,' while ensuring that 'every child will spend at least a portion of his education in either a neighborhood elementary school or a neighborhood junior and senior high school.' 402 F.Supp. 1096, 1116 (1975). By eschewing racial ratios for each school, the Board's plan contemplated transportation of fewer students for shorter distances than respondent Bradley's proposal.

In addition to student reassignments, the Board's plan called for implementation of 13 remedial or compensatory programs, referred to in the record as 'educational components.' These compensatory programs, which were proposed in addition to the plan's provisions for magnet schools and vocational high schools, included three of the four components at issue in this case in-service training for teachers and administrators, guidance and counseling programs, and revised testing procedures. . . .

Having established these general principles, the District Court formulated several 'remedial guidelines' to govern the Detroit Board's development of a final plan. Declining 'to substitute its authority for the authority of elected state and local officials to decide which educational components are beneficial to the school community,' *id.*, at 1145, the District Judge laid down the following guidelines with respect to each of the four educational components at issue here. [The District Court directed that the four components be implemented with the goal of eradicating the effects of past discrimination.]

. . . . Nine months later, on May 11, 1976, the District Court entered its final order. Emphasizing that it had 'been careful to order only what is essential for a school district undergoing desegregation,' App. to Pet. for Cert. 117a, the court ordered the Detroit Board and the state defendants to institute comprehensive programs as to the four educational components by the start of the September 1976 school term. The cost of these four programs, the court concluded, was to be equally borne by the Detroit School Board and the State. To carry out this cost sharing, the court directed the local board to calculate its highest budget allocation in any prior year for the several educational programs and, from that base, any excess cost attributable to the desegregation plan was to be paid equally by the two groups of defendants responsible for prior constitutional violations, i.e., the Detroit Board and the state defendants.

            . . . .

II

This Court has not previously addressed directly the question whether federal courts can order remedial education programs as part of a school desegregation decree. However, the general principles governing our resolution of this issue are well settled by the prior decisions of this Court. In the first case concerning federal courts' remedial powers in eliminating de jure school segregation, the Court laid down the basic rule which governs to this day: 'In fashioning and effectuating the [desegregation] decrees, the courts will be guided by equitable principles.' *Brown v. Board of Education*, 349 U.S. 294, 300, 75 S.Ct. 753, 756, 99 L.Ed. 1083 (1955) (*Brown II*).

A

Application of those 'equitable principles,' we have held, requires federal courts to focus upon three factors. In the first place, like other equitable remedies, the nature of the desegregation remedy is to be determined by the nature and scope of the constitutional violation. *Swann v. Charlotte-Mecklenburg Board of Education*, 402 U.S., at 16, 91 S.Ct., at 1276. The remedy must therefore be related to 'the condition alleged to offend the Constitution . . . .' *Milliken I*, 418 U.S., at 738, 94 S. Ct., at 3124. Second, the decree must indeed be remedial in nature, that is, it must be designed as nearly as possible 'to restore the victims of discriminatory conduct to the position they would have occupied in the absence of such conduct.' *Id.*, at 746, 94 S.Ct., at 3128. Third, the federal courts in devising a remedy must take into account the interests of state and local authorities in managing their own affairs, consistent with the Constitution. In *Brown II* the Court squarely held that '[s]chool authorities have the *primary* responsibility for elucidating, assessing, and solving these problems . . . .' 349 U.S., at 299, 75 S.Ct., at 756. (Emphasis supplied.) If, however, 'school authorities fail in their affirmative obligations . . . judicial authority may be invoked.' *Swann, supra*, 402 U.S., at 15, 91 S.Ct., at 1276. Once invoked, 'the scope of a district court's equitable powers to remedy past wrongs is broad, for breadth and flexibility are inherent in equitable remedies.' *Ibid.*

B

. . . . The well-settled principle that the nature and scope of the remedy are to be determined by the violation means simply that federal-court decrees must directly address and relate to the constitutional violation itself. Because of this inherent limitation upon federal judicial authority, federal-court decrees exceed appropriate limits if they are aimed at eliminating a condition that does not violate the Constitution or does not flow from such a violation, see *Pasadena City Board of Education v. Spangler*, 427 U.S. 424, 96 S.Ct. 2697, 49 L.Ed.2d 599 (1976), or if they are imposed upon governmental units that were neither involved in nor affected by the constitutional violation, as in *Milliken I, supra. Hills v. Gautreaux*, 425 U.S. 284, 292–296, 96 S.Ct. 1538, 1543–1545, 47 L.Ed.2d 792 (1976). But where, as here, a constitutional violation has been found, the remedy does not 'exceed' the violation if the remedy is tailored to cure the '*condition* that offends the Constitution.' *Milliken I, supra*, 418 U.S., at 738, 94 S.Ct., at 3124. (Emphasis supplied.)

The 'condition' offending the Constitution is Detroit's de jure segregated school system, which was so pervasively and persistently segregated that the District Court found that the need for the educational components flowed directly from constitutional violations by both state and local officials. These specific educational remedies, although normally left to the discretion of the elected school board and professional educators, were deemed necessary to restore the victims of discriminatory conduct to the position they would have enjoyed in terms of education had these four components been provided in a nondiscriminatory manner in a school system free from pervasive de jure racial segregation.

In the first case invalidating a de jure system, a unanimous Court, speaking through Mr. Chief Justice Warren, held in *Brown v. Board of Education*, 347 U.S. 483, 495, 74 S.Ct. 686, 692, 98 L.Ed. 873 (1954) (*Brown I*): 'Separate educational facilities are inherently unequal.' *Brown v. Board of Education*, 347 U.S. 483, 495, 74 S.Ct. 686, 692, 98 L.Ed. 873 (1954). And in *United States v. Montgomery County Board of Education*, 395 U.S. 225, 89 S.Ct. 1670, 23 L.Ed.2d 263 (1969), the Court concerned itself not with pupil assignment, but with the desegregation of faculty and staff as part of the process of dismantling a dual system. In doing so, the Court, there speaking through Mr. Justice Black, focused on the reason for judicial concerns going beyond pupil assignment: 'The dispute . . . deals with faculty and staff desegregation, a goal that we have recognized to be an important aspect of the basic task of achieving a public school system wholly free from racial discrimination.' *Id.*, at 231–232, 89 S.Ct., at 1674.

Montgomery County therefore stands firmly for the proposition that matters other than pupil assignment must on occasion be addressed by federal courts to eliminate the effects of prior segregation. Similarly, in *Swann* we reaffirmed the principle laid down in *Green v. County School Board*, 391 U.S. 430, 88 S.Ct. 1689, 20 L.Ed.2d 716 (1968), that 'existing policy and practice with regard to faculty, staff, transportation, extracurricular activities, and facilities were among the most important indicia of a segregated system.' 402 U.S., at 18, 91 S.Ct., at 1277. In a word, discriminatory student assignment policies can themselves manifest and breed other inequalities built into a dual system founded on racial discrimination. Federal courts need not, and cannot, close their eyes to inequalities, shown by the record, which flow from a longstanding segregated system.

C

In light of the mandate of *Brown I* and *Brown II*, federal courts have, over the years, often required the inclusion of remedial programs in desegregation plans to overcome the inequalities inherent in dual school systems. . . . [Prior cases] demonstrate that the District Court in the case now before us did not break new ground in approving the School Board's proposed plan. Quite the contrary, acting on abundant evidence in this record, the District Court approved a remedial plan going beyond mere pupil assignments, as expressly approved by *Swann* and Montgomery County. In so doing, the District Court was adopting specific programs proposed by local school authorities, who must be presumed to be familiar with the problems and the needs of a system undergoing desegregation.

We do not, of course, imply that the order here is a blueprint for other cases. That cannot be; in school desegregation cases, '[t]here is no universal answer to complex problems . . . ; there is obviously no one plan that will do the job in every case.' *Green*, 391 U.S., at 439, 88 S.Ct., at 1695. On this record, however, we are bound to conclude that the decree before us was aptly tailored to remedy the consequences of the constitutional violation. Children who have been thus educationally and culturally set apart from the larger community will inevitably acquire habits of speech, conduct, and attitudes reflecting their cultural isolation. They are likely to acquire speech habits, for example, which vary from the environment in which they must ultimately function and compete, if they are to enter and be a part of that community. This is not peculiar to race; in this setting, it can affect any children who, as a group, are isolated by force of law from the mainstream. Cf. *Lau v. Nichols*, 414 U.S. 563, 94 S.Ct. 786, 39 L.Ed.2d 1 (1974).

Pupil assignment alone does not automatically remedy the impact of previous, unlawful educational isolation; the consequences linger and can be dealt with only by independent measures. In short, speech habits acquired in a segregated system do not vanish simply by moving the child to a desegregated school. The root condition shown by this record must be treated directly by special training at the hands of teachers prepared for that task. This is what the District Judge in the case drew from the record before him as to the consequences of Detroit's de jure system, and we cannot conclude that the remedies decreed exceeded the scope of the violations found.

Nor do we find any other reason to believe that the broad and flexible equity powers of the court were abused in this case. The established role of local school authorities was maintained inviolate, and the remedy is indeed remedial. The order does not punish anyone, nor does it impair or jeopardize the educational system in Detroit . . . .

III

Petitioners also contend that the District Court's order, even if otherwise proper, violates the Eleventh Amendment. In their view, the requirement that the state defendants pay one-half the additional costs attributable to the four educational components is, 'in practical effect, indistinguishable from an award of money damages against the state based upon the asserted prior misconduct of state officials.' Brief for Petitioners 34. Arguing from this premise, petitioners conclude that the 'award' in this case is barred under this Court's holding in *Edelman v. Jordan*, 415 U.S. 651, 94 S.Ct. 1347, 39 L.Ed.2d 662 (1974).

Edelman involved a suit for money damages against the State, as well as for prospective injunctive relief. The suit was brought by an individual who claimed that Illinois officials had improperly withheld disability benefit payments from him and from the members of his class. Applying traditional Eleventh Amendment principles, we held that the suit was barred to the extent the suit sought 'the award of an *accrued* monetary liability . . .' which represented 'retroactive payments.' *Id.*, at 663–664, 94 S.Ct., at 1356. (Emphasis supplied.) Conversely, the Court held that the suit was proper to the extent it sought 'payment of state funds . . . as a necessary consequence of compliance *in the future* with a substantive federal-question determination . . . .' *Id.*, at 668, 94 S.Ct., at 1358. (Emphasis supplied.)

The decree to share the future costs of educational components in this case fits squarely within the prospective-compliance exception reaffirmed by *Edelman*. That exception, which had its genesis in *Ex parte Young*, 209 U.S. 123, 28 S.Ct. 441,

52 L.Ed. 714 (1908), permits federal courts to enjoin state officials to conform their conduct to requirements of federal law, notwithstanding a direct and substantial impact on the state treasury. 415 U.S., at 667, 94 S.Ct., at 1357. The order challenged here does no more than that. . . .

These programs were not, and as a practical matter could not be, intended to wipe the slate clean by one bold stroke, as could a retroactive award of money in *Edelman*. Rather, by the nature of the antecedent violation, which on this record caused significant deficiencies in communications skills reading and speaking the victims of Detroit's de jure segregated system will continue to experience the effects of segregation until such future time as the remedial programs can help dissipate the continuing effects of past misconduct. Reading and speech deficiencies cannot be eliminated by judicial fiat; they will require time, patience, and the skills of specially trained teachers. That the programs are also 'compensatory' in nature does not change the fact that they are part of a plan that operates prospectively to bring about the delayed benefits of a unitary school system. We therefore hold that such prospective relief is not barred by the Eleventh Amendment.

Finally, there is no merit to petitioners' claims that the relief ordered here violates the Tenth Amendment and general principles of federalism. The Tenth Amendment's reservation of nondelegated powers to the States is not implicated by a federal-court judgment enforcing the express prohibitions of unlawful state conduct enacted by the Fourteenth Amendment. Cf. *Fitzpatrick v. Bitzer*, 427 U.S. 445, 96 S.Ct. 2666, 49 L.Ed.2d 614 (1976). Nor are principles of federalism abrogated by the decree. The District Court has neither attempted to restructure local governmental entities nor to mandate a particular method or structure of state of local financing. Cf. *San Antonio Independent School Dist. v. Rodriguez*, 411 U.S. 1, 93 S. Ct. 1278, 36 L.Ed.2d 16 (1973). The District Court has, rather, properly enforced the guarantees of the Fourteenth Amendment consistent with our prior holdings, and in a manner that does not jeopardize the integrity of the structure or functions of state and local government.

The judgment of the Court of Appeals is therefore

Affirmed.

Missouri v. Jenkins

515 U.S. 70 (1995)

CHIEF JUSTICE REHNQUIST delivered the opinion of the Court.

As this school desegregation litigation enters its 18th year, we are called upon again to review the decisions of the lower courts. In this case, the State of Missouri has challenged the District Court's order of salary increases for virtually all instructional and noninstructional staff within the Kansas City, Missouri, School District (KCMSD) and the District Court's order requiring the State to continue to fund remedial "quality education" programs because student achievement levels were still "at or below national norms at many grade levels."

I

A general overview of this litigation is necessary for proper resolution of the issues upon which we granted certiorari. This case has been before the same United States District Judge since 1977. *Missouri v. Jenkins*, 491 U.S. 274, 276, 109 S.Ct. 2463, 2465, 105 L.Ed.2d 229 (1989) (*Jenkins I*). In that year, the KCMSD, the school board, and the children of two school board members brought suit against the State and other defendants. Plaintiffs alleged that the State, the surrounding suburban school districts (SSD's), and various federal agencies had caused and perpetuated a system of racial segregation in the schools of the Kansas City metropolitan area.

[In a portion of the opinion omitted here the Court details the sequence of remedies imposed by the District Court after findin that the Distrct Court had indeed maintained a segregated school system. Among the remedies were expansion of kindergarden and summer schools to all students, cash grants, state responsibility to fund programs in and out of the KCMSD district. Also, because the racial make up of the district remained majority black, the district court believed desegregation required state and district collaboration. Amog measures approved by the District Court were: renovation of approximately 55 schools, the closure of 18 facilities, and the construction of 17 new schools, salary assistance to all but three of the approximately 5,000 KCMSD employees. The total cost of this component of the desegregation remedy since 1987 is over $200 million. See Desegregation Expenditures.]

. . . As a result, the desegregation costs have escalated and now are approaching an annual cost of $200 million. These massive expenditures have financed

> "high schools in which every classroom will have air conditioning, an alarm system, and 15 microcomputers; a 2,000-square-foot planetarium; green houses and vivariums; a 25-acre farm with an air-conditioned meeting room for 104 people; a Model United Nations wired for language translation; broadcast capable radio and television studios with an editing and animation lab; a temperature controlled art gallery; movie editing and screening rooms; a 3,500-square-foot dust-free diesel mechanics room; 1,875-square-foot elementary school animal rooms for use in a zoo project; swimming pools; and numerous other facilities." *Jenkins II*, 495 U.S., at 77, 110 S.Ct., at 1676–1677 (Kennedy, J., concurring in part and concurring in judgment).

Not surprisingly, the cost of this remedial plan has "far exceeded KCMSD's budget, or for that matter, its authority to tax." *Id.*, at 60, 110 S.Ct., at 1668. The State, through the operation of joint-and-several liability, has borne the brunt of these costs. The District Court candidly has acknowledged that it has "allowed the District planners to dream" and "provided the mechanism for th[ose] dreams to be realized." App. to Pet. for Cert. A-133. In short, the District Court "has gone to great lengths to provide KCMSD with facilities and opportunities not available anywhere else in the country." *Id.,* at A-115.

II

. . .

Because of the importance of the issues, we granted certiorari to consider the following: (1) whether the District Court exceeded its constitutional authority when it granted salary increases to virtually all instructional and noninstructional employees of the KCMSD, and (2) whether the District Court properly relied upon the fact that student achievement test scores had failed to rise to some unspecified level when it declined to find that the State had achieved partial unitary status as to the quality education programs. 512 U.S. 1287, 115 S.Ct. 41, 129 L.Ed.2d 936 (1994).

. . . Almost 25 years ago, in *Swann v. Charlotte-Mecklenburg Bd. of Ed.,* 402 U.S. 1, 91 S.Ct. 1267, 28 L.Ed.2d 554 (1971), we dealt with the authority of a district court to fashion remedies for a school district that had been segregated in law in violation of the Equal Protection Clause of the Fourteenth Amendment. Although recognizing the discretion that must necessarily adhere in a district court in fashioning a remedy, we also recognized the limits on such remedial power:

> "[E]limination of racial discrimination in public schools is a large task and one that should not be retarded by efforts to achieve broader purposes lying beyond the jurisdiction of the school authorities. One vehicle can carry only a limited amount of baggage. It would not serve the important objective of *Brown* [*v. Board of Education,* 347 U.S. 483, 74 S.Ct. 686, 98 L.Ed.2d 873 (1954),*]* to seek to use school desegregation cases for purposes beyond their scope, although desegregation of schools ultimately will have impact on other forms of discrimination." *Id.,* at 22–23, 91 S.Ct., at 1279.

Three years later, in *Milliken I,* 418 U.S. 717, 94 S.Ct. 3112, 41 L.Ed.2d 1069 (1974), we held that a District Court had exceeded its authority in fashioning interdistrict relief where the surrounding school districts had not themselves been guilty of any constitutional violation. *Id.,* 418 U.S., at 746–747, 94 S.Ct., at 3128. We said that a desegregation remedy "is necessarily designed, as all remedies are, to restore the victims of discriminatory conduct to the position they would have occupied in the absence of such conduct." *Id.,* at 746, 94 S.Ct., at 3128. "[W]ithout an interdistrict violation and interdistrict effect, there is no constitutional wrong calling for an interdistrict remedy." *Id.,* at 745, 94 S.Ct., at 3127. We also rejected "[t]he suggestion . . . that schools which have a majority of Negro students are not 'desegregated,' whatever the makeup of the school district's population and however neutrally the district lines have been drawn and administered." *Id.,* at 747, n. 22, 94 S.Ct., at 3128, n. 22; see also *Freeman,* 503 U.S., at 474, 112 S.Ct., at 1437 ("[A] critical beginning point is the degree of racial imbalance in the school district, that is to say a comparison of the proportion of majority to minority students in individual schools with the proportions of the races in the district as a whole").

... In *Milliken v. Bradley,* 433 U.S. 267, 97 S.Ct. 2749, 53 L.Ed.2d 745 (1977) (*Milliken II*), we articulated a three-part framework derived from our prior cases to guide district courts in the exercise of their remedial authority.

"In the first place, like other equitable remedies, the nature of the desegregation remedy is to be determined by the nature and scope of the constitutional violation. *Swann v. Charlotte-Mecklenburg Board of Education,* 402 U.S., at 16 [91 S.Ct., at 1276]. The remedy must therefore be related to 'the *condition* alleged to offend the Constitution. . . .' *Milliken I,* 418 U.S., at 738 [94 S.Ct., at 3124]. Second, the decree must indeed be *remedial* in nature, that is, it must be designed as nearly as possible 'to restore the victims of discriminatory conduct to the position they would have occupied in the absence of such conduct.' *Id.,* at 746 [94 S.Ct., at 3128]. Third, the federal courts in devising a remedy must take into account the interests of state and local authorities in managing their own affairs, consistent with the Constitution." *Id.,* at 280–281, 97 S.Ct., at 2757 (footnotes omitted).

We added that the "principle that the nature and scope of the remedy are to be determined by the violation means simply that federal-court decrees must directly address and relate to the constitutional violation itself." *Id.,* at 281–282, 97 S.Ct., at 2758. In applying these principles, we have identified "student assignments, . . . 'faculty, staff, transportation, extracurricular activities and facilities'" as the most important indicia of a racially segregated school system. *Board of Ed. of Oklahoma City Public Schools v. Dowell,* 498 U.S. 237, 250, 111 S.Ct. 630, 638, 112 L.Ed.2d 715 (1991) (quoting *Green v. School Bd. of New Kent Cty.,* 391 U.S. 430, 435, 88 S.Ct. 1689, 1693, 20 L.Ed.2d 716 (1968)).

Because "federal supervision of local school systems was intended as a temporary measure to remedy past discrimination," *Dowell, supra,* at 247, 111 S.Ct., at 637, we also have considered the showing that must be made by a school district operating under a desegregation order for complete or partial relief from that order. In *Freeman,* we stated that

"[a]mong the factors which must inform the sound discretion of the court in ordering partial withdrawal are the following: [1] whether there has been full and satisfactory compliance with the decree in those aspects of the system where supervision is to be withdrawn; [2] whether retention of judicial control is necessary or practicable to achieve compliance with the decree in other facets of the school system; and [3] whether the school district has demonstrated, to the public and to the parents and students of the once disfavored race, its good-faith commitment to the whole of the courts' decree and to those provisions of the law and the Constitution that were the predicate for judicial intervention in the first instance." 503 U.S., at 491, 112 S. Ct., at 1446.

The ultimate inquiry is "'whether the [constitutional violator] ha[s] complied in good faith with the desegregation decree since it was entered, and whether the

vestiges of past discrimination ha[vc] been eliminated to the extent practicable.'"
Id., at 492, 112 S.Ct., at 1446 (quoting *Dowell, supra,* 498 U.S., at 249–250, 111 S.Ct.,
at 638).

. . . As noted in *Milliken I,* 418 U.S. 717, 94 S.Ct. 3112, 41 L.Ed.2d 1069 (1974), we
have rejected the suggestion "that schools which have a majority of Negro students
are not 'desegregated' whatever the racial makeup of the school district's population
and however neutrally the district lines have been drawn and administered." *Id.,*
418 U.S., at 747, n. 22, 94 S.Ct., at 3128, n. 22; see *Milliken II,* 433 U.S., at 280, n. 14,
97 S.Ct., at 2757, n. 14 ("[T]he Court has consistently held that the Constitution is
not violated by racial imbalance in the schools, without more"); *Spangler, supra,* 427
U.S., at 434, 96 S.Ct., at 2703–2704.

Instead of seeking to remove the racial identity of the various schools within the
KCMSD, the District Court has set out on a program to create a school district
that was equal to or superior to the surrounding SSD's. Its remedy has focused on
"desegregative attractiveness," coupled with "suburban comparability." Examination of the District Court's reliance on "desegregative attractiveness" and "suburban
comparability" is instructive for our ultimate resolution of the salary-order issue.

The purpose of desegregative attractiveness has been not only to remedy the
system wide reduction in student achievement, but also to attract nonminority
students not presently enrolled in the KCMSD. This remedy has included an elaborate program of capital improvements, course enrichment, and extracurricular
enhancement not simply in the formerly identifiable black schools, but in schools
throughout the district. The District Court's remedial orders have converted every
senior high school, every middle school, and one-half of the elementary schools in
the KCMSD into "magnet" schools. The District Court's remedial order has all but
made the KCMSD itself into a magnet district.

We previously have approved of intradistrict desegregation remedies involving
magnet schools. See, *e.g., Milliken II, supra,* 433 U.S., at 272, 97 S.Ct., at 2753. Magnet
schools have the advantage of encouraging voluntary movement of students within
a school district in a pattern that aids desegregation on a voluntary basis, without
requiring extensive busing and redrawing of district boundary lines. Cf. *Jenkins II,
supra,* 495 U.S., at 59–60, 110 S.Ct., at 1667–1668 (Kennedy, J., concurring in part
and concurring in judgment) (citing *Milliken II, supra,* 433 U.S., at 272, 97 S.Ct., at
2753). As a component in an intradistrict remedy, magnet schools also are attractive
because they promote desegregation while limiting the withdrawal of white student
enrollment that may result from mandatory student reassignment. See 639 F.Supp.,
at 37; cf. *United States v. Scotland Neck City Bd. of Ed.,* 407 U.S. 484, 491, 92 S.Ct.
2214, 2218, 33 L.Ed.2d 75 (1972).

The District Court's remedial plan in this case, however, is not designed solely
to redistribute the students within the KCMSD in order to eliminate racially identifiable schools within the KCMSD. Instead, its purpose is to attract nonminority
students from outside the KCMSD schools. But this *inter* district goal is beyond

the scope of the *intra*district violation identified by the District Court. In effect, the District Court has devised a remedy to accomplish indirectly what it admittedly lacks the remedial authority to mandate directly: the interdistrict transfer of students. 639 F.Supp., at 38 ("'[B]ecause of restrictions on this Court's remedial powers in restructuring the operations of local and state government entities,' any *mandatory* plan which would go beyond the boundary lines of KCMSD goes far beyond the nature and extent of the constitutional violation [that] this Court found existed").

In *Milliken I* we determined that a desegregation remedy that would require mandatory interdistrict reassignment of students throughout the Detroit metropolitan area was an impermissible interdistrict response to the intradistrict violation identified. 418 U.S., at 745, 94 S.Ct., at 3127–3128. In that case, the lower courts had ordered an interdistrict remedy because "'any less comprehensive a solution than a metropolitan area plan would result in an all-black school system immediately surrounded by practically all white suburban school systems, with an overwhelmingly white majority population in the total metropolitan area.'" *Id.,* at 735, 94 S.Ct., at 3122. We held that before a district court could order an interdistrict remedy, there must be a showing that "racially discriminatory acts of the state or local school districts, or of a single school district have been a substantial cause of interdistrict segregation." *Id.,* at 745, 94 S.Ct., at 3127. Because the record "contain[ed] evidence of *de jure* segregated conditions only in the Detroit Schools" and there had been "no showing of significant violation by the 53 outlying school districts and no evidence of interdistrict violation or effect," we reversed the District Court's grant of interdistrict relief. *Ibid.*

. . . What we meant in *Milliken I* by an interdistrict violation was a violation that caused segregation between adjoining districts. Nothing in *Milliken I* suggests that the District Court in that case could have circumvented the limits on its remedial authority by requiring the State of Michigan, a constitutional violator, to implement a magnet program designed to achieve the same interdistrict transfer of students that we held was beyond its remedial authority. Here, the District Court has done just that: created a magnet district of the KCMSD in order to serve the *inter*district goal of attracting nonminority students from the surrounding SSD's and redistributing them within the KCMSD. The District Court's pursuit of "desegregative attractiveness" is beyond the scope of its broad remedial authority. See *Milliken II,* 433 U.S., at 280, 97 S.Ct., at 2757.

. . .

Our decision today is fully consistent with *Gautreaux.* A district court seeking to remedy an *intra*district violation that has not "directly caused" significant interdistrict effects, *Milliken I, supra,* 418 U.S., at 744–745, 94 S.Ct., at 3126–3128, exceeds its remedial authority if it orders a remedy with an interdistrict purpose. This conclusion follows directly from *Milliken II,* decided one year after *Gautreaux,* where we reaffirmed the bedrock principle that "federal-court decrees exceed appropriate limits if they are aimed at eliminating a condition that does not violate the Constitution or does not flow from such a violation." 433 U.S., at 282, 97 S.Ct., at 2758. In *Milliken II,* we also emphasized that "federal courts in devising a remedy must take into account the interests of state and local authorities in managing their own affairs, consistent with the Constitution." *Id.,* at 280–281, 97 S.Ct., at 2757. *Gautreaux,* however, involved the imposition of a remedy upon a federal agency. See 425 U.S., at 292, n. 9, 96 S.Ct., at 1544, n. 9. Thus, it did not raise the same federalism concerns that are implicated when a federal court issues a remedial order against a State. See *Milliken II, supra,* 433 U.S., at 280–281, 97 S.Ct., at 2757–2758.

The District Court's pursuit of "desegregative attractiveness" cannot be reconciled with our cases placing limitations on a district court's remedial authority. It is certainly theoretically possible that the greater the expenditure per pupil within the KCMSD, the more likely it is that some unknowable number of nonminority students not presently attending schools in the KCMSD will choose to enroll in those schools . . . Nor are there limits to the duration of the District Court's involvement . . . Each additional program ordered by the District Court—and financed by the State—to increase the "desegregative attractiveness" of the school district makes the KCMSD more and more dependent on additional funding from the State; in turn, the greater the KCMSD's dependence on state funding, the greater its reliance on continued supervision by the District Court. But our cases recognize that local autonomy of school districts is a vital national tradition, *Dayton I,* 433 U.S., at 410, 97 S.Ct., at 2770, and that a district court must strive to restore state and local authorities to the control of a school system operating in compliance with the Constitution. See *Freeman,* 503 U.S., at 489, 112 S.Ct., at 1445; *Dowell,* 498 U.S., at 247, 111 S.Ct., at 636–637.

. . . In reconsidering . . . the District Court should apply our three-part test from *Freeman v. Pitts, supra,* 503 U.S., at 491, 112 S.Ct., at 1445–1446. The District Court should consider that the State's role with respect to the quality education programs has been limited to the funding, not the implementation, of those programs. As all the parties agree that improved achievement on test scores is not necessarily required for the State to achieve partial unitary status as to the quality education programs, the District Court should sharply limit, if not dispense with, its reliance on this factor. Brief for Respondents KCMSD et al. 34–35; Brief for Respondents Jenkins et al. 26. Just as demographic changes independent of *de jure* segregation will affect the racial composition of student assignments, *Freeman,* 503 U.S., at 494–495, 112 S.Ct., at 1447–1448, so too will numerous external factors beyond the control of the KCMSD and the State affect minority student achievement. So long as these external factors are not the result of segregation, they do not figure in the remedial calculus. See *Spangler,* 427 U.S., at 434, 96 S.Ct., at 2703–2704; *Swann,* 402 U.S., at 22, 91 S.Ct., at 1279. Insistence upon academic goals unrelated to the effects of legal segregation unwarrantably postpones the day when the KCMSD will be able to operate on its own.

The District Court also should consider that many goals of its quality education plan already have been attained: the KCMSD now is equipped with "facilities and opportunities not available anywhere else in the country." App. to Pet. for Cert. A-115. KCMSD schools received an AAA rating eight years ago, and the present remedial programs have been in place for seven years. See 19 F.3d, at 401 (Beam, J., dissenting from denial of rehearing en banc). It may be that in education, just as it may be in economics, a "rising tide lifts all boats," but the remedial quality education program should be tailored to remedy the injuries suffered by the victims of prior *de jure* segregation. See *Milliken II, supra,* 433 U.S., at 287, 97 S.Ct., at 2760–2761. Minority students in kindergarten through grade 7 in the KCMSD always have attended AAA-rated schools; minority students in the KCMSD that previously attended schools rated below AAA have since received remedial education programs for a period of up to seven years.

On remand, the District Court must bear in mind that its end purpose is not only "to remedy the violation" to the extent practicable, but also "to restore state and local authorities to the control of a school system that is operating in compliance with the Constitution." *Freeman, supra,* 503 U.S., at 489, 112 S.Ct., at 1445.

The judgment of the Court of Appeals is reversed.

It is so ordered.

Notes and Questions

1. In *Milliken II,* the Court reaffirms the power of federal courts to review plans to desegregate and to issue remedial plans to help address the school district's documented practice of de jure segregation. Note the following standard:

> Application of those 'equitable principles,' we have held, requires federal courts to focus upon three factors. In the first place, like other equitable remedies, the nature of the desegregation remedy is to be determined by the nature and scope of the constitutional violation. . . . The remedy must therefore be related to 'the condition alleged to offend the Constitution . . . .'

> Second, the decree must indeed be remedial in nature, that is, it must be designed as nearly as possible 'to restore the victims of discriminatory conduct to the position they would have occupied in the absence of such conduct.'

> Third, the federal courts in devising a remedy must take into account the interests of state and local authorities in managing their own affairs, consistent with the Constitution. In *Brown II* the Court squarely held that '[s]chool authorities have the primary responsibility for elucidating, assessing, and solving these problems . . . .'

> If, however, 'school authorities fail in their affirmative obligations . . . . Once invoked, 'the scope of a district court's equitable powers to remedy

past wrongs is broad, for breadth and flexibility are inherent in equitable remedies.'

How does the Court balance its obligation to desegregate with its concerns with federalism? Consider that school districts today, as is the case, for example, with Jefferson County, Alabama, are often reported as re-segregated. *See* Nikole Hannah-Jones, *The Resegregation of Jefferson County*, N.Y. TIMES (Sept. 6, 2017), https://www .nytimes.com/2017/09/06/magazine/the-resegregation-of-jefferson-county.html. Could the judiciary, in supervising desegregation post-*Brown*, have done more to prevent this pattern of resegregation in the United States?

2. What do you think of the Court's view regarding whether majority minority school districts are problematic: "We also reject . . . [t]he suggestion . . . that schools which have a majority of Negro students are not 'desegregated,' whatever the makeup of the school district's population and however neutrally the district lines have been drawn and administered.' *Milliken I*, 418 U.S. at 747, n. 22; *see also Freeman*, 503 U.S., at 474 ('[A] critical beginning point is the degree of racial imbalance in the school district, that is to say, a comparison of the proportion of majority to minority students in individual schools with the proportions of the races in the district as a whole')."

Do you agree that in districts formerly *de jure* segregated, majority minority school districts should not alone trigger concerns?

E. Statutory Avenues

1. Title VI

Thus far, we have reviewed desegregation efforts under the Equal Protection Clause of the Fourteenth Amendment of the Constitution, tracing back to *Brown II*'s implementation order. Title VI of the Civil Rights Act of 1964 provides an additional avenue for challenging unequal school policies. Title VI states: "No person in the United States shall, on the ground of race, color, or national origin, be excluded from participation in, or be denied the benefits of, or be subjected to discrimination under any program or activity receiving federal financial assistance." Claims filed under Title VI, unlike those filed under the Fourteenth Amendment, also apply to private parties receiving federal funding. *See Gratz v. Bollinger*, 539 U.S. 244 (2003); *Alexander v. Sandoval*, 532 U.S. 275 (2001). In *Fordice* below, the Court considers states' responsibility for historically Black colleges, many of which were created because of the segregatory policies of those states. Should the states that motivated the creation of these institutions bear a continuous fiscal obligation to them? And should states' duty to desegregate be different in the higher education context?

United States v. Fordice

505 U.S. 717 (1992)

JUSTICE WHITE delivered the opinion of the Court.

In 1954, this Court held that the concept of "'separate but equal'" has no place in the field of public education. *Brown v. Board of Education,* 347 U.S. 483, 495, 74 S.Ct. 686, 692, 98 L.Ed. 873 (*Brown I*). The following year, the Court ordered an end to segregated public education "with all deliberate speed." *Brown v. Board of Education,* 349 U.S. 294, 301, 75 S.Ct. 753, 756, 99 L.Ed. 1083 (1955) (*Brown II*). Since these decisions, the Court has had many occasions to evaluate whether a public school district has met its affirmative obligation to dismantle its prior *de jure* segregated system in elementary and secondary schools. In these cases we decide what standards to apply in determining whether the State of Mississippi has met this obligation in the university context.

I

Mississippi launched its public university system in 1848 by establishing the University of Mississippi, an institution dedicated to the higher education exclusively of white persons. In succeeding decades, the State erected additional postsecondary, single-race educational facilities. Alcorn State University opened its doors in 1871 as "an agricultural college for the education of Mississippi's black youth." *Ayers v. Allain,* 674 F.Supp. 1523, 1527 (ND Miss.1987). Creation of four more exclusively white institutions followed: Mississippi State University (1880), Mississippi University for Women (1885), University of Southern Mississippi (1912), and Delta State University (1925). The State added two more solely black institutions in 1940 and 1950: in the former year, Jackson State University, which was charged with training "black teachers for the black public schools," *id.,* at 1528; and in the latter year, Mississippi Valley State University, whose functions were to educate teachers primarily for rural and elementary schools and to provide vocational instruction to black students.

Despite this Court's decisions in *Brown I* and *Brown II,* Mississippi's policy of *de jure* segregation continued. The first black student was not admitted to the University of Mississippi until 1962, and then only by court order. See *Meredith v. Fair,* 306 F.2d 374 (CA5), cert. denied, 371 U.S. 828, 83 S.Ct. 49, 9 L.Ed.2d 66 enf'd, 313 F.2d 532 (1962) (en banc) (*per curiam*). For the next 12 years the segregated public university system in the State remained largely intact. Mississippi State University, Mississippi University for Women, University of Southern Mississippi, and Delta State University each admitted at least one black student during these years, but the student composition of these institutions was still almost completely white. During this period, Jackson State and Mississippi Valley State were exclusively black; Alcorn State had admitted five white students by 1968.

In 1969, the United States Department of Health, Education and Welfare (HEW) initiated efforts to enforce Title VI of the Civil Rights Act of 1964, 42 U.S.C. § 2000d.

HEW requested that the State devise a plan to disestablish the formerly *de jure* segregated university system. . . . But even the limited effects of [the approved] Plan in disestablishing the prior *de jure* segregated system were substantially constricted by the state legislature, which refused to fund it until fiscal year 1978, and even then at well under half the amount sought by the Board. App. 896–897, 1444–1445, 1448–1449.

Private petitioners initiated this lawsuit in 1975. They complained that Mississippi had maintained the racially segregative effects of its prior dual system of postsecondary education in violation of the Fifth, Ninth, Thirteenth, and Fourteenth Amendments, 42 U.S.C. §§ 1981 and 1983, and Title VI of the Civil Rights Act of 1964, 42 U.S.C. § 2000d. Shortly thereafter, the United States filed its complaint in intervention, charging that state officials had failed to satisfy their obligation under the Equal Protection Clause of the Fourteenth Amendment and Title VI to dismantle Mississippi's dual system of higher education.

After this lawsuit was filed, the parties attempted for 12 years to achieve a consensual resolution of their differences through voluntary dismantlement by the State of its prior separated system. The board of trustees implemented reviews of existing curricula and program "mission" at each institution. In 1981, the Board issued "Mission Statements" that identified the extant purpose of each public university. These "missions" were clustered into three categories: comprehensive, urban, and regional. "Comprehensive" universities were classified as those with the greatest existing resources and program offerings. All three such institutions (University of Mississippi, Mississippi State, and Southern Mississippi) were exclusively white under the prior *de jure* segregated system. The Board authorized each to continue offering doctoral degrees and to assert leadership in certain disciplines. Jackson State, the sole urban university, was assigned a more limited research and degree mission, with both functions geared toward its urban setting. It was exclusively black at its inception. The "regional" designation was something of a misnomer, as the Board envisioned those institutions primarily in an undergraduate role, rather than a "regional" one in the geographic sense of serving just the localities in which they were based. Only the universities classified as "regional" included institutions that, prior to desegregation, had been either exclusively white — Delta State and Mississippi University for Women — or exclusively black — Alcorn State and Mississippi Valley State.

By the mid-1980's, 30 years after *Brown,* more than 99 percent of Mississippi's white students were enrolled at University of Mississippi, Mississippi State, Southern Mississippi, Delta State, and Mississippi University for Women. The student bodies at these universities remained predominantly white, averaging between 80 and 91 percent white students. Seventy-one percent of the State's black students attended Jackson State, Alcorn State, and Mississippi Valley State, where the racial composition ranged from 92 to 99 percent black. *Ayers v. Allain,* 893 F.2d 732, 734–735 (CA5 1990) (panel decision).

II

By 1987, the parties concluded that they could not agree on whether the State had taken the requisite affirmative steps to dismantle its prior *de jure* segregated system. They proceeded to trial. Both sides presented voluminous evidence on a full range of educational issues spanning admissions standards, faculty and administrative staff recruitment, program duplication, on-campus discrimination, institutional funding disparities, and satellite campuses. . . .

When it addressed the same aspects of the university system covered by the findings of fact in light of the foregoing standard, the court found no violation of federal law in any of them. "In summary, the court finds that current actions on the part of the defendants demonstrate conclusively that the defendants are fulfilling their affirmative duty to disestablish the former *de jure* segregated system of higher education." *Id.,* at 1564.

The Court of Appeals reheard the action en banc and affirmed the decision of the District Court. *Ayers v. Allain,* 914 F.2d 676 (CA5 1990). With a single exception, see *infra,* at 2742, it did not disturb the District Court's findings of fact or conclusions of law. The en banc majority agreed that "Mississippi was . . . constitutionally required to eliminate invidious racial distinctions and dismantle its dual system." *Id.,* at 682. That duty, the court held, had been discharged since "the record makes clear that Mississippi has adopted and implemented race neutral policies for operating its colleges and universities and that all students have real freedom of choice to attend the college or university they wish. . . ." *Id.,* at 678.

We granted the respective writs of certiorari filed by the United States and the private petitioners. 499 U.S. 958, 111 S.Ct. 1579, 113 L.Ed.2d 644 (1991).

III

The District Court, the Court of Appeals, and respondents recognize and acknowledge that the State of Mississippi had the constitutional duty to dismantle the dual school system that its laws once mandated. Nor is there any dispute that this obligation applies to its higher education system. If the State has not discharged this duty, it remains in violation of the Fourteenth Amendment. *Brown v. Board of Education* and its progeny clearly mandate this observation. Thus, the primary issue in these cases is whether the State has met its affirmative duty to dismantle its prior dual university system.

Our decisions establish that a State does not discharge its constitutional obligations until it eradicates policies and practices traceable to its prior *de jure* dual system that continue to foster segregation. Thus we have consistently asked whether existing racial identifiability is attributable to the State, see, *e.g., Freeman v. Pitts,* 503 U.S. 467, 496, 112 S.Ct. 1430, 118 L.Ed.2d 108 (1992) . . . . Like the United States, we do not disagree with the Court of Appeals' observation that a state university system is quite different in very relevant respects from primary and secondary schools.

Unlike attendance at the lower level schools, a student's decision to seek higher education has been a matter of choice. The State historically has not assigned university students to a particular institution. Moreover, like public universities throughout the country, Mississippi's institutions of higher learning are not fungible—they have been designated to perform certain missions. Students who qualify for admission enjoy a range of choices of which institution to attend. Thus, as the Court of Appeals stated, "[i]t hardly needs mention that remedies common to public school desegregation, such as pupil assignments, busing, attendance quotas, and zoning, are unavailable when persons may freely choose whether to pursue an advanced education and, when the choice is made, which of several universities to attend." 914 F.2d, at 687.

We do not agree with the Court of Appeals or the District Court, however, that the adoption and implementation of race-neutral policies alone suffice to demonstrate that the State has completely abandoned its prior dual system. That college attendance is by choice and not by assignment does not mean that a race-neutral admissions policy cures the constitutional violation of a dual system. In a system based on choice, student attendance is determined not simply by admissions policies, but also by many other factors. Although some of these factors clearly cannot be attributed to state policies, many can be. . . .

IV

Had the Court of Appeals applied the correct legal standard, it would have been apparent from the undisturbed factual findings of the District Court that there are several surviving aspects of Mississippi's prior dual system which are constitutionally suspect; for even though such policies may be race neutral on their face, they substantially restrict a person's choice of which institution to enter, and they contribute to the racial identifiability of the eight public universities. Mississippi must justify these policies or eliminate them.

It is important to state at the outset that we make no effort to identify an exclusive list of unconstitutional remnants of Mississippi's prior *de jure* system. In highlighting, as we do below, certain remnants of the prior system that are readily apparent from the findings of fact made by the District Court and affirmed by the Court of Appeals, we by no means suggest that the Court of Appeals need not examine, in light of the proper standard, each of the other policies now governing the State's university system that have been challenged or that are challenged on remand in light of the standard that we articulate today. With this caveat in mind, we address four policies of the present system: admission standards, program duplication, institutional missions assignments, and continued operation of all eight public universities.

We deal first with the current admissions policies of Mississippi's public universities. As the District Court found, the three flagship historically white universities in the system—University of Mississippi, Mississippi State University, and University of Southern Mississippi—enacted policies in 1963 requiring all entrants to achieve a minimum composite score of 15 on the test administered by the American College Testing Program (ACT). 674 F.Supp., at 1531. The court described the "discriminatory taint" of this policy, *id.*, at 1557, an obvious reference to the fact that, at the time, the average ACT score for white students was 18 and the average score for blacks was 7. 893 F.2d, at 735. The District Court concluded, and the en banc Court of Appeals agreed, that present admissions standards derived from policies enacted in the 1970's to redress the problem of student unpreparedness. 914 F.2d, at 679; 674 F.Supp., at 1531. Obviously, this mid-passage justification for perpetuating a policy enacted originally to discriminate against black students does not make the present admissions standards any less constitutionally suspect.

The present admissions standards are not only traceable to the *de jure* system and were originally adopted for a discriminatory purpose, but they also have present discriminatory effects. Every Mississippi resident under 21 seeking admission to the university system must take the ACT test. Any applicant who scores at least 15 qualifies for automatic admission to any of the five historically white institutions except Mississippi University for Women, which requires a score of 18 for automatic admission unless the student has a 3.0 high school grade average. Those scoring less than 15 but at least 13 automatically qualify to enter Jackson State University, Alcorn State University, and Mississippi Valley State University. Without doubt, these requirements restrict the range of choices of entering students as to which institution they may attend in a way that perpetuates segregation. Those scoring 13 or 14, with some exceptions, are excluded from the five historically white universities and if they want a higher education must go to one of the historically black institutions or attend junior college with the hope of transferring to a historically white institution. Proportionately more blacks than whites face this choice: In 1985, 72 percent of Mississippi's white high school seniors achieved an ACT composite score of 15 or better, while less than 30 percent of black high school seniors earned that score. App. 1524–1525. It is not surprising then that Mississippi's universities remain predominantly identifiable by race.

The segregative effect of this automatic entrance standard is especially striking in light of the differences in minimum automatic entrance scores among the regional universities in Mississippi's system. The minimum score for automatic admission to Mississippi University for Women is 18; it is 13 for the historically black universities. Yet Mississippi University for Women is assigned the same institutional mission as two other regional universities, Alcorn State and Mississippi Valley State—that of providing quality undergraduate education. The effects of the policy fall disproportionately on black students who might wish to attend Mississippi University for Women; and though the disparate impact is not as great, the same is true of the minimum standard ACT score of 15 at Delta State University—the other "regional" university—as compared to the historically black "regional" universities where a score of 13 suffices for automatic admission. The courts below made little, if any, effort to justify in educational terms those particular disparities in entrance requirements or to inquire whether it was practicable to eliminate them.

We also find inadequately justified by the courts below or by the record before us the differential admissions requirements between universities with dissimilar programmatic missions. We do not suggest that absent a discriminatory purpose different programmatic missions accompanied by different admissions standards would be constitutionally suspect simply because one or more schools are racially identifiable. But here the differential admissions standards are remnants of the dual system with a continuing discriminatory effect, and the mission assignments "to some degree follow the historical racial assignments," 914 F.2d, at 692. . . .

Another constitutionally problematic aspect of the State's use of the ACT test scores is its policy of denying automatic admission if an applicant fails to earn the minimum ACT score specified for the particular institution, without also resorting to the applicant's high school grades as an additional factor in predicting college performance. The United States produced evidence that the American College Testing Program (ACTP), the administering organization of the ACT, discourages use of ACT scores as the sole admissions criterion on the ground that it gives an incomplete "picture" of the student applicant's ability to perform adequately in college. App. 1209–1210. One ACTP report presented into evidence suggests that "it would be foolish" to substitute a 3- or 4-hour test in place of a student's high school grades as a means of predicting college performance. *Id.*, at 193. The record also indicated that the disparity between black and white students' high school grade averages was much narrower than the gap between their average ACT scores, thereby suggesting that an admissions formula which included grades would increase the number of black students eligible for automatic admission to all of Mississippi's public universities.

The United States insists that the State's refusal to consider information which would better predict college performance than ACT scores alone is irrational in light of most States' use of high school grades and other indicators along with standardized test scores. . . . In our view, such justification is inadequate because the ACT requirement was originally adopted for discriminatory purposes, the current requirement is traceable to that decision and seemingly continues to have segregative effects, and the State has so far failed to show that the "ACT-only" admissions standard is not susceptible to elimination without eroding sound educational policy.

A second aspect of the present system that necessitates further inquiry is the widespread duplication of programs. "Unnecessary" duplication refers, under the District Court's definition, "to those instances where two or more institutions offer the same nonessential or noncore program. Under this definition, all duplication at the bachelor's level of nonbasic liberal arts and sciences course work and all duplication at the master's level and above are considered to be unnecessary." 674 F.Supp., at 1540. The District Court found that 34.6 percent of the 29 undergraduate programs at historically black institutions are "unnecessarily duplicated" by the historically white universities, and that 90 percent of the graduate programs at the historically black institutions are unnecessarily duplicated at the historically white institutions. *Id.,* at 1541. In its conclusions of law on this point, the District Court nevertheless determined that "there is no proof" that such duplication "is directly associated with the racial identifiability of institutions," and that "there is no proof that the elimination of unnecessary program duplication would be justifiable from an educational standpoint or that its elimination would have a substantial effect on student choice." *Id.,* at 1561.

... It can hardly be denied that such duplication was part and parcel of the prior dual system of higher education—the whole notion of "separate but equal" required duplicative programs in two sets of schools—and that the present unnecessary duplication is a continuation of that practice. *Brown* and its progeny, however, established that the burden of proof falls on the *State,* and not the aggrieved plaintiffs, to establish that it has dismantled its prior *de jure* segregated system. *Brown II,* 349 U.S., at 300, 75 S.Ct., at 756. The court's holding that petitioners could not establish the constitutional defect of unnecessary duplication, therefore, improperly shifted the burden away from the State. ...

We next address Mississippi's scheme of institutional mission classification, and whether it perpetuates the State's formerly *de jure* dual system. The District Court found that, throughout the period of *de jure* segregation, University of Mississippi, Mississippi State University, and University of Southern Mississippi were the flagship institutions in the state system. They received the most funds, initiated the most advanced and specialized programs, and developed the widest range of curricular functions. At their inception, each was restricted for the education solely of white persons. *Id.,* at 1526–1528. The missions of Mississippi University for Women and Delta State University, by contrast, were more limited than their other all-white counterparts during the period of legalized segregation. Mississippi University for Women and Delta State University were each established to provide undergraduate education solely for white students in the liberal arts and such other fields as music, art, education, and home economics. *Id.,* at 1527–1528. When they were founded, the three exclusively black universities were more limited in their assigned academic missions than the five all-white institutions. Alcorn State, for example, was designated to serve as "an agricultural college for the education of Mississippi's black youth." *Id.,* at 1527. Jackson State and Mississippi Valley State were established to train black teachers. *Id.,* at 1528. Though the District Court's findings do not make this point explicit, it is reasonable to infer that state funding and curriculum decisions throughout the period of *de jure* segregation were based on the purposes for which these institutions were established.

In 1981, the State assigned certain missions to Mississippi's public universities as they then existed. It classified University of Mississippi, Mississippi State, and Southern Mississippi as "comprehensive" universities having the most varied programs and offering graduate degrees. Two of the historically white institutions, Delta State University and Mississippi University for Women, along with two of the historically black institutions, Alcorn State University and Mississippi Valley State University, were designated as "regional" universities with more limited programs and devoted primarily to undergraduate education. Jackson State University was classified as an "urban" university whose mission was defined by its urban location.

The institutional mission designations adopted in 1981 have as their antecedents the policies enacted to perpetuate racial separation during the *de jure* segregated regime. . . . That different missions are assigned to the universities surely limits to some extent an entering student's choice as to which university to seek admittance. While the courts below both agreed that the classification and mission assignments were made without discriminatory purpose, the Court of Appeals found that the record "supports the plaintiffs' argument that the mission designations had the effect of maintaining the more limited program scope at the historically black universities." *Id.,* at 690. We do not suggest that absent discriminatory purpose the assignment of different missions to various institutions in a State's higher education system would raise an equal protection issue where one or more of the institutions become or remain predominantly black or white. But here the issue is whether the State has sufficiently dismantled its prior dual system; and when combined with the differential admission practices and unnecessary program duplication, it is likely that the mission designations interfere with student choice and tend to perpetuate the segregated system. On remand, the court should inquire whether it would be practicable and consistent with sound educational practices to eliminate any such discriminatory effects of the State's present policy of mission assignments.

Fourth, the State attempted to bring itself into compliance with the Constitution by continuing to maintain and operate all eight higher educational institutions. The existence of eight instead of some lesser number was undoubtedly occasioned by state laws forbidding the mingling of the races. And as the District Court recognized, continuing to maintain all eight universities in Mississippi is wasteful and irrational. The District Court pointed especially to the facts that Delta State and Mississippi Valley State are only 35 miles apart and that only 20 miles separate Mississippi State and Mississippi University for Women. 674 F.Supp., at 1563–1564. It was evident to the District Court that "the defendants undertake to fund more institutions of higher learning than are justified by the amount of financial resources available to the state," *id.,* at 1564, but the court concluded that such fiscal irresponsibility was a policy choice of the legislature rather than a feature of a system subject to constitutional scrutiny.

Unquestionably, a larger rather than a smaller number of institutions from which to choose in itself makes for different choices, particularly when examined in the light of other factors present in the operation of the system, such as admissions, program duplication, and institutional mission designations. Though certainly closure of one or more institutions would decrease the discriminatory effects of the present system, see, *e.g., United States v. Louisiana,* 718 F.Supp. 499, 514 (ED La.1989), based on the present record we are unable to say whether such action is constitutionally required. Elimination of program duplication and revision of admissions criteria may make institutional closure unnecessary. However, on remand this issue should be carefully explored by inquiring and determining whether retention of all eight institutions itself affects student choice and perpetuates the segregated higher education system, whether maintenance of each of the universities is educationally justifiable, and whether one or more of them can be practicably closed or merged with other existing institutions.

Because the former *de jure* segregated system of public universities in Mississippi impeded the free choice of prospective students, the State in dismantling that system must take the necessary steps to ensure that this choice now is truly free. The full range of policies and practices must be examined with this duty in mind. That an institution is predominantly white or black does not in itself make out a constitutional violation. But surely the State may not leave in place policies rooted in its prior officially segregated system that serve to maintain the racial identifiability of its universities if those policies can practicably be eliminated without eroding sound educational policies.

If we understand private petitioners to press us to order the upgrading of Jackson State, Alcorn State, and Mississippi Valley State *solely* so that they may be publicly financed, exclusively black enclaves by private choice, we reject that request. The State provides these facilities for *all* its citizens and it has not met its burden under *Brown* to take affirmative steps to dismantle its prior *de jure* system when it perpetuates a separate, but "more equal" one. Whether such an increase in funding is necessary to achieve a full dismantlement under the standards we have outlined, however, is a different question, and one that must be addressed on remand.

Because the District Court and the Court of Appeals failed to consider the State's duties in their proper light, the cases must be remanded. To the extent that the State has not met its affirmative obligation to dismantle its prior dual system, it shall be adjudged in violation of the Constitution and Title VI and remedial proceedings shall be conducted. The decision of the Court of Appeals is vacated, and the cases are remanded for further proceedings consistent with this opinion.

It is so ordered.

Notes and Questions

1. How were Mississippi's policies rooted in former racial policies in existence during segregation?

2. What made the admission policies problematic? What about the mission statements of the respective schools?

2. Title VI and Desegregation in Employment

The Court continued to flesh out the scope of Title VI in other contexts. In *Guardians Association v. Civil Service Commission of the City of New York*, 463 U.S. 582 (1983), the Court struggled to determine plaintiffs' specific rights under the statute. The Justices split on whether it gave plaintiffs a private right of action against disparate impact discrimination. Recall similar inquiries regarding Title IX, in Chapter 3, in the context of gender discrimination.

Specifically, in *Guardians*, "[t]he threshold issue before the Court [was]whether the private plaintiffs in this case need to prove discriminatory intent to establish a violation of Title VI of the Civil Rights Act of 1964, 42 U.S.C. § 2000d, *et seq.*, and administrative implementing regulations promulgated thereunder." In separate opinions, five Justices ruled that the Court of Appeals erred in requiring proof of discriminatory intent. They, however, based their rulings on different reasoning. For example, at least one Justice concluded that, "in the absence of proof of discriminatory animus, compensatory relief should not be awarded to private Title VI plaintiffs; unless discriminatory intent is shown, declaratory and limited injunctive relief should be the only available private remedies for Title VI violations."

After the split opinion in *Guardians*, the Court revisited the issue and, in *Alexander v. Sandoval*, below, clarified that private parties did not have a right of action to sue for enforcement of disparate impact regulations issued under Title VI. In other words, if plaintiffs suing under Title VI cannot show proof of intent to discriminate by defendant, they do not have a private right to sue. In those cases, standing to sue when alleging disparate impact remains with the federal government. Private parties, nonetheless, still can sue for intentional discrimination in violation of the language of Title VI itself. As a result, the only option left to private individuals desiring more rigorous enforcement of regulations related to impact discrimination is to pressure the enforcing agency through lobbying and the comment process.

What approach to statutory interpretation is the majority espousing in the following statement from *Alexander v. Sandoval*: "We have never accorded dispositive weight to context shorn of text. In determining whether statutes create private rights of action, as in interpreting statutes generally, see *Blatchford v. Native Village of Noatak*, 501 U.S. 775, 784, 111 S. Ct. 2578, 115 L.Ed.2d 686 (1991), legal context matters only to the extent it clarifies text."

Alexander v. Sandoval

532 U.S. 275 (2001)

Justice Scalia delivered the opinion of the Court.

This case presents the question whether private individuals may sue to enforce disparate-impact regulations promulgated under Title VI of the Civil Rights Act of 1964.

I

The Alabama Department of Public Safety (Department), of which petitioner James Alexander is the director, accepted grants of financial assistance from the United States Department of Justice (DOJ) and Department of Transportation (DOT) and so subjected itself to the restrictions of Title VI of the Civil Rights Act of 1964, 78 Stat. 252, as amended, 42 U.S.C. § 2000d *et seq.* Section 601 of that Title provides that no person shall, "on the ground of race, color, or national origin, be excluded from participation in, be denied the benefits of, or be subjected to discrimination under any program or activity" covered by Title VI. 42 U.S.C. § 2000d. Section 602 authorizes federal agencies "to effectuate the provisions of [§ 601] . . . by issuing rules, regulations, or orders of general applicability," 42 U.S.C. § 2000d-1, and the DOJ in an exercise of this authority promulgated a regulation forbidding funding recipients to "utilize criteria or methods of administration which have the effect of subjecting individuals to discrimination because of their race, color, or national origin . . . ." 28 CFR § 42.104(b)(2) (2000). See also 49 CFR § 21.5(b)(2) (2000) (similar DOT regulation).

The State of Alabama amended its Constitution in 1990 to declare English "the official language of the state of Alabama." Amdt. 509. Pursuant to this provision and, petitioners have argued, to advance public safety, the Department decided to administer state driver's license examinations only in English. Respondent Sandoval, as representative of a class, brought suit in the United States District Court for the Middle District of Alabama to enjoin the English-only policy, arguing that it violated the DOJ regulation because it had the effect of subjecting non-English speakers to discrimination based on their national origin. The District Court agreed. It enjoined the policy and ordered the Department to accommodate non-English speakers. *Sandoval v. Hagan*, 7 F.Supp.2d 1234 (M.D.Ala.1998). Petitioners appealed to the Court of Appeals for the Eleventh Circuit, which affirmed. *Sandoval v. Hagan*, 197 F.3d 484 (C.A.11 1999). Both courts rejected petitioners' argument that Title VI did not provide respondents a cause of action to enforce the regulation.

We do not inquire here whether the DOJ regulation was authorized by § 602, or whether the courts below were correct to hold that the English-only policy had the effect of discriminating on the basis of national origin. The petition for writ of certiorari raised, and we agreed to review, only the question posed in the first paragraph of this opinion: whether there is a private cause of action to enforce the regulation. 530 U.S. 1305, 121 S.Ct. 28, 147 L.Ed.2d 1051 (2000).

II

Although Title VI has often come to this Court, it is fair to say (indeed, perhaps an understatement) that our opinions have not eliminated all uncertainty regarding its commands. For purposes of the present case, however, it is clear from our decisions, from Congress's amendments of Title VI, and from the parties' concessions that three aspects of Title VI must be taken as given. First, private individuals may sue to enforce § 601 of Title VI and obtain both injunctive relief and damages. In *Cannon v. University of Chicago*, 441 U.S. 677, 99 S.Ct. 1946, 60 L.Ed.2d 560 (1979), the Court held that a private right of action existed to enforce Title IX of the Education Amendments of 1972, 86 Stat. 373, as amended, 20 U.S.C. § 1681 *et seq.* The reasoning of that decision embraced the existence of a private right to enforce Title VI as well. "Title IX," the Court noted, "was patterned after Title VI of the Civil Rights Act of 1964." 441 U.S., at 694, 99 S.Ct. 1946. And, "[i]n 1972 when Title IX was enacted, the [parallel] language in Title VI had already been construed as creating a private remedy." *Id.,* at 696, 99 S.Ct. 1946. That meant, the Court reasoned, that Congress had intended Title IX, like Title VI, to provide a private cause of action. . . .

Second, it is similarly beyond dispute—and no party disagrees—that §601 prohibits only intentional discrimination. In *Regents of Univ. of Cal. v. Bakke,* 438 U.S. 265, 98 S.Ct. 2733, 57 L.Ed.2d 750 (1978), the Court reviewed a decision of the California Supreme Court that had enjoined the University of California Medical School from "according any consideration to race in its admissions process." *Id.,* at 272, 98 S.Ct. 2733. Essential to the Court's holding reversing that aspect of the California court's decision was the determination that §601 "proscribe[s] only those racial classifications that would violate the Equal Protection Clause or the Fifth Amendment." *Id.,* at 287, 98 S.Ct. 2733 (opinion of Powell, J.); see also *id.,* at 325, 328, 352, 98 S.Ct. 2733 (opinion of Brennan, White, Marshall, and Blackmun, JJ.). In *Guardians Assn. v. Civil Serv. Comm'n of New York City,* 463 U.S. 582, 103 S.Ct. 3221, 77 L.Ed.2d 866 (1983), the Court made clear that under *Bakke* only intentional discrimination was forbidden by §601. 463 U.S., at 610–611, 103 S.Ct. 3221 (Powell, J., joined by Burger, C.J., and Rehnquist, J., concurring in judgment); *id.,* at 612, 103 S. Ct. 3221 (O'Connor, J., concurring in judgment); *id.,* at 642, 103 S.Ct. 3221 (Stevens, J., joined by Brennan and Blackmun, JJ., dissenting). What we said in *Alexander v. Choate,* 469 U.S. 287, 293, 105 S.Ct. 712, 83 L.Ed.2d 661 (1985), is true today: "Title VI itself directly reach[es] only instances of intentional discrimination."

Third, we must assume for purposes of deciding this case that regulations promulgated under §602 of Title VI may validly proscribe activities that have a disparate impact on racial groups, even though such activities are permissible under §601. Though no opinion of this Court has held that, five Justices in *Guardians* voiced that view of the law at least as alternative grounds for their decisions, see 463 U.S., at 591–592, 103 S.Ct. 3221 (opinion of White, J.); *id.,* at 623, n. 15, 103 S. Ct. 3221 (Marshall, J., dissenting); *id.,* at 643–645, 103 S.Ct. 3221 (Stevens, J., joined by Brennan and Blackmun, JJ., dissenting), and dictum in *Alexander v. Choate* is to the same effect, see 469 U.S., at 293, 295, n. 11, 105 S.Ct. 712. These statements are in considerable tension with the rule of *Bakke* and *Guardians* that §601 forbids only intentional discrimination, see, *e.g., Guardians Assn. v. Civil Serv. Comm'n of New York City, supra,* at 612–613, 103 S.Ct. 3221 (O'Connor, J., concurring in judgment), but petitioners have not challenged the regulations here. We therefore assume for the purposes of deciding this case that the DOJ and DOT regulations proscribing activities that have a disparate impact on the basis of race are valid.

Respondents assert that the issue in this case, like the first two described above, has been resolved by our cases. To reject a private cause of action to enforce the disparate-impact regulations, they say, we would "[have] to ignore the actual language of *Guardians* and *Cannon.*" Brief for Respondents 13. The language in *Cannon* to which respondents refer does not in fact support their position, as we shall discuss at length below, see *infra,* at 1521. But in any event, this Court is bound by holdings, not language. *Cannon* was decided on the assumption that the University of Chicago had intentionally discriminated against petitioner. See 441 U.S., at 680, 99 S.Ct. 1946 (noting that respondents "admitted *arguendo*" that petitioner's "applications for admission to medical school were denied by the respondents because she is a woman"). It therefore *held* that Title IX created a private right of action to enforce its ban on intentional discrimination, but had no occasion to consider whether the right reached regulations barring disparate-impact discrimination. In *Guardians,* the Court *held* that private individuals could not recover compensatory damages under Title VI except for intentional discrimination. Five Justices in addition voted to uphold the disparate-impact regulations (four would have declared them invalid, see 463 U.S., at 611, n. 5, 103 S.Ct. 3221 (Powell, J., concurring in judgment); *id.,* at 612–614, 103 S.Ct. 3221 (O'Connor, J., concurring in judgment)), but of those five, three expressly reserved the question of a direct private right of action to enforce the regulations, saying that "[w]hether a cause of action against private parties exists directly under the regulations . . . [is a] questio[n] that [is] not presented by this case." *Id.,* at 645, n. 18, 103 S.Ct. 3221 (Stevens, J., dissenting). Thus, only two Justices had cause to reach the issue that respondents say the "actual language" of *Guardians* resolves. Neither that case, nor any other in this Court, has held that the private right of action exists.

Nor does it follow straightaway from the three points we have taken as given that Congress must have intended a private right of action to enforce disparate-impact regulations. We do not doubt that regulations applying § 601's ban on intentional discrimination are covered by the cause of action to enforce that section. Such regulations, if valid and reasonable, authoritatively construe the statute itself, see *NationsBank of N.C., N.A. v. Variable Annuity Life Ins. Co.,* 513 U.S. 251, 257, 115 S. Ct. 810, 130 L.Ed.2d 740 (1995); *Chevron U.S.A. Inc. v. Natural Resources Defense Council, Inc.,* 467 U.S. 837, 843–844, 104 S.Ct. 2778, 81 L.Ed.2d 694 (1984), and it is therefore meaningless to talk about a separate cause of action to enforce the regulations apart from the statute. . . . The Title VI regulations at issue in *Lau,* similar to the ones at issue here, forbade funding recipients to take actions which had the effect of discriminating on the basis of race, color, or national origin. *Id.,* at 568, 94 S.Ct. 786. Unlike our later cases, however, the Court in *Lau* interpreted § 601 itself to proscribe disparate-impact discrimination, saying that it "rel[ied] solely on § 601 . . . to reverse the Court of Appeals," *id.,* at 566, 94 S.Ct. 786, and that the disparate-impact regulations simply "[made] sure that recipients of federal aid . . . conduct[ed] any federally financed projects consistently with § 601," *id.,* at 567, 94 S.Ct. 786.

We must face now the question avoided by Lau, because we have since rejected Lau's interpretation of § 601 as reaching beyond intentional discrimination. See supra, at 1516. It is clear now that the disparate-impact regulations do not simply apply § 601 — since they indeed forbid conduct that § 601 permits — and therefore clear that the private right of action to enforce § 601 does not include a private right to enforce these regulations. . . . If not, we must conclude that a failure to comply with regulations promulgated under § 602 that is not also a failure to comply with § 601 is not actionable.

Implicit in our discussion thus far has been a particular understanding of the genesis of private causes of action. Like substantive federal law itself, private rights of action to enforce federal law must be created by Congress. *Touche Ross & Co. v. Redington*, 442 U.S. 560, 578, 99 S.Ct. 2479, 61 L.Ed.2d 82 (1979) (remedies available are those "that Congress enacted into law"). The judicial task is to interpret the statute Congress has passed to determine whether it displays an intent to create not just a private right but also a private remedy.

. . . .

Nor do we agree with the Government that our cases interpreting statutes enacted prior to *Cort v. Ash* have given "dispositive weight" to the "expectations" that the enacting Congress had formed "in light of the 'contemporary legal context.'" Brief for United States 14. . . . We have never accorded dispositive weight to context shorn of text. In determining whether statutes create private rights of action, as in interpreting statutes generally, see *Blatchford v. Native Village of Noatak*, 501 U.S. 775, 784, 111 S.Ct. 2578, 115 L.Ed.2d 686 (1991), legal context matters only to the extent it clarifies text.

We therefore begin (and find that we can end) our search for Congress's intent with the text and structure of Title VI. Section 602 authorizes federal agencies "to effectuate the provisions of [§ 601] . . . by issuing rules, regulations, or orders of general applicability." 42 U.S.C. § 2000d-1. It is immediately clear that the "rights-creating" language so critical to the Court's analysis in *Cannon* of § 601, see 441 U.S., at 690, n. 13, 99 S.Ct. 1946, is completely absent from § 602. Whereas § 601 decrees that "[n]o person . . . shall . . . be subjected to discrimination," 42 U.S.C. § 2000d, the text of § 602 provides that "[e]ach Federal department and agency . . . is authorized and directed to effectuate the provisions of [§ 601]," 42 U.S.C. § 2000d-1. Far from displaying congressional intent to create new rights, § 602 limits agencies to "effectuat[ing]" rights already created by § 601. And the focus of § 602 is twice removed from the individuals who will ultimately benefit from Title VI's protection. Statutes that focus on the person regulated rather than the individuals protected create "no implication of an intent to confer rights on a particular class of persons." *California v. Sierra Club*, 451 U.S. 287, 294, 101 S.Ct. 1775, 68 L.Ed.2d 101 (1981). Section 602 is yet a step further removed: It focuses neither on the individuals protected nor even on the funding recipients being regulated, but on the agencies that will do the regulating. Like the statute found not to create a right of action in *Universities Research Assn., Inc. v. Coutu*, 450 U.S. 754, 101 S.Ct. 1451, 67 L. Ed.2d 662 (1981), § 602 is "phrased as a directive to federal agencies engaged in the distribution of public funds," *id.*, at 772, 101 S.Ct. 1451. When this is true, "[t]here [is] far less reason to infer a private remedy in favor of individual persons," *Cannon v. University of Chicago, supra,* at 690–691, 99 S.Ct. 1946. So far as we can tell, this authorizing portion of § 602 reveals no congressional intent to create a private right of action.

Nor do the methods that §602 goes on to provide for enforcing its authorized regulations manifest an intent to create a private remedy; if anything, they suggest the opposite. Section 602 empowers agencies to enforce their regulations either by terminating funding to the "particular program, or part thereof," that has violated the regulation or "by any other means authorized by law," 42 U.S.C. §2000d-1. No enforcement action may be taken, however, "until the department or agency concerned has advised the appropriate person or persons of the failure to comply with the requirement and has determined that compliance cannot be secured by voluntary means." *Ibid.* And every agency enforcement action is subject to judicial review. §2000d-2. If an agency attempts to terminate program funding, still more restrictions apply. The agency head must "file with the committees of the House and Senate having legislative jurisdiction over the program or activity involved a full written report of the circumstances and the grounds for such action." §2000d-1. And the termination of funding does not "become effective until thirty days have elapsed after the filing of such report." *Ibid.* Whatever these elaborate restrictions on agency enforcement may imply for the private enforcement of rights created *out-side* of §602, . . . they tend to contradict a congressional intent to create privately enforceable rights through §602 itself. The express provision of one method of enforcing a substantive rule suggests that Congress intended to preclude others. See, *e.g., Karahalios v. Federal Employees,* 489 U.S. 527, 533, 109 S.Ct. 1282, 103 L.Ed.2d 539 (1989); *Northwest Airlines, Inc. v. Transport Workers,* 451 U.S. 77, 93–94, 101 S. Ct. 1571, 67 L.Ed.2d 750 (1981); *Transamerica Mortgage Advisors, Inc. v. Lewis,* 444 U.S., at 19–20, 100 S.Ct. 242. Sometimes the suggestion is so strong that it precludes a finding of congressional intent to create a private right of action, even though other aspects of the statute (such as language making the would-be plaintiff "a member of the class for whose benefit the statute was enacted") suggest the con-trary. *Massachusetts Mut. Life Ins. Co. v. Russell,* 473 U.S., at 145, 105 S.Ct. 3085; see *id.,* at 146–147, 105 S.Ct. 3085. And as our Rev. Stat. §1979, 42 U.S.C. §1983, cases show, some remedial schemes foreclose a private cause of action to enforce even those statutes that admittedly create substantive private rights. See, *e.g., Middlesex County Sewerage Authority v. National Sea Clammers Assn.,* 453 U.S. 1, 19–20, 101 S. Ct. 2615, 69 L.Ed.2d 435 (1981). In the present case, the claim of exclusivity for the express remedial scheme does not even have to overcome such obstacles. The ques-tion whether §602's remedial scheme can overbear other evidence of congressional intent is simply not presented, since we have found no evidence anywhere in the text to suggest that Congress intended to create a private right to enforce regulations promulgated under §602.

Both the Government and respondents argue that the *regulations* contain rights-creating language and so must be privately enforceable, see Brief for United States 19–20; Brief for Respondents 31, but that argument skips an analytical step. Lan-guage in a regulation may invoke a private right of action that Congress through statutory text created, but it may not create a right that Congress has not. *Touche*

Ross & Co. v. Redington, 442 U.S., at 577, n. 18, 99 S.Ct. 2479 ("[T]he language of the statute and not the rules must control"). Thus, when a statute has provided a general authorization for private enforcement of regulations, it may perhaps be correct that the intent displayed in each regulation can determine whether or not it is privately enforceable. But it is most certainly incorrect to say that language in a regulation can conjure up a private cause of action that has not been authorized by Congress. Agencies may play the sorcerer's apprentice but not the sorcerer himself.

. . . .

Neither as originally enacted nor as later amended does Title VI display an intent to create a freestanding private right of action to enforce regulations promulgated under § 602. We therefore hold that no such right of action exists. Since we reach this conclusion applying our standard test for discerning private causes of action, we do not address petitioners' additional argument that implied causes of action against States (and perhaps nonfederal state actors generally) are inconsistent with the clear statement rule of *Pennhurst State School and Hospital v. Halderman,* 451 U.S. 1, 101 S.Ct. 1531, 67 L.Ed.2d 694 (1981). See *Davis v. Monroe County Bd. of Ed.,* 526 U.S. 629, 656–657, 684–685, 119 S.Ct. 1661, 143 L.Ed.2d 839 (1999) (Kennedy, J., dissenting).

The judgment of the Court of Appeals is reversed.

It is so ordered.

Chapter 5

Impasse in Access to Opportunity

A. Affirmative Action

1. Law as Power

Affirmative action benefitting key groups has a long-standing tradition in the United States. Laws and policies benefitting, for example, veterans and legacy students in the educational context, have prevailed for a long time.[1] Despite the long-standing existence of affirmative measures, racial affirmative action has been the source of intense social strife. After more than four centuries of systematic exclusion, the government was forced to consider measures to provide opportunities to African Americans. From Slavery to the failed Reconstruction, their meaningful and rewarding participation in society was made impossible by restrictive laws and oppressive tactics.[2] Undoing these oppressive methods first required leveling the playing field to facilitate equal access and equal opportunity for African Americans. Doing so opened the door to other traditionally excluded groups like women, Latinos, Asians, and, eventually, disabled persons.[3]

Unfortunately, nowhere has the underlying power dynamics of the status quo been more evident than regarding affirmative measures to remedy persistent and systemic racial discrimination in the United States. As with many other countries grappling with a deep history of institutionalized discrimination, changing the established power structures and footholds creates resentment and conflicts. The

---

1. *The Color of Perspective: Affirmative Action and the Constitutional Rhetoric of White Innocence*, 11 Mich. J. Race & L. 477, 537; *Doctrines of Delusion: How the History of the G.I. Bill and Other Inconvenient Truths Undermine the Supreme Court's Affirmative Action Jurisprudence*, 75 U. Pitt. L. Rev. 583; Ira Katznelson, *When Affirmative Action Was White: An Untold History of Racial Inequality in Twentieth-Century America*; http://www.nytimes.com/2005/08/28/books/review/when-affirmative -action-was-white-uncivil-rights.html.

2. Michael J. Klarman, *The Plessy Era*, 1998 Sup. Ct. Rev. 303 (1998); James W. Fox Jr., *Intimations of Citizenship: Repressions and Expressions of Equal Citizenship in the Era of Jim Crow*, 50 How. L.J. 113 (2006); Michelle Alexander, The New Jim Crow: Mass Incarceration in the Age of Colorblindness (The New Press, 2012).

3. *See* Dolores E. Janiewski, Sisterhood Denied: Race, Gender, and Class in a New South Community (1985); *see also* Peter Baker, *50 Years Later, Obama Salutes Effects of Civil Rights Act*, N.Y. Times (Apr. 10, 2014), http://www.nytimes.com/2014/04/11/us/politics/50-years-later-obama -salutes-passage-of-civil-rights-act.html; Herron Keyon Gaston, *Who Benefited from the Civil Rights Movement?*, Huff. Post (Feb. 9, 2015, 2:24 PM), http://www.huffingtonpost.com/herron-keyon -gaston/who-benefited-from-the-ci_b_6637798.html.

materials below reflect the tension around racial affirmative action and track the move toward a colorblind approach to remedying discrimination. In its recent ruling on the issue, the Supreme Court established that affirmative action measures based on race will trigger strict scrutiny, the highest standard of review under the 14th Amendment. Strict scrutiny requires that the governmental action be necessary to achieve a compelling interest. The only two justifications that could successfully ever support such measures are: 1) the achievement of diversity and 2) remedying legal segregation. Without one of these two justifications, a governmental entity might not even survive the first leg of the standard, which is to prove a compelling interest. As you map the trajectory leading to the current approach and investigate questions relating to affirmative action in the United States, consider whether the debate around affirmative action reflects a particular power dynamic. Also, how do the materials below provide insight as to the best way to remedy institutional wrongs and make whole traditionally excluded groups?[4]

2. Voluntary vs. Involuntary Affirmative Action

At its inception, affirmative action was achieved via governmental policies and laws, as well as through judicially issued consent decrees; all by-products of efforts to remedy de jure segregation. These cases are reviewed under either statutory laws or constitutional tenets. Cases reviewed under statutory laws apply the relevant standards applicable to the specific statutes. Those reviewed under constitutional standards are evaluated under the Fourteenth Amendment. Of particular interest in the latter setting are educational policies designed to promote diversity and remedy educational inequity. The *Fisher* decision, which appears later, forebodes ominous changes, in the near future, to the diversity rationale.

3. Voluntary Affirmative Action

a. Statutory Avenues

The Court's strict evaluation of past discrimination as a compelling interest is illustrated below in the context of city construction contracts and education. In *Croson*, the Court asserts that general evidence of past discrimination will not be sufficient to support governmental assertion of a compelling interest. In order to survive strict scrutiny, the discrimination the city seeks to remedy must be specifically proven. *Croson* and the current landscape of affirmative action, thus, signaled that remedying past and ongoing de facto discrimination would become extremely difficult.

---

4. Terry H. Anderson, The Pursuit of Fairness: A History of Affirmative Action (2005); Jason Levy, *Slavery Disclosure Laws: For Financial Reparations or for "Telling the Truth?"*, 2009 Colum. Bus. L. Rev. 468 (2009); Kim Forde-Mazrui, *Taking Conservatives Seriously: A Moral Justification for Affirmative Action and Reparations*, 92 Calif. L. Rev. 683 (2004).

City of Richmond v. J.A. Croson Company

488 U.S. 469 (1989)

Justice O'CONNOR announced the judgment of the Court and delivered the opinion of the Court with respect to Parts I, III-B, and IV, an opinion with respect to Part II, in which THE CHIEF JUSTICE and Justice WHITE join, and an opinion with respect to Parts III-A and V, in which THE CHIEF JUSTICE, Justice WHITE, and Justice KENNEDY join.

In this case, we confront once again the tension between the Fourteenth Amendment's guarantee of equal treatment to all citizens, and the use of race-based measures to ameliorate the effects of past discrimination on the opportunities enjoyed by members of minority groups in our society. In *Fullilove v. Klutznick,* 448 U.S. 448, 100 S.Ct. 2758, 65 L.Ed.2d 902 (1980), we held that a congressional program requiring that 10% of certain federal construction grants be awarded to minority contractors did not violate the equal protection principles embodied in the Due Process Clause of the Fifth Amendment. Relying largely on our decision in *Fullilove,* some lower federal courts have applied a similar standard of review in assessing the constitutionality of state and local minority set-aside provisions under the Equal Protection Clause of the Fourteenth Amendment. . . . Since our decision two Terms ago in *Wygant v. Jackson Board of Education,* 476 U.S. 267, 106 S.Ct. 1842, 90 L.Ed.2d 260 (1986), the lower federal courts have attempted to apply its standards in evaluating the constitutionality of state and local programs which allocate a portion of public contracting opportunities exclusively to minority-owned businesses. See, *e.g., Michigan Road Builders Assn., Inc. v. Milliken,* 834 F.2d 583 (CA6 1987), appeal docketed, No. 87-1860; *Associated General Contractors of Cal. v. City and Cty. of San Francisco,* 813 F.2d 922 (CA9 1987). We noted probable jurisdiction in this case to consider the applicability of our decision in *Wygant* to a minority set-aside program adopted by the city of Richmond, Virginia.

I

On April 11, 1983, the Richmond City Council adopted the Minority Business Utilization Plan (the Plan). The Plan required prime contractors to whom the city awarded construction contracts to subcontract at least 30% of the dollar amount of the contract to one or more Minority Business Enterprises (MBE's). Ordinance No. 83-69-59, codified in Richmond, Va., City Code, § 12-156(a) (1985). The 30% set-aside did not apply to city contracts awarded to minority-owned prime contractors. *Ibid.*

The Plan defined an MBE as "[a] business at least fifty-one (51) percent of which is owned and controlled . . . by minority group members." § 12-23, p. 941. "Minority group members" were defined as "[c]itizens of the United States who are Blacks, Spanish-speaking, Orientals, Indians, Eskimos, or Aleuts." *Ibid.* There was no geographic limit to the Plan; an otherwise qualified MBE from anywhere in the United States could avail itself of the 30% set-aside. The Plan declared that it was "remedial" in nature, and enacted "for the purpose of promoting wider participation by minority business enterprises in the construction of public projects." § 12-158(a). The Plan expired on June 30, 1988, and was in effect for approximately five years. *Ibid.*

The Plan authorized the Director of the Department of General Services to promulgate rules which "shall allow waivers in those individual situations where a contractor can prove to the satisfaction of the director that the requirements herein cannot be achieved." § 12-157. To this end, the Director promulgated Contract Clauses, Minority Business Utilization Plan (Contract Clauses). Paragraph D of these rules provided:

> "No partial or complete waiver of the foregoing [30% set-aside] requirement shall be granted by the city other than in exceptional circumstances. To justify a waiver, it must be shown that every feasible attempt has been made to comply, and it must be demonstrated that sufficient, relevant, qualified Minority Business Enterprises . . . are unavailable or unwilling to participate in the contract to enable meeting the 30% MBE goal." ¶ D, Record, Exh. 24, p. 1; see *J.A. Croson Co. v. Richmond,* 779 F.2d 181, 197 (CA4 1985) *(Croson I).*

The Director also promulgated "purchasing procedures" to be followed in the letting of city contracts in accordance with the Plan. *Id.,* at 194. Bidders on city construction contracts were provided with a "Minority Business Utilization Plan Commitment Form." Record, Exh. 24, p. 3. . . .

The Plan was adopted by the Richmond City Council after a public hearing. App. 9-50. Seven members of the public spoke to the merits of the ordinance: five were in opposition, two in favor. Proponents of the set-aside provision relied on a study which indicated that, while the general population of Richmond was 50% black, only 0.67% of the city's prime construction contracts had been awarded to minority businesses in the 5-year period from 1978 to 1983. It was also established that a variety of contractors' associations, whose representatives appeared in opposition to the ordinance, had virtually no minority businesses within their membership. See Brief for Appellant 22 (chart listing minority membership of six local construction industry associations). The city's legal counsel indicated his view that the ordinance was constitutional under this Court's decision in *Fullilove v. Klutznick,* 448 U.S. 448, 100 S.Ct. 2758, 65 L.Ed.2d 902 (1980). App. 24. . . .

On September 6, 1983, the city of Richmond issued an invitation to bid on a project for the provision and installation of certain plumbing fixtures at the city jail. On September 30, 1983, Eugene Bonn, the regional manager of J.A. Croson Company (Croson), a mechanical plumbing and heating contractor, received the bid forms. The project involved the installation of stainless steel urinals and water closets in the city jail. Products of either of two manufacturers were specified, Acorn Engineering Company (Acorn) or Bradley Manufacturing Company (Bradley). Bonn determined that to meet the 30% set-aside requirement, a minority contractor would have to supply the fixtures. The provision of the fixtures amounted to 75% of the total contract price.

. . . .

On September 30, Bonn contacted five or six MBE's that were potential suppliers of the fixtures, after contacting three local and state agencies that maintained lists of MBE's. No MBE expressed interest in the project or tendered a quote. On October 12, 1983, the day the bids were due, Bonn again telephoned a group of MBE's. This time, Melvin Brown, president of Continental Metal Hose (Continental), a local MBE, indicated that he wished to participate in the project. Brown subsequently contacted two sources of the specified fixtures in order to obtain a price quotation. One supplier, Ferguson Plumbing Supply, which is not an MBE, had already made a quotation directly to Croson, and refused to quote the same fixtures to Continental. Brown also contacted an agent of Bradley, one of the two manufacturers of the specified fixtures. The agent was not familiar with Brown or Continental, and indicated that a credit check was required which would take at least 30 days to complete.

On October 13, 1983, the sealed bids were opened. Croson turned out to be the only bidder, with a bid of $126,530. Brown and Bonn met personally at the bid opening, and Brown informed Bonn that his difficulty in obtaining credit approval had hindered his submission of a bid.

By October 19, 1983, Croson had still not received a bid from Continental. On that date it submitted a request for a waiver of the 30% set-aside. Croson's waiver request indicated that Continental was "unqualified" and that the other MBE's contacted had been unresponsive or unable to quote. Upon learning of Croson's waiver request, Brown contacted an agent of Acorn, the other fixture manufacturer specified by the city. Based upon his discussions with Acorn, Brown subsequently submitted a bid on the fixtures to Croson. Continental's bid was $6,183.29 higher than the price Croson had included for the fixtures in its bid to the city. This constituted a 7% increase over the market price for the fixtures. With added bonding and insurance, using Continental would have raised the cost of the project by $7,663.16. On the same day that Brown contacted Acorn, he also called city procurement officials and told them that Continental, an MBE, could supply the fixtures specified in the city jail contract. On November 2, 1983, the city denied Croson's waiver request, indicating that Croson had 10 days to submit an MBE Utilization Commitment Form, and warned that failure to do so could result in its bid being considered unresponsive.

Croson wrote the city on November 8, 1983. In the letter, Bonn indicated that Continental was not an authorized supplier for either Acorn or Bradley fixtures. He also noted that Acorn's quotation to Brown was subject to credit approval and in any case was substantially higher than any other quotation Croson had received. Finally, Bonn noted that Continental's bid had been submitted some 21 days after the prime bids were due. In a second letter, Croson laid out the additional costs that using Continental to supply the fixtures would entail, and asked that it be allowed to raise the overall contract price accordingly. The city denied both Croson's request for a waiver and its suggestion that the contract price be raised. The city informed Croson that it had decided to rebid the project. On December 9, 1983, counsel for Croson wrote the city asking for a review of the waiver denial. The city's attorney responded that the city had elected to rebid the project, and that there is no appeal of such a decision. Shortly thereafter Croson brought this action under 42 U.S.C. § 1983 in the Federal District Court for the Eastern District of Virginia, arguing that the Richmond ordinance was unconstitutional on its face and as applied in this case.

. . . .

II

The parties and their supporting *amici* fight an initial battle over the scope of the city's power to adopt legislation designed to address the effects of past discrimination. Relying on our decision in *Wygant,* appellee argues that the city must limit any race-based remedial efforts to eradicating the effects of its own prior discrimination. This is essentially the position taken by the Court of Appeals below. Appellant argues that our decision in *Fullilove* is controlling, and that as a result the city of Richmond enjoys sweeping legislative power to define and attack the effects of prior discrimination in its local construction industry. We find that neither of these two rather stark alternatives can withstand analysis.

In *Fullilove,* we upheld the minority set-aside contained in § 103(f)(2) of the Public Works Employment Act of 1977, Pub.L. 95-28, 91 Stat. 116, 42 U.S.C. § 6701 *et seq.* (Act) against a challenge based on the equal protection component of the Due Process Clause. The Act authorized a $4 billion appropriation for federal grants to state and local governments for use in public works projects. The primary purpose of the Act was to give the national economy a quick boost in a recessionary period; funds had to be committed to state or local grantees by September 30, 1977 . . . .

The principal opinion in *Fullilove,* written by Chief Justice Burger, did not employ "strict scrutiny" or any other traditional standard of equal protection review. The Chief Justice noted at the outset that although racial classifications call for close examination, the Court was at the same time "bound to approach [its] task with appropriate deference to the Congress, a co-equal branch charged by the Constitution with the power to 'provide for the . . . general Welfare of the United States' and 'to enforce by appropriate legislation,' the equal protection guarantees of the Fourteenth Amendment." 448 U.S., at 472, 100 S.Ct., at 2771 . . .

. . . .

Appellant and its supporting *amici* rely heavily on *Fullilove* for the proposition that a city council, like Congress, need not make specific findings of discrimination to engage in race-conscious relief. Thus, appellant argues "[i]t would be a perversion of federalism to hold that the federal government has a compelling interest in remedying the effects of racial discrimination in its own public works program, but a city government does not." Brief for Appellant 32 (footnote omitted).

What appellant ignores is that Congress, unlike any State or political subdivision, has a specific constitutional mandate to enforce the dictates of the Fourteenth Amendment. The power to "enforce" may at times also include the power to define situations which *Congress* determines threaten principles of equality and to adopt prophylactic rules to deal with those situations. See *Katzenbach v. Morgan*, 384 U.S., at 651, 86 S.Ct., at 1723 ("Correctly viewed, § 5 is a positive grant of legislative power authorizing Congress to exercise its discretion in determining whether and what legislation is needed to secure the guarantees of the Fourteenth Amendment"). See also *South Carolina v. Katzenbach*, 383 U.S. 301, 326, 86 S.Ct. 803, 817, 15 L.Ed.2d 769 (1966) (similar interpretation of congressional power under § 2 of the Fifteenth Amendment). The Civil War Amendments themselves worked a dramatic change in the balance between congressional and state power over matters of race. Speaking of the Thirteenth and Fourteenth Amendments in *Ex parte Virginia*, 100 U.S. 339, 345, 25 L.Ed. 676 (1880), the Court stated: "They were intended to be, what they really are, limitations of the powers of the States and enlargements of the power of Congress."

That Congress may identify and redress the effects of society-wide discrimination does not mean that, *a fortiori*, the States and their political subdivisions are free to decide that such remedies are appropriate. Section 1 of the Fourteenth Amendment is an explicit *constraint* on state power, and the States must undertake any remedial efforts in accordance with that provision. To hold otherwise would be to cede control over the content of the Equal Protection Clause to the 50 state legislatures and their myriad political subdivisions. The mere recitation of a benign or compensatory purpose for the use of a racial classification would essentially entitle the States to exercise the full power of Congress under § 5 of the Fourteenth Amendment and insulate any racial classification from judicial scrutiny under § 1. We believe that such a result would be contrary to the intentions of the Framers of the Fourteenth Amendment, who desired to place clear limits on the States' use of race as a criterion for legislative action, and to have the federal courts enforce those limitations. See *Associated General Contractors of Cal. v. City and Cty. of San Francisco*, 813 F.2d, at 929 (Kozinski, J.) ("The city is not just like the federal government with regard to the findings it must make to justify race-conscious remedial action"); see also Days, Fullilove, 96 Yale L.J. 453, 474 (1987) (hereinafter Days) ("*Fullilove* clearly focused on the constitutionality of a *congressionally* mandated set-aside program") (emphasis in original); Bohrer, *Bakke, Weber,* and *Fullilove:* Benign Discrimination and Congressional Power to Enforce the Fourteenth Amendment, 56 Ind. L.J. 473, 512–513 (1981) ("Congress may authorize, pursuant to section 5, state action that would be foreclosed to the states acting alone").

We do not, as Justice Marshall's dissent suggests, see *post*, at 755–757, find in § 5 of the Fourteenth Amendment some form of federal pre-emption in matters of race. We simply note what should be apparent to all—§ 1 of the Fourteenth Amendment stemmed from a distrust of state legislative enactments based on race; § 5 is, as the dissent notes, "'a *positive* grant of legislative power'" to Congress. *Post*, at 755, quoting *Katzenbach v. Morgan, supra*, 384 U.S., at 651, 86 S.Ct., at 1723 (emphasis in dissent). Thus, our treatment of an exercise of congressional power in *Fullilove* cannot be dispositive here. In the *Slaughter-House Cases*, 16 Wall. 36, 21 L.Ed. 394

(1873), cited by the dissent, *post,* at 756, the Court noted that the Civil War Amendments granted "additional powers to the Federal government," and laid "additional restraints upon those of the States." 16 Wall., at 68.

It would seem equally clear, however, that a state or local subdivision (if delegated the authority from the State) has the authority to eradicate the effects of private discrimination within its own legislative jurisdiction. . . . This authority must, of course, be exercised within the constraints of §1 of the Fourteenth Amendment. Our decision in *Wygant* is not to the contrary. *Wygant* addressed the constitutionality of the use of racial quotas by local school authorities pursuant to an agreement reached with the local teachers' union. It was in the context of addressing the school board's power to adopt a race-based layoff program affecting its own work force that the *Wygant* plurality indicated that the Equal Protection Clause required "some showing of prior discrimination by the governmental unit involved." *Wygant,* 476 U.S., at 274, 106 S.Ct., at 1847. As a matter of state law, the city of Richmond has legislative authority over its procurement policies, and can use its spending powers to remedy private discrimination, if it identifies that discrimination with the particularity required by the Fourteenth Amendment. To this extent, on the question of the city's competence, the Court of Appeals erred in following *Wygant* by rote in a case involving a state entity which has state-law authority to address discriminatory practices within local commerce under its jurisdiction.

Thus, if the city could show that it had essentially become a "passive participant" in a system of racial exclusion practiced by elements of the local construction industry, we think it clear that the city could take affirmative steps to dismantle such a system. It is beyond dispute that any public entity, state or federal, has a compelling interest in assuring that public dollars, drawn from the tax contributions of all citizens, do not serve to finance the evil of private prejudice. Cf. *Norwood v. Harrison,* 413 U.S. 455, 465, 93 S.Ct. 2804, 2810, 37 L.Ed.2d 723 (1973) ("Racial discrimination in state-operated schools is barred by the Constitution and [i]t is also axiomatic that a state may not induce, encourage or promote private persons to accomplish what it is constitutionally forbidden to accomplish") (citation and internal quotations omitted).

III

A

The Equal Protection Clause of the Fourteenth Amendment provides that "[n]o State shall . . . deny to *any person* within its jurisdiction the equal protection of the laws." (Emphasis added.) As this Court has noted in the past, the "rights created by the first section of the Fourteenth Amendment are, by its terms, guaranteed to the individual. The rights established are personal rights." *Shelley v. Kraemer,* 334 U.S. 1, 22, 68 S.Ct. 836, 846, 92 L.Ed. 1161 (1948). The Richmond Plan denies certain citizens the opportunity to compete for a fixed percentage of public contracts based solely upon their race. To whatever racial group these citizens belong, their "personal rights" to be treated with equal dignity and respect are implicated by a rigid rule erecting race as the sole criterion in an aspect of public decision-making.

Absent searching judicial inquiry into the justification for such race-based measures, there is simply no way of determining what classifications are "benign" or "remedial" and what classifications are in fact motivated by illegitimate notions of racial inferiority or simple racial politics. Indeed, the purpose of strict scrutiny is to "smoke out" illegitimate uses of race by assuring that the legislative body is pursuing a goal important enough to warrant use of a highly suspect tool. The test also ensures that the means chosen "fit" this compelling goal so closely that there is little or no possibility that the motive for the classification was illegitimate racial prejudice or stereotype.

Classifications based on race carry a danger of stigmatic harm. Unless they are strictly reserved for remedial settings, they may in fact promote notions of racial inferiority and lead to a politics of racial hostility. See *University of California Regents v. Bakke*, 438 U.S., at 298, 98 S.Ct., at 2752 (opinion of Powell, J.) ("[P]referential programs may only reinforce common stereotypes holding that certain groups are unable to achieve success without special protection based on a factor having no relation to individual worth"). We thus reaffirm the view expressed by the plurality in *Wygant* that the standard of review under the Equal Protection Clause is not dependent on the race of those burdened or benefited by a particular classification. . . .

Our continued adherence to the standard of review employed in *Wygant* does not, as Justice Marshall's dissent suggests, see *post,* at 752, indicate that we view "racial discrimination as largely a phenomenon of the past" or that "government bodies need no longer preoccupy themselves with rectifying racial injustice." As we indicate, see *infra,* at 730–731, States and their local subdivisions have many legislative weapons at their disposal both to punish and prevent present discrimination and to remove arbitrary barriers to minority advancement. Rather, our interpretation of § 1 stems from our agreement with the view expressed by Justice Powell in *Bakke* that "[t]he guarantee of equal protection cannot mean one thing when applied to one individual and something else when applied to a person of another color." *Bakke, supra,* 438 U.S., at 289–290, 98 S.Ct., at 2748.

. . . .

In *Bakke, supra,* the Court confronted a racial quota employed by the University of California at Davis Medical School. Under the plan, 16 out of 100 seats in each entering class at the school were reserved exclusively for certain minority groups. *Id.,* 438 U.S., at 288–289, 98 S.Ct., at 2747–2748. Among the justifications offered in support of the plan were the desire to "reduc[e] the historic deficit of traditionally disfavored minorities in medical school and the medical profession" and the need to "counte[r] the effects of societal discrimination." *Id.,* at 306, 98 S.Ct., at 2756 (citations omitted). Five Members of the Court determined that none of these interests could justify a plan that completely eliminated nonminorities from consideration for a specified percentage of opportunities. *Id.,* at 271–272, 98 S.Ct., at 2738 (Powell, J.) (addressing constitutionality of Davis plan); *id.,* at 408, 98 S.Ct., at 2808 (Stevens, J., joined by Burger, C.J. and Stewart and Rehnquist, JJ. concurring in judgment in part and dissenting in part) (addressing only legality of Davis admissions plan under Title VI of the Civil Rights Act of 1964).

Justice Powell's opinion applied heightened scrutiny under the Equal Protection Clause to the racial classification at issue. His opinion decisively rejected the first justification for the racially segregated admissions plan. The desire to have more black medical students or doctors, standing alone, was not merely insufficiently compelling to justify a racial classification, it was "discrimination for its own sake," forbidden by the Constitution. *Id.,* at 307, 98 S.Ct., at 2757. Nor could the second concern, the history of discrimination in society at large, justify a racial quota in medical school admissions. Justice Powell contrasted the "focused" goal of remedying "wrongs worked by specific instances of racial discrimination" with "the remedying of the effects of 'societal discrimination,' an amorphous concept of injury that may be ageless in its reach into the past." *Ibid.* He indicated that for the governmental interest in remedying past discrimination to be triggered "judicial, legislative, or administrative findings of constitutional or statutory violations" must be made. *Ibid.* Only then does the government have a compelling interest in favoring one race over another . . . .

B

We think it clear that the factual predicate offered in support of the Richmond Plan suffers from the same two defects identified as fatal in *Wygant.* The District Court found the city council's "findings sufficient to ensure that, in adopting the Plan, it was remedying the present effects of past discrimination in the *construction industry.*" Supp.App. 163 (emphasis added). Like the "role model" theory employed in *Wygant,* a generalized assertion that there has been past discrimination in an entire industry provides no guidance for a legislative body to determine the precise scope of the injury it seeks to remedy. It "has no logical stopping point." *Wygant, supra,* at 275, 106 S.Ct., at 1847 (plurality opinion). "Relief" for such an ill-defined wrong could extend until the percentage of public contracts awarded to MBE's in Richmond mirrored the percentage of minorities in the population as a whole.

. . . .

While there is no doubt that the sorry history of both private and public discrimination in this country has contributed to a lack of opportunities for black entrepreneurs, this observation, standing alone, cannot justify a rigid racial quota in the awarding of public contracts in Richmond, Virginia. Like the claim that discrimination in primary and secondary schooling justifies a rigid racial preference in medical school admissions, an amorphous claim that there has been past discrimination in a particular industry cannot justify the use of an unyielding racial quota.

It is sheer speculation how many minority firms there would be in Richmond absent past societal discrimination, just as it was sheer speculation how many minority medical students would have been admitted to the medical school at Davis absent past discrimination in educational opportunities. Defining these sorts of injuries as "identified discrimination" would give local governments license to create a patchwork of racial preferences based on statistical generalizations about any particular field of endeavor.

These defects are readily apparent in this case. The 30% quota cannot in any realistic sense be tied to any injury suffered by anyone. The District Court relied upon five predicate "facts" in reaching its conclusion that there was an adequate basis for the 30% quota: (1) the ordinance declares itself to be remedial; (2) several proponents of the measure stated their views that there had been past discrimination in the construction industry; (3) minority businesses received 0.67% of prime contracts from the city while minorities constituted 50% of the city's population; (4) there were very few minority contractors in local and state contractors' associations; and (5) in 1977, Congress made a determination that the effects of past discrimination had stifled minority participation in the construction industry nationally. Supp.App. 163–167.

None of these "findings," singly or together, provide the city of Richmond with a "strong basis in evidence for its conclusion that remedial action was necessary." *Wygant,* 476 U.S., at 277, 106 S.Ct., at 1849 (plurality opinion). There is nothing approaching a prima facie case of a constitutional or statutory violation by *anyone* in the Richmond construction industry. *Id.,* at 274–275, 106 S.Ct., at 1846–1847; see also *id.,* at 293, 106 S.Ct., at 1856 (O'Connor, J., concurring).

. . . .

Reliance on the disparity between the number of prime contracts awarded to minority firms and the minority population of the city of Richmond is similarly misplaced. There is no doubt that "[w]here gross statistical disparities can be shown, they alone in a proper case may constitute prima facie proof of a pattern or practice of discrimination" under Title VII. *Hazelwood School Dist. v. United States,* 433 U.S. 299, 307–308, 97 S.Ct. 2736, 2741, 53 L.Ed.2d 768 (1977). But it is equally clear that "[w]hen special qualifications are required to fill particular jobs, comparisons to the general population (rather than to the smaller group of individuals who possess the necessary qualifications) may have little probative value." *Id.,* at 308, n. 13, 97 S. Ct., at 2742, n. 13. See also *Mayor of Philadelphia v. Educational Equality League,* 415 U.S. 605, 620, 94 S.Ct. 1323, 1333, 39 L.Ed.2d 630 (1974) ("[T]his is not a case in which it can be assumed that all citizens are fungible for purposes of determining whether members of a particular class have been unlawfully excluded").

In the employment context, we have recognized that for certain entry level positions or positions requiring minimal training, statistical comparisons of the racial composition of an employer's work force to the racial composition of the relevant population may be probative of a pattern of discrimination. See *Teamsters v. United States,* 431 U.S. 324, 337–338, 97 S.Ct. 1843, 1855–1856, 52 L.Ed.2d 396 (1977) (statistical comparison between minority truck-drivers and relevant population probative of discriminatory exclusion). But where special qualifications are necessary, the relevant statistical pool for purposes of demonstrating discriminatory exclusion must be the number of minorities qualified to undertake the particular task. See *Hazelwood, supra,* 433 U.S., at 308, 97 S.Ct., at 2741; *Johnson v. Transportation Agency, Santa Clara County,* 480 U.S. 616, 651–652, 107 S.Ct. 1442, 1462, 94 L.Ed.2d 615 (1987) (O'Connor, J., concurring in judgment).

In this case, the city does not even know how many MBE's in the relevant market are qualified to undertake prime or subcontracting work in public construction projects. Cf. *Ohio Contractors Assn. v. Keip,* 713 F.2d, at 171 (relying on percentage of minority *businesses* in the State compared to percentage of state purchasing contracts awarded to minority firms in upholding set-aside). Nor does the city know what percentage of total city construction dollars minority firms now receive as subcontractors on prime contracts let by the city.

To a large extent, the set-aside of subcontracting dollars seems to rest on the unsupported assumption that white prime contractors simply will not hire minority firms. See *Associated General Contractors of Cal. v. City and Cty. of San Francisco,* 813 F.2d, at 933 ("There is no finding — and we decline to assume — that male caucasian contractors will award contracts only to other male caucasians"). Indeed, there is evidence in this record that overall minority participation in city contracts in Richmond is 7 to 8%, and that minority contractor participation in Community Block Development Grant *construction* projects is 17 to 22%. App. 16 (statement of Mr. Deese, City Manager). Without any information on minority participation in subcontracting, it is quite simply impossible to evaluate overall minority representation in the city's construction expenditures.

The city and the District Court also relied on evidence that MBE membership in local contractors' associations was extremely low. Again, standing alone this evidence is not probative of any discrimination in the local construction industry. There are numerous explanations for this dearth of minority participation, including past societal discrimination in education and economic opportunities as well as both black and white career and entrepreneurial choices. Blacks may be disproportionately attracted to industries other than construction. See The State of Small Business: A Report of the President 201 (1986) ("Relative to the distribution of all businesses, black-owned businesses are more than proportionally represented in the transportation industry, but considerably less than proportionally represented in the wholesale trade, manufacturing, and finance industries").

. . . .

IV

As noted by the court below, it is almost impossible to assess whether the Richmond Plan is narrowly tailored to remedy prior discrimination since it is not linked to identified discrimination in any way. We limit ourselves to two observations in this regard.

First, there does not appear to have been any consideration of the use of race-neutral means to increase minority business participation in city contracting. See

United States v. Paradise, 480 U.S. 149, 171, 107 S.Ct. 1053, 1066, 94 L.Ed.2d 203 (1987) ("In determining whether race-conscious remedies are appropriate, we look to several factors, including the efficacy of alternative remedies"). Many of the barriers to minority participation in the construction industry relied upon by the city to justify a racial classification appear to be race neutral. If MBE's disproportionately lack capital or cannot meet bonding requirements, a race-neutral program of city financing for small firms would, *a fortiori*, lead to greater minority participation. The principal opinion in *Fullilove* found that Congress had carefully examined and rejected race-neutral alternatives before enacting the MBE set-aside. See *Fullilove*, 448 U.S., at 463–467, 100 S.Ct., at 2767–2769; see also *id.*, at 511, 100 S.Ct., at 2792 (Powell, J., concurring) ("[B]y the time Congress enacted [the MBE set-aside] in 1977, it knew that other remedies had failed to ameliorate the effects of racial discrimination in the construction industry"). There is no evidence in this record that the Richmond City Council has considered any alternatives to a race-based quota.

Second, the 30% quota cannot be said to be narrowly tailored to any goal, except perhaps outright racial balancing. It rests upon the "completely unrealistic" assumption that minorities will choose a particular trade in lockstep proportion to their representation in the local population. See *Sheet Metal Workers v. EEOC*, 478 U.S. 421, 494, 106 S.Ct. 3019, 3059, 92 L.Ed.2d 344 (1986) (O'Connor, J., concurring in part and dissenting in part) ("[I]t is completely unrealistic to assume that individuals of one race will gravitate with mathematical exactitude to each employer or union absent unlawful discrimination").

Since the city must already consider bids and waivers on a case-by-case basis, it is difficult to see the need for a rigid numerical quota

V

Nothing we say today precludes a state or local entity from taking action to rectify the effects of identified discrimination within its jurisdiction. If the city of Richmond had evidence before it that nonminority contractors were systematically excluding minority businesses from subcontracting opportunities it could take action to end the discriminatory exclusion. . . . Nor is local government powerless to deal with individual instances of racially motivated refusals to employ minority contractors. Where such discrimination occurs, a city would be justified in penalizing the discriminator and providing appropriate relief to the victim of such discrimination. . . . Even in the absence of evidence of discrimination, the city has at its disposal a whole array of race-neutral devices to increase the accessibility of city contracting opportunities to small entrepreneurs of all races. Simplification of bidding procedures, relaxation of bonding requirements, and training and financial aid for disadvantaged entrepreneurs of all races would open the public contracting market to all those who have suffered the effects of past societal discrimination or neglect. . . .

In the case at hand, the city has not ascertained how many minority enterprises are present in the local construction market nor the level of their participation in city construction projects. The city points to no evidence that qualified minority contractors have been passed over for city contracts or subcontracts, either as a group or in any individual case. Under such circumstances, it is simply impossible to say that the city has demonstrated "a strong basis in evidence for its conclusion that remedial action was necessary." Wygant, 476 U.S., at 277, 106 S.Ct., at 1849.

. . . Because the city of Richmond has failed to identify the need for remedial action in the awarding of its public construction contracts, its treatment of its citizens on a racial basis violates the dictates of the Equal Protection Clause. Accordingly, the judgment of the Court of Appeals for the Fourth Circuit is

Affirmed.

Notes and Questions

1. How do you assess the Court's argument that Richmond's policy is overinclusive? Are you persuaded by the Court's emphasis on the unintended beneficiaries of affirmative action policies in Richmond, as opposed to policies exclusively benefitting African Americans?

2. Note the majority's requirement that "gross statistical disparities might not suffice when specific qualifications are required to fill the job. The majority quotes *Hazelwood*, covered in chapter 2, as confirmation of its approach to statistics to prove discrimination. Are you convinced by this approach?"

3. The majority also confirms that the 14th Amendment expanded the power of Congress to prevent discrimination. What facts and arguments in the opinion support this?"

4. What are the arguments for and against granting deference to Congress when it legislates to prevent discrimination? You will review these arguments again in *Shelby County v. Holder* and *Tennessee v. Lane* in the chapters on voting and disability. Track whether the Court's standard and reasoning are applied consistently in these cases.

5. See the Court's comment contradicting the dissent's claim of ongoing need for measures.

> Since 1975 the city of Richmond has had an ordinance on the books prohibiting both discrimination in the award of public contracts and employment discrimination by public contractors. See Reply Brief for Appellant 18, n. 42 (citing Richmond, Va., City Code, § 17.2 *et seq.* (1985)). The city points to no evidence that its prime contractors have been violating the ordinance in either their employment or subcontracting practices. The complete silence of the record concerning enforcement of the city's own antidiscrimination ordinance flies in the face of the dissent's vision of a "tight-knit industry" which has prevented blacks from obtaining the experience necessary to participate in construction contracting.

Could the city have done a better job showing ongoing need for affirmative measures?

6. The Court continues its application of strict scrutiny, below, and the requirement that government demonstrate a compelling interest when reviewing governmental contracts deliberately inclusive of minority bidders.

Adarand Constructors, Inc. v. Pena

515 U.S. 200 (1995)

Justice O'Connor announced the judgment of the Court and delivered an opinion with respect to Parts I, II, III-A, III-B, III-D, and IV, which is for the Court except insofar as it might be inconsistent with the views expressed in Justice SCALIA's concurrence, and an opinion with respect to Part III-C in which Justice Kennedy joins.

Petitioner Adarand Constructors, Inc., claims that the Federal Government's practice of giving general contractors on Government projects a financial incentive to hire subcontractors controlled by "socially and economically disadvantaged individuals," and in particular, the Government's use of race-based presumptions in identifying such individuals, violates the equal protection component of the Fifth Amendment's Due Process Clause. The Court of Appeals rejected Adarand's claim. We conclude, however, that courts should analyze cases of this kind under a different standard of review than the one the Court of Appeals applied. We therefore vacate the Court of Appeals' judgment and remand the case for further proceedings.

I

In 1989, the Central Federal Lands Highway Division (CFLHD), which is part of the United States Department of Transportation (DOT), awarded the prime contract for a highway construction project in Colorado to Mountain Gravel & Construction Company. Mountain Gravel then solicited bids from subcontractors for the guardrail portion of the contract. Adarand, a Colorado-based highway construction company specializing in guardrail work, submitted the low bid. Gonzales Construction Company also submitted a bid.

The prime contract's terms provide that Mountain Gravel would receive additional compensation if it hired subcontractors certified as small businesses controlled by "socially and economically disadvantaged individuals," App. 24. Gonzales is certified as such a business; Adarand is not. Mountain Gravel awarded the subcontract to Gonzales, despite Adarand's low bid, and Mountain Gravel's Chief Estimator has submitted an affidavit stating that Mountain Gravel would have accepted Adarand's bid, had it not been for the additional payment it received by hiring Gonzales instead. *Id.*, at 28–31. Federal law requires that a subcontracting clause similar to the one used here must appear in most federal agency contracts, and it also requires the clause to state that "[t]he contractor shall presume that socially and economically disadvantaged individuals include Black Americans, Hispanic Americans, Native Americans, Asian Pacific Americans, and other minorities, or any other individual found to be disadvantaged by the [Small Business] Administration pursuant to section 8(a) of the Small Business Act." 15 U.S.C. §§ 637(d)(2), (3). Adarand claims that the presumption set forth in that statute discriminates on the basis of race in violation of the Federal Government's Fifth Amendment obligation not to deny anyone equal protection of the laws.

These fairly straightforward facts implicate a complex scheme of federal statutes and regulations, to which we now turn. The Small Business Act (Act), 72 Stat. 384, as amended, 15 U.S.C. §631 *et seq.*, declares it to be "the policy of the United States that small business concerns, [and] small business concerns owned and controlled by socially and economically disadvantaged individuals, . . . shall have the maximum practicable opportunity to participate in the performance of contracts let by any Federal agency." §8(d)(1), 15 U.S.C. §637(d)(1). The Act defines "socially disadvantaged individuals" as "those who have been subjected to racial or ethnic prejudice or cultural bias because of their identity as a member of a group without regard to their individual qualities," §8(a)(5), 15 U.S.C. §637(a)(5), and it defines "economically disadvantaged individuals" as "those socially disadvantaged individuals whose ability to compete in the free enterprise system has been impaired due to diminished capital and credit opportunities as compared to others in the same business area who are not socially disadvantaged." §8(a)(6)(A), 15 U.S.C. §637(a)(6)(A).

In furtherance of the policy stated in §8(d)(1), the Act establishes "[t]he Government-wide goal for participation by small business concerns owned and controlled by socially and economically disadvantaged individuals" at "not less than 5 percent of the total value of all prime contract and subcontract awards for each fiscal year." 15 U.S.C. §644(g)(1). It also requires the head of each federal agency to set agency-specific goals for participation by businesses controlled by socially and economically disadvantaged individuals. *Ibid.*

. . . .

The other SBA program relevant to this case is the "8(d) subcontracting program," which unlike the 8(a) program is limited to eligibility for subcontracting provisions like the one at issue here. In determining eligibility, the SBA presumes social disadvantage based on membership in certain minority groups, just as in the 8(a) program, and again appears to require an individualized, although "less restrictive," showing of economic disadvantage, §124.106(b). A different set of regulations, however, says that members of minority groups wishing to participate in the 8(d) subcontracting program are entitled to a race-based presumption of social *and* economic disadvantage. 48 CFR §§ 19.001, 19.703(a)(2) (1994). We are left with some uncertainty as to whether participation in the 8(d) subcontracting program requires an individualized showing of economic disadvantage. In any event, in both the 8(a) and the 8(d) programs, the presumptions of disadvantage are rebuttable if a third party comes forward with evidence suggesting that the participant is not, in fact, either economically or socially disadvantaged. 13 CFR §§ 124.111(c)–(d), 124.601–124.609 (1994).

The contract giving rise to the dispute in this case came about as a result of the Surface Transportation and Uniform Relocation Assistance Act of 1987, Pub.L. 100-17, 101 Stat. 132 (STURAA), a DOT appropriations measure. Section 106(c)(1) of

STURAA provides that "not less than 10 percent" of the appropriated funds "shall be expended with small business concerns owned and controlled by socially and economically disadvantaged individuals." 101 Stat. 145. STURAA adopts the Small Business Act's definition of "socially and economically disadvantaged individual," including the applicable race-based presumptions, and adds that "women shall be presumed to be socially and economically disadvantaged individuals for purposes of this subsection." § 106(c)(2)(B), 101 Stat. 146. STURAA also requires the Secretary of Transportation to establish "minimum uniform criteria for State governments to use in certifying whether a concern qualifies for purposes of this subsection." § 106(c)(4), 101 Stat. 146.

. . . .

To benefit from [the statutory scheme], Mountain Gravel had to hire a subcontractor who had been certified as a small disadvantaged business by the SBA, a state highway agency, or some other certifying authority acceptable to the contracting officer. Any of the three routes to such certification described above—SBA's 8(a) or 8(d) program, or certification by a State under the DOT regulations—would meet that requirement. The record does not reveal how Gonzales obtained its certification as a small disadvantaged business.

After losing the guardrail subcontract to Gonzales, Adarand filed suit against various federal officials in the United States District Court for the District of Colorado, claiming that the race-based presumptions involved in the use of subcontracting compensation clauses violate Adarand's right to equal protection. . . .

The Court's failure to produce a majority opinion in *Bakke, Fullilove,* and *Wygant* left unresolved the proper analysis for remedial race-based governmental action. See *United States v. Paradise,* 480 U.S., at 166, 107 S.Ct., at 1063 (plurality opinion of Brennan, J.) ("[A]lthough this Court has consistently held that some elevated level of scrutiny is required when a racial or ethnic distinction is made for remedial purposes, it has yet to reach consensus on the appropriate constitutional analysis"); *Sheet Metal Workers v. EEOC,* 478 U.S. 421, 480, 106 S.Ct. 3019, 3052, 92 L.Ed.2d 344 (1986) (plurality opinion of Brennan, J.). Lower courts found this lack of guidance unsettling. See, *e.g., Kromnick v. School Dist. of Philadelphia,* 739 F.2d 894, 901 (CA3 1984) . . . .

The Court resolved the issue, at least in part, in 1989. *Richmond v. J.A. Croson Co.,* 488 U.S. 469, 109 S.Ct. 706, 102 L.Ed.2d 854 (1989), concerned a city's determination that 30% of its contracting work should go to minority-owned businesses. A majority of the Court in *Croson* held that "the standard of review under the Equal Protection Clause is not dependent on the race of those burdened or benefited by a particular classification," and that the single standard of review for racial classifications should be "strict scrutiny." *Id.,* at 493–494, 109 S.Ct., at 722 (opinion of O'Connor, J., joined by Rehnquist, C.J., and White and Kennedy, JJ.); *id.,* at 520, 109 S.Ct., at 735 (Scalia, J., concurring in judgment) ("I agree . . . with Justice O'Connor's conclusion that strict scrutiny must be applied to all governmental classification by race"). As to the classification before the Court, the plurality agreed that "a state or local subdivision . . . has the authority to eradicate the effects of private discrimination within its own legislative jurisdiction," *id.,* at 491–492, 109 S.Ct., at 720–721, but the Court thought that the city had not acted with "a 'strong basis in evidence for its conclusion that remedial action was necessary,'" *id.,* at 500, 109 S.Ct., at 725 (majority opinion) (quoting *Wygant, supra,* at 277, 106 S.Ct., at 1849 (plurality opinion)). The Court also thought it "obvious that [the] program is not narrowly tailored to remedy the effects of prior discrimination." 488 U.S., at 508, 109 S.Ct., at 729–730.

With *Croson,* the Court finally agreed that the Fourteenth Amendment requires strict scrutiny of all race-based action by state and local governments. But *Croson* of course had no occasion to declare what standard of review the Fifth Amendment requires for such action taken by the Federal Government. . . .

Despite lingering uncertainty in the details, however, the Court's cases through *Croson* had established three general propositions with respect to governmental racial classifications. First, skepticism: "'Any preference based on racial or ethnic criteria must necessarily receive a most searching examination,' . . ." . . . Second, consistency: "[T]he standard of review under the Equal Protection Clause is not dependent on the race of those burdened or benefited by a particular classification," *Croson,* 488 U.S., at 494, 109 S.Ct., at 722 (plurality opinion); *id.,* at 520, 109 S.Ct., at 735 (SCALIA, J., concurring in judgment); see also *Bakke,* 438 U.S., at 289–290, 98 S.Ct., at 2747–2748 (opinion of Powell, J.), *i.e.,* all racial classifications reviewable under the Equal Protection Clause must be strictly scrutinized. And third, congruence: "Equal protection analysis in the Fifth Amendment area is the same as that under the Fourteenth Amendment," *Buckley v. Valeo,* 424 U.S., at 93, 96 S.Ct., at 670; see also *Weinberger v. Wiesenfeld,* 420 U.S., at 638, n. 2, 95 S.Ct., at 1228, n. 2; *Bolling v. Sharpe,* 347 U.S., at 500, 74 S.Ct., at 694. Taken together, these three propositions lead to the conclusion that any person, of whatever race, has the right to demand that any governmental actor subject to the Constitution justify any racial classification subjecting that person to unequal treatment under the strictest judicial scrutiny.

. . . .

Our action today makes explicit what Justice Powell thought implicit in the *Fullilove* lead opinion: Federal racial classifications, like those of a State, must serve a compelling governmental interest, and must be narrowly tailored to further that interest. See *Fullilove,* 448 U.S., at 496, 100 S.Ct., at 2783–84 (concurring opinion). (Recall that the lead opinion in *Fullilove* "d[id] not adopt . . . the formulas of analysis articulated in such cases as [*Bakke*]." *Id.,* at 492, 100 S.Ct., at 2781 (opinion of Burger, C.J.).) Of course, it follows that to the extent (if any) that *Fullilove* held federal racial classifications to be subject to a less rigorous standard, it is no longer controlling. But we need not decide today whether the program upheld in *Fullilove* would survive strict scrutiny as our more recent cases have defined it.

. . . . We think that requiring strict scrutiny is the best way to ensure that courts will consistently give racial classifications that kind of detailed examination, both as to ends and as to means. *Korematsu* demonstrates vividly that even "the most rigid scrutiny" can sometimes fail to detect an illegitimate racial classification, compare *Korematsu*, 323 U.S., at 223, 65 S.Ct., at 197 ("To cast this case into outlines of racial prejudice, without reference to the real military dangers which were presented, merely confuses the issue. Korematsu was not excluded from the Military Area because of hostility to him or his race"), with Pub.L. 100-383, § 2(a), 102 Stat. 903–904 ("[T]hese actions [of relocating and interning civilians of Japanese ancestry] were carried out without adequate security reasons . . . and were motivated largely by racial prejudice, wartime hysteria, and a failure of political leadership"). Any retreat from the most searching judicial inquiry can only increase the risk of another such error occurring in the future.

[We] wish to dispel the notion that strict scrutiny is "strict in theory, but fatal in fact." *Fullilove, supra*, at 519, 100 S.Ct., at 2795 (Marshall, J., concurring in judgment). The unhappy persistence of both the practice and the lingering effects of racial discrimination against minority groups in this country is an unfortunate reality, and government is not disqualified from acting in response to it. As recently as 1987, for example, every Justice of this Court agreed that the Alabama Department of Public Safety's "pervasive, systematic, and obstinate discriminatory conduct" justified a narrowly tailored race-based remedy. See *United States v. Paradise*, 480 U.S., at 167, 107 S.Ct., at 1064 (plurality opinion of Brennan, J.); *id.*, at 190, 107 S.Ct., at 1076 (Stevens, J., concurring in judgment); *id.*, at 196, 107 S.Ct., at 1079–1080 (O'Connor, J., dissenting). When race-based action is necessary to further a compelling interest, such action is within constitutional constraints if it satisfies the "narrow tailoring" test this Court has set out in previous cases. . . .

Because our decision today alters the playing field in some important respects, we think it best to remand the case to the lower courts for further consideration in light of the principles we have announced. The Court of Appeals, following *Metro Broadcasting* and *Fullilove*, analyzed the case in terms of intermediate scrutiny. It upheld the challenged statutes and regulations because it found them to be "narrowly tailored to achieve [their] *significant governmental purpose* of providing subcontracting opportunities for small disadvantaged business enterprises." 16 F.3d, at 1547 (emphasis added). The Court of Appeals did not decide the question whether the interests served by the use of subcontractor compensation clauses are properly described as "compelling." It also did not address the question of narrow tailoring in terms of our strict scrutiny cases, by asking, for example, whether there was "any consideration of the use of race-neutral means to increase minority business participation" in government contracting, *Croson, supra*, at 507, 109 S.Ct., at 729, or whether the program was appropriately limited such that it "will not last longer than the discriminatory effects it is designed to eliminate," *Fullilove, supra*, at 513, 100 S.Ct., at 2792–2793 (Powell, J., concurring).

. . . .

Accordingly, the judgment of the Court of Appeals is vacated, and the case is remanded for further proceedings consistent with this opinion.

It is so ordered.

Personnel Administrator of Massachusetts v. Feeney
442 U.S. 256 (1979)

MR. JUSTICE STEWART delivered the opinion of the Court.

This case presents a challenge to the constitutionality of the Massachusetts veterans' preference statute, Mass.Gen.Laws Ann., ch. 31, § 23, on the ground that it discriminates against women in violation of the Equal Protection Clause of the Fourteenth Amendment. Under ch. 31, § 23, all veterans who qualify for state civil service positions must be considered for appointment ahead of any qualifying nonveterans. The preference operates overwhelmingly to the advantage of males.

The appellee Helen B. Feeney is not a veteran. She brought this action pursuant to 42 U.S.C. § 1983, alleging that the absolute preference formula established in ch. 31, § 23, inevitably operates to exclude women from consideration for the best Massachusetts civil service jobs and thus unconstitutionally denies them the equal protection of the laws. The three-judge District Court agreed, one judge dissenting. *Anthony v. Massachusetts*, 415 F.Supp. 485 (Mass.1976).

The District Court found that the absolute preference afforded by Massachusetts to veterans has a devastating impact upon the employment opportunities of women. Although it found that the goals of the preference were worthy and legitimate and that the legislation had not been enacted for the purpose of discriminating against women, the court reasoned that its exclusionary impact upon women was nonetheless so severe as to require the State to further its goals through a more limited form of preference. Finding that a more modest preference formula would readily accommodate the State's interest in aiding veterans, the court declared ch. 31, § 23, unconstitutional and enjoined its operation.

Upon an appeal taken by the Attorney General of Massachusetts, this Court vacated the judgment and remanded the case for further consideration in light of our intervening decision in *Washington v. Davis*, 426 U.S. 229, 96 S.Ct. 2040, 48 L. Ed.2d 597. *Massachusetts v. Feeney*, 434 U.S. 884, 98 S.Ct. 252, 54 L.Ed.2d 169. The *Davis* case held that a neutral law does not violate the Equal Protection Clause solely because it results in a racially disproportionate impact; instead the disproportionate impact must be traced to a purpose to discriminate on the basis of race. 426 U.S., at 238–244, 96 S.Ct., at 2046–2050.

Upon remand, the District Court, one judge concurring and one judge again dissenting, concluded that a veterans' hiring preference is inherently nonneutral because it favors a class from which women have traditionally been excluded, and that the consequences of the Massachusetts absolute-preference formula for the employment opportunities of women were too inevitable to have been "unintended." Accordingly, the court reaffirmed its original judgment. *Feeney v. Massachusetts*,

451 F.Supp. 143. The Attorney General again appealed to this Court pursuant to 28 U.S.C. § 1253, and probable jurisdiction of the appeal was noted. 439 U.S. 891, 99 S. Ct. 247, 58 L.Ed.2d 236.

I

A

The Federal Government and virtually all of the States grant some sort of hiring preference to veterans. The Massachusetts preference, which is loosely termed an "absolute lifetime" preference, is among the most generous. It applies to all positions in the State's classified civil service, which constitute approximately 60% of the public jobs in the State. It is available to "any person, male or female, including a nurse," who was honorably discharged from the United States Armed Forces after at least 90 days of active service, at least one day of which was during "wartime." Persons who are deemed veterans and who are otherwise qualified for a particular civil service job may exercise the preference at any time and as many times as they wish.

Civil service positions in Massachusetts fall into two general categories, labor and official. For jobs in the official service, with which the proofs in this action were concerned, the preference mechanics are uncomplicated. All applicants for employment must take competitive examinations. Grades are based on a formula that gives weight both to objective test results and to training and experience. Candidates who pass are then ranked in the order of their respective scores on an "eligible list." Chapter 31, § 23, requires, however, that disabled veterans, veterans, and surviving spouses and surviving parents of veterans be ranked—in the order of their respective scores—above all other candidates.

Rank on the eligible list and availability for employment are the sole factors that determine which candidates are considered for appointment to an official civil service position. When a public agency has a vacancy, it requisitions a list of "certified eligibles" from the state personnel division. Under formulas prescribed by civil service rules, a small number of candidates from the top of an appropriate list, three if there is only one vacancy, are certified. The appointing agency is then required to choose from among these candidates. Although the veterans' preference thus does not guarantee that a veteran will be appointed, it is obvious that the preference gives to veterans who achieve passing scores a well-nigh absolute advantage.

B

The appellee has lived in Dracut, Mass., most of her life. She entered the work force in 1948, and for the next 14 years worked at a variety of jobs in the private sector. She first entered the state civil service system in 1963, having competed successfully for a position as Senior Clerk Stenographer in the Massachusetts Civil Defense Agency. There she worked for four years. In 1967, she was promoted to the position of Federal Funds and Personnel Coordinator in the same agency. The agency, and with it her job, was eliminated in 1975.

During her 12-year tenure as a public employee, Ms. Feeney took and passed a number of open competitive civil service examinations. On several she did quite well, receiving in 1971 the second highest score on an examination for a job with the Board of Dental Examiners, and in 1973 the third highest on a test for an Administrative Assistant position with a mental health center. Her high scores, however, did not win her a place on the certified eligible list. Because of the veterans' preference, she was ranked sixth behind five male veterans on the Dental Examiner list. She was not certified, and a lower scoring veteran was eventually appointed. On the 1973 examination, she was placed in a position on the list behind 12 male veterans, 11 of whom had lower scores. Following the other examinations that she took, her name was similarly ranked below those of veterans who had achieved passing grades.

Ms. Feeney's interest in securing a better job in state government did not wane. Having been consistently eclipsed by veterans, however, she eventually concluded that further competition for civil service positions of interest to veterans would be futile. In 1975, shortly after her civil defense job was abolished, she commenced this litigation.

C

The veterans' hiring preference in Massachusetts, as in other jurisdictions, has traditionally been justified as a measure designed to reward veterans for the sacrifice of military service, to ease the transition from military to civilian life, to encourage patriotic service, and to attract loyal and well-disciplined people to civil service occupations. See, *e.g., Hutcheson v. Director of Civil Service*, 361 Mass. 480, 281 N.E.2d 53 (1972). The Massachusetts law dates back to 1884, when the State, as part of its first civil service legislation, gave a statutory preference to civil service applicants who were Civil War veterans if their qualifications were equal to those of nonveterans. 1884 Mass. Acts, ch. 320, § 14 (sixth). This tie-breaking provision blossomed into a truly absolute preference in 1895, when the State enacted its first general veterans' preference law and exempted veterans from all merit selection requirements. 1895 Mass. Acts, ch. 501, § 2. In response to a challenge brought by a male non-veteran, this statute was declared violative of state constitutional provisions guaranteeing that government should be for the "common good" and prohibiting hereditary titles. *Brown v. Russell*, 166 Mass. 14, 43 N.E. 1005 (1896).

The current veterans' preference law has its origins in an 1896 statute, enacted to meet the state constitutional standards enunciated in *Brown v. Russell*. That statute limited the absolute preference to veterans who were otherwise qualified. . . .

Since 1919, the preference has been repeatedly amended to cover persons who served in subsequent wars, declared or undeclared. . . . The current preference formula in ch. 31, § 23, is substantially the same as that settled upon in 1919. This absolute preference—even as modified in 1919—has never been universally popular. Over the years it has been subjected to repeated legal challenges . . . . The present case is apparently the first to challenge the Massachusetts veterans' preference on the simple ground that it discriminates on the basis of sex.

D

The first Massachusetts veterans' preference statute defined the term "veterans" in gender-neutral language. See 1896 Mass. Acts, ch. 517, § 1 ("a person" who served in the United States Army or Navy), and subsequent amendments have followed this pattern, see, *e.g.,* 1919 Mass. Acts, ch. 150, § 1 ("any person who has served . . ."); 1954 Mass. Acts, ch. 627, § 1 ("any person, male or female, including a nurse"). Women who have served in official United States military units during wartime, then, have always been entitled to the benefit of the preference. In addition, Massachusetts, through a 1943 amendment to the definition of "wartime service," extended the preference to women who served in unofficial auxiliary women's units. 1943 Mass. Acts, ch. 194.

When the first general veterans' preference statute was adopted in 1896, there were no women veterans. The statute, however, covered only Civil War veterans. Most of them were beyond middle age, and relatively few were actively competing for public employment. Thus, the impact of the preference upon the employment opportunities of nonveterans as a group and women in particular was slight.

Notwithstanding the apparent attempts by Massachusetts to include as many military women as possible within the scope of the preference, the statute today benefits an overwhelmingly male class. This is attributable in some measure to the variety of federal statutes, regulations, and policies that have restricted the number of women who could enlist in the United States Armed Forces, and largely to the simple fact that women have never been subjected to a military draft. See generally Binkin and Bach 4–21.

When this litigation was commenced, then, over 98% of the veterans in Massachusetts were male; only 1.8% were female. And over one-quarter of the Massachusetts population were veterans. During the decade between 1963 and 1973 when the appellee was actively participating in the State's merit selection system, 47,005 new permanent appointments were made in the classified official service. Forty-three percent of those hired were women, and 57% were men. Of the women appointed, 1.8% were veterans, while 54% of the men had veteran status. A large unspecified percentage of the female appointees were serving in lower paying positions for which males traditionally had not applied. On each of 50 sample eligible lists that are part of the record in this case, one or more women who would have been certified as eligible for appointment on the basis of test results were displaced by veterans whose test scores were lower.

At the outset of this litigation appellants conceded that for "many of the permanent positions for which males and females have competed" the veterans' preference has "resulted in a substantially greater proportion of female eligibles than male eligibles" not being certified for consideration. The impact of the veterans' preference law upon the public employment opportunities of women has thus been severe. This impact lies at the heart of the appellee's federal constitutional claim.

II

The sole question for decision on this appeal is whether Massachusetts, in granting an absolute lifetime preference to veterans, has discriminated against women in violation of the Equal Protection Clause of the Fourteenth Amendment.

A

The equal protection guarantee of the Fourteenth Amendment does not take from the States all power of classification. . . .

Certain classifications, however, in themselves supply a reason to infer antipathy. Race is the paradigm. A racial classification, regardless of purported motivation, is presumptively invalid and can be upheld only upon an extraordinary justification. . . . . This rule applies as well to a classification that is ostensibly neutral but is an obvious pretext for racial discrimination . . . . Even if a neutral law has a disproportionately adverse effect upon a racial minority, it is unconstitutional under the Equal Protection Clause only if that impact can be traced to a discriminatory purpose.

Classifications based upon gender, not unlike those based upon race, have traditionally been the touchstone for pervasive and often subtle discrimination. . . . . Although public employment is not a constitutional right, *Massachusetts Bd. of Retirement v. Murgia, supra,* and the States have wide discretion in framing employee qualifications, see, *e.g., New York City Transit Authority v. Beazer, supra,* these precedents dictate that any state law overtly or covertly designed to prefer males over females in public employment would require an exceedingly persuasive justification to withstand a constitutional challenge under the Equal Protection Clause of the Fourteenth Amendment.

B

The cases of *Washington v. Davis, supra,* and *Arlington Heights v. Metropolitan Housing Dev. Corp., supra,* recognize that when a neutral law has a disparate impact upon a group that has historically been the victim of discrimination, an unconstitutional purpose may still be at work. But those cases signaled no departure from the settled rule that the Fourteenth Amendment guarantees equal laws, not equal results. *Davis* upheld a job-related employment test that white people passed in proportionately greater numbers than Negroes, for there had been no showing that racial discrimination entered into the establishment or formulation of the test. *Arlington Heights* upheld a zoning board decision that tended to perpetuate racially segregated housing patterns, since, apart from its effect, the board's decision was shown to be nothing more than an application of a constitutionally neutral zoning policy. Those principles apply with equal force to a case involving alleged gender discrimination.

When a statute gender-neutral on its face is challenged on the ground that its effects upon women are disproportionably adverse, a twofold inquiry is thus appropriate. The first question is whether the statutory classification is indeed neutral in the sense that it is not gender-based. If the classification itself, covert of overt, is not based upon gender, the second question is whether the adverse effect reflects invidious gender-based discrimination. See *Arlington Heights v. Metropolitan Housing Dev. Corp., supra.* In this second inquiry, impact provides an "important starting point," 429 U.S., at 266, 97 S.Ct., at 564, but purposeful discrimination is "the condition that offends the Constitution." *Swann v. Charlotte-Mecklenburg Board of Education,* 402 U.S. 1, 16, 91 S.Ct. 1267, 1276, 28 L.Ed.2d 554.

It is against this background of precedent that we consider the merits of the case before us.

III

A

The question whether ch. 31, § 23, establishes a classification that is overtly or covertly based upon gender must first be considered. The appellee has conceded that ch. 31, § 23, is neutral on its face. She has also acknowledged that state hiring preferences for veterans are not *per se* invalid, for she has limited her challenge to the absolute lifetime preference that Massachusetts provides to veterans. The District Court made two central findings that are relevant here: first, that ch. 31, § 23, serves legitimate and worthy purposes; second, that the absolute preference was not established for the purpose of discriminating against women. The appellee has thus acknowledged and the District Court has thus found that the distinction between veterans and nonveterans drawn by ch. 31, § 23, is not a pretext for gender discrimination. The appellee's concession and the District Court's finding are clearly correct.

If the impact of this statute could not be plausibly explained on a neutral ground, impact itself would signal that the real classification made by the law was in fact not neutral. See *Washington v. Davis,* 426 U.S., at 242, 96 S.Ct., at 2049; *Arlington Heights v. Metropolitan Housing Dev. Corp., supra,* 429 U.S., at 266, 97 S.Ct., at 564. But there can be but one answer to the question whether this veteran preference excludes significant numbers of women from preferred state jobs because they are women or because they are nonveterans. Apart from the facts that the definition of "veterans" in the statute has always been neutral as to gender and that Massachusetts has consistently defined veteran status in a way that has been inclusive of women who have served in the military, this is not a law that can plausibly be explained only as a gender-based classification. Indeed, it is not a law that can rationally be explained on that ground. Veteran status is not uniquely male. Although few women benefit from the preference the nonveteran class is not substantially all female. To the contrary, significant numbers of nonveterans are men, and all nonveterans—male as well as female—are placed at a disadvantage. Too many men are affected by ch. 31, § 23, to permit the inference that the statute is but a pretext for preferring men over women.

Moreover, as the District Court implicitly found, the purposes of the statute provide the surest explanation for its impact. Just as there are cases in which impact alone can unmask an invidious classification, cf. *Yick Wo v. Hopkins,* 118 U.S. 356, 6 S. Ct. 1064, 30 L.Ed. 220, there are others, in which—notwithstanding impact—the legitimate noninvidious purposes of a law cannot be missed. This is one. The distinction made by ch. 31, § 23, is, as it seems to be, quite simply between veterans and nonveterans, not between men and women.

B

The dispositive question, then, is whether the appellee has shown that a gender-based discriminatory purpose has, at least in some measure, shaped the Massachusetts veterans' preference legislation. As did the District Court, she points to two basic factors which in her view distinguish ch. 31, § 23, from the neutral rules at issue in the *Washington v. Davis* and *Arlington Heights* cases. The first is the nature of the preference, which is said to be demonstrably gender-biased in the sense that it favors a status reserved under federal military policy primarily to men. The second concerns the impact of the absolute lifetime preference upon the employment opportunities of women, an impact claimed to be too inevitable to have been unintended. The appellee contends that these factors, coupled with the fact that the preference itself has little if any relevance to actual job performance, more than suffice to prove the discriminatory intent required to establish a constitutional violation.

1

The contention that this veterans' preference is "inherently nonneutral" or "gender-biased" presumes that the State, by favoring veterans, intentionally incorporated into its public employment policies the panoply of sex-based and assertively discriminatory federal laws that have prevented all but a handful of women from becoming veterans. There are two serious difficulties with this argument. First, it is wholly at odds with the District Court's central finding that Massachusetts has not offered a preference to veterans for the purpose of discriminating against women. Second, it cannot be reconciled with the assumption made by both the appellee and the District Court that a more limiting hiring preference for veterans could be sustained. Taken together, these difficulties are fatal.

To the extent that the status of veteran is one that few women have been enabled to achieve, every hiring preference for veterans, however, modest or extreme, is inherently gender-biased. If Massachusetts by offering such a preference can be said intentionally to have incorporated into its state employment policies the historical gender-based federal military personnel practices, the degree of the preference would or should make no constitutional difference. Invidious discrimination does not become less so because the discrimination accomplished is of a lesser magnitude. Discriminatory intent is simply not amenable to calibration. It either is a factor that has influenced the legislative choice or it is not. The District Court's conclusion that the absolute veterans' preference was not originally enacted or subsequently reaffirmed for the purpose of giving an advantage to males as such necessarily compels the conclusion that the State is intended nothing more than to prefer "veterans." Given this finding, simple logic suggests that an intent to exclude women from significant public jobs was not at work in this law. To reason that it was, by describing the preference as "inherently nonneutral" or "gender-biased," is merely to restate the fact of impact, not to answer the question of intent.

To be sure, this case is unusual in that it involves a law that by design is not neutral. The law overtly prefers veterans as such. As opposed to the written test at issue in *Davis,* it does not purport to define a job-related characteristic. To the contrary, it confers upon a specifically described group—perceived to be particularly deserving—a competitive head start. But the District Court found, and the appellee has not disputed, that this legislative choice was legitimate. The basic distinction between veterans and nonveterans, having been found not gender-based, and the goals of the preference having been found worthy, ch. 31 must be analyzed as is any other neutral law that casts a greater burden upon women as a group than upon men as a group. The enlistment policies of the Armed Services may well have discrimination on the basis of sex. See *Frontiero v. Richardson,* 411 U.S. 677, 93 S.Ct. 1764, 36 L.Ed.2d 583; cf. *Schlesinger v. Ballard,* 419 U.S. 498, 95 S.Ct. 572, 42 L.Ed.2d 610. But the history of discrimination against women in the military is not on trial in this case.

. . . .

"Discriminatory purpose," however, implies more than intent as volition or intent as awareness of consequences. See *United Jewish Organizations v. Carey,* 430 U.S. 144, 179, 97 S.Ct. 996, 1016, 51 L.Ed.2d 229 (concurring opinion). It implies that the decision maker, in this case a state legislature, selected or reaffirmed a particular course of action at least in part "because of," not merely "in spite of," its adverse effects upon an identifiable group. Yet, nothing in the record demonstrates that this preference for veterans was originally devised or subsequently re-enacted because it would accomplish the collateral goal of keeping women in a stereotypic and predefined place in the Massachusetts Civil Service.

To the contrary, the statutory history shows that the benefit of the preference was consistently offered to "any person" who was a veteran. That benefit has been extended to women under a very broad statutory definition of the term veteran. The preference formula itself, which is the focal point of this challenge, was first adopted—so it appears from this record—out of a perceived need to help a small group of older Civil War veterans. It has since been reaffirmed and extended only to cover new veterans. When the totality of legislative actions establishing and extending the Massachusetts veterans' preference are considered, see *Washington v. Davis,* 426 U.S., at 242, 96 S.Ct., at 2049, the law remains what it purports to be: a preference for veterans of either sex over nonveterans of either sex, not for men over women.

IV

Veterans' hiring preferences represent an awkward—and, many argue, unfair—exception to the widely shared view that merit and merit alone should prevail in the employment policies of government. After a war, such laws have been enacted virtually without opposition. During peacetime, they inevitable have come to be viewed in many quarters as undemocratic and unwise. Absolute and permanent preferences, as the troubled history of this law demonstrates, have always been subject to the objection that they give the veteran more than a square deal. But the Fourteenth Amendment "cannot be made a refuge from ill-advised . . . laws." *District of Columbia v. Brooke*, 214 U.S. 138, 150, 29 S.Ct. 560, 563, 53 L.Ed. 941. The substantial edge granted to veterans by ch. 31, § 23, may reflect unwise policy. The appellee, however, has simply failed to demonstrate that the law in any way reflects a purpose to discriminate on the basis of sex.

The judgment is reversed, and the case is remanded for further proceedings consistent with this opinion.

It is so ordered.

B. De Facto Segregation and the Struggle for Educational Equality

Educational inequality is an issue that plagues the United States. Despite formal integration, de facto segregation exists in public schools throughout the country. *See* GAO, *Better Use of Information Could Help Agencies Identify Disparities and Address Racial Discrimination* (Apr. 2016), https://www.gao.gov/assets/680/676745 .pdf; Richard Rothstein, *For Public Schools, Segregation then, Segregation Since: Education and the Unfinished March*, Econ. Policy Inst. (Aug. 27, 2013), http://www .epi.org/files/2013/Unfinished-March-School-Segregation.pdf. Immediately post-*Brown*, white flight to private schools and to exclusive neighborhoods depleted local resources and left public schools struggling. *See* Monique Langhorne, *The African American Community: Circumventing the Compulsory Education System*, 33 Beverly Hills B. Ass'n J. 12, 19 (2000); Robin D. Barnes, *Black America and School Choice: Charting A New Course*, 106 Yale L.J. 2375, 2383 (1997) (explaining how "court orders to desegregate city schools led most notably to white flight"); Paul Gewirtz, *Remedies and Resistance*, 92 Yale L.J. 585, 639 (1983). Today, schools in poor areas and in communities of color lag behind. *See* Bruce Baker et al., *Is School Funding Fair? A National Report Card*, Education Law Center & Rutgers (Jan. 2017), http://www.edlawcenter.org/assets/files/pdfs/publications /National_Report_Card_2017.pdf; Gary Orfield et al., *Brown at 62: School Segregation by Race, Poverty and State*, Civil Rights Project & UCLA (May 16, 2016), https://www.civilrightsproject.ucla.edu/research/k-12-education/integration-and -diversity/brown-at-62-school-segregation-by-race-poverty-and-state/Brown-at-62 -final-corrected-2.pdf. Meanwhile, the Court quickly moved away from endorsing governmental plans that hoped to rectify hundreds of years of inequality by making racial diversity subject to strict scrutiny. *See Brown v. Bd. of Ed. of Topeka, Shawnee Cty., Kan.*, 347 U.S. 483 (1954), *supplemented sub nom. Brown v. Bd. of Educ. of Topeka, Kan.*, 349 U.S. 294 (1955). Though women and other groups benefit concretely from diversity, Affirmative plans focusing on gender do not trigger strict scrutiny. Gender, therefore, benefits from a lower standard of review under the Fourteenth Amendment.

While the Court tolerated set-asides on the basis of race for a brief time after legal segregation, in *Regents of Univ. of Cal. v. Bakke*, 438 U.S. 265 (1978), the Court declared that quotas and set-asides are illegal and merit strict scrutiny. The Court's approach to the Fourteenth Amendment and affirmative action after *Bakke* consisted in the elimination of quotas and of explicit reliance on race in programs to remedy discrimination. Subsequently came *Grutter v. Bollinger*, 539 U.S. 306 (2003), and *Gratz v. Bollinger*, 539 U.S. 244 (2003), providing the Court the opportunity to determine whether race could ever be one of the factors used to achieve diversity.

In 2003, the Court reviewed two programs at the University of Michigan in *Gratz* and *Grutter*. In *Gratz*, the university allotted specific points in undergraduate admission for race as well as other characteristics (e.g., 5 pts for African Americans, 10 pts for being from the South or being an immigrant). The Court found the specific targeting of race in the program through awarding points was unconstitutional. In *Grutter*, on the other hand, the defendant's race was only one of many factors for admission to the law school. The university demonstrated that it did not rely on race alone, but on the whole individual package. The Court upheld the law school's plan because it showed that it did not rely on race. Grutter and Gratz confirmed that, moving forward, remedying the impact of discrimination and de facto segregation with a particular focus on race is now nearly impossible.

Gratz v. Bollinger
539 U.S. 244 (2003)

Chief Justice Rehnquist delivered the opinion of the Court.

We granted certiorari in this case to decide whether "the University of Michigan's use of racial preferences in undergraduate admissions violate[s] the Equal Protection Clause of the Fourteenth Amendment. . . . Because we find that the manner in which the University considers the race of applicants in its undergraduate admissions guidelines violates these constitutional and statutory provisions, we reverse that portion of the District Court's decision upholding the guidelines.

I

A

Petitioners Jennifer Gratz and Patrick Hamacher both applied for admission to the University of Michigan's (University) College of Literature, Science, and the Arts (LSA) as residents of the State of Michigan. Both petitioners are Caucasian. Gratz, who applied for admission for the fall of 1995, was notified in January of that year that a final decision regarding her admission had been delayed until April. This delay was based upon the University's determination that, although Gratz was "'well qualified,'" she was "'less competitive than the students who ha[d] been admitted on first review.'" App. to Pet. for Cert. 109a. Gratz was notified in April that the LSA was unable to offer her admission. She enrolled in the University of Michigan at Dearborn, from which she graduated in the spring of 1999.

Hamacher applied for admission to the LSA for the fall of 1997. A final decision as to his application was also postponed because, though his "'academic credentials [were] in the qualified range, they [were] not at the level needed for first review admission.'" *Ibid.* Hamacher's application was subsequently denied in April 1997, and he enrolled at Michigan State University.

In October 1997, Gratz and Hamacher filed a lawsuit in the United States District Court for the Eastern District of Michigan against the University, the LSA, James Duderstadt, and Lee Bollinger. Petitioners' complaint was a class-action suit alleging "violations and threatened violations of the rights of the plaintiffs and the class they represent to equal protection of the laws under the Fourteenth Amendment . . . , and for racial discrimination in violation of 42 U.S.C. §§ 1981, 1983 and 2000d *et seq.*" App. 33. Petitioners sought, *inter alia,* compensatory and punitive damages for past violations, declaratory relief finding that respondents violated petitioners' "rights to nondiscriminatory treatment," an injunction prohibiting respondents from "continuing to discriminate on the basis of race in violation of the Fourteenth Amendment," and an order requiring the LSA to offer Hamacher admission as a transfer student. *Id.,* at 40.

. . . .

B

The University has changed its admissions guidelines a number of times during the period relevant to this litigation, and we summarize the most significant of these changes briefly. The University's Office of Undergraduate Admissions (OUA) oversees the LSA admissions process. In order to promote consistency in the review of the large number of applications received, the OUA uses written guidelines for each academic year. Admissions counselors make admissions decisions in accordance with these guidelines.

OUA considers a number of factors in making admissions decisions, including high school grades, standardized test scores, high school quality, curriculum strength, geography, alumni relationships, and leadership. OUA also considers race. During all periods relevant to this litigation, the University has considered African-Americans, Hispanics, and Native Americans to be "underrepresented minorities," and it is undisputed that the University admits "virtually every qualified . . . applicant" from these groups. App. to Pet. for Cert. 111a.

During 1995 and 1996, OUA counselors evaluated applications according to grade point average combined with what were referred to as the "SCUGA" factors. These factors included the quality of an applicant's high school (S), the strength of an applicant's high school curriculum (C), an applicant's unusual circumstances (U), an applicant's geographical residence (G), and an applicant's alumni relationships (A). After these scores were combined to produce an applicant's "GPA 2" score, the reviewing admissions counselors referenced a set of "Guidelines" tables, which listed GPA 2 ranges on the vertical axis, and American College Test/Scholastic Aptitude Test (ACT/SAT) scores on the horizontal axis. Each table was divided into cells that included one or more courses of action to be taken, including admit, reject, delay for additional information, or postpone for reconsideration.

In both years, applicants with the same GPA 2 score and ACT/SAT score were subject to different admissions outcomes based upon their racial or ethnic status. For example, as a Caucasian in-state applicant, Gratz's GPA 2 score and ACT score placed her within a cell calling for a postponed decision on her application. An in-state or out-of-state minority applicant with Gratz's scores would have fallen within a cell calling for admission.

In 1997, the University modified its admissions procedure. Specifically, the formula for calculating an applicant's GPA 2 score was restructured to include additional point values under the "U" category in the SCUGA factors. Under this new system, applicants could receive points for underrepresented minority status, socioeconomic disadvantage, or attendance at a high school with a predominantly underrepresented minority population, or underrepresentation in the unit to which the student was applying (for example, men who sought to pursue a career in nursing). Under the 1997 procedures, Hamacher's GPA 2 score and ACT score placed him in a cell on the in-state applicant table calling for postponement of a final admissions decision. An underrepresented minority applicant placed in the same cell would generally have been admitted.

Beginning with the 1998 academic year, the OUA dispensed with the Guidelines tables and the SCUGA point system in favor of a "selection index," on which an applicant could score a maximum of 150 points. This index was divided linearly into ranges generally calling for admissions dispositions as follows: 100–150 (admit); 95–99 (admit or postpone); 90–94 (postpone or admit); 75–89 (delay or postpone); 74 and below (delay or reject).

Each application received points based on high school grade point average, standardized test scores, academic quality of an applicant's high school, strength or weakness of high school curriculum, in-state residency, alumni relationship, personal essay, and personal achievement or leadership. Of particular significance here, under a "miscellaneous" category, an applicant was entitled to 20 points based upon his or her membership in an underrepresented racial or ethnic minority group. The University explained that the "'development of the selection index for admissions in 1998 changed only the mechanics, not the substance, of how race and ethnicity [were] considered in admissions.'" App. to Pet. for Cert. 116a.

In all application years from 1995 to 1998, the guidelines provided that qualified applicants from underrepresented minority groups be admitted as soon as possible in light of the University's belief that such applicants were more likely to enroll if promptly notified of their admission. Also from 1995 through 1998, the University carefully managed its rolling admissions system to permit consideration of certain applications submitted later in the academic year through the use of "protected seats." Specific groups—including athletes, foreign students, ROTC candidates, and underrepresented minorities—were "protected categories" eligible for these seats. A committee called the Enrollment Working Group (EWG) projected how many applicants from each of these protected categories the University was likely to receive after a given date and then paced admissions decisions to permit full consideration of expected applications from these groups. If this space was not filled by qualified candidates from the designated groups toward the end of the admissions season, it was then used to admit qualified candidates remaining in the applicant pool, including those on the waiting list.

During 1999 and 2000, the OUA used the selection index, under which every applicant from an underrepresented racial or ethnic minority group was awarded 20 points. Starting in 1999, however, the University established an Admissions Review Committee (ARC), to provide an additional level of consideration for some applications. Under the new system, counselors may, in their discretion, "flag" an application for the ARC to review after determining that the applicant (1) is academically prepared to succeed at the University, (2) has achieved a minimum selection index score, and (3) possesses a quality or characteristic important to the University's composition of its freshman class, such as high class rank, unique life experiences, challenges, circumstances, interests or talents, socioeconomic disadvantage, and underrepresented race, ethnicity, or geography. After reviewing "flagged" applications, the ARC determines whether to admit, defer, or deny each applicant.

[Pursuant to the class action suit, the] District Court . . . certified two questions for interlocutory appeal to the Sixth Circuit pursuant to 28 U.S.C. § 1292(b). Both parties appealed aspects of the District Court's rulings, and the Court of Appeals heard the case en banc on the same day as *Grutter v. Bollinger.* The Sixth Circuit later issued an opinion in *Grutter*, upholding the admissions program used by the University of Michigan Law School, and the petitioner in that case sought a writ of certiorari from this Court. Petitioners asked this Court to grant certiorari in this case as well, despite the fact that the Court of Appeals had not yet rendered a judgment, so that this Court could address the constitutionality of the consideration of race in university admissions in a wider range of circumstances. We did so. See 537 U.S. 1044, 123 S.Ct. 617, 154 L.Ed.2d 514 (2002).

II

As they have throughout the course of this litigation, petitioners contend that the University's consideration of race in its undergraduate admissions decisions violates § 1 of the Equal Protection Clause of the Fourteenth Amendment, Title VI, and 42

U.S.C. § 1981. . . . [In a portion of the opinion, omitted here, the Court resolves that the parties meet the requirements for standing to bring their claim.]

. . . .

Petitioners argue, first and foremost, that the University's use of race in undergraduate admissions violates the Fourteenth Amendment. Specifically, they contend that this Court has only sanctioned the use of racial classifications to remedy identified discrimination, a justification on which respondents have never relied. Brief for Petitioners 15–16. Petitioners further argue that "diversity as a basis for employing racial preferences is simply too open-ended, ill-defined, and indefinite to constitute a compelling interest capable of supporting narrowly-tailored means." *Id.,* at 17–18, 40–41. But for the reasons set forth today in *Grutter v. Bollinger, ante,* 539 U.S., at 327–333, 123 S.Ct. 2325, 2003 WL 21433492, the Court has rejected these arguments of petitioners.

Petitioners alternatively argue that even if the University's interest in diversity can constitute a compelling state interest, the District Court erroneously concluded that the University's use of race in its current freshman admissions policy is narrowly tailored to achieve such an interest. Petitioners argue that the guidelines the University began using in 1999 do not "remotely resemble the kind of consideration of race and ethnicity that Justice Powell endorsed in *Bakke.*" Brief for Petitioners 18. Respondents reply that the University's current admissions program *is* narrowly tailored and avoids the problems of the Medical School of the University of California at Davis program (U.C. Davis) rejected by Justice Powell. They claim that their program "hews closely" to both the admissions program described by Justice Powell as well as the Harvard College admissions program that he endorsed. Brief for Respondent Bollinger et al 32. Specifically, respondents contend that the LSA's policy provides the individualized consideration that "Justice Powell considered a hallmark of a constitutionally appropriate admissions program." *Id.,* at 35. For the reasons set out below, we do not agree.

It is by now well established that "all racial classifications reviewable under the Equal Protection Clause must be strictly scrutinized." *Adarand Constructors, Inc. v. Peña,* 515 U.S. 200, 224, 115 S.Ct. 2097, 132 L.Ed.2d 158 (1995). This "'standard of review . . . is not dependent on the race of those burdened or benefited by a particular classification.'" *Ibid.* (quoting *Richmond v. J.A. Croson Co.,* 488 U.S. 469, 494, 109 S.Ct. 706, 102 L.Ed.2d 854 (1989) (plurality opinion)). Thus, "any person, of whatever race, has the right to demand that any governmental actor subject to the Constitution justify any racial classification subjecting that person to unequal treatment under the strictest of judicial scrutiny." *Adarand,* 515 U.S., at 224, 115 S.Ct. 2097.

To withstand our strict scrutiny analysis, respondents must demonstrate that the University's use of race in its current admissions program employs "narrowly tailored measures that further compelling governmental interests." *Id.,* at 227, 115 S. Ct. 2097. Because "[r]acial classifications are simply too pernicious to permit any but the most exact connection between justification and classification," *Fullilove v. Klutznick,* 448 U.S. 448, 537, 100 S.Ct. 2758, 65 L.Ed.2d 902 (1980) (Stevens, J., dissenting), our review of whether such requirements have been met must entail "'a most searching examination.'" *Adarand, supra,* at 223, 115 S.Ct. 2097 (quoting *Wygant v. Jackson Bd. of Ed.,* 476 U.S. 267, 273, 106 S.Ct. 1842, 90 L.Ed.2d 260 (1986) (plurality opinion of Powell, J.)). We find that the University's policy, which automatically distributes 20 points, or one-fifth of the points needed to guarantee admission, to every single "underrepresented minority" applicant solely because of race, is not narrowly tailored to achieve the interest in educational diversity that respondents claim justifies their program.

In *Bakke,* Justice Powell reiterated that "[p]referring members of any one group for no reason other than race or ethnic origin is discrimination for its own sake." 438 U.S., at 307, 98 S.Ct. 2733. He then explained, however, that in his view it would be permissible for a university to employ an admissions program in which "race or ethnic background may be deemed a 'plus' in a particular applicant's file." *Id.,* at 317, 98 S.Ct. 2733. He explained that such a program might allow for "[t]he file of a particular black applicant [to] be examined for his potential contribution to diversity without the factor of race being decisive when compared, for example, with that of an applicant identified as an Italian-American if the latter is thought to exhibit qualities more likely to promote beneficial educational pluralism." *Ibid.* Such a system, in Justice Powell's view, would be "flexible enough to consider all pertinent elements of diversity in light of the particular qualifications of each applicant." *Ibid.*

Justice Powell's opinion in *Bakke* emphasized the importance of considering each particular applicant as an individual, assessing all of the qualities that individual possesses, and in turn, evaluating that individual's ability to contribute to the unique setting of higher education. The admissions program Justice Powell described, however, did not contemplate that any single characteristic automatically ensured a specific and identifiable contribution to a university's diversity. See *id.,* at 315, 98 S.Ct. 2733. See also *Metro Broadcasting, Inc. v. FCC,* 497 U.S. 547, 618, 110 S.Ct. 2997, 111 L.Ed.2d 445 (1990) (O'Connor, J., dissenting) (concluding that the Federal Communications Commission's policy, which "embodie[d] the related notions . . . that a particular applicant, by virtue of race or ethnicity alone, is more valued than other applicants because [the applicant is] 'likely to provide [a] distinct perspective,'" "impermissibly value[d] individuals" based on a presumption that "persons think in a manner associated with their race"). Instead, under the approach Justice Powell described, each characteristic of a particular applicant was to be considered in assessing the applicant's entire application.

The current LSA policy does not provide such individualized consideration. The LSA's policy automatically distributes 20 points to every single applicant from an "underrepresented minority" group, as defined by the University. The only consideration that accompanies this distribution of points is a factual review of an application to determine whether an individual is a member of one of these minority groups. Moreover, unlike Justice Powell's example, where the race of a "particular black applicant" could be considered without being decisive, see *Bakke*, 438 U.S., at 317, 98 S.Ct. 2733, the LSA's automatic distribution of 20 points has the effect of making "the factor of race . . . decisive" for virtually every minimally qualified underrepresented minority applicant. *Ibid.*

Also instructive in our consideration of the LSA's system is the example provided in the description of the Harvard College Admissions Program, which Justice Powell both discussed in, and attached to, his opinion in *Bakke*. The example was included to "illustrate the kind of significance attached to race" under the Harvard College program. *Id.*, at 324, 98 S.Ct. 2733. It provided as follows:

> "The Admissions Committee, with only a few places left to fill, might find itself forced to choose between A, the child of a successful black physician in an academic community with promise of superior academic performance, and B, a black who grew up in an inner-city ghetto of semi-literate parents whose academic achievement was lower but who had demonstrated energy and leadership as well as an apparently abiding interest in black power. If a good number of black students much like A but few like B had already been admitted, the Committee might prefer B; and vice versa. If C, a white student with extraordinary artistic talent, were also seeking one of the remaining places, his unique quality might give him an edge over both A and B. Thus, the critical criteria are often individual qualities or experience *not dependent upon race but sometimes associated with it.*" *Ibid.* (emphasis added).

This example further demonstrates the problematic nature of the LSA's admissions system. Even if student C's "extraordinary artistic talent" rivaled that of Monet or Picasso, the applicant would receive, at most, five points under the LSA's system. See App. 234–235. At the same time, every single underrepresented minority applicant, including students A and B, would automatically receive 20 points for submitting an application. Clearly, the LSA's system does not offer applicants the individualized selection process described in Harvard's example. Instead of considering how the differing backgrounds, experiences, and characteristics of students A, B, and C might benefit the University, admissions counselors reviewing LSA applications would simply award both A and B 20 points because their applications indicate that they are African-American, and student C would receive up to 5 points for his "extraordinary talent."

Respondents emphasize the fact that the LSA has created the possibility of an applicant's file being flagged for individualized consideration by the ARC. We think that the flagging program only emphasizes the flaws of the University's system as a whole when compared to that described by Justice Powell. Again, students A, B, and C illustrate the point. First, student A would never be flagged. This is because, as the University has conceded, the effect of automatically awarding 20 points is that virtually every qualified underrepresented minority applicant is admitted. Student A, an applicant "with promise of superior academic performance," would certainly fit this description. Thus, the result of the automatic distribution of 20 points is that the University would never consider student A's individual background, experiences, and characteristics to assess his individual "potential contribution to diversity," *Bakke, supra,* at 317, 98 S.Ct. 2733. Instead, every applicant like student A would simply be admitted.

It is possible that students B and C would be flagged and considered as individuals. This assumes that student B was not already admitted because of the automatic 20-point distribution, and that student C could muster at least 70 additional points. But the fact that the "review committee can look at the applications individually and ignore the points," once an application is flagged, Tr. of Oral Arg. 42, is of little comfort under our strict scrutiny analysis. The record does not reveal precisely how many applications are flagged for this individualized consideration, but it is undisputed that such consideration is the exception and not the rule in the operation of the LSA's admissions program. See App. to Pet. for Cert. 117a ("The ARC reviews only a portion of all of the applications. The bulk of admissions decisions are executed based on selection index score parameters set by the EWG"). Additionally, this individualized review is only provided *after* admissions counselors automatically distribute the University's version of a "plus" that makes race a decisive factor for virtually every minimally qualified underrepresented minority applicant.

Respondents contend that "[t]he volume of applications and the presentation of applicant information make it impractical for [LSA] to use the . . . admissions system" upheld by the Court today in *Grutter.* Brief for Respondent Bollinger et al. 6, n. 8. But the fact that the implementation of a program capable of providing individualized consideration might present administrative challenges does not render constitutional an otherwise problematic system. See *J.A. Croson Co.,* 488 U.S., at 508, 109 S.Ct. 706 (citing *Frontiero v. Richardson,* 411 U.S. 677, 690, 93 S.Ct. 1764, 36 L.Ed.2d 583 (1973) (plurality opinion of Brennan, J.) (rejecting "'administrative convenience'" as a determinant of constitutionality in the face of a suspect classification)). Nothing in Justice Powell's opinion in *Bakke* signaled that a university may employ whatever means it desires to achieve the stated goal of diversity without regard to the limits imposed by our strict scrutiny analysis.

We conclude, therefore, that because the University's use of race in its current freshman admissions policy is not narrowly tailored to achieve respondents' asserted compelling interest in diversity, the admissions policy violates the Equal Protection Clause of the Fourteenth Amendment. We further find that the admissions policy also violates Title VI and 42 U.S.C. § 1981. Accordingly, we reverse that portion of the District Court's decision granting respondents summary judgment with respect to liability and remand the case for proceedings consistent with this opinion.

It is so ordered.

Grutter v. Bollinger

539 U.S. 306 (2003)

JUSTICE O'CONNOR delivered the opinion of the Court.

This case requires us to decide whether the use of race as a factor in student admissions by the University of Michigan Law School (Law School) is unlawful.

I

A

The Law School ranks among the Nation's top law schools. It receives more than 3,500 applications each year for a class of around 350 students. . . . In 1992, the dean of the Law School charged a faculty committee with crafting a written admissions policy to implement these goals. In particular, the Law School sought to ensure that its efforts to achieve student body diversity complied with this Court's most recent ruling on the use of race in university admissions. See *Regents of Univ. of Cal. v. Bakke,* 438 U.S. 265, 98 S.Ct. 2733, 57 L.Ed.2d 750 (1978). Upon the unanimous adoption of the committee's report by the Law School faculty, it became the Law School's official admissions policy.

The hallmark of that policy is its focus on academic ability coupled with a flexible assessment of applicants' talents, experiences, and potential "to contribute to the learning of those around them." App. 111. The policy requires admissions officials to evaluate each applicant based on all the information available in the file, including a personal statement, letters of recommendation, and an essay describing the ways in which the applicant will contribute to the life and diversity of the Law School. *Id.,* at 83–84, 114–121. In reviewing an applicant's file, admissions officials must consider the applicant's undergraduate grade point average (GPA) and Law School Admission Test (LSAT) score because they are important (if imperfect) predictors of academic success in law school. *Id.,* at 112. The policy stresses that "no applicant should be admitted unless we expect that applicant to do well enough to graduate with no serious academic problems." *Id.,* at 111.

The policy makes clear, however, that even the highest possible score does not guarantee admission to the Law School. *Id.,* at 113. Nor does a low score automatically disqualify an applicant. *Ibid.* Rather, the policy requires admissions officials to look beyond grades and test scores to other criteria that are important to the Law School's educational objectives. *Id.,* at 114. So-called "'soft' variables" such as "the enthusiasm of recommenders, the quality of the undergraduate institution, the quality of the applicant's essay, and the areas and difficulty of undergraduate course selection" are all brought to bear in assessing an "applicant's likely contributions to the intellectual and social life of the institution." *Ibid.*

The policy aspires to "achieve that diversity which has the potential to enrich everyone's education and thus make a law school class stronger than the sum of its parts." *Id.,* at 118. The policy does not restrict the types of diversity contributions eligible for "substantial weight" in the admissions process, but instead recognizes "many possible bases for diversity admissions." *Id.*, at 118, 120. The policy does, however, reaffirm the Law School's longstanding commitment to "one particular type of diversity," that is, "racial and ethnic diversity with special reference to the inclusion of students from groups which have been historically discriminated against, like African-Americans, Hispanics and Native Americans, who without this commitment might not be represented in our student body in meaningful numbers." *Id.*, at 120. By enrolling a "'critical mass' of [underrepresented] minority students," the Law School seeks to "ensur[e] their ability to make unique contributions to the character of the Law School." *Id.*, at 120–121.

The policy does not define diversity "solely in terms of racial and ethnic status." *Id.*, at 121. Nor is the policy "insensitive to the competition among all students for admission to the [L]aw [S]chool." *Ibid.* Rather, the policy seeks to guide admissions officers in "producing classes both diverse and academically outstanding, classes made up of students who promise to continue the tradition of outstanding contribution by Michigan Graduates to the legal profession." *Ibid.*

B

Petitioner Barbara Grutter is a white Michigan resident who applied to the Law School in 1996 with a 3.8 GPA and 161 LSAT score. The Law School initially placed petitioner on a waiting list, but subsequently rejected her application. In December 1997, petitioner filed suit in the United States District Court for the Eastern District of Michigan against the Law School, the Regents of the University of Michigan, Lee Bollinger (Dean of the Law School from 1987 to 1994, and President of the University of Michigan from 1996 to 2002), Jeffrey Lehman (Dean of the Law School), and Dennis Shields (Director of Admissions at the Law School from 1991 until 1998). Petitioner alleged that respondents discriminated against her on the basis of race in violation of the Fourteenth Amendment; Title VI of the Civil Rights Act of 1964, 78 Stat. 252, 42 U.S.C. § 2000d; and Rev. Stat. § 1977, as amended, 42 U.S.C. § 1981.

Petitioner further alleged that her application was rejected because the Law School uses race as a "predominant" factor, giving applicants who belong to certain minority groups "a significantly greater chance of admission than students with similar credentials from disfavored racial groups." App. 33–34. Petitioner also alleged that respondents "had no compelling interest to justify their use of race in the admissions process." *Id.*, at 34. Petitioner requested compensatory and punitive damages, an order requiring the Law School to offer her admission, and an injunction prohibiting the Law School from continuing to discriminate on the basis of race. *Id.*, at 36. Petitioner clearly has standing to bring this lawsuit. *Northeastern Fla. Chapter, Associated Gen. Contractors of America v. Jacksonville,* 508 U.S. 656, 666, 113 S.Ct. 2297, 124 L.Ed.2d 586 (1993).

The District Court granted petitioner's motion for class certification and for bifurcation of the trial into liability and damages phases. The class was defined as "'all persons who (A) applied for and were not granted admission to the University of Michigan Law School for the academic years since (and including) 1995 until the time that judgment is entered herein; and (B) were members of those racial or ethnic groups, including Caucasian, that Defendants treated less favorably in considering their applications for admission to the Law School.'" App. to Pet. for Cert. 191a–192a.

. . . .

In an attempt to quantify the extent to which the Law School actually considers race in making admissions decisions, the parties introduced voluminous evidence at trial. Relying on data obtained from the Law School, petitioner's expert, Dr. Kinley Larntz, generated and analyzed "admissions grids" for the years in question (1995–2000). These grids show the number of applicants and the number of admittees for all combinations of GPAs and LSAT scores. Dr. Larntz made "'cell-by-cell'" comparisons between applicants of different races to determine whether a statistically significant relationship existed between race and admission rates. He concluded that membership in certain minority groups "'is an extremely strong factor in the decision for acceptance,'" and that applicants from these minority groups "'are given an extremely large allowance for admission'" as compared to applicants who are members of nonfavored groups. *Id.,* at 218a–220a. Dr. Larntz conceded, however, that race is not the predominant factor in the Law School's admissions calculus. 12 Tr. 11–13 (Feb. 10, 2001).

Dr. Stephen Raudenbush, the Law School's expert, focused on the predicted effect of eliminating race as a factor in the Law School's admission process. In Dr. Raudenbush's view, a race-blind admissions system would have a "'very dramatic,'" negative effect on underrepresented minority admissions. App. to Pet. for Cert. 223a. He testified that in 2000, 35 percent of underrepresented minority applicants were admitted. *Ibid.* Dr. Raudenbush predicted that if race were not considered, only 10 percent of those applicants would have been admitted. *Ibid.* Under this scenario, underrepresented minority students would have constituted 4 percent of the entering class in 2000 instead of the actual figure of 14.5 percent. *Ibid.*

In the end, the District Court concluded that the Law School's use of race as a factor in admissions decisions was unlawful. Applying strict scrutiny, the District Court determined that the Law School's asserted interest in assembling a diverse student body was not compelling because "the attainment of a racially diverse class . . . was not recognized as such by *Bakke* and it is not a remedy for past discrimination." *Id.,* at 246a. The District Court went on to hold that even if diversity were compelling, the Law School had not narrowly tailored its use of race to further that interest. The District Court granted petitioner's request for declaratory relief and enjoined the Law School from using race as a factor in its admissions decisions. The Court of Appeals entered a stay of the injunction pending appeal.

Sitting en banc, the Court of Appeals reversed the District Court's judgment and vacated the injunction. . . .

We granted certiorari, 537 U.S. 1043, 123 S.Ct. 617, 154 L.Ed.2d 514 (2002), to resolve the disagreement among the Courts of Appeals on a question of national importance: Whether diversity is a compelling interest that can justify the narrowly tailored use of race in selecting applicants for admission to public universities. Compare *Hopwood v. Texas*, 78 F.3d 932 (C.A.5 1996) *(Hopwood I)* (holding that diversity is not a compelling state interest), with *Smith v. University of Wash. Law School*, 233 F.3d 1188 (C.A.9 2000) (holding that it is).

II

A

We last addressed the use of race in public higher education over 25 years ago. In the landmark *Bakke* case, we reviewed a racial set-aside program that reserved 16 out of 100 seats in a medical school class for members of certain minority groups. 438 U.S. 265, 98 S.Ct. 2733, 57 L.Ed.2d 750 (1978). The decision produced six separate opinions, none of which commanded a majority of the Court. Four Justices would have upheld the program against all attack on the ground that the government can use race to "remedy disadvantages cast on minorities by past racial prejudice." *Id.*, at 325, 98 S.Ct. 2733 (joint opinion of Brennan, White, Marshall, and Blackmun, JJ., concurring in judgment in part and dissenting in part). Four other Justices avoided the constitutional question altogether and struck down the program on statutory grounds. *Id.*, at 408, 98 S.Ct. 2733 (opinion of Stevens, J., joined by Burger, C.J., and Stewart and Rehnquist, JJ., concurring in judgment in part and dissenting in part). Justice Powell provided a fifth vote not only for invalidating the set-aside program, but also for reversing the state court's injunction against any use of race whatsoever. The only holding for the Court in *Bakke* was that a "State has a substantial interest that legitimately may be served by a properly devised admissions program involving the competitive consideration of race and ethnic origin." *Id.*, at 320, 98 S.Ct. 2733. Thus, we reversed that part of the lower court's judgment that enjoined the university "from any consideration of the race of any applicant." *Ibid.*

Since this Court's splintered decision in *Bakke*, Justice Powell's opinion announcing the judgment of the Court has served as the touchstone for constitutional analysis of race-conscious admissions policies. Public and private universities across the Nation have modeled their own admissions programs on Justice Powell's views on permissible race-conscious policies. See, *e.g.*, Brief for Judith Areen et al. as *Amici Curiae* 12–13 (law school admissions programs employ "methods designed from and based on Justice Powell's opinion in *Bakke*"); Brief for Amherst College et al. as *Amici Curiae* 27 ("After *Bakke,* each of the *amici* (and undoubtedly other selective colleges and universities as well) reviewed their admissions procedures in light of Justice Powell's opinion . . . and set sail accordingly"). We therefore discuss Justice Powell's opinion in some detail.

Justice Powell began by stating that "[t]he guarantee of equal protection cannot mean one thing when applied to one individual and something else when applied to a person of another color. If both are not accorded the same protection, then it is not equal." *Bakke*, 438 U.S., at 289–290, 98 S.Ct. 2733. In Justice Powell's view, when governmental decisions "touch upon an individual's race or ethnic background, he is entitled to a judicial determination that the burden he is asked to bear on that basis is precisely tailored to serve a compelling governmental interest." *Id.*, at 299, 98 S.Ct. 2733. Under this exacting standard, only one of the interests asserted by the university survived Justice Powell's scrutiny.

First, Justice Powell rejected an interest in "'reducing the historic deficit of traditionally disfavored minorities in medical schools and in the medical profession'" as an unlawful interest in racial balancing. *Id.*, at 306–307, 98 S.Ct. 2733. Second, Justice Powell rejected an interest in remedying societal discrimination because such measures would risk placing unnecessary burdens on innocent third parties "who bear no responsibility for whatever harm the beneficiaries of the special admissions program are thought to have suffered." *Id.*, at 310, 98 S.Ct. 2733. Third, Justice Powell rejected an interest in "increasing the number of physicians who will practice in communities currently underserved," concluding that even if such an interest could be compelling in some circumstances the program under review was not "geared to promote that goal." *Id.*, at 306, 310, 98 S.Ct. 2733.

Justice Powell approved the university's use of race to further only one interest: "the attainment of a diverse student body." *Id.*, at 311, 98 S.Ct. 2733. With the important proviso that "constitutional limitations protecting individual rights may not be disregarded," Justice Powell grounded his analysis in the academic freedom that "long has been viewed as a special concern of the First Amendment." *Id.*, at 312, 314, 98 S.Ct. 2733. Justice Powell emphasized that nothing less than the "'nation's future depends upon leaders trained through wide exposure' to the ideas and mores of students as diverse as this Nation of many peoples." *Id.*, at 313, 98 S.Ct. 2733 (quoting *Keyishian v. Board of Regents of Univ. of State of N. Y.*, 385 U.S. 589, 603, 87 S.Ct. 675, 17 L.Ed.2d 629 (1967)). In seeking the "right to select those students who will contribute the most to the 'robust exchange of ideas,'" a university seeks "to achieve a goal that is of paramount importance in the fulfillment of its mission." 438 U.S., at 313, 98 S.Ct. 2733. Both "tradition and experience lend support to the view that the contribution of diversity is substantial." *Ibid.*

Justice Powell was, however, careful to emphasize that in his view race "is only one element in a range of factors a university properly may consider in attaining the goal of a heterogeneous student body." *Id.*, at 314, 98 S.Ct. 2733. For Justice Powell, "[i]t is not an interest in simple ethnic diversity, in which a specified percentage of the student body is in effect guaranteed to be members of selected ethnic groups," that can justify the use of race. *Id.*, at 315, 98 S.Ct. 2733. Rather, "[t]he diversity that furthers a compelling state interest encompasses a far broader array of qualifications and characteristics of which racial or ethnic origin is but a single though important element." *Ibid.*

. . . .

B

The Equal Protection Clause provides that no State shall "deny to any person within its jurisdiction the equal protection of the laws." U.S. Const., Amdt. 14, § 2. Because the Fourteenth Amendment "protect[s] *persons,* not *groups,*" all "governmental action based on race — a *group* classification long recognized as in most circumstances irrelevant and therefore prohibited — should be subjected to detailed judicial inquiry to ensure that the *personal* right to equal protection of the laws has not been infringed." *Adarand Constructors, Inc. v. Peña,* 515 U.S. 200, 227, 115 S.Ct. 2097, 132 L.Ed.2d 158 (1995) (emphasis in original; internal quotation marks and citation omitted). We are a "free people whose institutions are founded upon the doctrine of equality." *Loving v. Virginia,* 388 U.S. 1, 11, 87 S.Ct. 1817, 18 L.Ed.2d 1010 (1967) (internal quotation marks and citation omitted). It follows from that principle that "government may treat people differently because of their race only for the most compelling reasons." *Adarand Constructors, Inc. v. Peña,* 515 U.S., at 227, 115 S. Ct. 2097.

We have held that all racial classifications imposed by government "must be analyzed by a reviewing court under strict scrutiny." *Ibid.* This means that such classifications are constitutional only if they are narrowly tailored to further compelling governmental interests. "Absent searching judicial inquiry into the justification for such race-based measures," we have no way to determine what "classifications are 'benign' or 'remedial' and what classifications are in fact motivated by illegitimate notions of racial inferiority or simple racial politics." *Richmond v. J.A. Croson Co.,* 488 U.S. 469, 493, 109 S.Ct. 706, 102 L.Ed.2d 854 (1989) (plurality opinion). We apply strict scrutiny to all racial classifications to "'smoke out' illegitimate uses of race by assuring that [government] is pursuing a goal important enough to warrant use of a highly suspect tool." *Ibid.*

Strict scrutiny is not "strict in theory, but fatal in fact." *Adarand Constructors, Inc. v. Peña, supra,* at 237, 115 S.Ct. 2097 (internal quotation marks and citation omitted). Although all governmental uses of race are subject to strict scrutiny, not all are invalidated by it. As we have explained, "whenever the government treats any person unequally because of his or her race, that person has suffered an injury that falls squarely within the language and spirit of the Constitution's guarantee of equal protection." 515 U.S., at 229–230, 115 S.Ct. 2097. But that observation "says nothing about the ultimate validity of any particular law; that determination is the job of the court applying strict scrutiny." *Id.,* at 230, 115 S.Ct. 2097. When race-based action is necessary to further a compelling governmental interest, such action does not violate the constitutional guarantee of equal protection so long as the narrow-tailoring requirement is also satisfied.

Context matters when reviewing race-based governmental action under the Equal Protection Clause. See *Gomillion v. Lightfoot,* 364 U.S. 339, 343–344, 81 S.Ct. 125, 5 L.Ed.2d 110 (1960) (admonishing that, "in dealing with claims under broad provisions of the Constitution, which derive content by an interpretive process of inclusion and exclusion, it is imperative that generalizations, based on and qualified by the concrete situations that gave rise to them, must not be applied out of context in disregard of variant controlling facts"). In *Adarand Constructors, Inc. v. Peña*, we made clear that strict scrutiny must take "'relevant differences' into account." 515 U.S., at 228, 115 S.Ct. 2097. Indeed, as we explained, that is its "fundamental purpose." *Ibid.* Not every decision influenced by race is equally objectionable, and strict scrutiny is designed to provide a framework for carefully examining the importance and the sincerity of the reasons advanced by the governmental decision maker for the use of race in that particular context.

III

A

With these principles in mind, we turn to the question whether the Law School's use of race is justified by a compelling state interest. Before this Court, as they have throughout this litigation, respondents assert only one justification for their use of race in the admissions process: obtaining "the educational benefits that flow from a diverse student body." Brief for Respondent Bollinger et al. i. In other words, the Law School asks us to recognize, in the context of higher education, a compelling state interest in student body diversity.

We first wish to dispel the notion that the Law School's argument has been foreclosed, either expressly or implicitly, by our affirmative-action cases decided since *Bakke*. It is true that some language in those opinions might be read to suggest that remedying past discrimination is the only permissible justification for race-based governmental action. See, *e.g., Richmond v. J.A. Croson Co., supra,* at 493, 109 S.Ct. 706 (plurality opinion) (stating that unless classifications based on race are "strictly reserved for remedial settings, they may in fact promote notions of racial inferiority and lead to a politics of racial hostility"). But we have never held that the only governmental use of race that can survive strict scrutiny is remedying past discrimination. Nor, since *Bakke*, have we directly addressed the use of race in the context of public higher education. Today, we hold that the Law School has a compelling interest in attaining a diverse student body.

The Law School's educational judgment that such diversity is essential to its educational mission is one to which we defer. The Law School's assessment that diversity will, in fact, yield educational benefits is substantiated by respondents and their *amici*. Our scrutiny of the interest asserted by the Law School is no less strict for taking into account complex educational judgments in an area that lies primarily within the expertise of the university. Our holding today is in keeping with our tradition of giving a degree of deference to a university's academic decisions, within constitutionally prescribed limits. See *Regents of Univ. of Mich. v. Ewing*, 474 U.S. 214, 225, 106 S.Ct. 507, 88 L.Ed.2d 523 (1985); *Board of Curators of Univ. of Mo. v. Horowitz*, 435 U.S. 78, 96, n. 6, 98 S.Ct. 948, 55 L.Ed.2d 124 (1978); *Bakke*, 438 U.S., at 319, n. 53, 98 S.Ct. 2733 (opinion of Powell, J.).

We have long recognized that, given the important purpose of public education and the expansive freedoms of speech and thought associated with the university environment, universities occupy a special niche in our constitutional tradition. See, *e.g., Wieman v. Updegraff,* 344 U.S. 183, 195, 73 S.Ct. 215, 97 L.Ed. 216 (1952) (Frankfurter, J., concurring); *Sweezy v. New Hampshire,* 354 U.S. 234, 250, 77 S.Ct. 1203, 1 L.Ed.2d 1311 (1957); *Shelton v. Tucker,* 364 U.S. 479, 487, 81 S.Ct. 247, 5 L.Ed.2d 231 (1960); *Keyishian v. Board of Regents of Univ. of State of N. Y.,* 385 U.S., at 603, 87 S.Ct. 675. In announcing the principle of student body diversity as a compelling state interest, Justice Powell invoked our cases recognizing a constitutional dimension, grounded in the First Amendment, of educational autonomy: "The freedom of a university to make its own judgments as to education includes the selection of its student body." *Bakke, supra,* at 312, 98 S.Ct. 2733. From this premise, Justice Powell reasoned that by claiming "the right to select those students who will contribute the most to the 'robust exchange of ideas,'" a university "seek[s] to achieve a goal that is of paramount importance in the fulfillment of its mission." 438 U.S., at 313, 98 S.Ct. 2733 (quoting *Keyishian v. Board of Regents of Univ. of State of N.Y., supra,* at 603, 87 S.Ct. 675). Our conclusion that the Law School has a compelling interest in a diverse student body is informed by our view that attaining a diverse student body is at the heart of the Law School's proper institutional mission, and that "good faith" on the part of a university is "presumed" absent "a showing to the contrary." 438 U.S., at 318–319, 98 S.Ct. 2733.

As part of its goal of "assembling a class that is both exceptionally academically qualified and broadly diverse," the Law School seeks to "enroll a 'critical mass' of minority students." Brief for Respondent Bollinger et al. 13. The Law School's interest is not simply "to assure within its student body some specified percentage of a particular group merely because of its race or ethnic origin." *Bakke,* 438 U.S., at 307, 98 S.Ct. 2733 (opinion of Powell, J.). That would amount to outright racial balancing, which is patently unconstitutional. *Ibid.; Freeman v. Pitts,* 503 U.S. 467, 494, 112 S.Ct. 1430, 118 L.Ed.2d 108 (1992) ("Racial balance is not to be achieved for its own sake"); *Richmond v. J.A. Croson Co.,* 488 U.S., at 507, 109 S.Ct. 706. Rather, the Law School's concept of critical mass is defined by reference to the educational benefits that diversity is designed to produce.

These benefits are substantial. As the District Court emphasized, the Law School's admissions policy promotes "cross-racial understanding," helps to break down racial stereotypes, and "enables [students] to better understand persons of different races." App. to Pet. for Cert. 246a. These benefits are "important and laudable," because "classroom discussion is livelier, more spirited, and simply more enlightening and interesting" when the students have "the greatest possible variety of backgrounds." *Id.,* at 246a, 244a.

The Law School's claim of a compelling interest is further bolstered by its *amici,* who point to the educational benefits that flow from student body diversity. In addition to the expert studies and reports entered into evidence at trial, numerous studies show that student body diversity promotes learning outcomes, and "better prepares students for an increasingly diverse workforce and society, and better prepares them as professionals." Brief for American Educational Research Association et al. as *Amici Curiae* 3; see, *e.g.*, W. Bowen & D. Bok, The Shape of the River (1998); Diversity Challenged: Evidence on the Impact of Affirmative Action (G. Orfield & M. Kurlaender eds.2001); Compelling Interest: Examining the Evidence on Racial Dynamics in Colleges and Universities (M. Chang, D. Witt, J. Jones, & K. Hakuta eds.2003).

These benefits are not theoretical but real, as major American businesses have made clear that the skills needed in today's increasingly global marketplace can only be developed through exposure to widely diverse people, cultures, ideas, and viewpoints. Brief for 3M et al. as *Amici Curiae* 5; Brief for General Motors Corp. as *Amicus Curiae* 3–4. What is more, high-ranking retired officers and civilian leaders of the United States military assert that, "[b]ased on [their] decades of experience," a "highly qualified, racially diverse officer corps . . . is essential to the military's ability to fulfill its principle mission to provide national security." Brief for Julius W. Becton, Jr., et al. as *Amici Curiae* 5. The primary sources for the Nation's officer corps are the service academies and the Reserve Officers Training Corps (ROTC), the latter comprising students already admitted to participating colleges and universities. *Ibid.* At present, "the military cannot achieve an officer corps that is *both* highly qualified *and* racially diverse unless the service academies and the ROTC used limited race-conscious recruiting and admissions policies." *Ibid.* (emphasis in original). To fulfill its mission, the military "must be selective in admissions for training and education for the officer corps, *and* it must train and educate a highly qualified, racially diverse officer corps in a racially diverse educational setting." *Id.,* at 29 (emphasis in original). We agree that "[i]t requires only a small step from this analysis to conclude that our country's other most selective institutions must remain both diverse and selective." *Ibid.*

We have repeatedly acknowledged the overriding importance of preparing students for work and citizenship, describing education as pivotal to "sustaining our political and cultural heritage" with a fundamental role in maintaining the fabric of society. *Plyler v. Doe,* 457 U.S. 202, 221, 102 S.Ct. 2382, 72 L.Ed.2d 786 (1982). This Court has long recognized that "education . . . is the very foundation of good citizenship." *Brown v. Board of Education,* 347 U.S. 483, 493, 74 S.Ct. 686, 98 L.Ed. 873 (1954). For this reason, the diffusion of knowledge and opportunity through public institutions of higher education must be accessible to all individuals regardless of race or ethnicity. The United States, as *amicus curiae,* affirms that "[e]nsuring that public institutions are open and available to all segments of American society, including people of all races and ethnicities, represents a paramount government objective." Brief for United States as *Amicus Curiae* 13. And, "[n]owhere is the importance of such openness more acute than in the context of higher education." *Ibid.* Effective participation by members of all racial and ethnic groups in the civic life of our Nation is essential if the dream of one Nation, indivisible, is to be realized.

Moreover, universities, and in particular, law schools, represent the training ground for a large number of our Nation's leaders. *Sweatt v. Painter,* 339 U.S. 629, 634, 70 S.Ct. 848, 94 L.Ed. 1114 (1950) (describing law school as a "proving ground for legal learning and practice"). Individuals with law degrees occupy roughly half the state governorships, more than half the seats in the United States Senate, and more than a third of the seats in the United States House of Representatives. See Brief for Association of American Law Schools as *Amicus Curiae* 5–6. The pattern is even more striking when it comes to highly selective law schools. A handful of these schools accounts for 25 of the 100 United States Senators, 74 United States Courts of Appeals judges, and nearly 200 of the more than 600 United States District Court judges. *Id.,* at 6.

In order to cultivate a set of leaders with legitimacy in the eyes of the citizenry, it is necessary that the path to leadership be visibly open to talented and qualified individuals of every race and ethnicity. All members of our heterogeneous society must have confidence in the openness and integrity of the educational institutions that provide this training. As we have recognized, law schools "cannot be effective in isolation from the individuals and institutions with which the law interacts." See *Sweatt v. Painter, supra,* at 634, 70 S.Ct. 848. Access to legal education (and thus the legal profession) must be inclusive of talented and qualified individuals of every race and ethnicity, so that all members of our heterogeneous society may participate in the educational institutions that provide the training and education necessary to succeed in America.

The Law School does not premise its need for critical mass on "any belief that minority students always (or even consistently) express some characteristic minority viewpoint on any issue." Brief for Respondent Bollinger et al. 30. To the contrary, diminishing the force of such stereotypes is both a crucial part of the Law School's mission, and one that it cannot accomplish with only token numbers of minority students. Just as growing up in a particular region or having particular professional experiences is likely to affect an individual's views, so too is one's own, unique experience of being a racial minority in a society, like our own, in which race unfortunately still matters. The Law School has determined, based on its experience and expertise, that a "critical mass" of underrepresented minorities is necessary to further its compelling interest in securing the educational benefits of a diverse student body.

B

Even in the limited circumstance when drawing racial distinctions is permissible to further a compelling state interest, government is still "constrained in how it may pursue that end: [T]he means chosen to accomplish the [government's] asserted purpose must be specifically and narrowly framed to accomplish that purpose." *Shaw v. Hunt,* 517 U.S. 899, 908, 116 S.Ct. 1894, 135 L.Ed.2d 207 (1996) (internal quotation marks and citation omitted). The purpose of the narrow tailoring requirement is to ensure that "the means chosen 'fit' th[e] compelling goal so closely that there is little or no possibility that the motive for the classification was illegitimate racial prejudice or stereotype." *Richmond v. J.A. Croson Co.,* 488 U.S., at 493, 109 S.Ct. 706 (plurality opinion).

Since *Bakke,* we have had no occasion to define the contours of the narrow-tailoring inquiry with respect to race-conscious university admissions programs. That inquiry must be calibrated to fit the distinct issues raised by the use of race to achieve student body diversity in public higher education. Contrary to Justice Kennedy's assertions, we do not "abando[n] strict scrutiny," see *post,* at 2374 (dissenting opinion). Rather, as we have already explained, *supra,* at 2338, we adhere to *Adarand*'s teaching that the very purpose of strict scrutiny is to take such "relevant differences into account." 515 U.S., at 228, 115 S.Ct. 2097 (internal quotation marks omitted).

To be narrowly tailored, a race-conscious admissions program cannot use a quota system—it cannot "insulat[e] each category of applicants with certain desired qualifications from competition with all other applicants." *Bakke,* 438 U.S., at 315, 98 S. Ct. 2733 (opinion of Powell, J.). Instead, a university may consider race or ethnicity only as a "'plus' in a particular applicant's file," without "insulat[ing] the individual from comparison with all other candidates for the available seats." *Id.,* at 317, 98 S. Ct. 2733. In other words, an admissions program must be "flexible enough to consider all pertinent elements of diversity in light of the particular qualifications of each applicant, and to place them on the same footing for consideration, although not necessarily according them the same weight." *Ibid.*

We find that the Law School's admissions program bears the hallmarks of a narrowly tailored plan. As Justice Powell made clear in *Bakke,* truly individualized consideration demands that race be used in a flexible, nonmechanical way. It follows from this mandate that universities cannot establish quotas for members of certain racial groups or put members of those groups on separate admissions tracks. See *id.,* at 315–316, 98 S.Ct. 2733. Nor can universities insulate applicants who belong to certain racial or ethnic groups from the competition for admission. *Ibid.* Universities can, however, consider race or ethnicity more flexibly as a "plus" factor in the context of individualized consideration of each and every applicant. *Ibid.*

We are satisfied that the Law School's admissions program, like the Harvard plan described by Justice Powell, does not operate as a quota. Properly understood, a "quota" is a program in which a certain fixed number or proportion of opportunities are "reserved exclusively for certain minority groups." *Richmond v. J.A. Croson Co., supra,* at 496, 109 S.Ct. 706 (plurality opinion). . . .

The Law School's goal of attaining a critical mass of underrepresented minority students does not transform its program into a quota. As the Harvard plan described by Justice Powell recognized, there is of course "some relationship between numbers and achieving the benefits to be derived from a diverse student body, and between numbers and providing a reasonable environment for those students admitted." *Id.,* at 323, 98 S.Ct. 2733. . . . To the contrary, the Law School's admissions officers testified without contradiction that they never gave race any more or less weight based on the information contained in these reports. Brief for Respondents Bollinger et al.

43, n. 70 (citing App. in Nos. 01-1447 and 01-1516(CA6), p. 7336). Moreover, as Justice Kennedy concedes, see *post,* at 2372, between 1993 and 1998, the number of African-American, Latino, and Native-American students in each class at the Law School varied from 13.5 to 20.1 percent, a range inconsistent with a quota.

. . . .

That a race-conscious admissions program does not operate as a quota does not, by itself, satisfy the requirement of individualized consideration. When using race as a "plus" factor in university admissions, a university's admissions program must remain flexible enough to ensure that each applicant is evaluated as an individual and not in a way that makes an applicant's race or ethnicity the defining feature of his or her application. The importance of this individualized consideration in the context of a race-conscious admissions program is paramount. See *Bakke,* 438 U.S., at 318, n. 52, 98 S.Ct. 2733 (opinion of Powell, J.) (identifying the "denial . . . of th[e] right to individualized consideration" as the "principal evil" of the medical school's admissions program).

Here, the Law School engages in a highly individualized, holistic review of each applicant's file, giving serious consideration to all the ways an applicant might contribute to a diverse educational environment. The Law School affords this individualized consideration to applicants of all races. There is no policy, either *de jure* or *de facto,* of automatic acceptance or rejection based on any single "soft" variable. Unlike the program at issue in *Gratz v. Bollinger, post,* 539 U.S. 244, 123 S.Ct. 2411, the Law School awards no mechanical, predetermined diversity "bonuses" based on race or ethnicity. . . .

We also find that, like the Harvard plan Justice Powell referenced in *Bakke,* the Law School's race-conscious admissions program adequately ensures that all factors that may contribute to student body diversity are meaningfully considered alongside race in admissions decisions. With respect to the use of race itself, all underrepresented minority students admitted by the Law School have been deemed qualified. By virtue of our Nation's struggle with racial inequality, such students are both likely to have experiences of particular importance to the Law School's mission, and less likely to be admitted in meaningful numbers on criteria that ignore those experiences. See App. 120.

The Law School does not, however, limit in any way the broad range of qualities and experiences that may be considered valuable contributions to student body diversity. To the contrary, the 1992 policy makes clear "[t]here are many possible bases for diversity admissions," and provides examples of admittees who have lived or traveled widely abroad, are fluent in several languages, have overcome personal adversity and family hardship, have exceptional records of extensive community service, and have had successful careers in other fields. *Id.,* at 118–119. The Law School seriously considers each "applicant's promise of making a notable contribution to the class by way of a particular strength, attainment, or characteristic— *e.g.,* an unusual intellectual achievement, employment experience, nonacademic performance, or personal background." *Id.,* at 83–84. All applicants have the opportunity to highlight their own potential diversity contributions through the submission of a personal statement, letters of recommendation, and an essay describing the ways in which the applicant will contribute to the life and diversity of the Law School.

What is more, the Law School actually gives substantial weight to diversity factors besides race. The Law School frequently accepts nonminority applicants with grades and test scores lower than underrepresented minority applicants (and other non-minority applicants) who are rejected. See Brief for Respondent Bollinger et al. 10; App. 121–122. This shows that the Law School seriously weighs many other diversity factors besides race that can make a real and dispositive difference for nonminority applicants as well. By this flexible approach, the Law School sufficiently takes into account, in practice as well as in theory, a wide variety of characteristics besides race and ethnicity that contribute to a diverse student body. . . .

Petitioner and the United States argue that the Law School's plan is not narrowly tailored because race-neutral means exist to obtain the educational benefits of student body diversity that the Law School seeks. We disagree. Narrow tailoring does not require exhaustion of every conceivable race-neutral alternative. Nor does it require a university to choose between maintaining a reputation for excellence or fulfilling a commitment to provide educational opportunities to members of all racial groups. . . . Narrow tailoring does, however, require serious, good faith consideration of workable race-neutral alternatives that will achieve the diversity the university seeks. See *id.,* at 507, 109 S.Ct. 706 (set-aside plan not narrowly tailored where "there does not appear to have been any consideration of the use of race-neutral means"); *Wygant v. Jackson Bd. of Ed., supra,* at 280, n. 6, 106 S.Ct. 1842 (narrow tailoring "require[s] consideration" of "lawful alternative and less restrictive means").

We agree with the Court of Appeals that the Law School sufficiently considered workable race-neutral alternatives. The District Court took the Law School to task for failing to consider race-neutral alternatives such as "using a lottery system" or "decreasing the emphasis for all applicants on undergraduate GPA and LSAT scores." App. to Pet. for Cert. 251a. But these alternatives would require a dramatic sacrifice of diversity, the academic quality of all admitted students, or both.

The Law School's current admissions program considers race as one factor among many, in an effort to assemble a student body that is diverse in ways broader than race. Because a lottery would make that kind of nuanced judgment impossible, it would effectively sacrifice all other educational values, not to mention every other kind of diversity. So too with the suggestion that the Law School simply lower admissions standards for all students, a drastic remedy that would require the Law School to become a much different institution and sacrifice a vital component of its educational mission. The United States advocates "percentage plans," recently adopted by public undergraduate institutions in Texas, Florida, and California, to guarantee admission to all students above a certain class-rank threshold in every high school in the State. Brief for United States as *Amicus Curiae* 14–18. The United

States does not, however, explain how such plans could work for graduate and professional schools. Moreover, even assuming such plans are race-neutral, they may preclude the university from conducting the individualized assessments necessary to assemble a student body that is not just racially diverse, but diverse along all the qualities valued by the university. We are satisfied that the Law School adequately considered race-neutral alternatives currently capable of producing a critical mass without forcing the Law School to abandon the academic selectivity that is the cornerstone of its educational mission.

We acknowledge that "there are serious problems of justice connected with the idea of preference itself." *Bakke,* 438 U.S., at 298, 98 S.Ct. 2733 (opinion of Powell, J.). Narrow tailoring, therefore, requires that a race-conscious admissions program not unduly harm members of any racial group. Even remedial race-based governmental action generally "remains subject to continuing oversight to assure that it will work the least harm possible to other innocent persons competing for the benefit." *Id.,* at 308, 98 S.Ct. 2733. To be narrowly tailored, a race-conscious admissions program must not "unduly burden individuals who are not members of the favored racial and ethnic groups." *Metro Broadcasting, Inc. v. FCC,* 497 U.S. 547, 630, 110 S. Ct. 2997, 111 L.Ed.2d 445 (1990) (O'Connor, J., dissenting).

We are satisfied that the Law School's admissions program does not. Because the Law School considers "all pertinent elements of diversity," it can (and does) select nonminority applicants who have greater potential to enhance student body diversity over underrepresented minority applicants. See *Bakke, supra,* at 317, 98 S.Ct. 2733 (opinion of Powell, J.). . . .

We agree that, in the context of its individualized inquiry into the possible diversity contributions of all applicants, the Law School's race-conscious admissions program does not unduly harm nonminority applicants.

We are mindful, however, that "[a] core purpose of the Fourteenth Amendment was to do away with all governmentally imposed discrimination based on race." *Palmore v. Sidoti,* 466 U.S. 429, 432, 104 S.Ct. 1879, 80 L.Ed.2d 421 (1984). Accordingly, race-conscious admissions policies must be limited in time. This requirement reflects that racial classifications, however compelling their goals, are potentially so dangerous that they may be employed no more broadly than the interest demands. Enshrining a permanent justification for racial preferences would offend this fundamental equal protection principle. We see no reason to exempt race-conscious admissions programs from the requirement that all governmental use of race must have a logical end point. The Law School, too, concedes that all "race-conscious programs must have reasonable durational limits." Brief for Respondent Bollinger et al. 32.

In the context of higher education, the durational requirement can be met by sunset provisions in race-conscious admissions policies and periodic reviews to determine whether racial preferences are still necessary to achieve student body diversity. Universities in California, Florida, and Washington State, where racial preferences in admissions are prohibited by state law, are currently engaged in experimenting with a wide variety of alternative approaches. Universities in other States can and should draw on the most promising aspects of these race-neutral alternatives as they develop. Cf. *United States v. Lopez,* 514 U.S. 549, 581, 115 S.Ct. 1624, 131 L.Ed.2d 626 (1995) (Kennedy, J., concurring) ("[T]he States may perform their role as laboratories for experimentation to devise various solutions where the best solution is far from clear").

. . . .

We take the Law School at its word that it would "like nothing better than to find a race-neutral admissions formula" and will terminate its race-conscious admissions program as soon as practicable. See Brief for Respondent Bollinger et al. 34; *Bakke, supra,* at 317–318, 98 S.Ct. 2733 (opinion of Powell, J.) (presuming good faith of university officials in the absence of a showing to the contrary). It has been 25 years since Justice Powell first approved the use of race to further an interest in student body diversity in the context of public higher education. Since that time, the number of minority applicants with high grades and test scores has indeed increased. See Tr. of Oral Arg. 43. We expect that 25 years from now, the use of racial preferences will no longer be necessary to further the interest approved today.

IV

In summary, the Equal Protection Clause does not prohibit the Law School's narrowly tailored use of race in admissions decisions to further a compelling interest in obtaining the educational benefits that flow from a diverse student body. Consequently, petitioner's statutory claims based on Title VI and 42 U.S.C. § 1981 also fail. See *Bakke, supra,* at 287, 98 S.Ct. 2733 (opinion of Powell, J.) ("Title VI . . . proscribe[s] only those racial classifications that would violate the Equal Protection Clause or the Fifth Amendment"); *General Building Contractors Assn., Inc. v. Pennsylvania,* 458 U.S. 375, 389–391, 102 S.Ct. 3141, 73 L.Ed.2d 835 (1982) (the prohibition against discrimination in § 1981 is co-extensive with the Equal Protection Clause). The judgment of the Court of Appeals for the Sixth Circuit, accordingly, is affirmed.

It is so ordered.

C. Application of the Diversity Rationale Exception to Strict Scrutiny to the K-12 Setting

Parents Involved in Community Schools v. Seattle School District No. 1

551 U.S. 701 (2007)

CHIEF JUSTICE ROBERTS announced the judgment of the Court, and delivered the opinion of the Court with respect to Parts I, II, III-A, and III-C, and an opinion with respect to Parts III-B and IV, in which JUSTICE SCALIA, JUSTICE THOMAS, and JUSTICE ALITO join.

The school districts in these cases voluntarily adopted student assignment plans that rely upon race to determine which public schools certain children may attend. The Seattle school district classifies children as white or nonwhite; the Jefferson County school district as black or "other." In Seattle, this racial classification is used to allocate slots in oversubscribed high schools. In Jefferson County, it is used to make certain elementary school assignments and to rule on transfer requests. In each case, the school district relies upon an individual student's race in assigning that student to a particular school, so that the racial balance at the school falls within a predetermined range based on the racial composition of the school district as a whole. Parents of students denied assignment to particular schools under these plans solely because of their race brought suit, contending that allocating children to different public schools on the basis of race violated the Fourteenth Amendment guarantee of equal protection. The Courts of Appeals below upheld the plans. We granted certiorari, and now reverse.

I

Both cases present the same underlying legal question — whether a public school that had not operated legally segregated schools or has been found to be unitary may choose to classify students by race and rely upon that classification in making school assignments. Although we examine the plans under the same legal framework, the specifics of the two plans, and the circumstances surrounding their adoption, are in some respects quite different.

A

Seattle School District No. 1 operates 10 regular public high schools. In 1998, it adopted the plan at issue in this case for assigning students to these schools. App. in No. 05-908, pp. 90a-92a. The plan allows incoming ninth graders to choose from among any of the district's high schools, ranking however many schools they wish in order of preference.

Some schools are more popular than others. If too many students list the same school as their first choice, the district employs a series of "tiebreakers" to determine who will fill the open slots at the oversubscribed school. The first tiebreaker selects for admission students who have a sibling currently enrolled in the chosen school. The next tiebreaker depends upon the racial composition of the particular school and the race of the individual student. In the district's public schools approximately 41 percent of enrolled students are white; the remaining 59 percent, comprising all other racial groups, are classified by Seattle for assignment purposes as nonwhite. *Id.,* at 38a, 103a. If an oversubscribed school is not within 10 percentage points of the district's overall white/nonwhite racial balance, it is what the district calls "integration positive," and the district employs a tiebreaker that selects for assignment students whose race "will serve to bring the school into balance." *Id.,* at 38a. See *Parents Involved VII,* 426 F.3d 1162, 1169–1170 (C.A.9 2005) (en banc). If it is still necessary to select students for the school after using the racial tiebreaker, the next tiebreaker is the geographic proximity of the school to the student's residence. App. in No. 05-908, at 38a.

Seattle has never operated segregated schools—legally separate schools for students of different races—nor has it ever been subject to court-ordered desegregation. It nonetheless employs the racial tiebreaker in an attempt to address the effects of racially identifiable housing patterns on school assignments. Most white students live in the northern part of Seattle, most students of other racial backgrounds in the southern part. *Parents Involved VII, supra,* at 1166. Four of Seattle's high schools are located in the north—Ballard, Nathan Hale, Ingraham, and Roosevelt—and five in the south—Rainier Beach, Cleveland, West Seattle, Chief Sealth, and Franklin. One school—Garfield—is more or less in the center of Seattle. App. in No. 05-908, at 38a-39a, 45a.

For the 2000–2001 school year, five of these schools were oversubscribed—Ballard, Nathan Hale, Roosevelt, Garfield, and Franklin—so much so that 82 percent of incoming ninth graders ranked one of these schools as their first choice. *Id.,* at 38a. Three of the oversubscribed schools were "integration positive" because the school's white enrollment the previous school year was greater than 51 percent—Ballard, Nathan Hale, and Roosevelt. Thus, more nonwhite students (107, 27, and 82, respectively) who selected one of these three schools as a top choice received placement at the school than would have been the case had race not been considered, and proximity been the next tiebreaker. *Id.,* at 39a-40a. Franklin was "integration positive" because its nonwhite enrollment the previous school year was greater than 69 percent; 89 more white students were assigned to Franklin by operation of the racial tiebreaker in the 2000–2001 school year than otherwise would have been. *Ibid.* Garfield was the only oversubscribed school whose composition during the 1999–2000 school year was within the racial guidelines, although in previous years Garfield's enrollment had been predominantly nonwhite, and the racial tiebreaker had been used to give preference to white students. *Id.,* at 39a.

Petitioner Parents Involved in Community Schools (Parents Involved) is a nonprofit corporation comprising the parents of children who have been or may be denied assignment to their chosen high school in the district because of their race. The concerns of Parents Involved are illustrated by Jill Kurfirst, who sought to enroll her ninth-grade son, Andy Meeks, in Ballard High School's special Biotechnology Career Academy. Andy suffered from attention deficit hyperactivity disorder and dyslexia, but had made good progress with hands-on instruction, and his mother and middle school teachers thought that the smaller biotechnology program held the most promise for his continued success. Andy was accepted into this selective program but, because of the racial tiebreaker, was denied assignment to Ballard High School. *Id.,* at 143a-146a, 152a-160a. Parents Involved commenced this suit in the Western District of Washington, alleging that Seattle's use of race in assignments violated the Equal Protection Clause of the Fourteenth Amendment, Title VI of the Civil Rights Act of 1964, and the Washington Civil Rights Act. *Id.,* at 28a-35a.

. . . .

B

Jefferson County Public Schools operates the public school system in metropolitan Louisville, Kentucky. In 1973 a federal court found that Jefferson County had maintained a segregated school system, *Newburg Area Council, Inc. v. Board of Ed. of Jefferson Cty.*, 489 F.2d 925, 932 (CA6), vacated and remanded, 418 U.S. 918, 94 S.Ct. 3208, 3209, 41 L.Ed.2d 1160, reinstated with modifications, 510 F.2d 1358, 1359 (C.A.6 1974), and in 1975 the District Court entered a desegregation decree. See *Hampton v. Jefferson Cty. Bd. of Ed.*, 72 F.Supp.2d 753, 762–764 (W.D.Ky.1999). Jefferson County operated under this decree until 2000, when the District Court dissolved the decree after finding that the district had achieved unitary status by eliminating "[t]o the greatest extent practicable" the vestiges of its prior policy of segregation. . . .

In 2001, after the decree had been dissolved, Jefferson County adopted the voluntary student assignment plan at issue in this case. App. in No. 05-915, p. 77. Approximately 34 percent of the district's 97,000 students are black; most of the remaining 66 percent are white. *McFarland v. Jefferson Cty. Public Schools*, 330 F.Supp.2d 834, 839–840, and n. 6 (W.D.Ky.2004) (*McFarland I*). The plan requires all nonmagnet schools to maintain a minimum black enrollment of 15 percent, and a maximum black enrollment of 50 percent. App. in No. 05-915, at 81; *McFarland I, supra*, at 842.

At the elementary school level, based on his or her address, each student is designated a "resides" school to which students within a specific geographic area are assigned; elementary resides schools are "grouped into clusters in order to facilitate integration." App. in No. 05-915, at 82. The district assigns students to nonmagnet schools in one of two ways: Parents of kindergartners, first graders, and students new to the district may submit an application indicating a first and second choice among the schools within their cluster; students who do not submit such an application are assigned within the cluster by the district. "Decisions to assign students to schools within each cluster are based on available space within the schools and the racial guidelines in the District's current student assignment plan." *Id.*, at 38. If a school has reached the "extremes of the racial guidelines," a student whose race would contribute to the school's racial imbalance will not be assigned there. *Id.*, at 38–39, 82. After assignment, students at all grade levels are permitted to apply to transfer between nonmagnet schools in the district. Transfers may be requested for any number of reasons, and may be denied because of lack of available space or on the basis of the racial guidelines. *Id.*, at 43.

When petitioner Crystal Meredith moved into the school district in August 2002, she sought to enroll her son, Joshua McDonald, in kindergarten for the 2002–2003 school year. His [residence] school was only a mile from his new home, but it had no available space—assignments had been made in May, and the class was full. Jefferson County assigned Joshua to another elementary school in his cluster, Young Elementary. This school was 10 miles from home, and Meredith sought to transfer Joshua to a school in a different cluster, Bloom Elementary, which—like his resides school—was only a mile from home. See Tr. in *McFarland I*, pp. 1–49 through 1–54

(Dec. 8, 2003). Space was available at Bloom, and intercluster transfers are allowed, but Joshua's transfer was nonetheless denied because, in the words of Jefferson County, "[t]he transfer would have an adverse effect on desegregation compliance" of Young. App. in No. 05-915, at 97.

. . . [Standing discussion omitted.]

III

A

It is well established that when the government distributes burdens or benefits on the basis of individual racial classifications, that action is reviewed under strict scrutiny. *Johnson v. California,* 543 U.S. 499, 505–506, 125 S.Ct. 1141, 160 L.Ed.2d 949 (2005); *Grutter v. Bollinger,* 539 U.S. 306, 326, 123 S.Ct. 2325, 156 L.Ed.2d 304 (2003); *Adarand, supra,* at 224, 115 S.Ct. 2097. As the Court recently reaffirmed, "'racial classifications are simply too pernicious to permit any but the most exact connection between justification and classification.'" *Gratz v. Bollinger,* 539 U.S. 244, 270, 123 S.Ct. 2411, 156 L.Ed.2d 257 (2003) (quoting *Fullilove v. Klutznick,* 448 U.S. 448, 537, 100 S.Ct. 2758, 65 L.Ed.2d 902 (1980) (Stevens, J., dissenting); brackets omitted). In order to satisfy this searching standard of review, the school districts must demonstrate that the use of individual racial classifications in the assignment plans here under review is "narrowly tailored" to achieve a "compelling" government interest. *Adarand, supra,* at 227, 115 S.Ct. 2097.

Without attempting in these cases to set forth all the interests a school district might assert, it suffices to note that our prior cases, in evaluating the use of racial classifications in the school context, have recognized two interests that qualify as compelling. The first is the compelling interest of remedying the effects of past intentional discrimination. See *Freeman v. Pitts,* 503 U.S. 467, 494, 112 S.Ct. 1430, 118 L.Ed.2d 108 (1992). Yet the Seattle public schools have not shown that they were ever segregated by law, and were not subject to court-ordered desegregation decrees. The Jefferson County public schools were previously segregated by law and were subject to a desegregation decree entered in 1975. In 2000, the District Court that entered that decree dissolved it, finding that Jefferson County had "eliminated the vestiges associated with the former policy of segregation and its pernicious effects," and thus had achieved "unitary" status. *Hampton,* 102 F.Supp.2d, at 360. Jefferson County accordingly does not rely upon an interest in remedying the effects of past intentional discrimination in defending its present use of race in assigning students. See Tr. of Oral Arg. in No. 05-915, at 38.

Nor could it. We have emphasized that the harm being remedied by mandatory desegregation plans is the harm that is traceable to segregation, and that "the Constitution is not violated by racial imbalance in the schools, without more." *Milliken v. Bradley,* 433 U.S. 267, 280, n. 14, 97 S.Ct. 2749, 53 L.Ed.2d 745 (1977). See also *Freeman, supra,* at 495–496, 112 S.Ct. 1430; *Dowell,* 498 U.S., at 248, 111 S.Ct. 630; *Milliken v. Bradley,* 418 U.S. 717, 746, 94 S.Ct. 3112, 41 L.Ed.2d 1069 (1974). Once Jefferson County achieved unitary status, it had remedied the constitutional wrong that allowed race-based assignments. Any continued use of race must be justified on some other basis.

The second government interest we have recognized as compelling for purposes of strict scrutiny is the interest in diversity in higher education upheld in *Grutter,* 539 U.S., at 328, 123 S.Ct. 2325. The specific interest found compelling in *Grutter* was student body diversity "in the context of higher education." *Ibid.* The diversity interest was not focused on race alone but encompassed "all factors that may contribute to student body diversity." *Id.,* at 337, 123 S.Ct. 2325. We described the various types of diversity that the law school sought:

> "[The law school's] policy makes clear there are many possible bases for diversity admissions, and provides examples of admittees who have lived or traveled widely abroad, are fluent in several languages, have overcome personal adversity and family hardship, have exceptional records of extensive community service, and have had successful careers in other fields." *Id.,* at 338, 123 S.Ct. 2325 (brackets and internal quotation marks omitted).

The Court quoted the articulation of diversity from Justice Powell's opinion in *Regents of Univ. of Cal. v. Bakke,* 438 U.S. 265, 98 S.Ct. 2733, 57 L.Ed.2d 750 (1978), noting that "it is not an interest in simple ethnic diversity, in which a specified percentage of the student body is in effect guaranteed to be members of selected ethnic groups, that can justify the use of race." *Grutter, supra,* at 324–325, 123 S.Ct. 2325 (citing and quoting *Bakke, supra,* at 314–315, 98 S.Ct. 2733 (opinion of Powell, J.); brackets and internal quotation marks omitted). Instead, what was upheld in *Grutter* was consideration of "a far broader array of qualifications and characteristics of which racial or ethnic origin is but a single though important element." 539 U.S., at 325, 123 S.Ct. 2325 (quoting *Bakke, supra,* at 315, 98 S.Ct. 2733 (opinion of Powell, J.); internal quotation marks omitted).

The entire gist of the analysis in *Grutter* was that the admissions program at issue there focused on each applicant as an individual, and not simply as a member of a particular racial group. The classification of applicants by race upheld in *Grutter* was only as part of a "highly individualized, holistic review," 539 U.S., at 337, 123 S. Ct. 2325. . . .

In the present cases, by contrast, race is not considered as part of a broader effort to achieve "exposure to widely diverse people, cultures, ideas, and viewpoints," *ibid.*; race, for some students, is determinative standing alone. The districts argue that other factors, such as student preferences, affect assignment decisions under their plans, but under each plan when race comes into play, it is decisive by itself. It is not simply one factor weighed with others in reaching a decision, as in *Grutter*; it is *the* factor. Like the University of Michigan undergraduate plan struck down in *Gratz,* 539 U.S., at 275, 123 S.Ct. 2411, the plans here "do not provide for a meaningful individualized review of applicants" but instead rely on racial classifications in a "nonindividualized, mechanical" way, *id.,* at 276, 280, 123 S.Ct. 2411 (O'Connor, J., concurring).

Even when it comes to race, the plans here employ only a limited notion of diversity, viewing race exclusively in white/nonwhite terms in Seattle and black/"other" terms in Jefferson County. But see *Metro Broadcasting, Inc. v. FCC,* 497 U.S. 547, 610, 110 S.Ct. 2997, 111 L.Ed.2d 445 (1990). . . .

B

Perhaps recognizing that reliance on *Grutter* cannot sustain their plans, both school districts assert additional interests, distinct from the interest upheld in *Grutter,* to justify their race-based assignments. In briefing and argument before this Court, Seattle contends that its use of race helps to reduce racial concentration in schools and to ensure that racially concentrated housing patterns do not prevent nonwhite students from having access to the most desirable schools. Brief for Respondents in No. 05-908, at 19. Jefferson County has articulated a similar goal, phrasing its interest in terms of educating its students "in a racially integrated environment." App. in No. 05-915, at 22. Each school district argues that educational and broader socialization benefits flow from a racially diverse learning environment, and each contends that because the diversity they seek is racial diversity—not the broader diversity at issue in *Grutter*—it makes sense to promote that interest directly by relying on race alone.

The parties and their *amici* dispute whether racial diversity in schools in fact has a marked impact on test scores and other objective yardsticks or achieves intangible socialization benefits. The debate is not one we need to resolve, however, because it is clear that the racial classifications employed by the districts are not narrowly tailored to the goal of achieving the educational and social benefits asserted to flow from racial diversity. In design and operation, the plans are directed only to racial balance, pure and simple, an objective this Court has repeatedly condemned as illegitimate.

The plans are tied to each district's specific racial demographics, rather than to any pedagogic concept of the level of diversity needed to obtain the asserted educational benefits. In Seattle, the district seeks white enrollment of between 31 and 51 percent (within 10 percent of "the district white average" of 41 percent), and nonwhite enrollment of between 49 and 69 percent (within 10 percent of "the district minority average" of 59 percent). App. in No. 05-908, at 103a. In Jefferson County, by contrast, the district seeks black enrollment of no less than 15 or more than 50 percent, a range designed to be "equally above and below Black student enrollment system wide," *McFarland I,* 330 F.Supp.2d, at 842, based on the objective of achieving at "all schools . . . an African-American enrollment equivalent to the average district-wide African-American enrollment" of 34 percent, App. in No. 05-915, at 81. In Seattle, then, the benefits of racial diversity require enrollment of at least 31 percent white students; in Jefferson County, at least 50 percent. There must be at least 15 percent nonwhite students under Jefferson County's plan; in Seattle, more than three times that figure. This comparison makes clear that the racial demographics in each district—whatever they happen to be—drive the required "diversity" numbers. The plans here are not tailored to achieving a degree of diversity necessary to realize the asserted educational benefits; instead the plans are tailored, in the words of Seattle's Manager of Enrollment Planning, Technical Support, and Demographics, to "the goal established by the school board of attaining a level of diversity within the schools that approximates the district's overall demographics." App. in No. 05-908, at 42a.

The districts offer no evidence that the level of racial diversity necessary to achieve the asserted educational benefits happens to coincide with the racial demographics of the respective school districts—or rather the white/nonwhite or black/"other" balance of the districts, since that is the only diversity addressed by the plans. Indeed, in its brief Seattle simply assumes that the educational benefits track the racial breakdown of the district.

In *Grutter,* the number of minority students the school sought to admit was an undefined "meaningful number" necessary to achieve a genuinely diverse student body. 539 U.S., at 316, 335–336, 123 S.Ct. 2325. Although the matter was the subject of disagreement on the Court, see *id.,* at 346–347, 123 S.Ct. 2325 (SCALIA, J., concurring in part and dissenting in part); *id.,* at 382–383, 123 S.Ct. 2325 (Rehnquist, C.J., dissenting); *id.,* at 388–392, 123 S.Ct. 2325 (Kennedy, J., dissenting), the majority concluded that the law school did not count back from its applicant pool to arrive at the "meaningful number" it regarded as necessary to diversify its student body. *Id.,* at 335–336, 123 S.Ct. 2325. Here the racial balance the districts seek is a defined range set solely by reference to the demographics of the respective school districts. . . .

This working backward to achieve a particular type of racial balance, rather than working forward from some demonstration of the level of diversity that provides the purported benefits, is a fatal flaw under our existing precedent. We have many times over reaffirmed that "[r]acial balance is not to be achieved for its own sake." *Freeman,* 503 U.S., at 494, 112 S.Ct. 1430. See also *Richmond v. J.A. Croson Co.,* 488 U.S. 469, 507, 109 S.Ct. 706, 102 L.Ed.2d 854 (1989); *Bakke,* 438 U.S., at 307, 98 S.Ct. 2733 (opinion of Powell, J.) . . . .

Accepting racial balancing as a compelling state interest would justify the imposition of racial proportionality throughout American society, contrary to our repeated recognition that "[a]t the heart of the Constitution's guarantee of equal protection lies the simple command that the Government must treat citizens as individuals, not as simply components of a racial, religious, sexual or national class." *Miller v. Johnson,* 515 U.S. 900, 911, 115 S.Ct. 2475, 132 L.Ed.2d 762 (1995) . . . .

The principle that racial balancing is not permitted is one of substance, not semantics. Racial balancing is not transformed from "patently unconstitutional" to a compelling state interest simply by relabeling it "racial diversity." While the school districts use various verbal formulations to describe the interest they seek to promote—racial diversity, avoidance of racial isolation, racial integration—they offer no definition of the interest that suggests it differs from racial balance. See, *e.g.,*

App. in No. 05-908, at 257a ("Q. What's your understanding of when a school suffers from racial isolation?" "A. I don't have a definition for that"); *id.*, at 228a-229a ("I don't think we've ever sat down and said, 'Define racially concentrated school exactly on point in quantitative terms.' I don't think we've ever had that conversation"); Tr. in *McFarland I,* at 1-90 (Dec. 8, 2003) ("Q." "How does the Jefferson County School Board define diversity . . . ?" "A. Well, we want to have the schools that make up the percentage of students of the population").

. . . .

C

The districts assert, as they must, that the way in which they have employed individual racial classifications is necessary to achieve their stated ends. The minimal effect these classifications have on student assignments, however, suggests that other means would be effective. Seattle's racial tiebreaker results, in the end, only in shifting a small number of students between schools. Approximately 307 student assignments were affected by the racial tiebreaker in 2000–2001; the district was able to track the enrollment status of 293 of these students. App. in No. 05-908, at 162a. Of these, 209 were assigned to a school that was one of their choices, 87 of whom were assigned to the same school to which they would have been assigned without the racial tiebreaker. Eighty-four students were assigned to schools that they did not list as a choice, but 29 of those students would have been assigned to their respective school without the racial tiebreaker, and 3 were able to attend one of the oversubscribed schools due to waitlist and capacity adjustments. *Id.*, at 162a–163a. In over one-third of the assignments affected by the racial tiebreaker, then, the use of race in the end made no difference, and the district could identify only 52 students who were ultimately affected adversely by the racial tiebreaker in that it resulted in assignment to a school they had not listed as a preference and to which they would not otherwise have been assigned.

. . . .

Similarly, Jefferson County's use of racial classifications has only a minimal effect on the assignment of students. Elementary school students are assigned to their first- or second-choice school 95 percent of the time, and transfers, which account for roughly 5 percent of assignments, are only denied 35 percent of the time—and presumably an even smaller percentage are denied on the basis of the racial guidelines, given that other factors may lead to a denial. *McFarland I,* 330 F.Supp.2d, at 844–845, nn. 16, 18. Jefferson County estimates that the racial guidelines account for only 3 percent of assignments. Brief in Opposition in No. 05-915, p. 7, n. 4; Tr. of Oral Arg. in No. 05-915, at 46. As Jefferson County explains, "the racial guidelines have minimal impact in this process, because they 'mostly influence student assignment in subtle and indirect ways.'" Brief for Respondents in No. 05-915, pp. 8–9.

While we do not suggest that *greater* use of race would be preferable, the minimal impact of the districts' racial classifications on school enrollment casts doubt on the necessity of using racial classifications. . . .

The districts have also failed to show that they considered methods other than explicit racial classifications to achieve their stated goals. Narrow tailoring requires "serious, good faith consideration of workable race-neutral alternatives," *Grutter, supra*, at 339, 123 S.Ct. 2325, and yet in Seattle several alternative assignment plans—many of which would not have used express racial classifications—were rejected with little or no consideration. See, *e.g.*, App. in No. 05-908, at 224a-225a, 253a-259a, 307a. Jefferson County has failed to present any evidence that it considered alternatives, even though the district already claims that its goals are achieved primarily through means other than the racial classifications. Brief for Respondents in No. 05-915, at 8–9. Cf. *Croson*, 488 U.S., at 519, 109 S.Ct. 706 (Kennedy, J., concurring in part and concurring in judgment) (racial classifications permitted only "as a last resort").

. . . .

Before *Brown*, schoolchildren were told where they could and could not go to school based on the color of their skin. The school districts in these cases have not carried the heavy burden of demonstrating that we should allow this once again—even for very different reasons. For schools that never segregated on the basis of race, such as Seattle, or that have removed the vestiges of past segregation, such as Jefferson County, the way "to achieve a system of determining admission to the public schools on a nonracial basis," *Brown II, supra*, at 300–301, 75 S.Ct. 753, is to stop assigning students on a racial basis. The way to stop discrimination on the basis of race is to stop discriminating on the basis of race.

The judgments of the Courts of Appeals for the Sixth and Ninth Circuits are reversed, and the cases are remanded for further proceedings.

It is so ordered.

Note

Note the majority's promulgation that 'racial balancing' is contrary to the goal of the Constitution. What does the majority mean by "racial balancing"?

What threats does the majority associate with this approach? Why does it deem it contrary to the Constitution?

D. Beyond Affirmative Action — What Models Should We Be Promoting Post-*Fisher*?

In 2009, in *Ricci v. DeStefano*, 557 U.S. 557, the Court addressed what affirmative steps, if any, employers might be able to implement to avoid discrimination. In *Ricci*, New Haven administered a civil service test to determine promotion of firefighters. Upon determination that the exam would result in a disproportionate impact on applicants of color, the department opted not to certify the results. Candidates for promotion sued. The Court ruled that raced-based remedial measures to prevent discrimination would only be constitutional with proof of "strong basis in evidence" proffered by the employer. Recall the discussion in the above cases, in which the Court leaves open the possibility that government might be able to adopt measures to remedy evidence of racial bias. *Ricci* makes clear that this evidence cannot be speculative. In fact, along with *Parents Involved*, *Ricci* limits the ability to remedy discrimination to actual segregation under the law. This makes it more likely that, absent proof that a governmental entity took intentional steps to segregate based on race, remedial measures to desegregate would not be upheld by the Court. In *Fisher*, below, the Court seems to impose a similar restriction on the diversity rationale, the only other justification recognized for government's consideration of race as a factor in decionmaking. How does *Fisher* alter *Grutter*?

The diversity rationale: As seen above, Justice O'Connor in *Grutter* contrasted two programs from the University of Michigan and viewed *Grutter* as exemplifying a program that, though race was one of many factors, could survive strict scrutiny. She compared to a program awarding points for certain characteristics, including race. Nonetheless, in approving the affirmative action plan in *Grutter*, Justice O'Connor stated that the Court was still uncomfortable with race and diversity being a consideration at all. She recognized that it was still needed, but in dicta (not rule), she stated that she hoped that we would, soon, no longer need (perhaps in 25 years) the *Grutter*/diversity measures. Still, *Grutter* confirmed diversity as a compelling interest in 2003. Fast forward 10 years; plaintiff filed *Fisher*, hoping to serve as the case to overrule *Grutter* and invalidate the diversity rationale. In its 2013 decision in *Fisher*, however, the Court avoids that central question and rules, instead, that the lower court misapplied the strict scrutiny standard:

> The University of Texas at Austin considers race as one of various factors in its undergraduate admissions process. Race is not itself assigned a numerical value for each applicant, but the University has committed itself to increasing racial minority enrollment on campus. It refers to this goal as a "critical mass." Petitioner, who is Caucasian, sued the University after her application was rejected. She contends that the University's use of race in the admissions process violated the Equal Protection Clause of the Fourteenth Amendment.

> The parties asked the Court to review whether the judgment below was consistent with "this Court's decisions interpreting the Equal Protection Clause of the Fourteenth Amendment, including *Grutter v. Bollinger*, 539 U. S. 306 (2003)." Pet. for Cert.

> [Consequently, the] Court concludes that the Court of Appeals did not hold the University to the demanding burden of strict scrutiny articulated in *Grutter* and *Regents of Univ. of Cal. v. Bakke*, 438 U. S. 265, 305 (1978) (opinion of Powell, J.). Because the Court of Appeals did not apply the correct standard of strict scrutiny, its decision affirming the District Court's grant of summary judgment to the University was incorrect. That decision is vacated, and the case is remanded for further proceedings.

Strict scrutiny is a searching examination, and it is the government that bears the burden to prove "'that the reasons for any [racial] classification [are] clearly identified and unquestionably legitimate,'" *Croson, supra,* at 505 (quoting *Fullilove,* 448 *supra,* at 533–535 (Stevens, J., dissenting)). *Grutter* made clear that racial "classifications are constitutional only if they are narrowly tailored to further compelling governmental interests." 539 U. S., at 326. And *Grutter* endorsed Justice Powell's conclusion in *Bakke* that "the attainment of a diverse student body . . . is a constitutionally permissible goal for an institution of higher education." 438 U.S., at 311–312 (separate opinion). Thus, under *Grutter,* strict scrutiny must be applied to any admissions program using racial categories or classifications. This reiterates what we have been applying thus far.

As long as the Court reviews the evidence and makes sure that the compelling interest asserted is supported and justified, the Court maintains, in theory, deference to the judgment of institutions as expert:

> According to *Grutter,* a university's "educational judgment that such diversity is essential to its educational mission is one to which we defer . . . ." *Grutter* concluded that the decision to pursue "the educational benefits that flow from student body diversity," that the University deems integral to its mission is, in substantial measure, an academic judgment to which some, but not complete, judicial deference is proper under *Grutter.*

The interest is strictly evaluated, but stands if supported:

> A court, of course, should ensure that there is a reasoned, principled explanation for the academic decision. On this point, the District Court and Court of Appeals were correct in finding that *Grutter* calls for deference to the University's conclusion, "'based on its experience and expertise'" . . . that a diverse student body would serve its educational goals.

The Court goes on to elaborate on narrow tailoring. Compare this reasoning on narrow tailoring and the University's obligation with Justice O'Connor's approach to the University's justification in *Grutter*:

> Once the University has established that its goal of diversity is consistent with strict scrutiny, however, there must still be a further judicial determination that the admissions process meets strict scrutiny in its implementation. The University must prove that the means chosen by the University to attain diversity are narrowly tailored to that goal. On this point, the University receives no deference. *Grutter* made clear that it is for the courts, not for university administrators, to ensure that "[t]he means chosen to accomplish the [government's] asserted purpose must be specifically and narrowly framed to accomplish that purpose . . . . True, a court can take account of a university's experience and expertise in adopting or rejecting certain admissions processes. But, as the Court said in *Grutter,* it remains

at all times the University's obligation to demonstrate, and the Judiciary's obligation to determine, that admissions processes "ensure that each applicant is evaluated as an individual and not in a way that makes an applicant's race or ethnicity the defining feature of his or her application.

Fisher v. University of Texas at Austin

132 S. Ct. 1536 (2013)

JUSTICE KENNEDY delivered the opinion of the Court.

The University of Texas at Austin considers race as one of various factors in its undergraduate admissions process. Race is not itself assigned a numerical value for each applicant, but the University has committed itself to increasing racial minority enrollment on campus. It refers to this goal as a "critical mass." Petitioner, who is Caucasian, sued the University after her application was rejected. She contends that the University's use of race in the admissions process violated the Equal Protection Clause of the Fourteenth Amendment.

The parties asked the Court to review whether the judgment below was consistent with "this Court's decisions interpreting the Equal Protection Clause of the Fourteenth Amendment, including *Grutter v. Bollinger,* 539 U.S. 306, 123 S.Ct. 2325, 156 L.Ed.2d 304 (2003)." Pet. for Cert. i. The Court concludes that the Court of Appeals did not hold the University to the demanding burden of strict scrutiny articulated in *Grutter* and *Regents of Univ. of Cal. v. Bakke,* 438 U.S. 265, 305, 98 S. Ct. 2733, 57 L.Ed.2d 750 (1978) (opinion of Powell, J.). Because the Court of Appeals did not apply the correct standard of strict scrutiny, its decision affirming the District Court's grant of summary judgment to the University was incorrect. That decision is vacated, and the case is remanded for further proceedings.

I

A

Located in Austin, Texas, on the most renowned campus of the Texas state university system, the University is one of the leading institutions of higher education in the Nation. Admission is prized and competitive. In 2008, when petitioner sought admission to the University's entering class, she was 1 of 29,501 applicants. From this group 12,843 were admitted, and 6,715 accepted and enrolled. Petitioner was denied admission.

In recent years the University has used three different programs to evaluate candidates for admission. The first is the program it used for some years before 1997, when the University considered two factors: a numerical score reflecting an applicant's test scores and academic performance in high school (Academic Index or AI), and the applicant's race. In 1996, this system was held unconstitutional by the United States Court of Appeals for the Fifth Circuit. It ruled the University's consideration of race violated the Equal Protection Clause because it did not further any compelling government interest. *Hopwood v. Texas,* 78 F.3d 932, 955 (1996).

The second program was adopted to comply with the *Hopwood* decision. The University stopped considering race in admissions and substituted instead a new holistic metric of a candidate's potential contribution to the University, to be used in conjunction with the Academic Index. This "Personal Achievement Index" (PAI) measures a student's leadership and work experience, awards, extra-curricular activities, community service, and other special circumstances that give insight into a student's background. These included growing up in a single-parent home, speaking a language other than English at home, significant family responsibilities assumed by the applicant, and the general socioeconomic condition of the student's family. Seeking to address the decline in minority enrollment after *Hopwood,* the University also expanded its outreach programs.

The Texas State Legislature also responded to the *Hopwood* decision. It enacted a measure known as the Top Ten Percent Law, codified at Tex. Educ.Code Ann. § 51.803 (West 2009). Also referred to as H.B. 588, the Top Ten Percent Law grants automatic admission to any public state college, including the University, to all students in the top 10% of their class at high schools in Texas that comply with certain standards.

The University's revised admissions process, coupled with the operation of the Top Ten Percent Law, resulted in a more racially diverse environment at the University. Before the admissions program at issue in this case, in the last year under the post-*Hopwood* AI/PAI system that did not consider race, the entering class was 4.5% African-American and 16.9% Hispanic. This is in contrast with the 1996 pre-*Hopwood* and Top Ten Percent regime, when race was explicitly considered, and the University's entering freshman class was 4.1% African-American and 14.5% Hispanic.

Following this Court's decisions in *Grutter v. Bollinger, supra,* and *Gratz v. Bollinger,*539 U.S. 244, 123 S.Ct. 2411, 156 L.Ed.2d 257 (2003), the University adopted a third admissions program, the 2004 program in which the University reverted to explicit consideration of race. This is the program here at issue. In *Grutter,* the Court upheld the use of race as one of many "plus factors" in an admissions program that considered the overall individual contribution of each candidate. In *Gratz,* by contrast, the Court held unconstitutional Michigan's undergraduate admissions program, which automatically awarded points to applicants from certain racial minorities.

The University's plan to resume race-conscious admissions was given formal expression in June 2004 in an internal document entitled Proposal to Consider Race and Ethnicity in Admissions (Proposal). Supp. App. 1a. The Proposal relied in substantial part on a study of a subset of undergraduate classes containing between 5 and 24 students. It showed that few of these classes had significant enrollment by members of racial minorities. In addition the Proposal relied on what it called "anecdotal" reports from students regarding their "interaction in the classroom." The Proposal concluded that the University lacked a "critical mass" of minority students and that to remedy the deficiency it was necessary to give explicit consideration to race in the undergraduate admissions program.

To implement the Proposal the University included a student's race as a component of the PAI score, beginning with applicants in the fall of 2004. The University asks students to classify themselves from among five predefined racial categories on the application. Race is not assigned an explicit numerical value, but it is undisputed that race is a meaningful factor.

Once applications have been scored, they are plotted on a grid with the Academic Index on the x-axis and the Personal Achievement Index on the y-axis. On that grid students are assigned to so-called cells based on their individual scores. All students in the cells falling above a certain line are admitted. All students below the line are not. Each college—such as Liberal Arts or Engineering—admits students separately. So a student is considered initially for her first-choice college, then for her second choice, and finally for general admission as an undeclared major.

Petitioner applied for admission to the University's 2008 entering class and was rejected. She sued the University and various University officials in the United States District Court for the Western District of Texas. She alleged that the University's consideration of race in admissions violated the Equal Protection Clause. . . .

B

Among the Court's cases involving racial classifications in education, there are three decisions that directly address the question of considering racial minority status as a positive or favorable factor in a university's admissions process, with the goal of achieving the educational benefits of a more diverse student body: *Bakke*, 438 U.S. 265, 98 S.Ct. 2733, 57 L.Ed.2d 750; *Gratz, supra*; and *Grutter*, 539 U.S. 306, 123 S.Ct. 2325, 156 L.Ed.2d 304. We take those cases as given for purposes of deciding this case.

We begin with the principal opinion authored by Justice Powell in *Bakke, supra*. In *Bakke*, the Court considered a system used by the medical school of the University of California at Davis. From an entering class of 100 students the school had set aside 16 seats for minority applicants. In holding this program impermissible under the Equal Protection Clause Justice Powell's opinion stated certain basic premises. First, "decisions based on race or ethnic origin by faculties and administrations of state universities are reviewable under the Fourteenth Amendment." *Id.*, at 287, 98 S.Ct. 2733 (separate opinion). The principle of equal protection admits no "artificial line of a 'two-class theory'" that "permits the recognition of special wards entitled to a degree of protection greater than that accorded others." *Id.*, at 295, 98 S.Ct. 2733. It is therefore irrelevant that a system of racial preferences in admissions may seem benign. Any racial classification must meet strict scrutiny, for when government decisions "touch upon an individual's race or ethnic background, he is entitled to a judicial determination that the burden he is asked to bear on that basis is precisely tailored to serve a compelling governmental interest." *Id.*, at 299, 98 S.Ct. 2733.

... The attainment of a diverse student body, by contrast, serves values beyond race alone, including enhanced classroom dialogue and the lessening of racial isolation and stereotypes. The academic mission of a university is "a special concern of the First Amendment." *Id.,* at 312, 98 S.Ct. 2733. Part of "'the business of a university [is] to provide that atmosphere which is most conducive to speculation, experiment, and creation,'" and this in turn leads to the question of "'who may be admitted to study.'" *Sweezy v. New Hampshire,* 354 U.S. 234, 263, 77 S.Ct. 1203, 1 L. Ed.2d 1311 (1957) (Frankfurter, J., concurring in judgment).

Justice Powell's central point, however, was that this interest in securing diversity's benefits, although a permissible objective, is complex. "It is not an interest in simple ethnic diversity, in which a specified percentage of the student body is in effect guaranteed to be members of selected ethnic groups, with the remaining percentage an undifferentiated aggregation of students. The diversity that furthers a compelling state interest encompasses a far broader array of qualifications and characteristics of which racial or ethnic origin is but a single though important element." *Bakke,* 438 U.S., at 315, 98 S.Ct. 2733 (separate opinion).

In *Gratz,* 539 U.S. 244, 123 S.Ct. 2411, 156 L.Ed.2d 257, and *Grutter, supra,* the Court endorsed the precepts stated by Justice Powell. In *Grutter,* the Court reaffirmed his conclusion that obtaining the educational benefits of "student body diversity is a compelling state interest that can justify the use of race in university admissions." *Id.,* at 325, 123 S.Ct. 2325.

As *Gratz* and *Grutter* observed, however, this follows only if a clear precondition is met: The particular admissions process used for this objective is subject to judicial review. Race may not be considered unless the admissions process can withstand strict scrutiny. "Nothing in Justice Powell's opinion in *Bakke* signaled that a university may employ whatever means it desires to achieve the stated goal of diversity without regard to the limits imposed by our strict scrutiny analysis." *Gratz, supra,* at 275, 123 S.Ct. 2411. . . .

To implement these canons, judicial review must begin from the position that "any official action that treats a person differently on account of his race or ethnic origin is inherently suspect." *Fullilove, supra,* at 523, 100 S.Ct. 2758 (Stewart, J., dissenting); *McLaughlin v. Florida,* 379 U.S. 184, 192, 85 S.Ct. 283, 13 L.Ed.2d 222 (1964). Strict scrutiny is a searching examination, and it is the government that bears the burden to prove "'that the reasons for any [racial] classification [are] clearly identified and unquestionably legitimate,'" *Croson, supra,* at 505, 109 S.Ct. 706 (quoting *Fullilove, supra,* 448 U.S., at 533–535, 100 S.Ct. 2758 (Stevens, J., dissenting)).

II

Grutter made clear that racial "classifications are constitutional only if they are narrowly tailored to further compelling governmental interests." 539 U.S., at 326, 123 S.Ct. 2325. And *Grutter* endorsed Justice Powell's conclusion in *Bakke* that "the attainment of a diverse student body . . . is a constitutionally permissible goal for an institution of higher education." 438 U.S., at 311–312, 98 S.Ct. 2733 (separate opinion). Thus, under *Grutter*, strict scrutiny must be applied to any admissions program using racial categories or classifications.

According to *Grutter*, a university's "educational judgment that such diversity is essential to its educational mission is one to which we defer." 539 U.S., at 328, 123 S. Ct. 2325. *Grutter* concluded that the decision to pursue "the educational benefits that flow from student body diversity," *id.*, at 330, 123 S.Ct. 2325, that the University deems integral to its mission is, in substantial measure, an academic judgment to which some, but not complete, judicial deference is proper under *Grutter*. A court, of course, should ensure that there is a reasoned, principled explanation for the academic decision. On this point, the District Court and Court of Appeals were correct in finding that *Grutter* calls for deference to the University's conclusion, "'based on its experience and expertise,'" 631 F.3d, at 230 (quoting 645 F.Supp.2d 587, 603 (W.D.Tex.2009)), that a diverse student body would serve its educational goals. There is disagreement about whether *Grutter* was consistent with the principles of equal protection in approving this compelling interest in diversity. See *post*, at 2422 (Scalia, J., concurring); *post*, at 2423–2424 (Thomas, J., concurring);*post*, at 2432–2433 (Ginsburg, J., dissenting). But the parties here do not ask the Court to revisit that aspect of *Grutter*'s holding.

A university is not permitted to define diversity as "some specified percentage of a particular group merely because of its race or ethnic origin." *Bakke, supra,* at 307, 98 S.Ct. 2733 (opinion of Powell, J.). "That would amount to outright racial balancing, which is patently unconstitutional." *Grutter, supra,* at 330, 123 S.Ct. 2325. "Racial balancing is not transformed from 'patently unconstitutional' to a compelling state interest simply by relabeling it 'racial diversity.'" *Parents Involved in Community Schools v. Seattle School Dist. No. 1*, 551 U.S. 701, 732, 127 S.Ct. 2738, 168 L. Ed.2d 508 (2007).

Once the University has established that its goal of diversity is consistent with strict scrutiny, however, there must still be a further judicial determination that the admissions process meets strict scrutiny in its implementation. The University must prove that the means chosen by the University to attain diversity are narrowly tailored to that goal. On this point, the University receives no deference. *Grutter* made clear that it is for the courts, not for university administrators, to ensure that "[t]he means chosen to accomplish the [government's] asserted purpose must be specifically and narrowly framed to accomplish that purpose." 539 U.S., at 333, 123 S. Ct. 2325 (internal quotation marks omitted). True, a court can take account of a university's experience and expertise in adopting or rejecting certain admissions processes. But, as the Court said in *Grutter*, it remains at all times the University's obligation to demonstrate, and the Judiciary's obligation to determine, that admissions processes "ensure that each applicant is evaluated as an individual and not in a way that makes an applicant's race or ethnicity the defining feature of his or her application." *Id.*, at 337, 123 S.Ct. 2325.

Narrow tailoring also requires that the reviewing court verify that it is "necessary" for a university to use race to achieve the educational benefits of diversity. *Bakke, supra,* at 305, 98 S.Ct. 2733 This involves a careful judicial inquiry into whether a university could achieve sufficient diversity without using racial classifications. Although "[n]arrow tailoring does not require exhaustion of every *conceivable* race-neutral alternative," strict scrutiny does require a court to examine with care, and not defer to, a university's "serious, good faith consideration of workable race-neutral alternatives." See *Grutter,* 539 U.S., at 339–340, 123 S.Ct. 2325 (emphasis added). Consideration by the university is of course necessary, but it is not sufficient to satisfy strict scrutiny: The reviewing court must ultimately be satisfied that no workable race-neutral alternatives would produce the educational benefits of diversity. If "'a nonracial approach . . . could promote the substantial interest about as well and at tolerable administrative expense,'" *Wygant v. Jackson Bd. of Ed.,* 476 U.S. 267, 280, n. 6, 106 S.Ct. 1842, 90 L.Ed.2d 260 (1986) (quoting Greenawalt, *Judicial Scrutiny of "Benign" Racial Preference in Law School Admissions,* 75 Colum. L.Rev. 559, 578–579 (1975)), then the university may not consider race. A plaintiff, of course, bears the burden of placing the validity of a university's adoption of an affirmative action plan in issue. But strict scrutiny imposes on the university the ultimate burden of demonstrating, before turning to racial classifications, that available, workable race-neutral alternatives do not suffice.

Rather than perform this searching examination, however, the Court of Appeals held petitioner could challenge only "whether [the University's] decision to reintroduce race as a factor in admissions was made in good faith." 631 F.3d, at 236. And in considering such a challenge, the court would "presume the University acted in good faith" and place on petitioner the burden of rebutting that presumption. *Id.,* at 231–232. The Court of Appeals held that to "second-guess the merits" of this aspect of the University's decision was a task it was "ill-equipped to perform" and that it would attempt only to "ensure that [the University's] decision to adopt a race-conscious admissions policy followed from [a process of] good faith consideration." *Id.,* at 231. The Court of Appeals thus concluded that "the narrow-tailoring inquiry—like the compelling-interest inquiry—is undertaken with a degree of deference to the Universit[y]." *Id.,* at 232. Because "the efforts of the University have been studied, serious, and of high purpose," the Court of Appeals held that the use of race in the admissions program fell within "a constitutionally protected zone of discretion." *Id.,* at 231.

These expressions of the controlling standard are at odds with *Grutter*'s command that "all racial classifications imposed by government 'must be analyzed by a reviewing court under strict scrutiny.'" 539 U.S., at 326, 123 S.Ct. 2325 (quoting *Adarand Constructors, Inc. v. Peña,* 515 U.S. 200, 227, 115 S.Ct. 2097, 132 L.Ed.2d 158 (1995)). In *Grutter,* the Court approved the plan at issue upon concluding that it was not a quota, was sufficiently flexible, was limited in time, and followed "serious, good faith consideration of workable race-neutral alternatives." 539 U.S., at 339,

123 S.Ct. 2325. As noted above, See *supra*, at 2415, the parties do not challenge, and the Court therefore does not consider, the correctness of that determination.

Grutter did not hold that good faith would forgive an impermissible consideration of race. It must be remembered that "the mere recitation of a 'benign' or legitimate purpose for a racial classification is entitled to little or no weight." *Croson*, 488 U.S., at 500, 109 S.Ct. 706. Strict scrutiny does not permit a court to accept a school's assertion that its admissions process uses race in a permissible way without a court giving close analysis to the evidence of how the process works in practice.

The higher education dynamic does not change the narrow tailoring analysis of strict scrutiny applicable in other contexts. "[The analysis and level of scrutiny applied to determine the validity of [a racial] classification do not vary simply because the objective appears acceptable. . . . While the validity and importance of the objective may affect the outcome of the analysis, the analysis itself does not change." *Mississippi Univ. for Women v. Hogan*, 458 U.S. 718, 724, n. 9, 102 S.Ct. 3331, 73 L.Ed.2d 1090 (1982).

The District Court and Court of Appeals confined the strict scrutiny inquiry in too narrow a way by deferring to the University's good faith in its use of racial classifications and affirming the grant of summary judgment on that basis. The Court vacates that judgment, but fairness to the litigants and the courts that heard the case requires that it be remanded so that the admissions process can be considered and judged under a correct analysis. See *Adarand, supra*, at 237, 115 S.Ct. 2097. Unlike *Grutter*, which was decided after trial, this case arises from cross-motions for summary judgment. In this case, as in similar cases, in determining whether summary judgment in favor of the University would be appropriate, the Court of Appeals must assess whether the University has offered sufficient evidence that would prove that its admissions program is narrowly tailored to obtain the educational benefits of diversity. Whether this record—and not "simple . . . assurances of good intention," *Croson, supra*, at 500, 109 S.Ct. 706—is sufficient is a question for the Court of Appeals in the first instance.

. . . .

Strict scrutiny must not be "'strict in theory, but fatal in fact,'" *Adarand, supra*, at 237, 115 S.Ct. 2097; see also *Grutter, supra*, at 326, 123 S.Ct. 2325. But the opposite is also true. Strict scrutiny must not be strict in theory but feeble in fact. In order for judicial review to be meaningful, a university must make a showing that its plan is narrowly tailored to achieve the only interest that this Court has approved in this context: the benefits of a student body diversity that "encompasses a . . . broa[d] array of qualifications and characteristics of which racial or ethnic origin is but a single though important element." *Bakke*, 438 U.S., at 315, 98 S.Ct. 2733 (opinion of Powell, J.). The judgment of the Court of Appeals is vacated, and the case is remanded for further proceedings consistent with this opinion.

It is so ordered.

JUSTICE THOMAS, concurring [omitted].

Notes and Questions

1. Laws designed to remedy racial discrimination are evaluated closely under the strict scrutiny standard (*Bakke, Adarand, Gratz, Fisher, Grutter*). Recall that according to the Court's analysis, the only two compelling interests that might survive strict scrutiny when race is a factor are: 1) remedying de jure discrimination; 2) fostering diversity. In addition, they must survive the narrow tailoring requirement as well as ensure that the least restrictive means are used (that there are no other race-neutral alternatives available).

2. Does the Court in *Fisher* depart further from *Grutter* and its precedents in the following statement?

> Narrow tailoring also requires that the reviewing court verify that it is "necessary" for a university to use race to achieve the educational benefits of diversity. This involves a careful judicial inquiry into whether a university could achieve sufficient diversity without using racial classifications. . . . Narrow tailoring does not require exhaustion of every *conceivable* race-neutral alternative, strict scrutiny does require a court to examine with care, and not defer to, a university's "serious, good faith consideration of workable race-neutral alternatives" . . . . Consideration by the university is of course necessary, but it is not sufficient to satisfy strict scrutiny: The reviewing court must ultimately be satisfied that no workable race-neutral alternatives would produce the educational benefits of diversity . . . then the university may not consider race.
>
> A plaintiff, of course, bears the burden of placing the validity of a university's adoption of an affirmative action plan at issue. But strict scrutiny imposes on the university the ultimate burden of demonstrating, before turning to racial classifications, that available, workable race-neutral alternatives do not suffice. *Fisher*

3. Where did the lower Court err according to *Fisher*?

> Rather than perform this searching examination, however, the Court of Appeals held petitioner could challenge only "whether [the University's] decision to reintroduce race as a factor in admissions was made in good faith." 631 F.3d, at 236. And in considering such a challenge, the court would "presume the University acted in good faith" and place on petitioner the burden of rebutting that presumption. The Court of Appeals held that to "second-guess the merits" of this aspect of the University's decision was a task it was "ill-equipped to perform" and that it would attempt only to "ensure that [the University's] decision to adopt a race-conscious admissions policy followed from [a process of] good faith consideration." The Court of Appeals thus concluded that "the narrow-tailoring inquiry—like

the compelling-interest inquiry—is undertaken with a degree of deference to the University."

4. Though the Court in Fisher did not overrule Grutter in substance, in its application of the strict scrutiny standard, it put institutions on notice that their programs will be examined very closely moving forward and that no deference will be accorded to them. In light of that, strict scrutiny now has the potential to be even more fatal post-*Fisher* than it had been under *Grutter*. In contrast, some argue that *Grutter* had left some room for institutions to carve out the programs in a way that suited their needs as long as race was not used as a determining factor.[5] The question remains, however, as to whether there is a form of strict scrutiny under which the government might prevail in the future, especially in light of indications that there might be no general deference accorded to institutions when applying the strict scrutiny standard.

Particularly, the interpretation of narrow tailoring as extensively searching raises the question as to whether, in practicality, narrow tailoring will require exhaustion of all alternatives in order for a governmental entity to prevail.

5. The aftermath of *Fisher*: Upon remand, the Fifth Circuit applied strict scrutiny at all levels as mandated by the Supreme Court and found that the Texas policy did not violate the Fourteenth Amendment. Shortly after, the Supreme Court surprised many by granting certiorari once more to Abigail Fisher to consider whether the affirmative action plan violated the Equal Protection Clause. This willingness to revisit the same issue so soon signaled, to many, a desire by the Court to perhaps do away with the diversity rationale altogether. The Supreme Court did not. Still, many wonder whether the final nail on diversity as a suitable compelling interest under the Fourteenth Amendment might be fast approaching.

6. Understanding the Court: Based on these line of cases, is the Court saying that diversity is a transient/temporary compelling interest? Or is the Court saying that narrow tailoring requires an end to diversity-based policies?

7. What other possibilities exist if diversity is eliminated? What might potential approaches to educational equality be post-*Fisher*? Were the Court to outlaw diversity as a rationale, and, considering the deeply segregated and unequal status of public schools in America, what might be some successful recommendations?

E. Under Statutory Law

Statutory violations can also provide avenues for affirmative action based remedies. These issues come up, for example, when an employer meets attempts to

---

5. Comment: *Admissions Rituals as Political Acts: Guardians at the Gates of our Democratic Ideals*, 117 HARV. L. REV. 113, 182; *Divisive Diversity at the University of Texas: An Opportunity for the Supreme Court to Overturn Its Flawed Decision in* Grutter, 15 TEX. REV. LAW & POL. 437.

remedy past discrimination. An employer seeking to justify the adoption of an affirmative action plan might need not point to its own prior discriminatory practices, but might only need to point to a conspicuous imbalance in traditionally segregated job categories. Voluntary remedial action by employers can play a crucial role in furthering Title VII's purpose of eliminating the effects of discrimination in the workplace. Does Title VII permit such efforts? In *Johnson*, below, the Court reasoned that an agency's plan to remedy imbalance did not unnecessarily trammel male employees' rights or create an absolute bar to their advancement. The plan did not set aside positions for women, and expressly stated that its goals should not be construed as "quotas" that must be met: "Denial of the promotion to petitioner unsettled no legitimate, firmly rooted expectation on his part, since the Agency Director was authorized to select any of the seven applicants deemed qualified for the job."

Johnson v. Transportation Agency, Santa Clara County, California
480 U.S. 616 (1987)

JUSTICE BRENNAN delivered the opinion of the Court.

Respondent, Transportation Agency of Santa Clara County, California, unilaterally promulgated an Affirmative Action Plan applicable, *inter alia,* to promotions of employees. In selecting applicants for the promotional position of road dispatcher, the Agency, pursuant to the Plan, passed over petitioner Paul Johnson, a male employee, and promoted a female employee applicant, Diane Joyce. The question for decision is whether in making the promotion the Agency impermissibly took into account the sex of the applicants in violation of Title VII of the Civil Rights Act of 1964, 42 U.S.C. § 2000e *et seq.* The District Court for the Northern District of California, in an action filed by petitioner following receipt of a right-to-sue letter from the Equal Employment Opportunity Commission (EEOC), held that respondent had violated Title VII. App. to Pet. for Cert. 1a. The Court of Appeals for the Ninth Circuit reversed. 770 F.2d 752 (1985). We granted certiorari, 478 U.S. 1019, 106 S.Ct. 3331, 92 L.Ed.2d 737 (1986). We affirm.

I

A

In December 1978, the Santa Clara County Transit District Board of Supervisors adopted an Affirmative Action Plan ("Plan") for the County Transportation Agency. The Plan implemented a County Affirmative Action Plan, which had been adopted, declared the County, because "mere prohibition of discriminatory practices is not enough to remedy the effects of past practices and to permit attainment of an equitable representation of minorities, women and handicapped persons." App. 31. Relevant to this case, the Agency Plan provides that, in making promotions to positions within a traditionally segregated job classification in which women have been significantly underrepresented, the Agency is authorized to consider as one factor the sex of a qualified applicant.

In reviewing the composition of its work force, the Agency noted in its Plan that women were represented in numbers far less than their proportion of the County labor force in both the Agency as a whole and in five of seven job categories. Specifically, while women constituted 36.4% of the area labor market, they composed only 22.4% of Agency employees. Furthermore, women working at the Agency were concentrated largely in EEOC job categories traditionally held by women: women made up 76% of Office and Clerical Workers, but only 7.1% of Agency Officials and Administrators, 8.6% of Professionals, 9.7% of Technicians, and 22% of Service and Maintenance Workers. As for the job classification relevant to this case, none of the 238 Skilled Craft Worker positions was held by a woman. *Id.*, at 49. The Plan noted that this underrepresentation of women in part reflected the fact that women had not traditionally been employed in these positions, and that they had not been strongly motivated to seek training or employment in them "because of the limited opportunities that have existed in the past for them to work in such classifications." *Id.*, at 57. The Plan also observed that, while the proportion of ethnic minorities in the Agency as a whole exceeded the proportion of such minorities in the County work force, a smaller percentage of minority employees held management, professional, and technical positions.

The Agency stated that its Plan was intended to achieve "a statistically measurable yearly improvement in hiring, training and promotion of minorities and women throughout the Agency in all major job classifications where they are underrepresented." *Id.*, at 43. As a benchmark by which to evaluate progress, the Agency stated that its long-term goal was to attain a work force whose composition reflected the proportion of minorities and women in the area labor force. *Id.*, at 54. Thus, for the Skilled Craft category in which the road dispatcher position at issue here was classified, the Agency's aspiration was that eventually about 36% of the jobs would be occupied by women.

The Plan acknowledged that a number of factors might make it unrealistic to rely on the Agency's long-term goals in evaluating the Agency's progress in expanding job opportunities for minorities and women. Among the factors identified were low turnover rates in some classifications, the fact that some jobs involved heavy labor, the small number of positions within some job categories, the limited number of entry positions leading to the Technical and Skilled Craft classifications, and the limited number of minorities and women qualified for positions requiring specialized training and experience. *Id.*, at 56–57. As a result, the Plan counseled that short-range goals be established and annually adjusted to serve as the most realistic guide for actual employment decisions. Among the tasks identified as important in establishing such short-term goals was the acquisition of data "reflecting the ratio of minorities, women and handicapped persons who are working in the local area in major job classifications relating to those utilized by the County Administration," so as to determine the availability of members of such groups who "possess the desired qualifications or potential for placement." *Id.*, at 64. These data on qualified group members, along with predictions of position vacancies, were to serve as the basis for "realistic yearly employment goals for women, minorities and handicapped persons in each EEOC job category and major job classification." *Ibid.*

The Agency's Plan thus set aside no specific number of positions for minorities or women, but authorized the consideration of ethnicity or sex as a factor when evaluating qualified candidates for jobs in which members of such groups were poorly represented. One such job was the road dispatcher position that is the subject of the dispute in this case.

B

On December 12, 1979, the Agency announced a vacancy for the promotional position of road dispatcher in the Agency's Roads Division. Dispatchers assign road crews, equipment, and materials, and maintain records pertaining to road maintenance jobs. *Id.,* at 23–24. The position requires a minimum four years of dispatch or road maintenance work experience for Santa Clara County. The EEOC job classification scheme designates a road dispatcher as a Skilled Craft Worker.

Twelve County employees applied for the promotion, including Joyce and Johnson. Joyce had worked for the County since 1970, serving as an account clerk until 1975. She had applied for a road dispatcher position in 1974, but was deemed ineligible because she had not served as a road maintenance worker. In 1975, Joyce transferred from a senior account clerk position to a road maintenance worker position, becoming the first woman to fill such a job. Tr. 83–84. During her four years in that position, she occasionally worked out of class as a road dispatcher.

Petitioner Johnson began with the County in 1967 as a road yard clerk, after private employment that included working as a supervisor and dispatcher. He had also unsuccessfully applied for the road dispatcher opening in 1974. In 1977, his clerical position was downgraded, and he sought and received a transfer to the position of road maintenance worker. *Id.,* at 127. He also occasionally worked out of class as a dispatcher while performing that job.

Nine of the applicants, including Joyce and Johnson, were deemed qualified for the job, and were interviewed by a two-person board. Seven of the applicants scored above 70 on this interview, which meant that they were certified as eligible for selection by the appointing authority. The scores awarded ranged from 70 to 80. Johnson was tied for second with a score of 75, while Joyce ranked next with a score of 73. A second interview was conducted by three Agency supervisors, who ultimately recommended that Johnson be promoted. Prior to the second interview, Joyce had contacted the County's Affirmative Action Office because she feared that her application might not receive disinterested review. The Office in turn contacted the Agency's Affirmative Action Coordinator, whom the Agency's Plan makes responsible for, *inter alia,* keeping the Director informed of opportunities for the Agency to accomplish its objectives under the Plan. At the time, the Agency employed no women in any Skilled Craft position, and had never employed a woman as a road dispatcher. The Coordinator recommended to the Director of the Agency, James Graebner, that Joyce be promoted.

Graebner, authorized to choose any of the seven persons deemed eligible, thus had the benefit of suggestions by the second interview panel and by the Agency Coordinator in arriving at his decision. After deliberation, Graebner concluded that the promotion should be given to Joyce. As he testified: "I tried to look at the whole picture, the combination of her qualifications and Mr. Johnson's qualifications, their test scores, their expertise, their background, affirmative action matters, things like that. . . . I believe it was a combination of all those." *Id.*, at 68.

The certification form naming Joyce as the person promoted to the dispatcher position stated that both she and Johnson were rated as well qualified for the job. The evaluation of Joyce read: "Well qualified by virtue of 18 years of past clerical experience including 3 ½ years at West Yard plus almost 5 years as a [road maintenance worker]." App. 27. The evaluation of Johnson was as follows: "Well qualified applicant; two years of [road maintenance worker] experience plus 11 years of Road Yard Clerk. Has had previous outside Dispatch experience but was 13 years ago." *Ibid.* Graebner testified that he did not regard as significant the fact that Johnson scored 75 and Joyce 73 when interviewed by the two-person board. Tr. 57–58.

Petitioner Johnson filed a complaint with the EEOC alleging that he had been denied promotion on the basis of sex in violation of Title VII. He received a right-to-sue letter from the EEOC on March 10, 1981, and on March 20, 1981, filed suit in the United States District Court for the Northern District of California. The District Court found that Johnson was more qualified for the dispatcher position than Joyce, and that the sex of Joyce was the "*determining factor* in her selection." App. to Pet. for Cert. 4a (emphasis in original). The court acknowledged that, since the Agency justified its decision on the basis of its Affirmative Action Plan, the criteria announced in *Steelworkers v. Weber,* 443 U.S. 193, 99 S.Ct. 2721, 61 L.Ed.2d 480 (1979), should be applied in evaluating the validity of the Plan. App. to Pet. for Cert. 5a. It then found the Agency's Plan invalid on the ground that the evidence did not satisfy *Weber's* criterion that the Plan be temporary. App. to Pet. for Cert. 6a. The Court of Appeals for the Ninth Circuit reversed, holding that the absence of an express termination date in the Plan was not dispositive, since the Plan repeatedly expressed its objective as the attainment, rather than the maintenance, of a work force mirroring the labor force in the County. 770 F.2d, at 756. The Court of Appeals added that the fact that the Plan established no fixed percentage of positions for minorities or women made it less essential that the Plan contain a relatively explicit deadline. 770 F.2d, at 757. The Court held further that the Agency's consideration of Joyce's sex in filling the road dispatcher position was lawful. The Agency Plan had been adopted, the court said, to address a conspicuous imbalance in the Agency's work force, and neither unnecessarily trammeled the rights of other employees, nor created an absolute bar to their advancement. *Id.*, at 757–759.

II

As a preliminary matter, we note that petitioner bears the burden of establishing the invalidity of the Agency's Plan. Only last Term, in *Wygant v. Jackson Board of*

Education, 476 U.S. 267, 277–278, 106 S.Ct. 1842, 1849, 90 L.Ed.2d 260 (1986), we held that "[t]he ultimate burden remains with the employees to demonstrate the unconstitutionality of an affirmative-action program," and we see no basis for a different rule regarding a plan's alleged violation of Title VII. This case also fits readily within the analytical framework set forth in *McDonnell Douglas Corp. v. Green,* 411 U.S. 792, 93 S.Ct. 1817, 36 L.Ed.2d 668 (1973). Once a plaintiff establishes a prima facie case that race or sex has been taken into account in an employer's employment decision, the burden shifts to the employer to articulate a nondiscriminatory rationale for its decision. The existence of an affirmative action plan provides such a rationale. If such a plan is articulated as the basis for the employer's decision, the burden shifts to the plaintiff to prove that the employer's justification is pretextual and the plan is invalid. As a practical matter, of course, an employer will generally seek to avoid a charge of pretext by presenting evidence in support of its plan. That does not mean, however, as petitioner suggests, that reliance on an affirmative action plan is to be treated as an affirmative defense requiring the employer to carry the burden of proving the validity of the plan. The burden of proving its invalidity remains on the plaintiff.

The assessment of the legality of the Agency Plan must be guided by our decision in *Weber, supra.* In that case, the Court addressed the question whether the employer violated Title VII by adopting a voluntary affirmative action plan designed to "eliminate manifest racial imbalances in traditionally segregated job categories." *Id.,* 443 U.S., at 197, 99 S.Ct. at 2724. . . .

We upheld the employer's decision to select less senior black applicants over the white respondent, for we found that taking race into account was consistent with Title VII's objective of "break[ing] down old patterns of racial segregation and hierarchy." *Id.,* at 208, 99 S.Ct., at 2730. As we stated:

> "It would be ironic indeed if a law triggered by a Nation's concern over centuries of racial injustice and intended to improve the lot of those who had 'been excluded from the American dream for so long' constituted the first legislative prohibition of all voluntary, private, race-conscious efforts to abolish traditional patterns of racial segregation and hierarchy." *Id.,* at 204, 99 S.Ct., at 2728 (quoting remarks of Sen. Humphrey, 110 Cong.Rec. 6552 (1964)).

We noted that the plan did not "unnecessarily trammel the interests of the white employees," since it did not require "the discharge of white workers and their replacement with new black hires." 443 U.S., at 208, 99 S.Ct., at 2730. Nor did the plan create "an absolute bar to the advancement of white employees," since half of those trained in the new program were to be white. *Ibid.* Finally, we observed that the plan was a temporary measure, not designed to maintain racial balance, but to "eliminate a manifest racial imbalance." *Ibid.* . . .

In reviewing the employment decision at issue in this case, we must first examine whether that decision was made pursuant to a plan prompted by concerns similar to those of the employer in *Weber*. Next, we must determine whether the effect of the Plan on males and nonminorities is comparable to the effect of the Plan in that case.

The first issue is therefore whether consideration of the sex of applicants for Skilled Craft jobs was justified by the existence of a "manifest imbalance" that reflected underrepresentation of women in "traditionally segregated job categories." *id.*, at 197, 99 S.Ct., at 2724. in determining whether an imbalance exists that would justify taking sex or race into account, a comparison of the percentage of minorities or women in the employer's work force with the percentage in the area labor market or general population is appropriate in analyzing jobs that require no special expertise, see *Teamsters v. United States*, 431 U.S. 324, 97 S.Ct. 1843, 52 L.Ed.2d 396 (1977) (comparison between percentage of blacks in employer's work force and in general population proper in determining extent of imbalance in truck driving positions), or training programs designed to provide expertise, see *Steelworkers v. Weber*, 443 U.S. 193, 99 S.Ct. 2721, 61 L.Ed.2d 480 (1979) (comparison between proportion of blacks working at plant and proportion of blacks in area labor force appropriate in calculating imbalance for purpose of establishing preferential admission to craft training program). Where a job requires special training, however, the comparison should be with those in the labor force who possess the relevant qualifications. See *Hazelwood School District v. United States*, 433 U.S. 299, 97 S.Ct. 2736, 53 L.Ed.2d 768 (1977) (must compare percentage of blacks in employer's work ranks with percentage of qualified black teachers in area labor force in determining underrepresentation in teaching positions). The requirement that the "manifest imbalance" relate to a "traditionally segregated job category" provides assurance both that sex or race will be taken into account in a manner consistent with Title VII's purpose of eliminating the effects of employment discrimination, and that the interests of those employees not benefiting from the plan will not be unduly infringed.

A manifest imbalance need not be such that it would support a prima facie case against the employer, as suggested in Justice O'Connor's concurrence, *post*, at —, since we do not regard as identical the constraints of Title VII and the Federal Constitution on voluntarily adopted affirmative action plans. Application of the "prima facie" standard in Title VII cases would be inconsistent with *Weber*'s focus on statistical imbalance, and could inappropriately create a significant disincentive for employers to adopt an affirmative action plan. See *Weber, supra*, 443 U.S., at 204, 99 S.Ct., at 2727–2728 (Title VII intended as a "catalyst" for employer efforts to eliminate vestiges of discrimination). A corporation concerned with maximizing return on investment, for instance, is hardly likely to adopt a plan if in order to do so it must compile evidence that could be used to subject it to a colorable Title VII suit.

It is clear that the decision to hire Joyce was made pursuant to an Agency plan that directed that sex or race be taken into account for the purpose of remedying underrepresentation. The Agency Plan acknowledged the "limited opportunities that have existed in the past," App. 57, for women to find employment in certain job classifications "where women have not been traditionally employed in significant numbers." *Id.,* at 51. As a result, observed the Plan, women were concentrated in traditionally female jobs in the Agency, and represented a lower percentage in other job classifications than would be expected if such traditional segregation had not occurred. Specifically, 9 of the 10 Para-Professionals and 110 of the 145 Office and Clerical Workers were women. By contrast, women were only 2 of the 28 Officials and Administrators, 5 of the 58 Professionals, 12 of the 124 Technicians, none of the Skilled Craft Workers, and 1—who was Joyce—of the 110 Road Maintenance Workers. *Id.,* at 51–52. The Plan sought to remedy these imbalances through "hiring, training and promotion of . . . women throughout the Agency in all major job classifications where they are underrepresented." *Id.,* at 43.

As an initial matter, the Agency adopted as a benchmark for measuring progress in eliminating underrepresentation the long-term goal of a work force that mirrored in its major job classifications the percentage of women in the area labor market. Even as it did so, however, the Agency acknowledged that such a figure could not by itself necessarily justify taking into account the sex of applicants for positions in all job categories. . . .

As the Agency Plan recognized, women were most egregiously underrepresented in the Skilled Craft job category, since *none* of the 238 positions was occupied by a woman. In mid-1980, when Joyce was selected for the road dispatcher position, the Agency was still in the process of refining its short-term goals for Skilled Craft Workers in accordance with the directive of the Plan. This process did not reach fruition until 1982, when the Agency established a short-term goal for that year of 3 women for the 55 expected openings in that job category—a modest goal of about 6% for that category.

We reject petitioner's argument that, since only the long-term goal was in place for Skilled Craft positions at the time of Joyce's promotion, it was inappropriate for the Director to take into account affirmative action considerations in filling the road dispatcher position. The Agency's Plan emphasized that the long-term goals were not to be taken as guides for actual hiring decisions, but that supervisors were to consider a host of practical factors in seeking to meet affirmative action objectives, including the fact that in some job categories women were not qualified in numbers comparable to their representation in the labor force.

By contrast, had the Plan simply calculated imbalances in all categories according to the proportion of women in the area labor pool, and then directed that hiring be governed solely by those figures, its validity fairly could be called into question. This is because analysis of a more specialized labor pool normally is necessary in determining underrepresentation in some positions. If a plan failed to take distinctions in qualifications into account in providing guidance for actual employment decisions, it would dictate mere blind hiring by the numbers, for it would hold supervisors to "achievement of a particular percentage of minority employment or membership . . . regardless of circumstances such as economic conditions or the number of available qualified minority applicants . . . ." *Sheet Metal Workers v. EEOC,* 478 U.S. 421, 495, 106 S.Ct. 3019, 3060, 92 L.Ed.2d 344 (1986) (O'connor, J., concurring in part and dissenting in part).

The Agency's Plan emphatically did *not* authorize such blind hiring. It expressly directed that numerous factors be taken into account in making hiring decisions, including specifically the qualifications of female applicants for particular jobs. Thus, despite the fact that no precise short-term goal was yet in place for the Skilled Craft category in mid-1980, the Agency's management nevertheless had been clearly instructed that they were not to hire solely by reference to statistics. The fact that only the long-term goal had been established for this category posed no danger that personnel decisions would be made by reflexive adherence to a numerical standard.

Furthermore, in considering the candidates for the road dispatcher position in 1980, the Agency hardly needed to rely on a refined short-term goal to realize that it had a significant problem of underrepresentation that required attention. Given the obvious imbalance in the Skilled Craft category, and given the Agency's commitment to eliminating such imbalances, it was plainly not unreasonable for the Agency to determine that it was appropriate to consider as one factor the sex of Ms. Joyce in making its decision. The promotion of Joyce thus satisfies the first requirement enunciated in *Weber,* since it was undertaken to further an affirmative action plan designed to eliminate Agency work force imbalances in traditionally segregated job categories.

We next consider whether the Agency Plan unnecessarily trammeled the rights of male employees or created an absolute bar to their advancement. In contrast to the plan in *Weber,* which provided that 50% of the positions in the craft training program were exclusively for blacks, and to the consent decree upheld last Term in *Firefighters v. Cleveland,* 478 U.S. 501, 106 S.Ct. 3063, 92 L.Ed.2d 405 (1986), which required the promotion of specific numbers of minorities, the Plan sets aside no positions for women. The Plan expressly states that "[t]he 'goals' established for each Division should not be construed as 'quotas' that must be met." App. 64. Rather, the Plan merely authorizes that consideration be given to affirmative action concerns when evaluating qualified applicants. As the Agency Director testified, the sex of Joyce was but one of numerous factors he took into account in arriving at his decision. Tr. 68. The Plan thus resembles the "Harvard Plan" approvingly noted by Justice Powell in *Regents of University of California v. Bakke,* 438 U.S. 265, 316–319, 98 S.Ct. 2733, 2761–2763, 57 L.Ed.2d 750 (1978), which considers race along with other criteria in determining admission to the college. As Justice Powell observed: "In such an admissions program, race or ethnic background may be deemed a 'plus' in a particular applicant's file, yet it does not insulate the individual from comparison with all other candidates for the available seats." *Id.,* at 317, 98 S.Ct., at 2762. Similarly, the Agency Plan requires women to compete with all other qualified applicants. *No* persons are automatically excluded from consideration; *all* are able to have their qualifications weighed against those of other applicants.

In addition, petitioner had no absolute entitlement to the road dispatcher position. Seven of the applicants were classified as qualified and eligible, and the Agency Director was authorized to promote any of the seven. Thus, denial of the promotion unsettled no legitimate, firmly rooted expectation on the part of petitioner. Furthermore, while petitioner in this case was denied a promotion, he retained his employment with the Agency, at the same salary and with the same seniority, and remained eligible for other promotions.

Finally, the Agency's Plan was intended to *attain* a balanced work force, not to maintain one. The Plan contains 10 references to the Agency's desire to "attain" such a balance, but no reference whatsoever to a goal of maintaining it. The Director testified that, while the "broader goal" of affirmative action, defined as "the desire to hire, to promote, to give opportunity and training on an equitable, non-discriminatory basis," is something that is "a permanent part" of "the Agency's operating philosophy," that broader goal "is divorced, if you will, from specific numbers or percentages." Tr. 48–49.

. . . [S]ubstantial evidence shows that the Agency has sought to take a moderate, gradual approach to eliminating the imbalance in its work force, one which establishes realistic guidance for employment decisions, and which visits minimal intrusion on the legitimate expectations of other employees. Given this fact, as well as the Agency's express commitment to "attain" a balanced work force, there is ample assurance that the Agency does not seek to use its Plan to maintain a permanent racial and sexual balance.

III

In evaluating the compliance of an affirmative action plan with Title VII's prohibition on discrimination, we must be mindful of "this Court's and Congress' consistent emphasis on 'the value of voluntary efforts to further the objectives of the law.'" *Wygant*, 476 U.S., at 290, 106 S.Ct., at 1855 (O'Connor, J., concurring in part and concurring in judgment) (quoting *Bakke, supra,* 438 U.S., at 364, 98 S.Ct., at 2785–86). The Agency in the case before us has undertaken such a voluntary effort, and has done so in full recognition of both the difficulties and the potential for intrusion on males and nonminorities. The Agency has identified a conspicuous imbalance in job categories traditionally segregated by race and sex. It has made clear from the outset, however, that employment decisions may not be justified solely by reference to this imbalance, but must rest on a multitude of practical, realistic factors. It has therefore committed itself to annual adjustment of goals so as to provide a reasonable guide for actual hiring and promotion decisions. The Agency earmarks no positions for anyone; sex is but one of several factors that may be taken into account in evaluating qualified applicants for a position. As both the Plan's language and its manner of operation attest, the Agency has no intention of establishing a work force whose permanent composition is dictated by rigid numerical standards.

We therefore hold that the Agency appropriately took into account as one factor the sex of Diane Joyce in determining that she should be promoted to the road dispatcher position. The decision to do so was made pursuant to an affirmative action plan that represents a moderate, flexible, case-by-case approach to effecting a gradual improvement in the representation of minorities and women in the Agency's work force. Such a plan is fully consistent with Title VII, for it embodies the contribution that voluntary employer action can make in eliminating the vestiges of discrimination in the workplace. Accordingly, the judgment of the Court of Appeals is *Affirmed.*

Notes and Questions

1. What is the difference between showing that one is rectifying a manifest imbalance and a prima facie case of discrimination? A manifest imbalance is rooted in the employer's statistical finding that representation in its workforce falls short of diversity goals. This is different from the elements required for a plantiff to make a case of discrimination under Title VII. As a result, when an employer moves to rectify manifest imbalance, it is implementing "voluntary affirmative action" steps rather than rectifying past wrongs. Whether these steps are permitted by Title VII is a source of contention between the majority and the dissent in *Johnson v. Transp. Agency.*

2. The majority cites *Weber* to illustrate the tools available to employers to rectify a manifest imbalance compared to those considered when defending against a prima facie claim of discrimination. Recall the employer's defense to the claim of statistical disproportionate impact in *Hazelwood* when we covered systematic disparate intent. Plaintiffs in those cases shoulder a much tougher burden. They have to show that the hires by employer are disproportionate compared to the relevant labor market. Here, the Court states that the standard for the employer implementing voluntary affirmative steps based on imbalance are less stringent. In the case of voluntary steps, the employer could consider data from its local workforce.

> *Weber* . . . focused on the disparity between the percentage of black skilled craft workers in Kaiser's ranks and the percentage of blacks in the area labor force. 443 U.S., at 198–199, 99 S.Ct., at 2724–2725. Such an approach reflected a recognition that the proportion of black craft workers in the local labor force was likely as miniscule as the proportion in Kaiser's work force. The Court realized that the lack of imbalance between these figures would mean that employers in precisely those industries in which discrimination has been most effective would be precluded from adopting training programs to increase the percentage of qualified minorities. Thus, in cases such as *Weber,* where the employment decision at issue involves the selection of unskilled persons for a training program, the "manifest imbalance" standard permits comparison with the general labor force. By contrast, the "prima facie" standard would require comparison with

the percentage of minorities or women qualified for the job for which the trainees are being trained, a standard that would have invalidated the plan in *Weber* itself.

In some cases, of course, the manifest imbalance may be sufficiently egregious to establish a prima facie case. However, as long as there is a manifest imbalance, an employer may adopt a plan even where the disparity is not so striking, without being required to introduce the nonstatistical evidence of past discrimination that would be demanded by the "prima facie" standard. See, *e.g., Teamsters v. United States*, 431 U.S. 324, 339, 97 S.Ct. 1843, 1856, 52 L.Ed.2d 396 (1977) (statistics in pattern and practice case supplemented by testimony regarding employment practices). Of course, when there is sufficient evidence to meet the more stringent "prima facie" standard, be it statistical, nonstatistical, or a combination of the two, the employer is free to adopt an affirmative action plan."

3. The majority and Justice Scalia disagreed on whether Congress intended voluntary affirmative steps as part of compliance to Title VII. Justice Scalia's "dissent maintains that *Weber*'s conclusion that Title VII does not prohibit voluntary affirmative action programs 'rewrote the statute it purported to construe.'" The majority, however, reads a "decisive rejection of the argument that the 'plain language' of the statute prohibits affirmative action [in] (1) legislative history indicating Congress' clear intention that employers play a major role in eliminating the vestiges of discrimination, 443 U.S., at 201–204, 99 S.Ct., at 2726–28, and (2) the language and legislative history of § 703(j) of the statute, which reflect a strong desire to preserve managerial prerogatives so that they might be utilized for this purpose. *Id.,* at 204–207, 99 S.Ct. at 2727–29."

The majority goes on to argue:

Justice Scalia's dissent faults the fact that we take note of the absence of congressional efforts to amend the statute to nullify *Weber.* It suggests that congressional inaction cannot be regarded as acquiescence under all circumstances, but then draws from that unexceptional point the conclusion that *any* reliance on congressional failure to act is necessarily a "canard." The fact that inaction may not always provide crystalline revelation, however, should not obscure the fact that it may be probative to varying degrees. *Weber,* for instance, was a widely publicized decision that addressed a prominent issue of public debate. Legislative inattention thus is not a plausible explanation for congressional inaction. Furthermore, Congress not only passed no contrary legislation in the wake of *Weber,* but not one legislator even proposed a bill to do so. The barriers of the legislative process therefore also seem a poor explanation for failure to act. By contrast, when Congress has been displeased with our interpretation of Title VII, it has not hesitated to amend the statute to tell us so. For instance, when Congress passed the Pregnancy Discrimination Act of 1978, 42 U.S.C. § 2000e(k), "it unambiguously expressed its disapproval of both the holding and the reasoning of the Court in [*General Electric Co. v. Gilbert*, 429 U.S. 125, 97 S.Ct. 401, 50 L.Ed.2d 343 (1976)]." *Newport News Shipbuilding & Dry Dock Co. v. EEOC*, 462 U.S. 669, 678, 103 S.Ct. 2622, 2628, 77 L.Ed.2d 89 (1983). Surely, it is appropriate to find some probative value in such radically different congressional reactions to this Court's interpretations of the same statute.

As one scholar has put it, "When a court says to a legislature: 'You (or your predecessor) meant X,' it almost invites the legislature to answer: 'We did not.'" G. Calabresi, A Common Law for the Age of Statutes 31–32 (1982). Any belief in the notion of a dialogue between the judiciary and the legislature must acknowledge that on occasion an invitation declined is as significant as one accepted.

Part II

Impact of Post-*Brown* Gains Benefiting Diverse Groups — Ongoing Limitations

Chapter 6

The Rights of Language Minorities

A. Historical Overview

This section intersects with a number of legal contexts and focuses on the protections afforded to individuals for whom English is not the first language spoken/learned. At its inception, the United States was a nation of immigrants. In addition to the settlers immigrating from Europe, the U.S. has experienced steady waves of immigration for the last two centuries.[1] As such, the United States is built on diversity. In fact, the framers of the Constitution were concerned about linguistic diversity and fostered multilingualism. The Constitution, for example, was translated into multiple languages.

Growing intolerance of immigrants risks obscuring the long history of multiculturalism in the United States. The framers of the Constitution are reported as having welcomed different languages. They also abstained from declaring English as the United States's only language. In addition, soldiers from various cultural backgrounds fought in our War of Independence. Arguably, in our tradition, commitment to religious freedom goes hand in hand with the desire to protect the rights of linguistic minorities. Today, the American demographic is the most diverse it has ever been. Populations of color have grown exponentially in the last few decades. With the Latino population rapidly growing, and the consistent influx of immigrants to the population, it is predicted that the U.S. population will be a majority of color by 2043.[2]

Some purport that anxiety over growing populations and changing demographics is responsible for current tensions and social conflicts. Raging debates over

---

1. *Immigration Waves*, http://immigrationtounitedstates.org/603-immigration-waves.html?newsid=603; Faye Hipsman & Doris Meissner *Immigration in the United States: New Economic, Social, Political Landscapes with Legislative Reform on the Horizon*, http://www.migrationpolicy.org/article/immigration-united-states-new-economic-social-political-landscapes-legislative-reform/; Luke Waggoner, *Immigration Reform 2013: 3 Waves of Immigration that Changed America*, http://mic.com/articles/44183/immigration-reform-2013-3-waves-of-immigration-that-changed-america#.FIPmTXj7c.

2. United States Census, *U.S. Census Bureau Projections Show a Slower Growing, Older, More Diverse Nation a Half Century from Now*, http://www.census.gov/newsroom/releases/archives/population/cb12-243.html; Michael Cooper, *Census Officials, Citing Increasing Diversity, Say U.S. Will Be a 'Plurality Nation'*, N.Y. TIMES, http://www.nytimes.com/2012/12/13/us/us-will-have-no-ethnic-majority-census-finds.html.

immigration reform, amnesty for undocumented immigrants, and the value of cultural sensitivity obscure the myriad of legal protections afforded to language minorities. In fact, the term "minority" itself is no longer suitable to the developing landscape.[3]

Language rights are part and parcel of civil rights. Inability to understand the directives and substance of regulations highly inhibit, for example, participation in the democratic process. Substantive language rights are also essential to providing adequate education to immigrant children. In addition, individuals of immigrant origin routinely experience discrimination based on national origin and alienage. Finally, issues of due process consistently arise in governmental treatment of immigrants, particularly in the context of immigration, investigation and raids.[4]

The debate over the value of multilingualism continues in the United States. While some fear that multilingualism might endanger national unity, others point to peers abroad as examples of thriving and stable multilingual societies. *See* Cristina M. Rodríguez, *Language and Participation*, 94 CAL. L. REV. 687 (2006). In the United States, educators continue to struggle to provide adequate resources, educational support and training to multilingual students. Christine Armario, *U.S. Bilingual Education Challenge: Students Learning English as Second Language at Risk*, HUFFINGTON POST (Apr. 14, 2013), http://www.huffingtonpost.com/2013/04/14/us -bilingual-education-_n_3079950.html; NAT'L CTR. EDUC. STAT., THE CONDITION OF EDUCATION: ENGLISH LANGUAGE LEARNERS, http://nces.ed.gov/programs/coe /indicator_cgf.asp (last updated May 2014); Juan F. Perea, *Buscando América: Why Integration and Equal Protection Fail to Protect Latinos*, 117 HARV. L. REV. 1420, 1420 (2005). As highlighted in *Plyler v. Doe*, below, education remains an important vehicle for raising independent and self-sustaining young adults. *See* Nina Rabin, Mary Carol Combs, Norma González, *Understanding Plyler's Legacy: Voices from Border Schools*, 37 J.L. & EDUC. 15, 19 (2008). For this reason, thoughtful educational models are crucial. As it stands, bilingual education presents great challenges. Over the last decades, school systems have struggled to find successful educational models. As a result, students enrolled in bilingual education fail disproportionately.[5]

---

3. *See* Howard Hogan et al., *Projecting Diversity: The Methods, Results, Assumptions and Limitations of the U.S. Census Bureau's Population Projections*, 117 W. VA. L. REV. 1047 (2015); Sandra L. Colby & Jennifer M. Ortman, *Projections of the Size and Composition of the U.S. Population: 2014 to 2060* (Mar. 2015), https://www.census.gov/content/dam/Census/library/publications/2015/demo /p25-1143.pdf.

4. *Fortieth Annual Administrative Law Issue: Immigration Law and Adjudication: A Diversion Of Attention? Immigration Courts and the Adjudication of Fourth and Fifth Amendment Rights*, 59 DUKE L.J. 1563; Note: *An Iowa Immigration Raid Leads to Unprecedented Criminal Consequences: Why ICE Should Rethink the Postville Model*, 95 IOWA L. REV. 323.

5. *See* Joseph A. Santosuosso, *When in California . . . In Defense of the Abolishment of Bilingual Education*, 33 NEW ENG. L. REV. 837 (1999); NAT'L ASS'N BILINGUAL EDUC., http://www.nabe .org/BilingualEducation (last visited Jan. 30, 2018); BURNHAM-MASSEY, L., & PINA, M., EFFECTS OF BILINGUAL INSTRUCTION ON ENGLISH ACADEMIC ACHIEVEMENT OF LEP STUDENTS. READING IMPROVEMENT, 27(2), 129–132 (1990); C. ROSSELL & R. BAKER, THE EDUCATIONAL EFFECTIVENESS

The materials below discuss the various protections and remedies available to bilingual students.[6]

B. Legal Protection in Bilingual Education

Do students have a right to be educated in their native language? What is the meaning of a quality educational model in the context of bilingual education? Title VI presents one of the legal avenues for protection in this area.

Title VI prohibits discrimination by all recipients of federal funding. Section 601 states (42 U.S.C. § 2000d):

> No person in the United States shall, on the ground of race, color, or national origin, be excluded from participation in, be denied the benefits of, or be subjected to discrimination under any program or activity receiving Federal financial assistance.

To enforce this mandate, Section 602 provides:

> Each Federal department and agency which is empowered to extend Federal financial assistance to any program or activity, by way of grant, loan, or contract other than a contract of insurance or guaranty, is authorized and directed to effectuate the provisions of section 2000d of this title with respect to such program or activity by issuing rules, regulations, or orders of general applicability which shall be consistent with achievement of the objectives of the statute authorizing the financial assistance in connection with which the action is taken. . . .

42 U.S.C. § 2000d-1.

OF BILINGUAL EDUCATION. RESEARCH IN THE TEACHING OF ENGLISH, 30(1), 7–74 (1996); Christine Armario, *U.S. Bilingual Education Challenge: Students Learning English as Second Language at Risk*, HUFFINGTON POST (Apr. 14, 2013), http://www.huffingtonpost.com/2013/04/14/us -bilingual-education-n_3079950.html; NAT'L CTR. EDUC. STAT., THE CONDITION OF EDUCATION: ENGLISH LANGUAGE LEARNERS, http://nces.ed.gov/programs/coe/indicator_cgf.asp (last updated May 2014); Juan F. Perea, *BuscandoAmérica: Why Integration and Equal Protection Fail to Protect Latinos*, 117 HARV. L. REV. 1420, 1420 (2005).

6. Cheryl A. Roberts, *Bilingual Education Program Models: A Framework for Understanding*, http://www.ncela.us/files/rcd/BE021127/Bilingual_Education_Program.pdf; Bethany Li, *From Bilingual Education to OELALEAALEPS: How the No Child Left Behind Act Has Undermined English Language Learners' Access to A Meaningful Education*, 14 GEO. J. ON POVERTY L. & POL'Y 539, 541, 543–44 (2007); INTERCULTURAL DEVELOPMENT RESEARCH ASS'N, *IDRA Newsletter*, http://www .idra.org/IDRA_Newsletter/April_2001_Self_Renewing_Schools_Early_Childhood/Boosting_Our _Understanding_of_Bilingual_Education/ (last visited Mar. 14, 2018). *See also* Adela Solís, Ph.D., *Boosting Our Understanding of Bilingual Education*, http://www.idra.org/resource-center/boosting -our-understanding-of-bilingual-education/ (last visited Jan. 30, 2018); José L. Rodríguez, *Defining Our Transitional Bilingual Program*, http://www.idra.org/resource-center/defining-our-transitional -bilingual-program/ (last visited Jan. 30, 2018).

Issues related to educational inequality go far beyond the black/white binary. Students of color of all backgrounds often face challenges in the public school system. Students for whom English is not the first language face unique challenges and have had to fight using Title VI to force schools to address their specific curricular needs. In *Lau*, below, for example, the historical exclusion faced by Asian American students in the San Francisco school system are at the center of the case. More specifically, San Francisco is challenged in *Lau* for failing to provide adequate bilingual education to nearly half of the Chinese students enrolled in the school system. To provide some context, note that "a report adopted by the Human Rights Commission of San Francisco and submitted to the Court by respondents after oral arguments [showed] that, as of April 1973, there were 3,457 Chinese students in the school system who spoke little or no English. The document further showed 2,136 students enrolled in Chinese special instruction classes, but at least 429 of the enrollees were not Chinese but were included for ethnic balance. Thus, as of April 1973, no more than 1,707 of the 3,457 Chinese students needing special English instruction were receiving it."

Lau v. Nichols

414 U.S. 563 (1974)

Mr. Justice Douglas delivered the opinion of the Court.

The San Francisco, California, school system was integrated in 1971 as a result of a federal court decree, 339 F.Supp. 1315. See *Lee v. Johnson*, 404 U.S. 1215, 92 S.Ct. 14, 30 L.Ed.2d 19. The District Court found that there are 2,856 students of Chinese ancestry in the school system who do not speak English. Of those who have that language deficiency, about 1,000 are given supplemental courses in the English language. About 1,800, however, do not receive that instruction.

This class suit brought by non-English-speaking Chinese students against officials responsible for the operation of the San Francisco Unified School District seeks relief against the unequal educational opportunities, which are alleged to violate, inter alia, the Fourteenth Amendment. No specific remedy is urged upon us. Teaching English to the students of Chinese ancestry who do not speak the language is one choice. Giving instructions to this group in Chinese is another. There may be others. Petitioners ask only that the Board of Education be directed to apply its expertise to the problem and rectify the situation.

The District Court denied relief. The Court of Appeals affirmed, holding that there was no violation of the Equal Protection Clause of the Fourteenth Amendment or of § 601 of the Civil Rights Act of 1964, 78 Stat. 252, 42 U.S.C. § 2000d, which excludes from participation in federal financial assistance, recipients of aid which discriminate against racial groups, 483 F.2d 791. One judge dissented. A hearing *en banc* was denied, two judges dissenting. *Id.*, at 805.

We granted the petition for certiorari because of the public importance of the question presented, 412 U.S. 938, 93 S.Ct. 2786, 37 L.Ed.2d 397.

The Court of Appeals reasoned that '[e]very student brings to the starting line of his educational career different advantages and disadvantages caused in part by social, economic and cultural background, created and continued completely apart from any contribution by the school system,' 483 F.2d, at 797. Yet in our view the case may not be so easily decided. This is a public school system of California and §71 of the California Education Code states that 'English shall be the basic language of instruction in all schools.' That section permits a school district to determine 'when and under what circumstances instruction may be given bilingually.' That section also states as 'the policy of the state' to insure 'the mastery of English by all pupils in the schools.' And bilingual instruction is authorized 'to the extent that it does not interfere with the systematic, sequential, and regular instruction of all pupils in the English language.'

Moreover, §8573 of the Education Code provides that no pupil shall receive a diploma of graduation from grade 12 who has not met the standards of proficiency in 'English,' as well as other prescribed subjects. Moreover, by §12101 of the Education Code (Supp. 1973) children between the ages of six and 16 years are (with exceptions not material here) 'subject to compulsory full-time education.'

Under these state-imposed standards there is no equality of treatment merely by providing students with the same facilities, textbooks, teachers, and curriculum; for students who do not understand English are effectively foreclosed from any meaningful education.

Basic English skills are at the very core of what these public schools teach. Imposition of a requirement that, before a child can effectively participate in the educational program, he must already have acquired those basic skills is to make a mockery of public education. We know that those who do not understand English are certain to find their classroom experiences wholly incomprehensible and in no way meaningful.

We do not reach the Equal Protection Clause argument which has been advanced but rely solely on §601 of the Civil Rights Act of 1964, 42 U.S.C. §2000d, to reverse the Court of Appeals.

That section bans discrimination based 'on the ground of race, color, or national origin,' in 'any program or activity receiving Federal financial assistance.' The school district involved in this litigation receives large amounts of federal financial assistance. The Department of Health, Education, and Welfare (HEW), which has authority to promulgate regulations prohibiting discrimination in federally assisted school systems, 42 U.S.C. §2000d-1, in 1968 issued one guideline that '[s]chool systems are responsible for assuring that students of a particular race, color, or national origin are not denied the opportunity to obtain the education generally obtained by other students in the system.' 33 Fed.Reg. 4955. In 1970 HEW made the guidelines more specific, requiring school districts that were federally funded 'to rectify the language deficiency in order to open' the instruction to students who had 'linguistic deficiencies,' 35 Fed.Reg. 11595.

By §602 of the Act HEW is authorized to issue rules, regulations, and orders to make sure that recipients of federal aid under its jurisdiction conduct any federally financed projects consistently with §601. HEW's regulations, 45 CFR 80.3(b)(1), specify that the recipients may not

'(ii) Provide any service, financial aid, or other benefit to an individual which is different, or is provided in a different manner, from that provided to others under the program;

'(iv) Restrict an individual in any way in the enjoyment of any advantage or privilege enjoyed by others receiving any service, financial aid, or other benefit under the program.'

Discrimination among students on account of race or national origin that is prohibited includes 'discrimination . . . in the availability or use of any academic . . . or other facilities of the grantee or other recipient.' *Id.*, § 80.5(b).

Discrimination is barred which has that effect even though no purposeful design is present: a recipient 'may not . . . utilize criteria or methods of administration which have the effect of subjecting individuals to discrimination' or have 'the effect of defeating or substantially impairing accomplishment of the objectives of the program as respect individuals of a particular race, color, or national origin.' *Id.*, § 80.3(b)(2).

It seems obvious that the Chinese-speaking minority receive fewer benefits than the English-speaking majority from respondents' school system which denies them a meaningful opportunity to participate in the educational program—all earmarks of the discrimination banned by the regulations. In 1970 HEW issued clarifying guidelines, 35 Fed.Reg. 11595, which include the following:

'Where inability to speak and understand the English language excludes national origin-minority group children from effective participation in the educational program offered by a school district, the district must take affirmative steps to rectify the language deficiency in order to open its instructional program to these students.

'Any ability grouping or tracking system employed by the school system to deal with the special language skill needs of national origin-minority group children must be designed to meet such language skill needs as soon as possible and must not operate as an educational dead-end or permanent track.'

Respondent school district contractually agreed to 'comply with title VI of the Civil Rights Act of 1964 . . . and all requirements imposed by or pursuant to the Regulation' of HEW (45 CFR pt. 80) which are 'issued pursuant to that title . . .' and also immediately to 'take any measures necessary to effectuate this agreement.' The Federal Government has power to fix the terms on which its money allotments to the States shall be disbursed. *Oklahoma v. United States Civil Service Commission,*

330 U.S. 127, 142–143, 67 S.Ct. 544, 552–554, 91 L.Ed. 794. Whatever may be the limits of that power, *Steward Machine Co. v. Davis*, 301 U.S. 548, 590, 57 S.Ct. 883, 892, 81 L.Ed. 1279 et seq., they have not been reached here. Senator Humphrey, during the floor debates on the Civil Rights Act of 1964, said:

> 'Simple justice requires that public funds, to which all taxpayers of all races contribute, not be spent in any fashion which encourages, entrenches, subsidizes, or results in racial discrimination.'

We accordingly reverse the judgment of the Court of Appeals and remand the case for the fashioning of appropriate relief.

Reversed and remanded.

––––––––––

Subsequently, the Supreme Court determined in *Alexander v. Sandoval* (discussed in Chapter 4's coverage of educational inequality) that disparate impact claims are not available to private individuals under Title VI.

Question

How does the extension of a private right of action under Title IX, covered in Chapter 3, compare to the Court's opinion here regarding the scope of a private right of action under Title VI?

C. The Equal Educational Opportunities Act

Another source of protection for limited proficiency communities is the Equal Educational Opportunities Act. Unlike Title VI, the Equal Educational Opportunities Act provides some flexibility regarding disparate impact claims:

No State shall deny equal educational opportunity to an individual on account of his or her race, color, sex, or national origin, by—

(a) the deliberate segregation by an educational agency of students on the basis of race, color, or national origin among or within schools;

(b) the failure of an educational agency which has formerly practiced such deliberate segregation to take affirmative steps, consistent with part 4 of this subchapter, to remove the vestiges of a dual school system;

(c) the assignment by an educational agency of a student to a school, other than the one closest to his or her place of residence within the school district in which he or she resides, if the assignment results in a greater degree of segregation of students on the basis of race, color, sex, or national origin among the schools of such agency than would result if such student were assigned to the school closest to his or her place of residence within the school district of such agency providing the appropriate grade level and type of education for such student;

(d) discrimination by an educational agency on the basis of race, color, or national origin in the employment, employment conditions, or assignment to schools of its faculty or staff, except to fulfill the purposes of subsection (f) below;

(e) the transfer by an educational agency, whether voluntary or otherwise, of a student from one school to another if the purpose and effect of such transfer is to increase segregation of students on the basis of race, color, or national origin among the schools of such agency; or

(f) the failure by an educational agency to take appropriate action to overcome language barriers that impede equal participation by its students in its instructional programs.

Pub. L. 93-380, title II, § 204, Aug. 21, 1974, 88 Stat. 515. See *Gomez*, below, for the relevant standard for contesting a school board approach to bilingual education.

Gomez v. Illinois State Board of Education

811 F.2d 1030 (7th Cir. 1987)

ESCHBACH, SENIOR CIRCUIT JUDGE.

The primary question presented in this appeal is whether the district court erred in dismissing the plaintiffs' complaint on the ground that it failed to state a claim under § 204(f) of the Equal Educational Opportunities Act of 1974 (codified at 20 U.S.C. § 1703(f)), the Fourteenth Amendment, and Title VI of the Civil Rights Act of 1964. For the reasons stated below, we find that the lower court's dismissal of the complaint under Fed.R.Civ.P. 12(b)(6) was improper and will remand the action for further proceedings consistent with this opinion.

I

On April 16, 1985, the plaintiffs filed in federal district court an action under 42 U.S.C. § 1983 and Fed.R.Civ.P. 23(b)(2) in which they sought injunctive and declaratory relief on behalf of all Spanish-speaking children of limited English proficiency "who have been, are, or will be enrolled in Illinois public schools, and who have been, should have been, or should be assessed as limited English-proficient." Complaint ¶ 6. (In this opinion, children of limited English proficiency will be referred to as "LEP children.") The six named plaintiffs—students enrolled in either the Iroquois West School District No. 10 or the Peoria School District No. 150—are Spanish speaking. Five are LEP children. The sixth has not yet had her English proficiency tested by her local school system. The complaint named as defendants the Illinois State Board of Education ("Board") and the State Superintendent of Education, Ted Sanders ("Superintendent").

In passing on the propriety of the district court's ruling under Fed.R.Civ.P. 12(b)(6), we must accept the well-pleaded factual allegations of the complaint as true. *Car Carriers, Inc. v. Ford Motor Co.,* 745 F.2d 1101, 1104 (7th Cir.1984), *cert. denied,* 470 U.S. 1054, 105 S.Ct. 1758, 84 L.Ed.2d 821 (1985). We are, of course, not bound by the plaintiffs' legal characterization of the facts. *Prudential Life Insurance Co. v. Sipula*, 776 F.2d 157, 159 (7th Cir.1985). Thus, the following fact recitation is drawn from the complaint. In that pleading, the plaintiffs alleged the following:

In general terms, the plaintiffs were injured because the Board and the Superintendent violated both federal and state law by failing to promulgate uniform and consistent guidelines for the identification, placement, and training of LEP children. As a direct result of the defendants' acts or omissions, the plaintiffs have been deprived of an equal education and have suffered economic hardship, undue delays in their educational progress, and in many cases exclusion from any educational opportunities.

Under Ill.Rev.Stat., ch. 122, ¶ 1A-4(C), the Board is responsible for the educational policies and guidelines for public and private schools from pre-school through grade 12. Under *id*. ¶ 14C-3, that state agency must prescribe regulations for local school districts to follow in ascertaining the number of LEP children within a given school district and for classifying these children according to the language in which they possess primary speaking ability and according to their grade level, age, or achievement level. The Board must also prescribe an annual examination for determining the level of the LEP children's oral comprehension, speaking, reading, and writing of English. The Board has received and continues to receive federal funding for the implementation of educational programs designed to benefit LEP children.

The Superintendent is the chief executive officer of the Board. Under Illinois law, the Board has delegated to the Superintendent the authority to act on its behalf. The Superintendent has also been delegated the authority to develop rules necessary to "carry into efficient and uniform effect all laws for establishing and maintaining" public schools in the state including, *inter alia*, "teaching and instruction, curriculum, library, operation, administration and supervision." State Board of Education, *The Illinois Program for Evaluation, Supervision, and Recognition of Schools* (Document No. 1) at i (1977). The Superintendent is specifically charged with establishing rules for the approval and reimbursement of local school districts that provide transitional bilingual educational programs. Ill.Rev.Stat., ch. 122, ¶ 14C-12.

The Board has promulgated regulations requiring every local school district in Illinois to identify LEP children. *Id*. ¶ 14C-1. The identification process is referred to as a "census." When a census at a particular school building identifies as LEP children 20 or more students who speak the same primary language, the local district is required to provide a transitional bilingual education program. *Id*. ¶ 14C-3. When the census discloses less than 20 such students, the Board does not conduct any review or supervision of the existence or adequacy of whatever services a district might provide to LEP children.

The plaintiffs allege that the Board and the Superintendent have failed to provide local districts with adequate, objective, and uniform guidelines for identifying LEP children. As a result, local districts perceive that they have unlimited discretion in selecting methods of identifying such children and as a result have been able to avoid transitional bilingual education requirements by identifying less than 20

LEP children of the same primary language in a particular building. In addition, because of the absence of proper guidelines, local districts have been found to use as many as 23 different language proficiency tests, 11 standardized English tests, 7 standardized reading tests, and many formal and informal teacher-developed tests. Some of these tests do not accurately measure language proficiency, so that LEP children are not properly identified. This array of tests has also, to the detriment of the plaintiffs, resulted in inconsistent results. . . .

As a result of the defendants' failure to prescribe the proper guidelines, LEP children throughout the state have been denied the appropriate educational services they are entitled to under federal and state law. Until the proper guidelines are promulgated, the local districts will continue to deny the plaintiffs such services. . . .

The plaintiffs, after alleging that they had no adequate remedy at law, sought declaratory and injunctive relief, as well as costs and attorney's fees under 42 U.S.C. § 1988. They requested that the class be certified, but the record before us does not indicate that the district court ever ruled on certification. The defendants did not answer the complaint, but filed a motion, pursuant to Fed.R.Civ.P. 12(b)(6), to dismiss for failure to state a claim upon which relief can be granted.

. . . .

II

. . . .

Equal Educational Opportunities Act of 1974

The relevant provisions of the EEOA are set forth in § II(A)(2)(a) of this opinion and will not be repeated herein. The EEOA was a floor amendment to the 1974 legislation amending the Elementary and Secondary Education Act of 1965. *See* Pub.L. No. 93-380, 93d Cong., 2d Sess., tit. II, 88 Stat. 484, 514 (codified in scattered sections of 20 U.S.C.). There is virtually no legislative history on the provision, and we agree with the observation of the Fifth Circuit in *Castaneda v. Pickard,* 648 F.2d 989, 1001 (5th Cir.1981), that in interpreting floor amendments unaccompanied by illuminating debate a court must adhere closely to the ordinary meaning of the amendment's language.

Congress has provided us with little guidance for the interpretation of § 1703(f). The term "appropriate action" used in that provision indicates that the federal legislature did not mandate a specific program for language instruction, but rather conferred substantial latitude on state and local educational authorities in choosing their programs to meet the obligations imposed by federal law. But, as noted in *Castaneda,* 648 F.2d at 1009, "Congress also must have intended to insure that schools made a genuine and good faith effort, consistent with local circumstances and resources, to remedy the language deficiencies of their students and deliberately placed on federal courts the difficult responsibility of determining whether that obligation had been met." In addition, it is clear that § 1703(f) places the obligation on *both* state and local educational agencies to provide equal educational opportunities to their students.

We are, of course, not unmindful of an important institutional limitation that is present even in the absence of the broad language of § 1703(f). Because of the nature of the judicial process, federal courts are poorly equipped to set substantive standards for institutions whose control is properly reserved to other branches and levels of government better able to assess and apply the knowledge of professionals in a given field (here elementary and secondary education). In such a situation, we must formulate legal rules that protect the plaintiffs' interests in obtaining equal educational opportunities (through the elimination of language barriers) and that give guidance to educational agencies in establishing programs to promote those interests. At the same time, we must be careful not to substitute our suppositions for the expert knowledge of educators or our judgment for the educational and political decisions reserved to the state and local agencies. *See Castaneda,* 648 F.2d at 1009.

It is for these reasons that we believe we should review a state's implementation of § 1703(f) in a manner similar to that which we employ in reviewing an administrative agency's interpretation and implementation of its legislative mandate. . . . Although Congress has provided in § 1703(f) that the spectrum of permissible choice for educational agencies would be broad, that does not mean that the spectrum is without discernible boundaries. This is not a case in which there are no substantive rules to apply, so that there is "neither legal right nor legal wrong." *Achacoso-Sanchez v. INS,* 779 F.2d 1260, 1265 (7th Cir.1985). The term "appropriate action" is not simply precatory, but must be given content with a mind to the EEOA's allocation of responsibilities between the courts and the schools. The duty remains upon us to interpret and enforce congressional enactments, and we cannot accord such sweeping deference to state and local agencies that judicial review becomes in practice judicial abdication.

We find that, as a general matter, the framework set out in *Castaneda,* 648 F.2d at 1009, provides the proper accommodation of the competing concerns identified above. *See also United States v. Texas,* 680 F.2d 356, 371 (5th Cir.1982). Of course, we do not mean to say that we are adopting without qualification the jurisprudence developed in the Fifth Circuit regarding the interpretation of the EEOA. However, the *Castaneda* decision provides a fruitful starting point for our analysis. The fine tuning must await future cases. We, for example, may find that the *Castaneda* guidelines, when applied to a broad range of cases, provide for either too much or too little judicial review. In the instant case, however, they give the proper initial direction for the inquiry.

First, we must examine carefully the evidence of record regarding the soundness of the educational theory or principles upon which the challenged program is based. The court's responsibility in this regard is to ascertain whether a school system is pursuing a program informed by an educational theory recognized as sound by experts in the field or at least considered a legitimate experimental strategy. *Castaneda,* 648 F.2d at 1009. Our function is not to resolve disputes among the competing bodies of expert educational opinion. So long as the chosen theory is sound, we must defer to the judgment of the educational agencies in adopting that theory, even though other theories may also seem appropriate.

Second, we must determine whether the programs actually used by a school system are reasonably calculated to implement effectively the educational theory adopted by the system. After providing substantial leeway for the school system to choose initially its program, we would not be assuring that "appropriate action" was being taken if we found that the school system, after adopting an acceptable theory of instruction, failed to provide the procedures, resources, and personnel necessary to apply that theory in the classroom. *Id.* To the contrary, practical effect must be given to the pedagogical method adopted.

Finally, we must decide whether a school's program, although ostensibly premised on a legitimate educational theory and adequately implemented initially, fails, after a period of time sufficient to give the plan a legitimate trial, to obtain results that would indicate that the language barriers confronting the students are actually being overcome. *Id.* at 1010. In other words, the program can pass the first two thresholds of *Castaneda,* yet may after a time no longer constitute appropriate action for the school system in question, either because the theory upon which it was based did not ultimately provide the desired results or because the authorities failed to adapt the program to the demands that arose in its application. Judicial deference to the school system is unwarranted if over a certain period the system has failed to make substantial progress in correcting the language deficiencies of its students.

The defendants maintain that the *Castaneda* decision applies only to local school districts. We disagree. There is certainly no language in that case to suggest that it is so limited. Indeed, the Fifth Circuit in a subsequent decision applied the *Castaneda* guidelines to an entire state school system. *See Texas,* 680 F.2d at 371–72. There will be, of course, differences in the application of the *Castaneda* analysis depending on whether a state or a local program is at issue. The question is primarily one of the intensity of judicial review. For example, the state school board and its superintendent are obviously not directly involved in the classroom education process. Thus, state educational agencies can only set general guidelines in establishing and assuring the implementation of the state's programs. That does not mean, however, that they have no obligations under the EEOA, for even those general measures must constitute "appropriate action." If a local district is involved, however, then a consideration of what actually occurs in the classroom might be appropriate.

In this case, the first step of the *Castaneda* analysis, *i.e.,* whether the program at issue is based on sound educational theory, is not implicated, because the plaintiffs have no quarrel with the basic "transitional bilingual" education program the state of Illinois has chosen for LEP children. The plaintiffs do maintain, however, that the defendants have failed to meet the second step of *Castaneda,* which relates to implementation. Obviously, then, if the defendants have failed to satisfy step two, we need not consider step three, because this final step assumes that there has been an adequate initial implementation of the program.

That brings us to the central issue of this dispute: What obligation does § 1703(f) impose on state (as opposed to local) educational agencies for the implementation of programs designed to provide LEP children with an equal educational opportunity?

Accepting (as we must) the plaintiffs' allegations as true, the district court's decision means that the defendants need only issue regulations that fail to provide local districts with adequate and uniform guidelines for identifying and placing LEP children in a transitional bilingual education program and that the defendants need not monitor and enforce the implementation of the program chosen by the state's legislature.

We cannot accept such an interpretation of the EEOA. Section 1703(f) could hardly be called detailed, but it does make clear, through the definition of the term "educational agency," that the obligation to take "appropriate action" falls on both state and local educational agencies. We concur in the conclusion of the Ninth Circuit in *Idaho Migrant Council v. Board of Education*, 647 F.2d 69 (9th Cir.1981), that § 1703(f) requires that state, as well as local, educational agencies ensure that the needs of LEP children are met. The plaintiffs in essence alleged that the defendants have only gone through the motions of solving the problem of language barriers. . . .

We must address two events that occurred after the district court rendered its decision in the instant case. First, we noted above that the plaintiffs in their complaint addressed the defendants' alleged failure to supervise, monitor, and enforce Illinois's transitional bilingual education legislation in those local districts required by state law to establish such programs and that the plaintiffs also complained of the lack of programs for those attendance centers with less than 20 LEP children. When this suit was filed, Ill.Rev.Stat. ch. 122, ¶ 14C-3 provided that "[a] school district *may* establish a program in transitional bilingual education with respect to any classification with less than 20 children therein" (emphasis added). The Illinois legislature added the following language on August 1, 1985 (to become effective on that date):

> but should a school district decide not to establish such a program, the school district *shall* provide a locally determined transitional program of instruction which, based upon an individual student language assessment, provides content area instruction in a language other than English to the extent necessary to ensure that each student can benefit from educational instruction and achieve an early and effective transition into the regular school curriculum.

(emphasis added). We reject the defendants' contention that this new legislation moots the plaintiffs' claim relating to those attendance centers with less than 20 LEP children. If anything, this new provision places an additional obligation (along with the general ones imposed by Ill.Rev.Stat. ch. 122, ¶ 2) on the defendants to ensure that students in these attendance centers are receiving a proper education. Indeed, the defendants in their brief to this court have informed us that they will be developing regulations for the implementation of these local programs mandated by the 1985 amendment. We cannot, of course, determine on the record before us the effect this new legislation will have on the actions of the defendants, but we can say that the plaintiffs' claims are not now moot.

That brings us to the second development. On April 4, 1986, the Board released proposed regulations for the implementation of Illinois's Transitional Bilingual

Education Act that, if adopted, would replace those in effect when this suit was filed. However, at the time of our decision, these remain only *proposed* regulations. We do not understand then the defendants' argument that this administrative proposal in April of 1986 provides the plaintiffs with the relief they seek. Not only have the proposed regulations not been adopted, but they have never been tested in practice. The defendants could issue administrative pronouncements that, although (in the district court's words) "detailed," have no practical value whatsoever. That the defendants have reconsidered the regulations about which the plaintiffs complain does not mean that the defendants have eliminated the alleged deficiencies in the education of LEP children. On remand, the district court will, of course, consider any new provisions the defendants may promulgate. In any event, a decision from us on this record about the proposed regulations would be premature.

To summarize, we hold that the plaintiffs' allegations relating to § 1703(f) state a claim upon which relief can be granted. The district court's dismissal of the complaint was, therefore, improper and is reversed.

2. Remaining Claims

As the district court noted in its decision, the plaintiffs sought to recover under the Equal Protection Clause of the Fourteenth Amendment and Title VI of the Civil Rights Act of 1964, codified as amended at 42 U.S.C. §§ 2000d to 2000d-4. The court correctly concluded that, because the plaintiffs did not allege that the defendants acted with a discriminatory intent, the Fourteenth Amendment claim and Title VI statutory claim must fail. *See Guardians Association v. Civil Service Commission,* 463 U.S. 582, 103 S.Ct. 3221, 77 L.Ed.2d 866 (1983); *Washington v. Davis,* 426 U.S. 229, 96 S.Ct. 2040, 48 L.Ed.2d 597 (1976).

. . . .

III

For the reasons stated above, the district court's dismissal of the complaint is AFFIRMED in part and REVERSED in part and the action is REMANDED for further proceedings consistent with this opinion.

Notes

1. Note the standard for evaluating bilingual programs: 1) a court must ascertain whether a school system is pursuing an educational program informed by educational theory recognized by experts in the field. As long as the educational theory proves to be sound, the Court indicates that it will otherwise defer to the educational agency on this point; 2) courts must further investigate whether the programs in the school system are calculated to effectively implement the educational theory adopted by the system; 3)finally, courts must determine if, despite meeting steps 1 and 2, the school district has failed to obtain results, even after sufficient time for trial. In *Gomez,* the Court stated:

> "the first step of the *Castaneda* analysis, *i.e.,* whether the program at issue is based on sound educational theory, is not implicated, because the plaintiffs

have no quarrel with the basic "transitional bilingual" education program the state of Illinois has chosen for LEP children. The plaintiffs do maintain, however, that the defendants have failed to meet the second step of *Castaneda,* which relates to implementation. Obviously, then, if the defendants have failed to satisfy step two, we need not consider step three, because this final step assumes that there has been an adequate initial implementation of the program."

Consider how this standard is litigated throughout lower courts with varying results. *See Issa v. Sch. Dist. of Lancaster,* 847 F.3d 121, 143 (3d Cir. 2017) (holding that the district court did not abuse discretion by issuing an injunction, because "the plaintiffs showed they're likely to succeed on the merits of their EEOA claims, they're likely to suffer irreparable harm without relief, the balance of harms favors them, and relief is in the public interest"); *Methelus v. Sch. Bd. of Collier Cty., Fla.,* 243 F. Supp. 3d 1266 (M.D. Fla. 2017) (denying defendant's motion to dismiss because "plaintiffs stated plausible claim for violation of the EEOA, plaintiffs stated plausible claim for violation of Title VI, plaintiffs sufficiently alleged that board policy resulted in constitutional violation, as required to state § 1983 claim against board, and 5 plaintiffs stated claim for violation of procedural due process"); *United States v. Texas,* 601 F.3d 354, 375 (5th Cir. 2010) (holding "that the district court abused its discretion in holding that defendants violated Section 1703(f) of the EEOA because the evidence presented does not establish that a student's right has been violated or that defendants' acts or omissions caused any claimed violation"); *Flores v. Huppenthal,* 789 F.3d 994, 1008 (9th Cir. 2015) (holding that the "Plaintiffs have not alleged a statewide violation of the EEOA that is adequate to justify the continued enforcement of a statewide injunction"); *McFadden v. Bd. of Educ. for Illinois Sch. Dist. U-46,* 984 F. Supp. 2d 882, 903 (N.D. Ill. 2013) (finding in "favor of plaintiffs and against the District with respect to the District's gifted elementary school program at the time discovery closed in 2009"); Verified Petition for Writ of Mandate and Complaint for Injunctive and Declaratory Relief, *DOE 1 v. California,* 2012 WL 1957463 (Cal. Super.).

2. The 12(b)(6) stage of litigation is one that we looked at when we covered Title VII claims above. As you might recall, the quintessential determination at that stage of litigation is whether plaintiff has made sufficient allegations to establish the elements of a claim. That stage is the most beneficial to the person against whom a motion to dismiss under 12(b)(6) is filed. In an omitted portion of the *Gomez* opinion, the Court lays out instructive reminders to the lower court as to the role of the 12(b)(6) stage of litigation compared to the summary judgment stage (Rule 56) of the Federal Rules of Civil Procedure. This is a crucial reminder for students and litigators. Confusing these two stages can cause extreme harm to the lifespan of the lawsuit. Thus, it is important for litigators to pinpoint when a court might be imposing a higher burden on plaintiffs than necessary at the early stage of the lawsuit. See below for the Court's analysis from *Gomez*:

In view of what transpired below, we will pause to review the function of Rule 12(b)(6) procedures and the scope of the record a court must consider in passing on a motion under that rule. If the Federal Rules of Civil Procedure required that every action filed in district court proceed to trial, the costs generated thereby would be enormous and there would be little benefit in the way of increased accuracy in the results. For many lawsuits, it is obvious well before trial that the defending party is entitled to judgment and that there is no need to expend further the resources of the parties and the court. Thus, the federal rules employ several filters for separating out those suits that should receive plenary consideration from those that should not. Rule 12(b) contains the first set of filters. By moving under subsection (6) of that rule, the defending party maintains that, accepting the plaintiff's allegations as true, the complaint fails to state a claim upon which relief can be granted. At this point in the proceedings, where the plaintiff is a master of his pleading, there is no need to continue the suit if the party initiating the action cannot unilaterally set forth the necessary allegations that entitle him to recovery; thus, judgment should be for the defending party. This is not a decision for the district court to make lightly, however, as the dismissal of the suit under 12(b)(6) could preclude another suit based on any theory that the plaintiff might have advanced on the basis of the facts giving rise to the first action. *American Nurses' Association v. State of Illinois,* 783 F.2d 716, 726–27 (7th Cir.1986).

Thus, in ruling on the 12(b)(6) motion, a district court must accept the well-pleaded allegations of the complaint as true. In addition, the court must view those allegations in the light most favorable to the plaintiff. *Car Carriers,* 745 F.2d at 1106. Similarly, the record under 12(b)(6) is limited to the language of the complaint and to those matters of which the court may take judicial notice. The complaint cannot be amended by the briefs filed by the plaintiff in opposition to a motion to dismiss. *Id.* at 1107. By the same token, the defendant cannot, in presenting its 12(b)(6) challenge, attempt to refute the complaint or to present a different set of allegations. The attack is on the sufficiency of the complaint, and the defendant cannot set or alter the terms of the dispute, but must demonstrate that the plaintiff's claim, as set forth by the complaint, is without legal consequence.

It has been said that the complaint should be dismissed only if it is clear that no relief could be granted under any set of facts that could be proved consistent with the allegations set forth in that pleading. *Hishon v. King & Spaulding,* 467 U.S. 69, 73, 104 S.Ct. 2229, 2233, 81 L.Ed.2d 59 (1984); *see also Conley v. Gibson,* 355 U.S. 41, 45–46, 78 S.Ct. 99, 102, 2 L.Ed.2d 80 (1957). However, this formulation has not been taken literally, *Car Carriers,* 745 F.2d at 1106, because it would permit the dismissal of only patently frivolous cases. *See American Nurses' Association,* 783 F.2d at 727. Nonetheless, although the articulation of the standard may vary, it is undisputed that the defendant must overcome a high barrier to prevail under Rule 12(b)(6).

The problem in the instant case is that, from our reading of the district court's decision dismissing the complaint, it appears that the court neither accepted the plaintiffs' allegations as true nor viewed the evidence in the light most favorable to the plaintiffs. For example, the court did not directly address the plaintiffs' assertion that, although the Board and the Superintendent had ostensibly issued regulations for the education of LEP children, those measures were ineffective in identifying and placing these students.

We also note that the plaintiffs, after the initial dismissal of the complaint, filed a motion for reconsideration to which they attached affidavits, including a rather lengthy one from F. Howard Nelson, an "independent research consultant and program evaluator." In that document, Mr. Nelson discussed the inadequacies of the Illinois educational system for LEP children. Affidavits, however, are the weapons of summary judgment, not of challenges to the sufficiency of the complaint. *See* Fed.R.Civ.P. 12(b), 12(c), 56. It is understandable that the plaintiffs would attempt to make such a showing given the court's reliance on factual inferences not present in the pleadings. Nonetheless, once the district court dismissed the complaint, the plaintiffs had either to amend the complaint or to appeal the judgment. *Cf. Car Carriers*, 745 F.2d at 1111. Attaching affidavits to the motion for reconsideration of the dismissal of the complaint is not appropriate, unless the district court converts the 12(b)(6) motion into one for summary judgment. That conversion was not accomplished below and, of course, cannot be done here because it would be unduly prejudicial to the parties in view of the paucity of this record.

See the following examples of cases where complaints were dismissed for failure to state a claim, pursuant to rule 12(b)(6): *Coleman v. Maryland Court of Appeals*, 626 F.3d 187, 191 (4th Cir. 2010), *aff'd sub nom. Coleman v. Court of Appeals of Maryland*, 566 U.S. 30 (2012) ("district court also correctly ruled that Coleman failed to state a Title VII retaliation claim. No facts in the complaint identify any protected activity by Coleman that prompted the retaliation of which he complains"); *Phillips v. Pub. Serv. Co. of New Mexico*, 58 Fed. App'x 407, 409 (10th Cir. 2003) (stating that "[w]e agree with the district court that Phillips's Notice, as currently drafted, fails to allege any protected activity").

Gomez fits in the larger debate regarding the best means of improving the persistent educational gap in the United States. In addition to mandating sound curricular approaches to bilingual students in public school systems or any private schools receiving Title VI federal funding, a number of initiatives, such as the No Child Left Behind Act,[7] and Common Core,[8] have been championed by federal and state

7. Every Student Succeeds Act, 114 P.L. 95, 129 Stat. 1802 (enacted Dec. 10, 2015) (replacing the No Child Left Behind Act).

8. *See* Joy Resmovits, *How the Common Core Became Education's Biggest Bogeyman*, HUFFINGTON POST (Jan. 30, 2014), https://www.huffingtonpost.com/2014/01/10/common-core_n_4537284

governments in the decades following Gomez.[9] Additionally, politically, the debate and litigation around the treatment of undocumented immigrants rages on.[10] *Plyler v. Doe* and proposed legislation to protect Dreamers are, again, at the center of the legal landscape, with the decision in August of 2017 to rescind the Obama Era Executive Order[11] to protect children of undocumented immigrants who arrived in the U.S. at age 15 or younger.[12] While awaiting legislative clarity on this issue,[13] legal instability as to the fate of this large group (approximately 800,000 individuals) remains.[14] In the meantime, in a few states like California, children of undocumented immigrants are afforded limited protections.[15] This move by states, however, is, not enough to shield these children from deportation and other actions by Immigration officials, because the authority to regulate and enforce immigration laws reside in the federal government, per the Constitution.

.html; Judson N. Kempson, Comment, *Star-Crossed Lovers: The Department of Education and the Common Core*, 67 Admin. L. Rev. 595 (2015); Nat'l Conf. St. Legis., Enacted Common Core State Standards Legislation (2012), https://docs.google.com/viewer?a=v&pid=sites&srcid=ZGVmYXVsdGRvbWF pbnxuY3NsY2Nzc3VwZGF0ZXxneDo0 YTA2NjRkOGRkNGVlNWU4.

9. *See id., see also* Digest Educ. Stat., Federal Programs for Education and Related Activities (2002), http://nces.ed.gov/pubs2003/20 03060d.pdf; No Child Left Behind Act of 2001, Pub. L. No. 107–110.

10. *See* DREAM Act, S. 1615, 115th Cong. (2017–2018); *see also* California Dream Act (AB 130 & 131) (effective 2012–2013).

11. Am. Immigration Couns., Who and Where the DREAMers Are, Revised Estimates: A Demographic Profile of Immigrants Who Might Benefit from the Obama Administration's Deferred Action Initiative (Oct. 2012), http://www.immigrationpolicy.org/just-facts /who-and-where-dreamers-are-revised-estimates; Alex Nowrasteh, *Obama's Immigration Executive Order—Policy Implications*, Cato Inst. (Nov. 19, 2014, 2:59 PM), http://www.cato.org/blog /obamas-immigration-executive-order-policy-implications.

12. *See* David Nakamura, *Trump administration announces end of immigration protection program for 'dreamers'*, Wash. Post (Sept. 5, 2017), https://www.washingtonpost.com/news/post-politics /wp/2017/09/05/trump-administration-announces-end-of-immigration-protection-program-for -dreamers/?utm_term=.66bbac85fd3e; Michael D. Shear & Julie Hirschfeld Davis, *Trump Moves to End DACA and Calls on Congress to Act*, N.Y. Times (Sept. 5, 2017), https://www.nytimes.com/2017 /09/05/us/politics/trump-daca-dreamers-immigration.html.

13. DREAM Act, S. 1615, 115th Cong. (2017–2018).

14. *See* Michael D. Shear & Julie Hirschfeld Davis, *Trump Moves to End DACA and Calls on Congress to Act*, N.Y. Times (Sept. 5, 2017), https://www.nytimes.com/2017/09/05/us/politics /trump-daca-dreamers-immigration.html; Eric Columbus, *DACA Isn't Dead. It's Undead.*, Politico (Jan. 22, 2018), https://www.politico.com/magazine/story/2018/01/22/government-shutdown -daca-donald-trump-216496.

15. *California Dream Act Guide*, UCLA: Undergraduate Admissions, http://www.admission .ucla.edu/CaliforniaDreamAct/ (last visited Mar. 14, 2018); California Dream Act (AB 130 & 131) (effective 2012–2013). *See also* California Legislative Information, http://leginfo.legislature.ca.gov /faces/billTextClient.xhtml?bill_id=201120120AB131 (last visited Mar. 14, 2018).

D. Employment Discrimination against Language Minorities

In addition to those in the education context, robust protections exist for language minorities in employment, with a few exceptions. One source of protection is the Fourteenth Amendment itself. Note the distinction below between discrimination based on alienage versus discrimination based on national origin. Are you convinced that discrimination based on citizenship is not inherently part of the concept of national origin under Title VII?

Espinoza v. Farah Manufacturing Company, Inc.
414 U.S. 86 (1973)

Mr. Justice Marshall delivered the opinion of the Court.

This case involves interpretation of the phrase 'national origin' in Tit. VII of the Civil Rights Act of 1964. Petitioner Cecilia Espinoza is a lawfully admitted resident alien who was born in and remains a citizen of Mexico. She resides in San Antonio, Texas, with her husband, Rudolfo Espinoza, a United States citizen. In July 1969, Mrs. Espinoza sought employment as a seamstress at the San Antonio division of respondent Farah Manufacturing Co. Her employment application was rejected on the basis of a longstanding company policy against the employment of aliens. After exhausting their administrative remedies with the Equal Employment Opportunity Commission, petitioners commenced this suit in the District Court alleging that respondent had discriminated against Mrs. Espinoza because of her 'national origin' in violation of § 703 of Tit. VII, 78 Stat. 255, 42 U.S.C. § 2000e-2(a)(1). The District Court granted petitioners' motion for summary judgment, holding that a refusal to hire because of lack of citizenship constitutes discrimination on the basis of 'national origin.' 343 F.Supp. 1205. The Court of Appeals reversed, concluding that the statutory phrase 'national origin' did not embrace citizenship. 462 F.2d 1331. We granted the writ to resolve this question of statutory construction, 411 U.S. 946, 93 S.Ct. 1920, 36 L.Ed.2d 408, and now affirm.

Section 703 makes it 'an unlawful employment practice for an employer . . . to fail or refuse to hire . . . any individual . . . because of such individual's race, color, religion, sex, or national origin.' Certainly the plain language of the statute supports the result reached by the Court of Appeals. The term 'national origin' on its face refers to the country where a person was born, or, more broadly, the country from which his or her ancestors came.

The statute's legislative history, though quite meager in this respect, fully supports this construction. The only direct definition given the phrase 'national origin' is the following remark made on the floor of the House of Representatives by Congressman Roosevelt, Chairman of the House Subcommittee which reported the bill: 'It means the country from which you or your forebears came. . . . You may come from Poland, Czechoslovakia, England, France, or any other country.' 110 Cong.Rec. 2549

(1964). We also note that an earlier version of § 703 had referred to discrimination because of 'race, color, religion, national origin, or *ancestry*.' H.R. 7152, 88th Cong., 1st Sess., § 804, Oct. 2, 1963 (Comm. print) (emphasis added). The deletion of the word 'ancestry' from the final version was not intended as a material change, see, H.R.Rep.No.914, 88th Cong., 1st See. 87 (1963), suggesting that the terms 'national origin' and 'ancestry' were considered synonymous.

There are other compelling reasons to believe that Congress did not intend the term 'national origin' to embrace citizenship requirements. Since 1914, the Federal Government itself, through Civil Service Commission regulations, has engaged in what amounts to discrimination against aliens by denying them the right to enter competitive examination for federal employment. Exec. Order No. 1997, H.R.Doc. No. 1258, 63d Cong., 3d Sess. 118 (1914); see 5 U.S.C. § 3301; 5 CFR § 338.101 (1972). But it has never been suggested that the citizenship requirement for federal employment constitutes discrimination because of national origin, even though since 1943, various Executive Orders have expressly prohibited discrimination on the basis of national origin in Federal Government employment. See, e.g., Exec. Order No. 9346, 3 CFR 1280 (Cum.Supp. 1938–1943); Exec. Order No. 11478, 3 CFR 446 (1970).

Moreover, § 701(b) of Tit. VII, in language closely paralleling § 703, makes it 'the policy of the United States to insure equal employment opportunities for Federal employees without discrimination because of . . . national origin . . . .' Civil Rights Act of 1964, Pub.L. 88-352, § 701(b), 78 Stat. 254, re-enacted, Pub.L. 89-554, 80 Stat. 523, 5 U.S.C. § 7151. The legislative history of that section reveals no mention of any intent on Congress' part to reverse the longstanding practice of requiring federal employees to be United States citizens. To the contrary, there is every indication that no such reversal was intended. Congress itself has on several occasions since 1964 enacted statutes barring aliens from federal employment. The Treasury, Postal Service, and General Government Appropriation Act, 1973, for example, provides that 'no part of any appropriation contained in this or any other Act shall be used to pay the compensation of any officer or employee of the Government of the United States . . . unless such person (1) is a citizen of the United States.' Pub.L. 92-351, § 602, 86 Stat. 487. See also Pub.L. 91-144, § 502, 83 Stat. 336; Pub.L. 91-439, § 502, 84 Stat. 902.

To interpret the term 'national origin' to embrace citizenship requirements would require us to conclude that Congress itself has repeatedly flouted its own declaration of policy. This Court cannot lightly find such a breach of faith. See *Bate Refrigerating Co. v. Sulzberger*, 157 U.S. 1, 38, 15 S.Ct. 508, 517, 39 L.Ed. 601 (1895). So far as federal employment is concerned, we think it plain that Congress has assumed that the ban on national-origin discrimination in § 701(b) did not affect the historical practice of requiring citizenship as a condition of employment. See *First National Bank in St. Louis v. Missouri*, 263 U.S. 640, 658, 44 S.Ct. 213, 215, 68 L.Ed. 486 (1924). And there is no reason to believe Congress intended the term 'national origin' in § 703 to have any broader scope. Cf. *King v. Smith*, 392 U.S. 309, 330–331, 88 S.Ct. 2128, 2140, 20 L.Ed.2d 1118 (1968).

Petitioners have suggested that the statutes and regulations discriminating against noncitizens in federal employment are unconstitutional under the Due Process Clause of the Fifth Amendment. We need not address that question here, for the issue presented in this case is not whether Congress has the power to discriminate against aliens in federal employment, but rather, whether Congress intended to prohibit such discrimination in private employment. Suffice it to say that we cannot conclude Congress would at once continue the practice of requiring citizenship as a condition of federal employment and, at the same time, prevent private employers from doing likewise. Interpreting § 703 as petitioners suggest would achieve the rather bizarre result of preventing Farah from insisting on United States citizenship as a condition of employment while the very agency charged with enforcement of Tit. VII would itself be required by Congress to place such a condition on its own personnel.

The District Court drew primary support for its holding from an interpretative guideline issued by the Equal Employment Opportunity Commission which provides:

> 'Because discrimination on the basis of citizenship has the effect of discriminating on the basis of national origin, a lawfully immigrated alien who is domiciled or residing in this country may not be discriminated against on the basis of his citizenship . . . .' 29 CFR § 1606.1(d) (1972).

Like the Court of Appeals, we have no occasion here to question the general validity of this guideline insofar as it can be read as an expression of the Commission's belief that there may be many situations where discrimination on the basis of citizenship would have the effect of discriminating on the basis of national origin. In some instances, for example, a citizenship requirement might be but one part of a wider scheme of unlawful national-origin discrimination. In other cases, an employer might use a citizenship test as a pretext to disguise what is in fact national-origin discrimination. Certainly Tit. VII prohibits discrimination on the basis of citizenship whenever it has the purpose or effect of discriminating on the basis of national origin. 'The Act proscribes not only overt discrimination but also practices that are fair in form, but discriminatory in operation.' *Griggs v. Duke Power Co.*, 401 U.S. 424, 431, 91 S.Ct. 849, 853, 28 L.Ed.2d 158 (1971).

It is equally clear, however, that these principles lend no support to petitioners in this case. There is no indication in the record that Farah's policy against employment of aliens had the purpose or effect of discriminating against persons of Mexican national origin. It is conceded that Farah accepts employees of Mexican origin, provided the individual concerned has become an American citizen. Indeed, the District Court found that persons of Mexican ancestry make up more than 96% of the employees at the company's San Antonio division, and 97% of those doing the work for which Mrs. Espinoza applied. While statistics such as these do not automatically shield an employer from a charge of unlawful discrimination, the plain fact of the matter is that Farah does not discriminate against persons of Mexican national origin with respect to employment in the job Mrs. Espinoza sought. She was denied employment, not because of the country of her origin, but because she had not yet achieved United States citizenship. In fact, the record shows that the worker hired in place of Mrs. Espinoza was a citizen with a Spanish surname.

The Commission's guideline may have significance for a wide range of situations, but not for a case such as this where its very premise—that discrimination on the basis of citizenship has the effect of discrimination on the basis of national origin—is not borne out. It is also significant to note that the Commission itself once held a different view as to the meaning of the phrase 'national origin.' When first confronted with the question, the Commission, through its General Counsel, said: "National origin' refers to the country from which the individual or his forebears came . . . , not to whether or not he is a United States citizen . . . .' EEOC General Counsel's Opinion Letter, 1 CCH Employment Prac. Guide 1220.20 (1967). The Commission's more recent interpretation of the statute in the guideline relied on by the District Court is no doubt entitled to great deference, *Griggs v. Duke Power Co.*, *supra*, 401 U.S., at 434, 91 S.Ct. at 855; *Phillips v. Martin Marietta Corp.*, 400 U.S. 542, 545, 91 S.Ct. 496, 498, 27 L.Ed. 613 (1971) (Marshall, J., concurring), but that deference must have limits where, as here, application of the guideline would be inconsistent with an obvious congressional intent not to reach the employment practice in question. Courts need not defer to an administrative construction of a statute where there are 'compelling indications that it is wrong.' *Red Lion Broadcasting Co. v. FCC*, 395 U.S. 367, 381, 89 S.Ct. 1794, 1802, 23 L.Ed.2d 371 (1969); see also *Zuber v. Allen*, 396 U.S. 168, 193, 90 S.Ct. 314, 328, 24 L.Ed.2d 345 (1969); *Volkswagenwerk Aktiengesellschaft v. FMC*, 390 U.S. 261, 272, 88 S.Ct. 929, 935, 19 L.Ed.2d 1090 (1968).

Finally, petitioners seek to draw support from the fact that Tit. VII protects all individuals from unlawful discrimination, whether or not they are citizens of the United States. We agree that aliens are protected from discrimination under the Act. That result may be derived not only from the use of the term 'any individual' in § 703, but also as a negative inference from the exemption in § 702, which provides that Tit. VII 'shall not apply to an employer with respect to the employment of aliens outside any State . . . .' 42 U.S.C. § 2000e-1. Title VII was clearly intended to apply with respect to the employment of aliens inside any State.

The question posed in the present case, however, is not whether aliens are protected from illegal discrimination under the Act, but what kinds of discrimination the Act makes illegal. Certainly it would be unlawful for an employer to discriminate against aliens because of race, color, religion, sex, or national origin—for example, by hiring aliens of Anglo-Saxon background but refusing to hire those of Mexican or Spanish ancestry. Aliens are protected from illegal discrimination under the Act, but nothing in the Act makes it illegal to discriminate on the basis of citizenship or alienage.

We agree with the Court of Appeals that neither the language of the Act, nor its history, nor the specific facts of this case indicate that respondent has engaged in unlawful discrimination because of national origin.

Affirmed.

MR. JUSTICE DOUGLAS, dissenting.

It is odd that the Court which holds that a State may not bar an alien from the practice of law or deny employment to aliens can read a federal statute that prohibits discrimination in employment on account of 'national origin' so as to permit discrimination against aliens.

Alienage results from one condition only: being born outside the United States. Those born within the country are citizens from birth. It could not be more clear that Farah's policy of excluding aliens is de facto a policy of preferring those who were born in this country. Therefore the construction placed upon the 'national origin' provision is inconsistent with the construction this Court has placed upon the same Act's protections for persons denied employment on account of race or sex.

In connection with racial discrimination we have said that the Act prohibits 'practices, procedures, or tests neutral on their face, and even neutral in terms of intent,' if they create 'artificial, arbitrary, and unnecessary barriers to employment when the barriers operate invidiously to discriminate on the basis of racial *or other impermissible classification.*' *Griggs v. Duke Power Co.*, 401 U.S. 424, 430–431, 91 S. Ct. 849, 28 L.Ed.2d 158 (1971) (emphasis added). There we found that the employer could not use test or diploma requirements which on their face were racially neutral, when in fact those requirements had a de facto discriminatory result and the employer was unable to justify them as related to job performance. The tests involved in *Griggs* did not eliminate all blacks seeking employment, just as the citizenship requirement here does not eliminate all applicants of foreign origin. Respondent here explicitly conceded that the citizenship requirement is imposed without regard to the alien's qualifications for the job.

These petitioners against whom discrimination is charged are Chicanos. But whether brown, yellow, black, or white, the thrust of the Act is clear: alienage is no barrier to employment here. *Griggs*, as I understood it until today, extends its protective principles to all, not to blacks alone. Our cases on sex discrimination under the Act yield the same result as *Griggs*. See *Phillips v. Martin Marietta Corp.*, 400 U.S. 542, 91 S.Ct. 496, 27 L.Ed.2d 613 (1971).

The construction placed upon the statute in the majority opinion is an extraordinary departure from prior cases, and it is opposed by the Equal Employment Opportunity Commission, the agency provided by law with the responsibility of enforcing the Act's protections. The Commission takes the only permissible position: that discrimination on the basis of alienage always has the effect of discrimination on the basis of national origin. Refusing to hire an individual because he is an alien 'is discrimination based on birth outside the United States and is thus discrimination based on national origin in violation of Title VII.' Brief for Commission as Amicus Curiae. The Commission's interpretation of the statute is entitled to great weight.

There is no legislative history to cast doubt on this construction. Indeed, any other construction flies in the face of the underlying congressional policy of removing 'artificial, arbitrary, and unnecessary barrier(s) to employment.' *McDonnell Douglas Corp. v. Green*, 411 U.S. 792, 806, 93 S.Ct. 1817, 1826, 36 L.Ed.2d 668 (1973).

Mrs. Espinoza is a permanent resident alien, married to an American citizen, and her children will be native-born American citizens. But that first generation has the greatest adjustments to make to their new country. Their unfamiliarity with America makes them the most vulnerable to exploitation and discriminatory treatment. They, of course, have the same obligation as American citizens to pay taxes, and they are subject to the draft on the same basis. But they have never received equal treatment in the job market. Writing of the immigrants of the late 1800's, Oscar Handlin has said:

> 'For want of alternative, the immigrants took the lowest places in the ranks of industry. They suffered in consequence from the poor pay and miserable working conditions characteristic of the sweat-shops and the homework in the garment trades and in cigar making. But they were undoubtedly better off than the Irish and Germans of the 1840's for whom there had been no place at all.' The Newcomers 24 (1959).

The majority decides today that in passing sweeping legislation guaranteeing equal job opportunities, the Congress intended to help only the immigrant's children, excluding those 'for whom there [is] no place at all.' I cannot impute that niggardly an intent to Congress.

Bernal v. Fainter

467 U.S. 216 (1984)

JUSTICE MARSHALL delivered the opinion of the Court.

The question posed by this case is whether a statute of the State of Texas violates the Equal Protection Clause of the Fourteenth Amendment of the United States Constitution by denying aliens the opportunity to become notaries public. The Court of Appeals for the Fifth Circuit held that the statute does not offend the Equal Protection Clause. We granted certiorari, 464 U.S. 1007, 104 S.Ct. 522, 78 L.Ed.2d 707 (1983), and now reverse.

I

Petitioner, a native of Mexico, is a resident alien who has lived in the United States since 1961. He works as a paralegal for Texas Rural Legal Aid, Inc., helping migrant farm-workers on employment and civil rights matters. In order to administer oaths to these workers and to notarize their statements for use in civil litigation, petitioner applied in 1978 to become a notary public. Under Texas law, notaries public authenticate written instruments, administer oaths, and take out-of-court depositions. The Texas Secretary of State denied petitioner's application because he failed to satisfy the statutory requirement that a notary public be a citizen of the

United States. Tex.Rev.Civ.Stat.Ann., Art. 5949(2) (Vernon Supp.1984) (hereafter Article 5949(2)). After an unsuccessful administrative appeal, petitioner brought suit in the Federal District Court, claiming that the citizenship requirement mandated by Article 5942(2) violated the Federal Constitution.

The District Court ruled in favor of petitioner. *Vargas v. Strake*, C.A. No. B-79-147 (SD Tex., Oct. 9, 1981) (mem.). It reviewed the State's citizenship requirement under a strict-scrutiny standard and concluded that the requirement violated the Equal Protection Clause. The District Court also suggested that even under a rational-relationship standard, the state statute would fail to pass constitutional muster because its citizenship requirement "is wholly unrelated to the achievement of any valid state interest." App. to Pet. for Cert. 11a. A divided panel of the Court of Appeals for the Fifth Circuit reversed, concluding that the proper standard for review was the rational-relationship test and that Article 5949(2) satisfied that test because it "bears a rational relationship to the state's interest in the proper and orderly handling of a countless variety of legal documents of importance to the state." *Vargas v. Strake*, 710 F.2d 190, 195 (1983).

II

As a general matter, a state law that discriminates on the basis of alienage can be sustained only if it can withstand strict judicial scrutiny. In order to withstand strict scrutiny, the law must advance a compelling state interest by the least restrictive means available. Applying this principle, we have invalidated an array of state statutes that denied aliens the right to pursue various occupations. In *Sugarman v. Dougall*, 413 U.S. 634, 93 S.Ct. 2842, 37 L.Ed.2d 853 (1973), we struck down a state statute barring aliens from employment in permanent positions in the competitive class of the state civil service. In *In re Griffiths*, 413 U.S. 717, 93 S.Ct. 2851, 37 L.Ed.2d 910 (1973), we nullified a state law excluding aliens from eligibility for membership in the State Bar. And in *Examining Board v. Flores de Otero*, 426 U.S. 572, 96 S.Ct. 2264, 49 L.Ed.2d 65 (1976), we voided a state law that excluded aliens from the practice of civil engineering.

We have, however, developed a narrow exception to the rule that discrimination based on alienage triggers strict scrutiny. This exception has been labeled the "political function" exception and applies to laws that exclude aliens from positions intimately related to the process of democratic self-government. The contours of the "political function" exception are outlined by our prior decisions. In *Foley v. Connelie*, 435 U.S. 291, 98 S.Ct. 1067, 55 L.Ed.2d 287 (1978), we held that a State may require police to be citizens because, in performing a fundamental obligation of government, police "are clothed with authority to exercise an almost infinite variety of discretionary powers" often involving the most sensitive areas of daily life. *Id.*, at 297, 98 S.Ct., at 1071. In *Ambach v. Norwick*, 441 U.S. 68, 99 S.Ct. 1589, 60 L.Ed.2d 49 (1979), we held that a State may bar aliens who have not declared their intent to become citizens from teaching in the public schools because teachers, like police, possess a high degree of responsibility and discretion in the fulfillment of a basic governmental obligation. They have direct, day-to-day contact with students, exercise unsupervised discretion over them, act as role models, and influence their students about the government and the political process. *Id.*, at 78–79, 99 S. Ct., at 1595–1596. Finally, in *Cabell v. Chavez-Salido*, 454 U.S. 432, 102 S.Ct. 735, 70 L.Ed.2d 677 (1982), we held that a State may bar aliens from positions as probation officers because they, like police and teachers, routinely exercise discretionary power, involving a basic governmental function, that places them in a position of direct authority over other individuals.

The rationale behind the political-function exception is that within broad boundaries a State may establish its own form of government and limit the right to govern to those who are full-fledged members of the political community. Some public positions are so closely bound up with the formulation and implementation of self-government that the State is permitted to exclude from those positions persons outside the political community, hence persons who have not become part of the process of democratic self-determination.

> "The exclusion of aliens from basic governmental processes is not a deficiency in the democratic system but a necessary consequence of the community's process of political self-definition. Self-government, whether direct or through representatives, begins by defining the scope of the community of the governed and thus of the governors as well: Aliens are by definition those outside of this community." *Id.*, at 439–440, 102 S.Ct., at 740.

We have therefore lowered our standard of review when evaluating the validity of exclusions that entrust only to citizens important elective and nonelective positions whose operations "go to the heart of representative government." *Sugarman v. Dougall, supra*, 413 U.S., at 647, 93 S.Ct., at 2850. "While not retreating from the position that restrictions on lawfully resident aliens that primarily affect economic interests are subject to heightened judicial scrutiny . . . we have concluded that strict scrutiny is out of place when the restriction primarily serves a political function. . . ." *Cabell v. Chavez-Salido, supra*, 454 U.S., at 439, 102 S.Ct., at 739 (citation omitted).

To determine whether a restriction based on alienage fits within the narrow political-function exception, we devised in *Cabell* a two-part test.

> "First, the specificity of the classification will be examined: a classification that is substantially over inclusive or under inclusive tends to undercut the governmental claim that the classification serves legitimate political ends. . . . Second, even if the classification is sufficiently tailored, it may be applied in the particular case only to 'persons holding state elective or important nonelective executive, legislative, and judicial positions,' those officers who 'participate directly in the formulation, execution, or review of broad public policy' and hence 'perform functions that go to the heart of representative government.'" 454 U.S., at 440, 102 S.Ct., at 740 (quoting *Sugarman v. Dougall, supra*, 413 U.S., at 647, 93 S.Ct., at 2850).

III

We now turn to Article 5949(2) to determine whether it satisfies the *Cabell* test. The statute provides that "[to be eligible for appointment as a Notary Public, a person shall be a resident citizen of the United States and of this state . . ." Unlike the statute invalidated in *Sugarman*, Article 5949(2) does not indiscriminately sweep within its ambit a wide range of offices and occupations but specifies only one particular post with respect to which the State asserts a right to exclude aliens. Clearly, then, the statute is not over inclusive; it applies narrowly to only one category of persons: those wishing to obtain appointments as notaries. Less clear is whether Article 5949(2) is fatally under inclusive. Texas does not require court reporters to be United States citizens even though they perform some of the same services as notaries. Nor does Texas require that its Secretary of State be a citizen, even though he holds the highest appointive position in the State and performs many important functions, including supervision of the licensing of all notaries public. We need not decide this issue, however, because of our decision with respect to the second prong of the *Cabell* test.

In support of the proposition that notaries public fall within that category of officials who perform functions that "go to the heart of representative government," the State emphasizes that notaries are designated as public officers by the Texas Constitution. Texas maintains that this designation indicates that the State views notaries as important officials occupying posts central to the State's definition of itself as a political community. This Court, however, has never deemed the source of a position—whether it derives from a State's statute or its Constitution—as the dispositive factor in determining whether a State may entrust the position only to citizens. Rather, this Court has always looked to the actual function of the position as the dispositive factor. The focus of our inquiry has been whether a position was such that the officeholder would necessarily exercise broad discretionary power over the formulation or execution of public policies importantly affecting the citizen population—power of the sort that a self-governing community could properly entrust only to full-fledged members of that community. As the Court noted in *Cabell*, in determining whether the function of a particular position brings the position within the narrow ambit of the exception, "the Court will look to the importance of the function as a factor giving substance to the concept of democratic self-government." 454 U.S., at 441, n. 7, 102 S.Ct., at 740, n. 7.

The State maintains that even if the actual function of a post is the touchstone of a proper analysis, Texas notaries public should still be classified among those positions from which aliens can properly be excluded because the duties of Texas notaries entail the performance of functions sufficiently consequential to be deemed "political." . . .

We recognize the critical need for a notary's duties to be carried out correctly and with integrity. But a notary's duties, important as they are, hardly implicate responsibilities that go to the heart of representative government. Rather, these duties are essentially clerical and ministerial. In contrast to state troopers, *Foley v. Connelie*,

435 U.S. 291, 98 S.Ct. 1067, 55 L.Ed.2d 287 (1978), notaries do not routinely exercise the State's monopoly of legitimate coercive force. Nor do notaries routinely exercise the wide discretion typically enjoyed by public school teachers when they present materials that educate youth respecting the information and values necessary for the maintenance of a democratic political system. See *Ambach v. Norwick*, 441 U.S., at 77, 99 S.Ct., at 1594. To be sure, considerable damage could result from the negligent or dishonest performance of a notary's duties. But the same could be said for the duties performed by cashiers, building inspectors, the janitors who clean up the offices of public officials, and numerous other categories of personnel upon whom we depend for careful, honest service. What distinguishes such personnel from those to whom the political-function exception is properly applied is that the latter are invested either with policy making responsibility or broad discretion in the execution of public policy that requires the routine exercise of authority over individuals. Neither of these characteristics pertains to the functions performed by Texas notaries.

The inappropriateness of applying the political-function exception to Texas notaries is further underlined by our decision in *In re Griffiths*, 413 U.S. 634, 93 S.Ct. 2851, 37 L.Ed.2d 910 (1973), in which we subjected to strict scrutiny a Connecticut statute that prohibited noncitizens from becoming members of the State Bar. Along with the usual powers and privileges accorded to members of the bar, Connecticut gave to members of its Bar additional authority that encompasses the very duties performed by Texas notaries—authority to "'sign writs and subpoenas, take recognizances, administer oaths and take depositions and acknowledgements of deeds.'" *Id.*, at 723, 93 S.Ct., at 2856 (quoting Connecticut statute). In striking down Connecticut's citizenship requirement, we concluded that "[i]t in no way denigrates a lawyer's high responsibilities to observe that [these duties] hardly involve matters of state policy or acts of such unique responsibility as to entrust them only to citizens." *Id.*, at 724, 93 S.Ct., at 2856. If it is improper to apply the political-function exception to a citizenship requirement governing eligibility for membership in a state bar, it would be anomalous to apply the exception to the citizenship requirement that governs eligibility to become a Texas notary. We conclude, then, that the "political function" exception is inapplicable to Article 5949(2) and that the statute is therefore subject to strict judicial scrutiny.

IV

To satisfy strict scrutiny, the State must show that Article 5949(2) furthers a compelling state interest by the least restrictive means practically available. Respondents maintain that Article 5949(2) serves its "legitimate concern that notaries be reasonably familiar with state law and institutions" and "that notaries may be called upon years later to testify to acts they have performed." Brief for Respondents 24–25. However, both of these asserted justifications utterly fail to meet the stringent requirements of strict scrutiny. There is nothing in the record that indicates that resident aliens, as a class, are so incapable of familiarizing themselves with

Texas law as to justify the State's absolute and class wide exclusion. The possibility that some resident aliens are unsuitable for the position cannot justify a wholesale ban against all resident aliens. Furthermore, if the State's concern with ensuring a notary's familiarity with state law were truly "compelling," one would expect the State to give some sort of test actually measuring a person's familiarity with the law. The State, however, administers no such test. To become a notary public in Texas, one is merely required to fill out an application that lists one's name and address and that answers four questions pertaining to one's age, citizenship, residency, and criminal record — nothing that reflects the State's asserted interest in insuring that notaries are familiar with Texas law. Similarly inadequate is the State's purported interest in insuring the later availability of notaries' testimony. This justification fails because the State fails to advance a factual showing that the unavailability of notaries' testimony presents a real, as opposed to a merely speculative, problem to the State. Without a factual underpinning, the State's asserted interest lacks the weight we have required of interests properly denominated as compelling.

V

We conclude that Article 5949(2) violates the Fourteenth Amendment of the United States Constitution. Accordingly the judgment of the Court of Appeals is reversed, and the case is remanded for further proceedings consistent with this opinion.

It is so ordered.

Notes and Questions

See below for limitations relating to the scope of protections available to undocumented immigrants. While the Court did determine that children of undocumented immigrants cannot be deprived access to public education in *Plyler v. Doe*, in *Hoffman Plastic Compounds v. National Labor Relations Board* (below), it ruled that the National Labor Relations Board's determination regarding grants of back pay to undocumented workers is preempted by immigration law. Since undocumented workers are not legally entitled to work in the United States, the Court reasoned, awards of back pay for employers' labor violations are not allowed. Consider the import of this reasoning for protection of undocumented workers in the workforce and for today's national debate on immigration reform.

Futhermore, note the specific protections provided to undocumented immigrants under the IRCA, in specific spheres of society. Classes of undocumented immigrants gained protection and a path for regularization through this statute. As you process the range of protections and obligations imposed by the statute, consider whether this model could be implemented today. What type of protections would need to be implemented to allow application of these protections for current undocumented immigrants? Do these cases demonstrate some gaps in protections for undocumented immigrants that an amended or subsequent statute could address?

The IRCA was passed as part of a comprehensive immigration reform to regularize the status of certain classes of undocumented immigrants in the U.S. and to provide needed due process and civil protections to immigrants in the United States. Section 274B(a), for example, states:

> It is an unfair immigration-related employment practice for a person or other entity to discriminate against any individual (other than an unauthorized alien) with respect to the hiring, or recruitment or referral for a fee, of the individual for employment or the discharging of the individual from employment—
>
> (A) because of such individual's national origin, or
>
> (B) in the case of a citizen or intending citizen . . . because of such individual's citizenship status.

Consider the issues raised under this portion of the statute. One major takeaway from these cases is that statutory reform is only one step to achieving protection and integration of undocumented immigrants, even after the enactment of an amnesty. An additional necessary step requires vigilant litigation and training in order to ensure that the new legal status of these workers is honored, as well as to prevent retaliation.

League of United Latin American Citizens v. Pasadena Independent School District

662 F. Supp. 443 (S.D. Tex. 1987)

McDonald, District Judge.

On November 6, 1986, the Immigration Reform and Control Act of 1986 ("IRCA") became law. This legislation was designed, in part, to allow hundreds of thousands of undocumented aliens now present in the United States to become citizens by proceeding through a several-step legalization process. In enacting this law Congress recognized that:

> The United States has a large undocumented alien population living and working within its borders. Many of these people have been here for a number of years and have become a part of their communities. Many have strong family ties here which include U.S. citizens and lawful residents. They have built social networks in this country. They have contributed to the United States in myriad ways, including providing their talents, labor and tax dollars. However, because of their undocumented status, these people live in fear, afraid to seek help when their rights are violated, when they are victimized by criminals, employers or landlords or when they become ill.
>
> Continuing to ignore this situation is harmful to both the United States and the aliens themselves.

H.R.Conf.Rep. No. 99-682(I), at 49, U.S. Code Cong. & Admin. News 1986, pp. 5649, 5653.

Only those undocumented aliens who can demonstrate that they have lived in the United States since prior to January 1, 1982, are protected under the Act and are eligible for legalization. IRCA also makes it illegal to hire unauthorized aliens after November 6, 1986, and provides for sanctions against an employer to enforce this provision. The period between November 6, 1986, and June 1, 1987, is to be a public information period during which the employer sanction provisions will not be enforced. Individuals cannot apply for legalization until May 5, 1987.

The Act also contains provisions against discrimination based on national origin or citizenship status that might result from the new law. The instant action calls upon the Court to determine, among other things, whether Defendant's termination of Plaintiffs violated these anti-discrimination provisions.

On March 27, 1987, this Court conducted a hearing on Plaintiffs' Motion for a Preliminary Injunction filed pursuant to Federal Rule of Civil Procedure 65. At that time, the Court received documentary and testimonial evidence. Having considered the pleadings on file, the arguments of counsel and the evidence adduced at trial, the Court hereby grants Plaintiffs' Motion for Preliminary Injunction.

Background

Plaintiff, League of United Latin American Citizens ("LULAC"), is a non-profit corporation organized under the laws of the state of Texas for benevolent, charitable, educational, and patriotic purposes. LULAC is the oldest national organization of persons of Hispanic descent in the United States and was founded for the express purpose of protecting, defending, and preserving the civil rights of Hispanics.

Plaintiffs Maria Olympia Hernandez, Reina Raquel Guillen, Blanca Lopez, and Maria Garza (the "individual Plaintiffs") are undocumented aliens, each of whom entered the United States before January 1, 1982. As undocumented aliens, the individual Plaintiffs are currently unable to obtain valid social security numbers.

The individual Plaintiffs were employed by the Pasadena Independent School District ("PISD") prior to November 6, 1986. At the time they applied for employment, each individual Plaintiff inserted an invalid social security number on her application form.

The individual Plaintiffs are eligible for the legalization program under Section 245A of IRCA. Each testified that she intends to submit an application for legalization once the program is initiated. Applications for this legalization program will not be accepted until May 5, 1987. The continued employment of the Plaintiffs is permitted under the Grandfather Clause of IRCA, Section 101(a)(3). Upon approval of their legalization applications, each individual Plaintiff will be authorized to secure a valid social security number.

On February 18, 1987, each of the individual Plaintiffs was terminated from her employment as a custodial worker by PISD on the ground that she had provided false information on the PISD employment application by giving an invalid social security number. The Defendant maintains a policy that falsifying information on an application constitutes grounds for refusal to hire or termination. (Defendant's Exhibit 1). This policy, although in operation when Plaintiffs applied for employment, was not stated on the application nor was it communicated to Plaintiffs by school district personnel.

As part of its stated hiring practices, PISD also declares that information contained in applications for non-contract employment "shall be verified" within a thirty-day probationary period. (Defendant's Exhibit 1). Contrary to this provision, Defendant failed to investigate the validity of social security numbers offered on Plaintiffs' applications. Plaintiffs had been assigned to the custodial staff of Defendant's Sam Rayburn High School. The Director of Operations, who is responsible for the custodial staff, testified that he would recommend rehiring the Plaintiffs notwithstanding their submission of false social security numbers if they secured valid numbers because they were "good people" who had performed their jobs satisfactorily, some for as long as seven years.

At no time during their stay in the United States have any of the Plaintiffs been arrested or convicted of a criminal offense. Of the approximately 321 employees in the PISD Operations Department, 89.4% are Hispanic.

Beginning sometime in late January or early February 1987, officials at the high school distributed new W-4 employee withholding forms as authorized by the Internal Revenue Service. One worker, Francisco Hernandez, provided a social security number on the new form that was different from the one that he had previously provided. He admitted that he had used a false number and was terminated. On or about February 11, 1987, six Hispanic workers at Sam Rayburn High School, including the Plaintiffs, were confronted with the fact that they had supplied false social security numbers. There is controverted evidence as to how these six individuals were identified.

The PISD Personnel Department authorized school officials to give the workers five days to secure a valid number. (Defendant's Exhibits 2–5). Plaintiffs were told that if they complied then they could keep their jobs. Since the mechanism for qualified undocumented aliens to obtain valid social security numbers has yet to be established, Plaintiffs could not comply with Defendants directive and were discharged. (Defendant's Exhibits 6–9). None of the Plaintiffs have been able to find employment since leaving PISD.

Jurisdiction, Venue, and Standing

. . . .

IRCA authorizes administrative remedies for violations of certain provisions of the Act. Once created, administrative remedies must usually be exhausted before a district or appellate court will intervene. This principle prevents premature interference with agency procedures and affords the courts with benefit of the agency's expertise and administrative record. *Weinberger v. Salfi,* 422 U.S. 749, 765, 95 S.Ct. 2457, 2467, 45 L. Ed.2d 522 (1975). The administrative structure established under IRCA, however, is not currently in place. The Court concludes that in the absence of such a structure, jurisdiction is proper in the district court pursuant to 8 U.S.C. § 1329.

LULAC District Eight acts herein by and through its president, Margaret Gonzales. The organization's membership includes persons who are threatened by Defendants actions, including some of the named Plaintiffs. LULAC has standing to assert the corresponding rights of its members and to be a party to this action. *NAACP v. Button,* 371 U.S. 415, 428, 83 S.Ct. 328, 335, 9 L.Ed.2d 405 (1963).

. . . .

There is a substantial likelihood, however, that Plaintiffs will prevail on their claim that actions taken by PISD in terminating Plaintiffs violate the anti-discrimination provision of IRCA Section 274B(a). Since this is a case of first impression, it is the Court's duty "to find that interpretation which can most fairly be said to be imbedded in the statute, in the sense of being most harmonious with its scheme and with the general purposes that Congress manifested." *C.I.R. v. Engle,* 464 U.S. 206, 217, 104 S.Ct. 597, 604, 78 L.Ed.2d 420 (1984) *quoting NLRB v. Lion Oil Co.,* 352 U.S. 282, 297, 77 S.Ct. 330, 338, 1 L.Ed.2d 331 (1957) (Frankfurter, J., concurring in part and dissenting in part).

The relevant portion of Section 274B(a) states:

It is an unfair immigration-related employment practice for a person or other entity to discriminate against any individual (other than an unauthorized alien) with respect to the hiring, or recruitment or referral for a fee, of the individual for employment or the discharging of the individual from employment—

(A) because of such individual's national origin, or

(B) in the case of a citizen or intending citizen . . . because of such individual's citizenship status.

When applied to those who are qualified for legalization, and who intend to become citizens, a policy of terminating undocumented aliens for no other reason than that they have given employers a false social security number constitutes an unfair immigration-related employment practice under § 274B(a) of the Act. Only because of Plaintiffs' citizenship status have they been unable to secure valid social security numbers.

Further, Defendant's stated practice clearly contravenes the intent of Congress in enacting this law. In reporting the bill favorably to Congress, the House Judiciary Committee said of the anti-discrimination provision:

> The Committee does not believe barriers should be placed in the path of permanent residents and other aliens who are authorized to work and who are seeking employment, particularly when such aliens have evidenced an intent to become U.S. citizens. It makes no sense to admit immigrants and refugees to this country, require them to work and then allow employers to refuse to hire them because of their immigration (non-citizenship) status. Since Title VII does not provide any protection against employment discrimination based on alienage or non-citizen status, the Committee is of the view that the instant legislation must do so.

H.R.Conf. Report No. 99-682(I), at 70, U.S. Code Cong. & Admin. News 1986, p. 5674. Similarly, the Act would be manifestly unjust if it encouraged qualified aliens to come forward and reveal their undocumented status only to have that very information serve as grounds for termination by employers. Under IRCA undocumented workers are given an opportunity to come forward, reveal their status, and apply for temporary residency, permanent residency and ultimately citizenship. The proposed application for legalization requires that candidates list *inter alia* their aliases, social security numbers used and employers. (Plaintiffs' Exhibit 1, questions number 4, 19 and 36 respectively). It seems only logical that the Immigration and Naturalization Service will seek to verify this information with the employers of undocumented workers. Such verification will inform employers of falsifications that these workers have made, and, in the case of PISD, the result will be that the workers will be automatically terminated. In short, the application for legalization will lead to a revelation of falsifications made by undocumented aliens. Such revelations will in many cases lead to terminations.

[Clearly], Congress did not intend to force qualified aliens to make the choice between exercising this right and risking termination of their employment. This Hobson's choice, however, is precisely the peril that Defendant and others with similar policies would have the intended beneficiaries of this new law face.

Though not before the Court, it is undoubtedly true that most employers have a policy of terminating employees who falsify their applications. Under ordinary circumstances, such a policy is justifiable and valid. It is an extraordinary circumstance, however, to have so many undocumented aliens working in the United States under false names and with invalid social security numbers. In the coming months and years, the administrative process established under Section 274B of the Act will have to reconcile many current employment practices with the new rights established under IRCA.

The second criterion in reviewing the request for preliminary injunction is the substantial likelihood of irreparable injury to Plaintiffs. The Fifth Circuit has stated: "When an injunction is explicitly authorized by statute, proper discretion usually requires its issuance if the prerequisites for the remedy have been demonstrated and the injunction would fulfill the legislative purpose." *Donovan v. Brown Equipment and Service Tools, Inc.*, 666 F.2d 148, 157 (5th Cir.1982). In other words, when a statute authorizes injunctive relief and the statutory conditions have been met, the requirement of irreparable injury will be presumed. *See United States v. Hayes International Corporation*, 415 F.2d 1038, 1045 (5th Cir.1969).

IRCA explicitly authorizes the Attorney General to seek injunctions against employers who engage in a pattern or practice of hiring aliens who are ineligible for legalization under the Act. Section 274A(f)(2). Similarly, an administrative law judge is empowered to issue cease and desist orders should he or she determine that an employer has engaged in an unfair immigration-related employment practice. Section 274B(g)(2)(A). The Court notes that irreparable injury is presumed where an employee, having exhausted all available administrative remedies, seeks a preliminary injunction in an employment discrimination action under Title VII. *Middleton-Keirn v. Stone*, 655 F.2d 609, 611 (5th Cir.1981). Exhaustion of administrative remedies is not a viable course of action for Plaintiffs since the administrative procedures established under the Act are not yet in place.

The Plaintiffs have demonstrated that they would likely suffer irreparable injury in the absence of an injunction. Leonel Castillo, a former Commissioner of the Immigration and Naturalization Service, testified that it has long been the policy of the United States to reject as candidates for citizenship aliens who are likely to become a public charge. That policy is modified by, but continues under Section 245A(d)(2)(B)(iii). He also testified that the more income that an applicant for legalization brings in support of his or her petition, the more favorably that petition will be viewed.

Defendant contends that in order to prevail under this prong of our analysis, Plaintiffs must affirmatively prove that the actions of the school district will render them public charges under the Act. It would be ludicrous to require that Plaintiffs show that they applied for legalization and were in fact rejected as potential public charges because of Defendant's actions before irreparable harm could be demonstrated. The procedures for evaluating applications have not been developed and the application process does not commence until May 5, 1987. Consequently, this would be an impossible burden for Plaintiffs to meet. The Court concludes that the proper burden is that Plaintiffs must show that actions of the Defendant will significantly increase the likelihood that they will be deemed potential public charges. Plaintiffs have met this burden. Discharging the Plaintiffs reduces, perhaps even eliminates, their income and increases the likelihood that they would be rejected for legalization as potential public charges.

In balancing the relative harm to the parties under the third prong of the criteria, the Court finds that the threatened injury to the Plaintiffs outweighs the potential harm to Defendant. In this regard, Defendant asserts that it has a significant interest in upholding the integrity of its employment practices and that the use of invalid social security numbers disrupts the clerical operation of the school district and can lead to inaccuracies in personnel-related reports.

376 6 · THE RIGHTS OF LANGUAGE MINORITIES

Although these are valid issues, the evidence adduced at trial reduces the gravity of these concerns. PISD has a policy of punishing employees who falsify employment applications, but it also has a policy that it will verify the information on such applications within the thirty-day probationary period. Defendant jeopardized the integrity of its own employment practices when it failed to verify Plaintiffs' applications in conformity with its stated policy. Furthermore, there was no evidence that the specific social security numbers given by Plaintiffs had caused disruption of clerical operations. Moreover, an assistant superintendent in charge of finance was unable to quantify the time school district personnel spent correcting inaccuracies in reports stemming from employees' use of false social security numbers.

In any event, these problems are temporary. Those aliens wishing to apply for legalization under IRCA must do so within one year of the date to be determined by the Attorney General under Section 245A(a)(1)(A). The designated date must be within 180 days of the law's enactment. Moreover, after a specified period of lawful permanent residency a legal alien must apply for naturalization within six months of becoming eligible and must, except in limited circumstances, be naturalized as a citizen within two years of making the application (excluding the time required to process the application). Section 274B(a)(3). Consequently, within a not unreasonable period of time, the legalization process will result in qualified aliens receiving valid social security numbers and becoming American citizens.

By contrast, the potential harm resulting from Defendant's actions could have lasting implications for the Plaintiffs. Indeed, the harm that PISD would suffer by waiting a few weeks until the machinery of the legalization process is in place is small compared to the damage Plaintiffs would suffer by being denied legalization.

Finally, the Court finds that the granting of the injunction will not disserve the public interest, but rather will advance it. The school district has urged that it has a legitimate and important role in inculcating and upholding the virtue of honesty to its students. *See Bethel School District No. 403 v. Fraser,* 478 U.S. 675, 106 S.Ct. 3159, 92 L.Ed.2d 549 (1986). The citizens, however, through their elected officials in Congress, have determined that the presence of large numbers of illegal aliens can no longer be ignored. Congress has determined that it can neither turn back the hands of time nor ignore reality. The purpose of the Act is to extend a welcome hand to those undocumented aliens who have lived in the United States for the requisite number of years and can meet the other requirements for citizenship. At the same time, the law seeks to discourage unregulated immigration by providing for future sanctions against employers who hire unauthorized aliens. Section 274A.

If Defendant's employment practice is allowed to stand, Plaintiffs and many others similarly situated would be placed in the unfortunate and untenable position of deciding between prospective citizenship and present employment. In order to qualify for legalization, they must come forward and reveal their past misdeeds, misstatements, and falsifications. Once made, these revelations will automatically result in the termination of any qualified alien now working with PISD. Other similarly situated individuals run the risk of being fired from their jobs, either for falsifying their employment applications or for having invalid social security numbers.

If the Court gives way to the Defendant's argument that the value of enforcing its employment policy should expressly reign supreme over Congressional legislation designed to cure a problem which affects all persons living in the United States, whether citizens or not, then the Act would be rendered ineffectual. Also many employers—some unabashedly, others with a wink and a nod—have in the past knowingly and unlawfully hired undocumented aliens who were in this country. It would reward hypocrisy to allow such employers now to terminate qualified undocumented aliens for the sole reason they have made false statements by presenting invalid social security cards.

The Immigration Reform and Control Act of 1986 bestows certain rights, including the right to apply for citizenship, upon a class of aliens who are in this country illegally and without proper documentation. Plaintiffs belong to this class. Current citizens are not similarly situated to this class, are not protected by IRCA, and therefore cannot point to this Act as justification for any falsifications they may have made. Defendant's actions have the effect of jeopardizing Plaintiffs' rights under IRCA before they have had an opportunity to exercise those rights. If the Act is to be given force and effect, obvious impediments to securing its benefits should not be sanctioned.

Accordingly, it is ORDERED, ADJUDGED, and DECREED that Plaintiffs' Motion for a Preliminary Injunction be and hereby is GRANTED.

Hoffman Plastic Compounds, Inc. v. National Labor Relations Board

535 U.S. 137 (2002)

CHIEF JUSTICE REHNQUIST delivered the opinion of the Court.

The National Labor Relations Board (Board) awarded back pay to an undocumented alien who has never been legally authorized to work in the United States. We hold that such relief is foreclosed by federal immigration policy, as expressed by Congress in the Immigration Reform and Control Act of 1986 (IRCA).

Petitioner Hoffman Plastic Compounds, Inc. (petitioner or Hoffman), customformulates chemical compounds for businesses that manufacture pharmaceutical, construction, and household products. In May 1988, petitioner hired Jose Castro to operate various blending machines that "mix and cook" the particular formulas per customer order. Before being hired for this position, Castro presented documents that appeared to verify his authorization to work in the United States. In December 1988, the United Rubber, Cork, Linoleum, and Plastic Workers of America, AFL-CIO, began a union-organizing campaign at petitioner's production plant. Castro and several other employees supported the organizing campaign and distributed authorization cards to co-workers. In January 1989, Hoffman laid off Castro and other employees engaged in these organizing activities.

Three years later, in January 1992, respondent Board found that Hoffman unlawfully selected four employees, including Castro, for layoff "in order to rid itself of known union supporters" in violation of § 8(a)(3) of the National Labor Relations Act (NLRA). 306 N.L.R.B. 100, 1992 WL 14561. To remedy this violation, the Board ordered that Hoffman (1) cease and desist from further violations of the NLRA, (2) post a detailed notice to its employees regarding the remedial order, and (3) offer reinstatement and back pay to the four affected employees. *Id.,* at 107–108. Hoffman entered into a stipulation with the Board's General Counsel and agreed to abide by the Board's order.

In June 1993, the parties proceeded to a compliance hearing before an Administrative Law Judge (ALJ) to determine the amount of back pay owed to each discriminatee. On the final day of the hearing, Castro testified that he was born in Mexico and that he had never been legally admitted to, or authorized to work in, the United States. 314 N.L.R.B. 683, 685, 1994 WL 397901 (1994). He admitted gaining employment with Hoffman only after tendering a birth certificate belonging to a friend who was born in Texas. *Ibid.* He also admitted that he used this birth certificate to fraudulently obtain a California driver's license and a Social Security card, and to fraudulently obtain employment following his layoff by Hoffman. *Ibid.* Neither Castro nor the Board's General Counsel offered any evidence that Castro had applied or intended to apply for legal authorization to work in the United States. *Ibid.* Based on this testimony, the ALJ found the Board precluded from awarding Castro back pay or reinstatement as such relief would be contrary to *Sure-Tan, Inc. v. NLRB,* 467 U.S. 883, 104 S.Ct. 2803, 81 L. Ed.2d 732 (1984), and in conflict with IRCA, which makes it unlawful for employers knowingly to hire undocumented workers or for employees to use fraudulent documents to establish employment eligibility. 314 N.L.R.B., at 685–686.

In September 1998, four years after the ALJ's decision, and nine years after Castro was fired, the Board reversed with respect to back pay. 326 N.L.R.B. 1060, 1998 WL 663933. Citing its earlier decision in *A.P.R.A. Fuel Oil Buyers Group, Inc.,* 320 N.L.R.B. 408, 1995 WL 803434 (1995), the Board determined that "the most effective way to accommodate and further the immigration policies embodied in [IRCA] is to provide the protections and remedies of the [NLRA] to undocumented workers in the same manner as to other employees." 326 N.L.R.B., at 1060. The Board thus found that Castro was entitled to $66,951 of back pay, plus interest. *Id.,* at 1062. It calculated this back pay award from the date of Castro's termination to the date Hoffman first learned of Castro's undocumented status, a period of 4½ years. *Id.,* at 1061. A dissenting Board member would have affirmed the ALJ and denied Castro all back pay. *Id.,* at 1062 (opinion of Hurtgen).

Hoffman filed a petition for review of the Board's order in the Court of Appeals. A panel of the Court of Appeals denied the petition for review. 208 F.3d 229 (C.A.D.C.2000). After rehearing the case en banc, the court again denied the petition for review and enforced the Board's order. 237 F.3d 639 (2001). We granted certiorari, 533 U.S. 976, 122 S.Ct. 23, 150 L.Ed.2d 804 (2001), and now reverse.

This case exemplifies the principle that the Board's discretion to select and fashion remedies for violations of the NLRA, though generally broad, see, *e.g., NLRB v. Seven-Up Bottling Co. of Miami, Inc.,* 344 U.S. 344, 346–347, 73 S.Ct. 287, 97 L.Ed. 377 (1953), is not unlimited. . . . Since the Board's inception, we have consistently set aside awards of reinstatement or back pay to employees found guilty of serious illegal conduct in connection with their employment. In *Fansteel,* the Board awarded reinstatement with back pay to employees who engaged in a "sit down strike" that led to confrontation with local law enforcement officials. . . .

With respect to the Board's selection of remedies, however, we found its authority limited by federal immigration policy. See *id.,* at 903, 104 S.Ct. 2803 ("In devising remedies for unfair labor practices, the Board is obliged to take into account another 'equally important Congressional objective'" (quoting *Southern S.S. Co., supra,* at 47, 62 S.Ct. 886)). For example, the Board was prohibited from effectively rewarding a violation of the immigration laws by reinstating workers not authorized to reenter the United States. *Sure-Tan,* 467 U.S., at 903, 104 S.Ct. 2803. Thus, to avoid "a potential conflict with the INA," the Board's reinstatement order had to be conditioned upon proof of "the employees' legal reentry." *Ibid.* "Similarly," with respect to back pay, we stated: "[T]he employees must be deemed 'unavailable' for work (and the accrual of back pay therefore tolled) during any period when they were not lawfully entitled to be present and employed in the United States." *Ibid.* "[I]n light of the practical workings of the immigration laws," such remedial limitations were appropriate even if they led to "[t]he probable unavailability of the [NLRA's] more effective remedies." *Id.,* at 904, 104 S.Ct. 2803.

The Board cites our decision in *ABF Freight System, Inc. v. NLRB,* 510 U.S. 317, 114 S.Ct. 835, 127 L.Ed.2d 152 (1994), as authority for awarding back pay to employees who violate federal laws. In *ABF Freight,* we held that an employee's false testimony at a compliance proceeding did not require the Board to deny reinstatement with back pay. The question presented was "a narrow one," *id.,* at 322, 114 S.Ct. 835, limited to whether the Board was obliged to "adopt a rigid rule" that employees who testify falsely under oath automatically forfeit NLRA remedies, *id.,* at 325, 114 S.Ct. 835. There are significant differences between that case and this. First, we expressly did not address whether the Board could award back pay to an employee who engaged in "serious misconduct" unrelated to internal Board proceedings, *id.,* at 322, n. 7, 114 S.Ct. 835, such as threatening to kill a supervisor, *ibid.* (citing *Precision Window Mfg. v. NLRB,* 963 F.2d 1105, 1110 (C.A.8 1992)), or stealing from an employer, 510 U.S., at 322, n. 7, 114 S.Ct. 835 (citing *NLRB v. Commonwealth Foods, Inc.,* 506 F.2d 1065, 1068 (C.A.4 1974)). Second, the challenged order did not implicate federal statutes or policies administered by other federal agencies, a "most delicate area" in which the Board must be "particularly careful in its choice of remedy." *Burlington Truck Lines, Inc. v. United States,* 371 U.S. 156, 172, 83 S.Ct. 239, 9 L.Ed.2d

207 (1962). Third, the employee misconduct at issue, though serious, was not at all analogous to misconduct that renders an underlying employment relationship illegal under explicit provisions of federal law. See, *e.g.,* 237 F.3d, at 657, n. 2 (Sentelle, J., dissenting) ("The perjury statute provides for criminal sanctions; it does not forbid a present or potential perjurer from obtaining a job" (distinguishing *ABF Freight*)). For these reasons, we believe the present case is controlled by the *Southern S.S. Co.* line of cases, rather than by *ABF Freight.*

. . . .

The *Southern S.S. Co.* line of cases established that where the Board's chosen remedy trenches upon a federal statute or policy outside the Board's competence to administer, the Board's remedy may be required to yield. Whether or not this was the situation at the time of *Sure-Tan,* it is precisely the situation today. In 1986, two years after *Sure-Tan,* Congress enacted IRCA, a comprehensive scheme prohibiting the employment of illegal aliens in the United States. § 101(a)(1), 100 Stat. 3360, 8 U.S.C. § 1324a. As we have previously noted, IRCA "forcefully" made combating the employment of illegal aliens central to "[t]he policy of immigration law." *INS v. National Center for Immigrants' Rights, Inc.,* 502 U.S. 183, 194, and n. 8, 112 S.Ct. 551, 116 L.Ed.2d 546 (1991). It did so by establishing an extensive "employment verification system," § 1324a(a)(1), designed to deny employment to aliens who (a) are not lawfully present in the United States, or (b) are not lawfully authorized to work in the United States, § 1324a(h)(3). This verification system is critical to the IRCA regime. To enforce it, IRCA mandates that employers verify the identity and eligibility of all new hires by examining specified documents before they begin work. § 1324a(b). If an alien applicant is unable to present the required documentation, the unauthorized alien cannot be hired. § 1324a(a)(1).

Similarly, if an employer unknowingly hires an unauthorized alien, or if the alien becomes unauthorized while employed, the employer is compelled to discharge the worker upon discovery of the worker's undocumented status. § 1324a(a)(2). Employers who violate IRCA are punished by civil fines, § 1324a(e)(4)(A), and may be subject to criminal prosecution, § 1324a(f)(1). IRCA also makes it a crime for an unauthorized alien to subvert the employer verification system by tendering fraudulent documents. § 1324c(a). It thus prohibits aliens from using or attempting to use "any forged, counterfeit, altered, or falsely made document" or "any document lawfully issued to or with respect to a person other than the possessor" for purposes of obtaining employment in the United States. §§ 1324c(a)(1)-(3). Aliens who use or attempt to use such documents are subject to fines and criminal prosecution. 18 U.S.C. § 1546(b). There is no dispute that Castro's use of false documents to obtain employment with Hoffman violated these provisions.

Under the IRCA regime, it is impossible for an undocumented alien to obtain employment in the United States without some party directly contravening explicit congressional policies. Either the undocumented alien tenders fraudulent identification, which subverts the cornerstone of IRCA's enforcement mechanism, or the employer knowingly hires the undocumented alien in direct contradiction of its IRCA obligations. The Board asks that we overlook this fact and allow it to award back pay to an illegal alien for years of work not performed, for wages that could not lawfully have been earned, and for a job obtained in the first instance by a criminal fraud. We find, however, that awarding back pay to illegal aliens runs counter to policies underlying IRCA, policies the Board has no authority to enforce or administer. Therefore, as we have consistently held in like circumstances, the award lies beyond the bounds of the Board's remedial discretion.

The Board contends that awarding limited back pay to Castro "reasonably accommodates" IRCA, because, in the Board's view, such an award is not "inconsistent" with IRCA. Brief for Respondent 29-42. The Board argues that because the back pay period was closed as of the date Hoffman learned of Castro's illegal status, Hoffman could have employed Castro during the back pay period without violating IRCA. *Id.*, at 37. The Board further argues that while IRCA criminalized the misuse of documents, "it did not make violators ineligible for back pay awards or other compensation flowing from employment secured by the misuse of such documents." *Id.*, at 38. This latter statement, of course, proves little: The mutiny statute in *Southern S.S. Co.*, and the INA in *Sure-Tan,* were likewise understandably silent with respect to such things as back pay awards under the NLRA. What matters here, and what sinks both of the Board's claims, is that Congress has expressly made it criminally punishable for an alien to obtain employment with false documents. There is no reason to think that Congress nonetheless intended to permit back pay where but for an employer's unfair labor practices, an alien-employee would have remained in the United States illegally, and continued to work illegally, all the while successfully evading apprehension by immigration authorities. Far from "accommodating" IRCA, the Board's position, recognizing employer misconduct but discounting the misconduct of illegal alien employees, subverts it.

Indeed, awarding back pay in a case like this not only trivializes the immigration laws, it also condones and encourages future violations. The Board admits that had the INS detained Castro, or had Castro obeyed the law and departed to Mexico, Castro would have lost his right to back pay. . . . Similarly, Castro cannot mitigate damages, a duty our cases require, see *Sure-Tan,* 467 U.S., at 901, 104 S.Ct. 2803 (citing *Seven-Up Bottling,* 344 U.S., at 346, 73 S.Ct. 287; *Phelps Dodge Corp. v. NLRB,* 313 U.S. 177, 198, 61 S.Ct. 845, 85 L.Ed. 1271 (1941)), without triggering new IRCA violations, either by tendering false documents to employers or by finding employers willing to ignore IRCA and hire illegal workers. The Board here has failed to even consider this tension. See 326 N.L.R.B., at 1063, n. 10 (finding that Castro adequately mitigated damages through interim work with no mention of ALJ findings that Castro secured interim work with false documents).

We therefore conclude that allowing the Board to award back pay to illegal aliens would unduly trench upon explicit statutory prohibitions critical to federal immigration policy, as expressed in IRCA. It would encourage the successful evasion of apprehension by immigration authorities, condone prior violations of the immigration laws, and encourage future violations. However broad the Board's discretion to fashion remedies when dealing only with the NLRA, it is not so unbounded as to authorize this sort of an award.

Lack of authority to award back pay does not mean that the employer gets off scot-free. The Board here has already imposed other significant sanctions against Hoffman—sanctions Hoffman does not challenge. See *supra*, at 1278–1279. These include orders that Hoffman cease and desist its violations of the NLRA, and that it conspicuously post a notice to employees setting forth their rights under the NLRA and detailing its prior unfair practices. 306 N.L.R.B., at 100–101. Hoffman will be subject to contempt proceedings should it fail to comply with these orders. *NLRB v. Warren Co.,* 350 U.S. 107, 112–113, 76 S.Ct. 185, 100 L.Ed. 96 (1955) (Congress gave the Board civil contempt power to enforce compliance with the Board's orders). We have deemed such "traditional remedies" sufficient to effectuate national labor policy regardless of whether the "spur and catalyst" of back pay accompanies them. *Sure-Tan,* 467 U.S., at 904, 104 S.Ct. 2803. See also *id.,* at 904, n. 13, 104 S.Ct. 2803 ("This threat of contempt sanctions . . . provides a significant deterrent against future violations of the [NLRA]"). As we concluded in *Sure-Tan,* "in light of the practical workings of the immigration laws," any "perceived deficienc[y] in the NLRA's existing remedial arsenal" must be "addressed by congressional action," not the courts. *Id.,* at 904, 104 S.Ct. 2803. In light of IRCA, this statement is even truer today.

The judgment of the Court of Appeals is reversed.

It is so ordered.

Raad v. Fairbanks North Star Borough School District
323 F.3d 1185 (9th Cir. 2003)

BETTY B. FLETCHER, CIRCUIT JUDGE.

Plaintiff-Appellant Nada Raad, an American citizen of Lebanese descent and Muslim faith, appeals the district court's order of summary judgment against her claims of workplace discrimination on the basis of national origin and religion, and her claims of retaliation, in violation of Title VII of the Civil Rights Act of 1964, 42 U.S.C. § 2000e *et seq.* Raad's allegations of discrimination stem from her employment as a substitute teacher by the Fairbanks North Star Borough School District (the "District"). Raad alleges that the District subjected her to disparate treatment because of her national origin when it refused to hire her as a permanent teacher during three consecutive hiring cycles, beginning in 1991. After her third rejection in August 1993, Raad made a statement that District administrative staff construed as a bomb threat and reported to the police. Raad denies having made such a threat, and instead alleges that the report to the police was fraudulently made because Raad is a Muslim of Lebanese descent. As a result of the perceived bomb threat, Raad was suspended from teaching within the District for one year. Raad also claims that the initial rejection of her application for permanent employment in 1993, as well as her discipline for allegedly making a bomb threat, constituted acts of retaliation for protected activity.

The district court granted summary judgment in favor of the District on all of Raad's claims. Because we conclude that the district court failed to consider the evidence in the record in the light most favorable to Raad, the nonmoving party, and because, when viewed in that light, the record reflects a genuine dispute of material fact, we reverse the district court's decision as to all of Raad's claims on appeal except one, and remand this case for further proceedings.

I. FACTS AND PROCEDURAL HISTORY

Born and raised in Beirut, Lebanon, Nada Raad obtained undergraduate and graduate degrees from the University of Illinois Urbana-Champaign. After returning to Beirut, Raad accepted a position with the American University of Beirut, preparing lectures and exhibits in connection with its natural history museum. Raad immigrated to Alaska in 1989, when her husband accepted a teaching position with the University of Alaska, Fairbanks ("UAF"), and obtained her certification to teach in Alaska public schools through the UAF teaching program. She maintained excellent academic records in both her graduate study and her teaching preparation at UAF, and graduated from the UAF program with outstanding faculty recommendations.

Raad made her first application for full-time teaching status in the District in January 1991. She received a "preliminary personal interview" on March 6, 1991, with area high school principal Andre Layral and was awarded the highest possible rating by the team of principals who interviewed her (i.e., 3 out of 3 points). Nonetheless, in his evaluation of Raad's interview, Layral noted her accent as a potential weakness in her candidacy, observing that Raad's "accent and soft spokenness may be a detractor to some instructional effectiveness. This could be addressed if hired." Layral's statement, which remained in Raad's personnel file throughout her employment with the District, marks the first in a series of statements over the next two years made by District officials referring to Raad's accent as an obstacle to her full-time employment as a teacher in math and science. However, there is no evidence in the summary judgment record that Raad's accent ever interfered with her performance while she served either as a substitute teacher or as a temporary full-time teacher in 1992–93. To the contrary, Raad's recommenders, both within the District and at UAF, consistently complimented her classroom performance, including her success at establishing "an excellent rapport with her students."

During the 1991–92 school year, Raad received numerous requests from full-time District teachers that she serve as a substitute teacher in their classes when they were absent. Raad requested and received from former Tanana Middle School principal Deborah Kerr-Carpenter an unqualified recommendation that she be retained in a full-time position. However, in July 1992, District staff told Raad that she had not been placed in the hiring pool for the 1992–93 school year because Kerr-Carpenter's recommendation had not been submitted on the proper form. Raad obtained Kerr-Carpenter's recommendation on the proper administrative form on July 21, 1992, but was not informed that she had been placed in the hiring pool until the end of August. Meanwhile, in an interview report dated August 18, 1992, Kerr-Carpenter noted as a weakness Raad's "[a]rticulation of English — needs to talk slower/enunciate words better." Kerr-Carpenter reiterated this rationale in her deposition testimony, where she admitted that she did not hire Raad for a full-time position in 1992 because of "her articulation and enunciation of words."

Between the time when Raad resubmitted Kerr-Carpenter's recommendation and the time when the District informed her that she was under consideration for a 1992–93 position, the District filled four full-time teaching positions in math and science. During August 1992, Raad learned that a specific biology position had become open at Tanana Middle School. Raad requested to be considered for that position. Although Raad produced evidence that she was highly qualified, she was not hired to fill the position.

As a result of her inability to secure a permanent position, Raad met with District EEO officer Charles Moore on September 23, 1992. Raad filed a complaint of unlawful discrimination based on national origin and religion. Two days later, during a follow-up meeting, Moore informed Raad that her credentials were outstanding and that the reason why she had not been hired for the Tanana position was that Tanana needed someone with credentials to double as a ski coach. Because Raad frequently substituted at Tanana, Raad knew that Tanana already had two ski coaches; she therefore suspected that this justification was false. Moore assured Raad that he would advise Jerry Hartsock, principal at Lathrop High School, to offer her a full-time position there beginning in the 1993–94 school year.

In March 1993, Moore discouraged Raad from accepting a long-term substitute position at Lathrop because she was going to be hired for a full-time, temporary position at Ryan Middle School, replacing a teacher who was leaving mid-year. Raad accepted and completed this temporary assignment. In August 1993, Raad was interviewed for the full-time science position at Lathrop. Despite Moore's initial assurance that she would receive the position, Raad was later informed by Hartsock that she had been rejected. When confronted, Moore denied that he had made any commitment to Raad that she would receive this job. He then informed Raad that the District declined to hire her because of her accent.

Also in early August 1993, Raad learned that Kerr-Carpenter had hired Pat Cromer to fill a health teaching position at Tanana, without any competitive interview, in September 1992. Cromer and Raad had both applied for the Tanana 1992 science position, and Raad surmised that Cromer had been hired for the health position following Raad's discrimination complaint to Moore. This chronology was corroborated by Kerr-Carpenter herself. Moore testified in his deposition that he knew of no set of circumstances in which a principal would be empowered to offer a position of this kind without engaging in competitive interviews.

On August 13, 1993, after hearing that she had been rejected for the Lathrop position, Raad insisted on speaking with Superintendent Cross. She went to his office in the District administration building, but was not permitted to meet with him. Raad said that she needed to speak with Cross about "a matter of life or death," but was told that Cross simply would not meet with an unsuccessful job applicant. Raad then made two statements in front of Cross's administrative staff, Pam Hallberg and Lynda Sather, that have become central to this litigation. First, Raad alleges that, in a state of extreme frustration, she said that she was very angry and did not want to "blow up." Hallberg and Sather apparently interpreted this as a threat to "blow up the building" if Raad were not allowed to speak with Cross. Raad, who had made arrangements to see her attorney later that day, then went to Moore's office to speak with him about the matter. The record on summary judgment reflects that Raad was not yelling or in any way acting out of control either at this time or during her initial encounter with Cross's staff. Raad made a statement to Moore to the effect that she did not want to see anyone "get hurt," by which she meant—and Moore understood—*legally* hurt by the filing of a civil complaint. She allegedly made this statement, while sitting with her arms folded and crying, after Moore informed her that the police had been called.

Hallberg and Sather denied knowing that Raad was Lebanese, but the police log report documenting the request for assistance at the administration building due to a bomb threat identified the suspect as a "Lebanese woman." In addition, Raad's ethnicity was known to the District through its personnel file, which contained her transcripts, in which Raad is listed as Lebanese. Police escorted Raad from the building, but the Fairbanks District Attorney declined to press charges against her. Hallberg and Sather were interviewed following the incident by a Fairbanks police officer. The officer alluded to Raad's accent and then asked Hallberg whether she might have misunderstood the reputed bomb threat. Hallberg replied that she was not mistaken, although she could not recall Raad's exact words. However, she also noted that Raad did not say or do anything else that was threatening, only that her "body language" (i.e., leaning over the counter to talk to Hallberg) was threatening.

Raad submitted her intake questionnaire to the Alaska State Commission for Human Rights ("ASCHR") on or about August 31, 1993. On September 8, 1993, Raad was informed by letter from Personnel Director Anita Gallentine that the District would not offer her a full-time position or hire her as a substitute during the 1993–94 school year. Gallentine had also issued a memorandum to all building administrators in the District, ordering that Raad was not to be hired by any school for an indefinite period of time. In a subsequent disciplinary hearing on September 29, 1993, Raad was not permitted to introduce evidence of discrimination against her, and the hearing concluded by affirming Gallentine's decision.

On September 16, 1993, Raad filed a formal charge with the ASCHR, alleging discrimination on the basis of her national origin and religion, and in retaliation for opposing such discrimination, in violation of Title VII of the Civil Rights Act of 1964, 42 U.S.C. § 2000e *et seq.,* and state antidiscrimination law, Alaska Stat. § 18.80.220. Raad filed her civil complaint in district court on October 14, 1997. Following several motions and extensive discovery, the District moved for summary judgment on February 9, 2000. The district court granted the District's motion on July 14, 2000. Raad filed a Rule 59 motion for reconsideration on July 24, 2000, which the district court construed as a motion alleging clear error in its ruling of July 14. The court denied that motion on October 10, 2000, and Raad filed this appeal.

II. ANALYSIS

A. *Disparate Treatment Claims: National Origin and Religion*

1. *1991–92 failure-to-hire claims: continuing violation*

Since the district court issued its decision in this case, the Supreme Court has overruled the "continuing violation" theory of Title VII liability as it was applied by the district court following prior Ninth Circuit authority. *See Nat'l R.R. Passenger Corp. v. Morgan,* 536 U.S. 101, 122 S.Ct. 2061, 153 L.Ed.2d 106 (2002), *overruling Morgan v. Nat'l R.R. Passenger Corp.,* 232 F.3d 1008 (9th Cir.2000). In reviewing whether the district court properly granted summary judgment against Raad's claims based on the District's refusal to hire her for a full-time position in 1991 and 1992, we are bound to apply current Supreme Court law.

In *Morgan,* the Court drew a distinction between harassment-based and non-harassment-based claims under Title VII: plaintiffs may not establish employer liability for events occurring prior to the statutory limitations period in non-harassment based claims, even if events occurring outside of the limitations period form part of a pattern extending to events that are not time-barred. *Morgan,* 122 S. Ct. at 2072 . . . . In other words, a discriminatory practice, although it may extend over time and through a series of related acts, remains divisible into a set of discrete acts, legal action on the basis of which must be brought within the statutory limitations period.

Here, Raad filed her EEO charge with the ASCHR on September 16, 1993. Because she filed her charge with the state agency, the 300-day limitations period governs her claim. Therefore, the District may be held liable only for discriminatory acts perpetrated within 300 days of September 16, 1993, counting backward from that date. As a result, Raad's claims based on the District's denial of her full-time application in August 1993 for the science position at Lathrop, as well as her claims based on the report of a bomb threat and ensuing disciplinary action, are not time-barred. The District may be held liable for damages caused by these acts, assuming that Raad is able to prove her case.

The failure-to-hire claims arising out of Raad's applications in 1991 and 1992 are time-barred; however, their supporting factual allegations may remain relevant to Raad's live claims. *See Morgan,* 122 S.Ct. at 2072; *United Air Lines, Inc. v. Evans,* 431 U.S. 553, 558, 97 S.Ct. 1885, 52 L.Ed.2d 571 (1977). Accordingly, while these claims are not independently actionable, evidence about the District's refusal to hire Raad for a full-time teaching position in 1991 and 1992 is relevant and admissible insofar as it bears on her claim that she was discriminatorily refused a full-time position in August 1993.

2. *1993 failure-to-hire claim*

In granting summary judgment to the District on Raad's claims of unlawful hiring discrimination on the basis of national origin and religion, the district court reasoned that Raad had "failed to come forward with any direct evidence of discriminatory animus nor has she come forward with specific and substantial circumstantial evidence that establishes that defendant's articulated reason for not hiring her was false or that the real reason was discrimination." *Raad v. Fairbanks N. Star Borough Sch. Dist.*, No. F97-0068-CV, slip op. at 43 (D.Alaska July 17, 2000). In so holding, the district court erroneously drew inferences in favor of the defendant's position that its decisions to deny Raad full-time employment were based solely on her qualifications. For example, the court observed:

> It is the court's experience with employment cases where discrimination has been found that the defendants invariably give away their motives and intent by disparaging remarks in speech or writing or by contrived reasons for the employer's conduct. They are dismissive or disparaging of the prospective employee's national origin, religion, or whatever the employer's special bias happens to be. Not so here . . . . There is no evidence of the usual snide, sarcastic, or demeaning comments.

Raad, slip op. at 26 n. 20. However, it is well-settled law in this Circuit, as elsewhere, that "[a] *prima facie* case of unlawful employment discrimination on the basis of protected characteristics may be established through indirect evidence under the familiar *McDonnell Douglas* four-part test." *Lam v. Univ. of Haw.*, 40 F.3d 1551, 1559 (9th Cir.1994).

. . . .

To the charge of hiring discrimination with regard to the Lathrop full-time position in August 1993, the District responds that Raad was legitimately denied that position on the basis of her qualifications, including her language and communications skills, in addition to her temperament. At this stage, the burden-shifting scheme of *McDonnell Douglas* requires that Raad raise a genuine factual question whether, viewing the evidence in the light most favorable to her, the District's proffered reasons are pretextual. *See Chuang*, 225 F.3d at 1126. This "shift" does not necessarily place a new burden of *production* on Raad. In *Reeves v. Sanderson Plumbing Products, Inc.*, 530 U.S. 133, 147, 120 S.Ct. 2097, 147 L.Ed.2d 105 (2000), the Court held that the fact finder may infer "the ultimate fact of intentional discrimination" without additional proof once the plaintiff has made out her *prima facie* case if the fact finder rejects the employer's proffered nondiscriminatory reasons as unbelievable. *Accord Chuang*, 225 F.3d at 1127 ("[A] disparate treatment plaintiff can survive summary judgment without producing any evidence of discrimination beyond that constituting his prima facie case, if that evidence raises a genuine issue of material fact regarding the truth of the employer's proffered reasons.").

Our inquiry is twofold: The plaintiff can prove pretext "(1) indirectly, by showing that the employer's proffered explanation is 'unworthy of credence' because it is internally inconsistent or otherwise not believable, or (2) directly, by showing that unlawful discrimination more likely motivated the employer." *Id.* (citing *Godwin,* 150 F.3d at 1220–22). All of the evidence—whether direct or indirect—is to be considered cumulatively. *Id.*

Here, the district court, like the Fifth Circuit in *Reeves,* misapplied the standard of review, failed to draw all reasonable inferences in favor of Raad, the nonmoving party, and impermissibly substituted its judgment concerning the weight of the evidence for the jury's. For example, the district court stated that "[t]he fact that both Kerr-Carpenter and Layral mentioned plaintiff's accent is not evidence of impermissible bias, particularly in light of the other favorable comments that both individuals made about plaintiff." At the summary judgment stage, however, when one draws all permissible inferences in favor of the nonmoving party, this is precisely the wrong approach.

Raad's claim of hiring discrimination in August 1993 stands primarily upon the following evidence: that she was substantially more qualified than the applicant who received the position, Rise Roy; that she had initially been told that the position would be a transfer (as a result of her temporary full-time position in 1992–93) for which she would not have to interview or compete; and that EEO officer Moore later informed her that she had not received the job because of her accent. In this Circuit, we have held that a finding "that a Title VII plaintiff's qualifications were clearly superior to the qualifications of the applicant selected is a proper basis for a finding of discrimination." *Odima v. Westin Tucson Hotel,* 53 F.3d 1484, 1492 (9th Cir.1995). In *Odima,* we held that the plaintiff's superior qualifications *standing alone* were enough to prove pretext and, on that basis, we affirmed the district court's entry of judgment for the plaintiff following a bench trial. *Id.* . . .

When considering the evidence as a whole, there are numerous other bases upon which a trier of fact could infer pretext. For example, Moore informed Raad that she had been denied the Lathrop position due to her accent. On this record, his statement should be viewed against the backdrop of Kerr-Carpenter's 1992 statements regarding Raad's accent, and Layral's statement regarding Raad's accent in his preliminary interview evaluation, which remained in her file with the District.

The close relationship between language and national origin led the EEOC to classify discrimination based on "linguistic characteristics" as unlawful under Title VII. *See* 29 C.F.R. § 1606.1 (2003); *cf. id.* § 1606.7(a) (noting, in the context of speak-English-only rules, that "[t]he primary language of an individual is often an essential national origin characteristic"). "Accent and national origin are obviously inextricably intertwined in many cases." *Fragante v. City & County of Honolulu,*

888 F.2d 591, 596 (9th Cir.1989). To be sure, we have held that adverse employment decisions may be predicated upon an individual's accent, but only if it interferes with the individual's job performance. *Id.* at 596–97; *see also Carino v. Univ. of Okla. Bd. of Regents,* 750 F.2d 815, 819 (10th Cir.1984) ("A foreign accent that does not interfere with a Title VII claimant's ability to perform duties of the position he has been denied is not a legitimate justification for adverse employment decisions."). Here, the summary judgment record contains evidence that Raad's accent did not impair her performance as a teacher (and therefore was not job-related), including recommendations written by her graduate school instructors, requests for her as a substitute by other teachers employed by the District, and the District's own continued employment of her as a substitute. Based on this evidence, it would be reasonable for a finder of fact to infer that the District used her accent as a pretext to deny her a full-time position because of her national origin.

In addition to the accent and qualifications evidence, under *Morgan* we also look to the District's past treatment of Raad's candidacy for full-time positions as background evidence of intent to discriminate. Specifically, Raad alleges that the District undervalued her G.P.A. and writing sample in 1991 in order to exclude her from the hiring pool for full-time positions and delayed her admission into the hiring pool in 1992 in order to dispense the majority of positions prior to her becoming eligible. Raad also alleges that Kerr-Carpenter manufactured false flow charts to indicate that she had conducted competitive interviews for positions that she had given to other applicants without conducting such interviews in the 1992–93 school year. The circumstances surrounding each of these questions involve factual disputes that should not have been resolved at summary judgment by the district court's weighing of the evidence.

3. *Disciplinary suspension: the alleged bomb threat*

The district court also granted summary judgment to the District on Raad's claim that, due to her alleged bomb threat, she was discriminatorily subjected to a disciplinary suspension in her eligibility to be hired either as a substitute or as a full-time teacher. The district court inappropriately concluded, again weighing the evidence, that "defendant's personnel legitimately believed that plaintiff had threatened to blow up the building."

In applying the *McDonnell Douglas* test to the facts of this claim, Raad may establish a *prima facie* case of discrimination by showing that (1) she is a member of a protected class, (2) she was adequately performing her job (prior to the alleged bomb threat), and (3) she suffered an adverse employment action or was treated differently from others who were similarly situated. *See* 411 U.S. at 802, 93 S.Ct. 1817; *see also Kortan v. Cal. Youth Auth.,* 217 F.3d 1104, 1113 (9th Cir.2000). "The requisite degree of proof necessary to establish a *prima facie* case for Title VII . . . claims on summary judgment is minimal and does not even need to rise to the level of a preponderance of the evidence." *Wallis v. J.R. Simplot Co.,* 26 F.3d 885, 889 (9th Cir.1994). "The plaintiff need only offer evidence which gives rise to an inference of unlawful discrimination." *Id.* (internal quotation marks and citation omitted).

Raad made out a prima facie case of discrimination with respect to the District's reaction to the alleged bomb threat. She showed that: (1) she is a member of a protected group, (2) she was performing her job adequately before the alleged bomb threat, and (3) she suffered an adverse employment action when the District issued its disciplinary suspension. Therefore, the burden of production shifted to the District to articulate a legitimate, non-discriminatory reason for its actions. *Chuang*, 225 F.3d at 1126.

The District asserts that it disciplined Raad because she made a bomb threat, and claims that it would have sanctioned similarly any other employee who made such a threat. Raad maintains that she did not make a bomb threat, but that fact is irrelevant at the *second* step of the *McDonnell Douglas* analysis, which focuses on the employer. To satisfy its burden, the District "need only produce admissible evidence which would allow the trier of fact rationally to conclude that the employment decision had not been motivated by discriminatory animus." *Burdine*, 450 U.S. at 257, 101 S.Ct. 1089. Here, the District presented sufficient evidence of a bomb threat to shift the burden back to Raad to show that the District's proffered reason is pretextual. *Chuang*, 225 F.3d at 1126.

Raad may prove pretext "either directly by persuading the court that a discriminatory reason more likely motivated the employer or indirectly by showing that the employer's proffered explanation is unworthy of credence." *Burdine*, 450 U.S. at 256, 101 S.Ct. 1089. As discussed above, Raad presented evidence tending to show that the District's bomb-threat explanation is unworthy of credence. She offered proof that she did not threaten to blow up the building but, instead, stated only that she was very angry and did not want to "blow up." Further, Raad presented evidence that the staff members may have misunderstood what she said because of their preconceptions regarding her religion and national origin.

Although the District presented evidence in support of its claim that Raad did, in fact, make a bomb threat, Raad presented evidence from which a rational jury could conclude that she made no bomb threat at all and that the District's contrary interpretation of the event was influenced by stereotypes about her religion or nationality. Thus, there is a genuine issue of fact as to whether the District's stated reason for disciplining Raad was pretextual, and the district court erred in granting summary judgment.

. . . .

III. CONCLUSION

For the foregoing reasons, the decision of the district court awarding summary judgment to the District on Raad's disparate treatment claims based on national origin and religion, and on Raad's claims of retaliation relating to her disciplinary suspension after the alleged bomb threat, is reversed. The district court's grant of summary judgment to the District on Raad's retaliation claim based on her complaints to the EEO counselor is affirmed [omitted here]. The case is remanded for further proceedings consistent with this opinion.

AFFIRMED IN PART, REVERSED IN PART, AND REMANDED.

Notes and Questions

1. Should the Court in *Hoffman Plastics* have maintained deference to the Board's decision here? Are you convinced that awarding backpay to undocumented immigrants would conflict with federal immigration laws and policies? Is the decision consistent with the goal of preventing discrimination against language minorities in the workplace, despite the restriction imposed on award to undocumented immigrant? How so?

2. Based on the majority's discussion, do you deem the employer sufficiently punished for targeting union participants? What if Hoffman had targeted Castro because it suspected him of being undocumented? What legal recourse would there have been against Hoffman? Today, the answer to this question might depend of Castro's status. It is illegal for employers to make employment decisions based on bias toward an employee's citizenship status. Thus, if an employee is legally in the United States, an employer is prohibited from denying them a position or retaliating against that person based on the fact that they are not U.S. citizens. Nor can they make decisions motivated by the fact that such employee's family is from a foreign nation. However, as seen in *Plyler v. Doe*, in the absence of amnesty programs for undocumented immigrants, the status of being undocumented does not trigger any heightened review under our laws. States, however, as the Court discussed in *Arizona v. United States*, 567 U.S. 387 (2012), are preempted from enacting their own laws to regulate or impose criminal sanctions against undocumented immigrants who seek employment in their state. With regard to *Hoffman* and private employers, the question is whether we should give employers free reign to discriminate and create pretext to delve into employees' immigration history. Should employers be free to inquire into employees' immigration status beyond the documents submitted at hiring to verify alienage status? Should such inquires be deemed reasonable and related to legitimate employment purposes or do these inquiries amount to harassment? For example, would *Hoffman Plastic Compounds, Inc. v. NLRB*, 535 U.S. 137 (2002) support an employer's questions and requests during discovery probing the immigration status of the plaintiffs?

3. *League of United Latin American Citizens v. Pasadena Independent School District*, 662 F. Supp. 443 (S.D. Tex. 1987), involves discrimination claims by immigrants given amnesty against employers' strict disclosure rules. Any relevance to today? What did the ruling state?

See Kenneth Juan Figueroa, *Immigrants and the Civil Rights Regime: Parens Patriae Standing, Foreign Governments and Protection from Private Discrimination*, 102 COLUM. L. REV. 408 (2002); Lucas Guttentag, *Immigration-Related Employment*

Discrimination: Irca's Prohibitions, Procedures, and Remedies, 37 FED. B. NEWS & J. 29 (1990); Janice D. Villiers, *Closed Borders, Closed Ports: The Plight of Haitians Seeking Political Asylum in the United States*, 60 BROOK. L. REV. 841, 841 (1994); Rachel Bloomekatz, *Rethinking Immigration Status Discrimination and Exploitation in the Low-Wage Workplace*, 54 UCLA L. REV. 1963 (2007); Rachel Feltman, *Undocumented Workers in the United States: Legal, Political, and Social Effects*, 7 RICH. J. GLOBAL L. & BUS. 65 (2008); Leticia M. Saucedo, *Employment Authorization, Alienage Discrimination and Executive Authority*, 38 BERKELEY J. EMP. & LAB. L. 183, 185 (2017).

4. Like the IRCA, Title VII actively protects the rights of language minorities and immigrants in the workforce. Recall our discussion of Title VII's evidentiary structure in Chapter 2. The plaintiff in *Raad* was successful in surviving this strict evidentiary structure by providing concrete evidence supporting each element of the standard. What was this evidence? What must a plaintiff make sure to do when bringing a claim of discrimination based on national origin so as to survive summary judgment?

5. Note the connection drawn by the EEOC in its regulations linking language characteristics to national origin in potential claims of discrimination based on national origin. How does language addressing alienage potentially connect to bias based on national origin? How do you define each? Do you make a distinction between alienage and national origin?

6. Recall the statute of limitations under Title VII: A plaintiff must file a charge within 180 days after the unlawful employment practice occurred if filing directly with the EEOC, or within 300 days if filing with a state agency possessing the authority to process and remedy such claims under state law. 42 U.S.C. § 2000e-5(e). Why did the Court of Appeals deem Raad to have met the standard on one claim, but not the other?

7. Recall that the Supreme Court held in *McDonnell Douglas Corp. v. Green*, 411 U.S. 792, 802 (1973), that a plaintiff can make a *prima facie* case of discrimination by showing that (1) she belongs to a protected class; (2) she applied for and was qualified for a job for which the employer was seeking applicants; (3) despite being qualified, she was rejected; and (4) after her rejection, the position remained open and the employer continued to seek applicants from people of comparable qualifications. How do these factors apply in these cases?

Rivera v. Nibco, Inc.

364 F.3d 1057 (9th Cir. 2004)

REINHARDT, CIRCUIT JUDGE:

Defendant NIBCO has brought this interlocutory appeal to challenge the validity of a protective order, fashioned by a federal magistrate and affirmed by the district court. The order prohibits NIBCO from using the discovery process to inquire into the plaintiffs' immigration status and eligibility for employment. Because NIBCO has failed to demonstrate that the protective order was either clearly erroneous or contrary to law, we affirm the district court's decision denying reconsideration of the order.

I. Factual and Procedural Background

The plaintiffs in this dispute are twenty-three Latina and Southeast Asian female immigrants once employed as production workers at NIBCO's factory in Fresno, California. All of the plaintiffs are of limited English proficiency, yet all allegedly performed their respective duties successfully during their tenure with NIBCO. Although the plaintiffs' job descriptions did not require English proficiency, sometime in 1997 or 1998, NIBCO required them to take basic job skills examinations given only in English. The plaintiffs performed poorly on the exams. NIBCO allegedly responded with a range of adverse employment consequences. Some plaintiffs were demoted or transferred to undesirable job assignments; eventually, all plaintiffs were terminated in the period between July 30, 1998 and September 24, 1998.

The plaintiffs requested and received right-to-sue letters from the EEOC and California's Department of Fair Employment and Housing ("DFEH"). Subsequently, the plaintiffs filed an action in federal court, alleging disparate impact discrimination based on national origin in violation of Title VII, 42 U.S.C. § 2000e *et seq.,* and the California Fair Employment and Housing Act ("FEHA"), Cal. Gov't Code § 12940, *et seq.* The plaintiffs sought reinstatement (and front pay for those not electing reinstatement), back pay, compensatory and punitive damages, and attorney's fees, as well as injunctive relief enjoining NIBCO from, *inter alia,* continuing its English-language testing policy, and compelling it to expunge any record of wrongdoing from personnel files.

This interlocutory appeal arises out of a discovery dispute in the above action. During the deposition of plaintiff Martha Rivera, NIBCO asked where she was married and where she was born. Although Rivera had specified that she was of "Mexican ancestry" in her answers to interrogatories, Rivera's counsel instructed her not to answer any further questions pertaining to her immigration status. The plaintiffs thereafter terminated the deposition. The plaintiffs then filed for a protective order against further questions pertaining to immigration status. Their request was predicated on the claim that—because each plaintiff had already been verified for employment at the time of hiring and because further questions pertaining to immigration status were not relevant to their claims—additional questioning would have a chilling effect on their pursuit of their workplace rights.

The magistrate judge presiding over discovery issued a protective order. The order granted the plaintiffs some discovery protection for three types of questions NIBCO sought to ask. With respect to questions relating to the plaintiffs' places of birth, the magistrate judge found that "there appears to be no dispute that each plaintiff is a member of a protected class, and [thus that] further questions regarding where each plaintiff was born has no further relevance to this action." *Rivera v. NIBCO, Inc.,* 204 F.R.D. 647, 649 (E.D.Cal.2001). The magistrate judge did, however, allow

NIBCO discovery concerning the plaintiffs' places of marriage, educational background, current and past employment, damages, date of birth, and criminal convictions, but limited disclosure of that information to the parties and their attorneys. *Id.* at 649. With regard to each plaintiff's immigration status, the magistrate judge barred all discovery into the matter, but did not preclude NIBCO from conducting its own independent investigation. She acknowledged that the "after-acquired" evidence doctrine could limit NIBCO's liability in the event that it discovered that some plaintiffs were not eligible for employment, but ruled that NIBCO under the circumstances did not have a right to use the discovery process to gain that information. *Id.* at 649–51 (citing *McKennon v. Nashville Banner Publishing Co.,* 513 U.S. 352, 362–63, 115 S.Ct. 879, 130 L.Ed.2d 852 (1995)). Allowing NIBCO to obtain such information through the discovery process, she found, would unnecessarily chill legitimate claims of undocumented workers under Title VII.

NIBCO filed a motion under Fed. R. Civ. P. 72(a), requesting that the district court reconsider the magistrate's ruling. The court denied the motion. *Rivera v. Nibco, Inc.,* 2001 WL 1688880 (E.D.Cal. Dec.21, 2001). It found that the defendant's various contentions misstated the magistrate's ruling, and held that it was neither clearly erroneous nor contrary to law. *Id.*

NIBCO subsequently filed a motion to certify the discovery ruling for interlocutory appeal. Before the district judge ruled on the motion, however, the United States Supreme Court issued its decision in *Hoffman Plastic Compounds, Inc. v. NLRB,* 535 U.S. 137, 122 S.Ct. 1275, 152 L.Ed.2d 271 (2002) [hereinafter *Hoffman*]. *Hoffman* held that the National Labor Relations Board lacks the discretion to award back pay to undocumented workers seeking relief for an employer's unlawful employment practices under the National Labor Relations Act. *Id.* at 151–52, 122 S.Ct. 1275. NIBCO immediately filed a second motion to reconsider, claiming that after *Hoffman*, each plaintiff's immigration status was discoverable because of its direct relevance to potential remedies. In response, the plaintiffs proposed a proceeding bifurcated into liability and damages phases. Under the plaintiffs' proposal, the case would proceed to trial on liability first. If the plaintiffs were able to prove NIBCO's liability for the alleged disparate impact violation, the court would then hold an *in camera* proceeding designed to preserve the plaintiffs' anonymity, protect their statutory rights, and avoid prejudicing the defense. The proceeding would allow each plaintiff to testify regarding her immigration status, provide documents supporting her entitlement to back pay, and provide a formal certification from the Social Security Administration attesting that she was authorized to work throughout the back pay period. The judge would make deductions from the aggregate award back pay for any plaintiff who failed to prove eligibility. Once the aggregate award was thus reduced to encompass only eligible plaintiffs, plaintiffs' counsel would then have the responsibility of giving each eligible plaintiff her share of the total.

The district court postponed its decision on whether to bifurcate the trial, denied NIBCO's request to reconsider, and granted NIBCO's motion to certify the post-*Hoffman* order denying reconsideration of the interlocutory appeal pursuant to 28 U.S.C. § 1292(b). We granted the petition for interlocutory appeal.

II. Standard and Scope of Review

District courts review magistrate judges' pretrial orders under a "clearly erroneous or contrary to law" standard. Fed. R. Civ. P. 72(a). This court reviews "a district court's denial of a motion to reconsider a magistrate's pretrial[protective discovery] order under that same standard." *Osband v. Woodford*, 290 F.3d 1036, 1041 (9th Cir.2002). We may not overturn a protective order simply because we might have weighed differently the various interests and equities; instead, we must ascertain whether the order was contrary to law.

We have jurisdiction to consider orders certified for interlocutory appeal under 28 U.S.C. § 1292(b). Our scope of review is broader than the specific issues the district court has designated for appellate review. "[T]he appellate court may address any issue fairly included within the certified order because 'it is the order that is appealable, and not the controlling question identified by the district court.'" *Yamaha Motor Corp., U.S.A. v. Calhoun*, 516 U.S. 199, 205, 116 S.Ct. 619, 133 L.Ed.2d 578 (1996) . . . . In this case, the order certified is the district court's post-*Hoffman* order denying reconsideration of the protective order granted by the magistrate judge. We now turn to whether the district court was required by law to overturn or modify the protective order.

III. Discussion

The magistrate judge granted the protective order at issue pursuant to Fed. R. Civ. P. 26. Rule 26 states that, in general, any matter relevant to a claim or defense is discoverable. Fed. R. Civ. P. 26(b). That principle is subject to limitation. After a showing of good cause, the district court may issue any protective order "which justice requires to protect a party or person from annoyance, embarrassment, oppression, or undue burden or expense," including any order prohibiting the requested discovery altogether, limiting the scope of the discovery, or fixing the terms of disclosure. Fed.R.Civ.P. 26(c). The burden is upon the party seeking the order to "show good cause" by demonstrating harm or prejudice that will result from the discovery. . . . In this case, the protective order was justified because the substantial and particularized harm of the discovery—the chilling effect that the disclosure of plaintiffs' immigration status could have upon their ability to effectuate their rights—outweighed NIBCO's interests in obtaining the information at this early stage in the litigation. We therefore hold that the district court's decision not to disturb the order was neither clearly erroneous nor contrary to law.

A. The Harm of Disclosure

The protective order at issue bars discovery into each plaintiff's immigration status on the basis that allowing NIBCO to use the discovery process to obtain such information would chill the plaintiffs' willingness and ability to bring civil rights claims. *Rivera*, 204 F.R.D. at 651. By revealing their immigration status, any plaintiffs found to be undocumented might face criminal prosecution and deportation. Although NIBCO has promised not to disclose the plaintiffs' immigration status to any outside party, the district court found that requiring the plaintiffs to answer such questions in the discovery process would likely deter them, and future plaintiffs, from bringing meritorious claims.

We agree with the district court. There are reportedly over 5.3 million workers in the "unauthorized labor" force. *See* Dean E. Murphy, *A New Order: Imagining Life Without Illegal Immigrants,* N.Y. Times, Jan. 11, 2004, §4, at 1. Many of these workers are willing to work for substandard wages in our economy's most undesirable jobs. While documented workers face the possibility of retaliatory discharge for an assertion of their labor and civil rights, undocumented workers confront the harsher reality that, in addition to possible discharge, their employer will likely report them to the INS and they will be subjected to deportation proceedings or criminal prosecution. . . .

As a result, most undocumented workers are reluctant to report abusive or discriminatory employment practices. *See United States v. Brignoni-Ponce,* 422 U.S. 873, 879, 95 S.Ct. 2574, 45 L.Ed.2d 607 (1975) ("The aliens themselves are vulnerable to exploitation because they cannot complain of substandard working conditions without risking deportation."); *see also* Michael J. Wishnie, *Immigrants and the Right to Petition,* 78 N.Y.U. L. Rev. 667, 676–79 (2003) (arguing that undocumented workers are reluctant to report a variety of labor and employment law violations). Granting employers the right to inquire into workers' immigration status in cases like this would allow them to raise implicitly the threat of deportation and criminal prosecution every time a worker, documented or undocumented, reports illegal practices or files a Title VII action. Indeed, were we to direct district courts to grant discovery requests for information related to immigration status in every case involving national origin discrimination under Title VII, countless acts of illegal and reprehensible conduct would go unreported.

Even documented workers may be chilled by the type of discovery at issue here. Documented workers may fear that their immigration status would be changed, or that their status would reveal the immigration problems of their family or friends; similarly, new legal residents or citizens may feel intimidated by the prospect of having their immigration history examined in a public proceeding. Any of these individuals, failing to understand the relationship between their litigation and immigration status, might choose to forego civil rights litigation.

The chilling effect such discovery could have on the bringing of civil rights actions unacceptably burdens the public interest. The Supreme Court has recognized that Congress intended to empower individuals to act as private attorneys general in enforcing the provisions of Title VII. *See N.Y. Gaslight Club, Inc. v. Carey,* 447 U.S. 54, 63, 100 S.Ct. 2024, 64 L.Ed.2d 723 (1980) (finding that "Congress has cast the Title VII plaintiff in the role of 'a private attorney general,' vindicating a policy 'of the highest priority'"); *Alexander v. Gardner-Denver Co.,* 415 U.S. 36, 45, 94 S.Ct. 1011, 39 L.Ed.2d 147 (1974) ("the private right of action remains an essential means of obtaining judicial enforcement of Title VII. . . . In such cases, the private litigant not only redresses his own injury but also vindicates the important congressional policy against discriminatory employment practices."); *see also* H.R. Rep. No. 102-40, pt. 2, at 34 (1991) (report of the committee on the judiciary describing how the failure to adequately compensate plaintiffs has a chilling effect on the 'private attorneys general' policy of the civil rights laws). Given Title VII's dependence on private enforcement, we find that the national effort to eradicate discrimination in the workplace would be hampered by the discovery practices NIBCO seeks to validate here. We therefore conclude that discovery of each plaintiff's immigration status constitutes a substantial burden, both on the plaintiffs themselves and on the public interest in enforcing Title VII and FEHA.

B. Balancing of Interests

Even if the discovery would burden plaintiffs and others with an interest in enforcing Title VII and FEHA, the burden must be "undue" in order to justify the protective order. *See* Fed. R. Civ. P. 26(c). We thus must examine NIBCO's various interests in discovering the immigration status information. NIBCO asserts that because each plaintiff's immigration status governs her entitlement to reinstatement, front pay, and back pay on Title VII claim, and governs any recovery on her FEHA claim, it must be permitted to discover this information. We consider NIBCO's contentions below.

1. The Relevance of *Hoffman Plastic*

NIBCO's principal argument is that the Supreme Court's decision in *Hoffman Plastic Compounds, Inc. v. NLRB,* 535 U.S. 137, 122 S.Ct. 1275, 152 L.Ed.2d 271 (2002), forecloses any award of back pay to an undocumented plaintiff and therefore discovery of documented or undocumented status is essential to its defense. We disagree.

In *Hoffman,* the Supreme Court reviewed an award of back pay to illegal immigrants who, in violation of § 8(a)(3) of the National Labor Relations Act ("NLRA"), were terminated because of their participation in the organization of a union. 535 U.S. at 140–41, 122 S.Ct. 1275. The National Labor Relations Board ("NLRB") based its decision to award back pay on its previous holding that the NLRA's protections applied to documented and undocumented workers alike. *Id.* at 141, 122 S.Ct. 1275. The Supreme Court reversed the Board's order. The precise question before the Court was whether the NLRB had the authority under the NLRA to award back pay to undocumented workers notwithstanding the prohibition on hiring such workers in the Immigration Reform and Control Act of 1986 ("IRCA"). Answering that question in the negative, the majority also strongly suggested that the policy goals of IRCA outweigh those of the NLRA, and therefore that IRCA would preclude any back pay award to illegal immigrants under the NLRA. *Id.* at 148–52, 122 S.Ct. 1275.

NIBCO would have us go further and hold that: (a) *Hoffman* precludes any award of back pay to an illegal immigrant, no matter what federal statute the employer may have violated; and (b) the district court is *required* to grant the request for pretrial discovery of the plaintiffs' immigration status.

We seriously doubt that *Hoffman* is as broadly applicable as NIBCO contends, and specifically believe it unlikely that it applies in Title VII cases. The NLRA and Title VII are different statutes in numerous respects. Congress gave them distinct remedial schemes and vested their enforcement agencies with different powers. For purposes of this opinion, we note at least three significant differences between the two statutes.

First, the NLRA authorizes only certain limited private causes of action, while Title VII depends principally upon private causes of action for enforcement. The NLRA is enforced primarily through actions of the NLRB—private actions are available only in exceptional circumstances. . . . *See N.Y. Gaslight Club,* 447 U.S. at 63, 100 S.Ct. 2024(finding that "Congress has cast the Title VII plaintiff in the role of 'a private attorney general,' vindicating a policy 'of the highest priority'"); *Alexander,* 415 U.S. at 45, 94 S.Ct. 1011 (holding that "the private right of action remains an essential means of obtaining judicial enforcement of Title VII" and noting that "the private litigant not only redresses his own injury but also vindicates the important congressional policy against discriminatory employment practices").

Second, Congress has armed Title VII plaintiffs with remedies designed to punish employers who engage in unlawful discriminatory acts, and to deter future discrimination both by the defendant and by all other employers. Title VII's enforcement regime includes not only traditional remedies for employment law violations, such as back pay, front pay, and reinstatement, but also full compensatory and punitive damages. 42 U.S.C. § 1981a; *see also Pollard v. E.I. du Pont de Nemours & Co.,* 532 U.S. 843, 851–52, 121 S.Ct. 1946, 150 L.Ed.2d 62 (2001). Congress added the latter types of damages to Title VII in 1991 in order to facilitate the deterrence of discrimination. *See* Civil Rights Act of 1991, § 3, 102 Pub.L. 166; 105 Stat. 1071, 1071. . . .

Third, under the NLRA, the NLRB may award back pay to workers when it has found that an employer has violated the Act. Under Title VII, a federal court decides whether a statutory violation warrants a back pay award. This difference is significant given that *Hoffman* held that the NLRB possesses only the discretion to "select and fashion remedies for violations of the NLRA," and that this discretion, "though broad, is not unlimited." 535 U.S. at 142–43, 122 S.Ct. 1275 (citations omitted). The Court held that, given the strong policies underlying IRCA and the Board's limited power to construe statutes outside of its authority, the NLRB's construction of the NLRA was impermissible. This limitation on the Board's authority says nothing regarding a *federal court's power* to balance IRCA against *Title VII* if the two statutes conflict. A district court has the very authority to interpret both Title VII and IRCA that the NLRB lacks. Thus, to the extent that *Hoffman* stands for a limitation on the NLRB's remedial discretion to interpret statutes other than the NLRA, the decision appears not to be relevant to a Title VII action. *Cf. Smith v. Nat'l Steel & Shipbuilding Co.,* 125 F.3d 751, 757 (9th Cir.1997) (holding that district courts have the authority to construe competing statutes even when the NLRB lacks it).

The differences between the two statutes persuade us that *Hoffman* does not resolve the question whether federal courts may award back pay to undocumented workers who have been discharged in violation of Title VII. Resolving the conflicting statutory policies involved in determining whether IRCA bars such awards to employees discriminated against on the basis of their national origin necessitates a different analysis than the Court undertook in *Hoffman*. As we have pointed out, in Title VII Congress has chosen to rely heavily on private actions that result in the imposition of severe remedies, including back pay, in order to deter future discrimination and vindicate national policy of the highest priority. It is far from evident to us that Congress intended to bar the use of one of the most critical of those remedies in the case of undocumented workers who are victims of invidious discrimination. In fact, given the importance of private actions to the enforcement scheme and of back pay to the bringing of private actions, we are strongly inclined to believe that it did not. We are influenced in this view by the Court's statement in *Albemarle Paper,* 422 U.S. at 417–18, 95 S.Ct. 2362, that it "is the reasonably certain prospect of a back pay award that provide(s) the spur or catalyst which causes employers and unions to self-examine and to self-evaluate their employment practices and to endeavor to eliminate, so far as possible, the last vestiges of an unfortunate and ignominious page in this country's history" (internal citation and quotation marks omitted). We are also influenced by our own court's conclusion that Title VII's "central statutory purpose" is "eradicating discrimination throughout the economy and making persons whole for injuries suffered through past discrimination." *McLean v. Runyon,* 222 F.3d 1150, 1155 (9th Cir.2000) (quoting *Albemarle Paper,* 422 U.S. at 421, 95 S. Ct. 2362). Finally, we find it significant that the courts that have considered *Hoffman* in analogous cases have thus far found it to be inapplicable or distinguishable. In sum, the overriding national policy against discrimination would seem likely to outweigh any bar against the payment of back wages to unlawful immigrants in Title VII cases. Thus, we seriously doubt that *Hoffman* applies in such actions.

We need not decide the *Hoffman* question in this case, however. Regardless whether *Hoffman* applies in Title VII cases, it is clear that it does not *require* a district court to allow the discovery sought here. No back pay award has been authorized in this litigation. Indeed, the plaintiffs have proposed several options for ensuring that, whether or not *Hoffman* applies, no award of back pay is given to any undocumented alien in this proceeding. Thus, the very problem NIBCO has identified may well never arise here.

. . . We recognize that discovering the various plaintiffs' eligibility for particular remedies would aid the defendant in making pre-trial estimates of the damage award for which it might be responsible if found liable. The convenience to NIBCO, however, is substantially outweighed by the harm the discovery would cause the plaintiffs. *See supra* at 1064–65. Moreover, other remedies clearly remain available and liability must be determined in any event. *See, e.g., Farrar v. Hobby,* 506 U.S. 103, 112–14, 113 S.Ct. 566, 121 L.Ed.2d 494 (1992) (holding that even an award of nominal damages is sufficient to allow an award of attorney's fees); *Ruffin v. Great*

Dane Trailers, 969 F.2d 989, 993 (9th Cir.1992) (holding that a Title VII plaintiff may recover attorney's fees despite not recovering monetary damages when he has prevailed in his request for injunctive relief), *cert. denied,* 507 U.S. 910, 113 S.Ct. 1257, 122 L.Ed.2d 655 (1993).

The district court has not yet ruled on the plaintiffs' proposed bifurcated proceedings. Although we do not order such proceedings here, it is clear that a separation between liability and damages would be consistent with our prior case law and would satisfy the concern that causes of action under Title VII not be dismissed, or lost through intimidation, on account of the existence of particular remedies. The principal question to be decided in the action before us is whether NIBCO violated Title VII. It makes no difference to the resolution of that question whether some of the plaintiffs are ineligible for certain forms of statutory relief. NIBCO's contention that discovery regarding the plaintiffs' immigration status is essential to its defense is therefore without merit. Accordingly, we hold that the district court did not err when it declined to modify the protective order.

2. The After-Acquired Evidence Doctrine

NIBCO argues that the "after-acquired evidence" doctrine requires the district court to approve its discovery request. The "after-acquired evidence" doctrine precludes or limits an employee from receiving remedies for wrongful discharge if the employer later "discovers" evidence of wrongdoing that would have led to the employee's termination had the employer known of the misconduct. *McKennon v. Nashville Banner Publishing Co.,* 513 U.S. 352, 360–63, 115 S.Ct. 879, 130 L.Ed.2d 852 (1995). As we have explained, "[a]n employer can avoid back pay and other remedies by coming forward with after-acquired evidence of an employee's misconduct, but only if it can prove by a preponderance of the evidence that it would have fired the employee for that misconduct." *O'Day v. McDonnell Douglas Helicopter Co.,* 79 F.3d 756, 761 (9th Cir.1996).

. . . .

In this case, NIBCO has failed to come forward with any evidence that would justify limiting the plaintiffs' remedies. NIBCO claims, instead, that the court was required to facilitate its discovery of any such evidence by granting its requests to interrogate the former employees regarding their immigration status. We reject NIBCO's claim. *McKennon* does not direct courts to authorize the type of discovery NIBCO seeks to conduct here. Although *McKennon* involved illegal conduct that was "after-acquired" during a deposition, the *McKennon* Court did not hold that depositions could be conducted for the purpose of uncovering illegal actions. . . . *Id.* at 363, 115 S.Ct. 879.

District courts need not condone the use of discovery to engage in "fishing expedition[s]." *See, e.g., Exxon Corp. v. Crosby-Mississippi Resources, Ltd.,* 40 F.3d 1474, 1487 (5th Cir.1995). . . . Moreover, we note that before an employer may use "after-acquired evidence," it must meet its burden of showing that, had it been aware of that evidence, it would have forthwith discharged the employee. *See O'Day,* 79 F.3d at

758–59. Regrettably, many employers turn a blind eye to immigration status during the hiring process; their aim is to assemble a workforce that is both cheap to employ and that minimizes their risk of being reported for violations of statutory rights. Therefore, employers have a perverse incentive to ignore immigration laws at the time of hiring but insist upon their enforcement when their employees complain. . . .

. . . .

We hold that the district court properly exercised its discretion in concluding that NIBCO's proposed discovery placed an "undue burden" on the plaintiffs. The court did not err in determining that it would substantially burden the plaintiffs to allow the defendant to use the discovery process to inquire into their immigration status—a status that NIBCO had the opportunity to examine upon hiring and that is irrelevant to the question of liability. We seriously doubt that *Hoffman*'s prohibition of NLRB-authorized back pay awards under the NLRA serves to prohibit a district court from awarding back pay to a Title VII plaintiff. But even if we were to conclude that *Hoffman* did preclude back pay awards to illegal immigrants under all federal statutes, it would not matter in this case. *Hoffman* does not make immigration status relevant to the determination whether a defendant has committed national origin discrimination under Title VII. If the district court decides to bifurcate the proceeding, as the plaintiffs have requested, the availability of back pay remedies for certain plaintiffs will be determined, if at all, only after the liability phase. Similarly, neither IRCA nor the after-acquired evidence doctrine requires the district court to allow NIBCO's requested discovery. It was neither erroneous nor contrary to law for the district court to protect the plaintiffs, and the public interest, from being unduly burdened by issuing the protective order.

We AFFIRM the decision of the district court and REMAND for further proceedings consistent with this opinion.

E. Voting and Language Minorities

Language minorities face substantial obstacles in voting. As seen in the above section, access to educational opportunities is still a major issue facing limited language proficiency communities. As a result, existing educational programs do not always adequately prepare them for the intricacies of the United States' electoral system. In addition, attempts to infringe on their fundamental rights and to prevent their meaningful participation in the electoral process continue. Furthermore, as the population of language minorities of voting age grows, some factions have pushed back against their full integration in the democratic process, attempting to restrict their participation via implementation of new restrictive laws.[16]

---

16. *Language Disenfranchisement in Juries: A Call for Constitutional Remediation*, 65 HASTINGS L.J. 811; *Enfranchising Language Minority Citizens: The Bilingual Election Provisions of the Voting Rights Act*, 10 N.Y.U. J. LEGIS. & PUB. POL'Y 195; Note and Comment, *"My English Is Good Enough"*

Congress protects these communities via various laws. One such source of protection is that provided to Puerto Rican Americans:

Section 4(f) of the Voting Rights Act provides:

(1) Congress hereby declares that to secure the rights under the fourteenth amendment of persons educated in American-flag schools in which the predominant classroom language was other than English, it is necessary to prohibit the States from conditioning the right to vote of such persons on ability to read, write, understand, or interpret any matter in the English language.

(2) No person who demonstrates that he has successfully completed the sixth primary grade in a public school in, or a private school accredited by, any State or territory, the District of Columbia, or the Commonwealth of Puerto Rico in which the predominant classroom language was other than English, shall be denied the right to vote in any Federal, State, or local election because of his inability to read, write, understand, or interpret any matter in the English language, except that in States in which State law provides that a different level of education is presumptive of literacy, he shall demonstrate that he has successfully completed an equivalent level of education in a public school in, or a private school accredited by, any State or territory, the District of Columbia, or the Commonwealth of Puerto Rico in which the predominant classroom language was other than English.

79 Stat. 439, 42 U.S.C. § 1973b(e) (1964 ed., Supp. I).

This provision was upheld as a valid exercise of Congressional power in *South Carolina vs Katzenbach*, below. Congress enacted additional protections in 1975 in response to findings showing systematic exclusion and targeting of individuals with limited English proficiency. As a result, Congress incorporated protections for bilingual citizens living in jurisdictions where 5% or 10,000 citizens of a voting age are members of a single language minority.

Section 203 provides:

Whenever any State or political subdivision [covered by the section] provides registration or voting notices, forms, instructions, assistance, or other materials or information relating to the electoral process, including ballots, it shall provide them in the language of the applicable minority group as well as in the English language.

These 1975 Amendments also require that these covered jurisdictions provide assistance and bilingual materials to voters with limited English proficiency. The Voting

---

for San Luis: Adopting a Two-Pronged Approach for Arizona's English Fluency Requirements for Candidates for Public Office, 22 J.L. & Pol'y 305; Note, *Language Accommodations and Section 203 of the Voting Rights Act: Reporting Requirements as a Potential Solution to the Compliance Gap*, 67 Stan. L. Rev. 917; Symposium: *Language Assistance and Local Voting Rights Law*, 44 Ind. L. Rev. 161.

Rights Act grants enforcement powers to the Department of Justice. *United States v. Metropolitan Dade County, Florida*, 815 F. sup. 1475, 1478 (S.D. Fla. 1993).[17] Courts have defined covered jurisdictions to include school boards and agricultural and power districts.[18] As such, literacy tests and English-only provisions may constitute violations of the bilingual provisions of the Voting Rights Act. *See also Veasey v. Abbott* 830 F.3d 216 (5th Cir. 2016) (appeal pending) (striking down voter identification law based on disparate impact); *North Carolina State Conference of NAACP v. McCrory*, 831 F.3d 204 (4th Cir. 2016) (finding that discriminatory intent motivated the enactment of the law requiring photo ID and changes to early voting, same-day registration, out-of-precinct voting, and preregistration); *Terrebonne Parish Branch NAACP v. Jindal*, 274 F. Supp. 3d 395 (M.D. La. 2017) (appeal pending) (holding the voting system had discriminatory or dilutive effect in violation of the Voting Rights Act); *Patino v. City of Pasadena*, 230 F. Supp. 3d 667 (S.D. Tex. 2017) (finding the city acted with discriminatory intent in violation of the Equal Protection Clause when it changed from eight single-member district and diluted Latino voting strength); *Oregon v. Mitchell*, 400 U.S. 112 (1970) (upholding Congressional suspension of literacy tests nationally); *Garza vs. Smith*, 401 U.S. 1006, (1970) (limiting voter assistance to persons with disability, finding that refusing assistance to illiterate voters violates the Equal Protection Clause).

Katzenbach v. Morgan

384 U.S. 641 (1966)

Mr. Justice Brennan delivered the opinion of the Court.

These cases concern the constitutionality of §4(e) of the Voting Rights Act of 1965. That law, in the respects pertinent in these cases, provides that no person who has successfully completed the sixth primary grade in a public school in, or a private school accredited by, the Commonwealth of Puerto Rico in which the language of instruction was other than English shall be denied the right to vote in any election because of his inability to read or write English. Appellees, registered voters in New York City, brought this suit to challenge the constitutionality of §4(e) insofar as it pro tanto prohibits the enforcement of the election laws of New York requiring an ability to read and write English as a condition of voting. Under these laws many

---

17. *Local Government Law Symposium: Ensuring That Florida's Language Minorities Have Access to the Ballot*, 36 Stetson L. Rev. 329; *The Patchwork of State and Federal Language Assistance for Minority Voters and a Proposal for Model State Legislation*, 65 N.Y.U. Ann. Surv. Am. L. 323; *Enfranchising Language Minority Citizens: The Bilingual Election Provisions of the Voting Rights Act*, 10 N.Y.U. J. Legis. & Pub. Pol'y 195.

18. School boards: Irby v. Virginia State Bd. of Elections, 889 F.2d 1352 (4th Cir. 1989); *Dougherty County Bd. of Ed. v. White*, 439 U.S. 32 (1978); *Freedom: Constitutional Law: Yes, But What Have They Done to Black People Lately? The Role of Historical Evidence in the Virginia School Board Case*, 70 Chi.-Kent L. Rev. 1275. Agricultural and power districts: *Smith v. Salt River Project Agric. Improvement & Power Dist.*, 109 F.3d 586 (9th Cir. 1997); *The Causal Context of Disparate Vote Denial*, 54 B.C. L. Rev. 579.

of the several hundred thousand New York City residents who have migrated there from the Commonwealth of Puerto Rico had previously been denied the right to vote, and appellees attack § 4(e) insofar as it would enable many of these citizens to vote. Pursuant to § 14(b) of the Voting Rights Act of 1965, appellees commenced this proceeding in the District Court for the District of Columbia seeking a declaration that § 4(e) is invalid and an injunction prohibiting appellants, the Attorney General of the United States and the New York City Board of Elections, from either enforcing or complying with § 4(e). A three-judge district court was designated. 28 U.S.C. §§ 2282, 2284 (1964 ed.). Upon cross motions for summary judgment, that court, one judge dissenting, granted the declaratory and injunctive relief appellees sought. The court held that in enacting § 4(e) Congress exceeded the powers granted to it by the Constitution and therefore usurped powers reserved to the States by the Tenth Amendment. 247 F.Supp. 196. Appeals were taken directly to this Court, 28 U.S.C. §§ 1252, 1253 (1964 ed.) and we noted probable jurisdiction. 382 U.S. 1007, 86 S.Ct. 621, 15 L.Ed.2d 524. We reverse. We hold that, in the application challenged in these cases, § 4(e) is a proper exercise of the powers granted to Congress by § 5 of the Fourteenth Amendment and that by force of the Supremacy Clause, Article VI, the New York English literacy requirement cannot be enforced to the extent that it is inconsistent with § 4(e).

Under the distribution of powers effected by the Constitution, the States establish qualifications for voting for state officers, and the qualifications established by the States for voting for members of the most numerous branch of the state legislature also determine who may vote for United States Representatives and Senators, Art. I, § 2; Seventeenth Amendment; *Ex parte Yarbrough*, 110 U.S. 651, 663, 4 S.Ct. 152, 28 L.Ed. 274. But, of course, the States have no power to grant or withhold the franchise on conditions that are forbidden by the Fourteenth Amendment, or any other provision of the Constitution. Such exercises of state power are no more immune to the limitations of the Fourteenth Amendment than any other state action. The Equal Protection Clause itself has been held to forbid some state laws that restrict the right to vote.

The Attorney General of the State of New York argues that an exercise of congressional power under § 5 of the Fourteenth Amendment that prohibits the enforcement of a state law can only be sustained if the judicial branch determines that the state law is prohibited by the provisions of the Amendment that Congress sought to enforce. More specifically, he urges that § 4(e) cannot be sustained as appropriate legislation to enforce the Equal Protection Clause unless the judiciary decides— even with the guidance of a congressional judgment—that the application of the English literacy requirement prohibited by § 4(e) is forbidden by the Equal Protection Clause itself. We disagree. Neither the language nor history of § 5 supports such a construction. As was said with regard to § 5 in *Ex parte Com. of Virginia*, 100 U.S. 339, 345, 25 L.Ed. 676. 'It is the power of Congress which has been enlarged. Congress is authorized to enforce the prohibitions by appropriate legislation. Some legislation is contemplated to make the amendments fully effective.' A construction of § 5 that would require a judicial determination that the enforcement of the state law precluded by Congress violated the Amendment, as a condition of sustaining the congressional enactment, would depreciate both congressional resourcefulness and congressional responsibility for implementing the Amendment. It would confine the legislative power in this context to the insignificant role of abrogating only those state laws that the judicial branch was prepared to adjudge unconstitutional, or of merely informing the judgment of the judiciary by particularizing the 'majestic generalities' of § 1 of the Amendment. See *Fay v. People of State of New York*, 332 U.S. 261, 282 — 284, 67 S.Ct. 1613, 1624 — 1625, 91 L.Ed. 2043.

Thus our task in this case is not to determine whether the New York English literacy requirement as applied to deny the right to vote to a person who successfully completed the sixth grade in a Puerto Rican school violates the Equal Protection Clause. Accordingly, our decision in *Lassiter v. Northampton County Bd. of Election*, 360 U.S. 45, 79 S.Ct. 985, 3 L.Ed.2d 1072, sustaining the North Carolina English literacy requirement as not in all circumstances prohibited by the first sections of the Fourteenth and Fifteenth Amendments, is inapposite. Compare also *Guinn v. United States*, 238 U.S. 347, 366, 35 S.Ct. 926, 931, 59 L.Ed. 1340; *Camacho v. Doe*, 31 Misc.2d 692, 221 N.Y.S.2d 262 (1958), aff'd 7 N.Y.2d 762, 194 N.Y.S.2d 33, 163 N.E.2d 140 (1959); *Camacho v. Rogers*, 199 F.Supp. 155 (D.C.S.D.N.Y.1961). Lassiter did not present the question before us here: Without regard to whether the judiciary would find that the Equal Protection Clause itself nullifies New York's English literacy requirement as so applied, could Congress prohibit the enforcement of the state law by legislating under § 5 of the Fourteenth Amendment? In answering this question, our task is limited to determining whether such legislation is, as required by § 5, appropriate legislation to enforce the Equal Protection Clause.

By including § 5 the draftsmen sought to grant to Congress, by a specific provision applicable to the Fourteenth Amendment, the same broad powers expressed in the Necessary and Proper Clause, Art. I, § 8, cl. 18. The classic formulation of the reach of those powers was established by Chief Justice Marshall in *McCulloch v. Maryland*, 4 Wheat. 316, 421, 4 L.Ed. 579:

> 'Let the end be legitimate, let it be within the scope of the constitution, and all means which are appropriate, which are plainly adapted to that end, which are not prohibited, but consist with the letter and spirit of the constitution, are constitutional.

Ex parte Com. of Virginia, 100 U.S., at 345–346, 25 L.Ed. 676, decided 12 years after the adoption of the Fourteenth Amendment, held that congressional power under § 5 had this same broad scope:

> 'Whatever legislation is appropriate, that is, adapted to carry out the objects the amendments have in view, whatever tends to enforce submission to the prohibitions they contain, and to secure to all persons the enjoyment of perfect equality of civil rights and the equal protection of the laws against

State denial or invasion, if not prohibited, is brought within the domain of congressional power.'

Strauder v. West Virginia, 100 U.S. 303, 311, 25 L.Ed. 664; *Virginia v. Rives*, 100 U.S. 313, 318, 25 L.Ed. 667. Section 2 of the Fifteenth Amendment grants Congress a similar power to enforce by 'appropriate legislation' the provisions of that amendment; and we recently held in *State of South Carolina v. Katzenbach*, 383 U.S. 301, 326, 86 S. Ct. 803, 817, 15 L.Ed.2d 769, that '[t]he basic test to be applied in a case involving §2 of the Fifteenth Amendment is the same as in all cases concerning the express powers of Congress with relation to the reserved powers of the States.' That test was identified as the one formulated in *McCulloch v. Maryland*. See also *James Everard's Breweries v. Day*, 265 U.S. 545, 558–559, 44 S.Ct. 628, 631, 68 L.Ed. 1174 (Eighteenth Amendment). Thus the *McCulloch v. Maryland* standard is the measure of what constitutes 'appropriate legislation' under §5 of the Fourteenth Amendment. Correctly viewed, §5 is a positive grant of legislative power authorizing Congress to exercise its discretion in determining whether and what legislation is needed to secure the guarantees of the Fourteenth Amendment.

We therefore proceed to the consideration whether §4(e) is 'appropriate legislation' to enforce the Equal Protection Clause, that is, under the *McCulloch v. Maryland* standard, whether §4(e) may be regarded as an enactment to enforce the Equal Protection Clause, whether it is 'plainly adapted to that end' and whether it is not prohibited by but is consistent with 'the letter and spirit of the constitution.'

There can be no doubt that §4(e) may be regarded as an enactment to enforce the Equal Protection Clause. Congress explicitly declared that it enacted §4(e) 'to secure the rights under the fourteenth amendment of persons educated in American-flag schools in which the predominant classroom language was other than English.' The persons referred to include those who have migrated from the Commonwealth of Puerto Rico to New York and who have been denied the right to vote because of their inability to read and write English, and the Fourteenth Amendment rights referred to include those emanating from the Equal Protection Clause. More specifically, §4(e) may be viewed as a measure to secure for the Puerto Rican community residing in New York nondiscriminatory treatment by government—both in the imposition of voting qualifications and the provision or administration of governmental services, such as public schools, public housing and law enforcement.

Section 4(e) may be readily seen as 'plainly adapted' to furthering these aims of the Equal Protection Clause. The practical effect of §4(e) is to prohibit New York from denying the right to vote to large segments of its Puerto Rican community. Congress has thus prohibited the State from denying to that community the right that is 'preservative of all rights.' *Yick Wo v. Hopkins*, 118 U.S. 356, 370, 6 S.Ct. 1064, 1071, 30 L.Ed. 220. This enhanced political power will be helpful in gaining nondiscriminatory treatment in public services for the entire Puerto Rican community. Section 4(e) thereby enables the Puerto Rican minority better to obtain 'perfect equality of civil rights and the equal protection of the laws.' It was well within congressional authority to say that this need of the Puerto Rican minority for the vote warranted federal intrusion upon any state interests served by the English literacy requirement. It was for Congress, as the branch that made this judgment, to assess and weigh the various conflicting considerations—the risk or pervasiveness of the discrimination in governmental services, the effectiveness of eliminating the state restriction on the right to vote as a means of dealing with the evil, the adequacy or availability of alternative remedies, and the nature and significance of the state interests that would be affected by the nullification of the English literacy requirement as applied to residents who have successfully completed the sixth grade in a Puerto Rican school. It is not for us to review the congressional resolution of these factors. It is enough that we be able to perceive a basis upon which the Congress might resolve the conflict as it did. There plainly was such a basis to support § 4(e) in the application in question in this case. Any contrary conclusion would require us to be blind to the realities familiar to the legislators.

The result is no different if we confine our inquiry to the question whether s 4(e) was merely legislation aimed at the elimination of an invidious discrimination in establishing voter qualifications. We are told that New York's English literacy requirement originated in the desire to provide an incentive for non-English speaking immigrants to learn the English language and in order to assure the intelligent exercise of the franchise. Yet Congress might well have questioned, in light of the many exemptions provided, and some evidence suggesting that prejudice played a prominent role in the enactment of the requirement, whether these were actually the interests being served. Congress might have also questioned whether denial of a right deemed so precious and fundamental in our society was a necessary or appropriate means of encouraging persons to learn English, or of furthering the goal of an intelligent exercise of the franchise. Finally, Congress might well have concluded that as a means of furthering the intelligent exercise of the franchise, an ability to read or understand Spanish is as effective as ability to read English for those to whom Spanish-language newspapers and Spanish-language radio and television programs are available to inform them of election issues and governmental affairs. Since Congress undertook to legislate so as to preclude the enforcement of the state law, and did so in the context of a general appraisal of literacy requirements for voting, see *State of South Carolina v. Katzenbach, supra,* to which it brought a specially informed legislative competence, it was Congress' prerogative to weigh these competing considerations. Here again, it is enough that we perceive a basis upon which Congress might predicate a judgment that the application of New York's English literacy requirement to deny the right to vote to a person with a sixth grade education in Puerto Rican schools in which the language of instruction was other than English constituted an invidious discrimination in violation of the Equal Protection Clause.

There remains the question whether the congressional remedies adopted in § 4(e) constitute means which are not prohibited by, but are consistent 'with the letter and spirit of the constitution.' The only respect in which appellees contend that § 4(e) fails in this regard is that the section itself works an invidious discrimination in violation of the Fifth Amendment by prohibiting the enforcement of the English literacy requirement only for those educated in American-flag schools (schools located within United States jurisdiction) in which the language of instruction was other than English, and not for those educated in schools beyond the territorial limits of the United States in which the language of instruction was also other than English. This is not a complaint that Congress, in enacting §4(e), has unconstitutionally denied or diluted anyone's right to vote but rather that Congress violated the Constitution by not extending the relief effected in §4(e) to those educated in non-American-flag schools. We need not pause to determine whether appellees have a sufficient personal interest to have §4(e) invalidated on this ground, see generally *United States v. Raines*, 362 U.S. 17, 80 S.Ct. 519, 4 L.Ed.2d 524, since the argument, in our view, falls on the merits.

Section 4(e) does not restrict or deny the franchise but in effect extends the franchise to persons who otherwise would be denied it by state law. Thus we need not decide whether a state literacy law conditioning the right to vote on achieving a certain level of education in an American-flag school (regardless of the language of instruction) discriminates invidiously against those educated in non-American-flag schools. We need only decide whether the challenged limitation on the relief effected in §4(e) was permissible. In deciding that question, the principle that calls for the closest scrutiny of distinctions in laws denying fundamental rights is inapplicable; for the distinction challenged by appellees is presented only as a limitation on a reform measure aimed at eliminating an existing barrier to the exercise of the franchise. Rather, in deciding the constitutional propriety of the limitations in such a reform measure we are guided by the familiar principles that a 'statute is not invalid under the Constitution because it might have gone farther than it did,' *Roschen v. Ward*, 279 U.S. 337, 339, 49 S.Ct. 336, 73 L.Ed. 722, that a legislature need not 'strike at all evils at the same time.' *Semler v. Oregon State Board of Dental Examiners*, 294 U.S. 608, 610, 55 S.Ct. 570, 571, 79 L.Ed. 1086 and that 'reform may take one step at a time, addressing itself to the phase of the problem which seems most acute to the legislative mind,' *Williamson v. Lee Optical Co.*, 348 U.S. 483, 489, 75 S.Ct. 461, 465, 99 L.Ed. 563.

Guided by these principles, we are satisfied that appellees' challenge to this limitation in §4(e) is without merit. In the context of the case before us, the congressional choice to limit the relief effected in §4(e) may, for example, reflect Congress' greater familiarity with the quality of instruction in American-flag schools, a recognition of the unique historic relationship between the Congress and the Commonwealth of Puerto Rico, an awareness of the Federal Government's acceptance of the desirability of the use of Spanish as the language of instruction in Commonwealth schools, and the fact that Congress has fostered policies encouraging migration from the Commonwealth to the States. We have no occasion to determine in this case whether such factors would justify a similar distinction embodied in a voting-qualification law that denied the franchise to persons educated in non-American-flag schools. We hold only that the limitation on relief effected in §4(e) does not constitute a forbidden discrimination since these factors might well have been the basis for the decision of Congress to go 'no farther than it did.'

We therefore conclude that §4(e), in the application challenged in this case, is appropriate legislation to enforce the Equal Protection Clause and that the judgment of the District Court must be and hereby is reversed.

Reversed.

Notes

In footnotes not included here, *Katzenbach* provides the text of the New York laws at issue. Article II, §1, of the New York Constitution provided:

> Notwithstanding the foregoing provisions, after January first, one thousand nine hundred twenty-two, no person shall become entitled to vote by attaining majority, by naturalization or otherwise, unless such person is also able, except for physical disability, to read and write English.

Section 150 of the New York Election Law, McKinney's Consol.Laws, c. 17, provided, in pertinent part:

> . . . In the case of a person who became entitled to vote in this state by attaining majority, by naturalization or otherwise after January first, nineteen hundred twenty-two, such person must, in addition to the foregoing provisions, be able, except for physical disability, to read and write English. A 'new voter,' within the meaning of this article, is a person who, if he is entitled to vote in this state, shall have become so entitled on or after January first, nineteen hundred twenty-two, and who has not already voted at a general election in the state of New York after making proof of ability to read and write English, in the manner provided in section one hundred sixty-eight.

Section 168 of the New York Election Law provided, in pertinent part:

> 1. The board of regents of the state of New York shall make provisions for the giving of literacy tests.
>
> 2. . . . But a new voter may present as evidence of literacy a certificate or diploma showing that he has completed the work up to and including the sixth grade of an approved elementary school or of an approved higher school in which English is the language of instruction or a certificate or diploma showing that he has completed the work up to and including the sixth grade in a public school or a private school accredited by the Commonwealth of Puerto Rico in which school instruction is carried on predominantly in the English language or a matriculation card issued by a college or university to a student then at such institution or a certificate or a letter signed by an official of the university or college certifying to such attendance.'

The version of Section 168 at issue in *Katzenbach* was enacted while §4(e) was under consideration in Congress. The law prior to that required the successful completion of the eighth rather than the sixth grade in a school in which the language of instruction was English. Does this fact change your evaluation of the state's position?

F. Public Benefits and Alienage

State programs that restrict participation based on citizenship status trigger strict scrutiny and will rarely be upheld, unless they are a public function. This approach differs, however, when restrictions are imposed by the federal government. What, in your assessment, justifies the greater discretion accorded to the federal government under the Fifth Amendment than that accorded to the states under the Fourteenth Amendment? Consider the Court's justification below.

Graham v. Richardson
403 U.S. 365 (1971)

Mr. Justice Blackmun delivered the opinion of the Court.

These are welfare cases. They provide yet another aspect of the widening litigation in this area. The issue here is whether the Equal Protection Clause of the Fourteenth Amendment prevents a State from conditioning welfare benefits either (a) upon the beneficiary's possession of United States citizenship, or (b) if the beneficiary is an alien, upon his having resided in this country for a specified number of years. The facts are not in dispute.

I

This case, from Arizona, concerns the State's participation in federal categorical assistance programs. These programs originate with the Social Security Act of 1935, 49 Stat. 620, as amended, 42 U.S.C., c. 7. . . . Arizona Rev.Stat.Ann. § 46-233 (Supp.1970–1971), as amended in 1962, reads:

> 'A. No person shall be entitled to general assistance who does not meet and maintain the following requirements:
>
> > '1. Is a citizen of the United States, or has resided in the United States a total of fifteen years? . . .'

A like eligibility provision conditioned upon citizenship or durational residence appears in § 46-252(2), providing old-age assistance, and in § 46-272(4), providing assistance to the needy blind. See 42 U.S.C. §§ 1201–1206, 1381–1385.

Appellee Carmen Richardson, at the institution of this suit in July 1969, was 64 years of age. She is a lawfully admitted resident alien. She emigrated from Mexico in 1956 and since then has resided continuously in Arizona. She became permanently and totally disabled. She also met all other requirements for eligibility for APTD benefits except the 15-year residency specified for aliens by § 46-233(a)(1). She applied for benefits but was denied relief solely because of the residency provision.

. . . This case, from Pennsylvania, concerns that portion of a general assistance program that is not federally supported. The relevant statute is §432(2) of the Pennsylvania Public Welfare Code, Pa.Stat.Ann., Tit. 62, §432(2) (1968), originally enacted in 1939. It provides that those eligible for assistance shall be (1) needy persons who qualify under the federally supported categorical assistance programs and (2) those other needy persons who are citizens of the United States. Assistance to the latter group is funded wholly by the Commonwealth.

Appellee Elsie Mary Jane Leger is a lawfully admitted resident alien. She was born in Scotland in 1937. She came to this country in 1965 at the age of 28 under contract for domestic service with a family in Havertown. She has resided continuously in Pennsylvania since then and has been a taxpaying resident of the Commonwealth. In 1967 she left her domestic employment to accept more remunerative work in Philadelphia. She entered into a common-law marriage with a United States citizen. In 1969 illness forced both Mrs. Leger and her husband to give up their employment. They applied for public assistance. Each was ineligible under the federal programs. Mr. Leger, however, qualified for aid under the state program. Aid to Mrs. Leger was denied because of her alienage. The monthly grant to Mr. Leger was less than the amount determined by both federal and Pennsylvania authorities as necessary for a minimum standard of living in Philadelphia for a family of two.

. . . Appellee Beryl Jervis was added as a party plaintiff to the Leger action. She was born in Panama in 1912 and is a citizen of that country. In March 1968, at the age of 55, she came to the United States to undertake domestic work under contract in Philadelphia. She has resided continuously in Pennsylvania since then and has been a taxpaying resident of the Commonwealth. After working as a domestic for approximately one year, she obtained other, more remunerative, work in the city. In February 1970 illness forced her to give up her employment. She applied for aid. However, she was ineligible for benefits under the federally assisted programs and she was denied general assistance solely because of her alienage.

. . . .

The Fourteenth Amendment provides, '[N]or shall any State deprive any person of life, liberty, or property, without due process of law; nor deny to any person within its jurisdiction the equal protection of the laws.' It has long been settled, and it is not disputed here, that the term 'person' in this context encompasses lawfully admitted resident aliens as well as citizens of the United States and entitles both citizens and aliens to the equal protection of the laws of the State in which they reside. *Yick Wo v. Hopkins*, 118 U.S. 356, 369, 6 S.Ct. 1064, 1070, 30 L.Ed. 220 (1886); *Truax v. Raich*, 239 U.S. 33, 39, 36 S.Ct. 7, 9, 60 L.Ed. 131 (1915); *Takahashi v. Fish & Game Comm'n*, 334 U.S., at 420, 68 S.Ct., at 1143. Nor is it disputed that the Arizona and Pennsylvania statutes in question create two classes of needy persons, indistinguishable except with respect to whether they are or are not citizens of this country. Otherwise qualified United States citizens living in Arizona are entitled to federally funded categorical assistance benefits without regard to length of national residency, but aliens must have lived in this country for 15 years in order to qualify for aid. United States citizens living in Pennsylvania, unable to meet the requirements for federally funded benefits, may be eligible for state-supported general assistance, but resident aliens as a class are precluded from that assistance.

Under traditional equal protection principles, a State retains broad discretion to classify as long as its classification has a reasonable basis. . . . But the Court's decisions have established that classifications based on alienage, like those based on nationality or race, are inherently suspect and subject to close judicial scrutiny. Aliens as a class are a prime example of a 'discrete and insular' minority (see *United States v. Carolene Products Co.*, 304 U.S. 144, 152–153, n. 4, 58 S.Ct. 778, 783–784, 82 L.Ed. 1234 (1938)) for whom such heightened judicial solicitude is appropriate. Accordingly, it was said in *Takahashi*, 334 U.S., at 420, 68 S.Ct., at 1143, that 'the power of a state to apply its laws exclusively to its alien inhabitants as a class is confined within narrow limits.'

Arizona and Pennsylvania seek to justify their restrictions on the eligibility of aliens for public assistance solely on the basis of a State's 'special public interest' in favoring its own citizens over aliens in the distribution of limited resources such as welfare benefits. It is true that this Court on occasion has upheld state statutes that treat citizens and noncitizens differently, the ground for distinction having been that such laws were necessary to protect special interests of the State or its citizens. Thus, in *Truax v. Raich*, 239 U.S. 33, 36 S.Ct. 7, 60 L.Ed. 131 (1915), the Court, in striking down an Arizona statute restricting the employment of aliens, emphasized that '[t]he discrimination defined by the act does not pertain to the regulation or distribution of the public domain, or of the common property or resources of the people of the state, the enjoyment of which may be limited to its citizens as against both aliens and the citizens of other states.' 239 U.S., at 39–40, 36 S.Ct., at 10. And in *Crane v. New York*, 239 U.S. 195, 36 S.Ct. 85, 60 L.Ed. 218 (1915), the Court affirmed the judgment in *People v. Crane*, 214 N.Y. 154, 108 N.E. 427 (1915), upholding a New York statute prohibiting the employment of aliens on public works projects. . . .

Takahashi v. Fish & Game Comm'n, 334 U.S. 410, 68 S.Ct. 1138, 92 L.Ed. 1478 (1948), however, cast doubt on the continuing validity of the special public-interest doctrine in all contexts. There the Court held that California's purported ownership of fish in the ocean off its shores was not such a special public interest as would justify prohibiting aliens from making a living by fishing in those waters while permitting all others to do so. It was said:

> 'The Fourteenth Amendment and the laws adopted under its authority thus embody a general policy that all persons lawfully in this country shall abide 'in any state' on an equality of legal privileges with all citizens under non-discriminatory laws.' 334 U.S., at 420, 68 S.Ct., at 1143.

Whatever may be the contemporary vitality of the special public-interest doctrine in other contexts after Takahashi, we conclude that a State's desire to preserve limited welfare benefits for its own citizens is inadequate to justify Pennsylvania's making noncitizens ineligible for public assistance, and Arizona's restricting benefits to citizens and longtime resident aliens. First, the special public interest doctrine was heavily grounded on the notion that '[w]hatever is a privilege, rather than a right, may be made dependent upon citizenship.' *People v. Crane*, 214 N.Y., at 164, 108 N.E., at 430. But this Court now has rejected the concept that constitutional rights turn upon whether a governmental benefit is characterized as a 'right' or as a 'privilege.' . . . Since an alien as well as a citizen is a 'person' for equal protection purposes, a concern for fiscal integrity is no more compelling a justification for the questioned classification in these cases than it was in Shapiro.

Appellants, however, would narrow the application of *Shapiro* to citizens by arguing that the right to travel, relied upon in that decision, extends only to citizens and not to aliens. While many of the Court's opinions do speak in terms of the right of 'citizens' to travel, the source of the constitutional right to travel has never been ascribed to any particular constitutional provision. See *Shapiro v. Thompson*, 394 U.S., at 630 n. 8, 89 S.Ct., at 1329; *United States v. Guest*, 383 U.S. 745, 757–758, 86 S.Ct. 1170, 1177–1178, 16 L.Ed.2d 239 (1966). The Court has never decided whether the right applies specifically to aliens, and it is unnecessary to reach that question here. It is enough to say that the classification involved in *Shapiro* was subjected to strict scrutiny under the compelling state interest test, not because it was based on any suspect criterion such as race, nationality, or alienage, but because it impinged upon the fundamental right of interstate movement. As was said there, 'The waiting-period provision denies welfare benefits to otherwise eligible applicants solely because they have recently moved into the jurisdiction. But in moving from State to State or to the District of Columbia appellees were exercising a constitutional right, and any classification which serves to penalize the exercise of that right, unless shown to be necessary to promote a compelling governmental interest, is unconstitutional.' 394 U.S., at 634, 89 S.Ct., at 1331. The classifications involved in the instant cases, on the other hand, are inherently suspect and are therefore subject to strict judicial scrutiny whether or not a fundamental right is impaired. Appellants' attempted reliance on *Dandridge v. Williams*, 397 U.S. 471, 90 S.Ct. 1153, 25 L.Ed.2d 491 (1970), is also misplaced, since the classification involved in that case (family size) neither impinged upon a fundamental constitutional right nor employed an inherently suspect criterion.

We agree with the three-judge court in the Pennsylvania case that the 'justification of limiting expenses is particularly inappropriate and unreasonable when the discriminated class consists of aliens. Aliens like citizens pay taxes and may be called into the armed forces. Unlike the short-term residents in Shapiro, aliens may live within a state for many years, work in the state and contribute to the economic growth of the state.' 321 F.Supp., at 253. See also *Purdy & Fitzpatrick v. California*,

71 Cal.2d 566, 581–582, 79 Cal.Rptr. 77, 456 P.2d 645, 656 (1969). There can be no 'special public interest' in tax revenues to which aliens have contributed on an equal basis with the residents of the State.

Accordingly, we hold that a state statute that denies welfare benefits to resident aliens and one that denies them to aliens who have not resided in the United States for a specified number of years violate the Equal Protection Clause.

III

An additional reason why the state statutes at issue in these cases do not withstand constitutional scrutiny emerges from the area of federal-state relations. The National Government has 'broad constitutional powers in determining what aliens shall be admitted to the United States, the period they may remain, regulation of their conduct before naturalization, and the terms and conditions of their naturalization.' *Takahashi v. Fish & Game Comm'n*, 334 U.S., at 419, 68 S.Ct., at 1142; *Hines v. Davidowitz*, 312 U.S. 52, 66, 61 S.Ct. 399, 403, 85 L.Ed. 581 (1941); see also *Chinese Exclusion Case*, 130 U.S. 581, 9 S.Ct. 623, 32 L.Ed. 1068 (1889); *United States ex rel. Turner v. Williams*, 194 U.S. 279, 24 S.Ct. 719, 48 L.Ed. 979 (1904); *Fong Yue Ting v. United States*, 149 U.S. 698, 13 S.Ct. 1016, 37 L.Ed. 905 (1893); *Harisiades v. Shaughnessy*, 342 U.S. 580, 72 S.Ct. 512, 96 L.Ed. 586 (1952). Pursuant to that power, Congress has provided, as part of a comprehensive plan for the regulation of immigration and naturalization, that '[a]liens who are paupers professional beggars, or vagrants' or aliens who 'are likely at any time to become public charges' shall be excluded from admission into the United States, 8 U.S.C. §§ 1182(a)(8) and 1182(a)(15), and that any alien lawfully admitted shall be deported who 'has within five years after entry become a public charge from causes not affirmatively shown to have arisen after entry. * * *' 8 U.S.C. § 1251(a)(8). Admission of aliens likely to become public charges may be conditioned upon the posting of a bond or cash deposit. 8 U.S.C. § 1183. But Congress has not seen fit to impose any burden or restriction on aliens who become indigent after their entry into the United States. Rather, it has broadly declared: 'All persons within the jurisdiction of the United States shall have the same right in every State and Territory * * * to the full and equal benefit of all laws and proceedings for the security of persons and property as is enjoyed by white citizens. * * *' 42 U.S.C. § 1981. The protection of this statute has been held to extend to aliens as well as to citizens. *Takahashi*, 334 U.S., at 419 n. 7, 68 S.Ct., at 1142. Moreover, this Court has made it clear that, whatever may be the scope of the constitutional right of interstate travel, aliens lawfully within this country have a right to enter and abide in any State in the Union 'on an equality of legal privileges with all citizens under nondiscriminatory laws.' *Takahashi*, 334 U.S., at 420, 68 S.Ct., at 1143.

State laws that restrict the eligibility of aliens for welfare benefits merely because of their alienage conflict with these overriding national policies in an area constitutionally entrusted to the Federal Government. In *Hines v. Davidowitz*, 312 U.S., at 66–67, 61 S.Ct., at 403–404, where this Court struck down a Pennsylvania alien registration statute (enacted in 1939, as was the statute under challenge in No. 727) on grounds of federal pre-emption. . . .

The same is true here, for in the ordinary case an alien, becoming indigent and unable to work, will be unable to live where, because of discriminatory denial of public assistance, he cannot 'secure the necessities of life, including food, clothing and shelter.' State alien residency requirements that either deny welfare benefits to noncitizens or condition them on longtime residency, equate with the assertion of a right, inconsistent with federal policy, to deny entrance and abode. Since such laws encroach upon exclusive federal power, they are constitutionally impermissible.

. . . .

The judgments appealed from are affirmed.

It is so ordered.

Notes and Questions

In a footnote omitted from the excerpt here, the *Graham* court quoted the requirement for eligibility for the social benefits at issue:

> Except as hereinafter otherwise provided . . . needy persons of the classes defined in clauses (1) and (2) of this section shall be eligible for assistance:
>
> (1) Persons for whose assistance Federal financial participation is available to the Commonwealth. . . .
>
> (2) Other persons who are citizens of the United States, or who, during the period January 1, 1938 to December 31, 1939, filed their declaration of intention to become citizens. . . .

Compare this to the facts in *Matthews v. Diaz* below, where the federal government conditioned participation in Medicare on admission as a permanent resident and residency in the United States for five years.

Mathews v. Diaz
426 U.S. 67 (1976)

MR. JUSTICE STEVENS delivered the opinion of the Court.

The question presented by the Secretary's appeal is whether Congress may condition an alien's eligibility for participation in a federal medical insurance program on continuous residence in the United States for a five-year period and admission for permanent residence. The District Court held that the first condition was unconstitutional and that it could not be severed from the second. Since we conclude that both conditions are constitutional, we reverse.

Each of the appellees is a resident alien who was lawfully admitted to the United States less than five years ago. Appellees Diaz and Clara are Cuban refugees who remain in this country at the discretion of the Attorney General; appellee Espinosa has been admitted for permanent residence. All three are over 65 years old and have been denied enrollment in the Medicare Part B supplemental medical insurance program established by § 1831 *et seq.* of the Social Security Act of 1935, 49 Stat. 620, as added, 79 Stat. 301, and as amended, 42 U.S.C. 1395j et seq. (1970 ed. and Supp. IV). They brought this action to challenge the statutory basis for that denial. Specifically, they attack 42 U.S.C. § 1395*o* (2) (1970 ed., Supp. IV), which grants eligibility to resident citizens who are 65 or older but denies eligibility to comparable aliens unless they have been admitted for permanent residence and also have resided in the United States for at least five years. Appellees Diaz and Clara meet neither requirement; appellee Espinosa meets only the first.

On August 18, 1972, Diaz filed a class action complaint in the United States District Court for the Southern District of Florida alleging that his application for enrollment had been denied on the ground that he was not a citizen and had neither been admitted for permanent residence nor resided in the United States for the immediately preceding five years. He further alleged that numerous other persons had been denied enrollment in the Medicare Part B program for the same reasons. He sought relief on behalf of a class of persons who have been or will be denied enrollment in the Medicare insurance program for failure to meet the requirements of 42 U.S.C. § 1395*o* (2) (1970 ed., Supp. IV). Since the complaint prayed for a declaration that § 1395*o* (2) was unconstitutional and for an injunction requiring the Secretary to approve all applicants who had been denied eligibility solely for failure to comply with its requirements, a three-judge court was constituted.

On September 28, 1972, the District Court granted leave to add Clara and Espinosa as plaintiffs and to file an amended complaint. That pleading alleged that Clara had been denied enrollment for the same reasons as Diaz, but explained that Espinosa, although a permanent resident since 1971, had not attempted to enroll because he could not meet the durational residence requirement, and therefore any attempt would have been futile. The amended complaint sought relief on behalf of a subclass represented by Espinosa that is, aliens admitted for permanent residence who have been or will be denied enrollment for failure to meet the five-year continuous residence requirement as well as relief on behalf of the class represented by Diaz and Clara.

On October 24, 1972, the Secretary moved to dismiss the complaint on the ground, among others, that the District Court lacked jurisdiction over the subject matter because none of the plaintiffs had exhausted his administrative remedies under the Social Security Act. Two days later, on October 26, 1972, Espinosa filed his application for enrollment with the Secretary. He promptly brought this fact to the attention of the District Court, without formally supplementing the pleadings.

. . . We now consider . . . whether Congress may discriminate in favor of citizens and against aliens in providing welfare benefits; and . . . if so, whether the specific discriminatory provisions in § 1395*o* (2)(B) are constitutional.

[In part I, omitted here, the Court finds that the District Court had jurisdiction over Espinosa's claim.]

. . . .

There are literally millions of aliens within the jurisdiction of the United States. The Fifth Amendment, as well as the Fourteenth Amendment, protects every one of these persons from deprivation of life, liberty, or property without due process of law. *Wong Yang Sung v. McGrath*, 339 U.S. 33, 48–51, 70 S.Ct. 445, 453–455, 94 L.Ed. 616, 627–629; *Wong Wing v. United States*, 163 U.S. 228, 238, 16 S.Ct. 977, 981, 41 L. Ed. 140, 143; see *Russian Fleet v. United States*, 282 U.S. 481, 489, 51 S.Ct. 229, 231, 75 L.Ed. 473, 476. Even one whose presence in this country is unlawful, involuntary, or transitory is entitled to that constitutional protection. *Wong Yang Sung, supra*; *Wong Wing, supra*.

The fact that all persons, aliens and citizens alike, are protected by the Due Process Clause does not lead to the further conclusion that all aliens are entitled to enjoy all the advantages of citizenship or, indeed, to the conclusion that all aliens must be placed in a single homogeneous legal classification. For a host of constitutional and statutory provisions rest on the premise that a legitimate distinction between citizens and aliens may justify attributes and benefits for one class not accorded to the other; and the class of aliens is itself a heterogeneous multitude of persons with a wide-ranging variety of ties to this country.

In the exercise of its broad power over naturalization and immigration, Congress regularly makes rules that would be unacceptable if applied to citizens. The exclusion of aliens and the reservation of the power to deport have no permissible counterpart in the Federal Government's power to regulate the conduct of its own citizenry. The fact that an Act of Congress treats aliens differently from citizens does not in itself imply that such disparate treatment is "invidious."

In particular, the fact that Congress has provided some welfare benefits for citizens does not require it to provide like benefits for all aliens. Neither the overnight visitor, the unfriendly agent of a hostile foreign power, the resident diplomat, nor the illegal entrant, can advance even a colorable constitutional claim to a share in the bounty that a conscientious sovereign makes available to its own citizens and Some of its guests. The decision to share that bounty with our guests may take into account the character of the relationship between the alien and this country: Congress may decide that as the alien's tie grows stronger, so does the strength of his claim to an equal share of that munificence.

The real question presented by this case is not whether discrimination between citizens and aliens is permissible; rather, it is whether the statutory discrimination [w]ithin the class of aliens allowing benefits to some aliens but not to others is permissible. We turn to that question.

. . . .

For reasons long recognized as valid, the responsibility for regulating the relationship between the United States and our alien visitors has been committed to the political branches of the Federal Government. Since decisions in these matters may implicate our relations with foreign powers, and since a wide variety of classifications must be defined in the light of changing political and economic circumstances, such decisions are frequently of a character more appropriate to either the Legislature or the Executive than to the Judiciary. This very case illustrates the need for flexibility in policy choices rather than the rigidity often characteristic of constitutional adjudication. Appellees Diaz and Clara are but two of over 440,000 Cuban refugees who arrived in the United States between 1961 and 1972. And the Cuban parolees are but one of several categories of aliens who have been admitted in order to make a humane response to a natural catastrophe or an international political situation. Any rule of constitutional law that would inhibit the flexibility of the political branches of government to respond to changing world conditions should be adopted only with the greatest caution. The reasons that preclude judicial review of political questions also dictate a narrow standard of review of decisions made by the Congress or the President in the area of immigration and naturalization.

Since it is obvious that Congress has no constitutional duty to provide all aliens with the welfare benefits provided to citizens, the party challenging the constitutionality of the particular line Congress has drawn has the burden of advancing principled reasoning that will at once invalidate that line and yet tolerate a different line separating some aliens from others. In this case the appellees have challenged two requirements first, that the alien be admitted as a permanent resident, and, second, that his residence be of a duration of at least five years. But if these requirements were eliminated, surely Congress would at least require that the alien's entry be lawful; even then, unless mere transients are to be held constitutionally entitled to benefits, Some durational requirement would certainly be appropriate. In short, it is unquestionably reasonable for Congress to make an alien's eligibility depend on both the character and the duration of his residence. Since neither requirement is wholly irrational, this case essentially involves nothing more than a claim that it would have been more reasonable for Congress to select somewhat different requirements of the same kind.

We may assume that the five-year line drawn by Congress is longer than necessary to protect the fiscal integrity of the program. We may also assume that unnecessary hardship is incurred by persons just short of qualifying. But it remains true that some line is essential, that any line must produce some harsh and apparently arbitrary consequences, and, of greatest importance, that those who qualify under the test Congress has chosen may reasonably be presumed to have a greater affinity with the United States than those who do not. In short, citizens and those who are most like citizens qualify. Those who are less like citizens do not.

The task of classifying persons for medical benefits, like the task of drawing lines for federal tax purposes, inevitably requires that some persons who have an almost equally strong claim to favored treatment be placed on different sides of the line; the differences between the eligible and the ineligible are differences in degree rather than differences in the character of their respective claims. When this kind of policy choice must be made, we are especially reluctant to question the exercise of congressional judgment. In this case, since appellees have not identified a principled basis for prescribing a different standard than the one selected by Congress, they have, in effect, merely invited us to substitute our judgment for that of Congress in deciding which aliens shall be eligible to participate in the supplementary insurance program on the same conditions as citizens. We decline the invitation.

The cases on which appellees rely are consistent with our conclusion that this statutory classification does not deprive them of liberty or property without due process of law.

Graham v. Richardson, 403 U.S. 365, 91 S.Ct. 1848, 29 L.Ed.2d 534, provides the strongest support for appellees' position. That case holds that state statutes that deny welfare benefits to resident aliens, or to aliens not meeting a requirement of durational residence within the United States, violate the Equal Protection Clause of the Fourteenth Amendment and encroach upon the exclusive federal power over the entrance and residence of aliens. Of course, the latter ground of decision actually supports our holding today that it is the business of the political branches of the Federal Government, rather than that of either the States or the Federal Judiciary, to regulate the conditions of entry and residence of aliens. The equal protection analysis also involves significantly different considerations because it concerns the relationship between aliens and the States rather than between aliens and the Federal Government.

Insofar as state welfare policy is concerned, there is little, if any, basis for treating persons who are citizens of another State differently from persons who are citizens of another country. Both groups are noncitizens as far as the State's interests in administering its welfare programs are concerned. Thus, a division by a State of the category of persons who are not citizens of that State into subcategories of United States citizens and aliens has no apparent justification, whereas, a comparable classification by the Federal Government is a routine and normally legitimate part of its business. Furthermore, whereas the Constitution inhibits every State's power to restrict travel across its own borders, Congress is explicitly empowered to exercise that type of control over travel across the borders of the United States.

The distinction between the constitutional limits on state power and the constitutional grant of power to the Federal Government also explains why appellees' reliance on *Memorial Hospital v. Maricopa County*, 415 U.S. 250, 94 S.Ct. 1076, 39 L. Ed.2d 306, is misplaced. That case involved Arizona's requirement of durational residence within a county in order to receive nonemergency medical care at the county's expense. No question of alienage was involved. Since the sole basis for the classification between residents impinged on the constitutionally guaranteed right to travel within the United States, the holding in *Shapiro v. Thompson*, 394 U.S. 618, 89 S.Ct. 1322, 22 L.Ed.2d 600, required that it be justified by a compelling state interest. Finding no such justification, we held that the requirement violated the Equal Protection Clause. This case, however, involves no state impairment of the right to travel nor indeed any impairment whatever of the right to travel within the United States; the predicate for the equal protection analysis in those cases is simply not present. Contrary to appellees' characterization, it is not "political hypocrisy" to recognize that the Fourteenth Amendment's limits on state powers are substantially different from the constitutional provisions applicable to the federal power over immigration and naturalization.

Finally, we reject the suggestion that *U.S. Dept. of Agriculture v. Moreno*, 413 U.S. 528, 93 S.Ct. 2821, 37 L.Ed.2d 782, lends relevant support to appellees' claim. No question involving alienage was presented in that case. Rather, we found that the denial of food stamps to households containing unrelated members was not only unsupported by any rational basis but actually was intended to discriminate against certain politically unpopular groups. This case involves no impairment of the freedom of association of either citizens or aliens.

We hold that § 1395*o* (2)(B) has not deprived appellees of liberty or property without due process of law.

The judgment of the District Court is Reversed.

Notes and Questions

1. Title 42 U.S.C. § 1395*o* (1970 ed. and Supp. IV), at issue in Matthews v. Diaz, provides:

> Every individual who (1) is entitled to hospital insurance benefits under part A, or (2) has attained age 65 and is a resident of the United States, and is either (A) a citizen or (B) an alien lawfully admitted for permanent residence who has resided in the United States continuously during the 5 years immediately preceding the month in which he applies for enrollment under this part, is eligible to enroll in the insurance program established by this part.

2. In footnote 13, not reproduced here, the *Mathews* Court noted the following:

> The classifications among aliens established by the Immigration and Nationality Act.... illustrate the diversity of aliens and their ties to this country. Aliens may be immigrants or non-immigrants. Immigrants, in turn, are divided into those who are subject to numerical limitations upon admissions and those who are not. The former are subdivided into preference classifications which include: grown unmarried children of citizens; spouses and grown unmarried children of aliens lawfully admitted for permanent residence; professionals and those with exceptional ability in the sciences or arts; grown married children of citizens; brothers and sisters of citizens; persons who perform specified permanent skilled or unskilled labor for which a labor shortage exists; and certain victims of persecution and catastrophic natural calamities who were granted conditional entry and remained in the United States at least two years. 8 U.S.C. §§ 1153(a) (1)-(7). Immigrants not subject to certain numerical limitations include: children and spouses of citizens and parents of citizens at least 21 years old; natives of independent countries of the Western Hemisphere; aliens

lawfully admitted for permanent residence returning from temporary visits abroad; certain former citizens who may reapply for acquisition of citizenship; certain ministers of religion; and certain employees or former employees of the United States Government abroad. 8 U.S.C. §§ 1101(a)(27), 1151(a), (b).

What policy rationale would support each of those various classifications?

In footnote 24, the Court said:

We have left open the question whether a State may prohibit aliens from holding elective or important nonelective positions or whether a State may, in some circumstances, consider the alien status of an applicant or employee in making an individualized employment decision. See *Sugarman v. Dougall*, 413 U.S. 634, 646–649, 93 S.Ct. 2842, 2849–2851, 37 L. Ed.2d 853, 862–864; *In re Griffiths*, 413 U.S. 717, 728–729 and n. 21.

3. The Supreme Court has a longstanding pattern of deferring to the authority of the federal government over immigration. In *Mathews v. Diaz*, 426 U.S. 67 (1976), above, the Court upheld federal legislation that restricted certain aliens' eligibility for a medical insurance program based on the duration of their residence in the United States and on their admission for permanent residence. The Court also stressed in *Matthews* that "responsibility for regulating the relationship between the United States and our alien visitors has been committed to the political branches of the Federal Government," and therefore, judicial review of decisions made by Congress or the President in the area of immigration and naturalization must be narrow. *See also Washington v. Legrant*, 394 U.S. 618, a case involving a congressionally imposed requirement of one year's residence within the District of Columbia for receipt of welfare benefits. Alienage was not an issue, but the Court held that the law violated the Due Process Clause of the Fifth Amendment for the same reasons that the state-imposed durational residency requirements violated the Equal Protection Clause of the Fourteenth Amendment. 394 U.S. at 641–642. Is the distinction between these cases that the durational residency requirement only deterred travel of undocumented immigrants into the United States? Consider the Court's statement that the "power of Congress to prevent the travel of aliens into this country cannot seriously be questioned."

In light of this line of cases and reasoning, what characteristics would a travel ban, prohibiting entry into the United States to individuals from specific countries, have to have to withstand legal challenges? What characteristics would such law have to have?

4. Note the 11th Circuit's distinction between state legislation and federal legislation:

[*Plyler v. Doe*] is inapposite because it deals with a Fourteenth Amendment challenge to a *state's* classification of aliens. Nothing in *Plyler* even arguably suggests that a heightened level of scrutiny would have applied if the challenged statute had been enacted by Congress, i.e., that *Mathews* would not have controlled had the same classification been prescribed by a federal statute. Indeed, the *Plyler* Court specifically cited *Mathews* for the purpose of noting that the deference which extends to Congress' power to govern aliens' "admission to our Nation and *status* within our borders," *id.* at 225, 102 S. Ct. at 2399 (emphasis added), does not extend to a state's classification of aliens. *Plyler* is entirely consistent with *Mathews*, which noted that while strict scrutiny is applicable to a state's classification of aliens, it does not apply to congressional classifications. *See Matthews,* 426 U.S. at 86–87, 96 S. Ct. at 1895 ("The Fourteenth Amendment's limits on state powers are substantially different from the constitutional provisions applicable to the federal power over immigration and naturalization."). *Rodriguez by Rodriguez v. United States*, 169 F.3d 1342, 1350 (11th Cir. 1999).

See generally *City of Chicago v. Shalala*, 189 F.3d. 598 (1999*)*, *United States vs. Rodriguez* (182 F. Supp. 479 (S.D. Cal 1960) for the deference accorded to the federal government when making distinctions based on citizenship status.[19] Consider the latest version of the Executive travel ban, the subject of intense litigation in 2017.[20]

G. Undocumented Immigrants' Rights

The section below deals with policing of undocumented immigrants and considers constitutional and statutory protections available in these contexts. Contrary to misconceptions, immigrants benefit from due process and basic rights that must be respected before detention and deportation. One such protection involves prohibiting the forced signing of departure agreements by detainees and the implementation of transfers disregarding attorney relationships. Although the Supreme Court does implement strict criteria for overruling deportation decisions, arbitrary decisions or disregard for immigrants' due process rights remain frequent.[21] See below

---

19. *Developments in the Law Immigration: Policy and the Rights of Aliens* (Part 2 of 2), 96 Harv. L. Rev. 1286, 1418; Note and Comment, . . . *And Health Care for All: Immigrants in the Shadow of the Promise of Universal Health Care*, 35 Am. J. L. and Med. 185; *Laboratories of Bigotry? Devolution of the Immigration Power, Equal Protection, and Federalism*, 76 N.Y.U. L. Rev. 493.

20. Exec. Order No. 13780, 82 Fed. Reg. 13209 (Mar. 9, 2017).

21. *Compare* Valencia v. Mukasey, 548 F.3d 1261 (9th Cir. 2008), Catholic Charities CYO v. Chertoff, 622 F. Supp. 2d 865 (N.D. Cal. 2008), *and* Ruiz-Diaz v. U.S., 703 F.3d 483 (9th Cir. 2012), *with* Leslie v. AG of the United States, 611 F. 3d 171 (2010), Walters v. Reno, 145 F.3d 1032 (1998), Sierra Forest Legacy v. Rey, 670 F. Supp. 2d 1106 (2009), *and* Doe v. Hagee, 473 F. Supp. 2d 989 (2007). *See also* Ingrid V. Eagly & Steven Shafer, *A National Study of Access to Counsel in Immigration Court*, 164 U. Pa. L. Rev. 1, 10 (2015) (discussing "immigration representation and the complexities of the relationships among representation, deportation, and courts"); Jennifer M. Chacón, *Privatized Immigration Enforcement*, 52 Harv. Civ. Rights & Civ. Liberties L. Rev. 1, 24 (2017) (discussing the due process concerns surrounding immigrant detention); David Hausman & Jayashri Srikantiah, *Time, Due Process, and Representation: An Empirical and Legal Analysis of Continuances in Immigration Court*, 84 Fordham L. Rev. 1823 (2016) (discussing immigrant due process consequences of denials and short continuances); Denise Gilman, *To Loose the Bonds: The Deceptive*

for the strict standard, set forth in *Lopez-Mendoza*, to overturn deportation orders. The Court considers, in that case, whether the exclusionary rule, designed to prevent submission of evidence improperly obtained by law enforcement in criminal proceedings, applies in deportation cases.

Immigration and Naturalization Service v. Lopez-Mendoza
468 U.S.1032 (1984)

Respondent Lopez-Mendoza was arrested in 1976 by INS agents at his place of employment, a transmission repair shop in San Mateo, Cal. Responding to a tip, INS investigators arrived at the shop shortly before 8 a.m. The agents had not sought a warrant to search the premises or to arrest any of its occupants. The proprietor of the shop firmly refused to allow the agents to interview his employees during working hours. Nevertheless, while one agent engaged the proprietor in conversation another entered the shop and approached Lopez-Mendoza. In response to the agent's questioning, Lopez-Mendoza gave his name and indicated that he was from Mexico with no close family ties in the United States. The agent then placed him under arrest. Lopez-Mendoza underwent further questioning at INS offices, where he admitted he was born in Mexico, was still a citizen of Mexico, and had entered this country without inspection by immigration authorities. Based on his answers, the agents prepared a "Record of Deportable Alien" (Form I-213), and an affidavit which Lopez-Mendoza executed, admitting his Mexican nationality and his illegal entry into this country.

A hearing was held before an Immigration Judge. Lopez-Mendoza's counsel moved to terminate the proceeding on the ground that Lopez-Mendoza had been arrested illegally. The judge ruled that the legality of the arrest was not relevant to the deportation proceeding and therefore declined to rule on the legality of Lopez-Mendoza's arrest. *Matter of Lopez-Mendoza*, No. A22 452 208 (INS, Dec. 21, 1977), reprinted in App. to Pet. for Cert. 97a. The Form I-213 and the affidavit executed by Lopez-Mendoza

---

Promise of Freedom from Pretrial Immigration Detention, 92 Ind. L.J. 157 (2016) (asserting "that the immigration custody determination process fails to preserve and protect the constitutional presumption of liberty applicable to all persons facing detention that is not imposed as punishment after a criminal conviction"); David Cole, *In Aid of Removal: Due Process Limits on Immigration Detention*, 51 Emory L.J. 1003, 1039 (2002) (underscoring "how radically disrespectful of due process the government's exercise of immigration authority has become"); Anil Kalhan, *Rethinking Immigration Detention*, 110 Colum. L. Rev. Sidebar 42 (2010); Anne R. Traum, *Constitutionalizing Immigration Law on Its Own Path*, 33 Cardozo L. Rev. 491 (2011); Jason A. Cade, *Judging Immigration Equity: Deportation and Proportionality in the Supreme Court*, 50 U.C. Davis L. Rev. 1029, 1107 (2017); *Immigration Law—Right to Counsel—California District Court Finds Due Process May Include Right of Access to Counsel for Detained Noncitizens.—Lyon v. ICE, 171 F. Supp. 3d 961 (N.D. Cal. 2016)*, 130 Harv. L. Rev. 1056 (2017); César Cuauhtémoc García Hernández, *Invisible Spaces and Invisible Lives in Immigration Detention*, 57 How. L.J. 869 (2014); Ingrid V. Eagly, *Gideon's Migration*, 122 Yale L.J. 2282, 2305 (2013); César Cuauhtémoc García Hernández, *Due Process and Immigrant Detainee Prison Transfers: Moving Lprs to Isolated Prisons Violates Their Right to Counsel*, 21 Berkeley La Raza L.J. 17, 60 (2011).

were received into evidence without objection from Lopez-Mendoza. On the basis of this evidence the Immigration Judge found Lopez-Mendoza deportable. Lopez-Mendoza was granted the option of voluntary departure.

The BIA dismissed Lopez-Mendoza's appeal. It noted that "[t]he mere fact of an illegal arrest has no bearing on a subsequent deportation proceeding," *In re Lopez-Mendoza*, No. A22 452 208 (BIA, Sept. 19, 1979), reprinted in App. to Pet. for Cert. 100a, 102a, and observed that Lopez-Mendoza had not objected to the admission into evidence of Form I-213 and the affidavit he had executed. Id., at 103a. The BIA also noted that the exclusionary rule is not applied to redress the injury to the privacy of the search victim, and that the BIA had previously concluded that application of the rule in deportation proceedings to deter unlawful INS conduct was inappropriate. *Matter of Sandoval*, 17 I. & N.Dec. 70 (BIA 1979).

The Court of Appeals vacated the order of deportation and remanded for a determination whether Lopez-Mendoza's Fourth Amendment rights had been violated when he was arrested.

B

Respondent Sandoval-Sanchez (who is not the same individual who was involved in *Matter of Sandoval, supra*) was arrested in 1977 at his place of employment, a potato processing plant in Pasco, Wash. INS Agent Bower and other officers went to the plant, with the permission of its personnel manager, to check for illegal aliens. During a change in shift, officers stationed themselves at the exits while Bower and a uniformed Border Patrol agent entered the plant. They went to the lunchroom and identified themselves as immigration officers. Many people in the room rose and headed for the exits or milled around; others in the plant left their equipment and started running; still others who were entering the plant turned around and started walking back out. The two officers eventually stationed themselves at the main entrance to the plant and looked for passing employees who averted their heads, avoided eye contact, or tried to hide themselves in a group. Those individuals were addressed with innocuous questions in English. Any who could not respond in English and who otherwise aroused Agent Bower's suspicions were questioned in Spanish as to their right to be in the United States.

Respondent Sandoval-Sanchez was in a line of workers entering the plant. Sandoval-Sanchez testified that he did not realize that immigration officers were checking people entering the plant, but that he did see standing at the plant entrance a man in uniform who appeared to be a police officer. Agent Bower testified that it was probable that he, not his partner, had questioned Sandoval-Sanchez at the plant, but that he could not be absolutely positive. The employee he thought he remembered as Sandoval-Sanchez had been "very evasive," had averted his head, turned around, and walked away when he saw Agent Bower. App. 137, 138. Bower was certain that no one was questioned about his status unless his actions had given the agents reason to believe that he was an undocumented alien.

Thirty-seven employees, including Sandoval-Sanchez, were briefly detained at the plant and then taken to the county jail. About one-third immediately availed themselves of the option of voluntary departure and were put on a bus to Mexico. Sandoval-Sanchez exercised his right to a deportation hearing. Sandoval-Sanchez was then questioned further, and Agent Bower recorded Sandoval-Sanchez' admission of unlawful entry. Sandoval-Sanchez contends he was not aware that he had a right to remain silent.

At his deportation hearing Sandoval-Sanchez contended that the evidence offered by the INS should be suppressed as the fruit of an unlawful arrest. The Immigration Judge considered and rejected Sandoval-Sanchez' claim that he had been illegally arrested, but ruled in the alternative that the legality of the arrest was not relevant to the deportation hearing. *Matter of Sandoval-Sanchez*, No. A22 346 925 (INS, Oct. 7, 1977), reprinted in App. to Pet. for Cert. 104a. Based on the written record of Sandoval-Sanchez' admissions the Immigration Judge found him deportable and granted him voluntary departure. The BIA dismissed Sandoval-Sanchez' appeal. *In re Sandoval-Sanchez*, No. A22 346 925 (BIA, Feb. 21, 1980). It concluded that the circumstances of the arrest had not affected the voluntariness of his recorded admission, and again declined to invoke the exclusionary rule, relying on its earlier decision in *Matter of Sandoval, supra*.

On appeal the Court of Appeals concluded that Sandoval-Sanchez' detention by the immigration officers violated the Fourth Amendment, that the statements he made were a product of that detention, and that the exclusionary rule barred their use in a deportation hearing. The deportation order against Sandoval-Sanchez was accordingly reversed.

II

A deportation proceeding is a purely civil action to determine eligibility to remain in this country, not to punish an unlawful entry, though entering or remaining unlawfully in this country is itself a crime. 8 U.S.C. §§ 1302, 1306, 1325. The deportation hearing looks prospectively to the respondent's right to remain in this country in the future. Past conduct is relevant only insofar as it may shed light on the respondent's right to remain. See 8 U.S.C. §§ 1251, 1252(b); *Bugajewitz v. Adams*, 228 U.S. 585, 591, 33 S.Ct. 607, 608, 57 L.Ed. 978 (1913); *Fong Yue Ting v. United States*, 149 U.S. 698, 730, 13 S.Ct. 1016, 1028, 37 L.Ed. 905 (1893).

A deportation hearing is held before an immigration judge. The judge's sole power is to order deportation; the judge cannot adjudicate guilt or punish the respondent for any crime related to unlawful entry into or presence in this country. Consistent with the civil nature of the proceeding, various protections that apply in the context of a criminal trial do not apply in a deportation hearing. The respondent must be given "a reasonable opportunity to be present at [the] proceeding," but if the respondent fails to avail himself of that opportunity the hearing may proceed in his absence. 8 U.S.C. § 1252(b). In many deportation cases the INS must show only identity and alienage; the burden then shifts to the respondent to prove the time, place, and manner of his entry. See 8 U.S.C. § 1361; *Matter of Sandoval*, 17 I. & N.Dec. 70 (BIA 1979). A decision of deportability need be based only on "reasonable, substantial, and probative evidence," 8 U.S.C. § 1252(b)(4). The BIA for its part has required only "clear, unequivocal and convincing" evidence of the respondent's deportability, not proof beyond a reasonable doubt. 8 CFR § 242.14(a) (1984).

. . .

III

The "body" or identity of a defendant or respondent in a criminal or civil proceeding is never itself suppressible . . . On this basis alone the Court of Appeals' decision as to respondent Lopez-Mendoza must be reversed. At his deportation hearing Lopez-Mendoza objected only to the fact that he had been summoned to a deportation hearing following an unlawful arrest; he entered no objection to the evidence offered against him. The BIA correctly ruled that "[t]he mere fact of an illegal arrest has no bearing on a subsequent deportation proceeding." *In re Lopez-Mendoza*, No. A22452208 (BIA, Sept. 19, 1979, reprinted in App. to Pet. for Cert. 102a.

IV

Respondent Sandoval-Sanchez has a more substantial claim. He objected not to his compelled presence at a deportation proceeding, but to evidence offered at that proceeding. The general rule in a criminal proceeding is that statements and other evidence obtained as a result of an unlawful, warrantless arrest are suppressible if the link between the evidence and the unlawful conduct is not too attenuated. *Wong Sun v. United States*, 371 U.S. 471, 83 S.Ct. 407, 9 L.Ed.2d 441 (1963). The reach of the exclusionary rule beyond the context of a criminal prosecution, however, is less clear. Although this Court has once stated in dictum that "[i]t may be assumed that evidence obtained by the [Labor] Department through an illegal search and seizure cannot be made the basis of a finding in deportation proceedings," *United States ex rel. Bilokumsky v. Tod, supra*, 263 U.S., at 155, 44 S.Ct., at 56, the Court has never squarely addressed the question before. Lower court decisions dealing with this question are sparse.

In *United States v. Janis*, 428 U.S. 433, 96 S.Ct. 3021, 49 L.Ed.2d 1046 (1976), this Court set forth a framework for deciding in what types of proceeding application of the exclusionary rule is appropriate. Imprecise as the exercise may be, the Court recognized in *Janis* that there is no choice but to weigh the likely social benefits of excluding unlawfully seized evidence against the likely costs. On the benefit side of the balance "the 'prime purpose' of the [exclusionary] rule, if not the sole one, 'is to deter future unlawful police conduct.'" *Id.*, at 446, 96 S.Ct., at 3028, quoting *United States v. Calandra*, 414 U.S. 338, 347, 94 S.Ct. 613, 619, 38 L.Ed.2d 561 (1974). On the cost side there is the loss of often probative evidence and all of the secondary costs that flow from the less accurate or more cumbersome adjudication that therefore occurs.

. . . .

While it seems likely that the deterrence value of applying the exclusionary rule in deportation proceedings would be higher than it was in *Janis*, it is also quite clear that the social costs would be very much greater as well. Applying the *Janis* balancing test to the benefits and costs of excluding concededly reliable evidence from a deportation proceeding, we therefore reach the same conclusion as in *Janis*.

The likely deterrence value of the exclusionary rule in deportation proceedings is difficult to assess. On the one hand, a civil deportation proceeding is a civil complement to a possible criminal prosecution, and to this extent it resembles the civil proceeding under review in *Janis*. The INS does not suggest that the exclusionary rule should not continue to apply in criminal proceedings against an alien who unlawfully enters or remains in this country, and the prospect of losing evidence that might otherwise be used in a criminal prosecution undoubtedly supplies some residual deterrent to unlawful conduct by INS officials. But it must be acknowledged that only a very small percentage of arrests of aliens are intended or expected to lead to criminal prosecutions. Thus the arresting officer's primary objective, in practice, will be to use evidence in the civil deportation proceeding. Moreover, here, in contrast to *Janis*, the agency officials who effect the unlawful arrest are the same officials who subsequently bring the deportation action. As recognized in *Janis*, the exclusionary rule is likely to be most effective when applied to such "intrasovereign" violations.

Nonetheless, several other factors significantly reduce the likely deterrent value of the exclusionary rule in a civil deportation proceeding. First, regardless of how the arrest is effected, deportation will still be possible when evidence not derived directly from the arrest is sufficient to support deportation. As the BIA has recognized, in many deportation proceedings "the sole matters necessary for the Government to establish are the respondent's identity and alienage—at which point the burden shifts to the respondent to prove the time, place and manner of entry." *Matter of Sandoval*, 17 I. & N.Dec., at 79. Since the person and identity of the respondent are not themselves suppressible, see *supra*, at 3485, the INS must prove only alienage, and that will sometimes be possible using evidence gathered independently of, or sufficiently attenuated from, the original arrest. See *Matter of Sandoval, supra*, at 79; see, *e.g., Avila-Gallegos v. INS*, 525 F.2d 666 (CA2 1975) . . .

The second factor is a practical one. In the course of a year the average INS agent arrests almost 500 illegal aliens. Brief for Petitioner 38. Over 97.5% apparently agree to voluntary deportation without a formal hearing. 705 F.2d, at 1071, n. 17. Among the remainder who do request a formal hearing (apparently a dozen or so in all, per officer, per year) very few challenge the circumstances of their arrests. As noted by the Court of Appeals, "the BIA was able to find only two reported immigration cases since 1899 in which the [exclusionary] rule was applied to bar unlawfully seized evidence, only one other case in which the rule's application was specifically addressed, and fewer than fifty BIA proceedings since 1952 in which a Fourth Amendment challenge to the introduction of evidence was even raised." *Id.*, at 1071. Every INS agent knows, therefore, that it is highly unlikely that any particular arrestee will end up challenging the lawfulness of his arrest in a formal deportation proceeding. When an occasional challenge is brought, the consequences from the point of view of the officer's overall arrest and deportation record will be trivial. In these circumstances, the arresting officer is most unlikely to shape his conduct in anticipation of the exclusion of evidence at a formal deportation hearing.

Third, and perhaps most important, the INS has its own comprehensive scheme for deterring Fourth Amendment violations by its officers. Most arrests of illegal aliens away from the border occur during farm, factory, or other workplace surveys. Large numbers of illegal aliens are often arrested at one time, and conditions are understandably chaotic. See Brief for Petitioner in *INS v. Delgado*, O.T.1983, No. 82-1271, pp. 3–5. To safeguard the rights of those who are lawfully present at inspected workplaces the INS has developed rules restricting stop, interrogation, and arrest practices. *Id.*, at 7, n. 7, 32–40, and n. 25. These regulations require that no one be detained without reasonable suspicion of illegal alienage, and that no one be arrested unless there is an admission of illegal alienage or other strong evidence thereof. New immigration officers receive instruction and examination in Fourth Amendment law, and others receive periodic refresher courses in law. Brief for Petitioner 39–40. Evidence seized through intentionally unlawful conduct is excluded by Department of Justice policy from the proceeding for which it was obtained. See Memorandum from Benjamin R. Civiletti to Heads of Offices, Boards, Bureaus and Divisions, Violations of Search and Seizure Law (Jan. 16, 1981). The INS also has in place a procedure for investigating and punishing immigration officers who commit Fourth Amendment violations. See Office of General Counsel, INS, U.S. Dept. of Justice, The Law of Arrest, Search, and Seizure for Immigration Officers 35 (Jan. 1983). The INS's attention to Fourth Amendment interests cannot guarantee that constitutional violations will not occur, but it does reduce the likely deterrent value of the exclusionary rule. Deterrence must be measured at the margin.

Finally, the deterrent value of the exclusionary rule in deportation proceedings is undermined by the availability of alternative remedies for institutional practices by the INS that might violate Fourth Amendment rights. The INS is a single agency, under central federal control, and engaged in operations of broad scope but highly repetitive character. The possibility of declaratory relief against the agency thus offers a means for challenging the validity of INS practices, when standing requirements for bringing such an action can be met. Cf. *INS v. Delgado*, 466 U.S. 210, 104 S.Ct. 1758, 80 L.Ed.2d 247 (1984).

... Important as it is to protect the Fourth Amendment rights of all persons, there is no convincing indication that application of the exclusionary rule in civil deportation proceedings will contribute materially to that end.

On the other side of the scale, the social costs of applying the exclusionary rule in deportation proceedings are both unusual and significant. The first cost is one that is unique to continuing violations of the law. Applying the exclusionary rule in proceedings that are intended not to punish past transgressions but to prevent their continuance or renewal would require the courts to close their eyes to ongoing violations of the law. This Court has never before accepted costs of this character in applying the exclusionary rule.

Presumably no one would argue that the exclusionary rule should be invoked to prevent an agency from ordering corrective action at a leaking hazardous waste dump if the evidence underlying the order had been improperly obtained, or to compel police to return contraband explosives or drugs to their owner if the contraband had been unlawfully seized. On the rare occasions that it has considered costs of this type the Court has firmly indicated that the exclusionary rule does not extend this far. See *United States v. Jeffers*, 342 U.S. 48, 54, 72 S.Ct. 93, 96, 96 L.Ed. 59 (1951); *Trupiano v. United States*, 334 U.S. 699, 710, 68 S.Ct. 1229, 1234, 92 L.Ed. 1663 (1948). The rationale for these holdings is not difficult to find. "Both *Trupiano* and *Jeffers* concerned objects the possession of which, without more, constitutes a crime. The repossession of such per se contraband by Jeffers and Trupiano would have subjected them to criminal penalties. The return of the contraband would clearly have frustrated the express public policy against the possession of such objects." *One 1958 Plymouth Sedan v. Pennsylvania*, 380 U.S. 693, 699, 85 S.Ct. 1246, 1250, 14 L.Ed.2d 170 (1965) (footnote omitted). Precisely the same can be said here. Sandoval-Sanchez is a person whose unregistered presence in this country, without more, constitutes a crime. His release within our borders would immediately subject him to criminal penalties. His release would clearly frustrate the express public policy against an alien's unregistered presence in this country. Even the objective of deterring Fourth Amendment violations should not require such a result. The constable's blunder may allow the criminal to go free, but we have never suggested that it allows the criminal to continue in the commission of an ongoing crime. When the crime in question involves unlawful presence in this country, the criminal may go free, but he should not go free within our borders.

Other factors also weigh against applying the exclusionary rule in deportation proceedings. The INS currently operates a deliberately simple deportation hearing system, streamlined to permit the quick resolution of very large numbers of deportation actions, and it is against this backdrop that the costs of the exclusionary rule must be assessed. The costs of applying the exclusionary rule, like the benefits, must be measured at the margin.

The average immigration judge handles about six deportation hearings per day. Brief for Petitioner 27, n. 16. Neither the hearing officers nor the attorneys participating in those hearings are likely to be well versed in the intricacies of Fourth Amendment law

. . . The BIA's concerns are reinforced by the staggering dimension of the problem that the INS confronts. Immigration officers apprehend over one million deportable aliens in this country every year. *Id.*, at 85. A single agent may arrest many illegal aliens every day. Although the investigatory burden does not justify the commission of constitutional violations, the officers cannot be expected to compile elaborate, contemporaneous, written reports detailing the circumstances of every arrest. At present an officer simply completes a "Record of Deportable Alien" that is introduced to prove the INS's case at the deportation hearing; the officer rarely must attend the hearing. Fourth Amendment suppression hearings would undoubtedly require considerably more, and the likely burden on the administration of the immigration laws would be correspondingly severe.

Finally, the INS advances the credible argument that applying the exclusionary rule to deportation proceedings might well result in the suppression of large amounts of information that had been obtained entirely lawfully. . . .

In these circumstances we are persuaded that the *Janis* balance between costs and benefits comes out against applying the exclusionary rule in civil deportation hearings held by the INS. By all appearances the INS has already taken sensible and reasonable steps to deter Fourth Amendment violations by its officers, and this makes the likely additional deterrent value of the exclusionary rule small. The costs of applying the exclusionary rule in the context of civil deportation hearings are high. In particular, application of the exclusionary rule in cases such as Sandoval-Sanchez', would compel the courts to release from custody persons who would then immediately resume their commission of a crime through their continuing, unlawful presence in this country. "There comes a point at which courts, consistent with their duty to administer the law, cannot continue to create barriers to law enforcement in the pursuit of a supervisory role that is properly the duty of the Executive and Legislative Branches." *United States v. Janis*, 428 U.S., at 459, 96 S.Ct., at 3034. That point has been reached here.

. . . .

The judgment of the Court of Appeals is therefore Reversed.

Notes and Questions

1. Should the exclusionary rule apply to deportation hearings? In other words, should an illegal arrest be grounds for stopping deportation? Are you convinced by the Court's argument that the costs to the INS would outweigh the benefits of imposing Fourth Amendment restrictions on INS officers?

2. In his dissent, Justice Brennan stated: "I fully agree with Justice White that under the analysis developed by the Court in such cases as *United States v. Janis*, 428 U.S. 433, 96 S.Ct. 3021, 49 L.Ed.2d 1046 (1976), and *United States v. Calandra*, 414 U.S. 338, 94 S.Ct. 613, 38 L.Ed.2d 561 (1974), the exclusionary rule must apply in civil deportation proceedings. However, for the reasons set forth today in my dissenting opinion in *United States v. Leon, ante*, 468 U.S. 897, 104 S.Ct. 3405, 82 L. Ed.2d 677, I believe the basis for the exclusionary rule does not derive from its effectiveness as a deterrent, but is instead found in the requirements of the Fourth Amendment itself." Do you agree?

H. Search and Seizure

What search and seizure procedures are due to immigrants in the context of INS searches?

Immigration and Naturalization Service v. Delgado
466 U.S. 210 (1984)

JUSTICE REHNQUIST delivered the opinion of the Court.

In the course of enforcing the immigration laws, petitioner Immigration and Naturalization Service (INS) enters employers' worksites to determine whether any illegal aliens may be present as employees. The Court of Appeals for the Ninth Circuit held that the "factory surveys" involved in this case amounted to a seizure of the entire work forces, and further held that the INS could not question individual employees during any of these surveys unless its agents had a reasonable suspicion that the employee to be questioned was an illegal alien. *International Ladies' Garment Worker's Union, AFL-CIO v. Sureck*, 681 F.2d 624 (9th Cir.1982). We conclude that these factory surveys did not result in the seizure of the entire work forces, and that the individual questioning of the respondents in this case by INS agents concerning their citizenship did not amount to a detention or seizure under the Fourth Amendment. Accordingly, we reverse the judgment of the Court of Appeals.

Acting pursuant to two warrants, in January and September 1977 the INS conducted a survey of the work force at Southern California Davis Pleating Co. (Davis Pleating) in search of illegal aliens. The warrants were issued on a showing of probable cause by the INS that numerous illegal aliens were employed at Davis Pleating, although neither of the search warrants identified any particular illegal aliens by name. A third factory survey was conducted with the employer's consent in October 1977, at Mr. Pleat, another garment factory.

At the beginning of the surveys several agents positioned themselves near the buildings' exits, while other agents dispersed throughout the factory to question most, but not all, employees at their work stations. The agents displayed badges, carried walkie-talkies, and were armed, although at no point during any of the surveys was a weapon ever drawn. Moving systematically through the factory, the agents approached employees and, after identifying themselves, asked them from one to three questions relating to their citizenship. If the employee gave a credible reply that he was a United States citizen, the questioning ended, and the agent moved on to another employee. If the employee gave an unsatisfactory response or admitted that he was an alien, the employee was asked to produce his immigration papers. During the survey, employees continued with their work and were free to walk around within the factory.

Respondents are four employees questioned in one of the three surveys. In 1978 respondents and their union representative, the International Ladies Garment Workers' Union, filed two actions, later consolidated, in the United States District

Court for the Central District of California challenging the constitutionality of INS factory surveys and seeking declaratory and injunctive relief. Respondents argued that the factory surveys violated their Fourth Amendment right to be free from unreasonable searches or seizures and the equal protection component of the Due Process Clause of the Fifth Amendment.

The District Court denied class certification and dismissed the union from the action for lack of standing, App. to Pet. for Cert. 58a-60a. In a series of cross-motions for partial summary judgment, the District Court ruled that respondents had no reasonable expectation of privacy in their workplaces which conferred standing on them to challenge entry by the INS pursuant to a warrant or owner's consent. Id., at 49a-52a, 53a-55a, 56a-57a. In its final ruling the District Court addressed respondents' request for injunctive relief directed at preventing the INS from questioning them personally during any future surveys. The District Court, with no material facts in dispute, found that each of the four respondents was asked a question or questions by an INS agent during one of the factory surveys. Id., at 46a. Reasoning from this Court's decision in *Terry v. Ohio*, 392 U.S. 1, 88 S.Ct. 1868, 20 L.Ed.2d 889 (1968), that law enforcement officers may ask questions of anyone, the District Court ruled that none of the respondents had been detained under the Fourth Amendment during the factory surveys, either when they were questioned or otherwise. App. to Pet. for Cert. 47a. Accordingly, it granted summary judgment in favor of the INS.

The Court of Appeals reversed. Applying the standard first enunciated by a Member of this Court in *United States v. Mendenhall*, 446 U.S. 544, 100 S.Ct. 1870, 64 L.Ed.2d 497 (1980) (opinion of Stewart, J.), the Court of Appeals concluded that the entire work forces were seized for the duration of each survey, which lasted from one to two hours, because the stationing of agents at the doors to the buildings meant that "a reasonable worker 'would have believed that he was not free to leave.'" 681 F.2d, at 634 (quoting *United States v. Anderson*, 663 F.2d 934, 939 (CA9 1981)). Although the Court of Appeals conceded that the INS had statutory authority to question any alien or person believed to be an alien as to his right to be or remain in the United States, see 66 Stat. 233, 8 U.S.C. § 1357(a)(1), it further held that under the Fourth Amendment individual employees could be questioned only on the basis of a reasonable suspicion that a particular employee being questioned was an alien illegally in the country. 681 F.2d, at 639–645. A reasonable suspicion or probable cause to believe that a number of illegal aliens were working at a particular factory site was insufficient to justify questioning any individual employee. *Id.*, at 643. Consequently, it also held that the individual questioning of respondents violated the Fourth Amendment because there had been no such reasonable suspicion or probable cause as to any of them.

We granted certiorari to review the decision of the Court of Appeals, 461 U.S. 904, 103 S.Ct. 1872, 76 L.Ed.2d 805 (1983), because it has serious implications for the enforcement of the immigration laws and presents a conflict with the decision reached by the Third Circuit in *Babula v. INS*, 665 F.2d 293 (1981).

The Fourth Amendment does not proscribe all contact between the police and citizens, but is designed "to prevent arbitrary and oppressive interference by enforcement officials with the privacy and personal security of individuals." *United States v. Martinez-Fuerte*, 428 U.S. 543, 554, 96 S.Ct. 3074, 3081, 49 L.Ed.2d 1116 (1976). Given the diversity of encounters between police officers and citizens, however, the Court has been cautious in defining the limits imposed by the Fourth Amendment on encounters between the police and citizens. As we have noted elsewhere: "Obviously, not all personal intercourse between policemen and citizens involves 'seizures' of persons. Only when the officer, by means of physical force or show of authority, has restrained the liberty of a citizen may we conclude that a 'seizure' has occurred." *Terry v. Ohio, supra*, 392 U.S., at 19, n. 16, 88 S.Ct., at 1879 n. 16. While applying such a test is relatively straightforward in a situation resembling a traditional arrest, see *Dunaway v. New York*, 442 U.S. 200, 212–216, 99 S.Ct. 2248, 2256–2258, 60 L.Ed.2d 824 (1979), the protection against unreasonable seizures also extends to "seizures that involve only a brief detention short of traditional arrest." *United States v. Brignoni-Ponce*, 422 U.S. 873, 878, 95 S.Ct. 2574, 2578, 45 L.Ed.2d 607 (1975). What has evolved from our cases is a determination that an initially consensual encounter between a police officer and a citizen can be transformed into a seizure or detention within the meaning of the Fourth Amendment, "if, in view of all the circumstances surrounding the incident, a reasonable person would have believed that he was not free to leave." *Mendenhall, supra*, 446 U.S. at 554, 100 S.Ct., at 1877 (footnote omitted); see *Florida v. Royer*, 460 U.S. 491, 502, 103 S.Ct. 1319, 1326, 75 L.Ed.2d 229 (1983) (plurality opinion).

Although we have yet to rule directly on whether mere questioning of an individual by a police official, without more, can amount to a seizure under the Fourth Amendment, our recent decision in *Royer, supra*, plainly implies that interrogation relating to one's identity or a request for identification by the police does not, by itself, constitute a Fourth Amendment seizure. In *Royer*, when Drug Enforcement Administration agents found that the respondent matched a drug courier profile, the agents approached the defendant and asked him for his airplane ticket and driver's license, which the agents then examined. A majority of the Court believed that the request and examination of the documents were "permissible in themselves." *Id.*, at 501, 103 S.Ct., at 1326 (plurality opinion), see *id.*, at 523, n. 3, 103 S.Ct., at 1337–1338, n. 3 (opinion of Rehnquist, J.). In contrast, a much different situation prevailed in *Brown v. Texas*, 443 U.S. 47, 99 S.Ct. 2637, 61 L.Ed.2d 357 (1979), when two policemen physically detained the defendant to determine his identity, after the defendant refused the officers' request to identify himself. The Court held that absent some reasonable suspicion of misconduct, the detention of the defendant to determine his identity violated the defendant's Fourth Amendment right to be free from an unreasonable seizure. *Id.*, at 52, 99 S.Ct. at 2641.

What is apparent from *Royer* and *Brown* is that police questioning, by itself, is unlikely to result in a Fourth Amendment violation. While most citizens will respond to a police request, the fact that people do so, and do so without being told they are free not to respond, hardly eliminates the consensual nature of the response. Cf. *Schneckloth v. Bustamonte*, 412 U.S. 218, 231–234, 93 S.Ct. 2041, 2049–2051, 36 L. Ed.2d 854 (1973). Unless the circumstances of the encounter are so intimidating as to demonstrate that a reasonable person would have believed he was not free to leave if he had not responded, one cannot say that the questioning resulted in a detention under the Fourth Amendment. But if the persons refuses to answer and the police take additional steps — such as those taken in *Brown* — to obtain an answer, then the Fourth Amendment imposes some minimal level of objective justification to validate the detention or seizure. *United States v. Mendenhall*, 446 U.S., at 554, 100 S.Ct., at 1877; see *Terry v. Ohio*, 392 U.S., at 21, 88 S.Ct., at 1879.

The Court of Appeals held that "the manner in which the factory surveys were conducted in this case constituted a seizure of the workforce" under the Fourth Amendment. 681 F.2d, at 634. While the element of surprise and the systematic questioning of individual workers by several INS agents contributed to the court's holding, the pivotal factor in its decision was the stationing of INS agents near the exits of the factory buildings. According to the Court of Appeals, the stationing of agents near the doors meant that "departures were not to be contemplated," and thus, workers were "not free to leave." *Ibid*. In support of the decision below, respondents argue that the INS created an intimidating psychological environment when it intruded unexpectedly into the workplace with such a show of officers. Besides the stationing of agents near the exits, respondents add that the length of the survey and the failure to inform workers they were free to leave resulted in a Fourth Amendment seizure of the entire work force.

We reject the claim that the entire work forces of the two factories were seized for the duration of the surveys when the INS placed agents near the exits of the factory sites. Ordinarily, when people are at work their freedom to move about has been meaningfully restricted, not by the actions of law enforcement officials, but by the workers' voluntary obligations to their employers. The record indicates that when these surveys were initiated, the employees were about their ordinary business, operating machinery and performing other job assignments. While the surveys did cause some disruption, including the efforts of some workers to hide, the record also indicates that workers were not prevented by the agents from moving about the factories.

Respondents argue, however, that the stationing of agents near the factory doors showed the INS's intent to prevent people from leaving. But there is nothing in the record indicating that this is what the agents at the doors actually did. The obvious purpose of the agents' presence at the factory doors was to insure that all persons in the factories were questioned. The record indicates that the INS agents' conduct in this case consisted simply of questioning employees and arresting those they had probable cause to believe were unlawfully present in the factory. This conduct should have given respondents no reason to believe that they would be detained if they gave truthful answers to the questions put to them or if they simply refused to answer. If mere questioning does not constitute a seizure when it occurs inside the factory, it is no more a seizure when it occurs at the exits.

A similar conclusion holds true for all other citizens or aliens lawfully present inside the factory buildings during the surveys. The presence of agents by the exits posed no reasonable threat of detention to these workers while they walked throughout the factories on job assignments. Likewise, the mere possibility that they would be questioned if they sought to leave the buildings should not have resulted in any reasonable apprehension by any of them that they would be seized or detained in any meaningful way. Since most workers could have had no reasonable fear that they would be detained upon leaving, we conclude that the work forces as a whole were not seized.

The Court of Appeals also held that "detentive questioning" of individuals could be conducted only if INS agents could articulate "objective facts providing investigators with a reasonable suspicion that each questioned person, so detained, is an alien illegally in this country." 681 F.2d, at 638. Under our analysis, however, since there was no seizure of the work forces by virtue of the method of conducting the factory surveys, the only way the issue of individual questioning could be presented would be if one of the named respondents had in fact been seized or detained. Reviewing the deposition testimony of respondents, we conclude that none were.

The questioning of each respondent by INS agents seems to have been nothing more than a brief encounter. None of the three Davis Pleating employees were questioned during the January survey. During the September survey at Davis Pleating, respondent Delgado was discussing the survey with another employee when two INS agents approached him and asked him where he was from and from what city. When Delgado informed them that he came from Mayaguez, Puerto Rico, the agent made an innocuous observation to his partner and left. App. 94. Respondent Correa's experience in the September survey was similar. Walking from one part of the factory to another, Correa was stopped by an INS agent and asked where she was born. When she replied, "Huntington Park, [California]," the agent walked away and Correa continued about her business. Id., 115. Respondent Labonte, the third Davis Pleating employee, was tapped on the shoulder and asked in Spanish, "Where are your papers?" Id., 138. Labonte responded that she had her papers and without any further request from the INS agents, showed the papers to the agents, who then left. Finally, respondent Miramontes, the sole Mr. Pleat employee involved in this case, encountered an agent en route from an office to her worksite. Questioned concerning her citizenship, Miramontes replied that she was a resident alien, and on the agent's request, produced her work permit. The agent then left. Id., at 120–121.

Respondents argue that the manner in which the surveys were conducted and the attendant disruption caused by the surveys created a psychological environment which made them reasonably afraid they were not free to leave. Consequently, when respondents were approached by INS agents and questioned concerning their citizenship and right to work, they were effectively detained under the Fourth Amendment, since they reasonably feared that refusing to answer would have resulted in their arrest. But it was obvious from the beginning of the surveys that the INS agents were only questioning people. Persons such as respondents who simply went about their business in the workplace were not detained in any way; nothing more occurred than that a question was put to them. While persons who attempted to flee or evade the agents may eventually have been detained for questioning, see *id.*, at 50, 81–84, 91–93, respondents did not do so and were not in fact detained. The manner in which respondents were questioned, given its obvious purpose, could hardly result in a reasonable fear that respondents were not free to continue working or to move about the factory. Respondents may only litigate what happened to them, and our review of their description of the encounters with the INS agents satisfies us that the encounters were classic consensual encounters rather than Fourth Amendment seizures. See *Florida v. Royer*, 460 U.S. 491, 103 S.Ct. 1319, 75 L.Ed.2d 229 (1983); *United States v. Mendenhall*, 446 U.S. 544, 100 S.Ct. 1870, 64 L.Ed.2d 497 (1980).

Accordingly, the judgment of the Court of Appeals is

Reversed.

JUSTICE BRENNAN, with whom JUSTICE MARSHALL joins, concurring in part and dissenting in part.

As part of its ongoing efforts to enforce the immigration laws, the Immigration and Naturalization Service (INS) conducts "surveys" of those workplaces that it has reason to believe employ large numbers of undocumented aliens who may be subject to deportation. This case presents the question whether the INS's method of carrying out these "factory surveys" violates the rights of the affected factory workers to be secure against unreasonable seizures of one's person as guaranteed by the Fourth Amendment. Answering that question, the Court today holds, first, that the INS surveys involved here did not result in the seizure of the entire factory work force for the complete duration of the surveys, ante, at 1763–1764, and, second, that the individual questioning of respondents by INS agents concerning their citizenship did not constitute seizures within the meaning of the Fourth Amendment, ante, at 1764–1765. Although I generally agree with the Court's first conclusion, I am convinced that a fair application of our prior decisions to the facts of this case compels the conclusion that respondents were unreasonably seized by INS agents in the course of these factory surveys.

At first blush, the Court's opinion appears unremarkable. But what is striking about today's decision is its studied air of unreality. Indeed, it is only through a considerable feat of legerdemain that the Court is able to arrive at the conclusion that the respondents were not seized. The success of the Court's sleight of hand turns on the proposition that the interrogations of respondents by the INS were merely brief, "consensual encounters," *ante*, at 1765, that posed no threat to respondents' personal security and freedom. The record, however, tells a far different story.

Contrary to the Court's suggestion, see ante, at 1762, we have repeatedly considered whether and, if so, under what circumstances questioning of an individual by law enforcement officers may amount to a seizure within the meaning of the Fourth Amendment. See, e.g., *Terry v. Ohio*, 392 U.S. 1, 88 S.Ct. 1868, 20 L.Ed.2d 889 (1968); *Davis v. Mississippi*, 394 U.S. 721, 89 S.Ct. 1394, 22 L.Ed.2d 676 (1969); *Adams v.*

Williams, 407 U.S. 143, 92 S.Ct. 1921, 32 L.Ed.2d 612 (1972); *Brown v. Texas*, 443 U.S. 47, 99 S.Ct. 2637, 61 L.Ed.2d 357 (1979); *United States v. Mendenhall*, 446 U.S. 544, 100 S.Ct. 1870, 64 L.Ed.2d 497 (1980); *Florida v. Royer*, 460 U.S. 491, 103 S.Ct. 1319, 75 L.Ed.2d 229 (1983). Of course, as these decisions recognize, the question does not admit of any simple answer. The difficulty springs from the inherent tension between our commitment to safeguarding the precious, and all too fragile, right to go about one's business free from unwarranted government interference, and our recognition that the police must be allowed some latitude in gathering information from those individuals who are willing to cooperate. Given these difficulties, it is perhaps understandable that our efforts to strike an appropriate balance have not produced uniform results. Nevertheless, the outline of what appears to be the appropriate inquiry has been traced over the years with some clarity.

The Court launched its examination of this issue in *Terry v. Ohio, supra*, by explaining that "the Fourth Amendment governs 'seizures' of the person which do not eventuate in a trip to the station house and prosecution for crime—'arrests' in traditional terminology. *It must be recognized that whenever a police officer accosts an individual and restrains his freedom to walk away, he has 'seized' that person.*" *Id.*, at 16, 88 S.Ct., at 1877 (emphasis added). Such a seizure, the Court noted, may be evidenced by either "physical force or show of authority" indicating that the individual's liberty has been restrained. *Id.*, at 19, n. 16, 88 S.Ct., at 1879, n. 16. The essential teaching of the Court's decision in *Terry*—that an individual's right to personal security and freedom must be respected even in encounters with the police that fall short of full arrest—has been consistently reaffirmed. In *Davis v. Mississippi*, 394 U.S., at 726–727, 89 S.Ct., at 1397–1398, for example, the Court confirmed that investigatory detentions implicate the protections of the Fourth Amendment and further explained that "while the police have the right to request citizens to answer voluntarily questions concerning unsolved crimes they have no right to compel them to answer." *Id.*, at 727, n. 6, 89 S.Ct., at 1397, n. 6. Similarly, in *Brown v. Texas, supra*, we overturned a conviction for refusing to stop and identify oneself to police, because, in making the stop, the police lacked any "reasonable suspicion, based on objective facts, that the individual [was] involved in criminal activity." *Id.*, at 51, 99 S.Ct., at 2641. The animating principle underlying this unanimous decision was that the Fourth Amendment protects an individual's personal security and privacy from unreasonable interference by the police, even when that interference amounts to no more than a brief stop and questioning concerning one's identity.

Although it was joined at the time by only one other Member of this Court, Part IIA of Justice Stewart's opinion in *United States v. Mendenhall, supra*, offered a helpful, preliminary distillation of the lessons of these cases. Noting first that "as long as the person to whom questions are put remains free to disregard the questions and walk away, there has been no intrusion upon that person's liberty or privacy," Justice Stewart explained that "a person has been 'seized' within the meaning of the Fourth Amendment only if, in view of all of the circumstances surrounding the incident, a reasonable person would have believed that he was not free to leave." *Id.*, at 554, 100 S.Ct., at 1877. The opinion also suggested that such circumstances might include "the threatening presence of several officers, the display of a weapon by an officer, some physical touching of the person of the citizen, or the use of language or tone of voice indicating that compliance with the officer's request might be compelled." *Ibid.*

A majority of the Court has since adopted that formula as the appropriate standard for determining when inquiries made by the police cross the boundary separating merely consensual encounters from forcible stops to investigate a suspected crime. See *Florida v. Royer,* 460 U.S., at 502, 103 S.Ct., at 1326 (plurality opinion); *id.,* at 511–512, 103 S.Ct., at 1331 (Brennan, J., concurring in result); *id.,* at 514, 103 S. Ct., at 1333 (Blackmun, J., dissenting). This rule properly looks not to the subjective impressions of the person questioned but rather to the objective characteristics of the encounter which may suggest whether or not a reasonable person would believe that he remained free during the course of the questioning to disregard the questions and walk away. See 3 W. LaFave, Search and Seizure §9.2, p. 52 (1978). The governing principles that should guide us in this difficult area were summarized in the Royer plurality opinion:

> "[L]aw enforcement officers do not violate the Fourth Amendment by merely approaching an individual on the street or in another public place, by asking him if he is willing to answer some questions, by putting questions to him if the person is willing to listen, or by offering in evidence in a criminal prosecution his voluntary answers to such questions. Nor would the fact that the officer identifies himself as a police officer, without more, convert the encounter into a seizure requiring some level of objective justification. The person approached, however, need not answer any question put to him; indeed, he may decline to listen to the questions at all and may go on his way. *He may not be detained even momentarily without reasonable, objective grounds for doing so; and his refusal to listen or answer does not, without more, furnish those grounds.*" 460 U.S., at 497–498, 103 S.Ct., at 1324 (citations omitted) (emphasis added).

... The Court's eagerness to conclude that these interrogations did not represent seizures is to some extent understandable, of course, because such a conclusion permits the Court to avoid the imposing task of justifying these seizures on the basis of reasonable, objective criteria as required by the Fourth Amendment.

The reasonableness requirement of the Fourth Amendment applies to all seizures of the person, including those that involve only a brief detention short of traditional arrest. But because the intrusion upon an individual's personal security and privacy is limited in cases of this sort, we have explained that brief detentions may be justified on "facts that do not amount to the probable cause required for an arrest." *United States v. Brignoni-Ponce,* 422 U.S. 873, 880, 95 S.Ct. 2574, 2580, 45 L.Ed.2d 607 (1975). Nevertheless, our prior decisions also make clear that investigatory stops of the kind at issue here "must be justified by some objective manifestation that the person stopped is, or is about to be, engaged in criminal activity." *United States v. Cortez*, 449 U.S. 411, 417, 101 S.Ct. 690, 695, 66 L.Ed.2d 621 (1981). As the Court stated in *Terry*, the "demand for specificity in the information upon which police action is predicated is the central teaching of this Court's Fourth Amendment jurisprudence." 392 U.S., at 21, n. 18, 88 S.Ct., at 1880, n. 18. Repeatedly, we have insisted that police may not detain and interrogate an individual unless they have reasonable grounds for suspecting that the person is involved in some unlawful activity. In *United States v. Brignoni-Ponce, supra*, for instance, the Court held that "[Border Patrol] officers on roving patrol may stop vehicles only if they are aware of specific articulable facts, together with rational inferences from those facts, that reasonably warrant suspicion that the vehicles contain aliens who may be illegally in the country." *Id.*, 422 U.S., at 884, 95 S.Ct., at 2581. See also *Michigan v. Summers*, 452 U.S. 692, 699–700, 101 S.Ct. 2587, 69 L.Ed.2d 340 (1981); *Ybarra v. Illinois*, 444 U.S. 85, 92–93, 100 S.Ct. 338, 342–343, 62 L.Ed.2d 238 (1979); *Brown v. Texas*, 443 U.S., at 51–52, 99 S.Ct., at 2640–2641; *Delaware v. Prouse*, 440 U.S. 648, 661, 99 S.Ct. 1391, 1400, 59 L.Ed.2d 660 (1979); *Adams v. Williams*, 407 U.S., at 146–149, 92 S.Ct., at 1923–1924; *Davis v. Mississippi*, 394 U.S., at 726–728, 1397–1398; *Terry v. Ohio*, 392 U.S., at 16–19, 88 S.Ct., at 1877–1878. This requirement of particularized suspicion provides the chief protection of lawful citizens against unwarranted governmental interference with their personal security and privacy.

In this case, the individual seizures of respondents by the INS agents clearly were neither "based on specific, objective facts indicating that society's legitimate interests require[d] the seizure," nor "carried out pursuant to a plan embodying explicit, neutral limitations on the conduct of individual officers." *Brown v. Texas, supra*, 443 U.S., at 51, 99 S.Ct., at 2640. It is undisputed that the vast majority of the undocumented aliens discovered in the surveyed factories had illegally immigrated from Mexico. Nevertheless, the INS agents involved in this case apparently were instructed, in the words of the INS Assistant District Director in charge of the operations, to interrogate "virtually all persons employed by a company." App. 49. See also *id.*, at 77, 85–86, 151–152, 155. Consequently, all workers, irrespective of whether they were American citizens, permanent resident aliens, or deportable aliens, were subjected to questioning by INS agents concerning their right to remain in the country. By their own admission, the INS agents did not selectively question persons in these surveys on the basis of any reasonable suspicion that the persons were illegal aliens. See *id.*, at 55, 155. That the INS policy is so indiscriminate should not be surprising, however, since many of the employees in the surveyed factories who are lawful residents of the United States may have been born in Mexico, have a Latin appearance, or speak Spanish while at work. See id., at 57, 73. What this means, of course, is that the many lawful workers who constitute the clear majority at the surveyed workplaces are subjected to surprise questioning under intimidating circumstances by INS agents who have no reasonable basis for suspecting that they have done anything wrong. To say that such an indiscriminate policy of mass interrogation is constitutional makes a mockery of the words of the Fourth Amendment.

. . . .

No one doubts that the presence of large numbers of undocumented aliens in this country creates law enforcement problems of titanic proportions for the INS. Nor does anyone question that this agency must be afforded considerable latitude in meeting its delegated enforcement responsibilities. I am afraid, however, that the Court has become so mesmerized by the magnitude of the problem that it has too easily allowed Fourth Amendment freedoms to be sacrificed. Before we discard all efforts to respect the commands of the Fourth Amendment in this troubling area, however, it is worth remembering that the difficulties faced by the INS today are partly of our own making.

The INS methods under review in this case are, in my view, more the product of expedience than of prudent law enforcement policy. The Immigration and Nationality Act establishes a quota-based system for regulating the admission of immigrants to this country which is designed to operate primarily at our borders. See 8 U.S.C. §§ 1151–1153, 1221–1225. See generally *Developments*, 96 Harv.L.Rev., at 1334–1369. With respect to Mexican immigration, however, this system has almost completely broken down. This breakdown is due in part, of course, to the considerable practical problems of patrolling a 2,000- mile border; it is, however, also the result of our failure to commit sufficient resources to the border patrol effort. See Administration's Proposals on Immigration and Refugee Policy: Joint Hearing before the Subcommittee on Immigration, Refugees, and International Law of the House Committee on the Judiciary, and the Subcommittee on Immigration and Refugee Policy of the Senate Committee on the Judiciary, 97th Cong., 1st Sess., 6 (1981) (statement of Attorney General Smith); see also *Developments*, 96 Harv.L.Rev., at 1439. Furthermore, the Act expressly exempts American businesses that employ undocumented aliens from all criminal sanctions, 8 U.S.C. § 1324(a), thereby adding to the already powerful incentives for aliens to cross our borders illegally in search of employment.

In the face of these facts, it seems anomalous to insist that the INS must now be permitted virtually unconstrained discretion to conduct wide-ranging searches for undocumented aliens at otherwise lawful places of employment in the interior of the United States. What this position amounts to, I submit, is an admission that since we have allowed border enforcement to collapse and since we are unwilling to require American employers to share any of the blame, we must, as a matter of expediency, visit all of the burdens of this jury-rigged enforcement scheme on the privacy interests of completely lawful citizens and resident aliens who are subjected to these factory raids solely because they happen to work alongside some undocumented aliens. The average American, as we have long recognized, see *Carroll v. United States*, 267 U.S. 132, 154, 45 S.Ct. 280, 285, 69 L.Ed. 543 (1925), expects some interference with his or her liberty when seeking to cross the Nation's borders, but until today's decision no one would ever have expected the same treatment while lawfully at work in the country's interior. Because the conditions which spawned such expedient solutions are in no sense the fault of these lawful workers, the Court, as the guardian of their constitutional rights, should attend to this problem with greater sensitivity before simply pronouncing the Fourth Amendment a dead letter in the context of immigration enforcement. The answer to these problems, I suggest, does not lie in abandoning our commitment to protecting the cherished rights secured by the Fourth Amendment, but rather may be found by reexamining our immigration policy.

I dissent.

Questions

1. What was the problem with the search according to the dissent? How is the dissent's argument connected to Fourth Amendment's expectation of privacy arguments which distinguish reasonable searches from unreasonable ones?

2. Are these Fourth Amendment issues confined to the context of undocumented immigrants? Which of these Fourth Amendment issues do you find applicable exclusively to undocumented immigrants and which to the population at large?

3. How does the conversation taking place among the Justices mirror today's discourse on the scope of rights for persons in the U.S., generally, and the scope of rights for undocumented persons in particular? In what way are the issues similar or different?

I. Integrated Litigation

To what extent does the Equal Protection Clause protect children of undocumented immigrants? See below for *Plyler v, Doe*, a landmark opinion asserting protection for the dignity of children of undocumented immigrants in the context of education. *Plyler* is also a useful precedent for combining equal protection and fundamental right analyses.[22]

Plyler v. Doe
457 U.S. 202 (1982)

JUSTICE BRENNAN delivered the opinion of the Court.

The question presented by these cases is whether, consistent with the Equal Protection Clause of the Fourteenth Amendment, Texas may deny to undocumented

---

22. Fact Sheet, *Public Education for Immigrant Students: Understanding* Plyler v. Doe, http:// immigrationpolicy.org/just-facts/public-education-immigrant-students-states-challenge-supreme -court%E2%80%99s-decision-plyler-v-do; Olivas, Plyler v. Doe: *Still Guaranteeing Unauthorized Immigrant Children's Right to Attend U.S. Public Schools*, http://www.migrationpolicy.org/article /plyler-v-doe-still-guaranteeing-unauthorized-immigrant-childrens-right-attend-us-public/; *Supreme Court Decision on Right to an Education: The Case of Illegal Alien Children, "Plyler v. Doe"*, http://eric.ed.gov/?id=ED218805.

school-age children the free public education that it provides to children who are citizens of the United States or legally admitted aliens.

I

Since the late 19th century, the United States has restricted immigration into this country. Unsanctioned entry into the United States is a crime, 8 U.S.C. § 1325, and those who have entered unlawfully are subject to deportation, 8 U.S.C. §§ 1251, 1252 (1976 ed. and Supp.IV). But despite the existence of these legal restrictions, a substantial number of persons have succeeded in unlawfully entering the United States, and now live within various States, including the State of Texas.

In May 1975, the Texas Legislature revised its education laws to withhold from local school districts any state funds for the education of children who were not "legally admitted" into the United States. The 1975 revision also authorized local school districts to deny enrollment in their public schools to children not "legally admitted" to the country. Tex.Educ.Code Ann. § 21.031 (Vernon Supp.1981). These cases involve constitutional challenges to those provisions.

Plyler v. Doe

This is a class action, filed in the United States District Court for the Eastern District of Texas in September 1977, on behalf of certain school-age children of Mexican origin residing in Smith County, Tex., who could not establish that they had been legally admitted into the United States. The action complained of the exclusion of plaintiff children from the public schools of the Tyler Independent School District. The Superintendent and members of the Board of Trustees of the School District were named as defendants; the State of Texas intervened as a party-defendant. After certifying a class consisting of all undocumented school-age children of Mexican origin residing within the School District, the District Court preliminarily enjoined defendants from denying a free education to members of the plaintiff class. In December 1977, the court conducted an extensive hearing on plaintiffs' motion for permanent injunctive relief.

In considering this motion, the District Court made extensive findings of fact. The court found that neither § 21.031 nor the School District policy implementing it had "either the purpose or effect of keeping illegal aliens out of the State of Texas." 458 F.Supp. 569, 575 (1978). Respecting defendants' further claim that § 21.031 was simply a financial measure designed to avoid a drain on the State's finances, the court recognized that the increases in population resulting from the immigration of Mexican nationals into the United States had created problems for the public schools of the State, and that these problems were exacerbated by the special educational needs of immigrant Mexican children. The court noted, however, that the increase in school enrollment was primarily attributable to the admission of children who were legal residents. *Id.*, at 575–576. It also found that while the "exclusion of all undocumented children from the public schools in Texas would eventually result in economies at some level," *id.*, at 576, funding from both the State and Federal Governments was based primarily on the number of children enrolled. In net effect then, barring undocumented children from the schools would save money, but it would "not necessarily" improve "the quality of education." *Id.*, at 577. The court further observed that the impact of § 21.031 was borne primarily by a very small subclass of illegal aliens, "entire families who have migrated illegally and — for all practical purposes — permanently to the United States." *Id.*, at 578.[3] Finally, the court noted that under current laws and practices "the illegal alien of today may well be the legal alien of tomorrow," and that without an education, these undocumented children, "[a]lready disadvantaged as a result of poverty, lack of English-speaking ability, and undeniable racial prejudices, . . . will become permanently locked into the lowest socio-economic class." *Id.*, at 577.

. . . .

The Court of Appeals for the Fifth Circuit upheld the District Court's injunction. 628 F.2d 448 (1980). The Court of Appeals held that the District Court had erred in finding the Texas statute pre-empted by federal law. With respect to equal protection, however, the Court of Appeals affirmed in all essential respects the analysis of the District Court, *id.*, at 454–458, concluding that § 21.031 was "constitutionally infirm regardless of whether it was tested using the mere rational basis standard or some more stringent test," *id.*, at 458. We noted probable jurisdiction. 451 U.S. 968, 101 S.Ct. 2044, 68 L.Ed.2d 347 (1981).

In re Alien Children Education Litigation

During 1978 and 1979, suits challenging the constitutionality of § 21.031 and various local practices undertaken on the authority of that provision were filed in the United States District Courts for the Southern, Western, and Northern Districts of Texas. Each suit named the State of Texas and the Texas Education Agency as defendants, along with local officials. In November 1979, the Judicial Panel on Multidistrict Litigation, on motion of the State, consolidated the claims against the state officials into a single action to be heard in the District Court for the Southern District of Texas. A hearing was conducted in February and March 1980. In July 1980, the court entered an opinion and order holding that § 21.031 violated the Equal Protection Clause of the Fourteenth Amendment. *In re Alien Children Education Litigation*, 501 F.Supp. 544. The court held that "the absolute deprivation of education should trigger strict judicial scrutiny, particularly when the absolute deprivation is the result of complete inability to pay for the desired benefit." *Id.*, at 582. The court determined that the State's concern for fiscal integrity was not a compelling state interest, *id.*, at 582–583; that exclusion of these children had not been shown to be necessary to improve education within the State, *id.*, at 583; and that the educational needs of the children statutorily excluded were not different from the needs of children not excluded, *ibid.* The court therefore concluded that § 21.031 was not carefully tailored to advance the asserted state interest in an acceptable manner. *Id.*, at 583–584. While appeal of the District Court's decision was pending, the Court of Appeals rendered its decision in No. 80-1538. Apparently on the strength of that opinion, the Court of Appeals, on February 23, 1981, summarily affirmed the decision of the Southern District. We noted probable jurisdiction, 452 U.S. 937, 101 S. Ct. 3078, 69 L.Ed.2d 950 (1981), and consolidated this case with No. 80-1538 for briefing and argument.

II

The Fourteenth Amendment provides that "[n]o State shall . . . deprive any person of life, liberty, or property, without due process of law; nor deny to *any person within its jurisdiction* the equal protection of the laws." (Emphasis added.) Appellants argue at the outset that undocumented aliens, because of their immigration status, are not "persons within the jurisdiction" of the State of Texas, and that they therefore have no right to the equal protection of Texas law. We reject this argument. Whatever his status under the immigration laws, an alien is surely a "person" in any ordinary sense of that term. Aliens, even aliens whose presence in this country is unlawful, have long been recognized as "persons" guaranteed due process of law by the Fifth and Fourteenth Amendments. *Shaughnessy v. Mezei*, 345 U.S. 206, 212, 73 S.Ct. 625, 629, 97 L.Ed. 956 (1953); *Wong Wing v. United States*, 163 U.S. 228, 238, 16 S.Ct. 977, 981, 41 L.Ed. 140 (1896); *Yick Wo v. Hopkins*, 118 U.S. 356, 369, 6 S.Ct. 1064, 1070, 30 L.Ed. 220 (1886). Indeed, we have clearly held that the Fifth Amendment protects aliens whose presence in this country is unlawful from invidious discrimination by the Federal Government. *Mathews v. Diaz*, 426 U.S. 67, 77, 96 S.Ct. 1883, 1890, 48 L.Ed.2d 478 (1976).

Appellants seek to distinguish our prior cases, emphasizing that the Equal Protection Clause directs a State to afford its protection to persons *within its jurisdiction* while the Due Process Clauses of the Fifth and Fourteenth Amendments contain no such assertedly limiting phrase. In appellants' view, persons who have entered the United States illegally are not "within the jurisdiction" of a State even if they are present within a State's boundaries and subject to its laws. Neither our cases nor the logic of the Fourteenth Amendment supports that constricting construction of the phrase "within its jurisdiction." We have never suggested that the class of persons who might avail themselves of the equal protection guarantee is less than coextensive with that entitled to due process. To the contrary, we have recognized that both provisions were fashioned to protect an identical class of persons, and to reach every exercise of state authority.

> "The Fourteenth Amendment to the Constitution is not confined to the protection of citizens. It says: 'Nor shall any state deprive any person of life, liberty, or property without due process of law; nor deny to any person within its jurisdiction the equal protection of the laws.' *These provisions are universal in their application, to all persons within the territorial jurisdiction,* without regard to any differences of race, of color, or of nationality; and the protection of the laws is a pledge of the protection of equal laws." *Yick Wo, supra,* at 369, 6 S.Ct., at 1070 (emphasis added).

In concluding that "all persons within the territory of the United States," including aliens unlawfully present, may invoke the Fifth and Sixth Amendments to challenge actions of the Federal Government, we reasoned from the understanding that the Fourteenth Amendment was designed to afford its protection to all within the boundaries of a State. *Wong Wing, supra*, at 238, 16 S.Ct., at 981. Our cases applying the Equal Protection Clause reflect the same territorial theme:

> "Manifestly, the obligation of the State to give the protection of equal laws can be performed only where its laws operate, that is, within its own jurisdiction. It is there that the equality of legal right must be maintained. That obligation is imposed by the Constitution upon the States severally as governmental entities,—each responsible for its own laws establishing the rights and duties of persons within its borders." *Missouri ex rel. Gaines v. Canada*, 305 U.S. 337, 350, 59 S.Ct. 232, 236, 83 L.Ed. 208 (1938).

There is simply no support for appellants' suggestion that "due process" is somehow of greater stature than "equal protection" and therefore available to a larger class of persons. To the contrary, each aspect of the Fourteenth Amendment reflects an elementary limitation on state power. To permit a State to employ the phrase "within its jurisdiction" in order to identify subclasses of persons whom it would define as beyond its jurisdiction, thereby relieving itself of the obligation to assure that its laws are designed and applied equally to those persons, would undermine the principal purpose for which the Equal Protection Clause was incorporated in the Fourteenth Amendment. The Equal Protection Clause was intended to work nothing less than the abolition of all caste-based and invidious class-based legislation. That objective is fundamentally at odds with the power the State asserts here to classify persons subject to its laws as nonetheless excepted from its protection.

Although the congressional debate concerning § 1 of the Fourteenth Amendment was limited, that debate clearly confirms the understanding that the phrase "within its jurisdiction" was intended in a broad sense to offer the guarantee of equal protection to all within a State's boundaries, and to all upon whom the State would impose the obligations of its laws. Indeed, it appears from those debates that Congress, by using the phrase "person within its jurisdiction," sought expressly to ensure that the equal protection of the laws was provided to the alien population. Representative Bingham reported to the House the draft resolution of the Joint Committee of Fifteen on Reconstruction (H.R. 63) that was to become the Fourteenth Amendment. Cong. Globe, 39th Cong., 1st Sess., 1033 (1866). Two days later, Bingham posed the following question in support of the resolution:

> "Is it not essential to the unity of the people that the citizens of each State shall be entitled to all the privileges and immunities of citizens in the several States? Is it not essential to the unity of the Government and the unity of the people that all persons, *whether citizens or strangers, within this land,* shall have equal protection in every State in this Union in the rights of life and liberty and property?" *Id.*, at 1090.

Senator Howard, also a member of the Joint Committee of Fifteen, and the floor manager of the Amendment in the Senate, was no less explicit about the broad objectives of the Amendment, and the intention to make its provisions applicable to all who "may happen to be" within the jurisdiction of a State:

> "The last two clauses of the first section of the amendment disable a State from depriving not merely a citizen of the United States, but *any person, whoever he may be*, of life, liberty, or property without due process of law, or from denying to him the equal protection of the laws of the State. This abolishes all class legislation in the States and does away with the injustice of subjecting one caste of persons to a code not applicable to another. . . . It will, if adopted by the States, forever disable every one of them from passing laws trenching upon those fundamental rights and privileges which pertain to citizens of the United States, *and to all persons who may happen to be within their jurisdiction.*" *Id.*, at 2766 (emphasis added).

Use of the phrase "within its jurisdiction" thus does not detract from, but rather confirms, the understanding that the protection of the Fourteenth Amendment extends to anyone, citizen or stranger, who *is* subject to the laws of a State, and reaches into every corner of a State's territory. That a person's initial entry into a State, or into the United States, was unlawful, and that he may for that reason be expelled, cannot negate the simple fact of his presence within the State's territorial perimeter. Given such presence, he is subject to the full range of obligations imposed by the State's civil and criminal laws. And until he leaves the jurisdiction — either voluntarily, or involuntarily in accordance with the Constitution and laws of the United States — he is entitled to the equal protection of the laws that a State may choose to establish.

Our conclusion that the illegal aliens who are plaintiffs in these cases may claim the benefit of the Fourteenth Amendment's guarantee of equal protection only begins the inquiry. The more difficult question is whether the Equal Protection Clause has been violated by the refusal of the State of Texas to reimburse local school boards for the education of children who cannot demonstrate that their presence within the United States is lawful, or by the imposition by those school boards of the burden of tuition on those children. It is to this question that we now turn.

III

The Equal Protection Clause directs that "all persons similarly circumstanced shall be treated alike." *F.S. Royster Guano Co. v. Virginia*, 253 U.S. 412, 415, 40 S.Ct. 560, 561, 64 L.Ed. 989 (1920). But so too, "[t]he Constitution does not require things which are different in fact or opinion to be treated in law as though they were the same." *Tigner v. Texas*, 310 U.S. 141, 147, 60 S.Ct. 879, 882, 84 L.Ed. 1124 (1940). The initial discretion to determine what is "different" and what is "the same" resides in the legislatures of the States. A legislature must have substantial latitude to establish classifications that roughly approximate the nature of the problem perceived, that accommodate competing concerns both public and private, and that account for limitations on the practical ability of the State to remedy every ill. In applying the

Equal Protection Clause to most forms of state action, we thus seek only the assurance that the classification at issue bears some fair relationship to a legitimate public purpose.

But we would not be faithful to our obligations under the Fourteenth Amendment if we applied so deferential a standard to every classification. The Equal Protection Clause was intended as a restriction on state legislative action inconsistent with elemental constitutional premises. Thus we have treated as presumptively invidious those classifications that disadvantage a "suspect class," or that impinge upon the exercise of a "fundamental right." With respect to such classifications, it is appropriate to enforce the mandate of equal protection by requiring the State to demonstrate that its classification has been precisely tailored to serve a compelling governmental interest. In addition, we have recognized that certain forms of legislative classification, while not facially invidious, nonetheless give rise to recurring constitutional difficulties; in these limited circumstances we have sought the assurance that the classification reflects a reasoned judgment consistent with the ideal of equal protection by inquiring whether it may fairly be viewed as furthering a substantial interest of the State. We turn to a consideration of the standard appropriate for the evaluation of § 21.031.

A

Sheer incapability or lax enforcement of the laws barring entry into this country, coupled with the failure to establish an effective bar to the employment of undocumented aliens, has resulted in the creation of a substantial "shadow population" of illegal migrants — numbering in the millions — within our borders. This situation raises the specter of a permanent caste of undocumented resident aliens, encouraged by some to remain here as a source of cheap labor, but nevertheless denied the benefits that our society makes available to citizens and lawful residents. The existence of such an underclass presents most difficult problems for a Nation that prides itself on adherence to principles of equality under law.

The children who are plaintiffs in these cases are special members of this underclass. Persuasive arguments support the view that a State may withhold its beneficence from those whose very presence within the United States is the product of their own unlawful conduct. These arguments do not apply with the same force to classifications imposing disabilities on the minor *children* of such illegal entrants. At the least, those who elect to enter our territory by stealth and in violation of our law should be prepared to bear the consequences, including, but not limited to, deportation. But the children of those illegal entrants are not comparably situated. Their "parents have the ability to conform their conduct to societal norms," and presumably the ability to remove themselves from the State's jurisdiction; but the children who are plaintiffs in these cases "can affect neither their parents' conduct nor their own status." *Trimble v. Gordon*, 430 U.S. 762, 770, 97 S.Ct. 1459, 1465, 52 L.Ed.2d 31 (1977). Even if the State found it expedient to control the conduct of adults by acting against their children, legislation directing the onus of a parent's misconduct against his children does not comport with fundamental conceptions of justice.

"[V]isiting . . . condemnation on the head of an infant is illogical and unjust. Moreover, imposing disabilities on the . . . child is contrary to the basic concept of our system that legal burdens should bear some relationship to individual responsibility or wrongdoing. Obviously, no child is responsible for his birth and penalizing the . . . child is an ineffectual—as well as unjust—way of deterring the parent." *Weber v. Aetna Casualty & Surety Co.*, 406 U.S. 164, 175, 92 S.Ct. 1400, 1406, 31 L.Ed.2d 768 (1972) (footnote omitted).

Of course, undocumented status is not irrelevant to any proper legislative goal. Nor is undocumented status an absolutely immutable characteristic since it is the product of conscious, indeed unlawful, action. But § 21.031 is directed against children, and imposes its discriminatory burden on the basis of a legal characteristic over which children can have little control. It is thus difficult to conceive of a rational justification for penalizing these children for their presence within the United States. Yet that appears to be precisely the effect of § 21.031.

Public education is not a "right" granted to individuals by the Constitution. *San Antonio Independent School Dist. v. Rodriguez*, 411 U.S. 1, 35, 93 S.Ct. 1278, 1298, 36 L.Ed.2d 16 (1973). But neither is it merely some governmental "benefit" indistinguishable from other forms of social welfare legislation. Both the importance of education in maintaining our basic institutions, and the lasting impact of its deprivation on the life of the child, mark the distinction. The "American people have always regarded education and [the] acquisition of knowledge as matters of supreme importance." *Meyer v. Nebraska*, 262 U.S. 390, 400, 43 S.Ct. 625, 627, 67 L.Ed. 1042 (1923). We have recognized "the public schools as a most vital civic institution for the preservation of a democratic system of government," *Abington School District v. Schempp*, 374 U.S. 203, 230, 83 S.Ct. 1560, 1575, 10 L.Ed.2d 844 (1963) (Brennan, J., concurring), and as the primary vehicle for transmitting "the values on which our society rests." *Ambach v. Norwick*, 441 U.S. 68, 76, 99 S.Ct. 1589, 1594, 60 L.Ed.2d 49 (1979). "[A]s . . . pointed out early in our history, . . . some degree of education is necessary to prepare citizens to participate effectively and intelligently in our open political system if we are to preserve freedom and independence." *Wisconsin v. Yoder*, 406 U.S. 205, 221, 92 S.Ct. 1526, 1536, 32 L.Ed.2d 15 (1972). And these historic "perceptions of the public schools as inculcating fundamental values necessary to the maintenance of a democratic political system have been confirmed by the observations of social scientists." *Ambach v. Norwick, supra*, 411 U.S., at 77, 99 S.Ct., at 1594. In addition, education provides the basic tools by which individuals might lead economically productive lives to the benefit of us all. In sum, education has a fundamental role in maintaining the fabric of our society. We cannot ignore the significant social costs borne by our Nation when select groups are denied the means to absorb the values and skills upon which our social order rests.

In addition to the pivotal role of education in sustaining our political and cultural heritage, denial of education to some isolated group of children poses an affront to one of the goals of the Equal Protection Clause: the abolition of governmental barriers presenting unreasonable obstacles to advancement on the basis of individual merit. Paradoxically, by depriving the children of any disfavored group of an education, we foreclose the means by which that group might raise the level of esteem in which it is held by the majority. But more directly, "education prepares individuals to be self-reliant and self-sufficient participants in society." *Wisconsin v. Yoder, supra*, 406 U.S., at 221, 92 S.Ct., at 1536. Illiteracy is an enduring disability. The inability to read and write will handicap the individual deprived of a basic education each and every day of his life. The inestimable toll of that deprivation on the social economic, intellectual, and psychological well-being of the individual, and the obstacle it poses to individual achievement, make it most difficult to reconcile the cost or the principle of a status-based denial of basic education with the framework of equality embodied in the Equal Protection Clause. What we said 28 years ago in *Brown v. Board of Education*, 347 U.S. 483, 74 S.Ct. 686, 98 L.Ed. 873 (1954), still holds true:

> "Today, education is perhaps the most important function of state and local governments. Compulsory school attendance laws and the great expenditures for education both demonstrate our recognition of the importance of education to our democratic society. It is required in the performance of our most basic public responsibilities, even service in the armed forces. It is the very foundation of good citizenship. Today it is a principal instrument in awakening the child to cultural values, in preparing him for later professional training, and in helping him to adjust normally to his environment. In these days, it is doubtful that any child may reasonably be expected to succeed in life if he is denied the opportunity of an education. Such an opportunity, where the state has undertaken to provide it, is a right which must be made available to all on equal terms." *Id.*, at 493, 74 S.Ct., at 691.

B

These well-settled principles allow us to determine the proper level of deference to be afforded § 21.031. Undocumented aliens cannot be treated as a suspect class because their presence in this country in violation of federal law is not a "constitutional irrelevancy." Nor is education a fundamental right; a State need not justify by compelling necessity every variation in the manner in which education is provided to its population. See *San Antonio Independent School Dist. v. Rodriguez, supra*, at 28–39, 93 S.Ct., at 1293–1300. But more is involved in these cases than the abstract question whether § 21.031 discriminates against a suspect class, or whether education is a fundamental right. Section 21.031 imposes a lifetime hardship on a discrete class of children not accountable for their disabling status. The stigma of illiteracy will mark them for the rest of their lives. By denying these children a basic education, we deny them the ability to live within the structure of our civic institutions, and foreclose any realistic possibility that they will contribute in even the smallest way to the progress of our Nation. In determining the rationality of § 21.031, we may appropriately take into account its costs to the Nation and to the innocent children who are its victims. In light of these countervailing costs, the discrimination contained in § 21.031 can hardly be considered rational unless it furthers some substantial goal of the State.

IV

It is the State's principal argument, and apparently the view of the dissenting Justices, that the undocumented status of these children *vel non* establishes a sufficient rational basis for denying them benefits that a State might choose to afford other residents. The State notes that while other aliens are admitted "on an equality of legal privileges with all citizens under non-discriminatory laws," *Takahashi v. Fish & Game Comm'n*, 334 U.S. 410, 420, 68 S.Ct. 1138, 1143, 92 L.Ed. 1478 (1948), the asserted right of these children to an education can claim no implicit congressional imprimatur. Indeed, in the State's view, Congress' apparent disapproval of the presence of these children within the United States, and the evasion of the federal regulatory program that is the mark of undocumented status, provides authority for its decision to impose upon them special disabilities. Faced with an equal protection challenge respecting the treatment of aliens, we agree that the courts must be attentive to congressional policy; the exercise of congressional power might well affect the State's prerogatives to afford differential treatment to a particular class of aliens. But we are unable to find in the congressional immigration scheme any statement of policy that might weigh significantly in arriving at an equal protection balance concerning the State's authority to deprive these children of an education.

The Constitution grants Congress the power to "establish an uniform Rule of Naturalization." Art. I., § 8, cl. 4. Drawing upon this power, upon its plenary authority with respect to foreign relations and international commerce, and upon the inherent power of a sovereign to close its borders, Congress has developed a complex scheme governing admission to our Nation and status within our borders. See *Mathews v. Diaz*, 426 U.S. 67, 96 S.Ct. 1883, 48 L.Ed.2d 478 (1976); *Harisiades v. Shaughnessy*, 342 U.S. 580, 588–589, 72 S.Ct. 512, 518–519, 96 L.Ed. 586 (1952). The obvious need for delicate policy judgments has counseled the Judicial Branch to avoid intrusion into this field. *Mathews, supra*, at 81, 96 S.Ct., at 1892. But this traditional caution does not persuade us that unusual deference must be shown the classification embodied in § 21.031. The States enjoy no power with respect to the classification of aliens. See *Hines v. Davidowitz*, 312 U.S. 52, 61 S.Ct. 399, 85 L.Ed. 581 (1941). This power is "committed to the political branches of the Federal Government." *Mathews*, 426 U.S., at 81, 96 S.Ct., at 1892. Although it is "a routine and normally legitimate part" of the business of the Federal Government to classify on the basis of alien status, *id.*, at 85, 96 S.Ct., at 1894, and to "take into account the character of the relationship between the alien and this country," *id.*, at 80, 96 S.Ct., at 1891, only rarely are such matters relevant to legislation by a State. See *Id.*, at 84–85, 96 S.Ct., at 1893–1894; *Nyquist v. Mauclet*, 432 U.S. 1, 7, n. 8, 97 S.Ct. 2120, 2124, n. 8, 53 L.Ed.2d 63 (1977).

As we recognized in *DeCanas v. Bica*, 424 U.S. 351, 96 S.Ct. 933, 47 L.Ed.2d 43 (1976), the States do have some authority to act with respect to illegal aliens, at least where such action mirrors federal objectives and furthers a legitimate state goal. In *DeCanas*, the State's program reflected Congress' intention to bar from employment all aliens except those possessing a grant of permission to work in this country. *Id.*, at 361, 96 S.Ct., at 939. In contrast, there is no indication that the disability imposed by § 21.031 corresponds to any identifiable congressional policy. The State does not claim that the conservation of state educational resources was ever a congressional concern in restricting immigration. More importantly, the classification reflected in § 21.031 does not operate harmoniously within the federal program.

To be sure, like all persons who have entered the United States unlawfully, these children are subject to deportation. 8 U.S.C. §§ 1251, 1252 (1976 ed. and Supp.IV). But there is no assurance that a child subject to deportation will ever be deported. An illegal entrant might be granted federal permission to continue to reside in this country, or even to become a citizen. See, *e.g.*, 8 U.S.C. §§ 1252, 1253(h), 1254 (1976 ed. and Supp.IV). In light of the discretionary federal power to grant relief from deportation, a State cannot realistically determine that any particular undocumented child will in fact be deported until after deportation proceedings have been completed. It would of course be most difficult for the State to justify a denial of education to a child enjoying an inchoate federal permission to remain.

We are reluctant to impute to Congress the intention to withhold from these children, for so long as they are present in this country through no fault of their own, access to a basic education. In other contexts, undocumented status, coupled with some articulable federal policy, might enhance state authority with respect to the treatment of undocumented aliens. But in the area of special constitutional sensitivity presented by these cases, and in the absence of any contrary indication fairly discernible in the present legislative record, we perceive no national policy that supports the State in denying these children an elementary education. The State may borrow the federal classification. But to justify its use as a criterion for its own discriminatory policy, the State must demonstrate that the classification is reasonably adapted to "*the purposes for which the state desires to use it.*" *Oyama v. California*, 332 U.S. 633, 664–665, 68 S.Ct. 269, 284, 92 L.Ed. 249 (1948) (Murphy, J., concurring) (emphasis added). We therefore turn to the state objectives that are said to support § 21.031.

V

Appellants argue that the classification at issue furthers an interest in the "preservation of the state's limited resources for the education of its lawful residents." Brief for Appellants 26. . . . Apart from the asserted state prerogative to act against undocumented children solely on the basis of their undocumented status—an asserted prerogative that carries only minimal force in the circumstances of these cases—we discern three colorable state interests that might support § 21.031.

First, appellants appear to suggest that the State may seek to protect itself from an influx of illegal immigrants. While a State might have an interest in mitigating the potentially harsh economic effects of sudden shifts in population, § 21.031 hardly offers an effective method of dealing with an urgent demographic or economic problem. There is no evidence in the record suggesting that illegal entrants impose any significant burden on the State's economy. To the contrary, the available evidence suggests that illegal aliens underutilize public services, while contributing their labor to the local economy and tax money to the state finances. 458 F.Supp., at 578; 501 F.Supp., at 570–571. The dominant incentive for illegal entry into the State of Texas is the availability of employment; few if any illegal immigrants come to this country, or presumably to the State of Texas, in order to avail themselves of a free education. Thus, even making the doubtful assumption that the net impact of illegal aliens on the economy of the State is negative, we think it clear that "[c]harging tuition to undocumented children constitutes a ludicrously ineffectual attempt to stem the tide of illegal immigration," at least when compared with the alternative of prohibiting the employment of illegal aliens. 458 F.Supp., at 585. See 628 F.2d, at 461; 501 F.Supp., at 579 and n. 88.

Second, while it is apparent that a State may "not . . . reduce expenditures for education by barring [some arbitrarily chosen class of] children from its schools," *Shapiro v. Thompson*, 394 U.S. 618, 633, 89 S.Ct. 1322, 1330, 22 L.Ed.2d 600 (1969), appellants suggest that undocumented children are appropriately singled out for exclusion because of the special burdens they impose on the State's ability to provide high-quality public education. But the record in no way supports the claim that exclusion of undocumented children is likely to improve the overall quality of education in the State. As the District Court in No. 80-1934 noted, the State failed to offer any "credible supporting evidence that a proportionately small diminution of the funds spent on each child [which might result from devoting some state funds to the education of the excluded group] will have a grave impact on the quality of education." 501 F.Supp., at 583. And, after reviewing the State's school financing mechanism, the District Court in No. 80-1538 concluded that barring undocumented children from local schools would not necessarily improve the quality of education provided in those schools. 458 F.Supp., at 577. Of course, even if improvement in the quality of education were a likely result of barring some *number* of children from the schools of the State, the State must support its selection of *this* group as the appropriate target for exclusion. In terms of educational cost and need, however, undocumented children are "basically indistinguishable" from legally resident alien children. *Id.*, at 589; 501 F.Supp., at 583, and n. 104.

Finally, appellants suggest that undocumented children are appropriately singled out because their unlawful within the United States renders them less likely than other children to remain within the boundaries of the State, and to put their education to productive social or political use within the State. Even assuming that such an interest is legitimate, it is an interest that is most difficult to quantify. The State has no assurance that any child, citizen or not, will employ the education provided by the State within the confines of the State's borders. In any event, the record is clear that many of the undocumented children disabled by this classification will remain in this country indefinitely, and that some will become lawful residents or citizens of the United States. It is difficult to understand precisely what the State hopes to achieve by promoting the creation and perpetuation of a subclass of illiterates within our boundaries, surely adding to the problems and costs of unemployment, welfare, and crime. It is thus clear that whatever savings might be achieved by denying these children an education, they are wholly insubstantial in light of the costs involved to these children, the State, and the Nation.

VI

If the State is to deny a discrete group of innocent children the free public education that it offers to other children residing within its borders, that denial must be justified by a showing that it furthers some substantial state interest. No such showing was made here. Accordingly, the judgment of the Court of Appeals in each of these cases is

Affirmed.

JUSTICE MARSHALL, concurring.

While I join the Court's opinion, I do so without in any way retreating from my opinion in *San Antonio Independent School District v. Rodriguez*, 411 U.S. 1, 70-133, 93 S.Ct. 1278, 1315-1348, 36 L.Ed.2d 16 (1973) (dissenting opinion). I continue to believe that an individual's interest in education is fundamental, and that this view is amply supported "by the unique status accorded public education by our society, and by the close relationship between education and some of our most basic constitutional values." *Id.*, at 111, 93 S.Ct., at 1336. Furthermore, I believe that the facts of these cases demonstrate the wisdom of rejecting a rigidified approach to equal protection analysis, and of employing an approach that allows for varying levels of scrutiny depending upon "the constitutional and societal importance of the interest adversely affected and the recognized invidiousness of the basis upon which the particular classification is drawn." *Id.*, at 99, 93 S.Ct., at 1330. See also *Dandridge v. Williams*, 397 U.S. 471, 519–521, 90 S.Ct. 1153, 1178–1180, 25 L.Ed.2d 491 (1970) (Marshall, J., dissenting). It continues to be my view that a class-based denial of public education is utterly incompatible with the Equal Protection Clause of the Fourteenth Amendment.

J. Asylum and Deportation

The cases below outline the type of process due to immigrants when facing deportation. These issues come up whether immigrants are at the border or whether they are discovered already in the country. Crises like the one involving unaccompanied minors from Latin America in 2014 and the recent family separation policy in 2018 have brought the issues discussed in these cases back to the national awareness. *Perez-Funez* below describes what process is due, for undocumented immigrants at the border, particularly minors, before deportation. Note that application for asylum and petition to withhold deportation are both pre-requisite processes available to immigrants before INS can complete deportation. As you review the materials, consider whether policy changes (restricting grounds for asylum, by eliminating domestic violence as a basis, for example) would change the scope of these protections.

Issues related to process due to unaccompanied minors have resurfaced recently in the context of mass migration of minors from Latin America to U.S. borders (see, for example, Lauren R. Aronson, *The Tipping Point: The Failure of Form Over Substance in Addressing the Needs of Unaccompanied Immigrant Children*, 18 HARV. LATINO L. REV. 1, 22 (2015)). Furthermore, increased raids and reports of aggressive enforcement of immigration laws separating minors from their parents reflect that immigrant minors are particularly vulnerable. *Perez-Funez* highlights the need for focused deportation procedures in cases involving minors. Arguably, these issues remain the same from one administration to the other. However, since President Reagan's administration, migration crises remains a fixture globally. *Perez-Funez* focuses on the duty of immigration officers to provide clear instructions and an opportunity for minors to understand as well as call for help. What specific protections and steps, if any, would you consider fundamental in deportation cases involving unaccompanied minors?[23]

Perez-Funez v. District Director, Immigration and Naturalization Service

619 F. Supp. 656 (C.D. Cal. 1985)

RAFEEDIE, DISTRICT JUDGE.

INTRODUCTION

These consolidated cases come before the Court on plaintiffs' class action challenge, primarily on due process grounds, to the way in which the Immigration and Naturalization Service (INS) implements its voluntary departure procedure concerning unaccompanied minor aliens. The principal allegation is that INS policy and practice coerces class members into unknowingly and involuntarily selecting

---

23. Lauren R. Aronson, *The Tipping Point: The Failure of Form Over Substance in Addressing the Needs of Unaccompanied Immigrant Children*, 18 HARV. LATINO L. REV. 1, 22 (2015); Scott Rempell, *Credible Fears, Unaccompanied Minors, and the Causes of the Southwestern Border Surge*, 18 CHAP. L. REV. 337, 350 (2015); Hannah Rappleye, *Undocumented and Unaccompanied: Facts, Figures on Children at the Border*, NBC NEWS (Jul. 9, 2014, 5:57 PM), http://www.nbcnews.com/storyline /immigration-border-crisis/undocumented-unaccompanied-facts-figures-children-border -n152221; NPR Staff, *Who Are The Kids Of The Migrant Crisis?*, NPR (July 24, 2014, 4:21 PM), http:// www.npr.org/sections/parallels/2014/07/24/334494493/who-are-the-kids-of-the-migrant-crisis; Ian Gordon, *70,000 Kids Will Show Up Alone at Our Border This Year. What Happens to Them?*, MOTHER JONES (July/Aug. 2014), http://www.motherjones.com/politics/2014/06/child-migrants -surge-unaccompanied-central-america; Halimah Abdullah, *Immigrants or refugees? A difference with political consequences*, CNN (July 17, 2014 2:31 PM), http://www.cnn.com/2014/07/17/politics /immigration-border-crisis-refugee-politics/index.html; UNICEF USA, CHILD REFUGEE CRISIS: SYRIAN CHILDREN UNDER SIEGE, https://www.unicefusa.org/mission/emergencies/child-refugees /syria-crisis (last visited Jan. 31, 2018); Laura King, *Drowned Syrian toddler embodies heartbreak of migrant crisis*, L.A. TIMES (Sept. 3, 2015, 3:09 AM), http://www.latimes.com/world/middleeast/la -fg-syria-drowned-toddler-20150902-htmlstory.html.

voluntary departure, thereby waiving their rights to a deportation hearing or any other form of relief.

The nationwide class seeks the following relief: (1) a judgment declaring the INS' practices violative of the due process clause of the Fifth Amendment to the Constitution; and (2) a permanent injunction prohibiting the INS from effectuating voluntary departure of class members without first providing certain procedural safeguards to ensure a valid waiver of rights.

. . . .

BACKGROUND

A. Factual

Plaintiff and class representative Perez-Funez was sixteen years old when the INS arrested him near the Mexican border in California on March 22, 1981. He claimed that the INS presented him with a voluntary departure consent form without advising him of his rights in a meaningful manner.

Although he claims that he did not want to return to El Salvador, he signed the form because: (1) an INS agent told him he might otherwise have a lengthy detention period and (2) an agent informed him that he could not afford bail. He testified that he did not read or understand the voluntary departure form. He was at Los Angeles International Airport, bound for El Salvador, when an attorney intervened to keep him in this country. . . . The other class representatives have similar stories. . . . Fourteen other class members testified at trial. Although their stories varied in some respects, all stated they signed the form unknowingly and involuntarily.

B. Procedural

Counsel originally filed the Perez-Funez case as a petition for habeas corpus, subsequently amending it into a class action seeking declaratory and injunctive relief. The Cruz children intervened as plaintiffs in October 1981.

The Penas filed a separate class action asking for identical relief. In January 1984 the Court consolidated the cases, certified a nationwide class, and granted certain preliminary injunctive relief. *See Perez-Funez,* 611 F.Supp. 990. The court tried the case in April 1985, ordered post-trial briefs, and heard closing arguments in August 1985.

VOLUNTARY DEPARTURE—THE CHALLENGED PROCEDURE

Voluntary departure is a procedure by which a qualifying alien may consent to summary removal from the United States, normally at the alien's expense. For the INS to implement this procedure, the alien must sign the voluntary departure form (form I-274), waiving the right to a deportation hearing and all alternative forms of relief.

INS policy concerning voluntary departure of unaccompanied minors varies according to the age, residence, and place of apprehension of the child. For class members age fourteen to sixteen, the INS first gathers extensive information regarding the child, using form I-213. Plaintiffs' Exhibit 5. The INS then notifies the minor of the opportunity for voluntary departure by means of the voluntary departure form. Plaintiffs' Exhibit 3. At the bottom of this form, the child can sign and request either a deportation hearing or voluntary departure. Since January of 1984, INS agents have been giving the so-called "Perez-Funez Advisals" prior to presentation of the form. Plaintiffs' Exhibit 13. The Court ordered the giving of this notice as part of the preliminary injunction. *See Perez-Funez v. District Director, INS*, 611 F. Supp. 990 (C.D.Cal.1984).

The INS, however, has a different policy for class members age fourteen through seventeen who are arrested near the Mexican or Canadian borders and whose permanent residence is in one of those two countries. In such cases, the INS temporarily detains the child until a foreign consulate official arrives. If the minor has requested voluntary departure and the official confirms that the child can be returned, transportation arrangements are made. If such an official is not readily available, the INS will take the child to a Mexican or Canadian immigration officer.

For class members under fourteen, the INS follows the same procedure as for fourteen to sixteen year olds with certain significant additions. First, the INS looks for an adult relative accompanying the child to act as a consultant. If none is found, the agency contacts the appropriate foreign consulate in an effort to locate friends or relatives. If necessary, the INS will then contact the American Embassy in an effort to arrange a reunion with relatives or friends. When the INS cannot locate a friend or relative, it will allow the foreign consul to represent the child. Once a representative for the minor is found, the INS notifies him or her of the right to a deportation hearing and the opportunity for voluntary departure. An exception to this adult consultation requirement exists for minors apprehended near the border and whose permanent residence is in Mexico or Canada.

Thus, the policy varies depending on the situation. Moreover, the INS retains the discretion to refuse voluntary departure whenever it believes this type of disposition is inappropriate. It exercises this discretion more frequently with class members under fourteen.

Although voluntary departure represents a waiver of rights, it is in many ways a privilege. *See Tzantarmas v. United States*, 402 F.2d 163, 165 n. 1 (9th Cir.1968). Its advantages to the alien are that it has no adverse impact upon future lawful attempts to enter the United States (as contrasted with a formal deportation order), and it normally reduces the alien's time in detention. The advantage to the INS is that voluntary departure allows for summary disposition of the case, averting the need for a deportation hearing.

Plaintiffs do not challenge the existence or fairness of voluntary departure *per se*. Rather, they assert that class members are coerced into choosing this option and waiving their rights, regardless of whether voluntary departure would be in the child's best interests.

LEGAL DISCUSSION

A. Introduction/Analytical Framework

The thrust of plaintiff's claim is that the INS' policy concerning voluntary departure deprives unaccompanied minor aliens of significant rights, thereby violating the due process guarantees of the Fifth Amendment to the United States Constitution.

Due process is a flexible concept, its requirements varying according to the time, place, and circumstances. *Cafeteria Workers v. McElroy,* 367 U.S. 886, 895, 81 S.Ct. 1743, 1748–49, 6 L.Ed.2d 1230 (1961). In *Mathews v. Eldridge,* 424 U.S. 319, 96 S.Ct. 893, 47 L.Ed.2d 18 (1976), the Supreme Court set forth a three-part balancing test for the resolution of procedural due process issues. First, the court must consider the private interest affected. Second, the court has to evaluate the risk of erroneous deprivations of rights under the challenged procedures and the probable value, if any, of additional or substitute procedural safeguards. Last, the court must balance the government's interest, which includes consideration of the function involved as well as the burdens that supplemental or substitute procedures would impose. *Id.* at 335, 96 S.Ct. at 903. This test provides a framework for the Court's analysis of plaintiffs' challenge.

B. Rights and Interests of Class Members

Unaccompanied alien children possess substantial constitutional and statutory rights. These rights exist in spite of the minors' illegal entry into the country. *See Mathews v. Diaz,* 426 U.S. 67, 77, 96 S.Ct. 1883, 1890, 48 L.Ed.2d 478 (1976). Further, the Court notes that "[c]hildren have a very special place in life which law should reflect." *May v. Anderson,* 345 U.S. 528, 536, 73 S.Ct. 840, 844, 97 L.Ed. 1221 (1953) (Frankfurter, J., concurring). *See also In re Gault,* 387 U.S. 1, 13, 87 S.Ct. 1428, 1436, 18 L.Ed.2d 527 (1967) ("neither the Fourteenth Amendment nor the Bill of Rights is for adults alone").

Plaintiffs, however, do not possess rights equivalent to those of criminal defendants. Deportation proceedings are civil in nature. *INS v. Lopez-Mendoza,*—U.S.—, 104 S.Ct. 3479, 3484 (1984). Thus, the exclusionary rule does not apply. *Id.* Moreover, *Miranda* warnings generally are inappropriate in the deportation context. *Trias-Hernandez v. INS,* 528 F.2d 366, 368 (9th Cir.1975). Finally, there is no due process or statutory right to appointed counsel. *Martin-Mendoza v. INS,* 499 F.2d 918, 922 (9th Cir.1974).

Nonetheless, plaintiff's rights are significant. Foremost among these is the right of every alien to a deportation hearing, which right is waived when a child signs the voluntary departure form. Obviously, this proceeding is critical in terms of the interests at stake. According to the Supreme Court in *Wong Yang Sung v. McGrath,* 339 U.S. 33, 50, 70 S.Ct. 445, 454, 94 L.Ed. 616 (1950), "A deportation hearing involves issues basic to human liberty and happiness and, in the present upheavals in lands to which aliens may be returned, perhaps to life itself." These words are no less applicable today.

Also reflective of the substantial nature of this right is the statutory provision for an evidentiary hearing in which the alien has a right to notice, to counsel (at no expense to the government), to present evidence and cross-examine witnesses, and to a decision based upon substantial evidence. 8 U.S.C. § 1252(b). Due process requires no less. *United States v. Gasca-Kraft,* 522 F.2d 149, 152 (9th Cir.1975).

In addition, when an unaccompanied minor waives the right to a deportation hearing, he or she effectively waives the right to various forms of relief from deportation: (1) adjustment of status (8 U.S.C. § 1254); (2) suspension of deportation (8 U.S.C. § 1254); (3) political asylum (8 U.S.C. § 1158) or withholding of deportation (8 U.S.C. § 1253(h)(1)); and (4) deferred action status (Operating Instruction 103.1). Although many class members are not eligible for such relief, the eligible child who instead signs for voluntary departure makes a grave mistake indeed.

Therefore, taken together, the right to a deportation hearing and the various rights associated therewith constitute a substantial liberty interest on the part of plaintiff class members. Given the interests at stake and the tender ages of the possessors of those interests, the Court must carefully scrutinize the risk of erroneous deprivation.

C. Risk of Erroneous Deprivation and Probable Value of Additional Procedural Safeguards

1. Risk of Erroneous Deprivation

A class member's signature on the voluntary departure form waives the various rights discussed in the preceding section. Accordingly, the risk of erroneous deprivation issue boils down to whether the INS' procedures concerning voluntary departure result in effective waivers.

A waiver is "an intentional relinquishment or abandonment of a known right or privilege." *Johnson v. Zerbst,* 304 U.S. 458, 464, 58 S.Ct. 1019, 1023, 82 L.Ed. 1461 (1938). A presumption against such an abandonment of rights exists in the civil as well as the criminal context. *See Fuentes v. Shevin,* 407 U.S. 67, 94 n. 31, 92 S.Ct. 1983, 2001 n. 31, 32 L.Ed.2d 556 n. 31 (1972).

In order for a criminal defendant to waive the right to counsel, the waiver must be voluntary as well as knowing and intelligent, an issue which depends in each case "upon the particular facts and circumstances surrounding that case, including the background, experience, and conduct of the accused." *Johnson,* 304 U.S. at 464, 58 S.Ct. at 1023. Although the instant proceedings are civil, it is nevertheless clear that "[w]hatever the right, the standard for waiver is whether the actor fully understands the right in question and voluntarily intends to relinquish it." *Edwards v. Arizona,* 451 U.S. 477, 489, 101 S.Ct. 1880, 1887, 68 L.Ed.2d 378 (1981) (Powell, J., with whom Rehnquist, J., joins, concurring in the result).

In addressing the question of whether plaintiffs proved that the waivers obtained by the INS are invalid, the Court first is compelled to comment upon what plaintiffs did not prove. One of plaintiffs' principal allegations throughout this litigation has been that the INS engages in a policy of overt coercion of unaccompanied minors that allegedly includes physical mistreatment and verbal abuse. . . .

Nevertheless, even if the trial proved nothing else, it demonstrated that, under the procedures currently employed, unaccompanied minors do not understand their rights when confronted with the voluntary departure form. This is the one inescapable conclusion to be drawn from this lawsuit.

The Court heard the testimony of a parade of class members, predominately Salvadoran, and the Court found them to be credible concerning their lack of understanding. Their absence of knowledge was clear, even in situations where they had read, or had read to them, the forms and advisals. In fact, at the time of trial, plaintiffs still did not understand their legal rights. Even defendants' own witnesses conceded that the children did not grasp the "legal language" in the forms and that they did not "know what to do."

Plaintiffs' expert witnesses buttressed this conclusion. The upshot of their testimony was that minors generally do not understand the concept of legal rights without explanation. Further, according to the experts, when children's rights are presented to them in a stressful situation in which they are separated from their close-knit families and faced with a new culture, they cannot make a knowing and voluntary choice. Rather, the natural tendency is to defer to the authority before them, especially for those children accustomed to autocratic governments.

The Court notes that, as discussed above, INS policy treats children fourteen years of age and older differently from younger class members. When older children are involved, the INS makes less of an effort to contact a parent or relative, and it usually will honor the child's voluntary departure selection. The agency bases this different treatment on an assumption that older children are better able to make important decisions. For this proposition, they rely primarily on certain sections of the Immigration and Nationality Act, which oblige children fourteen and older to register and be fingerprinted (8 U.S.C. § 1302(a), (b)) and to give notice of any change of address (8 U.S.C. § 1305). Section 1306 provides penalties for failure to comply with these requirements as well as for other offenses.

Although the Court does not lightly disregard agency policy preferences, it cannot agree with the INS' age distinctions. First, the statutes upon which the INS relies do not address the constitutional issue present in this case. Class members face a much more difficult task in comparison to the obligations imposed by the statutes.

Second, the Court heard testimony from class members of various ages, some under fourteen and some over, and the absence of understanding was consistent. Age apparently made little difference. Last, expert testimony indicated that, while the minors' ability to understand the semantic meaning of words increases with age, older children encountering the instant situation still would be incapable of making informed decisions concerning the exercise or waiver of individual rights.

All of the foregoing is consistent with common sense. As the Supreme Court noted in *Bellotti v. Baird,* 443 U.S. 622, 635, 99 S.Ct. 3035, 3044, 61 L.Ed.2d 797 (1979), "during the formative years of childhood, minors often lack the experience, perspective, and judgment to recognize and avoid choices that could be detrimental to them." *See also Eddings v. Oklahoma,* 455 U.S. 104, 116, 102 S.Ct. 869, 877, 71 L.Ed.2d 1 ("Even the normal 16 year-old customarily lacks the maturity of an adult"). In the instant case, unaccompanied children of tender years encounter a stressful situation in which they are forced to make critical decisions. Their interrogators are foreign and authoritarian. The environment is new and the culture completely different. The law is complex. The children generally are questioned separately. In short, it is obvious to the Court that the situation faced by unaccompanied minor aliens is inherently coercive. Moreover, the INS' policy of allowing border patrol agents to explain rights but prohibiting the giving of advice does nothing to alleviate the problem.

The major divergence from this pattern of unknowing waiver was the evidence presented concerning class members apprehended in the immediate vicinity of the border and whose permanent residence is in Mexico or Canada. Plaintiffs presented only one Mexican minor as a witness, and while he appeared to sign the voluntary departure form in ignorance, the INS offered substantial evidence that the risk of unknowing waiver is less for this portion of the class. First, simply because of the proximity of Mexico and Canada to the United States, these individuals are more informed concerning immigration matters. In fact, border patrol agents testified that some Mexican minors become impatient when agents read advisals to them because the minors are extremely familiar with such material. Second, the evidence indicated that many Mexican class members *want* to take voluntary departure following a short adventure into this country, and agents stationed near the border testified that it was not unusual to apprehend and process certain Mexican minors on a recurring basis. Thus, while these minors most certainly have the same rights as other class members and even though the possibility of coerced waiver still exists, the risk of deprivation appears to be significantly decreased. Indeed, at closing argument, plaintiffs' counsel conceded that procedures for these class members need not be as elaborate.

The other decreased risk scenario involves class members under fourteen who either are arrested outside the immediate vicinity of the border or are not permanent residents of Mexico or Canada. With these children, the INS policy is to make a strong effort to locate relatives or friends of the child to act as a representative. If the agency can locate no relative or friend, it will allow a consulate official from the minor's home country to act as the child's advisor. The INS also uses its discretion to refuse voluntary departure more often in such cases.

... The major flaw, however, arises when the INS cannot find a relative or friend and thus turns to a consulate official. While the Court cannot find fault with a practice of *notifying* foreign officials of their citizens' illegal presence in this country, the Court believes that allowing foreign consuls to *represent* the child in the deportation process creates a substantial risk of error. Class members from such countries as El Salvador and Guatemala often are fleeing political and military conditions in their homelands. Therefore, the foreign consul may well have a position adverse to that of the class member. Accordingly, the Court cannot assume that the foreign official would have the child's best interests at heart. Other than this problem, the Court believes this particular policy adequately ensures a valid waiver.

. . . .

In sum then, the risk of erroneous deprivation is great, especially with respect to class members who are not arrested near the border or are not permanent residents of Mexico or Canada. The processing environment is inherently coercive and current procedures do not address the problem adequately.

B. Probable Value of Additional or Substitute Safeguards

Mathews v. Eldridge next requires the Court to consider the probable value of additional or substitute safeguards in minimizing the aforementioned risk of deprivation. 424 U.S. at 335, 96 S.Ct. at 903. Along these lines, the Court notes that plaintiffs' demands have decreased measurably from the early stages of this litigation. At one time plaintiffs sought an injunction requiring an arraignment-type hearing and appointment of counsel. Before the waiver could become effective, plaintiffs demanded a requirement of representation by counsel or a determination by an immigration judge that the waiver was knowing, intelligent, and voluntary. *See Perez-Funez v. District Director, INS,* 611 F.Supp. 990, 1001 n. 25 (C.D.Cal.1984).

By the time the parties submitted this case for decision, the proposed safeguards had shrunk to the following: (1) simplified rights advisals; (2) a videotape advisal by a neutral third party; and (3) access to telephones so that the children can contact an attorney, parent, or close relative. Along with access to telephones, plaintiffs seek to require the INS to use an updated list of free legal services, which list plaintiffs prepared.

Addressing the proposed safeguards in order, the Court believes that a simplified advisal would be of some value. It was evident from the trial that class members understood neither the INS' notification of rights (form I-274) nor the Court's own so-called "Perez-Funez Advisals." Moreover, plaintiffs proposed simplified advisal (Plaintiffs' Exhibit 52) fared little better. The evidence was contradictory concerning its effectiveness, and in content, it is both incomplete and partially incorrect. Nonetheless, both sides seem to agree that a written advisal is appropriate, and thus the goal should be to devise the simplest and most accurate advisal possible.

However, the principal lesson learned from the testimony concerning the written advisals was that such advisals alone are insufficient to apprise class members of their rights. This was the case even when border patrol agents read and attempted to explain the advisals to the children. With that in mind, the Court now evaluates the videotape advisal.

. . . The Court [also] finds the videotape advisal to be of only limited value.

That brings the Court to plaintiffs' final proposal: early access to telephones and an updated list of legal services. In light of all the evidence presented, the Court has found that access to telephones prior to presentation of the voluntary departure form is the only way to ensure a knowing waiver of rights.

As developed more fully above, the limited understanding and decision-making ability of the class members, the critical importance of the decisions, and the inherently coercive nature of INS processing require that the children be given some assistance in understanding their rights. The written advisals alone are insufficient. Further, despite the good faith efforts of most INS agents to be of help, the fact remains that the agents are also the arresting or detaining officers and thus are in an adversary position *vis-a-vis* the children. *Cf. In re Gault,* 387 U.S. at 35–36, 87 S. Ct. at 1447–48 . . . .

The Court, however, is by no means ruling that unaccompanied minors have a right to appointed counsel. The case law clearly forecloses such a finding. *See, e.g., Martin-Mendoza v. INS,* 499 F.2d 918, 922 (9th Cir.1974).

Rather, access to legal advice is merely one way of removing class members from an overly coercive environment. The other alternative is to have children contact a parent, close adult relative, or adult friend who can put the child on a more equal footing with the INS. *See Eddings v. Oklahoma,* 455 U.S. 104, 115, 102 S.Ct. 869, 877, 71 L.Ed.2d 1 (1982). . . .

Making the policy concerning telephone calls uniform also would be of great value. The class members' testimony indicated that the INS either denied access to phones or allowed access only after execution of the voluntary departure form. . . . The Court believes that, with respect to class members not apprehended in the immediate area of the border or whose permanent residence is not Mexico or Canada, *mandatory* contact with either counsel, a close relative, or friend *prior* to presentation of the voluntary departure form is central to the success of the telephone proposal. The evidence makes it clear that, in the absence of such communication, the great majority of these class members will commit an unknowing and involuntary waiver.

. . . In sum then, the Court has found that there is some probable value in providing class members with a simplified rights advisal and at least a minimal amount of utility in developing a videotape presentation. However, access to telephones would provide by far the greatest benefits in the hopes of ensuring knowing and voluntary decision-making.

IV. Governmental Interests and Burdens/The Propriety of Injunctive Relief

Finally, *Mathews v. Eldridge* instructs the Court to balance the previously-discussed individual rights and proposed safeguards with the government's interests, including the function involved and the burden that additional procedures would impose. 424 U.S. at 335, 96 S.Ct. at 903. Relatedly, when the Court considers the governmental interest, it must consider the propriety of injunctive relief, keeping in mind that an injunction "should be no more burdensome to the defendant than necessary to provide complete relief to plaintiffs." *Califano v. Yamasaki,* 442 U.S. 682, 702, 99 S.Ct. 2545, 2558, 61 L.Ed.2d 176 (1979). Moreover, the Court wishes to defer to the INS' expertise when constitutionally permissible. Thus, any remedy should be "tailored to correct the specific violation and no more obtrusive than to satisfy the constitutional minima." *Hoptowit v. Ray,* 682 F.2d 1237, 1258 (9th Cir.1982). In addition, the Court is ever mindful that the INS is an agency of limited resources.

As an initial point, consistent with its national function and purpose, the INS has an interest in ensuring that class members make knowing and voluntary decisions. Thus, to the extent that additional safeguards preserve constitutional rights without unduly burdening the agency, such safeguards are consistent with the INS' interests and function.

. . . .

Having considered all of the foregoing factors, the Court believes that, in the case of class members who are not apprehended in the vicinity of the border or are not permanent residents of Mexico or Canada, requiring phone contact with a legal counselor, close relative, or friend prior to presentation of the voluntary departure form is not unduly burdensome. According to immigration attorney Della Bohen, it takes approximately ten minutes to discuss legal options with class members. This short length of time should not disrupt processing significantly, even at the high volume posts.

Additionally, the INS expressed concern that a requirement of immediate contact with counsel or a relative would prevent the agency from promptly obtaining the background information necessary for efficient processing (this involves filling out the I-213 form). Recognizing this concern, the Court sees no problem with allowing the INS to procure information for the I-213 before giving access to telephones. The only constitutional necessity is that the child make contact before presentation of the voluntary departure form since no waiver occurs until the child signs. Therefore, as long as the INS does not attempt to obtain a waiver at this high-risk stage, it is perfectly free to perform its information-gathering function.

Another INS concern is that allowing phone calls in certain areas will promote smuggling by class members. While the agency presented some evidence of such a problem, the evidence did not convince the Court that the practice is pervasive. However, in those situations in which the INS believes that systematic smuggling is occurring, the Court is not adverse to permitting the agency to place or monitor calls or adopt any alternative solution to protect against this perceived problem. Of course, any alternative procedure must provide for communication prior to presentation of the voluntary departure form.

The Court further notes that this requirement does little to increase the burden which the INS currently undertakes concerning class members under age fourteen. Under that policy, contact with some third person already is required. Thus, with respect to these class members, the Court is merely substituting contact with legal counsel in place of representation by a foreign consulate that might not have interests consistent with those of the child.

As for those class members apprehended in the immediate vicinity of the border and who are permanent residents of Mexico or Canada, the burden would be even less than it is for other class members since the INS would only have to *offer* a phone call. Given the evidence that these class members generally have a better understanding of their rights and genuinely desire to voluntarily return, most will no doubt forego the call. Thus, the Court's relief would impose virtually no additional burden. Since this group constitutes the great majority of the class, this less elaborate procedure should reduce greatly the overall burden of the Court's relief.

Updating and maintaining the legal service lists would burden the INS to a certain extent although plaintiffs presented evidence indicating that the effort required is rather slight. Further, pursuant to 8 C.F.R. § 292a.1, the INS district director has a duty to maintain the lists. Because accurate lists are indispensable to the smooth operation of the telephone remedy and since free legal services are indeed available, the need for updating and maintaining the lists far outweighs the slight burden.

. . . .

CONCLUSION

This case has presented a real dilemma to the Court since it is not easily moved to intervene in the operations of a well-intentioned agency with considerable expertise. Nonetheless, plaintiffs have shown a deprivation of rights and so reduced their demands that their proposed relief is, for the most part, not unduly burdensome. Balancing the private interests affected with the risk of deprivation, the probable value of additional safeguards and the government's interest, the Court has determined that past and current INS procedures violate the due process rights of plaintiff class.

Accordingly, the Court will enter a judgment declaring the original INS procedures to be unconstitutional and enjoining any return to those procedures. Further, the Court will make the preliminary injunction of January 24, 1984 permanent with the following modifications:

1. The language "employ threats, misrepresentations, subterfuge, or other forms of coercion or . . ." shall be stricken as no longer necessary.

2. The parties are to confer among themselves and with experts to prepare a simplified rights advisal consistent with the current law of this circuit. This advisal should be prepared within thirty days of the entry of this judgment and submitted to the Court for approval. Once approved, it shall be read and provided to class members in the same manner as the previous advisal, along with the free legal services list compiled pursuant to 8 C.F.R. § 292a.1.

3. With respect to class members apprehended in the immediate vicinity of the border and who reside permanently in Mexico or Canada, the INS shall inform the

class member that he or she may make a telephone call to a parent, close relative, or friend, or to an organization found on the free legal services list. The INS shall so inform the class member of this opportunity prior to presentation of the voluntary departure form.

4. With respect to all other class members, the INS shall provide access to telephones and ensure that the class member has in fact communicated, by telephone or otherwise, with a parent, close adult relative, friend, or with an organization found on the free legal services list. The INS shall provide such access and ensure communication prior to presentation of the voluntary departure form.

5. The INS shall obtain a signed acknowledgment from the class member on a separate copy of the simplified rights advisal showing that the INS has provided all notices and required information, including confirmation of communication with a parent, close adult relative, friend, or legal organization, when applicable.

6. The district director shall update and maintain the free legal services list compiled pursuant to 8 C.F.R. § 292a.1.

Any motion for attorneys' fees should be filed in accordance with the Local Rules.

IT IS SO ORDERED.

Orantes-Hernandez v. Thornburgh

919 F.2d 549 (9th Cir. 1990)

SCHROEDER, CIRCUIT JUDGE:

I. Introduction

This is an appeal from the entry of a permanent injunction in favor of the plaintiffs in a class action against United States government immigration officials. The plaintiff class is composed of Salvadoran nationals who are eligible to apply for political asylum, and who have been or will be taken into custody by the Immigration and Naturalization Service (INS). The district court's injunction, together with its extensive supporting findings of fact and conclusions of law, is reported in *Orantes-Hernandez v. Meese*, 685 F.Supp. 1488 (C.D.Cal.1988) (*Orantes II*).

The complaint alleged that INS officials and Border Patrol Agents prevented members of the class from exercising their statutory right to apply for asylum under the provisions of 8 U.S.C. § 1158(a) (1988). The complaint also alleged INS interference with plaintiffs' ability to obtain counsel, a right guaranteed by 8 U.S.C. § 1362 and the due process clause. *See United States v. Villa-Fabela*, 882 F.2d 434, 438 (9th Cir.1989).

The injunction appealed from requires the INS to notify Salvadoran detainees both of their right to apply for political asylum and of their right to be represented by counsel, though not at government expense. *Orantes II*, 685 F.Supp. at 1512. It enjoins the INS from coercing Salvadoran detainees into signing voluntary departure agreements and from interfering with detainees' ability to obtain counsel at their own expense. *Id.* at 1511–1513.

This injunction makes permanent a preliminary injunction imposing similar requirements. *See Orantes-Hernandez v. Smith,* 541 F.Supp. 351 (C.D.Cal.1982) (*Orantes I*). The preliminary injunction, entered in 1982, was not stayed and the government did not pursue an appeal. The preliminary injunction remained in effect for the six years preceding the entry of the permanent injunction in 1988.

Although the government has raised some legal questions on appeal, the main issue we must decide is factual in nature: whether certain findings of the district court regarding government interference with plaintiffs' rights to apply for asylum and to seek the assistance of counsel at non-government expense are clearly erroneous.

II. Legal Background

A. Asylum

Plaintiffs' action arises under the Refugee Act of 1980 in which Congress sought to bring United States refugee law into conformity with the 1967 United Nations Protocol Relating to the Status of Refugees (UN Protocol). The UN Protocol, to which the United States acceded in 1968, binds parties to comply with the substantive provisions of Articles 2 through 34 of the United Nations Convention Relating to the Status of Refugees (1951 Convention) with respect to "refugees" as defined in Article 1.2 of the UN Protocol. *INS v. Stevic,* 467 U.S. 407, 416, 104 S.Ct. 2489, 2494, 81 L.Ed.2d 321 (1984).

The Refugee Act was passed with the intention of codifying existing practices. It "place[d] into law what we do for refugees now by custom, and on an *ad hoc* basis. . . ." S.Rep. No. 256, 96th Cong., 2d Sess. 1, *reprinted in* 1980 U.S.Code Cong. & Admin.News 141, 141. The Act expressly declared that its purpose was to enforce the "historic policy of the United States to respond to the urgent needs of the persons subject to persecution in their homelands," and to provide "statutory meaning to our national commitment to human rights and humanitarian concerns."

Prior to passage of the Refugee Act, there was no specific statutory basis for United States asylum policy with respect to aliens already in this country. *See INS v. Cardoza-Fonseca,* 480 U.S. 421, 433, 107 S.Ct. 1207, 1214, 94 L.Ed.2d 434 (1987); *Carvajal-Munoz v. INS,* 743 F.2d 562, 564 n. 3 (7th Cir.1984). Congress, therefore, established for the first time a provision in federal law specifically relating to requests for asylum. *Carvajal-Munoz,* 743 F.2d at 564. Section 201(b) of the Refugee Act created section 208 of the Immigration and Naturalization Act (INA) directing the Attorney General to

> establish a procedure for an alien physically present in the United States or at a land border or port of entry, irrespective of such alien's status, to apply for asylum, and the alien may be granted asylum in the discretion of the Attorney General if the Attorney General determines that such alien is a refugee within the meaning of section 101(a)(42)(A) of this title.

INA § 208(a), 8 U.S.C. § 1158(a) (1988); *Cardoza-Fonseca,* 480 U.S. at 427, 107 S.Ct. at 1211. Congressional intent was to create a "uniform procedure" for consideration of asylum claims which would include an opportunity for aliens to have asylum applications "considered outside a deportation and/or exclusion hearing setting." *See* S.Rep. No. 256, 96th Cong., 2d Sess. 1, 9, *reprinted in* 1980 U.S.Code Cong. & Admin.News 141, 149.

Congress added a new statutory definition of "refugee" to the INA in order to eliminate the geographical and ideological restrictions then applicable under the INA. *See* S.Rep. No. 256, 96th Cong., 2d Sess. 1, 4, *reprinted in* 1980 U.S.Code Cong. & Admin.News 141, 144. In formulating this definition, Congress noted its intent to bring the definition of "refugee" under United States immigration law into conformity with the UN Protocol. *See id.* The definition adopted by Congress is virtually identical to the definition of "refugee" in the 1951 Convention, *see Cardoza-Fonseca,* 480 U.S. at 437, 107 S.Ct. at 1216, and is an expanded version of the UN Protocol definition of "refugee", *see Stevic,* 467 U.S. at 422, 104 S.Ct. at 2496–97.

Section 101(a)(42)(A) of the INA defines a refugee as

> any person who is outside any country of such person's nationality or, in the case of a person having no nationality, is outside any country in which such person last habitually resided, and who is unable or unwilling to return to, and is unable or unwilling to avail himself or herself of the protection of, that country because of persecution or a well-founded fear of persecution on account of race, religion, nationality, membership in a particular social group, or political opinion.

8 U.S.C. § 1101(a)(42)(A) (1988).

This litigation focuses on those provisions of the Refugee Act establishing the right of aliens to apply for asylum. It is undisputed that all aliens possess such a right under the Act. *See* 8 U.S.C. § 1158(a) (1988); *Jean v. Nelson,* 727 F.2d 957, 982 (11th Cir.1984) (en banc) (section 1158 confers upon all aliens the right to apply for asylum), *aff'd as modified,* 472 U.S. 846, 105 S.Ct. 2992, 86 L.Ed.2d 664 (1985); *Haitian Refugee Center v. Smith,* 676 F.2d 1023, 1038–39 (5th Cir.1982) (same). One of the major concerns of the plaintiffs-appellees has been to ensure their ability to apply for asylum pursuant to the provisions of the Act. Much of this litigation has centered around plaintiffs' contentions that the INS was forcing them to apply for "voluntary departure" and preventing them from making an application for refugee status. It is therefore necessary to have some understanding of "voluntary departure."

An alien who is in the United States illegally may be apprehended and taken into custody by INS officials. INA § 242, 8 U.S.C. § 1252(a) (1988). After an alien is apprehended, the alien is presented with a Notice and Request for Disposition Form I-274 which allows the alien to choose to depart voluntarily from the United States at the alien's own expense before deportation proceedings are instituted, or to request a deportation hearing. *United States v. Doe,* 862 F.2d 776, 778 (9th Cir.1988).

Section 242(b) of the INA vests the Attorney General with discretion to award voluntary departure in lieu of initiating deportation proceedings. 8 U.S.C. § 1252(b) (1988); *Contreras-Aragon v. INS,* 852 F.2d 1088, 1094 (9th Cir.1988). This voluntary departure procedure has been called a "rough immigration equivalent of a guilty plea," allowing an alien knowingly to waive his right to a hearing in exchange for being able to depart voluntarily instead of under an order of deportation. *Id.* (citation omitted).

An advantage of voluntary departure over deportation is that it "permits the alien to select his or her own destination." *Id.* at 1090. In addition, it "facilitates the possibility of return to the United States" because an alien who leaves under a grant of voluntary departure, unlike a deported alien, does not need special permission to reenter the United States and does not face criminal penalties for failure to obtain that permission. *Id.; see also* INA §§ 212(a)(17) and 276, 8 U.S.C. §§ 1182(a)(17) and 1326 (1988).

There are disadvantages to voluntary departure as well. Aliens who voluntarily depart this country lose the right to apply for asylum before deportation proceedings are initiated. They also give up their right to a deportation hearing at which they may also apply for and have their asylum claim considered before an Immigration Judge. Not only do aliens who accept voluntary departure lose these rights, they may leave the United States without even knowing of these rights and options.

An application for voluntary departure under section 242(b) of the INA must be made prior to the commencement of a deportation hearing and no appeal lies from the denial of the application. *Contreras-Aragon,* 852 F.2d at 1094. If an alien chooses not to depart voluntarily, a proceeding to determine the deportability of the alien is commenced by an immigration official who issues and files an order to show cause with the Office of the Immigration Judge. 8 C.F.R. § 242.1(a) (1990). INS regulations give exclusive jurisdiction to the Immigration Judge to consider asylum applications once an alien is in custody, the characteristic that defines the plaintiff class in this case. *See generally* 2 Gordon & Gordon, *Immigration Law and Procedure* § 18.04[1](a) (rev. ed. 1990).

B. Counsel

The INA also provides aliens with the right to be represented by counsel in deportation proceedings at no expense to the government. *See* INA § 292, 8 U.S.C. § 1362 (1988). The Act specifically requires the Attorney General to adopt regulations to assure the right of counsel of one's choice. *See* INA § 242(b)(2), 8 U.S.C. § 1252(b)(2) (1988). The INS has done so in a regulation requiring that upon personal service of an order to show cause why an alien should not be deported, the alien "shall . . . be advised of his right to representation by counsel of his own choice at no expense to the Government." 8 C.F.R. § 242.1(c) (1990). The regulations go on to describe persons and groups entitled to represent aliens in deportation proceedings, and make it possible for persons who are not attorneys to represent aliens in such proceedings. *See id.* § 292.1.

This court has held that aliens have a due process right to obtain counsel of their choice at their own expense. *Rios-Berrios v. INS,* 776 F.2d 859, 862 (9th Cir.1985). We have "consistently emphasized the critical role of counsel in deportation proceedings. . . .

III. The History of This Litigation

A. The Preliminary Injunction

This action was filed on March 4, 1982. The complaint alleged that INS officials were routinely coercing Salvadorans to "voluntarily depart" the United States in lieu of exercising their rights to a deportation hearing and to seek political asylum. According to plaintiffs' complaint the INS was failing to advise Salvadorans of their right to seek political asylum within the United States and was interfering with, or preventing, Salvadorans from exercising their right to assistance of counsel. The class members also claimed that the INS was failing to provide adequate telephone access to detained Salvadorans and prohibiting them from receiving or possessing any written material other than the New Testament. Finally, they alleged that the INS did not provide and maintain adequate law libraries at detention facilities and placed Salvadoran detainees in solitary confinement without notice and a hearing.

. . . The court granted provisional class certification and issued a preliminary injunction on April 30, 1982. The preliminary injunction prohibited the INS from coercing class members in any way when informing them of the availability of voluntary departure. The district court also ordered the INS to provide Salvadorans with two forms of notice of their rights before informing them of the availability of voluntary departure. . . .

The INS was also ordered to provide information on detained Salvadorans to interested relatives and counsel, and to provide an attorney who had filed written notice of appearance 24 hours advance notice before removal of a class member from the United States. The INS had to allow counsel to rescind voluntary departure agreements, and permit paralegals access to detainees. Two major INS detention centers where many class members were detained are located in El Centro and Chula Vista, California. The court ordered the INS to allow detainees at El Centro and Chula Vista to receive and possess legal materials and to install, or make available, telephones in the Chula Vista facility. The INS was also ordered to allow counsel reasonable access to detainees at El Centro. Finally, the INS was enjoined from placing any class member in solitary confinement for more than 24 hours, except upon good cause shown and unless the class member had written notice and a hearing. . . .

B. The Permanent Injunction

The preliminary injunction remained in effect while the district court heard testimony and received deposition and other evidence from approximately 175 witnesses. These witnesses included members of the plaintiff class, government agents and immigration attorneys representing aliens. . . . The court found that despite the existence of the preliminary injunction, the INS continued to engage in a pattern and practice of coercion and that the members of the plaintiff class continued to be prevented from exercising their rights both to apply for asylum and to obtain counsel. *See id.* . . .

In addition, the district court found that the government's partial compliance had not created any burden, and that full compliance would not result in any significant additional hardship. The court pointed out that "[a]fter nearly five years of operating under the preliminary injunction, the government was not able to present any evidence of such burden." *Id.* at 1508, conclusion 38.

The district court's extensive opinion with its findings of fact and conclusions of law supporting permanent injunctive relief was filed with the order imposing the permanent injunction on April 29, 1988, and this appeal followed.

IV. Legal Analysis

The district court's injunction is designed to ensure the ability of the plaintiff class members to exercise their rights to apply for political asylum and to seek the assistance of counsel. The existence of those rights is not seriously in issue. Hence, what is disputed is not rights but remedies.

With respect to asylum, the key remedy contained in the district court's injunction is the "*Orantes* advisal," the provision requiring the government to give members of the plaintiff class actual written notice of their right to apply for asylum. This remedy rests upon three alternative and independent legal bases. One is that notice is required as a matter of due process. *See Orantes II*, 685 F.Supp. at 1506–07, conclusions 24–25. The second is that notice is required in order to fully effectuate the intent of the Refugee Act. *See id.* at 1506, conclusions 19–23. The third is that such notice is required in this case as a remedial measure to counteract the pattern of interference by the INS with the plaintiff class members' ability to exercise their rights. *See id.* at 1507–08, conclusions 26–43.

The government's threshold attack on the injunction is focused on the first two bases for the injunction, namely that as a matter of law the INS is required to give notice of the right to apply for asylum to all aliens it processes. This court has not considered this issue, but other courts have. *See Jean*, 727 F.2d 957; *Ramirez-Osorio v. INS*, 745 F.2d 937 (5th Cir.1984). The decisions in those cases stop short of holding that aliens have a statutory or constitutional right to blanket notice of the right to apply for asylum. The decisions agree, however, that notice should be given to those aliens who indicate that they fear persecution if they were to be returned home. *See Jean*, 727 F.2d at 983 n. 35; *Ramirez-Osorio*, 745 F.2d at 943–44.

The issue of notice was discussed at some length in *Jean*. The Eleventh Circuit held that there is no notice requirement in the statute itself and further, that aliens have no due process right to notice of the right to apply for asylum. *See* 727 F.2d at 981–83. The court recognized, however, that the Act would be violated if aliens who indicated they feared persecution if returned home were not advised of the right to seek asylum. *See id.* at 983 n. 35. The court said that "if INS officials were refusing to inform aliens of their right to seek asylum even if they did indicate that they feared persecution if returned to their home countries . . . [t]his would constitute a clear violation of the Refugee Act, and remedial action would be justified. . . ." *Id.*

. . . The government has . . . appropriately conceded in oral argument that if the evidence in this case supports the district court's findings of a pattern of coercion and interference with the plaintiff class members' right to apply for asylum, then the INS would be violating the Act and remedial action would be justified.

Accordingly, it is not necessary for us to reach any constitutional or even statutory interpretation issues with regard to the notice requirement if the record in this case supports the district court's findings with regard to the INS's conduct and reflects the appropriateness of the injunctive relief ordered. Such an approach is consistent with the general principle that we should not reach constitutional issues if the case can be decided on another basis. A fundamental rule of judicial restraint requires courts to consider nonconstitutional grounds for decisions before reaching any constitutional questions. *Jean,* 472 U.S. at 854, 105 S.Ct. at 2996–97; *Gulf Oil Co. v. Bernard,* 452 U.S. 89, 99, 101 S.Ct. 2193, 2199, 68 L.Ed.2d 693 (1981). We therefore direct our focus to the district court's alternative grounds for ordering the INS to advise the plaintiff class members of the possibility of applying for refugee status.

Before turning to the district court's findings, we review the legal standards under which we weigh the appropriateness of injunctive relief against an agency of the federal government. . . .

Plaintiffs must demonstrate "'the likelihood of substantial and immediate irreparable injury and the inadequacy of remedies at law.'" *LaDuke,* 762 F.2d at 1330 (quoting *O'Shea v. Littleton,* 414 U.S. 488, 502, 94 S.Ct. 669, 679, 38 L.Ed.2d 647 (1974)). To satisfy this standard, plaintiffs must establish actual success on the merits, and that the balance of equities favors injunctive relief. *Id.* That is, the plaintiff seeking an injunction must prove the plaintiff's own case and adduce the requisite proof, by a preponderance of the evidence, of the conditions and circumstances upon which the plaintiff bases the right to and necessity for injunctive relief. *Citizens Concerned for Separation of Church & State v. Denver,* 628 F.2d 1289, 1299 (10th Cir.1980), *cert. denied,* 452 U.S. 963, 101 S.Ct. 3114, 69 L.Ed.2d 975 (1981).

Once plaintiffs establish they are entitled to injunctive relief, the district court has broad discretion in fashioning a remedy. *Lemon v. Kurtzman,* 411 U.S. 192, 200, 93 S.Ct. 1463, 1469, 36 L.Ed.2d 151 (1973) ("In shaping equity decrees, the trial court is vested with broad discretionary power; appellate review is correspondingly narrow") . . . .

In this case, the equities favor issuance of the injunction if the findings of the district court with respect to INS practices are supported by the evidence. The government has not pointed to any evidence in the record to show that the issuance of the preliminary injunction caused any additional burden to it or that compliance with the permanent injunction would result in any appreciable burden. The government has asserted that informing all aliens of the right to apply for asylum is "potentially" burdensome because it will foster frivolous claims. However, the government does not provide support for this supposition.

Our decision in this case therefore must focus on whether the court's factual findings concerning the conduct of INS agents are clearly erroneous. We thus must turn to the nature of the district court's findings and a more comprehensive description of the evidence in the case.

V. The District Court's Findings and Evidence Concerning INS Interference With the Right to Apply for Asylum

The injunction on appeal to this court made permanent a preliminary injunction based mainly upon the district court's findings of a pattern and practice of interference and coercion on the part of INS agents which prevented Salvadoran aliens who feared return to their country from exercising their right to apply for asylum. One of the government's major contentions on appeal is that the entry of the permanent injunction was unwarranted because there were significant changes in circumstances after the entry of the preliminary injunction which made a permanent injunction unnecessary. In order to analyze this contention, it is necessary to have some familiarity with the voluminous record in this case concerning conditions as they existed both before and after the preliminary injunction.

A. The Record Supporting the Preliminary Injunction

The district court found that prior to the issuance of the preliminary injunction, INS agents coerced Salvadorans who had not expressed a desire to return to El Salvador to sign Form I-274A for voluntary departure. *See Orantes II,* 685 F.Supp. at 1494, finding 33. The evidence supporting this finding is overwhelming.

Form I-274A contained only one signature line and once signed, the alien waived the rights to counsel and a deportation hearing and was processed for voluntary departure. The form did not discuss the alien's right to apply for asylum. However, by signing for voluntary departure, aliens also effectively waived their right to apply for asylum. Numerous class members testified of being forced or tricked into signing for voluntary departure. For example, Freddy Antonio Cartagena signed the voluntary departure form without being given a chance to read it and was just told to "sign here." Marta Ester Paniagua Vides was given a form. She asked the agents if the form was for voluntary departure and they assured her it was not. She signed the paper and it in fact turned out to be Form I-274A. Another witness, Martha Osorio Sandoval, testified she told the agents that she did not want to sign for voluntary departure after reading the form. The agents told her that she had to sign and if she did not, she would remain detained in jail for a long time. Juan Francisco Perez-Cruz, arrested in 1980, did not request asylum even though informed of it because the agent told him that asylum was only for people who were fleeing their country because they were an enemy of the government or an assassin. The agent also told Perez-Cruz that if he wanted asylum, it would be 3 to 6 months, he would be detained the entire time and that if he did not get asylum he would be deported. He was given Form I-274A and told to "sign where the mark is."

Other class members testified about being told that they must apply for voluntary departure even though they expressed fears about returning to El Salvador. Noe Castillo Nunez, apprehended in September 1981, told INS agents that he was afraid to go back to El Salvador because he had received death threats. The agents told Nunez the threats were his problem, that they did not care what happened to him, and that he should return because he would be deported anyway. Nunez was then given some forms and told to "sign here." The papers were quickly taken away and Nunez did not know what he signed. He told the agents that he wanted to apply for asylum, but they told him they did not know anything about it. Dora Alicia Ayala de Castillo was apprehended in September 1981 with 23 members of her family. She told the agents that she and her family were fleeing from the war and begged the agents to help them. She also told the agents that if they went back to their country they were in danger of dying. de Castillo signed for voluntary departure without ever being told about the right to apply for asylum.

Jorge Antonio Joya, apprehended on April 16, 1981, was given a voluntary departure form and told to "sign it." Joya could not read the form because it was in English, but the agent told him it was for his deportation to El Salvador. Joya begged the agent and told him that he could not go back. The agent laughed at Joya and told him to "just sign." Joya further testified that while he was detained in El Centro, an officer often told Salvadorans who had applied for asylum that their applications would never be granted and the best thing they could do would be to sign for voluntary departure.

Even those who asked expressly about political asylum were forced to sign the voluntary departure form. Gloria Esperanza Benitez de Flores was apprehended in March 1982. The day after her apprehension, INS agents requested more than five times that she sign for voluntary departure. The agents placed her in a jail cell and told her she would remain there for a long time if she did not sign. When Benitez de Flores asked the agents about asylum, she was told that the INS was not giving anyone asylum, that it would be useless for her to stay, and it would be better for her to sign for voluntary departure. Dora Elia Estrada, arrested in 1980, refused to sign a voluntary departure form and asked for asylum. The agent who arrested her told her that political asylum "wasn't given" in the United States, and that if she did not sign for voluntary departure she was going to be in detention for a long time in a jail where there were "only men." Another guard told Estrada that if she asked for asylum, the money she posted for bail would be lost and she would be returned to El Salvador; another agent told her that the information she gave them would be sent to El Salvador.

Many class members recounted similar stories of their experiences during the period before the preliminary injunction was entered. . . .

It is significant that the government offered no contradictory evidence to suggest these events did not occur. It is at least equally significant that the testimony of INS agents themselves confirmed it was their accepted practice not to inform

Salvadorans about asylum and to proffer only voluntary departure, even when the Salvadorans expressed fear of return. This practice was directly contrary to the stated policy of the head of the INS, who had represented that INS agents provide notice of the right to apply for asylum to aliens who indicate they fear persecution in their homeland. *See* Oversight Hearings, 96th Cong., 2d Sess. 225 (1980).

Examples of the agents' testimony in this case are as follows. Border Patrol Agent Michael Singh testified that prior to the *Orantes* injunction, he was instructed to continue processing an alien if, during processing, the alien says that he is afraid to return to his country. Singh would fill out an asylum application only if the alien used the words "I want political asylum." If the alien did not use those words, the general policy was to continue processing for deportation. Even if the alien said that he feared persecution on return to his country, processing continued and no asylum form would be proffered. Singh was aware of no policy that the INS had to inform Salvadorans of their right to asylum if they feared persecution. He testified that prior to the injunction it was not his practice or the practice of other agents to inform Salvadorans of their right to apply for asylum even when the Salvadorans expressed fear of persecution.

David Pfeifer, the Deputy Chief of Border Patrol since 1980, testified that prior to the injunction, agents were not required to explain anything to the alien other than what was stated in Form I-274A for voluntary departure. Jim Carter, a criminal investigator with the INS since 1977, testified that prior to the preliminary injunction in this case, he did not advise Salvadorans that they had a right to apply for asylum even if the alien said he was afraid to return to his country. Border Patrol Agent Ronald Knight testified that prior to the *Orantes* injunction, agents were not instructed to ask detainees whether they feared persecution if returned to their homeland.

Senior Border Patrol Agent John D. Edwards, an agent for 9 years, testified about a pre-injunction arrest of a number of Salvadoran women. He testified that he did not tell any of the women that they could apply for asylum if they feared returning to El Salvador. Discussing the same incident, Special Agent Johnny Mendez testified he did not tell one of the Salvadoran women that if she feared return to El Salvador she could apply for asylum because "[i]t wasn't within [his] authority or [his] job description to advise her." Agent Tracy L. Kirk testified that before the *Orantes* injunction, he processed hundreds of Salvadorans and never advised any of them of the right to apply for asylum, even if the aliens told Kirk they feared return to El Salvador.

In sum, the testimony of both members of the plaintiff class and INS agents demonstrated a pattern of INS interference with the class members' right to apply for asylum. The district court's order requiring the INS to provide the "*Orantes* advisal" to class members was to remedy this interference. Because the key issue in this appeal concerns whether the record supports the district court's decision to make that injunction permanent, we turn to the record with respect to the post-preliminary injunction period.

B. Post-preliminary Injunction Interference With the Right to Apply for Asylum

In entering the permanent injunction, the district court found that although the "*Orantes* advisal" had served to protect the rights of some class members, the INS did not in fact provide the advisal to many other class members. *See Orantes II*, 685 F.Supp. at 1498–99, findings 76 & 78. The court found that without continuing the advisal in effect, there was a substantial likelihood that class members would be deprived of their right to apply for asylum. *Id.* at 1499, finding 79. The court concluded that both before and after the issuance of the injunction, the INS had engaged in a pattern and practice of conduct encouraging voluntary departure and discouraging asylum. *Id.* at 1507, conclusion 28.

The government contends that these findings are unsupported by evidence in the record as to events which occurred after 1983 when its forms were changed in response to the preliminary injunction. The government asks us to judge its conduct from February 1983, when it revised its voluntary departure form, replacing the old I-274A with a new Form I-274. . . .

The new Form I-274 contains two signature lines permitting the alien to opt for voluntary departure or to request a deportation hearing. Yet the form itself does not say anything about the right to apply for asylum. The words "asylum" or "refugee" do not appear on it. . . .

Indeed, the evidence in the record shows that despite the change in forms, the pattern of inducing class members into accepting voluntary departure persisted, even where the alien expressed fear of returning to El Salvador or had specifically requested asylum. For example, there was testimony that on many occasions agents circled the signature line for voluntary departure or put an "X" on the form next to it, telling the alien to "sign here." There was also evidence that agents gave forms in English to class members who could not understand that language.

. . . .

The district court found that after the preliminary injunction was in effect, INS agents continued to tell Salvadorans that if they applied for asylum it would be denied, or that they would be deported regardless of their asylum application. *See Orantes II*, 685 F.Supp. at 1495, finding 40. The court found that INS agents were misrepresenting eligibility for asylum, telling class members that information on the application would be sent to El Salvador, and threatening to transfer class members to remote locations if they exercised their right to request a hearing or to apply for asylum. *See id.*, findings 40–42. The court also found that INS agents threatened the aliens by telling them that they would be detained a long time if they asked for asylum. *Id.* at 1494–95, finding 39. There is post-1983 evidence of INS agents making such representations in conjunction with the *Orantes* advisal and in contravention of its purpose. Some examples follow.

After Jose Hernan Sanchez-Velasquez was read the contents of the *Orantes* advisal, he asked what "asylum" was. An INS agent told him that he could only ask for asylum if he was a guard or a guerilla, and that he would be detained for ten years. Heber Reynaldo Santos was given the *Orantes* advisal and asked an INS agent for more information about the "situation for political refugees." The agent told him there were a lot of Salvadorans in jail waiting for asylum and that they had spent four to seven months there. The agent told Santos that those aliens would remain in jail and eventually be deported anyway because it was difficult to obtain asylum. Santos later received legal help and was granted asylum and withholding of deportation. Jaime Rodriguez Alas told an INS agent that he was being persecuted in his country and could not go back. The agent told him that he could apply for asylum but it would take a long time and Alas would have to remain detained for possibly a year or more. Miguel Enrique Avila-Ochoa, arrested in 1985, testified that INS officers commented that aliens who asked for asylum would "remain in El Centro maybe for six months or a year and it would come to no good anyway."

In addition, although INS agents were required to give aliens the "*Orantes* advisal" along with Form I-274, the record shows that some agents did not even show aliens the advisal. This was testified to by Jose Salomon Morales, Quiro Jaime Navarro, Juan Alfonso Peralta Escoto, Maria Santos Madril, Jaime Rodriguez Alas, and Ana Marina Flores. Their testimony is uncontradicted.

The district court also faulted the INS for its lack of corrective measures following the entry of the preliminary injunction, pointing out the lack of training, lack of discipline, and lack of uniform policies and procedures for processing aliens. *See Orantes II*, 685 F.Supp. at 1495–96, 1499–1500, findings 46–47, 49–50, 82–86. These findings also have full support in the record.

Harry F. Malone has been the supervisory detention and deportation officer at El Centro since March of 1981. His duties include ensuring that procedures at El Centro comport with INS regulations and policies. Malone testified that his supervisor, the district director, had never engaged in any formal review of the practices and procedures of El Centro to ensure that they comport with national policies and practices governing the operation of the center.

Jeffrey Parsons, a Border Patrol Agent in Calexico, testified that he did not recall attending classes where political asylum procedures and laws were discussed and that since attending the academy, he had not received any training or instruction on asylum procedures.

. . . .

There is, in short, a large volume of evidence in this record from both class members and INS agents documenting INS practices after the preliminary injunction was entered, including many episodes in which members of the plaintiff class experienced direct interference with their ability to apply for asylum.

The government's focus is not on the evidence of actual events, but rather on a claimed lack of statistical evidence to support the district court's finding "30" that the "vast majority of Salvadorans apprehended sign voluntary departure agreements. . . ." *Orantes II,* 685 F.Supp. at 1494, finding 30. The government does not dispute that this finding accurately describes the situation before the preliminary injunction but claims that it is not accurate with respect to the post-injunction era. The government, however, offers no evidence to refute its continuing accuracy.

The finding, when read in context, describes the situation throughout the litigation. The government stipulated in a pre-trial statement that, according to INS statistics for the period 1980 to April 1982, the majority of Salvadoran refugees who were arrested opted for voluntary departure. We do not find any basis for holding finding 30 to be clearly erroneous in the post-injunction period in light of the volume of evidence of the INS's conduct and plaintiff class members' experience after entry of the preliminary injunction. We cannot fault the plaintiffs for failing to produce exclusively post-injunction statistical evidence which the INS itself apparently did not maintain and has not produced.

In sum, the record consisting of evidence from both members of the plaintiff class and INS agents during the post-injunction period fully supports the district court's findings that there was continued INS interference with plaintiff class members' exercise of their right to apply for political asylum.

. . . .

VI. The District Court's Findings With Respect to INS Interference With the Right to Counsel

The permanent injunction dealt not only with the right to apply for asylum, but also with the related right to consult with counsel. The INA provides aliens a right to be represented by counsel at no expense to the government. *See* INA § 292, 8 U.S.C. § 1362 (1988). Regulations adopted to effectuate this section require INS officials to notify aliens of their right to counsel and the availability of free legal services programs, 8 C.F.R. § 242.1(c) (1990), and to maintain a current list of such programs and provide the list to aliens, *id.* §§ 292a.1, 292a.2. The regulations also expressly require that juvenile detainees must be given access to a telephone and cannot be presented with a voluntary departure form until they have communicated with a parent, adult relative, friend, or organization on the free legal services list. *Id.* § 242.24(g). *See Perez-Funez v. INS,* 619 F.Supp. 656, 670 (C.D.Cal.1985).

Some of the district court's most detailed findings faulted the government for the nature of the legal services lists provided to Salvadorans, pointing out that many did not contain accurate telephone numbers and that many of the offices were not located in the vicinity where the alien was being detained. *See Orantes II,* 685 F. Supp. at 1497–98, finding 67. Further, the district court found that the lists were not always provided or available to aliens during processing and that the INS routinely failed to make these lists available at detention centers. *See id.* at 1498, findings 71–72. These findings are also fully supported by testimony from many of the class members.

. . . .

Several immigration advocates undertook investigations to determine the accuracy of the legal services lists. The testimony of Juan Rascon provides but one example of the result of these investigations. Rascon found that of the eight organizations on the Arizona district's list, one had gone out of business a year before, three had no phone numbers listed, and one out-of-state organization's phone number was listed but not the area code. Of the two organizations Rascon was able to contact, neither represented Central Americans in asylum proceedings.

The government does not dispute the substance of these findings, but argues that the findings are "premised on a mistaken view of INS's legal obligations" because the pertinent regulation, 8 C.F.R. § 292a.2, requires only that INS provide lists containing organizations that provide "free legal services to indigent aliens." The government asks us to excuse the inaccuracies in the lists because legal services organizations typically do not inform INS of their changes in address, and the government asks us to find that INS had valid reasons for not including certain organizations on the list.

The government's contentions miss the mark. The district court's findings with respect to the legal services lists were but part of a series of findings which went to the ability of Salvadorans to exercise their constitutional and statutory right to counsel at non-government expense. These findings show that the faulty lists were but the first of numerous obstacles, the cumulative effect of which was to prevent aliens from contacting counsel and receiving any legal advice. Most of the findings are undisputed.

For example, the district court found that INS agents did not allow Salvadorans to consult with counsel before signing for voluntary departure. *See Orantes II,* 685 F.Supp. at 1495, finding 43. This finding is supported by the testimony of class members. . . .

The court also found that aliens were frequently detained far from where potential counsel or existing counsel were located. *See Orantes II,* 685 F.Supp. at 1500, finding 87. The government does not challenge this finding. The district court found that limited attorney visitation hours at several detention centers, long delays in bringing detainees to interviews, the inadequacy of systems used to apprise detainees of the presence of their attorneys, and INS's inadequate efforts to ensure the privacy of both in-person and telephonic attorney-client interviews interfered with the attorney-client relationship. *See id.* at 1501, findings 102–03. These findings are not challenged.

The government does challenge the district court's finding that INS routinely does not notify attorneys that their clients have been transferred. *Id.* at 1500, finding 94. Our review of the record leads us to conclude that the testimony in support of this finding is substantial.

Formal representation of an alien does not occur until counsel files a Form G-28, "Notice of Entry of Appearance as Attorney or Representative," with the INS. A number of immigration advocates testified that clients for whom they had filed Form G-28 were frequently transferred to remote detention centers without any notice to counsel. . . .

There were, in addition, extensive findings in this case on access to libraries and legal materials which are also not disputed. The district court found that detainees have no meaningful access to basic written legal materials, that the INS confiscated legal materials provided detainees by counsel or refugee organizations, that neither processing centers nor detention facilities had comprehensive law libraries, either in English or Spanish, and that the use of writing materials was restricted or banned at a number of detention facilities. *See Orantes II*, 685 F.Supp. at 1501–02, findings 105–109, 111.

. . . .

With respect to telephones, the district court found that processing officers deny class members access to telephones until after processing, and that despite the preliminary injunction in this case, INS continues to process aliens at locations where telephones are not available to them. *See id.* at 1497, findings 65–66. It also found detainee access to telephones at eight detention centers was severely limited due to time restrictions, the number of functioning telephones and restrictive INS procedures; that detained Salvadorans experienced difficulty reaching counsel when using collect call telephones; and, that the system of informing detainees of attorneys' phone calls was not reliable. *See id.* at 1502, finding 112.

The government does not dispute the fact that aliens are not provided access to telephones at some processing centers, but only challenges its significance. Telephones are important in detention centers because, given the pattern of INS misconduct, the only opportunity the alien may have to learn of rights and options in lieu of voluntary departure is by contacting an attorney or relative. The government makes no challenge to the other findings regarding telephones.

In sum, the record demonstrates that the provisions of the district court's injunction designed to ensure access to counsel were appropriate remedies for a pattern of practices which severely impeded class members from communicating with counsel.

. . . .

VIII. Conclusion

After careful study of the record in this case based upon the government's challenges to the district court's findings of fact, we conclude the challenged findings are not clearly erroneous. The district court's entry of this injunction, which makes permanent the preliminary injunction entered in 1982, was not an abuse of discretion.

AFFIRMED.

Notes and Questions

1. In footnote 5, not included here, the court stated:

Article 1.2 of the UN Protocol defines a "refugee" as an individual who

> owing to a well-founded fear of being persecuted, for reasons of race, religion, nationality, membership in a particular social group or political opinion, is outside the country of his nationality and is unable or, owing to such fear, is unwilling to avail himself of the protection of that country; or who, not having a nationality and being outside the country of former habitual residence, is unable or, owing to such fear, is unwilling to return to it.

See also UNHCR: THE UN REFUGEE AGENCY, CONVENTION AND PROTOCOL RELATING TO THE STATUS OF REFUGEES 14 (Dec. 2010), http://www.unhcr.org/en-us /3b66c2aa10.

2. In footnote 9, the court explained:

The INA provides two procedural paths by which deportable aliens may remain in this country to avoid persecution in another country. The first path is to apply for a grant of asylum pursuant to section 208 of the Act, 8 U.S.C. § 1158 (1988). In order to qualify for asylum, an alien must meet the definition of "refugee" as defined in the INA. *Stevic,* 467 U.S. at 423 n. 18, 104 S.Ct. 2497 n. 18. The alien must show a "well-founded fear" of persecution based on one of the five statutorily impermissible bases. *See* INA § 208(a), 8 U.S.C. § 1158(a) (1988); INA § 101(a)(42)(A), 8 U.S.C. § 1101(a) (42)(A) (1988). Even if an alien satisfies the definition of a refugee, he is not automatically granted asylum; the decision to grant a particular application rests in the discretion of the Attorney General granted under INA § 208(a). *Id.* § 1158(a).

The second path by which deportable aliens presently within the United States may remain here to avoid persecution is to apply for withholding of deportation. *See* INA § 243(h), 8 U.S.C. § 1253(h) (1988). To qualify for withholding, an alien must show a "clear probability" of persecution as opposed to the "well-founded fear" required for asylum. INA § 243(h), 8 U.S.C. § 1253(h) (1988). *See Cardoza-Fonseca,* 480 U.S. at 423, 107 S.Ct. at 1208–09, *Bolanos-Hernandez v. INS,* 767 F.2d 1277, 1281–82 (9th Cir.1984). Unlike the discretionary standard governing requests for asylum, however, if an alien qualifies for withholding, the Attorney General is prohibited from deporting the alien. *See Stevic,* 467 U.S. at 421 n. 15, 104 S.Ct. at 2496 n. 15; *Bolanos-Hernandez,* 767 F.2d at 1281–82. Asylum and withholding of deportation decisions made by immigration judges and reviewed by the Board of Immigration Appeals are subject to direct review by courts of appeal. *See* INA §§ 106(a), 242(b), 8 U.S.C. §§ 1105a(a), 1252(b) (1988).

3. What are the substantive liberty interests accorded to minors not afforded to other immigrants? What policy justifications underlie these distinctions?

Chapter 7

Disability Rights and Litigation

Law as power and reflection of the status quo:

> I used to have a service dog for a disability that didn't present itself out-wardly (he could sense when I was going to have a bradycardic episode and pass out before it happen, his official title was neurological response dog) anyway, it was horrible. I actually needed him but people treated me like [expletive]. I couldn't walk into a single business, get on the bus, go any-where with him without being stopped and hostilely questioned. It kind of turned me into a shut in, its emotionally tiring enough dealing with being sick all the time without dealing with [expletive] too.
>
> Some people in manual wheelchairs see them as an extension of their body—so pushing someone is as weird and infantilizing as picking up a stranger and carrying them.
>
> Years ago I had just finished working. I was putting the tools in the van when a man came by in an old wheel chair. We were on a very steep hill with a very broken and uneven sidewalk. The guy was really struggling to make his way along. I looked up the long shitty hill and thought he's going to have a really tough time. I didn't know if I should ask if he wanted an assist? Should I just start pushing and try to be funny asking "so . . . Where are we going today?" And keep pushing. In the end, I think I just asked if he wanted any help? He stopped completely. Slowly looking me up and down he asks if I have a whole bunch of money I can give him? I told him the truth which was "nope!" He chuckled and said he was good. Then slowly made his way up that nasty hill on a miserably hot summers day. I don't know why, but I wish he would've let me give him a push up the hill. I also don't know why I think of that little exchange so often. It had to have been at least twenty-five years ago! But it's almost always on my mind.[1]

A large segment of the population suffers from these disability-related issues or remains impacted by the act of caring for loved ones with a disability. Still, although disability is a common issue, it is one that is still difficult to integrate into main-stream concerns.

---

1. *A powerful reddit thread reveals what it's like to have a disability,* http://www.washington post.com/blogs/wonkblog/wp/2015/04/24/a-powerful-reddit-thread-reveals-what-its-like-to-be-disabled/.

The above testimonies were excerpted from an internet thread sharing the experiences of persons with disabilities and the failure of the mainstream population to view them as multi-dimensional human beings. If, as we've seen throughout this coverage, law is indeed a reflection of who is in power, rather than mere logic, then the story and cases of persons with disabilities in this country show that we have a long way to go to overcome that status quo. Persons with a disability make up almost 1/5 (about 56.7 million) of this country's population, with an estimate that undiagnosed cases make that number even higher.[2] Though disability affects all, no matter race, creed or social background, poor communities and communities of color are the most vulnerable, neglected, and make up a great deal of undiagnosed cases. In addition, much more needs to be done to address the issues related to mental disability plaguing millions of Americans.[3] And, for all of the unreported cases, millions more lack access to adequate health care. Even less has been done to provide for the additional millions who serve as caretakers and support system for these individuals.

In light of this, what then does the disability litigation landscape look like? Imagine needing to go to the courthouse to handle a business matter. Let's say you are a new homeowner and need to register your deed at the courthouse where the property is located. Imagine also that you have a disability, which confines you to a wheelchair. When you arrive at the courthouse to handle what you think is this simple matter, you are confronted with an elaborate set of stairs with no access constructed for wheel chairs and other forms of disability. What is more, there is no one around to help. And, even if there were people around whom you could ask, your sense of dignity is already assaulted by the dependency reinforced by the layout of the entrance. But, you still need to register your deed. So, you decide that the only way available to get into the building is for you to crawl your way up the entrance. So you do.

This might seem like a hyperbolic fact pattern. Tragically, it is not. This was the case for the plaintiff in *Tennessee v. Lane*, 541 U.S. 509 (2004), one of the pivotal

---

2. See *Nearly 1 in 5 People Have a Disability in the U.S., Census Bureau Reports*, https://www
.census.gov/newsroom/releases/archives/miscellaneous/cb12-134.html, reporting that "About 56.7
million people — 19 percent of the population — had a disability in 2010, according to a broad definition of disability, with more than half of them reporting the disability was severe . . . The report,
Americans with Disabilities: 2010, presents estimates of disability status and type and is the first
such report with analysis since the Census Bureau published statistics in a similar report about the
2005 population of people with disabilities. According to the report, the total number of people
with a disability increased by 2.2 million over the period, but the percentage remained statistically
unchanged. Both the number and percentage with a severe disability rose, however. Likewise, the
number and percentage needing assistance also both increased."
3. Bekiempis, Victoria. *Nearly 1 in 5 Americans Suffers From Mental Illness Each Year,* Newsweek. (February 28, 2014), http://www.newsweek.com/nearly-1-5-americans-suffer-mental-illness
-each-year-230608. See also for statistics and cost of untreated mental illness the homepage for the
National Alliance on Mental Illness at http://www.nami.org/Learn-More/Mental-Health-By-the
-Numbers.

cases of the disability rights canon, who was confronted with this reality when he attempted to enter a courthouse to conduct his affairs. As such, Mr. Lane represented the ideal test case for illustrating the indignities that persons with disabilities routinely endure.[4] We will see more on Mr. Lane and the case's contribution for viable avenues for legal remedies against public entities later in this coverage.

Still, as the cases in this chapter illustrate, the history of persons with disabilities in this country belie claims of law as anything but a reflection of the status quo. Disability is one of the most sweeping issues of our society. Its ramifications are pervasive and affect a huge number of Americans, Yet, until just four decades ago, not only were there few laws protecting individuals with disabilities, but persons with disabilities were targeted and often imprisoned as unsightly, ugly and disturbers of the peace.[5] So called "ugly" or "vagrancy" laws were directed at persons with physical disabilities, summarily placing them in jail or fining them if they were found in public places. In essence, for the poor and the otherly abled, their very being was deemed to be a legal violation. Though "ugly" laws were widely repealed not so long ago, vagrancy and loitering statutes are still routinely used to pick up and remove homeless, poor and disabled individuals from public places.[6]

For many, these three elements conflate in ways that make them routine victims of assaults by uniformed members of the public and law enforcement alike. Consider an example: "No person who is diseased, maimed, mutilated or in any way deformed so as to be an unsightly or disgusting object or improper person to be allowed in or on the public ways or other public places in this city, or shall therein or thereon expose himself to public view, under a penalty of not less than one dollar nor more than fifty dollars for each offense." (Former Chicago Municipal Code, sec. 36034.) These types of laws were deliberately drafted to keep people viewed as "deformed" and "unsightly" from public view. What is more, a number of them were not repealed until the 1970s. Not only did these laws ostracize and penalize individuals for being disabled, but in many cities, they gave citizens standing to arrest, report, or otherwise neutralize individuals they viewed as unsightly. It is also important to note that, though no longer in effect, vestiges of these laws remain throughout the nation in the form of vagrancy and "tramp" statutes, punishing beggars, who may or may not be disabled in similar fashion as the "ugly" laws.

---

4. Centers for Disease Control and Prevention, *Common Barriers to Participation Experienced by People with Disabilities,* https://www.cdc.gov/ncbddd/disabilityandhealth/disability-barriers.html.

5. Susan M. Schweik, The Ugly Laws: Disability in Public (New York U, 2009). *See also* Elizabeth Greiwe, *How an 'ugly law' stayed on Chicago's books for 93 years,* Chicago Tribune (June 23, 2016), http://www.chicagotribune.com/news/opinion/commentary/ct-ugly-laws-disabilities-chicago-history-flashback-perspec-0626-md-20160622-story.html.

6. Tasha Tsiaperas, *Tent City closed, so where do Dallas' homeless go from here,* Dallas News, http://www.dallasnews.com/news/news/2016/05/13/tent-city-closed-so-where-do-dallas-homeless-go-from-here; Laura Smith, *Denver Isn't the Only City Seizing Homeless People's Gear,* Mother Jones (December 16, 2016), http://www.motherjones.com/politics/2016/12/denver-homeless-survival-gear-seizures.

Furthermore, persons with mental or neurological disabilities were often incapacitated under awful conditions in state and private sponsored institutions.[7] To support the passage of the Americans with Disabilities Act (the "ADA"), the most sweeping civil rights statute protecting persons with disabilities, Congress documented systematic practices, neglect and harm conducted by state officials against persons with disability. It took a long time and the newfound awareness of the sanctity of civil liberties brought by the Civil Rights Movement to usher in better treatment of individuals with disabilities. However, as you consider the laws studied here, examine the cases and the role of courts in limiting scope of disability rights, consider whether we have really done all we can to address disability-related issues.

A. The Social Environment

Think, for example, about the perceptions attached to mental disability. Is it still viewed today as a stigma that could cause one to lose one's job and standing in society rather than a condition in need of treatment like any other? Think about your acquaintances, your communities: how many cases of mental disability might you be aware of that remain untreated? What would these individuals'/families' lives be with proper and ongoing treatment? What is the source of the stigma associated with disability? Are we a society dying to be so perfect that we remain blind to these issues? What laws would you design to protect and serve non-conforming individuals?

In thinking about these questions, consider the following cases, *Buck v. Bell* and *City of Cleburne*, two cases that capture, in different ways, social reluctance to respect and fully support the dignity of people with disabilities. First, Carrie Buck comes to the court challenging a Virginia statute that would force her to be sterilized based on a determination that she is classified as "feeble minded." Justice Holmes's treatment of this case and of Carrie lives down in infamy as one of our ugliest judicial legacies.[8] In the annals of legal history, next to Justice Taney's infamous statement in Dred Scott, stands Justice Holmes' statement in condoning the sterilization of Carrie, that "three generations of imbeciles is enough."[9]

These attitudes and barriers are unfortunately far from dead. In a 2012 report issued by the Census Bureau, it is documented that "41 percent of those age 21 to 64 with any disability were employed, compared with 79 percent of those with no disability. Along with the lower likelihood of having a job came the higher likelihood

---

7. *See Nellie's Madhouse Memoir,* detailing Nellie Bly's undercover investigation of a New York insane asylum in 1887. Online at http://www.pbs.org/wgbh/amex/world/sfeature/memoir.html. *See also Timeline: Treatments for Mental Illness, American Experience—A Brilliant Madness: Timeline 1992–2002,* PBS. 6 Nov. 2007, http://www.pbs.org/wgbh/amex/nash/timeline/index.html.

8. Erwin Chemerinsky, The Case against the Supreme Court (Viking, 2014).

9. Buck v. Bell, 274 U.S. 200, 207 (1927).

of experiencing persistent poverty; that is, continuous poverty over a 24-month period. Among people age 15 to 64 with severe disabilities, 10.8 percent experienced persistent poverty; the same was true for 4.9 percent of those with a non-severe disability and 3.8 percent of those with no disability."[10] Knowing this, then, part of the task of rectifying ills against persons with disabilities is to eliminate attitudes and biases that prevent them from meaningful access to employment, services and accommodation. See *Buck v. Bell* and *City of Cleburne* below for a reminder of how entrenched these stereotypical attitudes can be.

Buck v. Bell

274 U.S. 200 (1927)

MR. JUSTICE HOLMES delivered the opinion of the Court.

This is a writ of error to review a judgment of the Supreme Court of Appeals of the State of Virginia, affirming a judgment of the Circuit Court of Amherst County, by which the defendant in error, the superintendent of the State Colony for Epileptics and Feeble Minded, was ordered to perform the operation of salpingectomy upon Carrie Buck, the plaintiff in error, for the purpose of making her sterile. 143 Va. 310, 130 S. E. 516. The case comes here upon the contention that the statute authorizing the judgment is void under the Fourteenth Amendment as denying to the plaintiff in error due process of law and the equal protection of the laws.

Carrie Buck is a feeble-minded white woman who was committed to the State Colony above mentioned in due form. She is the daughter of a feeble-minded mother in the same institution, and the mother of an illegitimate feeble-minded child. She was eighteen years old at the time of the trial of her case in the Circuit Court in the latter part of 1924. An Act of Virginia approved March 20, 1924 (Laws 1924, c. 394) recites that the health of the patient and the welfare of society may be promoted in certain cases by the sterilization of mental defectives, under careful safeguard, etc.; that the sterilization may be effected in males by vasectomy and in females by salpingectomy, without serious pain or substantial danger to life; that the Commonwealth is supporting in various institutions many defective persons who if now discharged would become a menace but if incapable of procreating might be discharged with safety and become self-supporting with benefit to themselves and to society; and that experience has shown that heredity plays an important part in the transmission of insanity, imbecility, etc. The statute then enacts that whenever the superintendent of certain institutions including the above named State Colony shall be of opinion that it is for the best interest of the patients and of society that an inmate under his care should be sexually sterilized, he may have the operation performed upon any patient afflicted

---

10. United States Census Bureau, *Nearly 1 in 5 People Have a Disability in the U.S., Census Bureau Reports*, (July 25, 2012), https://www.census.gov/newsroom/releases/archives/miscellaneous/cb12 -134.html.

with hereditary forms of insanity, imbecility, etc., on complying with the very careful provisions by which the act protects the patients from possible abuse.

. . . .

The attack is not upon the procedure but upon the substantive law. It seems to be contended that in no circumstances could such an order be justified. It certainly is contended that the order cannot be justified upon the existing grounds. The judgment finds the facts that have been recited and that Carrie Buck 'is the probable potential parent of socially inadequate offspring, likewise afflicted, that she may be sexually sterilized without detriment to her general health and that her welfare and that of society will be promoted by her sterilization,' and thereupon makes the order. In view of the general declarations of the Legislature and the specific findings of the Court obviously we cannot say as matter of law that the grounds do not exist, and if they exist they justify the result. We have seen more than once that the public welfare may call upon the best citizens for their lives. It would be strange if it could not call upon those who already sap the strength of the State for these lesser sacrifices, often not felt to be such by those concerned, in order to prevent our being swamped with incompetence. It is better for all the world, if instead of waiting to execute degenerate offspring for crime, or to let them starve for their imbecility, society can prevent those who are manifestly unfit from continuing their kind. The principle that sustains compulsory vaccination is broad enough to cover cutting the Fallopian tubes. *Jacobson v. Massachusetts*, 197 U. S. 11, 25 S. Ct. 358, 49 L. Ed. 643, 3 Ann. Cas. 765. Three generations of imbeciles are enough.

But, it is said, however it might be if this reasoning were applied generally, it fails when it is confined to the small number who are in the institutions named and is not applied to the multitudes outside. It is the usual last resort of constitutional arguments to point out shortcomings of this sort. But the answer is that the law does all that is needed when it does all that it can, indicates a policy, applies it to all within the lines, and seeks to bring within the lines all similarly situated so far and so fast as its means allow. Of course so far as the operations enable those who otherwise must be kept confined to be returned to the world, and thus open the asylum to others, the equality aimed at will be more nearly reached.

Judgment affirmed.

City of Cleburne v. Cleburne Living Center, Inc.

473 U.S. 432 (1985)

JUSTICE WHITE delivered the opinion of the Court.

A Texas city denied a special use permit for the operation of a group home for the mentally retarded, acting pursuant to a municipal zoning ordinance requiring permits for such homes. The Court of Appeals for the Fifth Circuit held that mental retardation is a "quasi-suspect" classification and that the ordinance violated the Equal Protection Clause because it did not substantially further an important governmental purpose. We hold that a lesser standard of scrutiny is appropriate, but conclude that under that standard the ordinance is invalid as applied in this case.

I

In July 1980, respondent Jan Hannah purchased a building at 201 Featherston Street in the city of Cleburne, Texas, with the intention of leasing it to Cleburne Living Center, Inc. (CLC), for the operation of a group home for the mentally retarded. It was anticipated that the home would house 13 retarded men and women, who would be under the constant supervision of CLC staff members. The house had four bedrooms and two baths, with a half bath to be added. CLC planned to comply with all applicable state and federal regulations.

The city informed CLC that a special use permit would be required for the operation of a group home at the site, and CLC accordingly submitted a permit application. In response to a subsequent inquiry from CLC, the city explained that under the zoning regulations applicable to the site, a special use permit, renewable annually, was required for the construction of "[h]ospitals for the insane or feeble-minded, or alcoholic [*sic*] or drug addicts, or penal or correctional institutions."

The city had determined that the proposed group home should be classified as a "hospital for the feebleminded." After holding a public hearing on CLC's application, the City Council voted 3 to 1 to deny a special use permit.

CLC then filed suit in Federal District Court against the city and a number of its officials, alleging, *inter alia,* that the zoning ordinance was invalid on its face and as applied because it discriminated against the mentally retarded in violation of the equal protection rights of CLC and its potential residents. [T]he District Court held the ordinance and its application constitutional. Concluding that no fundamental right was implicated and that mental retardation was neither a suspect nor a quasi-suspect classification, the court employed the minimum level of judicial scrutiny applicable to equal protection claims. . . .

The Court of Appeals for the Fifth Circuit reversed, determining that mental retardation was a quasi-suspect classification and that it should assess the validity of the ordinance under intermediate-level scrutiny. 726 F.2d 191 (1984). Because mental retardation was in fact relevant to many legislative actions, strict scrutiny was not appropriate. But in light of the history of "unfair and often grotesque mistreatment" of the retarded, discrimination against them was "likely to reflect deep-seated prejudice." *Id.,* at 197. In addition, the mentally retarded lacked political power, and their condition was immutable. The court considered heightened scrutiny to be particularly appropriate in this case, because the city's ordinance withheld a benefit which, although not fundamental, was very important to the mentally retarded. Without group homes, the court stated, the retarded could never hope to integrate themselves into the community. Applying the test that it considered appropriate, the court held that the ordinance was invalid on its face because it did not substantially further any important governmental interests. . . .

II

The Equal Protection Clause of the Fourteenth Amendment commands that no State shall "deny to any person within its jurisdiction the equal protection of the laws," which is essentially a direction that all persons similarly situated should be treated alike. *Plyler v. Doe*, 457 U.S. 202, 216, 102 S.Ct. 2382, 2394, 72 L.Ed.2d 786 (1982). Section 5 of the Amendment empowers Congress to enforce this mandate, but absent controlling congressional direction, the courts have themselves devised standards for determining the validity of state legislation or other official action that is challenged as denying equal protection. The general rule is that legislation is presumed to be valid and will be sustained if the classification drawn by the statute is rationally related to a legitimate state interest. . . .

The general rule gives way, however, when a statute classifies by race, alienage, or national origin. These factors are so seldom relevant to the achievement of any legitimate state interest that laws grounded in such considerations are deemed to reflect prejudice and antipathy—a view that those in the burdened class are not as worthy or deserving as others. For these reasons and because such discrimination is unlikely to be soon rectified by legislative means, these laws are subjected to strict scrutiny and will be sustained only if they are suitably tailored to serve a compelling state interest. *McLaughlin v. Florida*, 379 U.S. 184, 192, 85 S.Ct. 283, 288, 13 L. Ed.2d 222 (1964); *Graham v. Richardson*, 403 U.S. 365, 91 S.Ct. 1848, 29 L.Ed.2d 534 (1971). Similar oversight by the courts is due when state laws impinge on personal rights protected by the Constitution. *Kramer v. Union Free School District No. 15*, 395 U.S. 621, 89 S.Ct. 1886, 23 L.Ed.2d 583 (1969); *Shapiro v. Thompson*, 394 U.S. 618, 89 S.Ct. 1322, 22 L.Ed.2d 600 (1969); *Skinner v. Oklahoma ex rel. Williamson*, 316 U.S. 535, 62 S.Ct. 1110, 86 L.Ed. 1655 (1942).

Legislative classifications based on gender also call for a heightened standard of review. That factor generally provides no sensible ground for differential treatment. "[W]hat differentiates sex from such nonsuspect statuses as intelligence or physical disability . . . is that the sex characteristic frequently bears no relation to ability to perform or contribute to society." *Frontiero v. Richardson*, 411 U.S. 677, 686, 93 S. Ct. 1764, 1770, 36 L.Ed.2d 583 (1973) (plurality opinion). Rather than resting on meaningful considerations, statutes distributing benefits and burdens between the sexes in different ways very likely reflect outmoded notions of the relative capabilities of men and women. A gender classification fails unless it is substantially related to a sufficiently important governmental interest. *Mississippi University for Women v. Hogan*, 458 U.S. 718, 102 S.Ct. 3331, 73 L.Ed.2d 1090 (1982); *Craig v. Boren*, 429 U.S. 190, 97 S.Ct. 451, 50 L.Ed.2d 397 (1976). Because illegitimacy is beyond the individual's control and bears "no relation to the individual's ability to participate in and contribute to society," *Mathews v. Lucas*, 427 U.S. 495, 505, 96 S.Ct. 2755, 2762, 49 L.Ed.2d 651 (1976), official discriminations resting on that characteristic are also subject to somewhat heightened review. Those restrictions "will survive equal protection scrutiny to the extent they are substantially related to a legitimate state interest." *Mills v. Habluetzel*, 456 U.S. 91, 99, 102 S.Ct. 1549, 1554, 71 L.Ed.2d 770 (1982).

We have declined, however, to extend heightened review to differential treatment based on age: . . . [W]here individuals in the group affected by a law have distinguishing characteristics relevant to interests the State has the authority to implement, the courts have been very reluctant, as they should be in our federal system and with our respect for the separation of powers, to closely scrutinize legislative choices as to whether, how, and to what extent those interests should be pursued. In such cases, the Equal Protection Clause requires only a rational means to serve a legitimate end.

III

Against this background, we conclude for several reasons that the Court of Appeals erred in holding mental retardation a quasi-suspect classification calling for a more exacting standard of judicial review than is normally accorded economic and social legislation. First, it is undeniable, and it is not argued otherwise here, that those who are mentally retarded have a reduced ability to cope with and function in the everyday world. Nor are they all cut from the same pattern: as the testimony in this record indicates, they range from those whose disability is not immediately evident to those who must be constantly cared for. They are thus different, immutably so, in relevant respects, and the States' interest in dealing with and providing for them is plainly a legitimate one. How this large and diversified group is to be treated under the law is a difficult and often a technical matter, very much a task for legislators guided by qualified professionals and not by the perhaps ill-informed opinions of the judiciary. Heightened scrutiny inevitably involves substantive judgments about legislative decisions, and we doubt that the predicate for such judicial oversight is present where the classification deals with mental retardation.

Second, the distinctive legislative response, both national and state, to the plight of those who are mentally retarded demonstrates not only that they have unique problems, but also that the lawmakers have been addressing their difficulties in a manner that belies a continuing antipathy or prejudice and a corresponding need for more intrusive oversight by the judiciary. Thus, the Federal Government has not only outlawed discrimination against the mentally retarded in federally funded programs, see § 504 of the Rehabilitation Act of 1973, 29 U.S.C. § 794, but it has also provided the retarded with the right to receive "appropriate treatment, services, and habilitation" in a setting that is "least restrictive of [their] personal liberty." Developmental Disabilities Assistance and Bill of Rights Act, 42 U.S.C. §§ 6010(1), (2). In addition, the Government has conditioned federal education funds on a State's assurance that retarded children will enjoy an education that, "to the maximum extent appropriate," is integrated with that of nonmentally retarded children. Education of the Handicapped Act, 20 U.S.C. § 1412(5)(B). The Government has also facilitated the hiring of the mentally retarded into the federal civil service by exempting them from the requirement of competitive examination. See 5 CFR § 213.3102(t) (1984). The State of Texas has similarly enacted legislation that acknowledges the special status of the mentally retarded by conferring certain rights upon them, such as "the right to live in the least restrictive setting appropriate to [their] individual needs and abilities," including "the right to live . . . in a group home." Mentally Retarded Persons Act of 1977, Tex.Rev.Civ.Stat.Ann., Art. 5547-300, § 7 (Vernon Supp.1985).

Such legislation thus singling out the retarded for special treatment reflects the real and undeniable differences between the retarded and others. That a civilized and decent society expects and approves such legislation indicates that governmental consideration of those differences in the vast majority of situations is not only legitimate but also desirable. It may be, as CLC contends, that legislation designed to benefit, rather than disadvantage, the retarded would generally withstand examination under a test of heightened scrutiny. See Brief for Respondents 38–41. The relevant inquiry, however, is whether heightened scrutiny is constitutionally mandated in the first instance. Even assuming that many of these laws could be shown to be substantially related to an important governmental purpose, merely requiring the legislature to justify its efforts in these terms may lead it to refrain from acting at all. Much recent legislation intended to benefit the retarded also assumes the need for measures that might be perceived to disadvantage them. The Education of the Handicapped Act, for example, requires an "appropriate" education, not one that is equal in all respects to the education of nonretarded children; clearly, admission to a class that exceeded the abilities of a retarded child would not be appropriate. Similarly, the Developmental Disabilities Assistance Act and the Texas Act give the retarded the right to live only in the "least restrictive setting" appropriate to their abilities, implicitly assuming the need for at least some restrictions that would not be imposed on others. Especially given the wide variation in the abilities and needs of the retarded themselves, governmental bodies must have a certain amount of flexibility and freedom from judicial oversight in shaping and limiting their remedial efforts.

Third, the legislative response, which could hardly have occurred and survived without public support, negates any claim that the mentally retarded are politically powerless in the sense that they have no ability to attract the attention of the lawmakers. Any minority can be said to be powerless to assert direct control over the legislature, but if that were a criterion for higher level scrutiny by the courts, much economic and social legislation would now be suspect.

Fourth, if the large and amorphous class of the mentally retarded were deemed quasi-suspect for the reasons given by the Court of Appeals, it would be difficult to find a principled way to distinguish a variety of other groups who have perhaps immutable disabilities setting them off from others, who cannot themselves mandate the desired legislative responses, and who can claim some degree of prejudice from at least part of the public at large. One need mention in this respect only the aging, the disabled, the mentally ill, and the infirm. We are reluctant to set out on that course, and we decline to do so.

Doubtless, there have been and there will continue to be instances of discrimination against the retarded that are in fact invidious, and that are properly subject to judicial correction under constitutional norms. But the appropriate method of reaching such instances is not to create a new quasi-suspect classification and subject all governmental action based on that classification to more searching evaluation.

Rather, we should look to the likelihood that governmental action premised on a particular classification is valid as a general matter, not merely to the specifics of the case before us. Because mental retardation is a characteristic that the government may legitimately take into account in a wide range of decisions, and because both State and Federal Governments have recently committed themselves to assisting the retarded, we will not presume that any given legislative action, even one that disadvantages retarded individuals, is rooted in considerations that the Constitution will not tolerate.

Our refusal to recognize the retarded as a quasi-suspect class does not leave them entirely unprotected from invidious discrimination. To withstand equal protection review, legislation that distinguishes between the mentally retarded and others must be rationally related to a legitimate governmental purpose. This standard, we believe, affords government the latitude necessary both to pursue policies designed to assist the retarded in realizing their full potential, and to freely and efficiently engage in activities that burden the retarded in what is essentially an incidental manner. The State may not rely on a classification whose relationship to an asserted goal is so attenuated as to render the distinction arbitrary or irrational. See *Zobel v. Williams,* 457 U.S. 55, 61–63, 102 S.Ct. 2309, 2313–2314, 72 L.Ed.2d 672 (1982); *United States Dept. of Agriculture v. Moreno,* 413 U.S. 528, 535, 93 S.Ct. 2821, 2826, 37 L.Ed.2d 782 (1973). Furthermore, some objectives—such as "a bare . . . desire to harm a politically unpopular group," *id.,* at 534, 93 S.Ct., at 2826—are not legitimate state interests. See also *Zobel, supra,* 457 U.S., at 63, 102 S.Ct., at 2314. Beyond that, the mentally retarded, like others, have and retain their substantive constitutional rights in addition to the right to be treated equally by the law.

IV

We turn to the issue of the validity of the zoning ordinance insofar as it requires a special use permit for homes for the mentally retarded. We inquire first whether requiring a special use permit for the Featherston home in the circumstances here deprives respondents of the equal protection of the laws. If it does, there will be no occasion to decide whether the special use permit provision is facially invalid where the mentally retarded are involved, or to put it another way, whether the city may never insist on a special use permit for a home for the mentally retarded in an R-3 zone. This is the preferred course of adjudication since it enables courts to avoid making unnecessarily broad constitutional judgments. *Brockett v. Spokane Arcades, Inc.,* 472 U.S. 491, 501–502, 105 S.Ct. 2794, —, 86 L.Ed.2d 394 (1985); *United States v. Grace,* 461 U.S. 171, 103 S.Ct. 1702, 75 L.Ed.2d 736 (1983); *NAACP v. Button,* 371 U.S. 415, 83 S.Ct. 328, 9 L.Ed.2d 405 (1963).

The constitutional issue is clearly posed. The city does not require a special use permit in an R-3 zone for apartment houses, multiple dwellings, boarding and lodging houses, fraternity or sorority houses, dormitories, apartment hotels, hospitals, sanitariums, nursing homes for convalescents or the aged (other than for the insane or feebleminded or alcoholics or drug addicts), private clubs or fraternal orders, and other specified uses. It does, however, insist on a special permit for the Featherston home, and it does so, as the District Court found, because it would be a facility for the mentally retarded. May the city require the permit for this facility when other care and multiple-dwelling facilities are freely permitted?

It is true, as already pointed out, that the mentally retarded as a group are indeed different from others not sharing their misfortune, and in this respect they may be different from those who would occupy other facilities that would be permitted in an R-3 zone without a special permit. But this difference is largely irrelevant unless the Featherston home and those who would occupy it would threaten legitimate interests of the city in a way that other permitted uses such as boarding houses and hospitals would not. Because in our view the record does not reveal any rational basis for believing that the Featherston home would pose any special threat to the city's legitimate interests, we affirm the judgment below insofar as it holds the ordinance invalid as applied in this case.

. . . .

In the courts below the city also urged that the ordinance is aimed at avoiding concentration of population and at lessening congestion of the streets. These concerns obviously fail to explain why apartment houses, fraternity and sorority houses, hospitals and the like, may freely locate in the area without a permit. So, too, the expressed worry about fire hazards, the serenity of the neighborhood, and the avoidance of danger to other residents fail rationally to justify singling out a home such as 201 Featherston for the special use permit, yet imposing no such restrictions on the many other uses freely permitted in the neighborhood.

The short of it is that requiring the permit in this case appears to us to rest on an irrational prejudice against the mentally retarded, including those who would occupy the Featherston facility and who would live under the closely supervised and highly regulated conditions expressly provided for by state and federal law.

The judgment of the Court of Appeals is affirmed insofar as it invalidates the zoning ordinance as applied to the Featherston home. The judgment is otherwise vacated, and the case is remanded.

It is so ordered.

. . . .

JUSTICE MARSHALL, with whom JUSTICE BRENNAN and JUSTICE BLACKMUN join, concurring in the judgment in part and dissenting in part.

The Court holds that all retarded individuals cannot be grouped together as the "feebleminded" and deemed presumptively unfit to live in a community. Underlying this holding is the principle that mental retardation *per se* cannot be a proxy for depriving retarded people of their rights and interests without regard to variations in individual ability. With this holding and principle I agree. The Equal Protection Clause requires attention to the capacities and needs of retarded people as individuals.

I cannot agree, however, with the way in which the Court reaches its result or with the narrow, as-applied remedy it provides for the city of Cleburne's equal protection violation. The Court holds the ordinance invalid on rational-basis grounds and disclaims that anything special, in the form of heightened scrutiny, is taking place. Yet Cleburne's ordinance surely would be valid under the traditional rational-basis test applicable to economic and commercial regulation. In my view, it is important to articulate, as the Court does not, the facts and principles that justify subjecting this zoning ordinance to the searching review—the heightened scrutiny—that actually leads to its invalidation. Moreover, in invalidating Cleburne's exclusion of the "feebleminded" only as applied to respondents, rather than on its face, the Court radically departs from our equal protection precedents. Because I dissent from this novel and truncated remedy, and because I cannot accept the Court's disclaimer that no "more exacting standard" than ordinary rational-basis review is being applied, *ante,* at 3256, I write separately.

I

At the outset, two curious and paradoxical aspects of the Court's opinion must be noted. First, because the Court invalidates Cleburne's zoning ordinance on rational-basis grounds, the Court's wide-ranging discussion of heightened scrutiny is wholly superfluous to the decision of this case. This "two for the price of one" approach to constitutional decision-making—rendering two constitutional rulings where one is enough to decide the case—stands on their head traditional and deeply embedded principles governing exercise of the Court's Article III power. Just a few weeks ago, the Court "call[ed] to mind two of the cardinal rules governing the federal courts: 'One, never to anticipate a question of constitutional law in advance of the necessity of deciding it; the other never to formulate a rule of constitutional law broader than is required by the precise facts to which it is to be applied.'" *Brockett v. Spokane Arcades, Inc.,* 472 U.S. 491, 501, 105 S.Ct. 2794,—, 86 L.Ed.2d 394 (1985) (White, J.) (quoting *Liverpool, New York & Philadelphia S.S. Co. v. Commissioners of Emigration,* 113 U.S. 33, 39, 5 S.Ct. 352, 355, 28 L.Ed. 899 (1885)). When a lower court correctly decides a case, albeit on what this Court concludes are unnecessary constitutional grounds, "our usual custom" is not to compound the problem by following suit but rather to affirm on the narrower, dispositive ground available. *Alexander v. Louisiana,* 405 U.S. 625, 633, 92 S.Ct. 1221, 1226, 31 L.Ed.2d 536 (1972). The Court offers no principled justification for departing from these principles, nor, given our equal protection precedents, could it. See *Mississippi University for Women v. Hogan,* 458 U.S. 718, 724, n. 9, 102 S.Ct. 3331, 3336, n. 9, 73 L.Ed.2d 1090 (1982) (declining to address strict scrutiny when heightened scrutiny sufficient to invalidate action challenged); *Stanton v. Stanton,* 421 U.S. 7, 13, 95 S.Ct. 1373, 1377, 43 L.Ed.2d 688 (1975) same); *Hooper v. Bernalillo County Assessor,* 472 U.S. 612, 618, 105 S.Ct. 2862,—, 86 L.Ed.2d 487 (1985) (declining to reach heightened scrutiny in review of residency-based classifications that fail rational-basis test); *Zobel v. Williams,* 457 U.S. 55, 60–61, 102 S.Ct. 2309, 2312–2313, 72 L.Ed.2d 672 (1982) (same); cf. *Mitchell v. Forsyth,* 472 U.S. 511, 537–538, 105 S.Ct. 2806,—, 86 L.Ed.2d 411 (1985) (O'Connor, J., concurring in part).

Second, the Court's heightened-scrutiny discussion is even more puzzling given that Cleburne's ordinance is invalidated only after being subjected to precisely the sort of probing inquiry associated with heightened scrutiny. To be sure, the Court does not label its handiwork heightened scrutiny, and perhaps the method employed must hereafter be called "second order" rational-basis review rather than "heightened scrutiny." But however labeled, the rational basis test invoked today is most assuredly not the rational-basis test of *Williamson v. Lee Optical of Oklahoma, Inc.,* 348 U.S. 483, 75 S.Ct. 461, 99 L.Ed. 563 (1955), *Allied Stores of Ohio, Inc. v. Bowers,* 358 U.S. 522, 79 S.Ct. 437, 3 L.Ed.2d 480 (1959), and their progeny.

. . . .

I share the Court's criticisms of the overly broad lines that Cleburne's zoning ordinance has drawn. But if the ordinance is to be invalidated for its imprecise classifications, it must be pursuant to more powerful scrutiny than the minimal rational-basis test used to review classifications affecting only economic and commercial matters. The same imprecision in a similar ordinance that required opticians but not optometrists to be licensed to practice, see *Williamson v. Lee Optical of Oklahoma, Inc., supra,* or that excluded new but not old businesses from parts of a community, see *New Orleans v. Dukes, supra,* would hardly be fatal to the statutory scheme.

The refusal to acknowledge that something more than minimum rationality review is at work here is, in my view, unfortunate in at least two respects. The suggestion that the traditional rational-basis test allows this sort of searching inquiry creates precedent for this Court and lower courts to subject economic and commercial classifications to similar and searching "ordinary" rational-basis review — a small and regrettable step back toward the days of *Lochner v. New York,* 198 U.S. 45, 25 S.Ct. 539, 49 L.Ed. 937 (1905). Moreover, by failing to articulate the factors that justify today's "second order" rational-basis review, the Court provides no principled foundation for determining when more searching inquiry is to be invoked. Lower courts are thus left in the dark on this important question, and this Court remains unaccountable for its decisions employing, or refusing to employ, particularly searching scrutiny. Candor requires me to acknowledge the particular factors that justify invalidating Cleburne's zoning ordinance under the careful scrutiny it today receives.

II

I have long believed the level of scrutiny employed in an equal protection case should vary with "the constitutional and societal importance of the interest adversely affected and the recognized invidiousness of the basis upon which the particular classification is drawn." *San Antonio Independent School District v. Rodriguez,* 411 U.S. 1, 99, 93 S.Ct. 1278, 1330, 36 L.Ed.2d 16 (1973) (Marshall, J., dissenting). See also *Plyler v. Doe,* 457 U.S. 202, 230–231, 102 S.Ct. 2382, 2401–2402, 72 L.Ed.2d 786 (1982) (Marshall, J., concurring); *Dandridge v. Williams,* 397 U.S. 471, 508, 90 S.Ct. 1153, 1173, 25 L.Ed.2d 491 (1970) (Marshall, J., dissenting). When a zoning ordinance works to exclude the retarded from all residential districts in a community, these two considerations require that the ordinance be convincingly justified as substantially furthering legitimate and important purposes. *Plyler, supra; Mississippi University for Women v. Hogan,* 458 U.S. 718, 102 S.Ct. 3331, 73 L.Ed.2d 1090 (1982); *Frontiero v. Richardson,* 411 U.S. 677, 93 S.Ct. 1764, 36 L.Ed.2d 583 (1973); *Mills v. Habluetzel,* 456 U.S. 91, 102 S.Ct. 1549, 71 L.Ed.2d 770 (1982); see also *Buchanan v. Warley,* 245 U.S. 60, 38 S.Ct. 16, 62 L.Ed. 149 (1917).

First, the interest of the retarded in establishing group homes is substantial. The right to "establish a home" has long been cherished as one of the fundamental liberties embraced by the Due Process Clause. See *Meyer v. Nebraska,* 262 U.S. 390, 399, 43 S.Ct. 625, 626, 67 L.Ed. 1042 (1923). For retarded adults, this right means living together in group homes, for as deinstitutionalization has progressed, group homes have become the primary means by which retarded adults can enter life in the community. The District Court found as a matter of fact that

> "[t]he availability of such a home in communities is an essential ingredient of normal living patterns for persons who are mentally retarded, and each factor that makes such group homes harder to establish operates to exclude persons who are mentally retarded from the community." App. to Pet. for Cert. A-8.

Excluding group homes deprives the retarded of much of what makes for human freedom and fulfillment — the ability to form bonds and take part in the life of a community.

Second, the mentally retarded have been subject to a "lengthy and tragic history," *University of California Regents v. Bakke,* 438 U.S. 265, 303, 98 S.Ct. 2733, 2755, 57 L. Ed.2d 750 (1978) (opinion of Powell, J.), of segregation and discrimination that can only be called grotesque. During much of the 19th century, mental retardation was viewed as neither curable nor dangerous and the retarded were largely left to their own devices. By the latter part of the century and during the first decades of the new one, however, social views of the retarded underwent a radical transformation. Fueled by the rising tide of Social Darwinism, the "science" of eugenics, and the extreme xenophobia of those years, leading medical authorities and others began to portray the "feeble-minded" as a "menace to society and civilization . . . responsible in a large degree for many, if not all, of our social problems." A regime of state-mandated segregation and degradation soon emerged that in its virulence and bigotry rivaled, and indeed paralleled, the worst excesses of Jim Crow. Massive custodial institutions were built to warehouse the retarded for life; the aim was to halt reproduction of the retarded and "nearly extinguish their race." Retarded children were categorically excluded from public schools, based on the false stereotype that all were ineducable and on the purported need to protect nonretarded children from them. State laws deemed the retarded "unfit for citizenship."

Segregation was accompanied by eugenic marriage and sterilization laws that extinguished for the retarded one of the "basic civil rights of man" — the right to marry and procreate. *Skinner v. Oklahoma ex rel. Williamson,* 316 U.S. 535, 541, 62 S.Ct. 1110,

1113, 86 L.Ed. 1655 (1942). Marriages of the retarded were made, and in some States continue to be, not only voidable but also often a criminal offense. The purpose of such limitations, which frequently applied only to women of child-bearing age, was unabashedly eugenic: to prevent the retarded from propagating. To assure this end, 29 States enacted compulsory eugenic sterilization laws between 1907 and 1931. J. Landman, Human Sterilization 302–303 (1932). See *Buck v. Bell,* 274 U.S. 200, 207, 47 S.Ct. 584, 584, 71 L.Ed. 1000 (1927) (Holmes, J.); cf. *Plessy v. Ferguson,* 163 U.S. 537, 16 S.Ct. 1138, 41 L.Ed. 256 (1896); *Bradwell v. Illinois,* 16 Wall. 130, 141, 21 L.Ed. 442 (1873) (Bradley, J., concurring in judgment).

Prejudice, once let loose, is not easily cabined. See *University of California Regents v. Bakke,* 438 U.S. 265, 395, 98 S.Ct. 2733, 2801, 57 L.Ed.2d 750 (opinion of Marshall, J.). As of 1979, most States still categorically disqualified "idiots" from voting, without regard to individual capacity and with discretion to exclude left in the hands of low-level election officials. Not until Congress enacted the Education of the Handicapped Act, 84 Stat. 175, as amended, 20 U.S.C. § 1400 *et seq.,* were "the door[s] of public education" opened wide to handicapped children. *Hendrick Hudson District Board of Education v. Rowley,* 458 U.S. 176, 192, 102 S.Ct. 3034, 3043, 73 L.Ed.2d 690 (1982). But most important, lengthy and continuing isolation of the retarded has perpetuated the ignorance, irrational fears, and stereotyping that long have plagued them.

In light of the importance of the interest at stake and the history of discrimination the retarded have suffered, the Equal Protection Clause requires us to do more than review the distinctions drawn by Cleburne's zoning ordinance as if they appeared in a taxing statute or in economic or commercial legislation. The searching scrutiny I would give to restrictions on the ability of the retarded to establish community group homes leads me to conclude that Cleburne's vague generalizations for classifying the "feeble-minded" with drug addicts, alcoholics, and the insane, and excluding them where the elderly, the ill, the boarder, and the transient are allowed, are not substantial or important enough to overcome the suspicion that the ordinance rests on impermissible assumptions or outmoded and perhaps invidious stereotypes. See *Plyler v. Doe,* 457 U.S. 202, 102 S.Ct. 2382, 72 L.Ed.2d 786 (1982); *Roberts v. United States Jaycees,* 468 U.S. 609, 104 S.Ct. 3244, 82 L.Ed.2d 462 (1984); *Mississippi University for Women v. Hogan,* 458 U.S. 718, 102 S.Ct. 3331, 73 L.Ed.2d 1090 (1982); *Mills v. Habluetzel,* 456 U.S. 91, 102 S.Ct. 1549, 71 L.Ed.2d 770 (1982).

. . . .

In my view, the Court's remedial approach is both unprecedented in the equal protection area and unwise. This doctrinal change of course was not sought by the parties, suggested by the various *amici,* or discussed at oral argument. Moreover, the Court does not persuasively reason its way to its novel remedial holding nor reconsider our prior cases directly on point. Instead, the Court simply asserts that "this is the preferred course of adjudication." Given that this assertion emerges only from today's decision, one can only hope it will not become entrenched in the law without fuller consideration.

V

The Court's opinion approaches the task of principled equal protection adjudication in what I view as precisely the wrong way. The formal label under which an equal protection claim is reviewed is less important than careful identification of the interest at stake and the extent to which society recognizes the classification as an invidious one. Yet in focusing obsessively on the appropriate label to give its standard of review, the Court fails to identify the interests at stake or to articulate the principle that classifications based on mental retardation must be carefully examined to assure they do not rest on impermissible assumptions or false stereotypes regarding individual ability and need. No guidance is thereby given as to when the Court's freewheeling, and potentially dangerous, "rational-basis standard" is to be employed, nor is attention directed to the invidiousness of grouping all retarded individuals together. Moreover, the Court's narrow, as-applied remedy fails to deal adequately with the overbroad presumption that lies at the heart of this case. Rather than leaving future retarded individuals to run the gauntlet of this overbroad presumption, I would affirm the judgment of the Court of Appeals in its entirety and would strike down on its face the provision at issue. I therefore concur in the judgment in part and dissent in part.

Notes and Questions

1. As documented above, much of the history of neglect and the discrimination experienced by persons with disabilities are based on long standing stereotypes. In addition, our society seems to struggle with any person or group viewed as nonconforming. As we explore the legal and civil rights advancements in this area, evaluate whether we have yet adopted the right perspective and approach for resolving disability issues. In other words, to what extent are our laws and their implementation still influenced by society's limited view of the potential contributions of persons with disabilities? In so doing, consider Michael Stein's call for a Human Rights based approach to disability which goes beyond mere access and legal remedies, but embraces the full dignity and holistic dimensions of persons with disabilities. *See* Michael Stein, *Disability Human Rights*, 95 CALIF. L. REV. 75 (2007).

2. Does the zoning law in *Cleburne* seem farfetched today? Are there parallels to today's local and national approaches?

3. How do you assess Justice Marshall's critique of the three tiers of scrutiny? Is his approach more honest and more effective? What do you think of his proposal for reviewing equal protection claims? Does Marshall's concurrence give fodder and support to those who criticize the three tiers of scrutiny and their application by the Court in the last few decades?

4. The above cases serve as examples of social attitudes toward individuals with disabilities at two different time periods. As a result, the following congressional findings as part of the American Disability Act of 1990 (as Amended by the ADA Amendments Act of 2008) should come as no surprise:

The Congress finds that —

(1) physical or mental disabilities in no way diminish a person's right to fully participate in all aspects of society, yet many people with physical or mental disabilities have been precluded from doing so because of discrimination; others who have a record of a disability or are regarded as having a disability also have been subjected to discrimination;

(2) historically, society has tended to isolate and segregate individuals with disabilities, and, despite some improvements, such forms of discrimination against individuals with disabilities continue to be a serious and pervasive social problem;

(3) discrimination against individuals with disabilities persists in such critical areas as employment, housing, public accommodations, education, transportation, communication, recreation, institutionalization, health services, voting, and access to public services;

(4) unlike individuals who have experienced discrimination on the basis of race, color, sex, national origin, religion, or age, individuals who have experienced discrimination on the basis of disability have often had no legal recourse to redress such discrimination;

(5) individuals with disabilities continually encounter various forms of discrimination, including outright intentional exclusion, the discriminatory effects of architectural, transportation, and communication barriers, overprotective rules and policies, failure to make modifications to existing facilities and practices, exclusionary qualification standards and criteria, segregation, and relegation to lesser services, programs, activities, benefits, jobs, or other opportunities;

(6) census data, national polls, and other studies have documented that people with disabilities, as a group, occupy an inferior status in our society, and are severely disadvantaged socially, vocationally, economically, and educationally;

(7) the Nation's proper goals regarding individuals with disabilities are to assure equality of opportunity, full participation, independent living, and economic self-sufficiency for such individuals; and

(8) the continuing existence of unfair and unnecessary discrimination and prejudice denies people with disabilities the opportunity to compete on an equal basis and to pursue those opportunities for which our free society is justifiably famous, and costs the United States billions of dollars in unnecessary expenses resulting from dependency and non-productivity.

5. Should we all be doing more socially to remedy discrimination against persons with disabilities? For example, how much of our language and common expressions could be interpreted as conveying contempt for persons with disabilities? Consider the majority's use of "mental retardation", commonly used at the time, compared to today's deliberate use of "intellectual disability."

6. Based on Cleburne, how would you argue today for heightened scrutiny for persons with disabilities? How would your arguments fare, in light of precedents, when applied to characteristics yet to be recognized?

B. The Statutory Era

It was not until the 1970s that we began to see meaningful changes in treatment and perceptions of persons with disabilities. Before 1973, legal efforts to protect them were scarce and shallow. In all, they tended to mirror social attitudes and views of disabled individuals as less than a person. With activism and growing understanding, laws protecting persons with disabilities were enacted. *Southeastern Community College v. Davis*, below, highlights the importance of the Rehabilitation Act of 1973[11] as a precursor to what we now know as the modern legal landscape for disability rights. Unlike prior limited statutes — the Social Security Act of 1935 (giving certain rights to medical services to disabled children), the La-Follette Barden Act of 1943, and the Vocational Rehabilitation Act of 1954 (providing employment rehabilitation to disabled individuals over the age of 15) — the Rehabilitation Act of 1973 was much broader and extensive in its reach. In that fact, it constitutes the most significant precursor to modern statutes like the ADA and the Individuals with Disabilities Education Act (IDEA). As a result, the Rehabilitation Act is still a viable source of protection, particularly in its unique function burdening recipients of federal funds.

The essential parts of the Rehabilitation Act consist of sections 501, 503 and 504. Section 501 anticipates Title I of the ADA by prohibiting federal agencies and contractors from discriminating against people with disabilities in employment and requiring them to develop affirmative action programs.[12] Section 504 extends beyond the federal employment context by prohibiting discrimination in any programs receiving federal funding.[13] The statute also allows for monetary damage awards, though punitive damages are limited to employment discrimination cases.[14] The statute is modeled after procedures in Title VII and Title VI for employment and remedies provided under Title VI for claims related to public services.[15] Furthermore, Section 504 expressly abrogates state immunity. Additionally, the Act also strengthens the protections in transportation by creating a board in Section 502 (Transportation Barriers Compliance Board) to enforce the Architectural barriers Act of 1968.

---

11. 29 U.S.C. § 701.
12. 29 U.S.C. § 791.
13. 29 U.S.C. § 794.
14. 29 U.S.C. § 794a.
15. 42 U.S.C. § 2000d et seq.

Consequently, though the later and more comprehensive ADA and IDEA became more frequent bases of litigation, the Rehabilitation Act remains a viable and useful source of protection. *Davis* below demonstrates a more serious approach to disability issues by the Court and Congress post-Civil Rights Movement than there ever was in our jurisprudence up to that point.

Also note that the definition of disability serves as a common basis between the Rehabilitation Act and later statutes, like the American Disabilities Act."

Southeastern Community College v. Davis
442 U.S. 397 (1979)

MR. JUSTICE POWELL delivered the opinion of the Court.

This case presents a matter of first impression for this Court: Whether § 504 of the Rehabilitation Act of 1973, which prohibits discrimination against an "otherwise qualified handicapped individual" in federally funded programs "solely by reason of his handicap," forbids professional schools from imposing physical qualifications for admission to their clinical training programs.

Respondent, who suffers from a serious hearing disability, seeks to be trained as a registered nurse. During the 1973–1974 academic year she was enrolled in the College Parallel program of Southeastern Community College, a state institution that receives federal funds. Respondent hoped to progress to Southeastern's Associate Degree Nursing program, completion of which would make her eligible for state certification as a registered nurse. In the course of her application to the nursing program, she was interviewed by a member of the nursing faculty. It became apparent that respondent had difficulty understanding questions asked, and on inquiry she acknowledged a history of hearing problems and dependence on a hearing aid. She was advised to consult an audiologist.

On the basis of an examination at Duke University Medical Center, respondent was diagnosed as having a "bilateral, sensori-neural hearing loss." App. 127a. A change in her hearing aid was recommended, as a result of which it was expected that she would be able to detect sounds "almost as well as a person would who has normal hearing." *Id.*, at 127a-128a. But this improvement would not mean that she could discriminate among sounds sufficiently to understand normal spoken speech. Her lip reading skills would remain necessary for effective communication: "While wearing the hearing aid, she is well aware of gross sounds occurring in the listening environment. However, she can only be responsible for speech spoken to her, when the talker gets her attention and allows her to look directly at the talker." *Id.*, at 128a.

Southeastern next consulted Mary McRee, Executive Director of the North Carolina Board of Nursing. On the basis of the audiologist's report, McRee recommended that respondent not be admitted to the nursing program. In McRee's view, respondent's hearing disability made it unsafe for her to practice as a nurse. In addition, it would be impossible for respondent to participate safely in the normal clinical training program, and those modifications that would be necessary to enable safe participation would prevent her from realizing the benefits of the program: "To adjust patient learning experiences in keeping with respondent's hearing limitations could, in fact, be the same as denying her full learning to meet the objectives of your nursing programs." *Id.*, at 132a-133a.

After respondent was notified that she was not qualified for nursing study because of her hearing disability, she requested reconsideration of the decision. The entire nursing staff of Southeastern was assembled, and McRee again was consulted. McRee repeated her conclusion that on the basis of the available evidence, respondent "has hearing limitations which could interfere with her safely caring for patients." *Id.*, at 139a. Upon further deliberation, the staff voted to deny respondent admission.

Respondent then filed suit in the United States District Court for the Eastern District of North Carolina, alleging both a violation of § 504 of the Rehabilitation Act of 1973, 87 Stat. 394, as amended, 29 U.S.C. 794 (1976 ed., Supp. II), and a denial of equal protection and due process. After a bench trial, the District Court entered judgment in favor of Southeastern. 424 F.Supp. 1341 (1976). It confirmed the findings of the audiologist that even with a hearing aid respondent cannot understand speech directed to her except through lip reading, and further found:

> "In many situations such as an operation room intensive care unit, or post-natal care unit, all doctors and nurses wear surgical masks which would make lip reading impossible. Additionally, in many situations a Registered Nurse would be required to instantly follow the physician's instructions concerning procurement of various types of instruments and drugs where the physician would be unable to get the nurse's attention by other than vocal means." *Id.*, at 1343.

Accordingly, the court concluded:

> "Respondent's handicap actually prevents her from safely performing in both her training program and her proposed profession. The trial testimony indicated numerous situations where respondent's particular disability would render her unable to function properly. Of particular concern to the court in this case is the potential of danger to future patients in such situations." *Id.*, at 1345.

Based on these findings, the District Court concluded that respondent was not an "otherwise qualified handicapped individual" protected against discrimination by § 504. In its view, "otherwise qualified, can only be read to mean otherwise able to function sufficiently in the position sought in spite of the handicap, if proper training and facilities are suitable and available." 424 F.Supp., at 1345. Because respondent's disability would prevent her from functioning "sufficiently" in Southeastern's nursing program, the court held that the decision to exclude her was not discriminatory within the meaning of § 504.

On appeal, the Court of Appeals for the Fourth Circuit reversed. 574 F.2d 1158 (1978). It did not dispute the District Court's findings of fact, but held that the court had misconstrued § 504. In light of administrative regulations that had been promulgated while the appeal was pending, see 42 Fed.Reg. 22676 (1977), the appellate court believed that § 504 required Southeastern to "reconsider plaintiff's application for admission to the nursing program without regard to her hearing ability." 574 F.2d, at 1160. It concluded that the District Court had erred in taking respondent's handicap into account in determining whether she was "otherwise qualified" for the program, rather than confining its inquiry to her "academic and technical qualifications." *Id.,* at 1161. The Court of Appeals also suggested that § 504 required "affirmative conduct" on the part of Southeastern to modify its program to accommodate the disabilities of applicants, "even when such modifications become expensive." 574 F.2d, at 1162.

Because of the importance of this issue to the many institutions covered by § 504, we granted certiorari. 439 U.S. 1065, 99 S.Ct. 830, 59 L.Ed.2d 30 (1979). We now reverse.

As previously noted, this is the first case in which this Court has been called upon to interpret § 504. It is elementary that "the starting point in every case involving construction of a statute is the language itself." *Blue Chip Stamps v. Manor Drug Stores,* 421 U.S. 723, 756, 95 S.Ct. 1917, 1935, 44 L.Ed.2d 539 (1975) (Powell, J., concurring); see *Greyhound Corp. v. Mt. Hood Stages, Inc.,* 437 U.S. 322, 330, 98 S.Ct. 2370, 2375, 57 L.Ed.2d 239 (1978); *Santa Fe Industries, Inc. v. Green,* 430 U.S. 462, 472, 97 S.Ct. 1292, 1300, 51 L.Ed.2d 480 (1977). Section 504 by its terms does not compel educational institutions to disregard the disabilities of handicapped individuals or to make substantial modifications in their programs to allow disabled persons to participate. Instead, it requires only that an "otherwise qualified handicapped individual" not be excluded from participation in a federally funded program "solely by reason of his handicap," indicating only that mere possession of a handicap is not a permissible ground for assuming an inability to function in a particular context. The court below, however, believed that the "otherwise qualified" persons protected by § 504 include those who would be able to meet the requirements of a particular program in every respect except as to limitations imposed by their handicap. See 574 F.2d, at 1160. Taken literally, this holding would prevent an institution from taking into account any limitation resulting from the handicap, however disabling. It assumes, in effect, that a person need not meet legitimate physical requirements in order to be "otherwise qualified." We think the understanding of the District Court is closer to the plain meaning of the statutory language. An otherwise qualified person is one who is able to meet all of a program's requirements in spite of his handicap.

The regulations promulgated by the Department of HEW to interpret § 504 reinforce, rather than contradict, this conclusion. According to these regulations, a "qualified handicapped person" is, "with respect to postsecondary and vocational education services, a handicapped person who meets the academic and technical standards requisite to admission or participation in the school's education program or activity . . . ." 45 CFR § 84.3(k)(3) (1978). An explanatory note states:

"The term 'technical standards' refers to *all* nonacademic admissions criteria that are essential to participation in the program in question." 45 CFR
pt. 84, App. A, p. 405 (1978) (emphasis supplied).

A further note emphasizes that legitimate physical qualifications may be essential to
participation in particular programs. We think it clear, therefore, that HEW inter-
prets the "other" qualifications which a handicapped person may be required to
meet as including necessary physical qualifications.

III

The remaining question is whether the physical qualifications Southeastern
demanded of respondent might not be necessary for participation in its nursing
program. It is not open to dispute that, as Southeastern's Associate Degree Nursing
program currently is constituted, the ability to understand speech without reliance
on lip reading is necessary for patient safety during the clinical phase of the program. As the District Court found, this ability also is indispensable for many of the
functions that a registered nurse performs.

Respondent contends nevertheless that §504, properly interpreted, compels
Southeastern to undertake affirmative action that would dispense with the need
for effective oral communication. First, it is suggested that respondent can be given
individual supervision by faculty members whenever she attends patients directly.
Moreover, certain required courses might be dispensed with altogether for respondent. It is not necessary, she argues, that Southeastern train her to undertake all the
tasks a registered nurse is licensed to perform. Rather, it is sufficient to make §504
applicable if respondent might be able to perform satisfactorily some of the duties
of a registered nurse or to hold some of the positions available to a registered nurse.

Respondent finds support for this argument in portions of the HEW regulations
discussed above. In particular, a provision applicable to postsecondary educational
programs requires covered institutions to make "modifications" in their programs
to accommodate handicapped persons, and to provide "auxiliary aids" such as sign-
language interpreters Respondent argues that this regulation imposes an obligation
to ensure full participation in covered programs by handicapped individuals and,
in particular, requires Southeastern to make the kind of adjustments that would be
necessary to permit her safe participation in the nursing program.

We note first that on the present record it appears unlikely respondent could
benefit from any affirmative action that the regulation reasonably could be interpreted as requiring. Section 84.44(d)(2), for example, explicitly excludes "devices
or services of a personal nature" from the kinds of auxiliary aids a school must
provide a handicapped individual. Yet the only evidence in the record indicates that
nothing less than close, individual attention by a nursing instructor would be sufficient to ensure patient safety if respondent took part in the clinical phase of the
nursing program. See 424 F.Supp., at 1346. Furthermore, it also is reasonably clear
that §84.44(a) does not encompass the kind of curricular changes that would be

necessary to accommodate respondent in the nursing program. In light of respondent's inability to function in clinical courses without close supervision, Southeastern, with prudence, could allow her to take only academic classes. Whatever benefits respondent might realize from such a course of study, she would not receive even a rough equivalent of the training a nursing program normally gives. Such a fundamental alteration in the nature of a program is far more than the "modification" the regulation requires.

Moreover, an interpretation of the regulations that required the extensive modifications necessary to include respondent in the nursing program would raise grave doubts about their validity. If these regulations were to require substantial adjustments in existing programs beyond those necessary to eliminate discrimination against otherwise qualified individuals, they would do more than clarify the meaning of § 504. Instead, they would constitute an unauthorized extension of the obligations imposed by that statute.

The language and structure of the Rehabilitation Act of 1973 reflect a recognition by Congress of the distinction between the evenhanded treatment of qualified handicapped persons and affirmative efforts to overcome the disabilities caused by handicaps. Section 501(b), governing the employment of handicapped individuals by the Federal Government, requires each federal agency to submit "an affirmative action program plan for the hiring, placement, and advancement of handicapped individuals . . . ." These plans "shall include a description of the extent to which and methods whereby the special needs of handicapped employees are being met." Similarly, § 503(a), governing hiring by federal contractors, requires employers to "take affirmative action to employ and advance in employment qualified handicapped individuals . . . ." The President is required to promulgate regulations to enforce this section.

Under § 501(c) of the Act, by contrast, state agencies such as Southeastern are only "encouraged . . . to adopt and implement such policies and procedures." Section 504 does not refer at all to affirmative action, and except as it applies to federal employers it does not provide for implementation by administrative action. A comparison of these provisions demonstrates that Congress understood accommodation of the needs of handicapped individuals may require affirmative action and knew how to provide for it in those instances where it wished to do so.

Although an agency's interpretation of the statute under which it operates is entitled to some deference, "this deference is constrained by our obligation to honor the clear meaning of a statute, as revealed by its language, purpose, and history." *Teamsters v. Daniel*, 439 U.S. 551, 566 n. 20, 99 S.Ct. 790, 800 n. 20, 58 L.Ed.2d 808 (1979). Here, neither the language, purpose, nor history of § 504 reveals an intent to impose an affirmative-action obligation on all recipients of federal funds. Accordingly, we hold that even if HEW has attempted to create such an obligation itself, it lacks the authority to do so.

IV

We do not suggest that the line between a lawful refusal to extend affirmative action and illegal discrimination against handicapped persons always will be clear. It is possible to envision situations where an insistence on continuing past requirements and practices might arbitrarily deprive genuinely qualified handicapped persons of the opportunity to participate in a covered program. Technological advances can be expected to enhance opportunities to rehabilitate the handicapped or otherwise to qualify them for some useful employment. Such advances also may enable attainment of these goals without imposing undue financial and administrative burdens upon a State. Thus, situations may arise where a refusal to modify an existing program might become unreasonable and discriminatory. Identification of those instances where a refusal to accommodate the needs of a disabled person amounts to discrimination against the handicapped continues to be an important responsibility of HEW.

In this case, however, it is clear that Southeastern's unwillingness to make major adjustments in its nursing program does not constitute such discrimination. The uncontroverted testimony of several members of Southeastern's staff and faculty established that the purpose of its program was to train persons who could serve the nursing profession in all customary ways. See, e. g., App. 35a, 52a, 53a, 71a, 74a. This type of purpose, far from reflecting any animus against handicapped individuals is shared by many if not most of the institutions that train persons to render professional service. It is undisputed that respondent could not participate in Southeastern's nursing program unless the standards were substantially lowered. Section 504 imposes no requirement upon an educational institution to lower or to effect substantial modifications of standards to accommodate a handicapped person.

One may admire respondent's desire and determination to overcome her handicap, and there well may be various other types of service for which she can qualify. In this case, however, we hold that there was no violation of §504 when Southeastern concluded that respondent did not qualify for admission to its program. Nothing in the language or history of §504 reflects an intention to limit the freedom of an educational institution to require reasonable physical qualifications for admission to a clinical training program. Nor has there been any showing in this case that any action short of a substantial change in Southeastern's program would render unreasonable the qualifications it imposed.

V

Accordingly, we reverse the judgment of the court below, and remand for proceedings consistent with this opinion.

So ordered.

Notes and Questions

1. How does the Court apply the rules of statutory construction here to determine the scope and nature of obligations regarding affirmative action benefitting persons with disabilities?

2. Why is it significant, according to the Court, that Congress did not incorporate reference to "affirmative action" in Section 504, "except as applied to federal employers"?

3. Note the importance of the "qualification" prong in plaintiff's ability to make a successful claim of discrimination. How does the determination of "substantial change in the program" play a role in the qualification analysis? In other words, would plaintiff have been qualified had the Court determined the accommodations requested to be reasonable?

4. Is the Court's determination of the requested accommodation as a substantial change correct? Is the goal of statutes like the Rehabilitation Act to provide a floor of access to persons with disabilities or a ceiling? Are there any modifications you could envision that would maintain both the integrity of the program and provide access to the plaintiffs in this case?

C. The Americans with Disabilities Act

A number of statutes were enacted during the two decades preceding the Americans with Disabilities Act. The first iteration of the Individuals with Disabilities Education Act (formerly the Education for All Handicapped Children Act) protecting children at various stages of education, including infants and preschoolers, was passed in 1975. Others, like the Voting Accessibility for the Elderly and Handicapped Act (1973), made polling places more accessible to the disabled and elderly. In 1986, the Carrier Access Act added airlines as additional areas covered by anti-discrimination laws. Similarly, Fair Housing Amendment Acts protected persons with disabilities in rental and purchase of housing, also requiring access and reasonable accommodation.

Still, it was not until the American with Disabilities Act of 1990 that robust, and comprehensive, layered and far-reaching protections arrived. Congressional authority to pass the ADA rests on its authority to regulate items with substantial economic effects on commerce pursuant to the Commerce Clause and on its authority under Section 5 of the Fourteenth Amendment.

The ADA's main components are Title I, II and III. Title I prohibits discrimination in employment,[16] Title II affects provision of public services,[17] and Title III regulates public accommodations.[18] Title IV and V cover miscellaneous issues like attorney's fees, retaliation, sovereign immunity, etc.[19]

Title I regulates discrimination in the public and private sphere. It does not, however, replace Section 504 of the Rehabilitation Act. The two statutes operate

16. 42 U.S.C. §§ 12111–12117.
17. 42 U.S.C. §§ 12131–12165.
18. 42 U.S.C. §§ 12181–12189.
19. Title IV: 47 U.S.C. § 225; Title V: 42 U.S.C. §§ 12201–12213.

separately, because one deals with recipient of federal funding and the other squarely focuses on employment. Thus the term employer in Title I is independent of federal funding. Consequently, Title I adopts Title II's definition of a covered employer: "15 or more employees for more than 20 calendar weeks." As with Title VII, the EEOC enforces Title I.

Title II of the ADA regulates access to programs, activities and any services provided by public entities. It covers all aspects of local channels, including public universities, local governments, and public buildings and facilities. Title II follows the administrative procedures of Title VI and Section 504 of the Rehabilitation Act, which means that, unlike with Title I, plaintiffs may file directly in federal court.[20] *See* Department of Justice Regulations.[21] But plaintiffs may not recover punitive damages under Title II. Title II is modeled after Section 504 of the Rehabilitation Act (*Notice of Proposed Rulemaking*, https://www.ada.gov/regs2016/504_nprm.html).[22] Such classification makes Title II contingent on the Spending Clause's contractual framework. Regulations deemed to be based on the Spending Clause are interpreted to prohibit the federal government from allowing individuals to recover money damages against states in the absence of a state's consent. Regulations purporting to do so are scrutinized strictly by the courts. *Barnes v. Gorman*, 536 U.S. 181 (2002). But see *Tennessee v. Lane*, 541 U.S. 509 (2004), which allowed recovery against Tennessee because of interference with a fundamental constitutional right (DOJ regulations, https://www.ada.gov/regs2016/504_nprm.html).

Lastly, Title III protects against discrimination in public accommodations, including private businesses and commercial facilities. This means that Title III binds private entities in construction and access in similar fashion that it does public entities in Title II. Attorneys' fees and monetary damages are allowed in actions brought by the Attorney General—*i.e.*, in pattern and practice cases. Otherwise, private individuals are allowed injunctive relief and costs, and can sue directly in federal courts. Private entities that fall under Title II of the ADA, are also required to provide reasonable accommodations, along with meeting building standards for accessibility. Additionally, like in the Civil Rights Act of 1964, Title III exempts private clubs. [23]

---

20. "Title II incorporates the enforcement procedures of the Rehabilitation Act, . . . which do not require exhaustion of administrative remedies for non-federal employees." Ethridge v. State of Alabama, 847 F. Supp. 903, 907 (M.D. Ala. 2013) (citing Smith v.Barton, 914 F.2d 1330 (9th Cir.1990), cert. denied, 501 U.S. 1217, 111 S. Ct. 2825, 115 L. Ed. 2d 995 (1991); Pushkin v. Regents of the University of Colorado, 658 F.2d 1372 (10th Cir.1981); Ali v. City of Clearwater, 807 F. Supp. 701 (M.D.Fla.1992)).

21. 28 C.F.R. §§ 35.170–178.

22. See DOJ Regulations stating: "Title II of the ADA prohibits discrimination on the basis of disability by public entities (*i.e.*, State and local governments and their agencies) and is modeled on section 504. 42 U.S.C. 12132"https://www.ada.gov/regs2016/504_nprm.html.

23. 42 U.S.C. Section 2000 (a)(e).

These requirements are not without pushback. There exists, for example, fear that the regulations might be too costly for private individuals, or that frivolous lawsuits might be unjustifiably filed by individuals claiming discrimination. The cases below illustrate the rigorous standards applied by the Supreme Court in evaluating claims of discrimination. For example, the Court has taken seriously the "reasonable" portion of the reasonable accommodation provision, determining often that costs and change in the nature of the business might not be reasonable. In addition, part of the basis of an ADA claim contemplates the qualification of the plaintiff to avail herself of the services, access, programs etc. in question. Finally, safety and hazard risks in the employment context are all concerns and defenses outlined in the statute and which, if supported, can negate an ADA claim. As seen in this brief preview, the ADA is a complex and mammoth statute. As a result, parts of its administration are delegated to numerous agencies in addition to the EEOC: the Department of Justice and the Department of Transportation. Consequently, ADA regulations and agency rules are promulgated across various registers. Part of an attorney's ADA practice is to keep track of these various sources and to periodically consult them to make sure the attorney remains updated.

The Supreme Court's limiting interpretations of the ADA rules eventually led Congress to enact the 2008 Amendments to the ADA. *Sutton*, duplicated below, is now reversed by the Amendments. Still, it serves as a reminder of the interconnectedness of all branches of government when it comes to meaningful protection of persons with disabilities.

Martinson v. Kinney

104 F.3d 683 (4th Cir. 1997)

The district court concluded that an employer did not violate the Americans with Disabilities Act, 42 U.S.C. §§ 12101–12213 (1994), when it discharged a shoe salesman who suffered from epilepsy. *EEOC v. Kinney Shoe Corp.*, 917 F. Supp. 419 (W.D. Va. 1996). The district court's analysis was flawed in some respects but much of its reasoning and the court's ultimate holding were correct. Accordingly, we affirm.

Because the district court fully set forth the facts, *id.* at 422–24, we relate here only those necessary to understand our holding.

Harald Martinson worked for Kinney as a shoe salesman in a Winchester, Virginia shopping mall at various times between 1989 and 1992. In January 1992, Kinney rehired Martinson as a full-time salesperson. Martinson suffers from epilepsy, which was first diagnosed in 1967. During previous periods of employment with Kinney, Martinson had experienced seizures at work, and Kinney rehired him with the knowledge that seizures could occur. The seizures that Martinson experienced during the work day were usually similar to fainting spells; his body would collapse to the ground and he would appear to be sleeping. He would remain in this state for five to ten minutes, after which he would "awake" and take a twenty to forty-five minute break from work to compose himself. Other than "a bump or a scratch," Martinson has never injured himself or anyone else during any of his seizures over the past twenty-nine years. Furthermore, Martinson has not requested any accommodation other than tolerance of his seizures.

Kinney supervisors acknowledged that Martinson was a good salesman; he received two "Employee of the Month" awards, one just before his final dismissal. They also admitted that his "sales book" was "better than average." One of his managers testified that but for the seizures, Martinson was fully capable of performing his job; he was a reliable employee and had very good knowledge of the merchandise. Moreover, although Martinson's supervisors disagreed about this, one conceded that Martinson's seizures did not cause Kinney to lose customers.

Between January and July 1992, Martinson "guess [ed]" that he had approximately five seizures at work but he explained that he did not remember his seizures and so had to rely on others as to their occurrence; Kinney maintained that he had approximately sixteen. In July 1992, a Kinney manager warned Martinson that he would be fired if he "had another seizure." When Martinson did have another seizure, Kinney discharged him. On Martinson's employee separation report, Kinney District Sales Manager, Allen Bosworth, wrote that Martinson's discharge was attributable to "[s]eizures in store, sales floor, and stockroom. Inability to control timing of same."

The EEOC initiated this suit against Kinney on Martinson's behalf, and Martinson intervened. The district court held that while there were material issues of fact with regard to whether Martinson was qualified to do his job, Kinney was entitled to summary judgment because it had not engaged in "unlawful discrimination." *Id.* at 430.

Title I of the Americans with Disabilities Act (ADA) provides that "[n]o covered entity shall discriminate against a qualified individual with a disability because of the disability of such individual in regard to . . . discharge of employees . . . and other terms, conditions, and privileges of employment." 42 U.S.C. § 12112(a) (1994). Therefore, to establish a prima facie case of discriminatory firing, a plaintiff must prove: (1) he has a "disability;" (2) he is a "qualified individual;" and (3) in "discharg[ing]" him, his employer "discriminate [d] against [him] because of [his] disability." *Id.*; see also *Doe v. University of Maryland Med. Sys. Corp.*, 50 F.3d 1261, 1264–65 (4th Cir. 1995).

For purposes of summary judgment, the district court concluded that Martinson had a disability and thus the first prong of this test had been satisfied, a conclusion that Kinney does not contest at this stage. *Kinney*, 917 F. Supp. at 425. Further, the court determined that the EEOC and Martinson had met the second prong by producing sufficient evidence at least to raise an issue of fact as to whether Martinson was qualified for his job despite his seizures. *Id.* at 425–29. However, the district court concluded that the EEOC and Martinson could not carry their burden on the third prong of the prima facie test. *Id.* at 430–32. The court reasoned that since Kinney did not discharge Martinson because he suffered from the "general disability" of epilepsy but rather "because of the specific attributes of [Martinson's] specific form of the disability," i.e., his seizures, Martinson could not prevail on the third prong. *Id.* at 430–31.

The district court erred with regard to its conclusion as to the third prong. When an employer concededly discharges an employee because of a disability, the employee need prove nothing more to meet the third prong of the prima facie test. See *Rizzo v. Children's World Learning Ctrs.*, 84 F.3d 758, 762 (5th Cir. 1996). Kinney concededly discharged Martinson because of his" [s]eizures in store, sales floor, and stockroom" and his "[i]nability to control timing of same." To fire for seizures is to fire for a disability. Seizures are "a physical or mental impairment that substantially limits one or more of [Martinson's] major life activities," i.e., a disability. See 42 U.S.C. § 12102(2) (A) (defining disability). Whether Kinney fired Martinson because he suffered from epilepsy or because of the "specific attributes" of his disease, i.e., his seizures, is immaterial—both are disabilities and an employer may not use either to justify discharging an employee so long as that employee is qualified for the job. Thus, the undisputed facts demonstrate that Kinney discharged Martinson because of a disability. This is all the EEOC and Martinson must prove to satisfy the third prong of the prima facie test.

Although the district court erred with regard to the third prong, we can affirm if its decision was correct for any other reason. See, e.g., *McMahan v. International Ass'n of Bridge, Structural & Ornamental Iron Workers Local 601*, 964 F.2d 1462, 1467 (4th Cir. 1992). Here, we believe the district court was correct for another reason. Specifically, we believe the undisputed facts establish that Martinson was not qualified to perform at least one essential function of his position with Kinney.

To satisfy the second prong of the prima facie test, an ADA plaintiff must demonstrate that "with or without reasonable accommodation, [he] can perform the essential functions of the employment position." 42 U.S.C. § 12111(8) (defining "qualified individual with a disability"). The Kinney managers repeatedly testified that maintaining store security was an essential function of a Kinney salesperson's job. Martinson offered no evidence to the contrary. Thus, the undisputed evidence demonstrated and the district court properly recognized that this was "an inherent part of a shoe salesperson's job given that Kinney does not hire security guards." *Kinney*, 917 F. Supp. at 426. See 29 C.F.R. § 1630.2(n)(2)(ii) (explaining that a job "function may be essential because of the limited number of employees available among whom the performance of that job function can be distributed").

Just as the evidence was uncontroverted that providing security was an "essential function" of a Kinney salesperson's job, so too the evidence was uncontroverted that Martinson was not qualified to perform this function. Kinney offered uncontradicted evidence that normally the Winchester store was manned by only two or three employees and that at least on some occasions, Martinson was the sole employee in the public areas of the store—and so the only one available to provide security to the store and its merchandise. Moreover, Kinney District Sales Manager

Bosworth testified that even when another employee was present on the sales floor, Martinson's seizures would attract the other employee's concern and attention and thus distract that employee from "maintaining a vigilance on the floor to make sure that" a thief did not "come in, take something . . . and walk off with it."

In view of the involved factual record, it is perhaps unsurprising that in finding a material factual dispute as to whether Martinson could perform the "essential functions" of his position, the district court apparently did not focus on the significance of this undisputed evidence. Instead, the court remarked "[a] shoe salesman . . . is charged with selling shoes, a task which if compromised, simply leaves customers without shoes for a brief period." *Id.* at 426. However, in light of the uncontroverted fact that Martinson was, at times, solely responsible for the security of the store and its merchandise, it is clear that when a seizure compromised Martinson's tasks as a shoe salesman, one of the tasks compromised was the provision of store security. Safeguarding the store and its goods is a task that cannot reasonably be abandoned for even "a brief period."

Even if a person is unable to perform the essential functions of the job in question, a "court must nevertheless determine whether the person could do the job with reasonable accommodation." *Myers v. Hose*, 50 F.3d 278, 281–82 (4th Cir. 1995) (citations omitted); see also *Doe*, 50 F.3d at 1264–66. Martinson never requested any accommodation (other than tolerance of his seizures), perhaps recognizing, as we conclude, that no reasonable accommodation was possible here. To accommodate Martinson adequately, Kinney would need to hire an additional person to perform the essential security function of Martinson's job. The ADA simply does not require an employer to hire an additional person to perform an essential function of a disabled employee's position. See 29 C.F.R. Pt. 1630, App. at § 1630.2(o) ("An employer or other covered entity is not required to reallocate essential functions.").

Our holding is a narrow one, quelling the fears of the district court as to the "natural consequence" of a conclusion that Martinson was not qualified for his position with Kinney, i.e., that such a conclusion would render "Martinson . . . unqualified as a matter of law to hold any position because Martinson obviously cannot discharge the 'essential functions' of any job during the time he is unconscious." *Id.* at 427. This is not the "consequence" of our holding here.

Certain jobs do require uninterrupted vigilance for discrete periods of time. Martinson, as his counsel acknowledged at oral argument, is not qualified to perform such jobs. The security function of the Kinney salesperson position places it in that category. However, Martinson may well be qualified for a range of other jobs, including jobs in retail sales, so long as store security did not depend exclusively on Martinson's vigilance. Cf. *Overton v. Reilly*, 977 F.2d 1190, 1195 (7th Cir. 1993) (finding issue of fact as to whether disability-related naps at work disqualified the employee from his administrative job at the Environmental Protection Agency).

In sum, the undisputed facts demonstrate that Martinson's disability left him unable to perform the essential security function of his position with Kinney. For this reason, he could not establish the second prong of his prima facie ADA case, i.e., that he was a "qualified individual." Accordingly, the district court's order granting summary judgment to Kinney is

Affirmed.

Sutton v. United Air Lines, Inc.
527 U.S. 471 (1999)

JUSTICE O'CONNOR delivered the opinion of the Court.

The Americans with Disabilities Act of 1990 (ADA or Act), 104 Stat. 328, 42 U.S.C. § 12101 *et seq.,* prohibits certain employers from discriminating against individuals on the basis of their disabilities. See § 12112(a). Petitioners challenge the dismissal of their ADA action for failure to state a claim upon which relief can be granted. We conclude that the complaint was properly dismissed. In reaching that result, we hold that the determination of whether an individual is disabled should be made with reference to measures that mitigate the individual's impairment, including, in this instance, eyeglasses and contact lenses. In addition, we hold that petitioners failed to allege properly that respondent "regarded" them as having a disability within the meaning of the ADA.

I

Petitioners' amended complaint was dismissed for failure to state a claim upon which relief could be granted. See Fed. Rule Civ. Proc. 12(b)(6). Accordingly, we accept the allegations contained in their complaint as true for purposes of this case. See *United States v. Gaubert*, 499 U. S. 315, 327 (1991).

Petitioners are twin sisters, both of whom have severe myopia. Each petitioner's uncorrected visual acuity is 20/200 or worse in her right eye and 20/400 or worse in her left eye, but "[w]ith the use of corrective lenses, each . . . has vision that is 20/20 or better." App. 23. Consequently, without corrective lenses, each "effectively cannot see to conduct numerous activities such as driving a vehicle, watching television or shopping in public stores," *id.,* at 24, but with corrective measures, such as glasses or contact lenses, both "function identically to individuals without a similar impairment," *ibid.*

In 1992, petitioners applied to respondent for employment as commercial airline pilots. They met respondent's basic age, education, experience, and FAA certification qualifications. After submitting their applications for employment, both petitioners were invited by respondent to an interview and to flight simulator tests. Both were told during their interviews, however, that a mistake had been made in inviting them to interview because petitioners did not meet respondent's minimum vision requirement, which was uncorrected visual acuity of 20/100 or better. Due to their failure to meet this requirement, petitioners' interviews were terminated, and neither was offered a pilot position.

In light of respondent's proffered reason for rejecting them, petitioners filed a charge of disability discrimination under the ADA with the Equal Employment Opportunity Commission (EEOC). After receiving a right to sue letter, petitioners filed suit in the United States District Court for the District of Colorado, alleging that respondent had discriminated against them "on the basis of their disability, or because [respondent] regarded [petitioners] as having a disability" in violation of the ADA. App. 26. Specifically, petitioners alleged that due to their severe myopia they actually have a substantially limiting impairment or are regarded as having such an impairment, See *id.*, at 23–26, and are thus disabled under the Act.

The District Court dismissed petitioners' complaint for failure to state a claim upon which relief could be granted. See Civ. A. No. 96-5-121 (Aug. 28, 1996), App. to Pet. for Cert. A-27. Because petitioners could fully correct their visual impairments, the court held that they were not actually substantially limited in any major life activity and thus had not stated a claim that they were disabled within the meaning of the ADA. *Id.*, at A-32 to A-36. The court also determined that petitioners had not made allegations sufficient to support their claim that they were "regarded" by the respondent as having an impairment that substantially limits a major life activity. *Id.*, at A-36 to A-37. The court observed that "[t]he statutory reference to a substantial limitation indicates . . . that an employer regards an employee as handicapped in his or her ability to work by finding the employee's impairment to foreclose generally the type of employment involved." *Id.*, at A36 to A37. But petitioners had alleged only that respondent regarded them as unable to satisfy the requirements of a particular job, global airline pilot. Consequently, the court held that petitioners had not stated a claim that they were regarded as substantially limited in the major life activity of working. Employing similar logic, the Court of Appeals for the Tenth Circuit affirmed the District Court's judgment. 130 F.3d 893 (1997).

The Tenth Circuit's decision is in tension with the decisions of other Courts of Appeals. See, *e.g., Bartlett v. New York State Bd. of Law Examiners*, 156 F. 3d 321, 329 (CA2 1998) (holding self-accommodations cannot be considered when determining a disability), cert. pending.

II

The ADA prohibits discrimination by covered entities, including private employers, against qualified individuals with a disability. Specifically, it provides that no covered employer "shall discriminate against a qualified individual with a disability because of the disability of such individual in regard to job application procedures, the hiring, advancement, or discharge of employees, employee compensation, job training, and other terms, conditions, and privileges of employment." 42 U.S.C. § 12112(a); see also § 12111(2) ("The term 'covered entity' means an employer, employment agency, labor organization, or joint labor-management committee"). A "qualified individual with a disability" is identified as "an individual with a disability who, with or without reasonable accommodation, can perform the essential functions of the employment position that such individual holds or desires." § 12111(8). In turn, a "disability" is defined as:

"(A) a physical or mental impairment that substantially limits one or more of the major life activities of such individual;

"(B) a record of such an impairment; or

"(C) being regarded as having such an impairment." § 12102(2).

Accordingly, to fall within this definition one must have an actual disability (subsection (A)), have a record of a disability (subsection (B)), or be regarded as having one (subsection (C)).

The parties agree that the authority to issue regulations to implement the Act is split primarily among three Government agencies. According to the parties, the EEOC has authority to issue regulations to carry out the employment provisions in Title I of the ADA, §§ 12111–12117, pursuant to § 12116 ("Not later than 1 year after [the date of enactment of this Act], the Commission shall issue regulations in an accessible format to carry out this subchapter in accordance with subchapter II of chapter 5 of title 5"). The Attorney General is granted authority to issue regulations with respect to Title II, subtitle A, §§ 12131–12134, which relates to public services. See § 12134 ("Not later than 1 year after [the date of enactment of this Act], the Attorney General shall promulgate regulations in an accessible format that implement this part"). Finally, the Secretary of Transportation has authority to issue regulations pertaining to the transportation provisions of Titles II and III. See § 12149(a) ("Not later than 1 year after [the date of enactment of this Act], the Secretary of Transportation shall issue regulations, in an accessible format, necessary for carrying out this subpart (other than section 12143 of this title)"); § 12164 (substantially same); § 12186(a)(1) (substantially same); § 12143(b) ("Not later than one year after [the date of enactment of this Act], the Secretary shall issue final regulations to carry out this section"). See also § 12204 (granting authority to the Architectural and Transportation Barriers Compliance Board to issue minimum guidelines to supplement the existing Minimum Guidelines and Requirements for Accessible Design). Moreover, each of these agencies is authorized to offer technical assistance regarding the provisions they administer. See § 12206(c)(1) ("Each Federal agency that has responsibility under paragraph (2) for implementing this chapter may render technical assistance to individuals and institutions that have rights or duties under the respective subchapter or subchapters of this chapter for which such agency has responsibility").

. . . .

The agencies have also issued interpretive guidelines to aid in the implementation of their regulations. For instance, at the time that it promulgated the above regulations, the EEOC issued an "Interpretive Guidance," which provides that "[t]he determination of whether an individual is substantially limited in a major life activity must be made on a case by case basis, without regard to mitigating measures such as medicines, or assistive or prosthetic devices." 29 CFR pt. 1630, App. § 1630.2(j) (1998) (describing § 1630.2(j)). . . .

III

With this statutory and regulatory framework in mind, we turn first to the question whether petitioners have stated a claim under subsection (A) of the disability definition, that is, whether they have alleged that they possess a physical impairment that substantially limits them in one or more major life activities. See 42 U.S.C. § 12102(2)(A). Because petitioners allege that with corrective measures their vision "is 20/20 or better," see App. 23, they are not actually disabled within the meaning of the Act if the "disability" determination is made with reference to these measures. Consequently, with respect to subsection (A) of the disability definition, our decision turns on whether disability is to be determined with or without reference to corrective measures.

Petitioners maintain that whether an impairment is substantially limiting should be determined without regard to corrective measures. They argue that, because the ADA does not directly address the question at hand, the Court should defer to the agency interpretations of the statute, which are embodied in the agency guidelines issued by the EEOC and the Department of Justice. These guidelines specifically direct that the determination of whether an individual is substantially limited in a major life activity be made without regard to mitigating measures. See 29 CFR pt. 1630, App. § 1630.2(j); 28 CFR pt. 35, App. A, § 35.104 (1998); 28 CFR pt. 36, App. B, § 36.104.

Respondent, in turn, maintains that an impairment does not substantially limit a major life activity if it is corrected. It argues that the Court should not defer to the agency guidelines cited by petitioners because the guidelines conflict with the plain meaning of the ADA. The phrase "substantially limits one or more major life activities," it explains, requires that the substantial limitations actually and presently exist. Moreover, respondent argues, disregarding mitigating measures taken by an individual defies the statutory command to examine the effect of the impairment on the major life activities "of such individual." And even if the statute is ambiguous, respondent claims, the guidelines' directive to ignore mitigating measures is not reasonable, and thus this Court should not defer to it.

We conclude that respondent is correct that the approach adopted by the agency guidelines—that persons are to be evaluated in their hypothetical uncorrected state—is an impermissible interpretation of the ADA. Looking at the Act as a whole, it is apparent that if a person is taking measures to correct for, or mitigate, a physical or mental impairment, the effects of those measures—both positive and negative—must be taken into account when judging whether that person is "substantially limited" in a major life activity and thus "disabled" under the Act. The dissent relies on the legislative history of the ADA for the contrary proposition that individuals should be examined in their uncorrected state. See *post*, at 10–18 (opinion of *Stevens*, J.). Because we decide that, by its terms, the ADA cannot be read in this manner, we have no reason to consider the ADA's legislative history.

Three separate provisions of the ADA, read in concert, lead us to this conclusion. The Act defines a "disability" as "a physical or mental impairment that *substantially limits* one or more of the major life activities" of an individual. § 12102(2) (A) (emphasis added). Because the phrase "substantially limits" appears in the Act in the present indicative verb form, we think the language is properly read as requiring that a person be presently—not potentially or hypothetically—substantially limited in order to demonstrate a disability. A "disability" exists only where an impairment "substantially limits" a major life activity, not where it "might," "could," or "would" be substantially limiting if mitigating measures were not taken. A person whose physical or mental impairment is corrected by medication or other measures does not have an impairment that presently "substantially limits" a major life activity. To be sure, a person whose physical or mental impairment is corrected by mitigating measures still has an impairment, but if the impairment is corrected it does not "substantially limi[t]" a major life activity.

The definition of disability also requires that disabilities be evaluated "with respect to an individual" and be determined based on whether an impairment substantially limits the "major life activities of such individual." § 12102(2). Thus, whether a person has a disability under the ADA is an individualized inquiry. See *Bragdon v. Abbott*, 524 U.S. 624 , ____ (1998) (declining to consider whether HIV infection is a *per se* disability under the ADA); 29 CFR pt. 1630, App. § 1630.2(j) ("The determination of whether an individual has a disability is not necessarily based on the name or diagnosis of the impairment the person has, but rather on the effect of that impairment on the life of the individual").

The agency guidelines' directive that persons be judged in their uncorrected or unmitigated state runs directly counter to the individualized inquiry mandated by the ADA. The agency approach would often require courts and employers to speculate about a person's condition and would, in many cases, force them to make a disability determination based on general information about how an uncorrected impairment usually affects individuals, rather than on the individual's actual condition. For instance, under this view, courts would almost certainly find all diabetics to be disabled, because if they failed to monitor their blood sugar levels and administer insulin, they would almost certainly be substantially limited in one or more major life activities. A diabetic whose illness does not impair his or her daily activities would therefore be considered disabled simply because he or she has diabetes. Thus, the guidelines approach would create a system in which persons often must be treated as members of a group of people with similar impairments, rather than as individuals. This is contrary to both the letter and the spirit of the ADA.

The guidelines approach could also lead to the anomalous result that in determining whether an individual is disabled, courts and employers could not consider any negative side effects suffered by an individual resulting from the use of mitigating measures, even when those side effects are very severe. See, *e.g.,* Johnson,

Antipsychotics: Pros and Cons of Antipsychotics, RN (Aug. 1997) . . . . This result is also inconsistent with the individualized approach of the ADA.

Finally, and critically, findings enacted as part of the ADA require the conclusion that Congress did not intend to bring under the statute's protection all those whose uncorrected conditions amount to disabilities. Congress found that "some 43,000,000 Americans have one or more physical or mental disabilities, and this number is increasing as the population as a whole is growing older." § 12101(a)(1). This figure is inconsistent with the definition of disability pressed by petitioners.

Although the exact source of the 43 million figure is not clear, the corresponding finding in the 1988 precursor to the ADA was drawn directly from a report prepared by the National Council on Disability. See Burgdorf, *The Americans with Disabilities Act: Analysis and Implications of a Second-Generation Civil Rights Statute*, 26 Harv. Civ. Rights-Civ. Lib. L. Rev. 413, 434, n. 117 (1991) (reporting, in an article authored by the drafter of the original ADA bill introduced in Congress in 1988, that the report was the source for a figure of 36 million disabled persons quoted in the versions of the bill introduced in 1988). That report detailed the difficulty of estimating the number of disabled persons due to varying operational definitions of disability. National Council on Disability, Toward Independence 10 (1986). It explained that the estimates of the number of disabled Americans ranged from an over inclusive 160 million under a "health conditions approach," which looks at all conditions that impair the health or normal functional abilities of an individual, to an under inclusive 22.7 million under a "work disability approach," which focuses on individuals' reported ability to work. *Id.*, at 10–11. It noted that "a figure of 35 or 36 million [was] the most commonly quoted estimate." *Id.*, at 10. The 36 million number included in the 1988 bill's findings thus clearly reflects an approach to defining disabilities that is closer to the work disabilities approach than the health conditions approach.

. . . .

Regardless of its exact source, however, the [figure] reflects an understanding that those whose impairments are largely corrected by medication or other devices are not "disabled" within the meaning of the ADA. The estimate is consistent with the numbers produced by studies performed during this same time period that took a similar functional approach to determining disability. For instance, Mathematica Policy Research, Inc., drawing on data from the National Center for Health Statistics, issued an estimate of approximately 31.4 million civilian noninstitutionalized persons with "chronic activity limitation status" in 1979. Digest of Data on Persons with Disabilities 25 (1984). The 1989 Statistical Abstract offered the same estimate based on the same data, as well as an estimate of 32.7 million noninstitutionalized persons with "activity limitation" in 1985. Statistical Abstract, *supra*, at 115 (Table 184). In both cases, individuals with "activity limitations" were those who, relative to their age-sex group could not conduct "usual" activities: *e.g.*, attending preschool, keeping house, or living independently. See National Center for Health Statistics, U.S. Dept. of

Health and Human Services, Vital and Health Statistics, Current Estimates from the National Health Interview Survey, 1989, Series 10, pp. 7–8 (1990).

By contrast, nonfunctional approaches to defining disability produce signifi-cantly larger numbers. As noted above, the 1986 National Council on Disability report estimated that there were over 160 million disabled under the "health condi-tions approach." Toward Independence, *supra* , at 10; see also Mathematica Policy Research , *supra,* at 3 (arriving at similar estimate based on same Census Bureau data). Indeed, the number of people with vision impairments alone is 100 million. See National Advisory Eye Council, U.S. Dept. of Health and Human Services, Vision Research—A National Plan: 1999–2003, p. 7 (1998) ("[M]ore than 100 mil-lion people need corrective lenses to see properly"). "It is estimated that more than 28 million Americans have impaired hearing." National Institutes of Health, National Strategic Research Plan: Hearing and Hearing Impairment v (1996). And there were approximately 50 million people with high blood pressure (hypertension). Tindall, Stalking a Silent Killer; Hypertension, Business & Health 37 (August 1998) ("Some 50 million Americans have high blood pressure").

Because it is included in the ADA's text, the finding that 43 million individuals are disabled gives content to the ADA's terms, specifically the term "disability." Had Congress intended to include all persons with corrected physical limitations among those covered by the Act, it undoubtedly would have cited a much higher number of disabled persons in the findings. That it did not is evidence that the ADA's cover-age is restricted to only those whose impairments are not mitigated by corrective measures.

IV

Our conclusion that petitioners have failed to state a claim that they are actually disabled under subsection (A) of the disability definition does not end our inquiry. Under subsection (C), individuals who are "regarded as" having a disability are disabled within the meaning of the ADA. See § 12102(2)(C). Subsection (C) pro-vides that having a disability includes "being regarded as having," § 12102(2)(C), "a physical or mental impairment that substantially limits one or more of the major life activities of such individual," § 12102(2)(A). There are two apparent ways in which individuals may fall within this statutory definition: (1) a covered entity mis-takenly believes that a person has a physical impairment that substantially limits one or more major life activities, or (2) a covered entity mistakenly believes that an actual, nonlimiting impairment substantially limits one or more major life activi-ties. In both cases, it is necessary that a covered entity entertain misperceptions about the individual—it must believe either that one has a substantially limiting impairment that one does not have or that one has a substantially limiting impair-ment when, in fact, the impairment is not so limiting. These misperceptions often "resul[t] from stereotypic assumptions not truly indicative of . . . individual abil-ity." See 42 U.S.C. § 12101(7). See also *School Bd. of Nassau Cty. v. Arline,* 480 U. S. 273, 284 (1987) . . . .

Considering the allegations of the amended complaint in tandem, petitioners have not stated a claim that respondent regards their impairment as *substantially limiting* their ability to work. The ADA does not define "substantially limits," but "substantially" suggests "considerable" or "specified to a large degree." See Webster's Third New International Dictionary 2280 (1976) (defining "substantially" as "in a substantial manner" and "substantial" as "considerable in amount, value, or worth" and "being that specified to a large degree or in the main"); see also 17 Oxford English Dictionary 66–67 (2d ed. 1989) ("substantial": "[r]elating to or proceeding from the essence of a thing; essential"; "of ample or considerable amount, quantity or dimensions"). The EEOC has codified regulations interpreting the term "substantially limits" in this manner, defining the term to mean "[u]nable to perform" or "[s]ignificantly restricted." See 29 CFR §§ 1630.2(j)(1)(i),(ii) (1998).

When the major life activity under consideration is that of working, the statutory phrase "substantially limits" requires, at a minimum, that plaintiffs allege they are unable to work in a broad class of jobs. . . .

The EEOC [identifies] several factors that courts should consider when determining whether an individual is substantially limited in the major life activity of working, including the geographical area to which the individual has reasonable access, and "the number and types of jobs utilizing similar training, knowledge, skills or abilities, within the geographical area, from which the individual is also disqualified." §§ 1630.2(j)(3)(ii)(A), (B). To be substantially limited in the major life activity of working, then, one must be precluded from more than one type of job, a specialized job, or a particular job of choice. If jobs utilizing an individual's skills (but perhaps not his or her unique talents) are available, one is not precluded from a substantial class of jobs. Similarly, if a host of different types of jobs are available, one is not precluded from a broad range of jobs.

Because the parties accept that the term "major life activities" includes working, we do not determine the validity of the cited regulations. We note, however, that there may be some conceptual difficulty in defining "major life activities" to include work, for it seems "to argue in a circle to say that if one is excluded, for instance, by reason of [an impairment, from working with others] . . . then that exclusion constitutes an impairment, when the question you're asking is, whether the exclusion itself is by reason of handicap." Tr. of Oral Arg. in *School Bd. of Nassau Co. v. Arline*, O.T. 1986, No. 85-1277, p. 15 (argument of Solicitor General). Indeed, even the EEOC has expressed reluctance to define "major life activities" to include working and has suggested that working be viewed as a residual life activity, considered, as a last resort, *only* "[i]f an individual is not substantially limited with respect to *any other* major life activity." 29 CFR pt. 1630, App. § 1630.2(j) (1998) (emphasis added) . . . .

. . . .

For these reasons, the decision of the Court of Appeals for the Tenth Circuit is affirmed.

It is so ordered.

Notes and Questions

1. To make a claim of violation under the ADA, claimant must prove:

(A) a physical or mental impairment that substantially limits one or more of the major life activities of such individual;

(B) a record of such an impairment; or

(C) being regarded as having such an impairment.

§ 12102(2). In addition, to make a successful claim under Title I, the individual must also be "qualified with or without the disability."

Why does the plaintiff not meet that requirement in *Martinson v. Kinney*?

2. The record showed that: "While employed by Kinney, Martinson broke a display table and shoe polish rack by falling on them during seizures. In addition, on one occasion, a supervisor discovered him lying on the floor in the stockroom with a lit cigarette on his chest and on another occasion, a supervisor found him supine behind the sales counter holding a charge slip. However, when preparing Martinson's employee separation report at the time of the discharge, District Sales Manager Bosworth did not state that Martinson was fired because of these incidents, or indeed even mention them." Do you deem this omission by the employer genuine or misleading?

3. Note these important distinctions highlighted by the Court:

"Both a disease and its physical manifestations can constitute disabilities. For example, both glaucoma and blindness, both Down's Syndrome and mental retardation, and both cerebral palsy and impaired speech can be disabilities. *See* H.R. Rep. No. 101-485(II), at 51 (1990), reprinted in 1990 U.S.C.C.A.N. 303, 333 (listing as impairments both diseases, like brain cancer, and resulting conditions, like a hearing impairment). *Cf. School Bd. of Nassau County v. Arline*, 480 U.S. 273, 282, 107 S. Ct. 1123, 1128, 94 L. Ed. 2d 307 (1987) ("We do not agree . . . that, in defining a handicapped individual under [the Rehabilitation Act], the contagious effects of a disease can be meaningfully distinguished from the disease's physical effects on a claimant. . . .").

By contrast, misconduct—even misconduct related to a disability—is not itself a disability, and an employer is free to fire an employee on that basis. *See, e.g., Tyndall v. National Educ. Ctrs.*, 31 F.3d 209, 214–15 (4th Cir. 1994) (finding no discrimination when firing because of disability-related absences); *Little v. FBI*, 1 F.3d 255, 259 (4th Cir. 1993) (finding no discrimination when firing for disability-related intoxication on duty)."

D. The Safety Concerns under Title II and Title III

The ADA adopted definitions and guidelines fleshed out by courts and agencies under the Rehabilitation Act. The ability to successfully evoke safety concerns as a legitimate defense to discrimination against someone with a disability was limited under the Rehabilitation Act, as seen below in *Arline*. That remained so under the ADA, as illustrated in *Bragdon*. The 2008 Amendments to the ADA further expanded protections for individuals with HIV and AIDS by classifying them almost always as disabled. In that sense, the Amendments went even further than *Bragdon* below. Can you imagine a scenario where the employer's behavior is so connected to a plaintiff's illness that it entitles the plaintiff to protection under the ADA? What defenses might you want to make available to an employer, under such scenario? See below for courts' discussion of available defenses for employers under disability statutes.

School Board of Nassau County v. Arline

480 U.S. 273 (1987)

JUSTICE BRENNAN delivered the opinion of the Court.

Section 504 of the Rehabilitation Act of 1973, 87 Stat. 394, as amended, 29 U.S.C. §794 (Act), prohibits a federally funded state program from discriminating against a handicapped individual solely by reason of his or her handicap. This case presents the questions whether a person afflicted with tuberculosis, a contagious disease, may be considered a "handicapped individual" within the meaning of §504 of the Act, and, if so, whether such an individual is "otherwise qualified" to teach elementary school.

From 1966 until 1979, respondent Gene Arline taught elementary school in Nassau County, Florida. She was discharged in 1979 after suffering a third relapse of tuberculosis within two years. After she was denied relief in state administrative proceedings, she brought suit in federal court, alleging that the school board's decision to dismiss her because of her tuberculosis violated §504 of the Act.

A trial was held in the District Court, at which the principal medical evidence was provided by Marianne McEuen, M. D., an assistant director of the Community Tuberculosis Control Service of the Florida Department of Health and Rehabilitative Services. According to the medical records reviewed by Dr. McEuen, Arline was hospitalized for tuberculosis in 1957. App. 11–12. For the next 20 years, Arline's disease was in remission. *Id.*, at 32. Then, in 1977, a culture revealed that tuberculosis was again active in her system; cultures taken in March 1978 and in November 1978 were also positive. *Id.*, at 12.

The superintendent of schools for Nassau County, Craig Marsh, then testified as to the school board's response to Arline's medical reports. After both her second relapse, in the spring of 1978, and her third relapse in November 1978, the school board suspended Arline with pay for the remainder of the school year. *Id.*, at 49–51.

At the end of the 1978–1979 school year, the school board held a hearing, after which it discharged Arline, "not because she had done anything wrong," but because of the "continued reoccurrence [*sic*] of tuberculosis." *Id.*, at 49–52.

In her trial memorandum, Arline argued that it was "not disputed that the [school board dismissed her] solely on the basis of her illness. Since the illness in this case qualifies the Plaintiff as a 'handicapped person' it is clear that she was dismissed solely as a result of her handicap in violation of Section 504." Record 119. The District Court held, however, that although there was "[n]o question that she suffers a handicap," Arline was nevertheless not "a handicapped person under the terms of that statute." App. to Pet. for Cert. C-2. The court found it "difficult . . . to conceive that Congress intended contagious diseases to be included within the definition of a handicapped person." The court then went on to state that, "even assuming" that a person with a contagious disease could be deemed a handicapped person, Arline was not "qualified" to teach elementary school. *Id.*, at C-2–C-3.

The Court of Appeals reversed, holding that "persons with contagious diseases are within the coverage of section 504," and that Arline's condition "falls . . . neatly within the statutory and regulatory framework" of the Act. 772 F.2d 759, 764 (CA11 1985). The court remanded the case "for further findings as to whether the risks of infection precluded Mrs. Arline from being 'otherwise qualified' for her job and, if so, whether it was possible to make some reasonable accommodation for her in that teaching position" or in some other position. *Id.*, at 765 (footnote omitted). We granted certiorari, 475 U.S. 1118 (1986), and now affirm.

II

In enacting and amending the Act, Congress enlisted all programs receiving federal funds in an effort "to share with handicapped Americans the opportunities for an education, transportation, housing, health care, and jobs that other Americans take for granted." 123 Cong. Rec. 13515 (1977) (statement of Sen. Humphrey). To that end, Congress not only increased federal support for vocational rehabilitation, but also addressed the broader problem of discrimination against the handicapped by including § 504, an antidiscrimination provision patterned after Title VI of the Civil Rights Act of 1964. Section 504 of the Rehabilitation Act reads in pertinent part:

> "No otherwise qualified handicapped individual in the United States, as defined in section 706(7) of this title, shall, solely by reason of his handicap, be excluded from participation in, be denied the benefits of, or be subjected to discrimination under any program or activity receiving Federal financial assistance . . . ." 29 U.S.C. § 794.

In 1974 Congress expanded the definition of "handicapped individual" for use in § 504 to read as follows:[3]

---

3. Footnote text missing.

[A]ny person who (i) has a physical or mental impairment which substantially limits one or more of such person's major life activities, (ii) has a record of such an impairment, or (iii) is regarded as having such an impairment. 29 U.S.C. § 706(7)(B).

The amended definition reflected Congress' concern with protecting the handicapped against discrimination stemming not only from simple prejudice, but also from "archaic attitudes and laws" and from "the fact that the American people are simply unfamiliar with and insensitive to the difficulties confront[ing] individuals with handicaps." S. Rep. No. 93-1297, p. 50 (1974). To combat the effects of erroneous but nevertheless prevalent perceptions about the handicapped, Congress expanded the definition of "handicapped individual" so as to preclude discrimination against "[a] person who has a record of, or is regarded as having, an impairment. [but who] may at present have no actual incapacity at all." *Southeastern Community College v. Davis,* 442 U.S. 397, 405–406, n. 6 (1979). http://www.leagle.com/decision /1987753480US273_1740/SCHOOL BD. OF NASSAU COUNTY v. ARLINE—fid5

In determining whether a particular individual is handicapped as defined by the Act, the regulations promulgated by the Department of Health and Human Services are of significant assistance. As we have previously recognized, these regulations were drafted with the oversight and approval of Congress, see *Consolidated Rail Corporation v. Darrone,* 465 U.S. 624, 634–635, and nn. 14–16 (1984); they provide "an important source of guidance on the meaning of § 504." *Alexander v. Choate,* 469 U.S. 287, 304, n. 24 (1985). The regulations are particularly significant here because they define two critical terms used in the statutory definition of handicapped individual. "Physical impairment" is defined as follows:

> "[A]ny physiological disorder or condition, cosmetic disfigurement, or anatomical loss affecting one or more of the following body systems: neurological; musculoskeletal; special sense organs; respiratory, including speech organs; cardiovascular; reproductive, digestive, genitourinary; hemic and lymphatic; skin; and endocrine." 45 CFR § 84.3(j)(2)(i) (1985).

In addition, the regulations define "major life activities" a functions such as caring for one's self, performing manual tasks, walking, seeing, hearing, speaking, breathing, learning, and working. § 84.3(j)(2)(ii).

III

Within this statutory and regulatory framework, then, we must consider whether Arline can be considered a handicapped individual. According to the testimony of Dr. McEuen, Arline suffered tuberculosis "in an acute form in such a degree that it affected her respiratory system," and was hospitalized for this condition. App. 11. Arline thus had a physical impairment as that term is defined by the regulations, since she had a "physiological disorder or condition ... affecting [her] ... respiratory [system]." 45 CFR § 84.3(j)(2)(i) (1985). This impairment was serious enough to require hospitalization, a fact more than sufficient to establish that one or more of her major life activities were substantially limited by her impairment. Thus, Arline's hospitalization for tuberculosis in 1957 suffices to establish that she has a "record of . . . impairment" within the meaning of 29 U.S.C. § 706(7)(B)(ii), and is therefore a handicapped individual.

Petitioners concede that a contagious disease may constitute a handicapping condition to the extent that it leaves a person with "diminished physical or mental capabilities," Brief for Petitioners 15, and concede that Arline's hospitalization for tuberculosis in 1957 demonstrates that she has a record of a physical impairment, see Tr. of Oral Arg. 52–53. Petitioners maintain, however, that Arline's record of impairment is irrelevant in this case, since the school board dismissed Arline not because of her diminished physical capabilities, but because of the threat that her relapses of tuberculosis posed to the health of others.

We do not agree with petitioners that, in defining a handicapped individual under § 504, the contagious effects of a disease can be meaningfully distinguished from the disease's physical effects on a claimant in a case such as this. Arline's contagiousness and her physical impairment each resulted from the same underlying condition, tuberculosis. It would be unfair to allow an employer to seize upon the distinction between the effects of a disease on others and the effects of a disease on a patient and use that distinction to justify discriminatory treatment.

Nothing in the legislative history of § 504 suggests that Congress intended such a result. That history demonstrates that Congress was as concerned about the effect of an impairment on others as it was about its effect on the individual. Congress extended coverage, in 29 U.S.C. § 706(7)(B)(iii), to those individuals who are simply "regarded as having" a physical or mental impairment. The Senate Report provides as an example of a person who would be covered under this subsection "a person with some kind of visible physical impairment which in fact does not substantially limit that person's functioning." S. Rep. No. 93-1297, at 64.http://www.leagle .com/decision/1987753480US273_1740/SCHOOL BD. OF NASSAU COUNTY v. ARLINE—fid10

Such an impairment might not diminish a person's physical or mental capabilities, but could nevertheless substantially limit that person's ability to work as a result of the negative reactions of others to the impairment.

Allowing discrimination based on the contagious effects of a physical impairment would be inconsistent with the basic purpose of § 504, which is to ensure that handicapped individuals are not denied jobs or other benefits because of the prejudiced attitudes or the ignorance of others. By amending the definition of "handicapped individual" to include not only those who are actually physically impaired, but also those who are regarded as impaired and who, as a result, are substantially limited in a major life activity, Congress acknowledged that society's accumulated myths and fears about disability and disease are as handicapping as are the physical limitations that flow from actual impairment. Few aspects of a handicap give rise to the same level of public fear and misapprehension as contagiousness. Even those who suffer or have recovered from such noninfectious diseases as epilepsy or cancer have faced discrimination based on the irrational fear that they might be contagious.

The Act is carefully structured to replace such reflexive reactions to actual or perceived handicaps with actions based on reasoned and medically sound judgments: the definition of "handicapped individual" is broad, but only those individuals who are both handicapped *and* otherwise qualified are eligible for relief. The fact that *some* persons who have contagious diseases may pose a serious health threat to others under certain circumstances does not justify excluding from the coverage of the Act *all* persons with actual or perceived contagious diseases. Such exclusion would mean that those accused of being contagious would never have the opportunity to have their condition evaluated in light of medical evidence and a determination made as to whether they were "otherwise qualified." Rather, they would be vulnerable to discrimination on the basis of mythology—precisely the type of injury Congress sought to prevent. We conclude that the fact that a person with a record of a physical impairment is also contagious does not suffice to remove that person from coverage under § 504.

IV

The remaining question is whether Arline is otherwise qualified for the job of elementary schoolteacher. To answer this question in most cases, the district court will need to conduct an individualized inquiry and make appropriate findings of fact. Such an inquiry is essential if § 504 is to achieve its goal of protecting handicapped individuals from deprivations based on prejudice, stereotypes, or unfounded fear, while giving appropriate weight to such legitimate concerns of grantees as avoiding exposing others to significant health and safety risks. The basic factors to be considered in conducting this inquiry are well established. In the context [480 U.S. 288]of the employment of a person handicapped with a contagious disease, we agree with *amicus* American Medical Association that this inquiry should include [findings of] facts, based on reasonable medical judgments given the state of medical knowledge, about (a) the nature of the risk (how the disease is transmitted), (b) the duration of the risk (how long is the carrier infectious), (c) the severity of the risk (what is the potential harm to third parties) and (d) the probabilities the disease will be transmitted and will cause varying degrees of harm. Brief for American Medical Association as Amicus Curiae 19.

In making these findings, courts normally should defer to the reasonable medical judgments of public health officials. The next step in the "otherwise-qualified" inquiry is for the court to evaluate, in light of these medical findings, whether the employer could reasonably accommodate the employee under the established standards for that inquiry. See n. 17, *supra.*

Because of the paucity of factual findings by the District Court, we, like the Court of Appeals, are unable at this stage of the proceedings to resolve whether Arline is "otherwise qualified" for her job. The District Court made no findings as to the duration and severity of Arline's condition, nor as to the probability that she would transmit the disease. Nor did the court determine whether Arline was contagious at the time she was discharged, or whether the School Board could have reasonably accommodated her. Accordingly, the resolution of whether Arline was otherwise qualified requires further findings of fact.

V

We hold that a person suffering from the contagious disease of tuberculosis can be a handicapped person within the meaning of § 504 of the Rehabilitation Act of 1973, and that respondent Arline is such a person. We remand the case to the District Court to determine whether Arline is otherwise qualified for her position. The judgment of the Court of Appeals is *Affirmed.*

Bragdon v. Abbott

524 U.S. 624 (1998)

Justice Kennedy delivered the opinion of the Court.

We address in this case the application of the Americans with Disabilities Act of 1990 (ADA), 104 Stat. 327, 42 U.S.C. § 12101 *et seq.,* to persons infected with the human immunodeficiency virus (HIV). We granted certiorari to review, first, whether HIV infection is a disability under the ADA when the infection has not yet progressed to the so-called symptomatic phase; and, second, whether the Court of Appeals, in affirming a grant of summary judgment, cited sufficient material in the record to determine, as a matter of law, that respondent's infection with HIV posed no direct threat to the health and safety of her treating dentist.

I

Respondent Sidney Abbott has been infected with HIV since 1986. When the incidents we recite occurred, her infection had not manifested its most serious symptoms. On September 16, 1994, she went to the office of petitioner Randon Bragdon in Bangor, Maine, for a dental appointment. She disclosed her HIV infection on the patient registration form. Petitioner completed a dental examination, discovered a cavity, and informed respondent of his policy against filling cavities of HIV-infected patients. He offered to perform the work at a hospital with no added fee for his services, though respondent would be responsible for the cost of using the hospital's facilities. Respondent declined.

Respondent sued petitioner under state law and § 302 of the ADA, 104 Stat. 355, 42 U.S.C. § 12182, alleging discrimination on the basis of her disability. The state law claims are not before us. Section 302 of the ADA provides:

> "No individual shall be discriminated against on the basis of disability in the full and equal enjoyment of the goods, services, facilities, privileges, advantages, or accommodations of any place of public accommodation by any person who . . . operates a place of public accommodation." § 12182(a).

The term "public accommodation" is defined to include the "professional office of a health care provider." § 12181(7)(F).

A later subsection qualifies the mandate not to discriminate. It provides:

"Nothing in this subchapter shall require an entity to permit an individual to participate in or benefit from the goods, services, facilities, privileges, advantages and accommodations of such entity where such individual poses a direct threat to the health or safety of others." § 12182(b)(3).

. . . .

[The District Court ruled in favor of plaintiff.] The Court of Appeals affirmed. It held respondent's HIV infection was a disability under the ADA, even though her infection had not yet progressed to the symptomatic stage. 107 F.3d 934, 939–943 (CA1 1997). The Court of Appeals also agreed that treating the respondent in petitioner's office would not have posed a direct threat to the health and safety of others. Id., at 943–948. Unlike the District Court, however, the Court of Appeals declined to rely on the Marianos affidavits. Id., at 946, n. 7. Instead the court relied on the 1993 CDC Dentistry Guidelines, as well as the Policy on AIDS, HIV Infection and the Practice of Dentistry, promulgated by the American Dental Association in 1991 (1991 American Dental Association Policy on HIV). 107 F.3d, at 945–946.

II

We first review the ruling that respondent's HIV infection constituted a disability under the ADA. The statute defines disability as:

"(A) a physical or mental impairment that substantially limits one or more of the major life activities of such individual;

"(B) a record of such an impairment; or

"(C) being regarded as having such impairment." § 12102(2).

We hold respondent's HIV infection was a disability under subsection (A) of the definitional section of the statute. In light of this conclusion, we need not consider the applicability of subsections (B) or (C).

Our consideration of subsection (A) of the definition proceeds in three steps. First, we consider whether respondent's HIV infection was a physical impairment. Second, we identify the life activity upon which respondent relies (reproduction and child bearing) and determine whether it constitutes a major life activity under the ADA. Third, tying the two statutory phrases together, we ask whether the impairment substantially limited the major life activity. In construing the statute, we are informed by interpretations of parallel definitions in previous statutes and the views of various administrative agencies which have faced this interpretive question.

A

The ADA's definition of disability is drawn almost verbatim from the definition of "handicapped individual" included in the Rehabilitation Act of 1973, 29 U.S.C. § 706(8)(B) (1988 ed.), and the definition of "handicap" contained in the Fair Housing Amendments Act of 1988, 42 U.S.C. § 3602(h)(1) (1988 ed.). Congress' repetition of a well-established term carries the implication that Congress intended the term to be construed in accordance with pre-existing regulatory interpretations. See *FDIC v. Philadelphia Gear Corp.*, 476 U.S. 426, 437—438 (1986); *Commissioner v. Estate of Noel,* 380 U.S. 678, 681–682 (1965); *ICC v. Parker,* 326 U.S. 60, 65 (1945). In this case, Congress did more than suggest this construction; it adopted a specific statutory provision in the ADA directing as follows:

> "Except as otherwise provided in this chapter, nothing in this chapter shall be construed to apply a lesser standard than the standards applied under title V of the Rehabilitation Act of 1973 (29 U.S.C. §790 et seq.) or the regulations issued by Federal agencies pursuant to such title." 42 U.S.C. §12201(a).

The directive requires us to construe the ADA to grant at least as much protection as provided by the regulations implementing the Rehabilitation Act.

1

The first step in the inquiry under subsection (A) requires us to determine whether respondent's condition constituted a physical impairment. The Department of Health, Education and Welfare (HEW) issued the first regulations interpreting the Rehabilitation Act in 1977. The regulations are of particular significance because, at the time, HEW was the agency responsible for coordinating the implementation and enforcement of §504. *Consolidated Rail Corporation v. Darrone,* 465 U.S. 624, 634, (1984) (citing Exec. Order No. 11914, 3 CFR 117 (1976–1980 Comp.)). The HEW regulations, which appear without change in the current regulations issued by the Department of Health and Human Services, define "physical or mental impairment" to mean:

> "(A) any physiological disorder or condition, cosmetic disfigurement, or anatomical loss affecting one or more of the following body systems: neurological; musculoskeletal; special sense organs; respiratory, including speech organs; cardiovascular; reproductive, digestive, genito-urinary; hemic and lymphatic; skin; and endocrine; or

> "(B) any mental or psychological disorder, such as mental retardation, organic brain syndrome, emotional or mental illness, and specific learning disabilities." 45 CFR §84.3(j)(2)(i) (1997).

In issuing these regulations, HEW decided against including a list of disorders constituting physical or mental impairments, out of concern that any specific enumeration might not be comprehensive. 42 Fed. Reg. 22685 (1977), reprinted in 45 CFR pt. 84, App. A, p. 334 (1997). The commentary accompanying the regulations, however, contains a representative list of disorders and conditions constituting physical impairments, including "such diseases and conditions as orthopedic, visual, speech, and hearing impairments, cerebral palsy, epilepsy, muscular dystrophy, multiple sclerosis, cancer, heart disease, diabetes, mental retardation, emotional illness, and . . . drug addiction and alcoholism." *Ibid.*

. . . .

HIV infection is not included in the list of specific disorders constituting physical impairments, in part because HIV was not identified as the cause of AIDS until 1983. . . . HIV infection does fall well within the general definition set forth by the regulations, however.

The disease follows a predictable and, as of today, an unalterable course. Once a person is infected with HIV, the virus invades different cells in the blood and in body tissues. Certain white blood cells, known as helper T-lymphocytes or CD4+ cells, are particularly vulnerable to HIV. The virus attaches to the CD4 receptor site of the target cell and fuses its membrane to the cell's membrane. HIV is a retrovirus, which means it uses an enzyme to convert its own genetic material into a form indistinguishable from the genetic material of the target cell. The virus' genetic material migrates to the cell's nucleus and becomes integrated with the cell's chromosomes. Once integrated, the virus can use the cell's own genetic machinery to replicate itself. Additional copies of the virus are released into the body and infect other cells in turn. Young, *The Replication Cycle of HIV-1*, in The AIDS Knowledge Base, pp. 3.1–2 to 3.1–7 (P. Cohen, M. Sande, & P. Volberding eds., 2d ed. 1994) . . . . Although the body does produce antibodies to combat HIV infection, the antibodies are not effective in eliminating the virus. Pantaleo et al., *Immunopathogenesis of Human Immunodeficiency Virus Infection*, in AIDS: Etiology 79; Garner, *HIV Vaccine Development*, in AIDS Knowledge Base 3.6–5; Haynes, *Immune Responses to Human Immunodeficiency Virus Infection*, in AIDS: Etiology 91.

The virus eventually kills the infected host cell. CD4+ cells play a critical role in coordinating the body's immune response system, and the decline in their number causes corresponding deterioration of the body's ability to fight infections from many sources. Tracking the infected individual's CD4+ cell count is one of the most accurate measures of the course of the disease. Greene, Medical Management of AIDS 19, 24. Osmond, *Classification and Staging of HIV Disease*, in AIDS Knowledge Base 1.1–8; Saag, *Clinical Spectrum of Human Immunodeficiency Virus Diseases*, in AIDS: Etiology 204.

The initial stage of HIV infection is known as acute or primary HIV infection. In a typical case, this stage lasts three months. The virus concentrates in the blood. The assault on the immune system is immediate. The victim suffers from a sudden and serious decline in the number of white blood cells. There is no latency period. Mononucleosis-like symptoms often emerge between six days and six weeks after infection, at times accompanied by fever, headache, enlargement of the lymph nodes (lymphadenopathy), muscle pain (myalgia), rash, lethargy, gastrointestinal disorders, and neurological disorders. . . .

After the symptoms associated with the initial stage subside, the disease enters what is referred to sometimes as its asymptomatic phase. The term is a misnomer, in some respects, for clinical features persist throughout, including lymphadenopathy, dermatological disorders, oral lesions, and bacterial infections. Although it varies with each individual, in most instances this stage lasts from 7 to 11 years. . . . [I]t is now known that the relative lack of symptoms is attributable to the virus' migration from the circulatory system into the lymph nodes. Cohen & Volberding, AIDS Knowledge Base 4.1–4. The migration reduces the viral presence in other parts of the body, with a corresponding diminution in physical manifestations of the disease. The virus, however, thrives in the lymph nodes, which, as a vital point of the body's immune response system, represents an ideal environment for the infection of other CD4+ cells. Strapans & Feinberg, Medical Management of AIDS 33–34. Studies have shown that viral production continues at a high rate. Cohen & Volberding, AIDS Knowledge Base 4.1–4; Strapans & Feinberg, Medical Management of AIDS 38. CD4+ cells continue to decline an average of 5% to 10% (40 to 80 cells/mm3) per year throughout this phase. Saag, AIDS: Etiology 207.

A person is regarded as having AIDS when his or her CD4+ count drops below 200 cells/mm3 of blood or when CD4+ cells comprise less than 14% of his or her total lymphocytes. . . . During this stage, the clinical conditions most often associated with HIV, such as *pneumocystis carninii* pneumonia, Kaposi's sarcoma, and non-Hodgkins lymphoma, tend to appear. In addition, the general systemic disorders present during all stages of the disease, such as fever, weight loss, fatigue, lesions, nausea, and diarrhea, tend to worsen. In most cases, once the patient's CD4+ count drops below 10 cells/mm3, death soon follows. Cohen & Volberding, AIDS Knowledge Base 4.1–9; Saag, AIDS: Etiology 207–209.

In light of the immediacy with which the virus begins to damage the infected person's white blood cells and the severity of the disease, we hold it is an impairment from the moment of infection. As noted earlier, infection with HIV causes immediate abnormalities in a person's blood, and the infected person's white cell count continues to drop throughout the course of the disease, even when the attack is concentrated in the lymph nodes. In light of these facts, HIV infection must be regarded as a physiological disorder with a constant and detrimental effect on the infected person's hemic and lymphatic systems from the moment of infection. HIV infection satisfies the statutory and regulatory definition of a physical impairment during every stage of the disease.

2

The statute is not operative, and the definition not satisfied, unless the impairment affects a major life activity. Respondent's claim throughout this case has been that the HIV infection placed a substantial limitation on her ability to reproduce and to bear children. App. 14; 912 F. Supp., at 586; 107 F.3d, at 939. Given the pervasive, and invariably fatal, course of the disease, its effect on major life activities of many sorts might have been relevant to our inquiry. Respondent and a number of *amici* make arguments about HIV's profound impact on almost every phase of the infected person's life. See Brief for Respondent Sidney Abbott 24–27; Brief for American Medical Association as *Amicus Curiae* 20; Brief for Infectious Diseases Society of America et al. as *Amici Curiae* 7–11. In light of these submissions, it may seem legalistic to circumscribe our discussion to the activity of reproduction. We have little doubt that had different parties brought the suit they would have maintained that an HIV infection imposes substantial limitations on other major life activities.

From the outset, however, the case has been treated as one in which reproduction was the major life activity limited by the impairment. It is our practice to decide cases on the grounds raised and considered in the Court of Appeals and included in the question on which we granted certiorari. See, *e.g., Blessing v. Freestone,* 520 U.S. 329, 340, n. 3 (1997) (citing this Court's Rule 14.1(a));*Capitol Square Review and Advisory Bd. v. Pinette,* 515 U.S. 753, 760 (1995). We ask, then, whether reproduction is a major life activity.

We have little difficulty concluding that it is. . . . While petitioner concedes the importance of reproduction, he claims that Congress intended the ADA only to cover those aspects of a person's life which have a public, economic, or daily character. Brief for Petitioner 14, 28, 30, 31; see also *id.,* at 36–37 (citing *Krauel v. Iowa Methodist Medical Center,* 95 F.3d 674, 677 (CA8 1996)). The argument founders on the statutory language. Nothing in the definition suggests that activities without a public, economic, or daily dimension may somehow be regarded as so unimportant or insignificant as to fall outside the meaning of the word "major." The breadth of the term confounds the attempt to limit its construction in this manner.

As we have noted, the ADA must be construed to be consistent with regulations issued to implement the Rehabilitation Act. See 42 U.S.C. §12201(a). Rather than enunciating a general principle for determining what is and is not a major life activity, the Rehabilitation Act regulations instead provide a representative list, defining term to include "functions such as caring for one's self, performing manual tasks, walking, seeing, hearing, speaking, breathing, learning, and working." 45 CFR §84.3(j)(2)(ii) (1997); 28 CFR §41.31(b)(2) (1997). As the use of the term "such as" confirms, the list is illustrative, not exhaustive.

These regulations are contrary to petitioner's attempt to limit the meaning of the term "major" to public activities. The inclusion of activities such as caring for one's self and performing manual tasks belies the suggestion that a task must have a public or economic character in order to be a major life activity for purposes of the ADA. On the contrary, the Rehabilitation Act regulations support the inclusion of reproduction as a major life activity, since reproduction could not be regarded as any less important than working and learning. Petitioner advances no credible basis for confining major life activities to those with a public, economic, or daily aspect. In the absence of any reason to reach a contrary conclusion, we agree with the Court of Appeals' determination that reproduction is a major life activity for the purposes of the ADA.

3

The final element of the disability definition in subsection (A) is whether respondent's physical impairment was a substantial limit on the major life activity she asserts. The Rehabilitation Act regulations provide no additional guidance. 45 CFR pt. 84, App. A, p. 334 (1997).

Our evaluation of the medical evidence leads us to conclude that respondent's infection substantially limited her ability to reproduce in two independent ways. First, a woman infected with HIV who tries to conceive a child imposes on the man a significant risk of becoming infected. The cumulative results of 13 studies collected in a 1994 textbook on AIDS indicates that 20% of male partners of women with HIV became HIV-positive themselves, with a majority of the studies finding a statistically significant risk of infection. Osmond & Padian, *Sexual Transmission of HIV*, in AIDS Knowledge Base 1.9–8, and tbl. 2; see also Haverkos & Battjes, *Female-to-Male Transmission of HIV*, 268 JAMA 1855, 1856, tbl. (1992) . . . .

Second, an infected woman risks infecting her child during gestation and childbirth, *i.e.,* perinatal transmission. Petitioner concedes that women infected with HIV face about a 25% risk of transmitting the virus to their children. 107 F.3d, at 942; 912 F. Supp., at 387, n. 6. Published reports available in 1994 confirm the accuracy of this statistic. Report of a Consensus Workshop, *Maternal Factors Involved in Mother-to-Child Transmission of HIV-1*, 5 J. Acquired Immune Deficiency Syndromes 1019, 1020 (1992) . . . .

The Act addresses substantial limitations on major life activities, not utter inabilities. Conception and childbirth are not impossible for an HIV victim but, without doubt, are dangerous to the public health. This meets the definition of a substantial limitation. The decision to reproduce carries economic and legal consequences as well. There are added costs for antiretroviral therapy, supplemental insurance, and long-term health care for the child who must be examined and, tragic to think, treated for the infection. The laws of some States, moreover, forbid persons infected with HIV from having sex with others, regardless of consent. Iowa Code §§ 139.1, 139.31 (1997); Md. Health Code Ann. § 18-601.1(a) (1994); Mont. Code Ann. §§ 50-18-101, 50-18-112 (1997); Utah Code Ann. § 26-6-3.5(3) (Supp. 1997); *id.,* § 26-6-5 (1995); Wash. Rev. Code § 9A.36.011(1)(b) (Supp. 1998); see also N.D. Cent. Code § 12.1-20-17 (1997).

In the end, the disability definition does not turn on personal choice. When significant limitations result from the impairment, the definition is met even if the difficulties are not insurmountable. For the statistical and other reasons we have cited, of course, the limitations on reproduction may be insurmountable here. Testimony from the respondent that her HIV infection controlled her decision not to have a child is unchallenged. App. 14; 912 F. Supp., at 587; 107 F.3d, at 942. In the context of reviewing summary judgment, we must take it to be true. Fed. Rule Civ. Proc. 56(e). We agree with the District Court and the Court of Appeals that no triable issue of fact impedes a ruling on the question of statutory coverage. Respondent's HIV infection is a physical impairment which substantially limits a major life activity, as the ADA defines it. In view of our holding, we need not address the second question presented, *i.e.,* whether HIV infection is a *per se* disability under the ADA.

B

Our holding is confirmed by a consistent course of agency interpretation before and after enactment of the ADA. Every agency to consider the issue under the Rehabilitation Act found statutory coverage for persons with asymptomatic HIV. Responsibility for administering the Rehabilitation Act was not delegated to a single agency, but we need not pause to inquire whether this causes us to withhold deference to agency interpretations under *Chevron U.S.A. Inc. v. Natural Resources Defense Council, Inc.,* 467 U.S. 837, 844 (1984). It is enough to observe that the well-reasoned views of the agencies implementing a statute "constitute a body of experience and informed judgment to which courts and litigants may properly resort for guidance." *Skidmore v. Swift & Co.,* 323 U.S. 134, 139–140 (1944).

One comprehensive and significant administrative precedent is a 1988 opinion issued by the Office of Legal Counsel of the Department of Justice (OLC) concluding that the Rehabilitation Act "protects symptomatic and asymptomatic HIV-infected individuals against discrimination in any covered program." Application of Section 504 of the Rehabilitation Act to HIV-Infected Individuals, 12 Op. Off. Legal Counsel 264, 264–265 (Sept. 27, 1988) (preliminary print) (footnote omitted). . . .

In addition, OLC indicated that "[t]he life activity of engaging in sexual relations is threatened and probably substantially limited by the contagiousness of the virus." *Id.,* at 274. Either consideration was sufficient to render asymptomatic HIV infection a handicap for purposes of the Rehabilitation Act. In the course of its Opinion, OLC considered, and rejected, the contention that the limitation could be discounted as a voluntary response to the infection. The limitation, it reasoned, was the infection's manifest physical effect. *Id.,* at 274, and n. 13. Without exception, the other agencies to address the problem before enactment of the ADA reached the same result. Federal Contract Compliance Manual App. 6D, 8 FEP Manual 405:352 (Dec. 23, 1988); *In re David Ritter,* No. 03890089, 1989 WL 609697, *10 (EEOC, Dec. 8, 1989); see also Comptroller General's Task Force on AIDS in the Workplace. . . .

Every court which addressed the issue before the ADA was enacted in July 1990, moreover, concluded that asymptomatic HIV infection satisfied the Rehabilitation Act's definition of a handicap. See *Doe v. Garrett,* 903 F.2d 1455, 1457 (CA11 1990), cert. denied, 499 U.S. 904 (1991); *Ray v. School Dist. of DeSoto County,* 666 F. Supp. 1524, 1536 (MD Fla. 1987). . . . We are aware of no instance prior to the enactment of the ADA in which a court or agency ruled that HIV infection was not a handicap under the Rehabilitation Act.

Had Congress done nothing more than copy the Rehabilitation Act definition into the ADA, its action would indicate the new statute should be construed in light of this unwavering line of administrative and judicial interpretation. All indications are that Congress was well aware of the position taken by OLC when enacting the ADA and intended to give that position its active endorsement. H. R. Rep. No. 101-485, pt. 2, p. 52 (1990) (endorsing the analysis and conclusion of the OLC Opinion); *id.,* pt. 3, at 28, n. 18 (same); S. Rep. No. 101–116, pp. 21, 22 (1989) (same). As noted earlier, Congress also incorporated the same definition into the Fair Housing Amendments Act of 1988. See 42 U.S.C. § 3602(h)(1). We find it significant that the implementing regulations issued by the Department of Housing and Urban Development (HUD) construed the definition to include infection with HIV. 54 Fed. Reg. 3232, 3245 (1989) (codified at 24 CFR § 100.201 (1997). . . .

. . . .

C

The regulatory authorities we cite are consistent with our holding that HIV infection, even in the so-called asymptomatic phase, is an impairment which substantially limits the major life activity of reproduction.

III

. . . .

Of the [questions presented], we granted certiorari only on question three. The question is phrased in an awkward way, for it conflates two separate inquiries. In asking whether it is appropriate to defer to petitioner's judgment, it assumes that petitioner's assessment of the objective facts was reasonable. The central premise of the question and the assumption on which it is based merit separate consideration.

Again, we begin with the statute. Notwithstanding the protection given respondent by the ADA's definition of disability, petitioner could have refused to treat her if her infectious condition "pose[d] a direct threat to the health or safety of others." 42 U.S.C. § 12182(b)(3). The ADA defines a direct threat to be "a significant risk to the health or safety of others that cannot be eliminated by a modification of policies, practices, or procedures or by the provision of auxiliary aids or services." *Ibid.* Parallel provisions appear in the employment provisions of Title I. §§ 12111(3), 12113(b).

The ADA's direct threat provision stems from the recognition in *School Bd. of Nassau Cty. v. Arline,* 480 U.S. 273, 287 (1987), of the importance of prohibiting discrimination against individuals with disabilities while protecting others from significant health and safety risks, resulting, for instance, from a contagious disease. In *Arline,* the Court reconciled these objectives by construing the Rehabilitation Act not to require the hiring of a person who posed "a significant risk of communicating an infectious disease to others." *Id.,* at 287, n. 16. Congress amended the Rehabilitation Act and the Fair Housing Act to incorporate the language. See 29 U.S.C. § 706(8)(D) (excluding individuals who "would constitute a direct threat to the health or safety of other individuals"); 42 U.S.C. § 3604(f)(9) (same). It later relied on the same language in enacting the ADA. See 28 CFR pt. 36, App. B, p. 626 (1997) (ADA's direct threat provision codifies *Arline*). Because few, if any, activities in life are risk free, *Arline* and the ADA do not ask whether a risk exists, but whether it is significant. *Arline, supra,* at 287, and n. 16; 42 U.S.C. § 12182(b)(3).

The existence, or nonexistence, of a significant risk must be determined from the standpoint of the person who refuses the treatment or accommodation, and the risk assessment must be based on medical or other objective evidence. *Arline, supra*, at 288; 28 CFR § 36.208(c) (1997); *id.*, pt. 36, App. B, p. 626. As a health care professional, petitioner had the duty to assess the risk of infection based on the objective, scientific information available to him and others in his profession. His belief that a significant risk existed, even if maintained in good faith, would not relieve him from liability. To use the words of the question presented, petitioner receives no special deference simply because he is a health care professional. It is true that *Arline* reserved "the question whether courts should also defer to the reasonable medical judgments of private physicians on which an employer has relied." 480 U.S., at 288, n. 18. At most, this statement reserved the possibility that employers could consult with individual physicians as objective third-party experts. It did not suggest that an individual physician's state of mind could excuse discrimination without regard to the objective reasonableness of his actions.

Our conclusion that courts should assess the objective reasonableness of the views of health care professionals without deferring to their individual judgments does not answer the implicit assumption in the question presented, whether petitioner's actions were reasonable in light of the available medical evidence. In assessing the reasonableness of petitioner's actions, the views of public health authorities, such as the U.S. Public Health Service, CDC, and the National Institutes of Health, are of special weight and authority. *Arline, supra*, at 288; 28 CFR pt. 36, App. B, p. 626 (1997). The views of these organizations are not conclusive, however. A health care professional who disagrees with the prevailing medical consensus may refute it by citing a credible scientific basis for deviating from the accepted norm. See W. Keeton, D. Dobbs, R. Keeton, & D. Owen, Prosser and Keeton on Law of Torts § 32, p. 187 (5th ed. 1984).

We have reviewed so much of the record as necessary to illustrate the application of the rule to the facts of this case. For the most part, the Court of Appeals followed the proper standard in evaluating the petitioner's position and conducted a thorough review of the evidence. Its rejection of the District Court's reliance on the Marianos affidavits was a correct application of the principle that petitioner's actions must be evaluated in light of the available, objective evidence. The record did not show that CDC had published the conclusion set out in the affidavits at the time petitioner refused to treat respondent. 107 F.3d, at 946, n. 7.

A further illustration of a correct application of the objective standard is the Court of Appeals' refusal to give weight to the petitioner's offer to treat respondent in a hospital. *Id.*, at 943, n. 4. Petitioner testified that he believed hospitals had safety measures, such as air filtration, ultraviolet lights, and respirators, which would reduce the risk of HIV transmission. App. 151. Petitioner made no showing, however, that any area hospital had these safeguards or even that he had hospital privileges. *Id.*, at 31. His expert also admitted the lack of any scientific basis for the conclusion that these measures would lower the risk of transmission. *Id.*, at 209. Petitioner failed to present any objective, medical evidence showing that treating respondent in a hospital would be safer or more efficient in preventing HIV transmission than treatment in a well-equipped dental office.

We are concerned, however, that the Court of Appeals might have placed mistaken reliance upon two other sources. In ruling no triable issue of fact existed on this point, the Court of Appeals relied on the 1993 CDC Dentistry Guidelines and the 1991 American Dental Association Policy on HIV. 107 F.3d, at 945–946. This evidence is not definitive. As noted earlier, the CDC Guidelines recommended certain universal precautions which, in CDC's view, "should reduce the risk of disease transmission in the dental environment." U.S. Dept. of Health and Human Services, Public Health Service, CDC, *Recommended Infection Control Practices for Dentistry*, 41 Morbidity & Mortality Weekly Rep. No. RR-18, p. 1 (May 28, 1993). . . . In our view, the Guidelines do not necessarily contain implicit assumptions conclusive of the point to be decided. The Guidelines set out CDC's recommendation that the universal precautions are the best way to combat the risk of HIV transmission. They do not assess the level of risk.

Nor can we be certain, on this record, whether the 1991 American Dental Association Policy on HIV carries the weight the Court of Appeals attributed to it. The Policy does provide some evidence of the medical community's objective assessment of the risks posed by treating people infected with HIV in dental offices. It indicates:

> "Current scientific and epidemiologic evidence indicates that there is little risk of transmission of infectious diseases through dental treatment if recommended infection control procedures are routinely followed. Patients with HIV infection may be safely treated in private dental offices when appropriate infection control procedures are employed. Such infection control procedures provide protection both for patients and dental personnel." App. 225.

We note, however, that the Association is a professional organization, which, although a respected source of information on the dental profession, is not a public health authority. It is not clear the extent to which the Policy was based on the Association's assessment of dentists' ethical and professional duties in addition to its scientific assessment of the risk to which the ADA refers. Efforts to clarify dentists' ethical obligations and to encourage dentists to treat patients with HIV infection with compassion may be commendable, but the question under the statute is one of statistical likelihood, not professional responsibility. Without more information on the manner in which the American Dental Association formulated this Policy, we are unable to determine the Policy's value in evaluating whether petitioner's assessment of the risks was reasonable as a matter of law.

. . . .

Our evaluation of the evidence is constrained by the fact that on these and other points we have not had briefs and arguments directed to the entire record. . . . We conclude the proper course is to give the Court of Appeals the opportunity to determine whether our analysis of some of the studies cited by the parties would change its conclusion that petitioner presented neither objective evidence nor a triable issue of fact on the question of risk. In remanding the case, we do not foreclose the possibility that the Court of Appeals may reach the same conclusion it did earlier. A remand will permit a full exploration of the issue through the adversary process.

The determination of the Court of Appeals that respondent's HIV infection was a disability under the ADA is affirmed. The judgment is vacated, and the case is remanded for further proceedings consistent with this opinion.

E. The Individuals with Disabilities in Education Act

As mentioned above, the IDEA protects individuals with disabilities in education. This is one of the hardest statutes to enforce, as enforcement often depends on both awareness by parents and resources from the school district. The cases below show that school districts and courts struggle with the very clear mandates of the statute. How do you assess the statute's goals compared to courts' resolution of these issues?

Cedar Rapids Community School Dist. v. Garret F.

526 U.S. 66 (1999)

. . . .

I

Respondent Garret F. is a friendly, creative, and intelligent young man. When Garret was four years old, his spinal column was severed in a motorcycle accident. Though paralyzed from the neck down, his mental capacities were unaffected. He is able to speak, to control his motorized wheelchair through use of a puff and suck straw, and to operate a computer with a device that responds to head movements. Garret is currently a student in the Cedar Rapids Community School District (District), he attends regular classes in a typical school program, and his academic performance has been a success. Garret is, however, ventilator dependent, and therefore requires a responsible individual nearby to attend to certain physical needs while he is in school.

Amendments of 1990, § 101(c), 104 Stat. 1103, the relevant language in § 1401(a)(17) has not been amended since 1975. All references to the IDEA herein are to the 1994 version as codified in Title 20 of the United States Code—the version of the statute in effect when this dispute arose. In his report in this case, the Administrative Law Judge explained:

> "Being ventilator dependent means that [Garret] breathes only with external aids, usually an electric ventilator, and occasionally by someone else's

manual pumping of an air bag attached to his tracheotomy tube when the ventilator is being maintained. This later procedure is called ambu bagging." App. to Pet. for Cert. 19a.

"He needs assistance with urinary bladder catheterization once a day, the suctioning of his tracheotomy tube as needed, but at least once every six hours, with food and drink at lunchtime, in getting into a reclining position for five minutes of each hour, and ambu bagging occasionally as needed when the ventilator is checked for proper functioning. He also needs assistance from someone familiar with his ventilator in the event there is a malfunction or electrical problem, and someone who can perform emergency procedures in the event he experiences autonomic hyperreflexia. Autonomic hyperreflexia is an uncontrolled visceral reaction to anxiety or a full bladder. Blood pressure increases, heart rate increases, and flushing and sweating may occur. Garret has not experienced autonomic hyperreflexia frequently in recent years, and it has usually been alleviated by catheterization. He has not ever experienced autonomic hyperreflexia at school. Garret is capable of communicating his needs orally or in another fashion so long as he has not been rendered unable to do so by an extended lack of oxygen." *Id.* at 20a.

During Garret's early years at school his family provided for his physical care during the school day. When he was in kindergarten, his 18-year-old aunt attended him; in the next four years, his family used settlement proceeds they received after the accident, their insurance, and other resources to employ a licensed practical nurse. In 1993, Garret's mother requested the District to accept financial responsibility for the health care services that Garret requires during the school day. The District denied the request, believing that it was not legally obligated to provide continuous one-on-one nursing services.

Relying on both the IDEA and Iowa law, Garret's mother requested a hearing before the Iowa Department of Education. An Administrative Law Judge (ALJ) received extensive evidence concerning Garret's special needs, the District's treatment of other disabled students, and the assistance provided to other ventilator-dependent children in other parts of the country. In his 47-page report, the ALJ found that the District has about 17,500 students, of whom approximately 2,200 need some form of special education or special services. Although Garret is the only ventilator-dependent student in the District, most of the health care services that he needs are already provided for some other students. "The primary difference between Garret's situation and that of other students is his dependency on his ventilator for life support." App. to Pet. for Cert. 28a. The ALJ noted that the parties disagreed over the training or licensure required for the care and supervision of such students, and that those providing such care in other parts of the country ranged from nonlicensed personnel to registered nurses. However, the District did not contend that only a licensed physician could provide the services in question.

The ALJ explained that federal law requires that children with a variety of health impairments be provided with "special education and related services" when their disabilities adversely affect their academic performance, and that such children should be educated to the maximum extent appropriate with children who are not disabled. In addition, the ALJ explained that applicable federal regulations distinguish between "school health services," which are provided by a "qualified school nurse or other qualified person," and "medical services," which are provided by a licensed physician. See 34 CFR §§ 300.16(a), (b)(4), (b)(ll) (1998). The District must provide the former, but need not provide the latter (except, of course, those "medical services" that are for diagnostic or evaluation purposes, 20 U.S.C. § 1401(a)(17)). According to the ALJ, the distinction in the regulations does not just depend on "the title of the person providing the service"; instead, the "medical services" exclusion is limited to services that are "in the special training, knowledge, and judgment of a physician to carry out." App. to Pet. for Cert. 51a. The ALJ thus concluded that the IDEA required the District to bear financial responsibility for all of the services in dispute, including continuous nursing services.

In addition, the ALJ's opinion contains a thorough discussion of "other tests and criteria" pressed by the District, *id.*, at 52a, including the burden on the District and the cost of providing assistance to Garret. Although the ALJ found no legal authority for establishing a cost-based test for determining what related services are required by the statute, he went on to reject the District's arguments on the merits. See *id.*, at 42a-53a. We do not reach the issue here, but the ALJ also found that Garret's in-school needs must be met by the District under an Iowa statute as well as the IDEA. *Id.*, at 54a-55a.

The District challenged the ALJ's decision in Federal District Court, but that court approved the ALJ's IDEA ruling and granted summary judgment against the District. *Id.*, at 9a, 15a. The Court of Appeals affirmed. 106 F.3d 822 (CA8 1997). It noted that, as a recipient of federal funds under the IDEA, Iowa has a statutory duty to provide all disabled children a "free appropriate public education," which includes "related services." See *id.*, at 824. The Court of Appeals read our opinion in *Irving Independent School Dist. v. Tatro*, 468 U.S. 883 (1984), to provide a two-step analysis of the "related services" definition in § 1401(a)(17) — asking first, whether the requested services are included within the phrase "supportive services"; and second, whether the services are excluded as "medical services." 106 F.3d, at 824–825. The Court of Appeals succinctly answered both questions in Garret's favor. The court found the first step plainly satisfied, since Garret cannot attend school unless the requested services are available during the school day. *Id.*, at 825. As to the second step, the court reasoned that *Tatro* "established a bright-line test: the services of a physician (other than for diagnostic and evaluation purposes) are subject to the medical services exclusion, but services that can be provided in the school setting by a nurse or qualified layperson are not." 106 F. 3d, at 825.

In its petition for certiorari, the District challenged only the second step of the Court of Appeals' analysis. The District pointed out that some federal courts have not asked whether the requested health services must be delivered by a physician, but instead have applied a multifactor test that considers, generally speaking, the nature and extent of the services at issue. See, *e.g., Neely v. Rutherford County School,* 68 F.3d 965, 972–973 (CA6 1995), cert. denied, 517 U.S. 1134 (1996); *Detsel v. Board of Ed. of Auburn Enlarged City School Dist.,* 820 F.2d 587, 588 (CA2) *(per curiam),* cert. denied, 484 U.S. 981 (1987). We granted the District's petition to resolve this conflict. 523 U. S. 1117 (1998).

II

The District contends that § 1401(a)(17) does not require it to provide Garret with "continuous one-on-one nursing services" during the school day, even though Garret cannot remain in school without such care. Brief for Petitioner 10. However, the IDEA's definition of "related services," our decision in *Irving Independent School Dist. v. Tatro,* 468 U.S. 883 (1984), and the overall statutory scheme all support the decision of the Court of Appeals.

The text of the "related services" definition, see n. 1, *supra,* broadly encompasses those supportive services that "may be required to assist a child with a disability to benefit from special education." As we have already noted, the District does not challenge the Court of Appeals' conclusion that the in-school services at issue are within the covered category of "supportive services." As a general matter, services that enable a disabled child to remain in school during the day provide the student with "the meaningful access to education that Congress envisioned." *Tatro,* 468 U.S., at 891 ("'Congress sought primarily to make public education available to handicapped children' and 'to make such access meaningful'" (quoting *Board of Ed. of Hendrick Hudson Central School Dist., Westchester Cty. v. Rowley,* 458 U.S. 176, 192 (1982))).

This general definition of "related services" is illuminated by a parenthetical phrase listing examples of particular services that are included within the statute's coverage. § 1401(a)(17). "[M]edical services" are enumerated in this list, but such services are limited to those that are "for diagnostic and evaluation purposes." *Ibid.* The statute does not contain a more specific definition of the "medical services" that are excepted from the coverage of § 1401(a)(17).

The scope of the "medical services" exclusion is not a matter of first impression in this Court. In *Tatro* we concluded that the Secretary of Education had reasonably determined that the term "medical services" referred only to services that must be performed by a physician, and not to school health services. 468 U.S., at 892–894. Accordingly, we held that a specific form of health care (clean intermittent catheterization) that is often, though not always, performed by a nurse is not an excluded medical service. We referenced the likely cost of the services and the competence of school staff as justifications for drawing a line between physician and other services, ibid., but our endorsement of that line was unmistakable. It is thus settled that the phrase

> "The regulations define 'related services' for handicapped children to include 'school health services,' 34 CFR § 300.13(a) (1983), which are defined in turn as 'services provided by a qualified school nurse or other qualified person,' § 300.13(b)(10). 'Medical services' are defined as 'services provided by a licensed physician.' § 300.13(b)(4). Thus, the Secretary has [reasonably] determined that the services of a school nurse otherwise qualifying as a 'related service' are not subject to exclusion as a 'medical service,' but that the services of a physician are excludable as such.

> "... *By limiting the 'medical services' exclusion to the services of a physician or hospital,* both far more expensive, the Secretary has given a permissible construction to the provision." 468 U.S., at 892–893 (emphasis added) (footnote omitted); see also *id.,* at 894 ("[T]he regulations state that school nursing services must be provided only if they can be performed by a nurse or other qualified person, not if they must be performed by a physician").

Based on certain policy letters issued by the Department of Education, it seems that the Secretary's *post-Tatro* view of the statute has not been entirely clear. *E.g.,* App. to Pet. for Cert. 64a. We may assume that the Secretary has authority under the IDEA to adopt regulations that define the "medical services" exclusion by more explicitly taking into account the nature and extent of the requested services; and the Secretary surely has the authority to enumerate the services that are, and are not, fairly included within the scope of § 1407(a)(17). But the Secretary has done neither; and, in this Court, he advocates affirming the judgment of the Court of Appeals. Brief for United States as *Amicus Curiae* 7–8, 30; see also *Auer v. Robbins,* 519 U.S. 452, 462 (1997) (an agency's views as *amicus curiae* may be entitled to deference). We obviously have no authority to rewrite the regulations, and we see no sufficient reason to revise *Tatro,* either.

> ... "medical services" in § 1401(a)(17) does not embrace all forms of care that might loosely be described as "medical" in other contexts, such as a claim for an income tax deduction. See 26 U.S.C. § 213(d)(1) (1994 ed. and Supp. II) (defining "medical care").

The District does not ask us to define the term so broadly.

Indeed, the District does not argue that any of the items of care that Garret needs, considered individually, could be excluded from the scope of 20 U.S.C. § 1401(a)(17). It could not make such an argument, considering that one of the services Garret needs (catheterization) was at issue in *Tatro,* and the others may be provided competently by a school nurse or other trained personnel. See App. to Pet. for Cert. 15a, 52a. As the ALJ concluded, most of the requested services are already provided by the District to other students, and the in-school care necessitated by Garret's ventilator dependency does not demand the training, knowledge, and judgment of a licensed physician. *Id.,* at 51a–52a. While more extensive, the in-school services Garret needs are no more "medical" than was the care sought in *Tatro.*

Instead, the District points to the combined and continuous character of the required care, and proposes a test under which the outcome in any particular case would "depend upon a series of factors, such as [1] whether the care is continuous or intermittent, [2] whether existing school health personnel can provide the service, [3] the cost of the service, and [4] the potential consequences if the service is not properly performed." Brief for Petitioner 11; see also *id.,* at 34–35.

The District's multifactor test is not supported by any recognized source of legal authority. The proposed factors can be found in neither the text of the statute nor the regulations that we upheld in *Tatro.* Moreover, the District offers no explanation why these characteristics make one service . . . any more "medical" than another. The continuous character of certain services associated with Garret's ventilator dependency has no apparent relationship to "medical" services, much less a relationship of equivalence. Continuous services may be more costly and may require additional school personnel, but they are not thereby more "medical." Whatever its imperfections, a rule that limits the medical services exemption to physician services is unquestionably a reasonable and generally workable interpretation of the statute. Absent an elaboration of the statutory terms plainly more convincing than that which we reviewed in *Tatro,* there is no good reason to depart from settled law.

Finally, the District raises broader concerns about the financial burden that it must bear to provide the services that Garret needs to stay in school. The problem for the District in providing these services is not that its staff cannot be trained to deliver them; the problem, the District contends, is that the existing school health staff cannot meet all of their [needs.]

. . . .

The District may have legitimate financial concerns, but our role in this dispute is to interpret existing law. Defining "related services" in a manner that *accommodates* the cost concerns Congress may have had, cf. *Tatro,* 468 U.S., at 892, is altogether different from using cost *itself* as the definition. Given that § 1401(a)(17) does not employ cost in its definition of "related services" or excluded "medical services," accepting the District's cost-based standard as the sole test for determining the scope of the provision would require us to engage in judicial lawmaking without any guidance from Congress. It would also create some tension with the purposes of the IDEA. The statute may not require public schools to maximize the potential of disabled students. See Tr. of Oral Arg. 4–5, 13; Brief for Petitioner 6–7, 9. The District, however, will not necessarily need to hire an additional employee to meet Garret's needs. The District already employs a one-on-one teacher associate (TA) who assists Garret during the school day. See App. to Pet. for Cert. 26a–27a. At one time, Garret's TA was a licensed practical nurse (LPN). In light of the state Board of Nursing's recent ruling that the District's registered nurses may decide to delegate Garret's care to an LPN, see Brief for United States as *Amicus Curiae* 9–10 (filed Apr. 22, 1998), the dissent's future-cost estimate is speculative. See App. to Pet. for Cert. 28a, 58a-60a (if the District could assign Garret's care to a TA who is also an LPN, there would be "a minimum of additional expense").

. . . .

Board of Education v. Rowley

458 U.S. 176 (1982)

JUSTICE REHNQUIST delivered the opinion of the Court.

This case presents a question of statutory interpretation. Petitioners contend that the Court of Appeals and the District Court misconstrued the requirements imposed by Congress upon States which receive federal funds under the Education of the Handicapped Act. We agree, and reverse the judgment of the Court of Appeals.

I

The Education of the Handicapped Act (Act), 84 Stat. 175, as amended, 20 U.S.C. § 1401 *et seq.* (1976 ed. and Supp. IV), provides federal money to assist state and local agencies in educating handicapped children, and conditions such funding upon a State's compliance with extensive goals and procedures. The Act represents an ambitious federal effort to promote the education of handicapped children, and was passed in response to Congress' perception that a majority of handicapped children in the United States

"were either totally excluded from schools or [were] sitting idly in regular classrooms awaiting the time when they were old enough to 'drop out.'"

H.R.Rep. No. 94 332, p. 2 (1975) (H.R.Rep.). The Act's evolution and major provisions shed light on the question of statutory interpretation which is at the heart of this case.

. . . .

. . . Congress in 1974 greatly increased federal funding for education of the handicapped and, for the first time, required recipient States to adopt "a goal of providing full educational opportunities to all handicapped children." Pub.L. 93-380, 88 Stat. 579, 583 (1974 statute). The 1974 statute was recognized as an interim measure only, adopted "in order to give the Congress an additional year in which to study what, if any, additional Federal assistance [was] required to enable the States to meet the needs of handicapped children."

H.R.Rep. at 4. The ensuing year of study produced the Education for All Handicapped Children Act of 1975. In order to qualify for federal financial assistance under the Act, a State must demonstrate that it "has in effect a policy that assures all handicapped children the right to a free appropriate public education." 20 U.S.C. § 1412(1). That policy must be reflected in a state plan submitted to and approved by the Secretary of Education, § 1413, which describes in detail the goals, programs, and timetables under which the State intends to educate handicapped children within its borders. §§ 1412, 1413. States receiving money under the Act must provide education to the handicapped by priority, first "to handicapped children who are not receiving an education" and second "to handicapped children . . . with the most severe handicaps who are receiving an inadequate education," § 1412(3), and, "to the maximum extent appropriate," must educate handicapped children "with children who are not handicapped." § 1412(5). The Act broadly defines "handicapped children" to include "mentally retarded, hard of hearing, deaf, speech impaired, visually handicapped, seriously emotionally disturbed, orthopedically impaired, [and] other health impaired children, [and] children with specific learning disabilities." § 1401(1).

The "free appropriate public education" required by the Act is tailored to the unique needs of the handicapped child by means of an "individualized educational program" (IEP). § 1401(18). The IEP, which is prepared at a meeting between a qualified representative of the local educational agency, the child's teacher, the child's parents or guardian, and, where appropriate, the child, consists of a written document containing "(A) a statement of the present levels of educational performance of such child, (B) a statement of annual goals, including short-term instructional objectives, (C) a statement of the specific educational services to be provided to such child, and the extent to which such child will be able to participate in regular educational programs, (D) the projected date for initiation and anticipated duration of such services, and (E) appropriate objective criteria and evaluation procedures and schedules for determining, on at least an annual basis, whether instructional objectives are being achieved." § 1401(19). Local or regional educational agencies must review, and, where appropriate, revise, each child's IEP at least annually. § 1414(a)(5). See also § 1413(a)(11).

In addition to the state plan and the IEP already described, the Act imposes extensive procedural requirements upon States receiving federal funds under its provisions. Parents or guardians of handicapped children must be notified of any proposed change in "the identification, evaluation, or educational placement of the child or the provision of a free appropriate public education to such child," and must be permitted to bring a complaint about "any matter relating to" such evaluation and education. §§ 1415(b)(1)(D) and (E).

Complaints brought by parents or guardians must be resolved at "an impartial due process hearing," and appeal to the state educational agency must be provided if the initial hearing is held at the local or regional level. §§ 1415(b)(2) and (C). Thereafter, "[a]ny party aggrieved by the findings and decision" of the state administrative hearing has "the right to bring a civil action with respect to the complaint . . . in any State court of competent jurisdiction or in a district court of the United States without regard to the amount in controversy." § 1415(e)(2).

Thus, although the Act leaves to the States the primary responsibility for developing and executing educational programs for handicapped children, it imposes significant requirements to be followed in the discharge of that responsibility. Compliance is assured by provisions permitting the withholding of federal funds upon determination that a participating state or local agency has failed to satisfy the requirements of the Act, §§ 1414(b)(2)(A), 1416, and by the provision for judicial review. At present, all States except New Mexico receive federal funds under the portions of the Act at issue today. Brief for United States as *Amicus Curiae* 2, n. 2.

II

This case arose in connection with the education of Amy Rowley, a deaf student at the Furnace Woods School in the Hendrick Hudson Central School District, Peekskill, N.Y. Amy has minimal residual hearing, and is an excellent lip-reader. During the year before she began attending Furnace Woods, a meeting between her parents and school administrators resulted in a decision to place her in a regular kindergarten class in order to determine what supplemental services would be necessary to her education. Several members of the school administration prepared for Amy's arrival by attending a course in sign-language interpretation, and a teletype machine was installed in the principal's office to facilitate communication with her parents, who are also deaf. At the end of the trial period, it was determined that Amy should remain in the kindergarten class, but that she should be provided with an FM hearing aid which would amplify words spoken into a wireless receiver by the teacher or fellow students during certain classroom activities. Amy successfully completed her kindergarten year.

As required by the Act, an IEP was prepared for Amy during the fall of her first-grade year. The IEP provided that Amy should be educated in a regular classroom at Furnace Woods, should continue to use the FM hearing aid, and should receive instruction from a tutor for the deaf for one hour each day and from a speech therapist for three hours each week. The Rowleys agreed with parts of the IEP, but insisted that Amy also be provided a qualified sign-language interpreter in all her academic classes in lieu of the assistance proposed in other parts of the IEP. Such an interpreter had been placed in Amy's kindergarten class for a 2-week experimental period, but the interpreter had reported that Amy did not need his services at that time. The school administrators likewise concluded that Amy did not need such an interpreter in her first-grade classroom. They reached this conclusion after consulting the school district's Committee on the Handicapped, which had received expert evidence from Amy's parents on the importance of a sign-language interpreter, received testimony from Amy's teacher and other persons familiar with her academic and social progress, and visited a class for the deaf.

When their request for an interpreter was denied, the Rowleys demanded and received a hearing before an independent examiner. After receiving evidence from both sides, the examiner agreed with the administrators' determination that an interpreter was not necessary, because "Amy was achieving educationally, academically, and socially" without such assistance. App. to Pet. for Cert. F-22. The examiner's decision was affirmed on appeal by the New York Commissioner of Education on the basis of substantial evidence in the record. *Id.* at E-4. Pursuant to the Act's provision for judicial review, the Rowleys then brought an action in the United States District Court for the Southern District of New York, claiming that the administrators' denial of the sign-language interpreter constituted a denial of the "free appropriate public education" guaranteed by the Act.

The District Court found that Amy "is a remarkably well-adjusted child" who interacts and communicates well with her classmates and has "developed an extraordinary rapport" with her teachers. 483 F.Supp. 528, 531 (1980). It also found that "she performs better than the average child in her class, and is advancing easily from grade to grade," *id.* at 534, but "that she understands considerably less of what goes on in class than she could if she were not deaf," and thus "is not learning as much, or performing as well academically, as she would without her handicap," *id.* at 532. This disparity between Amy's achievement and her potential led the court to decide that she was not receiving a "free appropriate public education," which the court defined as "an opportunity to achieve [her] full potential commensurate with the opportunity provided to other children." *Id.* at 534. . . .

A divided panel of the United States Court of Appeals for the Second Circuit affirmed. The Court of Appeals "agree[d] with the [D]istrict [C]ourt's conclusions of law," and held that its "findings of fact [were] not clearly erroneous." 632 F.2d 945, 947 (1980).

We granted certiorari to review the lower courts' interpretation of the Act. 454 U.S. 961 (1981). Such review requires us to consider two questions: what is meant by the Act's requirement of a "free appropriate public education"? And what is the role of state and federal courts in exercising the review granted by 20 U.S.C. § 1415? We consider these questions separately.

III

A

This is the first case in which this Court has been called upon to interpret any provision of the Act. As noted previously, the District Court and the Court of Appeals concluded that "[t]he Act itself does not define *appropriate education,*" 483 F.Supp. at 533, but leaves "to the courts and the hearing officers" the responsibility of "giv[ing] content to the requirement of an 'appropriate education.'" *Ibid.* See also 632 F.2d at 947. Petitioners contend that the definition of the phrase "free appropriate public education" used by the courts below overlooks the definition of that phrase actually found in the Act. Respondents agree that the Act defines "free appropriate public education," but contend that the statutory definition is not "functional," and thus "offers judges no guidance in their consideration of controversies involving 'the identification, evaluation, or educational placement of the child or the provision of a free appropriate public education.'" Brief for Respondents 28. The United States, appearing as *amicus curiae* on behalf of respondents, states that, "[a]lthough the Act includes definitions of a 'free appropriate public education' and other related terms, the statutory definitions do not adequately explain what is meant by 'appropriate.'"

We are loath to conclude that Congress failed to offer any assistance in defining the meaning of the principal substantive phrase used in the Act. It is beyond dispute that, contrary to the conclusions of the courts below, the Act does expressly define "free appropriate public education":

> "The term 'free appropriate public education' means *special education* and *related services* which (A) have been provided at public expense, under public supervision and direction, and without charge, (B) meet the standards of the State educational agency, (C) include an appropriate preschool, elementary, or secondary school education in the State involved, and (D) are provided in conformity with the individualized education program required under section 1414(a)(5) of this title." § 1401(18) (emphasis added).

"Special education," as referred to in this definition, means

> "specially designed instruction, at no cost to parents or guardians, to meet the unique needs of a handicapped child, including classroom instruction, instruction in physical education, home instruction, and instruction in hospitals and institutions." § 1401(16).

"Related services" are defined as

> "transportation, and such developmental, corrective, and other supportive services . . . as may be required to assist a handicapped child to benefit from special education." § 1401(17).

Like many statutory definitions, this one tends toward the cryptic, rather than the comprehensive, but that is scarcely a reason for abandoning the quest for legislative intent. Whether or not the definition is a "functional" one, as respondents contend it is not, it is the principal tool which Congress has given us for parsing the critical phrase of the Act. We think more must be made of it than either respondents or the United States seems willing to admit.

According to the definitions contained in the Act, a "free appropriate public education" consists of educational instruction specially designed to meet the unique needs of the handicapped child, supported by such services as are necessary to permit the child "to benefit" from the instruction. Almost as a checklist for adequacy under the Act, the definition also requires that such instruction and services be provided at public expense and under public supervision, meet the State's educational standards, approximate the grade levels used in the State's regular education, and comport with the child's IEP. Thus, if personalized instruction is being provided with sufficient supportive services to permit the child to benefit from the instruction, and the other items on the definitional checklist are satisfied, the child is receiving a "free appropriate public education" as defined by the Act.

Other portions of the statute also shed light upon congressional intent. Congress found that, of the roughly eight million handicapped children in the United States at the time of enactment, one million were "excluded entirely from the public school system," and more than half were receiving an inappropriate education. 89 Stat. 774, note following § 1401. In addition, as mentioned in Part I, the Act requires States to extend educational services first to those children who are receiving no education and second to those children who are receiving an "inadequate education." § 1412(3). When these express statutory findings and priorities are read together with the Act's extensive procedural requirements and its definition of "free appropriate public education," the face of the statute evinces a congressional intent to bring previously excluded handicapped children into the public education systems of the States and to require the States to adopt *procedures* which would result in individualized consideration of and instruction for each child.

Noticeably absent from the language of the statute is any substantive standard prescribing the level of education to be accorded handicapped children. Certainly the language of the statute contains no requirement like the one imposed by the lower courts — that States maximize the potential of handicapped children "commensurate with the opportunity provided to other children." 483 F.Supp. at 534. . . .

B

(i)

As suggested in Part I, federal support for education of the handicapped is a fairly recent development. Before passage of the Act, some States had passed laws to improve the educational services afforded handicapped children, but many of these children were excluded completely from any form of public education or were left to fend for themselves in classrooms designed for education of their nonhandicapped peers. . . .

[Two cases, *Pennsylvania Assn. for Retarded Children v. Commonwealth*, 334 F. Supp. 1257 (E.D. Pa. 1971), 343 F. Supp. 279 (1972) (*PARC*), and *Mills v. Board of Education of District of Columbia*, 348 F. Supp. 866 (D.D.C. 1972), inspired the legislation.] *Mills* and *PARC* both held that handicapped children must be given *access* to an adequate, publicly supported education. Neither case purports to require any particular substantive level of education. Rather, like the language of the Act, the cases set forth extensive procedures to be followed in formulating personalized educational programs for handicapped children. *See* 348 F.Supp. at 878–883; 334 F. Supp. at 1251267. The fact that both *PARC* and *Mills* are discussed at length in the legislative suggests that the principles which they established are the principles which, to a significant extent, guided the drafters of the Act. Indeed, immediately after discussing these cases, the Senate Report describes the 1974 statute as having "incorporated the major principles of the right to education cases." S.Rep. at 8. Those principles, in turn, became the basis of the Act, which itself was designed to effectuate the purposes of the 1974 statute. H.R.Rep. at 5.

That the Act imposes no clear obligation upon recipient States beyond the requirement that handicapped children receive some form of specialized education is perhaps best demonstrated by the fact that Congress, in explaining the need for the Act, equated an "appropriate education" to the receipt of some specialized educational services. . . .

It is evident from the legislative history that the characterization of handicapped children as "served" referred to children who were receiving some form of specialized educational services from the States, and that the characterization of children as "unserved" referred to those who were receiving no specialized educational services. For example, a letter sent to the United States Commissioner of Education by the House Committee on Education and Labor, signed by two key sponsors of the Act in the House, asked the Commissioner to identify the number of handicapped "children served" in each State. The letter asked for statistics on the number of children "being served" in various types of "special education program[s]" and the number of children who were not "receiving educational services." Hearings on S. 6 before the Subcommittee on the Handicapped of the Senate Committee on Labor and Public Welfare, 94th Cong., 1st Sess., 205–207 (1975) . . . .

(ii)

Respondents contend that "the goal of the Act is to provide each handicapped child with an equal educational opportunity." Brief for Respondents 35. We think, however, that the requirement that a State provide specialized educational services to handicapped children generates no additional requirement that the services so provided be sufficient to maximize each child's potential "commensurate with the opportunity provided other children." Respondents and the United States correctly note that Congress sought "to provide assistance to the States in carrying out their responsibilities under . . . the Constitution of the United States to provide equal protection of the laws." S.Rep. at 13. But we do not think that such statements imply a congressional intent to achieve strict equality of opportunity or services.

The educational opportunities provided by our public school systems undoubtedly differ from student to student, depending upon a myriad of factors that might affect a particular student's ability to assimilate information presented in the classroom. The requirement that States provide "equal" educational opportunities would thus seem to present an entirely unworkable standard requiring impossible measurements and comparisons. Similarly, furnishing handicapped children with only such services as are available to nonhandicapped children would in all probability fall short of the statutory requirement of "free appropriate public education"; to require, on the other hand, the furnishing of every special service necessary to maximize each handicapped child's potential is, we think, further than Congress intended to go. Thus, to speak in terms of "equal" services in one instance gives less than what is required by the Act, and in another instance, more. The theme of the Act is "free appropriate public education," a phrase which is too complex to be captured by the word "equal," whether one is speaking of opportunities or services.

. . . .

The District Court and the Court of Appeals thus erred when they held that the Act requires New York to maximize the potential of each handicapped child commensurate with the opportunity provided nonhandicapped children. Desirable though that goal might be, it is not the standard that Congress imposed upon States which receive funding under the Act. Rather, Congress sought primarily to identify and evaluate handicapped children, and to provide them with access to a free public education.

(iii)

Implicit in the congressional purpose of providing access to a "free appropriate public education" is the requirement that the education to which access is provided be sufficient to confer some educational benefit upon the handicapped child. It would do little good for Congress to spend millions of dollars in providing access to a public education only to have the handicapped child receive no benefit from that education. The statutory definition of "free appropriate public education," in addition to requiring that States provide each child with "specially designed instruction," expressly requires the provision of "such . . . supportive services . . . as may be required to assist a handicapped child *to benefit* from special education." § 1401(17) (emphasis added). We therefore conclude that the "basic floor of opportunity" provided by the Act consists of access to specialized instruction and related services which are individually designed to provide educational benefit to the handicapped child.

The determination of when handicapped children are receiving sufficient educational benefits to satisfy the requirements of the Act presents a more difficult problem. The Act requires participating States to educate a wide spectrum of handicapped children, from the marginally hearing-impaired to the profoundly retarded and palsied. It is clear that the benefits obtainable by children at one end of the spectrum will differ dramatically from those obtainable by children at the other end, with infinite variations in between. One child may have little difficulty competing successfully in an academic setting with nonhandicapped children, while another child may encounter great difficulty in acquiring even the most basic of self-maintenance skills. We do not attempt today to establish any one test for determining the adequacy of educational benefits conferred upon all children covered by the Act. Because in this case we are presented with a handicapped child who is receiving substantial specialized instruction and related services, and who is performing above average in the regular classrooms of a public school system, we confine our analysis to that situation.

The Act requires participating States to educate handicapped children with nonhandicapped children whenever possible. When that "mainstreaming" preference of the Act has been met and a child is being educated in the regular classrooms of a public school system, the system itself monitors the educational progress of the child. Regular examinations are administered, grades are awarded, and yearly advancement to higher grade levels is permitted for those children who attain an adequate knowledge of the course material. The grading and advancement system thus constitutes an important factor in determining educational benefit. Children who graduate from our public school systems are considered by our society to have been "educated" at least to the grade level they have completed, and access to an "education" for handicapped children is precisely what Congress sought to provide in the Act.

C

When the language of the Act and its legislative history are considered together, the requirements imposed by Congress become tolerably clear. Insofar as a State is required to provide a handicapped child with a "free appropriate public education," we hold that it satisfies this requirement by providing personalized instruction with sufficient support services to permit the child to benefit educationally from that instruction. Such instruction and services must be provided at public expense, must meet the State's educational standards, must approximate the grade levels used in the State's regular education, and must comport with the child's IEP. In addition, the IEP, and therefore the personalized instruction, should be formulated in accordance with the requirements of the Act and, if the child is being educated in the regular classrooms of the public education system, should be reasonably calculated to enable the child to achieve passing marks and advance from grade to grade.

IV

A

... But although we find that this grant of authority is broader than claimed by petitioners, we think the fact that it is found in § 1415, which is entitled "Procedural safeguards," is not without significance. When the elaborate and highly specific procedural safeguards embodied in § 1415 are contrasted with the general and somewhat imprecise substantive admonitions contained in the Act, we think that the importance Congress attached to these procedural safeguards cannot be gainsaid. . . .

[T]he provision that a reviewing court base its decision on the "preponderance of the evidence" is by no means an invitation to the courts to substitute their own notions of sound educational policy for those of the school authorities which they review. The very importance which Congress has attached to compliance with certain procedures in the preparation of an IEP would be frustrated if a court were permitted simply to set state decisions at naught. . . . . .

Therefore, a court's inquiry in suits brought under § 1415(e)(2) is twofold. First, has the State complied with the procedures set forth in the Act? And second, is the individualized educational program developed through the Act's procedures reasonably calculated to enable the child to receive educational benefits? If these requirements are met, the State has complied with the obligations imposed by Congress, and the courts can require no more.

B

In assuring that the requirements of the Act have been met, courts must be careful to avoid imposing their view of preferable educational methods upon the States. The primary responsibility for formulating the education to be accorded a handicapped child, and for choosing the educational method most suitable to the child's needs, was left by the Act to state and local educational agencies in cooperation with the parents or guardian of the child. The Act expressly charges States with the responsibility of "acquiring and disseminating to teachers and administrators of programs for handicapped children significant information derived from educational research, demonstration, and similar projects, and [of] adopting, where appropriate, promising educational practices and materials." § 1413(a)(3). In the face of such a clear statutory directive, it seems highly unlikely that Congress intended courts to overturn a State's choice of appropriate educational theories in a proceeding conducted pursuant to § 1415(e)(2).

We previously have cautioned that courts lack the "specialized knowledge and experience" necessary to resolve "persistent and difficult questions of educational policy." *San Antonio Independent School Dist. v. Rodriguez,* 411 U. S. 42. We think that Congress shared that view when it passed the Act. As already demonstrated, Congress' intention was not that the Act displace the primacy of States in the field of education, but that States receive funds to assist them in extending their educational systems to the handicapped. Therefore, once a court determines that the requirements of the Act have been met, questions of methodology are for resolution by the States.

V

Entrusting a child's education to state and local agencies does not leave the child without protection. Congress sought to protect individual children by providing for parental involvement in the development of state plans and policies, *supra,* at 458 U.S. 182–183, and n. 6, and in the formulation of the child's individual educational program . . .

Applying these principles to the facts of this case, we conclude that the Court of Appeals erred in affirming the decision of the District Court. Neither the District Court nor the Court of Appeals found that petitioners had failed to comply with the procedures of the Act, and the findings of neither court would support a conclusion that Amy's educational program failed to comply with the substantive requirements of the Act. On the contrary, the District Court found that the "evidence firmly establishes that Amy is receiving an 'adequate' education, since she performs better than the average child in her class and is advancing easily from grade to grade." 483 F.Supp. at 534. In light of this finding, and of the fact that Amy was receiving personalized instruction and related services calculated by the Furnace Woods school administrators to meet her educational needs, the lower courts should not have concluded that the Act requires the provision of a sign-language interpreter. Accordingly, the decision of the Court of Appeals is reversed, and the case is remanded for further proceedings consistent with this opinion.

So ordered.

Notes and Questions

1. What does the Court deem to be its role in reviewing school board's decisions under the IDEA? Does it conduct a de novo review? How does the Court reach its conclusion as to the appropriate standard of review?

2. Is this methodology likely to hinder or benefit plaintiffs in their quests to question school boards' decisions? Compare the results reached above with the most recent application of this standard by the Court in the case of a young girl, Ehlena Fry, being restricted from using her service dog in school. *Fry v. Napoleon Cmty. Sch.*, 137 S. Ct. 743 (2017). In that case, the Court ruled in favor Ehlena Fry, stating: "In its first section, the IDEA declares as its first purpose 'to ensure that all children with disabilities have available to them a free appropriate public education.' § 1400(d)(1)(A). That principal purpose then becomes the Act's principal command: A State receiving federal funding under the IDEA must make such an education 'available to all children with disabilities.' § 1412(a)(1)(A). The guarantee of a FAPE to those children gives rise to the bulk of the statute's more specific provisions. . . . And finally, as all the above suggests, the FAPE requirement provides the yardstick for measuring the adequacy of the education that a school offers to a child with a disability: Under that standard, this Court has held, a child is entitled to 'meaningful' access to education based on her individual needs. *Rowley*, 458 U.S., at 192, 102 S. Ct. 3034." *Fry v. Napoleon Cmty. Sch.*, 137 S. Ct. at 748–49. Do the justifications in overriding school board's decisions make sense when analogized with *Rowley*? Or, has the majority of the Court simply gained a better understanding of issues faced by children with disabilities in school?

Chapter 8

Constitutional Torts

A. Section 1983 and Other Remedial Statutes

1. Law as Power

Imagine being pulled over by a police officer while traveling in the car. What comes to mind at the moment? Is it annoyance that you might get a ticket or flashbacks to moments prior to the stop to determine what you might have done wrong? Do you sit in the car hoping that the police stop will take place quickly so you can make it to your next destination on time?

Now, imagine that, as black or latina/o persons routinely stopped by the police, those same thoughts and concerns take a backseat to automatic fear. A fear that the stop will go wrong, that the officer will be full of preconceived notions and quick to violence, that your rights as a citizen will be completely ignored at best, or at worst, that you will meet death. Imagine the fear of encountering the same fate of past victims, the fear engendered when recalling an officer threatening, "I will light you up" to a question asking the reason for the stop or arrest.[1] Or imagine your 15-year-old daughter, unarmed and in a bathing suit at a pool party, wrestled to the ground and assaulted by an officer because the officers disliked her responses or tone. Or even more, imagine the routine dread and fear experienced by parents of color when their children leave the house, the fear that law enforcement might react irrationally or disproportionally to their children based on stereotypes rather than on a reasonable assessment of a particular situation.[2]

These are scenarios from countless police brutality cases that are routine in American society. The use of deadly force by the police has been the subject of numerous lawsuits, with the number of incidents rising rather than decreasing. In

---

1. Ray Sanchez, *Who Was Sandra Bland?*, CNN (July 23, 2015, 9:17 PM), http://www.cnn.com/2015/07/22/us/sandra-bland/index.html.

2. The Leadership Conference, Justice on Trial: Racial Disparities in the American Criminal Justice System (2000), http://archives.civilrights.org/publications/justice-on-trial/; Frank Newport, *Gallup Review: Black and White Attitudes Toward Police*, Gallup (Aug. 20, 2014), http://www.gallup.com/poll/175088/gallup-review-black-white-attitudes-toward-police.aspx; Toluse Olorunnipa, *For many black families, distrust of police has decades of history*, Topeka Capital-Journal (Aug. 25, 2014, 1:07 PM), http://cjonline.com/news/2014-08-25/many-black-families-distrust-police-has-decades-history; CBS/AP, *Deep national mistrust of police by minorities exposed in Ferguson, Missouri*, CBS News (Aug. 19, 2014, 2:49 PM), http://www.cbsnews.com/news/ferguson-missouri-highlights-deep-national-mistrust-of-police-by-minorities.

fact, the United States has the dubious honor of being a leader in police brutality and cases of death at the hands of the police. As of October 13, 2015, for example, there were 902 cases of death-by-police in the U.S., with 416 of the victims being white and the rest of the victims predominantly black and latino/a.[3] Yet blacks and Latinos make up respectively only 13% and 17% of the population. With these numbers, it is, thus, not hard to believe statistics showing that victims of color have died at a rate of two per day since the beginning of the millennium.[4]

This is the modern context in which the issues discussed in this chapter often rear their heads. This section on constitutional torts covers to laws guiding claims alleging violations by governmental officials along with relevant doctrinal rules and guidelines for determining liability. To be sure, these types of violations are not limited to claims arising out of police brutality. In fact, that context is only one example in which citizens might have standing to seek liability for violations caused or facilitated by governmental officials. Other contexts include claims levied against school boards or other types of governmental employees claiming First Amendment violations in the form of sanctions or other restrictions on speech. Or they might include First Amendment claims against city officials in restricting groups' ability to protest or assemble in a public area. Or as seen below, Eighth Amendment claims levied against prison officials for permitting or failing to protect against particular harms.

As you can see, the legal practice involving constitutional torts is vast. Still, it is undeniable that a vast number of the cases and a substantial part of the public discourse in the last three decades have centered around police brutality. Cases alleging governmental brutality or improper use of force make up a large part of our jurisprudence, creating a schism between the purported legal approach and on the one hand, and the reality experienced by many, on the other.

As you proceed, consider that, despite the laws and doctrines outlined below, the legal framework will continue to be inadequate without a social commitment to answer the following question: How do we explain the prevalence of police brutality as our status quo? What do we make of the fact that this issue of brutality by law enforcement is a uniquely American phenomenon, that peer countries experience just a fraction of these cases in a 10–20 year time period, and some not at all?[5]

In this chapter on constitutional torts, we address these issues, using one of the most commonly used statutory frameworks for seeking remedies for violations by

---

3. THE GUARDIAN, THE COUNTED: PEOPLE KILLED BY POLICE IN THE U.S., http://www
.theguardian.com/us-news/ng-interactive/2015/jun/01/the-counted-police-killings-us-database
(last visited Feb. 1, 2016) (counting 217 blacks and 131 Latinos/as).

4. *US Police Kill More than Two People a Day: Report*, http://news.yahoo.com/us-police-kill
-more-two-people-day-report-063637174.html.

5. Jamiles Lartey, *By the Numbers: US Police Kill More in Days than Other Countries do in Years*,
THE GUARDIAN (June 9, 2015, 6:00 AM), http://www.theguardian.com/us-news/2015/jun/09/the
-counted-police-killings-us-vs-other-countries.

law enforcement, 42 U.S.C. § 1983. In reviewing the cases below, determine whether it is true that no other area of law better illustrates law as a reflection of power than 42 U.S.C. § 1983. This doctrine has served as a frequent vehicle for holding governmental entities accountable.

As such, consider whether the adjudication of claims of police brutality—such as in the cases of Michael Brown, Freddie Grey, Tamir Rice, Sandra Bland or the Floyd stop and frisk class action suit in New York—might be routine illustrations of law as protecting the interests of those in power, rather than an adequate remedy for unequal systems.[6]

Note also that this area remains one of the hardest areas of law for plaintiffs. The standards and burdens have been traditionally unfavorable to plaintiffs' claims. And, traditionally, juries have proved more sympathetic to police officers than victims.[7] At the core of this type of litigation is the weight of deference afforded to law enforcement in disproportion to their responsibility to their communities and the risks they encounter on the job. But first, as you read these cases, evaluate whether the standards and application of the doctrines fit the goal and spirit of the statutes. Do they rightly reflect law as protecting the status quo? What might it take to create a reversal of the current trend? Is a change through law and doctrine still a promising avenue? In other words, is law not enough? If not, what should the alternative to law be?

2. Historical Overview

This chapter focuses on two Reconstruction statutes passed just a few years after the Fourteenth Amendment, Sections 1983 and 1985(3). They were designed to enforce the tenets of civil rights agreed to after the Civil War, understanding that these gains would not happen on their own. Congress enacted these two statutes pursuant to its authority under Section 5 of the Fourteenth Amendment in the hope of curtailing the hate levied against newly freed blacks in the South.

It is significant that, enacted as part of the Civil Rights Act of 1871, 42 U.S.C. § 1983 was a direct Congressional response to state-sponsored brutality. Informally labeled as the Ku Klux Klan Act, Section 1983 is a Reconstruction effort to provide a remedy against the violence levied against African Americans by state-sponsored persons or entities and state-tolerated hate groups. Nonetheless, although hate

---

6. Nicole Flatow, *What Has Changed About Police Brutality in America, From Rodney King to Michael Brown*, THINK PROGRESS (Sept. 11, 2014, 5:02 PM), http://thinkprogress.org/justice/2014/09/11/3477520/whats-changed-and-what-hasnt-in-policing-the-police/; Eric F. Citron, *Right and Responsibility in Fourth Amendment Jurisprudence: The Problem with Pretext*, 116 YALE L.J. 1072 (2007); Susan Bandes, *Tracing the Pattern of No Pattern: Stories of Police Brutality*, 34 LOY. L.A. L. REV. 665 (2001).

7. Paul Butler, *Racially Based Jury Nullification: Black Power in the Criminal Justice System*, 105 YALE L.J. 677 (1995).

groups like the Ku Klux Klan were already systematically targeting blacks through lynchings, burning and rallies, 42 U.S.C. § 1983 laid dormant for nearly a century. The goodwill of the federal government was short-lived, and the statute was cast aside by officials unwilling to enforce it. Very soon, the federal government retreated from these efforts. The reign of Jim Crow was quickly solidified in the early Twentieth Century.

42 U.S.C. § 1983 provides:

> Every person who, under color of any statute, ordinance, regulation, custom, or usage, of any State or Territory or the District of Columbia, subjects, or causes to be subjected, any citizen of the United States or other person within the jurisdiction thereof to the deprivation of any rights, privileges, or immunities secured by the Constitution and laws, shall be liable to the party injured in an action at law, suit in equity, or other proper proceeding for redress, except that in any action brought against a judicial officer for an act or omission taken in such officer's judicial capacity, injunctive relief shall not be granted unless a declaratory decree was violated or declaratory relief was unavailable. For the purposes of this section, any Act of Congress applicable exclusively to the District of Columbia shall be considered to be a statute of the District of Columbia.[8]

The statute was not revived and given its full modern import until *Monroe v. Pape*, 365 U.S. 167 (1961). Before *Monroe*, the Supreme Court read the statute to reach only claims where the wrongful conduct was authorized by law. *Monroe* expanded this reading and deemed the statute to also reach individuals acting under the badge of state authority, regardless of legality of conduct.[9]

B. Rights Enforceable Under 42 U.S.C. § 1983

In order to prevail in a 42 U.S.C. § 1983 suit, a plaintiff must prove a violation of an underlying constitutional or statutory right. As such, 42 U.S.C. § 1983 is only a remedial statute, designed to correct and provide relief for wrongdoing, but not the main basis of any violation. To make a claim under § 1983, a plaintiff must show (1) that the conduct complained of was committed by a person acting under color of state law; and (2) that the conduct deprived the plaintiff of a constitutional or statutory right.

---

8. R.S. § 1979; Pub. L. 96-170, § 1, Dec. 29, 1979, 93 Stat. 1284; Pub. L. 104-317, title III, § 309(c), Oct. 19, 1996, 110 Stat. 3853.

9. Monroe v. Pape, 365 U.S. 167, 172 (1961), *overruled in part by* Monell v. Dep't of Soc. Servs. of City of New York, 436 U.S. 658 (1978) (holding that "Congress, in enacting [The Civil Rights Act], meant to give a remedy to parties deprived of constitutional rights, privileges and immunities by an official's abuse of his position").

This, of course, begs the question: How must a plaintiff prove the deprivation of constitutional/statutory right? To determine whether a constitutional violation exists, the plaintiff must look, based on the facts, to the specific doctrine that would trigger a claim of violation. For example, if the plaintiff wants to sue under 42 U.S.C. § 1983 for a policy mandating that inmates cut their hair in prison, then the plaintiff must show that the defendant violated the First Amendment or applicable statutes providing religious protections.[10] Over time, courts have clarified the application of specific standards appropriate for certain types of facts, with very precise lines of cases for different circumstances. For instance, official negligence under the Eighth Amendment may trigger a higher standard in the context of a prison riot than during the normal course of prison operation. See below for the Court's enunciation of the applicable standard for evaluating the use of deadly force by police officers in *Tennessee v. Garner*, 471 U.S. 1 (1985).

Tennessee v. Garner

471 U.S. 1 (1985)

JUSTICE WHITE delivered the opinion of the Court.

This case requires us to determine the constitutionality of the use of deadly force to prevent the escape of an apparently unarmed suspected felon. We conclude that such force may not be used unless it is necessary to prevent the escape and the officer has probable cause to believe that the suspect poses a significant threat of death or serious physical injury to the officer or others.

I

At about 10:45 p.m. on October 3, 1974, Memphis Police Officers Elton Hymon and Leslie Wright were dispatched to answer a "prowler inside call." Upon arriving at the scene they saw a woman standing on her porch and gesturing toward the adjacent house. She told them she had heard glass breaking and that "they" or "someone" was breaking in next door. While Wright radioed the dispatcher to say that they were on the scene, Hymon went behind the house. He heard a door slam and saw someone run across the backyard. The fleeing suspect, who was appellee-respondent's decedent, Edward Garner, stopped at a 6-feet-high chain link fence at the edge of the yard. With the aid of a flashlight, Hymon was able to see Garner's face and hands. He saw no sign of a weapon, and, though not certain, was "reasonably sure" and "figured" that Garner was unarmed. App. 41, 56; Record 219. He thought Garner was 17 or 18 years old and about 5'5"or 5'7" tall. While Garner was crouched at the base of the fence, Hymon called out "police, halt" and took a few steps toward him. Garner then began to climb over the fence. Convinced that if Garner made it over the fence he would elude capture, Hymon shot him. The bullet hit Garner in the back of the head. Garner was taken by ambulance to a hospital,

---

10. Lovelace v. Lee, 472 F.3d 174 (4th Cir. 2006); Shabazz v. Barnauskas, 600 F. Supp. 712 (M.D. Fla. 1985); Gartrell v. Ashcroft, 191 F. Supp. 2d 23 (D.D.C. 2002).

where he died on the operating table. Ten dollars and a purse taken from the house were found on his body.

In using deadly force to prevent the escape, Hymon was acting under the authority of a Tennessee statute and pursuant to Police Department policy. The statute provides that "[i]f, after notice of the intention to arrest the defendant, he either flee or forcibly resist, the officer may use all the necessary means to effect the arrest." Tenn.Code Ann. §40-7-108 (1982). The Department policy was slightly more restrictive than the statute, but still allowed the use of deadly force in cases of burglary. App. 140–144. The incident was reviewed by the Memphis Police Firearm's Review Board and presented to a grand jury. Neither took any action. *Id.,* at 57.

Garner's father then brought this action in the Federal District Court for the Western District of Tennessee, seeking damages under 42 U.S.C. §1983 for asserted violations of Garner's constitutional rights. The complaint alleged that the shooting violated the Fourth, Fifth, Sixth, Eighth, and Fourteenth Amendments of the United States Constitution. It named as defendants Officer Hymon, the Police Department, its Director, and the Mayor and city of Memphis. After a 3-day bench trial, the District Court entered judgment for all defendants. It dismissed the claims against the Mayor and the Director for lack of evidence. It then concluded that Hymon's actions were authorized by the Tennessee statute, which in turn was constitutional. Hymon had employed the only reasonable and practicable means of preventing Garner's escape. Garner had "recklessly and heedlessly attempted to vault over the fence to escape, thereby assuming the risk of being fired upon." App. to Pet. for Cert. A10.

The Court of Appeals for the Sixth Circuit affirmed with regard to Hymon, finding that he had acted in good-faith reliance on the Tennessee statute and was therefore within the scope of his qualified immunity. 600 F.2d 52 (1979). It remanded for reconsideration of the possible liability of the city, however, in light of *Monell v. New York City Dept. of Social Services,* 436 U.S. 658, 98 S.Ct. 2018, 56 L.Ed.2d 611 (1978), which had come down after the District Court's decision. The District Court was directed to consider whether a city enjoyed a qualified immunity, whether the use of deadly force and hollow point bullets in these circumstances was constitutional, and whether any unconstitutional municipal conduct flowed from a "policy or custom" as required for liability under *Monell.* 600 F.2d, at 54–55.

The District Court concluded that *Monell* did not affect its decision. While acknowledging some doubt as to the possible immunity of the city, it found that the statute, and Hymon's actions, were constitutional. Given this conclusion, it declined to consider the "policy or custom" question. App. to Pet. for Cert. A37-A39.

The Court of Appeals reversed and remanded. 710 F.2d 240 (1983). It reasoned that the killing of a fleeing suspect is a "seizure" under the Fourth Amendment, and is therefore constitutional only if "reasonable." The Tennessee statute failed as applied to this case because it did not adequately limit the use of deadly force by distinguishing between felonies of different magnitudes — "the facts, as found, did not justify the use of deadly force under the Fourth Amendment." *Id.,* at 246. Officers cannot resort to deadly force unless they "have probable cause . . . to believe that the suspect [has committed a felony and] poses a threat to the safety of the officers or a danger to the community if left at large." *Ibid.*

The State of Tennessee, which had intervened to defend the statute, see 28 U.S.C. § 2403(b), appealed to this Court. The city filed a petition for certiorari. We noted probable jurisdiction in the appeal and granted the petition. 465 U.S. 1098, 104 S.Ct. 1589, 80 L.Ed.2d 122 (1984).

II

Whenever an officer restrains the freedom of a person to walk away, he has seized that person. *United States v. Brignoni-Ponce,* 422 U.S. 873, 878, 95 S.Ct. 2574, 2578, 45 L.Ed.2d 607 (1975). While it is not always clear just when minimal police interference becomes a seizure, see *United States v. Mendenhall,* 446 U.S. 544, 100 S.Ct. 1870, 64 L.Ed.2d 497 (1980), there can be no question that apprehension by the use of deadly force is a seizure subject to the reasonableness requirement of the Fourth Amendment.

A

A police officer may arrest a person if he has probable cause to believe that person committed a crime. *E.g., United States v. Watson,* 423 U.S. 411, 96 S.Ct. 820, 46 L. Ed.2d 598 (1976). Petitioners and appellant argue that if this requirement is satisfied the Fourth Amendment has nothing to say about *how* that seizure is made. This submission ignores the many cases in which this Court, by balancing the extent of the intrusion against the need for it, has examined the reasonableness of the manner in which a search or seizure is conducted. To determine the constitutionality of a seizure "[w]e must balance the nature and quality of the intrusion on the individual's Fourth Amendment interests against the importance of the governmental interests alleged to justify the intrusion." *United States v. Place,* 462 U.S. 696, 703, 103 S.Ct. 2637, 2642, 77 L.Ed.2d 110 (1983); see *Delaware v. Prouse,* 440 U.S. 648, 654, 99 S. Ct. 1391, 1396, 59 L.Ed.2d 660 (1979); *United States v. Martinez-Fuerte,* 428 U.S. 543, 555, 96 S.Ct. 3074, 3081, 49 L.Ed.2d 1116 (1976). We have described "the balancing of competing interests" as "the key principle of the Fourth Amendment." *Michigan v. Summers,* 452 U.S. 692, 700, n. 12, 101 S.Ct. 2587, 2593, n. 12, 69 L.Ed.2d 340 (1981). See also *Camara v. Municipal Court,* 387 U.S. 523, 536–537, 87 S.Ct. 1727, 1734–1735, 18 L.Ed.2d 930 (1967). Because one of the factors is the extent of the intrusion, it is plain that reasonableness depends on not only when a seizure is made, but also how it is carried out. *United States v. Ortiz,* 422 U.S. 891, 895, 95 S.Ct. 2585, 2588, 45 L. Ed.2d 623 (1975); *Terry v. Ohio,* 392 U.S. 1, 28–29, 88 S.Ct. 1868, 1883–1884, 20 L. Ed.2d 889 (1968).

Applying these principles to particular facts, the Court has held that governmental interests did not support a lengthy detention of luggage, *United States v. Place, supra,* an airport seizure not "carefully tailored to its underlying justification," *Florida v. Royer,* 460 U.S. 491, 500, 103 S.Ct. 1319, 1325, 75 L.Ed.2d 229 (1983) (plurality opinion), surgery under general anesthesia to obtain evidence, *Winston v. Lee,* 470 U.S. 753, 105 S.Ct. 1611, 84 L.Ed.2d 662 (1985), or detention for fingerprinting without probable cause, *Davis v. Mississippi,* 394 U.S. 721, 89 S.Ct. 1394, 22 L.Ed.2d 676 (1969); *Hayes v. Florida,* 470 U.S. 811, 105 S.Ct. 1643, 84 L.Ed.2d 705 (1985). On the other hand, under the same approach it has upheld the taking of fingernail scrapings from a suspect, *Cupp v. Murphy,* 412 U.S. 291, 93 S.Ct. 2000, 36 L.Ed.2d 900 (1973), an unannounced entry into a home to prevent the destruction of evidence, *Ker v. California,* 374 U.S. 23, 83 S.Ct. 1623, 10 L.Ed.2d 726 (1963), administrative housing inspections without probable cause to believe that a code violation will be found, *Camara v. Municipal Court, supra,* and a blood test of a drunken-driving suspect, *Schmerber v. California,* 384 U.S. 757, 86 S.Ct. 1826, 16 L.Ed.2d 908 (1966). In each of these cases, the question was whether the totality of the circumstances justified a particular sort of search or seizure.

B

The same balancing process applied in the cases cited above demonstrates that, notwithstanding probable cause to seize a suspect, an officer may not always do so by killing him. The intrusiveness of a seizure by means of deadly force is unmatched. The suspect's fundamental interest in his own life need not be elaborated upon. The use of deadly force also frustrates the interest of the individual, and of society, in judicial determination of guilt and punishment. Against these interests are ranged governmental interests in effective law enforcement. It is argued that overall violence will be reduced by encouraging the peaceful submission of suspects who know that they may be shot if they flee. Effectiveness in making arrests requires the resort to deadly force, or at least the meaningful threat thereof. "Being able to arrest such individuals is a condition precedent to the state's entire system of law enforcement." Brief for Petitioners 14.

Without in any way disparaging the importance of these goals, we are not convinced that the use of deadly force is a sufficiently productive means of accomplishing them to justify the killing of nonviolent suspects. Cf. *Delaware v. Prouse, supra,* 440 U.S., at 659, 99 S.Ct., at 1399. The use of deadly force is a self-defeating way of apprehending a suspect and so setting the criminal justice mechanism in motion. If successful, it guarantees that that mechanism will not be set in motion. And while the meaningful threat of deadly force might be thought to lead to the arrest of more live suspects by discouraging escape attempts, the presently available evidence does not support this thesis. The fact is that a majority of police departments in this country have forbidden the use of deadly force against nonviolent suspects. See *infra,* at 1704–1705. If those charged with the enforcement of the criminal law have abjured the use of deadly force in arresting nondangerous felons, there is a substantial basis for doubting that the use of such force is an essential attribute of the arrest power in all felony cases. See *Schumann v. McGinn,* 307 Minn. 446, 472, 240 N.W.2d 525, 540 (1976) (Rogosheske, J., dissenting in part). Petitioners and appellant have not persuaded us that shooting nondangerous fleeing suspects is so vital as to outweigh the suspect's interest in his own life.

The use of deadly force to prevent the escape of all felony suspects, whatever the circumstances, is constitutionally unreasonable. It is not better that all felony suspects die than that they escape. Where the suspect poses no immediate threat to the officer and no threat to others, the harm resulting from failing to apprehend him does not justify the use of deadly force to do so. It is no doubt unfortunate when a suspect who is in sight escapes, but the fact that the police arrive a little late or are a little slower afoot does not always justify killing the suspect. A police officer may not seize an unarmed, nondangerous suspect by shooting him dead. The Tennessee statute is unconstitutional insofar as it authorizes the use of deadly force against such fleeing suspects.

It is not, however, unconstitutional on its face. Where the officer has probable cause to believe that the suspect poses a threat of serious physical harm, either to the officer or to others, it is not constitutionally unreasonable to prevent escape by using deadly force. Thus, if the suspect threatens the officer with a weapon or there is probable cause to believe that he has committed a crime involving the infliction or threatened infliction of serious physical harm, deadly force may be used if necessary to prevent escape, and if, where feasible, some warning has been given. As applied in such circumstances, the Tennessee statute would pass constitutional muster.

III

A

It is insisted that the Fourth Amendment must be construed in light of the common-law rule, which allowed the use of whatever force was necessary to effect the arrest of a fleeing felon, though not a misdemeanant. As stated in Hale's posthumously published Pleas of the Crown:

> "[I]f persons that are pursued by these officers for felony or the just suspicion thereof . . . shall not yield themselves to these officers, but shall either resist or fly before they are apprehended or being apprehended shall rescue themselves and resist or fly, so that they cannot be otherwise apprehended, and are upon necessity slain therein, because they cannot be otherwise taken, it is no felony." 2 M. Hale, Historia Placitorum Coronae 85 (1736).

See also 4 W. Blackstone, Commentaries. Most American jurisdictions also imposed a flat prohibition against the use of deadly force to stop a fleeing misdemeanant, coupled with a general privilege to use such force to stop a fleeing felon. *E.g., Holloway v. Moser,* 193 N.C. 185, 136 S.E. 375 (1927); *State v. Smith,* 127 Iowa 534, 535, 103 N.W. 944, 945 (1905); *Reneau v. State,* 70 Tenn. 720 (1879); *Brooks v. Commonwealth,* 61 Pa. 352 (1869); *Roberts v. State,* 14 Mo. 138 (1851); see generally R. Perkins & R. Boyce, Criminal Law 1098–1102 (3d ed. 1982); Day, *Shooting the Fleeing Felon: State of the Law,* 14 Crim.L.Bull. 285, 286–287 (1978); Wilgus, *Arrest Without a Warrant,* 22 Mich.L.Rev. 798, 807–816 (1924). But see *Storey v. State,* 71 Ala. 329 (1882); *State v. Bryant,* 65 N.C. 327, 328 (1871); *Caldwell v. State,* 41 Tex. 86 (1874).

The State and city argue that because this was the prevailing rule at the time of the adoption of the Fourth Amendment and for some time thereafter, and is still in force in some States, use of deadly force against a fleeing felon must be "reasonable." It is true that this Court has often looked to the common law in evaluating the reasonableness, for Fourth Amendment purposes, of police activity. See, *e.g., United States v. Watson,* 423 U.S. 411, 418–419, 96 S.Ct. 820, 825–826, 46 L.Ed.2d 598 (1976); *Gerstein v. Pugh,* 420 U.S. 103, 111, 114, 95 S.Ct. 854, 861, 863, 43 L.Ed.2d 54 (1975); *Carroll v. United States,* 267 U.S. 132, 149–153, 45 S.Ct. 280, 283–285, 69 L.Ed. 543 (1925). On the other hand, it "has not simply frozen into constitutional law those law enforcement practices that existed at the time of the Fourth Amendment's passage." *Payton v. New York,* 445 U.S. 573, 591, n. 33, 100 S.Ct. 1371, 1382, n. 33, 63 L.Ed.2d 639 (1980). Because of sweeping change in the legal and technological context, reliance on the common-law rule in this case would be a mistaken literalism that ignores the purposes of a historical inquiry.

B

It has been pointed out many times that the common-law rule is best understood in light of the fact that it arose at a time when virtually all felonies were punishable by death. "Though effected without the protections and formalities of an orderly trial and conviction, the killing of a resisting or fleeing felon resulted in no greater consequences than those authorized for punishment of the felony of which the individual was charged or suspected." American Law Institute, Model Penal Code § 3.07, Comment 3, p. 56 (Tentative Draft No. 8, 1958) (hereinafter Model Penal Code Comment). Courts have also justified the common-law rule by emphasizing the relative dangerousness of felons. See, *e.g., Schumann v. McGinn,* 307 Minn., at 458, 240 N.W.2d, at 533; *Holloway v. Moser, supra,* 193 N.C., at 187, 136 S.E., at 376 (1927).

Neither of these justifications makes sense today. Almost all crimes formerly punishable by death no longer are or can be. See, *e.g., Enmund v. Florida,* 458 U.S. 782, 102 S.Ct. 3368, 73 L.Ed.2d 1140 (1982); *Coker v. Georgia,* 433 U.S. 584, 97 S.Ct. 2861, 53 L.Ed.2d 982 (1977). And while in earlier times "the gulf between the felonies and the minor offences was broad and deep," 2 Pollock & Maitland 467, n. 3; *Carroll v. United States, supra,* 267 U.S., at 158, 45 S.Ct., at 287, today the distinction is minor and often arbitrary. Many crimes classified as misdemeanors, or nonexistent, at common law are now felonies. Wilgus, 22 Mich.L.Rev., at 572–573. These changes have undermined the concept, which was questionable to begin with, that use of deadly force against a fleeing felon is merely a speedier execution of someone who has already forfeited his life. They have also made the assumption that a "felon" is more dangerous than a misdemeanant untenable. Indeed, numerous misdemeanors involve conduct more dangerous than many felonies.

There is an additional reason why the common-law rule cannot be directly translated to the present day. The common-law rule developed at a time when weapons were rudimentary. Deadly force could be inflicted almost solely in a hand-to-hand struggle during which, necessarily, the safety of the arresting officer was at risk. Handguns were not carried by police officers until the latter half of the last century.

L. Kennett & J. Anderson, The Gun in America 150–151 (1975). Only then did it become possible to use deadly force from a distance as a means of apprehension. As a practical matter, the use of deadly force under the standard articulation of the common-law rule has an altogether different meaning—and harsher consequences—now than in past centuries. See Wechsler & Michael, *A Rationale for the Law of Homicide: I*, 37 Colum.L.Rev. 701, 741 (1937).

One other aspect of the common-law rule bears emphasis. It forbids the use of deadly force to apprehend a misdemeanant, condemning such action as disproportionately severe. See *Holloway v. Moser*, 193 N.C., at 187, 136 S.E., at 376; *State v. Smith*, 127 Iowa, at 535, 103 N.W., at 945. See generally Annot., 83 A.L.R.3d 238 (1978).

In short, though the common-law pedigree of Tennessee's rule is pure on its face, changes in the legal and technological context mean the rule is distorted almost beyond recognition when literally applied.

C

In evaluating the reasonableness of police procedures under the Fourth Amendment, we have also looked to prevailing rules in individual jurisdictions. See, *e.g.*, *United States v. Watson*, 423 U.S., at 421–422, 96 S.Ct., at 826–827. The rules in the States are varied. See generally Comment, 18 Ga.L.Rev. 137, 140–144 (1983). Some 19 States have codified the common-law rule, though in two of these the courts have significantly limited the statute. Four States, though without a relevant statute, apparently retain the common-law rule. Two States have adopted the Model Penal Code's provision verbatim. Eighteen others allow, in slightly varying language, the use of deadly force only if the suspect has committed a felony involving the use or threat of physical or deadly force, or is escaping with a deadly weapon, or is likely to endanger life or inflict serious physical injury if not arrested. Louisiana and Vermont, though without statutes or case law on point, do forbid the use of deadly force to prevent any but violent felonies. The remaining States either have no relevant statute or case law, or have positions that are unclear.

It cannot be said that there is a constant or overwhelming trend away from the common-law rule. In recent years, some States have reviewed their laws and expressly rejected abandonment of the common-law rule. Nonetheless, the long-term movement has been away from the rule that deadly force may be used against any fleeing felon, and that remains the rule in less than half the States.

This trend is more evident and impressive when viewed in light of the policies adopted by the police departments themselves. Overwhelmingly, these are more restrictive than the common-law rule. C. Milton, J. Halleck, J. Lardner, & G. Abrecht, Police Use of Deadly Force 45–46 (1977). The Federal Bureau of Investigation and the New York City Police Department, for example, both forbid the use of firearms except when necessary to prevent death or grievous bodily harm. *Id.*, at 40–41; App. 83. For accreditation by the Commission on Accreditation for Law Enforcement Agencies, a department must restrict the use of deadly force to situations where "the officer reasonably believes that the action is in defense of human life ... or in defense of any person in immediate danger of serious physical injury." Commission on Accreditation for Law Enforcement Agencies, Inc., Standards for Law Enforcement Agencies 1-2 (1983) (italics deleted). A 1974 study reported that the police department regulations in a majority of the large cities of the United States allowed the firing of a weapon only when a felon presented a threat of death or serious bodily harm. Boston Police Department, Planning & Research Division, The Use of Deadly Force by Boston Police Personnel (1974), cited in *Mattis v. Schnarr,* 547 F.2d 1007, 1016, n. 19 (CA8 1976), vacated as moot *sub nom. Ashcroft v. Mattis,* 431 U.S. 171, 97 S.Ct. 1739, 52 L.Ed.2d 219 (1977). Overall, only 7.5% of departmental and municipal policies explicitly permit the use of deadly force against any felon; 86.8% explicitly do not. K. Matulia, A Balance of Forces: A Report of the International Association of Chiefs of Police 161 (1982) (table). See also Record 1108-1368 (written policies of 44 departments). See generally W. Geller & K. Karales, Split-Second Decisions 33–42 (1981); Brief for Police Foundation et al. as *Amici Curiae.* In light of the rules adopted by those who must actually administer them, the older and fading common-law view is a dubious indicium of the constitutionality of the Tennessee statute now before us.

D

Actual departmental policies are important for an additional reason. We would hesitate to declare a police practice of long standing "unreasonable" if doing so would severely hamper effective law enforcement. But the indications are to the contrary. There has been no suggestion that crime has worsened in any way in jurisdictions that have adopted, by legislation or departmental policy, rules similar to that announced today. *Amici* noted that "[a]fter extensive research and consideration, [they] have concluded that laws permitting police officers to use deadly force to apprehend unarmed, non-violent fleeing felony suspects actually do not protect citizens or law enforcement officers, do not deter crime or alleviate problems caused by crime, and do not improve the crime-fighting ability of law enforcement agencies." *Id.,* at 11. The submission is that the obvious state interests in apprehension are not sufficiently served to warrant the use of lethal weapons against all fleeing felons. See *supra,* at 1700–1701, and n. 10.

Nor do we agree with petitioners and appellant that the rule we have adopted requires the police to make impossible, split-second evaluations of unknowable facts. See Brief for Petitioners 25; Brief for Appellant 11. We do not deny the practical difficulties of attempting to assess the suspect's dangerousness. However, similarly difficult judgments must be made by the police in equally uncertain circumstances. See, *e.g., Terry v. Ohio,* 392 U.S., at 20, 27, 88 S.Ct., at 1879, 1883. Nor is there any indication that in States that allow the use of deadly force only against dangerous suspects, see nn. 15, 17–19, *supra,* the standard has been difficult to apply or has led to a rash of litigation involving inappropriate second-guessing of police officers' split-second decisions. Moreover, the highly technical felony/misdemeanor distinction is equally, if not more, difficult to apply in the field. An officer is in no position to know, for example, the precise value of property stolen, or whether the crime was a first or second offense. Finally, as noted above, this claim must be viewed with suspicion in light of the similar self-imposed limitations of so many police departments.

IV

The District Court concluded that Hymon was justified in shooting Garner because state law allows, and the Federal Constitution does not forbid, the use of deadly force to prevent the escape of a fleeing felony suspect if no alternative means of apprehension is available. See App. to Pet. for Cert. A9-A11, A38. This conclusion made a determination of Garner's apparent dangerousness unnecessary. The court did find, however, that Garner appeared to be unarmed, though Hymon could not be certain that was the case. *Id.,* at A4, A23. See also App. 41, 56; Record 219. Restated in Fourth Amendment terms, this means Hymon had no articulable basis to think Garner was armed.

In reversing, the Court of Appeals accepted the District Court's factual conclusions and held that "the facts, as found, did not justify the use of deadly force." 710 F.2d, at 246. We agree. Officer Hymon could not reasonably have believed that Garner—young, slight, and unarmed—posed any threat. Indeed, Hymon never attempted to justify his actions on any basis other than the need to prevent an escape. The District Court stated in passing that "[t]he facts of this case did not indicate to Officer Hymon that Garner was 'non-dangerous.'" App. to Pet. for Cert. A34. This conclusion is not explained, and seems to be based solely on the fact that Garner had broken into a house at night. However, the fact that Garner was a suspected burglar could not, without regard to the other circumstances, automatically justify the use of deadly force. Hymon did not have probable cause to believe that Garner, whom he correctly believed to be unarmed, posed any physical danger to himself or others.

The dissent argues that the shooting was justified by the fact that Officer Hymon had probable cause to believe that Garner had committed a nighttime burglary. *Post,* at 1711, 1712. While we agree that burglary is a serious crime, we cannot agree that it is so dangerous as automatically to justify the use of deadly force. The FBI classifies burglary as a "property" rather than a "violent" crime. See Federal Bureau of Investigation, Uniform Crime Reports, Crime in the United States 1 (1984). Although the armed burglar would present a different situation, the fact that an unarmed suspect has broken into a dwelling at night does not automatically mean he is physically dangerous. This case demonstrates as much. See also *Solem v. Helm,* 463 U.S. 277, 296–297, and nn. 22–23, 103 S.Ct. 3001, 3012–3013, and nn. 22–23, 77 L.Ed.2d 637 (1983). In fact, the available statistics demonstrate that burglaries only rarely involve physical violence. During the 10-year period from 1973–1982, only 3.8% of all burglaries involved violent crime. Bureau of Justice Statistics, Household Burglary 4 (1985). See also T. Reppetto, Residential Crime 17, 105 (1974); Conklin & Bittner, *Burglary in a Suburb,* 11 Criminology 208, 214 (1973).

V

We wish to make clear what our holding means in the context of this case. The complaint has been dismissed as to all the individual defendants. The State is a party only by virtue of 28 U.S.C. § 2403(b) and is not subject to liability. The possible liability of the remaining defendants — the Police Department and the city of Memphis — hinges on *Monell v. New York City Dept. of Social Services,* 436 U.S. 658, 98 S.Ct. 2018, 56 L.Ed.2d 611 (1978), and is left for remand. We hold that the statute is invalid insofar as it purported to give Hymon the authority to act as he did. As for the policy of the Police Department, the absence of any discussion of this issue by the courts below, and the uncertain state of the record, preclude any consideration of its validity.

The judgment of the Court of Appeals is affirmed, and the case is remanded for further proceedings consistent with this opinion.

So ordered.

Notes and Questions

1. What facts and patterns could explain the disproportionate role of police brutality against communities of color? Does your analysis change when the infractions are committed by officers of color?

2. Some argue that the police brutality landscape is a reflection of an ongoing culture of violence in the United States. Do you agree?

3. How might we go about developing greater empathy for those impacted by issues of police and state connected violence? Do movements like the Black Lives-Matter movement help in that endeavor?

C. The Eighth Amendment and 42 U.S.C. § 1983

Prison reform litigation is an important and substantial part of 42 U.S.C. § 1983 litigation. The issue of what constitutes cruel and unusual conditions under the Eighth Amendment is one with which courts have struggled. Accordingly, the Court devised the deliberate indifference standard in *Estelle v. Gamble,* 429 U.S. 97 (1976), for determining whether disregard of a prisoner's condition is a violation of the Eighth Amendment. In so doing, the Court stressed that mere negligence, or simple failure to properly treat or diagnose an inmate, for example, might not rise to the level of a violation. The Court further created exceptions that trigger even higher standards for emergency circumstances, such as during prison riots, etc.[11]

---

11. Brittany Glidden, *Necessary Suffering?: Weighing Government And Prisoner Interests In Determining What Is Cruel And Unusual,* 49 Am. Crim. L. Rev. 1815; John V. Jacobi, *Prison Health Public Health: Obligations and Opportunities,* 31 Am. J. L. and Med. 447; James D. Maynard, *One Case for an Independent Federal Judiciary: Prison Reform Litigation Spurs Structural Change in California,* 37

See below for illustration of this strict approach to prisoners' claims.

Farmer v. Brennan

511 U.S. 825 (1994)

JUSTICE SOUTER delivered the opinion of the Court.

A prison official's "deliberate indifference" to a substantial risk of serious harm to an inmate violates the Eighth Amendment. See *Helling v. McKinney*, 509 U.S. 25, 113 S.Ct. 2475, 125 L.Ed.2d 22 (1993); *Wilson v. Seiter*, 501 U.S. 294, 111 S.Ct. 2321, 115 L.Ed.2d 271 (1991); *Estelle v. Gamble*, 429 U.S. 97, 97 S.Ct. 285, 50 L.Ed.2d 251 (1976). This case requires us to define the term "deliberate indifference," as we do by requiring a showing that the official was subjectively aware of the risk.

I

The dispute before us stems from a civil suit brought by petitioner, Dee Farmer, alleging that respondents, federal prison officials, violated the Eighth Amendment by their deliberate indifference to petitioner's safety. Petitioner, who is serving a federal sentence for credit card fraud, has been diagnosed by medical personnel of the Bureau of Prisons as a transsexual, one who has "[a] rare psychiatric disorder in which a person feels persistently uncomfortable about his or her anatomical sex," and who typically seeks medical treatment, including hormonal therapy and surgery, to bring about a permanent sex change. American Medical Association, Encyclopedia of Medicine 1006 (1989); see also American Psychiatric Association, Diagnostic and Statistical Manual of Mental Disorders 74–75 (3d rev. ed. 1987). For several years before being convicted and sentenced in 1986 at the age of 18, petitioner, who is biologically male, wore women's clothing (as petitioner did at the 1986 trial), underwent estrogen therapy, received silicone breast implants, and submitted to unsuccessful "black market" testicle-removal surgery. See *Farmer v. Haas*, 990 F.2d 319, 320 (CA7 1993). Petitioner's precise appearance in prison is unclear from the record before us, but petitioner claims to have continued hormonal treatment while incarcerated by using drugs smuggled into prison, and apparently wears clothing in a feminine manner, as by displaying a shirt "off one shoulder," App. 112. The parties agree that petitioner "projects feminine characteristics." *Id.*, at 51, 74.

The practice of federal prison authorities is to incarcerate preoperative transsexuals with prisoners of like biological sex, see *Farmer v. Haas, supra*, at 320, and over time authorities housed petitioner in several federal facilities, sometimes in the general male prison population but more often in segregation. While there is no dispute that petitioner was segregated at least several times because of violations of prison rules,

MCGEORGE L. REV. 419; Bailey W. Heaps, *The Most Adequate Branch: Courts as Competent Prison Reformers*, 9 STAN. J.C.R. & C.L. 281; James E. Robertson, *The Majority Opinion as the Social Construction of Reality: The Supreme Court and Prison Rules*, 53 OKLA. L. REV. 161.

neither is it disputed that in at least one penitentiary petitioner was segregated because of safety concerns. See *Farmer v. Carlson,* 685 F.Supp. 1335, 1342 (MD Pa.1988).

On March 9, 1989, petitioner was transferred for disciplinary reasons from the Federal Correctional Institute in Oxford, Wisconsin (FCI-Oxford), to the United States Penitentiary in Terre Haute, Indiana (USP-Terre Haute). Though the record before us is unclear about the security designations of the two prisons in 1989, penitentiaries are typically higher security facilities that house more troublesome prisoners than federal correctional institutes. See generally Federal Bureau of Prisons, Facilities 1990. After an initial stay in administrative segregation, petitioner was placed in the USP-Terre Haute general population. Petitioner voiced no objection to any prison official about the transfer to the penitentiary or to placement in its general population. Within two weeks, according to petitioner's allegations, petitioner was beaten and raped by another inmate in petitioner's cell. Several days later, after petitioner claims to have reported the incident, officials returned petitioner to segregation to await, according to respondents, a hearing about petitioner's HIV-positive status.

Acting without counsel, petitioner then filed a *Bivens* complaint, alleging a violation of the Eighth Amendment. See *Bivens v. Six Unknown Fed. Narcotics Agents,* 403 U.S. 388, 91 S.Ct. 1999, 29 L.Ed.2d 619 (1971); *Carlson v. Green,* 446 U.S. 14, 100 S. Ct. 1468, 64 L.Ed.2d 15 (1980). As defendants, petitioner named respondents: the warden of USP-Terre Haute and the Director of the Bureau of Prisons (sued only in their official capacities); the warden of FCI-Oxford and a case manager there; and the Director of the Bureau of Prisons North Central Region Office and an official in that office (sued in their official and personal capacities). As later amended, the complaint alleged that respondents either transferred petitioner to USP-Terre Haute or placed petitioner in its general population despite knowledge that the penitentiary had a violent environment and a history of inmate assaults, and despite knowledge that petitioner, as a transsexual who "projects feminine characteristics," would be particularly vulnerable to sexual attack by some USP-Terre Haute inmates. This allegedly amounted to a deliberately indifferent failure to protect petitioner's safety, and thus to a violation of petitioner's Eighth Amendment rights. Petitioner sought compensatory and punitive damages, and an injunction barring future confinement in any penitentiary, including USP-Terre Haute.

Respondents filed a motion for summary judgment supported by several affidavits, to which petitioner responded with an opposing affidavit and a cross-motion for summary judgment; petitioner also invoked Federal Rule of Civil Procedure 56(f), asking the court to delay its ruling until respondents had complied with petitioner's pending request for production of documents. Respondents then moved for a protective order staying discovery until resolution of the issue of qualified immunity, raised in respondents' summary judgment motion.

Without ruling on respondents' request to stay discovery, the District Court denied petitioner's Rule 56(f) motion and granted summary judgment to respondents, concluding that there had been no deliberate indifference to petitioner's safety. The failure of prison officials to prevent inmate assaults violates the Eighth Amendment, the court stated, only if prison officials were "reckless in a criminal sense," meaning that they had "actual knowledge" of a potential danger. App. 124. Respondents, however, lacked the requisite knowledge, the court found. "[Petitioner] never expressed any concern for his safety to any of [respondents]. Since [respondents] had no knowledge of any potential danger to [petitioner], they were not deliberately indifferent to his safety." *Ibid.*

The United States Court of Appeals for the Seventh Circuit summarily affirmed without opinion. We granted certiorari, 510 U.S. 811, 114 S.Ct. 56, 126 L.Ed.2d 26 (1993), because Courts of Appeals had adopted inconsistent tests for "deliberate indifference." Compare, for example, *McGill v. Duckworth,* 944 F.2d 344, 348 (CA7 1991) (holding that "deliberate indifference" requires a "subjective standard of recklessness"), cert. denied, 503 U.S. 907, 112 S.Ct. 1265, 117 L.Ed.2d 493 (1992), with *Young v. Quinlan,* 960 F.2d 351, 360–361 (CA3 1992) ("[A] prison official is deliberately indifferent when he knows or should have known of a sufficiently serious danger to an inmate").

II

A

The Constitution "does not mandate comfortable prisons," *Rhodes v. Chapman,* 452 U.S. 337, 349, 101 S.Ct. 2392, 2400, 69 L.Ed.2d 59 (1981), but neither does it permit inhumane ones, and it is now settled that "the treatment a prisoner receives in prison and the conditions under which he is confined are subject to scrutiny under the Eighth Amendment," *Helling,* 509 U.S., at 31, 113 S.Ct., at 2480. In its prohibition of "cruel and unusual punishments," the Eighth Amendment places restraints on prison officials, who may not, for example, use excessive physical force against prisoners. See *Hudson v. McMillian,* 503 U.S. 1, 112 S.Ct. 995, 117 L.Ed.2d 156 (1992). The Amendment also imposes duties on these officials, who must provide humane conditions of confinement; prison officials must ensure that inmates receive adequate food, clothing, shelter, and medical care, and must "take reasonable measures to guarantee the safety of the inmates," *Hudson v. Palmer,* 468 U.S. 517, 526–527, 104 S.Ct. 3194, 3200, 82 L.Ed.2d 393 (1984). See *Helling, supra,* 509 U.S., at 31–32, 113 S.Ct., at 2480; *Washington v. Harper,* 494 U.S. 210, 225, 110 S.Ct. 1028, 1038–1039, 108 L.Ed.2d 178 (1990); *Estelle,* 429 U.S., at 103, 97 S.Ct., at 290. Cf. *DeShaney v. Winnebago County Dept. of Social Servs.,* 489 U.S. 189, 198–199, 109 S. Ct. 998, 1004–1005, 103 L.Ed.2d 249 (1989).

In particular, as the lower courts have uniformly held, and as we have assumed, "prison officials have a duty . . . to protect prisoners from violence at the hands of other prisoners." *Cortes-Quinones v. Jimenez-Nettleship,* 842 F.2d 556, 558 (CA1) (internal quotation marks and citation omitted), cert. denied, 488 U.S. 823, 109 S.Ct. 68, 102 L.Ed.2d 45 (1988); see also *Wilson v. Seiter,* 501 U.S., at 303, 111 S.Ct., at 2326–2327 (describing "the protection [an inmate] is afforded against other inmates" as a "conditio[n] of confinement" subject to the strictures of the Eighth Amendment). Having incarcerated "persons [with] demonstrated proclivit[ies] for antisocial criminal, and often violent, conduct," *Hudson v. Palmer, supra,* 468 U.S., at 526, 104 S.Ct., at 3200, having stripped them of virtually every means of self-protection and foreclosed their access to outside aid, the government and its officials are not free to let the state of nature take its course. Cf. *DeShaney, supra,* 489 U.S., at 199–200, 109 S.Ct., at 3021–3022; *Estelle, supra,* 429 U.S., at 103–104, 97 S.Ct., at 290–291. Prison conditions may be "restrictive and even harsh," *Rhodes, supra,* 452 U.S., at 347, 101 S.Ct., at 2399, but gratuitously allowing the beating or rape of one prisoner by another serves no "legitimate penological objectiv[e]," *Hudson v. Palmer, supra,* 468 U.S., at 548, 104 S.Ct., at 3211 (Stevens, J., concurring in part and dissenting in part), any more than it squares with "'evolving standards of decency,'" *Estelle, supra,* 429 U.S., at 102, 97 S.Ct., at 290 (quoting *Trop v. Dulles,* 356 U.S. 86, 101, 78 S. Ct. 590, 598, 2 L.Ed.2d 630 (1958) (plurality opinion)). Being violently assaulted in prison is simply not "part of the penalty that criminal offenders pay for their offenses against society." *Rhodes, supra,* 452 U.S., at 347, 101 S.Ct., at 2399.

It is not, however, every injury suffered by one prisoner at the hands of another that translates into constitutional liability for prison officials responsible for the victim's safety. Our cases have held that a prison official violates the Eighth Amendment only when two requirements are met. First, the deprivation alleged must be, objectively, "sufficiently serious," *Wilson, supra,* 501 U.S., at 298, 111 S.Ct., at 2324; see also *Hudson v. McMillian, supra,* 503 U.S., at 5, 112 S.Ct., at 998; a prison official's act or omission must result in the denial of "the minimal civilized measure of life's necessities," *Rhodes, supra,* 452 U.S., at 347, 101 S.Ct., at 2399. For a claim (like the one here) based on a failure to prevent harm, the inmate must show that he is incarcerated under conditions posing a substantial risk of serious harm. See *Helling, supra,* 509 U.S., at 35, 113 S.Ct., at 2481.

The second requirement follows from the principle that "only the unnecessary and wanton infliction of pain implicates the Eighth Amendment." *Wilson,* 501 U.S., at 297, 111 S.Ct., at 2323 (internal quotation marks, emphasis, and citations omitted). To violate the Cruel and Unusual Punishments Clause, a prison official must have a "sufficiently culpable state of mind." *Ibid.;* see also *id.,* at 302–303, 111 S.Ct., at 2326; *Hudson v. McMillian, supra,* 503 U.S., at 8, 112 S.Ct., at 2480. In prison-conditions cases that state of mind is one of "deliberate indifference" to inmate health or safety, *Wilson, supra,* 501 U.S., at 302–303, 111 S.Ct., at 2326 see also *Helling, supra,* 509 U.S., at 34–35, 113 S.Ct., at 2481; *Hudson v. McMillian, supra,* 503 U.S., at 5, 112 S. Ct., at 998; *Estelle, supra,* 429 U.S., at 106, 97 S.Ct., at 292, a standard the parties agree governs the claim in this case. The parties disagree, however, on the proper test for deliberate indifference, which we must therefore undertake to define.

B

1

Although we have never paused to explain the meaning of the term "deliberate indifference," the case law is instructive. The term first appeared in the United States Reports in *Estelle v. Gamble,* 429 U.S., at 104, 97 S.Ct., at 291, and its use there shows that deliberate indifference describes a state of mind more blameworthy than negligence. In considering the inmate's claim in *Estelle* that inadequate prison medical care violated the Cruel and Unusual Punishments Clause, we distinguished "deliberate indifference to serious medical needs of prisoners," *ibid.,* from "negligen[ce] in diagnosing or treating a medical condition," *id.,* at 106, 97 S.Ct., at 292, holding that only the former violates the Clause. We have since read *Estelle* for the proposition that Eighth Amendment liability requires "more than ordinary lack of due care for the prisoner's interests or safety." *Whitley v. Albers,* 475 U.S. 312, 319, 106 S.Ct. 1078, 1084, 89 L.Ed.2d 251 (1986).

While *Estelle* establishes that deliberate indifference entails something more than mere negligence, the cases are also clear that it is satisfied by something less than acts or omissions for the very purpose of causing harm or with knowledge that harm will result. That point underlies the ruling that "application of the deliberate indifference standard is inappropriate" in one class of prison cases: when "officials stand accused of using excessive physical force." *Hudson v. McMillian,* 503 U.S., at 6–7, 112 S.Ct., at 999; see also *Whitley, supra,* 475 U.S., at 320, 106 S.Ct., at 1084–1085. In such situations, where the decisions of prison officials are typically made "'in haste, under pressure, and frequently without the luxury of a second chance,'" *Hudson v. McMillian, supra,* 503 U.S., at 6, 112 S.Ct., at 998 (quoting *Whitley, supra,* 475 U.S., at 320, 106 S.Ct., at 1084–1085), an Eighth Amendment claimant must show more than "indifference," deliberate or otherwise. The claimant must show that officials applied force "maliciously and sadistically for the very purpose of causing harm," 503 U.S., at 6, 112 S.Ct., at 998 (internal quotation marks and citations omitted), or, as the Court also put it, that officials used force with "a knowing willingness that [harm] occur," *id.,* at 7, 112 S.Ct., at 999 (internal quotation marks and citation omitted). This standard of purposeful or knowing conduct is not, however, necessary to satisfy the *mens rea* requirement of deliberate indifference for claims challenging conditions of confinement; "the very high state of mind prescribed by *Whitley* does not apply to prison conditions cases." *Wilson, supra,* 501 U.S., at 302–303, 111 S.Ct., at 2326.

With deliberate indifference lying somewhere between the poles of negligence at one end and purpose or knowledge at the other, the Courts of Appeals have routinely equated deliberate indifference with recklessness. See, *e.g., LaMarca v. Turner,* 995 F.2d 1526, 1535 (CA11 1993); *Manarite v. Springfield,* 957 F.2d 953, 957 (CA1 1992); *Redman v. County of San Diego,* 942 F.2d 1435, 1443 (CA9 1991); *McGill v. Duckworth,* 944 F.2d, at 347; *Miltier v. Beorn,* 896 F.2d 848, 851–852 (CA4 1990); *Martin v. White,* 742 F.2d 469, 474 (CA8 1984); see also *Springfield v. Kibbe,* 480 U.S.

257, 269, 107 S.Ct. 1114, 1120–1121, 94 L.Ed.2d 293 (1987) (O'CONNOR, J., dissenting). It is, indeed, fair to say that acting or failing to act with deliberate indifference to a substantial risk of serious harm to a prisoner is the equivalent of recklessly disregarding that risk.

That does not, however, fully answer the pending question about the level of culpability deliberate indifference entails, for the term recklessness is not self-defining. The civil law generally calls a person reckless who acts or (if the person has a duty to act) fails to act in the face of an unjustifiably high risk of harm that is either known or so obvious that it should be known. See Prosser and Keeton § 34, pp. 213–214; Restatement (Second) of Torts § 500 (1965). The criminal law, however, generally permits a finding of recklessness only when a person disregards a risk of harm of which he is aware. See R. Perkins & R. Boyce, Criminal Law 850–851 (3d ed. 1982); J. Hall, General Principles of Criminal Law 115–116, 120, 128 (2d ed. 1960) (hereinafter Hall); American Law Institute, Model Penal Code § 2.02(2)(c), and Comment 3 (1985); but see *Commonwealth v. Pierce,* 138 Mass. 165, 175–178 (1884) (Holmes, J.) (adopting an objective approach to criminal recklessness). The standards proposed by the parties in this case track the two approaches (though the parties do not put it that way): petitioner asks us to define deliberate indifference as what we have called civil-law recklessness, and respondents urge us to adopt an approach consistent with recklessness in the criminal law.

We reject petitioner's invitation to adopt an objective test for deliberate indifference. We hold instead that a prison official cannot be found liable under the Eighth Amendment for denying an inmate humane conditions of confinement unless the official knows of and disregards an excessive risk to inmate health or safety; the official must both be aware of facts from which the inference could be drawn that a substantial risk of serious harm exists, and he must also draw the inference. This approach comports best with the text of the Amendment as our cases have interpreted it. The Eighth Amendment does not outlaw cruel and unusual "conditions"; it outlaws cruel and unusual "punishments." An act or omission unaccompanied by knowledge of a significant risk of harm might well be something society wishes to discourage, and if harm does result society might well wish to assure compensation. The common law reflects such concerns when it imposes tort liability on a purely objective basis. See Prosser and Keeton §§ 2, 34, pp. 6, 213–214; see also Federal Tort Claims Act, 28 U.S.C. §§ 2671–2680; *United States v. Muniz,* 374 U.S. 150, 83 S.Ct. 1850, 10 L.Ed.2d 805 (1963). But an official's failure to alleviate a significant risk that he should have perceived but did not, while no cause for commendation, cannot under our cases be condemned as the infliction of punishment.

In *Wilson v. Seiter,* we rejected a reading of the Eighth Amendment that would allow liability to be imposed on prison officials solely because of the presence of objectively inhumane prison conditions. See 501 U.S., at 299–302, 111 S.Ct., at 2324–2326. As we explained there, our "cases mandate inquiry into a prison official's state of mind when it is claimed that the official has inflicted cruel and unusual punishment." *Id.,* at 299, 111 S.Ct., at 2324. Although "state of mind," like "intent," is an ambiguous term that can encompass objectively defined levels of blameworthiness, see 1 W. LaFave & A. Scott, Substantive Criminal Law §§ 3.4, 3.5, pp. 296–300, 313–314 (1986) (hereinafter LaFave & Scott); *United States v. Bailey*, 444 U.S. 394, 404, 100 S.Ct. 624, 631–632, 62 L.Ed.2d 575 (1980), it was no accident that we said in *Wilson* and repeated in later cases that Eighth Amendment suits against prison officials must satisfy a "subjective" requirement. See *Wilson, supra*, 501 U.S., at 298, 111 S.Ct., at 2324; see also *Helling*, 509 U.S., at 35, 113 S.Ct., at 2481; *Hudson v. McMillian*, 503 U.S., at 8, 112 S.Ct., at 2327. It is true, as petitioner points out, that *Wilson* cited with approval Court of Appeals decisions applying an objective test for deliberate indifference to claims based on prison officials' failure to prevent inmate assaults. See 501 U.S., at 303, 111 S.Ct., at 2327 (citing *Cortes-Quinones v. Jimenez-Nettleship*, 842 F.2d, at 560; and *Morgan v. District of Columbia*, 824 F.2d 1049, 1057–1058 (CADC 1987)). But *Wilson* cited those cases for the proposition that the deliberate indifference standard applies to all prison-conditions claims, not to undo its holding that the Eighth Amendment has a "subjective component." 501 U.S., at 298, 111 S.Ct., at 2324. Petitioner's purely objective test for deliberate indifference is simply incompatible with *Wilson*'s holding.

To be sure, the reasons for focusing on what a defendant's mental attitude actually was (or is), rather than what it should have been (or should be), differ in the Eighth Amendment context from that of the criminal law. Here, a subjective approach isolates those who inflict punishment; there, it isolates those against whom punishment should be inflicted. But the result is the same: to act recklessly in either setting a person must "consciously disregar[d]" a substantial risk of serious harm. Model Penal Code § 2.02(2)(c).

. . . .

2

Our decision that Eighth Amendment liability requires consciousness of a risk is thus based on the Constitution and our cases, not merely on a parsing of the phrase "deliberate indifference." And we do not reject petitioner's arguments for a thoroughly objective approach to deliberate indifference without recognizing that on the crucial point (whether a prison official must know of a risk, or whether it suffices that he should know) the term does not speak with certainty. Use of "deliberate," for example, arguably requires nothing more than an act (or omission) of indifference to a serious risk that is voluntary, not accidental. Cf. *Estelle*, 429 U.S., at 105, 97 S.Ct., at 291–292 (distinguishing "deliberate indifference" from "accident" or "inadverten[ce]"). And even if "deliberate" is better read as implying knowledge of a risk, the concept of constructive knowledge is familiar enough that the term "deliberate indifference" would not, of its own force, preclude a scheme that conclusively presumed awareness from a risk's obviousness.

Because "deliberate indifference" is a judicial gloss, appearing neither in the Constitution nor in a statute, we could not accept petitioner's argument that the test for "deliberate indifference" described in *Canton v. Harris*, 489 U.S. 378, 109 S.

Ct. 1197, 103 L.Ed.2d 412 (1989), must necessarily govern here. In *Canton*, interpreting Rev.Stat. § 1979, 42 U.S.C. § 1983, we held that a municipality can be liable for failure to train its employees when the municipality's failure shows "a deliberate indifference to the rights of its inhabitants." 489 U.S., at 389, 109 S.Ct., at 1205 (internal quotation marks omitted). In speaking to the meaning of the term, we said that "it may happen that in light of the duties assigned to specific officers or employees the need for more or different training is so obvious, and the inadequacy so likely to result in the violation of constitutional rights, that the policymakers of the city can reasonably be said to have been deliberately indifferent to the need." *Id.,* at 390, 109 S.Ct., at 1205; see also *id.,* at 390, n. 10, 109 S.Ct., at 1205, n. 10 (elaborating). Justice O'Connor's separate opinion for three Justices agreed with the Court's "obvious[ness]" test and observed that liability is appropriate when policymakers are "on actual or constructive notice" of the need to train, *id.,* at 396, 109 S.Ct., at 1208 (opinion concurring in part and dissenting in part). It would be hard to describe the *Canton* understanding of deliberate indifference, permitting liability to be premised on obviousness or constructive notice, as anything but objective.

Canton's objective standard, however, is not an appropriate test for determining the liability of prison officials under the Eighth Amendment as interpreted in our cases. 42 U.S.C. § 1983, which merely provides a cause of action, "contains no state-of-mind requirement independent of that necessary to state a violation of the underlying constitutional right." *Daniels v. Williams,* 474 U.S. 327, 330, 106 S.Ct. 662, 664, 88 L.Ed.2d 662 (1986).

. . . .

We are no more persuaded by petitioner's argument that, without an objective test for deliberate indifference, prison officials will be free to ignore obvious dangers to inmates. Under the test we adopt today, an Eighth Amendment claimant need not show that a prison official acted or failed to act believing that harm actually would befall an inmate; it is enough that the official acted or failed to act despite his knowledge of a substantial risk of serious harm. Cf. 1 C. Torcia, Wharton's Criminal Law § 27, p. 141 (14th ed. 1978); Hall 115. We doubt that a subjective approach will present prison officials with any serious motivation "to take refuge in the zone between 'ignorance of obvious risks' and 'actual knowledge of risks.'" Brief for Petitioner 27. Whether a prison official had the requisite knowledge of a substantial risk is a question of fact subject to demonstration in the usual ways, including inference from circumstantial evidence, cf. Hall 118 (cautioning against "confusing a mental state with the proof of its existence"), and a factfinder may conclude that a prison official knew of a substantial risk from the very fact that the risk was obvious. Cf. LaFave & Scott § 3.7, p. 335 ("[I]f the risk is obvious, so that a reasonable man would realize it, we might well infer that [the defendant] did in fact realize it; but the inference cannot be conclusive, for we know that people are not always conscious of what reasonable people would be conscious of"). For example, if an Eighth Amendment plaintiff presents evidence showing that a substantial risk of inmate attacks was "longstanding, pervasive, well-documented, or expressly noted by prison officials in the past, and the circumstances suggest that the defendant-official being sued had been exposed to information concerning the risk and thus 'must have known' about it, then such evidence could be sufficient to permit a trier of fact to find that the defendant-official had actual knowledge of the risk." Brief for Respondents 22.

Nor may a prison official escape liability for deliberate indifference by showing that, while he was aware of an obvious, substantial risk to inmate safety, he did not know that the complainant was especially likely to be assaulted by the specific prisoner who eventually committed the assault. The question under the Eighth Amendment is whether prison officials, acting with deliberate indifference, exposed a prisoner to a sufficiently substantial "risk of serious damage to his future health," *Helling*, 509 U.S., at 35, 113 S.Ct., at 2481, and it does not matter whether the risk comes from a single source or multiple sources, any more than it matters whether a prisoner faces an excessive risk of attack for reasons personal to him or because all prisoners in his situation face such a risk. See Brief for Respondents 15 (stating that a prisoner can establish exposure to a sufficiently serious risk of harm "by showing that he belongs to an identifiable group of prisoners who are frequently singled out for violent attack by other inmates"). If, for example, prison officials were aware that inmate "rape was so common and uncontrolled that some potential victims dared not sleep [but] instead . . . would leave their beds and spend the night clinging to the bars nearest the guards' station," *Hutto v. Finney*, 437 U.S. 678, 681–682, n. 3, 98 S.Ct. 2565, 2569, n. 3, 57 L.Ed.2d 522, n. 3 (1978), it would obviously be irrelevant to liability that the officials could not guess beforehand precisely who would attack whom. Cf. *Helling, supra*, 509 U.S., at 33, 113 S.Ct., at 2480 (observing that the Eighth Amendment requires a remedy for exposure of inmates to "infectious maladies" such as hepatitis and venereal disease "even though the possible infection might not affect all of those exposed"); *Commonwealth v. Welansky*, 316 Mass. 383, 55 N.E.2d 902 (1944) (affirming conviction for manslaughter under a law requiring reckless or wanton conduct of a nightclub owner who failed to protect patrons from a fire, even though the owner did not know in advance who would light the match that ignited the fire or which patrons would lose their lives); *State v. Julius*, 185 W. Va. 422, 431–432, 408 S.E.2d 1, 10–11 (1991) (holding that a defendant may be held criminally liable for injury to an unanticipated victim).

Because, however, prison officials who lacked knowledge of a risk cannot be said to have inflicted punishment, it remains open to the officials to prove that they were unaware even of an obvious risk to inmate health or safety. That a trier of fact may infer knowledge from the obvious, in other words, does not mean that it must do so. Prison officials charged with deliberate indifference might show, for example, that they did not know of the underlying facts indicating a sufficiently substantial danger and that they were therefore unaware of a danger, or that they knew the underlying facts but believed (albeit unsoundly) that the risk to which the facts gave rise was insubstantial or nonexistent.

In addition, prison officials who actually knew of a substantial risk to inmate health or safety may be found free from liability if they responded reasonably to the risk, even if the harm ultimately was not averted. A prison official's duty under the Eighth Amendment is to ensure "'reasonable safety,'" *Helling, supra,* at 33, 113 S. Ct., at 2481; see also *Washington v. Harper,* 494 U.S., at 225, 110 S.Ct., at 1038–1039; *Hudson v. Palmer,* 468 U.S., at 526–527, 104 S.Ct., at 3200–3201, a standard that incorporates due regard for prison officials' "unenviable task of keeping dangerous men in safe custody under humane conditions," *Spain v. Procunier,* 600 F.2d 189, 193 (CA9 1979) (Kennedy, J.); see also *Bell v. Wolfish,* 441 U.S. 520, 547–548, 562, 99 S.Ct. 1861, 1878–1879, 1886, 60 L.Ed.2d 447 (1979). Whether one puts it in terms of duty or deliberate indifference, prison officials who act reasonably cannot be found liable under the Cruel and Unusual Punishments Clause.

We address, finally, petitioner's argument that a subjective deliberate indifference test will unjustly require prisoners to suffer physical injury before obtaining court-ordered correction of objectively inhumane prison conditions. "It would," indeed, "be odd to deny an injunction to inmates who plainly proved an unsafe, life-threatening condition in their prison on the ground that nothing yet had happened to them." *Helling, supra,* 509 U.S., at 33, 113 S.Ct., at 2481. But nothing in the test we adopt today clashes with that common sense. Petitioner's argument is flawed for the simple reason that "[o]ne does not have to await the consummation of threatened injury to obtain preventive relief." *Pennsylvania v. West Virginia,* 262 U.S. 553, 593, 43 S.Ct. 658, 663, 67 L.Ed. 1117 (1923). Consistently with this principle, a subjective approach to deliberate indifference does not require a prisoner seeking "a remedy for unsafe conditions [to] await a tragic event [such as an] actua[l] assaul[t] before obtaining relief." *Helling, supra,* at 33–34, 113 S.Ct., at 2481.

In a suit such as petitioner's, insofar as it seeks injunctive relief to prevent a substantial risk of serious injury from ripening into actual harm, "the subjective factor, deliberate indifference, should be determined in light of the prison authorities' current attitudes and conduct," *Helling, supra,* at 36, 113 S.Ct., at 2482: their attitudes and conduct at the time suit is brought and persisting thereafter. An inmate seeking an injunction on the ground that there is "a contemporary violation of a nature likely to continue," *United States v. Oregon State Medical Soc.,* 343 U.S. 326, 333, 72 S.Ct. 690, 695, 96 L.Ed. 978 (1952), must adequately plead such a violation; to survive summary judgment, he must come forward with evidence from which it can be inferred that the defendant-officials were at the time suit was filed, and are at the time of summary judgment, knowingly and unreasonably disregarding an objectively intolerable risk of harm, and that they will continue to do so; and finally to establish eligibility for an injunction, the inmate must demonstrate the continuance of that disregard during the remainder of the litigation and into the future. In so doing, the inmate may rely, in the district court's discretion, on developments that postdate the pleadings and pretrial motions, as the defendants may rely on such developments to establish that the inmate is not entitled to an injunction.

. . . .

That prison officials' "current attitudes and conduct," *Helling*, 509 U.S., at 36, 113 S.Ct., at 2482, must be assessed in an action for injunctive relief does not mean, of course, that inmates are free to bypass adequate internal prison procedures and bring their health and safety concerns directly to court. "An appeal to the equity jurisdiction conferred on federal district courts is an appeal to the sound discretion which guides the determinations of courts of equity," *Meredith v. Winter Haven*, 320 U.S. 228, 235, 64 S.Ct. 7, 11, 88 L.Ed. 9 (1943), and any litigant making such an appeal must show that the intervention of equity is required. When a prison inmate seeks injunctive relief, a court need not ignore the inmate's failure to take advantage of adequate prison procedures, and an inmate who needlessly bypasses such procedures may properly be compelled to pursue them. Cf. 42 U.S.C. § 1997e (authorizing district courts in § 1983 actions to require inmates to exhaust "such plain, speedy, and effective administrative remedies as are available"). Even apart from the demands of equity, an inmate would be well advised to take advantage of internal prison procedures for resolving inmate grievances. When those procedures produce results, they will typically do so faster than judicial processes can. And even when they do not bring constitutionally required changes, the inmate's task in court will obviously be much easier.

Accordingly, we reject petitioner's arguments and hold that a prison official may be held liable under the Eighth Amendment for denying humane conditions of confinement only if he knows that inmates face a substantial risk of serious harm and disregards that risk by failing to take reasonable measures to abate it.

III

A

Against this backdrop, we consider whether the District Court's disposition of petitioner's complaint, summarily affirmed without briefing by the Court of Appeals for the Seventh Circuit, comports with Eighth Amendment principles. We conclude that the appropriate course is to remand.

In granting summary judgment to respondents on the ground that petitioner had failed to satisfy the Eighth Amendment's subjective requirement, the District Court may have placed decisive weight on petitioner's failure to notify respondents of a risk of harm. That petitioner "never expressed any concern for his safety to any of [respondents]," App. 124, was the only evidence the District Court cited for its conclusion that there was no genuine dispute about respondents' assertion that they "had no knowledge of any potential danger to [petitioner]," *ibid*. But with respect to each of petitioner's claims, for damages and for injunctive relief, the failure to give advance notice is not dispositive. Petitioner may establish respondents' awareness by reliance on any relevant evidence. See *supra*, at 1981.

The summary judgment record does not so clearly establish respondents' entitlement to judgment as a matter of law on the issue of subjective knowledge that we can simply assume the absence of error below. For example, in papers filed in opposition to respondents' summary-judgment motion, petitioner pointed to respondents' admission that petitioner is a "non-violent" transsexual who, because of petitioner's "youth and feminine appearance" is "likely to experience a great deal of sexual pressure" in prison. App. 50–51, 73–74. And petitioner recounted a statement by one of the respondents, then warden of the penitentiary in Lewisburg, Pennsylvania, who told petitioner that there was "a high probability that [petitioner] could not safely function at USP-Lewisburg," *id.*, at 109, an incident confirmed in a published District Court opinion. See *Farmer v. Carlson,* 685 F.Supp., at 1342; see also *ibid.* ("Clearly, placing plaintiff, a twenty-one year old transsexual, into the general population at [USP-]Lewisburg, a [high-]security institution, could pose a significant threat to internal security in general and to plaintiff in particular").

We cannot, moreover, be certain that additional evidence is unavailable to petitioner because in denying petitioner's Rule 56(f) motion for additional discovery the District Court may have acted on a mistaken belief that petitioner's failure to notify was dispositive. Petitioner asserted in papers accompanying the Rule 56(f) motion that the requested documents would show that "each defendant had knowledge that USP-Terre Haute was and is, a violent institution with a history of sexual assault, stabbings, etc., [and that] each defendant showed reckless disregard for my safety by designating me to said institution knowing that I would be sexually assaulted." App. 105–106. But in denying the Rule 56(f) motion, the District Court stated that the requested documents were "not shown by plaintiff to be necessary to oppose defendants' motion for summary judgment," *id.*, at 121, a statement consistent with the erroneous view that failure to notify was fatal to petitioner's complaint.

Because the District Court may have mistakenly thought that advance notification was a necessary element of an Eighth Amendment failure-to-protect claim, we think it proper to remand for reconsideration of petitioner's Rule 56(f) motion and, whether additional discovery is permitted or not, for application of the Eighth Amendment principles explained above.

. . . .

IV

The judgment of the Court of Appeals is vacated, and the case is remanded for further proceedings consistent with this opinion.

So ordered.

Notes and Questions

1. At what point should risk of inmate assault become sufficiently substantial for Eighth Amendment purposes? Does the Court provide a threshold standard to help would-be plaintiffs assess likelihood of success?

2. The Court elaborated in footnote 8, not included here:

> While the obviousness of a risk is not conclusive and a prison official may show that the obvious escaped him, he would not escape liability if the evidence showed that he merely refused to verify underlying facts that he

strongly suspected to be true, or declined to confirm inferences of risk that he strongly suspected to exist (as when a prison official is aware of a high probability of facts indicating that one prisoner has planned an attack on another but resists opportunities to obtain final confirmation; or when a prison official knows that some diseases are communicable and that a single needle is being used to administer flu shots to prisoners but refuses to listen to a subordinate who he strongly suspects will attempt to explain the associated risk of transmitting disease). When instructing juries in deliberate indifference cases with such issues of proof, courts should be careful to ensure that the requirement of subjective culpability is not lost. It is not enough merely to find that a reasonable person would have known, or that the defendant should have known, and juries should be instructed accordingly.

3. Should the inmate's failure to complain be dispositive? Note Justice Thomas's statement below from footnote 2 of his concurrence, not included above:

> I do not read the remand portion of the Court's opinion to intimate that the courts below reached the wrong result, especially because the Seventh Circuit has long followed the rule of law the Court lays down today. See *McGill v. Duckworth*, 944 F.2d 344 (CA7 1991); *Duckworth v. Franzen*, 780 F.2d 645 (CA7 1985). Rather, I regard it as a cautionary measure undertaken merely to give the Court of Appeals an opportunity to decide in the first instance whether the District Court erroneously gave dispositive weight to petitioner's failure to complain to prison officials that he believed himself at risk of sexual assault in the general prison population. If, on remand, the Seventh Circuit concludes that the District Court did not, nothing in the Court's opinion precludes the Seventh Circuit from summarily affirming the entry of summary judgment in respondents' favor.

4. Should the Court be worried about minimizing the number of cases from inmates? See the Prison Litigation Reform Act and its goals. 42 U.S.C. § 1997e (2013); *see also Woodford v. Ngo*, 548 U.S. 81 (2006) (discussing Congress's enactment of the PLRA, which contains various provisions designed to decrease prisoner litigation in the federal courts).

D. Substantive Due Process and 42 U.S.C. § 1983

The Substantive Due Process doctrine presents the greatest difficulty for proving a constitutional violation of the Fourteenth Amendment. In order to prove a violation under the Fourteenth Amendment's Due Process Clause, plaintiffs must demonstrate a deprivation of "life, liberty, and property." Whether a protection amounts to an entitlement, however, is a question to which the Court has answered in the negative at various times. Accordingly, the Court has said that there is no right to protection from officials against actions by private actors in *Deshaney v. Winnebago Cty. Dep't of Soc. Services*, 489 U.S. 189 (1989), and that there is no property interest created in a typical state statute granting the right to protective orders against a harasser, *Town of Castle Rock v. Gonzales*, 545 U.S. 748 (2005). Further, even in the event that such a right were to be recognized as an entitlement protected by the Due Process Clause, courts have imposed the extremely high requirement that the officials' actions "shock the conscience" (*County of Sacramento v. Lewis*, 523 U.S. 833 (1998)), so strictly that it remains very hard for plaintiffs to prevail under these standards.[12]

DeShaney v. Winnebago County Department of Social Services
489 U.S. 189 (1989)

CHIEF JUSTICE REHNQUIST delivered the opinion of the Court.

Petitioner is a boy who was beaten and permanently injured by his father, with whom he lived. Respondents are social workers and other local officials who received complaints that petitioner was being abused by his father and had reason to believe that this was the case, but nonetheless did not act to remove petitioner from his father's custody. Petitioner sued respondents claiming that their failure to act deprived him of his liberty in violation of the Due Process Clause of the Fourteenth Amendment to the United States Constitution. We hold that it did not.

I

The facts of this case are undeniably tragic. Petitioner Joshua DeShaney was born in 1979. In 1980, a Wyoming court granted his parents a divorce and awarded custody of Joshua to his father, Randy DeShaney. The father shortly thereafter moved to Neenah, a city located in Winnebago County, Wisconsin, taking the infant Joshua with him. There he entered into a second marriage, which also ended in divorce.

The Winnebago County authorities first learned that Joshua DeShaney might be a victim of child abuse in January 1982, when his father's second wife complained to the police, at the time of their divorce, that he had previously "hit the boy causing marks and [was] a prime case for child abuse." App. 152–153. The Winnebago County Department of Social Services (DSS) interviewed the father, but he denied the accusations, and DSS did not pursue them further. In January 1983, Joshua was admitted to a local hospital with multiple bruises and abrasions. The examining physician suspected child abuse and notified DSS, which immediately obtained an order from a Wisconsin juvenile court placing Joshua in the temporary custody of the hospital. Three days later, the county convened an ad hoc "Child Protection

12. *McClendon v. City of Columbia*, 305 F.3d 314 (5th Cir. 2002); *Singleton v. Cecil*, 176 F.3d 419 (8th Cir. 1999); *Crowe v. Cty. of San Diego*, 359 F. Supp. 2d 994 (S.D. Cal. 2005); *Harrington v. Portland*, 677 F. Supp. 1491 (D. Or. 1987); *McKinney v. Pate*, 20 F.3d 1550 (11th Cir. 1994).

Team"—consisting of a pediatrician, a psychologist, a police detective, the county's lawyer, several DSS caseworkers, and various hospital personnel—to consider Joshua's situation. At this meeting, the Team decided that there was insufficient evidence of child abuse to retain Joshua in the custody of the court. The Team did, however, decide to recommend several measures to protect Joshua, including enrolling him in a preschool program, providing his father with certain counselling services, and encouraging his father's girlfriend to move out of the home. Randy DeShaney entered into a voluntary agreement with DSS in which he promised to cooperate with them in accomplishing these goals.

Based on the recommendation of the Child Protection Team, the juvenile court dismissed the child protection case and returned Joshua to the custody of his father. A month later, emergency room personnel called the DSS caseworker handling Joshua's case to report that he had once again been treated for suspicious injuries. The caseworker concluded that there was no basis for action. For the next six months, the caseworker made monthly visits to the DeShaney home, during which she observed a number of suspicious injuries on Joshua's head; she also noticed that he had not been enrolled in school, and that the girlfriend had not moved out. The caseworker dutifully recorded these incidents in her files, along with her continuing suspicions that someone in the DeShaney household was physically abusing Joshua, but she did nothing more. In November 1983, the emergency room notified DSS that Joshua had been treated once again for injuries that they believed to be caused by child abuse. On the caseworker's next two visits to the DeShaney home, she was told that Joshua was too ill to see her. Still DSS took no action.

In March 1984, Randy DeShaney beat 4-year-old Joshua so severely that he fell into a life-threatening coma. Emergency brain surgery revealed a series of hemorrhages caused by traumatic injuries to the head inflicted over a long period of time. Joshua did not die, but he suffered brain damage so severe that he is expected to spend the rest of his life confined to an institution for the profoundly retarded. Randy DeShaney was subsequently tried and convicted of child abuse.

Joshua and his mother brought this action under 42 U.S.C. § 1983 in the United States District Court for the Eastern District of Wisconsin against respondents Winnebago County, DSS, and various individual employees of DSS. The complaint alleged that respondents had deprived Joshua of his liberty without due process of law, in violation of his rights under the Fourteenth Amendment, by failing to intervene to protect him against a risk of violence at his father's hands of which they knew or should have known. The District Court granted summary judgment for respondents.

The Court of Appeals for the Seventh Circuit affirmed, 812 F.2d 298 (1987), holding that petitioners had not made out an actionable § 1983 claim for two alternative reasons. First, the court held that the Due Process Clause of the Fourteenth Amendment does not require a state or local governmental entity to protect its citizens from "private violence, or other mishaps not attributable to the conduct of its employees."

Id., at 301. In so holding, the court specifically rejected the position endorsed by a divided panel of the Third Circuit in *Estate of Bailey by Oare v. County of York,* 768 F.2d 503, 510–511 (1985), and by dicta in *Jensen v. Conrad,* 747 F.2d 185, 190–194 (CA4 1984), cert. denied, 470 U.S. 1052, 105 S.Ct. 1754, 84 L.Ed.2d 818 (1985), that once the State learns that a particular child is in danger of abuse from third parties and actually undertakes to protect him from that danger, a "special relationship" arises between it and the child which imposes an affirmative constitutional duty to provide adequate protection. 812 F.2d, at 303–304. Second, the court held, in reliance on our decision in *Martinez v. California,* 444 U.S. 277, 285, 100 S.Ct. 553, 559, 62 L.Ed.2d 481 (1980), that the causal connection between respondents' conduct and Joshua's injuries was too attenuated to establish a deprivation of constitutional rights actionable under § 1983. 812 F.2d, at 301–303. The court therefore found it unnecessary to reach the question whether respondents' conduct evinced the "state of mind" necessary to make out a due process claim after *Daniels v. Williams,* 474 U.S. 327, 106 S.Ct. 662, 88 L.Ed.2d 662 (1986), and *Davidson v. Cannon,* 474 U.S. 344, 106 S.Ct. 668, 88 L.Ed.2d 677 (1986). 812 F.2d, at 302.

Because of the inconsistent approaches taken by the lower courts in determining when, if ever, the failure of a state or local governmental entity or its agents to provide an individual with adequate protective services constitutes a violation of the individual's due process rights, see *Archie v. Racine,* 847 F.2d 1211, 1220–1223, and n. 10 (CA7 1988) (en banc) (collecting cases), cert. pending, No. 88-576, and the importance of the issue to the administration of state and local governments, we granted certiorari. 485 U.S. 958, 108 S.Ct. 1218, 99 L.Ed.2d 419 (1988). We now affirm.

II

The Due Process Clause of the Fourteenth Amendment provides that "[n]o State shall . . . deprive any person of life, liberty, or property, without due process of law." Petitioners contend that the State deprived Joshua of his liberty interest in "free[dom] from . . . unjustified intrusions on personal security," see *Ingraham v. Wright,* 430 U.S. 651, 673, 97 S.Ct. 1401, 1413, 51 L.Ed.2d 711 (1977), by failing to provide him with adequate protection against his father's violence. The claim is one invoking the substantive rather than the procedural component of the Due Process Clause; petitioners do not claim that the State denied Joshua protection without according him appropriate procedural safeguards, see *Morrissey v. Brewer,* 408 U.S. 471, 481, 92 S.Ct. 2593, 2600, 33 L.Ed.2d 484 (1972), but that it was categorically obligated to protect him in these circumstances, see *Youngberg v. Romeo,* 457 U.S. 307, 309, 102 S.Ct. 2452, 2454, 73 L.Ed.2d 28 (1982).

But nothing in the language of the Due Process Clause itself requires the State to protect the life, liberty, and property of its citizens against invasion by private actors. The Clause is phrased as a limitation on the State's power to act, not as a guarantee of certain minimal levels of safety and security. It forbids the State itself to deprive individuals of life, liberty, or property without "due process of law," but its language cannot fairly be extended to impose an affirmative obligation on the State to ensure that those interests do not come to harm through other means. Nor does history support such an expansive reading of the constitutional text. Like its counterpart in the Fifth Amendment, the Due Process Clause of the Fourteenth Amendment was intended to prevent government "from abusing [its] power, or employing it as an instrument of oppression," *Davidson v. Cannon, supra,* 474 U.S., at 348, 106 S.Ct., at 670; see also *Daniels v. Williams, supra,* 474 U.S., at 331, 106 S.Ct., at 665 (""""to secure the individual from the arbitrary exercise of the powers of government,"""" and "to prevent governmental power from being 'used for purposes of oppression'") (internal citations omitted); *Parratt v. Taylor,* 451 U.S. 527, 549, 101 S.Ct. 1908, 1919, 68 L.Ed.2d 420 (1981) (Powell, J., concurring in result) (to prevent the "affirmative abuse of power"). Its purpose was to protect the people from the State, not to ensure that the State protected them from each other. The Framers were content to leave the extent of governmental obligation in the latter area to the democratic political processes.

Consistent with these principles, our cases have recognized that the Due Process Clauses generally confer no affirmative right to governmental aid, even where such aid may be necessary to secure life, liberty, or property interests of which the government itself may not deprive the individual. See, *e.g., Harris v. McRae,* 448 U.S. 297, 317–318, 100 S.Ct. 2671, 2688–2689, 65 L.Ed.2d 784 (1980) (no obligation to fund abortions or other medical services) (discussing Due Process Clause of Fifth Amendment); *Lindsey v. Normet,* 405 U.S. 56, 74, 92 S.Ct. 862, 874, 31 L.Ed.2d 36 (1972) (no obligation to provide adequate housing) (discussing Due Process Clause of Fourteenth Amendment); see also *Youngberg v. Romeo, supra,* 457 U.S., at 317, 102 S.Ct., at 2458 ("As a general matter, a State is under no constitutional duty to provide substantive services for those within its border"). As we said in *Harris v. McRae:* "Although the liberty protected by the Due Process Clause affords protection against unwarranted *government* interference . . . , it does not confer an entitlement to such [governmental aid] as may be necessary to realize all the advantages of that freedom." 448 U.S., at 317–318, 100 S.Ct., at 2688–2689 (emphasis added). If the Due Process Clause does not require the State to provide its citizens with particular protective services, it follows that the State cannot be held liable under the Clause for injuries that could have been averted had it chosen to provide them. As a general matter, then, we conclude that a State's failure to protect an individual against private violence simply does not constitute a violation of the Due Process Clause.

Petitioners contend, however, that even if the Due Process Clause imposes no affirmative obligation on the State to provide the general public with adequate protective services, such a duty may arise out of certain "special relationships" created or assumed by the State with respect to particular individuals. Brief for Petitioners 13–18. Petitioners argue that such a "special relationship" existed here because the State knew that Joshua faced a special danger of abuse at his father's hands, and specifically proclaimed, by word and by deed, its intention to protect him against that danger. *Id.,* at 18–20. Having actually undertaken to protect Joshua from this danger — which petitioners concede the State played no part in creating — the State acquired an affirmative "duty," enforceable through the Due Process Clause, to do so in a reasonably competent fashion. Its failure to discharge that duty, so the argument goes, was an abuse of governmental power that so "shocks the conscience," *Rochin v. California*, 342 U.S. 165, 172, 72 S.Ct. 205, 209, 96 L.Ed. 183 (1952), as to constitute a substantive due process violation. Brief for Petitioners 20.

We reject this argument. It is true that in certain limited circumstances the Constitution imposes upon the State affirmative duties of care and protection with respect to particular individuals. In *Estelle v. Gamble*, 429 U.S. 97, 97 S.Ct. 285, 50 L.Ed.2d 251 (1976), we recognized that the Eighth Amendment's prohibition against cruel and unusual punishment, made applicable to the States through the Fourteenth Amendment's Due Process Clause, *Robinson v. California*, 370 U.S. 660, 82 S.Ct. 1417, 8 L.Ed.2d 758 (1962), requires the State to provide adequate medical care to incarcerated prisoners. 429 U.S., at 103–104, 97 S.Ct., at 290–291. We reasoned that because the prisoner is unable "'by reason of the deprivation of his liberty [to] care for himself,'" it is only "'just'" that the State be required to care for him. *Ibid.*, quoting *Spicer v. Williamson*, 191 N.C. 487, 490, 132 S.E. 291, 293 (1926).

In *Youngberg v. Romeo*, 457 U.S. 307, 102 S.Ct. 2452, 73 L.Ed.2d 28 (1982), we extended this analysis beyond the Eighth Amendment setting, holding that the substantive component of the Fourteenth Amendment's Due Process Clause requires the State to provide involuntarily committed mental patients with such services as are necessary to ensure their "reasonable safety" from themselves and others. *Id.*, at 314–325, 102 S.Ct., at 2457–2463; see *id.*, at 315, 324, 102 S.Ct., at 2457, 2462 (dicta indicating that the State is also obligated to provide such individuals with "adequate food, shelter, clothing, and medical care"). As we explained: "If it is cruel and unusual punishment to hold convicted criminals in unsafe conditions, it must be unconstitutional [under the Due Process Clause] to confine the involuntarily committed—who may not be punished at all—in unsafe conditions." *Id.*, at 315–316, 102 S.Ct., at 2457–2458; see also *Revere v. Massachusetts General Hospital*, 463 U.S. 239, 244, 103 S.Ct. 2979, 2983, 77 L.Ed.2d 605 (1983) (holding that the Due Process Clause requires the responsible government or governmental agency to provide medical care to suspects in police custody who have been injured while being apprehended by the police).

But these cases afford petitioners no help. Taken together, they stand only for the proposition that when the State takes a person into its custody and holds him there against his will, the Constitution imposes upon it a corresponding duty to assume some responsibility for his safety and general well-being. See *Youngberg v. Romeo*, *supra*, 457 U.S., at 317, 102 S.Ct., at 2458 ("When a person is institutionalized—and wholly dependent on the State[,] . . . a duty to provide certain services and care does exist"). The rationale for this principle is simple enough: when the State by the affirmative exercise of its power so restrains an individual's liberty that it renders him unable to care for himself, and at the same time fails to provide for his basic human needs—*e.g.*, food, clothing, shelter, medical care, and reasonable safety—it transgresses the substantive limits on state action set by the Eighth Amendment and the Due Process Clause. See *Estelle v. Gamble, supra,* 429 U.S., at 103–104, 97 S.Ct., at 290–291; *Youngberg v. Romeo, supra,* 457 U.S., at 315–316, 102 S.Ct., at 2457–2458. The affirmative duty to protect arises not from the State's knowledge of the individual's predicament or from its expressions of intent to help him, but from the limitation which it has imposed on his freedom to act on his own behalf. See *Estelle v. Gamble, supra,* 429 U.S., at 103, 97 S.Ct., at 290 ("An inmate must rely on prison authorities to treat his medical needs; if the authorities fail to do so, those needs will not be met"). In the substantive due process analysis, it is the State's affirmative act of restraining the individual's freedom to act on his own behalf—through incarceration, institutionalization, or other similar restraint of personal liberty—which is the "deprivation of liberty" triggering the protections of the Due Process Clause, not its failure to act to protect his liberty interests against harms inflicted by other means.

The *Estelle-Youngberg* analysis simply has no applicability in the present case. Petitioners concede that the harms Joshua suffered occurred not while he was in the State's custody, but while he was in the custody of his natural father, who was in no sense a state actor. While the State may have been aware of the dangers that Joshua faced in the free world, it played no part in their creation, nor did it do anything to render him any more vulnerable to them. That the State once took temporary custody of Joshua does not alter the analysis, for when it returned him to his father's custody, it placed him in no worse position than that in which he would have been had it not acted at all; the State does not become the permanent guarantor of an individual's safety by having once offered him shelter. Under these circumstances, the State had no constitutional duty to protect Joshua.

It may well be that, by voluntarily undertaking to protect Joshua against a danger it concededly played no part in creating, the State acquired a duty under state tort law to provide him with adequate protection against that danger. See Restatement (Second) of Torts § 323 (1965) (one who undertakes to render services to another may in some circumstances be held liable for doing so in a negligent fashion); see generally W. Keeton, D. Dobbs, R. Keeton, & D. Owen, Prosser and Keeton on the Law of Torts § 56 (5th ed. 1984) (discussing "special relationships" which may give rise to affirmative duties to act under the common law of tort). But the claim here is based on the Due Process Clause of the Fourteenth Amendment, which, as we have said many times, does not transform every tort committed by a state actor into a constitutional violation. See *Daniels v. Williams,* 474 U.S., at 335–336, 106 S.Ct., at 667; *Parratt v. Taylor,* 451 U.S., at 544, 101 S.Ct., at 1917; *Martinez v. California,* 444 U.S. 277, 285, 100 S.Ct. 553, 559, 62 L.Ed.2d 481 (1980); *Baker v. McColl an,* 443 U.S. 137, 146, 99 S.Ct. 2689, 26, 61 L.Ed.2d 433 (1979); *Paul v. Davis,* 424 U.S. 693, 701, 96 S.Ct. 1155, 1160, 47 L.Ed.2d 405 (1976). A State may, through its courts and legislatures, impose such affirmative duties of care and protection upon its agents as it wishes. But not "all common-law duties owed by government actors were . . . constitutionalized by the Fourteenth Amendment." *Daniels v. Williams, supra,* 474 U.S., at 335, 106 S.Ct., at 667. Because, as explained above, the State had no constitutional duty to protect Joshua against his father's violence, its failure to do so—though calamitous in hindsight—simply does not constitute a violation of the Due Process Clause.

Judges and lawyers, like other humans, are moved by natural sympathy in a case like this to find a way for Joshua and his mother to receive adequate compensation for the grievous harm inflicted upon them. But before yielding to that impulse, it is well to remember once again that the harm was inflicted not by the State of Wisconsin, but by Joshua's father. The most that can be said of the state functionaries in this case is that they stood by and did nothing when suspicious circumstances dictated a more active role for them. In defense of them it must also be said that had they moved too soon to take custody of the son away from the father, they would likely have been met with charges of improperly intruding into the parent-child relationship, charges based on the same Due Process Clause that forms the basis for the present charge of failure to provide adequate protection.

The people of Wisconsin may well prefer a system of liability which would place upon the State and its officials the responsibility for failure to act in situations such as the present one. They may create such a system, if they do not have it already, by changing the tort law of the State in accordance with the regular lawmaking process. But they should not have it thrust upon them by this Court's expansion of the Due Process Clause of the Fourteenth Amendment.

Affirmed.

Notes and Questions

1. *DeShaney* held that as a general matter governments have no affirmative substantive due process duty to protect persons from private harm. Due to restrictions imposed by the Court on remedies under Section 1983's remedial scheme for allegations of substantive due process violations, plaintiffs generally fail when attempting to recover under that doctrine. Consider the following list of lower court rulings.

> Fifth Circuit: *Lance v. Lewisville Independent School District*: "Where a fourth grade special needs student who had been bullied locked himself inside the school nurse's bathroom and then took his own life, his parents and his estate sued the school district under §1983 and substantive due process. The Fifth Circuit affirmed the district court's grant of summary judgment to the school district. The Fifth Circuit rejected the application of the special relationship theory, the state danger-creation theory and the caused-to-be-subjected theory. No special relationship between the decedent and the school district existed in the case pursuant to the en banc decision of the Fifth Circuit in *Doe ex rel Magee*, 675 F.3d 849 (5th Cir. 2012)(en banc). Also, there was no genuine issue of material fact in dispute regarding the state-created danger theory even if that theory were to be applied: the school district did not affirmatively place the decedent in danger, there was no evidence that the school district knew that decedent's suicide was imminent and the plaintiffs did not show that the school district created a

dangerous environment for the decedent. Finally, the caused-to-be subject theory has not been adopted by the Fifth Circuit."

Eighth Circuit: *Montgomery v. City of Ames*: "The plaintiff sued a city, police officers and others alleging a substantive due process violation arising out of the shooting of the plaintiff by a third person who broke into her house and shot her three times. She alleged that the defendants created the danger that the assailant would attack her through their deliberate indifference." *Montgomery v. City of Ames*, 2014 WL 1387033 (8th Cir. 2014). "Police officer deemed not liable, even though they had spoken to assailants and were aware of the history of abuse."

Gladden v. Richbourg, 2014 WL 3608521 (8th Cir. 2014), "Lawsuit stemmed from plaintiff dying of hypothermia after officers left him outside the city limits instead of the restaurant where they found him. The Court determined that since the decedent was not in custody at the time of death, there was no special relationship. The Court also found that police officers did not act recklessly."

Gormley v. Wood-El, 2014 WL 2921824 (S. Ct. N.J. 2014): "Holding for an attorney attacked by his client while in a psychiatric hospital's unsupervised day room."

As seen with these examples, despite evidence of special relationship and potential creation of danger, these types of cases remain nearly impossible to win for plaintiffs. Only in *Gormley* did the danger-creation theory work in combination with the special relationship theory by virtue of the total control exercised by the hospital officials over the plaintiff attorney, as found by the Supreme Court of New Jersey.

2. How do you evaluate the limitations placed by courts on making successful claims of violations of the Substantive Due Process Clause? Should it be easier to state a claim of violation of the right to life in the context of police neglect and police misconduct without having to fit, instead, under the Fourth or Eighth Amendments?

E. Governmental Defendants and Their Immunities

Suing government officials under 42 U.S.C. § 1983 requires a unique set of pleadings based on specific doctrines developed by the Court. Depending on the nature of the office at issue, for example, different legal considerations and standards will apply. For example, although 42 U.S.C. § 1983 provides remedies for actions done under color of law, the Court has determined that that language does not change the Eleventh Amendment's immunity bar against monetary damages. Other than specific exceptions, *Ex Parte Young*, 209 U.S. 123 (1908) will apply dictating that only equitable damages may be sought when suing states.

In the context of 42 U.S.C. § 1983, courts have determined that suing a state employee in their official capacity is tantamount to suing the state institution. Consequently, a party might not be able to recover money damages by suing an employee in their official capacity. For this reason, it is often advised to sue governmental employees in their official and individual capacities, in the event that the facts might lend themselves better to recovery via personal liability. Thus, if desiring to sue the Sherriff of County X, in the complaint a plaintiff must list the defendant "Sheriff, in his official as well as his individual capacity" to ensure that the claim against the sheriff is not viewed as a suit against a state, and, thereby, thrown out as a violation of the 11th Amendment.

Additionally, the Court has deemed that a different set of rules applies when suing municipalities. As a result, it is harder to sue municipalities. However, the Court revisited the history of the Sherman Amendment in *Monell*, below, to expand capacity to sue municipalities under 42 U.S.C. § 1983. Departing from its earlier decision in *Monroe v. Pape*, 365 U.S. 167 (1961), the Court in *Monell* ruled that municipalities may be held liable under 42 U.S.C. § 1983, if plaintiffs are successful in showing "policy" or "custom." Consequently, one action by an individual employee might not be enough for liability. Plaintiff must be able to trace the claim back to a policy or custom perpetuated by the institution. *Monell* has given rise to complex and arduous litigation against cities in the 42 U.S.C. § 1983 context.

Monell v. Department of Social Services of the City of New York

436 U.S. 658 (1978)

Mr. Justice Brennan delivered the opinion of the Court.

Petitioners, a class of female employees of the Department of Social Services and of the Board of Education of the city of New York, commenced this action under 42 U.S.C. § 1983 in July 1971. The gravamen of the complaint was that the Board and the Department had as a matter of official policy compelled pregnant employees to take unpaid leaves of absence before such leaves were required for medical reasons. Cf. *Cleveland Board of Education v. LaFleur,* 414 U.S. 632, 94 S.Ct. 791, 39 L.Ed.2d 52 (1974). The suit sought injunctive relief and back pay for periods of unlawful forced leave. Named as defendants in the action were the Department and its Commissioner, the Board and its Chancellor, and the city of New York and its Mayor. In each case, the individual defendants were sued solely in their official capacities.

On cross-motions for summary judgment, the District Court for the Southern District of New York held moot petitioners' claims for injunctive and declaratory relief since the City of New York and the Board, after the filing of the complaint, had changed their policies relating to maternity leaves so that no pregnant employee would have to take leave unless she was medically unable to continue to perform her job. 394 F.Supp. 853, 855 (1975). No one now challenges this conclusion. The court did conclude, however, that the acts complained of were unconstitutional under

LaFleur, supra. 394 F.Supp., at 855. Nonetheless plaintiffs' prayers for back pay were denied because any such damages would come ultimately from the City of New York and, therefore, to hold otherwise would be to "circumven[t]" the immunity conferred on municipalities by *Monroe v. Pape,* 365 U.S. 167, 81 S.Ct. 473, 5 L.Ed.2d 492 (1961). See 394 F.Supp., at 855.

On appeal, petitioners renewed their arguments that the Board of Education was not a "municipality" within the meaning of *Monroe v. Pape, supra,* and that, in any event, the District Court had erred in barring a damages award against the individual defendants. The Court of Appeals for the Second Circuit rejected both contentions. The court first held that the Board of Education was not a "person" under § 1983 because "it performs a vital governmental function . . . , and, significantly, while it has the right to determine how the funds appropriated to it shall be spent . . . , it has no final say in deciding what its appropriations shall be." 532 F.2d 259, 263 (1976). The individual defendants, however, were "persons" under § 1983, even when sued solely in their official capacities. 532 F.2d, at 264. Yet, because a damages award would "have to be paid by a city that was held not to be amenable to such an action in *Monroe v. Pape,*" a damages action against officials sued in their official capacities could not proceed. *Id.,* at 265.

We granted certiorari in this case, 429 U.S. 1071, 97 S.Ct. 807, 50 L.Ed.2d 789, to consider

> "Whether local governmental officials and/or local independent school boards are 'persons' within the meaning of 42 U.S.C. § 1983 when equitable relief in the nature of back pay is sought against them in their official capacities?" Pet. for Cert. 8.

Although, after plenary consideration, we have decided the merits of over a score of cases brought under § 1983 in which the principal defendant was a school board—and, indeed, in some of which § 1983 and its jurisdictional counterpart, 28 U.S.C. § 1343, provided the only basis for jurisdiction—we indicated in *Mt. Healthy City Board of Education v. Doyle,* 429 U.S. 274, 279, 97 S.Ct. 568, 573, 50 L.Ed.2d 471 (1977), last Term that the question presented here was open and would be decided "another day." That other day has come and we now overrule *Monroe v. Pape, supra,* insofar as it holds that local governments are wholly immune from suit under § 1983.

I

In *Monroe v. Pape,* we held that "Congress did not undertake to bring municipal corporations within the ambit of [§ 1983]." 365 U.S., at 187, 81 S.Ct. at 484. The sole basis for this conclusion was an inference drawn from Congress' rejection of the "Sherman amendment" to the bill which became the Civil Rights Act of 1871, 17 Stat. 13, the precursor of § 1983. The Amendment would have held a municipal corporation liable for damage done to the person or property of its inhabitants by *private* persons "riotously and tumultuously assembled." Cong. Globe, 42d Cong., 1st Sess., 749 (1871) (hereinafter Globe). Although the Sherman amendment did not seek to amend § 1 of the Act, which is now § 1983, and although the nature of the obligation created by that amendment was vastly different from that created by § 1, the Court nonetheless concluded in *Monroe* that Congress must have meant to exclude municipal corporations from the coverage of § 1 because "'the House [in voting against the Sherman amendment] had solemnly decided that in their judgment Congress had no constitutional power to impose any *obligation* upon county and town organizations, the mere instrumentality for the administration of state law.'" 365 U.S., at 190, 81 S.Ct. at 485 (emphasis added), quoting Globe 804 (Rep. Poland). This statement, we thought, showed that Congress doubted its "constitutional power . . . to impose *civil liability* on municipalities," 365 U.S., at 190, 81 S.Ct. at 486 (emphasis added), and that such doubt would have extended to any type of civil liability.

A fresh analysis of the debate on the Civil Rights Act of 1871, and particularly of the case law which each side mustered in its support, shows, however, that *Monroe* incorrectly equated the "obligation" of which Representative Poland spoke with "civil liability."

A. An Overview

There are three distinct stages in the legislative consideration of the bill which became the Civil Rights Act of 1871. On March 28, 1871, Representative Shellabarger, acting for a House select committee, reported H.R. 320, a bill "to enforce the provisions of the fourteenth amendment to the Constitution of the United States, and for other purposes." H.R. 320 contained four sections. Section 1, now codified as 42 U.S.C. § 1983, was the subject of only limited debate and was passed without amendment. Sections 2 through 4 dealt primarily with the "other purpose" of suppressing Ku Klux Klan violence in the Southern States. The wisdom and constitutionality of these sections—not § 1, now § 1983—were the subject of almost all congressional debate and each of these sections was amended. The House finished its initial debates on H.R. 320 on April 7, 1871, and one week later the Senate also voted out a bill. Again, debate on § 1 of the bill was limited and that section was passed as introduced.

Immediately prior to the vote on H.R. 320 in the Senate, Senator Sherman introduced his amendment. This was *not* an amendment to § 1 of the bill, but was to be added as § 7 at the end of the bill. Under the Senate rules, no discussion of the amendment was allowed and, although attempts were made to amend the amendment, it was passed as introduced. In this form, the amendment did *not* place liability on municipal corporations, but made any inhabitant of a municipality liable for damage inflicted by persons "riotously and tumultuously assembled."

The House refused to acquiesce in a number of amendments made by the Senate, including the Sherman amendment, and the respective versions of H.R. 320 were therefore sent to a conference committee. Section 1 of the bill, however, was not a subject of this conference since, as noted, it was passed verbatim as introduced in both Houses of Congress.

On April 18, 1871, the first conference committee completed its work on H.R. 320. The main features of the conference committee draft of the Sherman amendment were these: First, a cause of action was given to persons injured by

> "any persons riotously and tumultuously assembled together . . . with intent to deprive any person of any right conferred upon him by the Constitution and laws of the United States, or to deter him or punish him for exercising such right, or by reason of his race, color, or previous condition of servitude . . . ."

Second, the bill provided that the action would be against the county, city, or parish in which the riot had occurred and that it could be maintained by either the person injured or his legal representative. Third, unlike the amendment as proposed, the conference substitute made the government defendant liable on the judgment if it was not satisfied against individual defendants who had committed the violence. If a municipality were liable, the judgment against it could be collected

> "by execution, attachment, mandamus, garnishment, or any other proceeding in aid of execution or applicable to the enforcement of judgments against municipal corporations; and such judgment [would become] a lien as well upon all moneys in the treasury of such county, city, or parish, as upon the other property thereof."

In the ensuing debate on the first conference report, which was the first debate of any kind on the Sherman amendment, Senator Sherman explained that the purpose of his amendment was to enlist the aid of persons of property in the enforcement of the civil rights laws by making their property "responsible" for Ku Klux Klan damage. Statutes drafted on a similar theory, he stated, had long been in force in England and were in force in 1871 in a number of States. Nonetheless there were critical differences between the conference substitute and extant state and English statutes: The conference substitute, unlike most state riot statutes, lacked a short statute of limitations and imposed liability on the government defendant whether or not it had notice of the impending riot, whether or not the municipality was authorized to exercise a police power, whether or not it exerted all reasonable efforts to stop the riot, and whether or not the rioters were caught and punished.

The first conference substitute passed the Senate but was rejected by the House. House opponents, within whose ranks were some who had supported § 1, thought the Federal Government could not, consistent with the Constitution, obligate municipal corporations to keep the peace if those corporations were neither so obligated nor so authorized by their state charters. And, because of this constitutional objection, opponents of the Sherman amendment were unwilling to impose damages liability for nonperformance of a duty which Congress could not require municipalities to perform. This position is reflected in Representative Poland's statement that is quoted in *Monroe*.

Because the House rejected the first conference report a second conference was called and it duly issued its report. The second conference substitute for the Sherman amendment abandoned municipal liability and, instead, made "any person or persons having knowledge [that a conspiracy to violate civil rights was afoot], and having power to prevent or aid in preventing the same," who did not attempt to stop the same, liable to any person injured by the conspiracy. The amendment in this form was adopted by both Houses of Congress and is not codified as 42 U.S.C. § 1986.

The meaning of the legislative history sketched above can most readily be developed by first considering the debate on the report of the first conference committee. This debate shows conclusively that the constitutional objections raised against the Sherman amendment—on which our holding in *Monroe* was based, see *supra*, at 2022–2023—would not have prohibited congressional creation of a civil remedy against state municipal corporations that infringed federal rights. Because § 1 of the Civil Rights Act does not state expressly that municipal corporations come within its ambit, it is finally necessary to interpret § 1 to confirm that such corporations were indeed intended to be included within the "persons" to whom that section applies.

B. Debate on the First Conference Report

The style of argument adopted by both proponents and opponents of the Sherman amendment in both Houses of Congress was largely legal, with frequent references to cases decided by this Court and the Supreme Courts of the several States. Proponents of the Sherman amendment did not, however, discuss in detail the argument in favor of its constitutionality. Nonetheless, it is possible to piece together such an argument from the debates on the first conference report and those on § 2 of the civil rights bill, which, because it allowed the Federal Government to prosecute crimes "in the States," had also raised questions of federal power. The account of Representative Shellabarger, the House sponsor of H.R. 320, is the most complete.

Shellabarger began his discussion of H.R. 320 by stating that "there is a domain of constitutional law involved in the right consideration of this measure which is wholly unexplored." Globe, App. 67. There were analogies, however. With respect to the meaning of § 1 of the Fourteenth Amendment, and particularly its Privileges or Immunities Clause, Shellabarger relied on the statement of Mr. Justice Washington in *Corfield v. Coryell*, 3 F.Cas. 230, 4 Wash.C.C. 371 (CC ED Pa.1825), which defined the privileges protected by Art. IV:

> "'What these fundamental privileges are[,] it would perhaps be more tedious than difficult to enumerate. They may, however, be all comprehended under the following general heads: protection by the Government;' —
>
> "*Mark that* —
>
> "'*protection by the Government;* the enjoyment of life and liberty, with the right to acquire and possess property of every kind, and to pursue and obtain happiness and safety . . . .'" Globe App. 69 (emphasis added), quoting 4 Wash.C.C., at 380–381.

Building on his conclusion that citizens were owed protection—a conclusion not disputed by opponents of the Sherman amendment—Shellabarger then considered Congress' role in providing that protection. Here again there were precedents:

"[Congress has always] assumed to enforce, as against the States, and also persons, every one of the provisions of the Constitution. Most of the provisions of the Constitution which restrain and directly relate to the States, such as those in [Art. I, § 10,] relate to the divisions of the political powers of the State and General Governments. . . . These prohibitions upon political powers of the States are all of such nature that they can be, and even have been, . . . enforced by the courts of the United States declaring void all State acts of encroachment on Federal powers. Thus, and thus sufficiently, has the United States 'enforced' these provisions of the Constitution. But there are some that are not of this class. These are where the court secures the rights or the liabilities of persons within the States, as between such persons and the States.

"These three are: first, that as to fugitives from justice; second, that as to fugitives from service, (or slaves;) third, that declaring that the 'citizens of each State shall be entitled to all the privileges and immunities of citizens in the several States.'

"And, sir, every one of these—the only provisions where it was deemed that legislation was required to enforce the constitutional provisions—the only three where the rights or liabilities of persons in the States, as between these persons and the States, are directly provided for, Congress has by legislation affirmatively interfered to protect . . . such persons." Globe App. 69–70.

Of legislation mentioned by Shellabarger, the closest analog of the Sherman amendment, ironically, was the statute implementing the fugitives from justice and fugitive slave provisions of Art. IV—the Act of Feb. 12, 1793, 1 Stat. 302—the constitutionality of which had been sustained in 1842, in *Prigg v. Pennsylvania*, 16 Pet. 539, 10 L.Ed. 1060. There, Mr. Justice Story, writing for the Court, held that Art. IV gave slave-owners a federal right to the unhindered possession of their slaves in whatever State such slaves might be found. 16 Pet., at 612. Because state process for recovering runaway slaves might be inadequate or even hostile to the rights of the slave-owner, the right intended to be conferred could be negated if left to state implementation. *Id.*, at 614. Thus, since the Constitution guaranteed the right and this in turn required a remedy, Story held it to be a "natural inference" that Congress had the power itself to ensure an appropriate (in the Necessary and Proper Clause sense) remedy for the right. *Id.*, at 615.

Building on *Prigg*, Shellabarger argued that a remedy against municipalities and counties was an appropriate—and hence constitutional—method for ensuring the protection which the Fourteenth Amendment made every citizen's federal right. This much was clear from the adoption of such statutes by the several States as devices for suppressing riot. Thus, said Shellabarger, the only serious question remaining was "whether, since a county is an integer or part of a State, the United States can impose upon it, as such, *any obligations to keep the peace* in obedience to United States laws." This he answered affirmatively, citing *Board of Comm'rs v. Aspinwall*, 24 How. 376, 16 L.Ed. 735 (1861), the first of many cases upholding the power of federal courts to enforce the Contract Clause against municipalities.

House opponents of the Sherman amendment—whose views are particularly important since only the House voted down the amendment—did not dispute Shellabarger's claim that the Fourteenth Amendment created a federal right to protection, but they argued that the local units of government upon which the amendment fastened liability were not obligated to keep the peace at state law and further that the Federal Government could not constitutionally require local governments to create police forces, whether this requirement was levied directly, or indirectly by imposing damages for breach of the peace on municipalities. The most complete statement of this position is that of Representative Blair:

> "The proposition known as the Sherman amendment . . . is entirely new. It is altogether without a precedent in this country. . . . That amendment claims the power in the General Government to go into the States of this Union and lay such obligations as it may please upon the municipalities, which are the creations of the States alone. . . .

> ". . . [H]ere it is proposed, not to carry into effect an obligation which rests upon the municipality, but to create that obligation, and that is the provision I am unable to assent to. The parallel of the hundred does not in the least meet the case. The power that laid the obligation upon the hundred first put the duty upon the hundred that it should perform in that regard, and failing to meet the obligation which had been laid upon it, it was very proper that it should suffer damage for its neglect. . . .

> ". . . [T]here are certain rights and duties that belong to the States, . . . there are certain powers that inhere in the State governments. They create these municipalities, they say what their powers shall be and what their obligations shall be. If the Government of the United States can step in and add to those obligations, may it not utterly destroy the municipality? If it can say that it shall be liable for damages occurring from a riot, . . . where [will] its power . . . stop and what obligations . . . might [it] not lay upon a municipality. . . .

> "Now, only the other day, the Supreme Court . . . decided [in *Collector v. Day*, 11 Wall. 113, 20 L.Ed. 122 (1871)] that there is no power in the Government of the United States, under its authority to tax, to tax the salary of a State officer. Why? Simply because the power to tax involves the power to destroy, and it was not the intent to give the Government of the United States power to destroy the government of the States in any respect. It was held also in the case of *Prigg v. Pennsylvania*, 16 Pet. 539, 10 L.Ed. 1060

(1842) that it is not within the power of the Congress of the United States to lay duties upon a State officer; that we cannot command a State officer to do any duty whatever, as such; and I ask . . . the difference between that and commanding a municipality, which is equally the creature of the State, to perform a duty." Globe 795.

Any attempt to impute a unitary constitutional theory to opponents of the Sherman amendment is, of course, fraught with difficulties, not the least of which is that most Members of Congress did not speak to the issue of the constitutionality of the amendment. Nonetheless, two considerations lead us to conclude that opponents of the Sherman amendment found it unconstitutional substantially because of the reasons stated by Representative Blair: First, Blair's analysis is precisely that of Poland, whose views were quoted as authoritative in *Monroe*, see *supra*, at 2022–2023, and that analysis was shared in large part by all House opponents who addressed the constitutionality of the Sherman amendment. Second, Blair's exegesis of the reigning constitutional theory of his day, as we shall explain, was clearly supported by precedent—albeit precedent that has not survived, see *Ex parte Virginia*, 100 U.S. 339, 347–348, 25 L.Ed. 676 (1880); *Graves v. New York ex rel. O'Keefe*, 306 U.S. 466, 486, 59 S.Ct. 595, 83 L.Ed. 927 (1939)—and no other constitutional formula was advanced by participants in the House debates.

Collector v. Day, cited by Blair, was the clearest and, at the time of the debates, the most recent pronouncement of a doctrine of coordinate sovereignty that, as Blair stated, placed limits on even the enumerated powers of the National Government in favor of protecting state prerogatives. There, the Court held that the United States could not tax the income of Day, a Massachusetts state judge, because the independence of the States within their legitimate spheres would be imperiled if the instrumentalities through which States executed their powers were "subject to the control of another and distinct government." 11 Wall., at 127. Although the Court in *Day* apparently rested this holding in part on the proposition that the taxing "power acknowledges no limits but the will of the legislative body imposing the tax," *id.*, at 125–126; cf. *McCulloch v. Maryland*, 17 U.S. 316, 4 Wheat. 316, 4 L.Ed. 579 (1819), the Court had in other cases limited other national powers in order to avoid interference with the States.

In *Prigg v. Pennsylvania*, for example, Mr. Justice Story, in addition to confirming a broad national power to legislate under the Fugitive Slave Clause, see *supra*, at 2026, held that Congress could not "insist that states . . . provide means to carry into effect the duties of the national government." 16 Pet., at 615–616. And Mr. Justice McLean agreed that, "[a]s a general principle," it was true "that Congress had no power to impose duties on state officers, as provided in the [Act of Feb. 12, 1793]." Nonetheless he wondered whether Congress might not impose "positive" duties on state officers where a clause of the Constitution, like the Fugitive Slave Clause, seemed to require affirmative government assistance, rather than restraint of government, to secure federal rights. See *id.*, at 664–665.

Had Mr. Justice McLean been correct in his suggestion that, where the Constitution envisioned affirmative government assistance, the States or their officers or instrumentalities could be required to provide it, there would have been little doubt that Congress could have insisted that municipalities afford by "positive" action the protection owed individuals under § 1 of the Fourteenth Amendment whether or not municipalities were obligated by state law to keep the peace. However, any such argument, largely foreclosed by *Prigg*, was made impossible by the Court's holding in *Kentucky v. Dennison*, 24 How. 66, 16 L.Ed. 717 (1861). There, the Court was asked to require Dennison, the Governor of Ohio, to hand over Lago, a fugitive from justice wanted in Kentucky, as required by § 1 of the Act of Feb. 12, 1793, which implemented Art. IV, § 2, cl. 2, of the Constitution. Mr. Chief Justice Taney, writing for a unanimous Court, refused to enforce that section of the Act:

> "[W]e think it clear, that the Federal Government, under the Constitution, has no power to impose on a State officer, as such, any duty whatever, and compel him to perform it; for if it possessed this power, it might overload the officer with duties which would fill up all his time, and disable him from performing his obligations to the State, and might impose on him duties of a character incompatible with the rank and dignity to which he was elevated by the State." 24 How., at 107–108.

The rationale of *Dennison*—that the Nation could not impose duties on state officers since that might impede States in their legitimate activities—is obviously identical to that which animated the decision in *Collector v. Day*. See *supra*, at 2028–2029. And, as Blair indicated, municipalities as instrumentalities through which States executed their policies could be equally disabled from carrying out state policies if they were also obligated to carry out federally imposed duties. Although no one cited *Dennison* by name, the principle for which it stands was well known to Members of Congress, many of whom discussed *Day* as well as a series of State Supreme Court cases in the mid-1860's which had invalidated a federal tax on the process of state courts on the ground that the tax threatened the independence of a vital state function. Thus, there was ample support for Blair's view that the Sherman amendment, by putting municipalities to the Hobson's choice of keeping the peace or paying civil damages, attempted to impose obligations on municipalities by indirection that could not be imposed directly, thereby threatening to "destroy the government of the States." Globe 795.

If municipal liability under § 1 of the Civil Rights Act of 1871 created a similar Hobson's choice, we might conclude, as *Monroe* did, that Congress could not have intended municipalities to be among the "persons" to which that section applied. But this is not the case.

First, opponents expressly distinguished between imposing an obligation to keep the peace and merely imposing civil liability for damages on a municipality that was obligated by state law to keep the peace, but which had not in violation of the Fourteenth Amendment. Representative Poland, for example, reasoning from

Contract Clause precedents, indicated that Congress could constitutionally confer jurisdiction on the federal courts to entertain suits seeking to hold municipalities liable for using their authorized powers in violation of the Constitution—which is as far as § 1 of the Civil Rights Act went:

> "I presume . . . that where a State had imposed a duty [to keep the peace] upon [a] municipality . . . an action would be allowed to be maintained against them in the courts of the United States under the ordinary restrictions as to jurisdiction. But the enforcing a liability, existing by their own contract, or by a State law, in the courts, is a very widely different thing from devolving a new duty or liability upon them by the national Government, which has no power either to create or destroy them, and no power or control over them whatever." Globe 794.

Representative Burchard agreed:

> "[T]here is no duty imposed by the Constitution of the United States, or usually by State laws, upon a county to protect the people of that county against the commission of the offenses herein enumerated, such as the burning of buildings or any other injury to property or injury to person. Police powers are not conferred upon counties as corporations; they are conferred upon cities that have qualified legislative power. And so far as cities are concerned, where the equal protection required to be afforded by a State is imposed upon a city by State laws, perhaps the United States courts could enforce its performance. But counties . . . do not have any control of the police . . . ." *Id.*, at 795.

Second, the doctrine of dual sovereignty apparently put no limit on the power of federal courts to enforce the Constitution against municipalities that violated it. Under the theory of dual sovereignty set out in *Prigg*, this is quite understandable. So long as federal courts were vindicating the Federal Constitution, they were providing the "positive" government action required to protect federal constitutional rights and no question was raised of enlisting the States in "positive" action. The limits of the principles announced in *Dennison* and *Day* are not so well defined in logic, but are clear as a matter of history. It must be remembered that the same Court which rendered *Day* also vigorously enforced the Contract Clause against municipalities—an enforcement effort which included various forms of "positive" relief, such as ordering that taxes be levied and collected to discharge federal-court judgments, once a constitutional infraction was found. Thus, federal judicial enforcement of the Constitution's express limits on state power, since it was done so frequently, must, notwithstanding anything said in *Dennison* or *Day*, have been permissible, at least so long as the interpretation of the Constitution was left in the hands of the judiciary. Since § 1 of the Civil Rights Act simply conferred jurisdiction on the federal courts to enforce § 1 of the Fourteenth Amendment—a situation precisely analogous to the grant of diversity jurisdiction under which the Contract Clause was enforced against municipalities is no reason to suppose that opponents of the Sherman amendment would have found any constitutional barrier to § 1 suits against municipalities.

Finally, the very votes of those Members of Congress, who opposed the Sherman amendment but who had voted for § 1, confirm that the liability imposed by § 1 was something very different from that imposed by the amendment. Section 1 without question could be used to obtain a damages judgment against state or municipal *officials* who violated federal constitutional rights while acting under color of law. However, for *Prigg-Dennison-Day* purposes, as Blair and others recognized, there was no distinction of constitutional magnitude between officers and agents— including corporate agents—of the State: Both were state instrumentalities and the State could be impeded no matter over which sort of instrumentality the Federal Government sought to assert its power. *Dennison* and *Day*, after all, were not suits against municipalities but against *officers*, and Blair was quite conscious that he was extending these cases by applying them to municipal corporations. Nonetheless, Senator Thurman, who gave the most exhaustive critique of § 1—*inter alia*, complaining that it would be applied to state officers, see Globe App. 217—and who opposed both § 1 and the Sherman amendment, the latter on *Prigg* grounds, agreed unequivocally that § 1 was constitutional. Those who voted for § 1 must similarly have believed in its constitutionality despite *Prigg, Dennison*, and *Day*.

C. Debate on § 1 of the Civil Rights Bill

From the foregoing discussion, it is readily apparent that nothing said in debate on the Sherman amendment would have prevented holding a municipality liable under § 1 of the Civil Rights Act for its own violations of the Fourteenth Amendment. The question remains, however, whether the general language describing those to be liable under § 1—"any person"—covers more than natural persons. An examination of the debate on § 1 and application of appropriate rules of construction show unequivocally that § 1 was intended to cover legal as well as natural persons.

Representative Shellabarger was the first to explain the function of § 1:

> "[Section 1] not only provides a civil remedy for persons whose former condition may have been that of slaves, but also to all people where, under color of State law, they or any of them may be deprived of rights to which they are entitled under the Constitution by reason and virtue of their national citizenship." Globe App. 68.

By extending a remedy to all people, including whites, § 1 went beyond the mischief to which the remaining sections of the 1871 Act were addressed. Representative Shellabarger also stated without reservation that the constitutionality of § 2 of the Civil Rights Act of 1866 controlled the constitutionality of § 1 of the 1871 Act, and that the former had been approved by "the supreme courts of at least three States of this Union" and by Mr. Justice Swayne, sitting on circuit, who had concluded: "'We have no doubt of the constitutionality of every provision of this act.'" Globe App.

68. Representative Shellabarger then went on to describe how the courts would and should interpret § 1:

> "This act is remedial, and in aid of the preservation of human liberty and human rights. All statutes and constitutional provisions authorizing such statutes are liberally and beneficently construed. It would be most strange and, in civilized law, monstrous were this not the rule of interpretation. As has been again and again decided by your own Supreme Court of the United States, and everywhere else where there is wise judicial interpretation, the largest latitude consistent with the words employed is uniformly given in construing such statutes and constitutional provisions as are meant to protect and defend and give remedies for their wrongs to all the people. . . . Chief Justice Jay and also Story say:
>
> > "'Where a power is remedial in its nature there is much reason to contend that it ought to be construed liberally, and it is generally adopted in the interpretation of laws.' — 1 *Story on Constitution,* sec. 429." Globe App., at 68.

The sentiments expressed in Representative Shellabarger's opening speech were echoed by Senator Edmunds, the manager of H.R. 320 in the Senate:

> "The first section is one that I believe nobody objects to, as defining the rights secured by the Constitution of the United States when they are assailed by any State law or under color of any State law, and it is merely carrying out the principles of the civil rights bill [of 1866], which have since become a part of the Constitution." Globe 568.
>
> "[Section 1 is] so very simple and really reenact[s] the Constitution." *Id.,* at 569.

And he agreed that the bill "secure[d] the rights of white men as much as of colored men." *Id.,* at 696.

In both Houses, statements of the supporters of § 1 corroborated that Congress, in enacting § 1, intended to give a broad remedy for violations of federally protected civil rights. Moreover, since municipalities through their official acts could, equally with natural persons, create the harms intended to be remedied by § 1, and, further, since Congress intended § 1 to be broadly construed, there is no reason to suppose that municipal corporations would have been excluded from the sweep of § 1. Cf., *e.g., Ex parte Virginia,* 100 U.S. 339, 346–347, 25 L.Ed. 676 (1880); *Home Tel. & Tel. Co. v. Los Angeles,* 227 U.S. 278, 286–287, 294–296, 33 S.Ct. 312, 57 L.Ed. 510 (1913). One need not rely on this inference alone, however, for the debates show that Members of Congress understood "persons" to include municipal corporations.

Representative Bingham, for example, in discussing § 1 of the bill, explained that he had drafted § 1 of the Fourteenth Amendment with the case of *Barron v. Mayor of Baltimore,* 7 Pet. 243, 8 L.Ed. 672 (1833), especially in mind. "In [that] case the *city* had taken private property for public use, without COMPENSATION . . . ,

AND THERE WAS NO REDRESS FOR THE wrong . . . ." globe App. 84 (emphasis added). Bingham's further remarks clearly indicate his view that such takings by cities, as had occurred in *Barron*, would be redressable under §1 of the bill. See Globe App. 85. More generally, and as Bingham's remarks confirm, §1 of the bill would logically be the vehicle by which Congress provided redress for takings, since that section provided the only civil remedy for Fourteenth Amendment violations and that Amendment unequivocally prohibited uncompensated takings. Given this purpose, it beggars reason to suppose that Congress would have exempted municipalities from suit, insisting instead that compensation for a taking come from an officer in his individual capacity rather than from the government unit that had the benefit of the property taken.

In addition, by 1871, it was well understood that corporations should be treated as natural persons for virtually all purposes of constitutional and statutory analysis. This had not always been so. When this Court first considered the question of the status of corporations, Mr. Chief Justice Marshall, writing for the Court, denied that corporations "as such" were persons as that term was used in Art. III and the Judiciary Act of 1789. See *Bank of the United States v. Deveaux*, 5 Cranch 61, 86, 3 L.Ed. 38 (1809). By 1844, however, the *Deveaux* doctrine was unhesitatingly abandoned:

> "[A] corporation created by and doing business in a particular state, is to be deemed *to all intents and purposes as a person*, although an artificial person, . . . capable of being treated as a citizen of that state, as much as a natural person." *Louisville R. Co. v. Letson*, 2 How. 497, 558, 11 L.Ed. 353 (1844) (emphasis added), discussed in Globe 752.

And only two years before the debates on the Civil Rights Act, in *Cowles v. Mercer County*, 7 Wall. 118, 121, 19 L.Ed. 86 (1869), the *Letson* principle was automatically and without discussion extended to municipal corporations. Under this doctrine, municipal corporations were routinely sued in the federal courts and this fact was well known to Members of Congress.

That the "usual" meaning of the word "person" would extend to municipal corporations is also evidenced by an Act of Congress which had been passed only months before the Civil Rights Act was passed. This Act provided that

> "in all acts hereafter passed . . . the word 'person' may extend and be applied to bodies politic and corporate . . . unless the context shows that such words were intended to be used in a more limited sense." Act of Feb. 25, 1871, §2, 16 Stat. 431.

Municipal corporations in 1871 were included within the phrase "bodies politic and corporate" and, accordingly, the "plain meaning" of §1 is that local government bodies were to be included within the ambit of the persons who could be sued under §1 of the Civil Rights Act. Indeed, a Circuit Judge, writing in 1873 in what is apparently the first reported case under §1, read the Dictionary Act in precisely this way in a case involving a corporate plaintiff and a municipal defendant. See

Northwestern Fertilizing Co. v. Hyde Park, 18 F.Cas. 393, 394 (No. 10,336) (CC ND Ill.1873).

II

Our analysis of the legislative history of the Civil Rights Act of 1871 compels the conclusion that Congress *did* intend municipalities and other local government units to be included among those persons to whom § 1983 applies. Local governing bodies, therefore, can be sued directly under § 1983 for monetary, declaratory, or injunctive relief where, as here, the action that is alleged to be unconstitutional implements or executes a policy statement, ordinance, regulation, or decision officially adopted and promulgated by that body's officers. Moreover, although the touchstone of the § 1983 action against a government body is an allegation that official policy is responsible for a deprivation of rights protected by the Constitution, local governments, like every other § 1983 "person," by the very terms of the statute, may be sued for constitutional deprivations visited pursuant to governmental "custom" even though such a custom has not received formal approval through the body's official decision-making channels. As Mr. Justice Harlan, writing for the Court, said in *Adickes v. S.H. Kress & Co.,* 398 U.S. 144, 167–168, 90 S.Ct. 1598, 1613, 26 L.Ed.2d 142 (1970): "Congress included customs and usages [in § 1983] because of the persistent and widespread discriminatory practices of state officials . . . . Although not authorized by written law, such practices of state officials could well be so permanent and well settled as to constitute a 'custom or usage' with the force of law."

On the other hand, the language of § 1983, read against the background of the same legislative history, compels the conclusion that Congress did not intend municipalities to be held liable unless action pursuant to official municipal policy of some nature caused a constitutional tort. In particular, we conclude that a municipality cannot be held liable *solely* because it employs a tortfeasor—or, in other words, a municipality cannot be held liable under § 1983 on a *respondeat superior* theory.

We begin with the language of § 1983 as originally passed:

> "*[A]ny person who,* under color of any law, statute, ordinance, regulation, custom, or usage of any State, *shall subject, or cause to be subjected,* any person . . . to the deprivation of any rights, privileges, or immunities secured by the Constitution of the United States, shall, any such law, statute, ordinance, regulation, custom, or usage of the State to the contrary notwithstanding, be liable to the party injured in any action at law, suit in equity, or other proper proceeding for redress . . . ." 17 Stat. 13. (emphasis added).

The italicized language plainly imposes liability on a government that, under color of some official policy, "causes" an employee to violate another's constitutional rights. At the same time, that language cannot be easily read to impose liability vicariously on governing bodies solely on the basis of the existence of an employer-employee relationship with a tortfeasor. Indeed, the fact that Congress did specifically provide that A's tort became B's liability if B "caused" A to subject another to a tort suggests that Congress did not intend § 1983 liability to attach where such causation was absent. See *Rizzo v. Goode,* 423 U.S. 362, 370–371, 96 S.Ct. 598, 602, 46 L.Ed.2d 561 (1976).

Equally important, creation of a federal law of *respondeat superior* would have raised all the constitutional problems associated with the obligation to keep the peace, an obligation Congress chose not to impose because it thought imposition of such an obligation unconstitutional. To this day, there is disagreement about the basis for imposing liability on an employer for the torts of an employee when the sole nexus between the employer and the tort is the fact of the employer-employee relationship. See W. Prosser, Law of Torts § 69, p. 459 (4th ed. 1971). Nonetheless, two justifications tend to stand out. First is the common-sense notion that no matter how blameless an employer appears to be in an individual case, accidents might nonetheless be reduced if employers had to bear the cost of accidents. See, *e.g., ibid.;* 2 F. Harper & F. James, Law of Torts, § 26.3, pp. 1368–1369 (1956). Second is the argument that the cost of accidents should be spread to the community as a whole on an insurance theory. See, *e. g., id.,* § 26.5; Prosser, *supra,* at 459.

The first justification is of the same sort that was offered for statutes like the Sherman amendment: "The obligation to make compensation for injury resulting from riot is, by arbitrary enactment of statutes, affirmatory law, and the reason of passing the statute is to secure a more perfect police regulation." Globe 777 (Sen. Frelinghuysen). This justification was obviously insufficient to sustain the amendment against perceived constitutional difficulties and there is no reason to suppose that a more general liability imposed for a similar reason would have been thought less constitutionally objectionable. The second justification was similarly put forward as a justification for the Sherman amendment: "we do not look upon [the Sherman amendment] as a punishment . . . . It is a mutual insurance." *Id.,* at 792 (Rep. Butler). Again, this justification was insufficient to sustain the amendment.

We conclude, therefore, that a local government may not be sued under § 1983 for an injury inflicted solely by its employees or agents. Instead, it is when execution of a government's policy or custom, whether made by its lawmakers or by those whose edicts or acts may fairly be said to represent official policy, inflicts the injury that the government as an entity is responsible under § 1983. Since this case unquestionably involves official policy as the moving force of the constitutional violation found by the District Court, see *supra,* at 2020–2021, and n. 2, we must reverse the judgment below. In so doing, we have no occasion to address, and do not address, what the full contours of municipal liability under § 1983 may be. We have attempted only to sketch so much of the § 1983 cause of action against a local government as is apparent from the history of the 1871 Act and our prior cases, and we expressly leave further development of this action to another day.

III

Although we have stated that *stare decisis* has more force in statutory analysis than in constitutional adjudication because, in the former situation, Congress can correct our mistakes through legislation, see, *e.g., Edelman v. Jordan,* 415 U.S. 651,

671, and n. 14, 94 S.Ct. 1347, 1365, 39 L.Ed.2d 662 (1974), we have never applied *stare decisis* mechanically to prohibit overruling our earlier decisions determining the meaning of statutes. See, *e.g., Continental T.V., Inc. v. GTE Sylvania, Inc.*, 433 U.S. 36, 47–49, 97 S.Ct. 2549, 2559, 53 L.Ed.2d 568 (1977); *Burnet v. Coronado Oil & Gas Co.*, 285 U.S. 393, 406 n. 1, 52 S.Ct. 443, 454, 76 L.Ed. 815 (1932) (Brandeis, J., dissenting) (collecting cases). Nor is this a case where we should "place on the shoulders of Congress the burden of the Court's own error." *Girouard v. United States*, 328 U.S. 61, 70, 66 S.Ct. 826, 830, 90 L.Ed. 1084 (1946).

First, *Monroe v. Pape*, insofar as it completely immunizes municipalities from suit under § 1983, was a departure from prior practice. See, *e. g., Northwestern Fertilizing Co. v. Hyde Park*, 18 Fed.Cas. 393 (No. 10,336) (CC ND Ill.1873); *City of Manchester v. Leiby*, 117 F.2d 661 (CA1 1941); *Hannan v. City of Haverhill*, 120 F.2d 87 (CA1 1941); *Douglas v. City of Jeannette*, 319 U.S. 157, 63 S.Ct. 877, 87 L.Ed. 1324 (1943); *Holmes v. City of Atlanta*, 350 U.S. 879, 76 S.Ct. 141, 100 L.Ed. 776 (1955), in each of which municipalities were defendants in § 1983 suits. Moreover, the constitutional defect that led to the rejection of the Sherman amendment would not have distinguished between municipalities and school boards, each of which is an instrumentality of state administration. See *supra*, at 2027–2032. For this reason, our cases—decided both before and after *Monroe*—holding school boards liable in § 1983 actions are inconsistent with *Monroe*, especially as *Monroe's* immunizing principle was extended to suits for injunctive relief in *City of Kenosha v. Bruno*, 412 U.S. 507, 93 S.Ct. 2222, 37 L.Ed.2d 109 (1973). And although in many of these cases jurisdiction was not questioned, we ought not "disregard the implications of an exercise of judicial authority assumed to be proper for [100] years." *Brown Shoe Co. v. United States*, 370 U.S. 294, 307, 82 S.Ct. 1502, 1514, 8 L.Ed.2d 510 (1962); see *Bank of the United States v. Deveaux*, 5 Cranch, at 88 (Marshall, C. J.) ("Those decisions are not cited as authority . . . but they have much weight as they show that this point neither occurred to the bar or the bench"). Thus, while we have reaffirmed *Monroe* without further examination on three occasions, it can scarcely be said that *Monroe* is so consistent with the warp and woof of civil rights law as to be beyond question.

Second, the principle of blanket immunity established in *Monroe* cannot be cabined short of school boards. Yet such an extension would itself be inconsistent with recent expressions of congressional intent. In the wake of our decisions, Congress not only has shown no hostility to federal-court decisions against school boards, but it has indeed rejected efforts to strip the federal courts of jurisdiction over school boards. Moreover, recognizing that school boards are often defendants in school desegregation suits, which have almost without exception been § 1983 suits, Congress has twice passed legislation authorizing grants to school boards to assist them in complying with federal-court decrees. Finally, in regard to the Civil Rights Attorney's Fees Awards Act of 1976, 90 Stat. 2641, 42 U.S.C. § 1988 (1976 ed.), which allows prevailing parties (in the discretion of the court) in § 1983 suits to obtain attorney's fees from the losing parties, the Senate stated:

> "[D]efendants in these cases are often State or local *bodies* or State or local officials. In such cases it is intended that the attorneys' fees, like other items of costs, will be collected either directly from the official, *in his official capacity,* from funds of his agency or under his control, or *from the State or local government (whether or not the agency or government is a named party).*" S.Rep.No.94-1011, p. 5 (1976); U.S.Code Cong. & Admin.News 1976, pp. 5908, 5913 (emphasis added; footnotes omitted).

Far from showing that Congress has relied on *Monroe,* therefore, events since 1961 show that Congress has refused to extend the benefits of *Monroe* to school boards and has attempted to allow awards of attorney's fees against local governments even though *Monroe, City of Kenosha v. Bruno,* and *Aldinger v. Howard,* 427 U.S. 1, 96 S.Ct. 2413, 49 L.Ed.2d 276 (1976), have made the joinder of such governments impossible.

Third, municipalities can assert no reliance claim which can support an absolute immunity. As Mr. Justice Frankfurter said in *Monroe,* "[t]his is not an area of commercial law in which, presumably, individuals may have arranged their affairs in reliance on the expected stability of decision." 365 U.S., at 221–222, 81 S.Ct., at 503 (dissenting in part). Indeed, municipalities simply cannot "arrange their affairs" on an assumption that they can violate constitutional rights indefinitely since injunctive suits against local officials under § 1983 would prohibit any such arrangement. And it scarcely need be mentioned that nothing in *Monroe* encourages municipalities to violate constitutional rights or even suggests that such violations are anything other than completely wrong.

Finally, even under the most stringent test for the propriety of overruling a statutory decision proposed by Mr. Justice Harlan in *Monroe*—"that it appear beyond doubt from the legislative history of the 1871 statute that [*Monroe*] misapprehended the meaning of the [section]," 365 U.S., at 192, 81 S.Ct., at 487 (concurring opinion)—the overruling of *Monroe* insofar as it holds that local governments are not "persons" who may be defendants in § 1983 suits is clearly proper. It is simply beyond doubt that, under the 1871 Congress' view of the law, were § 1983 liability unconstitutional as to local governments, it would have been equally unconstitutional as to state officers. Yet everyone—proponents and opponents alike—knew § 1983 would be applied to state officers and nonetheless stated that § 1983 was constitutional. See *supra,* at 2030–2032. And, moreover, there can be no doubt that § 1 of the Civil Rights Act was intended to provide a remedy, to be broadly construed, against all forms of official violation of federally protected rights. Therefore, absent a clear statement in the legislative history supporting the conclusion that § 1 was not to apply to the official acts of a municipal corporation—which simply is not present—there is no justification for excluding municipalities from the "persons" covered by § 1.

For reasons stated above, therefore, we hold that *stare decisis* does not bar our overruling of *Monroe* insofar as it is inconsistent with Parts I and II of this opinion.

IV

Since the question whether local government bodies should be afforded some form of official immunity was not presented as a question to be decided on this petition and was not briefed by the parties or addressed by the courts below, we express no views on the scope of any municipal immunity beyond holding that municipal bodies sued under § 1983 cannot be entitled to an absolute immunity, lest our decision that such bodies are subject to suit under § 1983 "be drained of meaning," *Scheuer v. Rhodes*, 416 U.S. 232, 248, 94 S.Ct. 1683, 40 L.Ed.2d 90 (1974). Cf. *Bivens v. Six Unknown Federal Narcotics Agents*, 403 U.S. 388, 397–398, 91 S.Ct. 1999, 29 L.Ed.2d 619 (1971).

V

For the reasons stated above, the judgment of the Court of Appeals is *Reversed*.

Pembaur v. City of Cincinnati
475 U.S. 469 (1986)

Justice Brennan delivered the opinion of the Court, except as to Part II-B.

In *Monell v. New York City Dept. of Social Services,* 436 U.S. 658, 98 S.Ct. 2018, 56 L.Ed.2d 611 (1978), the Court concluded that municipal liability under 42 U.S.C. § 1983 is limited to deprivations of federally protected rights caused by action taken "pursuant to official municipal policy of some nature. . . ." *Id.,* at 691, 98 S.Ct., at 2036. The question presented is whether, and in what circumstances, a decision by municipal policymakers on a single occasion may satisfy this requirement.

I

Bertold Pembaur is a licensed Ohio physician and the sole proprietor of the Rockdale Medical Center, located in the city of Cincinnati in Hamilton County. Most of Pembaur's patients are welfare recipients who rely on government assistance to pay for medical care. During the spring of 1977, Simon Leis, the Hamilton County Prosecutor, began investigating charges that Pembaur fraudulently had accepted payments from state welfare agencies for services not actually provided to patients. A grand jury was convened, and the case was assigned to Assistant Prosecutor William Whalen. In April, the grand jury charged Pembaur in a six-count indictment.

During the investigation, the grand jury issued subpoenas for the appearance of two of Pembaur's employees. When these employees failed to appear as directed, the Prosecutor obtained capiases for their arrest and detention from the Court of Common Pleas of Hamilton County.

On May 19, 1977, two Hamilton County Deputy Sheriffs attempted to serve the capiases at Pembaur's clinic. Although the reception area is open to the public, the rest of the clinic may be entered only through a door next to the receptionist's window. Upon arriving, the Deputy Sheriffs identified themselves to the receptionist and sought to pass through this door, which was apparently open. The receptionist blocked their way and asked them to wait for the doctor. When Pembaur appeared a moment later, he and the receptionist closed the door, which automatically locked from the inside, and wedged a piece of wood between it and the wall. Returning to the receptionist's window, the Deputy Sheriffs identified themselves to Pembaur, showed him the capiases and explained why they were there. Pembaur refused to let them enter, claiming that the police had no legal authority to be there and requesting that they leave. He told them that he had called the Cincinnati police, the local media, and his lawyer. The Deputy Sheriffs decided not to take further action until the Cincinnati police arrived.

Shortly thereafter, several Cincinnati police officers appeared. The Deputy Sheriffs explained the situation to them and asked that they speak to Pembaur. The Cincinnati police told Pembaur that the papers were lawful and that he should allow the Deputy Sheriffs to enter. When Pembaur refused, the Cincinnati police called for a superior officer. When he too failed to persuade Pembaur to open the door, the Deputy Sheriffs decided to call their supervisor for further instructions. Their supervisor told them to call Assistant Prosecutor Whalen and to follow his instructions. The Deputy Sheriffs then telephoned Whalen and informed him of the situation. Whalen conferred with County Prosecutor Leis, who told Whalen to instruct the Deputy Sheriffs to "go in and get [the witnesses]." Whalen in turn passed these instructions along to the Deputy Sheriffs.

After a final attempt to persuade Pembaur voluntarily to allow them to enter, the Deputy Sheriffs tried unsuccessfully to force the door. City police officers, who had been advised of the County Prosecutor's instructions to "go in and get" the witnesses, obtained an axe and chopped down the door. The Deputy Sheriffs then entered and searched the clinic. Two individuals who fit descriptions of the witnesses sought were detained, but turned out not to be the right persons.

After this incident, the Prosecutor obtained an additional indictment against Pembaur for obstructing police in the performance of an authorized act. Although acquitted of all other charges, Pembaur was convicted for this offense. The Ohio Court of Appeals reversed, reasoning that Pembaur was privileged under state law to exclude the deputies because the search of his office violated the Fourth Amendment. *State v. Pembaur,* No. C-790380 (Hamilton County Court of Appeals, Nov. 3, 1982). The Ohio Supreme Court reversed and reinstated the conviction. *State v. Pembaur,* 9 Ohio St.3d 136, 459 N.E.2d 217, cert. denied, 467 U.S. 1219, 104 S.C. 2668, 81 L.Ed.2d 373 (1984). The Supreme Court held that the state-law privilege applied only to bad-faith conduct by law enforcement officials, and that, under the circumstances of this case, Pembaur was obliged to acquiesce to the search and seek redress later in a civil action for damages. 9 Ohio St.3d, at 138, 459 N.E.2d, at 219.

On April 20, 1981, Pembaur filed the present action in the United States District Court for the Southern District of Ohio against the city of Cincinnati, the County of Hamilton, the Cincinnati Police Chief, the Hamilton County Sheriff, the members of the Hamilton Board of County Commissioners (in their official capacities only),

Assistant Prosecutor Whalen, and nine city and county police officers. Pembaur sought damages under 42 U.S.C. § 1983, alleging that the county and city police had violated his rights under the Fourth and Fourteenth Amendments. His theory was that, absent exigent circumstances, the Fourth Amendment prohibits police from searching an individual's home or business without a search warrant even to execute an arrest warrant for a third person. We agreed with that proposition in *Steagald v. United States*, 451 U.S. 204, 101 S.Ct. 1642, 68 L.Ed.2d 38 (1981), decided the day after Pembaur filed this lawsuit. Pembaur sought $10 million in actual and $10 million in punitive damages, plus costs and attorney's fees.

Much of the testimony at the 4-day trial concerned the practices of the Hamilton County police in serving capiases. Frank Webb, one of the Deputy Sheriffs present at the clinic on May 19, testified that he had previously served capiases on the property of third persons without a search warrant, but had never been required to use force to gain access. Assistant Prosecutor Whalen was also unaware of a prior instance in which police had been denied access to a third person's property in serving a capias and had used force to gain entry. Lincoln Stokes, the County Sheriff, testified that the Department had no written policy respecting the serving of capiases on the property of third persons and that the proper response in any given situation would depend upon the circumstances. He too could not recall a specific instance in which entrance had been denied and forcibly gained. Sheriff Stokes did testify, however, that it was the practice in his Department to refer questions to the County Prosecutor for instructions under appropriate circumstances and that "it was the proper thing to do" in this case.

The District Court awarded judgment to the defendants and dismissed the complaint in its entirety. The court agreed that the entry and search of Pembaur's clinic violated the Fourth Amendment under *Steagald, supra,* but held *Steagald* inapplicable since it was decided nearly four years after the incident occurred. Because it construed the law in the Sixth Circuit in 1977 to permit law enforcement officials to enter the premises of a third person to serve a capias, the District Court held that the individual municipal officials were all immune under *Harlow v. Fitzgerald*, 457 U.S. 800, 102 S.Ct. 2727, 73 L.Ed.2d 396 (1982).

The claims against the county and the city were dismissed on the ground that the individual officers were not acting pursuant to the kind of "official policy" that is the predicate for municipal liability under *Monell.* With respect to Hamilton County, the court explained that, even assuming that the entry and search were pursuant to a governmental policy, "it was not a policy of Hamilton County *per se*" because "[t]he Hamilton County Board of County Commissioners, acting on behalf of the county, simply does not establish or control the policies of the Hamilton County Sheriff." With respect to the city of Cincinnati, the court found that "the only policy or custom followed . . . was that of aiding County Sheriff's Deputies in the performance of their duties." The court found that any participation by city police in the entry and search of the clinic resulted from decisions by individual officers as to the permissible scope of assistance they could provide, and not from a city policy to provide this particular kind of assistance.

On appeal, Pembaur challenged only the dismissal of his claims against Whalen, Hamilton County, and the city of Cincinnati. The Court of Appeals for the Sixth Circuit upheld the dismissal of Pembaur's claims against Whalen and Hamilton County, but reversed the dismissal of his claim against the city of Cincinnati on the ground that the District Court's findings concerning the policies followed by the Cincinnati police were clearly erroneous. 746 F.2d 337 (1984).

The Court of Appeals affirmed the District Court's dismissal of Pembaur's claim against Hamilton County, but on different grounds. The court held that the County Board's lack of control over the Sheriff would not preclude county liability if "the nature and duties of the Sheriff are such that his acts may fairly be said to represent the county's official policy with respect to the specific subject matter." *Id.,* at 340–341. Based upon its examination of Ohio law, the Court of Appeals found it "clea[r]" that the Sheriff and the Prosecutor were both county officials authorized to establish "the official policy of Hamilton County" with respect to matters of law enforcement. *Id.,* at 341. Notwithstanding these conclusions, however, the court found that Pembaur's claim against the county had been properly dismissed:

> "We believe that Pembaur failed to prove the existence of a county policy in this case. Pembaur claims that the deputy sheriffs acted pursuant to the policies of the Sheriff and Prosecutor by forcing entry into the medical center. Pembaur has failed to establish, however, anything more than that, on this *one occasion,* the Prosecutor and the Sheriff decided to force entry into his office. . . . That single, discrete decision is insufficient, by itself, to establish that the Prosecutor, the Sheriff, or both were implementing a governmental policy." *Ibid.* (footnote omitted) (emphasis in original).

Pembaur petitioned for certiorari to review only the dismissal of his claim against Hamilton County. The decision of the Court of Appeals conflicts with holdings in several other Courts of Appeals, and we granted the petition to resolve the conflict. 472 U.S. 1016, 105 S.Ct. 3475, 87 L.Ed.2d 611 (1985). We reverse.

II

A

Our analysis must begin with the proposition that "Congress did not intend municipalities to be held liable unless action pursuant to official municipal policy of some nature caused a constitutional tort." *Monell v. New York City Dept. of Social Services,* 436 U.S., at 691, 98 S.Ct., at 2036. As we read its opinion, the Court of Appeals held that a single decision to take particular action, although made by municipal policymakers, cannot establish the kind of "official policy" required by *Monell* as a predicate to municipal liability under § 1983. The Court of Appeals reached this conclusion without referring to *Monell*—indeed, without any explanation at all. However, examination of the opinion in *Monell* clearly demonstrates that the Court of Appeals misinterpreted its holding.

Monell is a case about responsibility. In the first part of the opinion, we held that local government units could be made liable under § 1983 for deprivations of federal rights, overruling a contrary holding in *Monroe v. Pape,* 365 U.S. 167, 81 S. Ct. 473, 5 L.Ed.2d 492 (1961). In the second part of the opinion, we recognized a limitation on this liability and concluded that a municipality cannot be made liable by application of the doctrine of *respondeat superior.* See *Monell,* 436 U.S., at 691, 98 S.Ct., at 2036. In part, this conclusion rested upon the language of § 1983, which imposes liability only on a person who "subjects, or causes to be subjected," any individual to a deprivation of federal rights; we noted that this language "cannot easily be read to impose liability vicariously on government bodies solely on the basis of the existence of an employer-employee relationship with a tortfeasor." *Id.,* at 692, 98 S.Ct., at 2036. Primarily, however, our conclusion rested upon the legislative history, which disclosed that, while Congress never questioned its power to impose civil liability on municipalities for their *own* illegal acts, Congress did doubt its constitutional power to impose such liability in order to oblige municipalities to control the conduct of *others. Id.,* at 665–683, 98 S.Ct., at 2022–2032. We found that, because of these doubts, Congress chose not to create such obligations in § 1983. Recognizing that this would be the effect of a federal law of *respondeat superior,* we concluded that § 1983 could not be interpreted to incorporate doctrines of vicarious liability. *Id.,* at 692–694, and n. 57, 98 S.Ct., at 2036–2037, and n. 57.

The conclusion that tortious conduct, to be the basis for municipal liability under § 1983, must be pursuant to a municipality's "official policy" is contained in this discussion. The "official policy" requirement was intended to distinguish acts of the *municipality* from acts of *employees* of the municipality, and thereby make clear that municipal liability is limited to action for which the municipality is actually responsible. *Monell* reasoned that recovery from a municipality is limited to acts that are, properly speaking, acts "of the municipality"—that is, acts which the municipality has officially sanctioned or ordered.

With this understanding, it is plain that municipal liability may be imposed for a single decision by municipal policymakers under appropriate circumstances. No one has ever doubted, for instance, that a municipality may be liable under § 1983 for a single decision by its properly constituted legislative body—whether or not that body had taken similar action in the past or intended to do so in the future— because even a single decision by such a body unquestionably constitutes an act of official government policy. See, *e.g., Owen v. City of Independence,* 445 U.S. 622, 100 S.Ct. 1398, 63 L.Ed.2d 673 (1980) (City Council passed resolution firing plaintiff without a pretermination hearing); *Newport v. Fact Concerts, Inc.,* 453 U.S. 247, 101 S.Ct. 2748, 69 L.Ed.2d 616 (1981) (City Council canceled license permitting concert because of dispute over content of performance). But the power to establish policy is no more the exclusive province of the legislature at the local level than at the state or national level. *Monell*'s language makes clear that it expressly envisioned other officials "whose acts or edicts may fairly be said to represent official policy," *Monell, supra,* 436 U.S., at 694, 98 S.Ct., at 2037–2038, and whose decisions therefore may give rise to municipal liability under § 1983.

Indeed, any other conclusion would be inconsistent with the principles underlying § 1983. To be sure, "official policy" often refers to formal rules or understandings—often but not always committed to writing—that are intended to, and do, establish fixed plans of action to be followed under similar circumstances consistently and over time. That was the case in *Monell* itself, which involved a written rule requiring pregnant employees to take unpaid leaves of absence before such leaves were medically necessary. However, as in *Owen* and *Newport,* a government frequently chooses a course of action tailored to a particular situation and not intended to control decisions in later situations. If the decision to adopt that particular course of action is properly made by that government's authorized decision makers, it surely represents an act of official government "policy" as that term is commonly understood. More importantly, where action is directed by those who establish governmental policy, the municipality is equally responsible whether that action is to be taken only once or to be taken repeatedly. To deny compensation to the victim would therefore be contrary to the fundamental purpose of § 1983.

B

Having said this much, we hasten to emphasize that not every decision by municipal officers automatically subjects the municipality to § 1983 liability. Municipal liability attaches only where the decision maker possesses final authority to establish municipal policy with respect to the action ordered. The fact that a particular official—even a policymaking official—has discretion in the exercise of particular functions does not, without more, give rise to municipal liability based on an exercise of that discretion. See, *e.g., Oklahoma City v. Tuttle,* 471 U.S., at 822–824, 105 S.Ct., at 2435–2436. The official must also be responsible for establishing final government policy respecting such activity before the municipality can be held liable. Authority to make municipal policy may be granted directly by a legislative enactment or may be delegated by an official who possesses such authority, and of course, whether an official had final policymaking authority is a question of state law. However, like other governmental entities, municipalities often spread policymaking authority among various officers and official bodies. As a result, particular officers may have authority to establish binding county policy respecting particular matters and to adjust that policy for the county in changing circumstances. To hold a municipality liable for actions ordered by such officers exercising their policymaking authority is no more an application of the theory of *respondeat superior* than was holding the municipalities liable for the decisions of the City Councils in *Owen* and *Newport.* In each case municipal liability attached to a single decision to take unlawful action made by municipal policymakers. We hold that municipal liability under § 1983 attaches where—and only where—a deliberate choice to follow a course of action is made from among various alternatives by the official or officials responsible for establishing final policy with respect to the subject matter in question. See *Tuttle, supra,* at 823, 105 S.Ct., at 2436 ("'policy' generally implies a course of action consciously chosen from among various alternatives").

C

Applying this standard to the case before us, we have little difficulty concluding that the Court of Appeals erred in dismissing petitioner's claim against the county. The Deputy Sheriffs who attempted to serve the capiases at petitioner's clinic found themselves in a difficult situation. Unsure of the proper course of action to follow, they sought instructions from their supervisors. The instructions they received were to follow the orders of the County Prosecutor. The Prosecutor made a considered decision based on his understanding of the law and commanded the officers forcibly to enter petitioner's clinic. That decision directly caused the violation of petitioner's Fourth Amendment rights.

Respondent argues that the County Prosecutor lacked authority to establish municipal policy respecting law enforcement practices because only the County Sheriff may establish policy respecting such practices. Respondent suggests that the County Prosecutor was merely rendering "legal advice" when he ordered the Deputy Sheriffs to "go in and get" the witnesses. Consequently, the argument concludes, the action of the individual Deputy Sheriffs in following this advice and forcibly entering petitioner's clinic was not pursuant to a properly established municipal policy.

We might be inclined to agree with respondent if we thought that the Prosecutor had only rendered "legal advice." However, the Court of Appeals concluded, based upon its examination of Ohio law, that both the County Sheriff and the County Prosecutor could establish county policy under appropriate circumstances, a conclusion that we do not question here. Ohio Rev.Code Ann. § 309.09(A) (1979) provides that county officers may "require . . . instructions from [the County Prosecutor] in matters connected with their official duties." Pursuant to standard office procedure, the Sheriff's Office referred this matter to the Prosecutor and then followed his instructions. The Sheriff testified that his Department followed this practice under appropriate circumstances and that it was "the proper thing to do" in this case. We decline to accept respondent's invitation to overlook this delegation of authority by disingenuously labeling the Prosecutor's clear command mere "legal advice." In ordering the Deputy Sheriffs to enter petitioner's clinic the County Prosecutor was acting as the final decision maker for the county, and the county may therefore be held liable under § 1983.

The decision of the Court of Appeals is reversed, and the case is remanded for further proceedings consistent with this opinion.

It is so ordered.

Board of the County Commissioners of Bryan County, Oklahoma v. Brown

520 U.S. 397 (1997)

JUSTICE O'CONNOR delivered the opinion of the Court. JUSTICE SOUTER dissented and filed an opinion in which JUSTICE STEVENS and JUSTICE BREYER joined. JUSTICE BREYER dissented and filed an opinion in which JUSTICE STEVENS and JUSTICE GINSBURG joined.

Respondent Jill Brown brought a claim for damages against petitioner Bryan County under Rev. Stat. § 1979, 42 U.S.C. § 1983. She alleged that a county police officer used excessive force in arresting her, and that the county itself was liable for her injuries based on its sheriff's hiring and training decisions. She prevailed on her claims against the county following a jury trial, and the Court of Appeals for the Fifth Circuit affirmed the judgment against the county on the basis of the hiring claim alone. 67 F.3d 1174 (1995). We granted certiorari. We conclude that the Court of Appeals' decision cannot be squared with our recognition that, in enacting § 1983, Congress did not intend to impose liability on a municipality unless *deliberate* action attributable to the municipality itself is the "moving force" behind the plaintiff's deprivation of federal rights. *Monell v. New York City Dept. of Social Servs.*, 436 U.S. 658, 694, 98 S.Ct. 2018, 2027, 56 L.Ed.2d 611 (1978).

I

In the early morning hours of May 12, 1991, Jill Brown (hereinafter respondent) and her husband were driving from Grayson County, Texas, to their home in Bryan County, Oklahoma. After crossing into Oklahoma, they approached a police checkpoint. Mr. Brown, who was driving, decided to avoid the checkpoint and return to Texas. After seeing the Browns' truck turn away from the checkpoint, Bryan County Deputy Sheriff Robert Morrison and Reserve Deputy Stacy Burns pursued the vehicle. Although the parties' versions of events differ, at trial both deputies claimed that their patrol car reached speeds in excess of 100 miles per hour. Mr. Brown testified that he was unaware of the deputies' attempts to overtake him. The chase finally ended four miles south of the police checkpoint.

After he got out of the squad car, Deputy Sheriff Morrison pointed his gun toward the Browns' vehicle and ordered the Browns to raise their hands. Reserve Deputy Burns, who was unarmed, rounded the corner of the vehicle on the passenger's side. Burns twice ordered respondent from the vehicle. When she did not exit, he used an "arm bar" technique, grabbing respondent's arm at the wrist and elbow, pulling her from the vehicle, and spinning her to the ground. Respondent's knees were severely injured, and she later underwent corrective surgery. Ultimately, she may need knee replacements.

Respondent sought compensation for her injuries under 42 U.S.C. § 1983 and state law from Burns, Bryan County Sheriff B.J. Moore, and the county itself. Respondent claimed, among other things, that Bryan County was liable for Burns' alleged use of excessive force based on Sheriff Moore's decision to hire Burns, the son of his nephew. Specifically, respondent claimed that Sheriff Moore had failed to adequately review Burns' background. Burns had a record of driving infractions and had pleaded guilty to various driving-related and other misdemeanors, including assault and battery, resisting arrest, and public drunkenness. Oklahoma law does not preclude the hiring of an individual who has committed a misdemeanor to serve as a peace officer. See Okla. Stat., Tit. 70, § 3311(D)(2)(a) (1991) (requiring that the hiring agency certify that the prospective officer's records do not reflect a felony conviction). At trial, Sheriff Moore testified that he had obtained Burns' driving record and a report on Burns from the National Crime Information Center, but had not closely reviewed either. Sheriff Moore authorized Burns to make arrests, but not to carry a weapon or to operate a patrol car.

In a ruling not at issue here, the District Court dismissed respondent's § 1983 claim against Sheriff Moore prior to trial. App. 28. Counsel for Bryan County stipulated that Sheriff Moore "was the policy maker for Bryan County regarding the Sheriff's Department." *Id.*, at 30. At the close of respondent's case and again at the close of all of the evidence, Bryan County moved for judgment as a matter of law. As to respondent's claim that Sheriff Moore's decision to hire Burns triggered municipal liability, the county argued that a single hiring decision by a municipal policymaker could not give rise to municipal liability under § 1983. *Id.*, at 59–60. The District Court denied the county's motions. The court also overruled the county's objections to jury instructions on the § 1983 claim against the county. *Id.*, at 125–126, 132.

To resolve respondent's claims, the jury was asked to answer several interrogatories. The jury concluded that Stacy Burns had arrested respondent without probable cause and had used excessive force, and therefore found him liable for respondent's injuries. It also found that the "hiring policy" and the "training policy" of Bryan County "in the case of Stacy Burns as instituted by its policymaker, B.J. Moore," were each "so inadequate as to amount to deliberate indifference to the constitutional needs of the Plaintiff." *Id.*, at 135. The District Court entered judgment for respondent on the issue of Bryan County's § 1983 liability. The county appealed on several grounds, and the Court of Appeals for the Fifth Circuit affirmed. 67 F.3d 1174 (1995). The court held, among other things, that Bryan County was properly found liable under § 1983 based on Sheriff Moore's decision to hire Burns. *Id.*, at 1185. The court addressed only those points that it thought merited review; it did not address the jury's determination of county liability based on inadequate training of Burns, *id.*, at 1178, nor do we. We granted certiorari, 517 U.S. 1154, 116 S.Ct. 1540, 134 L.Ed.2d 645 (1996), to decide whether the county was properly held liable for respondent's injuries based on Sheriff Moore's single decision to hire Burns. We now reverse.

II

Title 42 U.S.C. § 1983 provides in relevant part:

"Every person who, under color of any statute, ordinance, regulation, custom, or usage, of any State or Territory or the District of Columbia, subjects, or causes to be subjected, any citizen of the United States or other person within the jurisdiction thereof to the deprivation of any rights, privileges, or immunities secured by the Constitution and laws, shall be liable to the party injured in an action at law, suit in equity, or other proper proceeding for redress."

We held in *Monell v. New York City Dept. of Social Servs.*, 436 U.S., at 689, 98 S. Ct., at 2035, that municipalities and other local governmental bodies are "persons" within the meaning of § 1983. We also recognized that a municipality may not be held liable under § 1983 solely because it employs a tortfeasor. Our conclusion rested partly on the language of § 1983 itself. In light of the statute's imposition of liability on one who "subjects [a person], or causes [that person] to be subjected," to a deprivation of federal rights, we concluded that it "cannot be easily read to impose liability vicariously on governing bodies solely on the basis of the existence of an employer-employee relationship with a tortfeasor." *Id.*, at 692, 98 S.Ct., at 2036. Our conclusion also rested upon the statute's legislative history. As stated in *Pembaur v. Cincinnati*, 475 U.S. 469, 479, 106 S.Ct. 1292, 1298, 89 L.Ed.2d 452 (1986), "while Congress never questioned its power to impose civil liability on municipalities for their *own* illegal acts, Congress did doubt its constitutional power to impose such liability in order to oblige municipalities to control the conduct of *others* " (citing *Monell, supra,* at 665–683, 98 S.Ct., at 2022–2032). We have consistently refused to hold municipalities liable under a theory of *respondeat superior.* See *Oklahoma City v. Tuttle,* 471 U.S. 808, 818, 105 S.Ct. 2427, 2433, 85 L.Ed.2d 791 (1985) (plurality opinion); *id.,* at 828, 105 S.Ct., at 2438 (opinion of Brennan, J.); *Pembaur, supra,* at 478–479, 106 S.Ct., at 1297–1298; *St. Louis v. Praprotnik,* 485 U.S. 112, 122, 108 S. Ct. 915, 923, 99 L.Ed.2d 107 (1988) (plurality opinion); *id.,* at 137, 108 S.Ct., at 931 (opinion of Brennan, J.); *Canton v. Harris,* 489 U.S. 378, 392, 109 S.Ct. 1197, 1206, 103 L.Ed.2d 412 (1989).

Instead, in *Monell* and subsequent cases, we have required a plaintiff seeking to impose liability on a municipality under § 1983 to identify a municipal "policy" or "custom" that caused the plaintiff's injury. See *Monell, supra,* at 694, 98 S.Ct., at 2027; *Pembaur, supra,* at 480–481, 106 S.Ct., at 1298–1299; *Canton, supra,* at 389, 109 S.Ct., at 1205. Locating a "policy" ensures that a municipality is held liable only for those deprivations resulting from the decisions of its duly constituted legislative body or of those officials whose acts may fairly be said to be those of the municipality. *Monell, supra,* at 694, 98 S.Ct., at 2027. Similarly, an act performed pursuant to a "custom" that has not been formally approved by an appropriate decision maker may fairly subject a municipality to liability on the theory that the relevant practice is so widespread as to have the force of law. 436 U.S., at 690–691, 98 S.Ct., at 2035–2036 (citing *Adickes v. S.H. Kress & Co.,* 398 U.S. 144, 167–168, 90 S.Ct. 1598, 1613–1614, 26 L.Ed.2d 142 (1970)).

The parties join issue on whether, under *Monell* and subsequent cases, a single hiring decision by a county sheriff can be a "policy" that triggers municipal liability. Relying on our decision in *Pembaur,* respondent claims that a single act by a decision maker with final authority in the relevant area constitutes a "policy" attributable to the municipality itself. So long as a § 1983 plaintiff identifies a decision properly attributable to the municipality, respondent argues, there is no risk of imposing *respondeat superior* liability. Whether that decision was intended to govern only the situation at hand or to serve as a rule to be applied over time is immaterial. Rather, under respondent's theory, identification of an act of a proper municipal decision maker is all that is required to ensure that the municipality is held liable only for its own conduct. The Court of Appeals accepted respondent's approach.

As our § 1983 municipal liability jurisprudence illustrates, however, it is not enough for a § 1983 plaintiff merely to identify conduct properly attributable to the municipality. The plaintiff must also demonstrate that, through its *deliberate* conduct, the municipality was the "moving force" behind the injury alleged. That is, a plaintiff must show that the municipal action was taken with the requisite degree of culpability and must demonstrate a direct causal link between the municipal action and the deprivation of federal rights.

Where a plaintiff claims that a particular municipal action *itself* violates federal law, or directs an employee to do so, resolving these issues of fault and causation is straightforward. 42 U.S.C. § 1983 itself "contains no state-of-mind requirement independent of that necessary to state a violation" of the underlying federal right. *Daniels v. Williams,* 474 U.S. 327, 330, 106 S.Ct. 662, 664, 88 L.Ed.2d 662 (1986). In any § 1983 suit, however, the plaintiff must establish the state of mind required to prove the underlying violation. Accordingly, proof that a municipality's legislative body or authorized decision maker has intentionally deprived a plaintiff of a federally protected right necessarily establishes that the municipality acted culpably. Similarly, the conclusion that the action taken or directed by the municipality or its authorized decision maker itself violates federal law will also determine that the municipal action was the moving force behind the injury of which the plaintiff complains.

Sheriff Moore's hiring decision was itself legal, and Sheriff Moore did not authorize Burns to use excessive force. Respondent's claim, rather, is that a single facially lawful hiring decision can launch a series of events that ultimately cause a violation of federal rights. Where a plaintiff claims that the municipality has not directly inflicted an injury, but nonetheless has caused an employee to do so, rigorous standards of culpability and causation must be applied to ensure that the municipality is not held liable solely for the actions of its employee. See *Canton, supra,* 489 U.S., at 391–392, 109 S.Ct., at 1206–1207; *Tuttle, supra,* at 824, 105 S.Ct., at 2436 (plurality opinion). See also *Springfield v. Kibbe,* 480 U.S. 257, 270–271, 107 S.Ct. 1114, 1121–1122, 94 L.Ed.2d 293 (1987) (*per curiam*) (dissent from dismissal of writ as improvidently granted).

In relying heavily on *Pembaur*, respondent blurs the distinction between § 1983 cases that present no difficult questions of fault and causation and those that do. To the extent that we have recognized a cause of action under § 1983 based on a single decision attributable to a municipality, we have done so only where the evidence that the municipality had acted and that the plaintiff had suffered a deprivation of federal rights also proved fault and causation. For example, *Owen v. Independence*, 445 U.S. 622, 100 S.Ct. 1398, 63 L.Ed.2d 673 (1980), and *Newport v. Fact Concerts, Inc.*, 453 U.S. 247, 101 S.Ct. 2748, 69 L.Ed.2d 616 (1981), involved formal decisions of municipal legislative bodies. In *Owen*, the city council allegedly censured and discharged an employee without a hearing. 445 U.S., at 627–629, 633, and n. 13, 100 S.Ct., at 1403–1404, 1406, and n. 13. In *Fact Concerts*, the city council canceled a license permitting a concert following a dispute over the performance's content. 453 U.S., at 252, 101 S.Ct., at 2752. Neither decision reflected implementation of a generally applicable rule. But we did not question that each decision, duly promulgated by city lawmakers, could trigger municipal liability if the decision itself were found to be unconstitutional. Because fault and causation were obvious in each case, proof that the municipality's decision was unconstitutional would suffice to establish that the municipality itself was liable for the plaintiff's constitutional injury.

Similarly, *Pembaur v. Cincinnati* concerned a decision by a county prosecutor, acting as the county's final decision maker, 475 U.S., at 485, 106 S.Ct., at 1301, to direct county deputies to forcibly enter petitioner's place of business to serve *capiases* upon third parties. Relying on *Owen* and *Newport*, we concluded that a final decision maker's adoption of a course of action "tailored to a particular situation and not intended to control decisions in later situations" may, in some circumstances, give rise to municipal liability under § 1983. 475 U.S., at 481, 106 S.Ct., at 1299. In *Pembaur*, it was not disputed that the prosecutor had specifically directed the action resulting in the deprivation of petitioner's rights. The conclusion that the decision was that of a final municipal decision maker and was therefore properly attributable to the municipality established municipal liability. No questions of fault or causation arose.

Claims not involving an allegation that the municipal action itself violated federal law, or directed or authorized the deprivation of federal rights, present much more difficult problems of proof. That a plaintiff has suffered a deprivation of federal rights at the hands of a municipal employee will not alone permit an inference of municipal culpability and causation; the plaintiff will simply have shown that the *employee* acted culpably. We recognized these difficulties in *Canton v. Harris*, where we considered a claim that inadequate training of shift supervisors at a city jail led to a deprivation of a detainee's constitutional rights. We held that, quite apart from the state of mind required to establish the underlying constitutional violation-in that case, a violation of due process, 489 U.S., at 388–389, n. 8, 109 S.Ct., at 1205, n. 8-a plaintiff seeking to establish municipal liability on the theory that a facially lawful municipal action has led an employee to violate a plaintiff's rights must demonstrate that the municipal action was taken with "deliberate indifference" as to its known or obvious consequences. *Id.,* at 388, 109 S.Ct., at 1204. A showing of simple or even heightened negligence will not suffice.

We concluded in *Canton* that an "inadequate training" claim could be the basis for §1983 liability in "limited circumstances." *Id.,* at 387, 109 S.Ct., at 1204. We spoke, however, of a deficient training "program," necessarily intended to apply over time to multiple employees. *Id.,* at 390, 109 S.Ct., at 1205. Existence of a "program" makes proof of fault and causation at least possible in an inadequate training case. If a program does not prevent constitutional violations, municipal decision makers may eventually be put on notice that a new program is called for. Their continued adherence to an approach that they know or should know has failed to prevent tortious conduct by employees may establish the conscious disregard for the consequences of their action-the "deliberate indifference"-necessary to trigger municipal liability. *Id.,* at 390, n. 10, 109 S.Ct., at 1205, n. 10 ("It could ... be that the police, in exercising their discretion, so often violate constitutional rights that the need for further training must have been plainly obvious to the city policymakers, who, nevertheless, are 'deliberately indifferent' to the need"); *id.,* at 397, 109 S. Ct., at 1209 (O'Connor, J., concurring in part and dissenting in part) ("[M]unicipal liability for failure to train may be proper where it can be shown that policymakers were aware of, and acquiesced in, a pattern of constitutional violations . . ."). In addition, the existence of a pattern of tortious conduct by inadequately trained employees may tend to show that the lack of proper training, rather than a one-time negligent administration of the program or factors peculiar to the officer involved in a particular incident, is the "moving force" behind the plaintiff's injury. See *id.,* at 390–391, 109 S.Ct., at 1205–1206.

Before trial, counsel for Bryan County stipulated that Sheriff Moore "was the policy maker for Bryan County regarding the Sheriff's Department." App. 30. Indeed, the county sought to avoid liability by claiming that its Board of Commissioners participated in no policy decisions regarding the conduct and operation of the office of the Bryan County Sheriff. *Id.,* at 32. Accepting the county's representations below, then, this case presents no difficult questions concerning whether Sheriff Moore has final authority to act for the municipality in hiring matters. Cf. *Jett v. Dallas Independent School Dist.,* 491 U.S. 701, 109 S.Ct. 2702, 105 L.Ed.2d 598 (1989); *St. Louis v. Praprotnik,* 485 U.S. 112, 108 S.Ct. 915, 99 L.Ed.2d 107 (1988). Respondent does not claim that she can identify any pattern of injuries linked to Sheriff Moore's hiring practices. Indeed, respondent does not contend that Sheriff Moore's hiring practices are generally defective. The only evidence on this point at trial suggested that Sheriff Moore had adequately screened the backgrounds of all prior deputies he hired. App. 106–110. Respondent instead seeks to trace liability to what can only be described as a deviation from Sheriff Moore's ordinary hiring practices. Where a claim of municipal liability rests on a single decision, not itself representing a violation of federal law and not directing such a violation, the danger that a municipality will be held liable without fault is high. Because the decision necessarily governs a single case, there can be no notice to the municipal decision maker, based on previous violations of federally protected rights, that his approach is inadequate. Nor will it be readily apparent that the municipality's action caused the injury in question, because the plaintiff can point to no other incident tending to make it more likely that the plaintiff's own injury flows from the municipality's action, rather than from some other intervening cause.

In *Canton*, we did not foreclose the possibility that evidence of a single violation of federal rights, accompanied by a showing that a municipality has failed to train its employees to handle recurring situations presenting an obvious potential for such a violation, could trigger municipal liability. 489 U.S., at 390, and n. 10, 109 S.Ct., at 1205, and n. 10 ("[I]t may happen that in light of the duties assigned to specific officers or employees the need for more or different training is so obvious . . . that the policymakers of the city can reasonably be said to have been deliberately indifferent to the need"). Respondent purports to rely on *Canton*, arguing that Burns' use of excessive force was the plainly obvious consequence of Sheriff Moore's failure to screen Burns' record. In essence, respondent claims that this showing of "obviousness" would demonstrate both that Sheriff Moore acted with conscious disregard for the consequences of his action and that the Sheriff's action directly caused her injuries, and would thus substitute for the pattern of injuries ordinarily necessary to establish municipal culpability and causation.

The proffered analogy between failure-to-train cases and inadequate screening cases is not persuasive. In leaving open in *Canton* the possibility that a plaintiff might succeed in carrying a failure-to-train claim without showing a pattern of constitutional violations, we simply hypothesized that, in a narrow range of circumstances, a violation of federal rights may be a highly predictable consequence of a failure to equip law enforcement officers with specific tools to handle recurring situations. The likelihood that the situation will recur and the predictability that an officer lacking specific tools to handle that situation will violate citizens' rights could justify a finding that policymakers' decision not to train the officer reflected "deliberate indifference" to the obvious consequence of the policymakers' choice-namely, a violation of a specific constitutional or statutory right. The high degree of predictability may also support an inference of causation-that the municipality's indifference led directly to the very consequence that was so predictable.

Where a plaintiff presents a § 1983 claim premised upon the inadequacy of an official's review of a prospective applicant's record, however, there is a particular danger that a municipality will be held liable for an injury not directly caused by a deliberate action attributable to the municipality itself. Every injury suffered at the hands of a municipal employee can be traced to a hiring decision in a "but-for" sense: But for the municipality's decision to hire the employee, the plaintiff would not have suffered the injury. To prevent municipal liability for a hiring decision from collapsing into *respondeat superior* liability, a court must carefully test the link between the policymaker's inadequate decision and the particular injury alleged.

In attempting to import the reasoning of *Canton* into the hiring context, respondent ignores the fact that predicting the consequence of a single hiring decision, even one based on an inadequate assessment of a record, is far more difficult than predicting what might flow from the failure to train a single law enforcement officer as to a specific skill necessary to the discharge of his duties. As our decision in *Canton* makes clear, "deliberate indifference" is a stringent standard of fault, requiring proof that a municipal actor disregarded a known or obvious consequence of his action. Unlike the risk from a particular glaring omission in a training regimen, the risk from a single instance of inadequate screening of an applicant's background is not "obvious" in the abstract; rather, it depends upon the background of the applicant. A lack of scrutiny may increase the likelihood that an unfit officer will be hired, and that the unfit officer will, when placed in a particular position to affect the rights of citizens, act improperly. But that is only a generalized showing of risk. The fact that inadequate scrutiny of an applicant's background would make a violation of rights more *likely* cannot alone give rise to an inference that a policymaker's failure to scrutinize the record of a particular applicant produced a specific constitutional violation. After all, a full screening of an applicant's background might reveal no cause for concern at all; if so, a hiring official who failed to scrutinize the applicant's background cannot be said to have consciously disregarded an obvious risk that the officer would subsequently inflict a particular constitutional injury.

We assume that a jury could properly find in this case that Sheriff Moore's assessment of Burns' background was inadequate. Sheriff Moore's own testimony indicated that he did not inquire into the underlying conduct or the disposition of any of the misdemeanor charges reflected on Burns' record before hiring him. But this showing of an instance of inadequate screening is not enough to establish "deliberate indifference." In layman's terms, inadequate screening of an applicant's record may reflect "indifference" to the applicant's background. For purposes of a legal inquiry into municipal liability under § 1983, however, that is not the *relevant* "indifference." A plaintiff must demonstrate that a municipal decision reflects deliberate indifference to the risk that a violation of a particular constitutional or statutory right will follow the decision. Only where adequate scrutiny of an applicant's background would lead a reasonable policymaker to conclude that the plainly obvious consequence of the decision to hire the applicant would be the deprivation of a third party's federally protected right can the official's failure to adequately scrutinize the applicant's background constitute "deliberate indifference."

Neither the District Court nor the Court of Appeals directly tested the link between Burns' actual background and the risk that, if hired, he would use excessive force. The District Court instructed the jury on a theory analogous to that reserved in *Canton*. The court required respondent to prove that Sheriff Moore's inadequate screening of Burns' background was "so likely to result in *violations of constitutional rights*" that the Sheriff could "reasonably [be] said to have been deliberately indifferent to the *constitutional needs* of the Plaintiff." App. 123 (emphasis added). The court also instructed the jury, without elaboration, that respondent was required to prove that the "inadequate hiring . . . policy directly caused the Plaintiff's injury." *Ibid.*

As discussed above, a finding of culpability simply cannot depend on the mere probability that any officer inadequately screened will inflict any constitutional injury. Rather, it must depend on a finding that *this* officer was highly likely to inflict the *particular* injury suffered by the plaintiff. The connection between the background of the particular applicant and the specific constitutional violation alleged must be strong. What the District Court's instructions on culpability, and therefore the jury's finding of municipal liability, failed to capture is whether Burns' background made his use of excessive force in making an arrest a plainly obvious consequence of the hiring decision. The Court of Appeals' affirmance of the jury's finding of municipal liability depended on its view that the jury could have found that "inadequate screening of *a deputy* could likely result in the violation of *citizens' constitutional rights.*" 67 F.3d, at 1185 (emphasis added). Beyond relying on a risk of violations of unspecified constitutional rights, the Court of Appeals also posited that Sheriff Moore's decision reflected indifference to "the public's welfare." *Id.,* at 1184.

Even assuming without deciding that proof of a single instance of inadequate screening could ever trigger municipal liability, the evidence in this case was insufficient to support a finding that, in hiring Burns, Sheriff Moore disregarded a known or obvious risk of injury. To test the link between Sheriff Moore's hiring decision and respondent's injury, we must ask whether a full review of Burns' record reveals that Sheriff Moore should have concluded that Burns' use of excessive force would be a plainly obvious consequence of the hiring decision. On this point, respondent's showing was inadequate. To be sure, Burns' record reflected various misdemeanor infractions. Respondent claims that the record demonstrated such a strong propensity for violence that Burns' application of excessive force was highly likely. The primary charges on which respondent relies, however, are those arising from a fight on a college campus where Burns was a student. In connection with this single incident, Burns was charged with assault and battery, resisting arrest, and public drunkenness. In January 1990, when he pleaded guilty to those charges, Burns also pleaded guilty to various driving-related offenses, including nine moving violations and a charge of driving with a suspended license. In addition, Burns had previously pleaded guilty to being in actual physical control of a vehicle while intoxicated.

The fact that Burns had pleaded guilty to traffic offenses and other misdemeanors may well have made him an extremely poor candidate for reserve deputy. Had Sheriff Moore fully reviewed Burns' record, he might have come to precisely that conclusion. But unless he would necessarily have reached that decision *because* Burns' use of excessive force would have been a plainly obvious consequence of the hiring decision, Sheriff Moore's inadequate scrutiny of Burns' record cannot constitute "deliberate indifference" to respondent's federally protected right to be free from a use of excessive force.

Justice Souter's reading of the case is that the jury believed that Sheriff Moore in fact read Burns' entire record. *Post,* at 1399. That is plausible, but it is also irrelevant. It is not sufficient for respondent to show that Sheriff Moore read Burns' record and therefore hired Burns with knowledge of his background. Such a decision may reflect indifference to Burns' *record,* but what is required is deliberate indifference to a plaintiff's constitutional right. That is, whether Sheriff Moore failed to examine Burns' record, partially examined it, or fully examined it, Sheriff Moore's hiring decision could not have been "deliberately indifferent" unless in light of that record Burns' use of excessive force would have been a plainly obvious consequence of the hiring decision. Because there was insufficient evidence on which a jury could base a finding that Sheriff Moore's decision to hire Burns reflected conscious disregard of an obvious risk that a use of excessive force would follow, the District Court erred in submitting respondent's inadequate screening claim to the jury.

III

Cases involving constitutional injuries allegedly traceable to an ill-considered hiring decision pose the greatest risk that a municipality will be held liable for an injury that it did not cause. In the broadest sense, every injury is traceable to a hiring decision. Where a court fails to adhere to rigorous requirements of culpability and causation, municipal liability collapses into *respondeat superior* liability. As we recognized in *Monell* and have repeatedly reaffirmed, Congress did not intend municipalities to be held liable unless *deliberate* action attributable to the municipality directly caused a deprivation of federal rights. A failure to apply stringent culpability and causation requirements raises serious federalism concerns, in that it risks constitutionalizing particular hiring requirements that States have themselves elected not to impose. Cf. *Canton v. Harris,* 489 U.S., at 392, 109 S.Ct., at 1206. Bryan County is not liable for Sheriff Moore's isolated decision to hire Burns without adequate screening, because respondent has not demonstrated that his decision reflected a conscious disregard for a high risk that Burns would use excessive force in violation of respondent's federally protected right. We therefore vacate the judgment of the Court of Appeals and remand this case for further proceedings consistent with this opinion.

It is so ordered.

F. Federal Officials

Although 42 U.S.C. § 1983 only purports to regulate state actors, the Court has crafted similar protections against federal officers. This judicially created remedy is known as the *Bivens* doctrine. In *Bivens,* the Supreme Court, held that a complaint alleging that agents of Federal Bureau of Narcotics, acting under color of federal authority, made a warrantless entry of petitioner's apartment, searched the apartment and arrested him on narcotics charges, all without probable cause, stated a cognizable federal cause of action under the Fourth Amendment for damages recoverable upon proof of injuries resulting from the agents' violation of that Amendment.

Bivens v. Six Unknown Named Agents of Federal Bureau of Narcotics

403 U.S. 388 (1971)

MR. JUSTICE BRENNAN delivered the opinion of the Court. MR. JUSTICE HARLAN concurred in the judgment and filed an opinion. MR. CHIEF JUSTICE BURGER, MR. JUSTICE BLACK and MR. JUSTICE BLACKMUN filed dissenting opinions.

The Fourth Amendment provides that:

'The right of the people to be secure in their persons, houses, papers, and effects, against unreasonable searches and seizures, shall not be violated. * * *'

In *Bell v. Hood*, 327 U.S. 678, 66 S.Ct. 773, 90 L.Ed. 939 (1946), we reserved the question whether violation of that command by a federal agent acting under color of his authority gives rise to a cause of action for damages consequent upon his unconstitutional conduct. Today we hold that it does.

This case has its origin in an arrest and search carried out on the morning of November 26, 1965. Petitioner's complaint alleged that on that day respondents, agents of the Federal Bureau of Narcotics acting under claim of federal authority, entered his apartment and arrested him for alleged narcotics violations. The agents manacled petitioner in front of his wife and children, and threatened to arrest the entire family. They searched the apartment from stem to stern. Thereafter, petitioner was taken to the federal courthouse in Brooklyn, where he was interrogated, booked, and subjected to a visual strip search.

On July 7, 1967, petitioner brought suit in Federal District Court. In addition to the allegations above, his complaint asserted that the arrest and search were effected without a warrant, and that unreasonable force was employed in making the arrest; fairly read, it alleges as well that the arrest was made without probable cause. Petitioner claimed to have suffered great humiliation, embarrassment, and mental suffering as a result of the agents' unlawful conduct, and sought $15,000 damages from each of them. The District Court, on respondents' motion, dismissed the complaint on the ground, inter alia, that it failed to state a cause of action. 276 F.Supp. 12 (EDNY 1967). The Court of Appeals, one judge concurring specially, affirmed on that basis. 409 F.2d 718 (CA2 1969). We granted certiorari. 399 U.S. 905, 90 S.Ct. 2203, 26 L.Ed.2d 559 (1970). We reverse.

I

Respondents do not argue that petitioner should be entirely without remedy for an unconstitutional invasion of his rights by federal agents. In respondents' view, however, the rights that petitioner asserts—primarily rights of privacy—are creations of state and not of federal law. Accordingly, they argue, petitioner may obtain money damages to redress invasion of these rights only by an action in tort, under state law, in the state courts. In this scheme, the Fourth Amendment would serve merely to limit the extent to which the agents could defend the state law tort suit by asserting that their actions were a valid exercise of federal power: if the agents were shown to have violated the Fourth Amendment, such a defense would be lost to them and they would stand before the state law merely as private individuals. Candidly admitting that it is the policy of the Department of Justice to remove all such suits from the state to the federal courts for decision, respondents nevertheless urge that we uphold dismissal of petitioner's complaint in federal court, and remit him to filing an action in the state courts in order that the case may properly be removed to the federal court for decision on the basis of state law.

We think that respondents' thesis rests upon an unduly restrictive view of the Fourth Amendment's protection against unreasonable searches and seizures by federal agents, a view that has consistently been rejected by this Court. Respondents seek to treat the relationship between a citizen and a federal agent unconstitutionally exercising his authority as no different from the relationship between two private citizens. In so doing, they ignore the fact that power, once granted, does not disappear like a magic gift when it is wrongfully used. An agent acting—albeit unconstitutionally—in the name of the United States possesses a far greater capacity for harm than an individual trespasser exercising no authority other than his own. Cf. *Amos v. United States*, 255 U.S. 313, 317, 41 S.Ct. 266, 267–268, 65 L.Ed. 654 (1921); *United States v. Classic*, 313 U.S. 299, 326, 61 S.Ct. 1031, 1043, 85 L.Ed. 1368 (1941). Accordingly, as our cases make clear, the Fourth Amendment operates as a limitation upon the exercise of federal power regardless of whether the State in whose jurisdiction that power is exercised would prohibit or penalize the identical act if engaged in by a private citizen. It guarantees to citizens of the United States the absolute right to be free from unreasonable searches and seizures carried out by virtue of federal authority. And 'where federally protected rights have been invaded, it has been the rule from the beginning that courts will be alert to adjust their remedies so as to grant the necessary relief.' *Bell v. Hood*, 327 U.S., at 684, 66 S.Ct., at 777 (footnote omitted); see *Bemis Bros. Bag Co. v. United States*, 289 U.S. 28, 36, 53 S.Ct. 454, 457, 77 L.Ed. 1011 (1933) (Cardozo, J.); *The Western Maid*, 257 U.S. 419, 433, 42 S.Ct. 159, 161, 66 L.Ed. 299 (1922) (Holmes, J.).

First. Our cases have long since rejected the notion that the Fourth Amendment proscribes only such conduct as would, if engaged in by private persons, be condemned by state law. Thus in *Gambino v. United States*, 275 U.S. 310, 48 S.Ct. 137, 72 L.Ed. 293 (1927), petitioners were convicted of conspiracy to violate the National Prohibition Act on the basis of evidence seized by state police officers incident to petitioners' arrest by those officers solely for the purpose of enforcing federal law. *Id.*, at 314, 48 S.Ct., at 137–138. Notwithstanding the lack of probable cause for the arrest, *id.*, at 313, 48 S.Ct., at 137, it would have been permissible under state law if effected by private individuals. It appears, moreover, that the officers were under direction from the Governor to aid in the enforcement of federal law. *Id.*, at

315–317, 48 S.Ct., at 138. Accordingly, if the Fourth Amendment reached only to conduct impermissible under the law of the State, the Amendment would have had no application to the case. Yet this Court held the Fourth Amendment applicable and reversed petitioners' convictions as having been based upon evidence obtained through an unconstitutional search and seizure. Similarly, in *Byars v. United States*, 273 U.S. 28, 47 S.Ct. 248, 71 L.Ed. 520 (1927), the petitioner was convicted on the basis of evidence seized under a warrant issued, without probable cause under the Fourth Amendment, by a state court judge for a state law offense. At the invitation of state law enforcement officers, a federal prohibition agent participated in the search. This Court explicitly refused to inquire whether the warrant was 'good under the state law * * * since in no event could it constitute the basis for a *federal* search and seizure.' *Id.*, at 29, 47 S.Ct., at 248 (emphasis added). And our recent decisions regarding electronic surveillance have made it clear beyond peradventure that the Fourth Amendment is not tied to the niceties of local trespass laws. *Katz v. United States*, 389 U.S. 347, 88 S.Ct. 507, 19 L.Ed.2d 576 (1967); *Berger v. New York*, 388 U.S. 41, 87 S.Ct. 1873, 18 L.Ed.2d 1040 (1967); *Silverman v. United States*, 365 U.S. 505, 511, 81 S.Ct. 679, 682–683, 5 L.Ed.2d 734 (1961). In light of these cases, respondents' argument that the Fourth Amendment serves only as a limitation on federal defenses to a state law claim, and not as an independent limitation upon the exercise of federal power, must be rejected.

Second. The interests protected by state laws regulating trespass and the invasion of privacy, and those protected by the Fourth Amendment's guarantee against unreasonable searches and seizures, may be inconsistent or even hostile. Thus, we may bar the door against an unwelcome private intruder, or call the police if he persists in seeking entrance. The availability of such alternative means for the protection of privacy may lead the State to restrict imposition of liability for any consequent trespass. A private citizen, asserting no authority other than his own, will not normally be liable in trespass if he demands, and is granted, admission to another's house. See W. Prosser, The Law of Torts § 18, pp. 109–110 (3d ed., 1964); 1 F. Harper & F. James, The Law of Torts § 1.11 (1956). But one who demands admission under a claim of federal authority stands in a far different position. Cf. *Amos v. United States*, 255 U.S. 313, 317, 41 S.Ct. 266, 267–268, 65 L.Ed. 654 (1921). The mere invocation of federal power by a federal law enforcement official will normally render futile any attempt to resist an unlawful entry or arrest by resort to the local police; and a claim of authority to enter is likely to unlock the door as well. See *Weeks v. United States*, 232 U.S. 383, 386, 34 S.Ct. 341, 342, 58 L.Ed. 652 (1914); *Amos v. United States, supra.* 'In such cases there is no safety for the citizen, except in the protection of the judicial tribunals, for rights which have been invaded by the officers of the government, professing to act in its name. There remains to him but the alternative of resistance, which may amount to crime.' *United States v. Lee*, 106 U.S. 196, 219, 1 S.Ct. 240, 259, 27 L.Ed. 171 (1882). Nor is it adequate to answer that state law may take into account the different status of one clothed with the authority of the Federal Government. For just as state law may not authorize federal agents to violate the Fourth Amendment, *Byars v. United States, supra*; *Weeks v. United States, supra*; *In re Ayers*, 123 U.S. 443, 507, 8 S.Ct. 164, 183–184, 31 L.Ed. 216 (1887), neither may state law undertake to limit the extent to which federal authority can be exercised. *In re Neagle*, 135 U.S. 1, 10 S.Ct. 658, 34 L.Ed. 55 (1890). The inevitable consequence of this dual limitation on state power is that the federal question becomes not merely a possible defense to the state law action, but an independent claim both necessary and sufficient to make out the plaintiff's cause of action. Cf. *International Brotherhood of Boilermakers, etc. v. Hardeman*, 401 U.S. 233, 241, 91 S.Ct. 609, 28 L. Ed.2d 10 (1971).

Third. That damages may be obtained for injuries consequent upon a violation of the Fourth Amendment by federal officials should hardly seem a surprising proposition. Historically, damages have been regarded as the ordinary remedy for an invasion of personal interests in liberty. See *Nixon v. Condon*, 286 U.S. 73, 52 S.Ct. 484, 76 L.Ed. 984 (1932); *Nixon v. Herndon*, 273 U.S. 536, 540, 47 S.Ct. 446, 71 L.Ed. 759 (1927); *Swafford v. Templeton*, 185 U.S. 487, 22 S.Ct. 783, 46 L.Ed. 1005 (1902); *Wiley v. Sinkler*, 179 U.S. 58, 21 S.Ct. 17, 45 L.Ed. 84 (1900); J. Landynski, Search and Seizure and the Supreme Court 28 et seq. (1966); N. Lasson, History and Development of the Fourth Amendment to the United States Constitution 43 et seq. (1937); Katz, *The Jurisprudence of Remedies: Constitutional Legality and the Law of Torts in Bell v. Hood*, 117 U.Pa.L.Rev. 1, 8-33 (1968); cf. *West v. Cabell*, 153 U.S. 78, 14 S.Ct. 752, 38 L.Ed. 643 (1894); *Lammon v. Feusier*, 111 U.S. 17, 4 S.Ct. 286, 28 L.Ed. 337 (1884). Of course, the Fourth Amendment does not in so many words provide for its enforcement by an award of money damages for the consequences of its violation. But 'it is * * * well settled that where legal rights have been invaded, and a federal statute provides for a general right to sue for such invasion, federal courts may use any available remedy to make good the wrong done.' *Bell v. Hood*, 327 U.S., at 684, 66 S.Ct., at 777 (footnote omitted.) The present case involves no special factors counseling hesitation in the absence of affirmative action by Congress. We are not dealing with a question of 'federal fiscal policy,' as in *United States v. Standard Oil Co.*, 332 U.S. 301, 311, 67 S.Ct. 1604, 1609–1610, 91 L.Ed. 2067 (1947). In that case we refused to infer from the Government-soldier relationship that the United States could recover damages from one who negligently injured a soldier and thereby caused the Government to pay his medical expenses and lose his services during the course of his hospitalization. Noting that Congress was normally quite solicitous where the federal purse was involved, we pointed out that 'the United States (was) the party plaintiff to the suit. And the United States has power at any time to create the liability.' *Id.*, at 316, 67 S.Ct., at 1612; see *United States v. Gilman*, 347 U.S. 507, 74 S.Ct. 695, 98 L.Ed. 898 (1954). Nor are we asked in this case to impose liability upon a congressional employee for actions contrary to no constitutional prohibition, but merely said to be in excess of the authority delegated to him by the Congress. *Wheeldin v. Wheeler*, 373 U.S. 647, 83 S.Ct. 1441, 10 L.Ed.2d 605 (1963). Finally, we cannot accept respondents' formulation of the question as whether the availability of money damages is necessary to enforce the Fourth Amendment. For we have here no explicit congressional declaration that persons injured by a federal officer's violation of the Fourth Amendment may not recover money damages from the agents, but must instead be remitted to another remedy, equally effective in the view of Congress. The question is merely whether petitioner, if he can demonstrate an injury consequent upon the violation by federal agents of his Fourth Amendment rights, is entitled to redress his injury through a particular remedial mechanism normally available in the federal courts. Cf. *J.I. Case Co. v. Borak*, 377 U.S. 426, 433, 84 S.Ct. 1555, 1560, 12 L.Ed.2d 423 (1964); *Jacobs v. United States*, 290 U.S. 13, 16, 54 S.Ct. 26, 27–28, 78 L.Ed. 142 (1933). 'The very essence of civil liberty certainly consists in the right of every individual to claim the protection of the laws, whenever he receives an injury.' *Marbury v. Madison*, 1 Cranch 137, 163, 2 L.Ed. 60 (1803). Having concluded that petitioner's complaint states a cause of action under the Fourth Amendment, *supra*, at 2001–2004, we hold that petitioner is entitled to recover money damages for any injuries he has suffered as a result of the agents' violation of the Amendment.

II

In addition to holding that petitioner's complaint had failed to state facts making out a cause of action, the District Court ruled that in any event respondents were immune from liability by virtue of their official position. 276 F.Supp., at 15. This question was not passed upon by the Court of Appeals, and accordingly we do not consider it here. The judgment of the Court of Appeals is reversed and the case is remanded for further proceedings consistent with this opinion.

So ordered.

Judgment reversed and case remanded.

Mr. Justice Harlan, concurring in the judgment.

My initial view of this case was that the Court of Appeals was correct in dismissing the complaint, but for reasons stated in this opinion I am now persuaded to the contrary. Accordingly, I join in the judgment of reversal.

Petitioner alleged, in his suit in the District Court for the Eastern District of New York, that the defendants, federal agents acting under color of federal law, subjected him to a search and seizure contravening the requirements of the Fourth Amendment. He sought damages in the amount of $15,000 from each of the agents. Federal jurisdiction was claimed, inter alia, under 28 U.S.C. § 1331(a) which provides:

> 'The district courts shall have original jurisdiction of all civil actions wherein the matter in controversy exceeds the sum or value of $10,000, exclusive of interest and costs, and arises under the Constitution, laws, or treaties of the United States.'

The District Court dismissed the complaint for lack of federal jurisdiction under 28 U.S.C. § 1331(a) and failure to state a claim for which relief may be granted. 276 F. Supp. 12 (EDNY 1967). On appeal, the Court of Appeals concluded, on the basis of this Court's decision in *Bell v. Hood*, 327 U.S. 678, 66 S.Ct. 773, 90 L.Ed. 939 (1946), that petitioner's claim for damages did '(arise) under the Constitution' within the meaning of 28 U.S.C. § 1331(a); but the District Court's judgment was affirmed on the ground that the complaint failed to state a claim for which relief can be granted. 409 F.2d 718 (CA2 1969).

In so concluding, Chief Judge Lumbard's opinion reasoned, in essence, that: (1) the framers of the Fourth Amendment did not appear to contemplate a 'wholly new federal cause of action founded directly on the Fourth Amendment,' *id.*, at 721, and (2) while the federal courts had power under a general grant of jurisdiction to imply a federal remedy for the enforcement of a constitutional right, they should do so only when the absence of alternative remedies renders the constitutional command a 'mere 'form of words.'" *Id.*, at 723. The Government takes essentially the same position here. Brief for Respondents 4–5. And two members of the Court add the contention that we lack the constitutional power to accord Bivens a remedy for damages in the absence of congressional action creating 'a federal cause of action for damages for an unreasonable search in violation of the Fourth Amendment.' Opinion of Mr. Justice Black, *post*, at 2020; see also opinion of The Chief Justice, *post*, at 2015, 2017.

For the reasons set forth below, I am of the opinion that federal courts do have the power to award damages for violation of 'constitutionally protected interests' and I agree with the Court that a traditional judicial remedy such as damages is appropriate to the vindication of the personal interests protected by the Fourth Amendment.

I

I turn first to the contention that the constitutional power of federal courts to accord Bivens damages for his claim depends on the passage of a statute creating a 'federal cause of action.' Although the point is not entirely free of ambiguity, I do not understand either the Government or my dissenting Brothers to maintain that Bivens' contention that he is entitled to be free from the type of official conduct prohibited by the Fourth Amendment depends on a decision by the State in which he resides to accord him a remedy. Such a position would be incompatible with the presumed availability of federal equitable relief, if a proper showing can be made in terms of the ordinary principles governing equitable remedies. See *Bell v. Hood*, 327 U.S. 678, 684, 66 S.Ct. 773, 776–777, 90 L.Ed. 939 (1946). However broad a federal court's discretion concerning equitable remedies, it is absolutely clear—at least after *Erie R. Co. v. Tompkins*, 304 U.S. 64, 58 S.Ct. 817, 82 L.Ed. 1188 (1938)—that in a nondiversity suit a federal court's power to grant even equitable relief depends on the presence of a substantive right derived from federal law. Compare *Guaranty Trust Co. v. York*, 326 U.S. 99, 105–107, 65 S.Ct. 1464, 1467–1469, 89 L.Ed. 2079 (1945). with *Holmberg v. Armbrecht*, 327 U.S. 392, 395, 66 S.Ct. 582, 584, 90 L.Ed. 743 (1946). See also H. Hart & H. Wechsler, The Federal Courts and the Federal System 818–819 (1953).

Thus the interest which Bivens claims—to be free from official conduct in contravention of the Fourth Amendment—is a federally protected interest. See generally Katz, *The Jurisprudence of Remedies: Constitutional Legality and the Law of Torts in* Bell v. Hood, 117 U.Pa.L.Rev. 1, 33–34 (1968). Therefore, the question of judicial power to grant Bivens damages is not a problem of the 'source' of the 'right'; instead, the question is whether the power to authorize damages as a judicial remedy for the vindication of a federal constitutional right is placed by the Constitution itself exclusively in Congress' hands.

II

The contention that the federal courts remedy in the absence of any express for a claimed invasion of his federal constitutional rights until Congress explicitly authorizes the remedy cannot rest on the notion that the decision to grant compensatory relief involves a resolution of policy considerations not susceptible of judicial discernment. Thus, in suits for damages based on violations of federal statutes lacking any express authorization of a damage remedy, this Court has authorized such relief where, in its view, damages are necessary to effectuate the congressional policy underpinning the substantive provisions of the statute. *J.I. Case Co. v. Borak*, 377 U.S. 426, 84 S.Ct. 1555, 12 L.Ed.2d 423 (1964); *Tunstall v. Brotherhood of Locomotive Firemen & Enginemen*, 323 U.S. 210, 213, 65 S.Ct. 235, 237, 89 L.Ed. 187 (1944). Cf. *Wyandotte Transportation Co. v. United States*, 389 U.S. 191, 201–204, 88 S.Ct. 379, 385–387, 19 L.Ed.2d 407 (1967).

If it is not the nature of the remedy which is thought to render a judgment as to the appropriateness of damages inherently 'legislative,' then it must be the nature of the legal interest offered as an occasion for invoking otherwise appropriate judicial relief. But I do not think that the fact that the interest is protected by the Constitution rather than statute or common law justifies the assertion that federal courts are powerless to grant damages in the absence of explicit congressional action authorizing the remedy. Initially, I note that it would be at least anomalous to conclude that the federal judiciary—while competent to choose among the range of traditional judicial remedies to implement statutory and common-law policies, and even to generate substantive rules governing primary behavior in furtherance of broadly formulated policies articulated by statute or Constitution, see *Textile Workers Union v. Lincoln Mills*, 353 U.S. 448, 77 S.Ct. 912, 923, 1 L.Ed.2d 972 (1957); *United States v. Standard Oil Co.*, 332 U.S. 301, 304–311, 67 S.Ct. 1604, 1606–1610, 91 L.Ed. 2067 (1947); *Clearfield Trust Co. v. United States*, 318 U.S. 363, 63 S.Ct. 573, 87 L.Ed. 838 (1943)—is powerless to accord a damages remedy to vindicate social policies which, by virtue of their inclusion in the Constitution, are aimed predominantly at restraining the Government as an instrument of the popular will.

More importantly, the presumed availability of federal equitable relief against threatened invasions of constitutional interests appears entirely to negate the contention that the status of an interest as constitutionally protected divests federal courts of the power to grant damages absent express congressional authorization. Congress provided specially for the exercise of equitable remedial powers by federal courts, see Act of May 8, 1792, §2, 1 Stat. 276; C. Wright, Law of Federal Courts

257 (2d ed., 1970), in part because of the limited availability of equitable remedies in state courts in the early days of the Republic. See *Guaranty Trust Co. v. York*, 326 U.S. 99, 104–105, 65 S.Ct. 1464, 1467–1468, 89 L.Ed. 2079 (1945). And this Court's decisions make clear that, at least absent congressional restrictions, the scope of equitable remedial discretion is to be determined according to the distinctive historical traditions of equity as an institution, *Holmberg v. Armbrecht*, 327 U.S. 392, 395–396, 66 S.Ct. 582, 584–585, 90 L.Ed. 743 (1946); *Sprague v. Ticonic National Bank*, 307 U.S. 161, 165–166, 59 S.Ct. 777, 779–780, 83 L.Ed. 1184 (1939). The reach of a federal district court's 'inherent equitable powers,' *Textile Workers Union v. Lincoln Mills*, 353 U.S. 448, 460, 77 S.Ct. 912, 919—920, 1 L.Ed.2d 972 (Burton, J., concurring in result), is broad indeed, e.g., *Swann v. Charlotte-Mecklenburg Board of Education*, 402 U.S. 1, 91 S.Ct. 1267, 28 L.Ed.2d 554 (1971); nonetheless, the federal judiciary is not empowered to grant equitable relief in the absence of congressional action extending jurisdiction over the subject matter of the suit. See *Textile Workers Union v. Lincoln Mills, supra*, 353 U.S., at 460, 77 S.Ct., at 919–920 (Burton, J., concurring in result); Katz, 117 U.Pa.L.Rev., at 43.

If explicit congressional authorization is an absolute prerequisite to the power of a federal court to accord compensatory relief regardless of the necessity or appropriateness of damages as a remedy simply because of the status of a legal interest as constitutionally protected, then it seems to me that explicit congressional authorization is similarly prerequisite to the exercise of equitable remedial discretion in favor of constitutionally protected interests. Conversely, if a general grant of jurisdiction to the federal courts by Congress is thought adequate to empower a federal court to grant equitable relief for all areas of subject-matter jurisdiction enumerated therein, see 28 U.S.C. § 1331(a), then it seems to me that the same statute is sufficient to empower a federal court to grant a traditional remedy at law. Of course, the special historical traditions governing the federal equity system, see *Sprague v. Ticonic National Bank*, 307 U.S. 161, 59 S.Ct. 777, 83 L.Ed. 1184 (1939), might still bear on the comparative appropriateness of granting equitable relief as opposed to money damages. That possibility, however, relates, not to whether the federal courts have the power to afford one type of remedy as opposed to the other, but rather to the criteria which should govern the exercise of our power. To that question, I now pass.

III

The major thrust of the Government's position is that, where Congress has not expressly authorized a particular remedy, a federal court should exercise its power to accord a traditional form of judicial relief at the behest of a litigant, who claims a constitutionally protected interest has been invaded, only where the remedy is 'essential,' or 'indispensable for vindicating constitutional rights.' Brief for Respondents 19, 24. While this 'essentially' test is most clearly articulated with respect to damage remedies, apparently the Government believes the same test explains the exercise of equitable remedial powers. *Id.*, at 17–18. It is argued that historically the Court has rarely exercised the power to accord such relief in the absence of an express congressional authorization and that '(i)f Congress had thought that federal officers should be subject to a law different than state law, it would have had no difficulty in saying so, as it did with respect to state officers * * *.' *Id.*, at 20–21; see 42 U.S.C. § 1983. Although conceding that the standard of determining whether a damage remedy should be utilized to effectuate statutory policies is one of 'necessity' or 'appropriateness,' see *J.I. Case Co. v. Borak*, 377 U.S. 426, 432, 84 S.Ct. 1555, 1559–1560, 12 L.Ed.2d 423 (1964); *United States v. Standard Oil Co.*, 332 U.S. 301, 307, 67 S.Ct. 1604 (1947), the Government contends that questions concerning congressional discretion to modify judicial remedies relating to constitutionally protected interests warrant a more stringent constraint on the exercise of judicial power with respect to this class of legally protected interests. Brief for Respondents at 21–22.

These arguments for a more stringent test to govern the grant of damages in constitutional cases seem to be adequately answered by the point that the judiciary has a particular responsibility to assure the vindication of constitutional interests such as those embraced by the Fourth Amendment. To be sure, 'it must be remembered that legislatures are ultimate guardians of the liberties and welfare of the people in quite as great a degree as the courts.' *Missouri, Kansas & Texas R. Co. of Texas v. May*, 194 U.S. 267, 270, 24 S.Ct. 638, 639, 48 L.Ed. 971 (1904). But it must also be recognized that the Bill of Rights is particularly intended to vindicate the interests of the individual in the face of the popular will as expressed in legislative majorities; at the very least, it strikes me as no more appropriate to await express congressional authorization of traditional judicial relief with regard to these legal interests than with respect to interests protected by federal statutes.

The question then, is, as I see it, whether compensatory relief is 'necessary' or 'appropriate' to the vindication of the interest asserted. Cf. *J.I. Case Co. v. Borak*, *supra*, 377 U.S., at 432, 84 S.Ct., at 1559–1560; *United States v. Standard Oil Co.*, *supra*, 332 U.S., at 307, 67 S.Ct., at 1607–1608; Hill, *Constitutional Remedies*, 69 Col.L.Rev. 1109, 1155 (1969); Katz, 117 U.Pa.L.Rev., at 72. In resolving that question, it seems to me that the range of policy considerations we may take into account is at least as broad as the range of a legislature would consider with respect to an express statutory authorization of a traditional remedy. In this regard I agree with the Court that the appropriateness of according Bivens compensatory relief does not turn simply on the deterrent effect liability will have on federal official conduct. Damages as a traditional form of compensation for invasion of a legally protected interest may be entirely appropriate even if no substantial deterrent effects on future official lawlessness might be thought to result. Bivens, after all, has invoked judicial processes claiming entitlement to compensation for injuries resulting from allegedly lawless official behavior, if those injuries are properly compensable in money damages. I do not think a court of law—vested with the power to accord a remedy—should deny him his relief simply because he cannot show that future lawless conduct will thereby be deterred.

And I think it is clear that Bivens advances a claim of the sort that, if proved, would be properly compensable in damages. The personal interests protected by the Fourth Amendment are those we attempt to capture by the notion of 'privacy'; while the Court today properly points out that the type of harm which officials can inflict when they invade protected zones of an individual's life are different from the types of harm private citizens inflict on one another, the experience of judges in dealing with private trespass and false imprisonment claims supports the conclusion that courts of law are capable of making the types of judgment concerning causation and magnitude of injury necessary to accord meaningful compensation for invasion of Fourth Amendment rights.

On the other hand, the limitations on state remedies for violation of common-law rights by private citizens argue in favor of a federal damages remedy. The injuries inflicted by officials acting under color of law, while no less compensable in damages than those inflicted by private parties, are substantially different in kind, as the Court's opinion today discusses in detail. See *Monroe v. Pape*, 365 U.S. 167, 195, 81 S.Ct. 473, 488, 5 L.Ed.2d 492 (1961) (Harlan, J., concurring). It seems to me entirely proper that these injuries be compensable according to uniform rules of federal law, especially in light of the very large element of federal law which must in any event control the scope of official defenses to liability. See *Wheeldin v. Wheeler*, 373 U.S. 647, 652, 83 S.Ct. 1441, 1445–1446, 10 L.Ed.2d 605 (1963); *Monroe v. Pape, supra*, 365 U.S., at 194–195, 81 S.Ct., at 487–488 (Harlan, J., concurring); *Howard v. Lyons*, 360 U.S. 593, 79 S.Ct. 1331, 3 L.Ed. 1454 (1959). Certainly, there is very little to be gained from the standpoint of federalism by preserving different rules of liability for federal officers dependent on the State where the injury occurs. Cf. *United States v. Standard Oil Co.*, 332 U.S. 301, 305–311, 67 S.Ct. 1604, 1606–1610, 91 L.Ed. 2067 (1947).

Putting aside the desirability of leaving the problem of federal official liability to the vagaries of common-law actions, it is apparent that some form of damages is the only possible remedy for someone in Bivens' alleged position. It will be a rare case indeed in which an individual in Bivens' position will be able to obviate the harm by securing injunctive relief from any court. However desirable a direct remedy against the Government might be as a substitute for individual official liability, the sovereign still remains immune to suit. Finally, assuming Bivens' innocence of the crime charged, the 'exclusionary rule' is simply irrelevant. For people in Bivens' shoes, it is damages or nothing.

The only substantial policy consideration advanced against recognition of a federal cause of action for violation of Fourth Amendment rights by federal officials is the incremental expenditure of judicial resources that will be necessitated by this class of litigation. There is, however, something ultimately self-defeating about this argument. For if, as the Government contends, damages will rarely be realized by plaintiffs in these cases because of jury hostility, the limited resources of the official concerned, etc., then I am not ready to assume that there will be a significant increase in the expenditure of judicial resources on these claims. Few responsible lawyers and plaintiffs are likely to choose the course of litigation if the statistical chances of success are truly de minimis. And I simply cannot agree with my Brother Black that the possibility of 'frivolous' claims — if defined simply as claims with no legal merit — warrants closing the courthouse doors to people in Bivens' situation. There are other ways, short of that, of coping with frivolous lawsuits.

On the other hand, if — as I believe is the case with respect, at least, to the most flagrant abuses of official power — damages to some degree will be available when the option of litigation is chosen, then the question appears to be how Fourth Amendment interests rank on a scale of social values compared with, for example, the interests of stockholders defrauded by misleading proxies. See *J.I. Case Co. v. Borak, supra.* Judicial resources, I am well aware, are increasingly scarce these days. Nonetheless, when we automatically close the courthouse door solely on this basis, we implicitly express a value judgment on the comparative importance of classes of legally protected interests. And current limitations upon the effective functioning of the courts arising from budgetary inadequacies should not be permitted to stand in the way of the recognition of otherwise sound constitutional principles.

Of course, for a variety of reasons, the remedy may not often be sought. See generally Foote, *Tort Remedies for Police Violations of Individual Rights*, 39 Minn.L.Rev. 493 (1955). And the countervailing interests in efficient law enforcement of course argue for a protective zone with respect to many types of Fourth Amendment violations. Cf. *Barr v. Matteo*, 360 U.S. 564, 79 S.Ct. 1335, 3 L.Ed.2d 1434 (1959) (opinion of Harlan, J.). But, while I express no view on the immunity defense offered in the instant case, I deem it proper to venture the thought that at the very least such a remedy would be available for the most flagrant and patently unjustified sorts of police conduct. Although litigants may not often choose to seek relief, it is important, in a civilized society, that the judicial branch of the Nation's government stand ready to afford a remedy in these circumstances. It goes without saying that I intimate no view on the merits of petitioner's underlying claim.

For these reasons, I concur in the judgment of the Court.

Note

Though promising, *Bivens* has been underused by the courts. Its import and application is thus limited. What types of claims might you foresee, in the near future, as potential expansion and solidification of the Bivens doctrine?

G. Color of State Law and State Action

In much of 1983 litigation, the initial issue often revolves around whether the defendants were in fact "state actors" or whether they were operating under the "color of state law." This is more and more an issue as more collaborations take place between private actors and local governments. As such, this begs the question: when do private actors become "state actors" for the purpose of Section 1983?

Lugar v. Edmonson Oil Co.

457 U.S. 922 (1982)

JUSTICE WHITE delivered the opinion of the Court.

The Fourteenth Amendment of the Constitution provides in part:

> "No State shall make or enforce any law which shall abridge the privileges
> or immunities of citizens of the United States; nor shall any State deprive
> any person of life, liberty, or property, without due process of law; nor deny
> to any person within its jurisdiction the equal protection of the laws."

Because the Amendment is directed at the States, it can be violated only by conduct
that may be fairly characterized as "state action."

Title 42 U.S.C. § 1983 provides a remedy for deprivations of rights secured by
the Constitution and laws of the United States when that deprivation takes place
"under color of any statute, ordinance, regulation, custom, or usage, of any State or
Territory. . . ." This case concerns the relationship between the § 1983 requirement
of action under color of state law and the Fourteenth Amendment requirement of
state action.

I

In 1977, petitioner, a lessee-operator of a truck stop in Virginia, was indebted to
his supplier, Edmondson Oil Co., Inc. Edmondson sued on the debt in Virginia state
court. Ancillary to that action and pursuant to state law, Edmondson sought prejudgment attachment of certain of petitioner's property. Va.Code § 8.01-533 (1977).
The prejudgment attachment procedure required only that Edmondson allege, in
an *ex parte* petition, a belief that petitioner was disposing of or might dispose of
his property in order to defeat his creditors. Acting upon that petition, a Clerk of
the state court issued a writ of attachment, which was then executed by the County
Sheriff. This effectively sequestered petitioner's property, although it was left in his
possession. Pursuant to the statute, a hearing on the propriety of the attachment
and levy was later conducted. Thirty-four days after the levy, a state trial judge
ordered the attachment dismissed because Edmondson had failed to establish the
statutory grounds for attachment alleged in the petition.

Petitioner subsequently brought this action under 42 U.S.C. § 1983 against
Edmondson and its president. His complaint alleged that in attaching his property
respondents had acted jointly with the State to deprive him of his property without
due process of law. The lower courts construed the complaint as alleging a due process violation both from a misuse of the Virginia procedure and from the statutory
procedure itself. He sought compensatory and punitive damages for specified financial loss allegedly caused by the improvident attachment.

Relying on *Flagg Brothers Inc. v. Brooks*, 436 U.S. 149, 98 S.Ct. 1729, 56 L.Ed.2d
185 (1978), the District Court held that the alleged actions of the respondents did
not constitute state action as required by the Fourteenth Amendment and that the

complaint therefore did not state a claim upon which relief could be granted under § 1983. Petitioner appealed; the Court of Appeals for the Fourth Circuit, sitting en banc, affirmed, with three dissenters. 639 F.2d 1058 (1981).

The Court of Appeals rejected the District Court's reliance on *Flagg Brothers* in finding that the requisite state action was missing in this case. The participation of state officers in executing the levy sufficiently distinguished this case from *Flagg Brothers.* The Court of Appeals stated the issue as follows:

> "[W]hether the mere institution by a private litigant of presumptively valid state judicial proceedings, without any prior or subsequent collusion or concerted action by that litigant with the state officials who then proceed with adjudicative, administrative, or executive enforcement of the proceedings, constitutes action under color of state law within contemplation of § 1983." 639 F.2d, at 1061–1062 (footnote omitted).

The court distinguished between the acts directly chargeable to respondents and the larger context within which those acts occurred, including the direct levy by state officials on petitioner's property. While the latter no doubt amounted to state action, the former was not so clearly action under color of state law. The court held that a private party acts under color of state law within the meaning of § 1983 only when there is a usurpation or corruption of official power by the private litigant or a surrender of judicial power to the private litigant in such a way that the independence of the enforcing officer has been compromised to a significant degree. Because the court thought none of these elements was present here, the complaint failed to allege conduct under color of state law.

Because this construction of the under-color-of-state-law requirement appears to be inconsistent with prior decisions of this Court, we granted certiorari. 452 U.S. 937, 101 S.Ct. 3078, 69 L.Ed.2d 951 (1981).

II

Although the Court of Appeals correctly perceived the importance of *Flagg Brothers* to a proper resolution of this case, it misread that case. It also failed to give sufficient weight to that line of cases, beginning with *Sniadach v. Family Finance Corp.*, 395 U.S. 337, 89 S.Ct. 1820, 23 L.Ed.2d 349 (1969), in which the Court considered constitutional due process requirements in the context of garnishment actions and prejudgment attachments. See *North Georgia Finishing, Inc. v. Di-Chem, Inc.*, 419 U.S. 601, 95 S.Ct. 719, 42 L.Ed.2d 751 (1975); *Mitchell v. W.T. Grant Co.*, 416 U.S. 600, 94 S.Ct. 1895, 40 L.Ed.2d 406 (1974); *Fuentes v. Shevin*, 407 U.S. 67, 92 S.Ct. 1983, 32 L.Ed.2d 556 (1972). Each of these cases involved a finding of state action as an implicit predicate of the application of due process standards. *Flagg Brothers* distinguished them on the ground that in each there was overt, official involvement in the property deprivation; there was no such overt action by a state officer in *Flagg Brothers.* 436 U.S., at 157, 98 S.Ct., at 1734. Although this case falls on the *Sniadach*, and not the *Flagg Brothers*, side of this distinction, the Court of Appeals thought the garnishment and attachment cases to be irrelevant because none but *Fuentes* arose under 42 U.S.C. § 1983 and because *Fuentes* was distinguishable. It determined that it could ignore all of them because the issue in this case was not whether there was state action, but rather whether respondents acted under color of state law.

As we see it, however, the two concepts cannot be so easily disentangled. Whether they are identical or not, the state-action and the under-color-of-state-law requirements are obviously related. Indeed, until recently this Court did not distinguish between the two requirements at all.

A

In *United States v. Price*, 383 U.S. 787, 794, n. 7, 86 S.Ct. 1152, 1157 n.7, 16 L.Ed.2d 267 (1966), we explicitly stated that the requirements were identical: "In cases under § 1983, 'under color' of law has consistently been treated as the same thing as the 'state action' required under the Fourteenth Amendment." In support of this proposition the Court cited *Smith v. Allwright*, 321 U.S. 649, 64 S.Ct. 757, 88 L.Ed. 987 (1944), and *Terry v. Adams*, 345 U.S. 461, 73 S.Ct. 809, 97 L.Ed. 1152 (1953). In both of these cases black voters in Texas challenged their exclusion from party primaries as a violation of the Fifteenth Amendment and sought relief under 8 U.S.C. § 43 (1946 ed.). In each case, the Court understood the problem before it to be whether the discriminatory policy of a private political association could be characterized as "state action within the meaning of the Fifteenth Amendment." *Smith, supra,* 321 U.S., at 664, 64 S.Ct., at 765. Having found state action under the Constitution, there was no further inquiry into whether the action of the political associations also met the statutory requirement of action "under color of state law."

Similarly, it is clear that in a § 1983 action brought against a state official, the statutory requirement of action "under color of state law" and the "state action" requirement of the Fourteenth Amendment are identical. The Court's conclusion in *United States v. Classic*, 313 U.S. 299, 326, 61 S.Ct. 1031, 1043, 85 L.Ed. 1368 (1941), that "[m]isuse of power, possessed by virtue of state law and made possible only because the wrongdoer is clothed with the authority of state law, is action taken 'under color of' state law," was founded on the rule announced in *Ex parte Virginia*, 100 U.S. 339, 346–347, 25 L.Ed. 676 (1880), that the actions of a state officer who exceeds the limits of his authority constitute state action for purposes of the Fourteenth Amendment.

The decision of the Court of Appeals rests on a misreading of *Flagg Brothers*. In that case the Court distinguished two elements of a § 1983 action:

> "[Plaintiffs] are first bound to show that they have been deprived of a right 'secured by the Constitution and the laws' of the United States. They must secondly show that *Flagg Brothers* deprived them of this right acting 'under color of any statute' of the State of New York. It is clear that these two elements denote two separate areas of inquiry. *Adickes v. S.H. Kress & Co.*, 398 U.S. 144, 150 [90 S.Ct. 1598, 1604, 26 L.Ed.2d 142] (1970)." 436 U.S., at 155–156, 98 S.Ct., at 1732–1733.

Plaintiffs' case foundered on the first requirement. Because a due process violation was alleged and because the Due Process Clause protects individuals only from governmental and not from private action, plaintiffs had to demonstrate that the sale of their goods was accomplished by state action. The Court concluded that the sale, although authorized by state law, did not amount to state action under the Fourteenth Amendment, and therefore set aside the Court of Appeals' contrary judgment.

There was no reason in *Flagg Brothers* to address the question whether there was action under color of state law. The Court expressly eschewed deciding whether that requirement was satisfied by private action authorized by state law. *Id.*, at 156, 98 S. Ct., at 1733. Although the state-action and under-color-of-state-law requirements are "separate areas of inquiry," *Flagg Brothers* did not hold nor suggest that state action, if present, might not satisfy the § 1983 requirement of conduct under color of state law. Nevertheless, the Court of Appeals relied on *Flagg Brothers* to conclude in this case that state action under the Fourteenth Amendment is not necessarily action under color of state law for purposes of § 1983. We do not agree.

The two-part approach to a § 1983 cause of action, referred to in *Flagg Brothers*, was derived from *Adickes v. S.H. Kress & Co.*, 398 U.S. 144, 150, 90 S.Ct. 1598, 1604, 26 L.Ed.2d 142 (1970). *Adickes* was a § 1983 action brought against a private party, based on a claim of racial discrimination in violation of the Equal Protection Clause of the Fourteenth Amendment. Although stating that the § 1983 plaintiff must show both that he has been deprived "of a right secured by the 'Constitution and laws' of the United States" and that the defendant acted "under color of any statute . . . of any State," *ibid.*, we held that the private party's joint participation with a state official in a conspiracy to discriminate would constitute both "state action essential to show a direct violation of petitioner's Fourteenth Amendment equal protection rights" and action "'under color' of law for purposes of the statute." *Id.*, at 152, 90 S.Ct., at 1606. In support of our conclusion that a private party held to have violated the Fourteenth Amendment "can be liable under § 1983," *ibid.*, we cited that part of *United States v. Price*, 383 U.S., at 794, n. 7, 86 S.Ct., at 1157, n. 7, in which we had concluded that state action and action under color of state law are the same (quoted above). *Adickes* provides no support for the Court of Appeals' novel construction of § 1983.

B

The decision of the Court of Appeals is difficult to reconcile with the Court's garnishment and prejudgment attachment cases and with the congressional purpose in enacting § 1983.

Beginning with *Sniadach v. Family Finance Corp.*, 395 U.S. 337, 89 S.Ct. 1820, 23 L.Ed.2d 349 (1969), the Court has consistently held that constitutional requirements of due process apply to garnishment and prejudgment attachment procedures whenever officers of the State act jointly with a creditor in securing the property in dispute. *Sniadach* and *North Georgia Finishing, Inc. v. Di-Chem, Inc.*, 419 U.S. 601, 95 S.Ct. 719, 42 L.Ed.2d 751 (1975), involved state-created garnishment procedures; *Mitchell v. W.T. Grant Co.*, 416 U.S. 600, 94 S.Ct. 1895, 40 L.Ed.2d 406 (1974), involved execution of a vendor's lien to secure disputed property. In each of these cases state agents aided the creditor in securing the disputed property; but in each case the federal issue arose in litigation between creditor and debtor in the state courts and no state official was named as a party. Nevertheless, in each case the Court entertained and adjudicated the defendant-debtor's claim that the procedure under which the private creditor secured the disputed property violated federal constitutional standards of due process. Necessary to that conclusion is the holding that private use of the challenged state procedures with the help of state officials constitutes state action for purposes of the Fourteenth Amendment.

Fuentes v. Shevin, 407 U.S. 67, 92 S.Ct. 1983, 32 L.Ed.2d 556 (1972), was a § 1983 action brought against both a private creditor and the State Attorney General. The plaintiff sought declaratory and injunctive relief, on due process grounds, from continued enforcement of state statutes authorizing prejudgment replevin. The plaintiff prevailed; if the Court of Appeals were correct in this case, there would have been no § 1983 cause of action against the private parties. Yet they remained parties, and judgment ran against them in this Court.

If a defendant debtor in state-court debt collection proceedings can successfully challenge, on federal due process grounds, the plaintiff creditor's resort to the procedures authorized by a state statute, it is difficult to understand why that same behavior by the state-court plaintiff should not provide a cause of action under § 1983. If the creditor-plaintiff violates the debtor-defendant's due process rights by seizing his property in accordance with statutory procedures, there is little or no reason to deny to the latter a cause of action under the federal statute, § 1983, designed to provide judicial redress for just such constitutional violations.

To read the "under color of any statute" language of the Act in such a way as to impose a limit on those Fourteenth Amendment violations that may be redressed by the § 1983 cause of action would be wholly inconsistent with the purpose of § 1 of the Civil Rights Act of 1871, 17 Stat. 13, from which § 1983 is derived. The Act was passed "for the express purpose of 'enforce[ing] the Provisions of the Fourteenth Amendment.'" *Lynch v. Household Finance Corp.*, 405 U.S. 538, 545, 92 S.Ct. 1113, 1118, 31 L.Ed.2d 424 (1972). The history of the Act is replete with statements indicating that Congress thought it was creating a remedy as broad as the protection that the Fourteenth Amendment affords the individual. Perhaps the most direct statement of this was that of Senator Edmunds, the manager of the bill in the Senate: "[Section 1 is] so very simple and really reenact[s] the Constitution." Cong. Globe, 42d Cong., 1st Sess., 569 (1871). Representative Bingham similarly stated that the bill's purpose was "the enforcement . . . of the Constitution on behalf of every individual citizen of the Republic . . . to the extent of the rights guaranteed to him by the Constitution." *Id.*, App. 81.

In sum, the line drawn by the Court of Appeals is inconsistent with our prior cases and would substantially undercut the congressional purpose in providing the

§ 1983 cause of action. If the challenged conduct of respondents constitutes state action as delimited by our prior decisions, then that conduct was also action under color of state law and will support a suit under § 1983.

III

As a matter of substantive constitutional law the state-action requirement reflects judicial recognition of the fact that "most rights secured by the Constitution are protected only against infringement by governments," *Flagg Brothers*, 436 U.S., at 156, 98 S.Ct., at 1733. As the Court said in *Jackson v. Metropolitan Edison Co.*, 419 U.S. 345, 349, 95 S.Ct. 449, 453, 42 L.Ed.2d 477 (1974):

> "In 1883, this Court in the *Civil Rights Cases*, 109 U.S. 3 [3 S.Ct. 18, 27 L. Ed. 835], affirmed the essential dichotomy set forth in [the Fourteenth] Amendment between deprivation by the State, subject to scrutiny under its provisions, and private conduct, 'however discriminatory or wrongful,' against which the Fourteenth Amendment offers no shield."

Careful adherence to the "state action" requirement preserves an area of individual freedom by limiting the reach of federal law and federal judicial power. It also avoids imposing on the State, its agencies or officials, responsibility for conduct for which they cannot fairly be blamed. A major consequence is to require the courts to respect the limits of their own power as directed against state governments and private interests. Whether this is good or bad policy, it is a fundamental fact of our political order.

Our cases have accordingly insisted that the conduct allegedly causing the deprivation of a federal right be fairly attributable to the State. These cases reflect a two-part approach to this question of "fair attribution." First, the deprivation must be caused by the exercise of some right or privilege created by the State or by a rule of conduct imposed by the state or by a person for whom the State is responsible. In *Sniadach, Fuentes, W.T. Grant*, and *North Georgia*, for example, a state statute provided the right to garnish or to obtain prejudgment attachment, as well as the procedure by which the rights could be exercised. Second, the party charged with the deprivation must be a person who may fairly be said to be a state actor. This may be because he is a state official, because he has acted together with or has obtained significant aid from state officials, or because his conduct is otherwise chargeable to the State. Without a limit such as this, private parties could face constitutional litigation whenever they seek to rely on some state rule governing their interactions with the community surrounding them.

Although related, these two principles are not the same. They collapse into each other when the claim of a constitutional deprivation is directed against a party whose official character is such as to lend the weight of the State to his decisions. See *Monroe v. Pape*, 365 U.S. 167, 172, 81 S.Ct. 473, 476, 5 L.Ed.2d 492 (1961). The two principles diverge when the constitutional claim is directed against a party without such apparent authority, *i.e.*, against a private party. The difference between the two inquiries is well illustrated by comparing *Moose Lodge No. 107 v. Irvis*, 407 U.S. 163, 92 S.Ct. 1965, 32 L.Ed.2d 627 (1972), with *Flagg Brothers, supra.*

In *Moose Lodge*, the Court held that the discriminatory practices of the appellant did not violate the Equal Protection Clause because those practices did not constitute "state action." The Court focused primarily on the question of whether the admittedly discriminatory policy could in any way be ascribed to a governmental decision. The inquiry, therefore, looked to those policies adopted by the State that were applied to appellant. The Court concluded as follows:

> "We therefore hold, that with the exception hereafter noted, the operation of the regulatory scheme enforced by the Pennsylvania Liquor Control Board does not sufficiently implicate the State in the discriminatory guest policies of Moose Lodge to . . . make the latter 'state action' within the ambit of the Equal Protection Clause of the Fourteenth Amendment." 407 U.S., at 177, 92 S.Ct., at 1973.

In other words, the decision to discriminate could not be ascribed to any governmental decision; those governmental decisions that did affect Moose Lodge were unconnected with its discriminatory policies.

Flagg Brothers focused on the other component of the state-action principle. In that case, the warehouseman proceeded under New York Uniform Commercial Code, § 7-210, and the debtor challenged the constitutionality of that provision on the grounds that it violated the Due Process and Equal Protection Clauses of the Fourteenth Amendment. Undoubtedly the State was responsible for the statute. The response of the Court, however, focused not on the terms of the statute but on the character of the defendant to the § 1983 suit: Action by a private party pursuant to this statute, without something more, was not sufficient to justify a characterization of that party as a "state actor." The Court suggested that that "something more" which would convert the private party into a state actor might vary with the circumstances of the case. This was simply a recognition that the Court has articulated a number of different factors or tests in different contexts: *e.g.,* the "public function" test, see *Terry v. Adams*, 345 U.S. 461, 73 S.Ct. 809, 97 L.Ed. 1152 (1953); *Marsh v. Alabama*, 326 U.S. 501, 66 S.Ct. 276, 90 L.Ed. 265 (1946); the "state compulsion" test, see *Adickes v. S.H. Kress & Co.*, 398 U.S. at 170, 90 S.Ct. at 1615; the "nexus" test, see *Jackson v. Metropolitan Edison Co.*, 419 U.S. 345, 95 S.Ct. 449, 42 L.Ed.2d 477 (1974); *Burton v. Wilmington Parking Authority*, 365 U.S. 715, 81 S.Ct. 856, 6 L. Ed.2d 45 (1961); and in the case of prejudgment attachments, a "joint action test," *Flagg Brothers*, 436 U.S., at 157, 98 S.Ct., at 1734. Whether these different tests are actually different in operation or simply different ways of characterizing the necessarily fact-bound inquiry that confronts the Court in such a situation need not be resolved here. See *Burton, supra*, 365 U.S., at 722, 81 S.Ct., at 860 ("Only by sifting facts and weighing circumstances can the nonobvious involvement of the State in private conduct be attributed its true significance").

IV

Turning to this case, the first question is whether the claimed deprivation has resulted from the exercise of a right or privilege having its source in state authority. The second question is whether, under the facts of this case, respondents, who are private parties, may be appropriately characterized as "state actors."

Both the District Court and the Court of Appeals noted the ambiguous scope of petitioner's contentions: "There has been considerable confusion throughout the litigation on the question whether Lugar's ultimate claim of unconstitutional deprivation was directed at the Virginia statute itself or only at its erroneous application to him." 639 F.2d, at 1060, n. 1. Both courts held that resolution of this ambiguity was not necessary to their disposition of the case: both resolved it, in any case, in favor of the view that petitioner was attacking the constitutionality of the statute as well as its misapplication. In our view, resolution of this issue is essential to the proper disposition of the case.

Petitioner presented three counts in his complaint. Count three was a pendent claim based on state tort law; counts one and two claimed violations of the Due Process Clause. Count two alleged that the deprivation of property resulted from respondents' "malicious, wanton, willful, oppressive [sic], [and] unlawful acts." By "unlawful," petitioner apparently meant "unlawful under state law." To say this, however, is to say that the conduct of which petitioner complained could not be ascribed to any governmental decision; rather, respondents were acting contrary to the relevant policy articulated by the State. Nor did they have the authority of state officials to put the weight of the State behind their private decision, *i.e.*, this case does not fall within the abuse of authority doctrine recognized in *Monroe v. Pape,* 365 U.S. 167, 81 S.Ct. 473, 5 L.Ed.2d 492 (1961). That respondents invoked the statute without the grounds to do so could in no way be attributed to a state rule or a state decision. Count two, therefore, does not state a cause of action under § 1983 but challenges only private action.

Count one is a different matter. That count describes the procedures followed by respondents in obtaining the prejudgment attachment as well as the fact that the state court subsequently ordered the attachment dismissed because respondents had not met their burden under state law. Petitioner then summarily states that this sequence of events deprived him of his property without due process. Although it is not clear whether petitioner is referring to the state-created procedure or the misuse of that procedure by respondents, we agree with the lower courts that the better reading of the complaint is that petitioner challenges the state statute as procedurally defective under the Fourteenth Amendment.

While private misuse of a state statute does not describe conduct that can be attributed to the State, the procedural scheme created by the statute obviously is the product of state action. This is subject to constitutional restraints and properly may be addressed in a § 1983 action, if the second element of the state-action requirement is met as well.

As is clear from the discussion in Part II, we have consistently held that a private party's joint participation with state officials in the seizure of disputed property is sufficient to characterize that party as a "state actor" for purposes of the Fourteenth Amendment. The rule in these cases is the same as that articulated in *Adickes v. S.H. Kress & Co., supra*, 398 U.S., at 152, 90 S.Ct., at 1605–1606, in the context of an equal protection deprivation:

> "'Private persons, jointly engaged with state officials in the prohibited action, are acting "under color" of law for purposes of the statute. To act "under color" of law does not require that the accused be an officer of the State. It is enough that he is a willful participant in joint activity with the State or its agents,'" quoting *United States v. Price*, 383 U.S., at 794, 86 S.Ct., at 1157.

The Court of Appeals erred in holding that in this context "joint participation" required something more than invoking the aid of state officials to take advantage of state-created attachment procedures. That holding is contrary to the conclusions we have reached as to the applicability of due process standards to such procedures. Whatever may be true in other contexts, this is sufficient when the State has created a system whereby state officials will attach property on the *ex parte* application of one party to a private dispute.

In summary, petitioner was deprived of his property through state action; respondents were, therefore, acting under color of state law in participating in that deprivation. Petitioner did present a valid cause of action under § 1983 insofar as he challenged the constitutionality of the Virginia statute; he did not insofar as he alleged only misuse or abuse of the statute.

The judgment is reversed in part and affirmed in part, and the case is remanded for further proceedings consistent with this opinion.

So ordered.

H. Examples of Remedies under 42 U.S.C. § 1983

The cases below document the trend toward restricting damage awards. For example, damages based on the abstract "value" or "importance" of a constitutional right are not a permissible element of compensatory damages in an action under the Civil Rights Act of 1871.

Memphis Community School District v. Stachura

477 U.S. 299 (1986)

JUSTICE POWELL delivered the opinion of the Court.

This case requires us to decide whether 42 U.S.C. § 1983 authorizes an award of compensatory damages based on the factfinder's assessment of the value or importance of a substantive constitutional right.

I

Respondent Edward Stachura is a tenured teacher in the Memphis, Michigan, public schools. When the events that led to this case occurred, respondent taught seventh-grade life science, using a textbook that had been approved by the School Board. The textbook included a chapter on human reproduction. During the 1978–1979 school year, respondent spent six weeks on this chapter. As part of their instruction, students were shown pictures of respondent's wife during her pregnancy. Respondent also showed the students two films concerning human growth and sexuality. These films were provided by the County Health Department, and the Principal of respondent's school had approved their use. Both films had been shown in past school years without incident.

After the showing of the pictures and the films, a number of parents complained to school officials about respondent's teaching methods. These complaints, which appear to have been based largely on inaccurate rumors about the allegedly sexually explicit nature of the pictures and films, were discussed at an open School Board meeting held on April 23, 1979. Following the advice of the School Superintendent, respondent did not attend the meeting, during which a number of parents expressed the view that respondent should not be allowed to teach in the Memphis school system. The day after the meeting, respondent was suspended with pay. The School Board later confirmed the suspension, and notified respondent that an "administration evaluation" of his teaching methods was underway. No such evaluation was ever made. Respondent was reinstated the next fall, after filing this lawsuit.

Respondent sued the School District, the Board of Education, various Board members and school administrators, and two parents who had participated in the April 23 School Board meeting. The complaint alleged that respondent's suspension deprived him of both liberty and property without due process of law and violated his First Amendment right to academic freedom. Respondent sought compensatory and punitive damages under 42 U.S.C. § 1983 for these constitutional violations.

At the close of trial on these claims, the District Court instructed the jury as to the law governing the asserted bases for liability. Turning to damages, the court instructed the jury that on finding liability it should award a sufficient amount to compensate respondent for the injury caused by petitioners' unlawful actions:

> "You should consider in this regard any lost earnings; loss of earning capacity; out-of-pocket expenses; and any mental anguish or emotional distress that you find the Plaintiff to have suffered as a result of conduct by the Defendants depriving him of his civil rights." App. 94.

In addition to this instruction on the standard elements of compensatory damages, the court explained that punitive damages could be awarded, and described the standards governing punitive awards. Finally, at respondent's request and over petitioners' objection, the court charged that damages also could be awarded based on the value or importance of the constitutional rights that were violated:

"If you find that the Plaintiff has been deprived of a Constitutional right, you may award damages to compensate him for the deprivation. Damages for this type of injury are more difficult to measure than damages for a physical injury or injury to one's property. There are no medical bills or other expenses by which you can judge how much compensation is appropriate. In one sense, no monetary value we place upon Constitutional rights can measure their importance in our society or compensate a citizen adequately for their deprivation. However, just because these rights are not capable of precise evaluation does not mean that an appropriate monetary amount should not be awarded.

"The precise value you place upon any Constitutional right which you find was denied to Plaintiff is within your discretion. You may wish to consider the importance of the right in our system of government, the role which this right has played in the history of our republic, [and] the significance of the right in the context of the activities which the Plaintiff was engaged in at the time of the violation of the right." *Id.,* at 96.

The jury found petitioners liable, and awarded a total of $275,000 in compensatory damages and $46,000 in punitive damages. The District Court entered judgment notwithstanding the verdict as to one of the defendants, reducing the total award to $266,750 in compensatory damages and $36,000 in punitive damages.

In an opinion devoted primarily to liability issues, the Court of Appeals for the Sixth Circuit affirmed, holding that respondent's suspension had violated both procedural due process and the First Amendment. *Stachura v. Truszkowski,* 763 F.2d 211 (1985). Responding to petitioners' contention that the District Court improperly authorized damages based solely on the value of constitutional rights, the court noted only that "there was ample proof of actual injury to plaintiff Stachura both in his effective discharge . . . and by the damage to his reputation and to his professional career as a teacher. Contrary to the situation in *Carey v. Piphus,* 435 U.S. 247, 98 S.Ct. 1042, 55 L.Ed.2d 252 (1978) . . . , there was proof from which the jury could have found, as it did, actual and important damages." *Id.,* at 214.

We granted certiorari limited to the question whether the Court of Appeals erred in affirming the damages award in the light of the District Court's instructions that authorized not only compensatory and punitive damages, but also damages for the deprivation of "any constitutional right." 474 U.S. 918, 106 S.Ct. 245, 88 L.Ed.2d 254 (1985). We reverse, and remand for a new trial limited to the issue of compensatory damages.

II

Petitioners challenge the jury instructions authorizing damages for violation of constitutional rights on the ground that those instructions permitted the jury to award damages based on its own unguided estimation of the value of such rights. Respondent disagrees with this characterization of the jury instructions, contending that the compensatory damages instructions taken as a whole focused solely on respondent's injury and not on the abstract value of the rights he asserted.

We believe petitioners more accurately characterize the instructions. The damages instructions were divided into three distinct segments: (i) compensatory damages for harm to respondent, (ii) punitive damages, and (iii) additional "compensat[ory]" damages for violations of constitutional rights. No sensible juror could read the third of these segments to modify the first. On the contrary, the damages instructions plainly authorized — in addition to punitive damages — two distinct types of "compensatory" damages: one based on respondent's actual injury according to ordinary tort law standards, and another based on the "value" of certain rights. We therefore consider whether the latter category of damages was properly before the jury.

III

A

We have repeatedly noted that 42 U.S.C. § 1983 creates "'a species of tort liability' in favor of persons who are deprived of 'rights, privileges, or immunities secured' to them by the Constitution." *Carey v. Piphus,* 435 U.S. 247, 253, 98 S.Ct. 1042, 1047, 55 L.Ed.2d 252 (1978), quoting *Imbler v. Pachtman,* 424 U.S. 409, 417, 96 S.Ct. 984, 988, 47 L.Ed.2d 128 (1976). See also *Smith v. Wade,* 461 U.S. 30, 34, 103 S.Ct. 1625, 1628, 75 L.Ed.2d 632 (1983); *Newport v. Fact Concerts, Inc.,* 453 U.S. 247, 258–259, 101 S.Ct. 2748, 2755–2756, 69 L.Ed.2d 616 (1981). Accordingly, when § 1983 plaintiffs seek damages for violations of constitutional rights, the level of damages is ordinarily determined according to principles derived from the common law of torts. See *Smith v. Wade, supra,* 461 U.S., at 34, 103 S.Ct., at 1628; *Carey v. Piphus, supra,* 435 U.S., at 257–258, 98 S.Ct., at 1048–1049; cf. *Monroe v. Pape,* 365 U.S. 167, 196, and n. 5, 81 S.Ct. 473, 488, and n. 5, 5 L.Ed.2d 492 (1961) (Harlan, J., concurring).

Punitive damages aside, damages in tort cases are designed to provide "*compensation* for the injury caused to plaintiff by defendant's breach of duty." 2 F. Harper, F. James, & O. Gray, Law of Torts § 25.1, p. 490 (2d ed. 1986) (emphasis in original), quoted in *Carey v. Piphus, supra,* 435 U.S., at 255, 98 S.Ct., at 1047. See also *Bivens v. Six Unknown Federal Narcotics Agents,* 403 U.S. 388, 395, 397, 91 S.Ct. 1999, 2004, 2005, 29 L.Ed.2d 619 (1971); *id.,* at 408–409, 91 S.Ct., at 2010–2011 (Harlan, J., concurring in judgment). To that end, compensatory damages may include not only out-of-pocket loss and other monetary harms, but also such injuries as "impairment of reputation . . . , personal humiliation, and mental anguish and suffering." *Gertz v. Robert Welch, Inc.,* 418 U.S. 323, 350, 94 S.Ct. 2997, 3012, 41 L.Ed.2d 789 (1974). See also *Carey v. Piphus, supra,* 435 U.S., at 264, 98 S.Ct., at 1052 (mental and emotional distress constitute compensable injury in § 1983 cases). Deterrence is also an important purpose of this system, but it operates through the mechanism of damages that are *compensatory* — damages grounded in determinations of plaintiffs' actual losses. *E.g.,* 4 Harper, James, & Gray *supra,* at § 25.3 (discussing need for certainty in damages determinations); D. Dobbs, Law of Remedies § 3.1, pp. 135–136 (1973). Congress adopted this common-law system of recovery when it established liability for "constitutional torts." Consequently, "the basic purpose" of § 1983 damages is "to *compensate persons for injuries* that are caused by the deprivation of constitutional rights." *Carey v. Piphus*, 435 U.S., at 254, 98 S.Ct., at 1047 (emphasis added). See also *id.,* at 257, 98 S.Ct., at 1049 ("damages awards under § 1983 should be governed by the principle of compensation").

Carey v. Piphus represents a straightforward application of these principles. *Carey* involved a suit by a high school student suspended for smoking marijuana; the student claimed that he was denied procedural due process because he was suspended without an opportunity to respond to the charges against him. The Court of Appeals for the Seventh Circuit held that even if the suspension was justified, the student could recover substantial compensatory damages simply because of the insufficient procedures used to suspend him from school. We reversed, and held that the student could recover compensatory damages only if he proved actual injury caused by the denial of his constitutional rights. *Id.,* at 264, 98 S.Ct., at 1052. We noted: "Rights, constitutional and otherwise, do not exist in a vacuum. Their purpose is to protect persons from injuries to particular interests. . . ." *Id.,* at 254, 98 S.Ct., at 1047. Where no injury was present, no "compensatory" damages could be awarded.

The instructions at issue here cannot be squared with *Carey,* or with the principles of tort damages on which *Carey* and § 1983 are grounded. The jurors in this case were told that, in determining how much was necessary to "compensate [respondent] for the deprivation" of his constitutional rights, they should place a money value on the "rights" themselves by considering such factors as the particular right's "importance . . . in our system of government," its role in American history, and its "significance . . . in the context of the activities" in which respondent was engaged. App. 96. These factors focus, not on compensation for provable injury, but on the jury's subjective perception of the importance of constitutional rights as an abstract matter. *Carey* establishes that such an approach is impermissible. The constitutional right transgressed in *Carey*—the right to due process of law—is central to our system of ordered liberty. See *In re Gault,* 387 U.S. 1, 20–21, 87 S.Ct. 1428, 1439–1440, 18 L.Ed.2d 527 (1967). We nevertheless held that *no* compensatory damages could be awarded for violation of that right absent proof of actual injury. *Carey,* 435 U.S., at 264, 98 S.Ct., at 1052. *Carey* thus makes clear that the abstract value of a constitutional right may not form the basis for § 1983 damages.

Respondent nevertheless argues that *Carey* does not control here, because in this case a *substantive* constitutional right—respondent's First Amendment right to academic freedom—was infringed. The argument misperceives our analysis in *Carey.* That case does not establish a two-tiered system of constitutional rights, with substantive rights afforded greater protection than "mere" procedural safeguards. We did acknowledge in *Carey* that "the elements and prerequisites for recovery of damages" might vary depending on the interests protected by the constitutional right at issue. *Id.,* at 264–265, 98 S.Ct., at 1053. But we emphasized that, whatever the constitutional basis for § 1983 liability, such damages must always be designed "to *compensate injuries* caused by the [constitutional] deprivation." *Id.,* at 265, 98 S.Ct., at 1053 (emphasis added). See also *Hobson v. Wilson,* 237 U.S.App.D.C. 219, 277–279, 737 F.2d 1, 59–61 (1984), cert. denied, 470 U.S. 1084, 105 S.Ct. 1843, 85 L.Ed.2d 142 (1985); cf. *Smith v. Wade,* 461 U.S. 30, 103 S.Ct. 1625, 75 L.Ed.2d 632 (1983). That conclusion simply leaves no room for non-compensatory damages measured by the jury's perception of the abstract "importance" of a constitutional right.

Nor do we find such damages necessary to vindicate the constitutional rights that § 1983 protects. See n. 11, *supra.* 42 U.S.C. § 1983 presupposes that damages that compensate for actual harm ordinarily suffice to deter constitutional violations. *Carey, supra,* 435 U.S., at 256–257, 98 S.Ct., at 1043 ("To the extent that Congress intended that awards under § 1983 should deter the deprivation of constitutional rights, there is no evidence that it meant to establish a deterrent more formidable than that inherent in the award of compensatory damages"). Moreover, damages based on the "value" of constitutional rights are an unwieldy tool for ensuring compliance with the Constitution. History and tradition do not afford any sound guidance concerning the precise value that juries should place on constitutional protections. Accordingly, were such damages available, juries would be free to award arbitrary amounts without any evidentiary basis, or to use their unbounded discretion to punish unpopular defendants. Cf. *Gertz,* 418 U.S., at 350, 94 S.Ct., at 3012. Such damages would be too uncertain to be of any great value to plaintiffs, and would inject caprice into determinations of damages in § 1983 cases. We therefore hold that damages based on the abstract "value" or "importance" of constitutional rights are not a permissible element of compensatory damages in such cases.

B

Respondent further argues that the challenged instructions authorized a form of "presumed" damages—a remedy that is both compensatory in nature and traditionally part of the range of tort law remedies. Alternatively, respondent argues that the erroneous instructions were at worst harmless error.

Neither argument has merit. Presumed damages are a *substitute* for ordinary compensatory damages, not a *supplement* for an award that fully compensates the alleged injury. When a plaintiff seeks compensation for an injury that is likely to have occurred but difficult to establish, some form of presumed damages may possibly be appropriate. See *Carey,* 435 U.S., at 262, 98 S.Ct., at 1051; cf. *Dun & Bradstreet, Inc. v. Greenmoss Builders,* 472 U.S. 749, 760–761, 105 S.Ct. 2939, 2946, 86 L. Ed.2d 593 (1985) (opinion of Powell, J.); *Gertz v. Robert Welch, Inc., supra,* 418 U.S., at 349, 94 S.Ct., at 3011. In those circumstances, presumed damages may roughly approximate the harm that the plaintiff suffered and thereby compensate for harms that may be impossible to measure. As we earlier explained, the instructions at issue in this case did not serve this purpose, but instead called on the jury to measure damages based on a subjective evaluation of the importance of particular constitutional values. Since such damages are wholly divorced from any compensatory purpose, they cannot be justified as presumed damages. Moreover, no rough substitute

for compensatory damages was required in this case, since the jury was fully authorized to compensate respondent for both monetary and nonmonetary harms caused
by petitioners' conduct.

Nor can we find that the erroneous instructions were harmless. See 28 U.S.C.
§ 2111; *McDonough Power Equipment, Inc. v. Greenwood,* 464 U.S. 548, 104 S.Ct.
845, 78 L.Ed.2d 663 (1984). When damages instructions are faulty and the verdict
does not reveal the means by which the jury calculated damages, "[the] error in the
charge is difficult, if not impossible, to correct without retrial, in light of the jury's
general verdict." *Newport v. Fact Concerts, Inc.,* 453 U.S., at 256, n. 12, 101 S.Ct., at
2754, n. 12. The jury was authorized to award three categories of damages: (i) compensatory damages for injury to respondent, (ii) punitive damages, and (iii) damages based on the jury's perception of the "importance" of two provisions of the
Constitution. The submission of the third of these categories was error. Although
the verdict specified an amount for punitive damages, it did not specify how much
of the remaining damages was designed to compensate respondent for his injury
and how much reflected the jury's estimation of the value of the constitutional rights
that were infringed. The effect of the erroneous instruction is therefore unknowable, although probably significant: the jury awarded respondent a very substantial
amount of damages, none of which could have derived from any monetary loss.
It is likely, although not certain, that a major part of these damages was intended
to "compensate" respondent for the abstract "value" of his due process and First
Amendment rights. For these reasons, the case must be remanded for a new trial on
compensatory damages.

IV

The judgment of the Court of Appeals is reversed, and the case is remanded for
further proceedings consistent with this opinion.

It is so ordered.

Note

Based on the preceding cases, consider the following mock hypo and complaint
in preparation for a suit against police officers for unlawful conduct in violation
of Section 1983. In what ways do the cases discussed above help support the standards and facts argued in the mock complaint? What might you change or add to
strengthen the claim?

STATEMENT OF FACTS

On August 1, 2015 at 7:30 p.m. Rashad Williams was returning home from a
political event at the University of Mississippi when he was pulled over by an officer
of the Oxford Police Department. This was part of a series of random and periodic
checkpoints, begun in the last few years by the Police in Oxford. Once approached
by the officer, Rashad asked the reason for the stop. He was told by Officer Jerkins
that he was being pulled over for making an illegal uturn. Rashad disagreed with
Officer Jerkins, explaining to the officer that the u-turn was legal and that he did

nothing wrong. At the time of the traffic stop, Rashad was on the phone with his brother Ken who heard everything. Officer Jerkins became increasingly annoyed and told Rashad to get out of his car. When Rashad got out of the car, his brother Ken could still hear Rashad asking for the reasoning of this added step. Rashad, then, announced to the officer that he was about to show him that he was harmless and was simply coming from a university event. At that time, Ken heard Officer Jerkins say, "Get your hands out of your pockets and put them up." Rashad replied, "I am only . . .", but Ken heard shots before he could finish the sentence.

Upon investigation, Ken found out that his brother had been shot three times, twice in the chest and once to the head. Rashad died immediately on the scene. Devastated, Ken and his family began a movement to demand answers from the police regarding his brother's death.

Ken is now filing a wrongful death suit in hopes of holding the City of Oxford and Officer Jerkins accountable in civil court.

COUNT ONE
Violation of Fourth Amendment: Unreasonable Use of Force

The plaintiff incorporates the foregoing paragraphs by reference.

Plaintiffs allege that defendant, Officer Jerkins, deprived decedent of his Fourth Amendment rights by using excessive, deadly force, the nature of which was far beyond that necessary to accomplish the interest at stake: i.e., policing a minor traffic violation.

Plaintiffs concede that, given the existence of a no u-turn sign at the site of the incident, Officer Jerkins had probable cause for stopping Rashad's vehicle. Beyond this, however, Rashad's compliance with the officer's demands and lack of aggression gave the officer no probable cause to escalate to violence.

The defendant's use of force was objectively unreasonable.

The force used was unreasonable even had circumstances existed justifying an arrest.

Rashad did not pose any threat to the defendant. No facts support the use of deadly force.

The defendant officer's unreasonable use of force violated the decedent's Fourth Amendment right to be free from illegal seizures.

COUNT TWO
Violation of Fourteenth Amendment: Deprivation of Life & Due Process

The plaintiff incorporates the foregoing paragraphs by reference.

The defendant officer's choice to use deadly force against decedent did not serve a legitimate governmental objective.

The choice to shoot an unarmed man without any probable cause is shocking to the conscience.

The use of deadly force was brutal and offensive. The defendant officer's unreasonable use of force violated the plaintiff's Fourteenth Amendment rights to due process.

As a proximate results of the defendants' acts and omissions, decedent was caused to suffer injuries resulting in death.

COUNT THREE
Policy and Custom of Discrimination

The Oxford Police Department has a widespread pattern, practice, and custom of police discrimination.

The defendant municipality knew about the widespread practice and custom of police discrimination but failed to stop it.

This policy of discrimination included the institution of "random" checkpoints disproportionately placed in locations known to be inhabited primarily by residents of color.

The Oxford Police Department also disproportionately stops students of color at random without probable cause on weekend nights to check for ID.

The defendant municipality's failure to act constituted deliberate indifference.

COUNT FOUR
Police Officer Individual Liability Under 42 U.S.C. § 1983

The plaintiff incorporates the foregoing paragraphs by reference.

Plaintiff brings a claim against Officer Jerkins, individually as well as in his official capacity, pursuant to 42 U.S.C. § 1983 and for punitive damages.

At all material times, Officer Jerkins was acting under color of state law as an agent and employee of Defendant, the City of Oxford ("City"). Defendant Officer Jerkins was wearing his official Oxford Police Department uniform, and was acting in the course and scope of his duties as an Oxford Police Officer at the time he shot and killed Rashad Williams.

For the reasons outlined in the Plaintiff's general allegations and under Count One, Plaintiffs assert that Officer Jerkins' use of force was excessive, and in violation of the Fourth Amendment, subjecting him to individual liability.

Officer Jerkins did not have a reasonable fear of imminent bodily harm when he shot and killed Rashad nor did Officer Jerkins have a reasonable belief that any other person was in danger of imminent bodily harm from Rashad.

Consequently, shooting and killing Rashad was unwarranted under these circumstances, and was objectively unreasonable when comparing or balancing the amount of force used against the need for the force.

Therefore, by using subjectively and objectively unreasonable deadly force while acting under the color of state law, Officer Jerkins violated Decedent's rights under the Fourth Amendment and caused his wrongful death.

COUNT FIVE
Municipal Liability Under 42 U.S.C. § 1983

The plaintiff incorporates the foregoing paragraphs by reference.

Plaintiff brings a claim against the City of Oxford pursuant to 42 U.S.C. § 1983 for illegal pattern and practice of discrimination, negligent training of officers, and deliberate indifference to the constitutional rights of those seized by law enforcement.

The City of Oxford Police Department's widespread constitutional abuses have flourished as a result of and are directly and proximately caused by policies, customs, and practices implemented and enforced by the City.

For the past few years, City of Oxford Police Department has methodically implemented random checkpoints in communities that are widely known to consist primarily of residents of color.

Defendants have implemented and are continuing to enforce, encourage and sanction a policy, practice and/or custom of unconstitutional assault, and excessive use of force against city residents, including plaintiff, by their police department without justification, or probable cause.

Additionally, the Oxford Police Department has disproportionately stopped and checked students of color for identification on weekend nights.

I. Section 1985

A long-neglected statute, Section 1985 provides protection for claims of conspiracy to commit racial discrimination or violence. This is one of the few statutes that allows causes of actions and protections against conspiratorial acts of private individuals. However, other than a few for exceptions, Section 1985 has remained dormant for the last few decades. One of those exceptions is the extension of the Emmett Till Unsolved Civil Rights Crime Act of 2007. Nonetheless, organizations and non profits dedicated to restorative justice are committing their resources to resolving cold cases involving conspiracies among private individuals with the tacit approval of governmental officials. Note the Court's specification that a conspiracy is actionable because it deprives the plaintiffs of the rights protected by the Thirteenth Amendment and of the right to travel guaranteed by the federal Constitution. Section 1985 "can and does protect plaintiffs from purely private conspiracies." As such, it is not constrained by the Fourteenth Amendment. (http://news.northeastern.edu/2017/01/05/bringing-justice-and-closure-in-civil-rights-cold-cases/).

Griffin v. Breckenridge

403 U.S. 88 (1971)

Mr. Justice Stewart delivered the opinion of the Court.

This litigation began when the petitioners filed a complaint in the United States District Court for the Southern District of Mississippi, seeking compensatory and punitive damages and alleging, in substantial part, as follows:

'The plaintiffs are Negro citizens of the United States and residents of Kemper County, Mississippi. * * *

'The defendants, Lavon Breckenridge and James Calvin Breckenridge, are white adult citizens of the United States residing in DeKalb, Kemper County, Mississippi.

'On July 2, 1966, the * * * plaintiffs * * * were passengers in an automobile belonging to and operated by R.G. Grady of Memphis, Tennessee. They were travelling upon the federal, state and local highways in and about DeKalb, Mississippi, performing various errands and visiting friends.

'On July 2, 1966 defendants, acting under a mistaken belief that R.G. Grady was a worker for Civil Rights for Negroes, wilfully and maliciously conspired, planned, and agreed to block the passage of said plaintiffs in said automobile upon the public highways, to stop and detain them and to assault, beat and injure them with deadly weapons. Their purpose was to prevent said plaintiffs and other Negro-Americans, through such force, violence and intimidation, from seeking the equal protection of the laws and from enjoying the equal rights, privileges and immunities of citizens under the laws of the United States and the State of Mississippi, including but not limited to their rights to freedom of speech, movement, association and assembly; their right to petition their government for redress of their grievances; their rights to be secure in their persons and their homes; and their rights not to be enslaved nor deprived of life and liberty other than by due process of law.

'Pursuant to their conspiracy, defendants drove their truck into the path of Grady's automobile and blocked its passage over the public road. Both defendants then forced Grady and said plaintiffs to get out of Grady's automobile and prevented said plaintiffs from escaping while defendant James Calvin Breckenridge clubbed Grady with a blackjack, pipe or other kind of club by pointing firearms at said plaintiffs and uttering threats to kill and injure them if defendants' orders were not obeyed, thereby terrorizing them to the utmost degree and depriving them of their liberty.

'Pursuant to their conspiracy, defendants wilfully, intentionally, and maliciously menaced and assaulted each of the said plaintiffs by pointing firearms and wielding deadly blackjacks, pipes or other kind of clubs, while uttering threats to kill and injure said plaintiffs, causing them to become stricken with fear of immediate injury and death and to suffer extreme terror, mental anguish, and emotional and physical distress.

'Pursuant to defendants' conspiracy, defendant James Calvin Breckenridge then wilfully, intentionally and maliciously clubbed each of said plaintiffs on and about the head, severely injuring all of them, while both defendants continued to assault said plaintiffs and prevent their escape by pointing their firearms at them.

. . . .

'By their conspiracy and acts pursuant thereto, the defendants have wilfully and maliciously, directly and indirectly, intimidated and prevented the * * * plaintiffs * * * and other Negro-Americans from enjoying and exercising their rights, privileges and immunities as citizens of the United States and the State of Mississippi, including but not limited to, their rights to freedom of speech, movement, association and assembly; the right to petition their government for redress of grievances; their right to be secure in their person; their right not to be enslaved nor deprived of life, liberty or property other than by due process of law, and their rights to travel the public highways without restraint in the same terms as white citizens in Kemper County, Mississippi * * *.'

The jurisdiction of the federal court was invoked under the language of Rev.Stat. § 1980, 42 U.S.C. § 1985(3), which that provides:

'If two or more persons in any State or Territory conspire or go in disguise on the highway or on the premises of another, for the purpose of depriving either directly or indirectly, any person or class of persons of the equal protection of the laws or of equal privileges and immunities under the laws (and) in any case of conspiracy set forth in this section, if one or more persons engaged therein do, or cause to be done, any act in furtherance of the object of such conspiracy, whereby another is injured in his person or property, or deprived of having and exercising any right or privilege of a citizen of the United States, the party so injured or deprived may have an action for the recovery of damages, occasioned by such injury or deprivation, against any one or more of the conspirators.'

The District Court dismissed the complaint for failure to state a cause of action, relying on the authority of this Court's opinion in *Collins v. Hardyman*, 341 U.S. 651, 71 S.Ct. 937, 95 L.Ed. 1253, which in effect construed the above language of § 1985(3) as reaching only conspiracies under color of state law. The Court of Appeals for the Fifth Circuit affirmed the judgment of dismissal. 410 F.2d 817. Judge Goldberg's thorough opinion for that court expressed 'serious doubts' as to the 'continued vitality' of *Collins v. Hardyman, id.*, at 823, and stated that 'it would not surprise us if *Collins v. Hardyman* were disapproved and if § 1985(3) were held to embrace private conspiracies to interfere with rights of national citizenship,' *id.*, at 825–826 (footnote omitted), but concluded that '(s)ince we may not adopt what the Supreme Court has expressly rejected, we obediently abide the mandate in *Collins,' id.*, at

826–827. We granted certiorari, 397 U.S. 1074, 90 S.Ct. 1525, 25 L.Ed.2d 808, to consider questions going to the scope and constitutionality of 42 U.S.C. § 1985(3).

I

Collins v. Hardyman was decided 20 years ago. The complaint in that case alleged that the plaintiffs were members of a political club that had scheduled a meeting to adopt a resolution opposing the Marshall Plan, and to send copies of the resolution to appropriate federal officials; that the defendants conspired to deprive the plaintiffs of their rights as citizens of the United States peaceably to assemble and to equal privileges and immunities under the laws of the United States; that, in furtherance of the conspiracy, the defendants proceeded to the meeting site and, by threats and violence, broke up the meeting, thus interfering with the right of the plaintiffs to petition the Government for the redress of grievances; and that the defendants did not interfere or conspire to interfere with the meetings of other political groups with whose opinions the defendants agreed. The Court held that this complaint did not state a cause of action under § 1985(3):

> 'The complaint makes no claim that the conspiracy or the overt acts involved any action by state officials, or that defendants even pretended to act under color of state law. It is not shown that defendants had or claimed any protection or immunity from the law of the State or that they in fact enjoyed such because of any act or omission by state authorities.' 341 U.S., at 655, 71 S.Ct., at 939.

> 'What we have here is not a conspiracy to affect in any way these plaintiffs' equality of protection by the law, or their equality of privileges and immunities under the law. There is not the slightest allegation that defendants were conscious of or trying to influence the law, or were endeavoring to obstruct or interfere with it. * * * Such private discrimination is not inequality before the law unless there is some manipulation of the law or its agencies to give sanction or sanctuary for doing so.' *Id.*, at 661, 71 S.Ct., at 942.

The Court was careful to make clear that it was deciding no constitutional question, but simply construing the language of the statute, or more precisely, determining the applicability of the statute to the facts alleged in the complaint:

> 'We say nothing of the power of Congress to authorize such civil actions as respondents have commenced or otherwise to redress such grievances as they assert. We think that Congress has not, in the narrow class of conspiracies defined by this statute, included the conspiracy charged here. We therefore reach no constitutional questions.' *Id.*, at 662, 71 S.Ct., at 942.

Nonetheless, the Court made equally clear that the construction it gave to the statute was influenced by the constitutional problems that it thought would have otherwise been engendered:

'It is apparent that, if this complaint meets the requirements of this Act, it raises constitutional problems of the first magnitude that, in the light of history, are not without difficulty. These would include issues as to congressional power under and apart from the Fourteenth Amendment, the reserved power of the States, the content of rights derived from national as distinguished from state citizenship, and the question of separability of the Act in its application to those two classes of rights.' *Id.*, at 659, 71 S.Ct., at 940.

Mr. Justice Burton filed a dissenting opinion, joined by Mr. Justice Black and Mr. Justice Douglas. The dissenters thought that '(t)he language of the statute refutes the suggestion that action under color of state law is a necessary ingredient of the cause of action which it recognizes.' *Id.*, at 663, 71 S.Ct., at 942. Further the dissenters found no constitutional difficulty in according to the statutory words their apparent meaning:

'Congress certainly has the power to create a federal cause of action in favor of persons injured by private individuals through the abridgment of federally created constitutional rights. It seems to me that Congress has done just this in (§ 1985(3)). This is not inconsistent with the principle underlying the Fourteenth Amendment. That amendment prohibits the respective states from making laws abridging the privileges or immunities of citizens of the United States or denying to any person within the jurisdiction of a state the equal protection of the laws. Cases holding that those clauses are directed only at state action are not authority for the contention that Congress may not pass laws supporting rights which exist apart from the Fourteenth Amendment.' *Id.*, at 664, 71 S.Ct., at 943.

II

Whether or not *Collins v. Hardyman* was correctly decided on its own facts is a question with which we need not here be concerned. But it is clear, in the light of the evolution of decisional law in the years that have passed since that case was decided, that many of the constitutional problems there perceived simply do not exist. Little reason remains, therefore, not to accord to the words of the statute their apparent meaning. That meaning is confirmed by judicial construction of related laws, by the structural setting of § 1995(3) itself, and by its legislative history. And a fair reading of the allegations of the complaint in this case clearly brings them within this meaning of the statutory language. As so construed, and as applied to this complaint, we have no doubt that the statute was within the constitutional power of Congress to enact.

III

We turn, then, to an examination of the meaning of § 1985(3). On their face, the words of the statute fully encompass the conduct of private persons. The provision speaks simply of 'two or more persons in any State or Territory' who 'conspire or go in disguise on the highway or on the premises of another.' Going in disguise, in particular, is in this context an activity so little associated with official action and so commonly connected with private marauders that this clause could almost never be applicable under the artificially restrictive construction of Collins. And since the 'going in disguise' aspect must include private action, it is hard to see how the conspiracy aspect, joined by a disjunctive, could be read to require the involvement of state officers.

The provision continues, specifying the motivation required 'for the purpose of depriving, either directly or indirectly, any person or class of persons of the equal protection of the laws, or of equal privileges and immunities under the laws.' This language is, of course, similar to that of § 1 of the Fourteenth Amendment, which in terms speaks only to the States, and judicial thinking about what can constitute an equal protection deprivation has, because of the Amendment's wording, focused almost entirely upon identifying the requisite 'state action' and defining the offending forms of state law and official conduct. A century of Fourteenth Amendment adjudication has, in other words, made it understandably difficult to conceive of what might constitute a deprivation of the equal protection of the laws by private persons. Yet there is nothing inherent in the phrase that requires the action working the deprivation to come from the State. See, e.g., *United States v. Harris*, 106 U.S. 629, 643, 1 S.Ct. 601, 612, 27 L.Ed. 290. Indeed, the failure to mention any such requisite can be viewed as an important indication of congressional intent to speak in § 1985(3) of all deprivations of 'equal protection of the laws' and 'equal privileges and immunities under the laws,' whatever their source.

The approach of this Court to other Reconstruction civil rights statutes in the years since *Collins* has been to 'accord (them) a sweep as broad as (their) language.' *United States v. Price*, 383 U.S. 787, 801, 86 S.Ct. 1152, 1160, 16 L.Ed.2d 267; *Jones v. Alfred H. Mayer Co.*, 392 U.S. 409, 437, 88 S.Ct. 2186, 2202, 20 L.Ed.2d 1189. Moreover, very similar language in closely related statutes has early and late received an interpretation quite inconsistent with that given to § 1985(3) in *Collins*. In construing the exact criminal counterpart of § 1985(3), the Court in *United States v. Harris, supra*, observed that the statute was 'not limited to take effect only in case (of state action),' *id.*, at 639, 1 S.Ct., at 609, but 'was framed to protect from invasion by private persons the equal privileges and immunities under the laws of all persons and classes of persons,' *id.*, at 637, 1 S.Ct., at 607. In *United States v. Williams*, 341 U.S. 70, 71 S.Ct. 581, 95 L.Ed. 758, the Court considered the closest remaining criminal analogue to § 1985(3), 18 U.S.C. § 241. Mr. Justice Frankfurter's plurality opinion, without contravention from the concurrence or dissent, concluded that 'if language is to carry any meaning at all it must be clear that the principal purpose of (§ 241), unlike (18 U.S.C. § 242), was to reach private action rather than officers of a State acting under its authority. Men who 'go in disguise upon the public highway, or upon the premises of another' are not likely to be acting in official capacities.' 341 U.S., at 76, 71 S.Ct., at 584. 'Nothing in (the) terms (of § 241) indicates that color of State law was to be relevant to prosecution under it.' Id., at 78, 71 S.Ct., at 585 (footnote omitted).

A like construction of § 1985(3) is reinforced when examination is broadened to take in its companion statutory provisions. There appear to be three possible forms for a state action limitation on § 1985(3) — that there must be action under color of state law, that there must be interference with or influence upon state authorities, or that there must be a private conspiracy so massive and effective that it supplants those authorities and thus satisfies the state action requirement. The Congress that passed the Civil Rights Act of 1871, 17 Stat. 13, § 2 of which is the parent of § 1985(3), dealt with each of these three situations in explicit terms in other parts of the same Act. An element of the cause of action established by the first section, now 42 U.S.C. § 1983, is that the deprivation complained of must have been inflicted under color of state law. To read any such requirement into § 1985(3) would thus deprive that section of all independent effect. As for interference with State officials, § 1985(3) itself contains another clause dealing explicitly with that situation. And § 3 of the 1871 Act provided for military action at the command of the President should massive private lawlessness render state authorities powerless to protect the federal rights of classes of citizens, such a situation being defined by the Act as constituting a state denial of equal protection. 17 Stat. 14. Given the existence of these three provisions, it is almost impossible to believe that Congress intended, in the dissimilar language of the portion of § 1985(3) now before us, simply to duplicate the coverage of one or more of them.

The final area of inquiry into the meaning of § 1985(2) lies in its legislative history. As originally introduced in the 42d Congress, the section was solely a criminal provision outlawing certain conspiratorial acts done with intent 'to do any act in violation of the rights, privileges, or immunities of another person * * *.' Cong. Globe, 42d Cong., 1st Sess., App. 68 (1871). Introducing the bill, the House sponsor, Representative Shellabarger stressed that 'the United States always has assumed to enforce, as against the States, *and also persons*, every one of the provisions of the Constitution.' *Id.*, at App. 69 (emphasis supplied). The enormous sweep of the original language led to pressures for amendment, in the course of which the present civil remedy was added. The explanations of the added language centered entirely on the animus or motivation that would be required, and there was no suggestion whatever that liability would not be imposed for purely private conspiracies. Representative Willard, draftsman of the limiting amendment, said that his version 'provid(ed) that the essence of the crime should consist in the intent to deprive a person of the equal protection of the laws and of equal privileges and immunities under the laws; in other words, that the Constitution secured, and was only intended to secure, equality of rights and immunities, and that we could only punish by United States laws a denial of that equality.' *Id.*, at App. 188. Representative Shellabarger's explanation of the amendment was very similar: 'The object of the amendment is * * * to confine the authority of this law to the prevention of deprivations which shall attack the equality of rights of American citizens; that any violation of the right, the animus and effect of which is to strike down the citizen, to the end that he may not enjoy equality of rights as contrasted with his and other citizens' rights, shall be within the scope of the remedies of this section.' *Id.*, at 478.

Other supporters of the bill were even more explicit in their insistence upon coverage of private action. Shortly before the amendment was introduced, Representative Shanks urged, 'I do not want to see (this measure) so amended that there shall be taken out of it the frank assertion of the power of the national Government to protect life, liberty, and property, irrespective of the act of the State. *Id.*, at App. 141. At about the same time, Representative Coburn asked: 'Shall we deal with individuals, or with the State as a State? If we can deal with individuals, that is a less radical course, and works less interference with local governments. * * * It would seem more accordant with reason that the easier, more direct, and more certain method of dealing with individual criminals was preferable, and that the more thorough method of superseding State authority should only be resorted to when the deprivation of rights and the condition of outlawry was so general as to prevail in all quarters in defiance of or by permission of the local government.' *Id.*, at 459. After the amendment had been proposed in the House, Senator Pool insisted in support of the bill during Senate debate that 'Congress must deal with individuals, not States. It must punish the offender against the rights of the citizen * * *.' *Id.*, at 608.

It is thus evident that all indicators—text, companion provisions, and legislative history—point unwaveringly to § 1985(3)'s coverage of private conspiracies. That the statute was meant to reach private action does not, however, mean that it was intended to apply to all tortious, conspiratorial interferences with the rights of others. For, though the supporters of the legislation insisted on coverage of private conspiracies, they were equally emphatic that they did not believe, in the words of Representative Cook, 'that Congress has a right to punish an assault and battery when committed by two or more persons within a State.' *Id.*, at 485. The constitutional shoals that would lie in the path of interpreting § 1985(3) as a general federal tort law can be avoided by giving full effect to the congressional purpose—by requiring, as an element of the cause of action, the kind of invidiously discriminatory motivation stressed by the sponsors of the limiting amendment. See the remarks of Representatives Willard and Shellabarger, quoted supra, at 1797. The language requiring intent to deprive of equal protection, or equal privileges and immunities, means that there must be some racial, or perhaps otherwise class-based, invidiously discriminatory animus behind the conspirators' action. The conspiracy, in other words, must aim at a deprivation of the equal enjoyment of rights secured by the law to all.

IV

We return to the petitioners' complaint to determine whether it states a cause of action under § 1985(3) as so construed. To come within the legislation a complaint must allege that the defendants did (1) 'conspire or go in disguise on the highway or on the premises of another' (2) 'for the purpose of depriving, either directly or indirectly, any person or class of persons of the equal protection of the laws, or of equal privileges and immunities under the laws.' It must then assert that one or more of the conspirators (3) did, or caused to be done, 'any act in furtherance of the object of (the) conspiracy,' whereby another was (4a) 'injured in his person or property' or (4b) 'deprived of having and exercising any right or privilege of a citizen of the United States.'

The complaint fully alleges, with particulars, that the respondents conspired to carry out the assault. It further asserts that '(t)heir purpose was to prevent (the) plaintiffs and other Negro-Americans, through * * * force, violence and intimidation, from seeking the equal protection of the laws and from enjoying the equal rights, privileges and immunities of citizens under the laws of the United States and the State of Mississippi,' including a long list of enumerated rights such as free speech, assembly, association, and movement. The complaint further alleges that the respondents were 'acting under a mistaken belief that R.G. Grady was a worker for Civil Rights for Negroes.' These allegations clearly support the requisite animus to deprive the petitioners of the equal enjoyment of legal rights because of their race. The claims of detention, threats, and battery amply satisfy the requirement of acts done in furtherance of the conspiracy. Finally, the petitioners—whether or not the nonparty Grady was the main or only target of the conspiracy—allege personal injury resulting from those acts. The complaint, then, states a cause of action under § 1985(3). Indeed, the conduct here alleged lies so close to the core of the coverage intended by Congress that it is hard to conceive of wholly private conduct that would come within the statute if this does not. We must, accordingly, consider whether Congress had constitutional power to enact a statute that imposes liability under federal law for the conduct alleged in this complaint.

V

The constitutionality of § 1985(3) might once have appeared to have been settled adversely by *United States v. Harris*, 106 U.S. 629, 1 S.Ct. 601, 27 L.Ed. 290, and *Baldwin v. Franks*, 120 U.S. 678, 7 S.Ct. 656, 32 L.Ed. 766, which held unconstitutional its criminal counterpart, then § 5519 of the Revised Statutes. The Court in those cases, however, followed a severability rule that required invalidation of an entire statute if any part of it was unconstitutionally overbroad, unless its different parts could be read as wholly independent provisions, E.g., *Baldwin v. Franks, supra*, at 685, 7 S.Ct., at 658. This Court has long since firmly rejected that rule in such cases as *United States v. Raines*, 362 U.S. 17, 20–24, 80 S.Ct. 519, 522–524, 4 L.Ed.2d 524. Consequently, we need not find the language of § 1985(3) now before us constitutional in all its possible applications in order to uphold its facial constitutionality and its application to the complaint in this case.

That § 1985(3) reaches private conspiracies to deprive others of legal rights can, of itself, cause no doubts of its constitutionality. It has long been settled that 18 U.S.C. s 241, a criminal statute of far broader phrasing, reaches wholly private conspiracies and is constitutional. E.g., *In re Quarles*, 158 U.S. 532, 15 S.Ct. 959, 39 L.

Ed. 1080; *Logan v. United States*, 144 U.S. 263, 293–295, 12 S.Ct. 617, 626–627, 36 L. Ed. 429; *United States v. Waddell*, 112 U.S. 76, 77–81, 5 S.Ct. 35, 36–38, 28 L.Ed. 673; *Ex parte Yarbrough*, 110 U.S. 651, 4 S.Ct. 152, 28 L.Ed. 274. See generally *Twining v. New Jersey*, 211 U.S. 78, 97–98, 29 S.Ct. 14, 18–20, 53 L.Ed. 97. Our inquiry, therefore, need go only to identifying a source of congressional power to reach the private conspiracy alleged by the complaint in this case.

A

Even as it struck down Rev.Stat. §5519 in *United States v. Harris*, the Court indicated that parts of its coverage would, if severable, be constitutional under the Thirteenth Amendment. 106 U.S., at 640–641, 1 S.Ct., at 610–611. And surely there has never been any doubt of the power of Congress to impose liability on private persons under §2 of that amendment, 'for the amendment is not a mere prohibition of state laws establishing or upholding slavery, but an absolute declaration that slavery or involuntary servitude shall not exist in any part of the United States.' *Civil Rights Cases*, 109 U.S. 3, 20, 3 S.Ct. 18, 28, 27 L.Ed. 835. See also *id.*, at 23, 3 S. Ct., at 30; *Clyatt v. United States*, 197 U.S. 207, 216, 218, 25 S.Ct. 429, 430, 431, 49 L. Ed. 726; *Jones v. Alfred H. Mayer Co.*, 392 U.S., at 437–440, 88 S.Ct., at 2202–2204, 20 L.Ed.2d 1189. Not only may Congress impose such liability, but the varieties of private conduct that it may make criminally punishable or civilly remediable extend far beyond the actual imposition of slavery or involuntary servitude. By the Thirteenth Amendment, we committed ourselves as a Nation to the proposition that the former slaves and their descendants should be forever free. To keep that promise, 'Congress has the power under the Thirteenth Amendment rationally to determine what are the badges and the incidents of slavery, and the authority to translate that determination into effective legislation.' *Jones v. Alfred H. Mayer Co., supra*, at 440, 88 S.Ct., at 2203. We can only conclude that Congress was wholly within its powers under §2 of the Thirteenth Amendment in creating a statutory cause of action for Negro citizens who have been the victims of conspiratorial, racially discriminatory private action aimed at depriving them of the basic rights that the law secures to all free men.

B

Our cases have firmly established that the right of interstate travel is constitutionally protected, does not necessarily rest on the Fourteenth Amendment, and is assertable against private as well as governmental interference. *Shapiro v. Thompson*, 394 U.S. 618, 629–631, 89 S.Ct. 1322, 1328–1330, 22 L.Ed.2d 600; id., at 642–644, 89 S.Ct., at 1335–1336 (concurring opinion); *United States v. Guest*, 383 U.S. 745, 757–760 and n. 17, 86 S.Ct. 1170, 1177–1180, 16 L.Ed.2d 239; *Twining v. New Jersey*, 211 U.S. 78, 97, 29 S.Ct. 14, 18, 53 L.Ed. 97; *Slaughter-House Cases*, 16 Wall. 36, 79–80, 21 L.Ed. 394; *Crandall v. Nevada*, 6 Wall. 35, 44, 48–49, 18 L.Ed. 744; *Passenger Cases (Smith v. Turner)*, 7 How. 283, 492, 12 L.Ed. 702 (Taney, C.J., dissenting). The 'right to pass freely from state to state' has been explicitly recognized as 'among the rights and privileges of national citizenship.' *Twining v. New Jersey, supra*, 211

U.S., at 97, 29 S.Ct., at 19. That right, like other rights of national citizenship, is within the power of Congress to protect by appropriate legislation. E.g., *United States v. Guest, supra*, 383 U.S., at 759, 86 S.Ct., at 1178; *United States v. Classic*, 313 U.S. 299, 314–315, 61 S.Ct. 1031, 1037–1038, 85 L.Ed. 1368; *Ex parte Yarbrough*, 110 U.S. 651, 4 S.Ct. 152, 28 L.Ed. 274; *Oregon v. Mitchell*, 400 U.S. 112, 285–287, 91 S.Ct. 260, 345–346, 27 L.Ed.2d 272 (concurring and dissenting opinion).

The complaint in this case alleged that the petitioners 'were travelling upon the federal, state and local highways in and about' DeKalb, Kemper County, Mississippi. Kemper County is on the Mississippi-Alabama border. One of the results of the conspiracy, according to the complaint, was to prevent the petitioners and other Negroes from exercising their 'rights to travel the public highways without restraint in the same terms as white citizens in Kemper County, Mississippi.' Finally, the conspiracy was alleged to have been inspired by the respondents' erroneous belief that Grady, a Tennessean, was a worker for Negro civil rights. Under these allegations it is open to the petitioners to prove at trial that they had been engaging in interstate travel or intended to do so, that their federal right to travel interstate was one of the rights meant to be discriminatorily impaired by the conspiracy, that the conspirators intended to drive out-of-state civil rights workers from the State, or that they meant to deter the petitioners from associating with such persons. This and other evidence could make it clear that the petitioners had suffered from conduct that Congress may reach under its power to protect the right of interstate travel.

C

In identifying these two constitutional sources of congressional power, we do not imply the absence of any other. More specifically, the allegations of the complaint in this case have not required consideration of the scope of the power of Congress under § 5 of the Fourteenth Amendment. By the same token, since the allegations of the complaint bring this cause of action so close to the constitutionally authorized core of the statute, there has been no occasion here to trace out its constitutionally permissible periphery.

The judgment is reversed, and the case is remanded to the United States District Court for the Southern District of Mississippi for further proceedings consistent with this opinion.

It is so ordered.

Reversed and remanded.

Note

Restrictions on the ability to bring a Section 1985 have limited litigation under this statute. The Court in the case below, for example, determined: (1) the civil rights conspiracy statute provides no substantial rights itself to the class conspired against, and thus the rights, privileges and immunities that it vindicates must be found elsewhere; (2) because the First Amendment restrains only official conduct, plaintiffs claiming infringement of a right which had its source in the First Amendment were required to prove that the state was somehow involved in or affected by the conspiracy; and (3) the civil rights conspiracy statute was not intended to reach conspiracies motivated by bias towards others on account of their economic views, status or activities, and cannot be construed to reach conspiracies motivated by economic or commercial animus. The restrictions have rendered Section 1985 practically ineffective as a sources of civil rights protection. After reading the United Brotherhood of Carpenters case below, consider which of the claims might be suitable for Section 1985 litigation in the current landscape.

United Brotherhood of Carpenters and Joiners of America, Local 610, AFL-CIO v. Scott
463 U.S. 825 (1983)

JUSTICE WHITE, delivered the opinion of the Court.

This case concerns the scope of the cause of action made available by 42 U.S.C. § 1985(3) (Supp.1981) to those injured by conspiracies formed "for the purpose of depriving, either directly or indirectly, any person or class of persons of the equal protection of the laws, or of equal privileges and immunities under the laws."

I

A.A. Cross Construction Co., Inc. (Cross), contracted with the Department of the Army to construct the Alligator Bayou Pumping Station and Gravity Drainage Structure on the Taylor Bayou Hurricane Levee near Port Arthur, Texas. In accordance with its usual practice, Cross hired workers for the project without regard to union membership. Some of them were from outside the Port Arthur area. Employees of Cross were several times warned by local residents that Cross's practice of hiring non-union workers was a matter of serious concern to many in the area and that it could lead to trouble. According to the District Court, the evidence showed that at a January 15, 1975, meeting of the Executive Committee of the Sabine Area Building and Construction Trades Council a citizen protest against Cross's hiring practices was discussed and a time and place for the protest were chosen. On the morning of January 17, a large group assembled at the entrance to the Alligator Bayou construction site. In the group were union members present at the January 15 meeting. From this gathering several truckloads of men emerged, drove on to the construction site, assaulted and beat Cross employees, and burned and destroyed construction equipment. The District Court found that continued violence was threatened "if the non-union workers did not leave the area or concede to union policies and principles." 461 F.Supp. 224, 227 (E.D.Tex.1978). The violence and vandalism delayed construction and led Cross to default on its contract with the Army.

The plaintiffs in this case, after amendment of the complaint, were respondents Scott and Matthews—two Cross employees who had been beaten, and the company itself. The Sabine Area Building and Trades Council, 25 local unions, and various individuals were named as defendants. Plaintiffs asserted that defendants had conspired to deprive plaintiffs of their legally protected rights, contrary to 42 U.S.C.

§ 1985(3) (Supp.1981). The case was tried to the court. A permanent injunction was entered, and damages were awarded against 11 of the local unions, $5000 each to the individual plaintiffs and $112,385.14 to Cross, plus attorney's fees in the amount of $25,000.

In arriving at its judgment, the District Court recognized that to make out a violation of § 1985(3), as construed in *Griffin v. Breckenridge,* 403 U.S. 88, 102–103, 91 S.Ct. 1790, 1798, 29 L.Ed.2d 338 (1971), the plaintiff must allege and prove four elements: (1) a conspiracy; (2) for the purpose of depriving, either directly or indirectly, any person or class of persons of the equal protection of the laws, or of equal privileges and immunities under the laws; and (3) an act in furtherance of the conspiracy; (4) whereby a person is either injured in his person or property or deprived of any right or privilege of a citizen of the United States. The District Court found that the first, third, and fourth of these elements were plainly established. The issue, the District Court thought, concerned the second element, for in construing that requirement in *Griffin,* we held that the conspiracy not only must have as its purpose the deprivation of "equal protection of the laws, or of equal privileges and immunities under the laws," but also must be motivated by "some racial, or perhaps otherwise class-based, invidiously discriminatory animus behind the conspirators' action." 403 U.S., at 102, 91 S.Ct., at 1798. *Griffin* having involved racial animus and interference with rights that Congress could unquestionably protect against private conspiracies, the issue the District Court identified was whether private conspiratorial discrimination against employees of a non-unionized entity is the kind of conduct that triggers the proscription of § 1985(3). The District Court concluded that the conspiracy encompassed violations of both the civil and criminal laws of the state of Texas, thus depriving plaintiff of the protections afforded by those laws, that § 1985(3) proscribes class-based animus other than racial bias, and that the class of non-union laborers and employers is a protected class under the section. The District Court believed that "men and women have the right to associate or not to associate with any group or class of individuals, and concomitantly, to be free of violent acts against their bodies and property because of such association or non-association." 461 F.Supp., at 230. The conduct evidenced a discriminatory animus against non-union workers hence, there had been a violation of the federal law.

The Court of Appeals, sitting en banc, except for setting aside for failure of proof the judgment against eight of the eleven local unions, affirmed the judgment of the District Court. 680 F.2d 979 (CA 5 1982). The Court of Appeals understood respondents' submission to be that petitioners' conspiracy was aimed at depriving respondents of their First Amendment right to associate with their fellow non-union employees and that this curtailment was a deprivation of the equal protection of the laws within the meaning of § 1985(3). The Court of Appeals agreed, for the most part, holding that the purpose of the conspiracy was to deprive plaintiffs of their First Amendment right not to associate with a union. The court rejected the argument that it was necessary to show some state involvement to demonstrate an infringement of First Amendment rights. This argument, it thought, had been expressly rejected in *Griffin*, and it therefore felt compelled to disagree with two decisions of the Court of Appeals for the Seventh Circuit espousing that position. *Murphy v. Mount Carmel High School*, 543 F.2d 1189 (1976); *Dombrowski v. Dowling*, 459 F.2d 190 (1972). The Court of Appeals went on to hold that § 1985(3) reached conspiracies motivated either by political or economic bias. Thus petitioners' conspiracy to harm the non-union employees of a non-unionized contractor embodied the kind of class-based animus contemplated by § 1985(3) as construed in *Griffin*. Because of the importance of the issue involved, we granted certiorari, 459 U.S. 1034, 103 S.Ct. 442, 74 L.Ed.2d 599. We now reverse.

II

We do not disagree with the District Court and the Court of Appeals that there was a conspiracy, an act done in furtherance thereof, and a resultant injury to persons and property. Contrary to the Court of Appeals, however, we conclude that an alleged conspiracy to infringe First Amendment rights is not a violation of § 1985(3) unless it is proved that the state is involved in the conspiracy or that the aim of the conspiracy is to influence the activity of the state. We also disagree with the Court of Appeals' view that there was present here the kind of animus that § 1985(3) requires.

A

The Equal Protection Clause of the Fourteenth Amendment prohibits any state from denying any person the equal protection of the laws. The First Amendment, which by virtue of the Due Process Clause of the Fourteenth Amendment now applies to state governments and their officials, prohibits either Congress or a state from making any "law . . . abridging the freedom of speech, . . . or the right of the people peaceably to assemble". Had § 1985(3) in so many words prohibited conspiracies to deprive any person of the Equal Protection of the laws guaranteed by the Fourteenth Amendment or of Freedom of Speech guaranteed by the First Amendment, it would be untenable to contend that either of those provisions could be violated by a conspiracy that did not somehow involve or affect a state.

> "It is a commonplace that rights under the Equal Protection Clause itself arise only where there has been involvement of the State or of one acting under the color of its authority. The Equal Protection Clause 'does not . . . add anything to the rights which one citizen has under the Constitution against another.' *United States v. Cruikshank*, 92 U.S. 542, 554–555 [23 L. Ed. 588]. As Mr. Justice Douglas more recently put it, 'The Fourteenth Amendment protects the individual against *state action*, not against wrongs done by *individuals*.' *United States v. Williams*, 341 U.S. 70, 92 [71 S.Ct. 581, 593, 95 L.Ed. 758] (dissenting opinion). This has been the view of the Court from the beginning. *United States v. Cruikshank, supra; United States v. Harris*, 106 U.S. 629 [1 S.Ct. 601, 27 L.Ed. 290]; *Civil Rights Cases*, 109 U.S. 3 [3 S.Ct. 18, 27 L.Ed. 835]; *Hodges v. United States*, 203 U.S. 1 [27 S.Ct. 6, 51 L.Ed. 65]; *United States v. Powell*, 212 U.S. 564 [29 S.Ct. 690, 53 L.Ed. 653].

It remains the Court's view today. See, *e.g., Evans v. Newton,* 382 U.S. 296 [86 S.Ct. 486, 15 L.Ed.2d 373]; *United States v. Price, post,* [383 U.S.] p. 787 [86 S.Ct. p. 1152, 16 L.Ed.2d p. 267]." *United States v. Guest,* 383 U.S. 745, 755, 86 S.Ct. 1170, 1176, 16 L.Ed.2d 239 (1966).

The opinion for the Court by Justice Fortas in the companion case characterized the Fourteenth Amendment rights in the same way:

"As we have consistently held 'The Fourteenth Amendment protects the individual against *state action,* not against wrongs done by *individuals.*' *Williams I,* 341 U.S., at 92 [71 S.Ct., at 593] (opinion of Douglas, J.)" *United States v. Price,* 383 U.S. 787, 799, 86 S.Ct. 1152, 1160, 16 L.Ed.2d 267 (1966).

In this respect, the Court of Appeals for the Seventh Circuit was thus correct in holding that a conspiracy to violate First Amendment rights is not made out without proof of state involvement. *Murphy v. Mount Carmel High School, supra,* at 1193.

Griffin v. Breckenridge is not to the contrary. There we held that § 1985(3) reaches purely private conspiracies and, as so interpreted, was not invalid on its face or as there applied. We recognized that the language of the section referring to deprivations of "equal protection" or of "equal privileges and immunities" resembled the language and prohibitions of the Fourteenth Amendment, and that if § 1985(3) was so understood, it would be difficult to conceive of a violation of the statute that did not involve the state in some respect. But we observed that the section does not expressly refer to the Fourteenth Amendment and that there is nothing "inherent" in the language used in § 1985(3) "that requires the action working the deprivation to come from the State." 403 U.S., at 97, 91 S.Ct., at 1796. This was a correct reading of the language of the Act; the section is not limited by the constraints of the Fourteenth Amendment. The broader scope of § 1985(3) became even more apparent when we explained that the conspiracy at issue was actionable because it was aimed at depriving the plaintiffs of the rights protected by the Thirteenth Amendment and the right to travel guaranteed by the Federal Constitution. Section 1985(3) constitutionally can and does protect those rights from interference by purely private conspiracies.

Griffin did not hold that even when the alleged conspiracy is aimed at a right that is by definition a right only against state interference the plaintiff in a § 1985(3) suit nevertheless need not prove that the conspiracy contemplated state involvement of some sort. The complaint in *Griffin* alleged, among other things, a deprivation of First Amendment rights, but we did not sustain the action on the basis of that allegation and paid it scant attention. Instead, we upheld the application of § 1985(3) to private conspiracies aimed at interfering with rights constitutionally protected against private, as well as official, encroachment.

Neither is respondents' position helped by the assertion that even if the Fourteenth Amendment does not provide authority to proscribe exclusively private conspiracies, precisely the same conduct could be proscribed by the Commerce

Clause. That is no doubt the case; but § 1985(3) is not such a provision, since it "provides no substantial rights itself" to the class conspired against. *Great American Fed. S. & L. Ass'n v. Novotny,* 442 U.S. 366, 372, 99 S.Ct. 2345, 2349, 60 L.Ed.2d 957 (1979). The rights, privileges, and immunities that § 1985(3) vindicates must be found elsewhere, and here the right claimed to have been infringed has its source in the First Amendment. Because that Amendment restrains only official conduct, to make out their § 1985(3) case, it was necessary for respondents to prove that the state was somehow involved in or affected by the conspiracy.

The Court of Appeals accordingly erred in holding that § 1985(3) prohibits wholly private conspiracies to abridge the right of association guaranteed by the First Amendment. Because of that holding the Court of Appeals found it unnecessary to determine whether respondents' action could be sustained under § 1985(3) as involving a conspiracy to deprive respondents of rights, privileges, or immunities under state law or those protected against private action by the Federal Constitution or federal statutory law. Conceivably, we could remand for consideration of these possibilities or we ourselves could consider them. We take neither course, for in our view the Court of Appeals should also be reversed on the dispositive ground that § 1985(3)'s requirement that there must be "some racial, or perhaps otherwise class-based, invidiously discriminatory animus behind the conspirators' action", *Griffin v. Breckenridge,* 403 U.S., at 102, 91 S.Ct., at 1798, was not satisfied in this case.

B

As indicated above, after examining the language, structure, and legislative history of § 1985(3), the *Griffin* opinion emphatically declared that the section was intended to reach private conspiracies that in no way involved the state. The Court was nevertheless aware that the sweep of § 1985 as originally introduced in the House provoked strong opposition in that chamber and precipitated the proposal and adoption of a narrowing amendment, which limited the breadth of the bill so that the bill did not provide a federal remedy for "all tortious, conspiratorial interferences with the rights of others." 403 U.S., at 101, 91 S.Ct., at 1798. In large part, opposition to the original bill had been motivated by a belief that Congress lacked the authority to punish every assault and battery committed by two or more persons. *Id.,* at 102, 91 S.Ct., at 1798; Cong. Globe, 42d Cong., 1st Sess., App. 68, 115, 153, 188, 315, 486, 514. As we interpreted the legislative history 12 years ago in *Griffin,* the narrowing amendment "centered entirely on the animus or motivation that would be required . . ." *Id.,* at 100, 91 S.Ct., at 1797. Thus:

> "The constitutional shoals that would lie in the path of interpreting § 1985(3) as a general federal tort law can be avoided by giving full effect to the congressional purpose—by requiring, as an element of the cause of action, the kind of invidiously discriminatory motivation stressed by the sponsors of the limiting amendment. See the remarks of Representatives Willard and Shellabarger, quoted *supra,* at 100. The language requiring intent to deprive of *equal* protection, or *equal* privileges and immunities,

means that there must be some racial, or perhaps otherwise class-based, invidiously discriminatory animus behind the conspirators' action. The conspiracy, in other words, must aim at a deprivation of the equal enjoyment of rights secured by the law to all." *Id.*, at 102, 91 S.Ct., at 1798 (footnotes omitted).

This conclusion was warranted by the legislative history, was reaffirmed in *Novotny, supra,* and we accept it as the authoritative construction of the statute.

Because the facts in *Griffin* revealed an animus against Negroes and those who supported them, a class-based, invidious discrimination which was the central concern of Congress in enacting § 1985(3), the Court expressly declined to decide "whether a conspiracy motivated by invidiously discriminatory intent other than racial bias would be actionable under the portion of § 1985(3) before us." 403 U.S., at 102 n. 9, 91 S.Ct., at 1798 n. 9. Both courts below answered that question; both held that the section not only reaches conspiracies other than those motivated by racial bias but also forbids conspiracies against workers who refuse to join a union. We disagree with the latter conclusion and do not affirm the former.

C

The Court of Appeals arrived at its result by first describing the Reconstruction-era Ku Klux Klan as a political organization that sought to deprive a large segment of the Southern population of political power and participation in the governance of those states and of the nation. The Court of Appeals then reasoned that because Republicans were among the objects of the Klan's conspiratorial activities, Republicans in particular and political groups in general were to be protected by § 1985(3). Finally, because it believed that an animus against an economic group such as those who preferred non-union association is "closely akin" to the animus against political association, the Court of Appeals concluded that the animus against non-union employees in the Port Arthur area was sufficiently similar to the animus against a political party to satisfy the requirements of § 1985(3).

We are unpersuaded. In the first place, it is a close question whether § 1985(3) was intended to reach any class-based animus other than animus against Negroes and those who championed their cause, most notably Republicans. The central theme of the bill's proponents was that the Klan and others were forcibly resisting efforts to emancipate Negroes and give them equal access to political power. The predominate purpose of § 1985(3) was to combat the prevalent animus against Negroes and their supporters. The latter included Republicans generally, as well as others, such as Northerners who came South with sympathetic views towards the Negro. Although we have examined with some care the legislative history that has been marshalled in support of the position that Congress meant to forbid wholly non-racial, but politically motivated conspiracies, we find difficult the question whether § 1985(3) provided a remedy for every concerted effort by one political group to nullify the influence of or do other injury to a competing group by use of otherwise unlawful means. To accede to that view would go far toward making the federal courts, by virtue of § 1985(3), the monitors of campaign tactics in both state and federal elections, a role that the courts should not be quick to assume. If respondents' submission were accepted, the proscription of § 1985(3) would arguably reach the claim that a political party has interfered with the freedom of speech of another political party by encouraging the heckling of its rival's speakers and the disruption of the rival's meetings.

We realize that there is some legislative history to support the view that § 1985(3) has a broader reach. Senator Edmunds's statement on the floor of the Senate is the clearest expression of this view. He said that if a conspiracy were formed against a man "because he was a Democrat, if you please, or because he was a Catholic, or because he was a Methodist, or because he was a Vermonter, . . . then this section could reach it." Cong. Globe, 42d Cong., 1st Sess. 567. The provision that is now § 1985(3), however, originated in the House. The narrowing amendment, which changed § 1985(3) to its present form, was proposed, debated, and adopted there, and the Senate made only technical changes to the bill. Senator Edmunds's views, since he managed the bill on the floor of the Senate, are not without weight. But we were aware of his views in *Griffin,* 403 U.S., at 102 n. 9, 91 S.Ct., at 1798 n. 9, and still withheld judgment on the question whether § 1985(3), as enacted, went any farther than its central concern—combatting the violent and other efforts of the Klan and its allies to resist and to frustrate the intended effects of the Thirteenth, Fourteenth, and Fifteenth Amendments. Lacking other evidence of congressional intention, we follow the same course here.

D

Even if the section must be construed to reach conspiracies aimed at any class or organization on account of its political views or activities, or at any of the classes posited by Senator Edmunds, we find no convincing support in the legislative history for the proposition that the provision was intended to reach conspiracies motivated by bias towards others on account of their *economic* views, status, or activities. Such a construction would extend § 1985(3) into the economic life of the country in a way that we doubt that the 1871 Congress would have intended when it passed the provision in 1871.

Respondents submit that Congress intended to protect two general classes of Republicans, Negroes and Northern immigrants, the latter because the Klan resented carpetbagger efforts to dominate the economic life of the South. Respondents rely on a series of statements made during the debates on the Civil Rights Act of 1871, of which § 1985 was a part, indicating that Northern laborers and businessmen who had come from the North had been the targets of Klan conspiracies. Brief of Respondents 42–44. As we understand these remarks, however, the speakers believed that these Northerners were viewed as suspect because they were Republicans and were thought to be sympathetic to Negroes. We do not interpret these parts of the debates as asserting that the Klan had a general animus against either labor or capital, or against persons from other states as such. Nor is it plausible that the Southern Democrats were prejudiced generally against enterprising persons trying to better themselves, even if those enterprising persons were from Northern states. The animus was against Negroes and their sympathizers, and perhaps against Republicans as a class, but not against economic groups as such. Senator Pool, on whom respondents rely, identified what he thought was the heart of the matter:

> "The truth is that whenever a northern man, who goes into a southern State, will prove a traitor to the principles which he entertained at home, when he will lend himself to the purposes of the Democracy or be purchased by them, they forget that he is a carpet-bagger and are ready to use him and elevate him to any office within their gift." Cong. Globe, 42nd Cong., 1st Sess., 607.

We thus cannot construe § 1985(3) to reach conspiracies motivated by economic or commercial animus. Were it otherwise, for example, § 1985(3) could be brought to bear on any act of violence resulting from union efforts to organize an employer or from the employer's efforts to resist it, so long as the victim merely asserted and proved that the conduct involved a conspiracy motivated by an animus in favor of unionization, or against it, as the case may be. The National Labor Relations Act, 29 U.S.C. §§ 151 *et seq.*, addresses in great detail the relationship between employer, employee, and union in a great variety of situations, and it would be an unsettling event to rule that strike and picket-line violence must now be considered in the light of the strictures of § 1985(3). Moreover, if anti-union, anti-nonunion, or anti-employer biases represent the kinds of animus that trigger § 1985(3), there would be little basis for concluding that the statute did not provide a cause of action in a variety of other situations where one economic group is pitted against another, each having the intent of injuring or destroying the economic health of the other. We think that such a construction of the statute, which is at best only arguable and surely not compelled by either its language or legislative history, should be eschewed and that group actions generally resting on economic motivations should be deemed beyond the reach of § 1985(3). Economic and commercial conflicts, we think, are best dealt with by statutes, federal or state, specifically addressed to such problems, as well as by the general law proscribing injuries to persons and property. If we have misconstrued the intent of the 1871 Congress, or, in any event, if Congress now prefers to take a different tack, the Court will, of course, enforce any statute within the power of Congress to enact.

Accordingly, the judgment of the Court of Appeals is

Reversed.

Chapter 9

Voting

A. Law as Power

The voting context is the epicenter of political power struggles. Who gets to set policy, which party controls the House or the Senate, those questions all serve as motivations for electoral and strategic decisions regarding voting. However, the power struggle in this area runs even deeper. Power battles also center on who the electorate should be and on who should vote. Who should vote is a question that has raged in different forms throughout American history. For a long time, institutions in America have reinforced oppressive rules that solidified power in the hands of whites only. The electoral process and voting are no exception to that pattern. Threats and racial policing became de facto and legal means for maintaining the racialized power structure. During slavery, voting laws, along with everything else, reflected the power structure in that only people with property and racial privilege had access to the vote.

During Jim Crow, despite the Fifteenth Amendment and, later, the Nineteenth Amendment, the laws still reflected the power structure. They dictated who was allowed to vote or not vote based on race. As a result, black men and women were harassed, threatened, and blocked from voting in many parts of the United States until the passage of the Voting Rights Act of 1965.

Though the Civil Rights Era ushered in new laws to remedy these inequities, old structures remain difficult to uproot. As a result, over time, terror tactics, used by organizations like the Ku Klux Klan and those in collusion with them, were replaced by gerrymandering efforts and financial manipulation. Furthermore, Supreme Court decisions like *Citizens United v. Federal Election Commission*, 558 U.S. 310 (2010), opened the floodgate to even more disproportionate influence by affluent groups in the electoral process.

As a result, today, money affects everything in elections and electoral politics, including party platforms. For example, compared to the last few decades, data shows that it takes the equivalent of small countries' budgets to run the average campaign for federal office.[1] Consider that the 2014 midterm elections cost the highest of all

---

1. David Knowles, *U.S. Senate seat now costs $10.5 million to win, on average, while US House seat costs, $1.7 million, new analysis of FEC data shows*, http://www.nydailynews.com/news/politics /cost-u-s-senate-seat-10-5-million-article-1.1285491.

time, with a total of 4 billion dollars spent by candidates.[2] Given these figures, what should be done to ensure that the electoral process reflects the interests of all, instead of only the interests of those with power and influence? And, for you, students of the law, what are the available legal avenues for checking the political system?

Are there checks and balances that could be implemented in order to prevent persistent undue influence? To help you think through these questions, consider the legal history and current application of voting rights law below, and, determine whether related laws and judicial decisions fall short of their stated goals.

1. Historical Overview

> Representatives and direct Taxes shall be apportioned among the several States which may be included within this Union, according to their respective umbers, which shall be determined by adding to the whole Number of free Persons, including those bound to Service for a Term of Years, and excluding Indians not taxed, three fifths of all other Persons. — U.S. Const. Article I, Sec. II. Article I Section II of the Constitution

In its original form, this provision serves as a vivid illustration of the danger of having law simply mimic the interests of those in power. Due to Slavery's reduction of humans to chattel, the interests of African Americans were completely subjugated to those of slave holders. It is also a reminder that, though the right to vote is now viewed as one of our sacrosanct principles, the history of voting in this country reflects a more complex relationship.

At the start of the American experiment, access to the vote was viewed much more differently than now is. Then, voting laws were crafted at a local level and were varied. Recall that one of the pivotal triggers for the American Revolution was the frustration at the lack of meaningful representation and self-governance in the colonies.[3] Thus, changing the colonial structure to a more autonomous representative government was a key goal. In that spirit, during early colonial history, before the stronghold of Slavery, certain localities even extended access to the vote to non-whites. For example, during at least part of the colonial period, African Americans could vote in 11 of the 13 colonies, and could hold minor elected offices.

That these gains were ephemeral and limited in nature is a pattern that permeates the American history of voting rights. As the institution of Slavery took hold, even among free states, by the end of the Civil War, only six states extended the right to vote to African Americans.[4] Consequently, in creating the new American

---

2. Chris Cillizza, *2014 will be the most expensive midterm election ever*, https://www.washington post.com/news/the-fix/wp/2014/10/22/2014-will-be-the-most-expensive-midterm-election-ever/

3. Jedidiah Morse, Annals of the American Revolution.

4. Kirk Harold Porter, A History of Suffrage in the United States 148 (Greenwood Press 1971) (1918); "Civil Death": The Ideological Paradox of Criminal Disenfranchisement Law in the United States, 2002 Wis. L. Rev. 1045.

structure, existing biases were simply integrated in the new system. For example, access to voting was, in great part, limited to white males. The framers' nefarious compromise over representation in slaveholding states sanctioned the legal dehumanization of blacks. En masse, for the first 100 years or so, African Americans, women of all races and the poor did not have a right to vote, which means that they in essence had no meaningful access to self-determination.[5]

For African Americans, Reconstruction, the period after emancipation, saw a temporary active effort to secure political rights and access to the vote.[6] Under the enforcement powers promulgated by the Fourteenth and Fifteenth Amendments, Congress passed laws prohibiting infringement of individuals' exercise of their right to vote and other civil rights. The presence of federal troops in the South facilitated supervision of the electoral processes to ensure equal access to blacks. The Fifteenth Amendment was also instrumental in rectifying voting inequities in the Northern states, as many states in the North had adopted repressive laws against African Americans after the Civil War.

Historians view Reconstruction as the period where blacks had the most access to political power and to the means of self-determination.[7] For example, it is reported that there were proportionally more black elected officials during Reconstructions than in our current electoral reality. During Reconstruction, African Americans were elected to serve as representatives in the United States House of Representative and United States Senate. In addition, they were active on the state level, directly shaping the governmental structure of their respective states.

Two key factors influenced this temporary reprieve for African Americans: 1) the strong support and presence of the federal government, and 2) the success of the Republican Party. As both of these elements disappeared, so too did the gains made during Reconstruction. Soon, in Alabama, Mississippi, and Georgia, physical violence and legal restrictions became hallmark tools for repressing individuals' civil liberties. Jim Crow laws were enacted in many jurisdictions forbidding blacks, for example, from looking whites in the eye, from passing them on a sidewalk or the highway, from drinking from the same fountain as them, etc.[8] Herein lived the Jim

---

5. Luther v. Borden, 48 U.S. (7 How.) 1 (1849); Protecting Political Participation Through the Voter Qualifications Clause of Article I, 56 B.C. L. Rev 159; Chilton Williamson, American Suffrage from Property to Democracy 1760–1860, at vii, 42 (1960).

6. Tempering Society's Looking Glass: Correcting Misconceptions About the Voting Rights Act of 1965 and Securing American Democracy, 76 La. L. Rev. 1; Richard M. Valelly, The Two Reconstructions 128 (2004); Black Leaders During Reconstruction, http://www.history .com/topics/american-civil-war/black-leaders-during-reconstruction.

7. Eric Foner, Freedom's Lawmakers: A Directory of Black Officeholders Duringreconstruction, at xiv (La. State Univ. Press rev. ed. 1996).

8. M. Alexander, The New Jim Crow: Mass Incarceration in the Age of Colorblindness (2010); Richard M. Valelly, The Two Reconstructions 128 (2004); CQ Press, American Political Leaders 1789–2005, at 378 (2005); Melissa Nobles, Face Up to the Violence of Jim Crow, http://www.nytimes.com/roomfordebate/2014/01/06/turning-away-from-painful-chapters

Crow system for another 100 or so years. Targeting the vote, and, with little federal
oversight, states also adopted blatantly racist measures. In Mississippi, for example,
S.S. Calhoun stated at the Mississippi Constitutional Convention in 1890: "We came
here to exclude the Negro. Nothing short of this will answer." (https://progressmatters
.org/2013/12/30/evaluating-the-need-for-the-voting-rights-act-a-case-study-of-
mississippi/) With that intent, states like Mississippi enacted voting restrictions
designed to be implemented against blacks, but appearing neutral enough that it
would not rouse Northern discomfort. For example, Mississippi laws provided that
to vote in Mississippi after July 1892, an adult male must have paid all taxes, including a two-dollar poll tax, must not have committed any crimes, and "must be able
to read . . . understand when read to him or give a reasonable interpretation" of the
Mississippi Constitution.[9] Literacy tests, poll taxes and unreasonable testing questions, combined with intimidation, became the norm. This was effective, especially
because in the beginning of the Twentieth Century, a majority of blacks were illiterate, many having spent most of their lifetime in bondage when literacy was prohibited. Even after Emancipation, the Southern states funded few public secondary
schools that blacks could attend. Instead, private schools were viewed as a method to
circumvent the obligation to provide education for all.[10]

As a result, though there were 30,000 more African Americans of voting age than
whites of voting age in Mississippi, for example, only 5.7% of eligible African Americans were registered to vote compared to 57.7% of eligible whites. Other means,
like grandfather clauses and poll taxes, took advantage of the economic disparities
between blacks and whites, while making sure to benefit poor whites by creating
exceptions to these rules. Additionally, white-only primaries made sure that African
Americans who were better situated would not be able to obtain political power.[11]

Pay attention to these repressive mechanisms as we work through the voting
rights cases in this chapter. How many of these strategies and tools still permeate
voting laws today? Even though access to the vote is less restrictive today, mostly
due to civil rights laws enacted in the 1960s, are there measures that still make it
difficult for certain groups to have an effective voice in governance? In a country
based on representative government, how can we make sure other groups have a
meaningful say in governance when they are minority groups in majority white
districts? Specific reform measures in the context of redistricting were endorsed by

/face-up-to-the-violence-of-jim-crow; Richard Wright, Native Son 85–87 (Perennial Classics
1998) (1940); *The Rise and Fall of Jim Crow*, http://www.pbs.org/wnet/jimcrow/stories.html.

    9. Miss. Const. art. XII, §244; *Mississippi: Subversion of the Right to Vote*, http://www.crmvet
.org/docs/msrv64.pdf; *Rehabilitating Unconstitutional Statutes: An Analysis of* Cotton v. Fordice,
157 F.3d 388 (5th Cir. 1998), 71 U. Cin. L. Rev. 421.

    10. *Our Children's Burden: The Many-Headed Hydra of the Educational Disenfranchisement of
Black Children*, 42 How. L.J. 133; Griffin v. Cnty. Sch. Bd. of Prince Edward Cnty., 377 U.S. 218,
224–25 (1964).

    11. *Colorblindness, Race Neutrality, and Voting Rights*, 51 Emory L.J. 1397; William Gillette,
The Right to Vote: Politics and the Passage of the Fifteenth Amendment 163 (1965).

the Supreme Court to address these concerns after passage of the Voting Rights Act. However, the Supreme Court has long indicated that these measures will no longer be permitted. As you read these cases, think about the nature of representation. Is it necessary for groups to be represented by someone like them in order to be able to participate meaningfully in government? Does your answer change depending on the time period you are evaluating?

2. The Legal Environment

a. The Fight for Equal and Meaningful Access to Political Power

Voting power and access to the vote are two key issues that have triggered extensive litigation to remedy the social environment described above. The first pivotal tool, which overtly declared African Americans as legitimately entitled to participate in governance, is the Fifteenth Amendment. Though dormant during much of Jim Crow, the Fifteenth Amendment is still instrumental for assessing the scope of power and governmental intent in voting rights related issues. The Fifteenth Amendment states:

> The right of the citizens of the United States to vote shall not be denied or abridged by the United States or by any state on account of race, color or previous condition of servitude.

Using the Fifteenth Amendment, early voting cases challenged grandfather clauses, for instance, arguing that allowance of illiterate whites to vote, while forbidding African Americans to vote whether literate or illiterate, amounted to a violation. The Supreme Court eventually struck down these grandfather clauses as violative of the Fifteenth Amendment. *Guinn v. United States*, 238 U.S. 347 (1915). The poll tax, however, was upheld in *Breedlove v. Suttles*, 302 U.S. 277 (1937), holding the economic charge valid. This interpretation continued until the passage of the Twenty-Fourth Amendment, categorically outlawing poll taxes in federal elections. Its use in state elections was finally prohibited in *Harper v. Virginia* in 1966. 383 U.S. 663. It was not, however, until the passage of the Voting Rights Act in 1965 that litigation and enforcement began to yield meaningful progress in the voting context. Documented violence against those lobbying for the vote triggered national and international scrutiny. Persistent activism from civil rights workers eventually made these abuses untenable. These issues came to a head in Selma, AL and soon after, the Voting Rights Act was passed.[12]

---

12. The Library of Congress, American Memory Section, *Today in History: March 7, at* http://www.memory.loc.gov/ammem/today/mar07.html (last visited March 3, 2003); *Edmund Pettus Bridge, 'Bloody Sunday' Site, Declared A Historic Landmark*, http://www.huffingtonpost.com/2013/03/11/edmund-pettus-bridge-bloody-sunday-landmark_n_2855083.html; Symposium: *Of John Brown: Lawyers, the Law, and Civil Disobedience: Sumter County, Alabama and the Origins of the Voting Rights Act*, 54 ALA. L. REV. 877; Lyndon B. Johnson, Special Message to the Congress: The American Promise (March 15, 1965), *in* 1 PUB. PAPERS 281 (1966).

The following case demonstrates courts' limited interpretation of the Fourteenth and Fifteenth Amendments, soon after Reconstruction. It illustrates, also, the many ways in which white women's interests and that of African Americans, particularly, that of African American women, intersected despite failure to maximize those connections over time.[13]

United States v. Anthony is a reminder that all women once faced obstacles to obtaining the right to vote. Women were an excluded group until the passage of the Nineteenth Amendment in 1920. Why did the Reconstruction Amendments, particularly the Fifteenth, not protect Susan B. Anthony, and women in general, in their exercise of the rights to vote? Based on the case below, why do you think the Nineteenth Amendment was necessary?

United States v. Anthony
24 F. Cas. 829 (Cir. Ct. N.Y. 1873)

HUNT, CIRCUIT JUSTICE, after argument had been heard on the legal questions involved, ruled as follows:

The defendant is indicted under the act of congress of May 31st, 1870, for having voted for a representative in congress, in November 1872. Among other things, that act makes it an offence for any person knowingly to vote for such representative without having a lawful right to vote. It is charged that the defendant thus voted, she not having a right to vote, because she is a woman. The defendant insists that she has a right to vote; and that the provision of the constitution of this state, limiting the right to vote to persons of the male sex, is in violation of the fourteenth amendment of the constitution of the United States, and is void.

The thirteenth, fourteenth and fifteenth amendments were designed mainly for the protection of the newly emancipated negroes, but full effect must, nevertheless, be given to the language employed. The thirteenth amendment provides, that 'neither slavery nor involuntary servitude, except as a punishment for crime, whereof the party shall have been duly convicted, shall exist within the United States or any place subject to their jurisdiction.' If honestly received and fairly applied, this provision would have been enough to guard the rights of the colored race. In some states it was attempted to be evaded by enactments cruel and oppressive in their nature—as, that colored persons were forbidden to appear in the towns, except in a menial capacity; that they should reside on and cultivate the soil without being allowed to own it; that they were not permitted to give testimony in cases where a white man was a party. They were excluded from performing particular kinds of business, profitable and reputable, and they were denied the right of suffrage. To

13. DOLORES E. JANIEWSKI, SISTERHOOD DENIED: RACE, GENDER, AND CLASS IN A NEW SOUTH COMMUNITY (1985); VICTORIA BYERLY, HARD TIMES COTTON MILL GIRLS: PERSONAL HISTORIES OF WOMANHOOD AND POVERTY IN THE SOUTH (1986); Martha R. Mahoney, *Whiteness and Women, in Practice and Theory: A Response to Catharine MacKinnon*, 5 YALE J.L. & FEMINISM 217 (1993).

meet the difficulties arising from this state of things, the fourteenth and fifteenth amendments were enacted.

The fourteenth amendment creates and defines citizenship of the United States. It had long been contended, and had been held by many learned authorities, and had never been judicially decided to the contrary, that there was no such thing as a citizen of the United States, except as that condition arose from citizenship of some state. No mode existed, it was said, of obtaining a citizenship of the United States, except by first becoming a citizen of some state. This question is now at rest. The fourteenth amendment defines and declares who shall be citizens of the United States, to wit, 'all persons born or naturalized in the United States, and subject to the jurisdiction thereof.' The latter qualification was intended to exclude the children of foreign representatives and the like. With this qualification, every person born in the United States or naturalized is declared to be a citizen of the United States and of the state wherein he resides.

After creating and defining citizenship of the United States, the fourteenth amendment provides, that 'no state shall make or enforce any law which shall abridge the privileges or immunities of citizens of the United States.' This clause is intended to be a protection, not to all our rights, but to our rights as citizens of the United States only; that is, to rights existing or belonging to that condition or capacity. The expression, citizen of a state, used in the previous paragraph, is carefully omitted here. In article 4, § 2, subd. 1, of the constitution of the United States, it had been already provided, that 'the citizens of each state shall be entitled to all privileges and immunities of citizens in the several states.' The rights of citizens of the states and of citizens of the United States are each guarded by these different provisions. That these rights are separate and distinct, was held in the *Slaughterhouse Cases*, 16 Wall. [83 U.S.] 36, recently decided by the supreme court. The rights of citizens of the state, as such, are not under consideration in the fourteenth amendment. They stand as they did before the adoption of the fourteenth amendment, and are fully guaranteed by other provisions. The rights of citizens of the states have been the subject of judicial decision on more than one occasion. *Corfield v. Coryell* [Case No. 3,230]; *Ward v. Maryland*, 12 Wall. [79 U.S.] 418, 430; *Paul v. Virginia*, 8 Wall. [75 U.S.] 168. These are the fundamental privileges and immunities belonging of right to the citizens of all free governments, such as the right of life and liberty, the right to acquire and possess property, to transact business, to pursue happiness in his own manner, subject to such restraint as the government may adjudge to be necessary for the general good. In *Crandall v. Nevada*, 6 Wall. [73 U.S.] 35, 44, is found a statement of some of the rights of a citizen of the United States, viz., to come to the seat of government to assert any claim he may have upon the government, to transact any business he may have with it, to seek its protection, to share its offices, to engage in administering its functions, and to have free access to its seaports, through which all the operations of foreign commerce are conducted, to the sub-treasuries, the land offices, the revenue offices, and the courts of justice in the several states. 'Another privilege of a citizen of the United States,' says Mr. Justice

Miller, in the *Slaughterhouse Cases* [*supra*], 'is to demand the care and protection of the federal government over his life, liberty, and property, when on the high seas or within the jurisdiction of a foreign government.' 'The right to peaceably assemble and petition for redress of grievances, the privilege of the writ of habeas corpus,' he says, 'are rights of the citizen guaranteed by the federal constitution.'

The right of voting, or the privilege of voting, is a right or privilege arising under the constitution of the state, and not under the constitution of the United States. The qualifications are different in the different states. Citizenship, age, sex, residence, are variously required in the different states, or may be so. If the right belongs to any particular person, it is because such person is entitled to it by the laws of the state where he offers to exercise it, and not because of citizenship of the United States. If the state of New York should provide that no person should vote until he had reached the age of thirty years, or after he had reached the age of fifty, or that no person having gray hair, or who had not the use of all his limbs, should be entitled to vote, I do not see how it could be held to be a violation of any right derived or held under the constitution of the United States. We might say that such regulations were unjust, tyrannical, unfit for the regulation of an intelligent state; but, if rights of a citizen are thereby violated, they are of that fundamental class, derived from his position as a citizen of the state, and not those limited rights belonging to him as a citizen of the United States; and such was the decision in *Corfield v. Coryell* [*supra*].

The United States rights appertaining to this subject are those, first, under article 1, §2, subd. 1, of the United States constitution, which provides, that electors of representatives in congress shall have the qualifications requisite for electors of the most numerous branch of the state legislature; and second, under the fifteenth amendment, which provides, that 'the right of citizens of the United States to vote shall not be denied or abridged by the United States, or by any state, on account of race, color, or previous condition of servitude.' If the legislature of the state of New York should require a higher qualification in a voter for a representative in congress than is required for a voter for a member of the house of assembly of the state, this would, I conceive, be a violation of a right belonging to a person as a citizen of the United States. That right is in relation to a federal subject or interest, and is guaranteed by the federal constitution. The inability of a state to abridge the right of voting on account of race, color, or previous condition of servitude, arises from a federal guaranty. Its violation would be the denial of a federal right—that is, a right belonging to the claimant as a citizen of the United States. This right, however, exists by virtue of the fifteenth amendment. If the fifteenth amendment had contained the word 'sex,' the argument of the defendant would have been potent. She would have said, that an attempt by a state to deny the right to vote because one is of a particular sex is expressly prohibited by that amendment. The amendment, however, does not contain that word. It is limited to race, color, or previous condition of servitude. The legislature of the state of New York has seen fit to say, that the franchise of voting shall be limited to the male sex. In saying this, there is, in my judgment, no violation of the letter, or of the spirit, of the fourteenth or of the fifteenth amendment.

This view is assumed in the second section of the fourteenth amendment, which enacts, that, if the right to vote for federal officers is denied by any state to any of the male inhabitants of such state, except for crime, the basis of representation of such state shall be reduced in a proportion specified. Not only does this section assume that the right of male inhabitants to vote was the especial object of its protection, but it assumes and admits the right of a state, notwithstanding the existence of that clause under which the defendant claims to the contrary, to deny to classes or portions of the male inhabitants the right to vote which is allowed to other male inhabitants. The regulation of the suffrage is thereby conceded to the states as a state's right.

The case of *Bradwell v. State*, 16 Wall. [83 U.S.] 130, decided at the recent term of the supreme court, sustains both of the positions above put forth, viz., first, that the rights referred to in the fourteenth amendment are those belonging to a person as a citizen of the United States and not as a citizen of a state; and second, that a right of the character here involved is not one connected with citizenship of the United States. Mrs. Bradwell made application to be admitted to practice as an attorney and counsellor at law in the courts of Illinois. Her application was denied, and, upon a writ of error, it was held by the supreme court, that, to give jurisdiction under the fourteenth amendment, the claim must be of a right pertaining to citizenship of the United States, and that the claim made by her did not come within that class of cases. Justices Bradley, Swayne, and Field held that a woman was not entitled to a license to practice law. It does not appear that the other judges passed upon that question. The fourteenth amendment gives no right to a woman to vote, and the voting by Miss Anthony was in violation of law.

If she believed she had a right to vote, and voted in reliance upon that belief, does that relieve her from the penalty? It is argued, that the knowledge referred to in the act relates to her knowledge of the illegality of the act, and not to the act of voting; for, it is said, that she must know that she voted. Two principles apply here: First, ignorance of the law excuses no one; second, every person is presumed to understand and to intend the necessary effects of his own acts. Miss Anthony knew that she was a woman, and that the constitution of this state prohibits her from voting. She intended to violate that provision — intended to test it, perhaps, but, certainly, intended to violate it. The necessary effect of her act was to violate it, and this she is presumed to have intended. There was no ignorance of any fact, but, all the facts being known, she undertook to settle a principle in her own person. She takes the risk, and she cannot escape the consequences. It is said, and authorities are cited to sustain the position, that there can be no crime unless there is a culpable intent, and that, to render one criminally responsible a vicious will must be present. A. commits a trespass on the land of B., and B., thinking and believing that he has a right to shoot an intruder upon his premises, kills A. on the spot. Does B.'s misapprehension of his rights justify his act? Would a judge be justified in charging the jury, that, if satisfied that B. supposed he had a right to shoot A., he was justified, and they should find a verdict of not guilty? No judge would make such a charge. To constitute a crime, it is true that there must be a criminal intent, but it is equally true that knowledge of the facts of the case is always held to supply this intent. An intentional killing bears with it evidence of malice in law [and a desire to promote the welfare of the deceased by his translation to a better world would be no justification of the act, were it committed by a sane man]. Whoever, without justifiable cause, intentionally kills his neighbor, is guilty of a crime. The principle is the same in the case before us, and in all criminal cases. The precise question now before me has been several times decided, viz., that one illegally voting was bound and was assumed to know the law, and that a belief that he had a right to vote gave no defense, if there was no mistake of fact. *Hamilton v. People*, 57 Barb. 625; *State v. Boyett*, 10 Ired. 336; *State v. Hart*, 6 Jones, 389; *McGuire v. State*, 7 Humph. 54; *State v. Sheeley*, 15 Iowa, 404. No system of criminal jurisprudence can be sustained upon any other principle. Assuming that Miss Anthony believed she had a right to vote, that fact constitutes no defense, if, in truth, she had not the right. She voluntarily gave a vote which was illegal, and thus is subject to the penalty of the law.

Upon the foregoing ruling, the counsel for the defendant requested the court to submit the case to the jury on the question of intent, and with the following instructions: (1) If the defendant, at the time of voting, believed that she had a right to vote, and voted in good faith in that belief, she is not guilty of the offence charged. (2) In determining the question whether the defendant did or did not believe that she had a right to vote, the jury may take into consideration, as bearing upon that question, the advice which she received from the counsel to whom she applied, and, also, the fact, that the inspectors of the election considered the question and came to the conclusion that she had a right to vote. (3) The jury have a right to find a general verdict of guilty or not guilty, as they shall believe that the defendant has or has not committed the offence described in the statute.

Notes and Questions

Note the distinction that the N.Y. Court makes between the *Anthony* case and *Bradwell*. The *Susan B. Anthony* case is a reminder that white women also struggled for the vote. The *Anthony* case and *Smith v. Allright*, 64 S. Ct. 757 (1944) (reviewing the issue of white only primaries under the Fourteenth Amendment) showcase efforts to dismantle institutions based on white and male early superiority. In *Smith v. Allright*, the Court revisited the legality of white only primaries. The Court noted that while political parties' right to organize is protected by the First Amendment, they cannot limit their membership based on race in contravention of the Equal Protection Clause of the Fourteenth Amendment. *See Smith v. Allright*, 64 S. Ct. 757 (1944). Still, though black males obtained the right to vote with the Fifteenth Amendment, the struggle for meaningful access to the vote continued for blacks while white women were eventually successful more permanently in 1920 with the Nineteenth Amendment. The suffrage of black males and the ratification of the Reconstruction Amendments undoubtedly opened the door to the eventual suffrage of women, a fact illustrated by Anthony's efforts to use the Fourteenth and Fifteenth Amendments to make the point that she and other women should be allowed to vote. As you read and weigh the materials in the chapter, think about why the right to vote for blacks was more of a struggle than the right to vote for women. Additionally, where do you think black women fall in this history?

1. How does the Court in *U.S. v. Anthony* define the role and purpose of the Reconstruction Amendments? Is that consistent with today's view of how they operate and who they protect?

2. Note Susan B. Anthony's exercise of civil disobedience in this context. Are there any parallels between her efforts and the systematic disobedience displayed during the Civil Rights Movement's fight for racial equality?

3. Are Justice Hunt's reasons for issuing a directed verdict and ignoring the defendant's motion to submit the issue of intent to the jury convincing?

4. Susan B. Anthony was born in 1820 to a Quaker family with long activist traditions. After her father's business failed in the late 1830s, Anthony found work as a teacher. In 1851, she attended an anti-slavery conference, where she met Elizabeth Cady Stanton, who was also involved in the temperance movement. The temperance movement was aimed at limiting or completely stopping the production and sale of alcohol. After Anthony was denied a chance to speak at a temperance convention because she was a woman, she realized that no one would take women in politics seriously unless they had the right to vote. This experience, and her acquaintance with Elizabeth Cady Stanton, led her to join the women's rights movement in 1852. She then dedicated her life to women's suffrage. Ignoring opposition and abuse, Anthony traveled, lectured, and canvassed across the nation for women's right to the vote. She also campaigned for the abolition of slavery, women's right to property and to retain their earnings, and for women's labor organizations.

In 1900, Anthony persuaded the University of Rochester to admit women. In 1869, Anthony and Elizabeth Stanton founded the National Woman Suffrage Association. In a brazen move, in 1872, Anthony voted illegally in the presidential election. Anthony was arrested and unsuccessfully fought the charges. She was fined $100, which she never paid. In 1905, she met with President Roosevelt to lobby for an amendment to give women the right to vote. Anthony died the following year, on March 13, 1906, at the age of 86, at her home in Rochester, New York. In 1920, 14 years after Anthony's death, the Nineteenth Amendment to the U.S. Constitution, giving all adult women the right to vote, was passed.[14]

---

14. United States v. Anthony, 24 F. Cas. 829 (C.C.N.D.N.Y. 1873); Comment: *Trial and Tribulation: The Story of* United States v. Anthony, 48 BUFFALO L. REV. 981; *A Revolution Too Soon: Woman Suffragists and the "Living Constitution"*, 76 N.Y.U. L. REV. 1456.

B. The Voting Rights Act and
Other Statutory Rights

It took nearly a century for the promise of the Reconstruction Amendments to become reality. Progress was made possible by the monumental legal shifts facilitated by the civil rights movement in the latter Twentieth Century. These legal shifts, however, were hard won and took even longer to implement. Consider that after the watershed moment ushered by *Brown vs. Board of Education* in 1954, integration and substantial legal change in various areas did not occur until much later. Resistance to equality saw civil rights battles play out in the courtroom, with lawyers calling on courts to extend civil rights gains to numerous segregated contexts.[15] Not only did implementation of *Brown*'s desegregation mandate take several decades, but, other issues—like integration of the transportation system and the invalidity of miscegenation statutes—had to be individually litigated.[16] Forcing governments and institutions to abandon the harmful endorsement of segregation and to adopt, instead, a civil rights framework took tremendous strategizing and consciousness raising.

Such are the hurdles that faced the enactment of a comprehensive Voting Rights Act. This historical reluctance to rectify the continuous and violent abrogation of blacks' right to vote caused civil rights leaders and allies to mount a massive campaign to convince the country and the federal government to pass an effective voting rights statute. These long-term efforts culminated finally in the Voting Rights Act of 1965. With this statute, for the first time since Reconstruction, the federal government committed to address the numerous hurdles to voting facing blacks around the country. Further, as seen in the chapter on language minorities, the Voting Rights Act of 1965 also effectively protects language minorities and Puerto Rico born citizens.[17] Two prior statutes were passed, in 1957 and 1960, but they only gave limited protection.[18]

In contrast, the Voting Rights Act of 1965 enacted sweeping protections related to voting. Two big sections are at issue below: Section 2 and Section 5. Section 2 of the Voting Rights Act prohibits voter dilution, giving citizens the right to sue for infringements and obstacles to voting. Section 5 gives supervisory power to the federal government, based on a formula outlined by Section 4 of the Act, over states or counties with voting practices and changes to practice that abridge access to voting. The Act also bans literacy tests and poll taxes.[19]

---

15. Brown v. Bd. of Educ., 349 U.S. 294 (1955); Bailey v. Patterson, 369 U.S. 31 1962); Katzenbach v. McClung, 379 U.S. 294 (1964); Jones v. Alfred H. Mayer Co., 392 U.S. 409 (1968); Griggs v. Duke Power Co., 401 U.S. 424 (1971).

16. Browder v. Gayle, 142 F. Supp. 707 (M.D. Ala. 1956); *Justice Alito's Dissent in* Loving v. Virginia, 55 B.C. L. Rev. 1563; Brown v. Bd. of Educ., 347 U.S. 483 (1954).

17. 42 U.S.C. § 1973; 52 U.S.C. § 10301.

18. 42 U.S.C. § 1971; 52 U.S.C. § 10101; United States v. Raines, 362 U.S. 17 (1960).

19. 52 U.S.C. § 10301; 52 U.S.C. § 10303; 52 U.S.C. § 10304.

The dispute over the validity of the Act, however, started from its very inception and continues today. What is more, over time, the Court has proved specifically ambivalent regarding the validity of Section 5. The cases below illustrate the Court's historical as well as current approach to Section 5, leaving us, unfortunately, with more questions than answers.

As you read the materials in this section, try to trace where Congress derives authority to pass the Voting Rights Act. What standard does the Supreme Court apply to determine if Congress's exercise of its authority is valid when it comes to Section 5 today? Is the Court consistent from one case to another?

Soon after the passage of the Voting Rights Act, South Carolina sued contesting the power of Congress to regulate states regarding voting. In *Katzenbach* below, the Court affirmed congressional power pursuant to Congress's authority under the Fifteenth Amendment.

South Carolina v. Katzenbach
383 U.S. 301 (1966)

MR. JUSTICE BLACK dissented in part. MR. CHIEF JUSTICE WARREN delivered the opinion of the Court.

By leave of the Court, 382 U.S. 898, 86 S.Ct. 229, South Carolina has filed a bill of complaint, seeking a declaration that selected provisions of the Voting Rights Act of 1965 violate the Federal Constitution, and asking for an injunction against enforcement of these provisions by the Attorney General. Original jurisdiction is founded on the presence of a controversy between a State and a citizen of another State under Art. III, § 2, of the Constitution. See *State of Georgia v. Pennsylvania, R. Co.*, 324 U.S. 439, 65 S.Ct. 716, 89 L.Ed. 1051. Because no issues of fact were raised in the complaint, and because of South Carolina's desire to obtain a ruling prior to its primary elections in June 1966, we dispensed with appointment of a special master and expedited our hearing of the case.

Recognizing that the questions presented were of urgent concern to the entire country, we invited all of the States to participate in this proceeding as friends of the Court. A majority responded by submitting or joining in briefs on the merits, some supporting South Carolina and others the Attorney General. Seven of these States also requested and received permission to argue the case orally at our hearing. Without exception, despite the emotional overtones of the proceeding, the briefs and oral arguments were temperate, lawyerlike and constructive. All viewpoints on the issues have been fully developed, and this additional assistance has been most helpful to the Court.

The Voting Rights Act was designed by Congress to banish the blight of racial discrimination in voting, which has infected the electoral process in parts of our country for nearly a century. The Act creates stringent new remedies for voting discrimination where it persists on a pervasive scale, and in addition the statute strengthens existing remedies for pockets of voting discrimination elsewhere in the country. Congress assumed the power to prescribe these remedies from § 2 of the Fifteenth Amendment, which authorizes the National Legislature to effectuate by 'appropriate' measures the constitutional prohibition against racial discrimination in voting. We hold that the sections of the Act which are properly before us are an appropriate means for carrying out Congress' constitutional responsibilities and are consonant with all other provisions of the Constitution. We therefore deny South Carolina's request that enforcement of these sections of the Act be enjoined.

I.

The constitutional propriety of the Voting Rights Act of 1965 must be judged with reference to the historical experience which it reflects. Before enacting the measure, Congress explored with great care the problem of racial discrimination in voting. The House and Senate Committees on the Judiciary each held hearings for nine days and received testimony from a total of 67 witnesses. More than three full days were consumed discussing the bill on the floor of the House, while the debate in the Senate covered 26 days in all. At the close of these deliberations, the verdict of both chambers was overwhelming. The House approved the bill by a vote of 328–74, and the measure passed the Senate by a margin of 79–18.

Two points emerge vividly from the voluminous legislative history of the Act contained in the committee hearings and floor debates. First: Congress felt itself confronted by an insidious and pervasive evil which had been perpetuated in certain parts of our country through unremitting and ingenious defiance of the Constitution. Second: Congress concluded that the unsuccessful remedies which it had prescribed in the past would have to be replaced by sterner and more elaborate measures in order to satisfy the clear commands of the Fifteenth Amendment. We pause here to summarize the majority reports of the House and Senate Committees, which document in considerable detail the factual basis for these reactions by Congress. See H.R.Rep. No. 439, 89th Cong., 1st Sess., 8-16 (hereinafter cited as House Report); S.Rep.No. 162, pt. 3, 89th Cong., 1st Sess., 3-16, U.S. Code Congressional and Administrative News, p. 2437 (hereinafter cited as Senate Report).

The Fifteenth Amendment to the Constitution was ratified in 1870. Promptly thereafter Congress passed the Enforcement Act of 1870, which made it a crime for public officers and private persons to obstruct exercise of the right to vote. The statute was amended in the following year to provide for detailed federal supervision of the electoral process, from registration to the certification of returns. As the years passed and fervor for racial equality waned, enforcement of the laws became spotty and ineffective, and most of their provisions were repealed in 1894. The remnants have had little significance in the recently renewed battle against voting discrimination.

Meanwhile, beginning in 1890, the States of Alabama, Georgia, Louisiana, Mississippi, North Carolina, South Carolina, and Virginia enacted tests still in use which were specifically designed to prevent Negroes from voting. Typically, they made the ability to read and write a registration qualification and also required completion of a registration form. These laws were based on the fact that as of 1890 in each of the named States, more than two-thirds of the adult Negroes were illiterate while less than one-quarter of the adult whites were unable to read or write. At the same time, alternate tests were prescribed in all of the named States to assure that white illiterates would not be deprived of the franchise. These included grandfather clauses, property qualifications, 'good character' tests, and the requirement that registrants 'understand' or 'interpret' certain matter.

The course of subsequent Fifteenth Amendment litigation in this Court demonstrates the variety and persistence of these and similar institutions designed to deprive Negroes of the right to vote. Grandfather clauses were invalidated in *Guinn v. United States*, 238 U.S. 347, and *Myers v. Anderson*, 238 U.S. 368. Procedural hurdles were struck down in *Lane v. Wilson*, 307 U.S. 268. The white primary was outlawed in *Smith v. Allwright*, 321 U.S. 649, and *Terry v. Adams*, 345 U.S. 461. Improper challenges were nullified in *United States v. Thomas*, 362 U.S. 58. Racial gerrymandering was forbidden by *Gomillion v. Lightfoot*, 364 U.S. 339. Finally, discriminatory application of voting tests was condemned in *Schnell v. Davis*, 336 U.S. 933; *Alabama v. United States*, 371 U.S. 37, and *Louisiana v. United States*, 380 U.S. 145.

According to the evidence in recent Justice Department voting suits, the latter stratagem is now the principal method used to bar Negroes from the polls. Discriminatory administration of voting qualifications has been found in all eight Alabama cases, in all nine Louisiana cases, and in all nine Mississippi cases which have gone to final judgment. Moreover, in almost all of these cases, the courts have held that the discrimination was pursuant to a widespread 'pattern or practice.' White applicants for registration have often been excused altogether from the literacy and understanding tests or have been given easy versions, have received extensive help from voting officials, and have been registered despite serious errors in their answers. Negroes, on the other hand, have typically been required to pass difficult versions of all the tests, without any outside assistance and without the slightest error. The good-morals requirement is so vague and subjective that it has constituted an open invitation to abuse at the hands of voting officials. Negroes obliged to obtain vouchers from registered voters have found it virtually impossible to comply in areas where almost no Negroes are on the rolls.

In recent years, Congress has repeatedly tried to cope with the problem by facilitating case-by-case litigation against voting discrimination. The Civil Rights Act of 1957 authorized the Attorney General to seek injunctions against public and private interference with the right to vote on racial grounds. Perfecting amendments in the Civil Rights Act of 1960 permitted the joinder of States as parties defendant, gave the Attorney General access to local voting records, and authorized courts to register voters in areas of systematic discrimination. Title I of the Civil Rights Act of 1964 expedited the hearing of voting cases before three-judge courts and outlawed some of the tactics used to disqualify Negroes from voting in federal elections.

Despite the earnest efforts of the Justice Department and of many federal judges, these new laws have done little to cure the problem of voting discrimination. According to estimates by the Attorney General during hearings on the Act, registration of voting-age Negroes in Alabama rose only from 14.2% to 19.4% between 1958 and 1964; in Louisiana it barely inched ahead from 31.7% to 31.8% between 1956 and 1965; and in Mississippi it increased only from 4.4% to 6.4% between 1954 and 1964. In each instance, registration of voting-age whites ran roughly 50 percentage points or more ahead of Negro registration.

The previous legislation has proved ineffective for a number of reasons. Voting suits are unusually onerous to prepare, sometimes requiring as many as 6,000 man-hours spent combing through registration records in preparation for trial. Litigation has been exceedingly slow, in part because of the ample opportunities for delay afforded voting officials and others involved in the proceedings. Even when favorable decisions have finally been obtained, some of the States affected have merely switched to discriminatory devices not covered by the federal decrees or have enacted difficult new tests designed to prolong the existing disparity between white and Negro registration. Alternatively, certain local officials have defied and evaded court orders or have simply closed their registration offices to freeze the voting rolls. The provision of the 1960 law authorizing registration by federal officers has had little impact on local maladministration because of its procedural complexities.

During the hearings and debates on the Act, Selma, Alabama, was repeatedly referred to as the pre-eminent example of the ineffectiveness of existing legislation. In Dallas County, of which Selma is the seat, there were four years of litigation by the Justice Department and two findings by the federal courts of widespread voting discrimination. Yet in those four years, Negro registration rose only from 156 to 383, although there are approximately 15,000 Negroes of voting age in the county. Any possibility that these figures were attributable to political apathy was dispelled by the protest demonstrations in Selma in the early months of 1965. The House Committee on the Judiciary summed up the reaction of Congress to these developments in the following words:

'The litigation in Dallas County took more than 4 years to open the door to the exercise of constitutional rights conferred almost a century ago. The problem on a national scale is that the difficulties experienced in suits in Dallas County have been encountered over and over again under existing voting laws. Four years is too long. The burden is too heavy—the wrong to our citizens is too serious—the damage to our national conscience is too great not to adopt more effective measures than exist today.

'Such is the essential justification for the pending bill.' House Report 11.

The Voting Rights Act of 1965 reflects Congress' firm intention to rid the country of racial discrimination in voting. The heart of the Act is a complex scheme of stringent remedies aimed at areas where voting discrimination has been most flagrant. Section 4(a)-(d) lays down a formula defining the States and political subdivisions to which these new remedies apply. The first of the remedies, contained in §4(a), is the suspension of literacy tests and similar voting qualifications for a period of five years from the last occurrence of substantial voting discrimination. Section 5 prescribes a second remedy, the suspension of all new voting regulations pending review by federal authorities to determine whether their use would perpetuate voting discrimination. The third remedy, covered in §§6(b), 7, 9, and 13(a), is the assignment of federal examiners on certification by the Attorney General to list qualified applicants who are thereafter entitled to vote in all elections.

Other provisions of the Act prescribe subsidiary cures for persistent voting discrimination. Section 8 authorizes the appointment of federal poll-watchers in places to which federal examiners have already been assigned. Section 10(d) excuses those made eligible to vote in sections of the country covered by §4(b) of the Act from paying accumulated past poll taxes for state and local elections. Section 12(e) provides for balloting by persons denied access to the polls in areas where federal examiners have been appointed.

The remaining remedial portions of the Act are aimed at voting discrimination in any area of the country where it may occur. Section 2 broadly prohibits the use of voting rules to abridge exercise of the franchise on racial grounds. Sections 3, 6(a), and 13(b) strengthen existing procedures for attacking voting discrimination by means of litigation. Section 4(e) excuses citizens educated in American schools conducted in a foreign language from passing English-language literacy tests. Section 10(a)-(c) facilitates constitutional litigation challenging the imposition of all poll taxes for state and local elections. Sections 11 and 12(a)-(d) authorize civil and criminal sanctions against interference with the exercise of rights guaranteed by the Act.

At the outset, we emphasize that only some of the many portions of the Act are properly before us. South Carolina has not challenged §§2, 3, 4(e), 6(a), 8, 10, 12(d) and (e), 13(b), and other miscellaneous provisions having nothing to do with this lawsuit. Judicial review of these sections must await subsequent litigation. In addition, we find that South Carolina's attack on §§11 and 12(a)-(c) is premature. No person has yet been subjected to, or even threatened with, the criminal sanctions which these sections of the Act authorize. See *United States v. Raines*, 362 U.S. 17, 20–24. Consequently, the only sections of the Act to be reviewed at this time are §§4(a)–(d), 5, 6(b), 7, 9, 13(a), and certain procedural portions of §14, all of which are presently in actual operation in South Carolina. We turn now to a detailed description of these provisions and their present status.

Coverage formula.

The remedial sections of the Act assailed by South Carolina automatically apply to any State, or to any separate political subdivision such as a county or parish, for which two findings have been made: (1) the Attorney General has determined that on November 1, 1964, it maintained a 'test or device,' and (2) the Director of the Census has determined that less than 50% of its voting age residents were registered on

November 1, 1964, or voted in the presidential election of November 1964. These findings are not reviewable in any court and are final upon publication in the Federal Register. §4(b). As used throughout the Act, the phrase 'test or device' means any requirement that a registrant or voter must '(1) demonstrate the ability to read, write, understand, or interpret any matter, (2) demonstrate any educational achievement or his knowledge of any particular subject, (3) possess good moral character, or (4) prove his qualifications by the voucher of registered voters or members of any other class.' §4(c).

Statutory coverage of a State or political subdivision under §4(b) is terminated if the area obtains a declaratory judgment from the District Court for the District of Columbia, determining that tests and devices have not been used during the preceding five years to abridge the franchise on racial grounds. The Attorney General shall consent to entry of the judgment if he has no reason to believe that the facts are otherwise. §4(a). For the purposes of this section, tests and devices are not deemed to have been used in a forbidden manner if the incidents of discrimination are few in number and have been promptly corrected, if their continuing effects have been abated, and if they are unlikely to recur in the future. §4(d). On the other hand, no area may obtain a declaratory judgment for five years after the final decision of a federal court (other than the denial of a judgment under this section of the Act), determining that discrimination through the use of tests or devices has occurred anywhere in the State or political subdivision. These declaratory judgment actions are to be heard by a three-judge panel, with direct appeal to this Court. §4(a).

South Carolina was brought within the coverage formula of the Act on August 7, 1965, pursuant to appropriate administrative determinations which have not been challenged in this proceeding. On the same day, coverage was also extended to Alabama, Alaska, Georgia, Louisiana, Mississippi, Virginia, 26 counties in North Carolina, and one county in Arizona. Two more counties in Arizona, one county in Hawaii, and one county in Idaho were added to the list on November 19, 1965. Thus far Alaska, the three Arizona counties, and the single county in Idaho have asked the District Court for the District of Columbia to grant a declaratory judgment terminating statutory coverage.

Suspension of tests.

In a State or political subdivision covered by §4(b) of the Act, no person may be denied the right to vote in any election because of his failure to comply with a 'test or device.' §4(a).

On account of this provision, South Carolina is temporarily barred from enforcing the portion of its voting laws which requires every applicant for registration to show that he:

> 'Can both read and write any section of (the State) Constitution submitted to (him) by the registration officer or can show that he owns, and has paid all taxes collectible during the previous year on, property in this

State assessed at three hundred dollars or more.' S.C.Code Ann. § 23-62(4) (1965 Supp.).

The Attorney General has determined that the property qualification is inseparable from the literacy test, and South Carolina makes no objection to this finding. Similar tests and devices have been temporarily suspended in the other sections of the country listed above.

Review of new rules.

In a State or political subdivision covered by § 4(b) of the Act, no person may be denied the right to vote in any election because of his failure to comply with a voting qualification or procedure different from those in force on November 1, 1964. This suspension of new rules is terminated, however, under either of the following circumstances: (1) if the area has submitted the rules to the Attorney General, and he has not interposed an objection within 60 days, or (2) if the area has obtained a declaratory judgment from the District Court for the District of Columbia, determining that the rules will not abridge the franchise on racial grounds. These declaratory judgment actions are to be heard by a three-judge panel, with direct appeal to this Court. § 5.

South Carolina altered its voting laws in 1965 to extend the closing hour at polling places from 6 p.m. to 7 p.m. The State has not sought judicial review of this change in the District Court for the District of Columbia, nor has it submitted the new rule to the Attorney General for this scrutiny, although at our hearing the Attorney General announced that he does not challenge the amendment. There are indications in the record that other sections of the country listed above have also altered their voting laws since November 1, 1964.

Federal examiners.

In any political subdivision covered by § 4(b) of the Act, the Civil Service Commission shall appoint voting examiners whenever the Attorney General certifies either of the following facts: (1) that he has received meritorious written complaints from at least 20 residents alleging that they have been disenfranchised under color of law because of their race, or (2) that the appointment of examiners is otherwise necessary to effectuate the guarantees of the Fifteenth Amendment. In making the latter determination, the Attorney General must consider, among other factors, whether the registration ratio of non-whites to whites seems reasonably attributable to racial discrimination, or whether there is substantial evidence of good-faith efforts to comply with the Fifteenth Amendment. § 6(b). These certifications are not reviewable in any court and are effective upon publication in the Federal Register. § 4(b).

. . . .

III.

These provisions of the Voting Rights Act of 1965 are challenged on the fundamental ground that they exceed the powers of Congress and encroach on an area reserved to the States by the Constitution. South Carolina and certain of the amici curiae also attack specific sections of the Act for more particular reasons. They argue that the coverage formula prescribed in § 4(a)-(d) violates the principle of the equality of States, denies due process by employing an invalid presumption and by barring judicial review of administrative findings, constitutes a forbidden bill of attainder, and impairs the separation of powers by adjudicating guilt through legislation. They claim that the review of new voting rules required in § 5 infringes Article III by directing the District Court to issue advisory opinions. They contend that the assignment of federal examiners authorized in § 6(b) abridges due process by precluding judicial review of administrative findings and impairs the separation of powers by giving the Attorney General judicial functions; also that the challenge procedure prescribed in § 9 denies due process on account of its speed. Finally, South Carolina and certain of the amici curiae maintain that §§ 4(a) and 5, buttressed by § 14(b) of the Act, abridge due process by limiting litigation to a distant forum.

Some of these contentions may be dismissed at the outset. The word 'person' in the context of the Due Process Clause of the Fifth Amendment cannot, by any reasonable mode of interpretation, be expanded to encompass the States of the Union, and to our knowledge this has never been done by any court. See *International Shoe Co. v. Cocreham*, 246 La. 244, 266, 164 So.2d 314, 322, n. 5, cf. *United States v. City of Jackson*, 318 F.2d 1, 8 (C.A.5th Cir.). Likewise, courts have consistently regarded the Bill of Attainder Clause of Article I and the principle of the separation of powers only as protections for individual persons and private groups, those who are peculiarly vulnerable to non-judicial determinations of guilt. See *United States v. Brown*, 381 U.S. 437, 85 S.Ct. 1707, 14 L.Ed.2d 484; *Ex parte Garland*, 4 Wall. 333, 18 L.Ed. 366. Nor does a State have standing as the parent of its citizens to invoke these constitutional provisions against the Federal Government, the ultimate parens patriae of every American citizen. *Com. of Massachusetts v. Mellon*, 262 U.S. 447, 485–486; *State of Florida v. Mellon*, 273 U.S. 12, 18. The objections to the Act which are raised under these provisions may therefore be considered only as additional aspects of the basic question presented by the case: Has Congress exercised its powers under the Fifteenth Amendment in an appropriate manner with relation to the States?

The ground rules for resolving this question are clear. The language and purpose of the Fifteenth Amendment, the prior decisions construing its several provisions, and the general doctrines of constitutional interpretation, all point to one fundamental principle. As against the reserved powers of the States, Congress may use any rational means to effectuate the constitutional prohibition of racial discrimination in voting. Cf. our rulings last Term, sustaining Title II of the Civil Rights Act of 1964, in *Heart of Atlanta Motel v. United States*, 379 U.S. 241, 258–259, 261–262, and *Katzenbach v. McClung*, 379 U.S. 294, 303–304. We turn now to a more detailed description of the standards which govern our review of the Act.

Section 1 of the Fifteenth Amendment declares that '(t)he right of citizens of the United States to vote shall not be denied or abridged by the United States or by any

State on account of race, color, or previous condition of servitude.' This declaration has always been treated as self-executing and has repeatedly been construed, without further legislative specification, to invalidate state voting qualifications or procedures which are discriminatory on their face or in practice. See *Neal v. Delaware*, 103 U.S. 370; *Guinn v. United States*, 238 U.S. 347; *Myers v. Anderson*, 238 U.S. 368; *Lane v. Wilson*, 307 U.S. 268; *Smith v. Allwright*, 321 U.S. 649; *Schnell v. Davis*, 336 U.S. 933; *Terry v. Adams*, 345 U.S. 461; *United States v. Thomas*, 362 U.S. 58; *Gomillion v. Lightfoot*, 364 U.S. 339; *Alabama v. United States*, 371 U.S. 37; *Louisiana v. United States*, 380 U.S. 145. These decisions have been rendered with full respect for the general rule, reiterated last Term in *Carrington v. Rash*, 380 U.S. 89, 91, that States 'have broad powers to determine the conditions under which the right of suffrage may be exercised.' The gist of the matter is that the Fifteenth Amendment supersedes contrary exertions of state power. 'When a State exercises power wholly within the domain of state interest, it is insulated from federal judicial review. But such insulation is not carried over when state power is used as an instrument for circumventing a federally protected right.' *Gomillion v. Lightfoot*, 364 U.S., at 347.

South Carolina contends that the cases cited above are precedents only for the authority of the judiciary to strike down state statutes and procedures—that to allow an exercise of this authority by Congress would be to rob the courts of their rightful constitutional role. On the contrary, §2 of the Fifteenth Amendment expressly declares that 'Congress shall have power to enforce this article by appropriate legislation.' By adding this authorization, the Framers indicated that Congress was to be chiefly responsible for implementing the rights created in §1. 'It is the power of Congress which has been enlarged. Congress is authorized to enforce the prohibitions by appropriate legislation. Some legislation is contemplated to make the (Civil War) amendments fully effective.' *Ex parte Virginia*, 100 U.S. 339, 345. Accordingly, in addition to the courts, Congress has full remedial powers to effectuate the constitutional prohibition against racial discrimination in voting.

Congress has repeatedly exercised these powers in the past, and its enactments have repeatedly been upheld. For recent examples, see the Civil Rights Act of 1957, which was sustained in *United States v. Raines*, 362 U.S. 17; *United States v. Thomas, supra*; and *Hannah v. Larche*, 363 U.S. 420; and the Civil Rights Act of 1960, which was upheld in *Alabama v. United States, supra*; *Louisiana v. United States, supra*; and *United States v. Mississippi*, 380 U.S. 128. On the rare occasions when the Court has found an unconstitutional exercise of these powers, in its opinion Congress had attacked evils not comprehended by the Fifteenth Amendment. See *United States v. Reese*, 92 U.S. 214; *James v. Bowman*, 190 U.S. 127.

The basic test to be applied in a case involving §2 of the Fifteenth Amendment is the same as in all cases concerning the express powers of Congress with relation to the reserved powers of the States. Chief Justice Marshall laid down the classic formulation, 50 years before the Fifteenth Amendment was ratified:

'Let the end be legitimate, let it be within the scope of the constitution, and all means which are appropriate, which are plainly adapted to that end, which are not prohibited, but consist with the letter and spirit of the constitution, are constitutional.' *McCulloch v. Maryland*, 4 Wheat. 316, 421, 4 L. Ed. 579.

The Court has subsequently echoed his language in describing each of the Civil War Amendments:

'Whatever legislation is appropriate, that is, adapted to carry out the objects the amendments have in view, whatever tends to enforce submission to the prohibitions they contain, and to secure to all persons the enjoyment of perfect equality of civil rights and the equal protection of the laws against State denial or invasion, if not prohibited, is brought within the domain of congressional power.' *Ex parte Virginia*, 100 U.S., at 345–346.

This language was again employed, nearly 50 years later, with reference to Congress' related authority under § 2 of the Eighteenth Amendment. *James Everard's Breweries v. Day*, 265 U.S. 545, 558–559.

We therefore reject South Carolina's argument that Congress may appropriately do no more than to forbid violations of the Fifteenth Amendment in general terms — that the task of fashioning specific remedies or of applying them to particular localities must necessarily be left entirely to the courts. Congress is not circumscribed by any such artificial rules under § 2 of the Fifteenth Amendment. In the oft-repeated words of Chief Justice Marshall, referring to another specific legislative authorization in the Constitution, 'This power, like all others vested in Congress, is complete in itself, may be exercised to its utmost extent, and acknowledges no limitations, other than are prescribed in the constitution.' *Gibbons v. Ogden*, 9 Wheat. 1, 196, 6 L.Ed. 23.

IV.

Congress exercised its authority under the Fifteenth Amendment in an inventive manner when it enacted the Voting Rights Act of 1965. First: The measure prescribes remedies for voting discrimination which go into effect without any need for prior adjudication. This was clearly a legitimate response to the problem, for which there is ample precedent under other constitutional provisions. See *Katzenbach v. McClung*, 379 U.S. 294, 302–304; *United States v. Darby*, 312 U.S. 100, 120–121. Congress had found that case-by-case litigation was inadequate to combat widespread and persistent discrimination in voting, because of the inordinate amount of time and energy required to overcome the obstructionist tactics invariably encountered in these lawsuits. After enduring nearly a century of systematic resistance to the Fifteenth Amendment, Congress might well decide to shift the advantage of time and inertia from the perpetrators of the evil to its victims. The question remains, of course, whether the specific remedies prescribed in the Act were an appropriate means of combatting the evil, and to this question we shall presently address ourselves.

Second: The Act intentionally confines these remedies to a small number of States and political subdivisions which in most instances were familiar to Congress by name. This, too, was a permissible method of dealing with the problem. Congress had learned that substantial voting discrimination presently occurs in certain sections of the country, and it knew no way of accurately forecasting whether the evil might spread elsewhere in the future. In acceptable legislative fashion, Congress chose to limit its attention to the geographic areas where immediate action seemed necessary. See *McGowan v. State of Maryland*, 366 U.S. 420, 427; *Salsburg v. State of Maryland*, 346 U.S. 545, 550–554. The doctrine of the equality of States, invoked by South Carolina, does not bar this approach, for that doctrine applies only to the terms upon which States are admitted to the Union, and not to the remedies for local evils which have subsequently appeared. See *Coyle v. Smith*, 221 U.S. 559, and cases cited therein.

Coverage formula.

We now consider the related question of whether the specific States and political subdivisions within §4(b) of the Act were an appropriate target for the new remedies. South Carolina contends that the coverage formula is awkwardly designed in a number of respects and that it disregards various local conditions which have nothing to do with racial discrimination. These arguments, however, are largely beside the point. Congress began work with reliable evidence of actual voting discrimination in a great majority of the States and political subdivisions affected by the new remedies of the Act. The formula eventually evolved to describe these areas was relevant to the problem of voting discrimination, and Congress was therefore entitled to infer a significant danger of the evil in the few remaining States and political subdivisions covered by §4(b) of the Act. No more was required to justify the application to these areas of Congress' express powers under the Fifteenth Amendment. Cf. *North American Co. v. S.E.C.*, 327 U.S. 686, 710–711; *Assigned Car Cases*, 274 U.S. 564, 582–583.

To be specific, the new remedies of the Act are imposed on three States—Alabama, Louisiana, and Mississippi—in which federal courts have repeatedly found substantial voting discrimination. Section 4(b) of the Act also embraces two other States—Georgia and South Carolina—plus large portions of a third State—North Carolina—for which there was more fragmentary evidence of recent voting discrimination mainly adduced by the Justice Department and the Civil Rights Commission. All of these areas were appropriately subjected to the new remedies. In identifying past evils, Congress obviously may avail itself of information from any probative source. See *Heart of Atlanta Motel v. United States*, 379 U.S. 241, 252–253; *Katzenbach v. McClung*, 379 U.S., at 299–301.

The areas listed above, for which there was evidence of actual voting discrimination, share two characteristics incorporated by Congress into the coverage formula: the use of tests and devices for voter registration, and a voting rate in the 1964 presidential election at least 12 points below the national average. Tests and devices are relevant to voting discrimination because of their long history as a tool for perpetrating the evil; a low voting rate is pertinent for the obvious reason that widespread disenfranchisement must inevitably affect the number of actual voters. Accordingly, the coverage formula is rational in both practice and theory. It was therefore permissible to impose the new remedies on the few remaining States and political subdivisions covered by the formula, at least in the absence of proof that they have been free of substantial voting discrimination in recent years. Congress is clearly not bound by the rules relating to statutory presumptions in criminal cases when it prescribes civil remedies against other organs of government under § 2 of the Fifteenth Amendment. Compare *United States v. Romano*, 382 U.S. 136; *Tot v. United States*, 319 U.S. 463.

It is irrelevant that the coverage formula excludes certain localities which do not employ voting tests and devices but for which there is evidence of voting discrimination by other means. Congress had learned that widespread and persistent discrimination in voting during recent years has typically entailed the misuse of tests and devices, and this was the evil for which the new remedies were specifically designed. At the same time, through §§ 3, 6(a), and 13(b) of the Act, Congress strengthened existing remedies for voting discrimination in other areas of the country. Legislation need not deal with all phases of a problem in the same way, so long as the distinctions drawn have some basis in practical experience. See *Williamson v. Lee Optical Co.*, 348 U.S. 483, 488–489; *Railway Express Agency v. People of State of New York*, 336 U.S. 106. There are no States or political subdivisions exempted from coverage under § 4(b) in which the record reveals recent racial discrimination involving tests and devices. This fact confirms the rationality of the formula.

Acknowledging the possibility of overbreadth, the Act provides for termination of special statutory coverage at the behest of States and political subdivisions in which the danger of substantial voting discrimination has not materialized during the preceding five years. Despite South Carolina's argument to the contrary, Congress might appropriately limit litigation under this provision to a single court in the District of Columbia, pursuant to its constitutional power under Art. III, § 1, to 'ordain and establish' inferior federal tribunals. See *Bowles v. Willingham*, 321 U.S. 503, 510–512; *Yakus v. United States*, 321 U.S. 414, 427–431; *Lockerty v. Phillips*, 319 U.S. 182.

. . . .

South Carolina contends that these termination procedures are a nullity because they impose an impossible burden of proof upon States and political subdivisions entitled to relief. As the Attorney General pointed out during hearings on the Act, however, an area need do no more than submit affidavits from voting officials, asserting that they have not been guilty of racial discrimination through the use of tests and devices during the past five years, and then refute whatever evidence to the contrary may be adduced by the Federal Government. Section 4(d) further assures that an area need not disprove each isolated instance of voting discrimination in order to obtain relief in the termination proceedings. The burden of proof is therefore quite bearable, particularly since the relevant facts relating to the conduct of voting officials are peculiarly within the knowledge of the States and political subdivisions themselves. See *United States v. New York, N.H. & R.R. Co.*, 355 U.S. 253, 256, n. 5; cf. *S.E.C. v. Ralston Purina Co.*, 346 U.S. 119, 126.

The Act bars direct judicial review of the findings by the Attorney General and the Director of the Census which trigger application of the coverage formula. We reject the claim by Alabama as amicus curiae that this provision is invalid because it allows the new remedies of the Act to be imposed in an arbitrary way. The Court has already permitted Congress to withdraw judicial review of administrative determinations in numerous cases involving the statutory rights of private parties. For example, see *United States v. California Eastern Line*, 348 U.S. 351; *Switchmen's Union v. National Mediation Bd.*, 320 U.S. 297. In this instance, the findings not subject to review consist of objective statistical determinations by the Census Bureau and a routine analysis of state statutes by the Justice Department. These functions are unlikely to arouse any plausible dispute, as South Carolina apparently concedes. In the event that the formula is improperly applied, the area affected can always go into court and obtain termination of coverage under §4(b), provided of course that it has not been guilty of voting discrimination in recent years. This procedure serves as a partial substitute for direct judicial review.

Suspension of tests.

South Carolina assails the temporary suspension of existing voting qualifications, reciting the rule laid down by *Lassiter v. Northampton County Bd. of Elections*, 360 U.S. 45, that literacy tests and related devices are not in themselves contrary to the Fifteenth Amendment. In that very case, however, the Court went on to say, 'Of course a literacy test, fair on its face, may be employed to perpetuate that discrimination which the Fifteenth Amendment was designed to uproot.' *Id.*, at 53. The record shows that in most of the States covered by the Act, including South Carolina, various tests and devices have been instituted with the purpose of disenfranchising Negroes, have been framed in such a way as to facilitate this aim, and have been administered in a discriminatory fashion for many years. Under these circumstances, the Fifteenth Amendment has clearly been violated. See *Louisiana v. United States*, 380 U.S. 145; *State of Alabama v. United States*, 371 U.S. 37; *Schnell v. Davis*, 336 U.S. 933.

The Act suspends literacy tests and similar devices for a period of five years from the last occurrence of substantial voting discrimination. This was a legitimate response to the problem, for which there is ample precedent in Fifteenth Amendment cases. *Ibid.* Underlying the response was the feeling that States and political subdivisions which had been allowing white illiterates to vote for years could not sincerely complain about 'dilution' of their electorates through the registration of Negro illiterates. Congress knew that continuance of the tests and devices in use at the present time, no matter how fairly administered in the future, would freeze the effect of past discrimination in favor of unqualified white registrants. Congress permissibly rejected the alternative of requiring a complete re-registration of all voters, believing that this would be too harsh on many whites who had enjoyed the franchise for their entire adult lives.

Review of new rules.

The Act suspends new voting regulations pending scrutiny by federal authorities to determine whether their use would violate the Fifteenth Amendment. This may have been an uncommon exercise of congressional power, as South Carolina contends, but the Court has recognized that exceptional conditions can justify legislative measures not otherwise appropriate. See *Home Bldg. & Loan Ass'n v. Blaisdell*, 290 U.S. 398; *Wilson v. New*, 243 U.S. 332. Congress knew that some of the States covered by §4(b) of the Act had resorted to the extraordinary stratagem of contriving new rules of various kinds for the sole purpose of perpetuating voting discrimination in the face of adverse federal court decrees. Congress had reason to suppose that these States might try similar maneuvers in the future in order to evade the remedies for voting discrimination contained in the Act itself. Under the compulsion of these unique circumstances, Congress responded in a permissibly decisive manner.

For reasons already stated, there was nothing inappropriate about limiting litigation under this provision to the District Court for the District of Columbia, and in putting the burden of proof on the areas seeking relief. Nor has Congress authorized the District Court to issue advisory opinions, in violation of the principles of Article III invoked by Georgia as amicus curiae. The Act automatically suspends the operation of voting regulations enacted after November 1, 1964, and furnishes mechanisms for enforcing the suspension. A State or political subdivision wishing to make use of a recent amendment to its voting laws therefore has a concrete and immediate 'controversy' with the Federal Government. Cf. *Public Utilities Comm. v. United States*, 355 U.S. 534, 536–539; *United States v. State of California*, 332 U.S. 19, 24–25. An appropriate remedy is a judicial determination that continued suspension of the new rule is unnecessary to vindicate rights guaranteed by the Fifteenth Amendment.

Federal examiners.

The Act authorizes the appointment of federal examiners to list qualified applicants who are thereafter entitled to vote, subject to an expeditious challenge procedure. This was clearly an appropriate response to the problem, closely related to remedies authorized in prior cases. See *Alabama v. United States, supra*; *United States v. Thomas*, 362 U.S. 58. In many of the political subdivisions covered by §4(b) of the Act, voting officials have persistently employed a variety of procedural tactics to deny Negroes the franchise, often in direct defiance or evasion of federal court decrees. Congress realized that merely to suspend voting rules which have been misused or are subject to misuse might leave this localized evil undisturbed. As for the briskness of the challenge procedure, Congress knew that in some of the areas affected, challenges had been persistently employed to harass registered Negroes. It chose to forestall this abuse, at the same time providing alternative ways for removing persons listed through error or fraud. In addition to the judicial challenge procedure, § 7(d) allows for the removal of names by the examiner himself, and § 11(c) makes it a crime to obtain a listing through fraud.

In recognition of the fact that there were political subdivisions covered by § 4(b) of the Act in which the appointment of federal examiners might be unnecessary, Congress assigned the Attorney General the task of determining the localities to which examiners should be sent. There is no warrant for the claim, asserted by Georgia as amicus curiae, that the Attorney General is free to use this power in an arbitrary fashion, without regard to the purposes of the Act. Section 6(b) sets adequate standards to guide the exercise of his discretion, by directing him to calculate the registration ratio of non-whites to whites, and to weigh evidence of good-faith efforts to avoid possible voting discrimination. At the same time, the special termination procedures of § 13(a) provide indirect judicial review for the political subdivisions affected, assuring the withdrawal of federal examiners from areas where they are clearly not needed. Cf. *Carlson v. Landon*, 342 U.S. 524, 542–544; *Mulford v. Smith*, 307 U.S. 38, 48–49.

After enduring nearly a century of widespread resistance to the Fifteenth Amendment, Congress has marshalled an array of potent weapons against the evil, with authority in the Attorney General to employ them effectively. Many of the areas directly affected by this development have indicated their willingness to abide by any restraints legitimately imposed upon them. We here hold that the portions of the Voting Rights Act properly before us are a valid means for carrying out the commands of the Fifteenth Amendment. Hopefully, millions of non-white Americans will now be able to participate for the first time on an equal basis in the government under which they live. We may finally look forward to the day when truly '(t)he right of citizens of the United States to vote shall not be denied or abridged by the United States or by any State on account of race, color, or previous condition of servitude.'

The bill of complaint is dismissed.

Bill dismissed.

Notes

1. See below for *Presley v. Etowah County Commission*, 502 U.S. 491 (1992), which discusses the meaning of Section 5 of the Voting Rights Act and what constitutes an "entity" under Section 5.

2. Section 5 provides authority to the federal government to monitor states with a record of wrongdoing in relation to voting. Being covered under the Act means that a state or locality may not make a decision or a change in regard to voting procedures without first seeking the authorization of the Department of Justice. The process of seeking that permission is called preclearance. Section 5's coverage formula, below, is the calculation that brings states or localities under the supervision of the Department of Justice.[20]

Coverage Formula

Section 5 applies to:

> any State, or to any separate political subdivision such as a county or par-
> ish, for which two findings have been made: (1) the Attorney General has
> determined that on November 1, 1964, it maintained a "test or device," and
> (2) the Director of the Census has determined that less than 50% of its
> voting age residents were registered on November 1,1964, or voted in the
> presidential election of November 1964. These findings are not reviewable
> in any court and are final upon publication in the Federal Register. § 4(b).
> As used throughout the Act, the phrase "test or device" means any require-
> ment that a registrant or voter must "(1) demonstrate the ability to read,
> write, understand, or interpret any matter, (2) demonstrate any educational
> achievement or his knowledge of any particular subject, (3) possess good
> moral character, or (4) prove his qualifications by the voucher of registered
> voters or members of any other class." § 4(c).

Katzenbach, 383 U.S. at 317.

Section 5 was initially enacted for a period of five years and was renewed periodically by Congress based upon empirical findings of ongoing problems related to
voting. The viability of this formula, despite the recent 2006 renewal, is the focus
of *Northwest Austin Mun. Util. Dist. No. One v. Holder* and *Shelby County v. Holder*
below. Section 5 oversight has been documented to be one of the most successful
tools for holding many governments accountable and preventing underhanded voting tactics. Part of the reason for its effectiveness lies in the breath of Section 5's
scope. The Court has been called to define the meaning of "political subdivision"
and has determined that political subdivision includes among many others, utilities
boards, state agencies, county commissions, school boards, etc. As a result, jurisdictions covered by Section 5 may need to obtain preclearance from the Department
of Justice when contemplating a voting change. Another issue of frequent consideration is what constitutes a "voting change" in a variety of contexts under Section 5.
Does changing the ways in which county commissioners make decisions or alter
financing distributions constitute a voting change?[21] See below.

---

20. 52 U.S.C. § 10304; Shelby Cty. v. Holder, 133 S. Ct. 2612 (2013).

21. Northwest Austin Mun. Util. Dist. No. One v. Holder, 557 U.S. 193 (2009); South Carolina
v. Katzenbach, 383 U.S. 301 (1966); Fannie Lou Hamer, Rosa Parks, and Coretta Scott King Voting
Rights Act Reauthorization and Amendments Act of 2006, 109 P.L. 246, 120 Stat. 577; *Election Law
Violations*, 51 Am. Crim. L. Rev. 963; Shelby Cty. v. Holder, 811 F. Supp. 2d 424 (D.D.C. 2011).

Presley v. Etowah County Commission

112 S. Ct. 820 (1992)

JUSTICE KENNEDY delivered the opinion of the Court.

In various Alabama counties voters elect members of county commissions whose principal function is to supervise and control the maintenance, repair, and construction of the county roads. See Ala.Code §§ 11-3-1, 11-3-10 (1975). The consolidated appeals now before us concern certain changes in the decision making authority of the elected members on two different county commissions, and the question to be decided is whether these were changes "with respect to voting" within the meaning of § 5 of the Voting Rights Act of 1965, 79 Stat. 439, as amended, 42 U.S.C. § 1973c. These cases have significance well beyond the two county commissions; for the appellants, and the United States as *amicus curiae,* ask us to adopt a rule embracing the routine actions of state and local governments at all levels. We must interpret the provisions of § 5, which require a jurisdiction covered by the Act to obtain either judicial or administrative preclearance before enforcing any new "voting qualification or prerequisite to voting, or standard, practice, or procedure with respect to voting."

I

To determine whether there have been changes with respect to voting, we must compare the challenged practices with those in existence before they were adopted. Absent relevant intervening changes, the Act requires us to use practices in existence on November 1, 1964, as our standard of comparison.

A

We consider first the Etowah County Commission. On November 1, 1964, commission members were elected at large under a "residency district" system. The entire electorate of Etowah County voted on candidates for each of the five seats. Four of the seats corresponded to the four residency districts of the county. Candidates were required to reside in the appropriate district. The fifth member, the chairman, was not subject to a district residency requirement, though residency in the county itself was a requirement.

Each of the four residency districts functioned as a road district. The commissioner residing in the district exercised control over a road shop, equipment, and road crew for that district. It was the practice of the commission to vote as a collective body on the division of funds among the road districts, but once funds were divided each commissioner exercised individual control over spending priorities within his district. The chairman was responsible for overseeing the solid waste authority, preparing the budget, and managing the courthouse building and grounds.

Under a consent decree issued in 1986, see *Dillard v. Crenshaw County,* Civ. Action No. 85-T-1332-N (MD Ala., Nov. 12, 1986), the commission is being restructured, so that after a transition period there will be a six-member commission, with each of the members elected by the voters of a different district. The changes required by the consent decree were precleared by the Attorney General. For present purposes, it suffices to say that when this litigation began the commission consisted of four holdover members who had been on the commission before the entry of the consent decree and two new members elected from new districts. Commissioner Williams, who is white, was elected from new district 6, and Commissioner Presley, who is black, was elected from new district 5. Presley is the principal appellant in the Etowah County case. His complaint relates not to the elections but to actions taken by the four holdover members when he and Williams first took office.

On August 25, 1987, the commission passed the "Road Supervision Resolution." It provided that each holdover commissioner would continue to control the workers and operations assigned to his respective road shop, which, it must be remembered, accounted for all the road shops the county had. It also gave the four holdovers joint responsibility for overseeing the repair, maintenance, and improvement of all the roads of Etowah County in order to pick up the roads in the districts where the new commissioners resided. The new commissioners, now foreclosed from exercising any authority over roads, were given other functions under the resolution. Presley was to oversee maintenance of the county courthouse and Williams the operation of the engineering department. The Road Supervision Resolution was passed by a 4-to-2 margin, with the two new commissioners dissenting.

The same day the Road Supervision Resolution was passed, the commission passed a second, the so-called "Common Fund Resolution." It provides in part that

> "all monies earmarked and budgeted for repair, maintenance and improvement of the streets, roads and public ways of Etowah County [shall] be placed and maintained in common accounts, [shall] not be allocated, budgeted or designated for use in districts, and [shall] be used county-wide in accordance with need, for the repair, maintenance and improvement of all streets, roads and public ways in Etowah County which are under the jurisdiction of the Etowah County Commission." App. to Juris. Statement in No. 90-711, p. 49a.

This had the effect of altering the prior practice of allowing each commissioner full authority to determine how to spend the funds allocated to his own district. The Etowah County Commission did not seek judicial or administrative preclearance of either the Road Supervision Resolution or the Common Fund Resolution. The District Court held that the Road Supervision Resolution was subject to preclearance but that the Common Fund Resolution was not. No appeal was taken from the first ruling, so only the Common Fund Resolution is before us in the Etowah County case.

B

We turn next to the background of the Russell County Commission. On November 1, 1964, it had three commissioners. Like the members of the Etowah County

Commission before the consent decree change, Russell County Commissioners were elected at large by the entire electorate, subject to a requirement that a candidate for commissioner reside in the district corresponding to the seat he or she sought. A 1972 federal court order, see *Anthony v. Russell County*, No. 961-E (MD Ala., Nov. 21, 1972), required that the commission be expanded to include five members. The two new members were both elected at large from one newly created residency district for Phoenix City, the largest city in Russell County. Following the implementation of the court order, each of the three rural commissioners had individual authority over his own road shop, road crew, and equipment. The three rural commissioners also had individual authority for road and bridge repair and construction within their separate residency districts. Although funding for new construction and major repair projects was subject to a vote by the entire commission, individual commissioners could authorize expenditures for routine repair and maintenance work as well as routine purchase orders without seeking approval from the entire commission.

Following the indictment of one commissioner on charges of corruption in Russell County road operations, in May 1979 the commission passed a resolution delegating control over road construction, maintenance, personnel, and inventory to the county engineer, an official appointed by the entire commission and responsible to it. The engineer's previous duties had been limited to engineering and surveying services for the separate road shops and running a small crew devoted to pothole repair. Although the May 1979 resolution may have sufficed for the necessary delegation of authority to the county engineer, compare Ala.Code § 23-1-80 (1975) with Ala.Code § 11-6-3 (1975), the commission also requested the state legislature to pass implementing legislation. The Alabama Legislature did so on July 30, 1979, when it enacted Act No. 79-652, 1979 Ala. Acts 1132. It provides in pertinent part:

> "Section 1. All functions, duties and responsibilities for the construction, maintenance and repair of public roads, highways, bridges and ferries in Russell County are hereby vested in the county engineer, who shall, insofar as possible, construct and maintain such roads, highways, bridges and ferries on the basis of the county as a whole or as a unit, without regard to district or beat lines."

The parties refer to abolition of the individual road districts and transfer of responsibility for all road operations to the county engineer as the adoption of a "Unit System." Neither the resolution nor the statute which authorized the Unit System was submitted for preclearance under § 5.

Litigation involving the Russell County Commission led to a 1985 consent decree, see *Sumbry v. Russell County*, No. 84-T-1386-E (MD Ala., Mar. 17, 1985), that enlarged the commission to seven members and replaced the at-large election system with elections on a district-by-district basis. Without any mention of the Unit System changes, the consent decree was precleared by the Department of Justice under § 5. Following its implementation, appellants Mack and Gosha were elected in 1986. They are Russell County's first black county commissioners in modern times.

C

In May 1989, appellants in both cases now before us filed a single complaint in the District Court for the Middle District of Alabama, alleging racial discrimination in the operation of the Etowah and Russell County Commissions in violation of prior court orders, the Constitution, Title VI of the Civil Rights Act of 1964, 42 U.S.C. §2000d, and §2 of the Voting Rights Act, 42 U.S.C. §1973. In a series of amended complaints, appellants added claims under §5. The §5 claims alleged that Etowah County had violated the Act by failing to obtain preclearance of the 1987 Road Supervision and Common Fund Resolutions, and that Russell County had failed to preclear the 1979 change to the Unit System. Pursuant to 28 U.S.C. §2284, a three-judge District Court was convened to hear appellants' §5 claims. The other claims still pend in the District Court.

With respect to the issues now before us, a majority of the District Court held that neither the Common Fund Resolution of the Etowah County Commission nor the adoption of the Unit System in Russell County was subject to §5 preclearance. The court held that changes in the responsibilities of elected officials are subject to preclearance when they "effect a significant relative change in the powers exercised by governmental officials elected by, or responsible to, substantially different constituencies of voters." App. to Juris. Statement in No. 90-711, pp. 13a-14a. Applying its test, the court found that the Common Fund Resolution in Etowah County did not effect a significant change and adoption of the Unit System in Russell County did not transfer authority among officials responsible to different constituencies. We noted probable jurisdiction. 500 U.S. 914, 111 S.Ct. 2007, 114 L.Ed.2d 96 (1991). We affirm the District Court but adopt a different interpretation of §5 as the rationale for our decision.

II

We first considered the Voting Rights Act in *South Carolina v. Katzenbach*, 383 U.S. 301, 86 S.Ct. 803, 15 L.Ed.2d 769 (1966). Although we acknowledged that suspension of new voting regulations pending preclearance was an extraordinary departure from the traditional course of relations between the States and the Federal Government, *id.*, at 334, 86 S.Ct. at 821–822, we held it constitutional as a permitted congressional response to the unremitting attempts by some state and local officials to frustrate their citizens' equal enjoyment of the right to vote. See *id.*, at 308–315, 86 S.Ct. at 808–811.

After *South Carolina v. Katzenbach* upheld the Voting Rights Act against a constitutional challenge, it was not until we heard *Allen v. State Bd. of Elections*, 393 U.S. 544, 89 S.Ct. 817, 22 L.Ed.2d 1 (1969), that we were called upon to decide whether particular changes were covered by §5. There we rejected a narrow construction, one which would have limited §5 to state rules prescribing who may register to vote. We held that the section applies also to state rules relating to the qualifications of candidates and to state decisions as to which offices shall be elective. *Id.*, at 564–565, 89 S. Ct., at 831. We observed that "[t]he Voting Rights Act was aimed at the subtle, as well as the obvious, state regulations which have the effect of denying citizens their right to vote because of their race." *Id.*, at 565, 89 S.Ct., at 831. Our decision, and its rationale, have proved sound, and we adhere to both.

In giving a broad construction to § 5 in *Allen,* we noted that "Congress intended to reach any state enactment which altered the election law of a covered State in even a minor way." *Id.*, at 566, 89 S.Ct., at 832. Relying on this language and its application in later cases, appellants and the United States now argue that because there is no *de minimis* exception to § 5, the changes at issue here must be subject to preclearance. *E.g.,* Brief for United States as *Amicus Curiae* 21–22. This argument, however, assumes the answer to the principal question in the case: whether the changes at issue are changes in voting, or as we phrased it in *Allen,* "election law."

We agree that all changes in voting must be precleared and with *Allen's* holding that the scope of § 5 is expansive within its sphere of operation. That sphere comprehends all changes to rules governing voting, changes effected through any of the mechanisms described in the statute. Those mechanisms are any "qualification or prerequisite" or any "standard, practice, or procedure with respect to voting."

The principle that § 5 covers voting changes over a wide range is well illustrated by the separate cases we considered in the single opinion for the Court in *Allen. Allen* involved four cases. The eponymous *Allen v. State Bd. of Elections* concerned a change in the procedures for the casting of write-in ballots. 393 U.S., at 570–571, 89 S.Ct., at 834. In *Whitley v. Williams,* there were changes in the requirements for independent candidates running in general elections. *Id.*, at 551, 89 S.Ct., at 824. The challenged procedure in *Fairley v. Patterson* resulted in a change from single-district voting to at-large voting. *Id.*, at 550, 89 S.Ct., at 823. The remaining case, *Bunton v. Patterson,* involved a statute which provided that officials who in previous years had been elected would be appointed. *Id.*, at 550–551, 89 S.Ct., at 823–824. We held that the changes in each of the four cases were covered by § 5.

Our cases since *Allen* reveal a consistent requirement that changes subject to § 5 pertain only to voting. Without implying that the four typologies exhaust the statute's coverage, we can say these later cases fall within one of the four factual contexts presented in the *Allen* cases. First, we have held that § 5 applies to cases like *Allen v. State Bd. of Elections* itself, in which the changes involved the manner of voting. See *Perkins v. Matthews,* 400 U.S. 379, 387, 91 S.Ct. 431, 436, 27 L.Ed.2d 476 (1971) (location of polling places). Second, we have held that § 5 applies to cases like *Whitley v. Williams,* which involve candidacy requirements and qualifications. See *NAACP v. Hampton County Election Comm'n,* 470 U.S. 166, 105 S.Ct. 1128, 84 L.Ed.2d 124 (1985) (change in filing deadline); *Hadnott v. Amos,* 394 U.S. 358, 89 S.Ct. 1101, 22 L.Ed.2d 336 (1969) (same); *Dougherty County Bd. of Ed. v. White,* 439 U.S. 32, 99 S.Ct. 368, 58 L.Ed.2d 269 (1978) (rule requiring board of education members to take unpaid leave of absence while campaigning for office). Third, we have applied § 5 to cases like *Fairley v. Patterson,* which concerned changes in the composition of the electorate that may vote for candidates for a given office. See *Perkins v. Matthews,*

400 U.S., at 394, 91 S.Ct., at 439–440 (change from ward to at-large elections); *id.*, at 388, 91 S.Ct., at 437 (boundary lines of voting districts); *City of Richmond v. United States,* 422 U.S. 358, 95 S.Ct. 2296, 45 L.Ed.2d 245 (1975) (same). Fourth, we have made clear that §5 applies to changes, like the one in *Bunton v. Patterson,* affecting the creation or abolition of an elective office. See *McCain v. Lybrand,* 465 U.S. 236, 104 S.Ct. 1037, 79 L.Ed.2d 271 (1984) (appointed officials replaced by elected officials); *Lockhart v. United States,* 460 U.S. 125, 103 S.Ct. 998, 74 L.Ed.2d 863 (1983) (increase in number of city councilors).

The first three categories involve changes in election procedures, while all the examples within the fourth category might be termed substantive changes as to which offices are elective. But whether the changes are of procedure or substance, each has a direct relation to voting and the election process.

III

A comparison of the changes at issue here with those in our prior decisions demonstrates that the present cases do not involve changes covered by the Act.

A

The Etowah County Commission's Common Fund Resolution is not a change within any of the categories recognized in *Allen* or our later cases. It has no connection to voting procedures: It does not affect the manner of holding elections, it alters or imposes no candidacy qualifications or requirements, and it leaves undisturbed the composition of the electorate. It also has no bearing on the substance of voting power, for it does not increase or diminish the number of officials for whom the electorate may vote. Rather, the Common Fund Resolution concerns the internal operations of an elected body.

Appellants argue that the Common Fund Resolution is a covered change because after its enactment each commissioner has less individual power than before the resolution. A citizen casting a ballot for a commissioner today votes for an individual with less authority than before the resolution, and so, it is said, the value of the vote has been diminished.

Were we to accept appellants' proffered reading of §5, we would work an unconstrained expansion of its coverage. Innumerable state and local enactments having nothing to do with voting affect the power of elected officials. When a state or local body adopts a new governmental program or modifies an existing one it will often be the case that it changes the powers of elected officials. So too, when a state or local body alters its internal operating procedures, for example by modifying its subcommittee assignment system, it "implicate[s] an elected official's *decision making authority.*" Brief for United States as *Amicus Curiae* 17–18 (emphasis in original).

Appellants and the United States fail to provide a workable standard for distinguishing between changes in rules governing voting and changes in the routine organization and functioning of government. Some standard is necessary, for in a real sense every decision taken by government implicates voting. This is but the felicitous consequence of democracy, in which power derives from the people. Yet no one would contend that when Congress enacted the Voting Rights Act it meant to subject all or even most decisions of government in covered jurisdictions to federal supervision. Rather, the Act by its terms covers any "voting qualification or prerequisite to voting, or standard, practice, or procedure with respect to voting." 42 U.S.C. § 1973c. A faithful effort to implement the design of the statute must begin by drawing lines between those governmental decisions that involve voting and those that do not.

A simple example shows the inadequacy of the line proffered by appellants and the United States. Under appellants' view, every time a covered jurisdiction passed a budget that differed from the previous year's budget it would be required to obtain preclearance. The amount of funds available to an elected official has a profound effect on the power exercised. A vote for an ill-funded official is less valuable than a vote for a well-funded one.

No doubt in recognition of the unacceptable consequences of their views, appellants take the position that while "some budget changes may affect the right to vote and, under particular circumstances, would be subject to preclearance," most budget changes would not. Postargument Letter from Counsel for Appellants, Nov. 13, 1991 (available in Clerk of Court's case file). Under their interpretation of § 5, however, appellants fail to give any workable standard to determine when preclearance is required. And were we to acknowledge that a budget adjustment is a voting change in even some instances, the likely consequence is that every budget change would be covered, for it is well settled that every voting change with a "potential for discrimination" must be precleared. *Dougherty County Bd. of Ed. v. White*, 439 U.S., at 42, 99 S.Ct., at 374.

Confronting this difficulty, at oral argument the United States suggested that we draw an arbitrary line distinguishing between budget changes and other changes, Tr. of Oral Arg. 21–23. There is no principled basis for the distinction, and it would be a marked departure from the statutory category of voting. If a diminution or increase in an elected official's powers is a change with respect to voting, then whether it is accomplished through an enactment or a budget shift should not matter. Even if we were willing to draw an unprincipled line excluding budgetary changes but no other changes in an elected official's decision-making authority, the result would expand the coverage of § 5 well beyond the statutory language and the intention of Congress.

Under the view advanced by appellants and the United States, every time a state legislature acts to diminish or increase the power of local officials, preclearance would be required. Governmental action decreasing the power of local officials could carry with it a potential for discrimination against those who represent racial minorities at the local level. At the same time, increasing the power of local officials will entail a relative decrease in the power of state officials, and that too could carry with it a potential for discrimination against state officials who represent racial minorities at the state level. The all but limitless minor changes in the allocation of power among officials and the constant adjustments required for the efficient governance of every covered State illustrate the necessity for us to formulate workable rules to confine the coverage of § 5 to its legitimate sphere: voting.

Changes which affect only the distribution of power among officials are not subject to § 5 because such changes have no direct relation to, or impact on, voting. The Etowah County Commission's Common Fund Resolution was not subject to the preclearance requirement.

B

We next consider Russell County's adoption of the Unit System and its concomitant transfer of operations to the county engineer. Of the four categories of changes in rules governing voting we have recognized to date, there is not even an arguable basis for saying that adoption of the Unit System fits within any of the first three. As to the fourth category, it might be argued that the delegation of authority to an appointed official is similar to the replacement of an elected official with an appointed one, the change we held subject to § 5 in *Bunton v. Patterson*. This approach, however, would ignore the rationale for our holding: "[A]fter the change, [the citizen] is prohibited from electing an officer formerly subject to the approval of the voters." *Allen*, 393 U.S., at 569–570, 89 S.Ct., at 833–834. In short, the change in *Bunton v. Patterson* involved a rule governing voting not because it effected a change in the relative authority of various governmental officials, but because it changed an elective office to an appointive one.

The change in Russell County does not prohibit voters "from electing an officer formerly subject to the[ir] approval." *Allen, supra*, 393 U.S., at 570, 89 S.Ct., at 834. Both before and after the change the citizens of Russell County were able to vote for the members of the Russell County Commission. To be sure, after the 1979 resolution each commissioner exercised less direct authority over road operations, that authority having been delegated to an official answerable to the commission. But as we concluded with respect to Etowah County, the fact that an enactment alters an elected official's powers does not in itself render the enactment a rule governing voting.

It is a routine part of governmental administration for appointive positions to be created or eliminated and for their powers to be altered. Each time this occurs the relative balance of authority is altered in some way. The making or unmaking of an appointive post often will result in the erosion or accretion of the powers of some official responsible to the electorate, but it does not follow that those changes are covered by § 5. By requiring preclearance of changes with respect to voting, Congress did not mean to subject such routine matters of governance to federal supervision. Were the rule otherwise, neither state nor local governments could exercise power in a responsible manner within a federal system.

The District Court, wrestling with the problem we now face and recognizing the need to draw principled lines, held that Russell County's adoption of the Unit System is not a covered change because it did not transfer power among officials answerable to different constituencies. Even upon the assumption (the assumption we reject in this case) that some transfers of power among government officials could be changes with respect to voting as that term is used in the Act, we disagree with the District Court's test. The question whether power is shifted among officials answerable to the same or different constituencies is quite distinct from the question whether the power voters exercise over elected officials is affected. Intraconstituency changes may have a large indirect effect on the voters while interconstituency changes may have a small indirect effect, but in neither case is the effect a change in voting for purposes of the Act. The test adopted by the District Court does not provide the workable rule we seek. In any event, because it proceeds from the faulty premise that reallocations of authority within government can constitute voting changes, we cannot accept its approach.

We need not consider here whether an otherwise uncovered enactment of a jurisdiction subject to the Voting Rights Act might under some circumstances rise to the level of a *de facto* replacement of an elective office with an appointive one, within the rule of *Bunton v. Patterson.* For present purposes it suffices to note that the Russell County Commission retains substantial authority, including the power to appoint the county engineer and to set his or her budget. The change at issue in Russell County is not a covered change.

IV

The United States urges that despite our understanding of the language of § 5, we should defer to its administrative construction of the provision. We have recognized that "the construction placed upon the [Voting Rights] Act by the Attorney General . . . is entitled to considerable deference." *NAACP v. Hampton County Election Comm'n,* 470 U.S., at 178–179, 105 S.Ct., at 1135–1136. See also *United States v. Sheffield Bd. of Comm'rs,* 435 U.S. 110, 131, 98 S.Ct. 965, 979, 55 L.Ed.2d 148 (1978). But the principle has its limits. Deference does not mean acquiescence. As in other contexts in which we defer to an administrative interpretation of a statute, we do so only if Congress has not expressed its intent with respect to the question, and then only if the administrative interpretation is reasonable. See, *e.g., Chevron U.S.A. Inc. v. Natural Resources Defense Council, Inc.,* 467 U.S. 837, 842–844, 104 S.Ct. 2778, 2781–2782, 81 L.Ed.2d 694 (1984). Because the first of these conditions is not satisfied in the cases before us we do not defer to the Attorney General's interpretation of the Act.

We do not believe that in its use of the phrase "voting qualification or prerequisite to voting, or standard, practice, or procedure with respect to voting," 42 U.S.C. § 1973c, the statute is ambiguous as to the question whether § 5 extends beyond changes in rules governing voting. To be sure, reasonable minds may differ as to whether some particular changes in the law of a covered jurisdiction should be classified as changes in rules governing voting. In that sense § 5 leaves a gap for interpretation to fill. See *Chevron, supra*, 467 U.S., at 843, 104 S.Ct., at 2782. When the Attorney General makes a reasonable argument that a contested change should be classified as a change in a rule governing voting, we can defer to that judgment. But § 5 is unambiguous with respect to the question whether it covers changes other than changes in rules governing voting: It does not. The administrative position in the present cases is not entitled to deference, for it suggests the contrary. The United States argues that the changes are covered by § 5 because they implicate the decision-making authority of elected officials, even though they are not changes in rules governing voting. This argument does not meet the express requirement of the statute.

V

Nothing we say implies that the conduct at issue in these cases is not actionable under a different remedial scheme. The Voting Rights Act is not an all-purpose antidiscrimination statute. The fact that the intrusive mechanisms of the Act do not apply to other forms of pernicious discrimination does not undermine its utility in combating the specific evils it was designed to address.

Our prior cases hold, and we reaffirm today, that every change in rules governing voting must be precleared. The legislative history we rehearsed in *South Carolina v. Katzenbach* was cited to demonstrate Congress' concern for the protection of voting rights. Neither the appellants nor the United States has pointed to anything we said there or in the statutes reenacting the Voting Rights Act to suggest that Congress meant other than what it said when it made § 5 applicable to changes "with respect to voting" rather than, say, changes "with respect to governance."

If federalism is to operate as a practical system of governance and not a mere poetic ideal, the States must be allowed both predictability and efficiency in structuring their governments. Constant minor adjustments in the allocation of power among state and local officials serve this elemental purpose.

Covered changes must bear a direct relation to voting itself. That direct relation is absent in both cases now before us. The changes in Etowah and Russell Counties affected only the allocation of power among governmental officials. They had no impact on the substantive question whether a particular office would be elective or the procedural question how an election would be conducted. Neither change involves a new "voting qualification or prerequisite to voting, or standard, practice, or procedure with respect to voting." 42 U.S.C. § 1973c.

The judgment of the District Court is affirmed.

It is so ordered.

Notes and Questions

1. The Court also stated: "The Constitution uses the words 'right to vote' in five separate places: The Fourteenth, Fifteenth, Nineteenth, Twenty-Fourth, and Twenty-Sixth Amendments. Each of these Amendments contains the same broad

empowerment of Congress to enact "appropriate legislation" to enforce the protected right." The implication is unmistakable: Under our constitutional structure, Congress holds the lead rein in making the right to vote equally real for all U.S. citizens. These Amendments are in line with the special role assigned to Congress in protecting the integrity of the democratic process in federal elections. U.S. Const., Art. I, §4 ("[T]he Congress may at any time by Law make or alter" regulations concerning the "Times, Places and Manner of holding Elections for Senators and Representatives"); *Arizona v. Inter Tribal Council of Ariz., Inc.*, 133 S. Ct. 2247, 2253 (2013).

a. What are the practical consequences of the voting change in *Presley*? Were the changes in *Presley* benign as the majority indicates or were they evidence of discrimination on the part of the government?

b. In the context of the facts of the case, is the dissent (not included here) correct that the timing of the changes, after the election of African American commissioners, should be determinative? Think about the role of county commissioners in making decisions affecting distribution of the funds necessary for the maintenance and smooth running of local government.

c. In what ways could the changes in *Presley* undermine the equal distribution of resources? Consider the documented history of manipulation and resources depletion by local authorities in defiance of *Brown*.

C. Section 5 Today and in the Future

The future of Section 5 is in serious question subsequent to the Court's decision in *Shelby County v. Holder*, declaring the coverage formula unconstitutional. Conjuring *Katzenbach* and its interpretation of federalism doctrine, the *Shelby* majority determined that the current formula is an improper exercise of congressional power. This approach was announced by the Court in dicta in *Northwest Austin*. Analyze the Court's reasoning below and compare it to the analysis in *Katzenbach v. South Carolina*, above. Did Justice Roberts overstep in *Northwest Austin* by indicating a willingness to strike down Section 5 in the future? Is the Court's analysis in *Shelby County* consistent with precedents and the tenets of the Fifteenth Amendment?

Northwest Austin Mun. Util. Dist. No. One v. Holder
557 U.S. 193 (2009)

CHIEF JUSTICE ROBERTS delivered the opinion of the Court.

The plaintiff in this case is a small utility district raising a big question—the constitutionality of §5 of the Voting Rights Act. The district has an elected board, and is required by §5 to seek preclearance from federal authorities in Washington, D. C., before it can change anything about those elections. This is required even though there has never been any evidence of racial discrimination in voting in the district.

The district filed suit seeking relief from these preclearance obligations under the "bailout" provision of the Voting Rights Act. That provision allows the release of a "political subdivision" from the preclearance requirements if certain rigorous conditions are met. The court below denied relief, concluding that bailout was unavailable to a political subdivision like the utility district that did not register its own voters. The district appealed, arguing that the Act imposes no such limitation on bailout, and that if it does, the preclearance requirements are unconstitutional.

That constitutional question has attracted ardent briefs from dozens of interested parties, but the importance of the question does not justify our rushing to decide it. Quite the contrary: Our usual practice is to avoid the unnecessary resolution of constitutional questions. We agree that the district is eligible under the Act to seek bailout. We therefore reverse, and do not reach the constitutionality of § 5.

I

A

The Fifteenth Amendment promises that the "right of citizens of the United States to vote shall not be denied or abridged . . . on account of race, color, or previous condition of servitude." U.S. Const., Amdt. 15, § 1. In addition to that self-executing right, the Amendment also gives Congress the "power to enforce this article by appropriate legislation." § 2. The first century of congressional enforcement of the Amendment, however, can only be regarded as a failure. Early enforcement Acts were inconsistently applied and repealed with the rise of Jim Crow. *South Carolina v. Katzenbach*, 383 U.S. 301, 310, 86 S. Ct. 803, 15 L. Ed. 2d 769 (1966); A. Keyssar, The Right to Vote 105–111 (2000). Another series of enforcement statutes in the 1950's and 1960's depended on individual lawsuits filed by the Department of Justice. But litigation is slow and expensive, and the States were creative in "contriving new rules" to continue violating the Fifteenth Amendment "in the face of adverse federal court decrees." *Katzenbach, supra*, at 335, 86 S. Ct. 803, 15 L. Ed. 2d 769; *Riley v. Kennedy*, 553 U.S. 406, 411, 128 S. Ct. 1970, 1977, 170 L. Ed. 2d 837, 845 (2008).

Congress responded with the Voting Rights Act. Section 2 of the Act operates nationwide; as it exists today, that provision forbids any "standard, practice, or procedure" that "results in a denial or abridgement of the right of any citizen of the United States to vote on account of race or color." 42 U.S.C. § 1973(a). Section 2 is not at issue in this case.

The remainder of the Act constitutes a "scheme of stringent remedies aimed at areas where voting discrimination has been most flagrant." *Katzenbach, supra*, at 315, 86 S. Ct. 803, 15 L. Ed. 2d 769. Rather than continuing to depend on case-by-case litigation, the Act directly pre-empted the most powerful tools of black disenfranchisement in the covered areas. All literacy tests and similar voting qualifications were abolished by § 4 of the Act. Voting Rights Act of 1965, §§ 4(a)-(d), 79

Stat. 438–439. Although such tests may have been facially neutral, they were easily manipulated to keep blacks from voting. The Act also empowered federal examiners to override state determinations about who was eligible to vote. §§ 6, 7, 9, 13, *id.,* at 439–442, 444–445.

These two remedies were bolstered by § 5, which suspended all changes in state election procedure until they were submitted to and approved by a three-judge Federal District Court in Washington, D. C., or the Attorney General. *Id.,* at 439, codified as amended at 42 U.S.C. § 1973c(a). Such preclearance is granted only if the change neither "has the purpose nor will have the effect of denying or abridging the right to vote on account of race or color." *Ibid.* We have interpreted the requirements of § 5 to apply not only to the ballot-access rights guaranteed by § 4, but to drawing district lines as well. *Allen v. State Bd. of Elections,* 393 U.S. 544, 564–565, 89 S. Ct. 817, 22 L. Ed. 2d 1 (1969).

To confine these remedies to areas of flagrant disenfranchisement, the Act applied them only to States that had used a forbidden test or device in November 1964, and had less than 50% voter registration or turnout in the 1964 Presidential election. § 4(b), 79 Stat. 438. Congress recognized that the coverage formula it had adopted "might bring within its sweep governmental units not guilty of any unlawful discriminatory voting practices." *Briscoe v. Bell,* 432 U.S. 404, 411, 97 S. Ct. 2428, 53 L. Ed. 2d 439 (1977). It therefore "afforded such jurisdictions immediately available protection in the form of . . . [a] 'bailout' suit." *Ibid.*

To bail out under the current provision, a jurisdiction must seek a declaratory judgment from a three-judge District Court in Washington, D.C. 42 U.S.C. §§ 1973b(a)(1), 1973c(a). It must show that for the previous 10 years it has not used any forbidden voting test, has not been subject to any valid objection under § 5, and has not been found liable for other voting rights violations; it must also show that it has "engaged in constructive efforts to eliminate intimidation and harassment" of voters, and similar measures. §§ 1973b(a)(1)(A)-(F). The Attorney General can consent to entry of judgment in favor of bailout if the evidence warrants it, though other interested parties are allowed to intervene in the declaratory judgment action. § 1973b(a)(9). There are other restrictions: To bail out, a covered jurisdiction must show that every jurisdiction in its territory has complied with all of these requirements. § 1973b(a)(3). The District Court also retains continuing jurisdiction over a successful bailout suit for 10 years, and may reinstate coverage if any violation is found. § 1973b(a)(5).

As enacted, §§ 4 and 5 of the Voting Rights Act were temporary provisions. They were expected to be in effect for only five years. § 4(a), 79 Stat. 438. We upheld the temporary Voting Rights Act of 1965 as an appropriate exercise of congressional power in *Katzenbach,* explaining that "[t]he constitutional propriety of the Voting Rights Act of 1965 must be judged with reference to the historical experience which it reflects." 383 U.S., at 308, 86 S. Ct. 803, 15 L. Ed. 2d 769. We concluded that the problems Congress faced when it passed the Act were so dire that "exceptional conditions [could] justify legislative measures not otherwise appropriate." *Id.*, at 334–335, 86 S. Ct. 803, 15 L. Ed. 2d 769 (citing *Home Building & Loan Assn. v. Blaisdell*, 290 U.S. 398, 54 S. Ct. 231, 78 L. Ed. 413 (1934), and *Wilson v. New*, 243 U.S. 332, 37 S. Ct. 298, 61 L. Ed. 755 (1917)).

Congress reauthorized the Act in 1970 (for 5 years), 1975 (for 7 years), and 1982 (for 25 years). The coverage formula remained the same, based on the use of voting-eligibility tests and the rate of registration and turnout among all voters, but the pertinent dates for assessing these criteria moved from 1964 to include 1968 and eventually 1972. 42 U.S.C. § 1973b(b). We upheld each of these reauthorizations against constitutional challenges, finding that circumstances continued to justify the provisions.... Most recently, in 2006, Congress extended § 5 for yet another 25 years. Fannie Lou Hamer, Rosa Parks, and Coretta Scott King Voting Rights Act Reauthorization and Amendments Act of 2006, 120 Stat. 577. The 2006 Act retained 1972 as the last baseline year for triggering coverage under § 5. It is that latest extension that is now before us.

B

Northwest Austin Municipal Utility District Number One was created in 1987 to deliver city services to residents of a portion of Travis County, Texas. It is governed by a board of five members, elected to staggered terms of four years. The district does not register voters but is responsible for its own elections; for administrative reasons, those elections are run by Travis County. Because the district is located in Texas, it is subject to the obligations of § 5, although there is no evidence that it has ever discriminated on the basis of race.

The district filed suit in the District Court for the District of Columbia, seeking relief under the statute's bailout provisions and arguing in the alternative that, if interpreted to render the district ineligible for bailout, § 5 was unconstitutional. The three-judge District Court rejected both claims. Under the statute, only a "State or political subdivision" is permitted to seek bailout, 42 U.S.C. § 1973b(a)(1)(A), and the court concluded that the district was not a political subdivision because that term includes only "counties, parishes, and voter-registering subunits," *Northwest Austin Municipal Util. Dist. No. One v. Mukasey*, 573 F. Supp. 2d 221, 232 (2008).... We noted probable jurisdiction, 555 U.S. 1091, 129 S. Ct. 894, 172 L. Ed. 2d 768 (2009), and now reverse.

II

The historic accomplishments of the Voting Rights Act are undeniable. When it was first passed, unconstitutional discrimination was rampant, and the "registration of voting-age whites ran roughly 50 percentage points or more ahead" of black registration in many covered States. *Katzenbach, supra*, at 313, 86 S. Ct. 803, 15 L. Ed. 2d 769; H. R. Rep. No. 109-478, p 12 (2006). Today, the registration gap between white and black voters is in single digits in the covered States; in some of those States, blacks now register and vote at higher rates than whites. *Id.*, at 12–13. Similar dramatic improvements have occurred for other racial minorities. *Id.,* at 18–20. "[M]any of the first generation barriers to minority voter registration and voter turnout that were in place prior to the [Voting Rights Act] have been eliminated." *Id.,* at 12; *Bartlett v. Strickland,* 556 U.S. 1, 10, 129 S. Ct. 1231, 1240, 173 L. Ed. 2d 173, 181 (2009)) (plurality opinion) ("Passage of the Voting Rights Act of 1965 was an important step in the struggle to end discriminatory treatment of minorities who seek to exercise one of the most fundamental rights of our citizens: the right to vote").

At the same time, § 5, "which authorizes federal intrusion into sensitive areas of state and local policymaking, imposes substantial 'federalism costs.'" *Lopez, supra,* at 282, 119 S. Ct. 693, 142 L. Ed. 2d 728 (quoting *Miller v. Johnson,* 515 U.S. 900, 926, 115 S. Ct. 2475, 132 L. Ed. 2d 762 (1995)). These federalism costs have caused Members of this Court to express serious misgivings about the constitutionality of § 5. . . . Section 5 goes beyond the prohibition of the Fifteenth Amendment by suspending *all* changes to state election law—however innocuous—until they have been precleared by federal authorities in Washington, D. C. The preclearance requirement applies broadly, *NAACP v. Hampton County Election Comm'n,* 470 U.S. 166, 175–176, 105 S. Ct. 1128, 84 L. Ed. 2d 124 (1985), and in particular to every political subdivision in a covered State, no matter how small, *United States v. Sheffield Bd. of Comm'rs,* 435 U.S. 110, 117–118, 98 S. Ct. 965, 55 L. Ed. 2d 148 (1978).

Some of the conditions that we relied upon in upholding this statutory scheme in *Katzenbach* and *City of Rome* have unquestionably improved. Things have changed in the South. Voter turnout and registration rates now approach parity. Blatantly discriminatory evasions of federal decrees are rare. And minority candidates hold office at unprecedented levels. See generally H. R. Rep. No. 109-478, at 12–18.

These improvements are no doubt due in significant part to the Voting Rights Act itself, and stand as a monument to its success. Past success alone, however, is not adequate justification to retain the preclearance requirements. See Issacharoff, *Is Section 5 of the Voting Rights Act a Victim of Its Own Success?* 104 Colum. L. Rev. 1710 (2004). It may be that these improvements are insufficient and that conditions continue to warrant preclearance under the Act. But the Act imposes current burdens and must be justified by current needs.

The Act also differentiates between the States, despite our historic tradition that all the States enjoy "equal sovereignty." *United States v. Louisiana,* 363 U.S. 1, 16, 80 S. Ct. 961, 4 L. Ed. 2d 1025 (1960) (citing *Lessee of Pollard v. Hagan,* 44 U.S. 212, 3 How. 212, 223, 11 L. Ed. 565 (1845)); see also *Texas v. White,* 74 U.S. 700, 7 Wall. 700, 725–726, 19 L. Ed. 227 (1869). Distinctions can be justified in some cases. "The doctrine of the equality of States . . . does not bar . . . remedies for *local* evils which have subsequently appeared." *Katzenbach, supra,* at 328–329, 86 S. Ct. 803, 15 L. Ed. 2d 769 (emphasis added). But a departure from the fundamental principle of equal sovereignty requires a showing that a statute's disparate geographic coverage is sufficiently related to the problem that it targets.

These federalism concerns are underscored by the argument that the preclearance requirements in one State would be unconstitutional in another. See *Georgia v. Ashcroft*, 539 U.S. 461, 491–492, 123 S. Ct. 2498, 156 L. Ed. 2d 428 (2003) (Kennedy, J., concurring) ("Race cannot be the predominant factor in redistricting under our decision in Miller v. Johnson, 515 U.S. 900, 115 S. Ct. 2475, 132 L. Ed. 2d 762 (1995). Yet considerations of race that would doom a redistricting plan under the Fourteenth Amendment or § 2 seem to be what save it under § 5"). Additional constitutional concerns are raised in saying that this tension between §§ 2 and 5 must persist in covered jurisdictions and not elsewhere.

The evil that § 5 is meant to address may no longer be concentrated in the jurisdictions singled out for preclearance. The statute's coverage formula is based on data that is now more than 35 years old, and there is considerable evidence that it fails to account for current political conditions. For example, the racial gap in voter registration and turnout is lower in the States originally covered by § 5 than it is nationwide. E. Blum & L. Campbell, Assessment of Voting Rights Progress in Jurisdictions Covered Under Section Five of the Voting Rights Act 3–6 (Am. Enterprise Inst., 2006). Congress heard warnings from supporters of extending § 5 that the evidence in the record did not address "systematic differences between the covered and the non-covered areas of the United States[,] . . . and, in fact, the evidence that is in the record suggests that there is more similarity than difference." The Continuing Need for Section 5 Pre-Clearance: Hearing before the Senate Committee on the Judiciary, 109th Cong., 2d Sess., 10 (2006) (statement of Richard H. Pildes). . . .

The parties do not agree on the standard to apply in deciding whether, in light of the foregoing concerns, Congress exceeded its Fifteenth Amendment enforcement power in extending the preclearance requirements. The district argues that "'[t]here must be a congruence and proportionality between the injury to be prevented or remedied and the means adopted to that end,'" Brief for Appellant 31, quoting *City of Boerne v. Flores*, 521 U.S. 507, 520, 117 S. Ct. 2157, 138 L. Ed. 2d 624 (1997); the Federal Government asserts that it is enough that the legislation be a "'rational means to effectuate the constitutional prohibition,'" Brief for Federal Appellee 6, quoting *Katzenbach, supra*, at 324, 86 S. Ct. 803, 15 L. Ed. 2d 769. That question has been extensively briefed in this case, but we need not resolve it. The Act's preclearance requirements and its coverage formula raise serious constitutional questions under either test.

In assessing those questions, we are keenly mindful of our institutional role. We fully appreciate that judging the constitutionality of an Act of Congress is "the gravest and most delicate duty that this Court is called on to perform." *Blodgett v. Holden*, 275 U.S. 142, 147–148, 48 S. Ct. 105, 72 L. Ed. 206, 1928-1 C.B. 324 (1927) (Holmes, J., concurring). . . .

We will not shrink from our duty "as the bulwar[k] of a limited constitution against legislative encroachments," The Federalist No. 78, p 526 (J. Cooke ed. 1961) (A. Hamilton). . . . Here, the district also raises a statutory claim that it is eligible to bail out under §§ 4 and 5. . . . We therefore turn to the district's statutory argument.

III

Section 4(b) of the Voting Rights Act authorizes a bailout suit by a "State or political subdivision." 42 U.S.C. § 1973b(a)(1)(A). There is no dispute that the district is a political subdivision of the State of Texas in the ordinary sense of the term. See, *e.g.*, Black's Law Dictionary 1197 (8th ed. 2004) ("A division of a state that exists primarily to discharge some function of local government"). The district was created under Texas law with "powers of government" relating to local utilities and natural resources. Tex. Const., Art. XVI, § 59(b); Tex. Water Code Ann. § 54.011 (West 2002); see also *Bennett v. Brown Cty. Water Improvement Dist. No. 1*, 153 Tex. 599, 272 S.W.2d 498, 500 (Tex. 1954) ("[W]ater improvement district[s] . . . are held to be political subdivisions of the State" (internal quotation marks omitted)).

The Act, however, also provides a narrower statutory definition in § 14(c)(2): "'[P]olitical subdivision' shall mean any county or parish, except that where registration for voting is not conducted under the supervision of a county or parish, the term shall include any other subdivision of a State which conducts registration for voting." 42 U.S.C. § 1973l(c)(2). The District Court concluded that this definition applied to the bailout provision in § 4(a), and that the district did not qualify, since it is not a county or parish and does not conduct its own voter registration. . . . Were the scope of § 4(a) considered in isolation from the rest of the statute and our prior cases, the District Court's approach might well be correct. But here specific precedent, the structure of the Voting Rights Act, and underlying constitutional concerns compel a broader reading of the bailout provision.

Importantly, we do not write on a blank slate. Our decisions have already established that the statutory definition in § 14(c)(2) does not apply to every use of the term "political subdivision" in the Act. We have, for example, concluded that the definition does not apply to the preclearance obligation of § 5. According to its text, § 5 applies only "[w]henever a [covered] State or political subdivision" enacts or administers a new voting practice. Yet in *Sheffield Bd. of Comm'rs*, 435 U.S. 110, 98 S. Ct. 965, 55 L. Ed. 2d 148, we rejected the argument by a Texas city that it was neither a State nor a political subdivision as defined in the Act, and therefore did not need to seek preclearance of a voting change. The dissent agreed with the city, pointing out that the city did not meet the statutory definition of "political subdivision" and therefore could not be covered. *Id.*, at 141–144, 98 S. Ct. 965, 55 L. Ed. 2d 148 (opinion of Stevens, J.). The majority, however, relying on the purpose and structure of the Act, concluded that the "definition was intended to operate only for purposes of determining which political units in nondesignated States may be separately designated for coverage under § 4(b)." *Id.*, at 128–129, 98 S. Ct. 965, 55 L. Ed. 2d 148; see also *id.*, at 130, n. 18, 98 S. Ct. 965, 55 L. Ed. 2d 148 . . . .

. . . .

According to these decisions, then, the statutory definition of "political subdivision" in § 14(c)(2) does not apply to every use of the term "political subdivision" in the Act. . . . In light of our holdings that the statutory definition does not constrict the scope of preclearance required by § 5, the district argues, it only stands to reason that the definition should not constrict the availability of bailout from those preclearance requirements either.

. . . In *City of Rome* we rejected the city's attempt to bail out from coverage under § 5, concluding that "political units of a covered jurisdiction cannot independently bring a § 4(a) bailout action." 446 U.S., at 167, 100 S. Ct. 1548, 64 L. Ed. 2d 119. . . . Political subdivisions covered because they were part of a covered State, rather than because of separate coverage determinations, could not separately bail out. As Justice Stevens put it, "[t]he political subdivisions of a covered State" were "not entitled to bail out in a piecemeal fashion." *Id.*, at 192, 100 S. Ct. 1548, 64 L. Ed. 2d 119 (concurring opinion).

In 1982, however, Congress expressly repudiated *City of Rome* and instead embraced "piecemeal" bailout. As part of an overhaul of the bailout provision, Congress amended the Voting Rights Act to expressly provide that bailout was also available to "political subdivisions" in a covered State, "though [coverage] determinations were *not* made with respect to such subdivision as a separate unit." Voting Rights Act Amendments of 1982, § 2(b), 96 Stat. 131, codified at 42 U.S.C. § 1973b(a)(1) (emphasis added). . . .

But after the 1982 amendments, the Government's position is untenable. If the district is considered the State, and therefore necessarily subject to preclearance so long as Texas is covered, then the same must be true of all other subdivisions of the State, including counties. That would render even counties unable to seek bailout so long as their State was covered. But that is the very restriction the 1982 amendments overturned. Nobody denies that counties in a covered State can seek bailout, as several of them have. See Voting Rights Act: Section 5 of the Act—History, Scope, and Purpose: Hearing before the Subcommittee on the Constitution of the House Committee on the Judiciary, 109th Cong., 1st Sess., 2599-2834 (2005) (detailing bailouts). Because such piecemeal bailout is now permitted, it cannot be true that § 5 treats every governmental unit as the State itself.

. . . We therefore hold that all political subdivisions—not only those described in § 14(c)(2)—are eligible to file a bailout suit.

. . . .

More than 40 years ago, this Court concluded that "exceptional conditions" prevailing in certain parts of the country justified extraordinary legislation otherwise unfamiliar to our federal system. *Katzenbach*, 383 U.S., at 334, 86 S. Ct. 803, 15 L. Ed. 2d 769. In part due to the success of that legislation, we are now a very different

Nation. Whether conditions continue to justify such legislation is a difficult constitutional question we do not answer today. We conclude instead that the Voting Rights Act permits all political subdivisions, including the district in this case, to seek relief from its preclearance requirements.

The judgment of the District Court is reversed, and the case is remanded for further proceedings consistent with this opinion.

It is so ordered.

Shelby County, Alabama v. Holder
133 S. Ct. 594 (2013)

CHIEF JUSTICE ROBERTS delivered the opinion of the Court.

The Voting Rights Act of 1965 employed extraordinary measures to address an extraordinary problem. Section 5 of the Act required States to obtain federal permission before enacting any law related to voting—a drastic departure from basic principles of federalism. And § 4 of the Act applied that requirement only to some States—an equally dramatic departure from the principle that all States enjoy equal sovereignty. This was strong medicine, but Congress determined it was needed to address entrenched racial discrimination in voting, "an insidious and pervasive evil which had been perpetuated in certain parts of our country through unremitting and ingenious defiance of the Constitution." *South Carolina* v. *Katzenbach*, 383 U.S. 301, 309 (1966). As we explained in upholding the law, "exceptional conditions can justify legislative measures not otherwise appropriate." *Id.,* at 334. Reflecting the unprecedented nature of these measures, they were scheduled to expire after five years. See Voting Rights Act of 1965, § 4(a), 79 Stat. 438.

Nearly 50 years later, they are still in effect; indeed, they have been made more stringent, and are now scheduled to last until 2031. There is no denying, however, that the conditions that originally justified these measures no longer characterize voting in the covered jurisdictions. By 2009, "the racial gap in voter registration and turnout [was] lower in the States originally covered by § 5 than it [was] nationwide." *Northwest Austin Municipal Util. Dist. No. One* v. *Holder*, 557 U.S. 193–204 (2009). Since that time, Census Bureau data indicate that African-American voter turnout has come to exceed white voter turnout in five of the six States originally covered by § 5, with a gap in the sixth State of less than one half of one percent. See Dept. of Commerce, Census Bureau, Re-ported Voting and Registration, by Sex, Race and His-panic Origin, for States (Nov. 2012) (Table 4b).

At the same time, voting discrimination still exists; no one doubts that. The question is whether the Act's extraordinary measures, including its disparate treatment of the States, continue to satisfy constitutional requirements. As we put it a short time ago, "the Act imposes current burdens and must be justified by current needs." *Northwest Austin*, 557 U.S., at 203.

I

A

The Fifteenth Amendment was ratified in 1870, in the wake of the Civil War. It provides that "[t]he right of citizens of the United States to vote shall not be denied or abridged by the United States or by any State on account of race, color, or previous condition of servitude," and it gives Congress the "power to enforce this article by appropriate legislation."

"The first century of congressional enforcement of the Amendment, however, can only be regarded as a failure." *Id.*, at 197. In the 1890s, Alabama, Georgia, Louisiana, Mississippi, North Carolina, South Carolina, and Virginia began to enact literacy tests for voter registration and to employ other methods designed to prevent African-Americans from voting. *Katzenbach*, 383 U.S., at 310. Congress passed statutes outlawing some of these practices and facilitating litigation against them, but litigation remained slow and expensive, and the States came up with new ways to discriminate as soon as existing ones were struck down. Voter registration of African-Americans barely improved. *Id.*, at 313–314.

Inspired to action by the civil rights movement, Congress responded in 1965 with the Voting Rights Act. Section 2 was enacted to forbid, in all 50 States, any "standard, practice, or procedure . . . imposed or applied . . . to deny or abridge the right of any citizen of the United States to vote on account of race or color." 79 Stat. 437. The current version forbids any "standard, practice, or procedure" that "results in a denial or abridgement of the right of any citizen of the United States to vote on account of race or color." 42 U.S.C. § 1973(a). Both the Federal Government and individuals have sued to enforce § 2, see, *e.g., Johnson* v. *De Grandy*, 512 U.S. 997 (1994), and injunctive relief is available in appropriate cases to block voting laws from going into effect, see 42 U.S.C. § 1973j(d). Section 2 is permanent, applies nationwide, and is not at issue in this case.

Other sections targeted only some parts of the country. At the time of the Act's passage, these "covered" jurisdictions were those States or political subdivisions that had maintained a test or device as a prerequisite to voting as of November 1, 1964, and had less than 50 percent voter registration or turnout in the 1964 Presidential election. § 4(b), 79 Stat. 438. Such tests or devices included literacy and knowledge tests, good moral character requirements, the need for vouchers from registered voters, and the like. § 4(c), *id.*, at 438–439. A covered jurisdiction could "bail out" of coverage if it had not used a test or device in the preceding five years "for the purpose or with the effect of denying or abridging the right to vote on account of race or color." § 4(a), *id.*, at 438. In 1965, the covered States included Alabama, Georgia, Louisiana, Mississippi, South Carolina, and Virginia. The additional covered subdivisions included 39 counties in North Carolina and one in Arizona. See 28 CFR pt. 51, App. (2012).

In those jurisdictions, § 4 of the Act banned all such tests or devices. § 4(a), 79 Stat. 438. Section 5 provided that no change in voting procedures could take effect until it was approved by federal authorities in Washington, D. C.—either the Attorney General or a court of three judges. *Id.*, at 439. A jurisdiction could obtain such "preclearance" only by proving that the change had neither "the purpose [nor] the effect of denying or abridging the right to vote on account of race or color." *Ibid.*

Sections 4 and 5 were intended to be temporary; they were set to expire after five years. See §4(a), *id.*, at 438; *Northwest Austin, supra*, at 199. In *South Carolina* v. *Katzenbach*, we upheld the 1965 Act against constitutional challenge, explaining that it was justified to address "voting discrimination where it persists on a pervasive scale." 383 U. S., at 308.

In 1970, Congress reauthorized the Act for another five years, and extended the coverage formula in §4(b) to jurisdictions that had a voting test and less than 50 percent voter registration or turnout as of 1968. Voting Rights Act Amendments of 1970, §§3–4, 84 Stat. 315. That swept in several counties in California, New Hampshire, and New York. See 28 CFR pt. 51, App. Congress also extended the ban in §4(a) on tests and devices nationwide. §6, 84 Stat. 315.

In 1975, Congress reauthorized the Act for seven more years, and extended its coverage to jurisdictions that had a voting test and less than 50 percent voter registration or turnout as of 1972. Voting Rights Act Amendments of 1975, §§101, 202, 89 Stat. 400, 401. Congress also amended the definition of "test or device" to include the practice of providing English-only voting materials in places where over five percent of voting-age citizens spoke a single language other than English. §203, *id.*, at 401–402. As a result of these amendments, the States of Alaska, Arizona, and Texas, as well as several counties in California, Florida, Michigan, New York, North Carolina, and South Dakota, became covered jurisdictions. See 28 CFR pt. 51, App. Congress correspondingly amended sections 2 and 5 to forbid voting discrimination on the basis of membership in a language minority group, in addition to discrimination on the basis of race or color. §§203, 206, 89 Stat. 401, 402. Finally, Congress made the nationwide ban on tests and devices permanent. §102, *id.*, at 400.

In 1982, Congress reauthorized the Act for 25 years, but did not alter its coverage formula. See Voting Rights Act Amendments, 96 Stat. 131. Congress did, however, amend the bailout provisions, allowing political subdivisions of covered jurisdictions to bail out. Among other prerequisites for bailout, jurisdictions and their subdivisions must not have used a forbidden test or device, failed to receive preclearance, or lost a §2 suit, in the ten years prior to seeking bailout. §2, *id.*, at 131–133.

We upheld each of these reauthorizations against constitutional challenge. See *Georgia* v. *United States*, 411 U.S. 526 (1973); *City of Rome* v. *United States*, 446 U.S. 156 (1980); Lopez v. Monterey *County*, 525 U.S. 266 (1999).

In 2006, Congress again reauthorized the Voting Rights Act for 25 years, again without change to its coverage formula. Fannie Lou Hamer, Rosa Parks, and Coretta Scott King Voting Rights Act Reauthorization and Amend-ments Act, 120 Stat. 577. Congress also amended §5 to prohibit more conduct than before. §5, *id.*, at

580–581; see *Reno v. Bossier Parish School Bd.*, 528 U.S. 320, 341 (2000) (*Bossier II*); *Georgia v. Ashcroft*, 539 U.S. 461, 479 (2003). Section 5 now forbids voting changes with "any discriminatory purpose" as well as voting changes that diminish the ability of citizens, on account of race, color, or language minority status, "to elect their preferred candidates of choice." 42 U.S.C. §§ 1973c(b)-(d).

Shortly after this reauthorization, a Texas utility district brought suit, seeking to bail out from the Act's cover-age and, in the alternative, challenging the Act's constitutionality. See *Northwest Austin*, 557 U.S., at 200–201. A three-judge District Court explained that only a State or political subdivision was eligible to seek bailout under the statute, and concluded that the utility district was not a political subdivision, a term that encompassed only "counties, parishes, and voter-registering sub-units." *Northwest Austin Municipal Util. Dist. No. One v. Mukasey*, 573 F. Supp. 2d 221, 232 (DC 2008). The District Court also rejected the constitutional challenge. *Id.*, at 283.

We reversed. We explained that "'normally the Court will not decide a constitutional question if there is some other ground upon which to dispose of the case.'" *Northwest Austin, supra*, at 205 (quoting *Escambia County v. McMillan*, 466 U.S. 48, 51 (1984) (*per curiam*)). Concluding that "underlying constitutional concerns," among other things, "compel[led] a broader reading of the bailout provision," we construed the statute to allow the utility district to seek bailout. *Northwest Austin*, 557 U.S., at 207. In doing so we expressed serious doubts about the Act's continued constitutionality.

We explained that § 5 "imposes substantial federalism costs" and "differentiates between the States, despite our historic tradition that all the States enjoy equal sovereignty." *Id.*, at 202, 203 (internal quotation marks omitted). We also noted that "[t]hings have changed in the South. Voter turnout and registration rates now approach parity. Blatantly discriminatory evasions of federal decrees are rare. And minority candidates hold office at unprecedented levels." *Id.*, at 202. Finally, we questioned whether the problems that § 5 meant to address were still "concentrated in the jurisdictions singled out for preclearance." *Id.*, at 203.

Eight Members of the Court subscribed to these views, and the remaining Member would have held the Act unconstitutional. Ultimately, however, the Court's construction of the bailout provision left the constitutional issues for another day.

B

Shelby County is located in Alabama, a covered jurisdiction. It has not sought bailout, as the Attorney General has recently objected to voting changes proposed from within the county. See App. 87a-92a. Instead, in 2010, the county sued the Attorney General in Federal District Court in Washington, D.C., seeking a declaratory judgment that sections 4(b) and 5 of the Voting Rights Act are facially unconstitutional, as well as a permanent injunction against their enforcement. The District Court ruled against the county and upheld the Act. 811 F. Supp. 2d 424, 508 (2011).

The court found that the evidence before Congress in 2006 was sufficient to justify reauthorizing § 5 and continuing the § 4(b) coverage formula.

The Court of Appeals for the D.C. Circuit affirmed. In assessing § 5, the D. C. Circuit considered six primary categories of evidence: Attorney General objections to voting changes, Attorney General requests for more information regarding voting changes, successful § 2 suits in covered jurisdictions, the dispatching of federal observers to monitor elections in covered jurisdictions, § 5 preclearance suits involving covered jurisdictions, and the deterrent effect of § 5. See 679 F.3d 848, 862–863 (2012). After extensive analysis of the record, the court accepted Congress's conclusion that § 2 litigation remained inadequate in the covered jurisdictions to protect the rights of minority voters, and that § 5 was therefore still necessary. *Id.,*at 873.

. . . We granted certiorari. 568 U.S. ___ (2012).

II

In *Northwest Austin*, we stated that "the Act imposes current burdens and must be justified by current needs." 557 U.S., at 203. And we concluded that "a departure from the fundamental principle of equal sovereignty requires a showing that a statute's disparate geographic coverage is sufficiently related to the problem that it targets." *Ibid.* These basic principles guide our review of the question before us.

A

The Constitution and laws of the United States are "the supreme Law of the Land." U.S. Const., Art. VI, cl. 2. State legislation may not contravene federal law. The Federal Government does not, however, have a general right to review and veto state enactments before they go into effect. A proposal to grant such authority to "negative" state laws was considered at the Constitutional Convention, but rejected in favor of allowing state laws to take effect, subject to later challenge under the Supremacy Clause. See 1 Records of the Federal Convention of 1787, pp. 21, 164–168 (M. Farrand ed. 1911); 2 *id.,* at 27–29, 390–392.

Outside the strictures of the Supremacy Clause, States retain broad autonomy in structuring their governments and pursuing legislative objectives. Indeed, the Constitution provides that all powers not specifically granted to the Federal Government are reserved to the States or citizens. Amdt. 10. This "allocation of powers in our federal system preserves the integrity, dignity, and residual sovereignty of the States." *Bond v. United States*, 564 U.S. ___, ___ (2011) (slip op., at 9). But the federal balance "is not just an end in itself: Rather, federalism secures to citizens the liberties that derive from the diffusion of sovereign power." *Ibid.* (internal quotation marks omitted).

More specifically, "'the Framers of the Constitution intended the States to keep for themselves, as provided in the Tenth Amendment, the power to regulate elections.'" *Gregory v. Ashcroft*, 501 U.S. 452–462 (1991) (quoting *Sugarman v. Dougall*, 413 U.S. 634, 647 (1973); some internal quotation marks omitted). Of course, the

Federal Government retains significant control over federal elections. For instance, the Constitution authorizes Congress to establish the time and manner for electing Senators and Representatives. Art. I, §4, cl. 1; see also *Arizona v. Inter Tribal Council of Ariz., Inc., ante,* at 4–6. But States have "broad powers to determine the conditions under which the right of suffrage may be exercised." *Carrington v. Rash,* 380 U. S. 89, 91 (1965) (internal quotation marks omitted); see also *Arizona, ante,* at 13–15. And "[e]ach State has the power to prescribe the qualifications of its officers and the manner in which they shall be chosen." *Boyd v. Nebraska ex rel. Thayer,* 143 U. S. 135, 161 (1892). Drawing lines for congressional districts is likewise "primarily the duty and responsibility of the State." *Perry v. Perez,* 565 U.S. ___, ___ (2012) (*per curiam*) (slip op., at 3) (internal quotation marks omitted).

Not only do States retain sovereignty under the Constitution, there is also a "fundamental principle of *equal* sovereignty" among the States. *Northwest Austin, supra,* at 203 (citing *United States v. Louisiana,* 363 U. S. 1, 16 (1960); *Lessee of Pollard v. Hagan,* 3 How. 212, 223 (1845); and *Texas v. White,* 7 Wall. 700, 725–726 (1869)) (emphasis added). Over a hundred years ago, this Court explained that our Nation "was and is a union of States, equal in power, dignity and authority." *Coyle v. Smith,* 221 U. S. 559, 567 (1911). Indeed, "the constitutional equality of the States is essential to the harmonious operation of the scheme upon which the Republic was organized." *Id.,* at 580. *Coyle* concerned the admission of new States, and *Katzenbach* rejected the notion that the principle operated as a *bar* on differential treatment outside that context. 383 U.S., at 328–329. At the same time, as we made clear in *Northwest Austin,* the fundamental principle of equal sovereignty remains highly pertinent in assessing subsequent disparate treatment of States. 557 U.S., at 203.

The Voting Rights Act sharply departs from these basic principles. It suspends "*all* changes to state election law—however innocuous—until they have been precleared by federal authorities in Washington, D.C." *Id.,* at 202. States must beseech the Federal Government for permission to implement laws that they would otherwise have the right to enact and execute on their own, subject of course to any injunction in a §2 action. The Attorney General has 60 days to object to a preclearance request, longer if he requests more information. See 28 CFR §§51.9, 51.37. If a State seeks preclearance from a three-judge court, the process can take years.

And despite the tradition of equal sovereignty, the Act applies to only nine States (and several additional counties). While one State waits months or years and expends funds to implement a validly enacted law, its neighbor can typically put the same law into effect immediately, through the normal legislative process. Even if a noncovered jurisdiction is sued, there are important differences between those proceedings and preclearance proceedings; the preclearance proceeding "not only switches the burden of proof to the supplicant jurisdiction, but also applies substantive standards quite different from those governing the rest of the nation." 679 F.3d, at 884 (Williams, J., dissenting) (case below).

All this explains why, when we first upheld the Act in 1966, we described it as "stringent" and "potent." *Katzenbach*, 383 U.S., at 308, 315, 337. We recognized that it "may have been an uncommon exercise of congressional power," but concluded that "legislative measures not otherwise appropriate" could be justified by "exceptional conditions." *Id.*, at 334. We have since noted that the Act "authorizes federal intrusion into sensitive areas of state and local policymaking," *Lopez*, 525 U.S., at 282, and represents an "extraordinary departure from the traditional course of relations between the States and the Federal Government," *Presley v. Etowah County Comm'n*, 502 U.S. 491–501 (1992). As we reiterated in *Northwest Austin*, the Act constitutes "extraordinary legislation otherwise unfamiliar to our federal system." 557 U.S., at 211.

B

In 1966, we found these departures from the basic features of our system of government justified. The "blight of racial discrimination in voting" had "infected the electoral process in parts of our country for nearly a century." *Katzenbach*, 383 U.S., at 308. Several States had enacted a variety of requirements and tests "specifically designed to prevent" African-Americans from voting. *Id.*, at 310. Case-by-case litigation had proved inadequate to prevent such racial discrimination in voting, in part because States "merely switched to discriminatory devices not covered by the federal decrees," "enacted difficult new tests," or simply "defied and evaded court orders." *Id.*, at 314. Shortly before enactment of the Voting Rights Act, only 19.4 percent of African-Americans of voting age were registered to vote in Alabama, only 31.8 percent in Louisiana, and only 6.4 percent in Mississippi. *Id.*, at 313. Those figures were roughly 50 percentage points or more below the figures for whites. *Ibid.*

In short, we concluded that "[u]nder the compulsion of these unique circumstances, Congress responded in a permissibly decisive manner." *Id.*, at 334, 335. We also noted then and have emphasized since that this extra-ordinary legislation was intended to be temporary, set to expire after five years. *Id.*, at 333; *Northwest Austin*, *supra*, at 199.

At the time, the coverage formula—the means of linking the exercise of the unprecedented authority with the problem that warranted it—made sense. We found that "Congress chose to limit its attention to the geographic areas where immediate action seemed necessary." *Katzenbach*, 383 U.S., at 328. . . . The formula ensured that the "stringent remedies [were] aimed at areas where voting discrimination ha[d] been most flagrant." *Id.*, at 315.

C

Nearly 50 years later, things have changed dramatically. Shelby County contends that the preclearance requirement, even without regard to its disparate coverage, is now unconstitutional. Its arguments have a good deal of force. In the covered jurisdictions, "[v]oter turnout and registration rates now approach parity. Blatantly discriminatory evasions of federal decrees are rare. And minority candidates hold office at unprecedented levels." *Northwest Austin*, 557 U.S., at 202. The tests and devices that blocked access to the ballot have been forbidden nationwide for over 40 years. See § 6, 84 Stat. 315; § 102, 89 Stat. 400.

Those conclusions are not ours alone. Congress said the same when it reauthorized the Act in 2006, writing that "[s]ignificant progress has been made in eliminating first generation barriers experienced by minority voters, including increased numbers of registered minority voters, minority voter turnout, and minority representation in Congress, State legislatures, and local elected offices." § 2(b)(1), 120 Stat. 577. The House Report elaborated that "the number of African-Americans who are registered and who turn out to cast ballots has increased significantly over the last 40 years, particularly since 1982," and noted that "[i]n some circumstances, minorities register to vote and cast ballots at levels that surpass those of white voters." H.R. Rep. No. 109-478, p. 12 (2006). That Report also explained that there have been "significant increases in the number of African-Americans serving in elected offices"; more specifically, there has been approximately a 1,000 percent increase since 1965 in the number of African-American elected officials in the six States originally covered by the Voting Rights Act. *Id.*, at 18.

. . . There is no doubt that these improvements are in large part *because of* the Voting Rights Act. The Act has proved immensely successful at redressing racial discrimination and integrating the voting process. See § 2(b)(1), 120 Stat. 577. During the "Freedom Summer" of 1964, in Philadelphia, Mississippi, three men were murdered while working in the area to register African-American voters. See *United States v. Price*, 383 U.S. 787, 790 (1966). On "Bloody Sunday" in 1965, in Selma, Alabama, police beat and used tear gas against hundreds marching in sup-port of African-American enfranchisement. See *Northwest Austin, supra*, at 220, n. 3 (Thomas, J., concurring in judgment in part and dissenting in part). Today both of those towns are governed by African-American mayors. Problems remain in these States and others, but there is no denying that, due to the Voting Rights Act, our Nation has made great strides.

Yet the Act has not eased the restrictions in § 5 or narrowed the scope of the coverage formula in § 4(b) along the way. Those extraordinary and unprecedented features were reauthorized — as if nothing had changed. In fact, the Act's unusual remedies have grown even stronger. When Congress reauthorized the Act in 2006, it did so for another 25 years on top of the previous 40 — a far cry from the initial five-year period. See 42 U.S.C. § 1973b(a)(8). Congress also expanded the prohibitions in § 5. We had previously interpreted § 5 to prohibit only those redistricting plans that would have the purpose or effect of worsening the position of minority groups. See *Bossier II*, 528 U.S., at 324, 335–336. In 2006, Congress amended § 5 to prohibit laws that could have favored such groups but did not do so because of a discriminatory purpose, see 42 U.S.C. § 1973c(c), even though we had stated that such broadening of § 5 coverage would "exacerbate the substantial federalism costs that the preclearance procedure already exacts, perhaps to the extent of raising concerns about § 5's constitutionality," *Bossier II, supra,* at 336 (citation and internal quotation marks omitted). In addition, Congress expanded § 5 to prohibit any voting law "that has the purpose of or will have the effect of diminishing the ability of any citizens of the United States," on account of race, color, or language minority status, "to elect their preferred candidates of choice." § 1973c(b). In light of those two amendments, the bar that covered jurisdictions must clear has been raised even as the conditions justifying that requirement have dramatically improved.

We have also previously highlighted the concern that "the preclearance requirements in one State [might] be unconstitutional in another." *Northwest Austin,* 557 U.S., at 203; see *Georgia v. Ashcroft,* 539 U.S., at 491 (Kennedy, J., concurring) ("considerations of race that would doom a redistricting plan under the Fourteenth Amendment or § 2 [of the Voting Rights Act] seem to be what save it under § 5"). Nothing has happened since to alleviate this troubling concern about the current application of § 5.

... The provisions of § 5 apply only to those jurisdictions singled out by § 4. We now consider whether that coverage formula is constitutional in light of current conditions.

III

A

When upholding the constitutionality of the coverage formula in 1966, we concluded that it was "rational in both practice and theory." *Katzenbach,* 383 U.S., at 330. The formula looked to cause (discriminatory tests) and effect (low voter registration and turnout), and tailored the remedy (preclearance) to those jurisdictions exhibiting both.

By 2009, however, we concluded that the "coverage formula raise[d] serious constitutional questions." *Northwest Austin,* 557 U.S., at 204. As we explained, a statute's "current burdens" must be justified by "current needs," and any "disparate geographic coverage" must be "sufficiently related to the problem that it targets." *Id.,* at 203. The coverage formula met that test in 1965, but no longer does so.

Coverage today is based on decades-old data and eradicated practices. The formula captures States by reference to literacy tests and low voter registration and turnout in the 1960s and early 1970s. But such tests have been banned nationwide for over 40 years. § 6, 84 Stat. 315; § 102, 89 Stat. 400. And voter registration and turnout numbers in the covered States have risen dramatically in the years since. H.R. Rep. No. 109-478, at 12. Racial disparity in those numbers was compelling evidence justifying the preclearance remedy and the coverage formula. See, *e.g., Katzenbach, supra,* at 313, 329–330. There is no longer such a disparity.

In 1965, the States could be divided into two groups: those with a recent history of voting tests and low voter registration and turnout, and those without those characteristics. Congress based its coverage formula on that distinction. Today the Nation is no longer divided along those lines, yet the Voting Rights Act continues to treat it as if it were.

B

... [H]istory did not end in 1965. By the time the Act was reauthorized in 2006, there had been 40 more years of it. In assessing the "current need[]" for a preclearance system that treats States differently from one another today, that history cannot be ignored. During that time, largely because of the Voting Rights Act, voting tests were abolished, disparities in voter registration and turnout due to race were erased, and African-Americans attained political office in record numbers. And yet the coverage formula that Congress reauthorized in 2006 ignores these developments, keeping the focus on decades-old data relevant to decades-old problems, rather than current data reflecting current needs.

The Fifteenth Amendment commands that the right to vote shall not be denied or abridged on account of race or color, and it gives Congress the power to enforce that command. The Amendment is not designed to punish for the past; its purpose is to ensure a better future. See *Rice v. Cayetano*, 528 U. S. 495, 512 (2000) ("Consistent with the design of the Constitution, the [Fifteenth] Amendment is cast in fundamental terms, terms transcending the particular controversy which was the immediate impetus for its enactment."). To serve that purpose, Congress—if it is to divide the States—must identify those jurisdictions to be singled out on a basis that makes sense in light of current conditions. It cannot rely simply on the past. We made that clear in *Northwest Austin*, and we make it clear again today.

C

In defending the coverage formula, the Government, the intervenors, and the dissent also rely heavily on data from the record that they claim justify disparate coverage. Congress compiled thousands of pages of evidence before reauthorizing the Voting Rights Act. The court below and the parties have debated what that record shows—they have gone back and forth about whether to compare covered to noncovered jurisdictions as blocks, how to disaggregate the data State by State, how to weigh § 2 cases as evidence of ongoing discrimination, and whether to consider evidence not before Congress, among other issues. Compare, *e.g.*, 679 F.3d, at 873–883 (case below), with *id.*, at 889–902 (Williams, J., dissenting). Regardless of how to look at the record, however, no one can fairly say that it shows anything approaching the "pervasive," "flagrant," "widespread," and "rampant" discrimination that faced Congress in 1965, and that clearly distinguished the covered jurisdictions from the rest of the Nation at that time. *Katzenbach*, *supra*, at 308, 315, 331; *Northwest Austin*, 557 U.S., at 201.

But a more fundamental problem remains: Congress did not use the record it compiled to shape a coverage formula grounded in current conditions. It instead reenacted a formula based on 40-year-old facts having no logical relation to the present day. The dissent relies on "second-generation barriers," which are not impediments to the casting of ballots, but rather electoral arrangements that affect the weight of minority votes. That does not cure the problem. Viewing the preclearance requirements as targeting such efforts simply highlights the irrationality of continued reliance on the §4 coverage formula, which is based on voting tests and access to the ballot, not vote dilution. We cannot pretend that we are reviewing an updated statute, or try our hand at updating the statute ourselves, based on the new record compiled by Congress. Contrary to the dissent's contention, see *post,* at 23, we are not ignoring the record; we are simply recognizing that it played no role in shaping the statutory formula before us today.

The dissent also turns to the record to argue that, in light of voting discrimination in Shelby County, the county cannot complain about the provisions that subject it to preclearance. *Post,* at 23–30. But that is like saying that a driver pulled over pursuant to a policy of stopping all redheads cannot complain about that policy, if it turns out his license has expired. Shelby County's claim is that the coverage formula here is unconstitutional in all its applications, because of how it selects the jurisdictions subjected to preclearance. The county was selected based on that formula, and may challenge it in court.

D

The dissent proceeds from a flawed premise. It quotes the famous sentence from *McCulloch v. Maryland,* 4 Wheat. 316, 421 (1819), with the following emphasis: "Let the end be legitimate, let it be within the scope of the constitution, and *all means which are appropriate, which are plainly adapted to that end,* which are not prohibited, but consist with the letter and spirit of the constitution, are constitutional." *Post,* at 9 (emphasis in dissent). But this case is about a part of the sentence that the dissent does not emphasize—the part that asks whether a legislative means is "consist[ent] with the letter and spirit of the constitution." The dissent states that "[i]t cannot tenably be maintained" that this is an issue with regard to the Voting Rights Act, *post,* at 9, but four years ago, in an opinion joined by two of today's dissenters, the Court expressly stated that "[t]he Act's preclearance requirement and its coverage formula raise serious constitutional questions." *Northwest Austin, supra,* at 204. The dissent does not explain how those "serious constitutional questions" became untenable in four short years.

. . . In other ways as well, the dissent analyzes the question presented as if our decision in *Northwest Austin* never happened. For example, the dissent refuses to consider the principle of equal sovereignty, despite *Northwest Austin*'s emphasis on its significance. *Northwest Austin* also emphasized the "dramatic" progress since 1965, 557 U.S., at 201, but the dissent describes current levels of discrimination as "flagrant," "widespread," and "pervasive," *post,* at 7, 17 (internal quotation marks omitted). Despite the fact that *Northwest Austin* requires an Act's "disparate geographic coverage" to be "sufficiently related" to its targeted problems, 557 U.S., at 203, the dissent maintains that an Act's limited coverage actually eases Congress's burdens, and suggests that a fortuitous relationship should suffice. Although *Northwest Austin* stated definitively that "current burdens" must be justified by "current needs," *ibid.,* the dissent argues that the coverage formula can be justified by history, and that the required showing can be weaker on reenactment than when the law was first passed.

There is no valid reason to insulate the coverage formula from review merely because it was previously enacted 40 years ago. If Congress had started from scratch in 2006, it plainly could not have enacted the present coverage formula. It would have been irrational for Congress to distinguish between States in such a fundamental way based on 40-year-old data, when today's statistics tell an entirely different story. And it would have been irrational to base coverage on the use of voting tests 40 years ago, when such tests have been illegal since that time. But that is exactly what Congress has done.

. . . .

Striking down an Act of Congress "is the gravest and most delicate duty that this Court is called on to perform." *Blodgett v. Holden*, 275 U. S. 142, 148 (1927) (Holmes, J., concurring). We do not do so lightly. That is why, in 2009, we took care to avoid ruling on the constitutionality of the Voting Rights Act when asked to do so, and instead resolved the case then before us on statutory grounds. But in issuing that decision, we expressed our broader concerns about the constitutionality of the Act. Congress could have updated the coverage formula at that time, but did not do so. Its failure to act leaves us today with no choice but to declare § 4(b) unconstitutional. The formula in that section can no longer be used as a basis for subjecting jurisdictions to preclearance.

Our decision in no way affects the permanent, nationwide ban on racial discrimination in voting found in § 2. We issue no holding on § 5 itself, only on the coverage formula. Congress may draft another formula based on current conditions. Such a formula is an initial prerequisite to a determination that exceptional conditions still exist justifying such an "extraordinary departure from the traditional course of relations between the States and the Federal Government." *Presley*, 502 U.S., at 500–501. Our country has changed, and while any racial discrimination in voting is too much, Congress must ensure that the legislation it passes to remedy that problem speaks to current conditions.

The judgment of the Court of Appeals is reversed.

It is so ordered.

D. Section 2 of the Voting Rights Act

Section 2 of the Voting Rights Act presents another basis for challenging governmental decisions related to voting. Inspired by the Fifteenth Amendment, Section 2 prohibits voter dilution. Despite the existence of the Fifteenth Amendment since Reconstruction, the Court did not afford substantive relief in relation to voting until the Civil Rights Movement. Until then, the Court had successfully avoided issues relating to the electoral process as political questions. With *Baker v. Carr*[22] and *Reynolds v. Sims*,[23] however, the Court abandoned its restraint and determined that re-apportionment claims and claims of voter dilution based on variations in the populations in legislative districts could be justiciable under the Equal Protection Clause.

These two decisions opened the door to a substantial amount of litigation related to voting. The Voting Rights Act later codified and elaborated on additional rights available in the voting context.[24] Claims brought under the Fourteenth and Fifteenth Amendments to the Constitution were restricted to actions where intent could be established, thereby limiting the types of claims that could be brought.[25] Efforts to expand the scope of these two constitutional Amendments to include an effect test have been generally unsuccessful.[26]

In response to the restrictive approach applied by the Court in *City of Mobile v. Bolden*,[27] however, Congress expanded the application of Section 2 to include an effects test. As a result, voting rights claims are now more robustly litigated under either the Fourteenth Amendment, Fifteenth Amendment, or Section 2 of the Voting Rights Act.

Section 2 provides:

(a) No voting qualification or prerequisite to voting or standard, practice, or procedure shall be imposed or applied by any State or political subdivision in a manner which results in a denial or abridgement of the right of any citizen of the United States to vote on account of race or color, or in

---

22. 369 U.S. 186 (1962) (holding allegations of a state statute effecting an apportionment that deprives plaintiffs equal protection under the Fourteenth Amendment "present a justiciable constitutional cause of action").

23. 377 U.S. 533 (1964) (finding proposed plans for apportionment of seats in the Alabama Legislature invalid under the Equal Protection Clause because the apportionment was not on a population basis and was completely lacking in rationality).

24. The Voting Rights Act of 1965, 52 U.S.C. §§ 10101-10702 (2017).

25. *See* Whitcomb v. Chavis, 403 U.S. 124 (1971); Burns v. Richardson, 384 U.S. 73 (1966); *see also* Henry L. Chambers, Jr., *Colorblindness, Race Neutrality, and Voting Rights*, 51 EMORY L.J. 1397, 1426–27 (2002) (stating that "it appears that constitutional voting rights claims—whether brought under the Fourteenth or Fifteenth Amendment—must involve intentional discrimination to be successful"); Darren Lenard Hutchinson, *Undignified: The Supreme Court, Racial Justice, and Dignity Claims*, 69 FLA. L. REV. 1, 16 (2017) (arguing that "[r]equiring discriminatory intent—even though racial discrimination occurs unintentionally or nonconsciously—substantially impedes the potency of the Equal Protection Clause as a remedy for racial inequality"). *But see* White v. Register, 412 U.S. 755 (1973).

26. *See* City of Mobile v. Bolden, 446 U.S. 55 (1980); *see also* Joshua P. Thompson, *Towards A Post-Shelby County Section 5 Where a Constitutional Coverage Formula Does Not Reauthorize the Effects Test*, 34 N. ILL. U. L. REV. 585 (2014).

27. 446 U.S. 55 (1980).

contravention of the guarantees set forth in section 4(f)(2), as provided in subsection (b).

(b) A violation of subsection (a) is established if, based on the totality of circumstances, it is shown that the political processes leading to nomination or election in the State or political subdivision are not equally open to participation by members of a class of citizens protected by subsection (a) in that its members have less opportunity than other members of the electorate to participate in the political process and to elect representatives of their choice. The extent to which members of a protected class have been elected to office in the State or political subdivision is one circumstance which may be considered: *Provided,* That nothing in this section establishes a right to have members of a protected class elected in numbers equal to their proportion in the population.

Codified at 42 U.S.C. § 1973, now 52 U.S.C. § 10301.

Permitting proof of discriminatory impact under Section 2 has given rise to healthy challenges to legislative redistricting. Central to these challenges are issues related to the racial make up of districts and the manner in which representatives are elected. For example, redistricting plans with single member districts and/or multimember districts can give rise to claims that the votes of the minority population in the district are so diluted that they have no chance to elect a candidate of their choice. In multimember districts, where multiple representatives serve the interests of one district, the minority population risks not being able to elect representatives that speak for their interests, if their numbers are completely swallowed up in the general demographic landscape. Single member districts, though potentially smaller in size, can also give rise to issues of dilution. Smaller single member districts may be designed in a way that the populations of color are so spread out across the districts that their voting power is reduced to nothing.[28]

Gerrymandering, or the use of race when designing districts, give rise to additional issues under Section 2. Historically, legislatures have used redistricting to obliterate the impact of voters with whom they might not be successful. Gerrymandering is strategy that was originally aggressively used to make sure that blacks would not have any voting power or influence once they obtained the right to vote. At the same time, because redistricting was necessary to correct gerrymandering, majority/minority districts and various other options were applied over time to correct the concentration of white voting power. In response to these historical and legal facts, the Court has crafted a standard for evaluating the design and shape of districts to prevent undue manipulation by legislatures. Nonetheless, the Court has

---

28. *State's Rights, Last Rites, and Voting Rights,* 47 Conn. L. Rev. 481; Steven Hill, *How the Voting Rights Act Hurts Democrats and Minorities,* http://www.theatlantic.com/politics/archive/2013/06 /how-the-voting-rights-act-hurts-democrats-and-minorities/276893/; Justin Levitt, *Why Does It Matter?,* http://redistricting.lls.edu/why.php; http://www.naacp.org/news/entry/lawsuit-filed-on -mississippi-redistricting-plan; http://www.naacp.org/pages/civic-engagement-about.

increasingly moved away from racial redistricting as a means of remedying voting inequity.

Such is the background that gives rise to the issues present in *Thornburg v. Gingles*, *Shaw v. Reno* and *Miller v. Johnson*, below. First, see *Thornburg* and its formulation of the relevant standard for voter dilution in the redistricting context.

Thornburg v. Gingles
478 U.S. 30 (1986)

JUSTICE BRENNAN announced the judgment of the Court and delivered the opinion of the Court with respect to Parts I, II, III-A, III-B, IV-A, and V, and an opinion with respect to Part III-C, in which JUSTICE MARSHALL, JUSTICE BLACKMUN, and JUSTICE STEVENS join, and an opinion with respect to Part IV-B, in which JUSTICE WHITE joins.

This case requires that we construe for the first time § 2 of the Voting Rights Act of 1965, as amended June 29, 1982. 42 U.S.C. § 1973. The specific question to be decided is whether the three-judge District Court, convened in the Eastern District of North Carolina pursuant to 28 U.S.C. § 2284(a) and 42 U.S.C. § 1973c, correctly held that the use in a legislative redistricting plan of multimember districts in five North Carolina legislative districts violated § 2 by impairing the opportunity of black voters "to participate in the political process and to elect representatives of their choice." § 2(b), 96 Stat. 134.

I

In April 1982, the North Carolina General Assembly enacted a legislative redistricting plan for the State's Senate and House of Representatives. Appellees, black citizens of North Carolina who are registered to vote, challenged seven districts, one single-member and six multimember districts, alleging that the redistricting scheme impaired black citizens' ability to elect representatives of their choice in violation of the Fourteenth and Fifteenth Amendments to the United States Constitution and of § 2 of the Voting Rights Act.

After appellees brought suit, but before trial, Congress amended § 2. The amendment was largely a response to this Court's plurality opinion in *Mobile v. Bolden*, 446 U.S. 55, 100 S.Ct. 1490, 64 L.Ed.2d 47 (1980), which had declared that, in order to establish a violation either of § 2 or of the Fourteenth or Fifteenth Amendments, minority voters must prove that a contested electoral mechanism was intentionally adopted or maintained by state officials for a discriminatory purpose. Congress substantially revised § 2 to make clear that a violation could be proved by showing discriminatory effect alone and to establish as the relevant legal standard the "results test," applied by this Court in *White v. Regester,* 412 U.S. 755, 93 S.Ct. 2332, 37 L.Ed.2d 314 (1973), and by other federal courts before *Bolden, supra.* S.Rep. No. 97-417, 97th Cong.2nd Sess. 28 (1982), U.S.Code Cong. & Admin.News 1982, pp. 177, 205 (hereinafter S.Rep.).

Section 2, as amended, 96 Stat. 134, reads as follows:

"(a) No voting qualification or prerequisite to voting or standard, practice, or procedure shall be imposed or applied by any State or political subdivision in a manner which results in a denial or abridgement of the right
of any citizen of the United States to vote on account of race or color, or in
contravention of the guarantees set forth in section 4(f)(2), as provided in
subsection (b).

"(b) A violation of subsection (a) is established if, based on the totality
of circumstances, it is shown that the political processes leading to nomination or election in the State or political subdivision are not equally open
to participation by members of a class of citizens protected by subsection
(a) in that its members have less opportunity than other members of the
electorate to participate in the political process and to elect representatives
of their choice. The extent to which members of a protected class have been
elected to office in the State or political subdivision is one circumstance
which may be considered: *Provided,* That nothing in this section establishes
a right to have members of a protected class elected in numbers equal to
their proportion in the population." Codified at 42 U.S.C. § 1973.

. . . .

The District Court applied the "totality of the circumstances" test set forth in
§ 2(b) to appellees' statutory claim, and, relying principally on the factors outlined in the Senate Report, held that the redistricting scheme violated § 2 because it
resulted in the dilution of black citizens' votes in all seven disputed districts. In light
of this conclusion, the court did not reach appellees' constitutional claims. *Gingles
v. Edmisten,* 590 F.Supp. 345 (EDNC 1984).

Preliminarily, the court found that black citizens constituted a distinct population and registered-voter minority in each challenged district. The court noted that
at the time the multimember districts were created, there were concentrations of
black citizens within the boundaries of each that were sufficiently large and contiguous to constitute effective voting majorities in single-member districts lying wholly
within the boundaries of the multimember districts. With respect to the challenged
single-member district, Senate District No. 2, the court also found that there existed
a concentration of black citizens within its boundaries and within those of adjoining
Senate District No. 6 that was sufficient in numbers and in contiguity to constitute
an effective voting majority in a single-member district. The District Court then
proceeded to find that the following circumstances combined with the multimember districting scheme to result in the dilution of black citizens' votes.

First, the court found that North Carolina had officially discriminated against
its black citizens with respect to their exercise of the voting franchise from approximately 1900 to 1970 by employing at different times a poll tax, a literacy test, a prohibition against bullet (single-shot) voting and designated seat plans for multimember

districts. The court observed that even after the removal of direct barriers to black voter registration, such as the poll tax and literacy test, black voter registration remained relatively depressed; in 1982 only 52.7% of age-qualified blacks statewide were registered to vote, whereas 66.7% of whites were registered. The District Court found these statewide depressed levels of black voter registration to be present in all of the disputed districts and to be traceable, at least in part, to the historical pattern of statewide official discrimination.

Second, the court found that historic discrimination in education, housing, employment, and health services had resulted in a lower socioeconomic status for North Carolina blacks as a group than for whites. The court concluded that this lower status both gives rise to special group interests and hinders blacks' ability to participate effectively in the political process and to elect representatives of their choice.

Third, the court considered other voting procedures that may operate to lessen the opportunity of black voters to elect candidates of their choice. It noted that North Carolina has a majority vote requirement for primary elections and, while acknowledging that no black candidate for election to the State General Assembly had failed to win solely because of this requirement, the court concluded that it nonetheless presents a continuing practical impediment to the opportunity of black voting minorities to elect candidates of their choice. The court also remarked on the fact that North Carolina does not have a subdistrict residency requirement for members of the General Assembly elected from multimember districts, a requirement which the court found could offset to some extent the disadvantages minority voters often experience in multimember districts.

Fourth, the court found that white candidates in North Carolina have encouraged voting along color lines by appealing to racial prejudice. It noted that the record is replete with specific examples of racial appeals, ranging in style from overt and blatant to subtle and furtive, and in date from the 1890's to the 1984 campaign for a seat in the United States Senate. The court determined that the use of racial appeals in political campaigns in North Carolina persists to the present day and that its current effect is to lessen to some degree the opportunity of black citizens to participate effectively in the political processes and to elect candidates of their choice.

Fifth, the court examined the extent to which blacks have been elected to office in North Carolina, both statewide and in the challenged districts. It found, among other things, that prior to World War II, only one black had been elected to public office in this century. While recognizing that "it has now become possible for black citizens to be elected to office at all levels of state government in North Carolina," 590 F.Supp., at 367, the court found that, in comparison to white candidates running for the same office, black candidates are at a disadvantage in terms of relative probability of success. It also found that the overall rate of black electoral success has been minimal in relation to the percentage of blacks in the total state population. For example, the court noted, from 1971 to 1982 there were at any given time only two-to-four blacks in the 120-member House of Representatives—that is, only 1.6% to 3.3% of House members were black. From 1975 to 1983 there were at any one time only one or two blacks in the 50-member State Senate—that is, only 2% to 4% of State Senators were black. By contrast, at the time of the District Court's opinion, blacks constituted about 22.4% of the total state population.

With respect to the success in this century of black candidates in the contested districts, see also Appendix B to opinion, *post*, p.—, the court found that only one black had been elected to House District 36—after this lawsuit began. Similarly, only one black had served in the Senate from District 22, from 1975–1980. Before the 1982 election, a black was elected only twice to the House from District 39 (part of Forsyth County); in the 1982 contest two blacks were elected. Since 1973 a black citizen had been elected each 2-year term to the House from District 23 (Durham County), but no black had been elected to the Senate from Durham County. In House District 21 (Wake County), a black had been elected twice to the House, and another black served two terms in the State Senate. No black had ever been elected to the House or Senate from the area covered by House District No. 8, and no black person had ever been elected to the Senate from the area covered by Senate District No. 2.

The court did acknowledge the improved success of black candidates in the 1982 elections, in which 11 blacks were elected to the State House of Representatives, including 5 blacks from the multimember districts at issue here. However, the court pointed out that the 1982 election was conducted after the commencement of this litigation. The court found the circumstances of the 1982 election sufficiently aberrational and the success by black candidates too minimal and too recent in relation to the long history of complete denial of elective opportunities to support the conclusion that black voters' opportunities to elect representatives of their choice were not impaired.

Finally, the court considered the extent to which voting in the challenged districts was racially polarized. Based on statistical evidence presented by expert witnesses, supplemented to some degree by the testimony of lay witnesses, the court found that all of the challenged districts exhibit severe and persistent racially polarized voting.

Based on these findings, the court declared the contested portions of the 1982 redistricting plan violative of §2 and enjoined appellants from conducting elections pursuant to those portions of the plan. Appellants, the Attorney General of North Carolina and others, took a direct appeal to this Court, pursuant to 28 U.S.C. §1253, with respect to five of the multimember districts—House Districts 21, 23, 36, and 39, and Senate District 22. Appellants argue, first, that the District Court utilized a legally incorrect standard in determining whether the contested districts exhibit racial bloc voting to an extent that is cognizable under §2. Second, they contend that the court used an incorrect definition of racially polarized voting and thus erroneously relied on statistical evidence that was not probative of polarized voting. Third, they maintain that the court assigned the wrong weight to evidence of some black candidates' electoral success. Finally, they argue that the trial court erred in concluding that these multimember districts result in black citizens having less opportunity than their white counterparts to participate in the political process and to elect representatives of their choice. We noted probable jurisdiction, 471 U.S. 1064, 105 S.Ct. 2137, 85 L.Ed.2d 495 (1985), and now affirm with respect to all of the districts except House District 23. With regard to District 23, the judgment of the District Court is reversed.

II

SECTION 2 AND VOTE DILUTION THROUGH USE OF MULTIMEMBER DISTRICTS

An understanding both of § 2 and of the way in which multimember districts can operate to impair blacks' ability to elect representatives of their choice is prerequisite to an evaluation of appellants' contentions. First, then, we review amended § 2 and its legislative history in some detail. Second, we explain the theoretical basis for appellees' claim of vote dilution.

A

SECTION 2 AND ITS LEGISLATIVE HISTORY

Subsection 2(a) prohibits all States and political subdivisions from imposing *any* voting qualifications or prerequisites to voting, or any standards, practices, or procedures which result in the denial or abridgment of the right to vote of any citizen who is a member of a protected class of racial and language minorities. Subsection 2(b) establishes that § 2 has been violated where the "totality of the circumstances" reveal that "the political processes leading to nomination or election . . . are not equally open to participation by members of a [protected class] . . . in that its members have less opportunity than other members of the electorate to participate in the political process and to elect representatives of their choice." While explaining that "[t]he extent to which members of a protected class have been elected to office in the State or political subdivision is one circumstance which may be considered" in evaluating an alleged violation, § 2(b) cautions that "nothing in [§ 2] establishes a right to have members of a protected class elected in numbers equal to their proportion in the population."

The Senate Report which accompanied the 1982 amendments elaborates on the nature of § 2 violations and on the proof required to establish these violations. First and foremost, the Report dispositively rejects the position of the plurality in *Mobile v. Bolden*, 446 U.S. 55, 100 S.Ct. 1490, 64 L.Ed.2d 47 (1980), which required proof that the contested electoral practice or mechanism was adopted or maintained with the intent to discriminate against minority voters. See, *e.g.,* S.Rep., at 2, 15–16, 27. The intent test was repudiated for three principal reasons—it is "unnecessarily divisive because it involves charges of racism on the part of individual officials or entire communities," it places an "inordinately difficult" burden of proof on plaintiffs, and it "asks the wrong question." *Id.,* at 36, U.S.Code Cong. & Admin. News 1982, p. 214. The "right" question, as the Report emphasizes repeatedly, is whether "as a result of the challenged practice or structure plaintiffs do not have an equal opportunity to participate in the political processes and to elect candidates of their choice." *Id.,* at 28, U.S.Code Cong. & Admin.News 1982, p. 206. See also *id.,* at 2, 27, 29, n. 118, 36.

In order to answer this question, a court must assess the impact of the contested structure or practice on minority electoral opportunities "on the basis of objective factors." *Id.,* at 27, U.S.Code Cong. & Admin.News 1982, p. 205. The Senate Report specifies factors which typically may be relevant to a § 2 claim: the history of voting-related discrimination in the State or political subdivision; the extent to which voting in the elections of the State or political subdivision is racially polarized; the extent to which the State or political subdivision has used voting practices or procedures that tend to enhance the opportunity for discrimination against the minority group, such as unusually large election districts, majority vote requirements, and prohibitions against bullet voting; the exclusion of members of the minority group from candidate slating processes; the extent to which minority group members bear the effects of past discrimination in areas such as education, employment, and health, which hinder their ability to participate effectively in the political process; the use of overt or subtle racial appeals in political campaigns; and the extent to which members of the minority group have been elected to public office in the jurisdiction. *Id.,* at 28–29; see also *supra,* at —. The Report notes also that evidence demonstrating that elected officials are unresponsive to the particularized needs of the members of the minority group and that the policy underlying the State's or the political subdivision's use of the contested practice or structure is tenuous may have probative value. *Id.,* at 29. The Report stresses, however, that this list of typical factors is neither comprehensive nor exclusive. While the enumerated factors will often be pertinent to certain types of § 2 violations, particularly to vote dilution claims, other factors may also be relevant and may be considered. *Id.,* at 29–30 . . . .

Although the Senate Report espouses a flexible, fact-intensive test for § 2 violations, it limits the circumstances under which § 2 violations may be proved in three ways. First, electoral devices, such as at-large elections, may not be considered *per se* violative of § 2. Plaintiffs must demonstrate that, under the totality of the circumstances, the devices result in unequal access to the electoral process. *Id.,* at 16. Second, the conjunction of an allegedly dilutive electoral mechanism and the lack of proportional representation alone does not establish a violation. *Ibid.* Third, the results test does not assume the existence of racial bloc voting; plaintiffs must prove it. *Id.,* at 33.

B

VOTE DILUTION THROUGH THE USE
OF MULTIMEMBER DISTRICTS

Appellees contend that the legislative decision to employ multimember, rather than single-member, districts in the contested jurisdictions dilutes their votes by submerging them in a white majority, thus impairing their ability to elect representatives of their choice.

The essence of a § 2 claim is that a certain electoral law, practice, or structure interacts with social and historical conditions to cause an inequality in the opportunities enjoyed by black and white voters to elect their preferred representatives. This Court has long recognized that multimember districts and at-large voting schemes may "'operate to minimize or cancel out the voting strength of racial [minorities in] the voting population. . . .'" Multimember districts and at-large election schemes, however, are not *per se* violative of minority voters' rights. S.Rep., at 16. Cf. *Rogers v. Lodge, supra,* 458 U.S., at 617, 102 S.Ct., at 3275; *Regester, supra,* 412 U.S., at 765, 93 S. Ct., at 2339; *Whitcomb, supra,* 403 U.S., at 142, 91 S.Ct., at 1868. Minority voters who contend that the multimember form of districting violates § 2, must prove that the use of a multimember electoral structure operates to minimize or cancel out their ability to elect their preferred candidates. See, *e.g.,* S.Rep., at 16.

While many or all of the factors listed in the Senate Report may be relevant to a claim of vote dilution through submergence in multimember districts, unless there is a conjunction of the following circumstances, the use of multimember districts generally will not impede the ability of minority voters to elect representatives of their choice. Stated succinctly, a bloc voting majority must *usually* be able to defeat candidates supported by a politically cohesive, geographically insular minority group. Bonapfel 355; Blacksher & Menefee 34; Butler 903; Carpeneti 696–699; Davidson, Minority Vote Dilution: An Overview (hereinafter Davidson), in Minority Vote Dilution 4; Grofman, Alternatives 117. Cf. *Bolden,* 446 U.S., at 105, n. 3, 100 S.Ct., at 1520, n. 3 (Marshall, J., dissenting). First, the minority group must be able to demonstrate that it is sufficiently large and geographically compact to constitute a majority in a single-member district. If it is not, as would be the case in a substantially integrated district, the *multi-member form* of the district cannot be responsible for minority voters' inability to elect its candidates. . . . Second, the minority group must be able to show that it is politically cohesive. If the minority group is not politically cohesive, it cannot be said that the selection of a multimember electoral structure thwarts distinctive minority group interests. Blacksher & Menefee 51–55, 58–60, and n. 344; Carpeneti 696–697; Davidson 4. Third, the minority must be able to demonstrate that the white majority votes sufficiently as a bloc to enable it—in the absence of special circumstances, such as the minority candidate running unopposed, see, *infra,* at—, and n. 26—usually to defeat the minority's preferred candidate. . . . In establishing this last circumstance, the minority group demonstrates that submergence in a white multimember district impedes its ability to elect its chosen representatives.

. . . .

III

. . . .

A

THE DISTRICT COURT'S TREATMENT OF
RACIALLY POLARIZED VOTING

The investigation conducted by the District Court into the question of racial bloc voting credited some testimony of lay witnesses, but relied principally on statistical evidence presented by appellees' expert witnesses, in particular that offered by Dr. Bernard Grofman. Dr. Grofman collected and evaluated data from 53 General Assembly primary and general elections involving black candidacies. These elections were held over a period of three different election years in the six originally challenged multimember districts. Dr. Grofman subjected the data to two complementary methods of analysis—extreme case analysis and bivariate ecological regression analysis—in order to determine whether blacks and whites in these districts differed in their voting behavior. These analytic techniques yielded data concerning the voting patterns of the two races, including estimates of the percentages of members of each race who voted for black candidates.

The court's initial consideration of these data took the form of a three-part inquiry: did the data reveal any correlation between the race of the voter and the selection of certain candidates; was the revealed correlation statistically significant; and was the difference in black and white voting patterns "substantively significant"? The District Court found that blacks and whites generally preferred different candidates and, on that basis, found voting in the districts to be racially correlated. The court accepted Dr. Grofman's expert opinion that the correlation between the race of the voter and the voter's choice of certain candidates was statistically significant. Finally, adopting Dr. Grofman's terminology, see Tr. 195, the court found that in all but 2 of the 53 elections the degree of racial bloc voting was "so marked as to be substantively significant, in the sense that the results of the individual election would have been different depending upon whether it had been held among only the white voters or only the black voters." 590 F.Supp., at 368.

The court also reported its findings, both in tabulated numerical form and in written form, that a high percentage of black voters regularly supported black candidates and that most white voters were extremely reluctant to vote for black candidates. The court then considered the relevance to the existence of legally significant white bloc voting of the fact that black candidates have won some elections. It determined that in most instances, special circumstances, such as incumbency and lack of opposition, rather than a diminution in usually severe white bloc voting, accounted for these candidates' success. The court also suggested that black voters' reliance on bullet voting was a significant factor in their successful efforts to elect candidates of their choice. Based on all of the evidence before it, the trial court concluded that each of the districts experienced racially polarized voting "in a persistent and severe degree." *Id.,* at 367.

B

THE DEGREE OF BLOC VOTING THAT IS LEGALLY SIGNIFICANT UNDER § 2

. . . .

2

The Standard for Legally Significant Racial Bloc Voting

. . . Because, as we explain below, the extent of bloc voting necessary to demonstrate that a minority's ability to elect its preferred representatives is impaired varies according to several factual circumstances, the degree of bloc voting which constitutes the threshold of legal significance will vary from district to district. Nonetheless, it is possible to state some general principles and we proceed to do so.

The purpose of inquiring into the existence of racially polarized voting is twofold: to ascertain whether minority group members constitute a politically cohesive unit and to determine whether whites vote sufficiently as a bloc usually to defeat the minority's preferred candidates. See *supra,* at—. Thus, the question whether a given district experiences legally significant racially polarized voting requires discrete inquiries into minority and white voting practices. A showing that a significant number of minority group members usually vote for the same candidates is one way of proving the political cohesiveness necessary to a vote dilution claim, Blacksher & Menefee 59–60, and n. 344, and, consequently, establishes minority bloc voting within the context of § 2. And, in general, a white bloc vote that normally will defeat the combined strength of minority support plus white "crossover" votes rise to the level of legally significant white bloc voting. *Id.,* at 60. The amount of white bloc voting that can generally "minimize or cancel," S.Rep., at 28, U.S.Code Cong. & Admin.News 1982, p. 205; *Regester,* 412 U.S., at 765, 93 S.Ct., at 2339, black voters' ability to elect representatives of their choice, however, will vary from district to district according to a number of factors, including the nature of the allegedly dilutive electoral mechanism; the presence or absence of other potentially dilutive electoral devices, such as majority vote requirements, designated posts, and prohibitions against bullet voting; the percentage of registered voters in the district who are members of the minority group; the size of the district; and, in multimember districts, the number of seats open and the number of candidates in the field. See, *e.g.,* Butler 874–876; Davidson 5; Jones, *The Impact of Local Election Systems on Black Political Representation,* 11 Urb.Aff.Q. 345 (1976); United States Commission on Civil Rights, The Voting Rights Act: Unfulfilled Goals 38–41 (1981).

Because loss of political power through vote dilution is distinct from the mere inability to win a particular election, *Whitcomb,* 403 U.S., at 153, 91 S.Ct., at 1874, a pattern of racial bloc voting that extends over a period of time is more probative of a claim that a district experiences legally significant polarization than are the results of a single election. Blacksher & Menefee 61; Note, *Geometry and Geography* 200, n. 66 ("Racial polarization should be seen as an attribute not of a single election, but rather of a polity viewed over time. The concern is necessarily temporal and the analysis historical because the evil to be avoided is the subordination of minority groups in American politics, not the defeat of individuals in particular electoral contests"). Also for this reason, in a district where elections are shown usually to be polarized, the fact that racially polarized voting is not present in one or a few individual elections does not necessarily negate the conclusion that the district experiences legally significant bloc voting. Furthermore, the success of a minority candidate in a particular election does not necessarily prove that the district did not experience polarized voting in that election; special circumstances, such as the absence of an opponent, incumbency, or the utilization of bullet voting, may explain minority electoral success in a polarized contest.

As must be apparent, the degree of racial bloc voting that is cognizable as an element of a § 2 vote dilution claim will vary according to a variety of factual circumstances. Consequently, there is no simple doctrinal test for the existence of legally significant racial bloc voting. However, the foregoing general principles should provide courts with substantial guidance in determining whether evidence that black and white voters generally prefer different candidates rises to the level of legal significance under § 2.

3

Standard Utilized by the District Court

. . . While the court did not phrase the standard for legally significant racial bloc voting exactly as we do, a fair reading of the court's opinion reveals that the court's analysis conforms to our view of the proper legal standard.

The District Court's findings concerning black support for black candidates in the five multimember districts at issue here clearly establish the political cohesiveness of black voters. As is apparent from the District Court's tabulated findings, reproduced in Appendix A to opinion, *post,* p.—, black voters' support for black candidates was overwhelming in almost every election. In all but 5 of 16 primary elections, black support for black candidates ranged between 71% and 92%; and in the general elections, black support for black Democratic candidates ranged between 87% and 96%.

In sharp contrast to its findings of strong black support for black candidates, the District Court found that a substantial majority of white voters would rarely, if ever, vote for a black candidate. In the primary elections, white support for black candidates ranged between 8% and 50%, and in the general elections it ranged between 28% and 49%. See *ibid.* The court also determined that, on average, 81.7% of white voters did not vote for any black candidate in the primary elections. In the general elections, white voters almost always ranked black candidates either last or next to last in the multicandidate field, except in heavily Democratic areas where white voters consistently ranked black candidates last among the Democrats, if not last or next to last among all candidates. The court further observed that approximately two-thirds of white voters did not vote for black candidates in general elections, even after the candidate had won the Democratic primary and the choice was to vote for a Republican or for no one.

While the District Court did not state expressly that the percentage of whites who refused to vote for black candidates in the contested districts would, in the usual course of events, result in the defeat of the minority's candidates, that conclusion is apparent both from the court's factual findings and from the rest of its analysis. First, with the exception of House District 23, see *infra*, at—, the trial court's findings clearly show that black voters have enjoyed only minimal and sporadic success in electing representatives of their choice. See Appendix B to opinion, *post*, p.—. Second, where black candidates won elections, the court closely examined the circumstances of those elections before concluding that the success of these blacks did not negate other evidence, derived from all of the elections studied in each district, that legally significant racially polarized voting exists in each district. For example, the court took account of the benefits incumbency and running essentially unopposed conferred on some of the successful black candidates, as well as of the very different order of preference blacks and whites assigned black candidates, in reaching its conclusion that *legally significant* [emphasis added] racial polarization exists in each district.

We conclude that the District Court's approach, which tested data derived from three election years in each district, and which revealed that blacks strongly supported black candidates, while, to the black candidates' usual detriment, whites rarely did, satisfactorily addresses each facet of the proper legal standard.

C

EVIDENCE OF RACIALLY POLARIZED VOTING

1

Appellants' Argument

North Carolina and the United States also contest the evidence upon which the District Court relied in finding that voting patterns in the challenged districts were racially polarized. They argue that the term "racially polarized voting" must, as a matter of law, refer to voting patterns for which the *principal cause* is race. They contend that the District Court utilized a legally incorrect definition of racially polarized voting by relying on bivariate statistical analyses which merely demonstrated a *correlation* between the race of the voter and the level of voter support for certain candidates, but which did not prove that race was the primary determinant of voters' choices. . . . Brief for United States as *Amicus Curiae* 30, n. 57, can prove that race was the primary determinant of voter behavior.

. . . [W]e disagree: For purposes of § 2, the legal concept of racially polarized voting incorporates neither causation nor intent. It means simply that the race of voters correlates with the selection of a certain candidate or candidates; that is, it refers to the situation where different races (or minority language groups) vote in blocs for different candidates. Grofman, Migalski, & Noviello 203. As we demonstrate *infra,* appellants' theory of racially polarized voting would thwart the goals Congress sought to achieve when it amended § 2 and would prevent courts from performing the "functional" analysis of the political process, S.Rep., at 30, n. 119, U.S.Code Cong. & Admin.News 1982, p. 208, and the "searching practical evaluation of the 'past and present reality,'" *id.,* at 30, U.S.Code Cong. & Admin.News 1982, p. 208 (footnote omitted), mandated by the Senate Report.

2

Causation Irrelevant to Section 2 Inquiry

The first reason we reject appellants' argument that racially polarized voting refers to voting patterns that are in some way *caused by race,* rather than to voting patterns that are merely *correlated with the race of the voter,* is that the reasons black and white voters vote differently have no relevance to the central inquiry of § 2. By contrast, the correlation between race of voter and the selection of certain candidates is crucial to that inquiry.

Both § 2 itself and the Senate Report make clear that the critical question in a § 2 claim is whether the use of a contested electoral practice or structure results in members of a protected group having less opportunity than other members of the electorate to participate in the political process and to elect representatives of their choice. See, *e.g.,* S.Rep., at 2, 27, 28, 29, n. 118, 36. As we explained, *supra,* at—, multimember districts may impair the ability of blacks to elect representatives of their choice where blacks vote sufficiently as a bloc as to be able to elect their preferred candidates in a black majority, single-member district and where a white majority votes sufficiently as a bloc usually to defeat the candidates chosen by blacks. It is the *difference* between the choices made by blacks and whites—not the reasons for that difference—that results in blacks having less opportunity than whites to elect their preferred representatives. Consequently, we conclude that under the "results test" of § 2, only the correlation between race of voter and selection of certain candidates, not the causes of the correlation, matters.

The irrelevance to a § 2 inquiry of the reasons why black and white voters vote differently supports, by itself, our rejection of appellants' theory of racially polarized voting. However, their theory contains other equally serious flaws that merit further attention. As we demonstrate below, the addition of irrelevant variables distorts the equation and yields results that are indisputably incorrect under § 2 and the Senate Report.

3

Race of Voter as Primary Determinant of Voter Behavior

. . . .

... [W]e would hold that the legal concept of racially polarized voting, as it relates to claims of vote dilution, refers only to the existence of a correlation between the race of voters and the selection of certain candidates. Plaintiffs need not prove causation or intent in order to prove a prima facie case of racial bloc voting and defendants may not rebut that case with evidence of causation or intent.

IV

THE LEGAL SIGNIFICANCE OF SOME BLACK CANDIDATES' SUCCESS

A

North Carolina and the United States maintain that the District Court failed to accord the proper weight to the success of some black candidates in the challenged districts. Black residents of these districts, they point out, achieved improved representation in the 1982 General Assembly election. They also note that blacks in House District 23 have enjoyed proportional representation consistently since 1973 and that blacks in the other districts have occasionally enjoyed nearly proportional representation. This electoral success demonstrates conclusively, appellants and the United States argue, that blacks in those districts do not have "less opportunity than other members of the electorate to participate in the political process and to elect representatives of their choice." 42 U.S.C. § 1973(b). Essentially, appellants and the United States contend that if a racial minority gains proportional or nearly proportional representation in a single election, that fact alone precludes, as a matter of law, finding a § 2 violation.

Section 2(b) provides that "[t]he extent to which members of a protected class have been elected to office . . . is one circumstance which may be considered." 42 U.S.C. § 1973(b). . . . [T]he language of § 2 and its legislative history plainly demonstrate that proof that some minority candidates have been elected does not foreclose a § 2 claim.

Moreover, in conducting its "independent consideration of the record" and its "searching practical evaluation of the 'past and present reality,'" the District Court could appropriately take account of the circumstances surrounding recent black electoral success in deciding its significance to appellees' claim. In particular, as the Senate Report makes clear, *id.,* at 29, n. 115, the court could properly notice the fact that black electoral success increased markedly in the 1982 election — an election that occurred after the instant lawsuit had been filed — and could properly consider to what extent "the pendency of this very litigation [might have] worked a one-time advantage for black candidates in the form of unusual organized political support by white leaders concerned to forestall single-member districting." 590 F.Supp., at 367, n. 27.

Nothing in the statute or its legislative history prohibited the court from viewing with some caution black candidates' success in the 1982 election, and from deciding on the basis of all the relevant circumstances to accord greater weight to blacks' relative lack of success over the course of several recent elections. Consequently, we hold that the District Court did not err, as a matter of law, in refusing to treat the fact that some black candidates have succeeded as dispositive of appellees' §2 claim. Where multimember districting generally works to dilute the minority vote, it cannot be defended on the ground that it sporadically and serendipitously benefits minority voters.

B

The District Court did err, however, in ignoring the significance of the *sustained* success black voters have experienced in House District 23. In that district, the last six elections have resulted in proportional representation for black residents. This persistent proportional representation is inconsistent with appellees' allegation that the ability of black voters in District 23 to elect representatives of their choice is not equal to that enjoyed by the white majority.

In some situations, it may be possible for §2 plaintiffs to demonstrate that such sustained success does not accurately reflect the minority group's ability to elect its preferred representatives, but appellees have not done so here. Appellees presented evidence relating to black electoral success in the last three elections; they failed utterly, though, to offer any explanation for the success of black candidates in the previous three elections. Consequently, we believe that the District Court erred, as a matter of law, in ignoring the sustained success black voters have enjoyed in House District 23, and would reverse with respect to that District.

V

ULTIMATE DETERMINATION OF VOTE DILUTION

Finally, appellants and the United States dispute the District Court's ultimate conclusion that the multimember districting scheme at issue in this case deprived black voters of an equal opportunity to participate in the political process and to elect representatives of their choice.

A

As an initial matter, both North Carolina and the United States contend that the District Court's ultimate conclusion that the challenged multimember districts operate to dilute black citizens' votes is a mixed question of law and fact subject to *de novo* review on appeal. In support of their proposed standard of review, they rely primarily on *Bose Corp. v. Consumers Union of U.S., Inc.,* 466 U.S. 485, 104 S. Ct. 1949, 80 L.Ed.2d 502 (1984), a case in which we reconfirmed that, as a matter of constitutional law, there must be independent appellate review of evidence of "actual malice" in defamation cases. Appellants and the United States argue that because a finding of vote dilution under amended §2 requires the application of a rule of law to a particular set of facts it constitutes a legal, rather than factual, determination. Reply Brief for Appellants 7; Brief for United States as *Amicus Curiae* 18–19. Neither appellants nor the United States cite our several precedents in which we have treated the ultimate finding of vote dilution as a question of fact subject to the clearly-erroneous standard of Rule 52(a). See, *e.g., Rogers v. Lodge,* 458 U.S., at 622–627, 102 S.Ct., at 3278–3281; *City of Rome v. United States,* 446 U.S. 156, 183, 100 S.Ct. 1548, 1564, 64 L.Ed.2d 119 (1980); *White v. Regester,* 412 U.S., at 765–770, 93 S.Ct., at 2339–2341. Cf. *Anderson v. Bessemer City,* 470 U.S. 564, 573, 105 S.Ct. 1504, 1511, 84 L.Ed.2d 518 (1985).

. . . [W]e expressly held in *Rogers v. Lodge, supra,* that the question whether an at-large election system was maintained for discriminatory purposes and subsidiary issues, which include whether that system had the effect of diluting the minority vote, were questions of fact, reviewable under Rule 52(a)'s clearly-erroneous standard. 458 U.S., at 622–623, 102 S.Ct., at 3278–3279. Similarly, in *City of Rome v. United States,* we declared that the question whether certain electoral structures had a "discriminatory effect," in the sense of diluting the minority vote, was a question of fact subject to clearly-erroneous review. 446 U.S., at 183, 100 S.Ct., at 1565.

We reaffirm our view that the clearly-erroneous test of Rule 52(a) is the appropriate standard for appellate review of a finding of vote dilution. As both amended § 2 and its legislative history make clear, in evaluating a statutory claim of vote dilution through districting, the trial court is to consider the "totality of the circumstances" and to determine, based "upon a searching practical evaluation of the 'past and present reality,'" S.Rep., at 30, U.S.Code Cong. & Admin.News 1982, p. 208 . . . and requires "an intensely local appraisal of the design and impact" of the contested electoral mechanisms. 458 U.S., at 622, 102 S.Ct., at 3278. The fact that amended § 2 and its legislative history provide legal standards which a court must apply to the facts in order to determine whether § 2 has been violated does not alter the standard of review. . . . Thus, the application of the clearly-erroneous standard to ultimate findings of vote dilution preserves the benefit of the trial court's particular familiarity with the indigenous political reality without endangering the rule of law.

B

The District Court in this case carefully considered the totality of the circumstances and found that in each district racially polarized voting; the legacy of official discrimination in voting matters, education, housing, employment, and health services; and the persistence of campaign appeals to racial prejudice acted in concert with the multimember districting scheme to impair the ability of geographically insular and politically cohesive groups of black voters to participate equally in the political process and to elect candidates of their choice. It found that the success a few black candidates have enjoyed in these districts is too recent, too limited, and, with regard to the 1982 elections, perhaps too aberrational, to disprove its conclusion. Excepting House District 23, with respect to which the District Court committed legal error, see *supra,* at—, we affirm the District Court's judgment. We cannot say that the District Court, composed of local judges who are well acquainted with the political realities of the State, clearly erred in concluding that use of a multimember electoral structure has caused black voters in the districts other than House District 23 to have less opportunity than white voters to elect representatives of their choice.

The judgment of the District Court is

Affirmed in part and reversed in part.

Notes and Questions

1. Why was the United States on the side of North Carolina instead of on the side of the plaintiffs? What role does the Department of Justice play in this type of litigation? Is it consistent with the mission of the agency?

2. How does Thornburg define the standard for determining voter dilution in a district? How are these factors still relevant to today's electoral realities?

E. Intersection of Section 2 and Section 5

In *Reno v. Bossier* below, the Supreme Court considered whether evidence that a new plan violates Section 2 of the Voting Rights Act could justify denial of preclearance under Section 5.

Reno v. Bossier Parish School Board
520 U.S. 471 (1997)

JUSTICE O'CONNOR delivered the opinion of the Court.

Today we clarify the relationship between § 2 and § 5 of the Voting Rights Act of 1965, 79 Stat. 437, 439, as amended, 42 U.S.C. §§ 1973, 1973c. Specifically, we decide two questions: (i) whether preclearance must be denied under § 5 whenever a covered jurisdiction's new voting "standard, practice, or procedure" violates § 2; and (ii) whether evidence that a new "standard, practice, or procedure" has a dilutive impact is always irrelevant to the inquiry whether the covered jurisdiction acted with "the purpose . . . of denying or abridging the right to vote on account of race or color" under § 5. We answer both in the negative.

I

Appellee Bossier Parish School Board ("Board") is a jurisdiction subject to the preclearance requirements of § 5 of the Voting Rights Act of 1965, 42 U.S.C. § 1973c, and must therefore obtain the approval of either the United States Attorney General or the United States District Court for the District of Columbia before implementing any changes to a voting "qualification, prerequisite, standard, practice, or procedure." The Board has 12 members who are elected from single-member districts by majority vote to serve 4-year terms. When the 1990 census revealed wide population disparities among its districts, see App. to Juris. Statement 93a (Stipulations of

Fact and Law ¶ 82), the Board decided to redraw the districts to equalize the population distribution.

During this process, the Board considered two redistricting plans. It considered, and initially rejected, the redistricting plan that had been recently adopted by the Bossier Parish Police Jury, the parish's primary governing body (the Jury plan), to govern its own elections. Just months before, the Attorney General had precleared the Jury plan, which also contained 12 districts. *Id.,* at 88a (Stipulations ¶ 68). None of the 12 districts in the Board's existing plan or in the Jury plan contained a majority of black residents. *Id.,* at 93a (Stipulations ¶ 82) (under 1990 population statistics in the Board's existing districts, the three districts with highest black concentrations contain 46.63%, 43.79%, and 30.13% black residents, respectively); *id.,* at 85a (Stipulations ¶ 59) (population statistics for the Jury plan, with none of the plan's 12 districts containing a black majority). Because the Board's adoption of the Jury plan would have maintained the status quo regarding the number of black-majority districts, the parties stipulated that the Jury plan was not "retrogressive." *Id.,* at 141a (Stipulations ¶ 252) ("The . . . plan is not retrogressive to minority voting strength compared to the existing benchmark plan . . ."). Appellant George Price, president of the local chapter of the National Association for the Advancement of Colored People (NAACP), presented the Board with a second option—a plan that created two districts each containing not only a majority of black residents, but a majority of voting-age black residents. *Id.,* at 98a (Stipulations ¶ 98). Over vocal opposition from local residents, black and white alike, the Board voted to adopt the Jury plan as its own, reasoning that the Jury plan would almost certainly be precleared again and that the NAACP plan would require the Board to split 46 electoral precincts.

But the Board's hopes for rapid preclearance were dashed when the Attorney General interposed a formal objection to the Board's plan on the basis of "new information" not available when the Justice Department had precleared the plan for the Police Jury—namely, the NAACP's plan, which demonstrated that "black residents are sufficiently numerous and geographically compact so as to constitute a majority in two single-member districts." *Id.,* at 155a-156a (Attorney General's August 30, 1993, objection letter). The objection letter asserted that the Board's plan violated § 2 of the Act, 42 U.S.C. § 1973, because it "unnecessarily limit[ed] the opportunity for minority voters to elect their candidates of choice," App. to Juris. Statement, at 156a, as compared to the new alternative. Relying on 28 CFR § 51.55(b)(2) (1996), which provides that the Attorney General shall withhold preclearance where "necessary to prevent a clear violation of amended Section 2 [42 U.S.C. § 1973]," the Attorney General concluded that the Board's redistricting plan warranted a denial of preclearance under § 5. App. to Juris. Statement 157a. The Attorney General declined to reconsider the decision. *Ibid.*

The Board then filed this action seeking preclearance under § 5 in the District Court for the District of Columbia. . . . We noted probable jurisdiction on June 3, 1996. 517 U.S. 1232, 116 S.Ct. 1874, 135 L.Ed.2d 171.

II

The Voting Rights Act of 1965 (Act), 42 U.S.C. § 1973 *et seq.*, was enacted by Congress in 1964 to "attac[k] the blight of voting discrimination" across the Nation. S.Rep. No. 97-417, 2d Sess., p. 4 (1982) U.S.Code Cong. & Admin.News 1982 pp. 177, 180; *South Carolina v. Katzenbach*, 383 U.S. 301, 308, 86 S.Ct. 803, 808, 15 L.Ed.2d 769 (1966). Two of the weapons in the Federal Government's formidable arsenal are § 5 and § 2 of the Act. Although we have consistently understood these sections to combat different evils and, accordingly, to impose very different duties upon the States, see *Holder v. Hall*, 512 U.S. 874, 883, 114 S.Ct. 2581, 2587, 129 L.Ed.2d 687 (1994) (plurality opinion) . . . . [W]e entertain little doubt that the Department of Justice or other litigants would "routinely" attempt to avail themselves of this new reason for denying preclearance, so that recognizing § 2 violations as a basis for denying § 5 preclearance would inevitably make compliance with § 5 contingent upon compliance with § 2. Doing so would, for all intents and purposes, replace the standards for § 5 with those for § 2. Because this would contradict our longstanding interpretation of these two sections of the Act, we reject appellants' position.

. . . In light of this limited purpose, § 5 applies only to certain States and their political subdivisions. Such a covered jurisdiction may not implement any change in a voting "qualification, prerequisite, standard, practice, or procedure" unless it first obtains either administrative preclearance of that change from the Attorney General or judicial preclearance from the District Court for the District of Columbia. 42 U.S.C. § 1973c. To obtain judicial preclearance, the jurisdiction bears the burden of proving that the change "does not have the purpose and will not have the effect of denying or abridging the right to vote on account of race or color." Ibid.; City of Rome v. United States, 446 U.S. 156, 183, n. 18, 100 S.Ct. 1548, 1565, n. 18, 64 L.Ed.2d 119 (1980) (covered jurisdiction bears burden of proof). Because § 5 focuses on "freez[ing] election procedures," a plan has an impermissible "effect" under § 5 only if it "would lead to a retrogression in the position of racial minorities with respect to their effective exercise of the electoral franchise." Beer v. United States, 425 U.S. 130, 141, 96 S.Ct. 1357, 1384 (1976)

Retrogression, by definition, requires a comparison of a jurisdiction's new voting plan with its existing plan. See Holder, supra, at 883, 114 S.Ct., at 2587 (plurality opinion) ("Under § 5, then, the proposed voting practice is measured against the existing voting practice to determine whether retrogression would result from the proposed change"). It also necessarily implies that the jurisdiction's existing plan is the benchmark against which the "effect" of voting changes is measured. [For example, if a new plan does not increase the degree of discrimination against the city's minority population when compared to existing plan, it might be entitled to § 5 preclearance because not retrogressive—Eds.]

Section 2, on the other hand, was designed as a means of eradicating voting practices that "minimize or cancel out the voting strength and political effectiveness of minority groups," S.Rep. No. 97-417, at 28, U.S.Code Cong. & Admin.News

1982 pp. 177, 205. Under this broader mandate, § 2 bars all States and their political subdivisions from maintaining any voting "standard, practice, or procedure" that "results in a denial or abridgement of the right . . . to vote on account of race or color." 42 U.S.C. § 1973(a). A voting practice is impermissibly dilutive within the meaning of § 2

> "if, based on the totality of the circumstances, it is shown that the politi-cal processes leading to nomination or election in the State or political subdivision are not equally open to participation by [members of a class defined by race or color] in that its members have less opportunity than other members of the electorate to participate in the political process and to elect representatives of their choice." 42 U.S.C. § 1973(b).

A plaintiff claiming vote dilution under § 2 must initially establish that: (i) "[the racial group] is sufficiently large and geographically compact to constitute a major-ity in a single-member district"; (ii) the group is "politically cohesive"; and (iii) "the white majority votes sufficiently as a bloc to enable it . . . usually to defeat the minor-ity's preferred candidate." Thornburg v. Gingles, 478 U.S. 30, 50–51, 106 S.Ct. 2752, 2766–2767, 92 L.Ed.2d 25 (1986); Growe v. Emison, 507 U.S. 25, 40, 113 S.Ct. 1075, 1084, 122 L.Ed.2d 388 (1993). The plaintiff must also demonstrate that the totality of the circumstances supports a finding that the voting scheme is dilutive . . . .

Appellants contend that preclearance must be denied under § 5 whenever a cov-ered jurisdiction's redistricting plan violates § 2. The upshot of this position is to shift the focus of § 5 from nonretrogression to vote dilution, and to change the § 5 benchmark from a jurisdiction's existing plan to a hypothetical, undiluted plan. [Quoting White v. Regester, the Court distinguishes constitional claims of voter dilution brought under the 14th or the 15th Amendments (both requiring proof of intent) from claims brought under Section 2 (which after amendment allow proof of effects). [The Court reasoned that, because constitutional standards are distinct from Section 2's, denying preclearance could not be viewed as necessarily prevent-ing such violation.]

. . . .

III

Appellants next contend that evidence showing that a jurisdiction's redistricting plan dilutes the voting power of minorities is at least relevant in a § 5 proceeding because it tends to prove that the jurisdiction enacted its plan with a discriminatory "purpose." . . . Because we hold that some of this "§ 2 evidence" may be relevant to establish a jurisdiction's "intent to retrogress" and cannot say with confidence that the District Court considered the evidence proffered to show that the Board's reap-portionment plan was dilutive, we vacate this aspect of the District Court's holding and remand. In light of this conclusion, we leave open for another day the question whether the § 5 purpose inquiry ever extends beyond the search for retrogressive intent. . . . The existence of such a purpose, and its relevance to § 5, are issues to be decided on remand.

Although § 5 warrants a denial of preclearance if a covered jurisdiction's voting change "ha[s] the purpose [or] . . . the effect of denying or abridging the right to vote on account of race or color," 42 U.S.C. § 1973c, we have consistently interpreted this language in light of the purpose underlying § 5 — "to insure that no voting-procedure changes would be made that would lead to a retrogression in the position of racial minorities." Beer, 425 U.S., at 141, 96 S.Ct., at 1364. Accordingly, we have adhered to the view that the only "effect" that violates § 5 is a retrogressive one. Ibid.; City of Lockhart, 460 U.S., at 134, 103 S.Ct., at 1004.

Evidence is "relevant" if it has "any tendency to make the existence of any fact that is of consequence to the determination of the action more probable or less probable than it would be without the evidence." Fed. Rule Evid. 401. As we observed in Arlington Heights, 429 U.S., at 266, 97 S.Ct., at 563–564, the impact of an official action is often probative of why the action was taken in the first place since people usually intend the natural consequences of their actions. Thus, a jurisdiction that enacts a plan having a dilutive impact is more likely to have acted with a discriminatory intent to dilute minority voting strength than a jurisdiction whose plan has no such impact. A jurisdiction that acts with an intent to dilute minority voting strength is more likely to act with an intent to worsen the position of minority voters — *i.e.,* an intent to retrogress — than a jurisdiction acting with no intent to dilute. The fact that a plan has a dilutive impact therefore makes it "more probable" that the jurisdiction adopting that plan acted with an intent to retrogress than "it would be without the evidence." To be sure, the link between dilutive impact and intent to retrogress is far from direct, but "the basic standard of relevance . . . is a liberal one," *Daubert v. Merrell Dow Pharmaceuticals, Inc.,* 509 U.S. 579, 587, 113 S. Ct. 2786, 2794, 125 L.Ed.2d 469 (1993), and one we think is met here.

That evidence of a plan's dilutive impact may be relevant to the § 5 purpose inquiry does not, of course, mean that such evidence is dispositive of that inquiry. In fact, we have previously observed that a jurisdiction's single decision to choose a redistricting plan that has a dilutive impact does not, without more, suffice to establish that the jurisdiction acted with a discriminatory purpose. *Shaw v. Hunt,* 517 U.S. 899, 914, n. 6, 116 S.Ct. 1894, 1904, n. 6, 135 L.Ed.2d 207 (1996) . . . .

As our discussion illustrates, assessing a jurisdiction's motivation in enacting voting changes is a complex task requiring a "sensitive inquiry into such circumstantial and direct evidence as may be available." *Arlington Heights,* 429 U.S., at 266, 97 S. Ct., at 564. In conducting this inquiry, courts should look to our decision in *Arlington Heights* for guidance. There, we set forth a framework for analyzing "whether invidious discriminatory purpose was a motivating factor" in a government body's decision-making. *Ibid.* In addition to serving as the framework for examining discriminatory purpose in cases brought under the Equal Protection Clause for over two decades, see, *e.g., Shaw v. Reno,* 509 U.S. 630, 644, 113 S.Ct. 2816, 2825, 125 L. Ed.2d 511 (1993) (citing *Arlington Heights* standard in context of Equal Protection Clause challenge to racial gerrymander of districts); *Rogers v. Lodge,* 458 U.S. 613, 618, 102 S.Ct. 3272, 3276, 73 L.Ed.2d 1012 (1982) (evaluating vote dilution claim under Equal Protection Clause using *Arlington Heights* test); *Mobile,* 446 U.S., at 70–74, 100 S.Ct., at 1501–1503 (same), the *Arlington Heights* framework has also been used, at least in part, to evaluate purpose in our previous § 5 cases. See *Pleasant Grove v. United States,* 479 U.S. 462, 469–470, 107 S.Ct. 794, 798–799, 93 L.Ed.2d 866 (1987) (considering city's history in rejecting annexation of black neighborhood and its departure from normal procedures when calculating costs of annexation alternatives); see also *Busbee v. Smith,* 549 F.Supp. 494, 516–517 (D.C. 1982), summarily aff'd, 459 U.S. 1166, 103 S.Ct. 809, 74 L.Ed.2d 1010 (1983) (referring to *Arlington Heights* test); *Port Arthur v. United States,* 517 F.Supp. 987, 1019, aff'd, 459 U.S. 159, 103 S.Ct. 530, 74 L.Ed.2d 334 (1982) (same).

The "important starting point" for assessing discriminatory intent under *Arlington Heights* is "the impact of the official action whether it 'bears more heavily on one race than another.'" 429 U.S., at 266, 97 S.Ct., at 564 (citing *Washington v. Davis,* 426 U.S. 229, 242, 96 S.Ct. 2040, 2048–2049, 48 L.Ed.2d 597 (1976)). In a § 5 case, "impact" might include a plan's retrogressive effect and, for the reasons discussed above, its dilutive impact. Other considerations relevant to the purpose inquiry include, among other things, "the historical background of the [jurisdiction's] decision"; "[t]he specific sequence of events leading up to the challenged decision"; "[d]epartures from the normal procedural sequence"; and "[t]he legislative or administrative history, especially . . . [any] contemporary statements by members of the decisionmaking body." 429 U.S., at 268, 97 S.Ct., at 565.

We are unable to determine from the District Court's opinion in this action whether it deemed irrelevant all evidence of the dilutive impact of the redistricting plan adopted by the Board. At one point, the District Court correctly stated that "the adoption of one nonretrogressive plan rather than another nonretrogressive plan that contains more majority-black districts cannot *by itself* give rise to the inference of discriminatory intent." 907 F.Supp., at 450 (emphasis added). This passage implies that the District Court believed that the existence of less dilutive options was at least relevant to, though not dispositive of, its purpose inquiry. While this language is consistent with our holding today, see *supra,* at 1501–1502, the District Court also declared that "we will not permit section 2 evidence to prove discriminatory purpose under section 5," *ibid.* With this statement, the District Court appears to endorse the notion that evidence of dilutive impact is irrelevant even to an inquiry into retrogressive intent, a notion we reject. See *supra,* at 1501–1502.

. . . Because we are not satisfied that the District Court considered evidence of the dilutive impact of the Board's redistricting plan, we vacate this aspect of the District Court's opinion. The District Court will have the opportunity to apply the *Arlington Heights* test on remand as well as to address appellants' additional arguments that it erred in refusing to consider evidence that the Board was in violation of an ongoing injunction "to 'remedy any remaining vestiges of [a] dual [school] system,'" 907 F.Supp., at 449, n. 18.

. . . .

The judgment of the District Court is vacated, and the case is remanded for further proceedings consistent with this decision.

It is so ordered.

Notes

1. As originally enacted, § 5 provided:

> Whenever a State or political subdivision with respect to which the prohibitions set forth in section 4(a) are in effect shall enact or seek to administer any voting qualification or prerequisite to voting, or standard, practice, or procedure with respect to voting different from that in force or effect on November 1, 1964, such State or subdivision may institute an action in the United States District Court for the District of Columbia for a declaratory judgment that such qualification, prerequisite, standard, practice, or procedure does not have the purpose and will not have the effect of denying or abridging the right to vote on account of race or color, and unless and until the court enters such judgment no person shall be denied the right to vote for failure to comply with such qualification prerequisite, standard, practice, or procedure: *Provided,* That such qualification, prerequisite, standard, practice, or procedure may be enforced without such proceeding if the qualification, prerequisite, standard, practice, or procedure has been submitted by the chief legal officer or other appropriate official of such State or subdivision to the Attorney General and the Attorney General has not interposed an objection within sixty days after such submission, except that neither the Attorney General's failure to object nor a declaratory judgment entered under this section shall bar a subsequent action to enjoin enforcement of such qualification, prerequisite, standard, practice, or procedure. Any action under this section shall be heard and determined by a court of three judges in accordance with the provisions of section 2284 of title 28 of the United States Code [28 U.S.C. § 2284] and any appeal shall lie to the Supreme Court.

What threshold question must be examined on remand, according to the Court? Is it whether evidence of voter dilution amounts to evidence of intent to cause retrogression? Note the distinction between intent to dilute the vote and intent to cause retrogression. What must plaintiffs show to demonstrate intent to cause retrogression when working with data showing voter dilution?

Why was the following not enough to make a claim of Section 5 violation? "The parties stipulated that there had been a long history of discrimination against black voters in Bossier Parish; that voting in Bossier Parish was racially polarized; and that it was possible to draw two majority black districts without violating traditional districting principles".

2. Section 4 of the Act sets forth the formula for identifying the jurisdictions in which such discrimination had occurred. *See South Carolina v. Katzenbach,* 383 U.S., at 317–318.

3. Title 28 CFR § 51.55 (1996) provides:

Consistency with constitutional and statutory requirements.

(a) *Consideration in general.* In making a determination the Attorney General will consider whether the change is free of discriminatory purpose and retrogressive effect in light of, and with particular attention being given to, the requirements of the 14th, 15th, and 24th amendments to the Constitution, 42 U.S.C. 1971(a) and (b), sections 2, 4(a), 4(f)(2), 4(f)(4), 201, 203(c), and 208 of the Act, and other constitutional and statutory provisions designed to safeguard the right to vote from denial or abridgment on account of race, color, or membership in a language minority group.

(b) *Section 2.*

(1) Preclearance under section 5 of a voting change will not preclude any legal action under section 2 by the Attorney General if implementation of the change subsequently demonstrates that such action is appropriate.

(2) In those instances in which the Attorney General concludes that, as proposed, the submitted change is free of discriminatory purpose and retrogressive effect, but also concludes that a bar to implementation of the change is necessary to prevent a clear violation of amended section 2, the Attorney General shall withhold section 5 preclearance.

When do proposed plans for designing districts violate standards of traditional districting plans? Below, we consider the specific standards promulgated by the Court for equitable and constititutional designs of districts. The operative question in *Shaw v. Reno* hones in on how to make a successful claim that a redistricting plan's proposed designs for specific districts are unconstitutional. At what point could a non-traditional design, gerrymandering, trigger a claim of equal protection violation? Note the Court's promulgation that "redistricting legislation that is so bizarre on its face that it is 'unexplainable on grounds other than race' ... demands the same close scrutiny that we give other state laws that classify citizens by race." Think of reapportionment plans in your own districts. How many might qualify as "so bizarre" that they should trigger strict scrutiny? Are legislators of both parties shortchanging the electorate by squeezing them all into predictable districts?

Shaw v. Reno

509 U.S. 630 (1993)

JUSTICE O'CONNOR delivered the opinion of the Court.

This case involves two of the most complex and sensitive issues this Court has faced in recent years: the meaning of the constitutional "right" to vote, and the propriety of race-based state legislation designed to benefit members of historically disadvantaged racial minority groups. As a result of the 1990 census, North Carolina became entitled to a 12th seat in the United States House of Representatives. The General Assembly enacted a reapportionment plan that included one majority-black congressional district. After the Attorney General of the United States objected to the plan pursuant to § 5 of the Voting Rights Act of 1965, 79 Stat. 439, as amended, 42 U.S.C. § 1973c, the General Assembly passed new legislation creating a second majority-black district. Appellants allege that the revised plan, which contains district boundary lines of dramatically irregular shape, constitutes an unconstitutional racial gerrymander. The question before us is whether appellants have stated a cognizable claim.

I

The voting age population of North Carolina is approximately 78% white, 20% black, and 1% Native American; the remaining 1% is predominantly Asian. App. to Brief for Federal Appellees 16a. The black population is relatively dispersed; blacks constitute a majority of the general population in only 5 of the State's 100 counties. Brief for Appellants 57. Geographically, the State divides into three regions: the eastern Coastal Plain, the central Piedmont Plateau, and the western mountains. H. Lefler & A. Newsom, The History of a Southern State: North Carolina 18–22 (3d ed. 1973). The largest concentrations of black citizens live in the Coastal Plain, primarily in the northern part. O. Gade & H. Stillwell, North Carolina: People and Environments 65–68 (1986). The General Assembly's first redistricting plan contained one majority-black district centered in that area of the State.

Forty of North Carolina's one hundred counties are covered by § 5 of the Voting Rights Act of 1965, 42 U.S.C. § 1973c, which prohibits a jurisdiction subject to its provisions from implementing changes in a "standard, practice, or procedure with respect to voting" without federal authorization, *ibid*. The jurisdiction must obtain either a judgment from the United States District Court for the District of Columbia declaring that the proposed change "does not have the purpose and will not have the effect of denying or abridging the right to vote on account of race or color" or administrative preclearance from the Attorney General. *Ibid*. Because the General Assembly's reapportionment plan affected the covered counties, the parties agree that § 5 applied. Tr. of Oral Arg. 14, 27–29. The State chose to submit its plan to the Attorney General for preclearance.

The Attorney General, acting through the Assistant Attorney General for the Civil Rights Division, interposed a formal objection to the General Assembly's plan. The Attorney General specifically objected to the configuration of boundary lines drawn in the south-central to southeastern region of the State. In the Attorney General's view, the General Assembly could have created a second majority-minority district "to give effect to black and Native American voting strength in this area" by using boundary lines "no more irregular than [those] found elsewhere in the proposed plan," but failed to do so for "pretextual reasons." See App. to Brief for Federal Appellees 10a-11a.

Under §5, the State remained free to seek a declaratory judgment from the District Court for the District of Columbia notwithstanding the Attorney General's objection. It did not do so. Instead, the General Assembly enacted a revised redistricting plan, 1991 N.C. Extra Sess.Laws, ch. 7, that included a second majority-black district. The General Assembly located the second district not in the south-central to southeastern part of the State, but in the north-central region along Interstate 85. See Appendix, *infra*.

The first of the two majority-black districts contained in the revised plan, District 1, is somewhat hook shaped. Centered in the northeast portion of the State, it moves southward until it tapers to a narrow band; then, with finger-like extensions, it reaches far into the southern-most part of the State near the South Carolina border. District 1 has been compared to a "Rorschach ink-blot test," *Shaw v. Barr*, 808 F. Supp. 461, 476 (EDNC 1992) (Voorhees, C.J., concurring in part and dissenting in part), and a "bug splattered on a windshield," Wall Street Journal, Feb. 4, 1992, p. A14.

The second majority-black district, District 12, is even more unusually shaped. It is approximately 160 miles long and, for much of its length, no wider than the I-85 corridor. It winds in snakelike fashion through tobacco country, financial centers, and manufacturing areas "until it gobbles in enough enclaves of black neighborhoods." 808 F.Supp., at 476–477 (Voorhees, C.J., concurring in part and dissenting in part). Northbound and southbound drivers on I-85 sometimes find themselves in separate districts in one county, only to "trade" districts when they enter the next county. Of the 10 counties through which District 12 passes, 5 are cut into 3 different districts; even towns are divided. At one point the district remains contiguous only because it intersects at a single point with two other districts before crossing over them. See Brief for Republican National Committee as *Amicus Curiae* 14–15. One state legislator has remarked that "'[i]f you drove down the interstate with both car doors open, you'd kill most of the people in the district.'" Washington Post, Apr. 20, 1993, p. A4. The district even has inspired poetry: "Ask not for whom the line is drawn; it is drawn to avoid thee." Grofman, Would Vince Lombardi Have Been Right If He Had Said: "When It Comes to Redistricting, Race Isn't Everything, It's the *Only* Thing"?, 14 Cardozo L.Rev. 1237, 1261, n. 96 (1993) (internal quotation marks omitted).

The Attorney General did not object to the General Assembly's revised plan. But numerous North Carolinians did. The North Carolina Republican Party and individual voters brought suit in Federal District Court, alleging that the plan constituted an unconstitutional political gerrymander under *Davis v. Bandemer*, 478 U.S. 109, 106 S.Ct. 2797, 92 L.Ed.2d 85 (1986). That claim was dismissed, see *Pope v. Blue*, 809 F.Supp. 392 (WDNC), and this Court summarily affirmed, 506 U.S. 801, 113 S. Ct. 30, 121 L.Ed.2d 3 (1992).

. . . . We noted probable jurisdiction. 506 U.S. 1019, 113 S.Ct. 653, 121 L.Ed.2d 580 (1992).

II

A

"The right to vote freely for the candidate of one's choice is of the essence of a democratic society. . . ." *Reynolds v. Sims,* 377 U.S., at 555, 84 S.Ct., at 1378. For much of our Nation's history, that right sadly has been denied to many because of race. The Fifteenth Amendment, ratified in 1870 after a bloody Civil War, promised unequivocally that "[t]he right of citizens of the United States to vote" no longer would be "denied or abridged . . . by any State on account of race, color, or previous condition of servitude." U.S. Const., Amdt. 15, § 1.

But "[a] number of states . . . refused to take no for an answer and continued to circumvent the fifteenth amendment's prohibition through the use of both subtle and blunt instruments, perpetuating ugly patterns of pervasive racial discrimination." Blumstein, Defining and Proving Race Discrimination: Perspectives on the Purpose Vs. Results Approach from the Voting Rights Act, 69 Va.L.Rev. 633, 637 (1983). Ostensibly race-neutral devices such as literacy tests with "grandfather" clauses and "good character" provisos were devised to deprive black voters of the franchise. Another of the weapons in the States' arsenal was the racial gerrymander—"the deliberate and arbitrary distortion of district boundaries . . . for [racial] purposes." *Bandemer,* 478 U.S., at 164, 106 S.Ct., at 2826 (Powell, J., concurring in part and dissenting in part) (internal quotation marks omitted). In the 1870's, for example, opponents of Reconstruction in Mississippi "concentrated the bulk of the black population in a 'shoestring' Congressional district running the length of the Mississippi River, leaving five others with white majorities." E. Foner, Reconstruction: America's Unfinished Revolution, 1863–1877, p. 590 (1988). Some 90 years later, Alabama redefined the boundaries of the city of Tuskegee "from a square to an uncouth twenty-eight-sided figure" in a manner that was alleged to exclude black voters, and only black voters, from the city limits. *Gomillion v. Lightfoot,* 364 U.S. 339, 340, 81 S.Ct. 125, 127, 5 L.Ed.2d 110 (1960).

Alabama's exercise in geometry was but one example of the racial discrimination in voting that persisted in parts of this country nearly a century after ratification of the Fifteenth Amendment. See *South Carolina v. Katzenbach,* 383 U.S. 301, 309–313, 86 S.Ct. 803, 808–811, 15 L.Ed.2d 769 (1966). In some States, registration of eligible black voters ran 50% behind that of whites. *Id.,* at 313, 86 S.Ct., at 811. Congress enacted the Voting Rights Act of 1965 as a dramatic and severe response to the situation. The Act proved immediately successful in ensuring racial minorities access to the voting booth; by the early 1970's, the spread between black and white registration in several of the targeted Southern States had fallen to well below 10%. A. Thernstrom, Whose Votes Count? Affirmative Action and Minority Voting Rights 44 (1987).

But it soon became apparent that guaranteeing equal access to the polls would not suffice to root out other racially discriminatory voting practices. Drawing on the "one person, one vote" principle, this Court recognized that "[t]he right to vote can be affected by a *dilution* of voting power as well as by an absolute prohibition on casting a ballot." *Allen v. State Bd. of Elections*, 393 U.S. 544, 569, 89 S.Ct. 817, 833, 22 L. Ed.2d 1 (1969) (emphasis added). Where members of a racial minority group vote as a cohesive unit, practices such as multimember or at-large electoral systems can reduce or nullify minority voters' ability, as a group, "to elect the candidate of their choice." *Ibid.* Accordingly, the Court held that such schemes violate the Fourteenth Amendment when they are adopted with a discriminatory purpose and have the effect of diluting minority voting strength. See, *e.g.*, *Rogers v. Lodge*, 458 U.S. 613, 616–617, 102 S.Ct. 3272, 3274–3275, 73 L.Ed.2d 1012 (1982); *White v. Regester*, 412 U.S. 755, 765–766, 93 S.Ct. 2332, 2339–2340, 37 L.Ed.2d 314 (1973). Congress, too, responded to the problem of vote dilution. In 1982, it amended § 2 of the Voting Rights Act to prohibit legislation that *results* in the dilution of a minority group's voting strength, regardless of the legislature's intent. 42 U.S.C. § 1973; see *Thornburg v. Gingles*, 478 U.S. 30, 106 S.Ct. 2752, 92 L.Ed.2d 25 (1986) (applying amended § 2 to vote-dilution claim involving multimember districts); see also *Voinovich v. Quilter*, 507 U.S. 146, 155, 113 S.Ct. 1149, —, 122 L.Ed.2d 500 (1993) (single-member districts).

B

It is against this background that we confront the questions presented here. . . . Our focus is on appellants' claim that the State engaged in unconstitutional racial gerrymandering. That argument strikes a powerful historical chord: It is unsettling how closely the North Carolina plan resembles the most egregious racial gerrymanders of the past.

An understanding of the nature of appellants' claim is critical to our resolution of the case. In their complaint, appellants did not claim that the General Assembly's reapportionment plan unconstitutionally "diluted" white voting strength. They did not even claim to be white. Rather, appellants' complaint alleged that the deliberate segregation of voters into separate districts on the basis of race violated their constitutional right to participate in a "color-blind" electoral process. Complaint ¶ 29, App. to Juris. Statement 89a-90a; see also Brief for Appellants 31–32.

Despite their invocation of the ideal of a "color-blind" Constitution, see *Plessy v. Ferguson*, 163 U.S. 537, 559, 16 S.Ct. 1138, 1146, 41 L.Ed. 256 (1896) (Harlan, J., dissenting), appellants appear to concede that race-conscious redistricting is not always unconstitutional. See Tr. of Oral Arg. 16–19. That concession is wise: This Court never has held that race-conscious state decision-making is impermissible in *all* circumstances. What appellants object to is redistricting legislation that is so extremely irregular on its face that it rationally can be viewed only as an effort to segregate the races for purposes of voting, without regard for traditional districting principles and without sufficiently compelling justification. For the reasons that follow, we conclude that appellants have stated a claim upon which relief can be granted under the Equal Protection Clause. See Fed.Rule Civ.Proc. 12(b)(6).

III

A

The Equal Protection Clause provides that "[n]o State shall . . . deny to any person within its jurisdiction the equal protection of the laws." U.S. Const., Amdt. 14, § 1. Its central purpose is to prevent the States from purposefully discriminating between individuals on the basis of race. *Washington v. Davis,* 426 U.S. 229, 239, 96 S.Ct. 2040, 2047, 48 L.Ed.2d 597 (1976). Laws that explicitly distinguish between individuals on racial grounds fall within the core of that prohibition.

No inquiry into legislative purpose is necessary when the racial classification appears on the face of the statute. See *Personnel Administrator of Mass. v. Feeney,* 442 U.S. 256, 272, 99 S.Ct. 2282, 2293, 60 L.Ed.2d 870 (1979). Accord, *Washington v. Seattle School Dist. No. 1,* 458 U.S. 457, 485, 102 S.Ct. 3187, 3203, 73 L.Ed.2d 896 (1982). Express racial classifications are immediately suspect because, "[a]bsent searching judicial inquiry . . . , there is simply no way of determining what classifications are 'benign' or 'remedial' and what classifications are in fact motivated by illegitimate notions of racial inferiority or simple racial politics." *Richmond v. J.A. Croson Co.,* 488 U.S. 469, 493, 109 S.Ct. 706, 721, 102 L.Ed.2d 854 (1989) (plurality opinion); *id.,* at 520, 109 S.Ct., at 736 (SCALIA, J., concurring in judgment); see also *UJO,* 430 U.S., at 172, 97 S.Ct., at 1013 (Brennan, J., concurring in part) ("[A] purportedly preferential race assignment may in fact disguise a policy that perpetuates disadvantageous treatment of the plan's supposed beneficiaries").

Classifications of citizens solely on the basis of race "are by their very nature odious to a free people whose institutions are founded upon the doctrine of equality." *Hirabayashi v. United States,* 320 U.S. 81, 100, 63 S.Ct. 1375, 1385, 87 L.Ed. 1774 (1943). Accord, *Loving v. Virginia,* 388 U.S. 1, 11, 87 S.Ct. 1817, 1823, 18 L.Ed.2d 1010 (1967). They threaten to stigmatize individuals by reason of their membership in a racial group and to incite racial hostility. *Croson, supra,* 488 U.S., at 493, 109 S.Ct., at 721 (plurality opinion); *UJO, supra,* 430 U.S., at 173, 97 S.Ct., at 1014 (Brennan, J., concurring in part) ("[E]ven in the pursuit of remedial objectives, an explicit policy of assignment by race may serve to stimulate our society's latent race consciousness, suggesting the utility and propriety of basing decisions on a factor that ideally bears no relationship to an individual's worth or needs"). Accordingly, we have held that the Fourteenth Amendment requires state legislation that expressly distinguishes among citizens because of their race to be narrowly tailored to further a compelling governmental interest. See, *e.g., Wygant v. Jackson Bd. of Ed.,* 476 U.S. 267, 277–278, 106 S.Ct. 1842, 1848–1849, 90 L.Ed.2d 260 (1986) (plurality opinion); *id.,* at 285, 106 S.Ct., at 1853 (O'Connor, J., concurring in part and concurring in judgment).

These principles apply not only to legislation that contains explicit racial distinctions, but also to those "rare" statutes that, although race neutral, are, on their face, "unexplainable on grounds other than race." *Arlington Heights v. Metropolitan Housing Development Corp.,* 429 U.S. 252, 266, 97 S.Ct. 555, 564, 50 L.Ed.2d 450 (1977). . . .

B

Appellants contend that redistricting legislation that is so bizarre on its face that it is "unexplainable on grounds other than race," *Arlington Heights, supra,* 429 U.S., at 266, 97 S.Ct., at 564, demands the same close scrutiny that we give other state laws that classify citizens by race. Our voting rights precedents support that conclusion.

In *Guinn v. United States,* 238 U.S. 347, 35 S.Ct. 926, 59 L.Ed. 1340 (1915), the Court invalidated under the Fifteenth Amendment a statute that imposed a literacy requirement on voters but contained a "grandfather clause" applicable to individuals and their lineal descendants entitled to vote "on [or prior to] January 1, 1866." *Id.,* at 357, 35 S.Ct., at 928 (internal quotation marks omitted). The determinative consideration for the Court was that the law, though ostensibly race neutral, on its face "embod[ied] no exercise of judgment and rest[ed] upon no discernible reason" other than to circumvent the prohibitions of the Fifteenth Amendment. *Id.,* at 363, 35 S.Ct. at 931. In other words, the statute was invalid because, on its face, it could not be explained on grounds other than race.

The Court applied the same reasoning to the "uncouth twenty-eight-sided" municipal boundary line at issue in *Gomillion.* Although the statute that redrew the city limits of Tuskegee was race neutral on its face, plaintiffs alleged that its effect was impermissibly to remove from the city virtually all black voters and no white voters. The Court reasoned:

> "If these allegations upon a trial remained uncontradicted or unqualified, the conclusion would be irresistible, tantamount for all practical purposes to a mathematical demonstration, that the legislation is solely concerned with segregating white and colored voters by fencing Negro citizens out of town so as to deprive them of their pre-existing municipal vote." 364 U.S., at 341, 81 S.Ct., at 127.

. . . .

The Court extended the reasoning of *Gomillion* to congressional districting in *Wright v. Rockefeller,* 376 U.S. 52, 84 S.Ct. 603, 11 L.Ed.2d 512 (1964). At issue in *Wright* were four districts contained in a New York apportionment statute. The plaintiffs alleged that the statute excluded nonwhites from one district and concentrated them in the other three. *Id.,* at 53–54, 84 S.Ct., at 603–604. Every Member of the Court assumed that the plaintiffs' allegation that the statute "segregate[d] eligible voters by race and place of origin" stated a constitutional claim. *Id.,* at 56, 84 S.Ct., at 605 (internal quotation marks omitted); *id.,* at 58, 84 S.Ct., at 606 (Harlan, J., concurring); *id.,* at 59–62, 84 S.Ct., at 606–609 (Douglas, J., dissenting). The Justices disagreed only as to whether the plaintiffs had carried their burden of proof at trial. The dissenters thought the unusual shape of the district lines could "be explained only in racial terms." *Id.,* at 59, 84 S.Ct., at 607. The majority, however, accepted the District Court's finding that the plaintiffs had failed to establish that the districts were in fact drawn on racial lines. Although the boundary lines were somewhat irregular, the majority reasoned, they were not so bizarre as to permit of no other conclusion. Indeed, because most of the nonwhite voters lived together in one area, it would have been difficult to construct voting districts without concentrations of nonwhite voters. *Id.*, at 56–58, 84 S.Ct., at 605–606.

Wright illustrates the difficulty of determining from the face of a single-member districting plan that it purposefully distinguishes between voters on the basis of race. A reapportionment statute typically does not classify persons at all; it classifies tracts of land, or addresses. Moreover, redistricting differs from other kinds of state decision-making in that the legislature always is *aware* of race when it draws district lines, just as it is aware of age, economic status, religious and political persuasion, and a variety of other demographic factors. That sort of race consciousness does not lead inevitably to impermissible race discrimination. As *Wright* demonstrates, when members of a racial group live together in one community, a reapportionment plan that concentrates members of the group in one district and excludes them from others may reflect wholly legitimate purposes. The district lines may be drawn, for example, to provide for compact districts of contiguous territory, or to maintain the integrity of political subdivisions. See *Reynolds,* 377 U.S., at 578, 84 S.Ct., at 1390 (recognizing these as legitimate state interests).

The difficulty of proof, of course, does not mean that a racial gerrymander, once established, should receive less scrutiny under the Equal Protection Clause than other state legislation classifying citizens by race. Moreover, it seems clear to us that proof sometimes will not be difficult at all. In some exceptional cases, a reapportionment plan may be so highly irregular that, on its face, it rationally cannot be understood as anything other than an effort to "segregat[e] . . . voters" on the basis of race. *Gomillion, supra,* 364 U.S., at 341, 81 S.Ct., at 127. *Gomillion,* in which a tortured municipal boundary line was drawn to exclude black voters, was such a case. So, too, would be a case in which a State concentrated a dispersed minority population in a single district by disregarding traditional districting principles such as compactness, contiguity, and respect for political subdivisions. We emphasize that these criteria are important not because they are constitutionally required—they are not, cf. *Gaffney v. Cummings,* 412 U.S. 735, 752, n. 18, 93 S.Ct. 2321, 2331, n. 18, 37 L.Ed.2d 298 (1973)—but because they are objective factors that may serve to defeat a claim that a district has been gerrymandered on racial lines. Cf. *Karcher v. Daggett,* 462 U.S. 725, 755, 103 S.Ct. 2653, 2672, 77 L.Ed.2d 133 (1983) (STEVENS, J., concurring) ("One need not use Justice Stewart's classic definition of obscenity—'I know it when I see it'—as an ultimate standard for judging the constitutionality of a gerrymander to recognize that dramatically irregular shapes may have sufficient probative force to call for an explanation" (footnotes omitted)).

Put differently, we believe that reapportionment is one area in which appearances do matter. A reapportionment plan that includes in one district individuals who belong to the same race, but who are otherwise widely separated by geographical and political boundaries, and who may have little in common with one another but the color of their skin, bears an uncomfortable resemblance to political apartheid.

It reinforces the perception that members of the same racial group—regardless of their age, education, economic status, or the community in which they live—think alike, share the same political interests, and will prefer the same candidates at the polls. We have rejected such perceptions elsewhere as impermissible racial stereotypes. See, *e.g., Holland v. Illinois*, 493 U.S. 474, 484, n. 2, 110 S.Ct. 803, 809, n. 2, 107 L.Ed.2d 905 (1990) ("[A] prosecutor's assumption that a black juror may be presumed to be partial simply because he is black . . . violates the Equal Protection Clause" (internal quotation marks omitted)); see also *Edmonson v. Leesville Concrete Co.*, 500 U.S. 614, 630–631, 111 S.Ct. 2077, 2088, 114 L.Ed.2d 660 (1991) ("If our society is to continue to progress as a multiracial democracy, it must recognize that the automatic invocation of race stereotypes retards that progress and causes continued hurt and injury"). By perpetuating such notions, a racial gerrymander may exacerbate the very patterns of racial bloc voting that majority-minority districting is sometimes said to counteract.

The message that such districting sends to elected representatives is equally pernicious. When a district obviously is created solely to effectuate the perceived common interests of one racial group, elected officials are more likely to believe that their primary obligation is to represent only the members of that group, rather than their constituency as a whole. This is altogether antithetical to our system of representative democracy. As Justice Douglas explained in his dissent in *Wright v. Rockefeller* nearly 30 years ago:

> "Here the individual is important, not his race, his creed, or his color. The principle of equality is at war with the notion that District A must be represented by a Negro, as it is with the notion that District B must be represented by a Caucasian, District C by a Jew, District D by a Catholic, and so on. . . . That system, by whatever name it is called, is a divisive force in a community, emphasizing differences between candidates and voters that are irrelevant in the constitutional sense. . . .

> . . . .

> "When racial or religious lines are drawn by the State, the multiracial, multireligious communities that our Constitution seeks to weld together as one become separatist; antagonisms that relate to race or to religion rather than to political issues are generated; communities seek not the best representative but the best racial or religious partisan. Since that system is at war with the democratic ideal, it should find no footing here." 376 U.S., at 66–67, 84 S.Ct., at 611 (dissenting opinion).

For these reasons, we conclude that a plaintiff challenging a reapportionment statute under the Equal Protection Clause may state a claim by alleging that the legislation, though race-neutral on its face, rationally cannot be understood as anything other than an effort to separate voters into different districts on the basis of race, and that the separation lacks sufficient justification. It is unnecessary for us to decide whether or how a reapportionment plan that, on its face, can be explained in nonracial terms successfully could be challenged. Thus, we express no view as to whether "the intentional creation of majority-minority districts, without more," always gives rise to an equal protection claim. *Post,* at 2839 (White, J., dissenting). We hold only that, on the facts of this case, appellants have stated a claim sufficient to defeat the state appellees' motion to dismiss.

C

... Before us, the state appellees contend that the General Assembly's revised plan was necessary not to prevent retrogression, but to avoid dilution of black voting strength in violation of § 2, as construed in *Thornburg v. Gingles,* 478 U.S. 30, 106 S.Ct. 2752, 92 L.Ed.2d 25 (1986). In *Gingles* the Court considered a multimember redistricting plan for the North Carolina State Legislature. The Court held that members of a racial minority group claiming § 2 vote dilution through the use of multimember districts must prove three threshold conditions: that the minority group "is sufficiently large and geographically compact to constitute a majority in a single-member district," that the minority group is "politically cohesive," and that "the white majority votes sufficiently as a bloc to enable it . . . usually to defeat the minority's preferred candidate." *Id.,* at 50–51, 106 S.Ct., at 2766–2767. We have indicated that similar preconditions apply in § 2 challenges to single-member districts. See *Voinovich v. Quilter,* 507 U.S., at 157–158, 113 S.Ct., at 1084–1085; *Growe v. Emison,* 507 U.S., at 40, 113 S.Ct., at—.

Appellants maintain that the General Assembly's revised plan could not have been required by § 2. They contend that the State's black population is too dispersed to support two geographically compact majority-black districts, as the bizarre shape of District 12 demonstrates, and that there is no evidence of black political cohesion. They also contend that recent black electoral successes demonstrate the willingness of white voters in North Carolina to vote for black candidates. Appellants point out that blacks currently hold the positions of State Auditor, Speaker of the North Carolina House of Representatives, and chair of the North Carolina State Board of Elections. They also point out that in 1990 a black candidate defeated a white opponent in the Democratic Party runoff for a United States Senate seat before being defeated narrowly by the Republican incumbent in the general election. Appellants further argue that if § 2 did require adoption of North Carolina's revised plan, § 2 is to that extent unconstitutional. These arguments were not developed below, and the issues remain open for consideration on remand.

The state appellees alternatively argue that the General Assembly's plan advanced a compelling interest entirely distinct from the Voting Rights Act. We previously have recognized a significant state interest in eradicating the effects of past racial discrimination. See, *e.g., Croson,* 488 U.S., at 491–493, 109 S.Ct., at 720–722 (opinion of O'Connor, J., joined by Rehnquist, C.J., and White, J. . . .

The state appellees submit that two pieces of evidence gave the General Assembly a strong basis for believing that remedial action was warranted here: the Attorney

General's imposition of the §5 preclearance requirement on 40 North Carolina counties, and the *Gingles* District Court's findings of a long history of official racial discrimination in North Carolina's political system and of pervasive racial bloc voting. The state appellees assert that the deliberate creation of majority-minority districts is the most precise way—indeed the only effective way—to overcome the effects of racially polarized voting. This question also need not be decided at this stage of the litigation. We note, however, that only three Justices in *UJO* were prepared to say that States have a significant interest in minimizing the consequences of racial bloc voting apart from the requirements of the Voting Rights Act. And those three Justices specifically concluded that race-based districting, as a response to racially polarized voting, is constitutionally permissible only when the State "employ[s] sound districting principles," and only when the affected racial group's "residential patterns afford the opportunity of creating districts in which they will be in the majority." 430 U.S., at 167–168, 97 S.Ct., at 1011 (opinion of White, J., joined by Stevens and Rehnquist, JJ.).

V

Racial classifications of any sort pose the risk of lasting harm to our society. They reinforce the belief, held by too many for too much of our history, that individuals should be judged by the color of their skin. Racial classifications with respect to voting carry particular dangers. Racial gerrymandering, even for remedial purposes, may balkanize us into competing racial factions; it threatens to carry us further from the goal of a political system in which race no longer matters—a goal that the Fourteenth and Fifteenth Amendments embody, and to which the Nation continues to aspire. It is for these reasons that race-based districting by our state legislatures demands close judicial scrutiny.

In this case, the Attorney General suggested that North Carolina could have created a reasonably compact second majority-minority district in the south-central to southeastern part of the State. We express no view as to whether appellants successfully could have challenged such a district under the Fourteenth Amendment. We also do not decide whether appellants' complaint stated a claim under constitutional provisions other than the Fourteenth Amendment. Today we hold only that appellants have stated a claim under the Equal Protection Clause by alleging that the North Carolina General Assembly adopted a reapportionment scheme so irrational on its face that it can be understood only as an effort to segregate voters into separate voting districts because of their race, and that the separation lacks sufficient justification. If the allegation of racial gerrymandering remains uncontradicted, the District Court further must determine whether the North Carolina plan is narrowly tailored to further a compelling governmental interest. Accordingly, we reverse the judgment of the District Court and remand the case for further proceedings consistent with this opinion.

It is so ordered.

F. Racial Redistricting and Limitations

As seen below, the shape of a district is only one of the means of triggering strict scrutiny under the Equal Protection Clause. Beyond the look of a district, any allegation of race conscious decision making might be sufficient to make a claim under the Equal Protection Clause, as seen below, in *Miller v. Johnson*.

Miller v. Johnson

115 S. Ct. 2475 (1995)

JUSTICE KENNEDY delivered the opinion of the Court.

The constitutionality of Georgia's congressional redistricting plan is at issue here. In *Shaw v. Reno,* 509 U.S. 630, 113 S.Ct. 2816, 125 L.Ed.2d 511 (1993), we held that a plaintiff states a claim under the Equal Protection Clause by alleging that a state redistricting plan, on its face, has no rational explanation save as an effort to separate voters on the basis of race. The question we now decide is whether Georgia's new Eleventh District gives rise to a valid equal protection claim under the principles announced in *Shaw,* and, if so, whether it can be sustained nonetheless as narrowly tailored to serve a compelling governmental interest.

The Equal Protection Clause of the Fourteenth Amendment provides that no State shall "deny to any person within its jurisdiction the equal protection of the laws." U.S. Const., Amdt. 14, § 1. Its central mandate is racial neutrality in governmental decision-making. See, *e.g., Loving v. Virginia,* 388 U.S. 1, 11, 87 S.Ct. 1817, 1823, 18 L.Ed.2d 1010 (1967); *McLaughlin v. Florida,* 379 U.S. 184, 191–192, 85 S. Ct. 283, 287–288, 13 L.Ed.2d 222 (1964); see also *Brown v. Board of Education,* 347 U.S. 483, 74 S.Ct. 686, 98 L.Ed. 873 (1954). Though application of this imperative raises difficult questions, the basic principle is straightforward: "Racial and ethnic distinctions of any sort are inherently suspect and thus call for the most exacting judicial examination. . . . This perception of racial and ethnic distinctions is rooted in our Nation's constitutional and demographic history." *Regents of Univ. of Cal. v. Bakke,* 438 U.S. 265, 291, 98 S.Ct. 2733, 2748, 57 L.Ed.2d 750 (1978) (opinion of Powell, J.). This rule obtains with equal force regardless of "the race of those burdened or benefited by a particular classification." . . . In *Shaw v. Reno, supra,* we recognized that these equal protection principles govern a State's drawing of congressional districts, though, as our cautious approach there discloses, application of these principles to electoral districting is a most delicate task. Our analysis began from the premise that "[l]aws that explicitly distinguish between individuals on racial grounds fall within the core of [the Equal Protection Clause's] prohibition." *Id.,* at 642, 113 S.Ct., at 2824. This prohibition extends not just to explicit racial classifications, but also to laws neutral on their face but "'unexplainable on grounds other than race.'" *Id.,* at 644, 113 S.Ct., at 2825 (quoting *Arlington Heights v. Metropolitan Housing Development Corp.,* 429 U.S. 252, 266, 97 S.Ct. 555, 563, 50 L.Ed.2d 450 (1977)). Applying this basic equal protection analysis in the voting rights context, we held that "redistricting legislation that is so bizarre on its face that it is 'unexplainable on grounds other than race,' . . . demands the same close scrutiny that we give other state laws that classify citizens by race." 509 U.S., at 644, 113 S.Ct., at 2825 (quoting *Arlington Heights, supra,* at 266, 97 S.Ct., at 563).

This litigation requires us to apply the principles articulated in *Shaw* to the most recent congressional redistricting plan enacted by the State of Georgia.

B

In 1965, the Attorney General designated Georgia a covered jurisdiction under §4(b) of the Voting Rights Act (*Act*), 79 Stat. 438, as amended, 42 U.S.C. §1973b(b). 30 Fed.Reg. 9897 (1965); see 28 CFR pt. 51, App.; see also *City of Rome v. United States,* 446 U.S. 156, 161, 100 S.Ct. 1548, 1553, 64 L.Ed.2d 119 (1980). In consequence, §5 of the Act requires Georgia to obtain either administrative preclearance by the Attorney General or approval by the United States District Court for the District of Columbia of any change in a "standard, practice, or procedure with respect to voting" made after November 1, 1964. 42 U.S.C. §1973c. The preclearance mechanism applies to congressional redistricting plans, see, *e.g., Beer v. United States,* 425 U.S. 130, 133, 96 S.Ct. 1357, 1360, 47 L.Ed.2d 629 (1976), and requires that the proposed change "not have the purpose and will not have the effect of denying or abridging the right to vote on account of race or color." 42 U.S.C. §1973c. "[T]he purpose of §5 has always been to insure that no voting-procedure changes would be made that would lead to a retrogression in the position of racial minorities with respect to their effective exercise of the electoral franchise." *Beer, supra,* at 141, 96 S. Ct., at 1363.

Between 1980 and 1990, one of Georgia's 10 congressional districts was a majority-black district, that is, a majority of the district's voters were black. The 1990 Decennial Census indicated that Georgia's population of 6,478,216 persons, 27% of whom are black, entitled it to an additional eleventh congressional seat, App. 9, prompting Georgia's General Assembly to redraw the State's congressional districts. Both the House and the Senate adopted redistricting guidelines which, among other things, required single-member districts of equal population, contiguous geography, nondilution of minority voting strength, fidelity to precinct lines where possible, and compliance with §§2 and 5 of the Act, 42 U.S.C. §§1973, 1973c. See App. 11–12. Only after these requirements were met did the guidelines permit drafters to consider other ends, such as maintaining the integrity of political subdivisions, preserving the core of existing districts, and avoiding contests between incumbents. *Id.,* at 12.

A special session opened in August 1991, and the General Assembly submitted a congressional redistricting plan to the Attorney General for preclearance on October 1, 1991. The legislature's plan contained two majority-minority districts, the Fifth and Eleventh, and an additional district, the Second, in which blacks comprised just over 35% of the voting age population. Despite the plan's increase in the number of majority-black districts from one to two and the absence of any evidence of an intent to discriminate against minority voters, 864 F.Supp. 1354, 1363, and n. 7 (SD Ga.1994), the Department of Justice refused preclearance on January 21, 1992. App. 99-107. The Department's objection letter noted a concern that Georgia had created only two majority-minority districts, and that the proposed plan did not "recognize" certain minority populations by placing them in a majority-black district. *Id.*, at 105, 105–106.

The General Assembly returned to the drawing board. A new plan was enacted and submitted for preclearance. This second attempt assigned the black population in Central Georgia's Baldwin County to the Eleventh District and increased the black populations in the Eleventh, Fifth, and Second Districts. The Justice Department refused preclearance again, relying on alternative plans proposing three majority-minority districts. *Id.*, at 120–126. One of the alternative schemes relied on by the Department was the so-called "max-black" plan, 864 F.Supp., at 1360, 1362–1363, drafted by the American Civil Liberties Union (ACLU) for the General Assembly's black caucus. The key to the ACLU's plan was the "Macon/Savannah trade." The dense black population in the Macon region would be transferred from the Eleventh District to the Second, converting the Second into a majority-black district, and the Eleventh District's loss in black population would be offset by extending the Eleventh to include the black populations in Savannah. *Id.*, at 1365–1366. Pointing to the General Assembly's refusal to enact the Macon/Savannah swap into law, the Justice Department concluded that Georgia had "failed to explain adequately" its failure to create a third majority-minority district. App. 125. The State did not seek a declaratory judgment from the District Court for the District of Columbia. 864 F. Supp., at 1366, n. 11.

Twice spurned, the General Assembly set out to create three majority-minority districts to gain preclearance. *Id.*, at 1366. Using the ACLU's "max-black" plan as its benchmark, *id.*, at 1366–1367, the General Assembly enacted a plan that

> "bore all the signs of [the Justice Department's] involvement: The black population of Meriwether County was gouged out of the Third District and attached to the Second District by the narrowest of land bridges; Effingham and Chatham Counties were split to make way for the Savannah extension, which itself split the City of Savannah; and the plan as a whole split 26 counties, 23 more than the existing congressional districts." *Id.*, at 1367. See Appendix A, *infra*, following p. 2494.

The new plan also enacted the Macon/Savannah swap necessary to create a third majority-black district. The Eleventh District lost the black population of Macon, but picked up Savannah, thereby connecting the black neighborhoods of metropolitan Atlanta and the poor black populace of coastal Chatham County, though 260 miles apart in distance and worlds apart in culture. In short, the social, political, and economic makeup of the Eleventh District tells a tale of disparity, not community. See 864 F.Supp. at 1376–1377, 1389–1390; Plaintiff's Exh. No. 85, pp. 10–27 (report of Timothy G. O'Rourke, Ph.D.). As the appendices to this opinion attest, "[t]he populations of the Eleventh are centered around four discrete, widely spaced urban centers that have absolutely nothing to do with each other, and stretch the district hundreds of miles across rural counties and narrow swamp corridors." 864 F.Supp., at 1389 (footnote omitted).

"The dense population centers of the approved Eleventh District were all majority-black, all at the periphery of the district, and in the case of Atlanta, Augusta and Savannah, all tied to a sparsely populated rural core by even less populated land bridges. Extending from Atlanta to the Atlantic, the Eleventh covered 6,784.2 square miles, splitting eight counties and five municipalities along the way." *Id.*, at 1367 (footnote omitted).

The Almanac of American Politics has this to say about the Eleventh District: "Geographically, it is a monstrosity, stretching from Atlanta to Savannah. Its core is the plantation country in the center of the state, lightly populated, but heavily black. It links by narrow corridors the black neighborhoods in Augusta, Savannah and southern DeKalb County." M. Barone & G. Ujifusa, Almanac of American Politics 356 (1994). Georgia's plan included three majority-black districts, though, and received Justice Department preclearance on April 2, 1992. Plaintiff's Exh. No. 6; see 864 F.Supp., at 1367.

Elections were held under the new congressional redistricting plan on November 4, 1992, and black candidates were elected to Congress from all three majority-black districts. *Id.*, at 1369. On January 13, 1994, appellees, five white voters from the Eleventh District, filed this action against various state officials (Miller Appellants) in the United States District Court for the Southern District of Georgia. *Id.*, at 1369, 1370. As residents of the challenged Eleventh District, all appellees had standing. See *United States v. Hays*, 515 U.S. 737, 744–745, 115 S.Ct. 2431, 2436, 132 L. Ed.2d 635 (1995). Their suit alleged that Georgia's Eleventh District was a racial gerrymander and so a violation of the Equal Protection Clause as interpreted in *Shaw v. Reno*. A three-judge court was convened pursuant to 28 U.S.C. § 2284, and the United States and a number of Georgia residents intervened in support of the defendant-state officials.

A majority of the District Court panel agreed that the Eleventh District was invalid under *Shaw*, with one judge dissenting. 864 F.Supp. 1354 (1994). . . .

Appellants filed notices of appeal and requested a stay of the District Court's judgment, which we granted pending the filing and disposition of the appeals in this litigation, *Miller v. Johnson*, 512 U.S. 1283, 115 S.Ct. 36, 129 L.Ed.2d 932 (1994). We later noted probable jurisdiction. 513 U.S. 1071, 115 S.Ct. 713, 130 L.Ed.2d 620 (1995); see 28 U.S.C. § 1253.

II

A

Finding that the "evidence of the General Assembly's intent to racially gerrymander the Eleventh District is overwhelming, and practically stipulated by the parties involved," the District Court held that race was the predominant, overriding factor in drawing the Eleventh District. 864 F.Supp., at 1374; see *id.,* at 1374–1378. Appellants do not take issue with the court's factual finding of this racial motivation. Rather, they contend that evidence of a legislature's deliberate classification of voters on the basis of race cannot alone suffice to state a claim under *Shaw.* They argue that, regardless of the legislature's purposes, a plaintiff must demonstrate that a district's shape is so bizarre that it is unexplainable other than on the basis of race, and that appellees failed to make that showing here. Appellants' conception of the constitutional violation misapprehends our holding in *Shaw* and the equal protection precedent upon which *Shaw* relied.

Shaw recognized a claim "analytically distinct" from a vote dilution claim. 509 U.S., at 652, 113S.Ct., at 2830; see *id.,* at 649–650, 113 S.Ct., at 2828. Whereas a vote dilution claim alleges that the State has enacted a particular voting scheme as a purposeful device "to minimize or cancel out the voting potential of racial or ethnic minorities," *Mobile v. Bolden,* 446 U.S. 55, 66, 100 S.Ct. 1490, 1499, 64 L.Ed.2d 47 (1980) (citing cases), an action disadvantaging voters of a particular race, the essence of the equal protection claim recognized in *Shaw* is that the State has used race as a basis for separating voters into districts. Just as the State may not, absent extraordinary justification, segregate citizens on the basis of race in its public parks, *New Orleans City Park Improvement Assn. v. Detiege,* 358 U.S. 54, 79 S.Ct. 99, 3 L. Ed.2d 46 (1958) *(per curiam),* buses, *Gayle v. Browder,* 352 U.S. 903, 77 S.Ct. 145, 1 L. Ed.2d 114 (1956) *(per curiam),* golf courses, *Holmes v. Atlanta,* 350 U.S. 879, 76 S.Ct. 141, 100 L.Ed. 776 (1955) *(per curiam),* beaches, *Mayor of Baltimore v. Dawson,* 350 U.S. 877, 76 S.Ct. 133, 100 L.Ed. 774 (1955) *(per curiam),* and schools, *Brown v. Board of Education,* 347 U.S. 483, 74 S.Ct. 686, 98 L.Ed. 873 (1954), so did we recognize in *Shaw* that it may not separate its citizens into different voting districts on the basis of race. The idea is a simple one: "At the heart of the Constitution's guarantee of equal protection lies the simple command that the Government must treat citizens 'as individuals, not "as simply components of a racial, religious, sexual or national class."'" *Metro Broadcasting, Inc. v. FCC,* 497 U.S. 547, 602, 110 S.Ct. 2997, 3028, 111 L.Ed.2d 445 (1990) (O'Connor, J., dissenting). . . .

Our observation in *Shaw*of the consequences of racial stereotyping was not meant to suggest that a district must be bizarre on its face before there is a constitutional violation. Nor was our conclusion in *Shaw* that in certain instances a district's appearance (or, to be more precise, its appearance in combination with certain demographic evidence) can give rise to an equal protection claim, 509 U.S., at 649, 113 S.Ct., at 2828, a holding that bizarreness was a threshold showing, as appellants believe it to be. Our circumspect approach and narrow holding in *Shaw* did not erect an artificial rule barring accepted equal protection analysis in other redistricting cases. Shape is relevant not because bizarreness is a necessary element of the constitutional wrong or a threshold requirement of proof, but because it may be persuasive circumstantial evidence that race for its own sake, and not other districting principles, was the legislature's dominant and controlling rationale in drawing its district lines. The logical implication, as courts applying *Shaw* have recognized, is that parties may rely on evidence other than bizarreness to establish race-based districting. See *Shaw v. Hunt*, 861 F.Supp. 408, 431 (EDNC 1994); *Hays v. Louisiana*, 839 F.Supp. 1188, 1195 (WD La.1993), vacated, 512 U.S. 1230, 114 S.Ct. 2731, 129 L.Ed.2d 853 (1994); but see *DeWitt v. Wilson*, 856 F.Supp. 1409, 1413 (ED Cal.1994).

Our reasoning in *Shaw* compels this conclusion. We recognized in *Shaw* that, outside the districting context, statutes are subject to strict scrutiny under the Equal Protection Clause not just when they contain express racial classifications, but also when, though race neutral on their face, they are motivated by a racial purpose or object. 509 U.S., at 644, 113 S.Ct., at 2825. In the rare case, where the effect of government action is a pattern "'unexplainable on grounds other than race,'" *ibid.* (quoting *Arlington Heights*, 429 U.S., at 266, 97 S.Ct., at 563), "[t]he evidentiary inquiry is . . . relatively easy," *Arlington Heights, supra,* at 266, 97 S.Ct., at 563 (footnote omitted). As early as *Yick Wo v. Hopkins*, 118 U.S. 356, 6 S.Ct. 1064, 30 L.Ed. 220 (1886), the Court recognized that a laundry permit ordinance was administered in a deliberate way to exclude all Chinese from the laundry business; and in *Gomillion v. Lightfoot*, 364 U.S. 339, 81 S.Ct. 125, 5 L.Ed.2d 110 (1960), the Court concluded that the redrawing of Tuskegee, Alabama's municipal boundaries left no doubt that the plan was designed to exclude blacks. Even in those cases, however, it was the presumed racial purpose of state action, not its stark manifestation, that was the constitutional violation. Patterns of discrimination as conspicuous as these are rare, and are not a necessary predicate to a violation of the Equal Protection Clause. Cf. *Arlington Heights, supra,* at 266, n. 14, 97 S.Ct., at 563, n. 14. In the absence of a pattern as stark as those in *Yick Wo* or *Gomillion*, "impact alone is not determinative, and the Court must look to other evidence" of race-based decision-making. *Arlington Heights, supra,* at 266, 97 S.Ct., at 563 (footnotes omitted).

Shaw applied these same principles to redistricting. "In some exceptional cases, a reapportionment plan may be so highly irregular that, on its face, it rationally cannot be understood as anything other than an effort to 'segregat[e] . . . voters' on the basis of race." *Shaw, supra,* at 646–647, 113 S.Ct., at 2826 (quoting *Gomillion, supra,* at 341, 81 S.Ct., at 127). In other cases, where the district is not so bizarre on its face that it discloses a racial design, the proof will be more "difficul[t]." 509 U.S., at 646, 113 S.Ct., at 2826. Although it was not necessary in *Shaw* to consider further the proof required in these more difficult cases, the logical import of our reasoning is that evidence other than a district's bizarre shape can be used to support the claim.

. . . In sum, we make clear that parties alleging that a State has assigned voters on the basis of race are neither confined in their proof to evidence regarding the district's geometry and makeup nor required to make a threshold showing of bizarreness. Today's litigation requires us further to consider the requirements of the proof necessary to sustain this equal protection challenge.

B

Federal-court review of districting legislation represents a serious intrusion on the most vital of local functions. It is well settled that "reapportionment is primarily the duty and responsibility of the State." *Chapman v. Meier,* 420 U.S. 1, 27, 95 S.Ct. 751, 766, 42 L.Ed.2d 766 (1975); see, *e.g., Voinovich v. Quilter,* 507 U.S. 146, 156–157, 113 S.Ct. 1149, 1156–1157, 122 L.Ed.2d 500 (1993); *Growe v. Emison,* 507 U.S. 25, 34, 113 S.Ct. 1075, 1081, 122 L.Ed.2d 388 (1993). Electoral districting is a most difficult subject for legislatures, and so the States must have discretion to exercise the political judgment necessary to balance competing interests. Although race-based decision-making is inherently suspect, *e.g., Adarand,* 515 U.S., at 218, 115 S.Ct., at 2108 (citing *Bakke,* 438 U.S., at 291, 98 S.Ct., at 2748 (opinion of Powell, J.)), until a claimant makes a showing sufficient to support that allegation the good faith of a state legislature must be presumed, see *id.* at 318–319, 98 S.Ct., at 2762–2763 (opinion of Powell, J.). The courts, in assessing the sufficiency of a challenge to a districting plan, must be sensitive to the complex interplay of forces that enter a legislature's redistricting calculus. Redistricting legislatures will, for example, almost always be aware of racial demographics; but it does not follow that race predominates in the redistricting process. *Shaw, supra,* at 646, 113 S.Ct., at 2826 . . . . The distinction between being aware of racial considerations and being motivated by them may be difficult to make. This evidentiary difficulty, together with the sensitive nature of redistricting and the presumption of good faith that must be accorded legislative enactments, requires courts to exercise extraordinary caution in adjudicating claims that a State has drawn district lines on the basis of race.

[T]he plaintiff's burden is to show, either through circumstantial evidence of a district's shape and demographics or more direct evidence going to legislative purpose, that race was the predominant factor motivating the legislature's decision to place a significant number of voters within or without a particular district. To make this showing, a plaintiff must prove that the legislature subordinated traditional race-neutral districting principles, including but not limited to compactness, contiguity, and respect for political subdivisions or communities defined by actual shared interests, to racial considerations. Where these or other race-neutral considerations are the basis for redistricting legislation, and are not subordinated to race, a State can "defeat a claim that a district has been gerrymandered on racial lines." *Shaw, supra,* 515 U.S., at 647, 113 S.Ct., at 2827. These principles inform the plaintiff's burden of proof at trial. Of course, courts must also recognize these principles, and the intrusive potential of judicial intervention into the legislative realm, when assessing under the Federal Rules of Civil Procedure the adequacy of a plaintiff's showing at the various stages of litigation and determining whether to permit discovery or trial to proceed. See, *e.g.,* Fed.Rules Civ.Proc. 12(b) and (e), 26(b)(2), 56; see also *Celotex Corp. v. Catrett,* 477 U.S. 317, 327, 106 S.Ct. 2548, 2554, 91 L.Ed.2d 265 (1986).

In our view, the District Court applied the correct analysis, and its finding that race was the predominant factor motivating the drawing of the Eleventh District was not clearly erroneous. The court found it was "exceedingly obvious" from the shape of the Eleventh District, together with the relevant racial demographics, that the drawing of narrow land bridges to incorporate within the district outlying append-ages containing nearly 80% of the district's total black population was a deliberate attempt to bring black populations into the district. 864 F.Supp., at 1375; see *id.*, at 1374–1376. Although by comparison with other districts the geometric shape of the Eleventh District may not seem bizarre on its face, when its shape is considered in conjunction with its racial and population densities, the story of racial gerryman-dering seen by the District Court becomes much clearer. See Appendix B, *infra*, at 2496; see also App. 133. Although this evidence is quite compelling, we need not determine whether it was, standing alone, sufficient to establish a *Shaw* claim that the Eleventh District is unexplainable other than by race. The District Court had before it considerable additional evidence showing that the General Assembly was motivated by a predominant, overriding desire to assign black populations to the Eleventh District and thereby permit the creation of a third majority-black district in the Second. 864 F.Supp., at 1372, 1378.

The court found that "it became obvious," both from the Justice Department's objection letters and the three preclearance rounds in general, "that [the Justice Department] would accept nothing less than abject surrender to its maximization agenda." *Id.*, at 1366, n. 11; see *id.*, at 1360–1367; see also *Arlington Heights,* 429 U.S., at 267, 97 S.Ct., at 564 ("historical background of the decision is one evidentiary source"). It further found that the General Assembly acquiesced and as a conse-quence was driven by its overriding desire to comply with the Department's maxi-mization demands. The court supported its conclusion not just with the testimony of Linda Meggers, the operator of "Herschel," Georgia's reapportionment computer, and "probably the most knowledgeable person available on the subject of Georgian redistricting," 864 F.Supp., at 1361, 1363, n. 6, 1366, but also with the State's own con-cessions. The State admitted that it "'would not have added those portions of Eff-ingham and Chatham Counties that are now in the [far southeastern extension of the] present Eleventh Congressional District but for the need to include additional black population in that district to offset the loss of black population caused by the shift of predominantly black portions of Bibb County in the Second Congressional District which occurred in response to the Department of Justice's March 20th, 1992, objection letter.'" *Id.*, at 1377. It conceded further that "[t]o the extent that precincts in the Eleventh Congressional District are split, a substantial reason for their being split was the objective of increasing the black population of that district." *Ibid.* And in its brief to this Court, the State concedes that "[i]t is undisputed that Georgia's eleventh is the product of a desire by the General Assembly to create a majority black district." Brief for Miller Appellants 30. Hence the trial court had little difficulty con-cluding that the Justice Department "spent months demanding purely race-based revisions to Georgia's redistricting plans, and that Georgia spent months attempt-ing to comply." 864 F.Supp., at 1377. On this record, we fail to see how the District Court could have reached any conclusion other than that race was the predominant factor in drawing Georgia's Eleventh District; and in any event, we conclude the court's finding is not clearly erroneous. Cf. *Wright v. Rockefeller,* 376 U.S. 52, 56–57, 84 S.Ct. 603, 605, 11 L.Ed.2d 512 (1964) (evidence presented "conflicting inferences" and therefore "failed to prove that the New York Legislature was either motivated by racial considerations or in fact drew the districts on racial lines").

In light of its well-supported finding, the District Court was justified in rejecting the various alternative explanations offered for the district. Although a legislature's compliance with "traditional districting principles such as compactness, contiguity, and respect for political subdivisions" may well suffice to refute a claim of racial gerrymandering, *Shaw,* 509 U.S., at 647, 113 S.Ct., at 2827, appellants cannot make such a refutation where, as here, those factors were subordinated to racial objectives. Georgia's Attorney General objected to the Justice Department's demand for three majority-black districts on the ground that to do so the State would have to "violate all reasonable standards of compactness and contiguity." App. 118. This statement from a state official is powerful evidence that the legislature subordinated traditional districting principles to race when it ultimately enacted a plan creating three majority-black districts, and justified the District Court's finding that "every [objective districting] factor that could realistically be subordinated to racial tinkering in fact suffered that fate." 864 F.Supp., at 1384; see *id.,* at 1364, n. 8; *id.,* at 1375 ("While the boundaries of the Eleventh do indeed follow many precinct lines, this is because Ms. Meggers designed the Eleventh District along racial lines, and race data was most accessible to her at the precinct level").

Nor can the State's districting legislation be rescued by mere recitation of purported communities of interest. The evidence was compelling "that there are no tangible 'communities of interest' spanning the hundreds of miles of the Eleventh District." *Id.,* at 1389–1390. A comprehensive report demonstrated the fractured political, social, and economic interests within the Eleventh District's black population. See Plaintiff's Exh. No. 85, pp. 10–27 (report of Timothy G. O'Rourke, Ph.D.). It is apparent that it was not alleged shared interests but rather the object of maximizing the district's black population and obtaining Justice Department approval that in fact explained the General Assembly's actions. 864 F.Supp., at 1366, 1378, 1380. A State is free to recognize communities that have a particular racial makeup, provided its action is directed toward some common thread of relevant interests. "[W]hen members of a racial group live together in one community, a reapportionment plan that concentrates members of the group in one district and excludes them from others may reflect wholly legitimate purposes." *Shaw,* 509 U.S., at 646, 113 S.Ct., at 2826. But where the State assumes from a group of voters' race that they "think alike, share the same political interests, and will prefer the same candidates at the polls," it engages in racial stereotyping at odds with equal protection mandates. *Id.,* at 647, 113 S.Ct., at 2827; cf. *Powers v. Ohio,* 499 U.S. 400, 410, 111 S. Ct. 1364, 1370, 113 L.Ed.2d 411 (1991) ("We may not accept as a defense to racial discrimination the very stereotype the law condemns").

Race was, as the District Court found, the predominant, overriding factor explaining the General Assembly's decision to attach to the Eleventh District various appendages containing dense majority-black populations. 864 F.Supp., at 1372, 1378. As a result, Georgia's congressional redistricting plan cannot be upheld unless it satisfies strict scrutiny, our most rigorous and exacting standard of constitutional review.

III

To satisfy strict scrutiny, the State must demonstrate that its districting legislation is narrowly tailored to achieve a compelling interest. *Shaw, supra,* at 653–657, 113 S.Ct., at 2830–2832; see also *Croson,* 488 U.S., at 494, 109 S.Ct., at 722 (plurality opinion); *Wygant,* 476 U.S., at 274, 280, and n. 6, 106 S.Ct., at 1847, 1850, and n. 6 (plurality opinion); cf. *Adarand,* 515 U.S., at 227, 115 S.Ct., at 2114. There is a "significant state interest in eradicating the effects of past racial discrimination." *Shaw, supra,* at 656, 113 S.Ct., at 2831. The State does not argue, however, that it created the Eleventh District to remedy past discrimination, and with good reason: There is little doubt that the State's true interest in designing the Eleventh District was creating a third majority-black district to satisfy the Justice Department's preclearance demands. 864 F.Supp., at 1378 ("[T]he only interest the General Assembly had in mind when drafting the current congressional plan was satisfying [the Justice Department's] preclearance requirements"); *id.,* at 1366; compare *Wygant, supra,* at 277, 106 S.Ct., at 1848 (plurality opinion) (under strict scrutiny, State must have convincing evidence that remedial action is necessary before implementing affirmative action), with *Heller v. Doe,* 509 U.S. 312, 320, 113 S.Ct. 2637, 2642, 125 L.Ed.2d 257 (1993) (under rational-basis review, legislature need not "'actually articulate at any time the purpose or rationale supporting its classification'") (quoting *Nordlinger v. Hahn,* 505 U.S. 1, 15, 112 S.Ct. 2326, 2334, 120 L.Ed.2d 1 (1992)). Whether or not in some cases compliance with the Act, standing alone, can provide a compelling interest independent of any interest in remedying past discrimination, it cannot do so here. As we suggested in *Shaw,* compliance with federal antidiscrimination laws cannot justify race-based districting where the challenged district was not reasonably necessary under a constitutional reading and application of those laws. See 509 U.S., at 653–655, 113 S.Ct., at 2830–2831. The congressional plan challenged here was not required by the Act under a correct reading of the statute.

The Justice Department refused to preclear both of Georgia's first two submitted redistricting plans. The District Court found that the Justice Department had adopted a "black-maximization" policy under § 5, and that it was clear from its objection letters that the Department would not grant preclearance until the State made the "Macon/Savannah trade" and created a third majority-black district. 864 F.Supp., at 1366, 1380. It is, therefore, safe to say that the congressional plan enacted in the end was required in order to obtain preclearance. It does not follow, however, that the plan was required by the substantive provisions of the Act.

We do not accept the contention that the State has a compelling interest in complying with whatever preclearance mandates the Justice Department issues. When a state governmental entity seeks to justify race-based remedies to cure the effects of past discrimination, we do not accept the government's mere assertion that the remedial action is required. Rather, we insist on a strong basis in evidence of the harm being remedied. See, *e.g., Shaw, supra,* at 656, 113 S.Ct., at 2831–2832; *Croson, supra,* at 500–501, 109 S.Ct., at 725; *Wygant, supra,* at 276–277, 106 S.Ct. at 1848 (plurality opinion). "The history of racial classifications in this country suggests that blind judicial deference to legislative or executive pronouncements of necessity has no place in equal protection analysis." *Croson, supra,* at 501, 109 S.Ct., at 725. Our presumptive skepticism of all racial classifications, see *Adarand, supra,* at 223–224, 115 S.Ct., at 2110–2111, prohibits us as well from accepting on its face the Justice Department's conclusion that racial districting is necessary under the Act. Where a State relies on the Department's determination that race-based districting is necessary to comply with the Act, the judiciary retains an independent obligation in adjudicating consequent equal protection challenges to ensure that the State's actions are narrowly tailored to achieve a compelling interest. See *Shaw, supra,* at 654, 113 S.Ct., at 2830–2831. . . .

For the same reasons, we think it inappropriate for a court engaged in constitutional scrutiny to accord deference to the Justice Department's interpretation of the Act. Although we have deferred to the Department's interpretation in certain statutory cases, see, *e.g., Presley v. Etowah County Comm'n,* 502 U.S. 491, 508–509, 112 S.Ct. 820, 831, 117 L.Ed.2d 51 (1992), and cases cited therein, we have rejected agency interpretations to which we would otherwise defer where they raise serious constitutional questions. *Edward J. DeBartolo Corp. v. Florida Gulf Coast Building & Constr. Trades Council,* 485 U.S. 568, 574–575, 108 S.Ct. 1392, 1396–1397, 99 L.Ed.2d 645 (1988). When the Justice Department's interpretation of the Act compels race-based districting, it by definition raises a serious constitutional question, see, *e.g., Bakke,* 438 U.S., at 291, 98 S.Ct., at 2748 (opinion of Powell, J.) ("Racial and ethnic distinctions of any sort are inherently suspect" under the Equal Protection Clause), and should not receive deference.

Georgia's drawing of the Eleventh District was not required under the Act because there was no reasonable basis to believe that Georgia's earlier enacted plans violated § 5. Wherever a plan is "ameliorative," a term we have used to describe plans increasing the number of majority-minority districts, it "cannot violate § 5 unless the new apportionment itself so discriminates on the basis of race or color as to violate the Constitution." *Beer,* 425 U.S., at 141, 96 S.Ct., at 1363. Georgia's first and second proposed plans increased the number of majority-black districts from 1 out of 10 (10%) to 2 out of 11 (18.18%). These plans were "ameliorative" and could not have violated § 5's nonretrogression principle. *Ibid.* Acknowledging as much, see Brief for United States 29; 864 F.Supp., at 1384–1385, the United States now relies on the fact that the Justice Department may object to a state proposal either on the ground that it has a prohibited purpose or a prohibited effect, see, *e.g., Pleasant Grove v. United States,* 479 U.S. 462, 469, 107 S.Ct. 794, 798, 93 L.Ed.2d 866 (1987). The Government justifies its preclearance objections on the ground that the submitted plans violated

§ 5's purpose element. The key to the Government's position, which is plain from its objection letters if not from its briefs to this Court, compare App. 105–106, 124–125 with Brief for United States 31–33, is and always has been that Georgia failed to proffer a nondiscriminatory purpose for its refusal in the first two submissions to take the steps necessary to create a third majority-minority district.

The Government's position is insupportable. "[A]meliorative changes, even if they fall short of what might be accomplished in terms of increasing minority representation, cannot be found to violate section 5 unless they so discriminate on the basis of race or color as to violate the Constitution." Days, Section 5 and the Role of the Justice Department, in B. Grofman & C. Davidson, Controversies in Minority Voting 56 (1992). Although it is true we have held that the State has the burden to prove a nondiscriminatory purpose under § 5, *e.g., Pleasant Grove, supra,* at 469, 107 S.Ct., at 798, Georgia's Attorney General provided a detailed explanation for the State's initial decision not to enact the max-black plan, see App. 117–119. The District Court accepted this explanation, 864 F.Supp., at 1365, and found an absence of any discriminatory intent, *id.,* at 1363, and n. 7. The State's policy of adhering to other districting principles instead of creating as many majority-minority districts as possible does not support an inference that the plan "so discriminates on the basis of race or color as to violate the Constitution," *Beer, supra,* at 141, 96 S.Ct., at 1363; see *Mobile v. Bolden,* 446 U.S. 55, 100 S.Ct. 1490, 64 L.Ed.2d 47 (1980) (plurality opinion), and thus cannot provide any basis under § 5 for the Justice Department's objection.

Instead of grounding its objections on evidence of a discriminatory purpose, it would appear the Government was driven by its policy of maximizing majority-black districts. Although the Government now disavows having had that policy, see Brief for United States 35, and seems to concede its impropriety, see Tr. of Oral Arg. 32–33, the District Court's well-documented factual finding was that the Department did adopt a maximization policy and followed it in objecting to Georgia's first two plans. One of the two Department of Justice line attorneys overseeing the Georgia preclearance process himself disclosed that "'what we did and what I did specifically was to take a . . . map of the State of Georgia shaded for race, shaded by minority concentration, and overlay the districts that were drawn by the State of Georgia and see how well those lines adequately reflected black voting strength.'" 864 F.Supp., at 1362, n. 4. In utilizing § 5 to require States to create majority-minority districts wherever possible, the Department of Justice expanded its authority under the statute beyond what Congress intended and we have upheld.

. . . [T]he purpose of § 5 has always been to insure that no voting-procedure changes would be made that would lead to a retrogression in the position of racial minorities with respect to their effective exercise of the electoral franchise." 425 U.S., at 141, 96 S.Ct., at 1363. The Justice Department's maximization policy seems quite far removed from this purpose. We are especially reluctant to conclude that § 5 justifies that policy given the serious constitutional concerns it raises. In *South Carolina v. Katzenbach,* 383 U.S. 301, 86 S.Ct. 803, 15 L.Ed.2d 769 (1966), we upheld § 5 as a necessary and constitutional response to some States' "extraordinary stratagem[s] of contriving new rules of various kinds for the sole purpose of perpetuating voting discrimination in the face of adverse federal court decrees." *Id.,* at 335, 86 S.Ct., at 822 (footnote omitted); see also *City of Rome v. United States,* 446 U.S., at 173–183, 100 S.Ct., at 1559–1564. But our belief in *Katzenbach* that the federalism costs exacted by § 5 preclearance could be justified by those extraordinary circumstances does not mean they can be justified in the circumstances of this litigation. And the Justice Department's implicit command that States engage in presumptively unconstitutional race-based districting brings the Act, once upheld as a proper exercise of Congress' authority under § 2 of the Fifteenth Amendment, *Katzenbach, supra,* at 327, 337, 86 S.Ct., at 818, 823, into tension with the Fourteenth Amendment. As we recalled in *Katzenbach* itself, Congress' exercise of its Fifteenth Amendment authority even when otherwise proper still must "'consist with the letter and spirit of the constitution.'" 383 U.S., at 326, 86 S.Ct., at 817 (quoting *McCulloch v. Maryland,* 4 Wheat. 316, 421, 4 L.Ed. 579 (1819)). We need not, however, resolve these troubling and difficult constitutional questions today. There is no indication Congress intended such a far-reaching application of § 5, so we reject the Justice Department's interpretation of the statute and avoid the constitutional problems that interpretation raises. See, *e.g., DeBartolo Corp. v. Florida Gulf Coast Trades Council,* 485 U.S., at 575, 108 S.Ct., at 1397.

IV

The Act, and its grant of authority to the federal courts to uncover official efforts to abridge minorities' right to vote, has been of vital importance in eradicating invidious discrimination from the electoral process and enhancing the legitimacy of our political institutions. Only if our political system and our society cleanse themselves of that discrimination will all members of the polity share an equal opportunity to gain public office regardless of race. As a Nation we share both the obligation and the aspiration of working toward this end. The end is neither assured nor well served, however, by carving electorates into racial blocs. "If our society is to continue to progress as a multi-racial democracy, it must recognize that the automatic invocation of race stereotypes retards that progress and causes continued hurt and injury." *Edmonson v. Leesville Concrete Co.,* 500 U.S. 614, 630–631, 111 S.Ct. 2077, 2088, 114 L.Ed.2d 660 (1991). It takes a shortsighted and unauthorized view of the Voting Rights Act to invoke that statute, which has played a decisive role in redressing some of our worst forms of discrimination, to demand the very racial stereotyping the Fourteenth Amendment forbids.

. . . .

The judgment of the District Court is affirmed, and the cases are remanded for further proceedings consistent with this decision.

It is so ordered.

JUSTICE O'CONNOR, concurring [omitted].

JUSTICE STEVENS, dissenting.

Justice Ginsburg has explained why the District Court's opinion on the merits was erroneous and why this Court's law-changing decision will breed unproductive litigation. I join her excellent opinion without reservation. I add these comments because I believe the appellees in these cases, like the appellees in *United States v. Hays,* 515 U.S. 737, 115 Ct. 2431, 132 L.Ed.2d 635, have not suffered any legally cognizable injury.

In *Shaw v. Reno,* 509 U.S. 630, 113 S.Ct. 2816, 125 L.Ed.2d 511 (1993), the Court crafted a new cause of action with two novel, troubling features. First, the Court misapplied the term "gerrymander," previously used to describe grotesque line-drawing by a dominant group to maintain or enhance its political power at a minority's expense, to condemn the efforts of a majority (whites) to share its power with a minority (African-Americans). Second, the Court dispensed with its previous insistence in vote dilution cases on a showing of injury to an identifiable group of voters, but it failed to explain adequately what showing a plaintiff must make to establish standing to litigate the newly minted *Shaw* claim. Neither in *Shaw* itself nor in the cases decided today has the Court coherently articulated what injury this cause of action is designed to redress. Because appellees have alleged no legally cognizable injury, they lack standing, and these cases should be dismissed. See *Hays,* 515 U.S., at 750–751, 115 S.Ct., at 2439 (Stevens, J., concurring in judgment).

Even assuming the validity of *Shaw,* I cannot see how appellees in these cases could assert the injury the Court attributes to them. Appellees, plaintiffs below, are white voters in Georgia's Eleventh Congressional District. The Court's conclusion that they have standing to maintain a *Shaw* claim appears to rest on a theory that their placement in the Eleventh District caused them "'representational harms.'" *Hays,* at 744, 115 S.Ct., at 2436, cited *ante,* at 2485. The *Shaw* Court explained the concept of "representational harms" as follows: "When a district obviously is created solely to effectuate the perceived common interests of one racial group, elected officials are more likely to believe that their primary obligation is to represent only the members of that group, rather than their constituency as a whole." *Shaw,* 509 U.S., at 648, 113 S.Ct., at 2827. Although the *Shaw* Court attributed representational harms solely to a message sent by the legislature's action, those harms can only come about if the message is received—that is, first, if all or most black voters support the same candidate, and, second, if the successful candidate ignores the interests of her white constituents. Appellees' standing, in other words, ultimately depends on the very premise the Court purports to abhor: that voters of a particular race "'think alike, share the same political interests, and will prefer the same candidates at the polls.'" *Ante,* at 2486 (quoting *Shaw,* 509 U.S., at 647, 113 S.Ct., at 2827). This generalization, as the Court recognizes, is "offensive and demeaning." *Ante,* at 2486.

In particular instances, of course, members of one race may vote by an overwhelming margin for one candidate, and in some cases that candidate will be of the same race. "Racially polarized voting" is one of the circumstances plaintiffs must prove to advance a vote dilution claim. *Thornburg v. Gingles,* 478 U.S. 30, 56–58, 106 S. Ct. 2752, 2769–2770, 92 L.Ed.2d 25 (1986). Such a claim allows voters to allege that gerrymandered district lines have impaired their ability to elect a candidate of their own race. The Court emphasizes, however, that a so-called *Shaw* claim is "'analytically distinct' from a vote dilution claim," *ante,* at 2485 (quoting *Shaw,* 509 U.S., at 652, 113 S.Ct., at 2830). Neither in *Shaw,* nor in *Hays,* nor in the instant cases has the Court answered the question its analytic distinction raises: If the *Shaw* injury does not flow from an increased probability that white candidates will lose, then how can the increased probability that black candidates will win cause white voters, such as appellees, cognizable harm?

The Court attempts an explanation in these cases by equating the injury it imagines appellees have suffered with the injuries African-Americans suffered under segregation. The heart of appellees' claim, by the Court's account, is that "a State's assignment of voters on the basis of race," *ante,* at 2487, violates the Equal Protection Clause for the same reason a State may not "segregate citizens on the basis of race in its public parks, *New Orleans City Park Improvement Assn. v. Detiege,* 358 U.S. 54, 79 S.Ct. 99, 3 L.Ed.2d 46 (1958) *(per curiam),* buses, *Gayle v. Browder,* 352 U.S. 903, 77 S.Ct. 145, 1 L.Ed.2d 114 (1956) *(per curiam),* golf courses, *Holmes v. Atlanta,* 350 U.S. 879, 76 S.Ct. 141, 100 L.Ed. 776 (1955) *(per curiam),* beaches, *Mayor of Baltimore v. Dawson,* 350 U.S. 877, 76 S.Ct. 133, 100 L.Ed. 774 (1955) *(per curiam),* and schools, *Brown v. Board of Education,* 347 U.S. 483, 74 S.Ct. 686, 98 L.Ed. 873 (1954)." *Ante,* at 2486. This equation, however, fails to elucidate the elusive *Shaw* injury. Our desegregation cases redressed the *exclusion* of black citizens from public facilities reserved for whites. In these cases, in contrast, any voter, black or white, may live in the Eleventh District. What appellees contest is the *inclusion* of too many black voters in the district as drawn. In my view, if appellees allege no vote dilution, that inclusion can cause them no conceivable injury.

The Court's equation of *Shaw* claims with our desegregation decisions is inappropriate for another reason. In each of those cases, legal segregation frustrated the public interest in diversity and tolerance by barring African-Americans from joining whites in the activities at issue. The districting plan here, in contrast, serves the interest in diversity and tolerance by increasing the likelihood that a meaningful number of black representatives will add their voices to legislative debates. See *post,* at 2506 (GINSBURG, J., dissenting). "There is no moral or constitutional equivalence between a policy that is designed to perpetuate a caste system and one that seeks to eradicate racial subordination." *Adarand Constructors, Inc. v. Peña,* 515 U.S., at 243, 115 S.Ct., at 2120 (Stevens, J., dissenting); see also *id.,* at 247–248, n. 5, 115 S. Ct., at 2122–2123, n. 5. That racial integration of the sort attempted by Georgia now appears more vulnerable to judicial challenge than some policies alleged to perpetuate racial bias, cf. *Allen v. Wright,* 468 U.S. 737, 104 S.Ct. 3315, 82 L.Ed.2d 556 (1984), is anomalous, to say the least.

Equally distressing is the Court's equation of traditional gerrymanders, designed to maintain or enhance a dominant group's power, with a dominant group's decision to share its power with a previously underrepresented group. In my view, districting plans violate the Equal Protection Clause when they "serve no purpose other than to favor one segment—whether racial, ethnic, religious, economic, or political—that may occupy a position of strength at a particular point in time, or to disadvantage a politically weak segment of the community." *Karcher v. Daggett*, 462 U.S. 725, 748, 103 S.Ct. 2653, 2668–2669, 77 L.Ed.2d 133 (1983) (Stevens, J., concurring). In contrast, I do not see how a districting plan that favors a politically weak group can violate equal protection. The Constitution does not mandate any form of proportional representation, but it certainly permits a State to adopt a policy that promotes fair representation of different groups. Indeed, this Court squarely so held in *Gaffney v. Cummings*, 412 U.S. 735, 93 S.Ct. 2321, 37 L.Ed.2d 298 (1973):

> "[N]either we nor the district courts have a constitutional warrant to invalidate a state plan, otherwise within tolerable population limits, because it undertakes, not to minimize or eliminate the political strength of any group or party, but to recognize it and, through districting, provide a rough sort of proportional representation in the legislative halls of the State." *Id.*, at 754, 93 S.Ct., at 2332.

The Court's refusal to distinguish an enactment that helps a minority group from enactments that cause it harm is especially unfortunate at the intersection of race and voting, given that African-Americans and other disadvantaged groups have struggled so long and so hard for inclusion in that most central exercise of our democracy. See *post*, at 2500–2501 (Ginsburg, J., dissenting). I have long believed that treating racial groups differently from other identifiable groups of voters, as the Court does today, is itself an invidious racial classification. Racial minorities should receive neither more nor less protection than other groups against gerrymanders. *A fortiori*, racial minorities should not be less eligible than other groups to benefit from districting plans the majority designs to aid them.

I respectfully dissent.

Notes and Questions

1. Note that the Court applies in *Miller* the strong basis in evidence standard it applied in *Ricci* in the above chapter. The strong basis in evidence standard requires government to show proof that they had reason to think that their race conscious decision was a justified action to prevent committing discrimination.

2. Assume that Comp County, Mississippi, is a county of 50,000 on the banks of the Mississippi River. Twenty thousand of Comp's residents are black; the other thirty thousand are white. Comp is governed by a five-member commission, which is elected from five districts in a county-wide election. The districts, and their demographic characteristics are as follows: District 1 is 60% white, 40% black; District 2 is 80% white, 20% black; District 3 is 65% white, 35% black; District 4 is 20% white, 80% black; and district 5 is 97% white and 3% black.

Although several black candidates have run for the county commission from Districts 1, 2, 3, and 5 and each of them garnered overwhelming support from black voters, the only blacks ever to have been elected to the Comp County Commission have all been elected from District 4. Comp's elected representatives desire to equalize the voting power of African Americans in the districts. They are considering racial redistricting and influence districts as two possible solutions.

In light of the goals of the Voting Rights Act, what are the policy considerations for and against racial redistricting in order to remedy discriminatory voting practices? What standard must Comp comply with if they decide to use racial redistricting? Which of the two options, racial redistricting or the use of influence districts, would you recommend to the representatives?

3. Does the Court's current position on racial redistricting serve the goals of the Voting Rights Act? Evaluate the Court's position in light of the dissenting opinions in the racial redistricting cases. Which arguments are more convincing? Why?

4. Assume further that before the legislators in Comp are able to adopt a change, a group of citizens from Districts 1, 2, 3 and 5 seek to sue for discrimination in voting practices in the election of commissioners to represent the various districts. They come to you pointing to the fact that in the past 75 years, no black candidate has ever been able to win a seat in the other four districts. They have gathered particular data from the 2008 and 2012 elections as evidence. They seek your advice on the likelihood of success of a claim alleging voter dilution based on these facts. What additional facts might you need to know?

Part III

New Frontiers — Emerging and Evolving Litigation

Chapter 10

Food Justice and Poverty

A. Law as Power

Food justice is turning out to be one of the most dominant and pressing civil rights issues of the twenty-first century. We make, generally, more food than we can consume, causing much of it to go to waste, and still, distinct segments of our population are unable to access basic and healthy food.[1] This lack has contributed to an acute health crisis in our nation. Limited access to food works in two ways: limited ability to grow one's own food because of legal favoritism of big farming as well as geographic and economic isolation impeding access to adequately sustainable food. A third category threatening food access lies in the growing control granted to bio-engineered companies by policy makers and food agencies. The status of law as a reflection of power and status quo is reflected in this area as well.

Consider that our current treatment of genetically modified foods, "GMOs," occurred primarily from a policy decision made by the President (in support) to treat these products as substantially equivalent to normal foods even before they were introduced into commerce. Statement of Policy: Foods Derived from New Plant Varieties, 57 Fed. Reg. 22,984-01 (Food & Drug Admin. May 29, 1992). This approach, unlike that adopted by the European Union, amounted to substantial deference granted to big food companies. This early decision really highlights the impact power can have on law and policy, considering the lobbying power of certain companies and their entanglement with the campaigns of various representatives. This power structure has continued to play out in courts' treatment of legal challenges to the use and impact of GMO foods.

Farming remains one of the most important sources of food production for the world. As a result, access to sustainable farming and the ability for populations of various income level to grow and sell their own foods highly impact individuals' and communities' quality of life. The cases in Section B showcase efforts to challenge the disproportionate power of GMO companies with lawsuits asking food agencies to implement more rigorous reviews of GMO products and to label them. It also,

---

1. Comment, *Nurturing the Seeds of Food Justice: Unearthing the Impact of Institutionalized Racism on Access to Healthy Food in Urban African-American Communities*, 15 Scholar 97; *An Analysis of the Relationship Between Food Deserts and Obesity Rates in the United States*, 9 Geo. Public Pol'y Rev. 65; *All (Food) Politics Is Local: Increasing Food Access Through Local Government Action*, 7 Harv. L. & Pol'y Rev. 321; Garrett Broad, *The Black Panther Party: A Food Justice Story*, http://www.huffingtonpost.com/garrett-broad/the-black-panther-party-a_b_9311436.html.

through cases involving lawsuits by GMO companies against farmers for accidental cross pollination with their crops, showcases how easily these GMO entities' power became solidified in this area. Section C covers the various class actions suits filed by farmers of color (African Americans, Latinos) along with a reverse discrimination law suit against the federal government alleging discrimination in the administration of USDA loans.

Discriminatory administration of loans caused the diminishment of the class of black farmers in the United States. The case of black farmers covered below provided equitable remedies when Presidents Clinton and Obama permitted relief to black farmers who suffered discrimination at the hands of the USDA. In addition to the plight of farmers, food justice issues include limited access to fresh foods in depleted regions that function as food deserts for many poor citizens. As you progress in this chapter, consider the legal and non-legal models which might provide food justice to poor populations. To what extent do particular zoning laws make local governments accountable in this area? What reform models might work best to provide lasting change in this area?

B. GMOs

One of the hurdles farmers face when challenging food regulators' approach to genetically modified foods is the high level of discretion accorded by the courts to agencies. Under the *Chevron* doctrine, decisions by administrative agencies are only reviewed pursuant to the "arbitrary and capricious" standard. Short of that, even evidence of harm to plaintiffs, as demonstrated below, might not be enough to overcome the judicial deference accorded to administrative agencies' decisions. *Monsanto v. Geertson Seed Farms,* below, illustrates the extent of that deference. Our food supply is regulated by the USDA (U.S. Department of Agriculture), the FDA (the Food and Drug Administration) and the EPA (The Environmental Protection Agency). Each has specific duties delegated to them by Congress. Compare the majority's approach In *Monsanto Co. v. Geertson Seed Farms* to the lower court's decision enjoining the agency's order to partially deregulate. How do you assess the dissent's approach, which finds evidence of harm to be strong support for the district court's order?

In 1992, the federal government issued its position on bioengineered foods in anticipation of their introduction to the market:

> Under this policy, foods, such as fruits, vegetables, grains, and their byproducts, derived from plant varieties developed by the new methods of genetic modification are regulated within the existing framework of the act, FDA's implementing regulations, and current practice, utilizing an approach identical in principle to that applied to foods developed by traditional plant breeding ... In most cases, the substances expected to become components of food as a result of genetic modification of a plant will be the same as or substantially similar to substances commonly found in food, such as proteins, fats and oils, and carbohydrates. As discussed in more detail in section

V.C., FDA has determined that such substances should be subject to regulation under section 409 of the act in those cases when the objective characteristics of the substance raise questions of safety sufficient to warrant formal
premarket review and approval by FDA. The objective characteristics that
will trigger regulation of substances as food additives are described in the
guidance section of this notice (section VII.).

Statement of Policy: Foods Derived from New Plant Varieties, 57 Fed. Reg. 22,984
-01 (Food & Drug Admin. May 29, 1992).

This approach continues today. The cases below discuss courts' authority to review
agencies' decisions to deregulate food products. As seen below, even when successful
in bringing a claim questioning agencies' deregulation of products, plaintiffs' claims
are unlikely to surmount federal courts' low standard of review for these decisions.

Monsanto Co. v. Geertson Seed Farms
561 U.S. 139 (2010)

JUSTICE ALITO delivered the opinion of the Court.

This case arises out of a decision by the Animal and Plant Health Inspection
Service (APHIS) to deregulate a variety of genetically engineered alfalfa. The District Court held that APHIS violated the National Environmental Policy Act of 1969
(NEPA), 83 Stat. 852, 42 U.S.C. § 4321 *et seq.*, by issuing its deregulation decision without first completing a detailed assessment of the environmental consequences of its
proposed course of action. To remedy that violation, the District Court vacated the
agency's decision completely deregulating the alfalfa variety in question; ordered
APHIS not to act on the deregulation petition in whole or in part until it had completed a detailed environmental review; and enjoined almost all future planting of
the genetically engineered alfalfa pending the completion of that review. The Court
of Appeals affirmed the District Court's entry of permanent injunctive relief. The
main issue now in dispute concerns the breadth of that relief. For the reasons set forth
below, we reverse and remand for further proceedings.

I

A

The Plant Protection Act (PPA), 114 Stat. 438, 7 U.S.C. § 7701 *et seq.*, provides that
the Secretary of the Department of Agriculture (USDA) may issue regulations "to
prevent the introduction of plant pests into the United States or the dissemination
of plant pests within the United States." § 7711(a). The Secretary has delegated that
authority to APHIS, a division of the USDA. 7 CFR §§ 2.22(a), 2.80(a)(36) (2010).
Acting pursuant to that delegation, APHIS has promulgated regulations governing
"the introduction of organisms and products altered or produced through genetic
engineering that are plant pests or are believed to be plant pests." See § 340.0(a)(2)
and n. 1. Under those regulations, certain genetically engineered plants are presumed
to be "plant pests"—and thus "regulated articles" under the PPA—until APHIS deter
mines otherwise. See *ibid.;* §§ 340.1, 340.2, 340.6; see also App. 183. However, any

person may petition APHIS for a determination that a regulated article does not present a plant pest risk and therefore should not be subject to the applicable regulations. 7 U.S.C. §7711(c)(2); 7 CFR §340.6. APHIS may grant such a petition in whole or in part. §340.6(d)(3).

In deciding whether to grant nonregulated status to a genetically engineered plant variety, APHIS must comply with NEPA, which requires federal agencies "to the fullest extent possible" to prepare an environmental impact statement (EIS) for "every recommendation or report on proposals for legislation and other major Federal actio[n] significantly affecting the quality of the human environment." 42 U.S.C. §4332(2)(C). The statutory text "speaks solely in terms of *proposed* actions; it does not require an agency to consider the possible environmental impacts of less imminent actions when preparing the impact statement on proposed actions." *Kleppe v. Sierra Club*, 427 U.S. 390, 410, n. 20 (1976).

An agency need not complete an EIS for a particular proposal if it finds, on the basis of a shorter "environmental assessment" (EA), that the proposed action will not have a significant impact on the environment. 40 CFR §§1508.9(a), 1508.13 (2009). Even if a particular agency proposal requires an EIS, applicable regulations allow the agency to take at least some action in furtherance of that proposal while the EIS is being prepared. See §1506.1(a) ("no action concerning the proposal shall be taken which would: (1) Have an adverse environmental impact; or (2) Limit the choice of reasonable alternatives"); §1506.1(c) ("While work on a required program environmental impact statement is in progress and the action is not covered by an existing program statement, agencies shall not undertake in the interim any major Federal action covered by the program which may significantly affect the quality of the human environment unless such action" satisfies certain requirements).

B

This case involves Roundup Ready Alfalfa (RRA), a kind of alfalfa crop that has been genetically engineered to be tolerant of glyphosate, the active ingredient of the herbicide Roundup. Petitioner Monsanto Company (Monsanto) owns the intellectual property rights to RRA. Monsanto licenses those rights to co-petitioner Forage Genetics International (FGI), which is the exclusive developer of RRA seed.

APHIS initially classified RRA as a regulated article, but in 2004 petitioners sought nonregulated status for two strains of RRA. In response, APHIS prepared a draft EA assessing the likely environmental impact of the requested deregulation. It then published a notice in the Federal Register advising the public of the deregulation petition and soliciting public comments on its draft EA. After considering the hundreds of public comments that it received, APHIS issued a Finding of No Significant Impact and decided to deregulate RRA unconditionally and without preparing an EIS. Prior to this decision, APHIS had authorized almost 300 field trials of RRA conducted over a period of eight years. App. 348.

Approximately eight months after APHIS granted RRA nonregulated status, respondents (two conventional alfalfa seed farms and environmental groups concerned with food safety) filed this action against the Secretary of Agriculture and certain other officials in Federal District Court, challenging APHIS's decision to completely deregulate RRA. Their complaint alleged violations of NEPA, the Endangered Species Act of 1973 (ESA), 87 Stat. 884, 16 U.S.C. § 1531 *et seq.*, and the PPA. Respondents did not seek preliminary injunctive relief pending resolution of those claims. Hence, RRA enjoyed nonregulated status for approximately two years. During that period, more than 3,000 farmers in 48 States planted an estimated 220,000 acres of RRA. App. 350.

In resolving respondents' NEPA claim, the District Court accepted APHIS's determination that RRA does not have any harmful health effects on humans or livestock. App. to Pet. for Cert. 43a; accord, *id.*, at 45a. Nevertheless, the District Court held that APHIS violated NEPA by deregulating RRA without first preparing an EIS. In particular, the court found that APHIS's EA failed to answer substantial questions concerning two broad consequences of its proposed action: first, the extent to which complete deregulation would lead to the transmission of the gene conferring glyphosate tolerance from RRA to organic and conventional alfalfa; and, second, the extent to which the introduction of RRA would contribute to the development of Roundup-resistant weeds. *Id.*, at 52a. In light of its determination that the deregulation decision ran afoul of NEPA, the District Court dismissed without prejudice respondents' claims under the ESA and PPA.

After these rulings, the District Court granted petitioners permission to intervene in the remedial phase of the lawsuit. The court then asked the parties to submit proposed judgments embodying their preferred means of remedying the NEPA violation. APHIS's proposed judgment would have ordered the agency to prepare an EIS, vacated the agency's deregulation decision, and replaced that decision with the terms of the judgment itself. *Id.*, at 184a (proposed judgment providing that "[the federal] defendants' [June 14,] 2005 Determination of Nonregulated Status for Alfalfa Genetically Engineered for Tolerance to the Herbicide Glyphosate is hereby vacated *and replaced by the terms of this judgment*" (emphasis added)). The terms of the proposed judgment, in turn, would have permitted the continued planting of RRA pending completion of the EIS, subject to six restrictions. Those restrictions included, among other things, mandatory isolation distances between RRA and non-genetically-engineered alfalfa fields in order to mitigate the risk of gene flow; mandatory harvesting conditions; a requirement that planting and harvesting equipment that had been in contact with RRA be cleaned prior to any use with conventional or organic alfalfa; identification and handling requirements for RRA seed; and a requirement that all RRA seed producers and hay growers be under contract with either Monsanto or FGI and that their contracts require compliance with the other limitations set out in the proposed judgment.

The District Court rejected APHIS's proposed judgment. In its preliminary injunction, the District Court prohibited almost all future planting of RRA pending APHIS's completion of the required EIS. But in order to minimize the harm to farmers who had relied on APHIS's deregulation decision, the court expressly allowed those who had already purchased RRA to plant their seeds until March 30, 2007. *Id.*, at 58.

In its subsequently entered permanent injunction and judgment, the court (1) vacated APHIS's deregulation decision; (2) ordered APHIS to prepare an EIS before it made any decision on Monsanto's deregulation petition; (3) enjoined the planting of any RRA in the United States after March 30, 2007, pending APHIS's completion of the required EIS; and (4) imposed certain conditions (suggested by APHIS) on the handling and identification of already-planted RRA. *Id.*, at 79a, 109a. The District Court denied petitioners' request for an evidentiary hearing.

The Government, Monsanto, and FGI appealed, challenging the scope of the relief granted but not disputing the existence of a NEPA violation. See *Geertson Seed Farms v. Johanns*, 570 F.3d 1130, 1136 (2009). A divided panel of the Court of Appeals for the Ninth Circuit affirmed. . . . We granted certiorari. 558 U. S. (2010).

II

A

[The Court determines that both parties have standing to have the Supreme Court review their claims.]

. . . .

III

A

The District Court sought to remedy APHIS's NEPA violation in three ways: First, it vacated the agency's decision completely deregulating RRA; second, it enjoined APHIS from deregulating RRA, in whole or in part, pending completion of the mandated EIS; and third, it entered a nationwide injunction prohibiting almost all future planting of RRA. *Id.*, at 108a-110a. Because petitioners and the Government do not argue otherwise, we assume without deciding that the District Court acted lawfully in vacating the deregulation decision. See Tr. of Oral Arg. 7 ("[T]he district court could have vacated the order in its entirety and sent it back to the agency"); accord, *id.*, at 15–16. We therefore address only the latter two aspects of the District Court's judgment. Before doing so, however, we provide a brief overview of the standard governing the entry of injunctive relief.

B

"[A] plaintiff seeking a permanent injunction must satisfy a four-factor test before a court may grant such relief. A plaintiff must demonstrate: (1) that it has suffered an irreparable injury; (2) that remedies available at law, such as monetary damages, are inadequate to compensate for that injury; (3) that, considering the balance of hardships between the plaintiff and defendant, a remedy in equity is warranted; and (4) that the public interest would not be disserved by a permanent injunction." *eBay Inc. v. MercExchange, L.L.C.*, 547 U.S. 388, 391 (2006). The traditional four-factor test applies when a plaintiff seeks a permanent injunction to remedy a NEPA violation. See *Winter v. Natural Resources Defense Council, Inc.*, 555 U.S. ___, ___ (2008) (slip op., at 21–23).

Petitioners argue that the lower courts in this case proceeded on the errone-ous assumption that an injunction is generally the appropriate remedy for a NEPA violation. In particular, petitioners note that the District Court cited pre- *Winter* Ninth Circuit precedent for the proposition that, in "'the run of the mill NEPA case,'" an injunction delaying the contemplated government project is proper "'until the NEPA violation is cured.'" App. to Pet. for Cert. 65a (quoting *Idaho Watersheds Project v. Hahn*, 307 F.3d 815, 833 (CA9 2002)); see also App. to Pet. for Cert. 55a (quoting same language in preliminary injunction order). In addition, petitioners observe, the District Court and the Court of Appeals in this case both stated that, "in unusual circumstances, an injunction may be withheld, or, more likely, limited in scope" in NEPA cases. *Id.*, at 66a (quoting *National Parks Conservation Assn. v. Babbitt*, 241 F.3d 722, 737, n. 18 (CA9 2001) (internal quotation marks omitted)); 570 F.3d, at 1137.

Insofar as the statements quoted above are intended to guide the determina-tion whether to grant injunctive relief, they invert the proper mode of analysis. An injunction should issue only if the traditional four-factor test is satisfied. See *Winter*, *supra*, at ___ (slip op., at 21–24). In contrast, the statements quoted above appear to presume that an injunction is the proper remedy for a NEPA violation except in unusual circumstances. No such thumb on the scales is warranted . . . . We need not decide whether respondents' characterization of the lower court opinions in this case is sound. Even if it is, the injunctive relief granted here cannot stand.

C

We first consider whether the District Court erred in enjoining APHIS from par-tially deregulating RRA during the pendency of the EIS process. . . . Petitioners focus their challenge on the part of the District Court's order prohibiting the plant-ing of RRA. As we explain below, however, the broad injunction against planting can-not be valid if the injunction against partial deregulation is improper. See *infra*, at 23; see also App. to Pet. for Cert. 64a . . . . The validity of the injunction prohibiting partial deregulation is therefore properly before us. Like the District Court, we use the term "partial deregulation" to refer to any limited or conditional deregulation. See *id.*, at 64a, 69a.

The relevant part of the District Court's judgment states that, "[b]efore granting Monsanto's deregulation petition, *even in part*, the federal defendants shall prepare an environmental impact statement." App. to Pet. for Cert. 108a (emphasis added); see also *id.*, at 79a ("The Court will enter a final judgment . . . ordering the govern-ment to prepare an EIS before it makes a decision on Monsanto's deregulation peti-tion"). The plain text of the order prohibits *any* partial deregulation, not just the particular partial deregulation embodied in APHIS's proposed judgment. We think it is quite clear that the District Court meant just what it said. The related injunction against planting states that "*no* [RRA] . . . may be planted" "[u]ntil the federal defen-dants prepare the EIS and decide the deregulation petition." *Id.*, at 108a (emphasis added). That injunction, which appears in the very same judgment and directly fol-lows the injunction against granting Monsanto's petition "even in part," does not carve out an exception for planting subsequently authorized by a valid partial deregulation decision.

In our view, none of the traditional four factors governing the entry of permanent injunctive relief supports the District Court's injunction prohibiting partial deregulation. To see why that is so, it is helpful to understand how the injunction prohibiting a partial deregulation fits into the broader dispute between the parties.

Respondents in this case brought suit under the APA to challenge a particular agency order: APHIS's decision to *completely* deregulate RRA. The District Court held that the order in question was procedurally defective, and APHIS decided not to appeal that determination. At that point, it was for the agency to decide whether and to what extent it would pursue a *partial* deregulation. If the agency found, on the basis of a new EA, that a limited and temporary deregulation satisfied applicable statutory and regulatory requirements, it could proceed with such a deregulation even if it had not yet finished the onerous EIS required for complete deregulation. If and when the agency were to issue a partial deregulation order, any party aggrieved by that order could bring a separate suit under the Administrative Procedure Act to challenge the particular deregulation attempted. See 5 U.S.C. § 702.

In this case, APHIS apparently sought to "streamline" the proceedings by asking the District Court to craft a remedy that, in effect, would have partially deregulated RRA until such time as the agency had finalized the EIS needed for a complete deregulation. See Tr. of Oral Arg. 16, 23–24; App. to Pet. for Cert. 69a. To justify that disposition, APHIS and petitioners submitted voluminous documentary submissions in which they purported to show that the risk of gene flow would be insignificant if the District Court allowed limited planting and harvesting subject to APHIS's proposed conditions. Respondents, in turn, submitted considerable evidence of their own that seemed to cut the other way. This put the District Court in an unenviable position. "The parties' experts disagreed over virtually every factual issue relating to possible environmental harm, including the likelihood of genetic contamination and why some contamination had already occurred." 570 F. 3d, at 1135.

The District Court may well have acted within its discretion in refusing to craft a judicial remedy that would have *authorized* the continued planting and harvesting of RRA while the EIS is being prepared. It does not follow, however, that the District Court was within its rights in *enjoining* APHIS from allowing such planting and harvesting pursuant to the authority vested in the agency by law.

[W]hen the District Court entered its permanent injunction, APHIS had not yet exercised its authority to partially deregulate RRA. Until APHIS actually seeks to affect a partial deregulation, any judicial review of such a decision is premature. NEPA provides that an EIS must be "include[d] in every recommendation or report on *proposals* for legislation and other major Federal actions significantly affecting the quality of the human environment." 42 U.S.C. § 4332(2)(C) (emphasis added); see also *Kleppe v. Sierra Club*, 427 U.S. 390, 406 (1976) ("A court has no authority to depart from the statutory language and . . . determine a point during the germination process of a *potential* proposal at which an impact statement *should be prepared*" (first emphasis added)). When a particular agency proposal exists and requires the preparation of an EIS, NEPA regulations allow the agency to take at least some action pertaining to that proposal during the pendency of the EIS process. See 40 CFR §§ 1506.1(a), (c) (2009).

We do not express any view on the Government's contention that a limited deregulation of the kind embodied in its proposed judgment would not require the prior preparation of an EIS. See Brief for Federal Respondents 21–22 (citing § 1506.1(a)); Tr. of Oral Arg. 20 ("what we were proposing for the interim, that is allowing continued planting subject to various protective measures, was fundamentally different from the action on which the EIS was being prepared"). Because APHIS has not yet invoked the procedures necessary to attempt a limited deregulation, any judicial consideration of such issues is not warranted at this time.

Nor can the District Court's injunction be justified as a prophylactic measure needed to guard against the possibility that the agency would seek to effect on its own the particular partial deregulation scheme embodied in the terms of APHIS's proposed judgment. Even if the District Court was not required to adopt that judgment, there was no need to stop the agency from effecting a partial deregulation in accordance with the procedures established by law. Moreover, the terms of the District Court's injunction do not just enjoin the *particular* partial deregulation embodied in APHIS's proposed judgment. Instead, the District Court barred the agency from pursuing *any* deregulation—no matter how limited the geographic area in which planting of RRA would be allowed, how great the isolation distances mandated between RRA fields and fields for growing non-genetically-engineered alfalfa, how stringent the regulations governing harvesting and distribution, how robust the enforcement mechanisms available at the time of the decision, and—consequently—no matter how small the risk that the planting authorized under such conditions would adversely affect the environment in general and respondents in particular.

. . . .

Based on the analysis set forth above, it is clear that the order enjoining any deregulation whatsoever does not satisfy the traditional four-factor test for granting permanent injunctive relief. Most importantly, respondents cannot show that they will suffer irreparable injury if APHIS is allowed to proceed with any partial deregulation, for at least two independent reasons.

First, if and when APHIS pursues a partial deregulation that arguably runs afoul of NEPA, respondents may file a new suit challenging such action and seeking appropriate preliminary relief. See 5 U.S.C. §§ 702, 705. Accordingly, a permanent injunction is not now needed to guard against any present or imminent risk of likely irreparable harm.

Second, a partial deregulation need not cause respondents any injury at all, much less irreparable injury; if the scope of the partial deregulation is sufficiently limited, the risk of gene flow to their crops could be virtually nonexistent. For example, suppose that APHIS deregulates RRA only in a remote part of the country in which respondents neither grow nor intend to grow non-genetically-engineered alfalfa, and in which no conventional alfalfa farms are currently located. Suppose further that APHIS issues an accompanying administrative order mandating isolation distances so great as to eliminate any appreciable risk of gene flow to the crops of conventional farmers who might someday choose to plant in the surrounding area. See, *e.g.*, Brief in Opposition 9, n. 6 (quoting study concluding "'that in order for there to be *zero* tolerance of any gene flow between a [RRA] seed field and a conventional seed field, those fields would have to have a five-mile isolation distance between them'"). . . .

Of course, APHIS might ultimately choose not to partially deregulate RRA during the pendency of the EIS, or else to pursue the kind of partial deregulation embodied in its proposed judgment rather than the very limited deregulation envisioned in the above hypothetical. Until such time as the agency decides whether and how to exercise its regulatory authority, however, the courts have no cause to intervene. Indeed, the broad injunction entered here essentially pre-empts the very procedure by which the agency could determine, independently of the pending EIS process for assessing the effects of a *complete* deregulation, that a *limited* deregulation would not pose any appreciable risk of environmental harm. See 40 CFR §§ 1501.4, 1508.9(a) (2009).

In sum, we do not know whether and to what extent APHIS would seek to effect a limited deregulation during the pendency of the EIS process if it were free to do so; we do know that the vacatur of APHIS's deregulation decision means that virtually no RRA can be grown or sold until such time as a new deregulation decision is in place, and we also know that any party aggrieved by a hypothetical future deregulation decision will have ample opportunity to challenge it, and to seek appropriate preliminary relief, if and when such a decision is made. In light of these particular circumstances, we hold that the District Court did not properly exercise its discretion in enjoining a partial deregulation of any kind pending APHIS's preparation of an EIS. It follows that the Court of Appeals erred in affirming that aspect of the District Court's judgment.

D

We now turn to petitioners' claim that the District Court erred in entering a nation-wide injunction against planting RRA. Petitioners argue that the District Court did not apply the right test for determining whether to enter permanent injunctive relief; that, even if the District Court identified the operative legal standard, it erred as a matter of law in applying that standard to the facts of this case; and that the District Court was required to grant petitioners an evidentiary hearing to resolve contested issues of fact germane to the remedial dispute between the parties. We agree that the District Court's injunction against planting went too far, but we come to that conclusion for two independent reasons.

First, the impropriety of the District Court's broad injunction against planting flows from the impropriety of its injunction against partial deregulation. If APHIS may partially deregulate RRA before preparing a full-blown EIS—a question that we need not and do not decide here—farmers should be able to grow and sell RRA in accordance with that agency determination. Because it was inappropriate for the District Court to foreclose even the possibility of a partial and temporary deregulation, it necessarily follows that it was likewise inappropriate to enjoin any and all parties from acting in accordance with the terms of such a deregulation decision.

Second, respondents have represented to this Court that the District Court's injunction against planting does not have any meaningful practical effect independent of its vacatur. See Brief for Respondents 24. . . . An injunction is a drastic and extraordinary remedy, which should not be granted as a matter of course. See, *e.g.*, *Weinberger v. Romero-Barcelo*, 456 U.S. 305, 311–312 (1982). If a less drastic remedy (such as partial or complete vacatur of APHIS's deregulation decision) was sufficient to redress respondents' injury, no recourse to the additional and extraordinary relief of an injunction was warranted. See *ibid.;* see also *Winter*, 555 U. S., at ___ (slip op., at 21–23).

E

In sum, the District Court abused its discretion in enjoining APHIS from effecting a partial deregulation and in prohibiting the possibility of planting in accordance with the terms of such a deregulation. Given those errors, this Court need not express any view on whether injunctive relief of some kind was available to respondents on the record before us. Nor does the Court address the question whether the District Court was required to conduct an evidentiary hearing before entering the relief at issue here. The judgment of the Ninth Circuit is reversed, and the case is remanded for further proceedings consistent with this opinion.

It is so ordered.

JUSTICE STEVENS, dissenting.

The Court does not dispute the District Court's critical findings of fact: First, Roundup Ready Alfalfa (RRA) can contaminate other plants. See App. to Pet. for Cert. 38a, 54a, 62a. Second, even planting in a controlled setting had led to contamination in some instances. See *id.*, at 69a-70a. Third, the Animal and Plant Health Inspection Service (APHIS) has limited ability to monitor or enforce limitations on planting. See *id.*, at 70a. And fourth, genetic contamination from RRA could decimate farmers' livelihoods and the American alfalfa market for years to come. See *id.*, at 71a; see also *id.*, at 29a-30a. Instead, the majority faults the District Court for "enjoining APHIS from partially deregulating RRA." *Ante*, at 16.

In my view, the District Court may not have actually ordered such relief, and we should not so readily assume that it did. Regardless, the District Court did not abuse its discretion when, after considering the voluminous record and making the aforementioned findings, it issued the order now before us.

I

To understand the District Court's judgment, it is necessary to understand the background of this litigation. Petitioner Monsanto Company (Monsanto) is a large corporation that has long produced a weed killer called Roundup. After years of experimentation, Monsanto and co-petitioner Forage Genetics International (FGI) genetically engineered a mutation in the alfalfa genome that makes the plant immune to Roundup. Monsanto and FGI's new product, RRA, is "the first crop that has been engineered to resist a[n] herbicide" and that can transmit the genetically engineered gene to other plants. See App. to Pet. for Cert. 45a.

In 2004, in the midst of a deregulatory trend in the agricultural sector, petitioners asked APHIS to deregulate RRA, thereby allowing it to be sold and planted nationwide. App. 101a. Rather than conducting a detailed analysis and preparing an "environmental impact statement" (EIS), as required by the National Environmental Policy Act of 1969 (NEPA) for every "major Federal actio[n] significantly affecting the quality of the human environment," 42 U.S.C. §4332(2)(C), APHIS merely conducted an abbreviated "environmental assessment" (EA). During the 6-month period in which APHIS allowed public comment on its EA, the agency received 663 comments, 520 of which opposed deregulation. App. to Pet. for Cert. 29a. Farmers and scientists opined that RRA could contaminate alfalfa that has not been genetically modified, destroying the American export market for alfalfa and, potentially, contaminating other plants and breeding a new type of pesticide-resistant weed. *Id.*, at 29a-30a.

Despite substantial evidence that RRA genes could transfer to other plants, APHIS issued a Finding of No Significant Impact and agreed to deregulate RRA "unconditionally," *ante*, at 4. With no EIS to wait for and no regulation blocking its path, petitioners began selling RRA. Farmers and environmental groups swiftly brought this lawsuit to challenge APHIS's decision to deregulate, raising claims under NEPA and other statutes.

The District Court carefully reviewed a long record and found that "APHIS's reasons for concluding" that the risks of genetic contamination are low were "not 'convincing.'" App. to Pet. for Cert. 38a. A review of APHIS's internal documents showed that individuals within the agency warned that contamination might occur. APHIS rested its decision to deregulate on its assertion that contamination risk is "not significant because it is the organic and conventional farmers' responsibility" to protect themselves and the environment. *Ibid.* Yet the agency drew this conclusion without having investigated whether such farmers "can, in fact, protect their crops from contamination." *Ibid.* The District Court likewise found that APHIS's reasons for disregarding the risk of pesticide-resistant weeds were speculative and "not convincing." *Id.*, at 46a. The agency had merely explained that if weeds acquire roundup resistance, farmers can use "'[a]lternative herbicides.'" *Ibid.* In light of the "acknowledged" risk of RRA gene transmission and the potential "impact on the development of Roundup resistant weeds," the court concluded that there was a significant possibility of serious environmental harm, and granted summary judgment for the plaintiffs. *Id.*, at 54a; see also *id.*, at 45a.

At this point, the question of remedy arose. The parties submitted proposed final judgments, and several corporations with an interest in RRA, including Monsanto, sought permission to intervene. The District Court granted their motion and agreed "to give them the opportunity to present evidence to assist the court in fashioning the appropriate scope of whatever relief is granted." *Id.*, at 54a (internal quotation marks omitted).

While the District Court considered the proposed judgments, it issued a preliminary injunction. Ordinarily, the court explained, the remedy for failure to conduct an EIS is to vacate the permit that was unlawfully given—the result of which, in this case, would be to prohibit any use of RRA. See *id.*, at 55a; see also *id.*, at 65a. But this case presented a special difficulty: Following APHIS's unlawful deregulation order, some farmers had begun planting genetically modified RRA. *Id.*, at 55a. In its preliminary injunction, the District Court ordered that no new RRA could be planted until APHIS completed the EIS or the court determined that some other relief was appropriate. But, so as to protect these farmers, the court declined to prohibit them from "harvesting, using, or selling" any crops they had already planted. *Id.*, at 56a. And "to minimize the harm to those growers who intend to imminently plant Roundup Ready alfalfa," the court permitted "[t]hose growers who intend to plant [RRA] in the next three weeks and have already purchased the seed" to go ahead and plant. *Id.*, at 58a (emphasis deleted). Essentially, the court grandfathered in those farmers who had relied, in good faith, on APHIS's actions.

Before determining the scope of its final judgment, the District Court invited the parties and intervenors to submit "whatever additional evidence" they "wish[ed] to provide," and it scheduled additional oral argument. *Id.*, at 58a-59a. The parties submitted "competing proposals for permanent injunctive relief." *Id.*, at 60a. The plaintiffs requested that no one—not even the grandfathered-in farmers—be allowed to plant, grow, or harvest RRA until the full EIS had been prepared. *Id.*, at 64a. APHIS and the intervenors instead sought a remedy that would "facilitat[e] the continued and dramatic growth" of RRA: a "partial deregulation" order that would permit planting subject to certain conditions, such as specified minimum distances between RRA and conventional alfalfa and special cleaning requirements for equipment used on the genetically modified crop. See *id.*, at 60a-64a.

The court adopted a compromise. First, it declined to adopt the APHIS-Monsanto proposal. APHIS itself had acknowledged that "gene transmission could and had occurred," and that RRA "could result in the development of Roundup-resistant weeds." *Id.*, at 61a-62a. In light of the substantial record evidence of these risks, the court would not agree to a nationwide planting scheme "without the benefit of the development of all the relevant data," as well as public comment about whether contamination could be controlled. *Id.*, at 68a. The "partial deregulation" proposed by petitioners, the court noted, was really "deregulation with certain conditions," *id.*, at 69a—which, for the same reasons given in the court's earlier order, requires an EIS, *ibid.* The court pointed out numerous problems with the APHIS-Monsanto proposal. Neither APHIS nor Monsanto had provided "evidence that suggests whether, and to what extent, the proposed interim conditions" would actually "be followed," and comparable conditions had failed to prevent contamination in certain limited settings. *Id.*, at 69a-70a. APHIS, moreover, conceded that "it does not have the resources to inspect" the RRA that had already been planted, and so could not possibly be expected "to adequately monitor the more than one million acres of [RRA] intervenors estimate [would] be planted" under their proposal. *Ibid.* That was especially problematic because any plan to limit contamination depended on rules about harvesting, and farmers were unlikely to follow those rules. *Id.*, at 71a. "APHIS ha[d] still not made any inquiry" into numerous factual concerns raised by the court in its summary judgment order issued several months earlier. *Id.*, at 70a.

Next, the court rejected the plaintiffs' proposed remedy of "enjoin[ing] the harvesting and sale of already planted" RRA. *Id.*, at 76a. Although any planting or harvesting of RRA poses a contamination risk, the court reasoned that the equities were different for those farmers who had already invested time and money planting RRA in good-faith reliance on APHIS's deregulation order. And small amounts of harvesting could be more easily monitored. Rather than force the farmers to tear up their crops, the court imposed a variety of conditions on the crops' handling and distribution. *Id.*, at 77a.

As to all other RRA, however, the court sided with the plaintiffs and enjoined planting during the pendency of the EIS. Balancing the equities, the court explained that the risk of harm was great. "[C]ontamination cannot be undone; it will destroy the crops of those farmers who do not sell genetically modified alfalfa." *Id.*, at 71a. And because those crops "cannot be replanted for two to four years," that loss will be even greater. *Ibid.* On the other side of the balance, the court recognized that some farmers may wish to switch to genetically modified alfalfa immediately, and some companies like Monsanto want to start selling it to them just as fast. But, the court noted, RRA is a small percentage of those companies' overall business; unsold seed can be stored; and the companies "'have [no] cause to claim surprise'" as to any loss of anticipated revenue, as they "were aware of plaintiffs' lawsuit" and "nonetheless chose to market" RRA. *Id.*, at 72a.

Thus, the District Court stated that it would "vacat[e] the June 2005 deregulation decision"; "enjoi[n] the planting of [RRA] in the United States after March 30, 2007," the date of the decision, "pending the government's completion of the EIS and decision on the deregulation petition"; and impose "conditions on the handling and identification of already-planted [RRA]." *Id.*, at 79a. On the same day, the court issued its judgment. In relevant part, the judgment states:

. . . .

II

Before proceeding to address the Court's opinion on its own terms, it is important to note that I have reservations about the validity of those terms. The Court today rests not only the bulk of its analysis but also the primary basis for our jurisdiction on the premise that the District Court enjoined APHIS from partially deregulating RRA in any sense. See *ante*, at 9–11, 16–23.1 That is a permissible, but not necessarily correct, reading of the District Court's judgment.

. . . .

III

Even assuming that the majority has correctly interpreted the District Court's judgment, I do not agree that we should reverse the District Court.

At the outset, it is important to observe that when a district court is faced with an unlawful agency action, a set of parties who have relied on that action, and a prayer for relief to avoid irreparable harm, the court is operating under its powers of equity. In such a case, a court's function is "to do equity and to mold each decree to the necessities of the particular case." *Hecht Co. v. Bowles*, 321 U.S. 321, 329 (1944). "Flexibility" and "practicality" are the touchstones of these remedial determinations, as "the public interest," "private needs," and "competing private claims" must all be weighed and reconciled against the background of the court's own limitations and its . . . particular familiarity with the case. *Id.*, at 329–330.

. . . .

When a district court takes on the equitable role of adjusting legal obligations, we review the remedy it crafts for abuse of discretion. "[D]eference," we have explained, "is the hallmark of abuse-of-discretion review." *General Elec. Co. v. Joiner*, 522 U.S. 136, 143 (1997). Although equitable remedies are "not left to a trial court's 'inclination,'" they are left to the court's "'judgment.'" *Albemarle Paper Co. v. Moody*, 422 U.S. 405, 416 (1975) (quoting *United States v. Burr*, 25 F. Cas. 30, 35 (No. 14,692d) (CC Va. 1807) (Marshall, C. J.)). The principles set forth in applicable federal statutes may inform that judgment. See *United States v. Oakland Cannabis Buyers' Cooperative*, 532 U.S. 483, 497 (2001) ("[A] court sitting in equity cannot ignore the judgment of Congress, deliberately expressed in legislation" (internal quotation marks omitted)). And historically, courts have had particularly broad equitable power—and thus particularly broad discretion—to remedy public nuisances and other "'purprestures upon public rights and properties,'" *Mugler v. Kansas*, 123 U.S. 623, 672 (1887), 3 which include environmental harms. . . . In my view, the District Court did not "unreasonably exercis[e]" its discretion, *Bennett v. Bennett*, 208 U.S. 505, 512 (1908), even if it did categorically prohibit partial deregulation pending completion of the EIS. Rather, the District Court's judgment can be understood as either of two reasonable exercises of its equitable powers.

Equitable Application of Administrative Law

First, the District Court's decision can be understood as an equitable application of administrative law. Faced with two different deregulation proposals, the District Court appears to have vacated the deregulation that had already occurred, made clear that NEPA requires an EIS for any future deregulation of RRA, and partially stayed the vacatur to the extent it affects farmers who had already planted RRA. See Reply Brief for Federal Respondents

There is an ongoing debate about the role of equitable adjustments in administrative law. See, *e.g.*, Levin, Vacation at Sea: Judicial Remedies and Equitable Discretion in Administrative Law, 53 Duke L.J. 291 (2003). The parties to this appeal and the majority assume that the District Court's remedy was crafted under its equity powers, and I will do the same.

Under NEPA, an agency must prepare an EIS for "every . . . major Federal actio[n] significantly affecting the quality of the human environment." 42 U.S.C. § 4332(2)(C). Recall that the District Court had found, on the basis of substantial evidence, that planting RRA can cause genetic contamination of other crops, planting in controlled settings had led to contamination, APHIS is unable to monitor or enforce limitations on planting, and genetic contamination could decimate the American alfalfa market. In light of that evidence, the court may well have concluded that any deregulation of RRA, even in a "limited . . . geographic area" with "stringent . . . regulations governing harvesting and distribution," *ante*, at 19–20, requires an EIS under NEPA. See generally D. Mandelker, NEPA Law and Litigation §§ 8:33–8:48 (2d ed. 2009) (describing when an EIS is required); cf. *Marsh v. Oregon Natural Resources Council*, 490 U.S. 360, 371 (1989) (NEPA embodies "sweeping commitment" to environmental safety and principle that "the agency will not act on incomplete information, only to regret its decision after it is too late to correct"). Indeed, it appears that any deregulation of a genetically modified, herbicide-resistant crop that can transfer its genes to other organisms and cannot effectively be monitored easily fits the criteria for when an EIS is required. That is especially so when, as in this case, the environmental threat is novel. See *Winter v. Natural Resources Defense Council, Inc.*, 555 U.S. ___, ___ (2008) (slip op., at 13) (EIS is more important when party "is conducting a new type of activity with completely unknown effects on the environment").

. . . .

Finally, it bears mention that the District Court's experience with the case may have given it grounds for skepticism about the representations made by APHIS and petitioners. Sometimes "one judicial actor is better positioned than another to decide the issue in question." *Miller v. Fenton*, 474 U.S. 104, 114 (1985). A "district court may have insights not conveyed by the record." *Pierce v. Underwood*, 487 U.S. 552, 560 (1988). In this case, the agency had attempted to deregulate RRA without an EIS in spite of ample evidence of potential environmental harms. And when the court made clear that the agency had violated NEPA, the agency responded by seeking to "'streamline'" the process, *ante*, at 18, submitting a deregulation proposal with Monsanto that suffered from some of the same legal and empirical holes as its initial plan to deregulate. Against that background, the court may have felt it especially prudent to wait for an EIS before concluding that APHIS could manage RRA's threat to the environment.

. . . .

The District Court in this case was put in an "unenviable position." *Ibid.* In front of it was strong evidence that RRA poses a serious threat to the environment and to American business, and that limits on RRA deregulation might not be followed or enforced—and that even if they were, the newly engineered gene might nevertheless spread to other crops. Confronted with those disconcerting submissions, with APHIS's unlawful deregulation decision, with a group of farmers who had staked their livelihoods on APHIS's decision, and with a federal statute that prizes informed decision making on matters that seriously affect the environment, the court did the best it could. In my view, the District Court was well within its discretion to order the remedy that the Court now reverses. Accordingly, I respectfully dissent.

Alliance for Bio-Integrity v. Shalala

116 F. Supp. 2d 166 (2000)

KOLLAR-KOTELLY, DISTRICT JUDGE.

Technological advances have dramatically increased our ability to manipulate our environment, including the foods we consume. One of these advances, recombinant deoxyribonucleic acid (rDNA) technology, has enabled scientists to alter the genetic composition of organisms by mixing genes on the cellular and molecular level in order to create new breeds of plants for human and animal consumption. *See* Pls.' Statement of Material Facts Not in Dispute ¶¶ 1–3 ["Pls.' Stmt."]; Defs.' Statement of Material Facts Not in Dispute ¶¶ 6–7 ["Defs.' Stmt."]. These new breeds may be designed to repel pests, retain their freshness for a longer period of time, or contain more intense flavor and/or nutritional value. *See* Pls.' Stmt. ¶¶ 5–6; Defs.' Stmt. ¶ 8. Much controversy has attended such developments in biotechnology, and in particular the production, sale, and trade of genetically modified organisms and foods. The above-captioned lawsuit represents one articulation of this controversy.

Among Plaintiffs, some fear that these new breeds of genetically modified food could contain unexpected toxins or allergens, and others believe that their religion forbids consumption of foods produced through rDNA technology. *See* Pls.' Cross Mot. for Summ.J. ["Pls.' Mot. Summ.J."], Ex. 2 (Fagan Aff.); Ex. 3 (Lacey Aff.); Ex. 4 (Regal Aff.); Ex. 5 (Speck Aff.), Ex. 6 (Jaworowsky Aff.), Ex. 7 (Kedala Aff.). Plaintiffs, a coalition of groups and individuals including scientists and religious leaders concerned about genetically altered foods, have brought this action to protest the Food and Drug Administration's ("FDA") policy on such foods in general, and in particular on various genetically modified foods that already have entered the marketplace. The parties have filed cross-motions for summary judgment on plaintiffs' multiple claims. Upon careful consideration of the parties' briefs and the entire record, the Court shall grant Defendants' motion as to all counts of Plaintiffs' Complaint.

I. BACKGROUND

On May 29, 1992, the FDA published a "Statement of Policy: Foods Derived From New Plant Varieties" (Statement of Policy). *See* 57 Fed.Reg. 22,984; Pls.' Stmt. ¶ 16; Defs.' Stmt. ¶ 14. In the Statement of Policy, FDA announced that the agency would presume that foods produced through the rDNA process were "generally recognized as safe" (GRAS) under the Federal Food, Drug and Cosmetic Act ("FDCA"), 21 U.S.C. § 321(s), and therefore not subject to regulation as food additives. *See* 57 Fed.Reg. 22,989–91. While FDA recommended that food producers consult with it before marketing rDNA-produced foods, the agency did not mandate such consultation. *See id.* at 22,991. In addition, FDA reserved the right to regulate any particular rDNA-developed food that FDA believed was unsafe on a case-by-case basis, just as FDA would regulate unsafe foods produced through conventional means. *See id.* at 22,990.

The Statement of Policy also indicated that rDNA modification was not a "material fact" under the FDCA, 21 U.S.C. § 321(n), and that therefore labeling of rDNA-produced foods was not necessarily required. *See id.* at 22,991. FDA did not engage in a formal notice-and-comment process on the Statement of Policy, nor did it prepare an Environmental Impact Statement or Environmental Assessment. *See id.* at 23,004–05; Pls.' Stmt. ¶ 23. At least thirty-six foods, genetically altered through rDNA technology, have been marketed since the Statement of Policy was issued. *See* Pls.' Stmt. ¶ 30; Defs.' Stmt. ¶ 21.

Plaintiffs filed a Complaint in this Court challenging the FDA's policy on six different grounds: (1) the Statement was not properly subjected to notice-and-comment procedures; (2) the FDA did not comply with the National Environmental Protection Act (NEPA) by compiling an Environmental Assessment or Environmental Impact Statement; (3) the FDA's presumption that rDNA-developed foods are GRAS and therefore do not require food additive petitions under 21 U.S.C. § 321(s) is arbitrary and capricious; (4) the FDA's decision not to require labeling for rDNA-developed foods is arbitrary and capricious; (5) the FDA's decision not to regulate or require labeling for rDNA-developed foods violates the Free Exercise Clause; and (6) the FDA's decision not to regulate or require labeling for rDNA-developed foods violates the Religious Freedom Restoration Act. *See* Pls.' Second Am.Compl. ¶¶ 129–159. Plaintiffs have also challenged on the third and fourth grounds each of FDA's specific decisions not to regulate 36 individual rDNA-produced products. *See id.* ¶¶ 160–696. The parties have filed cross-motions for summary judgment on all of Plaintiff's claims.

II. DISCUSSION

A litigant is entitled to summary judgment when "there is no genuine issue as to any material fact and the moving party is entitled to judgment as a matter of law." Fed.R.Civ.P. 56(c). Summary judgment is only warranted where "the record, viewed in the light most favorable to the nonmoving party, reveals that there is no genuine issue as to any material fact." *Aka v. Washington Hosp. Ctr.,* 156 F.3d 1284, 1288 (D.C.Cir.1998) (en banc).

A. Subject Matter Jurisdiction

Defendants contend that Court lacks jurisdiction to hear plaintiffs' claims. *See* Defs.' Mot. to Dismiss, or Alternatively for Summ.J. at 15–17 ("Defs.' Mot. Summ.J."). Although Defendants have not presented this argument as a threshold to the Court's consideration of the entire case, raising it instead after developing several other arguments, the Court must treat it as such. *See, e.g., Steel Co. v. Citizens for Better Env't,* 523 U.S. 83, 9495, 118 S. Ct. 1003, 140 L. Ed. 2d 210 (1998) ("The requirement that jurisdiction be established as a threshold matter springs from the nature and limits of the judicial power of the United States and is inflexible and without exception") (internal citation omitted). In particular, Defendants argue that the Statement of Policy functioned as a way for the agency to "set its own enforcement agenda," and therefore, that this enforcement action belongs to agency discretion by Congressional mandate and is not subject to judicial review. *See* Defs.' Mot.Summ.J. at 13. Although the Supreme Court held that *individual* enforcement decisions are not subject to judicial review in *Heckler v. Chaney,* 470 U.S. 821, 831, 105 S. Ct. 1649, 84 L. Ed. 2d 714 (1985), Defendants' attempt to extend this holding to agency decisions not to enforce against a whole *class* has not been accepted by this Circuit. *See Shell Oil Co. v. EPA,* 950 F.2d 741, 764 (D.C.Cir.1991).

The *Chaney* Court reasoned that courts reviewing agency action "need a meaningful standard against which to judge the agency's exercise of discretion." *Chaney,* 470 U.S. at 830, 105 S. Ct. 1649. Individual agency decisions not to enforce a statute "involve a complicated balancing of a number of factors," and courts do not have a meaningful standard with which to evaluate the agency's balancing. *Id.* at 831, 105 S. Ct. 1649. Therefore, these decisions are "committed to agency discretion by law" and are not subject to judicial review. 5 U.S.C. § 701(a)(2). The Court noted that an agency's enforcement discretion may be limited when Congress has "set[] substantive priorities, or . . . otherwise circumscrib[ed] an agency's power to discriminate among issues or cases it will pursue." *Id.* at 833, 105 S. Ct. 1649. When determining if an agency action is reviewable, courts looks to "whether the applicable statutes and regulations are drawn so that a court would have a meaningful standard against which to judge the agency's exercise of discretion." *Nat'l Fed'n of Fed. Employees v. United States,* 905 F.2d 400, 405 (D.C.Cir.1990); *C C Distrib., Inc. v. United States,* 883 F.2d 146, 153 (D.C.Cir.1989).

This Circuit has recognized a distinction between agency decisions not to regulate an entire class of conduct, which are essentially policy choices, and individual nonenforcement decisions. *See Shell Oil Co.,* 950 F.2d at 764. When an agency has employed a formal procedure, such as notice and comment rulemaking, to announce a major policy decision not to regulate certain conduct, courts can use this procedure as "a focal point for judicial review." *Nat'l Treasury Employees Union v. Horner,* 854 F.2d 490, 496 (D.C.Cir. 1988). In the instant case, even without actual notice and comment procedures, the FDA's formal publication of the Statement of Policy provides a focal point for this Court's review of the agency's action. Moreover, this Court has a meaningful standard against which to judge the Statement of Policy. Congress's passage of the various statutes on which Plaintiffs rely here the Administrative Procedure Act, the Federal Food Drug and Cosmetic Act, the National Environmental Protection Act, and the Religious Freedom Restoration Act has limited the FDA's enforcement discretion. Although the Court may not review FDA's policy-laden individual enforcement decisions, the Court has jurisdiction to review whether or not FDA's Statement of Policy comports with Congressional directives.

B. Notice and Comment

Plaintiffs argue that the Statement of Policy should be set aside because it was not subjected to notice and comment proceedings, as required under the Administrative

Procedure Act ("APA"), 5 U.S.C. § 553. *See* Pls.' Mot.Summ.J. at 9. While conceding that the Statement of Policy did not undergo a formal notice and comment process, Defendants maintain that the Statement of Policy is a policy statement or an interpretive rule not subject to notice and comment requirements. *See* Defs.' Opp'n to Pls.' Mot.Summ.J. ["Defs.' Opp'n"] at 2; *see also* 5 U.S.C. § 553(b)(3)(A) (1994) (exempting from notice and comment interpretive rules and general statements of policy). Plaintiffs contend instead that the Statement of Policy is a substantive rule, and that therefore it was improperly exempted from a formal notice and comment process. *See* Pls.' Mot.Summ.J. at 13.

A substantive rule, which must undergo a formal notice-and-comment process, is a rule that "implement[s]" a statute and has "the force and effect of law." *Chrysler Corp. v. Brown*, 441 U.S. 281, 302 n. 31, 99 S. Ct. 1705, 60 L. Ed. 2d 208 (1979). Policy statements, on the other hand, are "statements issued by an agency to advise the public prospectively of the manner in which the agency proposes to exercise a discretionary power." *Id.* Although the distinction between these categories is not entirely clear, in *American Bus. Ass'n v. United States*, 627 F.2d 525 (D.C.Cir.1980), the Court of Appeals articulated a two-part test for determining when an agency action is a policy statement. Policy statements (1) must not impose any new rights or obligations, and (2) must "genuinely leave the agency and its decision-makers free to exercise discretion." *Id.* at 529. In weighing these criteria, "the ultimate issue is the agency's intent to be bound." *Public Citizen v. United States Nuclear Regulatory Comm'n*, 940 F.2d 679, 682 (D.C.Cir.1991). An agency's own characterization of its statement deserves some weight, but it is not dispositive. *See Truckers United for Safety v. Fed'l Highway Admin.*, 1998 WL 151182 (D.C.Cir. 1998). Rather, courts will look to the actual language of the statement. *See Brock v. Cathedral Bluffs Shale Oil Co.*, 796 F.2d 533, 537–38 (D.C.Cir.1986).

By its very name, the Statement of Policy announces itself as a policy statement. More importantly, the plain language of the Statement suggests that it does not have a binding effect. For example, the Statement does not declare that transferred genetic material will be considered GRAS; rather, it announces that "such material is *presumed* to be GRAS." 57 Fed.Reg. 22989 (emphasis added). This presumption of safety is rebuttable, because FDA will "require food additive petitions in cases where safety questions exist sufficient to warrant formal premarket review by FDA to ensure public health protection." *Id.* at 22990. Rebuttable presumptions leave an agency free to exercise its discretion and may therefore properly be announced in policy statements. *See Panhandle Producers v. Econ. Regulatory Admin.*, 822 F.2d 1105, 1110 (D.C.Cir. 1987); *Mada-Luna v. Fitzpatrick*, 813 F.2d 1006, 1013 (9th Cir. 1987) ("To the extent that the directive merely provides guidance to agency officials in exercising their discretionary powers while preserving their flexibility and their opportunity to make individualized determination[s], it constitutes a general statement of policy"); *accord Ryder Truck Lines, Inc. v. United States*, 716 F.2d 1369, 1377 (11th Cir.1983) ("As long as the agency remains free to consider the individual facts in the various cases that arise, then the agency action in question has not established a binding norm.")

In response to the argument that the Policy Statement vests broad discretion with the agency, Plaintiffs contend that the FDA's application of the Statement has given it a "practical effect" that has effectively bound the agency's discretion, as evidenced by the thirty-six genetically engineered foods that are currently on the market and not regulated by the FDA. *See* Pls.' Reply to Defs.' Opp'n ["Pls.' Reply"] at 8–9. Although courts will look to the "agency's actual applications" to determine the nature of an agency statement, such an inquiry occurs "[w]here the language and context of a statement are inconclusive." *Public Citizen*, 940 F.2d at 682. Here, the plain language of the Statement clearly indicates that it is a policy statement that merely creates a presumption and does not ultimately bind the agency's discretion. *See Brock*, 796 F.2d at 537. Given this unambiguous language, this Court need not consider the agency's application of the Statement to determine the Statement's meaning.

Even if, as Plaintiffs argue, FDA has previously used notice-and-comment procedures to determine GRAS status, in the instant case FDA has not determined GRAS status but has rather announced a GRAS presumption. *See* Pls.' Mot. Summ.J. at 9; *Panhandle Producers*, 822 F.2d at 1110 ("This court and others have consistently stated that an agency may announce presumptions through policy statements rather than notice-and-comment rulemaking."). The Statement of Policy creates a rebuttable presumption of GRAS that does not constrain the FDA's ability to exercise its discretion. *See Panhandle Producers*, 822 F.2d at 1110 ("Presumptions, so long as rebuttable, leave such freedom [to exercise the agency's discretion]."). Because the Statement is a policy statement merely announcing a GRAS presumption, the omission of formal notice-and-comment procedures does not violate the Administrative Procedure Act.

C. NEPA

Plaintiffs have also alleged that FDA violated the National Environmental Protection Act (NEPA), 42 U.S.C. § 4321 *et seq.*, by not performing an Environmental Assessment (EA) or an Environmental Impact Statement (EIS) in conjunction with the Statement of Policy. *See* Pl.'s Mot.Summ.J. at 20. NEPA requires "all agencies of the Federal Government . . . [to] include in every recommendation or report on proposals for legislation and other major Federal actions significantly affecting the quality of the human environment, a detailed statement . . . on the environmental impact of the proposed action." 42 U.S.C. § 4332(2)(c)(i).

"Major federal action," as defined in the Code of Federal Regulations, includes actions such as "[a]doption of official policy . . . [a]doption of formal plans . . . [a]doption of programs . . . [and] [a]pproval of specific projects." 40 C.F.R. § 1508.18(b) (1–4). For major federal actions, agencies must either prepare an EIS examining the environmental impact of the proposed action, prepare an EA determining whether or not to prepare an EIS, or claim that the action falls within a Categorical Exclusion, "a category of actions which do not individually or cumulatively have a significant effect on the human environment." 40 C.F.R. § 1508.4 (1999). If the agency is not engaging in a major federal action, NEPA requirements do not apply. *See Macht v. Skinner,* 916 F.2d 13, 16 (D.C.Cir.1990); *see also* 42 U.S.C. § 4332(2)(c) (requiring compliance only for "proposals for legislation and other major federal actions").

In the Statement of Policy, FDA announces that "the activities [FDA] may undertake with respect to foods from new plant varieties . . . will [not] constitute agency action under NEPA." 57 Fed.Reg. 23005. FDA's determination that the Statement is not a major federal action is essentially an interpretation of the meaning of "major federal action" in 42 U.S.C. § 4332(2)(c) and 40 C.F.R. § 1508.18. Agencies enjoy wide discretion in interpreting regulations, and the agency's interpretation will be upheld unless it is arbitrary and capricious. *See United States v. Larionoff,* 431 U.S. 864, 872, 97 S. Ct. 2150, 53 L. Ed. 2d 48 (1977); *Nat'l Trust for Historic Preservation v. Dole,* 828 F.2d 776, 782 (D.C.Cir.1987).

The FDA's determination that the Statement was not a major federal action comports with the holdings of this Circuit, and is therefore neither arbitrary nor capricious. While declaring a rebuttable presumption that foods produced through rDNA technology are GRAS, the FDA has neither made a final determination that any particular food will be allowed into the environment, nor taken any particular regulatory actions that could affect the environment. In order to trigger the NEPA requirement of an EIS, the agency must be prepared to undertake an "'irreversible and irretrievable commitment of resources' to an action that will affect the environment." *Wyoming Outdoor Council v. U.S. Forest Service,* 165 F.3d 43, 49 (D.C.Cir. 1999) (quoting *Mobil Oil Corp. v. FTC,* 562 F.2d 170, 173 (2d Cir.1977)). Because the FDA's presumption does not bind its decision-making authority, it has neither taken nor prepared to take the irreversible action that is necessary to require preparation of an EIS under *Wyoming Outdoor Council. See id.* Evidencing this nonbinding effect is the FDA's 1993 decision to open the labeling issue for further discussion, requesting additional public comment on the possible implementation of a general labeling requirement. 58 Fed. Reg. 25,837 (1993).

Moreover, agency decisions that maintain the substantive status quo do not constitute major federal actions under NEPA. *See Fund for Animals, Inc. v. Thomas,* 127 F.3d 80, 84 (D.C.Cir.1997); *Committee for Auto Responsibility v. Solomon,* 603 F.2d 992, 1002–03 (D.C.Cir. 1979). Defendants maintain correctly that their actions have not altered the status quo because "rDNA modified foods . . . were regulated no differently before the publication of the Policy Statement than they are now." Def.'s Mot.Summ.J. at 44. Because the announcement of a rebuttable presumption of GRAS does not affect the substantive regulatory status quo, it is not a major federal action. *See Fund for Animals,* 127 F.3d at 84.

The Statement of Policy is not only reversible and consistent with the status quo ante; it is also not properly an "agency action." The core of Plaintiff's NEPA claim is that FDA has failed to regulate rDNA-modified foods, and that this failure to act engenders environmental consequences. But NEPA applies only to agency actions, "even if inaction has environmental consequences." *Defenders Wildlife v. Andrus,* 627 F.2d 1238, 1243 (D.C.Cir.1980). The *Defenders of Wildlife* court reasoned that Congress did not intend for agencies to perform environmental studies when the agencies were not acting. *See id.* at 1244. In certain cases, agencies may take action by authorizing private action, but in such cases the government still must undertake some overt act, such as issuing a permit or affirming a substance as GRAS. *See id.*

In the instant case, FDA has not taken an overt action, but instead has merely announced a presumption that certain foods do not require special regulation. This presumption against regulation does not constitute an overt action, and is therefore not subject to NEPA requirements. *See Cross-Sound Ferry Services, Inc. v. ICC,* 934 F.2d 327, 334 (D.C.Cir.1991) (upholding I.C.C. finding that "a conclusion that regulation is not necessary is not a federal action, but is simply a determination not to take action," 6 I.C.C.2d 228, 246 (1989)), *abrogated on other grounds by Steel Co. v. Citizens for a Better Environment,* 523 U.S. 83, 118 S. Ct. 1003, 140 L. Ed. 2d 210 (1998).

In sum, because FDA's Statement of Policy is reversible, maintains the substantive status quo, and takes no overt action, the Statement of Policy does not constitute a major federal action under NEPA. FDA was not required to compile an Environmental Assessment or an Environmental Impact Statement in conjunction with the Statement of Policy, and therefore its failure to do so does not violate NEPA.

D. GRAS Presumption

In their challenge to the FDA's Statement of Policy, Plaintiffs further claim that the Statement of Policy's presumption that rDNA-engineered foods are GRAS violates the GRAS requirements of the Federal Food, Drug, and Cosmetic Act ("FDCA"), 21 U.S.C. § 321(s), and is therefore arbitrary and capricious. *See* Pls.' Mot.Summ.J. at 27; *see also* 5 U.S.C. § 706(2)(A). The FDCA provides that any substance which may "becom[e] a component or otherwise affect[] the characteristics of any food" shall be deemed a food additive. *See* 21 U.S.C. § 321(s). A producer of a food additive must submit a food additive petition to FDA for approval unless FDA determines that the additive is "generally recognized [by qualified experts] . . . as having been adequately shown through scientific procedures . . . to be safe under the conditions of its intended use." *Id.*

In the Statement of Policy, FDA indicated that, under § 321(s),

> it is the intended or expected introduction of a substance into food that makes the substance potentially subject to food additive regulation. Thus, in the case of foods derived from new plant varieties, it is the transferred genetic material and the intended expression product or products that could be subject to food additive regulation, if such material or expression products are not GRAS.

57 Fed.Reg. at 22,990. Accordingly, FDA reasoned that the only substances added to rDNA engineered foods are nucleic acid proteins, generally recognized as not only safe but also necessary for survival. *See id.* ("Nucleic acids are present in the cells of every living organism, including every plant and animal used for food by humans or animals, and do not raise a safety concern as a component of food"). Therefore, FDA concluded that rDNA engineered foods should be presumed to be GRAS unless evidence arises to the contrary. *See id.* at 22,991 ("Ultimately, it is the food producer who is responsible for assuring safety."); *see also* Defs.' Mot.Summ.J. at 18–20. The Statement of Policy does acknowledge, however, that certain genetically modified substances might trigger application of the food additives petitioning process. In that vein, FDA recognized that "the intended expression product in a food could be a protein, carbohydrate, fat or oil, or other substance that differs significantly in structure, function, or composition from substances found currently in food. Such substances may not be GRAS and may require regulation as a food additive." *Id.* at 22,990.

This Court's evaluation of the FDA's interpretation of § 321(s) is framed by *Chevron, U.S.A. v. Natural Resources Defense Council,* 467 U.S. 837, 104 S. Ct. 2778, 81 L. Ed. 2d 694 (1984). Since "'statutory interpretation begins with the language of the statute itself,'" *Butler v. West,* 164 F.3d 634, 639 (D.C.Cir.1999) (quoting *Pennsylvania Dep't of Pub. Welfare v. Davenport,* 495 U.S. 552, 557–58, 110 S. Ct. 2126, 109 L. Ed. 2d 588 (1990)), as a general matter the Court first must determine whether Congress has spoken directly to the issue at hand, a line of analysis that has become known as *Chevron* step one. If, using "traditional tools of statutory construction," *Natural Resources Defense Council, Inc. v. Browner,* 57 F.3d 1122, 1125 (D.C.Cir.1995), the Court answers this inquiry in the affirmative, then "that is the end of the matter; for the court, as well as the agency, must give effect to the unambiguously expressed intent of Congress." *Chevron,* 467 U.S. at 842–43, 104 S. Ct. 2778.

But *Chevron* review also concerns itself with the extent and application of agency discretion in interpreting the statute at issue. In other words, "a reviewing court's inquiry under *Chevron* is rooted in statutory analysis and is focused on discerning the boundaries of Congress' delegation of authority to the agency." *Arent v. Shalala,* 70 F.3d 610, 615 (D.C.Cir.1995). To resolve the issue, "the question for the reviewing court is whether the agency's construction of the statute is faithful to its plain meaning, or, if the statute has no plain meaning, whether the agency's interpretation 'is based on a permissible construction of the statute.'" *Id.* (quoting *Chevron,* 467 U.S. at 843, 104 S.Ct. 2778). If this interpretation is "reasonable and consistent with the statutory scheme and legislative history." *Cleveland v. United States Nuclear Regulatory Comm'n,* 68 F.3d 1361, 1367 (D.C.Cir.1995), then the Court must defer to the agency. This inquiry into the agency's interpretation constitutes *Chevron* step two. *See id.*

When Congress passed the Food Additives Amendment in 1958, it obviously could not account for the late twentieth-century technologies that would permit the genetic modification of food. The "object and policy" of the food additive amendments, *Mova Pharm. Corp. v. Shalala,* 140 F.3d 1060, 1067 (D.C.Cir.1998), is to "require the processor who wants to add a new and unproven additive to accept the responsibility . . . of first proving it to be safe for ingestion by human beings." S.Rep. No. 85-2422, at 2 (1958). The plain language of § 321(s) fosters a broad reading of "food additive" and includes "any substance intended for use in producing, manufacturing, packing, processing, preparing, treating, packaging, transporting, or holding food; and . . . any source of radiation intended for any such use." § 321(s).

Nonetheless, the statute exempts from regulation as additives substances that are "generally recognized . . . to be safe under the conditions of its intended use. . . ." § 321(s). Plaintiffs have not disputed FDA's claim that nucleic acid proteins are generally recognized to be safe. *See* Pls.' Resp. to Defs.' Stmt. ¶ 1. Plaintiffs have argued, however, that significant disagreement exists among scientific experts as to whether or not nucleic acid proteins are generally recognized to be safe when they are used to alter organisms genetically. Having examined the record in this case, the Court cannot say that FDA's decision to accord genetically modified foods a presumption of GRAS status is arbitrary and capricious. "The rationale for deference is particularly strong when the [agency] is evaluating scientific data within its technical expertise." *International Fabricare Institute v. U.S.E.P.A.,* 972 F.2d 384, 389 (D.C.Cir.1992). "[I]n an area characterized by scientific and technological uncertainty[,] . . . this court must proceed with particular caution, avoiding all temptation to direct the agency in a choice between rational alternatives." *Environmental Defense Fund, Inc. v. Costle,* 578 F.2d 337, 339 (D.C.Cir.1978).

To be generally recognized as safe, a substance must meet two criteria: (1) it must have technical evidence of safety, usually in published scientific studies, and (2) this technical evidence must be generally known and accepted in the scientific community. *See* 21 C.F.R. § 170.30(a-b); 62 Fed.Reg. 18940. Although unanimity among scientists is not required, "a severe conflict among experts . . . precludes a finding of general recognition." 62 Fed.Reg. at 18939. Plaintiffs have produced several documents showing significant disagreements among scientific experts. However, this Court's review is confined to the record before the agency at the time it made its decision. *IMS, P.C. v. Alvarez,* 129 F.3d 618, 623 (D.C.Cir.1997); *Walter O. Boswell Mem'l Hosp. v. Heckler,* 749 F.2d 788, 792 (D.C.Cir.1984) ("If a court is to review an agency's record fairly, it should have before it neither more nor less information than did the agency when it made its decision."). Therefore, the affidavits submitted by Plaintiffs that are not part of the administrative record will not be considered.

Nonetheless, Plaintiffs, pointing to the critical comments of lower-level FDA officials insist that even the administrative record reveals a lack of general recognition of safety among qualified experts. *See* Pl's Mot. at 35. However, lower-level comments on a regulation "do[] not invalidate the agency's subsequent application and interpretation of its own regulation." *San Luis Obispo Mothers for Peace v. U.S. Nuclear Regulatory Comm'n,* 789 F.2d 26, 33 (D.C.Cir.1986). Moreover, pointing to a 44,000-page record, the FDA notes that Plaintiffs have chosen to highlight a selected few comments of FDA employees, which were ultimately addressed in the agency's final Policy Statement. As a result, Plaintiffs have failed to convince the Court that the GRAS presumption is inconsistent with the statutory requirements.

E. Labeling

Plaintiffs have also challenged the Statement of Policy's failure to require labeling for genetically engineered foods, for which FDA relied on the presumption that most genetically modified food ingredients would be GRAS. *See* Pl.'s Mot. at 39. Plaintiffs claim that FDA should have considered the widespread consumer interest in having genetically engineered foods labeled, as well as the special concerns of religious groups and persons with allergies in having these foods labeled. *See* Pl.'s Mot. at 51–54.

The FDCA, 21 U.S.C. § 321(n), grants the FDA limited authority to require labeling. In general, foods shall be deemed misbranded if their labeling "fails to reveal facts . . . material with respect to consequences which may result from the use of the article to which the labeling . . . relates under the conditions of use prescribed in the labeling . . . or under such conditions of use as are customary or usual." 21 U.S.C. § 321(n). Plaintiffs challenge the FDA's interpretation of the term "material." Thus, the question is again one of statutory interpretation. As is apparent from the statutory language, Congress has not squarely addressed whether materiality pertains only to safety concerns or whether it also includes consumer interest. Accordingly, interpretation of the § 321(n)'s broad language is left to the agency. *Cf. Community Nutrition Inst. v. Block*, 749 F.2d 50, 54 (D.C.Cir.1984) ("[T]he relatively unspecific nature of the labeling standard which Congress has prescribed . . . suggests that this is an area in which courts must give great deference to the Secretary [of Agriculture]'s judgments.").

Because Congress has not spoken directly to the issue, this Court must determine whether the agency's interpretation of the statute is reasonable. *See Chevron*, 467 U.S. at 864, 104 S. Ct. 2778. Agency interpretations receive substantial deference, particularly when the agency is interpreting a statute that it is charged with administering. *See Rust v. Sullivan*, 500 U.S. 173, 184, 111 S. Ct. 1759, 114 L. Ed. 2d 233 (1991). Even if the agency's interpretation is not "the best or most natural by grammatical or other standards," if the interpretation is reasonable, then it is entitled to deference. *Pauley v. BethEnergy Mines, Inc.*, 501 U.S. 680, 702, 111 S. Ct. 2524, 115 L. Ed. 2d 604 (1991).

The FDA takes the position that no "material change," under § 321(n), has occurred in the rDNA derived foods at issue here. Absent unique risks to consumer health or uniform changes to food derived through rDNA technology, the FDA does not read § 321(n) to authorize an agency imposed food labeling requirement. More specifically irksome to the Plaintiffs, the FDA does not read § 321(n) to authorize labeling requirements solely because of consumer demand. The FDA's exclusion of consumer interest from the factors which determine whether a change is "material" constitutes a reasonable interpretation of the statute. Moreover, it is doubtful whether the FDA would even have the power under the FDCA to require labeling in a situation where the sole justification for such a requirement is consumer demand. *See Stauber v. Shalala,* 895 F. Supp. 1178, 1193 (W.D.Wis.1995) ("In the absence of evidence of a material difference between [milk from cows treated with a synthetic hormone] and ordinary milk, the use of consumer demand as the rationale for labeling would violate the Food, Drug, and Cosmetic Act.").

Plaintiffs fail to understand the limitation on the FDA's power to consider consumer demand when making labeling decisions because they fail to recognize that the determination that a product differs materially from the type of product it purports to be is a factual predicate to the requirement of labeling. Only once materiality has been established may the FDA consider consumer opinion to determine whether a label is required to disclose a material fact. Thus, "if there is a [material] difference, and consumers would likely want to know about the difference, then labeling is appropriate. If, however, the product does not differ in any significant way from what it purports to be, then it would be misbranding to label the product as different, even if consumers misperceived the product as different." *Id.* The FDA has already determined that, in general, rDNA modification does not "materially" alter foods, and as discussed in Section II.E, *supra,* this determination is entitled to deference. Given these facts, the FDA lacks a basis upon which it can legally mandate labeling, regardless of the level of consumer demand.

Plaintiffs also contend that the *process* of genetic modification is a "material fact" under § 321(n) which mandates special labeling, implying that there are new risks posed to the consumer. However, the FDA has determined that foods produced through rDNA techniques do not "present any different or greater safety concern than foods developed by traditional plant breeding," and concluded that labeling was not warranted. 57 Fed.Reg. at 22991. That determination, unless irrational, is entitled to deference. *See Pauley v. BethEnergy Mines, Inc.,* 501 U.S. 680, 702, 111 S. Ct. 2524, 115 L. Ed. 2d 604 (1991). Accordingly, there is little basis upon which this Court could find that the FDA's interpretation of § 321(n) is arbitrary and capricious.

. . . .

CONCLUSION

For the foregoing reasons, the Court determines that Defendant's 1992 Policy Statement did not violate the Administrative Procedures Act, the National Environmental Policy Act, or the procedures mandated by the FDCA and FDA regulations. Furthermore, Defendant was not arbitrary and capricious in its finding that genetically modified foods need not be labeled because they do not differ "materially" from non-modified foods under 21 U.S.C. § 321(n). Finally, the Court finds that Defendant's Policy Statement does not violate the First Amendment Free Exercise Clause or RFRA, 42 U.S.C. § 2000bb-1(b). Hence, the Court denies Plaintiffs' motion for summary judgment and grants Defendant's motion for same. An appropriate order accompanies this memorandum opinion.

Notes

1. Note the dissent's equity-based argument as to why injunction is warranted. Is the dissent right that the majority disregards evidence of potential harm to crops and the environment?

2. Consider the following: Ten companies control most of the seed supply, and three companies trade most of it globally.[2] Consider also that U.N. reports concluded that biotechnology does not constitute a solution to poverty.[3] What legal framework(s) would you apply to solve the issue of food justice in America today? Would you keep our approach or would you advocate for a new model?

3. See Tempe Smith, *Going to Seed?: Using Monsanto as a Case Study to Examine the Patent and Antitrust, Implications of the Sale and Use of Genetically Modified Seeds*, 61 ALA. L. REV. 629, 632 (2010) (discussing the patent and antitrust issues surrounding seed company's prohibition of "saving seeds that are a natural byproduct of their harvest for use in subsequent years").

4. For a discussion on differing approaches between the E.U. and the United States, see Jamie E. Jorg Spence, Note, *Right to Know: A Diet of the Future Presently Upon Us*, 39 VAL. U. L. REV. 1009, 1023–24 (2005) ("The public perception of GM foods, like that of the scientific community, is certainly not uniform, especially across the Atlantic. In Europe the public sentiment has been quite negative. Between 1992 and 1996, consumers in Europe formed activist groups that protested the new foods, and by fall of 1999, successfully convinced the UK and EU regulatory agencies to place moratoriums on the growth of these products and to stifle their import. Furthermore, Europeans appear to be becoming less supportive of biotechnology in general."); J.M. Migai Akech, *Developing Countries at Crossroads: Aid, Public Participation, and the Regulation of Trade in Genetically Modified Foods*, 29 FORDHAM INT'L L.J. 265, 275–76 (2006) ("Unlike the United States, which encourages self-regulation among GM-producing firms, the EU has adopted a regulatory model, which requires prior governmental approval before GMOs can be released into the environment. Over the last decade or so, while the United States . . . has approved some one hundred GMOs for release into the environment, the EU has only approved fourteen GMOs. The EU's arduous approval process is thus being blamed for impeding trade in GM foods. By contrast, the U.S. approach is being extolled

---

2. *See* ETC GROUP, WHO OWNS NATURE?: CORPORATE POWER AND THE FINAL FRONTIER IN THE COMMODIFICATION OF LIFE (Nov. 2008), http://www.etcgroup.org/sites/www.etcgroup.org/files /publication/707/01/etc_won_report_final_color.pdf (reporting the world's top 10 seed companies control a total of 67% of the global seed market); ETC GROUP, WHO WILL CONTROL THE GREEN ECONOMY? (Dec. 2011), http://www.etcgroup.org/files/publication/pdf_file/ETC_wwctge_4web _Dec2011.pdf (stating that "[j]ust three companies control more than half (53%) of the global commercial market for seed").

3. *See* UNITED NATIONS, THE BIOTECHNOLOGY PROMISE: CAPACITY-BUILDING FOR PARTICIPATION OF DEVELOPING COUNTRIES IN THE BIOECONOMY 2 (2004), http://unctad.org/en/docs/iteipc20042 _en.pdf (reporting that the goals of biotechnology have not been met in developing countries and poverty still effects a huge portion of the human population).

since its liberal GMO approval process 'leads to increased profits for corporations, and, in turn, funds future research and development projects for GMO products'").

5. Beyond Seeds: With the approval of the first genetically modified salmon, what are the consequences for the food industry in the United States? Should the rules be different for plant GMOs vs. animal GMOs? Should the substantial equivalence test be abandoned when it comes to animals? If so, what should replace it?

C. The Rural Sector

After Reconstruction, land ownership became the main source of income and means of upward mobility for African Americans. A growing class of black farmers flourished during that time. Unfortunately, as the Ku Klux Klan and other terror organizations established their strongholds, land ownership became more precarious. Many farmers and land owners lost their property as a result of intimidation and other terror tactics. Furthermore, persistent discrimination from the government and a move toward subsidies for big farming helped to further shrink the class of the black farmers in the United States. *Pigford*, the law suit below, was filed in the 1990s as a class action suit to vindicate the claims of thousands of black farmers who lost their farms decades ago as a result of discrimination by the USDA. This contributed in part to depletion and brain drain in rural areas, with many migrating to urban areas to make a living. As industry also abandoned these areas, the rate of poverty consistently increased.[4] See below for *Pigford* (the Black Farmers Class Action) and its progeny.[5]

Pigford v. Glickman
185 F.R.D. 82 (D.D.C. 1999)

PAUL L. FRIEDMAN, DISTRICT JUDGE.

Forty acres and a mule. As the Civil War drew to a close, the United States government created the Freedmen's Bureau to provide assistance to former slaves. The government promised to sell or lease to farmers parcels of unoccupied land and land that had been confiscated by the Union during the war, and it promised the loan of a federal government mule to plow that land. Some African Americans took advantage of these programs and either bought or leased parcels of land. During Reconstruction, however, President Andrew Johnson vetoed a bill to enlarge the powers and activities of the Freedmen's Bureau, and he reversed many of the policies of the Bureau. Much of the promised land that had been leased to African American farmers was taken away and returned to Confederate loyalists. For most African

---

4. *Distancing Rural Poverty*, 13 GEO. J. POVERTY LAW & POL'Y 3; *Cities Inside Out: Race, Poverty, and Exclusion at the Urban Fringe*, 55 UCLA L. REV. 1095.

5. *From Reconstruction to Deconstruction: Undermining Black Landownership, Political Independence, and Community Through Partition Sales of Tenancies in Common*, 95 NW. U. L. REV. 505.

Americans, the promise of forty acres and a mule was never kept. Despite the government's failure to live up to its promise, African American farmers persevered. By 1910, they had acquired approximately 16 million acres of farmland. By 1920, there were 925,000 African American farms in the United States.

On May 15, 1862, as Congress was debating the issue of providing land for freed former slaves, the United States Department of Agriculture was created. The statute creating the Department charged it with acquiring and preserving "all information concerning agriculture" and collecting "new and valuable seeds and plants; to test, by cultivation, the value of such of them as may require such tests; to propagate such as may be worthy of propagation, and to distribute them among agriculturists." An Act to establish a Department of Agriculture, ch. 71, 12 Stat. 387 (1862). In 1889, the Department of Agriculture achieved full cabinet department status. Today, it has an annual budget of $67.5 billion and administers farm loans and guarantees worth $2.8 billion.

As the Department of Agriculture has grown, the number of African American farmers has declined dramatically. Today, there are fewer than 18,000 African American farms in the United States, and African American farmers now own less then 3 million acres of land. The United States Department of Agriculture and the county commissioners to whom it has delegated so much power bear much of the responsibility for this dramatic decline. The Department itself has recognized that there has always been a disconnect between what President Lincoln envisioned as "the people's department," serving all of the people, and the widespread belief that the Department is "the last plantation," a department "perceived as playing a key role in what some see as a conspiracy to force minority and disadvantaged farmers off their land through discriminatory loan practices." *See* Pls' Motion for Class Certification. Exh. B, Civil Rights at the United States Department of Agriculture: A Report by the Civil Rights Action Team (Feb.1997) ("CRAT Report") at 2.

For decades, despite its promise that "no person in the United States shall, on the ground of race, color, or national origin, be excluded from participation in, be denied the benefits of, or be otherwise subjected to discrimination under any program or activity of an applicant or recipient receiving Federal financial assistance from the Department of Agriculture," 7 C.F.R. § 15.1, the Department of Agriculture and the county commissioners discriminated against African American farmers when they denied, delayed or otherwise frustrated the applications of those farmers for farm loans and other credit and benefit programs. Further compounding the problem, in 1983 the Department of Agriculture disbanded its Office of Civil Rights and stopped responding to claims of discrimination. These events were the culmination of a string of broken promises that had been made to African American farmers for well over a century.

It is difficult to resist the impulse to try to undo all the broken promises and years of discrimination that have led to the precipitous decline in the number of African

American farmers in the United States. The Court has before it a proposed settlement of a class action lawsuit that will not undo all that has been done. Despite that fact, however, the Court finds that the settlement is a fair resolution of the claims brought in this case and a good first step towards assuring that the kind of discrimination that has been visited on African American farmers since Reconstruction will not continue into the next century. The Court therefore will approve the settlement.

I. BACKGROUND OF THE CASE

The plaintiffs in this case allege (1) that the United States Department of Agriculture ("USDA") willfully discriminated against them and other similarly situated African American farmers on the basis of their race when it denied their applications for credit and/or benefit programs or delayed processing their applications, and (2) that when plaintiffs filed complaints of discrimination with the USDA, the USDA failed properly to investigate and resolve those complaints. *See* Seventh Amended Complaint at 4–5. Plaintiffs allege that defendant's actions violated a number of statutes and the Constitution, but both sides agree that this case essentially is brought under the Equal Credit Opportunity Act, 15 U.S.C. § 1691 ("ECOA"). *See* Transcript of Hearing of March 2, 1999, at 19.

The Court certified this case as a class action on October 9, 1998, and preliminarily approved a Consent Decree on January 5, 1999. After a hearing held on March 2, 1999, the parties made some revisions to the proposed Consent Decree and filed a revised proposed Consent Decree with the Court on March 19, 1999. The Court now concludes that the revised proposed Consent Decree is fair, adequate and reasonable.

A. Factual Background

Farming is a hard way to make a living. Small farmers operate at the whim of conditions completely beyond their control; weather conditions from year to year and marketable prices of crops to a large extent determine whether an individual farmer will make a profit, barely break even or lose money. As a result, many farmers depend heavily on the credit and benefit programs of the United States Department of Agriculture to take them from one year to the next For instance, if an early freeze kills three-quarters of a farmer's crop one year, he may not have sufficient resources to buy seeds to plant in the following season. Or if a farmer needs to modernize his operations and buy a new grain harvester in order to make his operations profitable, he often cannot afford to buy the harvester without an extension of credit. Because of the seasonal nature of farming, it also is of utmost importance that credit and benefit applications be processed quickly or the farmer may lose all or most of his anticipated income for an entire year. It does a farmer no good to receive a loan to buy seeds after the planting season has passed.

The USDA's credit and benefit programs are federally funded programs, but the decisions to approve or deny applications for credit or benefits are made locally at the county level. In virtually every farming community, local farmers and ranchers elect three to five-member county committees. The county committee is responsible for approving or denying farm credit and benefit applications, as well as for appointing a county executive who is supposed to provide farmers with help in completing their credit and benefit applications. The county executive also makes recommendations to the county committee regarding which applications should be approved. The salaries of the county committee members and the county executives are paid from federal funds, but they are not considered federal government employees. Similarly, while federal money is used to fund the credit and benefit programs, the elected county officials, not federal officials, make the decision as to who gets the federal money and who does not.

The county committees do not represent the racial diversity of the communities they serve. In 1996, in the Southeast Region, the region in the United States with the most African American farmers, just barely over 1% of the county commissioners were African American (28 out of a total of 2469). *See* CRAT Report at 19. In the Southwest region, only 0.3% of the county commissioners were African American. In two of the remaining three regions, there was not a single African American county commissioner. Nationwide, only 37 county commissioners were African American out of a total of 8147 commissioners—approximately 0.45%. *Id.*

Throughout the country, African American farmers complain that county commissioners have discriminated against them for decades, denying their applications, delaying the processing of their applications or approving them for insufficient amounts or with restrictive conditions. In several southeastern states, for instance, it took three times as long on average to process the application of an African American farmer as it did to process the application of a white farmer. CRAT Report at 21. Mr. Alvin E. Steppes is an African American farmer from Lee County, Arkansas. In 1986. Mr. Steppes applied to the Farmers Home Administration ("FmHA") for an operating loan. Mr. Steppes fully complied with the application requirements, but his application was denied. As a result, Mr. Steppes had insufficient resources to plant crops, he could not buy fertilizer and crop treatment for the crops he did plant, and he ended up losing his farm. *See* Seventh Amended Complaint at ¶ 14.

Mr. Calvin Brown from Brunswick County, Virginia applied in January 1984 for an operating loan for that planting season. When he inquired later that month about the status of his loan application, a FmHA county supervisor told him that the application was being processed. The next month, the same FmHA county supervisor told him that there was no record of his application ever having been filed and that Mr. Brown had to reapply. By the time Mr. Brown finally received his loan in May or June 1984, the planting season was over, and the loan was virtually useless to him. In addition, the funds were placed in a "supervised" bank account, which required him to obtain the signature of a county supervisor before withdrawing any funds, a requirement frequently required of African American farmers but not routinely imposed on white farmers. *See* Seventh Amended Complaint at ¶ 11.

In 1994, the entire county of Greene County, Alabama where Mr. George Hall farmed was declared eligible for disaster payments on 1994 crop losses. Every single application for disaster payments was approved by the Greene County Committee except Mr. Hall's application for four of his crops. *See* Seventh Amended Complaint at ¶ 5. Mr. James Beverly of Nottaway County, Virginia was a successful small farmer before going to FmHA. To build on his success, in 1981 he began working with his FmHA office to develop a farm plan to expand and modernize his swine herd operations. The plan called for loans to purchase breeding stock and equipment as well as farrowing houses that were necessary for the breeding operations. FmHA approved his loans to buy breeding stock and equipment, and he was told that the loan for farrowing houses would be approved. After he already had bought the livestock and the equipment, his application for a loan to build the farrowing houses was denied. The livestock and equipment were useless to him without the farrowing houses. Mr. Beverly ended up having to sell his property to settle his debt to the FmHA. *See id.* at ¶ 12.

The denial of credit and benefits has had a devastating impact on African American farmers. According to the Census of Agriculture, the number of African American farmers has declined from 925,000 in 1920 to approximately 18,000 in 1992. CRAT Report at 14. The farms of many African American farmers were foreclosed upon, and they were forced out of farming. Those who managed to stay in farming often were subject to humiliation and degradation at the hands of the county commissioners and were forced to stand by powerless, as white farmers received preferential treatment. As one of plaintiffs' lawyers, Mr. J.L. Chestnut, aptly put it, African American farmers "learned the hard way that though the rules and the law may be colorblind, people are not." Transcript of Hearing of March 2, 1999, at 173.

Any farmer who believed that his application to those programs was denied on the basis of his race or for other discriminatory reasons theoretically had open to him a process for filing a civil rights complaint either with the Secretary of Agriculture or with the Office of Civil Rights Enforcement and Adjudication ("OCREA") at USDA. USDA regulations set forth a detailed process by which these complaints were supposed to be investigated and conciliated, and ultimately a farmer who was unhappy with the outcome was entitled to sue in federal court under ECOA. *See Pigford v. Glickman,* 182 F.R.D. 341, 342–44 (D.D.C.1998). All the evidence developed by the USDA and presented to the Court indicates, however, that this system was functionally nonexistent for well over a decade. In 1983, OCREA essentially was dismantled and complaints that were filed were never processed, investigated or forwarded to the appropriate agencies for conciliation. As a result, farmers who filed complaints of discrimination never received a response, or if they did receive a response it was a cursory denial of relief. In some cases, OCREA staff simply threw discrimination complaints in the trash without ever responding to or investigating them. In other cases, even if there was a finding of discrimination, the farmer never received any relief.

In December of 1996, Secretary of Agriculture Dan Glickman appointed a Civil Rights Action Team ("CRAT") to "take a hard look at the issues and make strong recommendations for change." *See* CRAT Report at 3. In February of 1997, CRAT concluded that "[m]inority farmers have lost significant amounts of land and potential farm income as a result of discrimination by FSA [Farm Services Agency] programs and the programs of its predecessor agencies, ASCS [Agricultural Stabilization and Conservation Service] and FmHA [Farmers Home Administration]. . . . The process for resolving complaints has failed. Minority and limited-resource customers believe USDA has not acted in good faith on the complaints. Appeals are too often delayed and for too long. Favorable decisions are too often reversed." *Id.* at 30–31.

Also in February of 1997, the Office of the Inspector General of the USDA issued a report to Secretary Glickman stating that the USDA had a backlog of complaints of discrimination that had never been processed, investigated or resolved. *See* Pls' Motion for Class Certification, Exh. A (Evaluation Report for the Secretary on Civil Rights Issues). The Report found that immediate action was needed to clear the backlog of complaints, that the "program discrimination complaint process at [the Farm Services Agency] lacks integrity, direction, and accountability," *id.* at 6, and that "[s]taffing problems, obsolete procedures, and little direction from management have resulted in a climate of disorder within the civil rights staff at FSA." *Id.* at 1.

The acknowledgment by the USDA that the discrimination complaints had never been processed, however, came too late for many African American farmers. ECOA has a two-year statute of limitations. *See* 15 U.S.C. § 1691e(f). If the underlying discrimination alleged by the farmer had taken place more than two years prior to the filing of an action in federal court, the government would raise a statute of limitations defense to bar the farmer's claims. For instance, some class members in this case had filed their complaints of discrimination with the USDA in 1983 for acts of discrimination that allegedly occurred in 1982 or 1983. If the farmer waited for the USDA to respond to his discrimination complaint and did not file an action in court until he discovered in 1997 that the USDA had stopped responding to discrimination complaints, the government would argue that any claim under ECOA was barred by the statute of limitations.

In 1998, Congress provided relief to plaintiffs with respect to the statute of limitations problem by passing legislation that tolls the statute of limitations for all those who filed discrimination complaints with the Department of Agriculture before July 1, 1997, and who allege discrimination at any time during the period beginning on January 1, 1981 and ending on or before December 31, 1996. *See* Agricultural, Rural Development, Food and Drug Administration, and Related Agencies Appropriations Act, 1999, Pub.L. No. 105-277, § 741, 112 Stat. 2681 (codified at 7 U.S.C. § 2297, Notes).

B. Procedural Background

. . . .

On October 9, 1998, the Court granted the motion for class certification in *Pigford*. The Court also ordered the parties jointly to file a draft notice to class members by October 30, 1998. At a status hearing on October 13, 1998, plaintiffs informed the Court that Congress had passed a bill that would toll the statute of limitations for African American farmers who had filed complaints of discrimination with the USDA and that they would be withdrawing their motion for partial summary judgment on the statute of limitations issue as soon as the President signed the bill into law because that motion then would be unnecessary. On October 21, 1998, President Clinton signed into law the bill tolling the statute of limitations that had been enacted by Congress. *See* Agricultural, Rural Development, Food and Drug Administration, and Related Agencies Appropriations Act, 1999, Pub.L. No. 105-277, § 741, 112 Stat. 2681 (codified at 7 U.S.C. § 2297, Notes). The waiver of the statute of limitations provides that "a civil action to obtain relief with respect to the discrimination alleged in an eligible complaint, if commenced not later than 2 years after the enactment of this Act, shall not be barred by any statute of limitations." An "eligible complaint" is defined, in relevant part, as "a nonemployment related complaint that was filed with the Department of Agriculture before July 1, 1997 and alleges discrimination at any time during the period beginning on January 1, 1981 and ending December 31, 1996" in violation of ECOA or "in the administration of a commodity program or a disaster assistance program." *See id.*

Faced with a February 1, 1999, trial date, the parties continued their efforts at mediation with the help of Mr. Lewis. At some point after the March 5, 1998 status hearing, the focus of negotiations shifted from case-by-case analysis to structuring a global resolution of the claims of all class members. By December 1998, the parties had informed the Court that they were very close to agreeing upon a global settlement of plaintiffs' claims in both *Pigford* and *Brewington*. Finally, on January 5, 1999, the parties filed with the Court (1) a motion to consolidate the two cases, (2) a motion to alter the definition of the class certified in *Pigford* to include members of the *Brewington* action and to certify the class pursuant to Rule 23(b)(3) of the Federal Rules of Civil Procedure, (3) a motion for preliminary approval of a proposed Consent Decree, and (4) a notice to class members. The Court consolidated the two cases, preliminarily approved the Consent Decree, approved the notice to class members, notified class members of their right to file written objections by February 15, 1999, and scheduled a fairness hearing for March 2, 1999.

Within ten days after the preliminary approval of the Consent Decree, the facilitator mailed a copy of the Notice of Class Certification and Proposed Class Settlement to all then-known members of the class.

. . . .

The USDA exerted efforts to obtain the assistance of community based organizations, including those organizations that focus on African American and/or agricultural issues, in communicating to class members and potential class members the fact that the Court had preliminarily approved the Consent Decree and the time and place of the fairness hearing. Def's Memorandum in Support of Consent Decree (Declaration of David H. Harris). USDA officials also were notified that, to the extent possible, they had an obligation to communicate to class members information about the Consent Decree and the fairness hearing. The Court posted a copy of the proposed Consent Decree and the Notice of Class Certification on the Internet Website of the United States District Court for the District of Columbia. Finally, class counsel held meetings in counties throughout the country, particularly in the South, to notify farmers of the settlement, the process for filing a claim package and the time, place and purpose of the fairness hearing.

. . . .

The Court conducted a fairness hearing on March 2, 1999, which lasted an entire day. The Court allocated time for all objectors who previously had filed written objections to the Consent Decree and also allocated time at the end of the day for others who wished to express their views. *See* Order of February 25, 1999. The Court provided time for class counsel and counsel for the government to explain the proposed Consent Decree and to discuss their view of its fairness. The Court heard from representatives of eight organizations that had filed written objections, six individuals who had filed written objections and ten individuals who had not filed written objections. The Court also heard from class counsel, counsel for the government and the mediator.

After the hearing, the Court sent a letter to the parties summarizing some of the objections that had been raised at the hearing and suggesting changes to the proposed Consent Decree that might alleviate some of the concerns raised. The Court indicated that it would not issue a final ruling on the fairness of the proposed Consent Decree until March 19, 1999, in the event that the parties wanted to file a revised proposed Consent Decree addressing the concerns raised at the hearing and by the Court. By letter of March 19, 1999, the parties transmitted to the Court a revised proposed Consent Decree which includes those changes or clarifications that the parties believed they could make to the proposed Consent Decree without fundamentally altering the framework and basis for their agreement. The Court posted the revised Consent Decree to the Court's Internet Website and issued an order granting any objector leave to file any comments with respect to the revisions to the proposed Consent Decree by March 29, 1999. The revised proposed Consent Decree now is before the Court to determine whether it is fair, reasonable and adequate.

II. CLASS CERTIFICATION

. . . By Order of January 5, 1999, upon motion of the parties, the Court vacated [a previous] Order certifying the class and certified a new class pursuant to Rule 23(b)(3) of the Federal Rules of Civil Procedure. The newly certified class is defined as:

> All African American farmers who (1) farmed, or attempted to farm, between January 1, 1981 and December 31, 1996; (2) applied to the United States Department of Agriculture (USDA) during that time period for participation in a federal farm credit or benefit program and who believed that they were discriminated against on the basis of race in USDA's response to that

application; and (3) filed a discrimination complaint on or before July 1, 1997, regarding USDA's treatment of such farm credit or benefit application.

Order of January 5, 1999.

There are three changes to the substantive definition of the class. The first change relates to the time frame within which a class member is required to have filed his or her discrimination complaint with the USDA . . . .

The definition of the class certified by Order of January 5, 1999, modifies the class definition so that the filing date is consistent with the recently-enacted legislation tolling the statute of limitations. *See* Agricultural, Rural Development, Food and Drug Administration, and Related Agencies Appropriations Act, 1999, Pub.L. No. 105-277, § 741, 112 Stat. 2681 (codified at 7 U.S.C. § 2297, Notes). The legislation specifies that in order to toll the statute of limitations, a farmer must have filed his complaint of discrimination with the USDA before July 1, 1997, and the new class definition includes the same cut-off date . . . .

The second change also involves timing issues. The original class definition specified that class members must have farmed between January 1, 1983, and February 21, 1997, and applied for a credit or benefit program during that same time period. The definition of the class certified by Order of January 5, 1999, requires class members to have farmed or attempted to farm between January 1, 1981, and December 31, 1996, and to have applied for a credit or benefit program during that time period. As with the changed discrimination complaint filing dates, this change in class definition is consistent with the recently-enacted legislation tolling the statute of limitations. *See* Agricultural, Rural Development, Food and Drug Administration, and Related Agencies Appropriations Act, 1999, Pub.L. No. 105-277, § 741, 112 Stat. 2681 (codified at 7 U.S.C. § 2297, Notes).

The third change relates to the way in which a class member's complaint of discrimination was transmitted to the USDA. Under the original class definition, a class member must have filed a "written" complaint of discrimination with the USDA. The revised class definition provides that the class member must have "filed a discrimination complaint," and under the terms of the proposed Consent Decree, class members who have participated in "listening sessions" or have complained to members of Congress in certain case are deemed to have "filed" a discrimination complaint. *See* Consent Decree at ¶ 1(h). None of the substantive changes to the class definition in any way affects the Court's analysis or conclusion that the case properly is certified as a class action. *See Pigford v. Glickman,* 182 F.R.D. at 344–45.

The primary difference between the class certified by the Court on October 9, 1998 and the class certified by the Court on January 5, 1999, is more procedural than substantive: the former was certified pursuant to Rule 23(b)(2) of the Federal Rules of Civil Procedure for purposes of determining whether the USDA is liable to class members and the latter was certified for all purposes pursuant to Rule 23(b)(3).

Rule 23 provides that all class members in a Rule 23(b)(3) class action are entitled to notice and an opportunity to exclude themselves from — or "opt out" of — the class and pursue individual remedies. *See* Rule 23(c)(2), Fed.R.Civ.P. The Rule contains no explicit opt-out provision with respect to a class certified pursuant to Rule 23(b)(1) or Rule 23(b)(2), although a court may have discretion to permit class members to opt out of the class in (b)(1) and (b)(2) actions. *See Eubanks v. Billington,* 110 F.3d at 92–95. The parties in this case agreed that it was more appropriate — and fairer to members of the class — to ask the Court to certify the class under Rule 23(b)(3) for all purposes, particularly since the proposed settlement involves primarily monetary relief. *See id.* at 95. The decision to certify the class pursuant to Rule 23(b)(3) was made largely in order to allow class members to opt out of the class if they wanted to pursue their remedies individually either before the USDA or by separate court action.

The Court already has determined that a class exists and that the class meets the four criteria of Rule 23(a) of the Federal Rules of Civil Procedure. *See Pigford v. Glickman,* 182 F.R.D. at 346–50. Because the Court has certified the class under Rule 23(b)(3) of the Federal Rules of Civil Procedure, it also must ensure that the separate and additional requirements of (b)(3) are satisfied before approving the proposed settlement. *See Amchem Products, Inc. v. Windsor,* 521 U.S. 591, 622, 117 S. Ct. 2231, 138 L.Ed.2d 689 (1997) (court's fairness analysis for settlement purposes under Rule 23(e) cannot substitute for determination whether class is appropriately certified in the first place); *Thomas v. Albright,* 139 F.3d 227, 234 (D.C.Cir.) (requirements of predominance and superiority in subsection (b)(3) are additional to requirements of subsection (a) which apply to all class actions), *cert. denied,* 525 U.S. 1033, 119 S.Ct. 576, 142 L.Ed.2d 480 (1998).

Rule 23(b)(3) requires the Court to find (1) that questions of law or fact common to members of the class predominate over questions affecting only individual members, and (2) that a class action is "superior to other available methods for the fair and efficient adjudication of the controversy." Rule 23(b)(3), Fed.R.Civ.P. It is designed to cover cases in which a class action would promote "'uniformity of decision as to persons similarly situated, without sacrificing procedural fairness or bringing about other undesirable results.' The Advisory Committee had dominantly in mind vindication of 'the right of groups of people who individually would be without effective strength to bring their opponents into court at all.'" *Amchem Products, Inc. v. Windsor,* 521 U.S. at 615, 617, 117 S.Ct. 2231 (quoting Rule 23, Fed.R.Civ.P., Adv.Comm. Notes). This is just such a case.

The ultimate settlement of this action envisions the creation of a mechanism on a class-wide basis that will then be utilized to resolve the individual claims of class members outside the traditional litigation process, most of them (Track A) in a rather formulaic way. Most members of the class lack documentation of the allegedly discriminatory transactions at issue. Without any documentation of those transactions, it would be difficult if not impossible for an individual farmer to prevail in a suit in federal court under a traditional preponderance of the evidence standard. The parties acknowledge, however, that it is not the fault of class members that they lack records. Since class members' lack of documentation is at least in part attributable to the passage of time which has been exacerbated by the USDA's failure to timely process complaints of discrimination, there is a common issue of whether and how best to provide relief to class members who lack documentation, and that common issue "predominate[s] over any questions affecting only individual members." *See* Rule 23(b)(3), Fed.R.Civ.P. This class action and its settlement as proposed in the Consent Decree provide a mechanism to address that common issue. *See Amchem Products, Inc. v. Windsor,* 521 U.S. at 619, 117 S.Ct. 2231 ("Settlement is relevant to a class certification").

In addition to the lack of documentation making individual adjudication of most claims so difficult, the sheer size of the class makes the prospect of individual adjudication of damages virtually unmanageable. For this or any other court to adjudicate the individual claims of the 15,000 to 20,000 African American farmers now estimated to be members of the class would take years or perhaps even a decade or more. Any "fair and efficient" resolution of the claims therefore necessitates the implementation of some sort of class-wide mechanism such as the creative and speedy Track A/Track B procedures proposed by the parties in the Consent Decree. The Court therefore finds that "a class action is superior to other available methods for the fair and efficient adjudication of the controversy." *See* Rule 23(b) (3), Fed.R.Civ.P. The Court concludes that this action appropriately is certified for resolution pursuant to Rule 23(b)(3) of the Federal Rules of Civil Procedure. The remaining question is whether the proposed Consent Decree is fair, adequate and reasonable under Rule 23(e).

III. PROVISIONS OF PROPOSED CONSENT DECREE

The proposed Consent Decree, as revised after the fairness hearing and jointly filed by the parties on March 19, 1999, is a negotiated settlement that resolves all of the claims raised by plaintiffs in the Seventh Amended Complaint. The purpose of the Consent Decree is to ensure that in the future all class members in their dealings with the USDA will "receive full and fair treatment" that is "the same as the treatment accorded to similarly situated white persons." Consent Decree at 1–2. As with all settlements, it does not provide the plaintiffs and the class they represent with everything they sought in the complaint. Instead it is a negotiated settlement intended to achieve much of what was sought without the need for lengthy litigation and uncertain results. *See Stewart v. Rubin,* 948 F.Supp. 1077, 1087 (D.D.C.1996) ("inherent in compromise is a yielding of absolutes and an abandoning of highest hopes"), *aff'd* 124 F.3d 1309 (D.C.Cir.1997). It is impossible to know precisely how much the overall settlement in this case will cost the government, in part because the exact size of the class has not been determined and because the Consent Decree provides for debt relief that is dependent on the amount of debt that individual class members owe to the USDA, but plaintiffs estimate that the settlement is worth at least $2.25 billion, the largest civil rights settlement in the history of this country. *See* Pls' Response to Post-Hearing Submissions at 7.

The Consent Decree accomplishes its purposes primarily through a two-track dispute resolution mechanism that provides those class members with little or no documentary evidence with a virtually automatic cash payment of $50,000, and forgiveness of debt owed to the USDA (Track A), while those who believe they can prove their cases with documentary or other evidence by a preponderance of the evidence—the traditional burden of proof in civil litigation—have no cap on the amount they may recover (Track B). Those who like neither option provided by the Consent Decree may opt out of the class and pursue their individual remedies in court or administratively before the USDA. The essential terms of the proposed Consent Decree and settlement are summarized below.

Under the terms of the proposed Consent Decree, any class member has the right to opt out of the class and pursue his remedies either administratively before the USDA or in a separate court action. *See* Consent Decree at ¶ 2(b). A class member who opts out of the class cannot collect any relief under the settlement, but he retains all of his legal rights to file his own action against the USDA. In other words, if a class member opts out of the class, nothing in this settlement affects him. Any class member who wishes to opt out of the class must file a written request with the facilitator within 120 days of the date on which the Consent Decree is entered. *See id.*

Those who choose to remain in the class have 180 days from the entry of the Consent Decree within which to file their claim packages with the facilitator. Consent Decree at ¶ 5(c). When a claimant submits his claim package, he must include evidence that he filed a discrimination claim with the USDA between January 1, 1981 and July 1, 1997. *See id.* at ¶ 5(b). In the absence of documentation that a complaint was filed with the USDA, a claimant may submit a declaration from "a person who is not a member of the claimant's family" stating that he or she has first-hand knowledge that the claimant filed the complaint. *See id.* A claimant also must include a certification from an attorney stating that the attorney has a good faith belief in the truth of the factual basis of the claim and that the attorney will not require compensation from the claimant for his or her assistance. *See id.* at ¶ 5(e).

At the time that they submit their claim packages, claimants asserting discrimination in credit transactions also must choose between two options: adjudication of their claims under the Track A mechanism or arbitration of their claims under the Track B mechanism. Consent Decree at ¶ 5(d). The choice made between Track A and Track B has enormous significance. Under Track A, the class member has a fairly low burden of proof but his recovery is limited. Under Track B, there is a higher burden of proof but the recovery is unlimited. The claims facilitator, the Poorman-Douglas Corporation, has 20 days after the filing of a claims package within which to determine whether the claimant is a member of the class and, if he is, to forward the materials to counsel for the USDA and to the appropriate Track A or Track B decision-maker. *Id.* at ¶ 5(f)

Under Track A, a claimant must submit "substantial evidence" demonstrating that he or she was the victim of race discrimination. *See* Consent Decree at ¶¶ 9(a)(i), 9(b)(i). Substantial evidence means something more than a "mere scintilla" of evidence but less than a preponderance. *See Burns v. Office of Workers' Compensation Programs,* 41 F.3d 1555, 1562 n. 10 (D.C.Cir.1994). Put another way, substantial evidence is such "relevant evidence as a reasonable mind might accept to support [the] conclusion," even when "a plausible alternative interpretation of the evidence would support a contrary view." *Secretary of Labor v. Federal Mine Safety and Health Review Comm'n,* 111 F.3d 913, 918 (D.C.Cir.1997).

A claimant asserting discrimination in a credit transaction can satisfy this burden by presenting evidence of four specific things: (1) that he owned or leased, or attempted to own or lease, farm land; (2) that he applied for a specific credit transaction at a USDA county office between January 1, 1981 and December 31, 1996; (3) that the loan was denied, provided late, approved for a lesser amount than requested, encumbered by restrictive conditions, or USDA failed to provide appropriate loan service, and such treatment was less favorable than that accorded specifically identified, similarly situated white farmers; and (4) that USDA's treatment of the loan application led to economic damage to the class member. *See* Consent Decree at ¶ 9(a)(i). A claimant asserting discrimination only in a non-credit benefit program can satisfy his burden by presenting evidence (1) that he applied for a specific non-credit benefit program at a USDA county office between January 1, 1981 and December 31, 1996, and (2) that his application was denied or approved for a lesser amount then requested and that such treatment was less favorable than that accorded to specifically identified, similarly situated white farmers. *See id.* at ¶ 9(b)(i).

The USDA has sixty days after it receives notice of a Track A referral to provide the adjudicator and class counsel with any information relevant to the issues of liability and damages. Consent Decree at ¶ 8. After receiving any material from the USDA, the facilitator will either make a recommendation with respect to whether the claim should be approved or indicate its inability to make a recommendation. The entire packet of material, including the submissions by the claimant and the USDA and the recommendation of the facilitator, then is referred to a member of JAMS-Endispute, Inc., for a decision which is to be made within 30 days. *See id.* at ¶ 9(a). That decision is final, except that the Monitor, whose responsibilities are discussed further below, shall direct the adjudicator to reexamine the claim if he determines that "a clear and manifest error has occurred" that is "likely to result in a fundamental miscarriage of justice." *See id.* at ¶¶ 9(a)(v), 9(b)(v), 12(b)(iii).

If the adjudicator finds in the claimant's favor and the claim involves discrimination in a credit transaction, the claimant will receive (1) a cash payment of $50,000; (2) forgiveness of all debt owed to the USDA incurred under or affected by the program that formed the basis of the claim; (3) a tax payment directly to the IRS in the amount of 25% of the total debt forgiveness and cash payment; (4) immediate termination of any foreclosure proceedings that USDA initiated in connection with the loan(s) at issue in the claim; and (5) injunctive relief including one-time priority loan consideration and technical assistance. Consent Decree at ¶¶ 9(a)(iii); 11. If the adjudicator finds in the claimant's favor and the claim involves discrimination in a benefit program, the claimant will receive a cash payment in the amount of the benefit wrongly denied and injunctive relief including one-time priority loan consideration and technical assistance. *Id.* at ¶ 9(b)(iii).

Track B arbitration is the option for those who have more extensive documentation of discrimination in a credit transaction. Under Track B, an arbitrator will hold a one day mini-trial and then decide whether the claimant has established discrimination by a preponderance of the evidence. Consent Decree at ¶ 10. Class counsel will represent any claimant who chooses Track B, or a claimant may be represented by counsel of his choice if he so desires. Track B is designed to balance the need for prompt resolution of the claim with the need to provide adequate discovery and a fair hearing. The entire Track B process will take a maximum of 240 days. During the first 180 days, there is a mechanism for limited discovery and depositions of witnesses. Following the one day mini-trial, the arbitrator will render a decision within 30 to 60 days. *Id.* at ¶ 10(g).

If the arbitrator finds that the claimant has demonstrated by a preponderance of the evidence that he was the victim of racial discrimination and that he suffered damages from that discrimination, the claimant will be entitled to actual damages, the return of inventory property that was foreclosed and other injunctive relief, including a one-time priority loan consideration. Consent Decree at ¶¶ 10(g), 11. As with Track A claims, the decision of the arbitrator is final except that the Monitor shall direct the arbitrator to reexamine the claim if he determines that "a clear and manifest error has occurred" that is "likely to result in a fundamental miscarriage of justice." *See id.* at ¶¶ 10, 12(b)(iii).

The proposed Consent Decree also provides for an independent Monitor who will serve for a period of five years following the entry of the decree. The Monitor will be appointed by the Court from a list of names proposed by the parties and cannot be removed "except upon good cause." Consent Decree at ¶ 12(a). The Monitor is responsible for making periodic written reports to the Court, the Secretary of Agriculture, counsel for the government and class counsel, reporting on the good faith implementation of the Consent Decree and efforts to resolve disputes that arise between the parties under the terms of the decree. *Id.* at ¶ 12(b). He or she will be available to class members and members of the public through a toll-free telephone number to facilitate the lodging of Consent Decree complaints and to expedite their resolution. *Id.* at ¶ 12(b)(iv).

The Court retains jurisdiction to enforce the Consent Decree through contempt proceedings. Consent Decree at ¶ 21. If one side believes that the other side has violated the terms of the Consent Decree, there is a mandatory procedure for attempting to resolve the problem with the assistance of the Monitor that the parties must follow before filing a contempt motion with the Court, but the Court remains available in the event that the terms of the decree are violated. *Id.* at ¶ 13. Finally, the Consent Decree provides that class counsel shall be entitled to reasonable attorneys' fees and costs under ECOA, 15 U.S.C. § 1691e(d), and under the Administrative Procedure Act, 28 U.S.C. § 2412(d), for the filing and litigation of this action and for implementation of the Consent Decree. *Id.* at ¶ 14(a).

IV. FAIRNESS OF PROPOSED CONSENT DECREE

Under Rule 23 of the Federal Rules of Civil Procedure, no class action may be dismissed, settled or compromised without the approval of the Court. Rule 23(e), Fed.R.Civ.P. Before giving its approval, the Court must provide adequate notice to all members of the class, *id.*, conduct a "fairness hearing," and find, after notice and hearing, that the "settlement is fair, adequate and reasonable and is not the product of collusion between the parties." *Thomas v. Albright,* 139 F.3d at 231. In performing this task, the Court must protect the interests of those unnamed class members whose rights may be affected by the settlement of the action.

In this circuit there is "no obligatory test" that the Court must use to determine whether a settlement is fair, adequate and reasonable. *Osher v. SCA Realty I, Inc.,* 945 F.Supp. 298, 303–04 (D.D.C.1996). Instead the Court must consider the facts and circumstances of the case, ascertain what factors are most relevant in the circumstances and exercise its discretion in deciding whether approval of the proposed settlement is fair. By far the most important factor is a comparison of the terms of the compromise or settlement with the likely recovery that plaintiffs would realize if the case went to trial. *See Thomas v. Albright,* 139 F.3d at 231 ("The court's primary task is to evaluate the terms of the settlement in relation to the strength of plaintiffs' case"); *Isby v. Bayh,* 75 F.3d 1191, 1199 (7th Cir.1996) ("the relative strength of plaintiffs' case on the merits as compared to what the defendants offer by way of settlement, is the most important consideration"); *Maywalt v. Parker and Parsley Petroleum Co.,* 67 F.3d 1072, 1079 (2nd Cir.1995) ("[t]he primary concern is with the substantive terms of the settlement: Basic to this is the need to compare the terms of the compromise with the likely rewards of litigation") (internal citations and quotations omitted). Having carefully considered all of the objections that have been filed with the Court or expressed at the fairness hearing in relation to the strength of plaintiffs' case, the Court concludes that the settlement is fair, adequate and reasonable and is not the product of collusion between the parties.

. . . .

D. Absence of Provisions Preventing Future Discrimination

The stated purpose of the Consent Decree is to "ensur[e] that in their dealings with the USDA, all class members receive full and fair treatment that is the same as the treatment accorded to similarly situated white persons." Consent Decree at 2. The Consent Decree does not, however, provide any forward-looking injunctive relief. It does not require the USDA to take any steps to ensure that county commissioners who have discriminated against class members in the past are no longer in the position of approving loans. Nor does it provide a mechanism to ensure that future discrimination complaints are timely investigated and resolved so that the USDA does not practice the same discrimination against African American farmers that led to the filing of this lawsuit. In fact, the Consent Decree stands absolutely mute on two critical points: the full implementation of the recommendations of the Civil Rights Action Team and the integration and reform of the county committee system to make it more accountable and representative. The absence of any such provisions has led to strong, heart-felt objections. It also has caused the Court concern. After comparing the terms of the settlement as a whole with the recovery that plaintiffs likely would have received after trial, however, the Court cannot conclude that the absence of any such prospective injunctive relief renders the settlement as a whole unfair.

There are several legal responses to the objections about the lack of forward-looking injunctive relief. First, while plaintiffs sought both declaratory and monetary relief in the complaint, they never sought an injunction requiring the USDA to restructure or to fire people who may have engaged in discrimination. *See* Complaint at 40–42; Seventh Amended Complaint at 60–63. All of the objectors who seek to have the USDA restructured therefore are going beyond the scope of the complaint in this case. The role of the Court in approving or disapproving a settlement is limited to determining whether the settlement of the case before it is fair, adequate and reasonable. The Court cannot reject the Consent Decree merely because it does not provide relief for some other hypothetical case that plaintiffs could have but did not bring. *Cf. United States v. Microsoft,* 56 F.3d at 1459–60 (court cannot "reformulate the issues" or "redraft the complaint").

Second, nothing in the Consent Decree authorizes the USDA to engage in illegal conduct in the future, and the Consent Decree therefore should not be rejected for its failure to include such prospective injunctive relief. *See Isby v. Bayh,* 75 F.3d at 1197 . . . .

Third, even if plaintiffs had prevailed on their ECOA claims at trial, it is not at all clear that the Court could have or would have granted the broad injunctive relief that the objectors now seek. The injunctive relief that the objectors seek, essentially an injunction requiring the USDA to change the way it processes credit applications, may be authorized where plaintiffs prove a constitutional violation, *see Hills v. Gautreaux,* 425 U.S. 284, 297, 96 S.Ct. 1538, 47 L.Ed.2d 792 (1976), but plaintiffs in their Seventh Amended Complaint do not allege a constitutional violation and they have not undertaken to prove one. . . .

Those legal responses, however, provide little comfort to those who have experienced discrimination at the hands of the USDA and who legitimately fear that they will continue to face such discrimination in the future. The objections arise from a deep and overwhelming sense that the USDA and all of the structures it has put in place have been and continue to be fundamentally hostile to the African American farmer. . . .

Most fundamentally, these objections result from a well-founded and deep-seated mistrust of the USDA. A mistrust borne of a long history of racial discrimination. A mistrust that is well-deserved. As Mr. Chestnut put it, these objections reflect "fear which reaches all the way back to slavery. . . . That objection, you heard it from many today, it really asks you to retain jurisdiction over this case in perpetuity. Otherwise they say USDA will default, ignore the lawful mandates of this Court, and in time march home scot-free while blacks are left holding the empty bag again." Transcript of Hearing of March 2, 1999 at 172. The Court cannot guarantee class members that they will never experience discrimination at the hands of the USDA again, and the Consent Decree does not purport to make such a guarantee. But the Consent Decree and the Court do provide certain assurances.

First, under the terms of this Consent Decree, the USDA is obligated to pay billions of dollars to African American farmers who have suffered discrimination. Those billions of dollars will serve as a reminder to the Department of Agriculture that its actions were unacceptable and should serve to deter it from engaging in the same conduct in the future.

Second, the USDA is not above the law. Like many of the objectors, the Court was surprised and disappointed by the government's response to the Court's modest proposal that the Consent Decree include a simple sentence that in the future the USDA shall exert "best efforts to ensure compliance with all applicable statutes and regulations prohibiting discrimination." Letter from the Court to Counsel, dated March 5, 1999; *see* Response Letter from the Parties to the Court, dated March 19, 1999. Whether or not the government explicitly states it in this Consent Decree, however, the Constitution and laws of the United States continue to forbid discrimination on the basis of race, *see, e.g.,* U.S. Const. amend. V; 15 U.S.C. § 1691; 42 U.S.C. § 2000d, as do the regulations of the USDA. *See* 7 C.F.R. §§ 15.1, 15.51. The actions of the USDA from now into the future will be scrutinized closely—by class members, by their now organized and vocal allies, by Congress and by the Court. If the USDA or members of the county committees are operating on the misapprehension that they ever again can repeat the events that led to this lawsuit, those forces will disabuse them of any such notion.

Most importantly, the farmers who have been a part of this lawsuit have demonstrated their power to bring about fundamental change to the Department of Agriculture, albeit more slowly than some would have wanted. Each individual farmer may feel powerless, but as a group they have planted seeds that are changing the landscape of the USDA. As a group, they spurred Secretary Glickman in 1996 to look inward at the practices of the USDA and to examine African American farmers' allegations that the discrimination of the USDA was leading them to the point of financial ruin. As a group, they led Secretary Glickman to create the Civil Rights Action Team, a team that recommended sweeping changes to the USDA and to the county committee system. Indeed, in February 1997, the USDA Civil Rights Action Team itself recommended that the county committee system be revised by converting all county non-federal positions, including the county executive directors, to federal status, that the committee selection process by changed, that voting members of underrepresented groups be appointed to state and county committees, and that county committees be removed from any farm loan determinations. CRAT Report at 64–65.

As a group, the farmers mobilized a broad coalition within Congress to take the unprecedented action of tolling the statute of limitations. As a group, they brought Secretary Glickman to the negotiating table in this case and achieved the largest civil rights settlement in history. And as a group, they have made implementation of the recommendations of the CRAT Report a priority within the USDA. *See* Statement of February 9, 1999, by Secretary Dan Glickman, Before the Subcommittee on Agriculture, Rural Development, and Related Agencies Committee on Appropriations, United States Senate ("I also want to emphasize the importance that the President and I have placed on USDA civil rights issues; this priority is reflected in the [FY 2000] budget. The President's budget provides the necessary funding to continue to carry out the recommendations of the Civil Rights Action Team (CRAT) as well as the recommendations of the National Commission on Small Farms which supports our civil rights agenda"). While the USDA landscape has remained resistant to change for many seasons, the labors of these farmers finally are beginning to bear fruit. This settlement represents one significant harvest. It is up to the Secretary of Agriculture and other responsible officials at the USDA to fulfill its promises, to ensure that this shameful period is never repeated and to bring the USDA into the twenty-first century.

V. CONCLUSION

Forty acres and a mule. The government broke that promise to African American farmers. Over one hundred years later, the USDA broke its promise to Mr. James Beverly. It promised him a loan to build farrowing houses so that he could breed hogs. Because he was African American, he never received that loan. He lost his farm because of the loan that never was. Nothing can completely undo the discrimination of the past or restore lost land or lost opportunities to Mr. Beverly or to all of the other African American farmers whose representatives came before this Court. Historical discrimination cannot be undone.

But the Consent Decree represents a significant first step. A first step that has been a long time coming, but a first step of immeasurable value. As Mr. Chestnut put it, "Who really knows the true value, if there is one, for returning a small army of poor black farmers to the business of farming by the year 2000 who otherwise would never make it back? I am not wise enough to put a dollar value on that and I don't think anybody on this planet is wise enough to reduce that to dollars and cents." Transcript of Hearing of March 2, 1999 at 171. The Consent Decree is a fair, adequate and reasonable settlement of the claims brought in this case. It therefore will be approved and entered.

SO ORDERED.

Garcia v. Veneman

224 F.R.D. 8 (D.D.C. 2004)

aff'd and remanded sub nom.

Garcia v. Johanns, 444 F.3d 625 (D.C. Cir. 2006)

MEMORANDUM ORDER DENYING CLASS CERTIFICATION

ROBERTSON, DISTRICT JUDGE.

This case presents claims of discrimination by Hispanic farmers nationwide who in various ways were denied USDA credit and non-credit benefits over a period of some twenty years. Before the Court for the second time is the question of whether the case may be certified as a class action. When the question was first presented, by a motion for class certification filed in April 2002, the answer was in the negative, because plaintiffs had not shown, nor did it appear from the record that they could show, a common question of law or fact within the meaning of Fed.R.Civ.P. 23(a). *Garcia v. Veneman,* 211 F.R.D. 15 (D.D.C.2002) (*"Garcia I"*). Plaintiffs noticed an appeal from that order but withdrew the appeal when they were given leave to conduct limited discovery and invited to supplement their motion, Tr. of Jan. 15, 2003 Status Hr'g, at 2. Plaintiffs have now conducted further discovery—although the discovery has by no means been as broad and searching as they wished—and they have presented a supplemental brief on the issue of commonality, which I have treated as a renewed motion for class certification. Because I have concluded that plaintiffs' showing is still insufficient to establish the prerequisites for class certification established by Rules 23(a)(2), 23(b)(2), and 23(b)(3), and that further discovery is unlikely to change the picture, I am today issuing a second order denying class certification. This ruling, taken together with my earlier ruling that plaintiffs' claim of failure to investigate did not state a claim under the Equal Credit Opportunity Act, 15 U.S.C. §§ 1691 *et. seq.* (ECOA), or the Administrative Procedure Act, 5 U.S.C. §§ 701 *et. seq., see* Mem. Order of Mar. 20, 2002, so fundamentally alters the posture of this case that plaintiffs will presumably seek an interlocutory appeal. I will accordingly issue a *sua sponte* order staying proceedings in this Court so that plaintiffs may seek appellate review of the class certification question. *See* Fed.R.Civ.P. 23(f). If asked to do so, I will also certify my Memorandum Order of March 20, 2002 pursuant to 28 U.S.C. § 1292(b).

Analysis

This Memorandum Order is intended to pick up where *Garcia I* left off, and it should be read in conjunction with that ruling.

1. Proceedings since *Garcia I*

In *Garcia I,* I acknowledged the possibility that statistical analysis demonstrating that Hispanic farmers were disproportionately denied credit or non-credit benefits on subjective grounds, such as "character" or "commitment," might support a finding of commonality. At a status conference held on December 18, 2002, shortly after the issuance of *Garcia I,* I noted that certification would require more than anecdotal evidence (the plural of "anecdotes" is not "data"). I said I thought there must be a way to test plaintiffs' hypothesis without inspecting the files of 2700 local offices, and I encouraged plaintiffs to develop a modest discovery plan designed to link USDA's data to what plaintiffs claimed were subjective USDA criteria. At a subsequent status conference, on January 15, 2003, plaintiffs asserted their need for up to 25 depositions and 50 interrogatories, stating that these would involve individuals in the six states where most of the named plaintiffs reside (Texas, California, New Mexico, Florida, Washington, and Colorado). Plaintiffs also wanted to take Rule 30(b)(6) depositions of USDA persons who designed the databases that USDA has said contain all the data that has been captured on its benefit programs, but that plaintiffs already considered nearly useless for their purposes. At that time, I noted that I was trying to find a balance between plaintiffs' legitimate need to take discovery, if they had a colorable commonality claim, and the government's legitimate assertion of burdensomeness. I directed plaintiffs to serve their discovery so that I could evaluate any government objections.

At a status conference held on April 29, 2003, I noted again that there had to be a way to develop a discovery plan that would produce a good random sample. On July 15, 2003, government counsel asserted an inability to fashion such a sample and pointed to the databases that the government had already produced. Plaintiffs' counsel complained that the databases were completely unhelpful because they did not indicate why a particular application had been denied. Tr. of Jan. 15, 2003 Status Hr'g, at 5–6. The government finally produced the loan and disaster benefit files of some 37 of the approximately 110 named plaintiffs. I instructed plaintiffs' counsel to examine those files and to advise me whether "there is in those materials a colorable basis on which plaintiffs can assert that . . . a substantial number of [the named plaintiffs] were rejected for loans or benefits on grounds that are the kinds of subjective grounds that plaintiff[s] assert[ ] [they] can establish commonality for." *Id.* at 22. I suggested that, upon such a showing, I might permit further discovery of other files to provide a basis for a more rigorous statistical comparison. I did not lay down a bright line definition of what I thought would be substantial, but I suggested that 25 out of 37 might be satisfactory while 5 out of 37 would probably not be. *Id.* at 22–23.

2. Plaintiffs' submission

In their supplemental brief on the issue of commonality filed on December 5, 2003, plaintiffs reviewed the results of the discovery they had taken. They submitted that they had demonstrated commonality with respect to both disparate impact and disparate treatment claims, and they urged that, should I find otherwise, they be permitted further, broad-ranging discovery.

Plaintiffs' disparate impact theory is that the overall operation of USDA's farm credit and non-credit benefit programs is "one practice" (or that it must be so considered because USDA's failure to collect and maintain data makes it impossible to analyze the effect of separate components); that this "one practice" has had an adverse impact upon Hispanic farmers, as shown by discovery to date; and that class certification is appropriate because this "one practice" is subjective enough to come within any but the most rigid construction of the Supreme Court's dicta in *General Telephone Co. of the Southwest v. Falcon*, 457 U.S. 147, 159 n. 15, 102 S.Ct. 2364, 72 L. Ed.2d 740 (1982). Plaintiffs' disparate treatment theory asserts that USDA is itself the "single actor" responsible for a pattern and practice of discrimination against Hispanic farmers (because USDA has acquiesced in or ratified notoriously subjective and discriminatory practices of local offices and county commissioners), and that the sampling of evidence plaintiffs have been able to gather from the files they have examined reveals five sub-patterns of discrimination, any one of which would also support a finding sufficient to satisfy the commonality requirement of Rule 23(a) (2): (i) refusal to provide Hispanic farmers with loan applications or assistance in completing applications; (ii) subjecting Hispanic farmers to protracted delays in processing and funding their loans; (iii) using subjective criteria to reject the applications of Hispanic farmers; (iv) unnecessarily subjecting Hispanic farmers to the inconvenience of supervised bank accounts; and (v) delaying or denying loan servicing for Hispanic farmers.

At the same time that they submitted their supplemental brief, plaintiffs moved for leave to file a third amended complaint, setting forth five subclasses of Hispanic farmers, drawn to fit the sub-patterns plaintiffs claim to have discovered. Pls.' Proposed Third Am. Class Action Compl., ¶ 103.

3. Disparate impact theory

The plaintiff in a disparate impact case must "isolat[e] and identif[y] the specific employment practices that are allegedly responsible for any observed statistical disparities," *Watson v. Fort Worth Bank and Trust*, 487 U.S. 977, 994, 108 S.Ct. 2777, 101 L.Ed.2d 827 (1988). Plaintiffs have sought to finesse that requirement by asserting that isolation and identification are impossible because USDA did not keep adequate records. I rejected a variant of that argument in *Garcia I* as "unsupported by case authority and unpersuasive," 211 F.R.D. at 21 n. 6, but now plaintiffs have invoked the 1991 amendments to Title VII, 42 U.S.C. § 2000e-2(k)(1)(B)(I) — Congress's response to the burden of proof holding in *Wards Cove Packing Co. v. Atonio*, 490 U.S. 642, 109 S.Ct. 2115, 104 L.Ed.2d 733 (1989) — to assert (by analogy to employment law) that USDA's entire decision-making process must be considered "one . . . practice" because its separate components cannot be analyzed. Pls.' Mem. in Resp. to Ct.'s July 15, 2003 Order With Respect to Commonality, at 8 ("Pls.' Mem."). It is a creative argument, but ultimately an unpersuasive one. Not only does it "leapfrog to the merits," contrary to the teaching of *Eisen v. Carlisle & Jacquelin*, 417 U.S. 156, 177, 94 S.Ct. 2140, 40 L.Ed.2d 732 (1974), as the Government observes, Def.'s Opp'n to Class Certification & Resp. to Pls.' Dec. 5, 2003 Mem. Regarding Commonality, at 4, but it also boils down to the proposition that unexplained discrepancies in the distribution of government benefits satisfy the commonality requirement of Rule 23(a)(2) without more. That proposition is untenable. Anecdotal proof of discrimination against Hispanic farmers, and even statistical proof that Hispanic farmers have received proportionally less assistance than others, will not be enough to support class certification. *Falcon* reminds us that the underlying purpose of the Rule 23(a)(2) commonality requirement is to permit the court to define the class and determine whether the representation is adequate, to let the defendant know how to defend, and "'most significant[ly]'" to guard against the "potential unfairness to the class members bound by the judgment if the framing of the class is overbroad." 457 U.S. at 161, 102 S.Ct. 2364, (quoting *Johnson v. Georgia Highway Express, Inc.,* 417 F.2d 1122(5th Cir.1969)). That is why "'precise pleadings'" with "'reasonable specificity'" are required. *Id.* at 160–01, 102 S.Ct. 2364. The plaintiffs in this case have not identified a USDA credit or disaster benefit practice established at the national level that comes close in specificity to the example of a common question offered by the Supreme Court in *Falcon* ("a biased testing procedure to evaluate both applicants for employment and incumbent employees," 457 U.S. at 159 n. 15, 102 S.Ct. 2364). Without such specificity, *Falcon* teaches against class certification, except possibly in the "conceivabl[e]" case where there is *both* "significant proof" that the defendant "operated under a general policy of discrimination" *and* "the discrimination manifested itself . . . in the same general fashion, such as through entirely subjective decision-making processes." *Id.* As discussed in later sections of this memorandum, plaintiffs have neither shown that they can satisfy that test nor established probable cause to believe that they could do so, if only they could take more discovery.

4. Disparate treatment theory

Plaintiffs assert (again "leapfrogging to the merits") that USDA was on notice of discrimination against Hispanic farmers and that the Secretary "acquiesced in and ratified" that discrimination by failing to take meaningful corrective measures. That construction of the alleged facts appears to be an effort to sidestep my conclusion in *Garcia I* that "[c]ommonality is defeated . . . by the large numbers and geographic dispersion of the decision-makers," 211 F.R.D. at 22, so that, having identified a "single actor," plaintiffs may go on to assert USDA's liability for a pattern and practice of discouraging Hispanic farmers from availing themselves of farm credit and non-credit programs. Pls.' Mem., at 30–32. (Plaintiffs then go on to identify five sub-patterns and practices by which USDA allegedly "discouraged" Hispanic farmers: denying applications and assistance, delaying processing, using "highly subjective criteria," subjecting them to supervised bank accounts, and delaying or denying loan servicing. These alleged practices have become the labels for the five subclasses plaintiffs now seek to represent.)

I will step over the threshold question of whether a private pattern and practice cause of action can ever be maintained under ECOA. Neither side has briefed the issue, and I will assume for the sake of argument that plaintiffs' pattern and practice claims are cognizable. On the other side of the threshold, however, lies a question that cannot be assumed away, namely, whether plaintiffs' sweeping allegations of departmental acquiescence and ratification will support class certification in view of *Falcon*'s concern about "across-the-board" discrimination claims and its insistence upon specificity in pleading. That question must again be answered in the negative. First, plaintiffs' reliance upon *EEOC v. Inland Marine Industries*, 729 F.2d 1229 (9th Cir.1984), *Baer v. First Options of Chicago, Inc.*, No. 90 C 7207, 1993 U.S. Dist. LEXIS 19489 (N.D.Ill.Dec. 3, 1993), and other similar cases is misplaced. Those cases do stand for the proposition that a pattern of notice and refusal to correct can serve as proof of the intent element in an employment discrimination case, but they do not address the implication of such a pattern upon class certification. The holdings of those cases would not support a conclusion that USDA's alleged acquiescence and ratification would be enough by itself to satisfy the commonality requirement. Proof of conscious inaction on the part of USDA (*i.e.*, acquiescence and ratification) in the face of numbers demonstrating that Hispanic farmers suffered disproportionately high loan rejection rates and received disproportionately low disaster benefit payments might satisfy the first *Falcon* requirement of a "general policy of discrimination," but it would be no help at all with respect to the second *Falcon* requirement of decision-making processes that were "entirely subjective." The common discriminatory practice that *Falcon* and its progeny requires is still missing.

5. Subjective decision-making process

The class that plaintiffs seek to represent would include Hispanic farmers who suffered discrimination at the hands of county agents or county committees—hundreds and perhaps thousands of decision-makers in who knows how many of the 2700 county offices nationwide that number Hispanic farmers among their clientele. *Garcia I*, 211 F.R.D. at 22. As so described, the class presents insurmountable problems for plaintiffs in meeting what the Fourth Circuit has called the "critical" need to identify "the locus of autonomy in making the challenged . . . decisions." *Stastny v. S. Bell Tel. & Tel. Co.*, 628 F.2d 267, 279 (4th Cir.1980). *Compare id. with Rossini v. Ogilvy & Mather, Inc.*, 798 F.2d 590, 598 (2d Cir.1986) (commonality supported where "evidence was offered to show that many of the decisions affecting employees' opportunities for transfer, training and promotion were made by the same, central group of people. . . ."). *See also Webb v. Merck & Co.*, 206 F.R.D. 399, 406 (E.D.Pa.2002) (finding class certification inappropriate where employment decisions were made by managers with varying authority in six facilities across five states); *Carson v. Giant Food, Inc.*, 187 F.Supp.2d 462, 471 (D.Md.2002) (finding class certification inappropriate when alleged discrimination involved thirteen facilities in five towns or cities), *aff'd sub nom Skipper v. Giant Food Inc.*, No. 02-1319, 2003 WL 21350730 (4th Cir. June 11, 2003), *cert. denied*, 540 U.S. 1074, 124 S.Ct. 929, 157 L.Ed.2d 744 (2003); *Zachery v. Texaco Exploration & Prod., Inc.*, 185 F.R.D. 230, 239 (W.D.Tex.1999) (finding class certification inappropriate when alleged discrimination made by five hundred and twenty-three autonomous supervisors in fifteen states). That is why plaintiffs' argument for commonality has focused from the beginning on the subjectivity of USDA's county committee decision-making process. Plaintiffs must either bring their claims under the "entirely subjective" rubric that the Supreme Court thought might "conceivably" satisfy Rule 23(a)—or fail on their class certification motion.

Before 1997, USDA's regulations set forth seven eligibility criteria:

> (1) United States citizenship;
>
> (2) Legal capacity to incur loan obligations;
>
> (3) Education and/or farming experience (at least "1 year's complete production and marketing cycle within the last 5 years");
>
> (4) Character (emphasizing credit history, past record of debt repayment, and reliability) and industry to carry out the proposed operation;
>
> (5) Commitment to carry out undertakings and obligations;
>
> (6) Inability to obtain "sufficient credit elsewhere to finance actual needs at reasonable rates and terms. . . ."; and
>
> (7) Farm size (not to be larger than a family farm).

7 C.F.R. § 1941.12 (1997). *See also* 7 C.F.R. § 1943.12 (1997).

In addition to satisfying those criteria, a farmer also had to submit a Farm and Home Plan, which had to meet with the approval of the loan officer. A feasible plan is defined as:

> [A] plan based upon the applicant/borrower's records that show the farming operation's actual production and expenses. These records will be used along with realistic anticipated prices, including farm program payments when available, to determine that the income from the farm operation, along with any other reliable off farm income, will provide the income necessary for an applicant/borrower to at least be able to:
>
>> (a) Pay all operating expenses and all taxes which are due during the projected farm budget period;
>>
>> (b) Meet necessary payments on all debts; and
>>
>> (c) Provide living expenses for the family members of an individual borrower or a wage for the farm operator in the case of an entity borrower which is in accordance with the essential family needs. Family members include the individual borrower of farm operator in the case of an entity, and the immediate members of the family who reside in the same household.

7 C.F.R. § 1941.4. I concluded in *Garcia I* that some of these eligibility criteria, such as "character" or "commitment," are obviously subjective, while others, such as citizenship, legal capacity, inability to obtain credit elsewhere, and farm size, should be classified as objective. I also ruled that the eligibility factors added in 1997 were objective: loan history, lack of previous debt forgiveness, and no delinquency on any federal debt. Overall, I concluded that, because the decision-making process was guided by a number of objective factors, footnote 15 was not triggered.

Plaintiffs ask me to reconsider that overall conclusion, insisting that, of the seven factors set forth in the pre-1997 regulations—citizenship, legal capacity, education/

experience, character, commitment, inability to obtain credit elsewhere, and farm size—only citizenship and legal capacity are truly objective. Plaintiffs argue that the "inability to obtain credit elsewhere" criterion, which I found to be objective in *Garcia I*, is actually open to subjective interpretation and application. The regulation provides that an applicant is eligible for a loan only if he or she could not obtain sufficient credit elsewhere to "finance . . . actual needs at reasonable rates and terms, taking into consideration prevailing private and cooperative rates and terms in the community in or near where the applicant resides for loans for similar purposes and periods of time." 7 C.F.R. § 1941.6. Plaintiffs argue that there was considerable room for local officials to interpret this factor, because, they assert, for most of the time period relevant to this suit, county committees were responsible for determining what were an applicant's "actual needs," what constituted "reasonable rates and terms," and which legal institutions were deemed "near" the applicant's residence. Plaintiffs also maintain that county officials had discretion to define what constituted a "family farm." The applicable regulation defines a family farm as one which, *inter alia*, "produces agricultural commodities for sale in sufficient quantities so that it is recognized in the community as a farm rather than a rural residence." 7 C.F.R. § 1941.4. Plaintiffs also assert that approximately one-third of the examined loan rejections were done "on the basis of character or other similarly highly subjective criteria." Pls.' Mem. Ex. 7. And, plaintiffs place considerable emphasis on the USDA requirement that Farm and Home Plans be "feasible." Infeasibility appears to have been the reason given for more than half of the loan rejections plaintiffs have been able to review. The feasibility determination is guided by a number of objective inputs, however, including the applicant's own records of the farming operation's actual production and expenses. 7 C.F.R. § 1941.4. These records are combined with other estimates of actual prices to determine feasibility. *Id.* Even plaintiffs' anecdotal evidence shows that feasibility was grounded, at least in many cases, on objective financial data. *See* Pls.' Mem. Ex. 7.

Many of plaintiffs' arguments for reconsideration of my commonality finding are well taken, and taken together they do increase the subjectivity quotient of the USDA processes. The question is, have plaintiffs succeeded in raising the subjectivity quotient to the point where it can be said to be "entirely subjective"? The answer is no. Am I treating the words "entirely subjective" literally, as revealed truth? Again, no. Indeed, there can be no satisfactory resolution to the dispute about just how subjective is "entirely subjective" within the meaning of the Supreme Court's oracular *Falcon* footnote (which is dicta anyway). Judge Huvelle recently found the test to have been met in *McReynolds v. Sodexho Marriott Services, Inc.*, 208 F.R.D. 428, 441–42 (D.D.C.2002), an employment case in which the choice of hiring and promotion criteria was left entirely to the individual discretion of thousands of decision-makers at thousands of sites across the country. The line may not be clear, but whatever can be said about the USDA processes for making loans and giving disaster relief to farmers, they are (or were) certainly not so subjective as that, or as the process recently described in *Dukes v. Wal-Mart Stores, Inc.*, No. C01-02252, 222 F.R.D. 137 (N.D.Cal.2004).

6. Commonality within proposed subclasses

Plaintiffs appear to be arguing that several of the subclasses they propose to define and seek to represent meet the standard for commonality wholly apart from any analysis of subjectivity. They assert that:

- "Thirty-four named plaintiffs were either denied applications altogether or refused requested assistance in completing the loan application." Pls.' Mem. Ex. 8.

The stories of those 34 plaintiffs include many variations. One plaintiff was told to apply first to private banks; another was told that he did not have enough collateral and was not "offered" an application; another was told no disaster relief funds were available; another was treated rudely and was refused assistance in filling out the necessary forms. These are, essentially, thirty-four anecdotes about poor treatment given to individual Hispanic farmers at eight of USDA's 2700 offices.

- USDA "discouraged Hispanic farmers from availing themselves of farm credit by delaying the processing of their loan applications." Pls.' Mem., at 34.

A narrative presented in Exhibit 9 of Plaintiffs' Memorandum asserts that 28 of the 35 named plaintiffs for whom discovery has been received experienced "significant delays in receiving benefits related to farm programs," and that these delays were "in violation of the dictates of law and the dictates of morality." The material submitted in support of this claim consists of stories of bureaucratic delays, each one different from the other.

- USDA "discouraged Hispanic farmers from availing themselves of farm credit by delaying or denying loan servicing." Pls.' Mem., at 37.

Here again the individual stories of the named plaintiffs are anecdotes of bureaucracy, geographically dispersed, and quite different one from another. *See* Pls.' Mem. Ex. 11.

- USDA "discriminated against Hispanic farmers through the misuse of supervised bank accounts." Pls.' Mem. Ex. 10.

The deposit of loan proceeds or disaster payments funds into supervised bank accounts ("SBAs") imposes significant burdens on farmers. SBA's should be used only temporarily "to help the borrower learn to properly manage his/her financial affairs" and normally not for more than a year. 7 C.F.R. § 1902.2(a)(6), (a)(4). Plaintiffs allege that SBA's are frequently imposed on Hispanic farmers only because they cannot speak English, for no reason related to their farming experience or ability to manage their financial affairs, and for periods of longer than a year. That allegation is serious and comes closer than any of the others to fulfilling the requirements for class treatment. It may be that, as the plaintiffs pursue their individual cases, facts will emerge that could support class treatment of this claim in individual offices or in larger districts. *Cf. Castano v. Am. Tobacco Co.,* 84 F.3d 734 (5th Cir.1996) (finding class certification inappropriate for "immature" tort that could best be first developed in individual litigation). On the basis of the record in its present state of development, however, even if the SBA issue provided the requisite commonality, the requirements of Rule 23(b) have not been satisfied.

7. Rule 23(b) questions

Even if plaintiffs' proposed subclasses satisfy the commonality requirement of Rule 23(a)(2), they do not pass muster under Rule 23(b)(2) or Rule 23(b)(3). Plaintiffs have done what they can to shore up their claim to represent a valid Rule 23(b)(2) class by seeking broad and carefully tailored injunctive relief in their proposed third amended complaint, but their assertion that USDA "has acted or refused to act on grounds generally applicable to the class" depends upon the same "one practice" and "single actor" theories by which plaintiffs have sought to establish Rule 23(a) commonality, and which have already been rejected. As for Rule 23(b)(3), the discovery difficulties that have been encountered in this case and the diversity of the plaintiffs' anecdotal support for their class certification motion underscore my observations in *Garcia I* that, if this case were permitted to proceed as a class action, it would "quickly devolve into hundreds or perhaps thousands of individual inquiries about each claimant's particular circumstances," and that "[e]ven if the presence of class wide discrimination were established, individual issues would be much more important to any claimant's recovery." 211 F.R.D. at 24. The history of the *Pigford* (black farmers) class action litigation amply demonstrates that the certification of a plaintiff class to resolve decades of disputes about loans made or not made and disaster relief provided or not provided to thousands of individual farmers, working under disparate conditions and submitting applications to hundreds of different decision-makers (to say nothing of loan applications offered or not offered, loan applications delayed or not delayed, supervised bank accounts required or not required, and loan servicing provided or not provided), would be only the beginning of a lengthy and difficult process in which, as it turns out, it is the "questions affecting only individual members" that predominate. *See* Fed.R.Civ.P. 23(b)(3).

8. Further discovery

Plaintiffs will object—have already objected—that the denial of class certification at this point is uninformed by the information they might be able to develop through the broad discovery program that has been denied them until now, and that to restrict their discovery to unhelpful and uninformative USDA databases and to the loan files of their own clients unreasonably limits their ability to demonstrate the broader pattern of discrimination that they believe has existed over the last twenty years of USDA administration of farmers' loan and disaster relief programs. That objection is overruled. What plaintiffs have been able to assemble and present so far does not give rise to probable cause to believe that a searching and expensive discovery program would unearth sufficient evidence of commonality to support class certification. The examination of individual loan files requested is labor intensive, time consuming, and is no different, or little different, from the kind of discovery that would be necessary to deal with these cases individually.

9. Amendment of the complaint

Plaintiffs' proposed Third Amended Complaint, as already noted, would add five subclasses of plaintiffs and assert prayers for injunctive relief. Leave to amend pleadings is to be "freely given when justice so requires." Fed.R.Civ.P. 15(a). Because the ruling set forth in this Memorandum Order alters the landscape of this case, however, the appropriate course is to deny leave to amend, without prejudice.

. . . .

For the reasons set forth above and in *Garcia I* it is

ORDERED that plaintiffs' motion for class certification, as renewed or supplemented by plaintiffs' memorandum on the subject of commonality, is **denied**. It is

FURTHER ORDERED that plaintiffs' motion for leave to file a third amended class action complaint is **denied without prejudice**. It is

FURTHER ORDERED that defendant's motion to strike is **denied**. And it is

FURTHER ORDERED that further proceedings in this case are **stayed** pending further order of the Court.

Keepseagle v. Veneman

2001 U.S. Dist. LEXIS 25220, 2001 WL 34676944

(D.D.C. Dec. 11, 2001)

MEMORANDUM OPINION AND ORDER

SULLIVAN, J.

Pending before the Court is plaintiffs' motion for class certification. The Court has considered plaintiffs' motion and proposed order, defendant's opposition, and plaintiffs' reply thereto, all pertinent portions of the record, counsels' representations at oral argument on July 13, 2001, and the relevant statutory and case law. Plaintiffs have fulfilled all the requirements to justify class certification of this action. Accordingly, on September 28, 2001, the Court granted plaintiffs' motion for class certification pursuant to Fed.R.Civ.P. 23(b)(2). This Memorandum Opinion and Order sets for the justification for the Court's September 28, 2001 Order, further orders plaintiffs to file a proposed order outlining appropriate sub-classes in accordance with this Memorandum Opinion, and denies defendant's motion for a stay of the Court's September 28, 2001 Order.

Introduction

Plaintiffs and the class of Native American farmers and ranchers (hereinafter "farmer(s)") that they seek to represent applied for United States Department of Agriculture ("USDA") farm loan and benefit programs between January 1, 1981 and November 24, 1999. Eight hundred and thirty-eight (838) plaintiffs named in the Fifth Amended Complaint, and the members of plaintiffs' proposed class, make two common claims: (1) USDA discriminated against them on the basis of race in processing their farm program applications; and (2) USDA did not investigate complaints of discrimination. *See* Pls.' Mot. for Class Cert. at 92. According to the plaintiffs and class members, the USDA discriminated against them by, *inter alia,* denying them access to the programs or treating them less favorably than non-Native American farmers in processing their applications, servicing loans, and/or administering benefits. *See* Fifth Am. Compl. at 108–109. The plaintiffs and class members also allege that they complained of this discrimination to USDA, but that USDA failed to properly process and investigate their complaints. *See id.*

The plaintiffs and class members allege that USDA's discrimination against them in the administration of farm loan and benefits programs violates the Equal Credit Opportunity Act ("ECOA"), 15 U.S.C. § 1691e, the Administrative Procedures Act ("APA"), 5 U.S.C. § 706(2)(A), and Title VI of the Civil Rights Act of 1964 ("Title VI"), 42 U.S.C.2000d, *et seq.* In particular, plaintiffs allege that the discrimination in USDA's processing of credit applications and its failure to investigate is a violation of ECOA, and that discrimination in the department's processing of applications for non-credit programs and its failure to investigate such discrimination is a violation of the APA. Pls.' Reply at 7.

Plaintiffs seek declaratory and injunctive relief and damages. Pursuant to the ECOA, plaintiffs request damages and injunctive relief. *See* Fifth Am. Compl. at 85. Under the APA, plaintiffs pray for "appropriate relief," "including (1) compensation to plaintiffs and Class members for there having been no proper investigation of their complaints, and (2) specific performance with respect to their program benefits." *Id.* at 86. Plaintiffs also request "appropriate relief" under Title VI, including equitable performance and specific performance of program benefits. Finally, pursuant to the Declaratory Judgment Act ("DJA"), 28 U.S.C. § 2201, plaintiffs request declaratory judgment as to plaintiffs' and class members' "rights under [USDA's] farm programs including their right to equal credit, equal participation in farm programs, and their right to full and timely enforcement of racial discrimination complaints" under the APA. *Id.* at 84–85.

I. BACKGROUND

A. USDA's Farm Programs and Determination Process

USDA administers a variety of farm credit and benefit programs. Until 1994, USDA divided its administration of these programs between the Farmers Home Administration ("FmHA") (credit programs) and the Agriculture Stabilization and Conservation Service ("ASCS") (non-credit programs). In 1994, USDA consolidated these programs into the Farm Service Agency ("FSA").

A farmer seeking a farm credit or benefit is required to submit an application pursuant to USDA program policies. The local county committee and USDA staff and officials determine initially if the farmer is eligible for the program, and USDA staff ultimately grants or denies the application. *See generally* 7 C.F.R. §§ 1910.5, 1910.4(g), 1941.30, 1943.30 (2001).

B. USDA's Civil Rights Enforcement Structure and Procedure

Any farmer who believes that USDA denied his or her application for a program loan or benefit on the basis of race, or some other prohibited basis, has the option of filing a civil rights complaint with the Secretary of USDA and/or with the USDA office charged with investigating civil rights violations. From January 1, 1981, through November 24, 1999, a number of USDA offices were involved with civil rights investigations, including, *inter alia,* the Office of Civil Rights Enforcement and Adjudication ("OCREA"). In processing these civil rights complaints, OCREA and the appropriate USDA agency were required to pursue conciliation, perform a preliminary inquiry, and make a final discrimination determination. If the farmer was dissatisfied with the final discrimination determination, the farmer was permitted to sue in federal court under the Equal Credit Opportunity Act ("ECOA"), 15 U.S.C. § 1691e. *See Pigford v. Glickman,* 82 F.R.D. 341, 342–344 (D.D.C.1997).

C. Failings of USDA's Civil Rights Enforcement Unit

The plaintiffs and class members allege that USDA dismantled its civil rights enforcement unit in 1983 and has not investigated discrimination complaints since that time. Plaintiffs and class members contend that USDA, in two internal reports, admitted its failure to account for and to investigate these discrimination complaints. *See* Civil Rights Action Team, United States Department of Agriculture, *Civil Rights at the United States Department of* Agriculture (1997) (the "CRAT Report"); Office of Inspector General, *U.S. Department of Agriculture Evaluation Report for the Secretary on Civil Rights — Phase I Report No. 50801-2-Hq(1)* (1997) ("OIG-Report").

In the CRAT Report, USDA concluded that "[m]inority farmers have lost significant amounts of land and potential farm income as a result of discrimination by FSA programs and the programs of its predecessor agencies, ASCS and FmHA." CRAT Report at 30. The report found that "[t]he process for resolving complaints has failed." *Id.* at 31. USDA also noted that disparities existed between "non-minority loan processing and American Indian loan processing." *Id.* at 21.

In the OIG Report, USDA found that a significant number of USDA discrimination complaints filed were not processed, investigated or resolved. *See* OIG Report at 6. USDA concluded that the "program discrimination complaint process at FSA lacks integrity, direction and accountability," and that OCREA "does not have controls in place to monitor and track discrimination complaints." *Id.* at 9. In March 2000, USDA's Office of Inspector General issued a supplemental report finding that USDA had not made any significant changes in its system of processing discrimination complaints. *See* Office of Inspector General Audit Report, *Office of Civil Rights Status of Implementation of Recommendations Made in Prior Evaluations of Program Complaints, Audit Report 60801-4-Hq,* at i. (Mar.2000).

D. Previous litigation involving requests for class certification by minority farmers alleging discrimination by USDA

Two cases involving claims by minority farmers against USDA have already been reviewed by judges of this Court. In *Williams v. Glickman,* Judge Flannery denied certification to a proposed class of African American and Hispanic American farmers. Memo. Op., Civil Action No. 95-1149 (Feb. 14, 1997). In *Williams,* the plaintiffs proposed a class of:

> All African American or Hispanic American persons who, between 1981 and the present, have suffered from racial or national origin discrimination in the application for or the servicing of loans or credit from the FmHA (now Farm Services Agency) of the USDA, which has caused them to sustain economic loss and/or mental anguish/emotion [sic] distress damages.

Id. at 7.

Judge Flannery held that the class was not readily ascertainable because the initial determination of who qualified as a class member would require an individualized inquiry. *Id.* at 8. In addition, the court found that the class did not meet the requirements of Fed.R.Civ.P. 23 because the class was overbroad and did not meet the standards of commonality and typicality.

In a subsequent case, *Pigford v. Glickman,* Judge Friedman certified a class of African American farmers. 182 F.R.D. 341 (D.D.C.1998). In *Pigford,* the court first certified a class for purposes of a liability determination. *Id.* at 351. This class included:

> All African-American farmers who (1) farmed between January 1, 1983, and February 21, 1997; and (2) applied, during that time period, for participation in a federal farm program with USDA, and as a direct response to said application, believed that they were discriminated against on the basis of race, and filed a written discrimination complaint with USDA in that time period.

Id. at 345. The court distinguished this class from that in *Williams* by finding that the "parameters of the proposed class . . . are sufficiently clear to make the proposed class administratively manageable." *Id.* at 346. The parties in *Pigford* subsequently settled the case. *See Pigford v. Glickman,* 185 F.R.D. 82 (D.D.C.1999). The Court is mindful of these cases in reviewing the instant motion for class certification. . . .

II. PLAINTIFFS' REQUEST FOR CLASS CERTIFICATION

Plaintiffs request that the Court certify this case as a class action because USDA's failure to properly process, account for, and/or investigate their complaints of racial discrimination presents common questions of law and fact. *See* Pl.'s Mot. for Class Cert. at 29–31. Plaintiffs also assert that USDA's alleged discrimination in denying them access to farm loans and benefits programs and/or treating them less favorably than non-Native-American farmers presents common questions of law and fact. *Id.* Plaintiffs maintain that class certification is in the best interest of justice because it will facilitate the efficient enforcement of rights and will conserve judicial resources by enabling the plaintiffs to establish USDA's discrimination on a systemic basis. *See* Pls.' Proposed Order at 4. Plaintiffs propose a class defined as:

> All Native-American farmers and ranchers who believe that USDA discriminated against them on account of their race in their applications for, or USDA's administration of, USDA farm programs between January 1, 1981

and November 24, 1999, and who complained of that discrimination to the USDA, individually or through a representative.

Id. Plaintiffs further propose four subclasses, depending on whether the applicant had complained orally or in writing, and whether the complaint is on file with USDA. *Id.*

Plaintiffs present seven proposed class representatives. All the proposed class representatives are farmers or ranchers. The representatives include members of four different tribes, who reside in three different reservations. *See* Pls.' Mot. for Class Cert. at 7, 10, 15, 18, 21; Pls.' Fifth Am. Compl. at 127. Plaintiffs have not categorized the proposed representatives' claims. However, it appears that at least five proposed class representatives allege discrimination in the processing of loan applications. All the proposed class representatives who are described in plaintiffs' motion allege that they have "timely filed, either directly or through [their] Tribal Council, complaints to the defendant regarding these acts of discrimination." *See* Pls.' Mot. for Class Cert. at 9–10, 15, 18, 20–21, 23.

III. DISCUSSION

A. Existence of the Class

Rule 23 of the Federal Rules of Civil Procedure governs any discussion of class certification. Fed.R.Civ.P. 23. While Rule 23 does not formally require plaintiffs to prove the existence of a class, some courts have found that "this is a common-sense requirement and . . . routinely require it." *Pigford v. Glickman,* 182 F.R.D. 341, 346 (D.D.C.1998); *see Lewis v. National Football League,* 146 F.R.D. 5, 8 (D.D.C.1992); *see also Simer v. Rios,* 661 F.2d 655, 669 (7th Cir.1981) ("it is axiomatic that for a class action to be certified a 'class' must exist"). Neither the D.C. Circuit nor the Supreme Court has engaged in this additional step of the class certification analysis. *See, e.g., Amchem Products, Inc. v. Windsor,* 521 U.S. 591, 613–14, 117 S.Ct. 2231 (1997); *General Telephone Co. of the Southwest v. Falcon,* 457 U.S. 147, 160–61, 102 S.Ct. 2364 (1982) (reviewing only the prerequisites set out in Rule 23(a)); *Eubanks v. Billington,* 110 F.3d 87, 92 n.6 (D.C.Cir.1997) (listing prerequisites for a class action). Nevertheless, the Court is persuaded that some initial review of the proposed class is appropriate to ascertain whether "the general outlines of the membership of the class are determinable at the outset of litigation." *Pigford,* 182 F.R.D. at 346. This inquiry is one concerned with the court's ability to clearly identify and manage the class, and thus does not involve a "particularly stringent test." *Id.* . . .

Here, as in *Pigford,* by limiting the class to plaintiffs who have filed discrimination complaints concerning alleged discrimination in USDA's administration and processing of their applications, the plaintiffs' proposed class has clearly defined parameters.

1. Class Definition

The Court *sua sponte* modifies the proposed class in two ways for clarity and ease of administration. . . .

First, the Court removes the requirement that members must "believe" that they have experienced discrimination. Plaintiffs' proposed class definition tracks the language of the *Pigford* class, where the court *sua sponte* replaced the provision that class members have experienced discrimination with a condition that class members believe that they have experienced discrimination. 182 F.R.D. at 347. In this manner, the court avoided a need to make any initial finding of discrimination in order to determine class membership. However, in the instant matter, plaintiffs propose a class that will be limited to individuals who have complained of discrimination. Thus, the requirement that class members believe that they have experienced discrimination is likely to be superfluous. . . . The Court concludes that the limitation imposed by the "complaint" requirement is fully sufficient to permit the Court to identify the class and its members.

Second, the Court follows *Pigford*'s lead in imposing concrete time periods on the time that class members farmed, the time during which they applied to USDA for participation in a federal farm program, and in which they filed a discrimination complaint with USDA. The plaintiffs' proposed class limits only the time period of participation in a USDA program from January 1, 1981 through November 24, 1999.

This Court, therefore, reviews the following class under Rule 23's requirements for certification:

> All Native-American farmers and ranchers, who (1) farmed or ranched between January 1, 1981 and November 24, 1999; (2) applied to the USDA for participation in a farm program during that time period; and (3) filed a discrimination complaint with the USDA individually or through a representative during the time period.

2. In Considering the Motion for Class Certification, the Court Does Not Evaluate the Merits of Plaintiffs' Claims

Defendant argues that plaintiffs' proposed class definition will not entitle them to money damages and that, therefore, the Court should not certify the class. *See* Def.'s Opp'n to Proposed Order at 5. Specifically, defendant contends that the APA does not permit monetary damages and that the plaintiffs' class, or a part of it, will be barred by the statute of limitations from seeking monetary damages pursuant to ECOA. *Id.* at 5, 16. In determining whether to certify a class, the Court should not examine the underlying merits of the claims. *See Eisen v. Carlisle & Jacquelin*, 417 U.S. 156, 177–78 (1974). The Supreme Court noted in *Eisen* that, "in determining the propriety of a class action, the question is not whether the . . . plaintiffs have stated a cause of action or will prevail on the merits, but rather whether the requirements of Rule 23 are met." *Id.* at 178.

Defendant notes that plaintiffs' claims may be barred by the statute of limitations. The proposed class encompasses members who allege discrimination that occurred between January 1, 1981 and November 24, 1999. In 1999, Congress passed legislation tolling the statute of limitations for complaints of discrimination against

USDA. *See* Agricultural, Rural Development, Food and Drug Administration, and Related Agencies Appropriations Act, 1999, Pub.L. No. 105-277, § 741, 112 Stat. 2681 (codified at 7 U.S.C. § 2297, Notes). The legislation requires that, in order for the statute of limitations to toll, a farmer must have filed his complaint of discrimination with USDA before July 1, 1997. Defendant argues that members of the proposed class will not benefit from this waiver.

In *Kifafi v. Hilton Hotels Retirement Plan,* the court recognized that, while the "class action mechanism cannot be used to resurrect stale claims," a "resolution of a statute of limitations issue at the class certification stage would impermissibly intrude upon the merits" of the class representative's claim. 189 F.R.D. 174, 177–78 (D.D.C.1999). In the course of the *Pigford* litigation, the court revised the definition of the already certified class in order to reflect the new legislation. 185 F.R.D. at 93. The 1999 legislation may seem sufficiently clear so as to allow this Court to make similar modifications to the class. However, the plaintiff's proposed class includes farmers who have made both "written" and "oral" complaints, a factor which may trigger different statutes of limitations. *See* Def.'s Opp'n to Pls.' Proposed Order at 16–17. Thus, it would be impermissible for this Court to revise the definition of the class so as to effectively rule on the merits of class representatives' claims.

Defendant further argues that farmers who have "filed" orally, or whose complaints are not on file with USDA, are not properly included in the class. Plaintiffs' proposed class would include all Native American farmers and ranchers who have lodged complaints, in writing or orally, with USDA, including those on file with USDA and those not on file. Individuals who made oral complaints, or whose complaints are not on file with USDA, may have a more difficult time succeeding on the merits of their claims. Obviously, an oral complaint, or one not on file, may also raise different questions of proof. Nevertheless, individuals making such complaints are clearly within the proposed class definition, and any further consideration of defendant's objection would constitute consideration of the merits. *See Eisen,* 417 U.S. at 177–78 (1974). Withholding judgment as to whether all class members are ultimately entitled to relief, the Court finds that a class including individuals who have filed both oral and written complaints individually or through a representative is clearly identifiable.

B. Rule 23(a)

The four prerequisites of Rule 23(a) require plaintiffs to demonstrate that:

(1) the class is so numerous that joinder of all members is impracticable, (2) there are questions of law or fact common to the class, (3) the claims or defenses of the representative parties are typical of the claims or defenses of the class, and (4) the representative parties will fairly and adequately protect the interests of the class.

Fed.R.Civ.P. 23(a); *see also General Tel. Co. v. Falcone,* 457 U.S. 147, 156, 102 S.Ct. 2364 (1982).

1. Numerosity

Plaintiffs' Fifth Amended Complaint identifies 838 Native-American farmers from more than a dozen states throughout the United States. *See* Pls.' Fifth Am. Compl. at 108. Based on farm census data and discussions with representatives from the Native-American community, plaintiffs estimate that the class may approach 19,000 members. Pls.' Mot. at 28. Defendant counters that plaintiffs' estimate of 19,000 members is based on "mere belief." Def.'s Opp'n at 33. However, the current number of plaintiffs fitting the class definition, approximately 814, is sufficient to meet the numerosity requirement. *See Pigford*, 182 F.R.D. at 347–48 ("Plaintiffs have provided the names of four hundred and one named plaintiffs who they claim fall within the class definition. That alone is sufficient to establish numerosity, especially when the class members are located in different states."); *see also Coleman v. Pension Benefit Guaranty Corp.*, 196 F.R.D. 193, 198 (D.D.C.2000) (noting that the numerosity requirement is satisfied where it is clear that joinder would be impracticable).

2. Commonality

Plaintiffs have established that common questions of law and fact predominate the determination of liability. *See* Fed.R.Civ.P. 23(a)(2); *Falcon*, 457 U.S. at 159 n.15. The primary concern in assessing the commonality and typicality requirements of Rule 23(a) is to ensure that "maintenance of a class action is economical and [that] the named plaintiff's claim and the class claims are so interrelated that the interests of the class members will be fairly and adequately protected in their absence." *Falcon*, 457 U.S. at 157 n.13 (noting that the commonality and typicality requirements of Rule 23(a) tend to merge). "The commonality test is met where there is at least one issue, the resolution of which will affect all or a significant number of the putative class members." *Lightbourne v. County of El Paso*, 118 F.3d 421, 426 (5th Cir.1997).

The existence of factual distinctions differences between the claims of putative class members will not preclude a finding of typicality. *See Prado-Steiman v. Bush*, 221 F.3d 1266, 1279 n.14 (11th Cir.2000). Here, USDA's alleged failure to properly process, account for, and/or investigate discrimination complaints affected each class member. The plaintiffs assert three common factual and legal issues arising from that failure:

1. Did the USDA have a legal obligation to process and investigate complaints of discrimination it received?

2. If the USDA had such a duty, was there a systemic failure properly to process complaints in the specified time period?

3. If there was such a systemic failure, do plaintiffs have a private cause of action against the USDA?

Common questions of law and fact are also present in the issues involving USDA's alleged discrimination in denying the Native-American farmers access to farm loan and benefits programs or treating them less favorably than non-Native-American farmers.

The *Pigford* court identified common issues almost identical to those presented by plaintiffs. 182 F.R.D. at 348. In contrast, in *Williams,* the court held that a "common thread of discrimination" did not satisfy the requirement that plaintiffs demonstrate the existence of a common legal question. *Williams,* Mem. Op. of Feb. 14, 1997, at 13 (citing *Hartman v. Duffey,* 19 F .3d 1459, 1472 (D.C.Cir.1994) for the proposition that "there is more to a showing of commonality than a demonstration that class plaintiffs suffered discrimination on the basis of membership in a particular group"). However, plaintiffs need only show a "common thread" underlying the legal issues presented; here, they have alleged the existence of a "unifying pattern of discrimination," which gives rise to their legal claims. *Pigford,* 182 F.R.D. at 348.

. . . .

Plaintiffs' claims are less varied than those presented by the *Marisol A.* plaintiffs. While it is true that plaintiffs allege a variety of forms of racial discrimination by USDA, the alleged absence of a functioning, effective mechanism for investigating and resolving complaints of discrimination against Native American farmers exacerbates and prolongs any discrimination in the administration of USDA programs. It is clear that the systematic failure to process complaints of discrimination is a unifying characteristic of the class and raises common questions of fact and law.

3. Typicality

Typicality focuses on the similarity of the legal and remedial theories behind the claims of named representatives and those of the putative class. *See Prado-Steiman,* 221 F.3d at 1278 n.14. Plaintiffs satisfy typicality if "each class member's claim arises from the same course of events that led to the claims of the representative parties and each class member makes similar legal arguments to prove the defendant's liability." *Baby Neal for and by Kanter v. Casey,* 43 F.3d 48, 58 (3d Cir.1994); *see also Pigford,* 182 F.R.D. at 349.

Plaintiffs' claims arise from the alleged dismantling of USDA's civil rights office, and the conduct of USDA in failing to process complaints of discrimination brought to its attention by the class members. The same course of events were at issue in *Pigford,* where the court found that plaintiffs' claims were typical. 182 F.R.D. at 349. The allegations set forth by the proposed class representatives clearly fulfill the typicality requirement, as they arise out of the same alleged events and conduct, namely the systematic failure of any mechanism for processing discrimination complaints at USDA.

4. Fair and Adequate Representation

Plaintiffs' proposed class meets the fourth prong of Rule 23(a). Fed.R.Civ.P. 23(a) (4). Adequacy of representation refers to both legal counsel and class representatives. Thus, "the named representative must not have antagonistic or conflicting interests with the unnamed members of the class," and "the representative must appear able to vigorously prosecute the interests of the class through qualified counsel." *Twelve*

John Does v. District of Columbia, 117 F.3d 571, 575 (D.C.Cir.1997), citing *Nat'l Ass'n of Regional Medical Programs, Inc. v. Mathews,* 551 F.2d 340, 345 (D.C.Cir.1976).

The proposed class representatives are able to "fairly and adequately protect the interests of the class." Fed.R.Civ.P. 23(a)(4). In *Pigford,* the court held that the breadth of situations and interests presented by the over four hundred named plaintiffs was an assurance that all class members' interests would be fairly represented. *See Pigford,* 182 F.R.D. at 350. With more than 800 named plaintiffs, plaintiffs' claims encompass a breadth of issues. However, Rule 23(a)(4) is concerned with the named representatives, and here plaintiffs have proposed seven representatives. Plaintiffs assert that the claims of the lead plaintiffs are representative of the class. Pls.' Proposed Order at 8. Specifically, plaintiffs claim:

> [A]s to all plaintiffs in this case, the allegations are similar, if not identical, to the allegations and causes of actions of the first five plaintiffs. Simply put, each and every plaintiff/class representative was denied a loan or program benefit or was denied a loan or program benefit on terms similar to those offered to white farmers, or was paid too late to properly farm, or was not given any assistance in the completion of FmHA forms/applications; and then each plaintiff complained on grounds of discrimination, but such discrimination complaint was never resolved pursuant to the law; and all of these events occurred during the period 1981–1999.

Pls.' Motion at 23. The Court does not have before it the factual allegations of all plaintiffs. Nevertheless, after a review of the 357 short questionnaires provided by plaintiffs, Exhibits 8–9, Pls.' Reply, and the allegations of the seven proposed class representatives contained in plaintiffs' motion for class certification, the Court finds that the proposed representatives present a broad range of alleged discrimination. The Court finds no disparity of interest between the representatives and the class as a whole.

The proposed class representatives have also demonstrated that they are able to actively prosecute the interests of the class through competent counsel. The D.C. Circuit has held that counsel's failure to communicate with class members may constitute inadequate representation. *Twelve John Does,* 117 F.3d at 576–77 (class dissenters alleged that class counsel was out of touch with class members). There have been no allegations of inadequate consultation in the instant case. Defendant asks the Court to consider counsel's other cases and concerns about quality of representation raised in those cases. The Court, however, finds no fault with plaintiffs' counsel in the instant matter, and will not engage in the speculation about potential future problems urged by defendant. In fact, the Court notes that lead counsel in this action, Alexander J. Pires, Jr. and Philip L. Fraas, successfully prosecuted *Pigford v. Glickman,* obtaining a settlement for class members that resulted in approximately $1 billion in damages and debt forgiveness to class members. Joining Mr. Pires and Mr. Fraas as of counsel are also several other distinguished attorneys. The Court concludes that plaintiffs' counsel is fully able to fairly and adequately represent the class in this matter.

. . . .

D. The Rule 23(b) Requirements

The Court finds that plaintiffs have met the requirements of Rule 23(b)(2).

1. Rule 23(b)(2)

Rule 23(b)(2) provides that a class may be certified where "the party opposing the class has acted or refused to act on grounds generally applicable to the class, thereby making appropriate final injunctive relief or corresponding declaratory relief with respect to the class as a whole." Fed.R.Civ.P. 23(b). As described above, plaintiffs contend that the defendant, by allegedly failing to enforce the civil rights laws, acted on grounds applicable to the whole class because the civil rights laws apply to each class member. *See Eubanks,* 110 F.3d at 92 ("Although the defining characteristic of the (b)(2) class is that it seeks declaratory or injunctive relief applicable to the class as a whole, it is not uncommon in employment discrimination cases for the class also to seek monetary relief, at least where the monetary relief does not predominate.").

Plaintiffs seek to remedy USDA's alleged racial discrimination through injunctive and declaratory relief, as contemplated by Rule 23(b)(2). The plaintiffs and class members request:

Declaratory relief under 28 U.S.C. § 2201;

Injunctive and declaratory relief under the Equal Credit Opportunity Act, 15 U.S.C. § 1691e(a) & (d);

Equitable relief under the Administrative Procedure Act, 5 U.S.C. § 706(2)(A); and

Equitable relief under the Civil Rights Act of 1964, 42 U.S.C. § 2000d, et seq.

See Fifth Am. Compl. at ¶¶ 150–64.

Should plaintiffs and class members prove their allegations, a declaration that USDA discriminated on a class-wide basis against Native-American farmers in the administration of USDA's farm programs and suitable injunctive relief would be proper. Plaintiffs point to the injunctive relief that African-American farmers obtained through a consent decree in *Pigford,* which included "priority status for lending, an affirmative bar against further discrimination, and the creation of the Office of the Monitor to oversee that the Consent Decree is properly executed." *See Pigford* Consent Decree at 19–20. In the instant matter, plaintiffs seek to give Native-American farmers the benefits of such injunctive relief and "any additional measures needed to ensure" the eradication of discrimination against Native Americans in the application/processing procedures at USDA. *See Marisol A.,* 126 F .3d at 378 (finding that, although children in New York's welfare system had suffered different harms requiring individual remedies, the system's deficiencies stemmed from central failures, and a 23(b)(2) class was appropriate).

Rule 23(b)(2) may not be invoked, however, where "the appropriate final relief relates exclusively or predominantly to money damages." Fed.R.Civ.P. 23(b)(2), Adv. Comm. Note (1966). Where monetary damages are incidental to a claim for injunctive relief, certification pursuant to subsection (b)(2) may be appropriate. *See Walsh v. Ford Motor Co.,* 807 F.2d 1000, 1003 n.7 (D.C.Cir.1986).

In *Pigford,* Judge Friedman held that injunctive relief predominated plaintiffs' claims, even though they also sought substantial damages. 182 F.R.D. at 351. However, the *Pigford* class was certified pursuant to Rule 23(b)(2) for purposes of "liability," with the court reserving the issue of damages for a later time.

Plaintiffs' claims for injunctive and declaratory relief may clearly be certified under Rule 23(b)(2). Plaintiffs allege that USDA has failed to provide a mechanism for processing discrimination claims, essentially leaving plaintiffs with no remedy for perceived discriminatory conduct by USDA. The Court certifies the class pursuant to Rule 23(b)(2) for purposes of declaratory and injunctive relief.

. . . .

Notice

Rule 23(c)(2) requires that "individual notice be sent out to all class members who can be identified with reasonable effort" to inform them of the class certification. *Eisen,* 417 U.S. at 177. The Court directs that notice be provided to all class members regarding the institution of this class action. In view of the fact that USDA has computerized records for most of the potential class members, the Court orders USDA to provide plaintiffs with a list of all Native American farmers who applied for USDA farm programs between January 1, 1981 and November 24, 1999.

CONCLUSION

The Court has considered plaintiffs' motion for class certification and proposed order, the response and reply thereto, counsels' representations at oral argument, defendant's motion for a stay of the Court's September 28, 2001 order and the response and reply thereto, and the relevant statutory and case law. For the foregoing reasons, it is hereby

ORDERED that plaintiffs' motion for class certification is GRANTED. The Court certifies the following class for plaintiffs' claims for declaratory and injunctive relief pursuant to Fed.R.Civ.P. 23(b)(2):

> All Native-American farmers and ranchers, who (1) farmed or ranched between January 1, 1981 and November 24, 1999; (2) applied to the USDA for participation in a farm program during that time period; and (3) filed a discrimination complaint with the USDA individually or through a representative during the time period.

It is FURTHER ORDERED that plaintiffs shall file a proposed order by no later than January 28, 2002, which outlines appropriate subclasses in accordance with this memorandum and identifies class representatives for each of the named subclasses; and it is

FURTHER ORDERED that defendant shall file its response to the proposed sub-classes by no later than February 28, 2002; and it is

FURTHER ORDERED that plaintiffs shall file its reply to defendant's response by no later than March 15, 2002; and it is

FURTHER ORDERED that defendant's motion for a stay of the Court's September 28, 2001 Order is DENIED; and it is

FURTHER ORDERED that USDA shall provide plaintiffs, by no later than January 28, 2002 a list of all Native American farmers who applied for USDA farm programs between January 1, 1981 and November 24, 1999; and it is

FURTHER ORDERED that the parties shall jointly file a proposed "Notice of Pendency of Class Action" for the Court's review by no later than January 28, 2002.

IT IS SO ORDERED.

Green v. Veneman

159 F. Supp. 2d 360 (S.D. Miss. 2001)

MEMORANDUM OPINION AND ORDER

TOM S. LEE, CHIEF JUDGE.

This cause is before the court on the motion of defendant Ann E. Veneman, Secretary of the United States Department of Agriculture, to dismiss plaintiffs' amended complaint or, in the alternative, to transfer venue. Plaintiffs have responded in opposition to the motion and the court, having considered defendant's motion, concludes that plaintiffs' complaint fails to state a cognizable claim for relief and accordingly should be dismissed.

Plaintiffs in this case are 147 "non-African American farmers" who complain that the United States Department of Agriculture (USDA or Department) has discriminated against them on account of their race by denying to them certain benefits that the Department has agreed to make available to similarly situated African American farmers. Plaintiffs charge that the USDA's discriminatory actions violate the Equal Credit Opportunity Act (ECOA), 15 U.S.C. § 1691 *et seq.;* 42 U.S.C. § 1981 and § 1982; Title VI of the Civil Rights Act, 42 U.S.C. § 2000d *et seq.;* and the guarantee of equal protection afforded by the Fifth Amendment to the United States Constitution. In addition, plaintiffs have asserted claims under the Administrative Procedures Act, 5 U.S.C. §§ 551–559, 701–706, relating to applications for loans and loan servicing which they contend the USDA arbitrarily and capriciously denied.

Pigford v. Glickman:

Although plaintiffs declare in their responsive memorandum that "[i]t would be easy enough for [them] to state their claims [in this case] making no mention of a case called *Pigford v. Glickman,*" that plainly is not the case, for *Pigford v. Glickman* is at the heart of this case. This case exists only because of *Pigford v. Glickman* and thus it is only with knowledge of what transpired in *Pigford* that one can understand the source of plaintiffs' claims against the USDA in this case, and likewise, only with a full understanding of *Pigford* is it possible to reasonably evaluate the viability of the claims of the plaintiffs herein.

Pigford was brought as a class action in the District Court for the District of Columbia by a class of certain African American farmers who alleged that they had been subjected to race discrimination in the USDA's administration of its loan programs in violation of, *inter alia,* the Equal Credit Opportunity Act. Following certification of the plaintiff class in *Pigford,* the parties undertook settlement negotiations which ultimately culminated in a settlement and the entry of a consent decree by the court following a "fairness hearing" as provided by Rule 23 of the Federal Rules of Civil Procedure. The consent decree provided for the creation of a two-track mechanism to resolve the discrimination claims of individual class members. *Pigford v. Glickman,* 185 F.R.D. 82 (D.D.C.1999). Any claimant who would elect to proceed under Track A, in order to prevail, would be required to submit to a neutral adjudicator "substantial evidence" that he was the victim of race discrimination, a burden which he could meet by showing that he applied to the USDA for a loan or sought loan servicing and that the loan was denied, provided late, approved for a lesser amount than requested, encumbered by restrictive conditions, or USDA failed to provide appropriate loan service, and such treatment was less favorable than that accorded specifically identified, similarly situated white farmers, as a result of which the plaintiff suffered economic damage. *Pigford,* 185 F.R.D. at 94. If the adjudicator were to find that the claimant had sustained his or her burden to present "substantial evidence" of discrimination in a credit transaction, then in accordance with the terms of the consent decree, the claimant would be entitled to receive

> (1) a cash payment of $52,000; (2) forgiveness of all debt owed to the USDA incurred under or affected by the program that formed the basis of the claim; (3) a tax payment directly to the IRS in the amount of 25% of the total debt forgiveness and cash payment; (4) immediate termination of any foreclosure proceedings that USDA initiated in connection with the loan(s) at issue in the claim; and (5) injunctive relief including one-time priority loan consideration and technical assistance.

Id. at 94. If the adjudicator were to find in the claimant's favor and the claim involved discrimination in a benefit program, "the claimant [would be entitled to] receive a cash payment in the amount of the benefit wrongly denied and injunctive relief including one-time priority loan consideration and technical assistance." *Id.*

The consent decree provided a Track B alternative for plaintiffs with more extensive documentation of discrimination. *Id.* at 94. For Track B claimants, after a period of time for discovery, an arbitrator "[would] hold a one day mini-trial and then decide whether the claimant ha[d] established discrimination by a preponderance of the evidence," *id.,* and if, following that mini-trial, the arbitrator were to find that the claimant had shown by a preponderance of the evidence that he was the victim of racial discrimination and that he had suffered damages from that discrimination, the claimant would be entitled to actual damages, the return of inventory property that was foreclosed and other injunctive relief, including a one-time priority loan consideration. *Id.* at 97.

Plaintiffs' Claims Herein

In the wake of the court's approval of the class action settlement in *Pigford*, the plaintiffs herein, 147 "non-African American farmers," filed a class-action complaint in this court charging that as a result of the settlement in *Pigford*, they are now the victims of unlawful race discrimination by the USDA. In a nutshell, these plaintiffs allege that from 1981 through 1996, the period of time covered by the consent decree in *Pigford*, they were subjected to the very same abusive treatment of which the plaintiff class of African American farmers complained in *Pigford*, and yet the USDA, by virtue of the *Pigford* settlement, has chosen to favor only African American farmers by agreeing to extend to them remedial credit opportunities which are not also being extended to "non-African American farmers" who experienced the same mistreatment. Plaintiffs contend, therefore, that because of the Department's racial discrimination in the administration of its loan and benefits programs, they are entitled to declaratory and injunctive relief requiring the USDA to provide to them access to the same benefits as have been extended to the plaintiff class in *Pigford*.

The Secretary's Motion

In its motion, defendant submits that for reasons of judicial comity, this court should dismiss plaintiffs' complaint altogether or should, alternatively, transfer the case to the United States District Court for the District of Columbia in the interest of justice pursuant to 28 U.S.C. § 1404(a) so as to avoid interference with the continuing jurisdiction and remedial authority of that court. Defendant reasons in this regard that plaintiffs' complaint is an obvious challenge to the court's decree in *Pigford* and that consequently, plaintiffs' claims must be, or at least should be, addressed to the court which entered the *Pigford* decree. Defendant urges further, though, that should the court not be inclined to divest itself of the case on comity grounds, the court should dismiss the case for a more fundamental reason, namely, that it fails to state any claim upon which relief can be granted and is thus subject to dismissal under Federal Rule of Civil Procedure 12(b)(6). Because the court agrees that the complaint fails to state a viable claim for relief, the court concludes that defendant's motion is well taken.

Discrimination:

The Pigford and Green Plaintiffs are Not Similarly Situated

Plaintiffs allege that the defendant has denied and continues to deny them substantial and valuable credit opportunities that have been made available to other American farmers who, except for their race, are similarly situated. All of plaintiffs' claims in Counts II, V, VI, VII and VIII (which charge violations of the ECOA, Title VI, § 1981, § 1982 and the equal protection guarantee of the Fifth Amendment), in fact, are grounded on this allegation, which is in turn grounded on the same factual predicate, namely, that the USDA has discriminated against non-African American farmers on the basis of their race by not making available to them those certain credit benefits that it has agreed to provide to certain African American farmers via the *Pigford* settlement. That is to say, all of plaintiffs' claims of discrimination are based on the same allegedly discriminatory act, namely, the creation of the dispute resolution mechanism to resolve the individual claims of race discrimination raised by the *Pigford* class members and the decision to award monetary and other relief to those who succeed on their claims.

According to plaintiffs, by reason of the racially preferential remedial credit opportunities that the USDA has agreed to provide to African American farmers but which it has failed and refused to provide to non-African American farmers who have suffered the same abuses by the USDA in their credit transactions, plaintiffs are the victims of race discrimination.

Plaintiffs readily acknowledge that to prove their case under any of the discrimination theories advanced in their complaint, they must prove, first and foremost, "that the African American farmers that [the USDA] has chosen to favor suffered the same pattern of Unlawful Practices and abuses as Plaintiffs; in other words, Plaintiffs must show that they are similarly situated before their proof of race based disparate treatment becomes a matter of interest." However, and notwithstanding plaintiffs' conclusory assertions to the contrary, it is manifest that they are not similarly situated to the African American farmers that the USDA has "chosen to favor" via the *Pigford* settlement.

While it is necessary to focus on the specific conduct that plaintiffs challenge as discriminatory in considering whether they have alleged any cognizable claim for relief, it is essential in this case to also recognize that the plaintiffs allege that the USDA engaged in misconduct which they do not contend was discriminatory—and which they, in fact, contend was *not* discriminatory. More to the point, these plaintiffs charge, as did the plaintiffs in *Pigford,* that for the twenty years since January 1, 1981, they were the victims of maladministration and abuse by the USDA. They submit that they, like the African American farmers in *Pigford,* "have been denied applications made to [the] Secretary . . . for farm ownership loans for which they had great need and for which they were wholly eligible", that they have been refused operating credit and denied appropriate application processing, and have suffered unreasonable and unnecessary crippling delays in processing their applications, and in receiving the proceeds of loans that have been approved and/or have received approvals of their applications but in impracticably insufficient amounts, and with unreasonably restrictive conditions and/or have thereafter been denied appropriate loan servicing. In short, then, the plaintiffs herein charge that prior to the entry of the consent decree in *Pigford,* the Secretary indiscriminately mistreated African American and non-African American farmers alike, subjecting both to the same or substantially similar unlawful practices. According to these plaintiffs, though, by virtue of, and in the wake of the settlement in *Pigford,* the Department of Agriculture has knowingly, intentionally and consistently engaged in unlawful racial discrimination because it has failed and refused to provide them with the substantial equivalent of alternative Track A and Track B credit opportunities that it has made available to African American farmers, and has provided them with less favorable opportunities than it has provided to African American farmers, notwithstanding that these plaintiffs are similarly situated to those African American farmers in all respects except for their race.

In making this charge, plaintiffs pointedly ignore the fact that the basis for the plaintiffs' claims in *Pigford* was not simply that their applications for loans or credit services had been denied or otherwise mishandled by the USDA—a claim also made by the plaintiffs herein—but that the USDA had denied or mishandled their applications because they were African American. Indeed, plaintiffs' claims are rooted in their insistence that both African American and non-African American farmers were mistreated by the USDA in the decades preceding *Pigford* and that African American farmers were not, in fact, victims of race discrimination at all. However, a review of the *Pigford* court's opinion approving the settlement leaves no doubt that the court believed otherwise. That court, in addressing the proposed settlement in light of the evidence and arguments presented at the fairness hearing, found that the USDA had discriminated against African American farmers *on the basis of race.* The court observed at the start of its opinion, that

> [f]or decades, despite its promise that "no person in the United States shall, on the ground of race, color, or national origin, be excluded from participation in, be denied the benefits of, or be otherwise subjected to discrimination under any program or activity of an applicant or recipient receiving Federal financial assistance from the Department of Agriculture," 7 C.F.R. § 15.1, the Department of Agriculture and the county commissioners discriminated against African American farmers when they denied, delayed or otherwise frustrated the applications of those farmers for farm loans and other credit and benefit programs. Further compounding the problem, in 1983 the Department of Agriculture disbanded its Office of Civil Rights and stopped responding to claims of discrimination. These events were the culmination of a string of broken promises that had been made to African American farmers for well over a century.

> It is difficult to resist the impulse to try to undo all the broken promises and years of discrimination that have led to the precipitous decline in the number of African American farmers in the United States. The Court has before it a proposed settlement of a class action lawsuit that will not undo all that has been done. Despite that fact, however, the Court finds that the settlement is a fair resolution of the claims brought in this case and a good first step towards assuring that the kind of discrimination that has been visited on African American farmers since Reconstruction will not continue into the next century. The Court therefore will approve the settlement.

185 F.R.D. at 85–86. En route to approving the settlement, the court specifically noted that the county committees which were responsible at the local level for approving or denying farm credit and benefit applications, "do not represent the racial diversity of the communities they serve," and the court observed that "[i]n several southeastern states, . . . it took three times as long on average to process the application of an African American farmer as it did to process the application of a white farmer." *Id.* at 87. The court also noted that "a requirement frequently required of African American farmers but not routinely imposed on white farmers" was placement of loaned funds in a "supervised" account that required the signature of the county supervisor for withdrawal, *Id.* The court then commented,

> . . . Plaintiffs' arguments in this case wholly fail to account for the *Pigford* court's findings of race discrimination as a basis for its approval of the consent decree. Furthermore, while the plaintiffs acknowledge that there exists substantial documentation which tends to show that there were "gross failures within the Office of Civil Rights Enforcement and Adjudication at USDA," plaintiffs' arguments in this case also entirely fail to consider that the plaintiffs in *Pigford* complained not only that they were the victims of race discrimination but also that the Secretary's gross mishandling of civil rights complaints filed by African American farmers with the Secretary resulted in the inability of these persons to timely pursue their claims of discrimination with the Secretary and contributed to what the *Pigford* court considered the potential inability of African American farmers to establish their discrimination claims through the usual judicial processes. Plaintiffs dismiss the problems with the civil rights complaint process as having little bearing on any evaluation of the circumstances of the respective parties in *Pigford* and in this case. Yet the admitted failure of the USDA's civil rights enforcement procedures, and the impact of that failure on the *Pigford* plaintiffs' claims, were among the principal considerations which led to the *Pigford* court's decision to certify the class and to approve the settlement. That is to say, the *Pigford* court determined that the remedy proposed by the parties was fair and reasonable not only because the record contained what it considered to be substantial evidence of racial discrimination in the Secretary's administration of the USDA's farm loan programs, but also because the USDA's discrimination complaint process was all but nonexistent.

In their insistence on the viability of their claims, plaintiffs also ignore the fact that the *Pigford* class did not even include all African American farmers whose applications for credit were denied, or even all African American farmers who may have believed that their applications were denied on account of race, but rather included *only* African American farmers whose claims were denied during the relevant time frame (January 1, 1981 through July 1, 1997) *and* who actually "filed a discrimination complaint on or before July 1, 1997, regarding USDA's treatment of such farm credit or benefit application."

Finally, and perhaps most significantly, plaintiffs fail to address at all the fact that while the USDA consented in *Pigford* to a dispute resolution process for the claims of all *Pigford* class members who wished to avail themselves of that process, it did not consent to provide all class members with any actual remedial relief. Rather, the USDA agreed only to provide a remedy to class members who are able to demonstrate, at least by substantial evidence, that the Department discriminated against them on account of their race. Thus, while the USDA may have agreed to provide remedial credit opportunities to certain specific identifiable African American farmers, many other African American farmers have been and will be denied such opportunities.

In sum, plaintiffs' arguments in this case completely ignore the fact that the issue in *Pigford* was not just mistreatment or abuse by the USDA of American farmers, but rather mistreatment and abuse of *African American* farmers *because of their race.* Thus, plaintiffs' position respecting the USDA's allegedly "discriminatory" act—i.e., its agreement to provide valuable benefits to African American farmers—is not well grounded, for it does not fully account for the context in which the *Pigford* consent decree came into existence and achieved court approval, nor does it take into account the precise parameters of the class certified in *Pigford* or the specific relief afforded by the consent decree or the fact that the valuable credit opportunities to which the plaintiffs seek access were not made available by the *Pigford* consent decree to all African American farmers or even all the class members, but only to class members who could establish that they were victims of racial discrimination.

The court's point is simply this: It is not race alone that distinguishes the plaintiffs in this case from the individuals to whom the USDA has agreed via the *Pigford* consent decree to provide remedial credit opportunities, but rather it is the fact that those individuals are African American *and* that they made a timely complaint of *race* discrimination to the USDA *and* that they are able to prove that the USDA denied them a benefit *because of* their race. In other words, it is *proof* of race discrimination, and not simply membership in a racial group, that distinguishes successful *Pigford* class members from the plaintiffs herein. The USDA has not merely chosen to favor African American farmers who prove that they were denied credit benefits, but instead, upon being confronted with what the *Pigford* court considered to be substantial evidence of a pattern and practice of racial discrimination against African Americans, has agreed to provide a remedy to African American farmers within the class who are able to make the requisite showing of discrimination. Thus, as plaintiffs do not allege that the USDA ever denied them credit or credit services on account of their race at any time prior to the *Pigford* consent decree, and they do not allege that they filed prior to this lawsuit any claim of race discrimination regarding the USDA's treatment of any farm credit or benefit application, then they cannot show that they are similarly situated to the *Pigford* farmers to whom the USDA agreed to provide valuable credit opportunities as a remedy for race discrimination practiced against them.

. . . For the foregoing reasons, the court concludes that plaintiffs'. discrimination claims against defendant should be dismissed.

. . . .

Accordingly, the court concludes that these Counts should be dismissed.

Declaratory Judgment:

As Count I of plaintiffs' complaint seeks relief under the Declaratory Judgment Act and does not state a claim independent of plaintiffs' other counts, then given the failure of those other counts, this count, too, is due to be dismissed.

Conclusion:

Irrespective of what the attorneys involved in this suit may have understood, believed or expected with regard to the outcome of the present motion, the court has little doubt that many of the plaintiffs and potential plaintiffs may not have anticipated this result. The court also recognizes that many, most or all of these plaintiffs and potential plaintiffs may well believe that they have been grievously wronged by actions by the USDA in connection not only with their own loans but relative to the disposition of the *Pigford* case. While the court in that respect is regretful of the decision it makes today, the court is nevertheless of the view that under the law, the conclusion it has reached to dismiss the case is the correct conclusion.

Accordingly, it is ordered that defendant's motion to dismiss is granted.

Lea v. United States Department of Agriculture

2011 U.S. Dist. LEXIS 4825, 2011 WL 182698 (W.D. Ky. Jan. 19, 2011)

MEMORANDUM OPINION AND ORDER

Joseph H. Mckinley, Jr., District Judge.

This matter is before the Court on a motion to dismiss by Defendants Farmers National Bank ("FNB") and Larry Hinton and a motion to dismiss by Defendants United States Department of Agriculture ("USDA"), Michael Spalding, and Tom Vilsack. Fully briefed, the matters are ripe for decision. For the reasons that follow, the motions are granted.

I. STANDARD OF REVIEW

Upon a motion to dismiss for failure to state a claim pursuant to Fed.R.Civ.P. 12(b)(6), a court "must construe the complaint in the light most favorable to plaintiff," *League of United Latin Am. Citizens v. Bredesen,* 500 F.3d 523, 527 (6th Cir.2007) (citation omitted), "accept all well-pled factual allegations as true[,]" *id.,* and determine whether the "complaint states a plausible claim for relief[,]" *Ashcroft v. Iqbal,* — U.S. —, —, 129 S.Ct. 1937, 1950, 173 L.Ed.2d 868 (2009). Under this standard, the plaintiff must provide the grounds for its entitlement to relief, which "requires more than labels and conclusions, and a formulaic recitation of the elements of a cause of action." *Bell Atl. Corp. v. Twombly,* 550 U.S. 544, 555, 127 S.Ct. 1955, 167 L.Ed.2d 929 (2007). A plaintiff satisfies this standard only when it "pleads factual content that allows the court to draw the reasonable inference that the defendant is liable for the misconduct alleged." *Iqbal,* 129 S.Ct. at 1949. A complaint falls short if it pleads facts "merely consistent with a defendant's liability" or if the alleged facts do not "permit the court to infer more than the mere possibility of misconduct." *Id.* at 1949–50 .Instead, the allegations must "'show[] that the pleader is entitled to relief.'" *Id.* at 1950 (quoting Fed.R.Civ.P. 8(a)(2)).

II. BACKGROUND FACTS

The USDA, through the USDA Farm Service Agency ("FSA"), acts as a guarantor on loans issued by approved banking institutions to allow farmers to acquire funds to own and/or operate farm property. Plaintiff Corey Lea is an African American, financially disadvantaged farmer who owns and operates a farm located in Warren, Kentucky through such an arrangement with FNB. Pursuant to the loan guarantee program, FSA has a second mortgage on Plaintiffs' real property and FNB holds a first mortgage.

On December 21, 2007, Plaintiffs requested a loan subordination from the USDA after Plaintiffs secured a loan with Independence Bank ("Independence") to refinance Plaintiffs' outstanding loans and to fund the cost of building a new house on the property. On February 28, 2008, the loan subordination request was denied because the USDA appraisal valued Plaintiffs' property at $18,035 less than the proposed total debt. The USDA valuation of Plaintiffs' property was approximately $73,000 less than the appraisal performed by Independence's private appraiser. Following the denial, Plaintiffs filed a discrimination complaint with the USDA alleging that the denial of the loan resulted from Mr. Lea's status as an African American farmer. The USDA accepted Plaintiffs' discrimination claim as valid, but subsequently dismissed the claim following initiation of this suit.

On February 10, 2009, FNB initiated foreclosure proceedings on the loan guaranteed by the USDA because Plaintiffs failed to make payments on the loan for 5 months. FNB was granted a Judgment and Order of Sale on October 5, 2009, as to Plaintiffs' farm property. On November 4, 2009, Defendant Larry Hinton, FNB's attorney, and Defendant Michael Spalding, an Assistant United States Attorney, agreed to waive the one year right of redemption held in favor of the USDA. FNB has not yet instructed the Warren Circuit Court to sell Plaintiffs' property.

III. DISCUSSION

Plaintiffs initiated this action to enjoin FNB from foreclosing on Plaintiffs' real property and to recover damages for the alleged discrimination. Plaintiffs' Amended Complaint cites three causes of action: (1) violation of the Equal Credit Opportunity Act ("ECOA"); (2) violation of the Food, Conservation, and Energy Act ("FCEA"); and (3) violation of 42 U.S.C. § 1985(3). Defendants claim that their actions were in compliance with federal law. The Court will address each cause of action in turn.

A. Violation of ECOA

"An act done with discriminatory intent is not illegal unless it falls within the scope of a federal statute or runs afoul of the Constitution." *Michigan Prot. & Advocacy*

Serv., Inc. v. Babin, 18 F.3d 337, 345–46 (6th Cir.1994). Here, Plaintiffs allege that Defendants violated the ECOA which prohibits "any creditor" from discriminating against "any applicant, with respect to any aspect of a credit transaction . . . on the basis of race."15 U.S.C. § 1691(a). Defendants claim that the accusation is without merit because Plaintiffs do not meet the definition of an "applicant" under the Act, Plaintiffs cannot show they applied and were qualified for "an extension of credit," and Plaintiffs have failed to show that other similar credit applicants were treated more favorably.

In *Hood v. Midwest Sav. Bank,* 95 F. App'x 768 (6th Cir.2004), the court provided the elements necessary to establish a prima facie ECOA claim:

> [A] plaintiff must demonstrate that: (1) he is a member of a protected class; (2) he applied for and was qualified for a loan; (3) the loan application was rejected despite his or her qualifications; and (4) the lender continued to approve loans for applicants with qualifications similar to those of the plaintiff.

Id. at 788 (citing *Babin,* 18 F.3d at 346; *Ward v. Union Planters Nat'l Bank,* 113 F.3d 1236, at *2 (6th Cir.1997) (unpublished table decision)).

Plaintiffs rely on *Mays v. Buckeye Rural Elec. Co-op., Inc.,* 277 F.3d 873 (6th Cir.2002) for the proposition that the Sixth Circuit has not adopted the fourth, the "disparate treatment" element. Plaintiffs claim that because the *Mays* court neglected to include the "disparate treatment" element when reciting the elements necessary to an ECOA claim, this showing is not required. The court in *Hood* rejected this identical argument:

> [Plaintiff] argues that a plaintiff can establish a prima facie case of credit discrimination by showing the following four elements: (1) plaintiff was a member of the protected class; (2) plaintiff applied for credit from defendants; (3) plaintiff was qualified for the credit; and (4) despite plaintiff's qualifications, defendant denied her credit application. [Plaintiff] cites *Mays v. Buckeye Rural Elec. Co-op.,* 277 F.3d 873, 877 (6th Cir.2002), as authority for this statement of the elements. This reliance, however, is misplaced. [Plaintiff] relies on a Tenth Circuit case, *Matthiesen v. Banc One Mortgage Corp.,* 173 F.3d 1242, 1246 (10th Cir.1999), for this statement of the elements. The elements of the test, however, had already been set forth by the Sixth Circuit by the time *Matthiesen* was decided. *See Michigan Prot. & Advocacy Serv., Inc.,* 18 F.3d at 346. Since the *Matthiesen* court did not acknowledge *Michigan Protection & Advocacy Service* or attempt to distinguish it in any way, it appears likely that an exact statement of the elements was not critical to the decision in *Mays* and that the court simply overlooked the existing Sixth Circuit formulation.

Hood, 95 F. App'x at 778 n. 7.

Hood made clear that the test articulated in *Michigan Protection* is the appropriate test in the Sixth Circuit to determine whether an ECOA claim has been properly made. Therefore, facts supporting "disparate treatment" must be plead. *See Sanders v. USDA Rural Housing,* 2008 WL 2097386 (M.D.Tenn. May 16, 2008) ("disparate treatment" element applied to ECOA claim); *Jat, Inc. v. Nat'l City Bank of the Midwest,* 2008 WL 2397657 (E.D.Mich. June 10, 2008) (same). Plaintiffs have failed to advance any facts indicating "disparate treatment" and therefore the claim must be dismissed.

B. Violation of FCEA

Plaintiffs allege that because of the pending discrimination claim with the USDA, the FCEA's moratorium on foreclosure proceedings prevented FNB from obtaining the Judgment and Order of Sale. Defendants allege that the moratorium only prevented the USDA from initiating foreclosure proceedings, not private institutions like FNB.

In cases of statutory construction, the Court begins "by analyzing the statutory language, 'assuming that the ordinary meaning of that language accurately expresses the legislative purpose.'" *Hardt v. Reliance Standard Life Ins. Co.,* — U.S. — , —, 130 S.Ct. 2149, 2156, 176 L.Ed.2d 998 (2010) (quoting *Gross v. FBL Fin. Servs., Inc.,* — U.S. —, —, 129 S.Ct. 2343, 2350, 174 L.Ed.2d 119 (2009)). In the absence of ambiguity, the Court must enforce the statute according to its terms. *Hardt,* 130 S. Ct. at 2156.

7 U.S.C. § 1981a(b)(1) provides:

> Subject to the other provisions of this subsection, effective beginning on the date of the enactment of this subsection, there shall be in effect a moratorium, with respect to farmer program loans made under subchapter I, II, or III of this chapter on all acceleration and foreclosure proceedings *instituted by the Department of Agriculture* against any farmer or rancher who—
>
> (A) has pending against the Department a claim of program discrimination that is accepted by the Department as valid; or
>
> (B) files a claim of program discrimination that is accepted by the Department as valid.

(emphasis added). The Court is not persuaded that 7 U.S.C. § 1981a(b)(1) was intended to prevent loans guaranteed by the USDA from being foreclosed on by private institutions. To the contrary, 7 U.S.C. § 1981a(b)(1) unambiguously limits foreclosure proceedings only to those "instituted by the Department of Agriculture." This language would be superfluous if Congress intended for the moratorium to apply to all foreclosure proceedings, including those initiated by private banking institutions. Here, the foreclosure was not initiated by the USDA and therefore the moratorium is not applicable. Accordingly, FNB, as a private party, was free to begin foreclosure proceedings on the guaranteed loan regardless of whether a discrimination claim was pending.

Plaintiffs cite 7 C.F.R. § 762.143 for the suggestion that Congress intended for 7 U.S.C. § 1981a(b)(1) to apply to guaranteed loans. The relevant language of 7 C.F.R.

§ 762.143, which tracks that of 7 U.S.C. § 1999(g), states: "[t]he lender may not initi-ate foreclosure action on the [guaranteed] loan until 60 days after eligibility of the borrower to participate in the interest assistance programs has been determined by the Agency." The Court presumes that, "where words differ as they differ here, 'Congress acts intentionally and purposely in the disparate inclusion or exclusion.'" *Burlington N. & Santa Fe Ry. Co. v. White,* 548 U.S. 53, 63, 126 S.Ct. 2405, 165 L. Ed.2d 345 (2006) (quoting *Russello v. United States,* 464 U.S. 16, 23, 104 S.Ct. 296, 78 L.Ed.2d 17 (1983)). It is evident that "Congress intended the differences that its language suggests, for the two provisions differ not only in language but in purpose as well." *White,* 548 U.S. at 63. 7 U.S.C. § 1981a(b)(1) places a moratorium on fore-closures of farmer program loans initiated by the USDA, where 7 C.F.R. § 762.143 places a temporary hold on liquidation proceedings by a private lender of a guar-anteed loan until eligibility to participate in the Interest Rate Reduction Program has been established. Therefore, in crafting section 1981a(b)(1), Congress limited the moratorium solely to those foreclosures "instituted by the Department of Agri-culture," and the Court must enforce the provision according to its unambiguous terms. Because there have been no allegations that the USDA instituted the foreclo-sure proceedings, Plaintiffs' FCEA claim is dismissed.

C. 42 U.S.C. § 1985(3)

Lastly, Plaintiffs claim that Defendants engaged in a conspiracy of discrimina-tion which allowed FNB to improperly begin foreclosure proceedings on Plaintiffs' property. Specifically, Plaintiffs allege that the conspiracy is evidenced by the fol-lowing: (1) FNB and USDA failed to comply with 7 C.F.R. § 762.143 which requires USDA approval before a lender may initiate a foreclosure proceeding; (2) FNB and USDA violated 7 C.F.R. § 762.149 by failing to pursue mediation and submit a liquidation plan prior to seeking foreclosure; and (3) Mr. Hinton and Mr. Spald-ing violated 28 U.S.C. § 2410 by improperly waiving the USDA's one year right of redemption to allow FNB to begin foreclosure proceedings. Defendants assert that the Amended Complaint fails to state a valid section 1985(3) claim because: (1) the Amended Complaint is void of any facts to support the contention that Defendants acted with "class based animus"; (2) Plaintiffs' claim is barred by res judicata; (3) initiation of the foreclosure proceedings was lawful and therefore Defendants can-not establish a conspiracy; and (4) Defendants are protected by qualified immunity.

The Sixth Circuit has held that a viable 42 U.S.C. § 1985(3) claim must contain:

> (1) [A] conspiracy involving two or more persons (2) for the purpose of depriving, directly or indirectly, a person or class of persons of the equal protection of the laws and (3) an act in furtherance of the conspiracy (4) which causes injury to a person or property, or a deprivation of any right or privilege of a citizen of the United States.

Johnson v. Hills & Dales Gen. Hosp., 40 F.3d 837, 839 (6th Cir .1994) (citing *Hilliard v. Ferguson,* 30 F.3d 649, 652–53 (5th Cir .1994)). A plaintiff "must also establish that the conspiracy was motivated by a class-based animus." *Johnson,* 40 F.3d at 839.

The Court agrees with Defendants in that Plaintiffs failed to appropriately plead the "class-based animus" element. The inquiry is twofold. First, in order to be "[a] class protected by section 1985(3)[, the plaintiff] must possess the characteristics of a discrete and insular minority, such as race, national origin, or gender." *Haverstick Enters., Inc. v. Fin. Fed. Credit, Inc.,* 32 F.3d 989, 994 (6th Cir.1994). Secondly, the plaintiff must put forth specific facts indicating that the conspiracy was motivated by "'some racial or perhaps otherwise class-based, invidiously discriminatory animus.'" *Bartell v. Lohiser,* 215 F.3d 550, 559–60 (6th Cir.2000) (quoting *United Bhd. of Carpenters & Joiners of Am. v. Scott,* 463 U.S. 825, 829, 103 S.Ct. 3352, 77 L.Ed.2d 1049 (1983)). In other words, "as the Supreme Court recently held, a complaint that includes conclusory allegations of discriminatory intent without additional supporting details does not sufficiently show that the pleader is entitled to relief. . . . [A section 1985] claim can survive only if [the plaintiff] pleaded facts supporting that conclusion." *Nali v. Ekman,* 335 F. App'x 909, 913 (6th Cir.2009).

Defendants concede that Mr. Lea is a member of a protected class. To support the argument that Defendants were motivated by class-based animus, Plaintiffs rely on the following quote from *Pigford v. Glickman,* 185 F.R.D. 82 (D.D.C.1999):

> For decades, despite its promise that 'no person in the United States shall, on the ground of race, color, or national origin, be excluded from participation in, be denied the benefits of, or be otherwise subjected to discrimination under any program or activity of an applicant or recipient receiving Federal financial assistance from the Department of Agriculture,' 7 C.F.R. § 15.1, the Department of Agriculture and the county commissioners discriminated against African American farmers when they denied, delayed or otherwise frustrated the applications of those farmers for farm loans and other credit and benefit programs.

Id. at 85.

However, in order to overcome a 12(b)(6) motion, Plaintiffs must "*plead*[] *factual content* that allows the court to draw the reasonable inference that the defendant is liable for the misconduct alleged." *Iqbal,* 129 S.Ct. at 1949 (emphasis added). *See Nali,* 335 F. App'x at 913 (Where no facts were presented to show motivation to discriminate, plaintiff's section 1985(3) claim was dismissed); *Anthony v. Ranger,* 2010 WL 1268031, at *13 (E.D.Mich. March 30, 2010) (Section 1985(3) claim dismissed where court found that "[p]laintiff sets forth no plausible facts showing that the alleged conspiracy was motivated by racial or other class based animus, other than stating that Plaintiff is black"); *Phifer v. City of Grand Rapids, Michigan,* 657 F. Supp.2d 867, 876 (W.D.Mich.2009) (Section 1985 claim appropriately dismissed where "[plaintiff has neither shown the existence of a conspiracy nor alleged any fact suggesting that the conduct she complains of was motivated by racial or any other class-based animus"). A review of the Amended Complaint reveals that Plaintiffs have failed to put forth any plausible facts showing that the alleged conspiracy was motivated by racial animus. Simply citing *Pigford* for the proposition that the

USDA had engaged in a pattern of discrimination against African American farmers over a decade ago does not constitute evidence of discrimination in this case. Furthermore, the fact that Defendants waived the right of redemption also does not support an allegation of discrimination absent facts tending to show that the USDA had done just the opposite for those of a different race.

Because there have been no specific facts presented to allow the Court to reasonably conclude that the alleged discrimination was motivated by a class-based animus, Plaintiffs' claim is dismissed and the Court need not address the remainder of Defendants' arguments.

IV. CONCLUSION

For the reasons set forth above, **IT IS HEREBY ORDERED** that Defendants' motions to dismiss are **GRANTED.**

Notes

1. What did the Judge determine was missing from the claims of white farmers alleging discrimination? On what basis were the claims thrown out? How did their claims compare to those of the black farmers in the *Pigford* class action suit?

2. What is the standard for a successful Rule 23(b)(3) class? What function does class certification serve as compared to individual cases? How does class certification strengthen the adjudication process in each of the cases?

3. Consider Judge Friedman's response to plaintiffs' request for future looking resolutions to prevent discrimination by the USDA. How does Judge Freidman's reasoning resemble or differ from the Supreme Court's when overseeing desegregation in education post-*Brown*?

Chapter 11

Sexual Orientation and Gender Identity

A. Law as Power

The strategies that helped obtain meaningful civil rights in the racial context have been instrumental in many others, including some still emerging and shaping. Thus far, the Road to *Brown* framework, made so successful by Charles Hamilton Houston in the twentieth century, still serves as an effective strategic basis in the twenty-first. Still, ongoing realities and legal obstacles make civil rights litigation ever so challenging. As longstanding excluded groups are able to develop strategies for challenging restrictive legal constructs, the underlying layers of power supporting these laws are increasingly laid bare.

In the evolving case of sexual identity and sexual orientation, for example, litigation has only begun scratching the surface of issues affecting Lesbian, Gay, Bisexual, Transsexual, and Queer, "LGBTQ," communities. The layers of power are unraveling as these legal issues shape up. Among other dynamics, they reveal the deep impact of judges' education, social awareness and political leanings on their decisions. Critical scholars have long showcased law as a product of subjective elements and adjudication. Nowhere is this more evident than in the context of sexuality and identity. Additionally, this area fully illustrates the nature of law as evolving and contingent on deeper understanding of and exposure to issues faced by various communities.

One of these legal changes occurred progressively around sodomy laws. Intolerance and disapproval of same-sex intimacy led states to pass anti-sodomy laws. Over time, however, as attitudes changed, these laws became unpopular and largely unenforced in later decades. As national discourse focused attention on stereotypes burdening same-sex partners, the litigation of cases challenging the legality of sodomy laws began. The Supreme Court first reviewed the issue in *Bowers v. Hardwick*[1] to consider whether a state sodomy statute violated the Substantive Due Process Clause of the Fourteenth Amendment. The Court then, infamously, reasoned that the law was constitutional and that tradition supported the prohibition of same-sex intimacy.

---

1. Bowers v. Hardwick, 478 U.S. 186 (1986).

Nearly twenty years later, however, sweeping changes in views had swept the nation. Campaigns to educate the public on the rights and dignity of gay and lesbian citizens bore fruit.[2] At the beginning of the millennium, states began to allow same sex unions through community partnership agreements. It was still a long way to marriage equality, but a movement had undeniably started. Such is the social backdrop of *Lawrence v. Texas,* below. *Lawrence* reversed *Bowers* and redefined our tradition as one which now rejects anti-sodomy laws. Justice Kennedy, who penned the opinion, came to forge a significant legacy fleshing out the scope of protection, regarding sexual autonomy, for gay citizens under Substantive Due Process Clause. *Windsor* and *Obergefell,* below, continued that legacy.

Lawrence v. Texas

539 U.S. 558 (2003)

Justice Kennedy delivered the opinion of the Court.

Liberty protects the person from unwarranted government intrusions into a dwelling or other private places. In our tradition the State is not omnipresent in the home. And there are other spheres of our lives and existence, outside the home, where the State should not be a dominant presence. Freedom extends beyond spatial bounds. Liberty presumes an autonomy of self that includes freedom of thought, belief, expression, and certain intimate conduct. The instant case involves liberty of the person both in its spatial and in its more transcendent dimensions.

I

The question before the Court is the validity of a Texas statute making it a crime for two persons of the same sex to engage in certain intimate sexual conduct.

In Houston, Texas, officers of the Harris County Police Department were dispatched to a private residence in response to a reported weapons disturbance. They entered an apartment where one of the petitioners, John Geddes Lawrence, resided. The right of the police to enter does not seem to have been questioned. The officers observed Lawrence and another man, Tyron Garner, engaging in a sexual act. The two petitioners were arrested, held in custody overnight, and charged and convicted before a Justice of the Peace.

The complaints described their crime as "deviate sexual intercourse, namely anal sex, with a member of the same sex (man)." App. to Pet. for Cert. 127a, 139a. The applicable state law is Tex. Penal Code Ann. § 21.06(a) (2003). It provides: "A person commits an offense if he engages in deviate sexual intercourse with another individual of the same sex." The statute defines "[d]eviate sexual intercourse" as follows:

---

2. Marriage Center, http://www.hrc.org/campaigns/marriage-center; *LGBT Relationships,* https://www.aclu.org/issues/lgbt-rights/lgbt-relationships; Pride, http://www.pride.com/.

"(A) any contact between any part of the genitals of one person and the mouth or anus of another person; or

"(B) the penetration of the genitals or the anus of another person with an object." § 21.01(1).

The petitioners exercised their right to a trial *de novo* in Harris County Criminal Court. They challenged the statute as a violation of the Equal Protection Clause of the Fourteenth Amendment and of a like provision of the Texas Constitution. Tex. Const., Art. 1, § 3a. Those contentions were rejected. The petitioners, having entered a plea of *nolo contendere,* were each fined $200 and assessed court costs of $141.25. App. to Pet. for Cert. 107a-110a.

The Court of Appeals for the Texas Fourteenth District considered the petitioners' federal constitutional arguments under both the Equal Protection and Due Process Clauses of the Fourteenth Amendment. After hearing the case en banc the court, in a divided opinion, rejected the constitutional arguments and affirmed the convictions. 41 S.W.3d 349 (2001). The majority opinion indicates that the Court of Appeals considered our decision in *Bowers v. Hardwick,* 478 U.S. 186, 106 S.Ct. 2841, 92 L.Ed.2d 140 (1986), to be controlling on the federal due process aspect of the case. *Bowers* then being authoritative, this was proper.

We granted certiorari, 537 U.S. 1044, 123 S.Ct. 661, 154 L.Ed.2d 514 (2002), to consider three questions:

1. Whether petitioners' criminal convictions under the Texas 'Homosexual Conduct' law—which criminalizes sexual intimacy by same-sex couples, but not identical behavior by different-sex couples—violate the Fourteenth Amendment guarantee of equal protection of the laws.

2. Whether petitioners' criminal convictions for adult consensual sexual intimacy in the home violate their vital interests in liberty and privacy protected by the Due Process Clause of the Fourteenth Amendment.

3. Whether *Bowers v. Hardwick, supra,* should be overruled. See Pet. for Cert. i.

The petitioners were adults at the time of the alleged offense. Their conduct was in private and consensual.

II

We conclude the case should be resolved by determining whether the petitioners were free as adults to engage in the private conduct in the exercise of their liberty under the Due Process Clause of the Fourteenth Amendment to the Constitution. For this inquiry we deem it necessary to reconsider the Court's holding in *Bowers.*

There are broad statements of the substantive reach of liberty under the Due Process Clause in earlier cases, including *Pierce v. Society of Sisters,* 268 U.S. 510, 45 S. Ct. 571, 69 L.Ed. 1070 (1925), and *Meyer v. Nebraska,* 262 U.S. 390, 43 S.Ct. 625, 67 L. Ed. 1042 (1923); but the most pertinent beginning point is our decision in *Griswold v. Connecticut,* 381 U.S. 479, 85 S.Ct. 1678, 14 L.Ed.2d 510 (1965).

In *Griswold* the Court invalidated a state law prohibiting the use of drugs or devices of contraception and counseling or aiding and abetting the use of contraceptives. The Court described the protected interest as a right to privacy and placed emphasis on the marriage relation and the protected space of the marital bedroom. *Id.,* at 485, 85 S.Ct. 1678.

After *Griswold* it was established that the right to make certain decisions regarding sexual conduct extends beyond the marital relationship. In *Eisenstadt v. Baird,* 405 U.S. 438, 92 S.Ct. 1029, 31 L.Ed.2d 349 (1972), the Court invalidated a law prohibiting the distribution of contraceptives to unmarried persons. The case was decided under the Equal Protection Clause, *id.,* at 454, 92 S.Ct. 1029; but with respect to unmarried persons, the Court went on to state the fundamental proposition that the law impaired the exercise of their personal rights, *ibid*. It quoted from the statement of the Court of Appeals finding the law to be in conflict with fundamental human rights, and it followed with this statement of its own:

> "It is true that in *Griswold* the right of privacy in question inhered in the marital relationship . . . . If the right of privacy means anything, it is the right of the *individual,* married or single, to be free from unwarranted governmental intrusion into matters so fundamentally affecting a person as the decision whether to bear or beget a child." *Id.,* at 453, 92 S.Ct. 1029.

The opinions in *Griswold* and *Eisenstadt* were part of the background for the decision in *Roe v. Wade,* 410 U.S. 113, 93 S.Ct. 705, 35 L.Ed.2d 147 (1973). As is well known, the case involved a challenge to the Texas law prohibiting abortions, but the laws of other States were affected as well. Although the Court held the woman's rights were not absolute, her right to elect an abortion did have real and substantial protection as an exercise of her liberty under the Due Process Clause. The Court cited cases that protect spatial freedom and cases that go well beyond it. *Roe* recognized the right of a woman to make certain fundamental decisions affecting her destiny and confirmed once more that the protection of liberty under the Due Process Clause has a substantive dimension of fundamental significance in defining the rights of the person.

In *Carey v. Population Services Int'l,* 431 U.S. 678, 97 S.Ct. 2010, 52 L.Ed.2d 675 (1977), the Court confronted a New York law forbidding sale or distribution of contraceptive devices to persons under 16 years of age. Although there was no single opinion for the Court, the law was invalidated. Both *Eisenstadt* and *Carey,* as well as the holding and rationale in *Roe,* confirmed that the reasoning of *Griswold* could not be confined to the protection of rights of married adults. This was the state of the law with respect to some of the most relevant cases when the Court considered *Bowers v. Hardwick.*

The facts in *Bowers* had some similarities to the instant case. A police officer, whose right to enter seems not to have been in question, observed Hardwick, in his own bedroom, engaging in intimate sexual conduct with another adult male. The conduct was in violation of a Georgia statute making it a criminal offense to engage in sodomy. One difference between the two cases is that the Georgia statute prohibited the conduct whether or not the participants were of the same sex, while the Texas statute, as we have seen, applies only to participants of the same sex. Hardwick was not prosecuted, but he brought an action in federal court to declare the state statute invalid. He alleged he was a practicing homosexual and that the criminal prohibition violated rights guaranteed to him by the Constitution. The Court, in an opinion by Justice White, sustained the Georgia law. Chief Justice Burger and Justice Powell joined the opinion of the Court and filed separate, concurring opinions. Four Justices dissented. 478 U.S., at 199, 106 S.Ct. 2841 (opinion of Blackmun, J., joined by Brennan, Marshall, and Stevens, JJ.); *id.*, at 214, 106 S.Ct. 2841 (opinion of Stevens, J., joined by Brennan and Marshall, JJ.).

The Court began its substantive discussion in *Bowers* as follows: "The issue presented is whether the Federal Constitution confers a fundamental right upon homosexuals to engage in sodomy and hence invalidates the laws of the many States that still make such conduct illegal and have done so for a very long time." *Id.*, at 190, 106 S.Ct. 2841. That statement, we now conclude, discloses the Court's own failure to appreciate the extent of the liberty at stake. To say that the issue in *Bowers* was simply the right to engage in certain sexual conduct demeans the claim the individual put forward, just as it would demean a married couple were it to be said marriage is simply about the right to have sexual intercourse. The laws involved in *Bowers* and here are, to be sure, statutes that purport to do no more than prohibit a particular sexual act. Their penalties and purposes, though, have more far-reaching consequences, touching upon the most private human conduct, sexual behavior, and in the most private of places, the home. The statutes do seek to control a personal relationship that, whether or not entitled to formal recognition in the law, is within the liberty of persons to choose without being punished as criminals.

This, as a general rule, should counsel against attempts by the State, or a court, to define the meaning of the relationship or to set its boundaries absent injury to a person or abuse of an institution the law protects. It suffices for us to acknowledge that adults may choose to enter upon this relationship in the confines of their homes and their own private lives and still retain their dignity as free persons. When sexuality finds overt expression in intimate conduct with another person, the conduct can be but one element in a personal bond that is more enduring. The liberty protected by the Constitution allows homosexual persons the right to make this choice.

Having misapprehended the claim of liberty there presented to it, and thus stating the claim to be whether there is a fundamental right to engage in consensual sodomy, the *Bowers* Court said: "Proscriptions against that conduct have ancient roots." *Id.*, at 192, 106 S.Ct. 2841. In academic writings, and in many of the scholarly *amicus* briefs filed to assist the Court in this case, there are fundamental criticisms of the historical premises relied upon by the majority and concurring opinions in *Bowers*. Brief for Cato Institute as *Amicus Curiae* 16–17; Brief for American Civil Liberties Union et al. as *Amici Curiae* 15–21; Brief for Professors of History et al. as *Amici Curiae* 3–10. We need not enter this debate in the attempt to reach a definitive historical judgment, but the following considerations counsel against adopting the definitive conclusions upon which *Bowers* placed such reliance.

At the outset it should be noted that there is no longstanding history in this country of laws directed at homosexual conduct as a distinct matter. Beginning in colonial times there were prohibitions of sodomy derived from the English criminal laws passed in the first instance by the Reformation Parliament of 1533. The English prohibition was understood to include relations between men and women as well as relations between men and men. See, *e.g., King v. Wiseman,* 92 Eng. Rep. 774, 775 (K.B.1718) (interpreting "mankind" in Act of 1533 as including women and girls). Nineteenth-century commentators similarly read American sodomy, buggery, and crime-against-nature statutes as criminalizing certain relations between men and women and between men and men. See, *e.g.,* 2 J. Bishop, Criminal Law § 1028 (1858); 2 J. Chitty, Criminal Law 47–50 (5th Am. ed. 1847); R. Desty, A Compendium of American Criminal Law 143 (1882); J. May, The Law of Crimes § 203 (2d ed. 1893). The absence of legal prohibitions focusing on homosexual conduct may be explained in part by noting that according to some scholars the concept of the homosexual as a distinct category of person did not emerge until the late 19th century. See, e.g., J. Katz, The Invention of Heterosexuality 10 (1995); J. D'Emilio & E. Freedman, Intimate Matters: A History of Sexuality in America 121 (2d ed. 1997) ("The modern terms *homosexuality* and *heterosexuality* do not apply to an era that had not yet articulated these distinctions"). Thus early American sodomy laws were not directed at homosexuals as such but instead sought to prohibit nonprocreative sexual activity more generally. This does not suggest approval of homosexual conduct. It does tend to show that this particular form of conduct was not thought of as a separate category from like conduct between heterosexual persons.

Laws prohibiting sodomy do not seem to have been enforced against consenting adults acting in private. A substantial number of sodomy prosecutions and convictions for which there are surviving records were for predatory acts against those who could not or did not consent, as in the case of a minor or the victim of an assault. As to these, one purpose for the prohibitions was to ensure there would be no lack of coverage if a predator committed a sexual assault that did not constitute rape as defined by the criminal law. Thus the model sodomy indictments presented in a 19th-century treatise, see 2 Chitty, *supra,* at 49, addressed the predatory acts of an adult man against a minor girl or minor boy. Instead of targeting relations between consenting adults in private, 19th-century sodomy prosecutions typically involved relations between men and minor girls or minor boys, relations between adults involving force, relations between adults implicating disparity in status, or relations between men and animals.

To the extent that there were any prosecutions for the acts in question, 19th-century evidence rules imposed a burden that would make a conviction more difficult to obtain even taking into account the problems always inherent in prosecuting consensual acts committed in private. Under then-prevailing standards, a man could not be convicted of sodomy based upon testimony of a consenting partner, because the partner was considered an accomplice. A partner's testimony, however, was admissible if he or she had not consented to the act or was a minor, and therefore incapable of consent. See, *e.g.,* F. Wharton, Criminal Law 443 (2d ed. 1852); 1 F. Wharton, Criminal Law 512 (8th ed. 1880). The rule may explain in part the infrequency of these prosecutions. In all events that infrequency makes it difficult to say that society approved of a rigorous and systematic punishment of the consensual acts committed in private and by adults. The longstanding criminal prohibition of homosexual sodomy upon which the *Bowers* decision placed such reliance is as consistent with a general condemnation of nonprocreative sex as it is with an established tradition of prosecuting acts because of their homosexual character.

The policy of punishing consenting adults for private acts was not much discussed in the early legal literature. We can infer that one reason for this was the very private nature of the conduct. Despite the absence of prosecutions, there may have been periods in which there was public criticism of homosexuals as such and an insistence that the criminal laws be enforced to discourage their practices. But far from possessing "ancient roots," *Bowers,* 478 U.S., at 192, 106 S.Ct. 2841, American laws targeting same-sex couples did not develop until the last third of the 20th century. The reported decisions concerning the prosecution of consensual, homosexual sodomy between adults for the years 1880–1995 are not always clear in the details, but a significant number involved conduct in a public place. See Brief for American Civil Liberties Union et al. as *Amici Curiae* 14–15, and n. 18.

It was not until the 1970's that any State singled out same-sex relations for criminal prosecution, and only nine States have done so. See 1977 Ark. Gen. Acts no. 828; 1983 Kan. Sess. Laws p. 652; 1974 Ky. Acts p. 847; 1977 Mo. Laws p. 687; 1973 Mont. Laws p. 1339; 1977 Nev. Stats. p. 1632; 1989 Tenn. Pub. Acts ch. 591; 1973 Tex. Gen. Laws ch. 399; see also *Post v. State,* 715 P.2d 1105 (Okla.Crim.App.1986) (sodomy law invalidated as applied to different-sex couples). Post-*Bowers* even some of these States did not adhere to the policy of suppressing homosexual conduct. Over the course of the last decades, States with same-sex prohibitions have moved toward abolishing them. See, *e.g., Jegley v. Picado,* 349 Ark. 600, 80 S.W.3d 332 (2002); *Gryczan v. State,* 283 Mont. 433, 942 P.2d 112 (1997); *Campbell v. Sundquist,* 926 S.W.2d 250 (Tenn.App.1996); *Commonwealth v. Wasson,* 842 S.W.2d 487 (Ky.1992); see also 1993 Nev. Stats. p. 518 (repealing Nev.Rev.Stat. § 201.193).

In summary, the historical grounds relied upon in *Bowers* are more complex than the majority opinion and the concurring opinion by Chief Justice Burger indicate. Their historical premises are not without doubt and, at the very least, are overstated.

It must be acknowledged, of course, that the Court in *Bowers* was making the broader point that for centuries there have been powerful voices to condemn homosexual conduct as immoral. The condemnation has been shaped by religious beliefs, conceptions of right and acceptable behavior, and respect for the traditional family. For many persons these are not trivial concerns but profound and deep convictions accepted as ethical and moral principles to which they aspire and which thus determine the course of their lives. These considerations do not answer the question before us, however. The issue is whether the majority may use the power of the State to enforce these views on the whole society through operation of the criminal law. "Our obligation is to define the liberty of all, not to mandate our own moral code." *Planned Parenthood of Southeastern Pa. v. Casey*, 505 U.S. 833, 850, 112 S.Ct. 2791, 120 L.Ed.2d 674 (1992).

Chief Justice Burger joined the opinion for the Court in *Bowers* and further explained his views as follows: "Decisions of individuals relating to homosexual conduct have been subject to state intervention throughout the history of Western civilization. Condemnation of those practices is firmly rooted in Judeao-Christian moral and ethical standards." 478 U.S., at 196, 106 S.Ct. 2841. As with Justice White's assumptions about history, scholarship casts some doubt on the sweeping nature of the statement by Chief Justice Burger as it pertains to private homosexual conduct between consenting adults. See, *e.g.,* Eskridge, Hardwick and Historiography, 1999 U. Ill. L.Rev. 631, 656. In all events we think that our laws and traditions in the past half century are of most relevance here. These references show an emerging awareness that liberty gives substantial protection to adult persons in deciding how to conduct their private lives in matters pertaining to sex. "[H]istory and tradition are the starting point but not in all cases the ending point of the substantive due process inquiry." *County of Sacramento v. Lewis*, 523 U.S. 833, 857, 118 S.Ct. 1708, 140 L. Ed.2d 1043 (1998) (Kennedy, J., concurring).

This emerging recognition should have been apparent when *Bowers* was decided. In 1955 the American Law Institute promulgated the Model Penal Code and made clear that it did not recommend or provide for "criminal penalties for consensual sexual relations conducted in private." ALI, Model Penal Code § 213.2, Comment 2, p. 372 (1980). It justified its decision on three grounds: (1) The prohibitions undermined respect for the law by penalizing conduct many people engaged in; (2) the statutes regulated private conduct not harmful to others; and (3) the laws were arbitrarily enforced and thus invited the danger of blackmail. ALI, Model Penal Code, Commentary 277–280 (Tent. Draft No. 4, 1955). In 1961 Illinois changed its laws to conform to the Model Penal Code. Other States soon followed. Brief for Cato Institute as *Amicus Curiae* 15–16.

In *Bowers* the Court referred to the fact that before 1961 all 50 States had outlawed sodomy, and that at the time of the Court's decision 24 States and the District of Columbia had sodomy laws. 478 U.S., at 192–193, 106 S.Ct. 2841. Justice Powell pointed out that these prohibitions often were being ignored, however. Georgia, for instance, had not sought to enforce its law for decades. *Id.,* at 197–198, n. 2, 106 S. Ct. 2841 ("The history of nonenforcement suggests the moribund character today of laws criminalizing this type of private, consensual conduct").

The sweeping references by Chief Justice Burger to the history of Western civilization and to Judeo-Christian moral and ethical standards did not take account of other authorities pointing in an opposite direction. A committee advising the British Parliament recommended in 1957 repeal of laws punishing homosexual conduct. The Wolfenden Report: Report of the Committee on Homosexual Offenses and Prostitution (1963). Parliament enacted the substance of those recommendations 10 years later. Sexual Offences Act 1967, § 1.

Of even more importance, almost five years before *Bowers* was decided the European Court of Human Rights considered a case with parallels to *Bowers* and to today's case. An adult male resident in Northern Ireland alleged he was a practicing homosexual who desired to engage in consensual homosexual conduct. The laws of Northern Ireland forbade him that right. He alleged that he had been questioned, his home had been searched, and he feared criminal prosecution. The court held that the laws proscribing the conduct were invalid under the European Convention on Human Rights. *Dudgeon v. United Kingdom*, 45 Eur. Ct. H.R. (1981) & ¶ 52. Authoritative in all countries that are members of the Council of Europe (21 nations then, 45 nations now), the decision is at odds with the premise in *Bowers* that the claim put forward was insubstantial in our Western civilization.

In our own constitutional system the deficiencies in *Bowers* became even more apparent in the years following its announcement. The 25 States with laws prohibiting the relevant conduct referenced in the *Bowers* decision are reduced now to 13, of which 4 enforce their laws only against homosexual conduct. In those States where sodomy is still proscribed, whether for same-sex or heterosexual conduct, there is a pattern of nonenforcement with respect to consenting adults acting in private. The State of Texas admitted in 1994 that as of that date it had not prosecuted anyone under those circumstances. *State v. Morales*, 869 S.W.2d 941, 943.

Two principal cases decided after *Bowers* cast its holding into even more doubt. In *Planned Parenthood of Southeastern Pa. v. Casey*, 505 U.S. 833, 112 S.Ct. 2791, 120 L. Ed.2d 674 (1992), the Court reaffirmed the substantive force of the liberty protected by the Due Process Clause. The *Casey* decision again confirmed that our laws and tradition afford constitutional protection to personal decisions relating to marriage, procreation, contraception, family relationships, child rearing, and education. *Id.*, at 851, 112 S.Ct. 2791. In explaining the respect the Constitution demands for the autonomy of the person in making these choices, we stated as follows:

> "These matters, involving the most intimate and personal choices a person may make in a lifetime, choices central to personal dignity and autonomy, are central to the liberty protected by the Fourteenth Amendment. At the heart of liberty is the right to define one's own concept of existence, of meaning, of the universe, and of the mystery of human life. Beliefs about these matters could not define the attributes of personhood were they formed under compulsion of the State." *Ibid.*

Persons in a homosexual relationship may seek autonomy for these purposes, just as heterosexual persons do. The decision in *Bowers* would deny them this right.

The second post-*Bowers* case of principal relevance is *Romer v. Evans*, 517 U.S. 620, 116 S.Ct. 1620, 134 L.Ed.2d 855 (1996). There the Court struck down class-based legislation directed at homosexuals as a violation of the Equal Protection Clause. *Romer* invalidated an amendment to Colorado's Constitution which named as a solitary class persons who were homosexuals, lesbians, or bisexual either by "orientation, conduct, practices or relationships," *id.*, at 624, 116 S.Ct. 1620 (internal quotation marks omitted), and deprived them of protection under state antidiscrimination laws. We concluded that the provision was "born of animosity toward the class of persons affected" and further that it had no rational relation to a legitimate governmental purpose. *Id.*, at 634, 116 S.Ct. 1620.

As an alternative argument in this case, counsel for the petitioners and some *amici* contend that *Romer* provides the basis for declaring the Texas statute invalid under the Equal Protection Clause. That is a tenable argument, but we conclude the instant case requires us to address whether *Bowers* itself has continuing validity. Were we to hold the statute invalid under the Equal Protection Clause some might question whether a prohibition would be valid if drawn differently, say, to prohibit the conduct both between same-sex and different-sex participants.

Equality of treatment and the due process right to demand respect for conduct protected by the substantive guarantee of liberty are linked in important respects, and a decision on the latter point advances both interests. If protected conduct is made criminal and the law which does so remains unexamined for its substantive validity, its stigma might remain even if it were not enforceable as drawn for equal protection reasons. When homosexual conduct is made criminal by the law of the State, that declaration in and of itself is an invitation to subject homosexual persons to discrimination both in the public and in the private spheres. The central holding of *Bowers* has been brought in question by this case, and it should be addressed. Its continuance as precedent demeans the lives of homosexual persons.

The stigma this criminal statute imposes, moreover, is not trivial. The offense, to be sure, is but a class C misdemeanor, a minor offense in the Texas legal system. Still, it remains a criminal offense with all that imports for the dignity of the persons charged. The petitioners will bear on their record the history of their criminal convictions. Just this Term we rejected various challenges to state laws requiring the registration of sex offenders. *Smith v. Doe*, 538 U.S. 84, 123 S.Ct. 1140, 155 L.Ed.2d 164 (2003); *Connecticut Dept. of Public Safety v. Doe*, 538 U.S. 1, 123 S.Ct. 1160, 155 L.Ed.2d 98 (2003). We are advised that if Texas convicted an adult for private, consensual homosexual conduct under the statute here in question the convicted person would come within the registration laws of at least four States were he or she to be subject to their jurisdiction. Pet. for Cert. 13, and n. 12 (citing Idaho Code §§ 18-8301 to 18-8326 (Cum.Supp.2002); La.Code Crim. Proc. Ann. §§ 15:540-15:549 West 2003); Miss.Code Ann. §§ 45-33-21 to 45-33-57 (Lexis 2003); S.C.Code Ann. §§ 23-3-400 to 23-3-490 (West 2002)). This underscores the consequential nature of the punishment and the state-sponsored condemnation attendant to the criminal prohibition. Furthermore, the Texas criminal conviction carries with it the other collateral consequences always following a conviction, such as notations on job application forms, to mention but one example.

The foundations of *Bowers* have sustained serious erosion from our recent decisions in *Casey* and *Romer*. When our precedent has been thus weakened, criticism from other sources is of greater significance. In the United States criticism of *Bowers* has been substantial and continuing, disapproving of its reasoning in all respects, not just as to its historical assumptions. See, *e.g.*, C. Fried, Order and Law: Arguing the Reagan Revolution — A Firsthand Account 81–84 (1991); R. Posner, Sex and Reason 341–350 (1992). The courts of five different States have declined to follow it in interpreting provisions in their own state constitutions parallel to the Due Process Clause of the Fourteenth Amendment, see *Jegley v. Picado,* 349 Ark. 600, 80 S.W.3d 332 (2002); *Powell v. State,* 270 Ga. 327, 510 S.E.2d 18, 24 (1998); *Gryczan v. State,* 283 Mont. 433, 942 P.2d 112 (1997); *Campbell v. Sundquist,* 926 S.W.2d 250 (Tenn.App.1996); *Commonwealth v. Wasson,* 842 S.W.2d 487 (Ky.1992).

To the extent *Bowers* relied on values we share with a wider civilization, it should be noted that the reasoning and holding in *Bowers* have been rejected elsewhere. The European Court of Human Rights has followed not *Bowers* but its own decision in *Dudgeon v. United Kingdom.* See *P.G. & J.H. v. United Kingdom,* App. No. 00044787/98, & ¶ 56 (Eur.Ct.H. R., Sept. 25, 2001); *Modinos v. Cyprus,* 259 Eur. Ct. H.R. (1993); *Norris v. Ireland,* 142 Eur. Ct. H.R. (1988). Other nations, too, have taken action consistent with an affirmation of the protected right of homosexual adults to engage in intimate, consensual conduct. See Brief for Mary Robinson et al. as *Amici Curiae* 11–12. The right the petitioners seek in this case has been accepted as an integral part of human freedom in many other countries. There has been no showing that in this country the governmental interest in circumscribing personal choice is somehow more legitimate or urgent.

The doctrine of *stare decisis* is essential to the respect accorded to the judgments of the Court and to the stability of the law. It is not, however, an inexorable command. *Payne v. Tennessee,* 501 U.S. 808, 828, 111 S.Ct. 2597, 115 L.Ed.2d 720 (1991) ("*Stare decisis* is not an inexorable command; rather, it 'is a principle of policy and not a mechanical formula of adherence to the latest decision'" (quoting *Helvering v. Hallock,* 309 U.S. 106, 119, 60 S.Ct. 444, 84 L.Ed. 604 (1940))). In *Casey* we noted that when a court is asked to overrule a precedent recognizing a constitutional liberty interest, individual or societal reliance on the existence of that liberty cautions with particular strength against reversing course. 505 U.S., at 855–856, 112 S.Ct. 2791; see also *id.,* at 844, 112 S.Ct. 2791 ("Liberty finds no refuge in a jurisprudence of doubt"). The holding in *Bowers,* however, has not induced detrimental reliance comparable to some instances where recognized individual rights are involved. Indeed, there has been no individual or societal reliance on *Bowers* of the sort that could counsel against overturning its holding once there are compelling reasons to do so. *Bowers* itself causes uncertainty, for the precedents before and after its issuance contradict its central holding.

The rationale of *Bowers* does not withstand careful analysis. In his dissenting opinion in *Bowers* Justice Stevens came to these conclusions:

"Our prior cases make two propositions abundantly clear. First, the fact that the governing majority in a State has traditionally viewed a particular practice as immoral is not a sufficient reason for upholding a law prohibiting the practice; neither history nor tradition could save a law prohibiting miscegenation from constitutional attack. Second, individual decisions by married persons, concerning the intimacies of their physical relationship, even when not intended to produce offspring, are a form of 'liberty' protected by the Due Process Clause of the Fourteenth Amendment. Moreover, this protection extends to intimate choices by unmarried as well as married persons." 478 U.S., at 216, 106 S.Ct. 2841 (footnotes and citations omitted).

Justice Stevens' analysis, in our view, should have been controlling in *Bowers* and should control here.

Bowers was not correct when it was decided, and it is not correct today. It ought not to remain binding precedent. *Bowers v. Hardwick* should be and now is overruled.

The present case does not involve minors. It does not involve persons who might be injured or coerced or who are situated in relationships where consent might not easily be refused. It does not involve public conduct or prostitution. It does not involve whether the government must give formal recognition to any relationship that homosexual persons seek to enter. The case does involve two adults who, with full and mutual consent from each other, engaged in sexual practices common to a homosexual lifestyle. The petitioners are entitled to respect for their private lives. The State cannot demean their existence or control their destiny by making their private sexual conduct a crime. Their right to liberty under the Due Process Clause gives them the full right to engage in their conduct without intervention of the government. "It is a promise of the Constitution that there is a realm of personal liberty which the government may not enter." *Casey, supra,* at 847, 112 S.Ct. 2791. The Texas statute furthers no legitimate state interest which can justify its intrusion into the personal and private life of the individual.

Had those who drew and ratified the Due Process Clauses of the Fifth Amendment or the Fourteenth Amendment known the components of liberty in its manifold possibilities, they might have been more specific. They did not presume to have this insight. They knew times can blind us to certain truths and later generations can see that laws once thought necessary and proper in fact serve only to oppress. As the Constitution endures, persons in every generation can invoke its principles in their own search for greater freedom.

The judgment of the Court of Appeals for the Texas Fourteenth District is reversed, and the case is remanded for further proceedings not inconsistent with this opinion.

It is so ordered.

Note

Justice Kennedy deliberately emphasized that *Lawrence* did not extend to the issue of marriage equality, anticipating perhaps the forthcoming struggles around the issue. Justice Scalia, on the other hand, called the majority disingenuous for claiming to limit the opinion. Many interpreted the majority's reluctance as indicative of the Court's unwillingness to take up the issue of marriage equality for a long time. That time came more quickly than predicted, in 2013, thanks to massively successful activism around the issue. Changing technology also facilitated widespread education and awareness of the deplorable impact of marriage inequality on individuals' lives. See *Windsor* and *Obergefell*, below, for the Court's approach to the rights of same sex couples regarding marriage in the state and federal context.

Bipartisan Legal Advisory Group of the United States House of Representatives v. Windsor

133 S. Ct. 2885 (2013)

JUSTICE KENNEDY delivered the opinion of the Court.

Two women then resident in New York were married in a lawful ceremony in Ontario, Canada, in 2007. Edith Windsor and Thea Spyer returned to their home in New York City. When Spyer died in 2009, she left her entire estate to Windsor. Windsor sought to claim the estate tax exemption for surviving spouses. She was barred from doing so, however, by a federal law, the Defense of Marriage Act, which excludes a same-sex partner from the definition of "spouse" as that term is used in federal statutes. Windsor paid the taxes but filed suit to challenge the constitutionality of this provision. The United States District Court and the Court of Appeals ruled that this portion of the statute is unconstitutional and ordered the United States to pay Windsor a refund. This Court granted certiorari and now affirms the judgment in Windsor's favor.

I

In 1996, as some States were beginning to consider the concept of same-sex marriage, see, e.g., *Baehr v. Lewin*, 74 Haw. 530, 852 P.2d 44 (1993), and before any State had acted to permit it, Congress enacted the Defense of Marriage Act (DOMA), 110 Stat. 2419. DOMA contains two operative sections: Section 2, which has not been challenged here, allows States to refuse to recognize same-sex marriages performed under the laws of other States. See 28 U.S.C. § 1738C.

Section 3 is at issue here. It amends the Dictionary Act in Title 1, § 7, of the United States Code to provide a federal definition of "marriage" and "spouse." Section 3 of DOMA provides as follows:

> "In determining the meaning of any Act of Congress, or of any ruling, regulation, or interpretation of the various administrative bureaus and agencies of the United States, the word 'marriage' means only a legal union between

one man and one woman as husband and wife, and the word 'spouse' refers only to a person of the opposite sex who is a husband or a wife." 1 U.S.C. § 7.

The definitional provision does not by its terms forbid States from enacting laws permitting same-sex marriages or civil unions or providing state benefits to residents in that status. The enactment's comprehensive definition of marriage for purposes of all federal statutes and other regulations or directives covered by its terms, however, does control over 1,000 federal laws in which marital or spousal status is addressed as a matter of federal law. See GAO, D. Shah, Defense of Marriage Act: Update to Prior Report 1 (GAO-04-353R, 2004).

Edith Windsor and Thea Spyer met in New York City in 1963 and began a long-term relationship. Windsor and Spyer registered as domestic partners when New York City gave that right to same-sex couples in 1993. Concerned about Spyer's health, the couple made the 2007 trip to Canada for their marriage, but they continued to reside in New York City. The State of New York deems their Ontario marriage to be a valid one. See 699 F.3d 169, 177–178 (CA2 2012).

Spyer died in February 2009, and left her entire estate to Windsor. Because DOMA denies federal recognition to same-sex spouses, Windsor did not qualify for the marital exemption from the federal estate tax, which excludes from taxation "any interest in property which passes or has passed from the decedent to his surviving spouse." 26 U.S.C. § 2056(a). Windsor paid $363,053 in estate taxes and sought a refund. The Internal Revenue Service denied the refund, concluding that, under DOMA, Windsor was not a "surviving spouse." Windsor commenced this refund suit in the United States District Court for the Southern District of New York. She contended that DOMA violates the guarantee of equal protection, as applied to the Federal Government through the Fifth Amendment.

While the tax refund suit was pending, the Attorney General of the United States notified the Speaker of the House of Representatives, pursuant to 28 U.S.C. § 530D, that the Department of Justice would no longer defend the constitutionality of DOMA's § 3. Noting that "the Department has previously defended DOMA against . . . challenges involving legally married same-sex couples," App. 184, the Attorney General informed Congress that "the President has concluded that given a number of factors, including a documented history of discrimination, classifications based on sexual orientation should be subject to a heightened standard of scrutiny." *Id.*, at 191. The Department of Justice has submitted many § 530D letters over the years refusing to defend laws it deems unconstitutional, when, for instance, a federal court has rejected the Government's defense of a statute and has issued a judgment against it. This case is unusual, however, because the § 530D letter was not preceded by an adverse judgment. The letter instead reflected the Executive's own conclusion, relying on a definition still being debated and considered in the courts, that heightened equal protection scrutiny should apply to laws that classify on the basis of sexual orientation.

Although "the President . . . instructed the Department not to defend the statute in *Windsor*," he also decided "that Section 3 will continue to be enforced by the Executive Branch" and that the United States had an "interest in providing Congress a full and fair opportunity to participate in the litigation of those cases." *Id.*, at 191–193. The stated rationale for this dual-track procedure (determination of unconstitutionality coupled with ongoing enforcement) was to "recogniz[e] the judiciary as the final arbiter of the constitutional claims raised." *Id.*, at 192.

In response to the notice from the Attorney General, the Bipartisan Legal Advisory Group (BLAG) of the House of Representatives voted to intervene in the litigation to defend the constitutionality of §3 of DOMA. The Department of Justice did not oppose limited intervention by BLAG. The District Court denied BLAG's motion to enter the suit as of right, on the rationale that the United States already was represented by the Department of Justice. The District Court, however, did grant intervention by BLAG as an interested party. See Fed. Rule Civ. Proc. 24(a)(2).

On the merits of the tax refund suit, the District Court ruled against the United States. It held that §3 of DOMA is unconstitutional and ordered the Treasury to refund the tax with interest. Both the Justice Department and BLAG filed notices of appeal, and the Solicitor General filed a petition for certiorari before judgment. Before this Court acted on the petition, the Court of Appeals for the Second Circuit affirmed the District Court's judgment. It applied heightened scrutiny to classifications based on sexual orientation, as both the Department and Windsor had urged. The United States has not complied with the judgment. Windsor has not received her refund, and the Executive Branch continues to enforce §3 of DOMA.

In granting certiorari on the question of the constitutionality of §3 of DOMA, the Court requested argument on two additional questions: whether the United States' agreement with Windsor's legal position precludes further review and whether BLAG has standing to appeal the case. All parties agree that the Court has jurisdiction to decide this case; and, with the case in that framework, the Court appointed Professor Vicki Jackson as amicus curiae to argue the position that the Court lacks jurisdiction to hear the dispute. 568 U.S. ___ (2012). She has ably discharged her duties.

In an unrelated case, the United States Court of Appeals for the First Circuit has also held §3 of DOMA to be unconstitutional. A petition for certiorari has been filed in that case. Pet. for Cert. in *Bipartisan Legal Advisory Group v. Gill*, O.T. 2012, No. 12–13.

II

It is appropriate to begin by addressing whether either the Government or BLAG, or both of them, were entitled to appeal to the Court of Appeals and later to seek certiorari and appear as parties here.

There is no dispute that when this case was in the District Court it presented a concrete disagreement between opposing parties, a dispute suitable for judicial resolution. "[A] taxpayer has standing to challenge the collection of a specific tax assessment as unconstitutional; being forced to pay such a tax causes a real and immediate economic injury to the individual taxpayer." *Hein v. Freedom From Religion Foundation, Inc.*, 551 U.S. 587, 599 (2007) (plurality opinion) (emphasis deleted). Windsor suffered a redressable injury when she was required to pay estate taxes from which, in her view, she was exempt but for the alleged invalidity of § 3 of DOMA.

The decision of the Executive not to defend the constitutionality of § 3 in court while continuing to deny refunds and to assess deficiencies does introduce a complication. Even though the Executive's current position was announced before the District Court entered its judgment, the Government's agreement with Windsor's position would not have deprived the District Court of jurisdiction to entertain and resolve the refund suit; for her injury (failure to obtain a refund allegedly required by law) was concrete, persisting, and unredressed. The Government's position— agreeing with Windsor's legal contention but refusing to give it effect—meant that there was a justiciable controversy between the parties, despite what the claimant would find to be an inconsistency in that stance. Windsor, the Government, BLAG, and the amicus appear to agree upon that point. The disagreement is over the standing of the parties, or aspiring parties, to take an appeal in the Court of Appeals and to appear as parties in further proceedings in this Court.

The amicus' position is that, given the Government's concession that § 3 is unconstitutional, once the District Court ordered the refund the case should have ended; and the amicus argues the Court of Appeals should have dismissed the appeal. The amicus submits that once the President agreed with Windsor's legal position and the District Court issued its judgment, the parties were no longer adverse. From this standpoint the United States was a prevailing party below, just as Windsor was. Accordingly, the amicus reasons, it is inappropriate for this Court to grant certiorari and proceed to rule on the merits; for the United States seeks no redress from the judgment entered against it.

[The Court reasons that the new plaintffs have standing because the United States maintained a stake in the lawsuit, since the lower court ordered it to pay a refund.]

III

When at first Windsor and Spyer longed to marry, neither New York nor any other State granted them that right. After waiting some years, in 2007 they traveled to Ontario to be married there. It seems fair to conclude that, until recent years, many citizens had not even considered the possibility that two persons of the same sex might aspire to occupy the same status and dignity as that of a man and woman in lawful marriage. For marriage between a man and a woman no doubt had been thought of by most people as essential to the very definition of that term and to its role and function throughout the history of civilization. That belief, for many who long have held it, became even more urgent, more cherished when challenged. For others, however, came the beginnings of a new perspective, a new insight.

Accordingly some States concluded that same-sex marriage ought to be given recognition and validity in the law for those same-sex couples who wish to define themselves by their commitment to each other. The limitation of lawful marriage to heterosexual couples, which for centuries had been deemed both necessary and fundamental, came to be seen in New York and certain other States as an unjust exclusion.

Slowly at first and then in rapid course, the laws of New York came to acknowledge the urgency of this issue for same-sex couples who wanted to affirm their commitment to one another before their children, their family, their friends, and their community. And so New York recognized same-sex marriages performed elsewhere; and then it later amended its own marriage laws to permit same-sex marriage. New York, in common with, as of this writing, 11 other States and the District of Columbia, decided that same-sex couples should have the right to marry and so live with pride in themselves and their union and in a status of equality with all other married persons. After a statewide deliberative process that enabled its citizens to discuss and weigh arguments for and against same- sex marriage, New York acted to enlarge the definition of marriage to correct what its citizens and elected representatives perceived to be an injustice that they had not earlier known or understood. See Marriage Equality Act, 2011 N.Y. Laws 749 (codified at N.Y. Dom. Rel. Law Ann. §§ 10-a, 10-b, 13 (West 2013)).

Against this background of lawful same-sex marriage in some States, the design, purpose, and effect of DOMA should be considered as the beginning point in deciding whether it is valid under the Constitution. By history and tradition the definition and regulation of marriage, as will be discussed in more detail, has been treated as being within the authority and realm of the separate States. Yet it is further established that Congress, in enacting discrete statutes, can make determinations that bear on marital rights and privileges. Just this Term the Court upheld the authority of the Congress to pre-empt state laws, allowing a former spouse to retain life insurance proceeds under a federal program that gave her priority, because of formal beneficiary designation rules, over the wife by a second marriage who survived the husband. *Hillman v. Maretta*, 569 U. S. ___ (2013); see also *Ridgway v. Ridgway*, 454 U. S. 46 (1981); *Wissner v. Wissner*, 338 U. S. 655 (1950). This is one example of the general principle that when the Federal Government acts in the exercise of its own proper authority, it has a wide choice of the mechanisms and means to adopt. See *McCulloch v. Maryland*, 4 Wheat. 316, 421 (1819). Congress has the power both to ensure efficiency in the administration of its programs and to choose what larger goals and policies to pursue.

Other precedents involving congressional statutes which affect marriages and family status further illustrate this point. In addressing the interaction of state domestic relations and federal immigration law Congress determined that marriages "entered into for the purpose of procuring an alien's admission [to the United States] as an immigrant" will not qualify the noncitizen for that status, even if the noncitizen's marriage is valid and proper for state-law purposes. 8 U.S.C. § 1186a(b)

(1) (2006 ed. and Supp. V). And in establishing income-based criteria for Social Security benefits, Congress decided that although state law would determine in general who qualifies as an applicant's spouse, common-law marriages also should be recognized, regardless of any particular State's view on these relationships. 42 U.S.C. § 1382c(d)(2).

Though these discrete examples establish the constitutionality of limited federal laws that regulate the meaning of marriage in order to further federal policy, DOMA has a far greater reach; for it enacts a directive applicable to over 1,000 federal statutes and the whole realm of federal regulations. And its operation is directed to a class of persons that the laws of New York, and of 11 other States, have sought to protect. See *Goodridge v. Department of Public Health*, 440 Mass. 309, 798 N.E.2d 941 (2003); An Act Implementing the Guarantee of Equal Protection Under the Constitution of the State for Same Sex Couples, 2009 Conn. Pub. Acts no. 09–13; *Varnum v. Brien*, 763 N.W.2d 862 (Iowa 2009); Vt. Stat. Ann., Tit. 15, § 8 (2010); N.H. Rev. Stat. Ann. § 457:1-a (West Supp. 2012); Religious Freedom and Civil Marriage Equality Amendment Act of 2009, 57 D.C. Reg. 27 (Dec. 18, 2009); N.Y. Dom. Rel. Law Ann. § 10-a (West Supp. 2013); Wash. Rev. Code § 26.04.010 (2012). . . .

In order to assess the validity of that intervention it is necessary to discuss the extent of the state power and authority over marriage as a matter of history and tradition. State laws defining and regulating marriage, of course, must respect the constitutional rights of persons, see, e.g., *Loving v. Virginia*, 388 U. S. 1 (1967); but, subject to those guarantees, "regulation of domestic relations" is "an area that has long been regarded as a virtually exclusive province of the States." *Sosna v. Iowa*, 419 U.S. 393, 404 (1975).

The recognition of civil marriages is central to state domestic relations law applicable to its residents and citizens. See *Williams v. North Carolina*, 317 U.S. 287, 298 (1942) ("Each state as a sovereign has a rightful and legitimate concern in the marital status of persons domiciled within its borders"). The definition of marriage is the foundation of the State's broader authority to regulate the subject of domestic relations with respect to the "[p]rotection of offspring, property interests, and the enforcement of marital responsibilities." *Ibid.* "[T]he states, at the time of the adoption of the Constitution, possessed full power over the subject of marriage and divorce . . . [and] the Constitution delegated no authority to the Government of the United States on the subject of marriage and divorce." *Haddock v. Haddock*, 201 U.S. 562, 575 (1906); see also *In re Burrus*, 136 U.S. 586–594 (1890) ("The whole subject of the domestic relations of husband and wife, parent and child, belongs to the laws of the States and not to the laws of the United States").

Consistent with this allocation of authority, the Federal Government, through our history, has deferred to state-law policy decisions with respect to domestic relations. In *De Sylva v. Ballentine*, 351 U.S. 570 (1956), for example, the Court held that, "[t]o decide who is the widow or widower of a deceased author, or who are his executors or next of kin," under the Copyright Act "requires a reference to the law of the State which created those legal relationships" because "there is no federal law of domestic relations." *Id.*, at 580. In order to respect this principle, the federal courts, as a general rule, do not adjudicate issues of marital status even when there might otherwise be a basis for federal jurisdiction. See *Ankenbrandt v. Richards*, 504 U.S. 689, 703 (1992). Federal courts will not hear divorce and custody cases even if they arise in diversity because of "the virtually exclusive primacy . . . of the States in the regulation of domestic relations." *Id.*, at 714 (Blackmun, J., concurring in judgment).

The significance of state responsibilities for the definition and regulation of marriage dates to the Nation's beginning; for "when the Constitution was adopted the common understanding was that the domestic relations of husband and wife and parent and child were matters reserved to the States." *Ohio ex rel. Popovici v. Agler*, 280 U.S. 379–384 (1930). Marriage laws vary in some respects from State to State. For example, the required minimum age is 16 in Vermont, but only 13 in New Hampshire. Compare Vt. Stat. Ann., Tit. 18, § 5142 (2012), with N.H. Rev. Stat. Ann. § 457:4 (West Supp. 2012). Likewise the permissible degree of consanguinity can vary (most States permit first cousins to marry, but a handful—such as Iowa and Washington, see Iowa Code § 595.19 (2009); Wash. Rev. Code § 26.04.020 (2012)—prohibit the practice). But these rules are in every event consistent within each State.

Against this background DOMA rejects the long-established precept that the incidents, benefits, and obligations of marriage are uniform for all married couples within each State, though they may vary, subject to constitutional guarantees, from one State to the next. Despite these considerations, it is unnecessary to decide whether this federal intrusion on state power is a violation of the Constitution because it disrupts the federal balance. The State's power in defining the marital relation is of central relevance in this case quite apart from principles of federalism. Here the State's decision to give this class of persons the right to marry conferred upon them a dignity and status of immense import. When the State used its historic and essential authority to define the marital relation in this way, its role and its power in making the decision enhanced the recognition, dignity, and protection of the class in their own community. DOMA, because of its reach and extent, departs from this history and tradition of reliance on state law to define marriage. "'[D]iscriminations of an unusual character especially suggest careful consideration to determine whether they are obnoxious to the constitutional provision.'" *Romer v. Evans*, 517 U.S. 620, 633 (1996) (quoting *Louisville Gas & Elec. Co. v. Coleman*, 277 U.S. 32–38 (1928)).

The Federal Government uses this state-defined class for the opposite purpose—to impose rstrictions and disabilities. That result requires this Court now to address whether the resulting injury and indignity is a deprivation of an essential part of the liberty protected by the Fifth Amendment. What the State of New York treats as alike the federal law deems unlike by a law designed to injure the same class the State seeks to protect.

In acting first to recognize and then to allow same-sex marriages, New York was responding "to the initiative of those who [sought] a voice in shaping the destiny of their own times." *Bond v. United States*, 564 U.S. ___, ___ (2011) (slip op., at 9). These actions were without doubt a proper exercise of its sovereign authority within our federal system, all in the way that the Framers of the Constitution intended. The dynamics of state government in the federal system are to allow the formation of consensus respecting the way the members of a discrete community treat each other in their daily contact and constant interaction with each other.

The States' interest in defining and regulating the marital relation, subject to constitutional guarantees, stems from the understanding that marriage is more than a routine classification for purposes of certain statutory benefits. Private, consensual sexual intimacy between two adult persons of the same sex may not be punished by the State, and it can form "but one element in a personal bond that is more enduring." *Lawrence v. Texas*, 539 U.S. 558, 567 (2003). By its recognition of the validity of same-sex marriages performed in other jurisdictions and then by authorizing same-sex unions and same-sex marriages, New York sought to give further protection and dignity to that bond. For same-sex couples who wished to be married, the State acted to give their lawful conduct a lawful status. This status is a far-reaching legal acknowledgment of the intimate relationship between two people, a relationship deemed by the State worthy of dignity in the community equal with all other marriages. It reflects both the community's considered perspective on the historical roots of the institution of marriage and its evolving understanding of the meaning of equality.

IV

DOMA seeks to injure the very class New York seeks to protect. By doing so it violates basic due process and equal protection principles applicable to the Federal Government. See U.S. Const., Amdt. 5; *Bolling v. Sharpe*, 347 U.S. 497 (1954). The Constitution's guarantee of equality "must at the very least mean that a bare congressional desire to harm a politically unpopular group cannot" justify disparate treatment of that group. *Department of Agriculture v. Moreno*, 413 U.S. 528–535 (1973). In determining whether a law is motived by an improper animus or purpose, "'[d]iscriminations of an unusual character'" especially require careful consideration. *Supra*, at 19 (quoting *Romer, supra*, at 633). DOMA cannot survive under these principles. The responsibility of the States for the regulation of domestic relations is an important indicator of the substantial societal impact the State's classifications have in the daily lives and customs of its people. DOMA's unusual deviation from the usual tradition of recognizing and accepting state definitions of marriage here operates to deprive same-sex couples of the benefits and responsibilities that come with the federal recognition of their marriages. This is strong evidence of a law having the purpose and effect of disapproval of that class. The avowed purpose and practical effect of the law here in question are to impose a disadvantage, a separate status, and so a stigma upon all who enter into same-sex marriages made lawful by the unquestioned authority of the States.

The history of DOMA's enactment and its own text demonstrate that interference with the equal dignity of same-sex marriages, a dignity conferred by the States in the exercise of their sovereign power, was more than an incidental effect of the federal statute. It was its essence. The House Report announced its conclusion that "it is both appropriate and necessary for Congress to do what it can to defend the institution of traditional heterosexual marriage. . . . H.R. 3396 is appropriately entitled the 'Defense of Marriage Act.' The effort to redefine 'marriage' to extend to homosexual couples is a truly radical proposal that would fundamentally alter the institution of marriage." H.R. Rep. No. 104-664, pp. 12–13 (1996). The House concluded that DOMA expresses "both moral disapproval of homosexuality, and a moral conviction that heterosexuality better comports with traditional (especially Judeo-Christian) morality." *Id.*, at 16 (footnote deleted). The stated purpose of the law was to promote an "interest in protecting the traditional moral teachings reflected in heterosexual-only marriage laws." *Ibid*. Were there any doubt of this far-reaching purpose, the title of the Act confirms it: The Defense of Marriage.

The arguments put forward by BLAG are just as candid about the congressional purpose to influence or interfere with state sovereign choices about who may be married. As the title and dynamics of the bill indicate, its purpose is to discourage enactment of state same-sex marriage laws and to restrict the freedom and choice of couples married under those laws if they are enacted. The congressional goal was "to put a thumb on the scales and influence a state's decision as to how to shape its own marriage laws." *Massachusetts*, 682 F.3d, at 12–13. The Act's demonstrated purpose is to ensure that if any State decides to recognize same-sex marriages, those unions will be treated as second-class marriages for purposes of federal law. This raises a most serious question under the Constitution's Fifth Amendment.

DOMA's operation in practice confirms this purpose. When New York adopted a law to permit same-sex marriage, it sought to eliminate inequality; but DOMA frustrates that objective through a system-wide enactment with no identified connection to any particular area of federal law. DOMA writes inequality into the entire United States Code. The particular case at hand concerns the estate tax, but DOMA is more than a simple determination of what should or should not be allowed as an estate tax refund. Among the over 1,000 statutes and numerous federal regulations that DOMA controls are laws pertaining to Social Security, housing, taxes, criminal sanctions, copyright, and veterans' benefits.

DOMA's principal effect is to identify a subset of state-sanctioned marriages and make them unequal. The principal purpose is to impose inequality, not for other reasons like governmental efficiency. Responsibilities, as well as rights, enhance the dignity and integrity of the person. And DOMA contrives to deprive some couples married under the laws of their State, but not other couples, of both rights and responsibilities. By creating two contradictory marriage regimes within the same State, DOMA forces same-sex couples to live as married for the purpose of state law but unmarried for the purpose of federal law, thus diminishing the stability and predictability of basic personal relations the State has found it proper to acknowledge and protect. By this dynamic DOMA undermines both the public and private significance of state-sanctioned same-sex marriages; for it tells those couples, and all the world, that their otherwise valid marriages are unworthy of federal recognition. This places same-sex couples in an unstable position of being in a second-tier marriage. The differentiation demeans the couple, whose moral and sexual choices the Constitution protects, see *Lawrence*, 539 U.S. 558, and whose relationship the State has sought to dignify. And it humiliates tens of thousands of children now being raised by same-sex couples. The law in question makes it even more difficult for the children to understand the integrity and closeness of their own family and its concord with other families in their community and in their daily lives.

Under DOMA, same-sex married couples have their lives burdened, by reason of government decree, in visible and public ways. By its great reach, DOMA touches many aspects of married and family life, from the mundane to the profound. It prevents same-sex married couples from obtaining government healthcare benefits they would otherwise receive. See 5 U.S.C. §§ 8901(5), 8905. It deprives them of the Bankruptcy Code's special protections for domestic-support obligations. See 11 U.S.C. §§ 101(14A), 507(a)(1)(A), 523(a)(5), 523(a)(15). It forces them to follow a complicated procedure to file their state and federal taxes jointly. Technical Bulletin TB-55, 2010 Vt. Tax LEXIS 6 (Oct. 7, 2010); Brief for Federalism Scholars as Amici Curiae 34. It prohibits them from being buried together in veterans' cemeteries. National Cemetery Administration Directive 3210/1, p. 37 (June 4, 2008).

For certain married couples, DOMA's unequal effects are even more serious. The federal penal code makes it a crime to "assaul[t], kidna[p], or murde[r] . . . a member of the immediate family" of "a United States official, a United States judge, [or] a Federal law enforcement officer," 18 U.S.C. § 115(a)(1)(A), with the intent to influence or retaliate against that official, § 115(a)(1). Although a "spouse" qualifies as a member of the officer's "immediate family," § 115(c)(2), DOMA makes this protection inapplicable to same-sex spouses.

DOMA also brings financial harm to children of same-sex couples. It raises the cost of health care for families by taxing health benefits provided by employers to their workers' same-sex spouses. See 26 U.S.C. § 106; Treas. Reg. § 1.106-1, 26 CFR § 1.106-1 (2012); IRS Private Letter Ruling 9850011 (Sept. 10, 1998). And it denies or reduces benefits allowed to families upon the loss of a spouse and parent, benefits that are an integral part of family security. See Social Security Administration, Social Security Survivors Benefits 5 (2012) (benefits available to a surviving spouse caring for the couple's child), online at http://www.ssa.gov/pubs/EN-05-10084.pdf.

DOMA divests married same-sex couples of the duties and responsibilities that are an essential part of married life and that they in most cases would be honored to accept were DOMA not in force. For instance, because it is expected that spouses will support each other as they pursue educational opportunities, federal law takes into consideration a spouse's income in calculating a student's federal financial aid eligibility. See 20 U.S.C. § 1087nn(b). Same-sex married couples are exempt from this requirement. The same is true with respect to federal ethics rules. Federal executive and agency officials are prohibited from "participat[ing] personally and substantially" in matters as to which they or their spouses have a financial interest. 18 U.S.C. § 208(a). A similar statute prohibits Senators, Senate employees, and their spouses from accepting high-value gifts from certain sources, see 2 U.S.C. § 31-2(a)(1), and another mandates detailed financial disclosures by numerous high-ranking officials and their spouses. See 5 U.S.C. App. §§ 102(a), (e). Under DOMA, however, these Government-integrity rules do not apply to same-sex spouses.

. . . .

The power the Constitution grants it also restrains. And though Congress has great authority to design laws to fit its own conception of sound national policy, it cannot deny the liberty protected by the Due Process Clause of the Fifth Amendment.

What has been explained to this point should more than suffice to establish that the principal purpose and the necessary effect of this law are to demean those persons who are in a lawful same-sex marriage. This requires the Court to hold, as it now does, that DOMA is unconstitutional as a deprivation of the liberty of the person protected by the Fifth Amendment of the Constitution.

The liberty protected by the Fifth Amendment's Due Process Clause contains within it the prohibition against denying to any person the equal protection of the laws. See *Bolling*, 347 U.S., at 499–500; *Adarand Constructors, Inc. v. Peña*, 515 U.S. 200–218 (1995). While the Fifth Amendment itself withdraws from Government the power to degrade or demean in the way this law does, the equal protection guarantee of the Fourteenth Amendment makes that Fifth Amendment right all the more specific and all the better understood and preserved.

The class to which DOMA directs its restrictions and restraints are those persons who are joined in same-sex marriages made lawful by the State. DOMA singles out a class of persons deemed by a State entitled to recognition and protection to enhance their own liberty. It imposes a disability on the class by refusing to acknowledge a status the State finds to be dignified and proper. DOMA instructs all federal officials, and indeed all persons with whom same-sex couples interact, including their own children, that their marriage is less worthy than the marriages of others. The federal statute is invalid, for no legitimate purpose overcomes the purpose and effect to disparage and to injure those whom the State, by its marriage laws, sought to protect in personhood and dignity. By seeking to displace this protection and treating those persons as living in marriages less respected than others, the federal statute is in violation of the Fifth Amendment. This opinion and its holding are confined to those lawful marriages.

The judgment of the Court of Appeals for the Second Circuit is affirmed.

It is so ordered.

JUSTICE SCALIA, with whom JUSTICE THOMAS joins, and with whom THE CHIEF JUS-
TICE joins as to Part I, dissenting.

This case is about power in several respects. It is about the power of our people
to govern themselves, and the power of this Court to pronounce the law. Today's
opinion aggrandizes the latter, with the predictable consequence of diminishing the
former. We have no power to decide this case. And even if we did, we have no power
under the Constitution to invalidate this democratically adopted legislation. The
Court's errors on both points spring forth from the same diseased root: an exalted
conception of the role of this institution in America.

I

A

The Court is eager—hungry—to tell everyone its view of the legal question at
the heart of this case. Standing in the way is an obstacle, a technicality of little interest to anyone but the people of We the People, who created it as a barrier against
judges' intrusion into their lives. They gave judges, in Article III, only the "judicial Power," a power to decide not abstract questions but real, concrete "Cases" and
"Controversies." Yet the plaintiff and the Government agree entirely on what should
happen in this lawsuit. They agree that the court below got it right; and they agreed
in the court below that the court below that one got it right as well. What, then, are
we doing here?

The answer lies at the heart of the jurisdictional portion of today's opinion,
where a single sentence lays bare the majority's vision of our role. The Court says
that we have the power to decide this case because if we did not, then our "primary
role in determining the constitutionality of a law" (at least one that "has inflicted
real injury on a plaintiff") would "become only secondary to the President's." *Ante*,
at 12. But wait, the reader wonders—Windsor won below, and so cured her injury,
and the President was glad to see it. True, says the majority, but judicial review must
march on regardless, lest we "undermine the clear dictate of the separation-of-
powers principle that when an Act of Congress is alleged to conflict with the Constitution, it is emphatically the province and duty of the judicial department to say
what the law is." Ibid. (internal quotation marks and brackets omitted).

That is jaw-dropping. It is an assertion of judicial supremacy over the people's
Representatives in Congress and the Executive. It envisions a Supreme Court standing (or rather enthroned) at the apex of government, empowered to decide all constitutional questions, always and everywhere "primary" in its role.

This image of the Court would have been unrecognizable to those who wrote
and ratified our national charter. They knew well the dangers of "primary" power,
and so created branches of government that would be "perfectly co-ordinate by
the terms of their common commission," none of which branches could "pretend
to an exclusive or superior right of settling the boundaries between their respective powers." The Federalist, No. 49, p. 314 (C. Rossiter ed. 1961) (J. Madison). The

people did this to protect themselves. They did it to guard their right to self-rule against the black-robed supremacy that today's majority finds so attractive. So it was that Madison could confidently state, with no fear of contradiction, that there was nothing of "greater intrinsic value" or "stamped with the authority of more enlightened patrons of liberty" than a government of separate and coordinate powers. *Id.*, No. 47, at 301.

For this reason we are quite forbidden to say what the law is whenever (as today's opinion asserts) "'an Act of Congress is alleged to conflict with the Constitution.'" *Ante*, at 12. We can do so only when that allegation will determine the outcome of a lawsuit, and is contradicted by the other party. The "judicial Power" is not, as the majority believes, the power "'to say what the law is,'" *ibid.*, giving the Supreme Court the "primary role in determining the constitutionality of laws." The majority must have in mind one of the foreign constitutions that pronounces such primacy for its constitutional court and allows that primacy to be exercised in contexts other than a lawsuit. See, e.g., Basic Law for the Federal Republic of Germany, Art. 93. The judicial power as Americans have understood it (and their English ancestors before them) is the power to adjudicate, with conclusive effect, disputed government claims (civil or criminal) against private persons, and disputed claims by private persons against the government or other private persons. Sometimes (though not always) the parties before the court disagree not with regard to the facts of their case (or not only with regard to the facts) but with regard to the applicable law — in which event (and only in which event) it becomes the "'province and duty of the judicial department to say what the law is.'" *Ante*, at 12.

In other words, declaring the compatibility of state or federal laws with the Constitution is not only not the "primary role" of this Court, it is not a separate, free-standing role at all. We perform that role incidentally — by accident, as it were — when that is necessary to resolve the dispute before us. Then, and only then, does it become "'the province and duty of the judicial department to say what the law is.'" That is why, in 1793, we politely declined the Washington Administration's request to "say what the law is" on a particular treaty matter that was not the subject of a concrete legal controversy. 3 Correspondence and Public Papers of John Jay 486–489 (H. Johnston ed. 1893). And that is why, as our opinions have said, some questions of law will never be presented to this Court, because there will never be anyone with standing to bring a lawsuit. See *Schlesinger v. Reservists Comm. to Stop the War*, 418 U.S. 208, 227 (1974); *United States v. Richardson*, 418 U.S. 166, 179 (1974). As Justice Brandeis put it, we cannot "pass upon the constitutionality of legislation in a friendly, non-adversary, proceeding"; absent a "'real, earnest and vital controversy between individuals,'" we have neither any work to do nor any power to do it. *Ashwander v. TVA*, 297 U.S. 288, 346 (1936) (concurring opinion) (quoting *Chicago & Grand Trunk R. Co. v. Wellman*, 143 U.S. 339, 345 (1892)). Our authority begins and ends with the need to adjudge the rights of an injured party who stands before us seeking redress. *Lujan v. Defenders of Wildlife*, 504 U.S. 555, 560 (1992).

That is completely absent here. Windsor's injury was cured by the judgment in her favor. And while, in ordinary circumstances, the United States is injured by a directive to pay a tax refund, this suit is far from ordinary. Whatever injury the United States has suffered will surely not be redressed by the action that it, as a litigant, asks us to take. The final sentence of the Solicitor General's brief on the merits reads: "For the foregoing reasons, the judgment of the court of appeals should be affirmed." Brief for United States (merits) 54. That will not cure the Government's injury, but carve it into stone. One could spend many fruitless afternoons ransacking our library for any other petitioner's brief seeking an affirmance of the judgment against it. What the petitioner United States asks us to do in the case before us is exactly what the respondent Windsor asks us to do: not to provide relief from the judgment below but to say that that judgment was correct. And the same was true in the Court of Appeals: Neither party sought to undo the judgment for Windsor, and so that court should have dismissed the appeal (just as we should dismiss) for lack of jurisdiction. Since both parties agreed with the judgment of the District Court for the Southern District of New York, the suit should have ended there. The further proceedings have been a contrivance, having no object in mind except to elevate a District Court judgment that has no precedential effect in other courts, to one that has precedential effect throughout the Second Circuit, and then (in this Court) precedential effect throughout the United States.

We have never before agreed to speak — to "say what the law is" — where there is no controversy before us. In the more than two centuries that this Court has existed as an institution, we have never suggested that we have the power to decide a question when every party agrees with both its nominal opponent and the court below on that question's answer. The United States reluctantly conceded that at oral argument. See Tr. of Oral Arg. 19–20.

The closest we have ever come to what the Court blesses today was our opinion in *INS v. Chadha*, 462 U.S. 919 (1983). But in that case, two parties to the litigation disagreed with the position of the United States and with the court below: the House and Senate, which had intervened in the case. Because Chadha concerned the validity of a mode of congressional action — the one-house legislative veto — the House and Senate were threatened with destruction of what they claimed to be one of their institutional powers. The Executive choosing not to defend that power, we permitted the House and Senate to intervene. Nothing like that is present here.

. . . The majority's discussion of the requirements of Article III bears no resemblance to our jurisprudence. It accuses the amicus (appointed to argue against our jurisdiction) of "elid[ing] the distinction between . . . the jurisdictional requirements of Article III and the prudential limits on its exercise." *Ante*, at 6. It then proceeds to call the requirement of adverseness a "prudential" aspect of standing. Of standing. That is incomprehensible. A plaintiff (or appellant) can have all the standing in the world — satisfying all three standing requirements of *Lujan* that the majority so carefully quotes, *ante*, at 7 — and yet no Article III controversy may be before the court. Article III requires not just a plaintiff (or appellant) who has standing to complain but an opposing party who denies the validity of the complaint. It is not the amicus that has done the eliding of distinctions, but the majority, calling the quite separate Article III requirement of adverseness between the parties an element (which it then pronounces a "prudential" element) of standing. The question here is not whether, as the majority puts it, "the United States retains a stake sufficient to support Article III jurisdiction," *ibid*. the question is whether there is any controversy (which requires contradiction) between the United States and Ms. Windsor. There is not.

. . . Given that the majority has volunteered its view of the merits, however, I proceed to discuss that as well.

A

There are many remarkable things about the majority's merits holding. The first is how rootless and shifting its justifications are. For example, the opinion starts with seven full pages about the traditional power of States to define domestic relations—initially fooling many readers, I am sure, into thinking that this is a federalism opinion. But we are eventually told that "it is unnecessary to decide whether this federal intrusion on state power is a violation of the Constitution," and that "[t]he State's power in defining the marital relation is of central relevance in this case quite apart from principles of federalism" because "the State's decision to give this class of persons the right to marry conferred upon them a dignity and status of immense import." *Ante*, at 18. But no one questions the power of the States to define marriage (with the concomitant conferral of dignity and status), so what is the point of devoting seven pages to describing how long and well established that power is? Even after the opinion has formally disclaimed reliance upon principles of federalism, mentions of "the usual tradition of recognizing and accepting state definitions of marriage" continue. See, e.g., *ante*, at 20. What to make of this? The opinion never explains. My guess is that the majority, while reluctant to suggest that defining the meaning of "marriage" in federal statutes is unsupported by any of the Federal Government's enumerated powers, nonetheless needs some rhetorical basis to support its pretense that today's prohibition of laws excluding same-sex marriage is confined to the Federal Government (leaving the second, state-law shoe to be dropped later, maybe next Term). But I am only guessing.

Equally perplexing are the opinion's references to "the Constitution's guarantee of equality." *Ibid*. Near the end of the opinion, we are told that although the "equal protection guarantee of the Fourteenth Amendment makes [the] Fifth Amendment [due process] right all the more specific and all the better understood and preserved"—what can that mean?—"the Fifth Amendment itself withdraws from Government the power to degrade or demean in the way this law does." *Ante*, at 25. The only possible interpretation of this statement is that the Equal Protection Clause, even the Equal Protection Clause as incorporated in the Due Process Clause, is not the basis for today's holding. But the portion of the majority opinion that explains why DOMA is unconstitutional (Part IV) begins by citing *Bolling v. Sharpe*, 347 U.S. 497 (1954), *Department of Agriculture v. Moreno*, 413 U.S. 528 (1973), and *Romer v. Evans*, 517 U.S. 620 (1996) — all of which are equal-protection cases. And those three cases are the only authorities that the Court cites in Part IV about the Constitution's meaning, except for its citation of *Lawrence v. Texas*, 539 U.S. 558 (2003) (not an equal-protection case) to support its passing assertion that the Constitution protects the "moral and sexual choices" of same-sex couples, *ante*, at 23.

Moreover, if this is meant to be an equal-protection opinion, it is a confusing one. The opinion does not resolve and indeed does not even mention what had been the central question in this litigation: whether, under the Equal Protection Clause, laws restricting marriage to a man and a woman are reviewed for more than mere rationality. That is the issue that divided the parties and the court below, compare Brief for Respondent Bipartisan Legal Advisory Group of U. S. House of Representatives (merits) 24–28 (no), with Brief for Respondent Windsor (merits) 17–31 and Brief for United States (merits) 18–36 (yes); and compare 699 F.3d 169, 180–185 (CA2 2012) (yes), with *id.*, at 208–211 (Straub, J., dissenting in part and concurring in part) (no). In accord with my previously expressed skepticism about the Court's "tiers of scrutiny" approach, I would review this classification only for its rationality. See *United States v. Virginia*, 518 U. S. 515–570 (1996) (Scalia, J., dissenting). As nearly as I can tell, the Court agrees with that; its opinion does not apply strict scrutiny, and its central propositions are taken from rational-basis cases like *Moreno*. But the Court certainly does not apply anything that resembles that deferential framework. See *Heller v. Doe*, 509 U.S. 312, 320 (1993) (a classification "'must be upheld . . . if there is any reason- ably conceivable state of facts'" that could justify it).

The majority opinion need not get into the strict-vs.-rational-basis scrutiny question, and need not justify its holding under either, because it says that DOMA is unconstitutional as "a deprivation of the liberty of the person protected by the Fifth Amendment of the Constitution," *ante*, at 25; that it violates "basic due process" principles, *ante*, at 20; and that it inflicts an "injury and indignity" of a kind that denies "an essential part of the liberty protected by the Fifth Amendment," *ante*, at 19. The majority never utters the dread words "substantive due process," perhaps sensing the disrepute into which that doctrine has fallen, but that is what those statements mean. Yet the opinion does not argue that same-sex marriage is "deeply rooted in this Nation's history and tradition," *Washington v. Glucksberg*, 521 U.S. 702–721 (1997), a claim that would of course be quite absurd. So would the further suggestion (also necessary, under our substantive-due-process precedents) that a world in which DOMA exists is one bereft of "'ordered liberty.'" *Id.*, at 721 (quoting *Palko v. Connecticut*, 302 U.S. 319, 325 (1937)).

Some might conclude that this loaf could have used a while longer in the oven. But that would be wrong; it is already overcooked. The most expert care in preparation cannot redeem a bad recipe. The sum of all the Court's nonspecific handwaving is that this law is invalid (maybe on equal-protection grounds, maybe on substantive-due-process grounds, and perhaps with some amorphous federalism component playing a role) because it is motivated by a "'bare . . . desire to harm'" couples in same-sex marriages. *Ante*, at 20. It is this proposition with which I will therefore engage.

B

As I have observed before, the Constitution does not forbid the government to enforce traditional moral and sexual norms. See *Lawrence v. Texas*, 539 U.S. 558, 599 (2003) (Scalia, J., dissenting). I will not swell the U.S. Reports with restatements of that point. It is enough to say that the Constitution neither requires nor forbids our society to approve of same-sex marriage, much as it neither requires nor forbids us to approve of no-fault divorce, polygamy, or the consumption of alcohol. . . .

Laying such a charge against them should require the most extraordinary evidence, and I would have thought that every attempt would be made to indulge a more anodyne explanation for the statute. The majority does the opposite — affirmatively concealing from the reader the arguments that exist in justification. It makes only a passing mention of the "arguments put forward" by the Act's defenders, and does not even trouble to paraphrase or describe them. See *ante*, at 21. I imagine that this is because it is harder to maintain the illusion of the Act's supporters as unhinged members of a wild-eyed lynch mob when one first describes their views as they see them.

. . . .

The penultimate sentence of the majority's opinion is a naked declaration that "[t]his opinion and its holding are confined" to those couples "joined in same-sex marriages made lawful by the State." *Ante*, at 26, 25. I have heard such "bald, unreasoned disclaimer[s]" before. *Lawrence*, 539 U.S., at 604. When the Court declared a constitutional right to homosexual sodomy, we were assured that the case had nothing, nothing at all to do with "whether the government must give formal recognition to any relationship that homosexual persons seek to enter." *Id.*, at 578. Now we are told that DOMA is invalid because it "demeans the couple, whose moral and sexual choices the Constitution protects," *ante*, at 23 — with an accompanying citation of *Lawrence*. It takes real cheek for today's majority to assure us, as it is going out the door, that a constitutional requirement to give formal recognition to same-sex marriage is not at issue here — when what has preceded that assurance is a lecture on how superior the majority's moral judgment in favor of same-sex marriage is to the Congress's hateful moral judgment against it. I promise you this: The only thing that will "confine" the Court's holding is its sense of what it can get away with.

I do not mean to suggest disagreement with The Chief Justice's view, *ante*, p. 2–4 (dissenting opinion), that lower federal courts and state courts can distinguish today's case when the issue before them is state denial of marital status to same-sex couples — or even that this Court could theoretically do so. Lord, an opinion with such scatter-shot rationales as this one (federalism noises among them) can be distinguished in many ways. And deserves to be. State and lower federal courts should take the Court at its word and distinguish away.

In my opinion, however, the view that this Court will take of state prohibition of same-sex marriage is indicated beyond mistaking by today's opinion. As I have said, the real rationale of today's opinion, whatever disappearing trail of its legalistic argle-bargle one chooses to follow, is that DOMA is motivated by "'bare . . . desire to harm'" couples in same-sex marriages. Supra, at 18. How easy it is, indeed how inevitable, to reach the same conclusion with regard to state laws denying same-sex couples marital status. . . .

. . . Few public controversies touch an institution so central to the lives of so many, and few inspire such attendant passion by good people on all sides. Few public controversies will ever demonstrate so vividly the beauty of what our Framers gave us, a gift the Court pawns today to buy its stolen moment in the spotlight: a system of government that permits us to rule ourselves. Since DOMA's passage, citizens on all sides of the question have seen victories and they have seen defeats. There have been plebiscites, legislation, persuasion, and loud voices—in other words, democracy. Victories in one place for some, see North Carolina Const., Amdt. 1 (providing that "[m]arriage between one man and one woman is the only domestic legal union that shall be valid or recognized in this State") (approved by a popular vote, 61% to 39% on May 8, 2012), are offset by victories in other places for others, see Maryland Question 6 (establishing "that Maryland's civil marriage laws allow gay and lesbian couples to obtain a civil marriage license") (approved by a popular vote, 52% to 48%, on November 6, 2012). Even in a sin- gle State, the question has come out differently on different occasions. Compare Maine Question 1 (permitting "the State of Maine to issue marriage licenses to same-sex couples") (approved by a popular vote, 53% to 47%, on November 6, 2012) with Maine Question 1 (rejecting "the new law that lets same-sex couples marry") (approved by a popular vote, 53% to 47%, on November 3, 2009).

In the majority's telling, this story is black-and-white: Hate your neighbor or come along with us. The truth is more complicated. It is hard to admit that one's political opponents are not monsters, especially in a struggle like this one, and the challenge in the end proves more than today's Court can handle. Too bad. A reminder that dis- agreement over something so fundamental as marriage can still be politically legitimate would have been a fit task for what in earlier times was called the judicial temperament. We might have covered ourselves with honor today, by promising all sides of this debate that it was theirs to settle and that we would respect their resolution. We might have let the People decide.

But that the majority will not do. Some will rejoice in today's decision, and some will despair at it; that is the nature of a controversy that matters so much to so many. But the Court has cheated both sides, robbing the winners of an honest victory, and the losers of the peace that comes from a fair defeat. We owed both of them better. I dissent.

Notes

1. What is the basis of the majority's ruling, the Equal Protection Clause or Substantive Due Process Clause? Does the majority provide a standard of review for either?

2. Consider the dissent's claim that the majority departs from Justice Marshall in this opinion. Is the majority's interpretation of the Constitution really less sound than Justice Marshall's reasoning for finding a constitutional basis for judicial review in *Marbury v. Madison*?

––––––––––

The *Windsor* opinion left open how its ruling might apply to states prohibiting same sex marriage. Two years later, the Court picked up that issue in *Obergefell*.

Obergefell v. Hodges

135 S. Ct. 2584 (2015)

JUSTICE KENNEDY delivered the opinion of the Court.

The Constitution promises liberty to all within its reach, a liberty that includes certain specific rights that allow persons, within a lawful realm, to define and express their identity. The petitioners in these cases seek to find that liberty by marrying someone of the same sex and having their marriages deemed lawful on the same terms and conditions as marriages between persons of the opposite sex.

I

These cases come from Michigan, Kentucky, Ohio, and Tennessee, States that define marriage as a union between one man and one woman. See, *e.g.,* Mich. Const., Art. I, § 25; Ky. Const. § 233A; Ohio Rev. Code Ann. § 3101.01 (Lexis 2008); Tenn. Const., Art. XI, § 18. The petitioners are 14 same-sex couples and two men whose same-sex partners are deceased. The respondents are state officials responsible for enforcing the laws in question. The petitioners claim the respondents violate the Fourteenth Amendment by denying them the right to marry or to have their marriages, lawfully performed in another State, given full recognition.

Petitioners filed these suits in United States District Courts in their home States. Each District Court ruled in their favor. Citations to those cases are in Appendix A, *infra* [omitted]. The respondents appealed the decisions against them to the United States Court of Appeals for the Sixth Circuit. It consolidated the cases and reversed the judgments of the District Courts. *DeBoer v. Snyder,* 772 F.3d 388 (2014). The Court of Appeals held that a State has no constitutional obligation to license same-sex marriages or to recognize same-sex marriages performed out of State.

The petitioners sought certiorari. This Court granted review, limited to two questions. 574 U.S. ___ (2015). The first, presented by the cases from Michigan and Kentucky, is whether the Fourteenth Amendment requires a State to license a marriage between two people of the same sex. The second, presented by the cases from

Ohio, Tennessee, and, again, Kentucky, is whether the Fourteenth Amendment requires a State to recognize a same-sex marriage licensed and performed in a State which does grant that right.

II

Before addressing the principles and precedents that govern these cases, it is appropriate to note the history of the subject now before the Court.

A

From their beginning to their most recent page, the annals of human history reveal the transcendent importance of marriage. The lifelong union of a man and a woman always has promised nobility and dignity to all persons, without regard to their station in life. Marriage is sacred to those who live by their religions and offers unique fulfillment to those who find meaning in the secular realm. Its dynamic allows two people to find a life that could not be found alone, for a marriage becomes greater than just the two persons. Rising from the most basic human needs, marriage is essential to our most profound hopes and aspirations.

The centrality of marriage to the human condition makes it unsurprising that the institution has existed for millennia and across civilizations. Since the dawn of history, marriage has transformed strangers into relatives, binding families and societies together. Confucius taught that marriage lies at the foundation of government. 2 Li Chi: Book of Rites 266 (C. Chai & W. Chai eds., J. Legge transl. 1967). This wisdom was echoed centuries later and half a world away by Cicero, who wrote, "The first bond of society is marriage; next, children; and then the family." See De Officiis 57 (W. Miller transl. 1913). There are untold references to the beauty of marriage in religious and philosophical texts spanning time, cultures, and faiths, as well as in art and literature in all their forms. It is fair and necessary to say these references were based on the understanding that marriage is a union between two persons of the opposite sex.

That history is the beginning of these cases. The respondents say it should be the end as well. To them, it would demean a timeless institution if the concept and lawful status of marriage were extended to two persons of the same sex. Marriage, in their view, is by its nature a gender-differentiated union of man and woman. This view long has been held—and continues to be held—in good faith by reasonable and sincere people here and throughout the world.

The petitioners acknowledge this history but contend that these cases cannot end there. Were their intent to demean the revered idea and reality of marriage, the petitioners' claims would be of a different order. But that is neither their purpose nor their submission. To the contrary, it is the enduring importance of marriage that underlies the petitioners' contentions. This, they say, is their whole point. Far from seeking to devalue marriage, the petitioners seek it for themselves because of their respect—and need—for its privileges and responsibilities. And their immutable nature dictates that same-sex marriage is their only real path to this profound commitment.

Recounting the circumstances of three of these cases illustrates the urgency of the petitioners' cause from their perspective. Petitioner James Obergefell, a plaintiff in the Ohio case, met John Arthur over two decades ago. They fell in love and started a life together, establishing a lasting, committed relation. In 2011, however, Arthur was diagnosed with amyotrophic lateral sclerosis, or ALS. This debilitating disease is progressive, with no known cure. Two years ago, Obergefell and Arthur decided to commit to one another, resolving to marry before Arthur died. To fulfill their mutual promise, they traveled from Ohio to Maryland, where same-sex marriage was legal. It was difficult for Arthur to move, and so the couple were wed inside a medical transport plane as it remained on the tarmac in Baltimore. Three months later, Arthur died. Ohio law does not permit Obergefell to be listed as the surviving spouse on Arthur's death certificate. By statute, they must remain strangers even in death, a state-imposed separation Obergefell deems "hurtful for the rest of time." App. in No. 14-556 etc., p. 38. He brought suit to be shown as the surviving spouse on Arthur's death certificate.

April DeBoer and Jayne Rowse are co-plaintiffs in the case from Michigan. They celebrated a commitment ceremony to honor their permanent relation in 2007. They both work as nurses, DeBoer in a neonatal unit and Rowse in an emergency unit. In 2009, DeBoer and Rowse fostered and then adopted a baby boy. Later that same year, they welcomed another son into their family. The new baby, born prematurely and abandoned by his biological mother, required around-the-clock care. The next year, a baby girl with special needs joined their family. Michigan, however, permits only opposite-sex married couples or single individuals to adopt, so each child can have only one woman as his or her legal parent. If an emergency were to arise, schools and hospitals may treat the three children as if they had only one parent. And, were tragedy to befall either DeBoer or Rowse, the other would have no legal rights over the children she had not been permitted to adopt. This couple seeks relief from the continuing uncertainty their unmarried status creates in their lives.

Army Reserve Sergeant First Class Ijpe DeKoe and his partner Thomas Kostura, co-plaintiffs in the Tennessee case, fell in love. In 2011, DeKoe received orders to deploy to Afghanistan. Before leaving, he and Kostura married in New York. A week later, DeKoe began his deployment, which lasted for almost a year. When he returned, the two settled in Tennessee, where DeKoe works full-time for the Army Reserve. Their lawful marriage is stripped from them whenever they reside in Tennessee, returning and disappearing as they travel across state lines. DeKoe, who served this Nation to preserve the freedom the Constitution protects, must endure a substantial burden.

The cases now before the Court involve other petitioners as well, each with their own experiences. Their stories reveal that they seek not to denigrate marriage but rather to live their lives, or honor their spouses' memory, joined by its bond.

B

The ancient origins of marriage confirm its centrality, but it has not stood in isolation from developments in law and society. The history of marriage is one of both continuity and change. That institution—even as confined to opposite-sex relations—has evolved over time.

For example, marriage was once viewed as an arrangement by the couple's parents based on political, religious, and financial concerns; but by the time of the Nation's founding it was understood to be a voluntary contract between a man and a woman. See N. Cott, Public Vows: A History of Marriage and the Nation 9–17 (2000); S. Coontz, Marriage, A History 15–16 (2005). As the role and status of women changed, the institution further evolved. Under the centuries-old doctrine of coverture, a married man and woman were treated by the State as a single, male-dominated legal entity. See 1 W. Blackstone, Commentaries on the Laws of England 430 (1765). As women gained legal, political, and property rights, and as society began to understand that women have their own equal dignity, the law of coverture was abandoned. See Brief for Historians of Marriage et al. as *Amici Curiae* 16–19. These and other developments in the institution of marriage over the past centuries were not mere superficial changes. Rather, they worked deep transformations in its structure, affecting aspects of marriage long viewed by many as essential. See generally N. Cott, Public Vows; S. Coontz, Marriage; H. Hartog, Man & Wife in America: A History (2000).

These new insights have strengthened, not weakened, the institution of marriage. Indeed, changed understandings of marriage are characteristic of a Nation where new dimensions of freedom become apparent to new generations, often through perspectives that begin in pleas or protests and then are considered in the political sphere and the judicial process.

This dynamic can be seen in the Nation's experiences with the rights of gays and lesbians. Until the mid-20th century, same-sex intimacy long had been condemned as immoral by the state itself in most Western nations, a belief often embodied in the criminal law. For this reason, among others, many persons did not deem homosexuals to have dignity in their own distinct identity. A truthful declaration by same-sex couples of what was in their hearts had to remain unspoken. Even when a greater awareness of the humanity and integrity of homosexual persons came in the period after World War II, the argument that gays and lesbians had a just claim to dignity was in conflict with both law and widespread social conventions. Same-sex intimacy remained a crime in many States. Gays and lesbians were prohibited from most government employment, barred from military service, excluded under immigration laws, targeted by police, and burdened in their rights to associate. See Brief for Organization of American Historians as *Amicus Curiae* 5–28.

For much of the 20th century, moreover, homosexuality was treated as an illness. When the American Psychiatric Association published the first Diagnostic and Statistical Manual of Mental Disorders in 1952, homosexuality was classified as a mental disorder, a position adhered to until 1973. See Position Statement on Homosexuality and Civil Rights, 1973, in 131 Am. J. Psychiatry 497 (1974). Only in more recent years have psychiatrists and others recognized that sexual orientation is both a normal expression of human sexuality and immutable. See Brief for American Psychological Association et al. as *Amici Curiae* 7–17.

In the late 20th century, following substantial cultural and political developments, same-sex couples began to lead more open and public lives and to establish families. This development was followed by a quite extensive discussion of the issue in both governmental and private sectors and by a shift in public attitudes toward greater tolerance. As a result, questions about the rights of gays and lesbians soon reached the courts, where the issue could be discussed in the formal discourse of the law.

This Court first gave detailed consideration to the legal status of homosexuals in *Bowers v. Hardwick*, 478 U.S. 186 (1986). There it upheld the constitutionality of a Georgia law deemed to criminalize certain homosexual acts. Ten years later, in *Romer v. Evans*, 517 U.S. 620 (1996), the Court invalidated an amendment to Colorado's Constitution that sought to foreclose any branch or political subdivision of the State from protecting persons against discrimination based on sexual orientation. Then, in 2003, the Court overruled *Bowers*, holding that laws making same-sex intimacy a crime "demea[n] the lives of homosexual persons." *Lawrence v. Texas*, 539 U.S. 558.

Against this background, the legal question of same-sex marriage arose. In 1993, the Hawaii Supreme Court held Hawaii's law restricting marriage to opposite-sex couples constituted a classification on the basis of sex and was therefore subject to strict scrutiny under the Hawaii Constitution. *Baehr v. Lewin*, 74 Haw. 530, 852 P.2d 44. Although this decision did not mandate that same-sex marriage be allowed, some States were concerned by its implications and reaffirmed in their laws that marriage is defined as a union between opposite-sex partners. So too in 1996, Congress passed the Defense of Marriage Act (DOMA), 110Stat. 2419, defining marriage for all federal-law purposes as "only a legal union between one man and one woman as husband and wife." 1 U.S.C. §7.

The new and widespread discussion of the subject led other States to a different conclusion. In 2003, the Supreme Judicial Court of Massachusetts held the State's Constitution guaranteed same-sex couples the right to marry. See *Goodridge v. Department of Public Health*, 440 Mass. 309, 798 N.E.2d 941 (2003). After that ruling, some additional States granted marriage rights to same-sex couples, either through judicial or legislative processes. These decisions and statutes are cited in Appendix B, *infra* [omitted]. Two Terms ago, in *United States v. Windsor*, 570 U.S. ___ (2013), this Court invalidated DOMA to the extent it barred the Federal Government from treating same-sex marriages as valid even when they were lawful in the State where they were licensed. DOMA, the Court held, impermissibly disparaged those same-sex couples "who wanted to affirm their commitment to one another before their children, their family, their friends, and their community." *Id.,* at ___ (slip op., at 14).

Numerous cases about same-sex marriage have reached the United States Courts of Appeals in recent years. In accordance with the judicial duty to base their decisions on principled reasons and neutral discussions, without scornful or disparaging commentary, courts have written a substantial body of law considering all sides of these issues. That case law helps to explain and formulate the underlying principles this Court now must consider. With the exception of the opinion here under review and one other, see *Citizens for Equal Protection v. Bruning*, 455 F.3d 859, 864–868 (CA8 2006), the Courts of Appeals have held that excluding same-sex couples from marriage violates the Constitution. There also have been many thoughtful District Court decisions addressing same-sex marriage — and most of them, too, have concluded same-sex couples must be allowed to marry. In addition the highest courts of many States have contributed to this ongoing dialogue in decisions interpreting their own State Constitutions. These state and federal judicial opinions are cited in Appendix A, *infra.*

After years of litigation, legislation, referenda, and the discussions that attended these public acts, the States are now divided on the issue of same-sex marriage. See Office of the Atty. Gen. of Maryland, The State of Marriage Equality in America, State-by-State Supp. (2015).

III

Under the Due Process Clause of the Fourteenth Amendment, no State shall "deprive any person of life, liberty, or property, without due process of law." The fundamental liberties protected by this Clause include most of the rights enumerated in the Bill of Rights. See *Duncan v. Louisiana*, 391 U.S. 145 -149 (1968). In addition these liberties extend to certain personal choices central to individual dignity and autonomy, including intimate choices that define personal identity and beliefs. See, *e.g., Eisenstadt v. Baird*, 405 U.S. 438, 453 (1972); *Griswold v. Connecticut*, 381 U.S. 479–486 (1965).

The identification and protection of fundamental rights is an enduring part of the judicial duty to interpret the Constitution. That responsibility, however, "has not been reduced to any formula." *Poe v. Ullman*, 367 U.S. 497, 542 (1961) (Harlan, J., dissenting). Rather, it requires courts to exercise reasoned judgment in identifying interests of the person so fundamental that the State must accord them its respect. See *ibid.* That process is guided by many of the same considerations relevant to analysis of other constitutional provisions that set forth broad principles rather than specific requirements. History and tradition guide and discipline this inquiry but do not set its outer boundaries. See *Lawrence, supra,* at 572. That method respects our history and learns from it without allowing the past alone to rule the present.

The nature of injustice is that we may not always see it in our own times. The generations that wrote and ratified the Bill of Rights and the Fourteenth Amendment did not presume to know the extent of freedom in all of its dimensions, and so they entrusted to future generations a charter protecting the right of all persons to enjoy liberty as we learn its meaning. When new insight reveals discord between the Constitution's central protections and a received legal stricture, a claim to liberty must be addressed.

Applying these established tenets, the Court has long held the right to marry is protected by the Constitution. In *Loving v. Virginia*, 388 U.S. 1, 12 (1967), which invalidated bans on interracial unions, a unanimous Court held marriage is "one of the vital personal rights essential to the orderly pursuit of happiness by free men." The Court reaffirmed that holding in *Zablocki v. Redhail*, 434 U.S. 374, 384 (1978), which held the right to marry was burdened by a law prohibiting fathers who were behind on child support from marrying. The Court again applied this principle in *Turner v. Safley*, 482 U.S. 78, 95 (1987), which held the right to marry was abridged by regulations limiting the privilege of prison inmates to marry. Over time and in other contexts, the Court has reiterated that the right to marry is fundamental under the Due Process Clause. See, *e.g., M.L.B. v. S.L.J.*, 519 U.S. 102, 116 (1996); *Cleveland Bd. of Ed. v. LaFleur*, 414 U.S. 632–640 (1974); *Griswold, supra*, at 486; *Skinner v. Oklahoma ex rel. Williamson*, 316 U.S. 535, 541 (1942); *Meyer v. Nebraska*, 262 U.S. 390, 399 (1923).

It cannot be denied that this Court's cases describing the right to marry presumed a relationship involving opposite-sex partners. The Court, like many institutions, has made assumptions defined by the world and time of which it is a part. This was evident in *Baker v. Nelson*, 409 U.S. 810, a one-line summary decision issued in 1972, holding the exclusion of same-sex couples from marriage did not present a substantial federal question.

Still, there are other, more instructive precedents. This Court's cases have expressed constitutional principles of broader reach. In defining the right to marry these cases have identified essential attributes of that right based in history, tradition, and other constitutional liberties inherent in this intimate bond. See, *e.g., Lawrence*, 539 U.S., at 574; *Turner, supra*, at 95; *Zablocki, supra*, at 384; *Loving, supra*, at 12; *Griswold, supra*, at 486. And in assessing whether the force and rationale of its cases apply to same-sex couples, the Court must respect the basic reasons why the right to marry has been long protected. See, *e.g., Eisenstadt, supra*, at 453–454; *Poe, supra*, at 542–553 (Harlan, J., dissenting).

This analysis compels the conclusion that same-sex couples may exercise the right to marry. The four principles and traditions to be discussed demonstrate that the reasons marriage is fundamental under the Constitution apply with equal force to same-sex couples.

A first premise of the Court's relevant precedents is that the right to personal choice regarding marriage is inherent in the concept of individual autonomy. This abiding connection between marriage and liberty is why *Loving* invalidated interracial marriage bans under the Due Process Clause. See 388 U.S., at 12; see also

Zablocki, supra, at 384 (observing *Loving* held "the right to marry is of fundamental importance for all individuals"). Like choices concerning contraception, family relationships, procreation, and childrearing, all of which are protected by the Constitution, decisions concerning marriage are among the most intimate that an individual can make. See *Lawrence, supra,* at 574. Indeed, the Court has noted it would be contradictory "to recognize a right of privacy with respect to other matters of family life and not with respect to the decision to enter the relationship that is the foundation of the family in our society." *Zablocki, supra,* at 386.

Choices about marriage shape an individual's destiny. As the Supreme Judicial Court of Massachusetts has explained, because "it fulfils yearnings for security, safe haven, and connection that express our common humanity, civil marriage is an esteemed institution, and the decision whether and whom to marry is among life's momentous acts of self-definition." *Goodridge,* 440 Mass., at 322, 798 N.E.2d, at 955.

The nature of marriage is that, through its enduring bond, two persons together can find other freedoms, such as expression, intimacy, and spirituality. This is true for all persons, whatever their sexual orientation. See *Windsor,* 570 U.S., at ___- ___ (slip op., at 22–23). There is dignity in the bond between two men or two women who seek to marry and in their autonomy to make such profound choices. Cf. *Loving, supra,* at 12 ("[T]he freedom to marry, or not marry, a person of another race resides with the individual and cannot be infringed by the State").

A second principle in this Court's jurisprudence is that the right to marry is fundamental because it supports a two-person union unlike any other in its importance to the committed individuals. This point was central to *Griswold v. Connecticut,* which held the Constitution protects the right of married couples to use contraception. 381 U.S., at 485. Suggesting that marriage is a right "older than the Bill of Rights," *Griswold* described marriage this way:

> "Marriage is a coming together for better or for worse, hopefully enduring, and intimate to the degree of being sacred. It is an association that promotes a way of life, not causes; a harmony in living, not political faiths; a bilateral loyalty, not commercial or social projects. Yet it is an association for as noble a purpose as any involved in our prior decisions. " *Id.,* at 486.

And in *Turner,* the Court again acknowledged the intimate association protected by this right, holding prisoners could not be denied the right to marry because their committed relationships satisfied the basic reasons why marriage is a fundamental right. See 482 U.S., at 95–96. The right to marry thus dignifies couples who "wish to define themselves by their commitment to each other." *Windsor, supra,* at ___ (slip op., at 14). Marriage responds to the universal fear that a lonely person might call out only to find no one there. It offers the hope of companionship and understanding and assurance that while both still live there will be someone to care for the other.

As this Court held in *Lawrence,* same-sex couples have the same right as opposite-sex couples to enjoy intimate association. *Lawrence* invalidated laws that made same-sex intimacy a criminal act. And it acknowledged that "[w]hen sexuality finds overt expression in intimate conduct with another person, the conduct can be but one element in a personal bond that is more enduring." 539 U.S., at 567. But while *Lawrence* confirmed a dimension of freedom that allows individuals to engage in intimate association without criminal liability, it does not follow that freedom stops there. Outlaw to outcast may be a step forward, but it does not achieve the full promise of liberty.

A third basis for protecting the right to marry is that it safeguards children and families and thus draws meaning from related rights of childrearing, procreation, and education. See *Pierce v. Society of Sisters*, 268 U.S. 510 (1925); *Meyer*, 262 U.S., at 399. The Court has recognized these connections by describing the varied rights as a unified whole: "[T]he right to 'marry, establish a home and bring up children' is a central part of the liberty protected by the Due Process Clause." *Zablocki*, 434 U.S., at 384 (quoting *Meyer, supra*, at 399). Under the laws of the several States, some of marriage's protections for children and families are material. But marriage also confers more profound benefits. By giving recognition and legal structure to their parents' relationship, marriage allows children "to understand the integrity and closeness of their own family and its concord with other families in their community and in their daily lives." *Windsor, supra*, at ___ (slip op., at 23). Marriage also affords the permanency and stability important to children's best interests. See Brief for Scholars of the Constitutional Rights of Children as *Amici Curiae* 22–27.

As all parties agree, many same-sex couples provide loving and nurturing homes to their children, whether biological or adopted. And hundreds of thousands of children are presently being raised by such couples. See Brief for Gary J. Gates as *Amicus Curiae* 4. Most States have allowed gays and lesbians to adopt, either as individuals or as couples, and many adopted and foster children have same-sex parents, see *id.*, at 5. This provides powerful confirmation from the law itself that gays and lesbians can create loving, supportive families.

Excluding same-sex couples from marriage thus conflicts with a central premise of the right to marry. Without the recognition, stability, and predictability marriage offers, their children suffer the stigma of knowing their families are somehow lesser. They also suffer the significant material costs of being raised by unmarried parents, relegated through no fault of their own to a more difficult and uncertain family life. The marriage laws at issue here thus harm and humiliate the children of same-sex couples. See *Windsor, supra*, at ___ (slip op., at 23).

That is not to say the right to marry is less meaningful for those who do not or cannot have children. An ability, desire, or promise to procreate is not and has not been a prerequisite for a valid marriage in any State. In light of precedent protecting the right of a married couple not to procreate, it cannot be said the Court or the States have conditioned the right to marry on the capacity or commitment to procreate. The constitutional marriage right has many aspects, of which childbearing is only one.

Fourth and finally, this Court's cases and the Nation's traditions make clear that marriage is a keystone of our social order. Alexis de Tocqueville recognized this truth on his travels through the United States almost two centuries ago:

> "There is certainly no country in the world where the tie of marriage is so much respected as in America ... [W]hen the American retires from the turmoil of public life to the bosom of his family, he finds in it the image of order and of peace .... [H]e afterwards carries [that image] with him into public affairs." 1 Democracy in America 309 (H. Reeve transl., rev. ed. 1990).

In *Maynard v. Hill*, 125 U.S. 190, 211 (1888), the Court echoed de Tocqueville, explaining that marriage is "the foundation of the family and of society, without which there would be neither civilization nor progress." Marriage, the *Maynard* Court said, has long been "'a great public institution, giving character to our whole civil polity.'" *Id.*, at 213. This idea has been reiterated even as the institution has evolved in substantial ways over time, superseding rules related to parental consent, gender, and race once thought by many to be essential. See generally N. Cott, Public Vows. Marriage remains a building block of our national community.

For that reason, just as a couple vows to support each other, so does society pledge to support the couple, offering symbolic recognition and material benefits to protect and nourish the union. Indeed, while the States are in general free to vary the benefits they confer on all married couples, they have throughout our history made marriage the basis for an expanding list of governmental rights, benefits, and responsibilities. These aspects of marital status include: taxation; inheritance and property rights; rules of intestate succession; spousal privilege in the law of evidence; hospital access; medical decision-making authority; adoption rights; the rights and benefits of survivors; birth and death certificates; professional ethics rules; campaign finance restrictions; workers' compensation benefits; health insurance; and child custody, support, and visitation rules. See Brief for United States as *Amicus Curiae* 6–9; Brief for American Bar Association as *Amicus Curiae* 8-29. Valid marriage under state law is also a significant status for over a thousand provisions of federal law. See *Windsor*, 570 U.S., at ___ - ___ (slip op., at 15–16). The States have contributed to the fundamental character of the marriage right by placing that institution at the center of so many facets of the legal and social order.

There is no difference between same- and opposite-sex couples with respect to this principle. Yet by virtue of their exclusion from that institution, same-sex couples are denied the constellation of benefits that the States have linked to marriage. This harm results in more than just material burdens. Same-sex couples are consigned to an instability many opposite-sex couples would deem intolerable in their own lives. As the State itself makes marriage all the more precious by the significance it attaches to it, exclusion from that status has the effect of teaching that gays and lesbians are unequal in important respects. It demeans gays and lesbians for the State to lock them out of a central institution of the Nation's society. Same-sex couples, too, may aspire to the transcendent purposes of marriage and seek fulfillment in its highest meaning.

The limitation of marriage to opposite-sex couples may long have seemed natural and just, but its inconsistency with the central meaning of the fundamental right to marry is now manifest. With that knowledge must come the recognition that laws excluding same-sex couples from the marriage right impose stigma and injury of the kind prohibited by our basic charter.

Objecting that this does not reflect an appropriate framing of the issue, the respondents refer to *Washington v. Glucksberg*, 521 U.S. 702, 721 (1997), which called for a "'careful description'" of fundamental rights. They assert the petitioners do not seek to exercise the right to marry but rather a new and nonexistent "right to same-sex marriage." Brief for Respondent in No. 14-556, p. 8. *Glucksberg* did insist that liberty under the Due Process Clause must be defined in a most circumscribed manner, with central reference to specific historical practices. Yet while that approach may have been appropriate for the asserted right there involved (physician-assisted suicide), it is inconsistent with the approach this Court has used in discussing other fundamental rights, including marriage and intimacy. *Loving* did not ask about a "right to interracial marriage"; *Turner* did not ask about a "right of inmates to marry"; and *Zablocki* did not ask about a "right of fathers with unpaid child support duties to marry." Rather, each case inquired about the right to marry in its comprehensive sense, asking if there was a sufficient justification for excluding the relevant class from the right. See also *Glucksberg*, 521 U.S., at 752–773 (Souter, J., concurring in judgment); *id.*, at 789–792 (Breyer, J., concurring in judgments).

That principle applies here. If rights were defined by who exercised them in the past, then received practices could serve as their own continued justification and new groups could not invoke rights once denied. This Court has rejected that approach, both with respect to the right to marry and the rights of gays and lesbians. See *Loving* 388 U.S., at 12; *Lawrence*, 539 U.S., at 566–567.

The right to marry is fundamental as a matter of history and tradition, but rights come not from ancient sources alone. They rise, too, from a better-informed understanding of how constitutional imperatives define a liberty that remains urgent in our own era. Many who deem same-sex marriage to be wrong reach that conclusion based on decent and honorable religious or philosophical premises, and neither they nor their beliefs are disparaged here. But when that sincere, personal opposition becomes enacted law and public policy, the necessary consequence is to put the imprimatur of the State itself on an exclusion that soon demeans or stigmatizes those whose own liberty is then denied. Under the Constitution, same-sex couples seek in marriage the same legal treatment as opposite-sex couples, and it would disparage their choices and diminish their personhood to deny them this right.

The right of same-sex couples to marry that is part of the liberty promised by the Fourteenth Amendment is derived, too, from that Amendment's guarantee of the equal protection of the laws. The Due Process Clause and the Equal Protection

Clause are connected in a profound way, though they set forth independent principles. Rights implicit in liberty and rights secured by equal protection may rest on different precepts and are not always co-extensive, yet in some instances each may be instructive as to the meaning and reach of the other. In any particular case one Clause may be thought to capture the essence of the right in a more accurate and comprehensive way, even as the two Clauses may converge in the identification and definition of the right. See *M.L.B.*, 519 U.S., at 120–121; *id.*, at 128–129 (Kennedy, J., concurring in judgment); *Bearden v. Georgia*, 461 U.S. 660, 665 (1983). This interrelation of the two principles furthers our understanding of what freedom is and must become.

The Court's cases touching upon the right to marry reflect this dynamic. In *Loving* the Court invalidated a prohibition on interracial marriage under both the Equal Protection Clause and the Due Process Clause. The Court first declared the prohibition invalid because of its un-equal treatment of interracial couples. It stated: "There can be no doubt that restricting the freedom to marry solely because of racial classifications violates the central meaning of the Equal Protection Clause." 388 U.S., at 12. With this link to equal protection the Court proceeded to hold the prohibition offended central precepts of liberty: "To deny this fundamental freedom on so unsupportable a basis as the racial classifications embodied in these statutes, classifications so directly subversive of the principle of equality at the heart of the Fourteenth Amendment, is surely to deprive all the State's citizens of liberty without due process of law." *Ibid*. The reasons why marriage is a fundamental right became more clear and compelling from a full awareness and understanding of the hurt that resulted from laws barring interracial unions.

The synergy between the two protections is illustrated further in *Zablocki*. There the Court invoked the Equal Protection Clause as its basis for invalidating the challenged law, which, as already noted, barred fathers who were behind on child-support payments from marrying without judicial approval. The equal protection analysis depended in central part on the Court's holding that the law burdened a right "of fundamental importance." 434 U.S., at 383. It was the essential nature of the marriage right, discussed at length in *Zablocki*, see *id.*, at 383–387, that made apparent the law's incompatibility with requirements of equality. Each concept—liberty and equal protection—leads to a stronger understanding of the other.

Indeed, in interpreting the Equal Protection Clause, the Court has recognized that new insights and societal understandings can reveal unjustified inequality within our most fundamental institutions that once passed unnoticed and unchallenged. To take but one period, this occurred with respect to marriage in the 1970's and 1980's. Notwithstanding the gradual erosion of the doctrine of coverture, see *supra*, at 6, invidious sex-based classifications in marriage remained common through the mid-20th century. See App. to Brief for Appellant in *Reed v. Reed*, O.T. 1971, No. 70-4, pp. 69–88 (an extensive reference to laws extant as of 1971 treating women as unequal to men in marriage). These classifications denied the equal dignity of men and women. One State's law, for example, provided in 1971 that "the husband is the head of the family and the wife is subject to him; her legal civil existence is merged in the husband, except so far as the law recognizes her separately, either for her own protection, or for her benefit." Ga. Code Ann. § 53-501 (1935). Responding to a new awareness, the Court invoked equal protection principles to invalidate laws imposing sex-based inequality on marriage. See, *e.g., Kirchberg v. Feenstra*, 450 U.S. 455 (1981); *Wengler v. Druggists Mut. Ins. Co.*, 446 U.S. 142 (1980); *Califano v. Westcott*, 443 U.S. 76 (1979); *Orr v. Orr*, 440 U.S. 268 (1979); *Califano v. Goldfarb*, 430 U.S. 199 (1977) (plurality opinion); *Weinberger v. Wiesenfeld*, 420 U.S. 636 (1975); *Frontiero v. Richardson*, 411 U.S. 677 (1973). Like *Loving* and *Zablocki*, these precedents show the Equal Protection Clause can help to identify and correct inequalities in the institution of marriage, vindicating precepts of liberty and equality under the Constitution.

Other cases confirm this relation between liberty and equality. In *M.L.B. v. S.L.J.*, the Court invalidated under due process and equal protection principles a statute requiring indigent mothers to pay a fee in order to appeal the termination of their parental rights. See 519 U.S., at 119–124. In *Eisenstadt* v. *Baird*, the Court invoked both principles to invalidate a prohibition on the distribution of contraceptives to unmarried persons but not married persons. See 405 U.S., at 446–454. And in *Skinner v. Oklahoma ex rel. Williamson*, the Court invalidated under both principles a law that allowed sterilization of habitual criminals. See 316 U.S., at 538–543.

In *Lawrence* the Court acknowledged the interlocking nature of these constitutional safeguards in the context of the legal treatment of gays and lesbians. See 539 U.S., at 575. Although *Lawrence* elaborated its holding under the Due Process Clause, it acknowledged, and sought to remedy, the continuing inequality that resulted from laws making intimacy in the lives of gays and lesbians a crime against the State. See *ibid. Lawrence* therefore drew upon principles of liberty and equality to define and protect the rights of gays and lesbians, holding the State "cannot demean their existence or control their destiny by making their private sexual conduct a crime." *Id.*, at 578.

This dynamic also applies to same-sex marriage. It is now clear that the challenged laws burden the liberty of same-sex couples, and it must be further acknowledged that they abridge central precepts of equality. Here the marriage laws enforced by the respondents are in essence unequal: same-sex couples are denied all the benefits afforded to opposite-sex couples and are barred from exercising a fundamental right. Especially against a long history of disapproval of their relationships, this denial to same-sex couples of the right to marry works a grave and continuing harm. The imposition of this disability on gays and lesbians serves to disrespect and subordinate them. And the Equal Protection Clause, like the Due Process Clause, prohibits this unjustified infringement of the fundamental right to marry. See, *e.g., Zablocki, supra*, at 383–388; *Skinner*, 316 U.S., at 541.

These considerations lead to the conclusion that the right to marry is a fundamental right inherent in the liberty of the person, and under the Due Process and

Equal Protection Clauses of the Fourteenth Amendment couples of the same-sex may not be deprived of that right and that liberty. The Court now holds that same-sex couples may exercise the fundamental right to marry. No longer may this liberty be denied to them. *Baker v. Nelson* must be and now is overruled, and the State laws challenged by Petitioners in these cases are now held invalid to the extent they exclude same-sex couples from civil marriage on the same terms and conditions as opposite-sex couples.

IV

There may be an initial inclination in these cases to proceed with caution — to await further legislation, litigation, and debate. The respondents warn there has been insufficient democratic discourse before deciding an issue so basic as the definition of marriage. In its ruling on the cases now before this Court, the majority opinion for the Court of Appeals made a cogent argument that it would be appropriate for the respondents' States to await further public discussion and political measures before licensing same-sex marriages. See *DeBoer*, 772 F.3d, at 409.

Yet there has been far more deliberation than this argument acknowledges. There have been referenda, legislative debates, and grassroots campaigns, as well as countless studies, papers, books, and other popular and scholarly writings. There has been extensive litigation in state and federal courts. See Appendix A, *infra*. Judicial opinions addressing the issue have been informed by the contentions of parties and counsel, which, in turn, reflect the more general, societal discussion of same-sex marriage and its meaning that has occurred over the past decades. As more than 100 *amici* make clear in their filings, many of the central institutions in American life — state and local governments, the military, large and small businesses, labor unions, religious organizations, law enforcement, civic groups, professional organizations, and universities — have devoted substantial attention to the question. This has led to an enhanced understanding of the issue — an understanding reflected in the arguments now presented for resolution as a matter of constitutional law.

Of course, the Constitution contemplates that democracy is the appropriate process for change, so long as that process does not abridge fundamental rights. Last Term, a plurality of this Court reaffirmed the importance of the democratic principle in *Schuette v. BAMN*, 572 U.S. ___ (2014), noting the "right of citizens to debate so they can learn and decide and then, through the political process, act in concert to try to shape the course of their own times." *Id.*, at ___ - ___ (slip op., at 15–16). Indeed, it is most often through democracy that liberty is preserved and protected in our lives. But as *Schuette* also said, "[t]he freedom secured by the Constitution consists, in one of its essential dimensions, of the right of the individual not to be injured by the unlawful exercise of governmental power." *Id.*, at ___ (slip op., at 15). Thus, when the rights of persons are violated, "the Constitution requires redress by the courts," notwithstanding the more general value of democratic decision-making. *Id.*, at ___ (slip op., at 17). This holds true even when protecting individual rights affects issues of the utmost importance and sensitivity.

The dynamic of our constitutional system is that individuals need not await legislative action before asserting a fundamental right. The Nation's courts are open to injured individuals who come to them to vindicate their own direct, personal stake in our basic charter. An individual can invoke a right to constitutional protection when he or she is harmed, even if the broader public disagrees and even if the legislature refuses to act. The idea of the Constitution "was to withdraw certain subjects from the vicissitudes of political controversy, to place them beyond the reach of majorities and officials and to establish them as legal principles to be applied by the courts." *West Virginia Bd. of Ed. v. Barnette*, 319 U.S. 624, 638 (1943). This is why "fundamental rights may not be submitted to a vote; they depend on the outcome of no elections." *Ibid.* It is of no moment whether advocates of same-sex marriage now enjoy or lack momentum in the democratic process. The issue before the Court here is the legal question whether the Constitution protects the right of same-sex couples to marry.

This is not the first time the Court has been asked to adopt a cautious approach to recognizing and protecting fundamental rights. In *Bowers*, a bare majority upheld a law criminalizing same-sex intimacy. See 478 U.S., at 186, 190–195. That approach might have been viewed as a cautious endorsement of the democratic process, which had only just begun to consider the rights of gays and lesbians. Yet, in effect, *Bowers* upheld state action that denied gays and lesbians a fundamental right and caused them pain and humiliation. As evidenced by the dissents in that case, the facts and principles necessary to a correct holding were known to the *Bowers* Court. See *id.*, at 199 (Blackmun, J., joined by Brennan, Marshall, and Stevens, JJ., dissenting); *id.*, at 214 (Stevens, J., joined by Brennan and Marshall, JJ., dissenting). That is why *Lawrence* held *Bowers* was "not correct when it was decided." 539 U.S., at 578. Although *Bowers* was eventually repudiated in *Lawrence*, men and women were harmed in the interim, and the substantial effects of these injuries no doubt lingered long after *Bowers* was overruled. Dignitary wounds cannot always be healed with the stroke of a pen.

A ruling against same-sex couples would have the same effect—and, like *Bowers*, would be unjustified under the Fourteenth Amendment. The petitioners' stories make clear the urgency of the issue they present to the Court. James Obergefell now asks whether Ohio can erase his marriage to John Arthur for all time. April DeBoer and Jayne Rowse now ask whether Michigan may continue to deny them the certainty and stability all mothers desire to protect their children, and for them and their children the childhood years will pass all too soon. Ijpe DeKoe and Thomas Kostura now ask whether Tennessee can deny to one who has served this Nation the basic dignity of recognizing his New York marriage. Properly presented with the petitioners' cases, the Court has a duty to address these claims and answer these questions.

Indeed, faced with a disagreement among the Courts of Appeals—a disagreement that caused impermissible geographic variation in the meaning of federal law—the Court granted review to determine whether same-sex couples may exercise the right to marry. Were the Court to uphold the challenged laws as constitutional, it would teach the Nation that these laws are in accord with our society's most basic compact. Were the Court to stay its hand to allow slower, case-by-case determination of the required availability of specific public benefits to same-sex couples, it still would deny gays and lesbians many rights and responsibilities intertwined with marriage.

The respondents also argue allowing same-sex couples to wed will harm marriage as an institution by leading to fewer opposite-sex marriages. This may occur, the respondents contend, because licensing same-sex marriage severs the connection between natural procreation and marriage. That argument, however, rests on a counterintuitive view of opposite-sex couple's decision-making processes regarding marriage and parenthood. Decisions about whether to marry and raise children are based on many personal, romantic, and practical considerations; and it is unrealistic to conclude that an opposite-sex couple would choose not to marry simply because same-sex couples may do so. See *Kitchen v. Herbert*, 755 F.3d 1193, 1223 (CA10 2014) ("[I]t is wholly illogical to believe that state recognition of the love and commitment between same-sex couples will alter the most intimate and personal decisions of opposite-sex couples"). The respondents have not shown a foundation for the conclusion that allowing same-sex marriage will cause the harmful outcomes they describe. Indeed, with respect to this asserted basis for excluding same-sex couples from the right to marry, it is appropriate to observe these cases involve only the rights of two consenting adults whose marriages would pose no risk of harm to themselves or third parties.

Finally, it must be emphasized that religions, and those who adhere to religious doctrines, may continue to advocate with utmost, sincere conviction that, by divine precepts, same-sex marriage should not be condoned. The First Amendment ensures that religious organizations and persons are given proper protection as they seek to teach the principles that are so fulfilling and so central to their lives and faiths, and to their own deep aspirations to continue the family structure they have long revered. The same is true of those who oppose same-sex marriage for other reasons. In turn, those who believe allowing same-sex marriage is proper or indeed essential, whether as a matter of religious conviction or secular belief, may engage those who disagree with their view in an open and searching debate. The Constitution, however, does not permit the State to bar same-sex couples from marriage on the same terms as accorded to couples of the opposite sex.

V

These cases also present the question whether the Constitution requires States to recognize same-sex marriages validly performed out of State. As made clear by the case of Obergefell and Arthur, and by that of DeKoe and Kostura, the recognition bans inflict substantial and continuing harm on same-sex couples.

Being married in one State but having that valid marriage denied in another is one of "the most perplexing and distressing complication[s]" in the law of domestic relations. *Williams v. North Carolina*, 317 U.S. 287, 299 (1942) (internal quotation marks omitted). Leaving the current state of affairs in place would maintain and promote instability and uncertainty. For some couples, even an ordinary drive into a neighboring State to visit family or friend's risks causing severe hardship in the event of a spouse's hospitalization while across state lines. In light of the fact that many States already allow same-sex marriage—and hundreds of thousands of these marriages already have occurred—the disruption caused by the recognition bans is significant and ever-growing.

As counsel for the respondents acknowledged at argument, if States are required by the Constitution to issue marriage licenses to same-sex couples, the justifications for refusing to recognize those marriages performed elsewhere are undermined. See Tr. of Oral Arg. on Question 2, p. 44. The Court, in this decision, holds same-sex couples may exercise the fundamental right to marry in all States. It follows that the Court also must hold—and it now does hold—that there is no lawful basis for a State to refuse to recognize a lawful same-sex marriage performed in another State on the ground of its same-sex character.

. . . .

No union is more profound than marriage, for it embodies the highest ideals of love, fidelity, devotion, sacrifice, and family. In forming a marital union, two people become something greater than once they were. As some of the petitioners in these cases demonstrate, marriage embodies a love that may endure even past death. It would misunderstand these men and women to say they disrespect the idea of marriage. Their plea is that they do respect it, respect it so deeply that they seek to find its fulfillment for themselves. Their hope is not to be condemned to live in loneliness, excluded from one of civilization's oldest institutions. They ask for equal dignity in the eyes of the law. The Constitution grants them that right.

The judgment of the Court of Appeals for the Sixth Circuit is reversed.

It is so ordered.

Note

Neither *Windsor* nor *Obergefell* go as far as to create a new suspect/quasi-suspect classification for sexual orientation under the Equal Protection Clause, leaving many to wonder whether the Court will ever address this issue. The fact is that there remains a need for legal protections to be extended to LGBTQ communities beyond marriage. Many forms of discrimination and hurdles facing transsexual communities, for example, are begging for judicial scrutiny. Additionally, potential application of the Equal Protection Clause to gender identity has not even begun in Supreme Court jurisprudence. As you read the lower court decisions below, consider how these groups might be protected under the Equal Protection Clause. Consider whether Gavin Grimm's suit against the State of Virginia over its bathroom laws is indicative of the need for further litigation under both constitutional doctrines and statutory protections. The case, remanded to the federal district court for determination of the agencies' power to expand the meaning of sex discrimination relating

to gender identity under Title IX, exposes issues left open by the gender jurisprudence.[3] *Gloucester Cty. Sch. Bd. v. G.G.* and *Michael M. v. Superior Court of Sonoma
County*, 450 U.S. 464 (1981). *Michael M.* validated states' ability to separate people
based on reproductive criteria. Specifically, the Supreme Court ruled in *Michael M.*
that states could provide different punishment for men who commit statutory rape
than for women doing the same, because of states' interest in preventing teen pregnancy and because of "biological differences" between men and women. Consider
how you might bring a claim of violation of the Equal Protection Clause challenging the requirement that access to facilities be based on gender identity at birth.

The case of Gavin Grimm exemplifies the legal landscape facing trans children in
schools and public spaces. Similar issues burden adults prohibited from using bathroom or locker room facilities based on their chosen gender.[4]

B. Epilogue

The meaning of sex discrimination, especially as applied to gender identity issues,
and the scope of protection accorded to sexual orientation remain unclear. These
issues are being resolved issue by issue by the Court. For example, in June of 2017,
the Supreme Court deemed that the State of Arkansas violated the Substantive Due
Process Clause by denying lesbian couples the same right to be on a child's birth
certificate as was extended to heterosexual couples. *Pavan v. Smith*, 137 S. Ct. 2075
(2017). It adjudicated the issue under *Obergefell*'s Substantive Due Process analysis,
and yet declined, again, to address the whether sexual orientation merits heightened
protection under the Equal Protection Clause. This issue remains one of the most
pressing and evolving individual rights issues of the early twenty-first century.

In similar fashion, the debate regarding grooming standards, outlined in Chapter
3, rages on. For example, lower courts, particularly, have failed to extend protection
under Title VII for employment decisions based on African American employees'
hairstyles. This issue even reached the Pentagon, which was recently forced to alter
its policies on braids in the military, after public outcry on the impact of the ban
on African American women in the military. *E.E.O.C. vs. Catastrophe Management
Solutions* below captures this debate. In the case below, the 11th Circuit declines to
protect against an employer's failure to hire because of the plaintiff's locks. This
issue has garnered a number of petitions seeking Supreme Court review of the

---

3. Gloucester Cty. Sch. Bd. v. G.G., 137 S. Ct. 1239 (2017). *See also* Moriah Balingit, *Gavin
Grimm just wanted to use the bathroom. He didn't think the nation would debate it.*, Wash. Post
(Aug. 30, 2016), https://www.washingtonpost.com/local/education/gavin-grimm-just-wanted-to
-use-the-bathroom-he-didnt-think-the-nation-would-debate-it/2016/08/30/23fc9892-6a26-11e6
-ba32-5a4bf5aad4fa_story.html?utm_term=.420c90652206.
4. Etsitty v. Utah Transit Auth., 502 F.3d 1215 (10th Cir. 2007); Johnston v. Univ. of Pittsburgh
of the Commonwealth Sys. of Higher Educ., 97 F. Supp. 3d 657 (W.D. Pa. 2015).

issue. Do you agree with the court that Title VII does not contemplate protection against dislike of African American hairstyles? What are the arguments supporting Substantive Due Process analyses? See Paulette M. Caldwell, A Hair Piece: Perspectives on the Intersection of Race and Gender, 1991 *Duke Law Journal* 365–396.

E.E.O.C. v. Catastrophe Management Solutions
837 F.3d 1156 (11th Cir. 2016)

JORDAN, CIRCUIT JUDGE:

The Equal Employment Opportunity Commission filed suit on behalf of Chastity Jones, a black job applicant whose offer of employment was rescinded by Catastrophe Management Solutions pursuant to its race-neutral grooming policy when she refused to cut off her dreadlocks. The EEOC alleged that CMS' conduct constituted discrimination on the basis of Ms. Jones' race in violation of Title VII of the Civil Rights Act of 1964, 42 U.S.C. §§ 2000e-2(a)(1) & 2000e-2(m). The district court dismissed the complaint under Federal Rule of Civil Procedure 12(b)(6) because it did not plausibly allege intentional racial discrimination by CMS against Ms. Jones. *See E.E.O.C. v. Catastrophe Mgmt. Solutions,* 11 F.Supp.3d 1139, 1142–44 (S.D. Ala. 2014). The district court also denied the EEOC's motion for leave to amend, concluding that the proposed amended complaint would be futile. The EEOC appealed.

With the benefit of oral argument, we affirm. First, the EEOC—in its proposed amended complaint and in its briefs—conflates the distinct Title VII theories of disparate treatment (the sole theory on which it is proceeding) and disparate impact (the theory it has expressly disclaimed). Second, our precedent holds that Title VII prohibits discrimination based on immutable traits, and the proposed amended complaint does not assert that dreadlocks—though culturally associated with race—are an immutable characteristic of black persons. Third, we are not persuaded by the guidance in the EEOC's Compliance Manual because it conflicts with the position taken by the EEOC in an earlier administrative appeal, and because the EEOC has not offered any explanation for its change in course. Fourth, no court has accepted the EEOC's view of Title VII in a scenario like this one, and the allegations in the proposed amended complaint do not set out a plausible claim that CMS intentionally discriminated against Ms. Jones on the basis of her race.

. . . .

A

CMS, a claims processing company located in Mobile, Alabama, provides customer service support to insurance companies. In 2010, CMS announced that it was seeking candidates with basic computer knowledge and professional phone skills to work as customer service representatives. CMS' customer representatives do not have contact with the public, as they handle telephone calls in a large call room.

Ms. Jones, who is black, completed an online employment application for the customer service position in May of 2010, and was selected for an in-person interview. She arrived at CMS for her interview several days later dressed in a blue business suit and wearing her hair in short dreadlocks.

After waiting with a number of other applicants, Ms. Jones interviewed with a company representative to discuss the requirements of the position. A short time later, Ms. Jones and other selected applicants were brought into a room as a group.

CMS' human resources manager, Jeannie Wilson—who is white—informed the applicants in the room, including Ms. Jones, that they had been hired. Ms. Wilson also told the successful applicants that they would have to complete scheduled lab tests and other paperwork before beginning their employment, and she offered to meet privately with anyone who had a conflict with CMS' schedule. As of this time no one had commented on Ms. Jones' hair.

Following the meeting, Ms. Jones met with Ms. Wilson privately to discuss a scheduling conflict she had and to request to change her lab test date. Ms. Wilson told Ms. Jones that she could return at a different time for the lab test.

Before Ms. Jones got up to leave, Ms. Wilson asked her whether she had her hair in dreadlocks. Ms. Jones said yes, and Ms. Wilson replied that CMS could not hire her "with the dreadlocks." When Ms. Jones asked what the problem was, Ms. Wilson said "they tend to get messy, although I'm not saying yours are, but you know what I'm talking about." Ms. Wilson told Ms. Jones about a male applicant who was asked to cut off his dreadlocks in order to obtain a job with CMS.

When Ms. Jones said that she would not cut her hair, Ms. Wilson told her that CMS could not hire her, and asked her to return the paperwork she had been given. Ms. Jones did as requested and left.

At the time, CMS had a race-neutral grooming policy which read as follows: "All personnel are expected to be dressed and groomed in a manner that projects a professional and businesslike image while adhering to company and industry standards and/or guidelines. . . . [H]airstyle should reflect a business/professional image. No excessive hairstyles or unusual colors are acceptable[.]"

. . . .

Dreadlocks, according to the proposed amended complaint, are "a manner of wearing hair that is common for black people and suitable for black hair texture. Dreadlocks are formed in a black person's hair naturally, without any manipulation, or by manual manipulation of hair into larger coils."

The EEOC alleged that the term dreadlock originated during the slave trade in the early history of the United States. "During the forced transportation of Africans across the ocean, their hair became matted with blood, feces, urine, sweat, tears, and dirt. Upon observing them, some slave traders referred to the slaves' hair as 'dreadful,'" and dreadlock became a "commonly used word to refer to the locks that had formed during the slaves' long trips across the ocean."

. . . Playing off these legal conclusions, the . . . amended complaint set out allegations about black persons and their hair. The hair of black persons grows "in very tight coarse coils," which is different than the hair of white persons. "Historically, the texture of hair has been used as a substantial determiner of race," and "dreadlocks are a method of hair styling suitable for the texture of black hair and [are] culturally associated" with black persons. When black persons "choose to wear and display their hair in its natural texture in the workplace, rather than straightening it or hiding it, they are often stereotyped as not being 'teamplayers,' 'radicals,' 'troublemakers,' or not sufficiently assimilated into the corporate and professional world of employment." Significantly, the proposed amended complaint did not allege that dreadlocks are an immutable characteristic of black persons.

II

Our review in this appeal is plenary. Like the district court, we accept as true the well-pleaded factual allegations in the proposed amended complaint and draw all reasonable inferences in the EEOC's favor. *See, e.g., Ellis v. Cartoon Network, Inc.,* 803 F.3d 1251, 1255 (11th Cir. 2015) (dismissal of a complaint for failure to state a claim); *St. Charles Foods, Inc. v. America's Favorite Chicken Co.,* 198 F.3d 815, 822 (11th Cir. 1999) (denial of a motion for leave to amend due to futility). The legal conclusions in the proposed amended complaint, however, are not presumed to be true. *See Ashcroft v. Iqbal,* 556 U.S. 662, 679–81, 129 S.Ct. 1937, 173 L.Ed.2d 868 (2009); *Franklin v. Curry,* 738 F.3d 1246, 1248 n.1 (11th Cir. 2013).

A complaint must contain sufficient factual allegations to "state a claim to relief that is plausible on its face." *Bell Atl. Corp. v. Twombly,* 550 U.S. 544, 570, 127 S.Ct. 1955, 167 L.Ed.2d 929 (2007). In a Title VII case like this one, the EEOC had to set out enough "factual content t[o] allow[] [a] court to draw the reasonable inference" that CMS is liable for the intentional racial discrimination alleged. *See Iqbal,* 556 U.S. at 678–79, 129 S.Ct. 1937 (explaining that the "plausibility standard" requires more than a "mere possibility" but is "not akin to a 'probability requirement'").

. . . .

The EEOC claimed in its proposed amended complaint that a "prohibition of dreadlocks in the workplace constitutes race discrimination because dreadlocks are a manner of wearing the hair that is physiologically and culturally associated with people of African descent." So, according to the EEOC, the decision of CMS to "interpret its race-neutral written grooming policy to ban the wearing of dreadlocks constitutes an employment practice that discriminates on the basis of race."

. . . The question in a disparate treatment case is "whether the protected trait actually motivated the employer's decision." *Raytheon,* 540 U.S. at 52, 124 S.Ct. 513 (ellipses and internal quotation marks omitted). Generally speaking, "[a] plaintiff can prove disparate treatment . . . by direct evidence that a workplace policy, practice, or decision relies expressly on a protected characteristic, or . . . by [circumstantial evidence] using the burden-shifting framework set forth in *McDonnell.*

. . . Title VII does not define the term "race." And, in the more than 50 years since Title VII was enacted, the EEOC has not seen fit to issue a regulation defining the term. *See* EEOC Compliance Manual, § 15-II, at 4 (2006) ("Title VII does not contain a definition of 'race,' nor has the Commission adopted one."). This appeal requires us to consider, at least in part, what "race" encompasses under Title VII because the EEOC maintains that "if [] individual expression is tied to a protected trait, such as race, discrimination based on such expression is a violation of the law." Br. of EEOC at 20.

"The meaning of the word 'race' in Title VII is, like any other question of statutory interpretation, a question of law for the court." *Village of Freeport v. Barrella*, 814 F.3d 594, 607 (2d Cir. 2016). When words are not defined in a statute, they are "interpreted as taking their ordinary, contemporary, common meaning," *Sandifer v. U.S. Steel Corp.*, ___ U.S. ___, 134 S.Ct. 870, 876, 187 L.Ed.2d 729 (2014) (citation and internal quotation marks omitted), and one of the ways to figure out that meaning is by looking at dictionaries in existence around the time of enactment. *See, e.g., St. Francis College v. Al-Khazraji*, 481 U.S. 604, 609–12, 107 S.Ct. 2022, 95 L.Ed.2d 582 (1987) (consulting 19th century dictionaries to determine the meaning of "race" in a case arising under 42 U.S.C. § 1981, which became law in 1866).

In the 1960s, as today, "race" was a complex concept that defied a single definition. Take, for example, the following discussion in a leading 1961 dictionary: "In technical discriminations, all more or less controversial and often lending themselves to great popular misunderstanding or misuse, RACE is anthropological and ethnological in force, usu[ally] implying a physical type with certain underlying characteristics, as a particular color of skin or shape of skull . . . although sometimes, and most controversially, other presumed factors are chosen, such as place of origin . . . or common root language." Webster's Third New International Dictionary of the English Language 1870 (unabridged 1961).

Nevertheless, most dictionaries at that time tied "race" to common physical characteristics or traits existing through ancestry, descent, or heredity. *See id.* (defining "race" as "the descendants of a common ancestor: a family, tribe, people, or nation belonging to the same stock" or "a class or kind of individuals with common characteristics, interests, appearance, or habits as if derived from a common ancestor," or "a division of mankind possessing traits that are transmissible by descent and sufficient to characterize it as a distinct human type (Caucasian =) (Mongoloid =)"); A Dictionary of the Social Sciences 569 (Julius Gould & William Kolb eds. 1964) ("A *race* is a subdivision of a species, individual members of which display with some frequency a number of hereditary attributes that have become associated with one another in some measure through considerable degree of in-breeding among the ancestors of the group during a substantial part of their recent evolution."); A Dictionary of Sociology 142 (G. Duncan Mitchell ed. 1968) ("Biologically speaking the concept of *race* refers to a population sharing a gene-pool giving rise to a characteristic distribution of physical characteristics determined by heredity. There are no clear cut boundaries between racial groups thus defined and considerable variations may be exhibited within races."). One specialty dictionary, while defining "race" as an "anthropological term denoting a large group of persons distinguished by significant hereditary physical traits," cautioned that "[a] common misconception is that cultural traits sufficiently differentiate races." Dictionary of Political Science 440 (Joseph Dunne ed. 1964).

From the sources we have been able to review, it appears more likely than not that "race," as a matter of language and usage, referred to common physical characteristics shared by a group of people and transmitted by their ancestors over time. Although the period dictionaries did not use the word "immutable" to describe such common characteristics, it is not much of a linguistic stretch to think that such characteristics are a matter of birth, and not culture.

There is little support for the position of the EEOC that the 1964 Congress meant for Title VII to protect "individual expression . . . tied to a protected race." Br. of EEOC at 20. Indeed, from a legal standpoint, it appears that "race" was then mostly understood in terms of inherited physical characteristics. *See* Black's Law Dictionary 1423 (4th ed. 1951) ("Race. An ethnical stock; a great division of mankind having in common certain distinguishing physical peculiarities constituting a comprehensive class appearing to be derived from a distinct primitive source. A tribal or national stock, a division or subdivision of one of the great racial stocks of mankind distinguished by minor peculiarities. Descent.") (citing cases).

It may be that today "race" is recognized as a "social construct," *Ho by Ho v. San Francisco Unified Sch. Dist.*, 147 F.3d 854, 863 (9th Cir. 1998), rather than an absolute biological truth. *See also Al-Khazraji*, 481 U.S. at 610 n.4, 107 S.Ct. 2022 (noting that some, but not all, scientists have concluded that "racial classifications are for the most part sociopolitical, rather than biological, in nature"); The American Heritage Dictionary of the English Language 1441 (4th ed. 2009) (usage note for "race": "The notion of race is nearly as problematic from a scientific point of view as it is from a social one."). But our possible current reality does not tell us what the country's collective zeitgeist was when Congress enacted Title VII half a century ago. "That race is essentially only a very powerful idea and not at all a biological fact is, again, an emerging contemporary understanding of the meaning of race." Rhonda V. Magee Andrews, *The Third Reconstruction: An Alternative to Race Consciousness and Colorblindness in Post-Slavery America*, 54 Ala. L. Rev. 483, 515 (2003).

. . . .

If we assume, however, that the quest for the ordinary understanding of "race" in the 1960s does not have a clear winner, then we must look for answers elsewhere. Some cases from the former Fifth Circuit provide us with binding guidance, giving some credence to Felix Frankfurter's adage that "[n]o judge writes on a wholly clean slate." Walter Hamilton, *Preview of a Justice*, 48 YALE L.J. 819, 821 (1939) (quoting Felix Frankfurter, The Commerce Clause Under Marshall, Taney, and Waite 12 (1937)). As we explain below, those cases teach that Title VII protects against discrimination based on immutable characteristics.

In *Willingham v. Macon Tel. Publ'g Co.*, 507 F.2d 1084 (5th Cir. 1975) (en banc), we addressed a Title VII sex discrimination claim by a male job applicant who was denied a position because his hair was too long. Although the employer interpreted its neutral dress/grooming policy to prohibit the wearing of long hair only by men, and although the plaintiff argued that he was the victim of sexual stereotyping (i.e., the view that only women should have long hair), we affirmed the grant of summary judgment in favor of the employer. *See id.* at 1092–93.

We held in *Willingham* that "[e]qual employment opportunity," which was the purpose of Title VII, "may be secured only when employers are barred from discriminating against employees on the basis of immutable characteristics, such as race and national origin. Similarly, an employer cannot have one hiring policy for men and another for women *if* the distinction is based on some fundamental right. But a hiring policy that distinguishes on some other ground, such as grooming or length of hair, is related more closely to the employer's choice of how to run his business than equality of employment opportunity." *Id.* at 1091. We "adopt[ed] the view . . . that distinctions in employment practices between men and women on the basis of something other than immutable or protected characteristics do not inhibit employment *opportunity* in violation of [Title VII]." *Id.* at 1092. And we approved the district court's alternative ground for affirming the grant of summary judgment in favor of the employer — that because grooming and hair standards were also imposed on female employees, men and women were treated equally. *See id.*In closing, we reiterated that "[p]rivate employers are prohibited from using different hiring policies for men and women only when the distinctions used relate to immutable characteristics or legally protected rights." *Id.*

Willingham involved hair length in the context of a sex discrimination claim, but in *Garcia v. Gloor*, 618 F.2d 264 (5th Cir. 1980), we applied the immutable characteristic limitation to national origin, another of Title VII's protected categories. In *Garcia* a bilingual Mexican-American employee who worked as a salesperson was fired for speaking Spanish to a co-worker on the job in violation of his employer's English-only policy, and he alleged that his termination was based on his national origin in violation of Title VII (which we referred to as the "EEO Act"). We affirmed the district court's judgment in favor of the employer following a bench trial . . .

. . . Title VII protects persons in covered categories with respect to their immutable characteristics, but not their cultural practices. *See Willingham*, 507 F.2d at 1092; *Garcia*, 618 F.2d at 269. And although these two decisions have been criticized by some, *see, e.g.*, Camille Gear Rich, *Performing Racial and Ethnic Identity: Discrimination by Proxy and the Future of Title VII*, 79 N.Y.U. L. REV. 1134, 1213–21 (2004), we are not free, as a later panel, to discard the immutable/mutable distinction they set out. *See Cohen v. Office Depot, Inc.*, 204 F.3d 1069, 1076 (11th Cir. 2000) ("[T]he prior panel precedent rule is not dependent upon a subsequent panel's appraisal of the initial decision's correctness. Nor is the application of the rule dependent upon the skill of the attorneys or wisdom of the judges involved in the prior decision — upon what was argued or considered.").

We recognize that the distinction between immutable and mutable characteristics of race can sometimes be a fine (and difficult) one, but it is a line that courts have drawn. So, for example, discrimination on the basis of black hair texture (an immutable characteristic) is prohibited by Title VII, while adverse action on the basis of black hairstyle (a mutable choice) is not. *Compare, e.g., Jenkins v. Blue Cross Mut. Hosp. Ins., Inc.,* 538 F.2d 164, 168 (7th Cir. 1976) (en banc) (recognizing a claim for racial discrimination based on the plaintiff's allegation that she was denied a promotion because she wore her hair in a natural Afro), *with, e.g., Rogers v. Am. Airlines, Inc.,* 527 F.Supp. 229, 232 (S.D.N.Y. 1981) (holding that a grooming policy prohibiting an all-braided hairstyle did not constitute racial discrimination, and distinguishing policies that prohibit Afros, because braids are not an immutable characteristic but rather "the product of . . . artifice"). As one commentator has put it, "the concept of immutability," though not perfect, "provides a rationale for the protected categories encompassed within the antidiscrimination statutes." Sharona Hoffman, *The Importance of Immutability in Employment Discrimination Law,* 52 Wm. & Mary L. Rev. 1483, 1514 (2011).

Critically, the EEOC's proposed amended complaint did not allege that dreadlocks themselves are an immutable characteristic of black persons, and in fact stated that black persons choose to wear dreadlocks because that hairstyle is historically, physiologically, and culturally associated with their race. That dreadlocks are a "natural outgrowth" of the texture of black hair does not make them an immutable characteristic of race. Under *Willingham* and *Garcia,* the EEOC failed to state a plausible claim that CMS intentionally discriminated against Ms. Jones on the basis of her race by asking her to cut her dreadlocks pursuant to its race-neutral grooming policy. The EEOC's allegations—individually or collectively—do not suggest that CMS used that policy as proxy for intentional racial discrimination.

. . . .

As far as we can tell, every court to have considered the issue has rejected the argument that Title VII protects hairstyles culturally associated with race. *See Cooper v. Am. Airlines, Inc.,* 149 F.3d 1167, at *1 (4th Cir.1998) (upholding district court's 12(b)(6) dismissal of claims based on a grooming policy requiring that braided hairstyles be secured to the head or at the nape of the neck); *Campbell v. Alabama Dep't of Corr.,* No. 2:13-CV-00106-RDP, 2013 WL 2248086, at *2 (N.D. Ala. May 20, 2013) ("A dreadlock hairstyle, like hair length, is not an immutable characteristic."); *Pitts v. Wild Adventures, Inc.,* No. CIV.A.7:06-CV-62-HL, 2008 WL 1899306, at *5–6 (M.D. Ga. Apr. 25, 2008) (holding that a grooming policy which prohibited dreadlocks and cornrows was outside the scope of federal employment discrimination statutes because it did not discriminate on the basis of immutable characteristics); *Eatman v. United Parcel Serv.,* 194 F.Supp.2d 256, 259–67 (S.D.N.Y. 2002) (holding that an employer's policy prohibiting "unconventional" hairstyles, including dreadlocks, braids, and cornrows, was not racially discriminatory in violation of Title VII); *McBride v. Lawstaf, Inc.,* No. CIV. A.1:96-CV-0196C, 1996 WL 755779, at *2 (N.D. Ga. Sept. 19, 1996) (holding that a grooming policy prohibiting braided hairstyles does not violate Title VII); *Rogers,* 527 F.Supp. at 232 (holding that a grooming policy prohibiting an all-braided hairstyle did not constitute racial discrimination, and distinguishing policies that prohibit Afros, because braids are not an immutable characteristic but rather "the product of . . . artifice"); *Carswell v. Peachford Hosp.,*No. C80-222A, 1981 WL 224, at *2 (N.D. Ga. May 26, 1981) ("There is no evidence, and this court cannot conclude, that the wearing of beads in one's hair is an immutable characteristic, such as national origin, race, or sex. Further, this court cannot conclude that the prohibition of beads in the hair by an employer is a subterfuge for discrimination."); *Wofford v. Safeway Stores, Inc.,* 78 F.R.D. 460, 470 (N.D. Cal. 1978) (explaining that the "even-handed application of reasonable grooming regulations has uniformly been held not to constitute discrimination on the basis of race") (internal citations omitted); *Thomas v. Firestone Tire & Rubber Co.,* 392 F.Supp. 373, 375 (N.D. Tex. 1975) (holding that a grooming policy regulating hair length and facial hair, which was applied even-handedly to employees of all races, did not violate Title VII or 42 U.S.C. § 1981). *See also Brown v. D.C. Transit System,* 523 F.2d 725, 726 (D.C. Cir. 1975) (rejecting claim by black male employees that race-neutral grooming regulation, which prohibited most facial hair, violated Title VII despite contention by employees that the regulation was "an 'extreme and gross suppression of them as black men and (was) a badge of slavery' depriving them 'of their racial identity and virility'").

. . . .

We would be remiss if we did not acknowledge that, in the last several decades, there have been some calls for courts to interpret Title VII more expansively by eliminating the biological conception of "race" and encompassing cultural characteristics associated with race. But even those calling for such an interpretive change have different visions (however subtle) about how "race" should be defined. *Compare, e.g.,* Ian F. Haney Lopez, *The Social Construction of Race: Some Observations on Illusion, Fabrication, and Choice,* 29 Harv. C.R.C.L. L. Rev. 1, 7 (1994) (defining "race" as "a vast group of people loosely bound together by historically contingent, socially significant elements of their morphology and/or ancestry"), and Rich, *Performing Racial and Ethnic Identity,* 79 N.Y.U. L. Rev. at 1142 ("There is an urgent need to redefine Title VII's definition of race and ethnicity to include both biological, visible racial/ethnic features and performed features associated with racial and ethnic identity."), *with, e.g.,* D. Wendy Greene, *Title VII: What's Hair (and Other Race-Based Characteristics) Got to Do With It?,* 79 U. Colo. L. Rev. 1355, 1385 (2008) ("Race includes physical appearances and behaviors that society, historically and presently, commonly associates with a particular racial group, even when the physical appearances and behavior are not 'uniquely' or 'exclusively' 'performed' by, or attributed to a particular racial group."), and Barbara J. Flagg, *Fashioning a Title VII Remedy for Transparently White Subjective Decisionmaking,* 104 Yale L.J. 2009, 2012 (1995) (suggesting that discrimination on the basis of race might include "personal characteristics that . . . intersect seamlessly with [one's racial] self-definition").

Yet the call for interpreting "race" as including culture has not been unanimous. This is in part because culture itself is (or can be) a very broad and ever-changing concept. *See, e.g.,* Richard T. Ford, *Race as Culture: Why Not?*, 47 U.C.L.A. L. Rev.1803, 1813 (2000) ("Culture is a much more problematic category for legal intervention than race, because culture in a broad sense encompasses almost any possible motivation for human behavior."). *Cf.* Annelise Riles, *Cultural Conflicts*, 71 L. & Contemp. Probs. 273, 285 (2008) ("[C]ultures are hybrid, overlapping, and creole: forces from trade to education to migration to popular culture and transnational law ensure that all persons participate in multiple cultures at once. Cultural elements circulate globally, and they are always changing. From this point of view, 'culture' is more of a constant act of translation and re-creation or re-presentation than it is a fixed and given thing.").

... We cannot, and should not, forget that we—and courts generally—are tasked with interpreting Title VII, a statute enacted by Congress, and not with grading competing doctoral theses in anthropology or sociology. Along these lines, consider the critique by Richard Ford of the attempt to have Title VII protect cultural characteristics or traits associated with race:

Once a status is ascribed, it is immutable in the pragmatic sense that the individual cannot readily alter it. This is the sense in which immutability is relevant to anti-discrimination law.The mutability of a racial characteristic then, is strictly speaking, irrelevant, but not because—as difference discourse would have it—anti-discrimination law should prohibit discrimination based on mutable as well as immutable racial characteristics, but rather because racial characteristics generally are irrelevant. And it is quite right to say that anti-discrimination law prohibits discrimination on the basis of immutable characteristics. But it does not follow that the immutable characteristics in question are characteristics of race; instead they are any characteristic of potential plaintiffs that may be proxies for racial status. This cuts against some common locutions that the law prohibits discrimination against racial groups; that it prohibits discrimination on the basis of racial characteristics; that it protects racial minorities; worst of all that it protects race. On my formulation it does none of these. Indeed it could not do these things because to do them it would first require a definition of a racial group, racial characteristic, and/ or race—none of which courts have readily [at] hand. Instead, law prohibits discrimination on the basis of race—something it can do without knowing what race is and indeed without accepting that race is something that is knowable. To prohibit discrimination on the basis of race, we need only know that there is a set of ideas about race that many people accept and decide to prohibit them from acting on the basis of these ideas.Richard Ford, Racial Culture: A Critique 103 (2005).

Our point is not to take a stand on any side of this debate—we are, after all, bound ...

Ms. Jones told CMS that she would not cut her dreadlocks in order to secure a job, and we respect that intensely personal decision and all it entails. But, for the reasons we have set out, the EEOC's original and proposed amended complaint did not state a plausible claim that CMS intentionally discriminated against Ms. Jones because of her race. The district court therefore did not err in dismissing the original complaint and in concluding that the proposed amended complaint was futile.

AFFIRMED.

Note

The Courts' failure to fully understand the way the law impacts lived experiences, especially those intersecting in multiple identities, is still one of the main challenges plaintiffs face in twenty-first century litigation. What might you suggest as potential means for bridging the understanding gap exhibited in these cases?

Conclusion: Law as Power

The materials discussed in this textbook are crucial reminders about the role of law and its operation, particularly as the law relates to those at the margins. One lesson is that law does not operate in a vacuum. Instead, it is the result of specific context and of the collection of individual backgrounds and biases. For that reason, it is a tool that is to be perfected and crafted to address the complex realities facing all, rather than to just mirror the interests of some in society.

Additionally, the dark periods of Jim Crow and Slavery (*Dred Scott*, *Plessy*, among many) remind us that, when unchecked, that law is the most effective duplicator of patterns favoring the powerful interests at the expense of the less powerful. These facts should not cause disappointment. Instead, the danger they portray should galvanize vigilance and constant interrogation, particularly from students of the law. This vigilance should cause everyone to verify that lawmaking and interpretation remain consistent with the spirit of equity and fairness in all aspects of society. This is one of the most sacred and thrilling tasks for any lawyer. Embrace it proudly.

Index